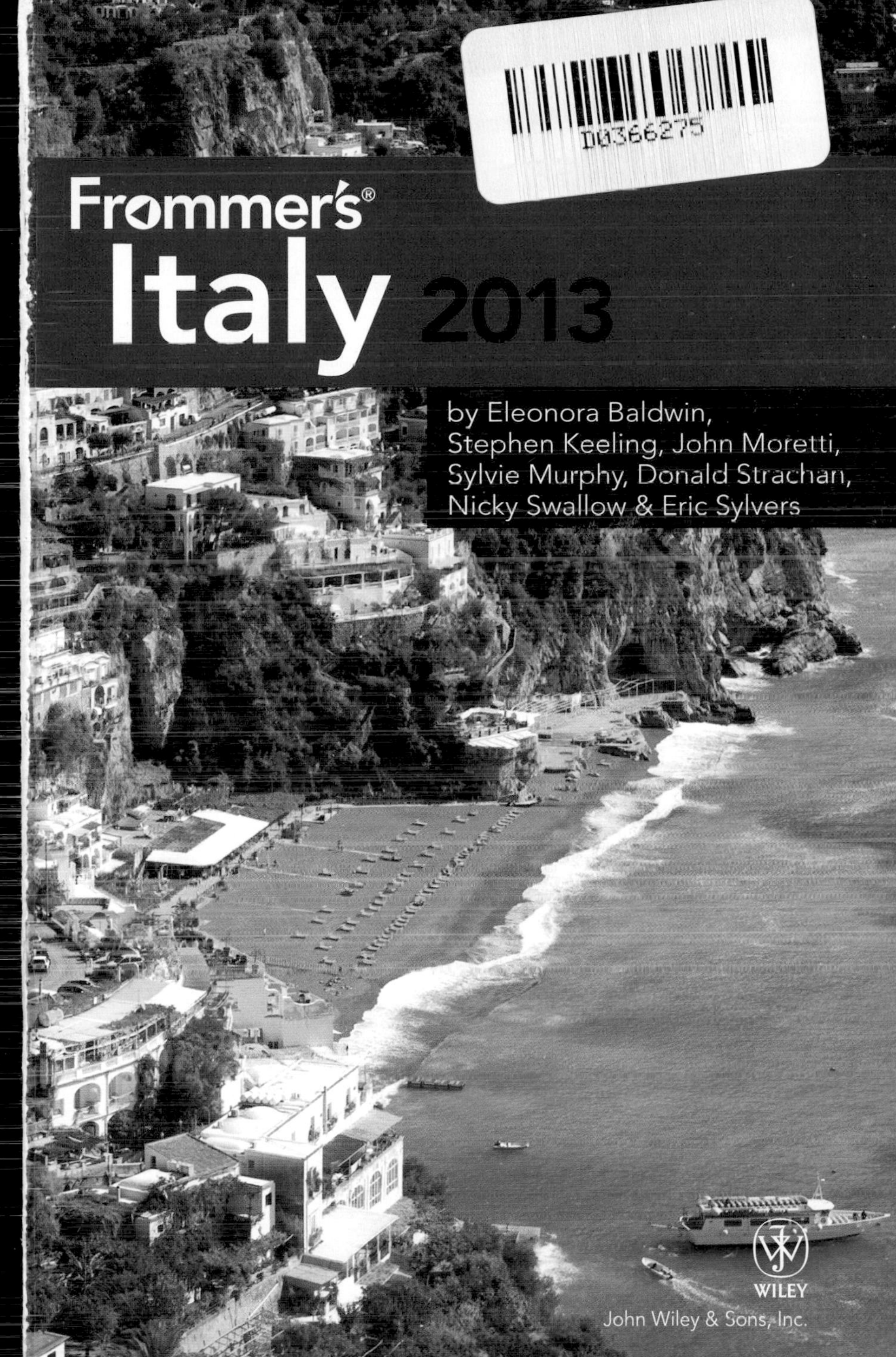

Frommer's® Italy 2013

by Eleonora Baldwin, Stephen Keeling, John Moretti, Sylvie Murphy, Donald Strachan, Nicky Swallow & Eric Sylvers

WILEY
John Wiley & Sons, Inc.

Published by:
JOHN WILEY & SONS, INC.
111 River St.
Hoboken, NJ 07030-5774

ISBN 978-1-118-27846-8 (paper); ISBN 978-1-118-39284-3 (ebk); ISBN 978-1-118-39286-7 (ebk)

Editors: Linda Barth & Ian Skinnari
Production Editor: Lindsay Conner
Cartographer: Andrew Murphy
Photo Editors: Cherie Cincilla & Richard Fox
Production by Wiley Indianapolis Composition Services

Front Cover Photo: Monte Titano (Mount Titan) in San Marino © nagelestock.com / Alamy Images
Back Cover Photos: left to right: Detail of the mosaics on the facade of St. Frediano's Basilica, Lucca, Tuscany © Riccardo de Luca; a kayak in Capri's bay © Raffaele Capasso; the Colosseum in Rome © Vanessa Berberian

For information on our other products and services or to obtain technical support, please contact our Customer Care Department within the U.S. at 877/762-2974, outside the U.S. at 317/572-3993 or fax 317/572-4002.

Wiley also publishes its books in a variety of electronic formats. Some content that appears in print may not be available in electronic formats.

Manufactured in China

5 4 3 2 1

CONTENTS

8 VENICE 424

9 THE VENETO & THE DOLOMITES 502

10 MILAN, LOMBARDY & THE LAKES 557

15 SICILY 822

16 SARDINIA 898

17 PLANNING YOUR TRIP TO ITALY 921

18 MOLTO ITALIANO 943

LIST OF MAPS

ABOUT THE AUTHORS

Eleonora Baldwin (chapter 4) is an American-born, Italian-raised, global citizen. As a food and travel writer, and wanderlust addict living in Rome, she divides her time between guiding foodie adventures, writing food stories and columns, traveling, and designing custom culinary vacations in Italy. She is the author/editor of four blogs in which she writes about Italian lifestyle, reviews restaurants, provides useful tools for parents traveling with kids in Rome, and captures the Eternal City's essence in her photography.

Stephen Keeling (chapter 7) was a financial journalist who lived and worked in Asia for almost a decade. Despite attempts to kick his gelato addiction, he has been to Italy many times. He is the coauthor of the award-winning *Frommer's Tuscany, Umbria & Florence With Your Family* and currently lives in New York City.

A freelance writer based in Italy, **John Moretti** (chapter 9) has written for *The International Herald Tribune, The Independent on Sunday, Italy Daily, The Associated Press*, and www.ft.com (*Financial Times* online). He is the author of *Living Abroad in Italy*, coeditor of *Rome in Detail*, and a contributor to Time Out's Milan and Naples city guides.

Sylvie Murphy (chapters 14, 15, and 16) has been dutifully traipsing the *bel paese*, in the name of research for American and British travel guides, for the past decade. The Eternal City and all things ancient Roman are her first love, though she also confesses a serious weakness for the natural splendor of the Bay of Naples and the wine of southern Tuscany. Sylvie lives in Kansas City, Missouri, with her husband, Tim.

Donald Strachan (chapters 1, 2, 3, 5, and 6) is a London-based writer, editor, and copywriter. He is the coauthor of *Frommer's The Balearics With Your Family* and *Florence & Tuscany Day by Day*, 2nd Edition. He has written for the *Sunday Telegraph*, the *Observer*, the *Independent on Sunday*, and the *Sydney Morning Herald*, among others.

A musician by training, **Nicky Swallow** (chapter 13) moved to Florence in 1981 to play in the opera orchestra. Her freelance musical career in the late '80s and early '90s took her all over Italy, and it was during this time that her enthusiasm for the diverse regional food, wine, and culture of the country found its roots. She has been writing about Italy, with a special emphasis on Florence and Tuscany, for ten years. She is editor of the *Charming Small Hotel Guide to Tuscany and Umbria* and Italian editor of the new on-line hotel guide, the Hotel Guru.

Eric Sylvers (chapters 8, 10, 11, 12, and 17) has worked as a journalist and writer for more than a decade in Italy, where he has written about everything from the country's economic woes to bike racing, climbing volcanoes, and a scooter ride on a remote island. The California native, outdoor enthusiast, and avid biker has traveled up and down the peninsula many times, including once on foot from the Swiss border to the far southeastern coast (the heel of the boot). He also worked on Frommer's Northern Italy guide. Eric blogs about Italian food, wine, and culture at www.foodieinitaly.com.

HOW TO CONTACT US

In researching this book, we discovered many wonderful places—hotels, restaurants, shops, and more. We're sure you'll find others. Please tell us about them, so we can share the information with your fellow travelers in upcoming editions. If you were disappointed with a recommendation, we'd love to know that, too. Please write to:

Frommer's Italy 2013
John Wiley & Sons, Inc. • 111 River St. • Hoboken, NJ 07030-5774
frommersfeedback@wiley.com

ADVISORY & DISCLAIMER

Travel information can change quickly and unexpectedly, and we strongly advise you to confirm important details locally before traveling, including information on visas, health and safety, traffic and transport, accommodation, shopping and eating out. We also encourage you to stay alert while traveling and to remain aware of your surroundings. Avoid civil disturbances, and keep a close eye on cameras, purses, wallets and other valuables.

While we have endeavored to ensure that the information contained within this guide is accurate and up-to-date at the time of publication, we make no representations or warranties with respect to the accuracy or completeness of the contents of this work and specifically disclaim all warranties, including without limitation warranties of fitness for a particular purpose. We accept no responsibility or liability for any inaccuracy or errors or omissions, or for any inconvenience, loss, damage, costs or expenses of any nature whatsoever incurred or suffered by anyone as a result of any advice or information contained in this guide.

The inclusion of a company, organization or Website in this guide as a service provider and/or potential source of further information does not mean that we endorse them or the information they provide. Be aware that information provided through some Websites may be unreliable and can change without notice. Neither the publisher or author shall be liable for any damages arising herefrom.

FROMMER'S STAR RATINGS, ICONS & ABBREVIATIONS

Every hotel, restaurant, and attraction listing in this guide has been ranked for quality, value, service, amenities, and special features using a **star-rating system.** In country, state, and regional guides, we also rate towns and regions to help you narrow down your choices and budget your time accordingly. Hotels and restaurants are rated on a scale of zero (recommended) to three stars (exceptional). Attractions, shopping, nightlife, towns, and regions are rated according to the following scale: zero stars (recommended), one star (highly recommended), two stars (very highly recommended), and three stars (must-see).

In addition to the star-rating system, we also use **seven feature icons** that point you to the great deals, in-the-know advice, and unique experiences that separate travelers from tourists. Throughout the book, look for:

special finds—those places only insiders know about

fun facts—details that make travelers more informed and their trips more fun

kids—best bets for kids and advice for the whole family

special moments—those experiences that memories are made of

overrated—places or experiences not worth your time or money

insider tips—great ways to save time and money

great values—where to get the best deals

The following abbreviations are used for credit cards:

AE	American Express	**DISC**	Discover	**V**	Visa
DC	Diners Club	**MC**	MasterCard		

TRAVEL RESOURCES AT FROMMERS.COM

Frommer's travel resources don't end with this guide. Frommer's website, **www.frommers.com**, has travel information on more than 4,000 destinations. We update features regularly, giving you access to the most current trip-planning information and the best airfare, lodging, and car-rental bargains. You can also listen to podcasts, connect with other Frommers.com members through our active-reader forums, share your travel photos, read blogs from guidebook editors and fellow travelers, and much more.

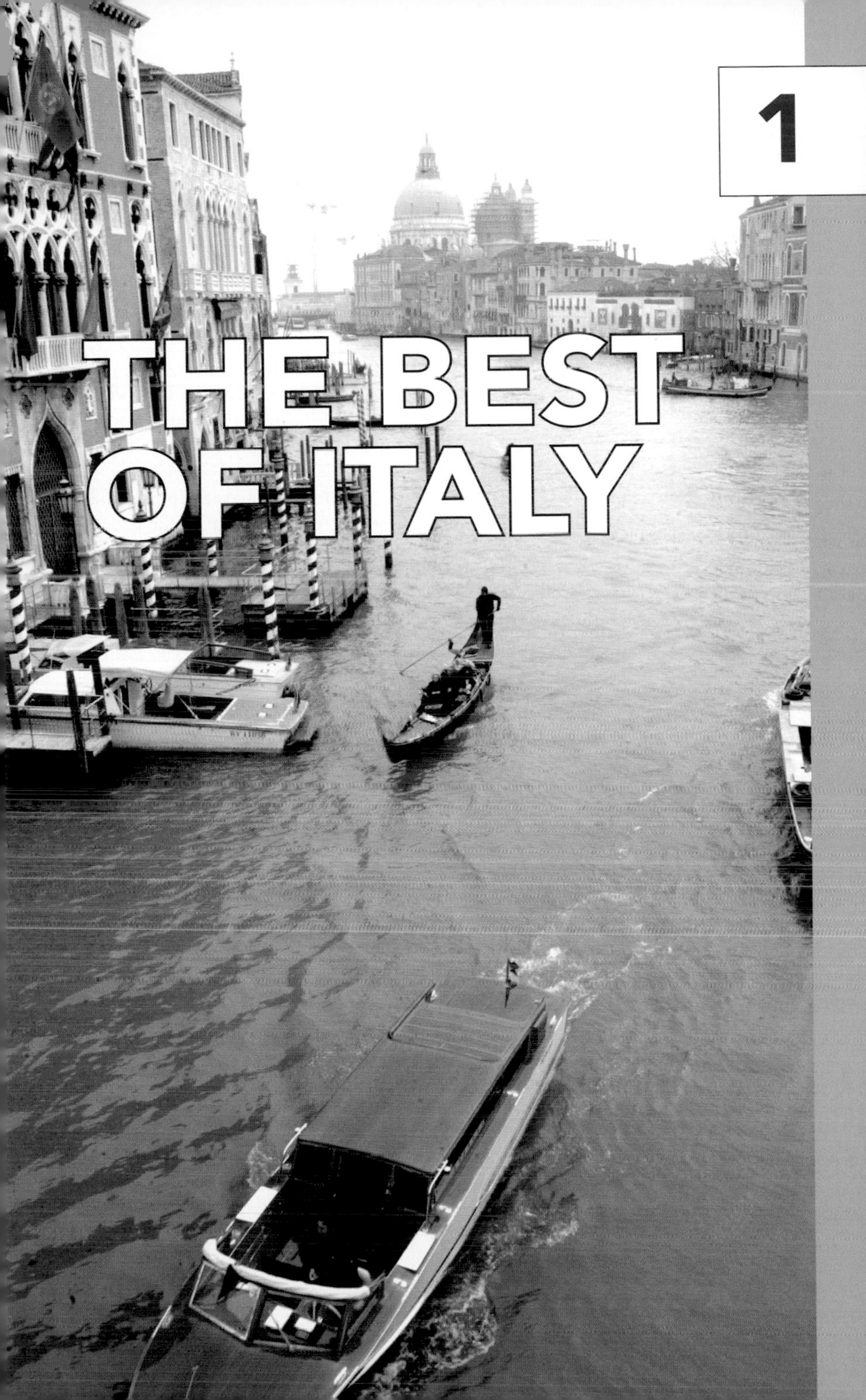

1

THE BEST OF ITALY

Italy is not a country that needs a great fanfare to introduce it. The mere mention of the word conjures up vivid images: the beguiling romance and ancient ruins of Rome; the Renaissance art and architecture of Florence; the azure waters of Mediterranean islands like Sicily, Capri, and Sardinia. For centuries, visitors have headed here looking for their own slice of the good life.

Cities Long before Italy was a country, it was a loose collection of city-states. Centuries of alliance and rivalry left a legacy that you can witness in the former maritime republic of **Venice,** in Gothic **Siena,** and in the Renaissance princedoms of **Mantua** and **Urbino. Lecce** is the great baroque city of the Italian heel, while **Naples** is the south's hectic and historic "capital."

Countryside The rolling, vine-clad hills of the **Chianti** and the cypress-studded, emerald-green expanses of the Tuscan **Val d'Orcia** serve up iconic images of the Italian countryside. Neighboring **Umbria** has a gentler rural beauty, and affords opportunities to lodge in a rural *agriturismo,* or farm-stay accommodation. Adventurous walkers of all ages can hike between the coastal villages of the **Cinque Terre** that remain untroubled by 21st-century chaos.

Eating & Drinking Italy doesn't have a truly national cuisine. The gastronomic capital, **Bologna,** is home to many of the world's favorite pasta dishes, and nearby **Parma** is famous for prosciutto and tangy cheese. Northern mountain dwellers carb-load on risotto, or polenta served with hearty stews. In the south, you'll find the freshest seafood along the coasts of **Sicily** and **Puglia.** Italy's best wines are generally red—Barolo and Barbaresco hail from **Piedmont,** and Tuscany is home to chianti and Vino Nobile di Montepulciano.

Mountains & Lakes The Italian north is embraced by a semicircle of peaks stretching from the **Alps** in the northwest to the **Dolomites** in the northeast. Head here for dramatic views, hiking, climbing, and wild winter sports galore. In the south, active volcanoes Vesuvius and Etna tower over Naples and Sicily, respectively. Europe's most famously photogenic lakes are scattered across the northern regions of Piedmont, Lombardy, and the Veneto: **Lake Como** has the chic resorts and cachet, and **Lake Garda** is the place to head for a family adventure.

THE most unforgettable ITALY EXPERIENCES

- **Visiting the smaller art cities:** For centuries, Italy wasn't a country, but dozens of principalities and city-states, each usually blessed (or cursed) with the patronage of a pope or ducal family. Consequently, these cities became treasure-troves of exquisite paintings and statues displayed in churches and grandiose palaces, and of handsome architecture lining the city streets. You'll find stunning examples in cities from Mantua and Vicenza in the north, to Siracusa and Taormina in Sicily.

PREVIOUS PAGE: **Venice.**

Vicenza.

- **Dining Italian style:** The most cherished pastime of most Italians is eating and each region has its own recipes, many handed down through generations. If the weather is fine and you're dining outdoors, perhaps with a view of a medieval church or piazza, you'll find your experience the closest thing to food heaven. *Buon appetito!*
- **Riding Venice's Grand Canal:** A ride on the S-shaped Grand Canal, which curves for 3.3km (2 miles) past Gothic and Renaissance buildings, will give you ever-changing glimpses of Venice's poignant beauty. Your ride doesn't have to be on a gondola; any public *vaporetto* (motorboat) sailing between Venice's rail station and Piazza San Marco will provide a heart-stopping view. See p. 447.
- **Spending a night at the opera:** You don't have to be a fan of Verdi, Rossini, or Puccini to appreciate the splendor of a night at Milan's **La Scala,** among the most prestigious houses in the world. Italy has other great opera houses—Venice's La Fenice and Verona's Arena to name two—but only one La Scala. See p. 585.
- **Being embraced by the art at Padova's Chapel of the Scrovegni:** Step aside, Sistine Chapel. Art lovers armed with binoculars behold this scene in awe—the recently renovated cycle of vibrant frescoes by Giotto that revolutionized 14th-century painting. It is considered one of the most important pieces of art leading up to the Renaissance, and visiting is an unforgettable, intimate experience. See p. 511

THE best CITY EXPERIENCES

- **Surrendering to the madness of a Palermo street market:** In Sicily's capital, which has been a crossroads between the East and the West for thousands of years, the chaotic, colorful, theatrical street markets are a priceless vignette of a living culture that can often feel more Middle Eastern than Italian. See p. 866.

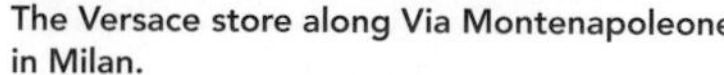
The Versace store along Via Montenapoleone in Milan.

The Mole Antonelliana in Turin.

- **Exploring underground Naples:** There is more to Naples than you can see at eye level. Head below its maze of historic streets to see evidence of its past, from the remains of the ancient Greek and Roman city, to the catacombs used for centuries to bury the dead, and the tunnels that sheltered refugees from the cholera epidemic of 1884. See p. 714.
- **Shopping the boutiques of Milan:** Milan is one of the world's hottest fashion capitals. You'll find a range of shoes, clothing, and accessories unequaled anywhere else. Even if you weren't born to shop, stroll along the streets bordering Via Montenapoleone and check out the elegant offerings from Europe's most celebrated designers. See p. 581.
- **Attending a soccer match in Rome:** Forget lions battling gladiators in the Colosseum. For real Roman thrills, hit a soccer game. Home sides Roma and Lazio play Series A matches at the Stadio Olimpico, Viale dello Stadio Olimpico (✆ **06-36851;** Bus: 32, 271, or 280), every weekend, from September to June, and twice yearly they compete against each other in a heated "derby," painting the stands with the red-yellow flags of Roma and the white-pale blue of Lazio. Tickets to Roma and Lazio soccer matches can be purchased on game day at the Stadio Olimpico for 20€ to 120€. They are also sold at Lottomatica spots, at the official Roma Store, Piazza Colonna 360 (www.asroma.it; ✆ **06-69200642**), or the Lazio Style shop, Via G. Calderini 66C (www.sslazio.it; ✆ **06-32541745**).
- **Ascending the Mole Antonelliana in a glass elevator:** Every great city has a great building with a great view, and Turin is no different. But what's special about a ride up the glass elevator of the Mole Antonelliana, one of the oddest looking buildings you'll see in Italy, is the combination of the view of the

inside (of the National Film Museum) and then the outside from the observation deck (of the city and the encircling Alps). See p. 633.

- **Catching an opera at Verona's Arena:** Summertime opera festivals here are produced on a scale more human than those in cities such as Milan are—and, best of all, they are held under the stars. The setting is the ancient **Arena di Verona,** a site that's grand enough to accommodate as many elephants as might be needed for a performance of *Aïda*. See p. 524.

THE best FOOD & DRINK EXPERIENCES

- **The gastronomic wonders of Parma:** Meet master butchers of dry-cured and subtly aged prosciutto, and producers of the world champion of cheese, Parmigiano-Reggiano, 25-year-old barrels of balsamic vinegar, and the vineyards of Colli di Parma. Taste, sip, and sample it all on your own culinary tour of Parma. See p. 419.
- **A visit to a Tuscan winery:** The rolling, vine-clad hills south of Florence nurture some of the world's best wine grapes. Oenophiles particularly appreciate the robust yet refined reds made from the sangiovese grape, and could spend a lifetime touring the cantinas and sampling the product. See "The Chianti" and "Montepulciano" in chapter 6.
- **A real Neapolitan pizza:** Naples invented the pizza, and there's no better place to sample one of Italy's great gastronomic exports. Pizza in these parts should be baked in a wood-fired oven and have a light base with a puffy rim that holds just the right amount of topping, consisting of local tomatoes and the best mozzarella. The only authentic additions are capers, anchovies, and fresh basil. *Deliziosa!* See p. 717.
- **A Bicerin at a Turin cafe:** Equal parts coffee, hot chocolate, and cream give the Bicerin enough calories to allow you to skip your next meal. You won't, of course, but you'll still be happy you had this decadent Torinese specialty, and will immediately be planning how to get one more before leaving town. See p. 639.
- **Cicchetti and a spritz in Venice:** *Cicchetti*—tapaslike small servings, usually eaten while standing at a bar—are a Venetian tradition. Accompanying the *cicchetti* with a spritz made with wine from the Veneto makes the experience

Tuscan wineries are among the world's finest.

Authentic Neapolitan pizza.

complete. While your options are numerous, some of the best spots to indulge are on the San Polo side of the Rialto bridge. See p. 476.

- **The sweets in Sicily:** Between cannoli, cassata, and countless local pastries tempting you at every turn, get ready to be in a constant state of hyperglycemia. Even if you're normally nauseated by such generous use of sugar, the insane deliciousness of these freshly made goodies is so extreme, the chemical dependence they engender so immediate, that you'll find yourself needing a *cannolo,* you know, for survival, at 4pm sharp every day. See chapter 15.

THE best WAYS TO SEE ITALY LIKE A LOCAL

- **Drinking your coffee *al banco:*** Italians—especially city dwellers—don't often linger at a piazza table sipping their morning cappuccino. For them, a *caffè* is a pit stop: They order at the bar *(al banco),* throw back the bitter elixir, and continue on their way. You'll also save a chunk of change drinking Italian style—your coffee should cost 50% less than the sit-down price.
- **Hitting the insider aperitivo spots in Rome:** Don't confuse *aperitivo* with happy hour: Predinner cocktails tickle appetites, induce conversation and flirting, and allow free access to all-you-can-eat buffets on the strength of one drink. **Freni e Frizioni** (p. 157) owns the best mixology department, **Etablì** (p. 154) rocks the top fireplace winter scene, **Société Lutece** (p. 154) boasts a superlative outdoor vibe, and **Salotto 42** (p. 155) claims the tastiest snacks and prettiest location. See "Entertainment & Nightlife" in chapter 4.
- **Renting a bike to see Ferrara from the saddle:** Join hundreds of bike-mad Ferrarese as they zip along narrow, cycle-friendly lanes that snake through the city's old center, weaving between the awe-inspiring Castello Estense and the Renaissance elegance of the Palazzo Schifanoia. You can also take bikes on a circuit of the city on top of the medieval walls. See p. 393.

- **Hitting the slopes away from the holiday season:** As spring gets closer and the days get longer, the skiing in Italy's Alps gets better, cheaper, and less crowded. Early February through mid-March can be the best time to hit the ski resorts in Valle d'Aosta, and if you go midweek you may wonder why you're never waiting in a lift-line. See p. 649.
- **Eating and partying on Florence's Left Bank:** Most Florentines have abandoned their *centro storico* to the visitors, but south of the Arno in the areas of Oltrarno, San Frediano, and San Niccolò, you'll find local after-dark fun. Stop in for an *aperitivo* at **Zoe** (p. 247), dine at **iO** (p. 237), slurp a gelato at **La Carraia** (p. 234), and drink until late at **Volume** (p. 246). See "Where to Eat" and "Entertainment & Nightlife" in chapter 5.

THE best FAMILY EXPERIENCES

- **Climbing Pisa's wonky tower:** Are we walking up or down? Pleasantly disoriented kids are bound to ask as you spiral your way to the rooftop viewing balcony atop one of the world's most famous pieces of botched engineering. Just be aware that 8 is the minimum age for heading up Pisa's Torre Pendente, or "Leaning Tower." See p. 318.
- **Relaxing poolside at your Pugliese trullo:** Hundreds of Puglia's fairy-tale *trulli* (stone huts with conical roofs) have been remade as holiday homes, complete with luxurious amenities and blissful country vistas. The equally lovely *masserie* (converted farmhouse accommodations) offer a bit more space. And in Puglia, you don't have to worry about dragging the kids to

Gelato.

museums and churches—the attraction in this undervisited, authentic pocket of Italy is simply being there. See chapter 14.

- **Boat tripping on Lake Garda:** Who doesn't like a day boating on a lake, any lake? Throw in Lake Garda's fiordlike appearance, Alpine peaks on the horizon, and splendid little towns, and you have the makings of a perfect outing with interest for everyone. See p. 602.
- **Walking the Cinque Terre:** Scrambling up and down the Cinque Terre's vineyard-covered hillsides, which afford breathtaking views of the surrounding coast, will excite anybody, from 7 to 70, who is up for a healthy workout. Add a tasty focaccia stop in each town and a plate of pasta *al pesto* in the evening, and you've got bliss. To avoid the crowds, go midweek—and avoid July and August altogether. See p. 689.
- **Taking a trip to the artisan gelateria:** Fluffy heaps of gelato, however pretty, are built with additives, stabilizers, and air pumped into the blend. Blue "Smurf" or bubble-gum-pink flavors denote chemical color enhancement, and ice crystals or grainy texture are telltale signs of engineered gelato—so steer clear. Authentic artisan *gelaterie* produce good stuff from scratch daily, with fresh ingredients and less bravado.
- **Hitting the beach in Sardinia:** The island's 1,800km (1,116-mile) coastline is packed with idyllic coves, or vast expanses of golden sand, where you can sunbathe, swim, and play, largely unencumbered by the "beach club" phenomenon that spoils many shores of mainland Italy. There's a good reason why Sardinia is sometimes called the "Italian Caribbean." See chapter 16.
- **Spending an undersea afternoon at the Genoa Aquarium:** Genoa's aquarium, the biggest in Europe, will put smiles on your kiddies' faces—and you're likely to be just as intrigued yourself by the sharks, seals, penguins, piranhas, and tiny orange frogs. Especially the frogs. See p. 666.

THE best MUSEUMS

- **Vatican Museums** (Rome): The 100 galleries that constitute the Musei Vaticani are loaded with papal treasures accumulated over the centuries. Musts include the Sistine Chapel, ancient Greek and Roman sculptures as *Laocoön* and *Belvedere Apollo,* the frescoed Stanze executed by Raphael (among which is the majestic *School of Athens*), and endless collections of pagan Greco-Roman antiquities and Renaissance art by European masters. See p. 95.
- **Galleria degli Uffizi** (Florence): This U-shaped High Renaissance building designed by Giorgio Vasari was the administrative headquarters, or *uffizi* (offices), for the dukes of Tuscany when the Medici called the shots round here. It's now the crown jewel of Europe's art museums, housing the world's greatest collection of Renaissance paintings. See p. 206.
- **Accademia** (Venice): One of Europe's great museums, the Accademia houses an incomparable collection of Venetian painting, exhibited chronologically from the 13th to the 18th century. It's one of the most richly stocked museums in Italy, boasting works by Bellini, Carpaccio, Giorgione, Titian, and Tintoretto. See p. 453.

Laocoön at the Vatican Museum.

- **Brera Picture Gallery** (Milan): The foremost place to see Milan's artistic treasures is the Brera Picture Gallery, whose collection—shown in a 17th-century palace—is especially rich in paintings from the schools of Lombardy and Venice. Three of the most important prizes are Mantegna's *Dead Christ*, Raphael's *Betrothal of the Virgin*, and Piero della Francesca's *Madonna with Saints*. See p. 574.
- **Galleria Borghese** (Rome): Housed amid the frescoes and decor of a 1613 palace in the heart of the Borghese Gardens, this gem of a building is merely the backdrop for the collections, which include masterpieces of baroque sculpture by a young Bernini and Canova, and paintings by Caravaggio and Raphael. See p. 120.
- **Galleria Nazionale** (Perugia): Umbrian art has a few art stars of its own—notably Perugino and Pinturicchio, both of whom are well represented in the region's marquee museum inside the crenellated Palazzo dei Priori. Also here are works of national importance by Duccio, Piero della Francesca, and others. See p. 333.
- **National Archaeological Museum** (Naples): Thanks to the vicinity of Pompeii and Herculaneum, Naples is home to one of the most important collections of ancient art and artifacts in the world. The vast rooms and halls house a unique haul of statuary, mosaics, wall-paintings, bronzes, and ceramics that make a visit here unmissable. See p. 710.

THE best HISTORIC EXPERIENCES

- **Getting Gothic on the streets of Siena:** One of Italy's most famous piazzas, the shell-shaped Campo stands at the heart of one of Europe's best-preserved medieval cities. Steep, canyonlike streets, icons of Gothic architecture like the Palazzo Pubblico, and ethereal Madonnas painted on shimmering gold altarpieces transport you back to a time before the Renaissance. See "Siena" in chapter 6.
- **Following in the footsteps of the dukes of Urbino:** Urbino's mighty Palazzo Ducale—and indeed the flowering of Urbino throughout the Renaissance—is the legacy of Duke Federico da Montefeltro, a patron of arts and letters. Wander the lavishly painted halls and apartments where he and his ancestors

Pompeii's Villa of Mysteries.

entertained (and employed) the likes of painters Raphael and Piero della Francesca. See p. 363.

- **Chasing the ghosts in Pompeii and Herculaneum:** When Vesuvius erupted in A.D. 79, it buried Herculaneum and Pompeii under molten lava and ash, truncating the lives of thousands and suspending the two cities in a sort of time capsule. Today, still under the shadow of the menacing volcano, these are poignant ghost towns that can be coaxed into life with a little imagination.

The ruins at Segesta, in Sicily.

- **Discovering Byzantine beauty in Ravenna:** Italy's unspoiled city of mosaics was once the capital of the Western Roman Empire and the seat of the Byzantine governor of Italy, periods that left a trove of ancient churches and glittering Byzantine-style mosaics, the finest anywhere outside Istanbul. See p. 400.
- **Going gaga for Greeks in Sicily:** From Agrigento's majestic Valley of the Temples to the theaters of Siracusa and Taormina, and the perfect lone temple at Segesta, Sicily packs an awesome punch of stunningly atmospheric and well-preserved archaeological sites. See chapter 15.

THE best CHARMING SMALL-TOWN EXPERIENCES

- **Roaming and grazing in Todi:** Famed for its simple, graceful Piazza del Popolo, the small hilltop town of Todi, in Umbria, transports you back to the Middle Ages. Lose yourself in its tangle of ancient streets and wine-dark alleys, then dine on its truffle-rich cuisine. See "A Side Trip to Todi" on p. 354.

One of Todi's ancient alleys

- **Wandering Etruscan Civita di Bagnoregio:** The climb up the bluff on a steep volcanic path, across an incongruous concrete bridge to the ancient Etruscan town may discourage you, but it's well worth it. You'll tread silent cobbled alleys, overwhelmed by the age and rustic beauty of the buildings, cozy main square, church of San Donato, and hospitable locals.
- **Relaxing lakeside in Bellagio:** Bellagio is the loveliest town in Italy's Lake District. Its promenade follows the shores of Lake Como and is perfect for meandering away your day. You'll want to

Bellagio, on Lake Como.

Taormina.

drag yourself away from the water long enough to explore the arcaded streets and little shops, visit lush gardens, and relax in the sunshine. See p. 614.

- **Exploring the other side of Taormina:** Although international tourism has touched Sicily's most beautiful town for centuries, lofty Taormina somehow remains grounded. Venture off the main tourist drag to the little shops where Taorminese do their business. In the city's drop-dead gorgeous Villa Comunale, stroll among real Taorminese *mamme* and their *bambini*. See "Taormina" in chapter 15.
- **Feasting on art and architecture in Bergamo's Città Alta:** Wandering the streets of Bergamo's phenomenally well-preserved Città Alta, which is perched on a hill above the surrounding plain, will give you an idea of what it was like to live in a northern Italian town in the 15th century. Picturesque *piazze, palazzi,* and churches abound. See p. 592.

THE best FREE EXPERIENCES

- **Driving the Amalfi Coast:** The SS. 163, "the road of 1,000 bends," hugs vertical cliffsides and deep gorges, cutting through olive groves, lemon terraces, and whitewashed villages—against a background of the bluest sea you can imagine. One of the world's most magnificent coastal drives provokes fear, nausea, and wonder in equal doses; the secret is to make sure that someone else is at the wheel for this nail-biting roller coaster of a drive. See chapter 13.
- **Getting lost in Venice:** You haven't experienced Venice until you've turned a corner convinced you're on the way somewhere, only to find yourself smack against a canal with no bridge or in a little courtyard with no way out. All you can do is shrug, smile, and give the city's maze of narrow streets another try, because getting lost in Venice is a pleasure. See p. 424.

- **Gazing in wonder at Assisi's Basilica di San Francesco:** Intimate, dark, and Romanesque downstairs, while soaringly Gothic above, Assisi's two-story church is perhaps the finest building in Italy dedicated to a medieval saint. Inside the Upper Church, Giotto's frescoes reached a new kind of figurative realism in Italian art around 1300, long before the painters of the Renaissance carried his technique further. See p. 338.
- **Getting rained on in Rome's Pantheon:** People often wonder whether the 9m (30-ft.) oculus in the middle of the Pantheon's dome has a glass covering. Visit the ancient temple in the middle of a downpour for your answer: The oculus is open to the elements, transforming the Pantheon into a giant shower on wet days. In light rain, the building fills with mist, but during a full-fledged thunderstorm, the drops come down in a perfect 9m-wide shaft, splattering loudly on the polychrome marble floor. See p. 112.
- **Hiking up to the Rifugio Menaggio, above Lake Como:** Need a workout and a breath of fresh air? Hike up to the Rifugio Menaggio, and take in spectacular vistas of Lake Como and into Switzerland. It's an idyllic family day trip through forest and Alpine fields like something out of *Heidi*. At the summit the *rifugio*, or lodge, serves a scrumptious, well-earned plate of risotto. See p. 618.

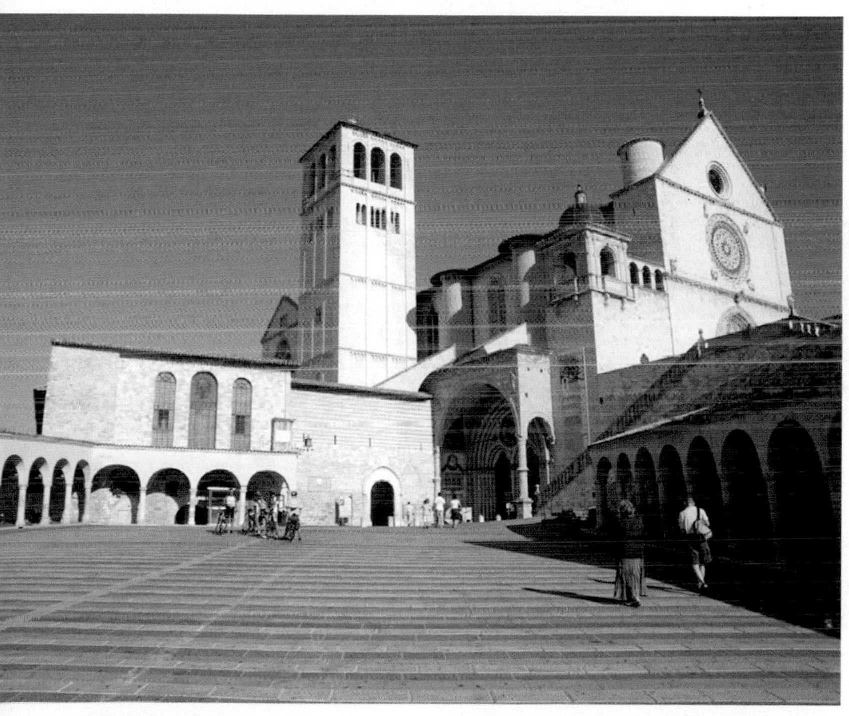

The Basilica di San Francesco in Assisi.

THE best GIFTS TO TAKE HOME

- **Ceramics:** Little Faenza, in Emilia-Romagna, was the original center of pottery making, especially majolica, during the Renaissance. (Majolica, also known as "faience," is a type of hand-painted, glazed, and heavily ornamented earthenware.) Tuscany and Umbria are also known for earthenware pottery, carried by stores in Florence, the Chianti, Gubbio, and Orvieto.
- **Fashion:** Italian fashion is world-renowned. Pucci and Valentino led the parade, followed by Armani, Gucci, and Versace. Milan's Quadrilatero d'Oro (p. 581) dominates the Italian scene, with the largest selection of haute couture boutiques, followed by Rome and Florence. Look out, too, for vintage threads, as the craze for finding that classic style has hit Italy.
- **Glass:** Venice's glass is world famous and you'll find hundreds of stores peddling it, across a range of qualities and prices. Production has been centered on Murano, an island in the Venetian lagoon, since the 14th century. You'll still find glass factories there, although many are now storefronts selling imported glass. Finding real Murano glass can be difficult, and when you succeed it will be expensive. See "Shopping" in chapter 8.
- **Lace:** For centuries, Italy has been known for its exquisite and delicate lace, fashioned into everything from women's undergarments to heirloom tablecloths. Venetian artisan lace is the most famous, and includes some of the finest products in the world, especially *tombolo* (pillow lace), macramé, and an expensive lace known as *chiacchierino*.
- **Leather:** The Italians craft the finest leather in the world. From boots to luggage, from leather clothing to purses (or wallets), Italian cities—especially Florence and Milan—abound in leather shops selling quality goods. This remains one of Italy's best values, in spite of some substandard work that is now appearing.

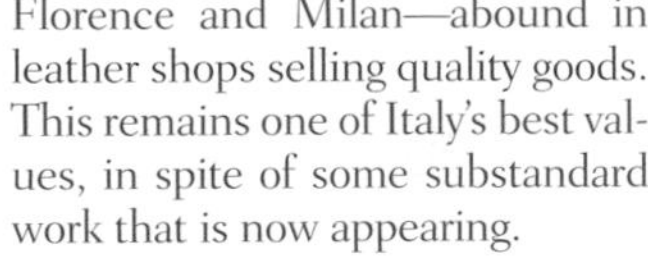

- **Prints & engravings:** Wood engravings, mezzotints, zinc and copperplate engravings—you name it and you'll find it, especially in **Rome** and **Florence,** but also in the small Tuscan town of **Volterra** (p. 300). You have to be a careful shopper: Some prints are genuine works of artisanship, but others are rushed off an assembly line.

Murano glass being made in Venice.

* **Kitchen gadgets:** Maybe bringing home a $7,000 La Marzocco espresso machine is out of the question, but even the most basic home wares stores sell small, inexpensive, packable, yet unmistakably Italian items for your *cucina.* Perhaps a dish for grated cheese in the shape of a wheel of Parmigiano-Reggiano, or an obscure ravioli cutter will delight foodie friends back home.

Leather goods for sale in Florence.

2

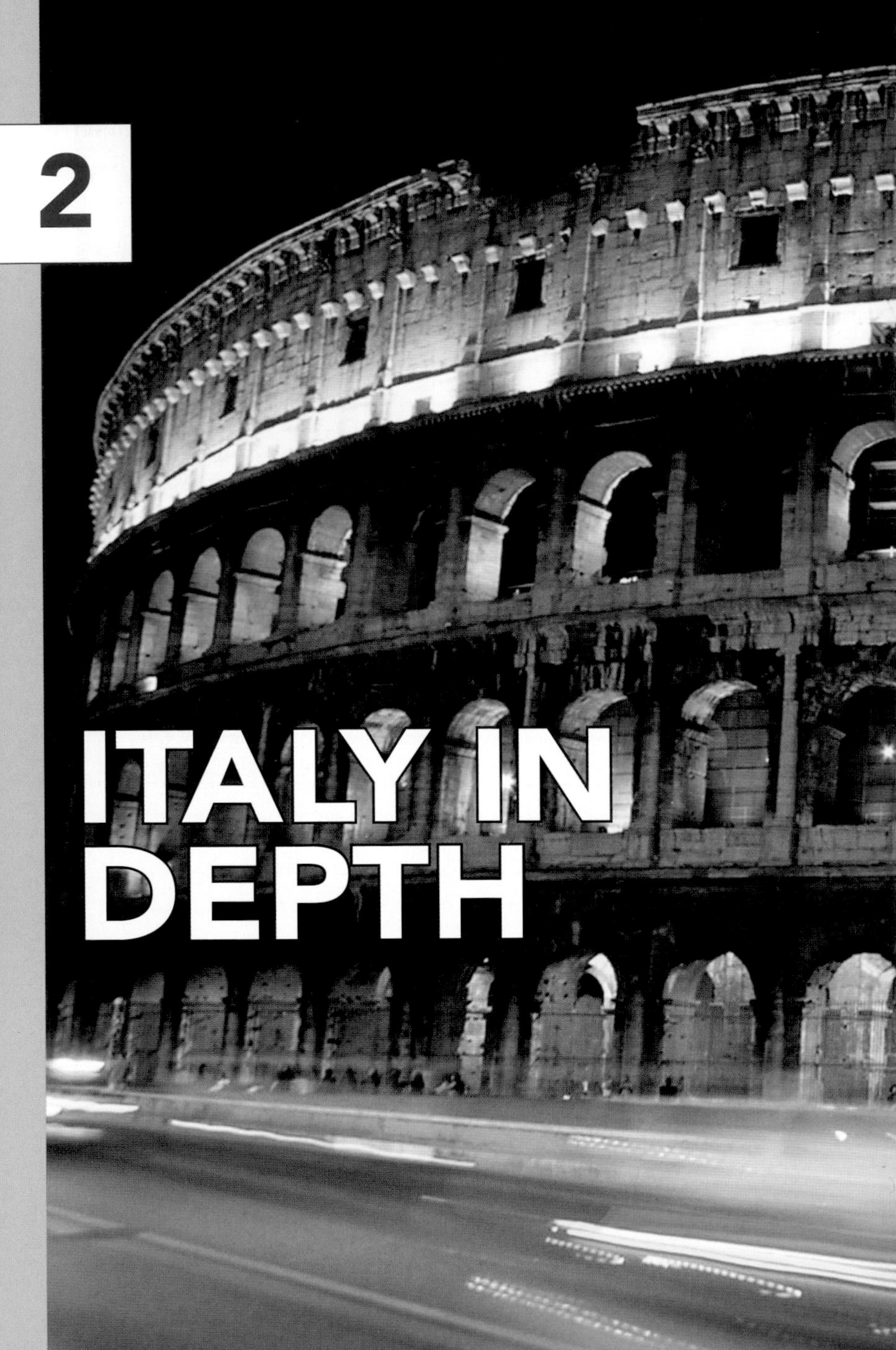

ITALY IN DEPTH

As with any destination, a little background reading can help you to understand more about Italy. It's a complex country, certainly, but not totally opaque. Many of the stereotypes are accurate—children are feted wherever they go, food is almost a religion, the north–south divide is real, officialdom and bureaucracy are part of daily life. Some are wide of the mark—not every Italian you meet will be open and effusive. Occasionally they do taciturn pretty well, too.

The most important thing to remember is that, for a country with so much history—three millennia and counting—Italy has only a short history *as a country.* Only in 2011 did it celebrate its 150th birthday. Prior to 1861, the map of the peninsula was in constant flux. War, alliance, invasion, and disputed successions caused that map to change color as often as a chameleon crossing a field of wildflowers. Republics, minimonarchies, client states, papal states, and city-states, as well as Islamic emirates, colonies, dukedoms, and Christian theocracies, roll onto and out of the pages of Italian history with regularity. The island of Sicily is, perhaps, the most invaded and occupied lump of rock on the planet—and as a visitor, you can enjoy the legacy of that history. In some regions, you'll hear languages and dialects other than Italian spoken everywhere. It's often part of an identity that is as regional as it is national.

This confusing history explains why your Italian experience will differ wildly if you visit, say, Naples rather than Venice. (And why you should visit both, if you can.) The architecture is different; the food is different; the important historical figures are different, as are often the local issues of the day. And the people are different. More than just geography, climate, and a 12-hour train ride separate the Valle d'Aosta, in the northwest, from Puglia, the heel of Italy's boot. And while the north–south schism is the divide most often written about, cities as close together as Lucca and Pisa can feel very dissimilar. This chapter should help you understand why.

ITALY TODAY

As in most of the Western world, the recent global financial crisis—known here simply as the *crisi*—had a disastrous effect on Italy's economy, causing the deepest recession since World War II. Public debt had grown to alarming levels—as high as 1,900 billion euros—and for a decade economic growth has been slow. As a result, late 2011 and 2012 saw Italy pitched into the center of a dramatic European currency crisis, which almost brought on the collapse of the euro. It still might. Once one of the world's strongest economies and a European Union powerhouse, Italy now seems to live on the verge of financial meltdown.

It's no coincidence, then, that the same period saw the third, and perhaps final, end of a government led by right-wing media magnate Silvio Berlusconi.

PREVIOUS PAGE: **Rome's Colosseum.**

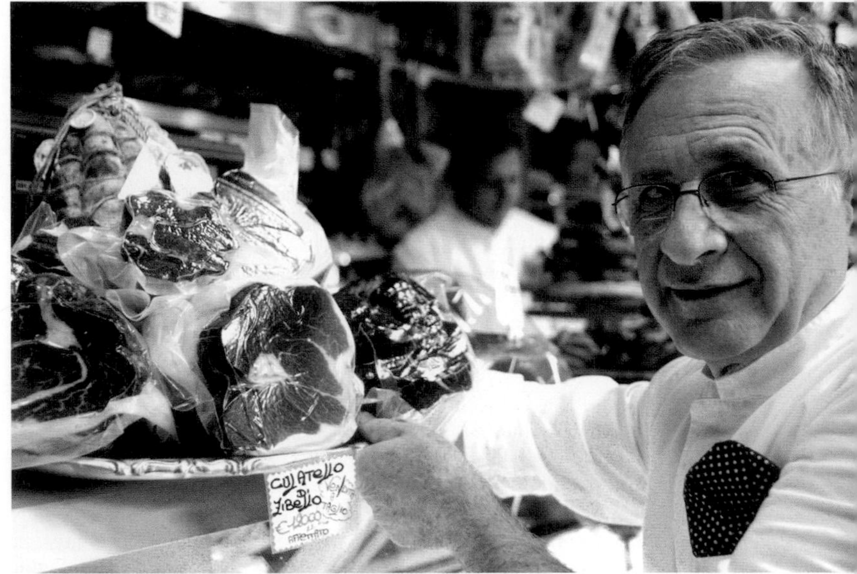

A Roman deli.

Italians seemed ready to forgive his "relaxed" attitude to corporate law, to overlook the occasional sex scandal, but leading them to the point of financial ruin was one blunder too far. Late 2011 saw the installation of a government of independent technocrats led by economist and former university professor Mario Monti. The prescribed economic medicine, dubbed *"La Manovra,"* hasn't been universally popular—car fuel is now the most expensive in Europe, and wholesale tax evasion among the super-rich has become a hot issue as the country seeks to balance the books. Every level of Italian government, from *comune* (local community), through *provincia* (province) and *regione* (region), to *lo stato* (the central state) has felt the pinch. Meanwhile, Berlusconi hasn't gone away completely, and continues to chip in from the sidelines.

Italy's population is declining, with its birthrate of around 9.1 per 1,000 people insufficient to keep pace with a death rate of 9.9 per 1,000. The population is also aging, and a youth vacuum is being filled by immigrants, especially those from Eastern Europe, notably Romania (whose language is similar to Italian) and Albania, as well as from North Africa. Italy doesn't have the colonial experience of Britain and France, or the "melting pot" history of the New World; tensions were inevitable, and discrimination is a daily fact of life for many minorities. The 2011 shooting of five Senegalese market traders by a Florentine far-right extremist is just one sign of a deeper malaise.

A "brain drain" continues to push young Italians to seek opportunities abroad. The problem is especially bad in rural communities and on the islands, where the old maxim, "it's not what you know, it's who you know" applies more strongly than ever in these straitened times.

Despite turmoil below the surface, however, the rituals of daily life persist almost unscathed. Family bonds and civic pride are as strong as ever, and chain stores remain the exception rather than the rule in many a *centro storico*. As the evening bells strike 7, locals gather in piazza cafes for an *aperitivo*—perhaps a vermouth in Piedmont, where it was invented, or a Campari and soda in Milan, or an Aperol spritz in the Veneto. Dinner begins with antipasti, starter plates, before moving on to *primo* ("first," usually a pasta or risotto dish), *secondo* ("second," often meat or fish served with a *contorno,* or side, on request), and finally *dolce,* a dessert. You're not obliged to eat all four, obviously, and at lunch few locals do, preferring a sandwich or value *menu del lavoro* (a worker's set-price lunch).

Pop culture remains a mix of the parochial and the international. The music charts still feature stalwarts like rapper Jovanotti and pop-rocker Laura Pausini—although thanks to online streaming services like Spotify (www.spotify.com) and Soundtracker (www.soundtracker.fm), started in 2010 by two Italian entrepreneurs, outsiders have easier access to Italian music. Prime-time TV centers around *calcio* (soccer) and global phenomena like *The X Factor.* The beautiful people still cherish upscale Italian fashion and sharp design; the Vespa rules on the city streets. Young Italians remain as attached as ever to their graffiti, and its subject matter hasn't changed for decades. So-and-so *"ti amo,"* the mayor is a *fascista* or *comunista,* and inhabitants of the rival town are . . . something completely unrepeatable. *Campanilismo*—literally, loyalty to one's bell tower—is as strong as ever.

One gastronomic trend to watch out for as you travel is the growth in popularity of artisanal beer, especially among the young. Although supermarket shelves are still stacked with mainstream brands Peroni and Moretti, smaller stores and bars increasingly offer craft microbrews. Italy had fewer than 50 breweries in

Vespas are ubiquitous in major Italian cities.

cuisine AROUND THE COUNTRY

Italians know how to cook—just ask one. But be sure to leave plenty of time: Once an Italian starts talking food, it's a while before he or she pauses for breath. Italy doesn't really have a unified, national cuisine; it's more a loose grouping of regional cuisines that share a few staples, notably pasta, bread, tomatoes, and pig meat cured in many ways. **Rome** can be the best place to introduce yourself to Italian food, because it boasts restaurants from every region. Throughout a Roman holiday, you'll also encounter authentic local specialties such as *saltimbocca alla romana* (literally "jump-in-your-mouth"—thin slices of veal with sage, cured ham, and cheese), *fritto alla romana* (a mixed fry likely to include everything from brains to artichokes), *carciofi alla romana* (tender artichokes cooked with herbs such as mint and garlic), and a dish that's become ubiquitous, *spaghetti alla carbonara*—pasta coated in a white sauce of pancetta (smoked, cured ham), egg, and *pecorino romano* (a hard ewe's milk cheese).

To the north, in **Tuscany,** you'll find seasonal ingredients served simply; it's almost the antithesis of "French" cooking, with its multiple processes. The main ingredient for almost any savory dish is the local olive oil, adored for its low acidity. Olives here are handpicked off the trees so that they don't get bruised (ensuring lower acidity and milder aroma). The typical Tuscan pasta is wide, flat *pappardelle,* generally tossed with a game sauce such as *lepre* (hare) or *cinghiale* (boar). Tuscans are fond of their own strong ewe's milk cheese, pecorino, made most famously around the Val d'Orcia town of Pienza. Meat is usually the centerpiece of any *secondo:* a *bistecca alla fiorentina* is the classic main dish, a T-bone-like wedge of meat. An authentic *fiorentina* should be cut only from the white Chianina breed of cattle. Sweet treats are also good here, particularly Siena's *panforte* (a dense, sticky cake), *biscotti di Prato* (also known as *cantuccini,* hard, almond-flour biscuits for dipping in dessert wine), and the *miele* (honey) of Montalcino.

Venice is rarely celebrated for its cuisine. Fresh seafood is usually excellent, however, and figures heavily in the Venetian diet. Grilled fish is often served with the red radicchio, a bitter lettuce that grows best in nearby Treviso. Two typical nonfish dishes are *fegato alla veneziana* (liver and onions) and *risi e bisi* (rice and fresh peas).

On the plains of **Piedmont** and **Lombardy,** the cooking is more refined. No dish is more famous than *cotoletta alla milanese* (veal dipped in egg and bread crumbs and fried in olive oil)—the Germans call it Wiener schnitzel. *Osso buco* is the other famous Lombard dish; this is shin of veal cooked in a ragout sauce. Turin's classic dish is *bagna càuda*—literally "hot bath" in the Piedmontese language, a sauce made with olive oil, garlic, butter, and anchovies, into which you dip raw vegetables. Piedmont is also the spiritual home of risotto, particularly the town of Vercelli, which is surrounded by rice paddies.

Farther north, food in the **Valle d'Aosta** is different from that in the rest of Italy—a hearty, mountain cuisine based around strong Fontina cheese and stews of game, often *cervo* (deer), served with polenta (a cornmeal mush). A typical starter might be *crespelle alla valdostana* (thin pancakes served in a sizzling béchamel sauce with Fontina and cooked ham). In another mountain region, the **Trentino–Alto Adige,** the cooking is influenced by the traditions of Austrian and Germanic kitchens. **South Tyrol** used to belong to Austria, and here you find tasty strudel pastries. The same is true of **Friuli,** where you'll also be served one of Italy's best cured hams, *prosciutto di San Daniele*.

Liguria turns to the sea for its inspiration, as reflected by its version of bouillabaisse, a *burrida* flavored with spices that's also popular in **Sardinia.** But its most famous food item is pesto, a paste-sauce made with fresh basil, garlic, hard cheese, and crushed pine nuts, which is used to dress pasta, fish, and many other dishes.

Emilia-Romagna is the country's great gastronomic center. Rich in produce, its school of cooking first created many pastas now common around Italy: *tagliatelle, tortellini,* and *cappelletti* (made in the shape of "little hats"). The best-known sausage of the area is mortadella, and equally famous is a *cotoletta alla bolognese* (veal cutlet fried with a slice of ham or bacon). The distinctive and famous cheese Parmigiano-Reggiano is a product of Parma and Reggio Emilia. *Zampone* (stuffed pig's foot) is a specialty of Modena. Parma is also known for its ham, which is fashioned into air-cured *prosciutto di Parma*. Served in paper-thin slices, it's deliciously sweet.

Much of the cookery of **Campania**—including spaghetti with clam sauce and pizza—is very familiar to North Americans, because so many Neapolitans moved to the New World and opened restaurants. Mozzarella is the classic local cheese, the best of it *mozzarella di bufala,* made with milk of buffalo, a species first introduced to Campania from Asia in the Middle Ages. Mixed fish fries (a *fritto misto*) are a staple of nearly every lunch table, both here and in **Puglia.** The latter was a poor agricultural region for centuries, and its cooking centers around the simple yet delicious pleasures of fine durum wheat pasta and specialties like *burrata,* a creamy cheese. By the coast, the catch of the day, prepared simply, is divine.

Sicily has a distinctive cuisine, with strong flavors and aromatic sauces. One staple primo is *maccheroni con le sarde* (pasta with pine nuts, fennel, spices, chopped sardines, and olive oil). In fact, fish is good and fresh pretty much everywhere (try local swordfish). The desserts and homemade pastries are excellent, including cannoli, cylindrical pastry cases stuffed with ricotta and candied fruit (or chocolate). Sicilian gelato is among the best in Italy.

If you want to cook Italian dishes at home, your best buy is *The Silver Spoon,* the bible of Italian cooking which was for decades a traditional wedding present for a new wife. You'll find all our favorite eating spots in the chapters that follow, but anyone who reads Italian and is planning a foodie trip around the country should also seek out the annual *Osterie d'Italia* or *Mangiarozzo* dining guides. They're widely available in Italian bookshops.

Books for Getting Acquainted with Italy and the Italians

A little in-flight reading before you land will enhance your visit. There have been many books written in English about the country and its people: Where to begin? It's anecdotal and broad-brush, certainly, but Luigi Barzini's *The Italians* (1964) remains the most readable introduction to the "national character," if such a thing really exists. For an outsider's view, the books of expat Brit Tim Parks are hard to beat for humor and razor-sharp insight. His *A Season with Verona* (2002) recounts a year following the local soccer team around the country, but is about way more than sport. In fact, the sport plays sidekick to Parks's finely tuned people-watching. The best recent history book is Dan Gilmour's *The Pursuit of Italy* (2011)—it's scholarly but totally readable.

2000. By 2011, that figure was 385, and rising fast. You'll even find quality beers on the hallowed shelves of the occasional enoteca.

It's not all doom and gloom on the political front, either. Among the young, social media tools like Twitter and Facebook have helped chase away the political apathy that has been entrenched for decades. A 2011 opposition proposal to halt Italy's nuclear fuel program triumphed in a referendum, thanks largely to online activism. It was the first time since 1995 that the legal threshold of 50% to make a referendum binding had been surpassed. *"Italiani pazzi per Twitter,"* a headline in Rome daily *La Repubblica* hollered.

THE MAKING OF ITALY

Etruscans & Latins: From Prehistory to the Rise of Rome

Of all the early inhabitants of Italy, the most significant legacy was left by the **Etruscans.** No one knows exactly where they came from, and the inscriptions that they left behind (often on graves in necropoli) are of little help—the Etruscan language has never been fully deciphered by scholars. It's thought they first appeared by the eastern coast of central Italy several centuries before Rome was built, around 800 B.C. Their religious rites and architecture show traces of contact with Mesopotamia; the Etruscans might have been refugees from Asia Minor who traveled west about 1200 to 1000 B.C.—this was the theory suggested by Greek historian Herodotus in his *Histories.* Whatever their origins, within 2 centuries, they had subjugated the lands now known as **Tuscany** (to which they left their name) and Campania, along with the **Villanovan** tribes that lived there.

It was the Etruscans who brought the first truly impressive art and architecture to mainland Italy, although the **Greeks** had left behind some monuments, notably the **Valley of the Temples** at Agrigento, Sicily (p. 857), and **Paestum,** in Campania (p. 786). However, while the Etruscans were building at **Tarquinia** (p. 187) and Caere (present-day **Cerveteri;** p. 187), the few nervous Latin tribes that remained outside their sway were gravitating to **Rome,** then little more than a village of sheepherders.

From their base at Rome, the Latins remained free of the Etruscans until about 600 B.C. As Rome's power grew, it increasingly profited from the strategically important Tiber crossing, where the ancient salt road (Via Salaria) turned northeastward toward the central Apennines. But the Etruscan advance was unstoppable, and although the Latin tribes concentrated their forces at Rome for a last stand, they were swept away by sophisticated conquerors. The new overlords introduced gold tableware and jewelry, bronze urns, and terracotta statuary, and the art and culture of Greece and Asia Minor. They also made Rome the governmental seat of Latium. "Roma" is an Etruscan name, and the ancient kings of Rome had Etruscan names: Numa, Ancus, Tarquinius, and even Romulus.

The Etruscans ruled until the **Roman revolt** around 510 B.C., and by 250 B.C. the Romans and their allies had vanquished or assimilated the Etruscans, wiping out their language and religion. However, many of the former rulers' manners and beliefs remained, and became integral to what we now understand as "Roman culture."

The best places to see the legacy left by the mysterious Etruscans are in Cerveteri and Tarquinia, outside Rome. Especially interesting is the latter's **Etruscan Necropolis** (p. 188), where thousands of tombs have been discovered. Central Italy preserves many sites and museum pieces that help visitors understand the Etruscan civilization. The Etruscan collection in Rome's **Vatican Museums** (p. 95) is a logical start point. There are further significant museums in **Orvieto** (p. 356) and **Volterra** (p. 300). As well as a collection strong on alabaster cinerary urns, Volterra has one surviving Etruscan town gate, the **Porta all'Arco** (p. 304). Florence's **Museo Archeologico** (p. 218) houses one of the greatest Etruscan bronzes yet unearthed, the *Arezzo Chimera*.

An Etruscan painting at the Tomb of the Panthers in Tarquinia.

The Roman Republic: ca. 510–27 B.C.

After the Roman Republic was established around 510 B.C., the Romans continued to increase their power by conquering neighboring communities in the highlands and forming alliances with other Latins in the lowlands. They gave to their allies, and then to conquered peoples, partial or complete Roman citizenship, with the obligation of military service. Citizen colonies were set up as settlements of Roman farmers, and many of the most famous cities of Italy originated as colonies—including both **Florence** and **Siena.** For the most part, these colonies were fortified and linked to Rome by military roads.

The stern Roman Republic was characterized by a belief in the gods, the necessity of learning from the past, the strength of the family, education through reading books and performing public service, and, most important, obedience. The all-powerful Senate presided as Rome defeated rival powers one after the other and came to rule the Mediterranean. The Punic Wars with **Carthage** (in modern-day Tunisia) in the 3rd century B.C. cleared away a major obstacle, although it wasn't all plain sailing for the Republic. Carthaginian general **Hannibal** (247–182 B.C.) conducted a devastating campaign across the Italian peninsula, crossing the Alps with his elephants into what's now the **Valle d'Aosta** (p. 649) and winning bloody battles by the shore of Lago Trasimeno, in Umbria, and at Cannae, in Puglia. Rome eventually prevailed in a war of attrition, but people said later that Rome's breaking of its treaty with Carthage (which led to that city's total destruction) put a curse on Rome.

No figure was more towering during the late Republic, or more instrumental in its transformation into the Empire (see below), than **Julius Caesar,** the charismatic conqueror of Gaul—"the wife of every husband and the husband of every wife." After defeating the last resistance of the Pompeians in 45 B.C., he came to Rome and was made dictator and consul for 10 years. Conspirators, led by Marcus Junius Brutus, stabbed him to death in the Senate on March 15, 44 B.C., the "Ides of March."

The view from Rome's Capitoline Hill.

Their motivation was to restore the power of the Republic, and topple dictatorship. But it failed: **Mark Antony,** a Roman general, assumed control. Intent on expansion, Antony met with the Egyptian queen, Cleopatra, at Tarsus in 41 B.C. She seduced him, and he stayed in Egypt for a year. When Antony eventually returned to Rome, still smitten with Cleopatra, he made peace with Caesar's willed successor, **Octavian,** and, after the Treaty of Brundisium which dissolved the Republic, found himself married to Octavian's sister, Octavia. This marriage, however, didn't prevent him from

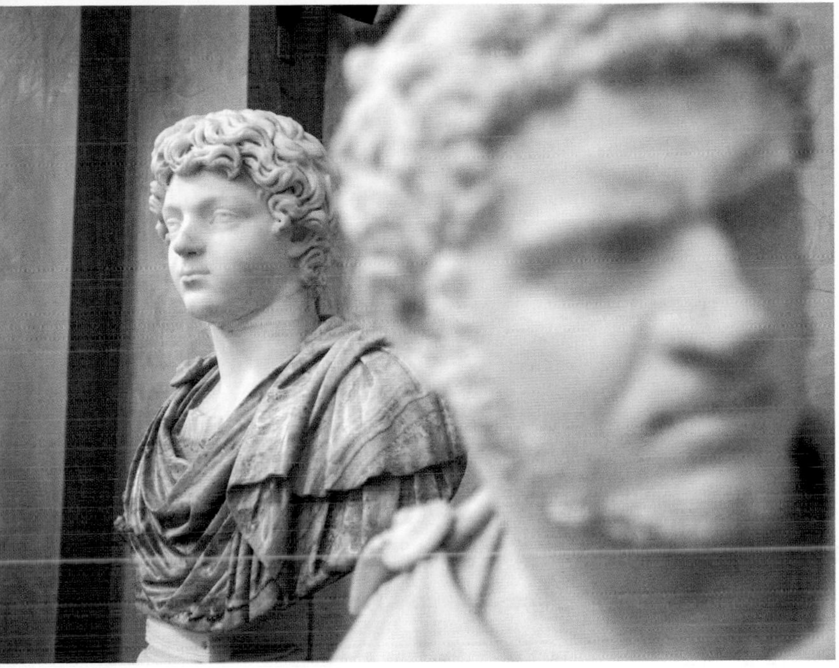

Roman bust.

marrying Cleopatra in 36 B.C. The furious Octavian gathered western legions and defeated Antony at the **Battle of Actium** on September 2, 31 B.C. Cleopatra fled to Egypt, followed by Antony, who committed suicide in disgrace a year later. Cleopatra, unable to seduce his successor and thus retain her rule of Egypt, followed suit with the help of an asp. The permanent end of the Republic was nigh.

Many of the standing buildings of ancient Rome date to periods after the Republic, but standing parts of the **Roman Forum** (p. 106) date from the Republic, including the **Temple of Saturn** and **Temple of Julius Caesar.** The adjacent **Capitoline Hill** and **Palatine Hill** have been sacred religious and civic places since the earliest days of Rome. Rome's best artifacts from the days of the Republic are housed inside the **Capitoline Museums** (p. 100). The greatest exponent of political oratory in the period was **Marcus Tullius Cicero** (106–43 B.C.), who wrote widely on philosophy and statesmanship, and was killed after expressing outspoken opposition to Mark Antony in his *Philippics.* The Republic's most prominent poet was **Catullus** (84–54 B.C.).

The Roman Empire in Its Pomp: 27 B.C.–A.D. 395

Born Gaius Octavius in 63 B.C., and later known as Octavian, **Augustus** became the first Roman emperor in 27 B.C. and reigned until A.D. 14. His autocratic reign, called "the golden age of Rome," ushered in the Pax Romana, 2 centuries of peace. He had been adopted by, and eventually became the heir of, his great-uncle Julius Caesar. In Rome you can still visit the remains of the **Forum of Augustus** (p. 104) and see his statue in the **Vatican Museums** (p. 95).

By now, Rome ruled the entire Mediterranean world, either directly or indirectly, because all political, commercial, and cultural pathways led straight to Rome, the sprawling city set on seven hills. On the eve of the birth of Christ, Rome was a mighty empire whose generals had brought the Western world under the sway of Roman law and civilization. It was in this period that **Virgil** wrote his best-loved epic poem, *The Aeneid,* which supplied a grandiose founding myth for the great city and empire; **Ovid** composed his erotic poetry; and **Horace** wrote his *Odes.*

The emperors, whose succession started with Augustus's principate, brought Rome to new heights. Augustus transformed the city from brick to marble, much the way Napoleon III transformed Paris many centuries later. But, shorn of the countervailing power of the Senate and legislatures of the Republican era, success led to corruption. The emperors wielded autocratic power, and the centuries witnessed a steady decay in the ideals and traditions on which the Empire had been founded. The army became a fifth column of barbarian mercenaries, the tax collector became the scourge of the countryside, and for every good emperor (Augustus, Claudius, Trajan, Vespasian, and Hadrian, to name a few) there were three or four debased heads of state (Caligula, Nero, Caracalla, and others).

After Augustus died (by poison, perhaps), his widow, **Livia**—a crafty social climber who had divorced her first husband to marry Augustus—set up her son, **Tiberius,** as ruler through a number of intrigues and poisonings. A long series of murders ensued, and Tiberius, who ruled during Pontius Pilate's trial and crucifixion of Christ, was eventually murdered in an uprising of landowners. In fact, murder was so common that a short time later, **Domitian** (A.D. 81–96) became so obsessed with the possibility of assassination that he had the walls of his palace covered in mica so that he could see behind him at all times. (He was killed anyway.)

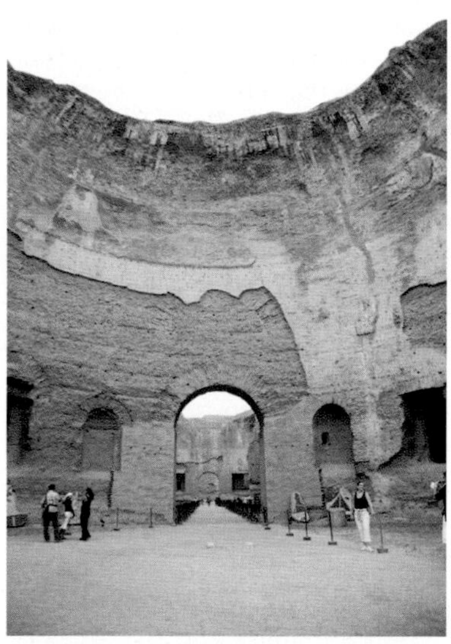
The Baths of Caracalla in Rome.

Excesses and scandal ruled the day—at least, if you believe surviving tracts written by contemporary chroniclers infused with all kinds of bias: **Caligula** supposedly committed incest with his sister, Drusilla, appointed his horse a lifetime member of the Senate, lavished money on foolish projects, and proclaimed himself a god. Caligula's successor, his uncle **Claudius,** was deceived and publicly humiliated by one of his wives, the lascivious Messalina (he had her killed for her trouble); he was then poisoned by his final wife, his niece Agrippina, to secure the succession of **Nero,** her son by a previous marriage. Nero's thanks were later to murder not only his mother but also his wife, Claudius's daughter, and his rival, Claudius's son. The disgraceful Nero, an enthusiastic persecutor of Christians, committed suicide with the cry, "What an artist I destroy!" Robert Graves's novels *I, Claudius* (1934) and *Claudius the God* (1935)—later made into an award-winning BBC TV miniseries that is still available on DVD—paint an entertaining picture of the intrigues of this era.

By the 3rd century A.D., corruption had become so prevalent there were 23 emperors in 73 years. Few, however, were as twisted and debased as **Caracalla** who, to secure control of the Empire, had his brother Geta slashed to pieces while Geta was lying in his mother's arms. (Rome's **Baths of Caracalla,** p. 100, were built during his reign.) Rule of the Empire changed hands so frequently that news of the election of a new emperor commonly reached the provinces together with a report of that emperor's assassination.

The 4th-century reforms of **Diocletian** held the Empire together—just about. He reinforced imperial power while paradoxically weakening Roman dominance and prestige by dividing the Empire into Eastern and Western halves, and establishing administrative capitals at outposts such as Milan and Trier, Germany. He instituted not only heavy taxes but also a socioeconomic system that made professions hereditary. This edict was so strictly enforced that the son of a silversmith could be tried as a criminal if he attempted to become a sculptor instead.

Constantine the Great became emperor in A.D. 306, and in 330, he made Constantinople (or Byzantium) the new capital of the Empire, moving the administrative functions away from Rome altogether, partly because the menace of possible barbarian attacks in the west had increased greatly. Constantine was the first Christian emperor, allegedly converting after he saw the True Cross in a dream, accompanied by the legend IN THIS SIGN SHALL YOU CONQUER. He quickly defeated rival emperor Maxentius and his followers at the **Battle of the Milivan Bridge** (A.D. 312), a scene that's illustrated in Piero della Francesca's 15th-century *Legend of the True Cross* frescoes, in **Arezzo** (p. 324).

It was during the Imperial period that Rome flourished magnificently in architecture, advancing in size and majesty far beyond earlier examples set by the Greeks. (The finest surviving examples of Hellenistic art and architecture are to be found on **Sicily** and in Rome's **Vatican Museums.**) **Classical orders** were simplified into types of column capitals, with the least ornate used on a building's ground level and the most ornate used on the top: **Doric** (a plain capital), **Ionic** (a capital with a scroll), and **Corinthian** (a capital with flowering acanthus leaves). Much of this development in building prowess was because of the discovery of a primitive form of concrete and the fine-tuning of the arch, which was used with a logic, rhythm, and ease never before seen. Monumental buildings were erected, each an embodiment of the strength, power, and organization of the Empire itself. Some of the best examples still stand in Rome, notably **Trajan's Forum** (p. 105), the **Colosseum** (p. 103), and Hadrian's **Pantheon** (p. 112), among many others. Elsewhere in Italy, Verona's **Arena** (p. 524) bears witness to the kinds of crowds that the brutal sport of gladiatorial combat could draw—Ridley Scott's 2000 Oscar-winning movie *Gladiator* isn't all fiction. Spoleto's **Casa Romana** (p. 350) and Sicily's **Villa Romana del Casale** (p. 854) provide insights into domestic Roman architecture, the latter with especially memorable **mosaic** work. Three **Roman cities** have been preserved, with street plans and, in some cases, even buildings remaining intact: doomed **Pompeii** (p. 735) and its neighbor **Herculaneum** (p. 733), both buried by Vesuvius's massive A.D. 79 eruption, and Rome's ancient seaport, **Ostia Antica** (p. 184). It was at Herculaneum that one of Rome's greatest writers perished, **Pliny the Elder** (A.D. 23–79). It's thanks to him, his nephew, **Pliny the Younger,** the historians **Tacitus** and **Livy,** and satirist **Juvenal** that much of our knowledge of ancient Roman life and history was not lost.

A plaster cast, meant to show what one of the victims at Pompeii may have looked like.

Much of the surviving Roman **art** had a major influence on the painters and sculptors of the Renaissance (see below). In Rome itself, look for the marble bas-reliefs (sculptures that project slightly from a flat surface) on the **Arch of Casa Romana Constantine** (p. 103), the sculpture and mosaic collections at the **Museo Nazionale Romano** (p. 110), and the gilded equestrian statue of Marcus Aurelius at the **Capitoline Museums** (p. 100). The Florentine Medici were avid collectors of Roman statuary, some of it now displayed in the corridors of the **Uffizi** (p. 206). Southern Italy's best museum for seekers of the ancients is Naples's **Museo Archeologico Nazionale** (p. 710).

To read more (*much* more) about this period, Edward Gibbon's 1776 *The History of the Decline and Fall of the Roman Empire* is published in six volumes, but Penguin issues a manageable abridgement. It deserves its reputation as one of the greatest histories ever written.

The Fall of the Empire, Byzantine Italy & the "Dark Ages"

The Eastern and Western sections of the Roman Empire split in A.D. 395, leaving the Italian peninsula without the support it had once received from east of the Adriatic. When the **Goths** moved toward Rome in the early 5th century, citizens in the provinces, who had grown to hate the bureaucracy set up by Diocletian and followed by succeeding emperors, welcomed the invaders. And then the pillage began.

Rome was first sacked by **Alaric I,** king of the Visigoths, in 410. The populace made no attempt to defend the city (other than trying vainly to buy him off, a tactic that had worked 3 years earlier); most people fled into the hills, or headed to their country estates if they were rich. The feeble Western emperor **Honorius** hid out in **Ravenna** the entire time, which from 402 he had made the new capital of the Western Roman Empire. The mausoleum of his sister, **Galla Placidia** (p. 404), remains a highlight of any visit to Ravenna.

More than 40 troubled years passed. Then **Attila the Hun** invaded Italy to besiege Rome. Attila was dissuaded from attacking, thanks largely to a peace mission headed by Pope Leo I in 452. Yet relief was short-lived: In 455, **Gaiseric,** king of the Vandals, carried out a 2-week sack that was unparalleled in its savagery. The empire of the West lasted for only another 20 years; finally, in 476, the sacks and chaos ended the once-mighty city, and Rome itself was left to the popes, though ruled nominally from Ravenna by an Exarch from Byzantium (aka Constantinople).

The last would-be Caesars to walk the streets of Rome were both "barbarians": The first was **Theodoric,** who established an Ostrogoth kingdom at Ravenna from 493 to 526; the second was Totilla, who held the last chariot races in Rome's **Circus Maximus** (p. 102) in 549. Totilla was engaged in an ongoing battle with Belisarius, the general of the Eastern emperor Justinian, who sought to regain Rome for the Eastern empire. The city changed hands several times, recovering some of its ancient pride by resisting Totilla's forces, but eventually it was entirely depopulated by the continuing battles. Much of the northern part of the peninsula was from the 560s ruled from **Pavia** by the **Lombards** whose name was supposedly an ancient corruption of "long beards," and was subsequently bequeathed to the northern Italian region of Lombardy, whose principal city is Milan.

Although little of the detailed history of Italy in this period is known and few buildings survive—it's certain that the spread of **Christianity** was gradually creating a new society. The religion was probably founded in Rome about a decade after the death of Jesus, and gradually gained strength despite early (and enthusiastic) persecution by the Romans. It was accepted as the official religion during the 4th-century reign of Constantine the Great (see above). The best way today to relive the early Christian era is to visit Rome's Appian Way and its Catacombs, along **Via Appia Antica** (p. 121), built in 312 B.C. According to Christian tradition, it was here that an escaping Peter encountered the vision of Christ. The **Catacombs of Callixtus** (p. 122) form the first cemetery of the Christian community of Rome, and once housed the remains of early popes and martyrs.

We have Christianity, along with the influence of Byzantium, to thank for the appearance of Italy's next great artistic style: the **Byzantine.** Painting and mosaic work in this era was very stylized and static, but also ornate and ethereal. Faces (and eyes) were almond shaped with pointy little chins; noses were long, with a spoonlike depression at the top; and folds in robes (always blue over red) were represented by stylized crosshatching in gold leaf. The most accomplished examples of Byzantine art are found in the churches of **Ravenna,** reflecting its status as the premier outpost of Byzantium on the Italian peninsula. The mosaics of the **Basilica di San Vitale** (p. 403) honor Byzantine Emperor Justinian I (483–565) and his wife, Theodora. Later churches in the Byzantine style include Venice's **Basilica di San Marco** (p. 439) and the 12th-century **Cappella Palatina** (p. 871) in Palermo, Sicily.

The Middle Ages: From the 9th Century to the 14th Century

A ravaged Rome entered the Middle Ages, its once-proud people scattered and unrecognizable in rustic exile. A modest population started life again in the swamps of the **Campus Martius,** while the seven hills, now without water because the aqueducts were cut, stood abandoned and crumbling.

The pope turned toward Europe, where he found a powerful ally in **Charlemagne,** king of the Franks. In 800, he was crowned emperor by Pope Leo III. Although Charlemagne pledged allegiance to the church and looked to Rome and its pope as the final arbiter in most religious and cultural affairs, he launched northwestern Europe on a course toward bitter opposition to the meddling of the papacy in temporal affairs.

The successor to Charlemagne's empire was a political entity known as the **Holy Roman Empire** (962–1806). The new Empire defined the end of the Dark Ages but ushered in a long period of bloody warfare. The Lombard League battled the Franks, defeating them at the **Battle of Legnano** (1176). Magyars from Hungary invaded northeastern Lombardy and, in turn, were defeated by an increasingly powerful **Venice.** This was the great era of Venetian preeminence in the eastern Mediterranean; it defeated naval rival Genoa in the 1380 Battle of Chioggia; its merchants reigned over most of the eastern Mediterranean, and presided over a Republic that lasted for a millennium; great buildings like the **Doge's Palace** (p. 447) were built; and the groundwork for the city's dominance of northeastern Italy was laid. You'll find the Lion of St. Mark, symbol of the city, lording it over piazzas from **Udine** to **Bergamo** (p. 592).

Normans gained military control of Sicily from the Arabs in the 11th century, divided it from the rest of Italy, and altered forever the island's racial and ethnic makeup. The reign of **Roger II of Sicily** (1130–54) is remembered for its religious tolerance and the multiethnic nature of the court—as well as its architecture. The **Palazzo dei Normanni** (p. 871), in Palermo, and nearby **Monreale** (p. 881) are just two among many great projects the Normans left behind. Italy had essentially dissolved into a fragmented, ever shifting collection of rival city-states, among them a fiefdom known as the **Papal States,** ruled by popes from Rome and covering present-day Latium, Umbria, the Marches, San Marino, and Romagna (the eastern half of Emilia-Romagna).

Rome during the Middle Ages was a quaint, rural town. Narrow lanes with overhanging buildings filled many areas that had once been showcases of imperial power. The forums, mercantile exchanges, temples, and theaters of the Imperial era slowly disintegrated and collapsed. (And not just in Rome: Lucca's **Piazza Anfiteatro,** remains as an outline where once stood the town's amphitheater, before its masonry was raided by church builders.) The decay of ancient Rome was assisted by periodic earthquakes, centuries of neglect, and the growing need for building materials. Rome receded into a dusty provincialism. As the seat of the Roman Catholic church, the state was almost completely controlled by priests, and began an aggressive expansion of church influence and acquisitions. The result was an endless series of power struggles.

The 1065 fall of the Holy Land to the Turks had catapulted the papacy into the forefront of world politics, primarily because of the **Crusades,** many of which the popes encouraged, but most of which were military and economic

Lucca's Piazza Anfiteatro.

disasters. During the 12th and 13th centuries, the bitter rivalries that rocked Europe's secular and spiritual bastions took their toll on the Holy Roman Empire, which grew weaker as city-states, buttressed by mercantile and trade-related prosperity, grew stronger and as France emerged as a potent nation in its own right. Conflict with France reached an impasse between 1305 and 1378, when the papacy moved to the French city of Avignon. Worse still, between 1378 and 1417, viciously competing popes—one in Rome, another **"antipope"** under the protection of French kings in Avignon—made simultaneous claims to the legacy of St. Peter.

In the mid–14th century, the **Black Death** ravaged Europe, killing perhaps a third of Italy's population, the unique preservation of Tuscan settlements like **San Gimignano** (p. 295) and **Siena** (p. 281) owes much to the fact that they never fully recovered after the devastation dished out by the 1348 plague. Despite such setbacks, the northern Italian city-states grew wealthy from Crusade booty, trade with one another and with the Middle East, and **banking.** These wealthy principalities and pseudo-republics ruled by merchant or noble elites flexed their muscles in the absence of any central authority. The south, meanwhile, was another country altogether: Nancy Goldstone's *The Lady Queen: The Notorious Reign of Joanna I, Queen of Naples, Jerusalem, and Sicily* (2009) entertainingly retells one extraordinary period. Italy at this time didn't exist.

The medieval period marks the beginning of building in stone on a mass scale. Flourishing from A.D. 800 to 1300, **Romanesque** architecture took its inspiration and rounded arches from ancient Rome. Its architects concentrated on building large churches with wide aisles to accommodate the masses. Modena's 12th century **Duomo** (p. 409) marks one of the earliest appearances of rounded arches, and its facade is covered with great Romanesque reliefs. Milan's **Basilica di Sant'Ambrogio** (p. 569) is festooned with the tiered loggias and arcades that became hallmarks of the Lombard Romanesque.

Pisa's **Piazza dei Miracoli** (1153–1360s; p. 316) is typical of the Pisan-Romanesque style, with stacked arcades of mismatched columns in the cathedral's facade (and wrapping around the famous **Leaning Tower of Pisa**), and blind arcading set with lozenges. The influence of Arab architecture is obvious—Pisa was a city of seafaring merchants. Nearby Lucca's **Cattedrale di San Martino** and **San Michele in Foro** (11th–14th c.) are two more examples of a local variant of the style.

Romanesque **sculpture** was fluid but still far from naturalistic. Often wonderfully childlike in its narrative simplicity, the work frequently mixes biblical scenes with the myths and motifs of local pagan traditions that were being incorporated into medieval Christianity. The 48 relief panels of the bronze doors of the **Basilica di San Zeno Maggiore** in Verona (p. 524) are among the greatest remaining examples of Romanesque sculpture in Italy, dating from the 9th to the 11th centuries. The exterior of Parma's **Baptistery** (p. 416) sports a series of Romanesque allegorical friezes, masterpieces by Benedetto Antelami (1150–1230).

As the appeal of Romanesque and the Byzantine faded, the **Gothic** style flourished from the 13th to the 15th centuries. In architecture, the Gothic was characterized by ceiling cross vaults, flying buttresses, pointed arches, and delicate stained-glass windows. These engineering developments freed architecture from the heavy, thick walls of the Romanesque and allowed ceilings to soar, walls to thin, and windows to proliferate. There's no better elaboration of what Gothic architecture is all about than Victorian critic John Ruskin's essay, *The Nature of Gothic* (1854)—it's freely available online.

The only truly French-style Gothic church in Italy is Milan's massive **Duomo** and **Baptistery** (p. 570), a lacy festival of pinnacles, buttresses, and pointy arches. Although the Gothic age continued to be religious, many secular buildings also arose, including an array of palazzos showing off the prestige and wealth of various ruling dynasties. Siena's civic **Palazzo Pubblico** (p. 283) and many of the great buildings of **Venice** (see chapter 8) date from this period. **San Gimignano** (p. 295), in Tuscany, has a uniquely preserved Gothic center.

Painters such as **Cimabue** (1251–1302) and **Giotto** (1266–1337), in Florence, and **Duccio di Buoninsegna** (ca. 1255–1319) in Siena, began to lift art from its Byzantine rigidity and set it on the road to realism. Giotto's finest work is his fresco cycle at Padua's **Cappella degli Scrovegni** (p. 511); he was the true harbinger of the oncoming Renaissance, which would forever change art and architecture. Duccio's 1311 *Maestà,* now in Siena's **Museo dell'Opera Metropolitana** (p. 290), influenced Sienese painters for centuries. Ambrogio Lorenzetti painted the greatest civic frescoes of the Middle Ages, his *Allegories of Good and Bad Government* in Siena's **Palazzo Pubblico** (p. 283), before he succumbed to the Black Death, along with almost every great Sienese artist of his generation. Tim Hyman's *Sienese Painting: The Art of a City Republic* (2003) is the best introduction in print.

The unfinished Gothic facade of the Basilica di San Petronio, Bologna.

The medieval period also saw the birth of literature in the Italian language—which itself was a written version of the **Tuscan dialect,** primarily because the great writers of the age were all Tuscans. Florentine **Dante Alighieri** wrote his *Divine Comedy* in the 1310s. Boccaccio's *Decameron*—kind of a Florentine *Canterbury Tales*—appeared in the 1350s. Aretine scholar **Petrarch** (1304–74) was Italy's founding father of humanism.

Renaissance & Baroque Italy: The 1400s to the 1700s

The story of Italy from the dawn of the Renaissance in the early 15th century to the Age of Enlightenment in the 17th and 18th centuries is as fascinating and complicated as that of the rise and fall of the Roman Empire. The seat of the papacy returned to Rome after the **Western Schism** (see above), where successive popes were every bit as interesting as the Roman emperors they had in effect replaced. The great Italian Renaissance families (the Barberini, Medici, Borgia, and Farnese) enhanced their status and fortunes impressively when one of their sons was elected pope. For a look at life during this tumultuous period, visit Rome's **Castel Sant'Angelo** (p. 99), which became a papal residence in the 14th century.

Despite the centuries that had passed since the collapse of the Roman Empire, the age of siege wasn't yet over. On one notorious occasion, in 1527, **Charles V, King of Spain,** carried out the worst sack Rome ever experienced. To the horror of Pope Clement VII (a Florentine of the Medici family), the entire city was brutally pillaged by the man who was to be crowned Holy Roman Emperor the next year. Three years later Charles and Clement together crushed republican resistance to the Empire and papacy in the **Siege of Florence** (1530).

During this period, **Rome** underwent major physical changes. The old centers of culture reverted to pastures and fields, and great churches and palaces were built with the stones of ancient Rome. This construction boom did more damage to the temples of the Caesars than any barbarian sack had done. Rare marbles were stripped from the imperial baths and used as altarpieces or sent to limekilns. So enthusiastic was the papal destruction of Imperial Rome that it's a miracle anything is left.

Rome was far from the only power in Italy. This was the height of the Venetian Republic's pomp. **Milan** was a glorious Renaissance capital, particularly under the Sforza dynasty and Ludovico "Il Moro" (1452–1508), patron of Leonardo da Vinci. Smaller but still significant centers of power included Gonzaga **Mantua** (p. 597), Este **Ferrara** (p. 393), and **Urbino,** in the Marches, especially under the stewardship of Federico da Montefeltro (1422–82).

This era is best remembered because of its art, however, and around 1400 the most significant power in Italy was the city where the Renaissance began: **Florence** (see chapter 5). Slowly but surely, the **Medici** family rose to become the most powerful of the city's ruling oligarchy, gradually usurping the powers of the guilds and the republicans. They reformed law and commerce, expanded the city's power by taking control of neighbors such as **Pisa,** and also sparked a "renaissance," a rebirth, in painting, sculpture, and architecture. Christopher Hibbert's *The Rise and Fall of the House of Medici* (2001) is the most readable historical account of the era.

Under the patronage of the Medici (as well as other powerful Florentine families), innovative young painters and sculptors broke with medieval traditions in pursuit of a greater degree of expressiveness and naturalism. **Donatello** (1386–1466) cast the first free-standing nude since antiquity (a bronze now in Florence's **Museo Nazionale del Bargello,** p. 210, along with others of his masterpieces). **Lorenzo Ghiberti** (1378–1455) labored for 50 years on two set of doors on Florence's **Baptistery** (p. 199), the most famous of which were dubbed the "Gates of Paradise." **Masaccio** (1401–28) produced the first painting that realistically portrayed linear perspective, on the nave wall of **Santa Maria Novella** (p. 216).

A close-up of Michelangelo's marble statue of David, in Florence.

Next followed the brief period that's become known as the **High Renaissance:** The epitome of the Renaissance man, Florentine **Leonardo da Vinci** (1452–1519), painted his *Last Supper,* in Milan's **Santa Maria delle Grazie** (p. 575), and an *Annunciation* (1481), now hanging in Florence's **Uffizi** (p. 206) alongside countless Renaissance masterpieces from such great painters as Paolo Uccello, Sandro Botticelli, and Piero della Francesca. **Raphael** (1483–1520) produced a sublime body of work in 37 short years: See his Madonnas and papal portraits in museums in Florence and Rome.

Skilled in sculpture, painting, and architecture, **Michelangelo** (1475–1564) and his career marked the apogee of the Renaissance. His giant *David* at

A detail of God giving life to Adam, from Michelangelo's ceiling of the Sistine Chapel in Rome.

the **Galleria dell'Accademia** (p. 217) in Florence is the world's most famous statue, and the **Sistine Chapel** frescoes have lured millions to the **Vatican Museums** (p. 95) in Rome. Michelangelo's life was novelized (and later made into a movie) by Irving Stone in *The Agony and the Ecstasy* (1961), which also offers insight into the Florentine politics of the day.

The father of the Venetian High Renaissance was **Titian** (1485–1576); known for his mastery of color and tonality, he was the true heir to great Venetian painters **Gentile Bellini** (1429–1507), **Giorgione** (1477–1510), and **Vittore Carpaccio** (1465–1525). Many of their masterpieces can be seen throughout **Venice** (see chapter 8).

As in painting, Renaissance architectural rules stressed proportion, order, classical inspiration, and mathematical precision to create unified, balanced structures. **Filippo Brunelleschi** (1377–1446), in the early 1400s, grasped the concept of "perspective" and provided artists with ground rules for creating the illusion of three dimensions on a flat surface. Ross King's *Brunelleschi's Dome* (2000) tells the story of his greatest achievement, the crowning of Florence's cathedral with that iconic ocher dome. Brunelleschi studied Rome's **Pantheon** (p. 112) to unlock the engineering secrets of its vast dome to build his own.

Michelangelo (1475–1564) took up architecture late in life, designing the Laurentian Library (1524) and New Sacristy (1524–34) at Florence's **Basilica di San Lorenzo**. He moved south (just as art's center of gravity did) to complete his crowning glory, the soaring dome of Rome's **St. Peter's Basilica** (p. 93).

The third great Renaissance architect—the most influential of them all—was **Andrea Palladio** (1508–80), who worked in a classical mode of columns, porticoes, pediments, and other ancient temple–inspired features. His masterpieces litter the streets of **Vicenza** (p. 516) and the surrounding countryside.

Whole libraries have been written on the Renaissance. The most accessible introductions include Peter and Linda Murray's *The Art of the Renaissance* (1963), Michael Levey's *Early Renaissance* (1967), and Evelyn Welch's *Art in Renaissance Italy 1350–1500* (2000)—it's certainly worth acquainting yourself with some of the themes and styles before you visit. Giorgio Vasari's *Lives of the Artists* was first published in 1550, and it remains the definitive work on the Renaissance artists—by one who knew some of them personally. It's also surprisingly readable. On the buildings, Peter Murray's *The Architecture of the Italian Renaissance* (1969) is a good read. In *The Stones of Florence* (1956), Mary McCarthy mixes architectural insight with no-holds-barred opinions.

In time, the High Renaissance stagnated, paving the way for the next great style: **baroque.** More than any previous movement, the baroque aimed toward a seamless meshing of architecture and art. Stuccoes, sculptures, and paintings were carefully designed to complement each other—and the space itself—to create a unified whole. It's spiritual home was Rome, and its towering figure was **Gian Lorenzo Bernini** (1598–1680), the greatest baroque sculptor, a fantastic architect, and no mean painter. Among many fine sculptures, you'll find his greatest in Rome's **Galleria Borghese** (p. 120). Though relatively sedate, Carlo Maderno's facade and Bernini's sweeping elliptical colonnade for Rome's **St. Peter's Square** make one of Italy's most famous baroque assemblages.

Outside the capital, one of the quirkiest baroque styles flourished in the churches of the Puglian city of **Lecce** (p. 808). **Siracusa** (p. 842) and **Ragusa**, in Sicily, are also fine, small baroque cities. In Turin, the stately baroque architecture of **Filippo Juvarra** (1678–1736), particularly his facade for the **Palazzo Madama** (p. 636) and hilltop **Basilica di Superga** (p. 632), contributes to the city's regal air.

In **music,** the baroque period is remembered fondly. The *Madrigals* of **Claudio Monteverdi** (1567–1643), who worked for the Gonzaga court at **Mantua** (p. 599), heralded the new style; his *Orfeo* is among the earliest operas ever written. Composer **Arcangelo Corelli** (1653–1713) was feted in Rome; his *Complete Works* are still widely available. Most famous of them all is Venetian **Antonio Vivaldi** (1678–1741), whose *Four Seasons* is among the most regularly performed classical compositions of all time.

In painting, the baroque offered a more theatrical and decorative take on the Renaissance, mixing a kind of super-realism based on using peasants as models and an exaggerated use of light and dark—a technique called chiaroscuro—with compositional complexity and explosions of dynamic fury, movement, color, and figures. The period produced many fine artists, but only a few true geniuses, most notably **Caravaggio** (1571–1610). Among his masterpieces are the *St. Matthew* (1599) cycle in Rome's **San Luigi dei Francesi**. The baroque also produced an outstanding female painter, in **Artemisia Gentileschi** (1593–1652): Check our her brutal *Judith Slaying Holofernes* (1620) in Florence's **Uffizi** (p. 206).

Frothy, ornate, and chaotic, **rococo** art was the baroque gone awry—and has few serious proponents in Italy. **Giambattista Tiepolo** (1696–1770) was arguably the best of the rococo painters, and specialized in ceiling frescoes and canvases with cloud-filled heavens of light, angels, and pale, early morning colors. He worked extensively in Venice and the Veneto, and left some seminal early works in **Udine**, in the far northeast. Roberto Calasso's *Tiepolo Pink* (2011) is the best recent book on the artist. For rococo building—more a decorative than architectural movement—look no further than Rome's **Spanish Steps** (p. 115) or the **Trevi Fountain** (p. 116).

At Last, a United Italy: The 1800s

By the 1800s, the glories of the Renaissance were already a fading memory. From Turin to Naples, chunks of Italy had changed hands many, many times—between the Austrians, the Spanish, and the French, among autocratic thugs and

Five English-Language Movies Set in Italy

- *The English Patient,* directed by Anthony Minghella (1996), set in various Italian locations, notably Sant'Anna in Camprena, just outside Pienza, Tuscany
- *Tea with Mussolini,* directed by Franco Zeffirelli (1999), set in Florence, San Gimignano, and Rome
- *A Room with a View,* directed by James Ivory (1985), set in Florence
- *The Talented Mr. Ripley,* directed by Anthony Minghella (1999), set in various coastal locations, including Ischia and Positano
- *Roman Holiday,* directed by William Wyler (1953), set in Rome

enlightened princes, between the noble and the merchant classes. The 19th century witnessed the final collapse of many of the Renaissance city-states. The last of the Medici, Gian Gastone, had died in 1737, leaving Tuscany in the hands of Lorraine and Habsburg princes. The Estes, dukes of Ferrara and Modena, were finally deposed in 1796, then later assimilated into a branch of the Habsburg family. The Visconti and Sforzas of Milan were long gone.

French emperor **Napoleon** made a bid for power in Italy beginning in 1796, fueling his war machines with what was a relatively easy victory. He brought an end to a millennium of Republic in **Venice** in 1797, and installed puppet or client rulers across the Italian peninsula. During the **Congress of Vienna** (1814–15), which followed Napoleon's defeat by an alliance of British, Prussians, and Dutch, Italy was once again divided among many factions: Austria was given a new kingdom of **Lombardy–Venetia,** and the Papal States were returned to the pope. Duchies including Parma were put back into the hands of former hereditary rulers; and southern Italy and Sicily, where Spain had held sway for centuries, went to a Bourbon dynasty, to be ruled from Naples as the **Kingdom of the Two Sicilies.** One historic move, which contributed to the later unification of Italy, was the gifting of the former republic of Genoa to Sardinia, which, at the time, was governed by **Piedmont** and its House of Savoy.

Political unrest became a fact of Italian life, some of it spurred by the industrialization of the north and some by the encouragement of energetic insurrectionaries like **Giuseppe Mazzini** (1805–72). Europe's year of revolutions, **1848,** rocked Italy, too, with violent risings in Lombardy and Sicily. After decades of political machinations and intrigue, and thanks to the brilliant efforts of statesman **Camillo Cavour** (1810–61) and rebel general **Giuseppe Garibaldi** (1807–82), the Kingdom of Italy was proclaimed in 1861 and **Victor Emmanuel (Vittorio Emanuele) II** of Savoy became its first monarch. Over 150 years later, the names still resonate as patriots—though whether they were patriots of Italy, or of an ambitious and expansionary kingdom of Piedmont, remains an open question. (The bloody Piedmontese **Sack of Genoa,** in 1849, suggests the latter was at least part of the story.)

Although the hope, promoted by Europe's theocrats and some of its devout Catholics, of attaining one empire ruled by the pope and the church had long faded, there was still a fight, followed by generations of hard feelings, when the Papal States were also confiscated by the new Italy. The kingdom's first capital was **Turin** (1861–65), seat of the victorious Piedmontese, followed by **Florence** (1865–71).

The establishment of the kingdom, however, didn't signal a complete unification of Italy because Latium (including Rome) was still under papal control and Venetia was held by Austria. This was partially resolved in 1866, when Venetia joined the rest of Italy after the **Seven Weeks' War** between Austria and Prussia. In 1871, Rome became the capital of the newly formed country, after the city was retaken on September 20, 1870. Present-day **Via XX Settembre** is the very street up which patriots advanced after breaching the city gates. The **Risorgimento**—the "resurgence," Italian unification—was complete.

Political heights in Italy seemed to correspond to historic depths in art and architecture. After carrying the banner of innovation for more than a millennium, Italians began to run out of creative steam. Among the more notable practitioners

The A-List of Italian Novels Available in English

Alessandro Manzoni, *The Betrothed* (1827)

Alberto Moravia, *The Conformist* (1951)

Giuseppe Tomasi di Lampedusa, *The Leopard* (1958)

Elsa Morante, *History: A Novel* (1974)

Italo Calvino, *If on a Winter's Night a Traveler* (1979)

Umberto Eco, *Foucault's Pendulum* (1988)

Niccolo Ammaniti, *I'm Not Scared* (2001)

was Venetian **Antonio Canova** (1757–1822), Italy's major neoclassical sculptor, who became notorious for painting both Napoleon and his sister Pauline as nudes. His best work is in Rome's **Galleria Borghese** (p. 120). Tuscany also bred a late-19th-century precursor to French Impressionism, the **Macchiaioli** movement; see their works in the "modern art" galleries at Florence's **Palazzo Pitti** (p. 222).

As a backlash against the excesses of the baroque and rococo, architects began turning to the austere simplicity and grandeur of the classical age, and inaugurated the **neoclassical** style by the middle of the 18th century. Their work was further inspired by the rediscovery of Pompeii and other ancient sites. The fervor for neoclassicism also created monstrous errors like Florence's Piazza della Repubblica, described by Mary McCarthy in her seminal *Stones of Florence* as "the ugliest in Italy." The end of the 19th century saw the first steel constructions piercing Italian skylines, with the most spectacular silhouette being cut by Turin's **Mole Antonelliana** (p. 633). The end of the century saw small incursions of Art Nouveau, known in Italy as **Liberty.** This highly decorative style made only a fraction of the impact here that it did in other European countries, but you can still get a sniff of it in the shopping arcades of **Turin** and the handsome storefronts of **Lucca** (p. 306).

If art was hitting an all-time low, **music** was experiencing its Italian golden age. **Giovanni Bottesini** (1821–89) was a renowned composer and musician: His *Virtuoso Works for Double-Bass and Strings,* conducted by Vittorio Antonelli, might be one of the finest showcases ever for the double bass. **Luigi Cherubini** (1760–1842) was more famous in France, where he worked. His *Harpsichord Sonatas Nos. 1–6* provides a genteel and restrained insight into the work of a conservative Italian classicist.

But it's bel canto **opera** for which the 19th century will largely be remembered. **Gioachino Rossini** (1792–1868) was born in Pesaro, in the Marches, and found fame with his 1816 *The Barber of Seville.* The fame of **Gaetano Donizetti** (1797–1848), a prolific native of Bergamo, was assured when his *Anna Bolena* premiered in 1830. Sicilian **Vincenzo Bellini** (1801–35) was the third great name in bel canto. All were perhaps overshadowed later in the century by **Giuseppe Verdi** (1813–1901), whose works such as *Rigoletto* and *La Traviata* have become some of the most whistled on the planet. Opera houses like Venice's **La Fenice** (p. 484) and Milan's **Teatro alla Scala** (p. 585) became sacred temples of the popular imagination.

The Early 20th Century: Two World Wars and One Duce

In 1915, Italy entered **World War I** on the side of the Allies, joining Britain, Russia, and France to help defeat Germany and the traditional enemy to the north, now the Austro-Hungarian Empire. If an Allied victory could be achieved—as it was by November 1918—Italy would be in pole position to claim **Trentino,** the **South Tyrol,** and the Austrian port of **Trieste.** (Jan Morris's melancholic 2001 *Trieste and the Meaning of Nowhere* remains the best book yet written on Italy's unique northeastern city.) These territories, however, came at a high cost: Italy suffered mass casualties on its northern front; **Friuli** and parts of the Veneto spent much of the war under Austrian occupation, only returning to Italy after the decisive **Battle of Vittorio Veneto** in October 1918.

In the aftermath of war, Italians suffered with rising unemployment and horrendous inflation. As in Germany, this deep political crisis led to the emergence of a dictator. On October 28, 1922, **Benito Mussolini,** who had started his Fascist Party in 1919, knew the country was ripe for change. He gathered 30,000 Black Shirts for his **March on Rome.** Inflation was soaring and workers had just called a general strike, so rather than recognizing a state under siege, **King Victor Emmanuel III** (1900–46) proclaimed Mussolini as the new government leader. In 1929, Il Duce—a moniker Mussolini began using from 1925—defined the divisions between the Italian government and the pope by signing the Lateran Treaty, which granted political, territorial, and fiscal autonomy to the microstate of **Vatican City.** The agreement also made Roman Catholicism the official state religion, though that designation was removed in 1978.

Wine bottles featuring former dictator Benito Mussolini on their labels.

Mussolini's rule was defined by thuggery, oppression, and fear. Newly claimed lands in the north—including South Tyrol and territory that now lies in both Croatia and Slovenia—were subjected to forced "Italianization," as regional languages were suppressed. Outspoken opponents, like socialist parliamentarian **Giacomo Matteotti** (1885–1924), were assassinated—you'll encounter many streets named in honor of Matteotti as you tour the country. During the Spanish Civil War (1936–39), Mussolini's support of Franco's Fascists, who had staged a coup against the elected government of Spain, helped seal the Axis alliance between Italy and Nazi Germany. Italy was inexorably sucked into **World War II.**

Despite having outdated military equipment, Italy had added to the general horror of the era by invading Abyssinia (Ethiopia) in 1935. In 1940, Italy invaded Greece through Albania; 1991 Oscar-winning movie *Mediterraneo* is a fictionalized (and comic) tale of everyday Italians thrust into an Adriatic war that few wanted. In 1942, thousands of Italian troops joined Hitler's disastrous campaign on the Russian front. All the while, armed, anti-Fascist **partisans** harried and harassed Mussolini's war machine at home. In 1943, Allied forces, under the command of U.S. Gen. Patton and British Gen. Montgomery, invaded Sicily, quickly secured the island, and prepared to move north toward Rome.

In the face of likely humiliation, Mussolini was overthrown by his Grand Council. The Allies cut a deal with Victor Emmanuel III, who had essentially collaborated with the Fascists and easily shifted allegiances. The Germans, however, weren't prepared to surrender Italy so easily. They annexed the north, and fought tooth and nail for every inch—prolonging the war in Italy until April 1945, committing several notorious massacres of civilians, and destroying every bridge in Florence bar the **Ponte Vecchio** (p. 212) as they slowly retreated. They even released Mussolini from his Italian jail cell to establish the short-lived, brutal **Republic of Salò,** headquartered on the shore of Lake Garda. Mussolini had hoped for a groundswell of popular opinion in favor of Italian Fascism, but events proved this to be a futile dream. In April 1945, Mussolini was captured by partisans as he tried to flee to Switzerland. Along with his mistress, Claretta Petacci, and several others, he was shot and strung upside-down in Milan's **Piazzale Loreto.**

Several fine English-language **memoirs** paint the horror of daily life in wartime Italy. Norman Lewis's brilliant *Naples '44* (1978) recounts the autobiographical experiences of a young British intelligence officer in just-liberated Naples. The everyday reality of the ground war in Tuscany is vividly brought to life by expat Iris Origo's diarized *War in Val d'Orcia* (1947). In *Love and War in the Apennines* (1971), English travel writer Eric Newby tells the story of his escape from a POW camp, his experiences running and hiding from pursuing Fascists, and the help he received from locals—including his future wife, Wanda. Primo Levi's *If This Is a Man* (1947) retells the Jewish-Italian writer's harrowing experiences as a prisoner in Auschwitz. Another Torinese Jew, Carlo Levi wrote *Christ Stopped at Eboli* (1945) as an account of his 1930s banishment to southern Italy for anti-Fascist activism. Available in translation, Giorgio Bassani's novel *The Garden of the Finzi-Continis* (1962) sets the lives of Ferrarese Jews against the creeping menace of interwar and wartime Fascism.

Several postwar **movies** also dealt with the Italian experience of Fascism and war. Roberto Rossellini's *Rome, Open City* (1946) influenced Hollywood film noir of the late 1940s. Set in occupied Rome, it tells the story of a partisan priest and a Communist who aid the resistance. Federico Fellini's *Amarcord* (1973) takes a comic swipe at Fascists and the Church with a tale set in 1930s Romagna.

Deeply unpleasant though their politics was, the Fascist regime did sponsor some remarkable **architecture.** You can see it at its best in Rome's planned satellite community called **EUR,** which includes a multistory "square Colosseum" so funky that it has been featured in many a film and music video. In a city famed for more venerable works, Florence's **Santa Maria Novella station** (1934) is a masterpiece of modernism. The station houses a plaque commemorating the many Jews who were sent to their deaths in Nazi Germany from the terminus. Dating from just prior to Mussolini's takeover, Turin's **Lingotto** factory (p. 634)—built for the city's giant car manufacturer, Fiat—was an icon of the industrial age. Its cult status was assured when its rooftop test track starred in *The Italian Job* (1969). You can still ride to the roof and walk around the track.

The early 20th century also saw a partial rediscovery of kudos for Italian art. The largely Italian **Futurist** movement flourished, as a rejection of the old, favoring the technology of the future and extolling the glories of the industrial age. **Umberto Boccioni** (1882–1916), a painter and sculptor, was perhaps its purest exponent, capturing speed, technology, and dynamism in his output. Among other artists emerging from this period was **Giorgio de Chirico** (1888–1978). He was hailed for his oneiric cityscapes, but after 1918 he became a classicist, claiming he was the heir to Titian. **Amedeo Modigliani** (1884–1920) bridged the gap between Frenchman Toulouse-Lautrec and the 1920s Art Deco painters. The victim of a tragic life, he excelled in both painting and sculpture. He was not really part of any movement, but highly individualistic in his vast output before an early death. The era's towering figure in music was **Giacomo Puccini** (1858–1924); operas like *Tosca* (1900) and *Madam Butterfly* (1904) still pack houses worldwide. You can hear his music performed every day of the year in his hometown, **Lucca** (p. 306).

Postwar Italy: From 1945 to the Present Day

Italy's citizens quickly voiced dissatisfaction with the monarchy and its identification with the Fascists. In 1946, they voted for the establishment of the **First Republic**—overwhelmingly so in northern and central Italy, which helped to counterbalance a southern majority in favor of keeping the monarchy. The major political party that emerged was the **Christian Democrats (DC),** a moderately right-of-center group whose first leader, Alcide De Gasperi (1881–1954), served as premier until 1953. The party dominated politics and government until it dissolved, in a perfect storm of corruption scandals, in the early 1990s.

Five Great Postwar Italian Movies

The Bicycle Thief, directed by Vittorio De Sica (1948)
8½, directed by Federico Fellini (1963)
Cinema Paradiso, directed by Giuseppe Tornatore (1988)
Life Is Beautiful, directed by Roberto Benigni (1997)
Gomorrah, directed by Matteo Garrone (2008)

Milan's Pirelli Tower is a striking example of Italian postwar architecture.

The other great political pole in Italian politics was occupied by the **Communist Party (PCI),** founded by philosopher Antonio Gramsci in 1921 in Livorno, Tuscany, and more active than any other organization in the fight against Fascism. Originally democratic-revolutionary and pro-Soviet, by the mid-1970s, it had abandoned this stance in favor of "Eurocommunism"—the moment of the **Historic Compromise** between Christian democracy and Communism in Italy. The power base of leftism in Italy was—and to a degree, still is—its "red heart," particularly the regions of Emilia-Romagna and Tuscany.

After the war, Italy quickly succeeded in rebuilding its economy, in part because of U.S. aid under the **Marshall Plan** (1948–52). By the 1960s, as a member of the European Economic Community (founded by the **Treaty of Rome** in 1957), Italy had become one of the world's leading industrialized nations, and prominent in the manufacture of automobiles and office equipment. Fiat (from Turin), Ferrari (from Emilia-Romagna), and Olivetti (from northern Piedmont) were brands known around the world. Confident industrialists commissioned daring buildings such as Milan's **Pirelli Tower** (1958), a collaboration between two of Italy's leading postwar architects, Gio Ponte (1891–1979) and Pier Luigi Nervi (1891–1979).

The country continued to be plagued by economic inequality between the industrially prosperous north and the depressed south. It suffered unprecedented capital flight (aided by Swiss banks only too willing to accept discreet deposits from wealthy Italians), inflation (almost 20% during much of the 1970s), and unemployment. During the late 1970s and early 1980s, it was rocked by domestic terrorism: These were the so-called **Anni di Piombo (Years of Lead),** during which extremists of the left and right bombed and assassinated with impunity. Conspiracy theories became the Italian staple diet; everyone from the state to shady Masonic lodges to the CIA was accused of involvement in what became in effect an undeclared civil war. Decades later it's still not clear even which side was responsible for deadly bombings such as the one that killed 17 in Milan's **Piazza Fontana** in 1969, or that which in 1980 slew 85 in **Bologna Central Station**—the station clock remains stuck at 10:25am, the time of the bombing. The most notorious incident of the Anni di Piombo was the kidnap and murder of Prime Minister **Aldo Moro** in 1978. You'll find a succinct account of these murky years in Tobias Jones's *The Dark Heart of Italy* (2003).

The postwar Italian **film industry** became respected above all for its innovative directors. **Federico Fellini** (1920–93) burst onto the scene with his highly individual style, beginning with *La Strada* (1954) and going on to such classics as *The City of Women* (1980). His *La Dolce Vita* (1961) seemingly defined an era. Marxist, homosexual, and practicing Catholic, **Pier Paolo Pasolini** (1922–75) was the most controversial of filmmakers until his mysterious murder. **Bernardo Bertolucci** (b. 1941), once an assistant to Pasolini, achieved international fame with such films as *The Conformist* (1970) and *Last Tango in Paris* (1971), starring Marlon Brando. (See "Five Great Postwar Italian Movies," above, for more on Italian film.)

In the early 1990s, Italians reeled as many of the country's leading politicians were accused of endemic corruption. These scandals uncovered as a result of the judiciary's **Mani Pulite (Clean Hands)** investigations—often dubbed **Tangentopoli** (approximately, "Bribesville")—provoked a constitutional crisis, caused the end of the First Republic, and ushered in the **Second Republic** in 1992.

The political system was turned on its head: A right-wing coalition, led by media mogul and A.C. Milan president **Silvio Berlusconi**'s new Forza Italia! party, swept to victory in 1994's general election. Berlusconi became prime minister, the first of three spells he spent in the post between 1994 and 2011. Along with **Romano Prodi,** who led center-left coalitions twice in-between, he has been the towering figure in recent Italian politics—and seemingly permanently embroiled in scandals involving sex, money, or both. Berlusconi blamed most of his woes on "vindictive left-wing prosecutors" or the media, much of which was in fact under the control of his own business empire.

Other resonant events in recent Italian history have centered on the country's twin religions: Catholicism and *calcio* (soccer). As much of the world watched and prayed, **Pope John Paul II** died in April 2005, at the age of 84, ending a reign of 26 years as pope. Worldwide mourning was proclaimed among Catholics. Later in the month, a new pope, Cardinal Joseph Ratzinger, was elected by his fellow cardinals. The Vatican's hard-liner on church doctrine took the papal throne as **Pope Benedict XVI.** The country's national sport has also had a roller coaster ride. Italy hosted the F.I.F.A. World Cup 1990, played sublime football, but fell at the semifinal stage. Rockier still was 2006. Bribery scandals **(Calciopoli)** implicated match officials and domestic club presidents, and led to the country's most storied club, **Juventus,** being relegated from the top division. However, the 2006 season ended with Italy's national side winning the

F.I.F.A. World Cup. For the first time since 1982, they were *campioni del mondo* (champions of the world).

Damaging earthquakes in Umbria in 1997—which seriously damaged Assisi's **Basilica di San Francesco** (p. 338)—Friuli in 1976, Campania in 1980, and L'Aquila in 2009, killed hundreds, and reminded Italians that their country lies in one of Europe's most active seismic zones.

WHEN TO GO

The best months for traveling in Italy are from **April to June** and **mid-September to October**—temperatures are usually comfortable, rural colors are richer and more pronounced, and the crowds aren't too intense. Starting in mid-June, the summer rush picks up, and from **July through early September** the country's busy spots teem with visitors. **August** is the worst month in most places: Not only does it get uncomfortably hot, muggy, and crowded, but seemingly the entire country goes on vacation, at least from August 15 onward—and many Italians take off the entire month. Many family-run hotels, restaurants, and shops are closed (except at the spas, beaches, and islands, where most Italians head). Paradoxically, you will have many urban places almost to yourself if you visit in August—Florence and the cities of Lombardy and Piedmont can seem virtual ghost towns, and hotels there are heavily discounted, but be aware that fashionable restaurants and nightspots are usually closed for the whole month.

From **late October to Easter,** many attractions operate on shorter (sometimes *much* shorter) winter hours, and some hotels are closed for renovation or redecoration, especially in seasonal resorts. Many family-run accommodations and restaurants take a month or two off sometime between **November and February;** spa and beach destinations become padlocked ghost towns. Of course, it's only then that winter sports destinations in the Alps and the Dolomites really come alive.

Weather

It's warm all over Italy in summer; it can be very hot in the south, and almost anywhere inland—landlocked cities on the northern plains and in central Umbria and Tuscany can feel stifling during a July or August hot spell. The higher temperatures (measured in Italy in degrees Celsius) usually begin everywhere in May, often lasting until sometime in October. Winters in the north of Italy are cold, with rain and snow, and a biting wind whistles over the mountains into cities from Venice in the east to Turin in the west. In the south, the weather is warm (or at least, warm-ish) all year, averaging 10°C (50°F) in winter. Southern summers are most pleasant by the coast.

For the most part, it's quite dry once you get away from the coast in Italy, so high temperatures don't seem as bad because the humidity is lower. In Rome, Naples, the central regions of Tuscany and Umbria, and the entire south, temperatures can stay in the 30s Celsius (90s Fahrenheit) for days, but nights are usually comfortably cooler. The rainiest months almost everywhere are October and November.

Italy's Average Daily High Temperature & Monthly Rainfall

ROME

	JAN	FEB	MAR	APR	MAY	JUNE	JULY	AUG	SEPT	OCT	NOV	DEC
TEMP. (°F)	55	56	59	63	71	77	83	83	79	71	62	57
TEMP. (°C)	12	13	15	17	21	25	28	28	26	21	16	13
RAINFALL (IN.)	3.2	2.8	2.7	2.6	2	1.3	.6	1	2.7	4.5	4.4	3.8

FLORENCE

	JAN	FEB	MAR	APR	MAY	JUNE	JULY	AUG	SEPT	OCT	NOV	DEC
TEMP. (°F)	49	53	60	68	75	84	89	88	81	69	58	50
TEMP. (°C)	9	11	15	20	23	28	31	31	27	20	14	10
RAINFALL (IN.)	1.9	2.1	2.7	2.9	3	2.7	1.5	1.9	3.3	4	3.9	2.8

NAPLES

	JAN	FEB	MAR	APR	MAY	JUNE	JULY	AUG	SEPT	OCT	NOV	DEC
TEMP. (°F)	54	55	60	64	72	79	85	85	80	71	62	56
TEMP. (°C)	12	12	15	17	22	26	29	29	26	21	16	13
RAINFALL (IN.)	3.8	3.2	3	3	2	1.5	.9	1.2	3.1	5.2	5	4.7

Public Holidays

Offices, government buildings (though not usually tourist offices), and shops in Italy are generally closed on: January 1 (Capodanno, or New Year); January 6 (La Befana, or Epiphany); Easter Sunday (Pasqua); Easter Monday (Pasquetta); April 25 (Liberation Day); May 1 (Festa del Lavoro, or Labor Day); June 2 (Festa della Repubblica, or Republic Day); August 15 (Ferragosto, or the Assumption of the Virgin); November 1 (All Saints' Day), December 8 (L'Immacolata, or the Immaculate Conception); December 25 (Natale, Christmas Day); December 26 (Santo Stefano, or St. Stephen's Day). You'll also often find businesses closed for the annual daylong celebration dedicated to the local saint (for example, on January 31 in San Gimignano, Tuscany).

Italy Calendar of Events

For an exhaustive list of events beyond those listed here, check http://events.frommers.com, where you'll find a searchable, up-to-the-minute roster of what's happening in cities all over the world.

JANUARY

Epiphany celebrations, nationwide. All cities, towns, and villages in Italy stage Roman Catholic Epiphany observances, which celebrate the visit of the Magi to the infant Jesus. One of the most extensive celebrations is the Festa Nazionale della Befana in Urbania, Le Marche. www.labefana.com. January 6.

Festa di Sant'Agnese, Sant'Agnese Fuori le Mura, Rome. In this ancient ceremony, two lambs are blessed and shorn; their wool is used later for *palliums* (Roman Catholic vestments). January 21.

Fiera di Sant'Orso, Aosta, Valle d'Aosta. Observing a tradition that has existed for 10 centuries, artisans from the mountain valleys display their wares—often made of wood, lace, or wrought iron—created during the long winter. www.fieradisantorso.it. Late January.

FEBRUARY

Almond Blossom Festival, Agrigento, Sicily. This folk festival welcomes spring with song, dance, costumes, and fireworks in Sicily's Valley of the Temples. First half of February.

Carnevale, Venice. At this riotous time, theatrical presentations and masked balls take place throughout Venice and on the islands in the lagoon. The balls are by invitation only (except the Doge's Ball), but the street events and fireworks are open to everyone. www.carnevale.venezia.it. The week before Ash Wednesday, the beginning of Lent.

MARCH

Festival della Canzone Italiana (Festival of Italian Popular Song), San Remo, Liguria. At this 5-day competition, major artists perform the latest Italian song releases. www.sanremo.rai.it. Early March.

Festa di San Giuseppe, the Trionfale Quarter, north of the Vatican, Rome. The heavily decorated statue of the saint is brought out at a fair with food stalls, concerts, and sporting events. Usually March 19.

APRIL

Holy Week, nationwide. Processions and age-old ceremonies—some from pagan days, some from the Middle Ages—are staged. The most notable procession is led by the pope, passing the Colosseum and the Roman Forum up to Palatine Hill; a torch-lit parade caps the observance. Sicily's observances are also noteworthy. Beginning 4 days before Easter Sunday; sometimes at the end of March but often in April.

Easter Sunday (Pasqua), Piazza di San Pietro, Rome. In an event broadcast around the world, the pope gives his blessing from the balcony of St. Peter's.

Scoppio del Carro (Explosion of the Cart), Florence. At this ancient observance, a cart laden with flowers and fireworks is drawn by three white oxen to the Duomo, where at the noon Mass a mechanical dove detonates it from the altar. Easter Sunday.

Maggio Musicale Fiorentino (Florentine Musical May), Florence. Italy's oldest and most prestigious music festival emphasizes music from the 14th to the 20th centuries, but also presents ballet and opera. www.maggiofiorentino.com. Late April to end of June.

MAY

Concorso Ippico Internazionale (International Horse Show), Piazza di Siena, Rome. Top-flight international show jumping at the Villa Borghese. www.piazzadisiena.com. Late May.

Corsa dei Ceri (Race of the Candles), Gubbio, Umbria. In this centuries-old ceremony celebrating the feast day of St. Ubaldo, the town's patron saint, 1,000-pound, 9m (30-ft.) wooden "candles" *(ceri)* are raced through the steep streets of this perfectly preserved medieval hill town. www.festadeiceri.it. May 15.

JUNE

Festa di San Ranieri, Pisa, Tuscany. The city honors its patron saint with candlelit parades, followed the next day by eight-rower teams competing in 16th-century costumes. June 16 and 17.

Festival di Ravenna, Ravenna, Emilia-Romagna. This classical festival of international renown draws world-class performers. A wide range of performances are staged, including operas, ballets, theater, symphonic music concerts, solo and chamber pieces, oratorios, and sacred music. Advance tickets are needed for the most popular events. www.ravennafestival.org. Mid-June to July.

Calcio Storico (Historic Football), Florence. This is a revival of a raucous 15th-century form of football, pitting four teams in medieval costumes against one another in a minitournament. The matches usually culminate on June 24, the feast day of St. John the Baptist. Late June.

Gioco del Ponte, Pisa, Tuscany. Teams in Renaissance costume take part in a long-contested push-of-war on the Ponte di Mezzo, which spans the Arno River. Last Sunday in June.

La Biennale di Venezia (International Exposition of Contemporary Art), Venice. One of the most famous regular art events in the world takes place during alternate odd-numbered years. www.labiennale.org. June to November.

La Giostra del Saracino (Joust of the Saracen), Arezzo, Tuscany. A colorful procession in full historical regalia precedes the tilting contest dating from the 13th century, with knights in armor in the town's sloping main piazza. www.giostradelsaracino.arezzo.it. Mid-June.

Festival Pucciniano, Torre del Lago, Tuscany. Puccini operas are performed in this Tuscan lakeside town's open-air theater, near the celebrated composer's former summertime villa. www.puccinifestival.it. Mid-June to mid-September.

JULY

Il Palio, Piazza del Campo, Siena, Tuscany. Palio fever grips this Tuscan hill town for a wild and exciting horse race from the Middle Ages. Pageantry, costumes, and the celebrations of the victorious *contrada* (sort of a neighborhood social club) mark the spectacle. It's a "no rules" event: Even a horse without a rider can win the race. July 2 and August 16.

International Opera Festival, Arena di Verona, Verona, Veneto. Culture buffs flock to the 20,000-seat Roman amphitheater, one of the world's best preserved, for monumental outdoor opera performances. www.arena.it. July to September.

Festa de' Noantri, Rome. Trastevere, the capital's most colorful quarter, becomes a gigantic outdoor restaurant, with tables lining the streets, and merrymakers and musicians providing the entertainment. After reaching the quarter, find the first empty table and try to get a waiter. Mid-July.

Umbria Jazz, Perugia, Umbria. The Umbrian region hosts the country's (and one of Europe's) top jazz festivals, featuring world-class artists. www.umbriajazz.com. Mid-July.

Festa del Redentore (Feast of the Redeemer), Venice. This festival marks the lifting of the plague in 1576, with fireworks, pilgrimages, and boating. www.redentorevenezia.it. Third Saturday and Sunday in July.

Festival Internazionale di Musica Antica, Urbino, the Marches. At this cultural extravaganza, international performers converge on Raphael's birthplace. It's the most important Renaissance and baroque music festival in Italy. www.fima-online.org. Mid-July.

AUGUST

Rossini Opera Festival, Pesaro, the Marches. The world's top bel canto specialists perform Rossini's operas and choral works at this seaside festival. www.rossinioperafestival.it. Throughout August.

Venice International Film Festival, Venice. Ranking after Cannes, this festival brings together stars, directors, producers, and filmmakers from all over the world. Films are shown between 9am and 3am in various areas of the Palazzo del Cinema on the Lido. Although many of the seats are reserved for international jury members, the public can attend whenever they want, if there are available seats. www.labiennale.org. Late August to early September.

SEPTEMBER

Regata Storica, Grand Canal, Venice. A maritime spectacular: Many gondolas participate in the canal procession, although gondolas don't race in the regatta itself. www.regatastoricavenezia.it. First Sunday in September.

Partita a Scacchi con Personaggi Viventi (Living Chess Game), Marostica, Veneto. This chess game is played in the town square by living chess pieces in period costumes. www.marosticascacchi.it. Second Saturday/Sunday of September during even-numbered years.

Festa di San Gennaro, Naples, Campania. The Duomo is the focal point for the festival in honor of the city's patron saint. Twice a year a solemn procession is followed by the miraculous "liquefaction" of the saint's blood. September 19 and May.

OCTOBER

Fiera Internazionale del Tartufo Bianco d'Alba, Alba, Piedmont. This festival honors the white truffle in Alba, Italy's truffle capital, with contests, truffle-hound competitions, and tastings of this ugly but very expensive and delectable fungus. www.fieradeltartufo.org. October to mid-November.

DECEMBER

La Scala Opera Season Opening, Teatro alla Scala, Milan. At the most famous opera house of them all, the season opens on December 7, the feast day of Milan's patron St. Ambrose, and runs into July, and September to mid-November. Even though opening-night tickets are close to impossible to get, it's worth a try. www.teatroallascala.org.

Christmas Blessing of the Pope, Piazza di San Pietro, Rome. Delivered at noon from the balcony of St. Peter's Basilica, the pope's words are broadcast to the faithful around the globe. December 25.

RESPONSIBLE TRAVEL IN ITALY

Eco-awareness in Italy is on the rise. But even the concept of taking a "responsible," "green," or "environmentally friendly" trip here isn't without controversy, particularly if you're arriving by plane. However, there are everyday things you can do to minimize the impact—and especially the carbon footprint—of your travels. Remove chargers from cellphones, laptops, and anything else that draws from the mains, once the gadget is fully charged. If you're shopping, buy seasonal fruit and vegetables, or local cheeses and meats, from markets, rather than produce sourced by supermarkets from distant lands. Eat seasonally in a family-run trattoria rather than at chain outfits (you'll want to anyway). Buy authentic gifts from back-street artisan shops, rather than mass-produced items from catch-all gift stores right on the main piazza. Most importantly, use public transportation to get around the country. Italy's **trains** are easy to use and efficient, its high-speed lines are among the best in Europe, and there's really no reason to take an internal flight unless you're visiting the islands. (And even then, if you have time, investigate ferry crossings.) For a comprehensive guide to navigating the country quickly and cost-effectively, see "Getting Around" in chapter 17.

Italy not only protects its historic monuments, but it also preserves its landscapes with two dozen **national parks,** as well as several regional parks and nature reserves. In all, nearly 5% of the landmass is under government protection, and you'll struggle to find a greener holiday than one in which you rely mostly on your two feet for getting around. If you plan to tour the parks, a good source of information is **Federparchi** (www.parks.it; ✆ **06-51604940**), the Italian Federation for Parks and Nature Reserves. The website is packed with information on the parks, and suggests multiple itineraries. These parks encompass lakes, forests, mountains, and even the sea. Among our favorites are the

Fresh tomatoes for sale at a Roman market.

Parco Nazionale d'Abruzzo, Lazio e Molise (www.parcoabruzzo.it), which contains the highest peaks in the Apennines and is the home of the brown bear and the chamois (hoofed, goatlike animals with long horns). The **Parco Nazionale delle Cinque Terre** (www.parconazionale5terre.it) is in a seaside setting scattered with olive groves, vineyards, rainbow-hued houses, and fishing villages. After damaging floods and mudslides in late 2011, it's now back in business. Straddling Piedmont and the Valle d'Aosta, the **Parque Nazionale Gran Paradiso** (www.pngp.it; p. 652) is high, rugged terrain and home to the Alpine ibex, which has been rescued from the brink of extinction in Europe. Before you go, it's worth checking out the website of the **Leave No Trace Center for Outdoor Ethics** (http://lnt.org), which has drawn up a code for outdoor travelers who want to protect the wilderness for future generations.

Bird-watchers should consult the website for the **Lega Italiana Protezione Uccelli (LIPU;** www.lipu.it), the Italian League for Bird Protection, a charitable organization founded in 1965 and devoted to the protection of the country's birdlife. The organization maintains a network of *oasi* (reserves) where you can roam in peace. Many have education centers attached, so visitors can learn what species they can expect to see, and when. If you read Italian, bookmark **www.lipu.it/oasi**.

There are a growing number of websites offering sustainable **accommodations** in Italy. **It's a Green Green World** (www.itsagreengreenworld.com) reviews green hotels across Italy, from an ancient family wine production factory converted to receive guests in Sicily to an Umbrian inn opening onto a panoramic view of Lago Trasimeno. **EcoLux Hotels** (www.ecoluxhotels.com) concentrates on upscale properties, and submits them to a thorough audit by

ALL ABOUT vino

Italy is the largest **wine**-producing country in the world; as far back as 800 B.C. the Etruscans were vintners. However, it wasn't until 1965 that laws were enacted to guarantee consistency in winemaking. Quality wines are labeled **"DOC"** (Denominazione di Origine Controllata). If you see **"DOCG"** on a label (the "G" means *garantita*), that denotes an even better-quality wine region. **"IGT"** (Indicazione Geografica Tipica) indicates a more general wine zone—for example, Umbria—but still with some quality control.

You can sometimes save money by buying directly from a producer—signs beside the highway of any wine-producing zone advertise VENDITA DIRETTA. Useful vocabulary words are *bottiglieria* (a simple wine shop) and enoteca (a more upscale store where vintages from several growers are sold).

Below we cite a few of the best Italian wines. Rest assured that there are hundreds more, and you'll have a great time sampling them to find your own favorites. Sometimes you don't want the marquee labels: A pitcher of the local *vino della casa* (house wine) to wash down lunch in a country trattoria can be a delight.

Tuscany: Tuscan red wines rank with some of the finest in world. **Sangiovese** is the king of grapes here, and **chianti** (p. 272) is the most widely known sangiovese wine. The best zone is **Chianti Classico,** where a lively ruby-red wine partners a bouquet of violets. The Tuscan south houses two even finer DOCGs: mighty, robust **Brunello di Montalcino,** a garnet red ideal for roasts and game; and almost purple **Vino Nobile di Montepulciano,** which has a rich, velvet body. Neighboring Umbria has a beefy red of its own, best drunk aged: **Sagrantino di Montefalco.** End a meal with the Tuscan dessert wine called **vin santo,** which is usually accompanied by *biscotti* that you dunk into your glass.

The Veneto: Reds here vary from light and lunchtime-friendly **Bardolino** to **Valpolicella,** which can be particularly intense if the grapes are partly dried before fermentation to make an **Amarone.** White, Garganega-based **Soave** has a pale amber color and a velvety flavor. **Prosecco** is the prototype Italian sparkling white, and the base for both a Bellini and a Spritz—any upscale joints that use champagne are doing it wrong.

Trentino–Alto Adige: This area (also **Südtirol**) produces wine influenced by Austria, and its crisp, mineraly whites are especially sought after. Look out for those made with slightly pale-green

environmental professionals. The **Travelife Collection** (www.travelifecollection.com) lists accommodations that are assessed on the basis of their social and environmental impact. The current offering is small, but is scheduled to expand through 2013.

Staying in an *agriturismo* (or farm-stay) is often a green option. These establishments are generally small businesses that live in harmony with their environment, make (and sell) some of their own produce, and employ local people. For more on finding suitable *agriturismo* accommodations, see p. 931. Adventurous campers should consider an *agricampeggio* (a rural campsite working with similar principles to an *agriturismo*).

Riesling and aromatic Gewürztraminer grapes. East of here, the wines of Friuli (notably the Colli Orientali DOC) are equally sublime, and not widely known outside the country. Sauvignon blanc and pinot bianco perform well here, too, but better still are the indigenous grapes: Tocai friuliano (a flinty, aromatic white), Schioppettino (a rich red), and Terrano (another full-bodied, savory red which picks up a distinctive flavor from the limestone karst terrain on which it grows).

Piedmont: The finest reds in Italy probably hail from the vine-clad slopes of Piedmont, particularly those made from the late ripening **Nebbiolo** grape in the Langhe hills south of Alba. The big names—with big flavors and big price tags—are **Barbaresco** (brilliant ruby red with a delicate flavor) and **Barolo** (also brilliant ruby red, and gaining finesse when it mellows into a velvety old age). Farther north, the **Valle d'Aosta** is home to a dry **Moscato di Chambave** with a powerful aroma and real zing, as well as interesting autochthonous varieties like meaty, dark-red **Fumin.**

Latium: Many of Rome's local wines come from the Castelli Romani, the hill towns around the capital. These wines are best drunk when young, and they're most often white, mellow, and dry. The golden wines of **Frascati** are the most famous, and are produced in both a demi-sec and a sweet variety, the latter served with dessert.

The South and islands: From the volcanic soil of Vesuvius, the wines of **Campania** have been extolled for 2,000 years. Homer praised the glory of **Falerno,** straw yellow in color. The key DOCG wines from Campania these days are **Greco di Tufo** (a mouth-filling, full white) and **Fiano di Avellino** (subtler and more floral). The heel of the Italian boot, **Puglia** used to produce more wine than any other part of Italy—most of it undistinguished. One of its most interesting DOCs is **Castel del Monte,** which comes in shades of pink, white, and red. The classic Puglian red is **Primitivo,** a full-bodied wine made from a grape that's genetically identical to California's zinfandel. The wines of **Sicily,** once called a "paradise of the grape," were extolled by the ancient poets, and table wines here are improving after a drop in quality (though not quantity). Sicily is also home to **Marsala,** a fortified wine first popularized by British port traders and now served with desserts; it also makes a great sauce for veal. **Sardinia** also has varieties of its own. **Cannonau** (a variant of Grenache) partners lamb well. With seafood, it's hard to beat the peachy freshness of a fine **Vermentino di Sardegna.**

Anyone serious about the environmental credentials of his or her hotel or guesthouse could ask if it is part of the **Legambiente Turismo** sustainability scheme. Businesses are only granted the eco-label if they meet criteria including use of clean energy, recycling technology, and organic ingredients. See **www.legambienteturismo.it**.

For Italy packages and tours with responsible credentials, consult the search engine at online agent **ResponsibleVacation.com** (known as Responsible-Travel.com in the U.K.). You'll find an explanation of how each tour or hotel offered makes a difference to the local community and environment as part of detailed product descriptions. **MuchBetterAdventures.com** focuses on

Cheese for sale in Pienza.

outdoor and activity holidays, such as cycling tours of Umbria and winter sports in the Dolomites. **Tourdust** (www.tourdust.com) is another small, Web-based agent offering "responsible" vacations in Italy. The boutique offerings include horseback riding and cycling in the Chianti and photography courses in Umbria.

In addition to the resources for Italy listed above, see **www.frommers.com/planning** for more tips on responsible travel.

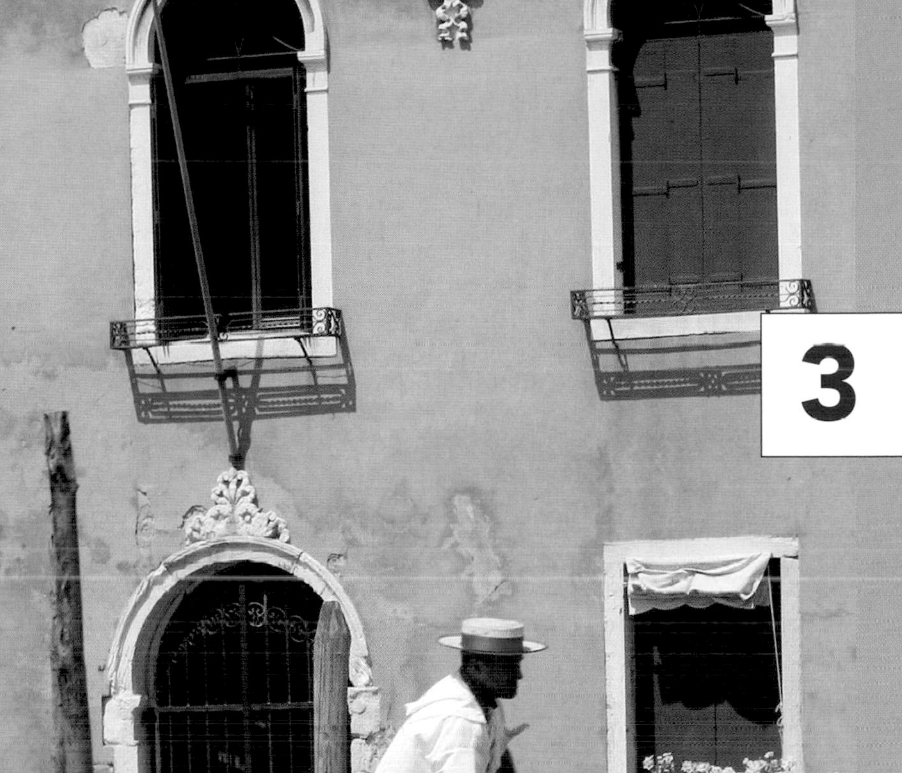

3

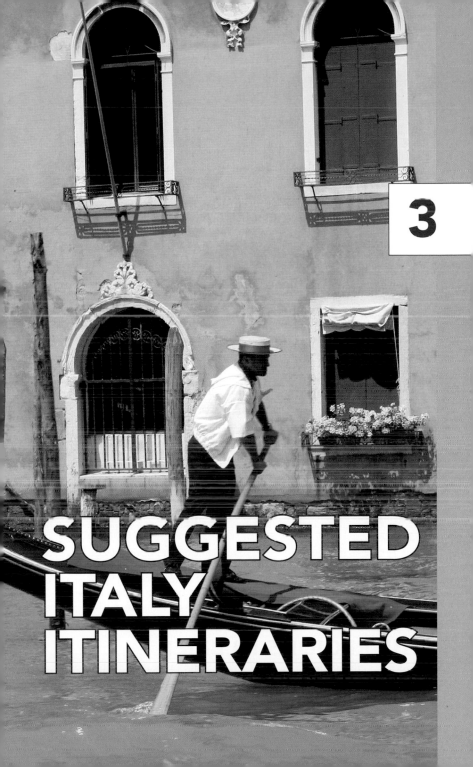

SUGGESTED ITALY ITINERARIES

I t would be a pleasure to get delightfully "lost" in Italy, wandering about at your leisure, melting into the rhythms of daily life in unspoiled villages miles away from the usual trails. But few of us have such a generous amount of time, and a lean-and-mean schedule is called for if you want to experience the best of the country as efficiently as possible.

Italy is so vast and treasure-filled that it's hard to resist the temptation to pack in too much in too short a time. It's a dauntingly diverse and complex destination, and you can't even skim the surface in 1 or 2 weeks—so relax, don't try. If you're a first-time visitor with very little touring time on your hands, we suggest you go just for the classic nuggets: Rome, Siena, Florence, and Venice could be packed into 1 very busy week, if that's really all the time you have.

Italy ranks with Germany and France in offering mainland Europe's best-maintained superhighways (called autostrade). You'll pay a toll to drive on them (p. 925), but it's much quicker to use them than to trust your limited time to the array of minor roads, which can be *much* slower going.

The country also boasts one of the fastest and most efficient high-speed rail networks in the world. Rome and Milan are the key hubs of this 21st-century transportation empire—for example, from Rome's Termini station, Florence can be reached in only 95 minutes, and Naples in 70 minutes. In fact, if you're city-hopping your way round Italy, you need never rent a car. Upgrades to the rail network mean that key routes are served by comfortable, fast trains; the key connections include the Turin–Milan–Bologna–Florence–Rome–Naples line, the Venice–Florence–Rome line, and (since 2012) the Milan–Venice line. You'll only really require a rental car if you plan rural detours, whether that's into the vineyards of Tuscany or around the lakes and mountains of the north.

Internal flights should be very much a last resort, but are probably unavoidable for getting to Palermo, in Sicily, or destinations in Puglia or Sardinia. Buses can be perfectly pleasant for short hops between small towns—but you'll need to plan routes carefully, because services are rarely as frequent as on the train network. One exception is Siena, which is most easily reached from Florence by express bus.

The itineraries that follow take you to some of our favorite places. The pace may be a bit breathless for some visitors, so skip a stop occasionally to have some chill-out time—after all, you're on vacation. Of course, you can also use any of our itineraries as a jumping-off point to develop your own custom-made adventure—review chapter 1 to see what experiences or sights might have special appeal to you.

THE REGIONS IN BRIEF

Bordered on the northwest by France, on the north by Switzerland and Austria, and on the east by Slovenia, Italy is a land largely surrounded by the sea. It isn't enormous, but the peninsula's shape gives you the impression of a much larger

PREVIOUS PAGE: **Gondola, Venice.**

The Regions of Italy
Turin
Como
Vercelli
Asti
Milan
Bergamo
Brescia
Lake Garda
Trent
Dolomites
Vicenza
PIEDMONT
Cremona
Verona
VENETO
Udine
Parma
Treviso
Mantua
Padua
SLOVENIA
Savona
Genoa
Ferrara
Venice
Trieste
LIGURIA
Modena
San Remo
Gulf of Genoa
Rapallo
EMILIA-ROMAGNA
Gulf of Venice
La Spezia
Bologna
Ravenna
CROATIA
Ligurian Sea
Lucca
Pisa
Northern Appennines
SAN MARINO
Rimini
Livorno
Florence
BOSNIA
TUSCANY
Pesaro
Siena
Gubbio
Ancona
Elba
Corsica (France)
Perugia
LE MARCHE
45 N.
Orvieto
Assisi
Viterbo
UMBRIA
Spoleto
Terni
Terano
Civitavecchia
L'Aquila
Pescara
VATICAN CITY
ROME
Chieti
ADRIATIC SEA
LATIUM
ABRUZZI
Ólbia
Sassari
Campobasso
MOLIZE
Nuoro
Gulf of Gaeta
Caserta
Benevento
Foggia
41 N.
Sardinia
Naples
Mt. Vesuvius
Ischia
PUGLIA
Pompeii
Sorrento
Capri
Amalfi
Salerno
Bari
Cagliari
Paestum
Southern Appennines
CAMPANIA
Brindisi
9 E.
Tyrrhenian Sea
BASILICATA
Taranto
Gulf of Taranto
Ustica
Cosenza
CALABRIA
Trapani
Aeolian Islands
Egadi Is.
Stromboli
Catanzaro
Palermo
Marsala
Lipari
40 N.
Selinunte
Messina
Ionian Sea
Reggio di Calabria
Enna
Taormina
Agrigento
Mt. Etna
Pantelleria
Catania
MEDITERRANEAN SEA
Sicily
0
100 mi
100 km
Syracuse
Ragusa

Enjoying an evening stroll near the Pantheon in Rome.

area; the ever-changing seacoast contributes to this feeling, as do the large islands of Sicily and Sardinia.

Two areas within Italy's boundaries aren't under the control of the Italian government: the **State of Vatican City** and the **Republic of San Marino.** Vatican City's 44 hectares (109 acres) were established in 1929 by a concordat between Pope Pius XI and Benito Mussolini, acting as head of the Italian government; the agreement also gave Roman Catholicism special status in Italy. The pope is the sovereign of the State of Vatican City, which has its own legal system and post office. The Republic of San Marino, with a capital of the same name, sits astride the slopes of Mount Titano, 23km (14 miles) from Rimini. It's small and completely surrounded by Italy.

Here's a brief rundown of the cities and regions covered in this guide:

Rome & Latium

The region of **Latium** (Lazio in Italian) is dominated by **Rome,** capital of the ancient empire and modern Italy. Much of the "civilized world" was once ruled from here, from the days when Romulus and Remus are said to have founded Rome in 753 B.C. Its fortunes have fallen, of course, but it remains a timeless city: There's no place with more artistic monuments—not even Venice or Florence. How much time should you allocate for the capital? As Italian writer Silvio Negro said, "A lifetime is not enough."

Florence, Tuscany & Umbria

Tuscany is one of the most culturally and politically influential provinces—the development of Italy without Tuscany is simply unthinkable (and the Italian language was a merely standardized version of the Florentine dialect). Tuscany, with its sun-warmed vineyards and stately cypresses, inspired the artists of the

Renaissance. Nowhere in the world is the impact of the Renaissance still felt more fully than in its birthplace, **Florence,** the repository of artistic works left by Masaccio, Leonardo, Michelangelo, and others. The main Tuscan destinations beyond Florence are the smaller cities of **Lucca, Pisa,** and especially **Siena,** Florence's great historical rival with a Gothic center that appears caught in a time warp.

Pastoral, hilly, and fertile, **Umbria** is similar to Tuscany, but less showy, with fewer blockbuster "sights," certainly, and consequently with fewer tourists. Nicknamed the "land of shadows," Umbria often seems covered in a bluish haze that gives the landscape an ethereal look. Cities particularly worth a visit are **Perugia, Gubbio, Assisi, Spoleto** (site of a renowned annual arts festival), and **Orvieto,** a lofty citadel once a key stronghold of the Etruscans. If you're short on time, concentrate on Assisi to check out Giotto's frescoes at the Basilica di San Francesco, and Perugia, the most vibrant city in the region, with outstanding art treasures of its own.

Bologna & Emilia-Romagna

Italians don't agree on much, but the national consensus is that the food in **Emilia-Romagna** is the best in Italy. The region's capital, **Bologna,** boasts a Renaissance core with plenty of churches and arcades, a fine university with roots in the Middle Ages, and a wealthy populace with a reputation for leftist leanings. Other art cities abound—none nobler than Byzantine **Ravenna,** with its stunning mosaics dating to the time when it was capital of the declining Roman Empire.

If you can make only one more stop in the region, make it **Parma,** to tour the city center with its Duomo and baptistery and to view its National Gallery. This is also the true home of Parmigiano-Reggiano cheese and, of course, Prosciutto di Parma. Also noteworthy is the hometown of the late opera star Luciano Pavarotti, **Modena,** known for its cuisine, its cathedral, and its Este Gallery. The Adriatic resort of **Rimini** and the medieval stronghold of **San Marino** are at the eastern periphery of Emilia-Romagna.

The narrow streets of Bologna.

The Piazza San Marco in Venice, with a view of St. Mark's Cathedral.

Venice, the Veneto & the Dolomites

Northeastern Italy is one of Europe's treasure-troves, encompassing **Venice** (certainly the world's most unusual city), the surrounding **Veneto** region, and the mighty **Dolomites** (including the **South Tyrol,** which Italy annexed from Austria after World War I). Aging, decaying, and sinking into the sea, Venice is so alluring we almost want to say, visit it even if you have to skip Rome and Florence. Also recommended are three fabled art cities in the "Venetian Arc": **Verona,** with its romance and its intact Roman Arena; **Vicenza,** where 16th-century aristocrats lived in villas designed by revolutionary architect Andrea Palladio; and **Padua,** with its sublime Giotto frescoes.

The most interesting base in the neighboring region of **Trentino–Alto Adige** (especially if you want to see the Austrian version of Italy) is **Trent (Trento),** the capital of Trentino. Bordering Austria and Slovenia, the region of **Friuli-Venezia Giulia** is, in its own way, one of the most cosmopolitan and culturally sophisticated in Italy. Its capital is **Trieste,** which was the key mercantile port for the Austro-Hungarian Empire, and many of its public buildings might remind you of Vienna.

Milan, Lombardy & the Lakes

Flat, fertile, prosperous, and politically conservative, **Lombardy** is dominated by **Milan** just as Latium is dominated by Rome. Lombardy is one of the world's leading commercial and cultural centers, and it has been ever since Milan developed into Italy's gateway to northern German-speaking Europe in the early Middle Ages. However, despite Leonardo's *Last Supper,* the La Scala opera house, and some major museums, Milan doesn't have the sights and tourist interest of Rome, Florence, or Venice. Visit Milan if you have the time, though you'll find more charm (and a more manageable area to cover) in the neighboring art cities of **Bergamo** and **Mantua.** Also competing for your time should be the photogenic lakes of **Como, Garda,** and **Maggiore.**

Piedmont & Valle d'Aosta

At Italy's extreme northwestern edge, sharing a set of Alpine peaks with France, **Piedmont** was the district from which Italy's campaign for unification spread in 1861. Its largest city, **Turin,** is sometimes called the "Detroit of Italy" because it's the home of the Fiat empire (and vermouth). Turin's most controversial sight is the Sacra Sindone (Holy Shroud), which many Catholics believe is the cloth in which Christ's body was wrapped when lowered from the cross.

A window on both Switzerland and France, the **Valle d'Aosta** (Italy's smallest region) often serves as an introduction to the country, especially for those journeying from France through the Mont Blanc tunnel. The introduction is misleading, however, because Valle d'Aosta stands apart from the rest of Italy, a semi-autonomous region of towering peaks and valleys in the northwestern corridor. The most important city in this region is the old Roman garrison of **Aosta.** More lively are two of Italy's major ski resorts, **Courmayeur** and **Breuil-Cervinia.** The best time to visit is in summer or the deep of a white winter—late spring and fall get rather sleepy in this part of the world.

Genoa & Liguria

Comprising most of the **Italian Riviera,** the region of **Liguria** incorporates the major historical seaport of **Genoa,** charming, upscale harbors such as the one at **Portofino,** and Italy's best coastal hiking, among the traditional communities of

Portofino.

the **Cinque Terre.** There's also a series of beach resorts (including **Rapallo** and **Santa Margherita Ligure**) that stretch east and west of Genoa: the **Riviera di Ponente** to the west, which runs from the French border, and the **Riviera di Levante** to the east. Faced with a choice, we gravitate toward the more glamorous and cosmopolitan Riviera di Levante.

Naples & Campania

Campania reverberates with the memories of the ancient Romans, who favored its strong sunlight, fertile soil, and bubbling sulfurous springs. It encompasses both the fascinating anarchy of **Naples** and the elegant beauty of **Capri** and the **Amalfi Coast.** The region also contains sites specifically identified in ancient mythology (lakes defined as the entrance to the Kingdom of the Dead, for example) and some of the world's most renowned ruins (including **Pompeii, Herculaneum,** and **Paestum**). Campania is overrun, overcrowded, and over-everything, but it still has a certain lure for visitors. The major resorts along the Amalfi Drive—not exactly undiscovered—are **Ravello** (not on the sea) and **Positano** (on the sea). **Amalfi** and **Sorrento** also have beautiful seaside settings.

Puglia

Sun-drenched and poor, **Puglia** (depending on the dialect, Le Puglie or Puglia) forms the heel of the Italian boot. It's the most frequently visited province of Italy's far south: The *trulli* houses of **Alberobello** are photographers' favorites for their unique cylindrical shapes and conical flagstone-sheathed roofs. Among the region's largest cities are **Bari** (the capital), **Foggia** (gateway to the stunning Gargano Peninsula), and **Brindisi** (gateway to Greece, by ferry). Each of these is a modern disaster, stuffed with tawdry buildings and groaning under heavy traffic: Puglia is a region where you should stick to the magnificent countryside, with the exception of the glories of baroque **Lecce.**

Fresh seafood is just one of many reasons to visit Italy's coasts.

Sicily

The largest island in the Mediterranean Sea, **Sicily** is a land of beauty, mystery, and world-class monuments. It's a bizarre mix of bloodlines and architecture from medieval Normandy, Aragónese Spain, Moorish North Africa, ancient Greece, Phoenicia, and Rome. The island's reputation for "primitiveness" has faded, as thousands of cars and fashionable people clog the lanes of its most dynamic and culturally fascinating city, **Palermo.** On the eastern edge of the island is Mount Etna, the tallest active volcano in Europe. Areas of ravishing beauty and eerie historical interest include the towns of **Syracuse** (Siracusa in Italian) and

Taormina, and the ruins at **Agrigento** and **Selinunte.** Sicily's ruins are rivaled only by those of Rome itself, and the Valley of the Temples is worth the trip here alone. For pure seaside serenity, plan a side-trip by boat to the **Aeolian Islands,** a couple of hours' ferry ride offshore.

Sardinia

Sardinia (Sardegna) is sometimes called Italy's best-kept secret. It's part of Italy, of course, but has its own unique landscape, culture, language (Sardo), and cuisine. For centuries it was fought over by major seafaring powers, ranging from the Romans and Phoenicians right up to the Genoese and the Aragonese. The **Costa Smeralda** (Emerald Coast) is perhaps the most desirable place to be in summer, when the rich and famous descend on its posh resorts. But Sardinia is a year-round destination; if you want to explore its culture and heritage, base yourself in **Cagliari,** Sardinia's capital.

ITALY HIGHLIGHTS

It's impossible to see a country the size of Italy in a couple of weeks. In this tour, we lead you around the best of it in 14 days. We go beyond the well-trodden (and spectacular) Rome–Florence–Venice trail to include the southern region of Campania: Naples (with its great archaeological treasures), Pompeii (with Italy's most spectacular ruins), and the stunning Amalfi Drive (the most thrilling but hair-raising road in the country). Additional stops in the Italian north are Bologna (a gourmet city); Padua (with its Giotto frescoes); Verona, of *Romeo and Juliet* fame; and the industrial city of Milan, with its great cathedral and sublime works of art.

DAYS 1 & 2: Rome ★★★

You could spend a lifetime in the Eternal City, but 2 days is enough to get a flavor of it. There are two major areas to focus on in a short visit: the legacy of Imperial Rome, such as the **Forum, Campidoglio** (remodeled by Michelangelo in the 1500s), and **Colosseum;** plus **St. Peter's Basilica** and the **Vatican Museums,** with a collection unlike any other in the world that, of course, includes Michelangelo's frescoed **Sistine Chapel.** Spend your evenings in the bars of **Campo de' Fiori** and the restaurants of **Trastevere.**

DAY 3: Naples ★★

Leave Rome as early in the morning as you can in order to take in the major attractions of Naples: the unparalleled collection of ancient artifacts at the **Museo Archeologico Nazionale;** the Titians and Caravaggios at the **Museo e Gallerie Nazionale di Capodimonte;** and, if time remains, the calm and beauty of the **Certosa di San Martino** and **Museo Nazionale di San Martino.** Wander **Spaccanapoli,** then make a date with a **pizzeria** that night—Neapolitans stake a reasonable claim that pizza was invented here. Stay overnight in Naples to end Day 3.

DAY 4: Pompeii: Europe's Best-Preserved Roman Ruins ★★★

On **DAY 4,** take the Circumvesuviana train 24km (15 miles) south of Naples to spend a day wandering the archaeological remains at **Pompeii.** Make sure you've packed water and a snack, because on-site services aren't great. The city was buried for 2,000 years, having suffered devastation when nearby Vesuvius erupted in A.D. 79. Some of the great treasures of southern Italy—including the remarkable patrician villa **Casa dei Vettii** and the frescoed **Villa dei Misteri**—are found here. Return to Naples for overnighting.

DAY 5: The Amalfi Coast & Its Death-Defying Drive ★★

On the morning of **DAY 5,** drive 49km (30 miles) south of Naples along A3 until you see the turnoff for **Sorrento.** At Sorrento, head east along the curvy Amalfi Drive, of which Andre Gide said "[there is] nothing more beautiful on this earth." The drive winds around the twisting, steep coastline, to the southern resorts of **Positano** and **Amalfi,** either of which would make an idyllic stopover. Allow at least 3 hours for this drive because it is slow moving.

DAY 6: North to Siena ★★★

It's a long day and a long drive, but head north up the A1 autostrada to Rome, bypassing it and continuing north to Siena. You'll arrive in the afternoon and set out right away for **Piazza del Campo,** the shell-shaped main square, including its art-filled **Museo Civico** (inside the **Palazzo Pubblico**). It's a flying visit, but you probably still have time to squeeze in a visit to the **Duomo** and **Museo dell'Opera Metropolitana,** where you'll find Sienese master Duccio's giant *Maestà.* Dinner right on the Campo can be expensive and unsatisfying; stop in there for an early evening drink and then head to a restaurant in Siena's atmospheric back streets.

DAYS 7 & 8: Florence: Cradle of the Renaissance ★★★

It's only 1 hour from Siena to Florence, so you have almost 2 whole days to explore the city of Giotto, Leonardo, Botticelli, and Michelangelo. Start with their masterpieces at the **Uffizi** (you should have booked ahead), followed by the **Duomo** complex: Scale Brunelleschi's ochre dome, and follow up with a visit to the adjoining **Battistero di San Giovanni, Museo dell'Opera del Duomo,** and **Campanile di Giotto.** Start the next day with *David* at the **Accademia.** For the rest of your time focus on the art at the **Palazzo Pitti, San Marco,** and the **Cappella Brancacci.** In the evenings, head south of the Arno for lively wine bars and generally better food.

DAY 9: Bologna: Gastronomic Capital of Italy ★★

The major sights here lie in the immediate center. The best of them are the **Basilica di San Petronio;** the **Pinacoteca Nazionale di Bologna,** with the world's best collection of works by baroque painter Guido Reni; and the **Torre della Garisenda,** all of which can be seen in one afternoon. But you're not just here for the sights. The real pleasures of Bologna are wandering its arcaded streets and finding the next food experience. This is Italy's food capital. Book a table and stay overnight in the city to end Day 9.

DAYS 10 & 11: Venice: City That Defies the Sea ★★★

You'll ride into the heart of Venice on a *vaporetto* (water bus), taking in the **Grand Canal,** the world's greatest thoroughfare. Begin your sightseeing at **Piazza San Marco:** The **Basilica di San Marco** is right there, and after exploring it, visit the nearby **Palazzo Ducale (Doge's Palace)** before walking over the **Bridge of Sighs.** Begin your evening with the classic Venetian *aperitivo,* an Aperol spritz (Aperol with sparkling wine) followed by *cicchetti* (Venetian tapas) before dinner. Make your second day all about the city's unique art: Take in the **Gallerie dell'Accademia,** the more modern **Peggy Guggenheim Collection,** and **San Rocco.**

DAY 12: Padua & Its Giotto Frescoes ★

You needn't check out from your lodgings in Venice to explore Padua. Lying only 40km (25 miles) to the west, it's a straightforward day trip by car or train. In one fairly relaxed day, you can visit the **Basilica di Sant'Antonio** with its Donatello bronzes and the **Cappella degli Scrovegni,** or Arena Chapel, with its Giotto frescoes—perhaps the most important paintings in the history of Italian art. Also look almost next door at the **Chiesa degli Eremitani** as well. One of the saddest sights in Italian art is here, the Ovetari Chapel, where Mantegna's frescoes were almost totally destroyed by a World War II bomb. Return to Venice for the night.

DAY 13: Verona: City of Lovers & Gladiators ★★★

Although he likely never set foot in the place, Shakespeare set the world's most famous love story here, *Romeo and Juliet.* Wander **Piazza dei Signori** and take in another square, **Piazza delle Erbe,** before descending on the **Arena di Verona:** Evoking Rome's Colosseum, it's the world's best-preserved gladiatorial arena, still used for monumental opera performances in summer months. The other architectural highlight is the Romanesque **Basilica San Zeno Maggiore.** Spend the night in Verona's old center.

DAY 14: Milan: Italy's Economic Powerhouse ★★★

The most bustling city in Italy isn't only about industry and commerce. Milan possesses one of the great Gothic cathedrals, the **Duomo.** Its **Biblioteca-Pinacoteca Ambrosiana,** with cartoons by Raphael, is one of the great galleries of Italy. The city of St. Ambrose also hosts the **Pinacoteca di Brera,** a treasure-trove of art, laden with masterpieces from the likes of Mantegna and Piero della Francesca. Book ahead, too, to view Leonardo's fading but still magnificent ***Last Supper.*** Stay overnight here: It is one of the major transportation hubs of Europe, ideal for departures for your next destination.

ITALY FOR FAMILIES

Italy offers hundreds of attractions that kids enjoy. It is, in fact, probably the friendliest family vacation destination in all of Europe. Practically, Italy presents few unexpected challenges. If you're traveling by rental car with young children, be sure to request safety car seats ahead of time. Let the rental company know the age of your child (up to 12) and they will arrange for a seat that complies with E.U. regulations. Rail travelers should remember that reduced-price family fares are available on much of the high-speed rail network; ask when you buy your tickets. As you tour, don't go hunting for "child-friendly" restaurants or special kids' menus. There's always plenty available for little ones—even dishes that aren't on offer to grown-up patrons! Never be afraid to ask if you have a fussy eater in the family. Pretty much any request is met with a smile.

Perhaps the main issue for travelers with children is pacing your museum visits so that you get a chance to see the masterpieces without having young kids suffer a meltdown after too many paintings of saints and bambini.

Our suggestion for this tour is to mix your time between the great art cities—some of which have attractions and activities tailored to kids—and the turquoise waters of the Mediterranean and Lake Garda. Start with 2 days in Rome, followed by a night in Siena, then 2 days in Florence, detouring via Pisa's Leaning Tower to Liguria and Lombardy. End your trip in Venice, which many children will think was created by Walt Disney anyway.

DAY 1: Rome's Ancient Ruins ★★★

History is on your side here: The wonders of ancient Rome should appeal as much to kids (of almost any age) as to adults. The ruins of the **Imperial Forums** do not depend on opening hours but can be viewed at any time. There's plenty of gory tales to tell at the **Colosseum,** after which kids can

St. Peter's Basilica, Rome.

let off a lot of steam wandering the **Roman Forum** and the **Palatine Hill.** Cap the afternoon by exploring the **Villa Borghese,** a monumental park in the heart of Rome. You can rent bikes for rides in the park. There is also a small zoo in the northeast of the grounds.

DAY 2: Rome: Living History ★★★

Head early to **St. Peter's Basilica.** They'll find it spooky wandering the Vatican grottoes, and few kids can resist climbing up to Michelangelo's dome at 114m (375 ft.). After time out for lunch, begin your assault on the **Vatican Museums** and the **Sistine Chapel.** Even if your kids don't like art museums, they will probably gawk at the grandeur. Later in the day head for the **Spanish Steps** before wandering over to the **Trevi Fountain.** Here, give the kids coins to toss into the fountain, which is said to ensure their return to Rome—perhaps when they are older and can better appreciate the city's many more artistic attractions.

DAY 3: Gothic Siena ★★★

Count yourself lucky if you're here in July or August for the famous 4-day **Palio** celebration, when horses race at breakneck speed around **Piazza del Campo.** Year-round, a couple of epic climbs will thrill them. The **Torre del Mangia,** the bell tower of the **Palazzo Pubblico,** ends in a dramatic view of the city and the enveloping countryside. Through the **Museo dell'Opera Metropolitana,** they can scale the Facciatone for an alternative view down into the Campo. At **Santa Maria della Scala,** they'll find **Bambimus,** the art museum for kids, where paintings are hung at child-friendly heights. The zebra-striped **Duomo** is jazzy enough to pique their curiosity. Siena's many bakeries are famed for their sweet treats.

DAYS 4 & 5: Florence: City of the Renaissance ★★★

Florence is usually thought of as more of an adult city, but there's at least enough here to fill 2 family days. Begin with the city's monumental main square, **Piazza della Signoria,** now an open-air museum of statues. The **Palazzo Vecchio** dominates one side; you can all tour it with a docent dressed as Cosimo de' Medici. You won't want to miss the **Uffizi.** With young children, you could turn your visit into a treasure trail of the museum's collection. Kids will delight in climbing to the top of the Brunelleschi's dome on the **Duomo** for a classic panorama. You'll still have time to climb the 414 steps up to the **Campanile di Giotto,** run around in the **Giardino di Boboli,** and stroll the **Ponte Vecchio** at dusk.

DAY 6: Pisa & Its Leaning Tower ★★

If your kids are 7 or under, you should consider skipping this stop: 8 is the minimum age for the disorienting ascent up the bell tower of Pisa's cathedral, which more commonly goes by the name the **Leaning Tower.** Elsewhere in the city, kids will love the hyperrealist monuments of the **Campo dei Miracoli** and learning about the city's Galileo links: He was born here, and supposedly discovered his law of pendulum motion while watching a swinging lamp inside the **Cattedrale.** In the evening, take them to taste a local specialty, *cecina*—a pizzalike garbanzo-bean flatbread served warm—at popular slice parlor, **Il Montino.**

DAY 7: Genoa & the Riviera di Levante ★★

The industrial city-seaport of Genoa isn't the obvious choice for the kids, but it's here you'll find one of Italy's most enticing family attractions. The **Acquario di Genova** is Europe's largest aquarium, where you can all enjoy a trip around the world's oceans. It requires a half-day to see properly, so get in early and you'll have time left to head out to the **Riviera di Levante,** a coastline of pretty ports and rocky coves east of the city. Our favorite base for overnighting around here is romantic **Portofino.**

DAYS 8 & 9: Lake Garda ★★★

Slow down for a couple of days by Italy's biggest inland lake. Take a boat trip, hire a pedal boat or kayak, and generally enjoy lakeside life. Most of the shore towns are seasonal resorts, and the most interesting for families is **Sirmione.** Here you can scramble up high on the ramparts of the **Castello Scaligero** and ride the little train out to the Roman ruins at the **Grotte di Catullo,** once a villa inhabited by poet Catullus (c. 84–54 B.C.). Look out for lake fish on local menus.

DAYS 10 & 11: Venice, City on the Lagoon ★★★

Venice is the great kid-pleaser of Italy, the fun beginning the moment you arrive and take a *vaporetto* ride along the **Grand Canal.** Head straight for **Piazza San Marco,** where children delight in feeding the pigeons and riding the elevator up the great **Campanile.** Catch the mosaics inside the **Basilica di San Marco,** which dominates the square. At the **Palazzo Ducale,** your kids can walk over the infamous **Bridge of Sighs.** As in Florence, make time for some art: Visit the **Gallerie dell'Accademia** and **San Rocco,** where kids view the episodic Tintoretto paintings like a picture book. If it's summer, save time for the beach, at the **Lido.**

AN ART LOVER'S WEEK IN TUSCANY BEYOND FLORENCE

The true devotees of Renaissance art will inevitably spend much of their time exploring the churches and *palazzi* of Florence. However, the smaller towns and cities of this exquisite Italian region are not short of masterpieces of their own. The city of Siena, Florence's traditional rival, contains ethereal art from the Sienese School of the Middle Ages. Pisa was home to the greatest Gothic sculptors in Italy. And smaller towns from Pienza to Arezzo have treasures that would be the pride of any city on earth.

DAY 1: Lucca: Elegant Walled City ★★

Leave Florence early and drive 72km (45 miles) west on the A11. (Ask your accommodations ahead of time about parking deals.) Inside its thick swath of Renaissance walls, bordered by gardens, the narrow streets of Lucca still follow a medieval plan. Lucca's main architectural attractions are its memorable facades, in the Luccan-Romanesque style. The **Duomo,** or **Cattedrale di San Martino,** has a green-and-white marble facade designed by Guidetto da Como. **San Michele in Foro** has one of the most beautiful church facades in all of Tuscany, with its delicately twisted columns and arcades. Dating from slightly earlier, the facade of **San Frediano** sports a shimmering golden mosaic by Berlinghieri. You'll get the best view of the whole place when you circumnavigate the walls by **bicycle.**

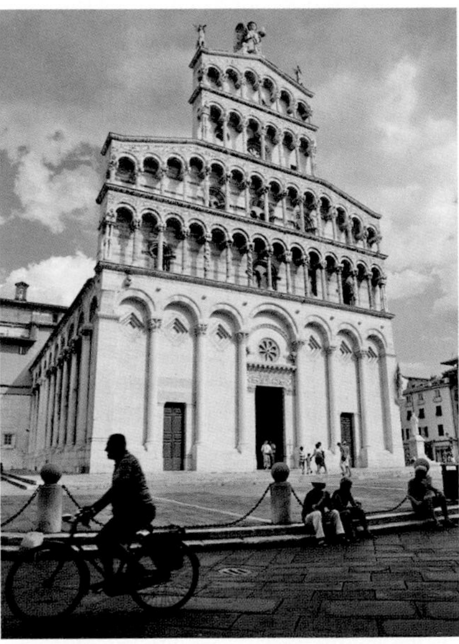

The towering facade of Lucca's San Michele in Foro.

DAY 2: Pisa: City of the Romanesque ★★★

Lucca lies only 21km (13 miles) northeast of Pisa. You could drive, but it's perhaps easier to visit as a day trip by rail. (Alight at Pisa San Rossore, not Pisa Centrale.) Pisa's unmissable monuments center around its **Campo dei Miracoli (Field of Miracles),** so touring is easy. Start with the **Leaning Tower** (for which you should book tickets ahead of time), whose six floors of columned galleries wind around the spiral. Next, prioritize the **Duomo** and **Battistero,** both stellar examples of the Pisan-Romanesque style, and housing two of the four great Pisano carved pulpits. If time remains, head across town to explore the haphazard but rewarding **Museo Nazionale di San Matteo.**

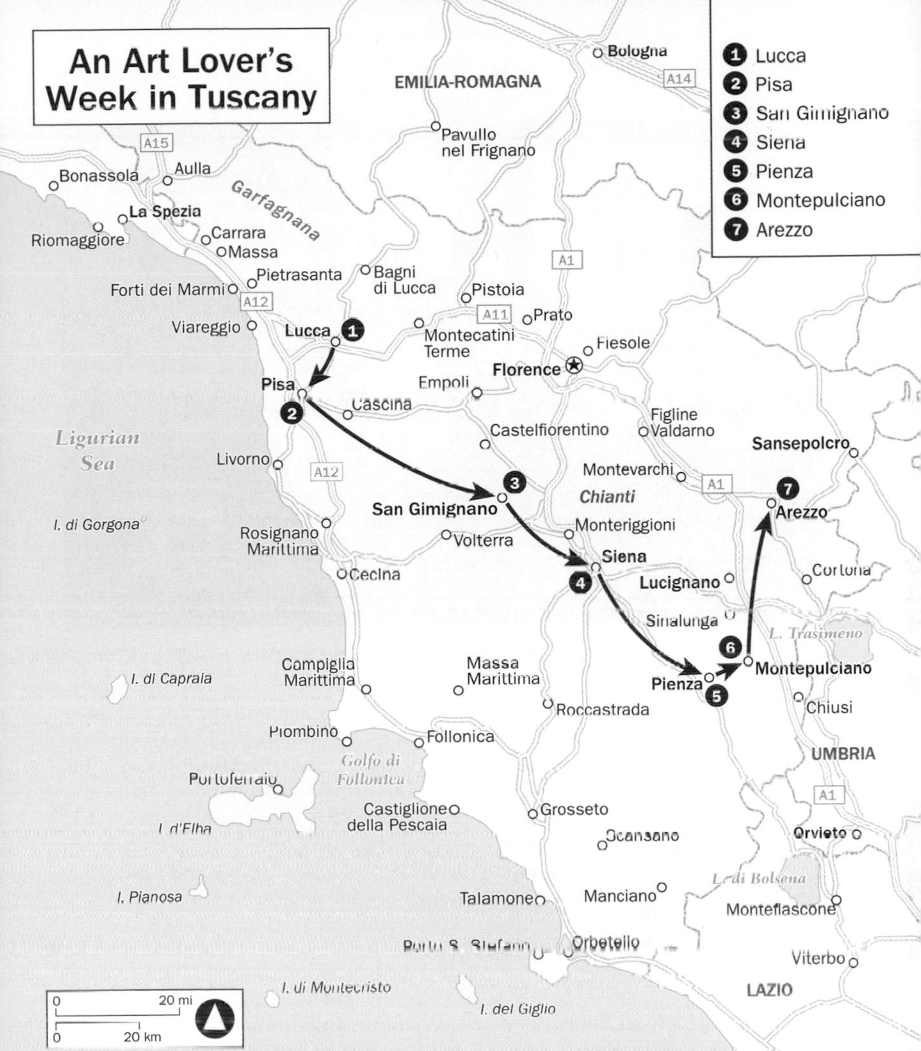

DAY 3: San Gimignano & Its Medieval Towers ★★★

This city lies 92km (57 miles) southeast of Pisa. For the architectural enthusiast, wandering through the gates of San Gimignano is the start of a journey back to the Middle Ages. This is Italy's best-preserved medieval town, and some one dozen of the original 70-plus towers remain. At **San Gimignano 1300,** you'll see a faithful re-creation of the town as it was 700 years ago. The town's art highlight is Domenico Ghirlandaio's Santa Fina frescoes in the **Collegiata.** There's more painting—and a great view across the vineyards surrounding the town—at the **Museo Civico & Torre Grossa.**

DAY 4: Siena: Homage to the Middle Ages ★★★

Siena (42km/26 miles southeast of San Gimignano) caters amply to the lover of both art and architecture. With time pressed, base your visit around

San Gimignano.

two key piazzas. The famous **Campo** is where you'll find the city's **Museo Civico,** home to monumental frescoes by Simone Martini and Ambrogio Lorenzetti. Uphill, around Piazza del Duomo, visit the **Duomo** itself (for Pinturicchio's Piccolomini Library and the Renaissance intarsia floor), the **Museo dell'Opera Metropolitana** (for Duccio's 1311 *Maestà*), and **Santa Maria della Scala,** the city's frescoed former hospital-turned-museum. If you still have time, dig deeper into the history of Sienese art at the **Pinacoteca Nazionale.** Although our breakneck tour calls for only 1 day here, 2 days is preferable if your schedule can accommodate it.

DAY 5: Pienza: Ideal Renaissance City ★

The village of Pienza lies 55km (33 miles) southeast of Siena. It owes its overall look to its homegrown son, Pope Pius II, born here in 1405. He set out to transform Pienza into a model Renaissance village—and got as far as overseeing one elegant piazza. Bernardo Rossellino, a protégé of the great Renaissance theorist Leon Battista Alberti, carried out the mandate of the pope, creating a **Cattedrale** with a Renaissance facade and its original altarpieces still displayed in situ (a rarity in Tuscany), the **Palazzo Piccolomini** (Rossellino's masterpiece), and a main square, **Piazza Pio II,** which remains a Renaissance jewel.

DAY 6: Montepulciano & Its Noble Wine ★★

On the morning of the following day, drive a mere 13km (8 miles) east to Montepulciano. Begin your visit to Tuscany's highest hill town with the parade of handsome *palazzi* flanking its steep main street, the Corso. The chief attractions for the devotee of Renaissance architecture are the **Palazzo Nobili-Tarugi** and **Tempio di San Biagio.** Everything centers around the monumental **Piazza Grande,** where you'll also find a rather plain **Duomo** with a huge Taddeo di Bartolo altarpiece inside. Leave some late afternoon and evening time for visiting a couple of tasting rooms and drinking the elegant local red wine, **Vino Nobile di Montepulciano,** at an enoteca.

The Museo dell'Opera in Siena.

DAY 7: Arezzo: The Piero della Francesca Capital ★★

Piero della Francesca was a visionary artist, one of the towering figures of the Italian Quattrocento (1400s). You'll find his masterpiece, the frescoes depicting *Legend of the True Cross* (1452–66), on the walls of the apse chapel at the **Basilica di San Francesco,** in Arezzo. Piero also frescoed a *Mary Magdalene* inside the town's **Duomo**—also famed for its stained glass by Guillaume de Marcillat. Piero fans could detour east along S73 for 39km (64 miles) to his birthplace, Sansepolcro, where the **Museo Civico,** Via Aggiunti 65 (✆ **0575-732218**), houses the master's *Resurrection*.

A WHISTLE-STOP WEEK IN ITALY FOR FOOD & WINE LOVERS

Alongside France, Italy has one of Europe's great cuisines. In fact, the country harbors several very different cuisines; its history as a collection of independent city states and noble fiefdoms has left a legacy in food as diverse as its architectural and cultural leftovers. Each, however, shares a commitment to local and regional produce, and treasures recipes that have been handed down through generations. Italy is also the world's biggest wine producer. While much of the output is undistinguished, if perfectly drinkable, table wine, some of the icons of world wine hail from the peninsula. Our itinerary takes in just three of the great Italian red wine zones: **Montepulciano,** whose noble wine was known to the Etruscans; the **Chianti,** probably the first properly codified wine zone in the world; and **Piedmont,** whose robust reds, Barolo and Barbaresco, command top prices at restaurants across the globe.

DAYS 1 & 2: Rome ★★★

Italy's capital is packed with restaurants offering cuisine from across the peninsula—**Trastevere** is a great spot for dining and drinks after dark.

While here, look out for traditional Roman dishes like pasta with *cacio e pepe* (sheep's milk cheese and black pepper) or *saltimbocca alla Romana*—literally, "jump in the mouth," a veal cutlet with prosciutto and sage. **Gelato** is either Florentine or Sicilian in origin, depending on whom you speak to, but it's in Rome you'll find some of the country's best. You'll need a rental car for your next leg. Collect it on your second afternoon and head north to Tuscany, to leave you a full day at your next stop.

DAY 3: Montepulciano ★★

Begin with a walk up the handsome, steep Corso, from the town gate to **Piazza Grande,** monumental heart of the *comune*. Here you'll find the **Palazzo Comunale** (climb it for a panorama over the surrounding vineyards) and **Cattedrale.** Oenophiles should make a beeline for the **Consorzio del Vino Nobile di Montepulciano** office, where you can taste vintages from small producers and seek advice for nearby wineries to visit. Our favorite cellar in the center is **Gattavecchi.** End the evening at **Acquacheta,** where the menu's all about beef—*"bistecca numero uno,"* is how Contucci winemaker Adamo describes it. Other local delicacies include sheep's milk cheese, *pecorino di Pienza.*

DAYS 4 & 5: The Chianti ★★★

Pick a base close to **Greve in Chianti** to lodge right at the heart of Tuscany's largest quality wine region. Sangiovese-based chianti is a diverse wine: Chianti Classico denotes grapes from the original (and best) growing zone, and tasting opportunities abound at cellars such as **Villa Vignamaggio** and **Castello di Volpaia**—book ahead if you require a tour. The Chianti is also famed for its butchers, selling everything from cuts of fresh beef (ideal if you're staying in a villa) to salami made from the local breed of pig, Cinta Senese. **Falorni,** in Greve, is outshone perhaps only by **Dario Cecchini,** in nearby Panzano. Also look for extra-virgin olive oil—the local elixir is among Italy's best.

DAY 6: Bologna ★★

You've arrived in Italy's gastronomic capital; leave the rental car here—it's easy to continue onward by train. The agricultural plains of Emilia-Romagna are Italy's breadbasket. So much of the produce we think of as typical "Italian food" originally hails from here: cured prosciutto and Parmigiano-Reggiano cheese from Parma, the finest balsamic vinegar from Modena, mortadella and *tortellini* (filled pasta) from Bologna itself. Foodies should browse Bologna's markets, the **Pescherie Vecchie** and **Mercato delle Erbe.** Make an evening reservation at a restaurant that specializes in classic Bolognese cooking.

DAY 7: Turin ★

Lofty peaks dot the horizon north and west of the Piedmontese capital, and the cooking in Italy's northwest reflects the heartier and hardier mountain folk who live on the doorstep. Nearby Vercelli is Italy's rice capital—the town is surrounded by paddy fields—and risotto is at its best here. There's also a noticeable Ligurian current in Torinese food: The basil-based pesto is superb and the favorite slice on the go isn't pizza but *farinata* (garbanzo-bean flour flatbread dusted with rosemary or pepper). **Eataly,** in the Lingotto neighborhood, stocks delicacies from across Italy. Sweet vermouth was also invented here; the classic local label is Punt e Mes ("point and a half" in Piedmontese dialect).

SMALL CITIES OF THE ITALIAN NORTH IN 6 DAYS

Often overshadowed by blockbusters like Rome and Florence, the small cities of northern Italy make an excellent itinerary for second-time visitors to the country. Each city on our tour has a center with refined Renaissance architecture, and a history of independence—as well as struggles with, and eventual subjection to, the great regional powers, such as Venice. The logical start-point is Milan, gateway to Italy for flights from across the globe. Sleep overnight there, collect your rental car or rail ticket—all the train connections on this tour are easy—and set off early. The endpoint is just a short drive or train ride from Venice, where we recommend you extend your stay by as many days as you can; see chapter 8 for full coverage of the city.

DAY 1: Bergamo ★★

Whether you arrive by train or car, alight in the **Lower Town** (Città Bassa) and ascend to the **Upper Town** (Città Alta) in style, on the town's century-old funicular railway. **Piazza Vecchia** is the architectural heart of the Upper Town. Beyond the arcades, you'll find the Romanesque **Basilica di Santa Maria Maggiore** and the Renaissance **Cappella Colleoni,** with its frescoed ceiling by Venetian painter Tiepolo. You should also make time for the **Galleria dell'Accademia Carrara,** with its exceptional collection of northern Italian painting. The town was the birthplace of composer Donizetti and has a lively cultural (largely operatic) program.

DAY 2: Verona ★★★

A visit to northern Italy's most renowned small city is less about ticking off sights than about soaking up the elegance of a place eternally (and fictionally) associated with Shakespeare's doomed lovers, *Romeo and Juliet.* If you're here in summer, make straight for the box office at the **Arena di Verona;** Italy's most intact amphitheatre still hosts monumental outdoor operatic productions, which you shouldn't miss. Your roaming should also take you to the **Castelvecchio,** fortified home of the Della Scala family, who ruled here in the 13th and 14th centuries, and **San Zeno Maggiore,** one of Italy's most appealing Romanesque churches.

DAY 3: Mantua ★★

Landlocked it may be, but the Renaissance city of Mantua is almost completely, romantically surrounded by water—lakes fed by the River Mincio. It owes its grandeur almost entirely to one family, the Gonzaga dynasty, who built piazzas and palaces, and filled them with art by the greatest masters of the period, such as Mantegna. One day is just enough to see L. B. Alberti's **Basilica di Sant Andrea,** the frescoed **Palazzo Ducale,** and the Room of Giants inside the **Palazzo Te.**

DAY 4: Vicenza ★★

Few cities in the world have been so shaped by the vision of one architect as Vicenza. Andrea Palladio was actually born in nearby Padua, but his vision for the reinvention of classical architecture was dramatically realized in Renaissance Vicenza. The prosperous, atmospheric streets are littered with his creations (and later buildings inspired by him). Visit the **Basilica Palladiana,** subject to a massive restoration project between 2007 and 2012, and Palladio's **Teatro Olimpico,** where you can still attend orchestral concerts. On a quiet hill outside of the center, Palladio's **Villa Rotonda** was the template for later state capitol buildings across the U.S.

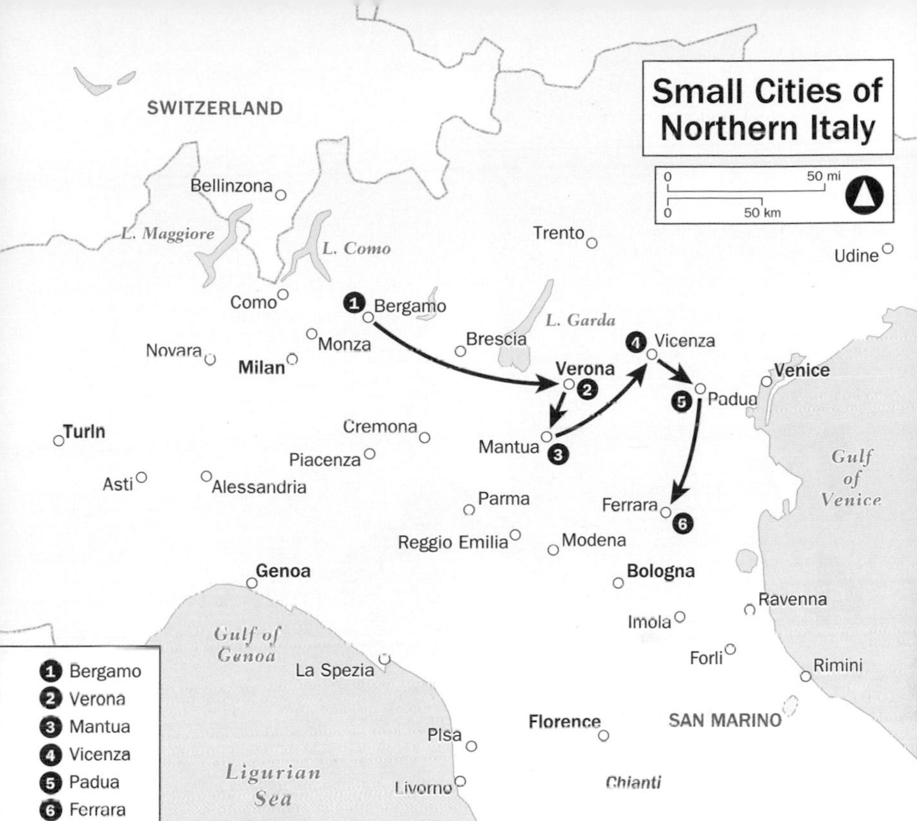

DAY 5: Padua ★

The most important art stop in northern Italy is Giotto's frescoed **Cappella degli Scrovegni,** but before you head there, stop in at the tourist office to buy a Padova Card—a discount ticket that buys you entrance to almost everything in town plus free public transportation or parking. The city is also the final resting place of St. Anthony of Padua, the second-most preeminent Franciscan saint after St. Francis himself. Inside the **Basilica di Sant'Antonio,** you'll find his tomb and some Donatello bronzes. Much of the city outskirts were unaesthetically rebuilt after sustaining massive damage during World War II; head to the Ovetari Chapel inside the **Chiesa degli Eremitani** to see what a direct hit from a bomb could do to irreplaceable frescoes by Mantegna. It's a tragic, moving sight.

DAY 6: Ferrara ★

This small, stately city of cyclists owes its grandeur as much to one despotic family as does nearby Mantua. In Ferrara, it was the Este dukes who held sway from the 1200s to the 1500s. They ruled the city from the **Castello Estense.** Elsewhere in the center, check out the famous facade of the Gothic-Romanesque **Duomo** and the **Palazzo dei Diamanti,** another Este creation and named for the 9,000 diamond-shaped stones adorning its facade. From Ferrara, it's a direct, 90-minute train journey to Venice.

4

ROME

Rome is a city of images and sounds, all vivid and all unforgettable. You can see one of the most striking images at dawn—ideally from Janiculum Hill (Gianicolo)—when the Roman skyline, with its bell towers and cupolas, gradually comes into focus. As the sun rises, the Roman symphony begins. First come the peals of church bells calling the faithful to Mass. Then the streets fill with cars, taxis, tour buses, and Vespas, the drivers gunning their engines and blaring their horns. Next the sidewalks are overrun with office workers, chattering as they rush off to their desks, but not before ducking into a cafe for their first cappuccino. Shop owners loudly throw up the metal grilles protecting their stores; the fruit-and-vegetable stands are crowded with Romans out to buy the day's supply of fresh produce, haggling over prices and caviling over quality.

Around 10am, the visitors—you included, with your guidebook in hand—take to the streets, battling the crowds and traffic as they wend from Renaissance palaces and baroque buildings to ancient ruins like the Colosseum and the Forum. After you've spent a long day in the sun, marveling at the sights you've seen millions of times in photos and movies, you can pause to experience the charm of Rome at dusk.

Find a cafe at summer twilight, and watch the shades of pink and rose turn to gold and copper as night falls. That's when a new Rome awakens. The cafes and restaurants grow more animated, especially if you've found one in an ancient piazza or along a narrow alley deep in Trastevere. After dinner, you can stroll by the lighted fountains and monuments (Trevi Fountain and the Colosseum look magical at night) or through Piazza Navona and have a gelato. The night is yours.

THE BEST ROME TRAVEL EXPERIENCES

- **Having breakfast with Marcus Aurelius:** Begin the day climbing up the steps of the stunning Michelangelo-designed Campidoglio square, sidle to the right and uphill to the **Capitoline Museum** side entrance for an early breakfast at Terrazza Caffarelli. Enjoy your cappuccino and flaky croissant with sweeping views of the Victor Emanuel monument, the Santa Maria in Ara Coeli church, and the Jewish ghetto, with a pink sky and dovetailed rooftops beyond.
- **Spelunking in the Appian Way underworld:** Explore Rome's biggest and most popular catacombs, the **Catacombs of St. Callixtus,** walking through an intricate network of galleries about 19km (12 miles) long and 20m (65 ft.)

PREVIOUS PAGE: **Fountain of the Four Rivers.**

deep. Highlights of the underground funerary tunnels include the crypt of the nine popes and impressive early Christian frescoes, paintings, and sculptures. See p. 122.

- **Ascending the Vittoriano in a glass lift:** For a breathtaking view of the Eternal City, climb past the flame guarded by soldiers burning on the front terrace which marks the grave of an unknown World War I soldier, and more monumental staircases up to where a 7€ ticket grants access to a glass elevator that rides up to the very top of the "Quadriga" terrace, allowing a view of the Imperial Fora, the Trajan Markets, the Colosseum, and the urban trident offered by Via del Corso and the adjoining streets.
- **Enjoying an aperitivo with Raphael's *Sibyls* at the Hotel Raphael's rooftop cafe:** After a day of sightseeing around the ruins, people-watching in Piazza Navona, and shopping at the Spanish Steps, take a break—and a predinner drink—in one of Rome's most unique cafes. Located in the Bramante Cloister, visitors can admire the famous Raphael frescoes of the *Sibyls and Angels* thanks to large glass partitions that overlook the church of Santa Maria della Pace.
- **Kissing your loved one at sunset on Ponte Sisto:** The footbridge that connects Campo de' Fiori to the bohemian Trastevere district is the perfect backdrop for romance. Above Piazza Trilussa where all the nightlife action is, lovers can admire the quiet and beautifully lit Fontanone, or choose any cobbled alley for a typical Roman trattoria to hide in.

ESSENTIALS

Getting There

BY PLANE Chances are, you'll arrive at Rome's **Leonardo da Vinci International Airport** (www.adr.it; ✆ **06-65951**), popularly known as **Fiumicino,** 30km (19 miles) from the city center. (If you're flying by charter, you might land at Ciampino Airport, discussed below.) There is a tourist information office at the airport's Terminal B, International arrival, open daily 9am to 6:30pm.

A ***cambio*** (money exchange) operates daily from 7:30am to 11pm, offering surprisingly good rates, and there are ATMs in the airport.

There's a **train station** in the airport. To get into the city, follow the signs marked TRENI for the 30-minute shuttle to Rome's main station, **Stazione Termini.** The shuttle (the Leonardo Express) runs from 5:52am to 11:36pm for 14€ one-way. On the way, you'll pass a machine dispensing tickets, or you can buy them in person near the tracks if you don't have small bills on you. When you arrive at Termini, get out of the train quickly and grab a baggage cart. (It's a long schlep from the track to the exit or to the other train connections, and baggage carts can be scarce.)

A **taxi** from da Vinci airport to the city costs 40€ and up for the 1-hour trip, depending on traffic. The expense might be worth it if you have a lot of luggage. Call ✆ **06-6645,** 06-3570, or 06-4994 for information. Note that the flat rate of 40€ is applicable from the airport to central Rome and vice versa, but only if your central Rome location is inside the Aurelian Walls (most hotels are). Otherwise, standard metered rates apply, which can be 75€ higher.

If you arrive on a charter flight at **Ciampino Airport** (www.adr.it; ✆ **06-65951**), you can take a Terravision bus (✆ **06-4880086**) to Stazione Termini. Trip time is about 45 minutes and costs 4€. A **taxi** from here to Rome costs 30€, a flat rate that applies as long as you're going to a destination within the old Aurelian Walls. Otherwise, you'll pay the metered fare, but the trip is shorter (about 40 min.).

BY TRAIN OR BUS Trains and buses (including trains from the airport) arrive in the center of old Rome at the silver **Stazione Termini,** Piazza dei Cinquecento (✆ **06-478411**). This is the train, bus, and subway transportation hub for all Rome, and it is surrounded by many hotels (especially cheaper ones).

If you're taking the **Metropolitana** (subway), follow the illuminated red-and-white M signs. To catch a bus, go straight through the outer hall and enter the sprawling bus lot of **Piazza dei Cinquecento.** You'll also find **taxis** there.

The station is filled with services. At a branch of the Intesasanpaolo bank (at tracks 1 and 24), you can exchange money. **Informazioni Ferroviarie** (in the outer hall) dispenses information on rail travel to other parts of Italy. There are also a **tourist information booth,** baggage services, newsstands, and snack bars.

BY CAR From the north, the main access route is the **Autostrada del Sole (A1).** Called "Motorway of the Sun," the highway links Milan with Naples via Bologna, Florence, and Rome. At 754km (469 miles), it is the longest Italian autostrada and is the "spinal cord" of Italy's road network. All the autostrade join with the **Grande Raccordo Anulare,** a ring road encircling Rome, channeling traffic into the congested city. Long before you reach this road, you should study a map carefully to see what part of Rome you plan to enter and mark your route accordingly. Route markings along the ring road tend to be confusing.

Warning: Return your rental car immediately, or at least get yourself to a hotel, park your car, and leave it there until you leave Rome. Don't even think about driving in Rome—the traffic is just too nightmarish.

Getting Around

Rome is excellent for walking, with sites of interest often clustered together. Much of the inner core is traffic-free, so you'll need to walk whether you like it or not. However, in many parts of the city it's hazardous and uncomfortable because of the crowds, heavy traffic, and narrow sidewalks. Sometimes sidewalks don't exist at all, and it becomes a sort of free-for-all with pedestrians competing for space against vehicular traffic (the traffic always seems to win). Always be on your guard. The hectic crush of urban Rome is considerably less during August, when many Romans leave town for vacation.

BY SUBWAY The **Metropolitana,** or **Metro,** for short, is the fastest means of transportation, operating 5:30am to 11:30pm Sunday to Thursday, and until 1:30am on Friday and Saturday. A big red M indicates the entrance to the subway.

Tickets are 1€ and are available from *tabacchi* (tobacco shops), many newsstands, and vending machines at all stations. Some stations have managers, but they won't make change. Booklets of tickets are available at

tabacchi and in some terminals. You can also buy a **tourist pass** on either a daily or a weekly basis (see "By Bus & Tram," below).

Building a subway system for Rome hasn't been easy because every time workers start digging, they discover an old temple or other archaeological treasure, and heavy earth moving has to cease for a while.

BY BUS & TRAM Roman buses and trams are operated by an organization known as **ATAC** (Agenzia del Trasporto Autoferrotranviario del Comune di Roma; www.atacmobile.it; ✆ **06-57003**), Piazzale degli Archivi 40, in the Eur suburb of Rome.

For 1€ you can ride to most parts of Rome, although it can be slow going in all that traffic, and the buses are often very crowded. Your ticket is valid for 75 minutes, and you can get on many buses and trams during that time by using the same ticket (as well as one run on the Metro). You can buy tickets in *tabacchi* or bus terminals. You must have your ticket before boarding because there are no ticket-issuing machines on the vehicles.

At Stazione Termini, you can buy a special **tourist pass,** which costs 4€ for a day or 16€ for a week. This pass allows you to ride on the ATAC network without bothering to buy individual tickets. The tourist pass is also valid on the subway—but never ride the trains when the Romans are going to or from work, or you'll be smashed flatter than fettuccine. On the first bus you board, you place your ticket in a small machine, which prints the day and hour you boarded, and then you withdraw it. You do the same on the

Two Bus Warnings

Any map of the Roman bus system will likely be outdated before it's printed. Many buses listed on the "latest" map no longer exist; others are enjoying a much-needed rest, and new buses suddenly appear without warning. There's also talk of completely renumbering the whole system soon, so be aware that the route numbers we've listed might have changed by the time you travel.

Take extreme caution when riding Rome's overcrowded buses—pickpockets abound! This is particularly true on bus no. 64, a favorite of visitors because of its route through the historic districts and thus also a favorite of Rome's pickpocketing community. This bus has earned various nicknames, including the "Pickpocket Express" and "Wallet Eater."

last bus you take during the valid period of the ticket. One-day and weekly tickets are also available at *tabacchi,* many newsstands, and at vending machines at all stations.

Buses and trams stop at areas marked FERMATA. At most of these, a yellow sign will display the numbers of the buses that stop there and a list of all the stops along each bus's route in order so you can easily search out your destination. In general, they're in service daily from 5am to midnight. After that and until dawn, you can ride on special night buses (they have an N in front of their bus number), which run only on main routes. It's best to take a taxi in the wee hours—if you can find one.

At the **bus information booth** at Piazza dei Cinquecento, in front of the Stazione Termini, you can purchase a directory with maps of the routes.

Although routes change often, a few old reliable routes have remained valid for years, such as **no. 75** from Stazione Termini to the Colosseum, **H** from Stazione Termini to Trastevere, and **no. 40** from Stazione Termini to the Vatican. But if you're going somewhere and are dependent on the bus, be sure to carefully check where the bus stop is and exactly which bus goes there—don't assume that it'll be the same bus the next day.

BY TAXI If you're accustomed to hopping a cab in New York or London, then do so in Rome. But don't count on hailing a taxi on the street or even getting one at a stand. If you're going out, have your hotel call one. At a restaurant, ask the waiter or cashier to dial for you. If you want to phone for yourself, try one of these numbers: © **06-6645,** 06-3570, or 06-4994.

The meter begins at 2.80€ for the first 3km (1¾ miles) and then rises .92€ per kilometer. The first suitcase is free. Every additional piece of luggage costs 1€. There's another 5.80€ supplement from 10pm to 7am. Avoid paying your fare with large bills; invariably, taxi drivers claim that they don't have change, hoping for a bigger tip (stick to your guns and give only about 15%).

BY CAR All roads might lead to Rome, but you don't want to drive once you get here. Because the reception desks of most Roman hotels have at least one English-speaking person, call ahead to find out the best route into Rome from wherever you're starting out. You're usually allowed to park in front of the hotel long enough to unload your luggage. You'll want to get rid of your rental car as soon as possible, or park in a garage.

You might want to rent a car to explore the countryside around Rome or drive to another city. You'll save the most money if you reserve before leaving home. But if you want to book a car here, know that **Hertz** is at Via Giovanni Giolitti 34 (www.hertz.com; ✆ **06-4740389;** Metro: Termini), and **Avis** is at Stazione Termini (www.avis.com; ✆ **06-4814373;** Metro: Termini). **Maggiore,** an Italian company, has an office at Stazione Termini (www.maggiore.it; ✆ **06-4880049;** Metro: Termini). There are also branches of the major rental agencies at the airport.

BY BIKE Other than walking, the best way to get through the medieval alleys and small piazzas of Rome is perched on the seat of a bicycle. The heart of ancient Rome is riddled with bicycle lanes to get you through the murderous traffic. The most convenient place to rent bikes is **Bici & Baci,** Via del Viminale 5 (www.bicibaci.com; ✆ **06-4828443**), lying 2 blocks west of Stazione Termini, the main rail station. Prices start at 4€ per hour or 11€ per day.

Visitor Information

Information is available at **Azienda Provinciale di Turismo** (APT; www.aptprovroma.it; ✆ **06-421381**), Via XX Settembre 26. The headquarters is open Monday to Friday 9am to 1pm. On Monday and Thursday it also is open 2 to 4pm.

More helpful, and stocking maps and brochures, are the offices maintained by the **Comune di Roma** at various sites around the city. They're staffed daily from 9:30am to 7pm, except the one at Termini (daily 8am–8:30pm). Here are the addresses of others in Stazione Termini: at Piazza Pia near the Castel Sant'Angelo; on Via Nazionale 183, near the Palazzo delle Esposizioni; on Piazza Sonnino, in Trastevere; on Piazza Cinque Lune, near Piazza Navona; and on Via dell'Olmata, near Piazza Santa Maria Maggiore. All phone calls for Comune di Roma are directed through a centralized number: ✆ **06-060608** (www.060608.it). Call daily 9am to 9pm.

Enjoy Rome, Via Marghera 8A (www.enjoyrome.com; ✆ **06-4451843**), was begun by an English-speaking couple, Fulvia and Pierluigi. They dispense information about almost everything in Rome and are far more pleasant and organized than the Board of Tourism. They'll also help you find a hotel room, with no service charge (in anything from a hostel to a three-star hotel). Hours are Monday to Friday 8:30am to 5pm, and Saturday 8:30am to 2pm.

City Layout

Arm yourself with a detailed street map, not the general overview handed out free at tourist offices. Most hotels hand out a pretty good version at their front desks.

The bulk of ancient, Renaissance, and baroque Rome (as well as the train station) lies on the east side of the **Tiber River (Fiume Tevere),** which meanders through town. However, several important landmarks are on the other side: **St. Peter's Basilica** and the **Vatican,** the **Castel Sant'Angelo,** and the colorful **Trastevere** neighborhood.

The city's various quarters are linked by large boulevards (large, at least, in some places) that have mostly been laid out since the late 19th century. Starting from the **Vittorio Emanuele Monument,** a controversial pile of snow-white Brescian marble that's often compared to a wedding cake, there's a street running practically due north to **Piazza del Popolo** and the city wall. This is **Via del Corso,** one of the main streets of Rome—noisy, congested, crowded with buses and shoppers, and called simply "Il Corso." To its left (west) lie the Pantheon, Piazza Navona, Campo de' Fiori, and the Tiber. To its right (east) you'll find the Spanish Steps, the Trevi Fountain, the Borghese Gardens, and Via Veneto.

One of Rome's many markets.

Back at the Vittorio Emanuele Monument, the major artery going west (and ultimately across the Tiber to St. Peter's) is **Corso Vittorio Emanuele.** Behind you to your right, heading toward the Colosseum, is **Via dei Fori Imperiali,** laid out in the 1930s by Mussolini to show off the ruins of the Imperial Forums he had excavated, which line it on either side. Yet another central conduit is **Via Nazionale,** running from **Piazza Venezia** (just in front of the Vittorio Emanuele Monument) east to **Piazza della Repubblica** (near Stazione Termini). The final lap of Via Nazionale is called **Via Quattro Novembre.**

THE NEIGHBORHOODS IN BRIEF

This section will give you some idea of where you might want to stay and where the major attractions are. It might be hard to find a specific address, because of the narrow streets of old Rome and the little, sometimes hidden, *piazze* (squares). Numbers usually run consecutively, with odd numbers on one side of the street and evens on the other. However, in the old districts the numbers sometimes run up one side and then run back in the opposite direction on the other side. Therefore, no. 50 could be opposite no. 308.

NEAR STAZIONE TERMINI The main train station, **Stazione Termini,** adjoins **Piazza della Repubblica,** and most likely this will be your introduction to Rome. Much of the area is seedy and filled with gas fumes from all the buses and cars, but it has been improving. If you stay here, you might not get a lot of atmosphere, but you'll have a lot of affordable options and a convenient location, near the transportation hub of the city and not far from ancient Rome. There's a lot to see here, including the **Basilica di Santa Maria Maggiore** and the **Baths of Diocletian.** Some high-class hotels are sprinkled in the area, including the **Grand,** but many are long past their heyday.

The neighborhoods on either side of Termini have been improving greatly, and some streets are now attractive. The best-looking area is ahead and to your right as you exit the station on the Via Marsala side. Most budget hotels here occupy a floor or more of a *palazzo* (palace); many of their entryways are drab, although upstairs they're often charming or at least clean and livable. In the area to the left of the station as you exit, the streets are wider, the traffic is heavier, and the noise level is higher. This area off Via

Giolitti is being redeveloped, and now most streets are in good condition. A few still need improvement; take caution at night.

VIA VENETO & PIAZZA BARBERINI In the 1950s and early 1960s, **Via Veneto** was the swinging place to be, as the likes of King Farouk, Frank Sinatra, and Swedish actress Anita Ekberg paraded up and down the boulevard to the delight of the paparazzi. The street is still here and is still the site of luxury hotels and elegant cafes and restaurants, though it's no longer the happening place to be. It's lined with restaurants catering to those visitors who've heard of this boulevard from decades past, but the restaurants are mostly overpriced and overcrowded tourist traps. Rome city authorities would like to restore this street to some of its former glory by banning vehicular traffic on the top half. It still makes for a pleasant stroll.

To the south, Via Veneto comes to an end at **Piazza Barberini,** dominated by the 1642 **Triton Fountain (Fontana del Tritone),** a baroque celebration with four dolphins holding up an open scallop shell in which a triton sits blowing into a conch. Overlooking the square is the **Palazzo Barberini.** In 1623, when Cardinal Maffeo Barberini became Pope Urban VIII, he ordered Carlo Maderno to build a palace here; it was later completed by Bernini and Borromini.

ANCIENT ROME Most visitors explore this area first, taking in the **Colosseum, Palatine Hill, Roman Forum, Imperial Forums,** and **Circus Maximus.** The area forms part of the *centro storico* (historic district)—along with **Campo de' Fiori** and **Piazza Navona** and the **Pantheon,** which are described below (we've considered them separately for the purposes of helping you locate hotels and restaurants). Because of its ancient streets, airy squares, classical atmosphere, and heartland location, this is a good place to stay. If you base yourself here, you can walk to the monuments and avoid Rome's inadequate public transportation.

This area offers only a few hotels—most of them inexpensive to moderate in price—and not a lot of great restaurants. Many restaurant owners have their eyes on the cash register and the tour-bus crowd, whose passengers are often hustled in and out of these restaurants so fast that they don't know whether the food is any good.

CAMPO DE' FIORI & THE JEWISH GHETTO South of Corso Vittorio Emanuele and centered on **Piazza Farnese** and the market square of **Campo de' Fiori,** many buildings in this area were constructed in Renaissance times as private homes. Stroll along **Via Giulia**—Rome's most fashionable street in the 16th century—with its antiques stores, hotels, and modern art galleries.

West of Via Arenula lies one of the city's most intriguing districts, the old Jewish **Ghetto,** where the dining options far outnumber the hotel options. In 1556, Pope Paul IV ordered the Jews, about 8,000 at the time, to move here. The walls weren't torn down until 1849. Although ancient and medieval Rome has more atmosphere, this working-class area is close to many attractions. You're more likely to dine here than stay here.

PIAZZA NAVONA & THE PANTHEON One of the most desirable areas of Rome, this district is a maze of narrow streets and alleys dating from the Middle Ages. It is filled with churches and palaces built during the Renaissance and baroque eras, often with rare marble and other materials stripped from ancient Rome. The only way to explore it is on foot. Its heart is **Piazza Navona,** built over Emperor Domitian's stadium and bustling with sidewalk cafes, *palazzi,* street artists, musicians, and pickpockets. There are several hotels in the area and plenty of *trattorie.*

Rivaling Piazza Navona—in general activity, the cafe scene, and the nightlife—is the area around the **Pantheon,** which remains from ancient Roman times and is surrounded by a district built much later. (This "pagan" temple was turned into a church and rescued, but the buildings that once surrounded it are long gone.)

PIAZZA DEL POPOLO & THE SPANISH STEPS **Piazza del Popolo** was laid out by Giuseppe Valadier and is one of Rome's largest squares. It's characterized by an obelisk brought from Heliopolis in lower Egypt during the reign of Augustus. At the end of the square is the **Porta del Popolo,** the gateway in the 3rd-century Aurelian wall. In the mid–16th century, this was one of the major gateways into the old city. If you enter the piazza along Via del Corso from the south, you'll see twin churches, **Santa Maria dei Miracoli** and **Santa Maria in Montesanto,** flanking the street. But the square's major church is **Santa Maria del Popolo** (1442–47), one of the best examples of a Renaissance church in Rome.

Since the 17th century, the **Spanish Steps** (the former site of the Spanish ambassador's residence) have been a meeting place for visitors. Some of Rome's most upscale shopping streets fan out from it, including **Via Condotti.** The elegant **Hassler,** one of Rome's grandest hotels, lies at the top of the steps. This is the most upscale part of Rome, full of expensive hotels, designer boutiques, and chic restaurants.

AROUND VATICAN CITY Across the Tiber, **Vatican City** is a small city-state, but its influence extends around the world. The **Vatican Museums, St. Peter's,** and the **Vatican Gardens** take up most of the land area, and the popes have lived here for 6 centuries. The neighborhood around the Vatican—called the "Borgo"—contains some good hotels (and several bad ones), but it's removed from the more happening scene of ancient and Renaissance Rome and getting to and from it can be time-consuming. The area is rather dull at night and contains few, if any, of Rome's finest restaurants. For the average visitor, Vatican City and its surrounding area are best for exploring during the day. Nonetheless, the area is popular for those whose sightseeing or business interests center around the Vatican.

TRASTEVERE In Roman dialect, Trastevere means "across the Tiber." For visitors arriving in Rome decades ago, it might as well have meant Siberia. All that has changed. This once medieval working-class district has been gentrified and overrun with visitors from all over the world. It started to change in the 1970s when expats and others discovered its rough charm. Since then Trastevere has been filling up with tour buses, dance clubs, offbeat shops, sidewalk vendors, pubs, and little *trattorie* with menus printed in English. There are even places to stay, but as of yet it hasn't burgeoned into a major hotel district. There are some excellent restaurants here as well.

The original people of the district—and there are still some of them left—are of mixed ancestry, mainly Jewish, Roman, and Greek. For decades they were known for speaking their own dialect in a language rougher than that spoken in central Rome. Even their cuisine was spicier.

The area centers on the ancient churches of **Santa Cecilia** and **Santa Maria.** It remains one of Rome's most colorful quarters, even if a bit overrun. Known as a "city within a city," it is at least a village within a city.

St. Peter's Basilica in Rome.

TESTACCIO & THE AVENTINE In A.D. 55, Nero ordered that Rome's thousands of broken amphorae and terra-cotta roof tiles be stacked in a carefully designated pile to the east of the Tiber, just west of Pyramide and today's Ostia Railway Station. Over the centuries, the mound grew to a height of around 61m (200 ft.) and then was compacted to form the centerpiece for one of the city's most unusual working-class neighborhoods, **Testaccio.** Eventually, houses were built on the terra-cotta mound and caves were dug into its mass to store wine and foodstuffs. Once home to the slaughterhouses of Rome and its former port on the Tiber, Testaccio means "ugly head" in Roman dialect. Bordered by the Protestant cemetery, Testaccio is known for its authentic Roman restaurants. Chefs here still cook as they always did, satisfying local—not tourist—palates. Change is on the way, however, and this is a neighborhood on the rise. Nightclubs have sprung up in the old warehouses, although they come and go rather quickly.

Another offbeat section of Rome is **Aventine Hill,** south of the Palatine and close to the Tiber. According to records, in 186 B.C. thousands of residents of the area were executed for joining in "midnight rituals of Dionysos and Bacchus." These bloody orgies are a thing of the past, and the Aventine area is now a leafy and rather posh residential quarter.

THE APPIAN WAY **Via Appia Antica** is a 2,300-year-old road that has witnessed much of the history of the ancient world. By 190 B.C., it extended from Rome to Brindisi on the southeast coast. Its most famous sights are the **Catacombs,** the graveyards of patrician families (despite what it says in *Quo Vadis* they weren't used as a place for Christians to hide while fleeing persecution). This is one of the most historically rich areas of Rome, but it's not a good place to stay. It does contain some restaurants where you can have lunch after your visit to the Catacombs.

PRATI The little-known **Prati** district is a middle-class suburb north of the Vatican. It has been discovered by budget travelers because of its affordable hotels, although it's not conveniently located for sightseeing. The **Trionfale flower-and-food market** is worth the trip. The area abounds in shopping streets less expensive than in central Rome, and street crime isn't much of a problem.

PARIOLI Rome's most elegant residential section, Parioli is framed by the green spaces of the **Villa Borghese** to the south and the **Villa Glori** and **Villa Ada** to the north. It's a setting for some of the city's finest restaurants, hotels, and nightclubs. It's not exactly central, however, and it can be a hassle if you're dependent on public transportation. Parioli lies adjacent to Prati but across the Tiber to the east; this is one of the safer districts. We'd call Parioli an area for connoisseurs, attracting those who shun the Spanish Steps and the overly commercialized Via Veneto, and those who'd never admit to having been in the Termini area.

MONTE MARIO On the northwestern precincts of Rome, **Monte Mario** is the site of the deluxe **Cavalieri Hilton,** an excellent stop to enjoy a drink and the panorama of Rome. If you plan to spend a lot of time shopping and sightseeing in the heart of Rome, it's a difficult and often expensive commute. The area is north of Prati, away from the bustle of central Rome. Bus no. 913 runs from Piazza Augusto Imperatore near Piazza del Popolo to Monte Mario.

Organized Tours

Because of the sheer number of sights to see, some first-time visitors like to start out with an organized tour. While few things can really be covered in any depth on these overview tours, they're sometimes useful for getting your bearings.

One of the leading tour operators is **American Express,** Piazza di Spagna 38 (**✆ 06-67641;** Metro: Piazza di Spagna). One popular tour is a 4-hour orientation to Rome and the Vatican, which departs most mornings at 9:30am or afternoons at 2:20pm and costs 75€ per person. Another 4-hour tour, which focuses on the Rome of antiquity (including visits to the Colosseum, the Roman Forum, the ruins of the Imperial Palace, and St. Peter in Chains), costs 75€. From April to October, a popular excursion outside Rome is a 5 hour bus tour to Tivoli, where tours are conducted of the Villa d'Este and its spectacular gardens and the ruins of the Villa Adriana, all for 65€ per person. The American Express Travel Office is open Monday to Friday 9am to 5:30pm and Saturday 9am to 12:30pm.

Context Rome, Via Santa Maria Maggiore 145 (www.contexttravel.com; **✆ 800/691-6036** in the U.S., or 06-97625204), is a collaborative of scholars. Guides offer small-group tours, including visits to monuments, museums, and historic piazzas, as well as culinary walks and meals in neighborhood *trattorie*. Custom-designed tours are also available. Prices of the regular tours begin at 30€. There is also a special kids' program, including treasure hunts and other experiences that feature visits to museums of appeal to the younger set.

[FastFACTS] ROME

American Express
The Rome offices are at Piazza di Spagna 38 (**✆ 06-67641;** Metro: Piazza di Spagna). The travel service is open Monday to Friday 9am to 5:30pm, Saturday 9am to 12:30pm. Hours for the financial and mail services are Monday to Friday 9am to 5pm. The tour desk is open all year-round Monday to Friday 9am to 5:30pm, Saturday 9am to 12:30pm.

Banks In general, banks are open Monday to Friday 8:30am to 1:30pm and 3 to 4pm. Some banks keep afternoon hours from 2:45 to 3:45pm. The bank office is open Monday to Friday 8:30am to 1:30pm.

Currency Exchange
There are exchange offices throughout the city. They're also at all major rail and air terminals, including Stazione Termini, where the *cambio* beside the rail information

booth is open daily 8am to 8pm. At some *cambio*, you'll have to pay commissions, often 1½%. Likewise, banks often charge commissions. ATMs, with multilingual prompts, are commonplace throughout Rome.

Dentists For dental work, go to **American Dental Arts Rome,** Via del Governo Vecchio 73 (www.adadentistsrome.com; ✆ **06-6832613;** bus: 41, 44, or 46B), which uses all the latest technology, including laser dental techniques. There is also a 24-hour **G. Eastman Dental Hospital** at Viale Regina Elena 287B (✆ **06-844831;** Metro: Policlinico).

Doctors Call the U.S. Embassy at ✆ **06-46741** for a list of doctors who speak English. All big hospitals have a 24-hour first-aid service (go to the emergency room, *pronto soccorso*). You'll find English-speaking doctors at the privately run **Salvator Mundi International Hospital,** Viale delle Mura Gianicolensi 67 (✆ **06-588961;** bus: 75). For medical assistance, the **International Medical Center** is on 24-hour duty at Via Firenze 47 (www.imc84.com; ✆ **06-4882371;** Metro: Piazza Repubblica). You could also contact the **Rome American Hospital,** Via Emilio Longoni 69 (www.rah.it; ✆ **06-22551**), with English-speaking doctors on duty 24 hours. A more personalized service is provided 24 hours by **MEDI-CALL,** Studio Medico, Via Cremera 8 (www.medi-call.it; ✆ **06-8840113;** bus: 86). It can arrange for a qualified doctor to make a house call at your hotel or anywhere in Rome. In most cases, the doctor will be a general practitioner who can refer you to a specialist if needed. Fees begin at around 100€ per visit and can go higher if a specialist or specialized treatments are necessary.

Drugstores A reliable pharmacy is **Farmacia Internazionale,** Piazza Barberini 49 (✆ **06-4825456;** Metro: Barberini), open day and night. Most pharmacies are open from 8:30am to 1pm and 4 to 7:30pm. In general, pharmacies follow a rotation system, so several are always open on Sunday.

Embassies & Consulates See chapter 17.

Emergencies To call the police, dial ✆ **113;** for an ambulance ✆ **118;** for a fire ✆ **115.**

Internet Access You can log onto the Web in central Rome at **Internet Train,** Via dei Marrucini 12 (www.internetcafe.it; ✆ **06-4454953;** bus: 3, 71, or 492). It is open Monday to Friday 9:30am to 1am, Saturday 10am to 1am, and Sunday 2pm to midnight. A 30-minute visit costs 1.50€.

Mail It's easiest to buy stamps and mail letters and postcards at your hotel's front desk. Stamps *(francobolli)* can also be bought at *tabacchi*. You can buy special stamps at the **Vatican City Post Office,** adjacent to the information office in St. Peter's Square; it's open Monday to Friday 8:30am to 7pm and Saturday 8:30am to 6pm. Letters mailed from Vatican City often arrive far more quickly than mail sent from Rome for the same cost.

Newspapers & Magazines You can buy major publications, including the *International Herald Tribune*, the *New York Times*, and the London *Times* at most newsstands. The expat magazine (in English), *Wanted in Rome*, comes out monthly and lists current events and shows. If you want to try your hand at reading Italian, *Time Out* now has a Rome edition.

Police Dial ✆ **113.**

Safety Pickpocketing is the most common problem. Men should keep their wallets in their front pocket or inside jacket pocket. Purse snatching is also commonplace, with young men on Vespas who ride past you and grab your purse. To avoid trouble, stay away from the curb and keep your purse on the wall side of your body and place the strap across your chest. Don't lay anything valuable on tables or chairs, where it can be grabbed up. Groups of child pickpockets have long been a particular menace, although the problem isn't as severe as in years past. If they completely surround you, you'll often literally have to fight them off. They might approach you with pieces of cardboard hiding their stealing hands. Just keep repeating a firm *no!*

Telephone The **country code** for Italy is **39.** The **city code** for Rome is **06;** use this code when calling from *anywhere* outside or inside Italy—you must add it within Rome itself (and you must include the 0 every time, even when calling from abroad). See chapter 17 for complete details on how to call Italy, how to place calls within Italy, and how to call home once you're in Italy.

Toilets Facilities are found near many of the major sights and often have attendants, as do those at bars, clubs, restaurants, cafes, and hotels, plus the airports and the rail station. (There are public restrooms near the Spanish Steps, or you can stop at the McDonald's there—it's one of the nicest branches of the Golden Arches you'll ever see!) The price for most public toilets is 1€. It's not a bad idea to carry some tissues in your pocket when you're out and about as well.

EXPLORING ROME

Rome's ancient monuments, whether time-blackened or gleaming white in the wake of a recent restoration, are a constant reminder that Rome was one of the greatest centers of Western civilization. In the heyday of the Empire, all roads led to Rome, with good reason. It was one of the first cosmopolitan cities, importing slaves, gladiators, great art, and even citizens from the far corners of the world. Despite its carnage and corruption, Rome left a legacy of law, a heritage of great art, architecture, and engineering, and an uncanny lesson in how to conquer enemies by absorbing their cultures.

But ancient Rome is only part of the spectacle. The Vatican has had a tremendous influence on making the city a tourism center. Although Vatican architects stripped down much of the city's glory, looting ancient ruins for their precious marble, they created great Renaissance treasures and even occasionally incorporated the old into the new—as Michelangelo did when turning the Baths of Diocletian into a church. And in the years that followed, Bernini adorned the city with the wonders of the baroque, especially his glorious fountains.

St. Peter's & the Vatican

If you want to know more about the Vatican, check out its website at **www.vatican.va**.

IN VATICAN CITY

In 1929, the Lateran Treaty between Pope Pius XI and the Italian government created the **Vatican,** the world's smallest sovereign state. It has only a few hundred citizens and is protected (theoretically) by its own militia, the curiously uniformed (some say by Michelangelo) Swiss guards (a tradition dating from the days when the Swiss, known as brave soldiers, were often hired out as mercenaries for foreign armies).

The only entrance to the Vatican for the casual visitor is through one of the glories of the Western world: Bernini's **St. Peter's Square (Piazza San Pietro).** As you stand in the huge piazza, you'll be in the arms of an ellipse partly enclosed by a majestic **Doric-pillared colonnade.** Atop it stands a gesticulating crowd of some 140 saints. Straight ahead is the facade of **St. Peter's Basilica ★★★** (Sts. Peter and Paul are represented by statues in front, with Peter carrying the keys to the kingdom), and, to the right, above the colonnade, are the dark brown buildings

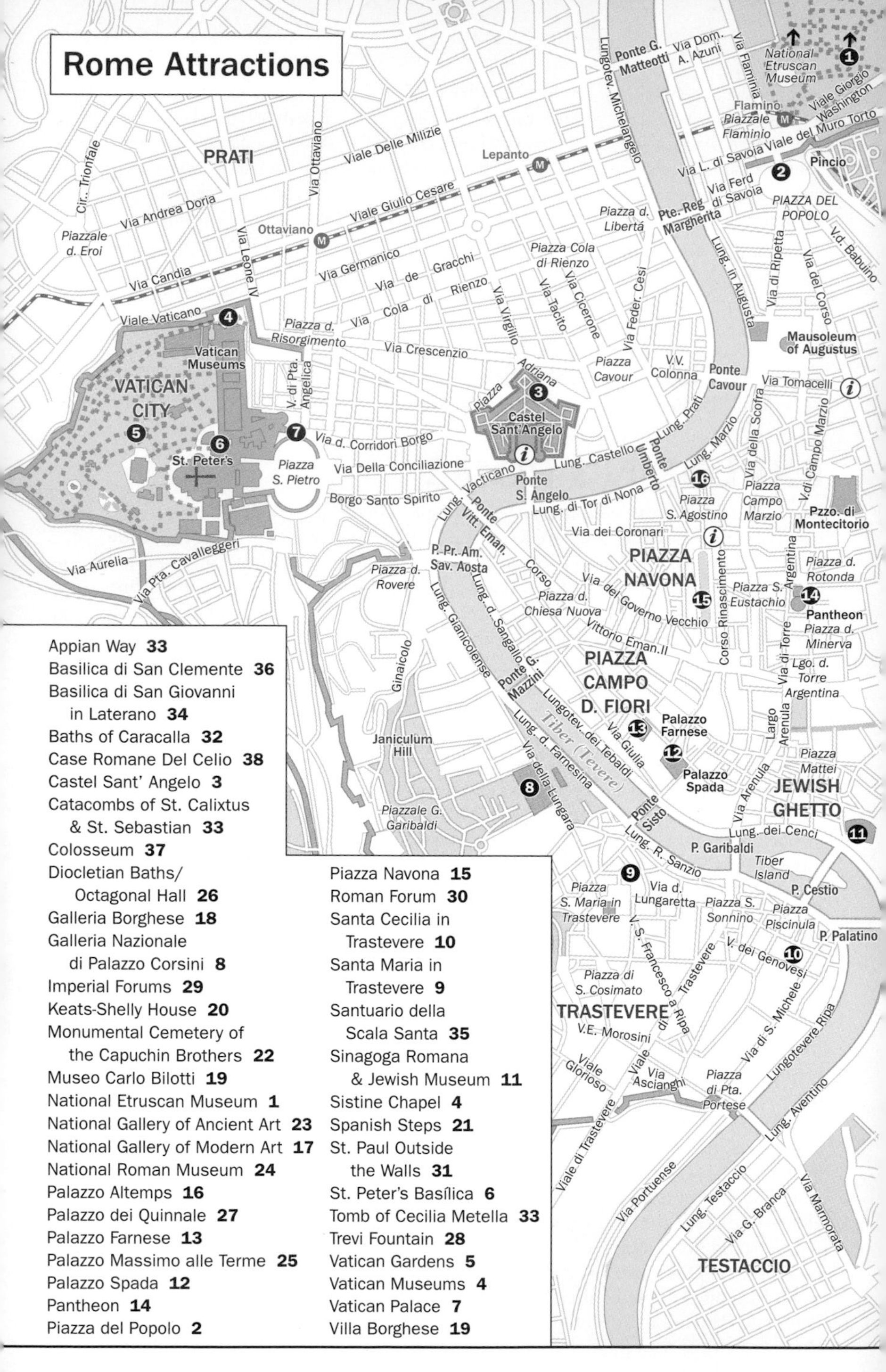
Rome Attractions
PRATI
VATICAN CITY
Vatican Museums
St. Peter's
Piazza S. Pietro
Castel Sant'Angelo
Ottaviano
Lepanto
Flaminio
Piazzale Flaminio
National Etruscan Museum
Pincio
PIAZZA DEL POPOLO
Mausoleum of Augustus
PIAZZA NAVONA
Pzzo. di Montecitorio
Pantheon
PIAZZA CAMPO D. FIORI
Palazzo Farnese
Palazzo Spada
JEWISH GHETTO
Tiber Island
Tiber (Tevere)
Janiculum Hill
Piazzale G. Garibaldi
TRASTEVERE
TESTACCIO
Viale Delle Milizie
Viale Giulio Cesare
Via Andrea Doria
Via Candia
Viale Vaticano
Via Germanico
Via Cola di Rienzo
Via Crescenzio
Via Della Conciliazione
Borgo Santo Spirito
Via Aurelia
Corso Vittorio Eman. II
Via del Governo Vecchio
Via dei Coronari
Corso Rinascimento
Via Giulia
Via della Lungara
Viale di Trastevere
Via Portuense
Via Marmorata
Appian Way 33
Basilica di San Clemente 36
Basilica di San Giovanni in Laterano 34
Baths of Caracalla 32
Case Romane Del Celio 38
Castel Sant' Angelo 3
Catacombs of St. Calixtus & St. Sebastian 33
Colosseum 37
Diocletian Baths/ Octagonal Hall 26
Galleria Borghese 18
Galleria Nazionale di Palazzo Corsini 8
Imperial Forums 29
Keats-Shelly House 20
Monumental Cemetery of the Capuchin Brothers 22
Museo Carlo Bilotti 19
National Etruscan Museum 1
National Gallery of Ancient Art 23
National Gallery of Modern Art 17
National Roman Museum 24
Palazzo Altemps 16
Palazzo dei Quinnale 27
Palazzo Farnese 13
Palazzo Massimo alle Terme 25
Palazzo Spada 12
Pantheon 14
Piazza del Popolo 2
Piazza Navona 15
Roman Forum 30
Santa Cecilia in Trastevere 10
Santa Maria in Trastevere 9
Santuario della Scala Santa 35
Sinagoga Romana & Jewish Museum 11
Sistine Chapel 4
Spanish Steps 21
St. Paul Outside the Walls 31
St. Peter's Basílica 6
Tomb of Cecilia Metella 33
Trevi Fountain 28
Vatican Gardens 5
Vatican Museums 4
Vatican Palace 7
Villa Borghese 19

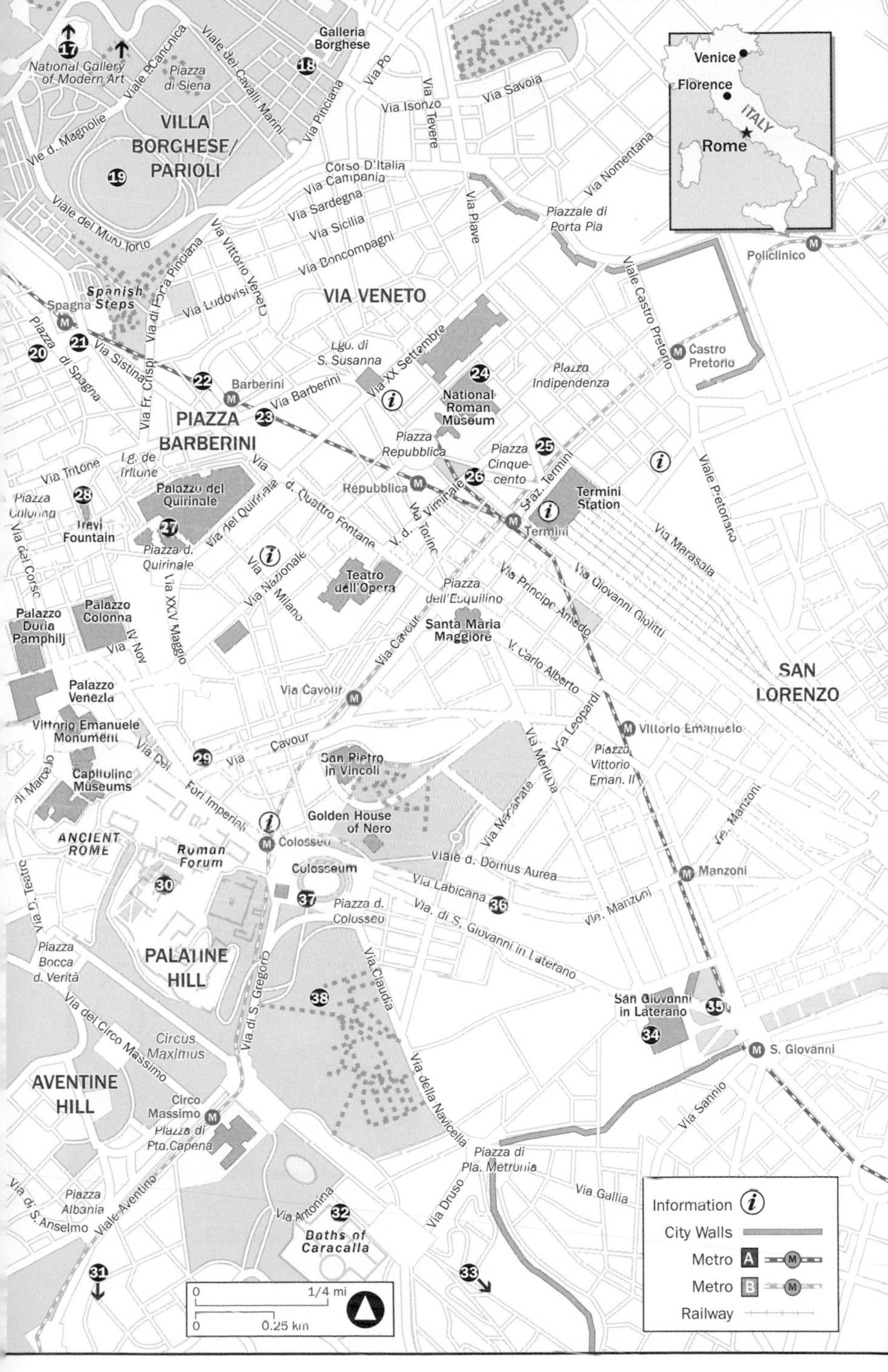

VILLA BORGHESE/ PARIOLI
VIA VENETO
PIAZZA BARBERINI
SAN LORENZO
ANCIENT ROME
PALATINE HILL
AVENTINE HILL
Galleria Borghese
National Gallery of Modern Art
Spanish Steps
National Roman Museum
Termini Station
Palazzo del Quirinale
Trevi Fountain
Teatro dell'Opera
Santa Maria Maggiore
Palazzo Colonna
Palazzo Doria Pamphilj
Palazzo Venezia
Vittorio Emanuele Monument
Capitoline Museums
San Pietro in Vincoli
Golden House of Nero
Roman Forum
Colosseum
Circus Maximus
Baths of Caracalla
San Giovanni in Laterano
Venice
Florence
ITALY
Rome
Information
City Walls
Metro A
Metro B
Railway
1/4 mi
0.25 km

THE ETERNAL drinking water CITY

There's no excuse for being dehydrated in Rome.

At the height of the Roman Empire, 11 aqueducts brought the city 25 million gallons of water a day for its baths, ornamental fountains, and basic utilities. That tradition of hydroabundance continues in modern Rome: There are monumental fountains everywhere you look, and one of the city's most generous gifts to tourists and citizens alike is its free, perfectly drinkable spring water, in the form of *nasoni.*

In almost every piazza in town, on countless side streets, and in archaeological sites, you'll see these cast-iron hydrants marked SPQR, whose curved pipes emit a continuous stream of water into a drain below. These hydrants are properly called *fontanelle* ("little fountains") but in Roman slang, they're *nasoni* ("big noses"), for the shape of the spigots.

Naturally, many newcomers' first question is: Is it really safe to drink this water? The answer is an emphatic yes. *Fontanelle* draw on spring water in the hills outside the city—the same sources the ancients tapped for their aqueducts, minus the lead pipes—that tastes better and is cleaner than Rome's tap water, which is also potable. (Only a handful of fountains around town, mostly in the parks, are not potable, in which case they're clearly marked *acqua non potabile.*) What's more, the water issuing from the *fontanelle* is always ice-cold, even in the height of summer.

Once you have a plastic water bottle, you can just keep refilling it at *nasoni* all over town—for free. If you don't have a bottle handy, here's how the pros do it: Simply block up the bottom of the spigot with your finger, and the stream of water will come out a small hole in the top of the curved pipe, like a drinking fountain. Be careful with this method, though, as some *nasoni* are quite powerful and will shoot water all over you if you completely block up the bottom of the pipe. Of course, in July or August, this might feel very refreshing.

When you master drinking from a *nasone,* it's time to move onto the big, ornamental fountains of Rome. No, we're not recommending you drink from their dirty basins, but from the side jets of water that feed fountains such as the Trevi and the Barcaccia at Piazza di Spagna. These jets are the same as *nasone* water, fresh and clean. Tradition even holds that the water supply for the Barcaccia guarantees eternal youth for all who drink it.

—Sylvie Murphy

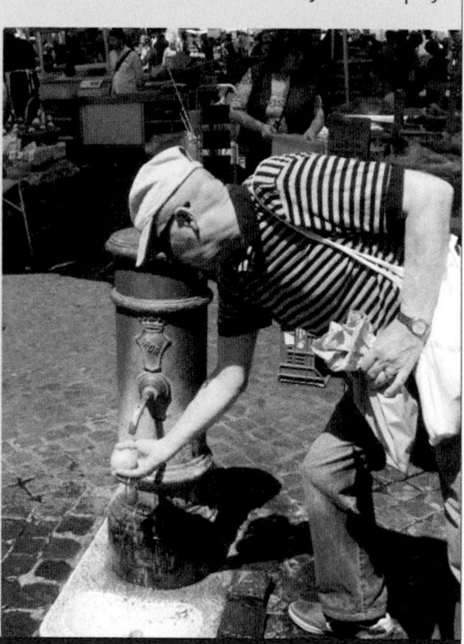

of the **papal apartments** and the **Vatican Museums ★★★**. In the center of the square is an **Egyptian obelisk,** brought from the ancient city of Heliopolis on the Nile delta. Flanking the obelisk are two 17th-century **fountains.** The one on the right (facing the basilica), by Carlo Maderno, who designed the facade of St. Peter's, was placed here by Bernini himself; the other is by Carlo Fontana.

The Vatican's famed spiral ramp.

On the left side of Piazza San Pietro is the **Vatican Tourist Office** (**✆ 06-69882019;** Mon–Sat 8:30am–6:30pm). It sells maps and guides that'll help you make more sense of the riches you'll be seeing in the museums. It also accepts reservations for tours of the Vatican Gardens and tries to answer questions.

St. Peter's Basilica ★★★ In ancient times, the Circus of Nero, where St. Peter is said to have been crucified, was slightly to the left of where the basilica is now located. Peter was allegedly buried here in A.D. 64 near the site of his execution, and in 324 Constantine commissioned a basilica to be built over Peter's tomb. That structure stood for more than 1,000 years, until it verged on collapse. The present basilica, mostly completed in the 1500s and 1600s, is predominantly High Renaissance and baroque. Inside, the massive scale is almost too much to absorb, showcasing some of Italy's greatest artists: Bramante, Raphael, Michelangelo, and Maderno. In a church of such grandeur—overwhelming in its detail of gilt, marble, and mosaic—you can't expect much subtlety. It's meant to be overpowering.

In the nave on the right (the first chapel) stands one of the Vatican's greatest treasures: Michelangelo's exquisite ***Pietà* ★★★**, created while the master was still in his 20s but clearly showing his genius for capturing the human form. (The sculpture has been kept behind reinforced glass since a madman's act of vandalism in the 1970s.) Note the lifelike folds of Mary's robes and her youthful features, although she would've been middle-aged at the time of the Crucifixion, Michelangelo portrayed her as a young woman to convey her purity.

Much farther on, in the right wing of the transept near the Chapel of St. Michael, rests Canova's neoclassical **sculpture of Pope Clement XIII ★★**. The truly devout stop to kiss the feet of the 13th-century **bronze of St. Peter ★**, attributed to Arnolfo di Cambio (at the far reaches of the nave, against a corner pillar on the right). Under Michelangelo's dome is the celebrated twisty-columned **baldacchino ★★** (1524), by Bernini, resting over the papal altar. The 29m-high (96-ft.) ultrafancy canopy was created in part, so it's said, from bronze stripped from the Pantheon, although that's up for debate.

In addition, you can visit the **treasury ★**, which is filled with jewel-studded chalices, reliquaries, and copes. One robe worn by Pius XII strikes a simple note in these halls of elegance. The sacristy contains a **Historical Museum (Museo Storico) ★** displaying Vatican treasures, including the large 1400s bronze tomb of Pope Sixtus V by Antonio Pollaiuolo and several antique chalices.

You can head downstairs to the **Vatican grottoes ★★**, with their tombs of the popes, both ancient and modern (Pope John XXIII got the most adulation until the recent interment of Pope John Paul II). Behind a wall of glass is what's assumed to be the tomb of St. Peter himself.

Michelangelo's *Pietà*.

To go even farther down, to the **Necropolis Vaticana ★★**, the area around St. Peter's tomb, you must send a fax or e-mail 3 weeks beforehand, or apply in advance in person at the Ufficio Scavi (✆/fax **06-69873017;** e-mail: scavi@fsp.va), through the arch to the left of the stairs up the basilica. You specify your name, the number in your party, your language, and dates you'd like to visit. When you apply at the Ufficio Scavi by fax or e-mail you also need to specify how you would like to be contacted (by e-mail, fax, or postal address). For details, check **www.vatican.va**. Children 14 and under are not admitted to the Necropolis Vaticana.

After you leave the grottoes, you'll find yourself in a courtyard and ticket line for the grandest sight: the climb to **Michelangelo's dome ★★★**, about 114m (375 ft.) high. You can walk up all the steps or take the elevator as far as it goes. The elevator saves you 171 steps, and you'll *still* have 320 to go after getting off. After you've made it to the top, you'll have an astounding view over the rooftops of Rome and even the Vatican Gardens and papal apartments—a photo op, if ever there was one.

Piazza San Pietro. ✆ **06-69881662.** Basilica (including grottoes) free admission. Guided tour of excavations around St. Peter's tomb 12€; children 14 and younger are not admitted. Stairs to the dome 5€; elevator to the dome 7€; sacristy (with Historical Museum) free. Basilica (including the sacristy and treasury) daily 9am–6pm. Grottoes daily 8am–5pm. Dome Oct–Mar daily 7am–6:30pm; Apr–Sept daily 7am–7pm. Bus: 49. Metro: Cipro, Ottaviano/San Pietro, then a long stroll.

Vatican Gardens ★ Separating the Vatican from the secular world on the north and west are 23 hectares (58 acres) of lush gardens filled with winding paths, brilliantly colored flowers, groves of massive oaks, and ancient fountains and pools. In the midst of this pastoral setting is a small summer house, Villa Pia, built for Pope Pius IV in 1560 by Pirro Ligorio. The gardens contain medieval fortifications from the 9th century to the present. Water spouts from a variety of fountains.

To make a reservation to visit the Vatican Gardens, you must book through the Vatican website at www.vatican.va. Once the reservation is accepted, you must go to

A St. Peter's Warning

St. Peter's has a strict dress code: no shorts, no skirts above the knee, and no bare shoulders and arms. ***Note:*** *You will not be let in if you come dressed inappropriately.* In a pinch, men and women alike can buy a big, cheap scarf from a nearby souvenir stand and wrap it around their legs as a long skirt or throw it over their shoulders as a shawl. If you're still showing too much skin, a guard hands out blue paper capes similar to what you wear in a doctor's office. Only limited photography is permitted inside.

the Vatican information office (at Piazza San Pietro, on the left side looking at the facade of St. Peter's) and pick up the tickets 2 or 3 days before your visit.

North and west of the Vatican. Tours of the gardens Mon–Tues and Thurs–Sun 10am (2 hr.; first half-hour by bus). Tour 31€. For further information, contact the Vatican Tourism Office (✆ **06-69883145**).

Vatican Museums (Musei Vaticani) & the Sistine Chapel (Cappella Sistina) ★★★ The Vatican Museums boast one of the world's greatest art collections. It's a gigantic repository of treasures from antiquity and the Renaissance, housed in a labyrinthine series of lavishly adorned palaces, apartments, and galleries leading you to the real gem: the Sistine Chapel. The Vatican Museums occupy a part of the papal palaces built from the 1200s on. From the former papal private apartments, the museums were created over a period of time to display the vast treasure-trove of art acquired by the Vatican.

You'll climb a magnificent spiral ramp to get to the ticket windows. After you're admitted, you can choose your route through the museum from **four color-coded itineraries** (A, B, C, D) according to the time you have (1½–5 hr.) and your interests. You determine your choice by consulting panels on the wall and then following the letter/color of your choice. All four itineraries culminate in the Sistine Chapel. Obviously, 1, 2, or even 20 trips will not be enough to see the wealth of the Vatican, much less to digest it. With that in mind, we've previewed only a representative sampling of the masterpieces on display (in alphabetical order).

Borgia Apartments ★: Frescoed with biblical scenes by Pinturicchio of Umbria and his assistants, these rooms were designed for Pope Alexander VI (the infamous Borgia pope). They may be badly lit, but they boast great splendor and style. At the end of the Raphael Rooms (see below) is the Chapel of Nicholas V, an intimate room frescoed by the Dominican monk Fra Angelico, the most saintly of all Italian painters.

Chiaramonti Museum: Founded by Pope Pius VII, also known as Chiaramonti, the museum includes the Corridoio (Corridor), the Galleria Lapidaria, and the Braccio Nuovo (New Side). The Corridor hosts an exposition of more than 800 Greek-Roman works, including statues, reliefs, and sarcophagi. In the Galleria Lapidaria are about 5,000 Christian and pagan inscriptions. You'll find a dazzling array of Roman sculpture and copies of Greek originals in these galleries. In the Braccio Nuovo, built as an extension of the Chiaramonti, you can admire the ***Nile*** **★**, a magnificent reproduction of a long-lost Hellenistic original and one of the most remarkable pieces of sculpture from antiquity. The imposing statue of Augustus of Prima Porta presents him as a regal commander.

Collection of Modern Religious Art: This museum, opened in 1973, represents American artists' first invasion of the Vatican. Of the 55 rooms, at least 12 are devoted to American artists. All the works chosen were judged on their "spiritual and religious values." Among the American works is Leonard Baskin's 1.5m (5-ft.) bronze sculpture of *Isaac*. Modern Italian artists such as de Chirico and Manzù are also displayed, and there's a special room for the paintings of the Frenchman Georges Rouault. You'll also see works by Picasso, Gauguin, Guttuso, Chagall, Henry Moore, Kandinsky, and others.

Egyptian-Gregorian Museum: Experience the grandeur of the pharaohs by studying sarcophagi, mummies, statues of goddesses, vases, jewelry, sculptured pink-granite statues, and hieroglyphics.

Detail from the ceiling of the Sistine Chapel, painted by Michelangelo.

Etruscan-Gregorian Museum ★: This was founded by Gregory XIV in 1837 and then enriched year after year, becoming one of the most important and complete collections of Etruscan art. With sarcophagi, a chariot, bronzes, urns, jewelry, and terra-cotta vases, this gallery affords remarkable insights into an ancient civilization. One of the most acclaimed exhibits is the Regolini-Galassi tomb, unearthed in the 19th century at Cerveteri. It shares top honors with the *Mars of Todi,* a bronze sculpture probably dating from the 5th century B.C.

Ethnological Museum: This is an assemblage of works of art and objects of cultural significance from all over the world. The principal route is a 1km (½-mile) walk through 25 geographical sections, displaying thousands of objects covering 3,000 years of world history. The section devoted to China is especially interesting.

Historical Museum: This museum tells the history of the Vatican. It exhibits arms, uniforms, and armor, some dating from the early Renaissance. The carriages displayed are those used by the popes and cardinals in religious processions.

Pinacoteca (Picture Gallery) ★★★: The Pinacoteca houses paintings and tapestries from the 11th to the 19th centuries. As you pass through Room 1, note the oldest picture at the Vatican, a keyhole-shaped wood panel of the *Last Judgment* from the 11th century. In Room 2 is one of the finest pieces—the *Stefaneschi Triptych* (six panels) by Giotto and his assistants. Bernardo Daddi's masterpiece of early Italian Renaissance art, *Madonna del Magnificat,* is also here. And you'll see works by Fra Angelico, the 15th-century Dominican monk who distinguished himself as a miniaturist (his *Virgin with Child* is justly praised—check out the Madonna's microscopic eyes).

In the **Raphael salon ★★★** (Room 8), you can view three paintings by the Renaissance giant himself: the *Coronation of the Virgin,* the *Virgin of Foligno,* and the massive *Transfiguration* (completed shortly before his death). There are also eight tapestries made by Flemish weavers from cartoons by Raphael. In Room 9, seek out Leonardo da Vinci's masterful but uncompleted ***St. Jerome with the Lion*** **★★**, as well as Giovanni Bellini's *Pietà* and one of Titian's greatest works, the *Virgin of Frari.* Finally, in Room 10, feast your eyes on one of the masterpieces of the baroque, Caravaggio's ***Deposition from the Cross*** **★★**.

Buy the Book

In the Vatican Museums you'll find many overpacked galleries and few labels on the works. To help you make sense of the incredible riches you'll be seeing here, buy the **detailed guide** sold at the Vatican Tourist Office (mentioned above), on the left side of the Piazza San Pietro.

Pio Clementino Museum ★★★: Here you'll find Greek and Roman sculptures, many of which are immediately recognizable. The rippling muscles of the ***Belvedere Torso*** **★★★**, a partially preserved Greek statue (1st c. B.C.) much admired by the artists of the Renaissance, especially Michelangelo, reveal an intricate knowledge of the human body. In the rotunda is a large gilded bronze of *Hercules* from the late 2nd century B.C. Other major sculptures are under porticoes opening onto the Belvedere courtyard. From the 1st century B.C., one sculpture shows ***Laocoön*** **★★★** and his two sons locked in an eternal struggle with the serpents. The incomparable ***Apollo Belvedere*** **★★★** (a late Roman reproduction of an authentic Greek work from the 4th c. B.C.) has become the symbol of classic male beauty, rivaling Michelangelo's *David*.

Raphael Rooms ★★: While still a young man, Raphael was given one of the greatest assignments of his short life: to decorate a series of rooms in the apartments of Pope Julius II. The decoration was carried out by Raphael and his workshop from 1508 to 1524. In these works, Raphael achieves the Renaissance aim of blending classic beauty with realism. In the first chamber, the Stanza dell'Incendio, you'll see much of the work of Raphael's pupils but little of the master—except in the fresco across from the window. The figure of the partially draped Aeneas rescuing his father (to the left of the fresco) is sometimes attributed to Raphael, as is the woman with a jug on her head to the right.

The Stanza della Segnatura.

Raphael reigns supreme in the next and most important salon, the Stanza della Segnatura, the first room decorated by the artist, where you'll find the majestic ***School of Athens*** **★★★**, one of his best-known works, depicting philosophers from the ages such as Aristotle, Plato, and Socrates. Many of the figures are actually portraits of some of the greatest artists of the Renaissance, including Bramante (on the right as Euclid, bent over and balding as he draws on a chalkboard), Leonardo da Vinci (as Plato, the bearded man in the center pointing heavenward), and even Raphael himself (looking out at you from the lower-right corner). While he was painting this masterpiece, Raphael stopped work to walk down the hall for the unveiling of Michelangelo's newly finished Sistine Chapel ceiling. He was so impressed that he returned to his *School of Athens* and added to his design a sulking Michelangelo sitting on the steps. Another well-known masterpiece here is the *Disputa del Sacramento.*

The *Stanza d'Eliodoro,* also by the master, manages to flatter Raphael's papal patrons (Julius II and Leo X) without compromising his art (although one rather fanciful fresco depicts the pope driving Attila from Rome). Finally, there's the *Sala di Constantino,* which was completed by his students after Raphael's death. The loggia, frescoed with more than 50 scenes from the Bible, was designed by Raphael, but the actual work was done by his loyal students.

A priest in Vatican City.

Sistine Chapel ★★★: Michelangelo considered himself a sculptor, not a painter. While in his 30s, he was commanded by Julius II to stop work on the pope's tomb and to devote his considerable talents to painting ceiling frescoes (an art form of which the Florentine master was contemptuous). Michelangelo labored for 4 years (1508–12) over this epic project, which was so physically taxing that it permanently damaged his eyesight. All during the task, he had to contend with the pope's urging him to hurry up; at one point, Julius threatened to topple Michelangelo from the scaffolding—or so Vasari relates in his *Lives of the Artists.*

It's ironic that a project undertaken against the artist's wishes would form his most enduring legend. Glorifying the human body as only a sculptor could, Michelangelo painted nine panels, taken from the pages of Genesis, and surrounded them with prophets and sibyls. The most notable panels detail the expulsion of Adam and Eve from the Garden of Eden and the creation of man; you'll recognize the image of God's outstretched hand as it imbues Adam with spirit. (You might want to bring along binoculars so you can see the details.)

The Florentine master was in his 60s when he began the masterly ***Last Judgment* ★★★** on the altar wall. Again working against his wishes, Michelangelo presented a more jaundiced view of people and their fate; God sits in judgment and sinners are plunged into the mouth of hell. A master of ceremonies under Paul III, Monsignor Biagio da Cesena, protested to the pope about the "shameless nudes." Michelangelo showed that he wasn't above petty revenge by painting the prudish monsignor, with the ears of a jackass, in hell. When Biagio complained to the pope, Paul III maintained that he had no jurisdiction in hell. However, Daniele da Volterra was summoned to drape clothing over some of the bare figures, thus earning for himself a dubious distinction as a haberdasher.

On the side walls are frescoes by other Renaissance masters, such as Botticelli, Perugino, Signorelli, Pinturicchio, Roselli, and Ghirlandaio, but because they must compete unfairly with the artistry of Michelangelo, they're virtually ignored by most visitors.

The restoration of the Sistine Chapel in the 1990s touched off a worldwide debate among art historians. The chapel was on the verge of collapse, from both

papal AUDIENCES

When the pope is in Rome, he gives a public audience every Wednesday beginning at 10:30am (sometimes at 10am in summer). It takes place in the Paul VI Hall of Audiences, although sometimes St. Peter's Basilica and St. Peter's Square are used to accommodate a large attendance. With the ascension of Benedict XVI to the Throne of Peter, this tradition continues. You can check on the pope's appearances and ceremonies he presides over (including celebrations of Mass) on the Vatican website (www.vatican.va). Anyone is welcome, but you must first obtain a **free ticket** from the office of the Prefecture of the Papal Household, accessible from St. Peter's Square by the Bronze Door, where the colonnade on the right (as you face the basilica) begins. The office is open Monday through Saturday from 9am to 1pm. Tickets are available on Monday and Tuesday; sometimes you won't be able to get into the office on Wednesday morning. Occasionally, if there's enough room, you can attend without a ticket.

You can also write ahead to the **Prefecture of the Papal Household,** 00120 Città del Vaticano (✆ **06-69885863**), indicating your language, the dates of your visit, and the number of people in your party. Tickets can be picked up at the office located just inside the Bronze Door (by the right colonnade of St. Peter's Sq.) at the following times: for general audiences from 3 to 7:30pm on the preceding day or on the morning of the audience from 8 to 10:30am.

At noon on Sunday, the pope speaks briefly from his study window and gives his blessing to the visitors and pilgrims gathered in St. Peter's Square. From about mid-July to mid-September, the Angelus and blessing take place at the summer residence at Castelgandolfo, some 26km (16 miles) out of Rome and accessible by Metro and bus.

its age and the weather, and restoration took years, as restorers used advanced computer analyses in their painstaking and controversial work. They reattached the fresco and repaired the ceiling, ridding the frescoes of their dark and shadowy look. Critics claim that in addition to removing centuries of dirt and grime—and several of the added "modesty" drapes—the restorers removed a vital second layer of paint as well. Purists argue that many of the restored figures seem flat compared with the originals, which had more shadow and detail. Others have hailed the project for saving Michelangelo's masterpiece for future generations to appreciate and for revealing the vibrancy of his color palette.

Vatican City, Viale Vaticano (a long walk around the Vatican walls from St. Peter's Sq.). ✆ **06-69884676.** Admission 15€ adults, 8€ children 6–13, free for children 5 and under. Mon–Sat 9am–4pm. Closed Jan 1 and 6, Feb 11, Mar 19, Easter, May 1, June 29, Aug 14–15, Nov 1, and Dec 8 and 25–26. Reservations for guided tours 31€ per person through Vatican website at www.vatican.va. Metro: Cipro–Musei Vaticani.

NEAR VATICAN CITY

Castel Sant'Angelo ★ This overpowering castle on the Tiber was built in the 2nd century as a tomb for Emperor Hadrian; it continued as an imperial mausoleum until the time of Caracalla. If it looks like a fortress, it should—that was its function in the Middle Ages. It was built over the Roman walls and linked to the Vatican by an underground passage that was used by the fleeing Pope Clement VII, who escaped from unwanted visitors such as Charles V during his 1527 sack of the city. In the 14th century, it became a papal residence, enjoying various connections with Boniface IX, Nicholas V, and Julius II, patron of Michelangelo and Raphael.

But its legend rests largely on its link with Pope Alexander VI, whose mistress bore him two children (those darlings of debauchery, Cesare and Lucrezia Borgia). Even those on a rushed visit might want to budget time for a stopover here because it's a most intriguing sight, an imposing fortress that has seen more blood, treachery, and turmoil than any other left in Rome. An audio guide is available to help you understand what you're seeing.

The highlight here is a trip through the Renaissance apartments with their coffered ceilings and lush decoration. Their walls have witnessed some of the most diabolical plots and intrigues of the High Renaissance. Later, you can go through the dank cells that once echoed with the screams of Cesare's victims of torture. The most famous figure imprisoned here was Benvenuto Cellini, the eminent sculptor/goldsmith, remembered chiefly for his *Autobiography.* Now an art museum, the castle halls display the history of the Roman mausoleum, along with a wide-ranging selection of ancient arms and armor. You can climb to the top terrace for another one of those dazzling views of the Eternal City.

The bumper-to-bumper cars and buses that once roared around Castel Sant'Angelo are now gone. The area around the castle has been turned into a pedestrian zone. Visitors can walk in peace through the landscaped section with a tree-lined avenue above the Tiber and a formal garden. In 2000, the moat under the ramparts was opened to the public for the first time. You can wander the footpaths and enjoy the beeches providing shade in the sweltering summer.

Lungotevere Castello 50. www.castelsantangelo.com. ✆ **06-6819111.** Admission 8.50€. Tues–Sun 9am–7pm. Bus: 23, 34, 40, 46, 49, 62, 64, 87, 280, 492, or 926, 982, 990. Metro: Cipro or Ottaviano, then a long stroll.

The Colosseum, the Roman Forum & Highlights of Ancient Rome

THE TOP SIGHTS IN ANCIENT ROME

Baths of Caracalla (Terme di Caracalla) ★ Named for the emperor Caracalla, the baths were completed in the early 3rd century. The richness of decoration has faded, and the lushness can be judged only from the shell of brick ruins that remain. In their heyday, they sprawled across 11 hectares (27 acres) and could handle 1,600 bathers at one time. A circular room, the ruined caldarium for very hot baths, is the traditional setting for operatic performances in Rome.

Via delle Terme di Caracalla 52. ✆ **06-39967700.** Admission 6€. Oct daily 9am–6:00pm; Nov–Feb 15 daily 9am–4:30pm; Feb 16–Mar 15 daily 9am–5pm; Mar 16–24 daily 9am–5:30pm; Mar 25–Aug daily 9am–7:15pm; Sept daily 9am–7pm. Last admission 1 hr. before closing. Closed holidays. Bus: 118, 160, or 628.

Capitoline Museum (Museo Capitolino) and Palazzo dei Conservatori ★★ Of Rome's seven hills, the Capitoline (Campidoglio) is the most sacred: Its origins stretch from antiquity; an Etruscan temple to Jupiter once stood on this spot. The approach is dramatic as you climb the long, sloping steps

The Colosseum, the Forum & Ancient Rome Attractions
Palazzo Venezia
Pza. Venezia
Vittorio Emanuele II Monument
Santa Maria in Aracoeli
Musei Capitolini
Palazzo dei Conservatori
CAPITOLINE HILL
Via dei Fori Imperiali
Via Cavour
di Marcello
Via d. Teatro
Colosseo
Colosseum
Pza. d. Colosseo
ROMAN FORUM
Forum Entrance
P. Palatino
Piazza Bocca d. Verità
Santa Maria in Cosmedin
Tiber (Tevere)
Lung. Aventino
Via dei Cerchi
Circus Maximus
Via dei Circo Massimo
PALATINE HILL
Via di S. Gregorio
0 1/8 mi
0 125 meters
Antiquarium Comunale
Circo Massimo
Pza. di Pta. Capena
Viale Aventino
Via d. Terme di Caracalla
Metro Stop
Antiquarium Forense / Antiquarium Palatino 19
Arco di Costantino (Arch of Constantine) 20
Arco di Settimio Severo (Arch of Septimius Severus) 8
Arco di Tito (Arch of Titus) 24
Basilica di Massenzio e di Costantino (Basilica of Constantine & Maxentius) 17
Basilica Julia 14
Casa delle Vestali (House of the Vestals) 25
Casa di Livia (Livia's House) 22
Casa Romane Del Celio 31
Colonna Traiana (Trajan's Column) 1
Curia 7
Foro di Augusto (Forum of Augustus) 4
Foro di Cesare (Forum of Julius Caesar) 6
Foro di Nerva (Forum of Nerva) 5
Foro di Traiano (Forum of Trajan) 2
Giardino Farnese (Farnese Garden) 23
Ippodromo (Hippodrome) 21
Mercati Traianoi (Trajan's Markets) 3
Palazzo Senatorio 11
Tabularium 10
Teatro di Pompeo (Theater of Pompey) 28
Tempio dei Dioscuri (Temple of the Dioscuri) 27
Tempio della Fortuna Virile (Temple of Fortuna Virile) 29
Tempio di Antonino e Faustina (Temple of Antoninus and Faustina) 16
Tempio di Ercole (Temple of Hercules) 30
Tempio di Romolo (Temple of Romulus) 18
Tempio di Saturno (Temple of Saturn) 13
Tempio di Vespasiano (Temple of Vespasian) 12
Tempio di Vesta (Temple of Vesta) 26
Umbilicus Urbus/ Imperial Rostra 9
Via Sacra 15

by Michelangelo. At the top is a perfectly proportioned square, **Piazza del Campidoglio ★★**, also laid out by the Florentine artist. Michelangelo positioned the bronze equestrian statue of Marcus Aurelius in the center, but it has now been moved inside for protection from pollution (a copy is on the pedestal). The other steps adjoining Michelangelo's approach will take you to Santa Maria d'Aracoeli (p. 110).

One side of the piazza is open; the others are bounded by the **Senatorium (Town Council),** the statuary-filled **Palace of the Conservatori (Curators),** and the **Capitoline Museum.** These museums house some of the greatest pieces of classical sculpture in the world.

The **Capitoline Museum,** built in the 17th century, was based on an architectural sketch by Michelangelo. In the first room is ***The Dying Gaul* ★★**, a work of majestic skill that's a copy of a Greek original dating from the 3rd century B.C. In a special gallery all her own is the ***Capitoline Venus* ★★**, who demurely covers herself. This statue was the symbol of feminine beauty and charm down through the centuries (it's a Roman copy of a 3rd-c.-B.C. Greek original). *Amore* (Cupid) and *Psyche* are up to their old tricks near the window.

The **equestrian statue of Marcus Aurelius ★★**, whose years in the piazza made it a victim of pollution, has been restored and is now kept in the museum for protection. This is the only such equestrian statue to have survived from ancient Rome, mainly because it was thought for centuries that the statue was that of Constantine the Great, and papal Rome respected the memory of the first Christian emperor. It's beautiful, although the perspective is rather odd. The statue is housed in a glassed-in room on the street level, the Cortile di Marforio; it's a kind of Renaissance greenhouse, surrounded by windows.

A **bronze horse ★★★**, possibly the work of a Parthenon sculptor, has gone on display after a decades-long restoration. Leaning on its hind legs with its head held back as if preparing to break into a wild dash, the horse is one of the few surviving bronze equestrian statues from Greek times—and it could be the most ancient. Some experts date it to the 5th century B.C. and attribute it to Phidias, who carved the frieze and the statue of the goddess Athene on the Parthenon in Athens. The life-size bronze once carried a figure on its back, perhaps a statue of Alexander the Great.

Palace of the Conservatori ★★, across the way, was also based on a Michelangelo architectural plan and is rich in classical sculpture and paintings. One of the most notable bronzes, a Greek work of incomparable beauty dating from the 1st century B.C., is ***Lo Spinario* ★★★** (a little boy picking a thorn from his foot). In addition, you'll find ***Capitoline Wolf (Lupa Capitolina)* ★★★**, a rare Etruscan bronze that may date from the 5th century B.C. (Romulus and Remus, the legendary twins who were suckled by the wolf, were added at a later date.) The palace also contains a Pinacoteca (Picture Gallery)—mostly works from the 16th and 17th centuries. Notable canvases are Caravaggio's *Fortune-Teller* and his curious *John the Baptist;* the *Holy Family,* by Dosso Dossi; *Romulus and Remus,* by Rubens; and Titian's *Baptism of Christ*. The entrance courtyard is lined with the remains (head, hands, a foot, and a kneecap) of an ancient colossal statue of Constantine the Great.

Piazza del Campidoglio 1. www.museicapitolini.org. ✆ **060608.** Admission 8.50€. Tues–Sun 9am–9pm. Bus: 44, 81, 95, 160, 170, 715, or 780.

Circus Maximus (Circo Massimo) The Circus Maximus, with its elongated oval proportions and ruined tiers of benches, still evokes the setting for *Ben-Hur* on the late show. Today a formless ruin, the once-grand circus was pilfered repeatedly by medieval and Renaissance builders in search of marble and stone. At one time, 250,000 Romans could assemble on the marble seats while the emperor observed the games from his box high on the Palatine Hill. What the Romans called a "circus" was a large arena enclosed by tiers of seats on three or four sides, used especially for sports or spectacles.

The circus lies in a valley formed by the Palatine on the left and the Aventine on the right. Next to the Colosseum, it was the most impressive structure in ancient Rome, in one of the most exclusive neighborhoods. For centuries, the pomp and ceremony of chariot races filled it with the cheers of thousands.

When the dark days of the 5th and 6th centuries fell, the Circus Maximus seemed a symbol of the ruination of Rome. The last games were held in A.D. 549 on the orders of Totilla the Goth, who seized Rome in 547 and established himself as emperor. He lived in the still-glittering ruins on the Palatine and apparently thought the chariot races in the Circus Maximus would lend credibility to his charade of an empire. It must've been a miserable show because the decimated population numbered something like 500 when Totilla recaptured the city. The Romans of these times were caught between Belisarius, the imperial general from Constantinople, and Totilla the Goth, both of whom fought bloodily for control of Rome. After the travesty of 549, the Circus Maximus was never used again, and the demand for building materials reduced it, like so much of Rome, to a great dusty field.

Btw. Via dei Cerchi and Via del Circo Massimo. Metro: Circo Massimo.

The Colosseum (Colosseo) ★★★ Now a mere shell, the Colosseum still remains the greatest architectural legacy from ancient Rome. Vespasian ordered the construction of the elliptical bowl, called the Amphitheatrum Flavium, in A.D. 72, it was inaugurated by Titus in A.D. 80 with a bloody combat, lasting many weeks, between gladiators and wild beasts. At its peak, under the cruel Domitian, the Colosseum could seat 50,000. The Vestal Virgins from the temple screamed for blood, as exotic animals were shipped in from the far corners of the Empire to satisfy jaded tastes (lion vs. bear, two humans vs. hippopotamus). Not-so-mock naval battles were staged (the canopied Colosseum could be flooded), and the defeated combatants might have their lives spared if they put up a good fight. Many historians now believe that one of the most enduring legends about the Colosseum—that Christians were fed to the lions—is unfounded.

Long after the Colosseum ceased to be an arena to amuse sadistic Romans, it was struck by an earthquake. Centuries later it was used as a quarry, its rich marble facing stripped away to build palaces and churches. On one side, part of the original four tiers remains; the first three levels were constructed in Doric, Ionic, and Corinthian styles, respectively, to lend variety. Inside, the seats are gone, as is the wooden floor.

Arch of Constantine ★★, the highly photogenic memorial next to the Colosseum, was erected by the Senate in A.D. 315 to honor Constantine's defeat of the pagan Maxentius (A.D. 306). Many of the reliefs have nothing whatsoever to do with Constantine or his works, but they tell of the victories of earlier Antonine rulers (apparently lifted from other, long-forgotten memorials).

Historically, the arch marks a period of great change in the history of Rome and thus the history of the world. Converted to Christianity by a vision on the battlefield, Constantine ended the centuries-long persecution of the Christians (during which many devout followers of the new religion had often been put to

Detail of the Siege of Verona from the Arch of Constantine.

death in a most gruesome manner). While Constantine didn't ban paganism (which survived officially until the closing of the temples more than half a century later), he espoused Christianity himself and began the inevitable development that culminated in the conquest of Rome by the Christian religion.

The same ticket that you buy for the Colosseum includes the visit to the Palatine Hill and the Palatine Museum.

Piazzale del Colosseo, Via dei Fori Imperiali. ✆ **06-39967700.** Admission 12€ all levels. Nov–Feb 15 daily 8:30am–4:30pm; Feb 16–Mar 15 daily 8:30am–5pm; Mar 16–27 daily 8:30am–5:30pm; Mar 28–Aug daily 8:30am–7:15pm; Sept daily 9am–7pm; Oct daily 8:30am–7pm. Guided tours in English year-round daily at 10:15, 11:15am, 12:30, 3, 4:15, and 5:15pm. Tours 4€. Admission to Colosseo includes visit to Palatine Hill.

Imperial Forums (Fori Imperiali) and Trajan's Market ★★ Mussolini issued the controversial orders to cut through centuries of debris and junky buildings to carve out Via dei Fori Imperiali, thereby linking the Colosseum to the grand 19th-century monuments of Piazza Venezia. Excavations under his Fascist regime began at once, and many archaeological treasures were revealed.

Begun by Julius Caesar as an answer to the overcrowding of Rome's older forums, the Imperial Forums were, at the time of their construction, flashier, bolder, and more impressive than the buildings in the Roman Forum. This site conveyed the unquestioned authority of the emperors at the height of their absolute power. On the street's north side, you'll come to a large outdoor restaurant, where Via Cavour joins the boulevard. Just beyond the small park across Via Cavour are the remains of the **Forum of Nerva,** built by the emperor whose 2-year reign (A.D. 96–98) followed that of the paranoid Domitian. You'll be struck by how much the ground level has risen in 19 centuries. The only really recognizable remnant is a wall of the Temple of Minerva with two fine Corinthian columns. This forum was once flanked by that of Vespasian, which is now gone. It's possible to enter the Forum of Nerva from the other side, but you can see it just as well from the railing.

The next forum you approach is the **Forum of Augustus ★★**, built before the birth of Christ to commemorate the emperor's victory over the assassins Cassius and Brutus in the Battle of Philippi (42 B.C.). Like the Forum of Nerva, you can enter this forum from the other side (cut across the wee footbridge).

Continuing along the railing, you'll see the vast semicircle of **Trajan's Market ★★**, whose teeming arcades stocked with merchandise from the far corners of the Roman world collapsed long ago, leaving only a few cats to watch after things. The shops once covered a multitude of levels. The historic market has reopened in Rome after years of restoration and now boasts the new Imperial Forums Museum.

Over two floors and more than 2,000 sq. m (21, 528 sq. ft.), visitors can roam through the Grande Aula and Corpo Centrale buildings. The buildings are home to 172 original marble fragments from the Fori Imperiali and here are also original remnants from the Foro di Augusto and the Foro di Nerva.

The museum occupies the ruins of boutiques, food stores, and workshops that formed Emperor Trajan's Market (nicknamed "the World's First Shopping Mall"). Across the street from the Roman Forum, the installation occupies the Great Hall and part of the central body of the market (built A.D. 100–110), and is designed to illustrate the history of ancient Rome's public meeting areas. Having fallen into total ruin, this once-bustling market was built over in the Middle Ages and then extensively excavated under Mussolini, who created Via dei Fori Imperiali to connect the Colosseum with Piazza Venezia.

Today it is one of Rome's main thoroughfares, cutting right through the heart of the classical remains. As a consequence, the Imperial Forums, many of which are still being excavated, are hard for ordinary visitors to understand, so the new Imperial Forums Museum uses replicas to help visitors orientate themselves, and has different galleries dedicated to forums and temples. It also houses a giant head of Constantine, found in 2005 in an old sewer, and 172 large marble fragments from the Imperial Forums, most of which had been in storage for years. They are also shown with drawings to illustrate where they fitted into the overall scheme. Also on view are 15 plaster models and 12 life-size re-creations of parts of Augustus's and Nerva's Forums next door. The models are painted in brilliant colors, which was typical in ancient Roman.

Admission to both Trajan's Market and the Imperial Forums Museum costs 9€, and the site is open Tuesday to Sunday 9am to 7pm. The website is www.mercatiditraiano.it.

Before you head down through the labyrinthine passages, you might like to climb the **Tower of the Milizie ★**, a 12th-century structure that was part of the medieval headquarters of the Knights of Rhodes. The view from the top (if it's open) is well worth the climb.

You can enter the **Forum of Trajan ★★** on Via Quattro Novembre near the steps of Via Magnanapoli. Once through the tunnel, you'll emerge into the newest and most beautiful of the Imperial Forums, built between A.D. 107 and 113, and designed by Greek architect Apollodorus of Damascus (who laid out the adjoining market). There are many statue fragments and pedestals bearing still-legible inscriptions, but more interesting is the great Basilica Ulpia, whose gray marble columns rise roofless into the sky. This forum was once regarded as one of the architectural wonders of the world.

Beyond the Basilica Ulpia is **Trajan's Column ★★★**, in magnificent condition, with an intricate bas-relief sculpture depicting Trajan's victorious campaign (though, from your vantage point, you'll be able to see only the earliest stages). The next stop is the **Forum of Julius Caesar ★★**, the first of the Imperial Forums. It lies on the opposite side of Via dei Fori Imperiali. This was the site of the Roman stock exchange, as well as the Temple of Venus.

After you've seen the wonders of ancient Rome, you might continue up Via dei Fori Imperiali to **Piazza Venezia ★★**, where the white Brescian marble **Vittorio Emanuele Monument** dominates the scene. (You can't miss it.) Italy's most flamboyant landmark, it was built in the late 1800s to honor the first king of Italy. It has been compared to everything from a wedding cake to a Victorian typewriter and has been ridiculed because of its harsh white color in a city of

No More Lines

The endless lines outside Italian museums and attractions are a fact of life. But new reservation services can help you avoid the wait, at least for some of the major museums.

Select Italy allows you to reserve your tickets for the Colosseum, the Roman Forum, Palatine Hill, the Galleria Borghese, and more, plus many other museums in Florence and Venice. The cost varies from 18€ to 35€, depending on the museum, and several combination passes are available. Contact Select Italy at ✆ **800/877-1755** in the U.S., or buy your tickets online at **www.selectitaly.com**.

honey-gold tones. An eternal flame burns at the Tomb of the Unknown Soldier. The interior of the monument has been closed for years, but you'll come to use it as a landmark as you figure your way around the city.

Via IV Novembre 94. www.mercatiditraiano.it. ✆ **06-0608.** Admission 11€. Tues–Sun 9am–7pm. Closed Dec 25, Jan 1, May 1. Metro: Colosseo. Keep to the right side of the street.

Roman Forum (Foro Romano), Palatine Hill (Palatino) & Palatine Museum (Museo Palatino) ★★★ When it came to cremating Caesar, purchasing a harlot for the night, sacrificing a naked victim, or just discussing the day's events, the Roman Forum was the place to be. Traversed by the **Via Sacra (Sacred Way) ★**, the main thoroughfare of ancient Rome, the Forum was built in the marshy land between the Palatine and Capitoline hills, and flourished as the center of Roman life in the days of the Republic, before it gradually lost prestige to the Imperial Forums.

You'll see only ruins and fragments, an arch or two, and lots of overturned boulders, but with some imagination you can feel the rush of history here. That any semblance of the Forum remains today is miraculous because it was used for years as a quarry (as was the Colosseum). Eventually it reverted to what the Italians call a *campo vaccino* (cow pasture). But excavations in the 19th century began to bring to light one of the world's most historic spots.

By day, the columns of now-vanished temples and the stones from which long-forgotten orators spoke are mere shells. Bits of grass and weeds grow where a triumphant Caesar was once lionized. But at night, when the Forum is silent in the moonlight, it isn't difficult to imagine Vestal Virgins still guarding the sacred temple fire. The best view of the Roman Forum at night is from Campidoglio or Capitoline Hill, Michelangelo's piazza from the Renaissance, which overlooks the Forum.

You can spend at least a morning wandering through the ruins of the Forum. If you're content with just looking, you can do so at your leisure. But if you want the stones to have some meaning, buy a detailed plan at the gate (the temples are hard to locate otherwise).

Turn right at the bottom of the entrance slope to walk west along the old Via Sacra toward the arch. Just before it on your right is the large brick **Curia ★★**, the main seat of the Roman Senate, built by Julius Caesar. Pop inside to see the 3rd-century marble inlay floor.

The triumphal **Arch of Septimius Severus ★★** (A.D. 203) displays time-bitten reliefs of the emperor's victories in what are today Iran and Iraq. During the Middle Ages, Rome became a provincial backwater, and frequent flooding of the nearby river helped bury most of the Forum. This former center of the Empire became a cow pasture. Some bits did still stick out aboveground, including the top half of this arch, which was used to shelter a barbershop! It wasn't until the 19th century that people really became interested in excavating these ancient ruins to see what Rome in its glory must have been like.

Just to the left of the arch, you can make out the remains of a cylindrical lump of rock with some marble steps curving off it. That round stone was the **Umbilicus Urbus,** considered the center of Rome and of the entire Roman Empire; the curving steps are those of the **Imperial Rostra ★**, where great orators and legislators stood to speak and the people gathered to listen. Nearby, the much-photographed trio of fluted columns with Corinthian capitals supporting a bit of architrave form the corner of the **Temple of Vespasian and Titus ★★** (emperors were routinely turned into gods upon dying).

Start heading to your left toward the eight Ionic columns marking the front of the **Temple of Saturn ★★** (rebuilt in 42 B.C.), which housed the first treasury of republican Rome. It was also the site of one of the Roman year's biggest annual blowout festivals, the December 17 feast of Saturnalia, which, after a bit of tweaking, Christians now celebrate as Christmas. Turn left to start heading back east, past the worn steps and stumps of brick pillars outlining the enormous **Basilica Julia ★★**, built by Julius Caesar. Past it are the three Corinthian columns of the **Temple of the Dioscuri ★★★**, dedicated to the Gemini twins, Castor and Pollux. Forming one of the most celebrated sights of the Roman Forum, a trio of columns supports an architrave fragment. The founding of this temple dates from the 5th century B.C.

Beyond the bit of curving wall that marks the site of the little round **Temple of Vesta** (rebuilt several times after fires started by the sacred flame within), you'll find the partially reconstructed **House of the Vestal Virgins ★★** (3rd–4th c. A.D.) against the south side of the grounds. This was the home of the consecrated young women who tended the sacred flame in the Temple of Vesta. Vestals were girls chosen from patrician families to serve a 30-year-long priesthood. During their tenure, they were among Rome's most venerated citizens, with unique powers such as the ability to pardon condemned criminals. The cult was quite serious about the "virgin" part of the job description—if one of Vesta's

Taking in the view of the Roman Forum from the Capitoline.

A View to Remember for a Lifetime

Standing on Piazza del Campidoglio, walk around the right side of the Palazzo Senatorio to a terrace overlooking the city's best panorama of the Roman Forum, with the Palatine Hill and the Colosseum as a backdrop. At night, the Forum is dramatically floodlit and the ruins look even more impressive and haunting.

earthly servants was found to have "misplaced" her virginity, the miscreant Vestal was buried alive. (Her amorous accomplice was merely flogged to death.) The overgrown rectangle of their gardens is lined with broken, heavily worn statues of senior Vestals on pedestals.

The path dovetails back to join Via Sacra at the entrance. Turn right and then left to enter the massive brick remains and coffered ceilings of the 4th-century **Basilica of Constantine and Maxentius ★★**. These were Rome's public law courts, and their architectural style was adopted by early Christians for their houses of worship (the reason so many ancient churches are called "basilicas").

Return to the path and continue toward the Colosseum. Veer right to the second great surviving triumphal arch, the **Arch of Titus ★★** (A.D. 81), on which one relief depicts the carrying off of treasures from Jerusalem's temple. Look closely and you'll see a menorah among the booty. The war that this arch glorifies ended with the expulsion of Jews from the colonized Judea, signaling the beginning of the Jewish Diaspora throughout Europe. From here you can enter and climb the **Palatine Hill ★** (with the same hours as the Forum; the same ticket will get you into both the Forum and Palatine Hill).

The Palatine, tradition tells us, was the spot on which the first settlers built their huts under the direction of Romulus. In later years, the hill became a patrician residential district that attracted such citizens as Cicero. In time, however, the area was gobbled up by imperial palaces and drew a famous and infamous roster of tenants, such as Livia (some of the frescoes in the House of Livia are in miraculous condition), Tiberius, Caligula (murdered here by members of his Praetorian Guard), Nero, and Domitian.

Only the ruins of its former grandeur remain today. You really need to be an archaeologist to make sense of them; they're more difficult to understand than those in the Forum. But even if you're not interested in the past, it's worth the climb for the panoramic view of both the Roman and the Imperial Forums, as well as the Capitoline Hill and the Colosseum.

The **Palatine Museum (Museo Palatino) ★** displays a good collection of Roman sculpture from the digs in the Palatine villas. In summer you can take guided tours in English daily at 11, 11:45am, and 4:15pm for 4€; call in winter to see if they're still available. If you ask the custodian, he might take you to one of the nearby locked villas and let you in for a peek at surviving frescoes and stuccoes. The same ticket that you buy for the Palatine Hill and the Palatine Museum includes the visit to the Colosseum.

Via della Salara Vecchia 5/6. ✆ **06-39967700.** Forum and Palatine Hill admission 12€. Oct 30–Dec and Jan 2–Feb 15 daily 8:30am–4:30pm; Feb 16–Mar 15 daily 8:30am–5pm; Mar 16–24 daily 8:30am–5:30pm; Mar 25–Aug daily 8:30am–7:15pm; Sept daily 8:30am–7pm; Oct 1–29 daily 8:30am–6:30pm. Last admission 1 hr. before closing. Guided tours are given daily at 11am, lasting 1 hr., costing 4€. Closed holidays. Metro: Colosseo. Bus: 75 or 84.

OTHER ATTRACTIONS NEAR ANCIENT ROME

Basilica di San Clemente ★ From the Colosseum, head up Via San Giovanni in Laterano to this basilica. It isn't just another Roman church—far from it. In this church-upon-a-church, centuries of history peel away. In the 4th century A.D., a church was built over a secular house from the 1st century, beside which stood a pagan temple dedicated to Mithras (god of the sun). Down in the eerie grottoes (which you can explore on your own), you'll discover well-preserved frescoes from the 9th to the 11th centuries. The Normans destroyed the lower church, and a new one was built in the 12th century. Its chief attraction is the bronze-orange mosaic from that period adorning the apse, as well as a chapel honoring St. Catherine of Alexandria with frescoes by Masolino.

Via San Giovanni in Laterano at Piazza San Clemente. www.basilicasanclemente.com. ✆ **06-7740021.** Basilica free admission; excavations 5€. Mon–Sat 9am–12:30pm and 3–6pm; Sun noon–6pm. Metro: Colosseo or Manzoni. Bus: 85, 87, 571, or 850.

Basilica di San Giovanni in Laterano ★ This church (not St. Peter's) is the cathedral of the diocese of Rome, where the pope comes to celebrate Mass on certain holidays. Built in A.D. 314 by Constantine, it has suffered the vicissitudes of Rome, forcing it to be rebuilt many times. Only fragmented parts of the baptistery remain from the original.

The present building is characterized by its 18th-century facade by Alessandro Galilei (statues of Christ and the Apostles ring the top). A 1993 terrorist bomb caused severe damage, especially to the facade. Borromini gets the credit (some say blame) for the interior, built for Innocent X. It's said that, in the misguided attempt to redecorate, frescoes by Giotto were destroyed (remains believed to have been painted by Giotto were discovered in 1952 and are now on display against a column near the entrance on the right inner pier). In addition, look for the unusual ceiling and the sumptuous transept, and explore the 13th-century cloisters with twisted double columns. Next door, **Palazzo Laterano** (no admission) was the original home of the popes before they became voluntary "Babylonian captives" in Avignon, France, in 1309.

Across the street is the **Palace of the Holy Steps (Santuario della Scala Santa),** Piazza San Giovanni in Laterano (✆ **06-7726641**). Allegedly, the 28 marble steps here (now covered with wood for preservation) were originally at Pontius Pilate's villa in Jerusalem, and Christ climbed them the day he was brought before Pilate. According to a medieval tradition, the steps were brought from Jerusalem to Rome by Constantine's mother, Helen, in 326, and they've been in this location since 1589. Today pilgrims from all over come here to climb the steps on their knees. This is one of the holiest sites in Christendom, although some historians say the stairs might date only from the 4th century.

Piazza San Giovanni in Laterano 4. ✆ **06-69886493.** Basilica free admission; cloisters 2€. Summer daily 7am–6:45pm (off season to 6pm). Metro: San Giovanni. Bus: 16, 81, 85, 87, 186, 218, or 650.

Case Romane del Celio ★ 🎁 The 5th-century Basilica of SS. Giovanni e Paolo stands over a residential complex consisting of several Roman houses of different periods. According to tradition, this was the dwelling of two Roman officers, John and Paul (not the Apostles), who were beheaded during the reign of Julian the Apostate (361–362), when they refused to serve in a military campaign. They were later made saints, and their bones were said to have been buried at this site. A visit here will provide you with a unique picture of how several generations of Romans lived. Preserved at the site is a residence from the 2nd century A.D., a single home of a wealthy family, and a 3rd-century-A.D. apartment building for artisans. A religious sect, the Passionists, excavated the site in 1887, discovering naked genii figures painted on the walls. Scandalized at such a realistic depiction of male genitalia, they blurred some of the most obvious anatomical details. The two-story construction, with some 20 rooms, also contains a labyrinth of well-preserved pagan and Christian paintings.

Piazza Santi Giovanni e Paolo 13 (entrance on Clivo di Scauro). www.caseromane.it. ✆ **06-70454544.** Admission 6€ adults, 4€ ages 12–18, free 11 and under. Thurs–Mon 10am–1pm and 3–6pm. Bus: 60, 75, 81, 175, 673, or Tram 3. Metro: Colosseo or Circo Massimo.

National Museum of Palazzo Venezia (Museo Nazionale di Palazzo di Venezia) ★ The Palazzo Venezia, in the geographic heart of Rome near Piazza Venezia, served as the seat of the Austrian Embassy until the end of World War I. During the Fascist regime (1928–43), it was the seat of the Italian government. The balcony from which Mussolini used to speak to the people was built in the 15th century. You can now visit the rooms and halls containing oil paintings, porcelain, tapestries, ivories, and ceramics. No one particular exhibit stands out—it's the sum total that adds up to a major attraction. The State Rooms occasionally open to host temporary exhibits.

Via del Plebiscito 118. ✆ **06-6780131.** Admission 4€. Tues–Sun 8:30am–7:00pm. Bus: 40, 63, 70, 75, or 81.

St. Peter in Chains (San Pietro in Vincoli) ★ This church, which has undergone recent renovations, was founded in the 5th century to house the chains that bound St. Peter in Palestine (they're preserved under glass). But the drawing card is the tomb of Pope Julius II, which features one of the world's most famous sculptures: **Michelangelo's *Moses* ★★★**. Michelangelo was to have carved 44 magnificent figures for the tomb. That didn't happen, of course, but the pope was given a great consolation prize—a figure intended to be "minor" that's now numbered among Michelangelo's masterpieces. In the *Lives of the Artists,* Vasari wrote about the stern father symbol of Michelangelo's *Moses:* "No modern work will ever equal it in beauty, no, nor ancient either."

Piazza San Pietro in Vincoli 4A (off Via degli Annibaldi). ✆ **06-97844950.** Free admission. Spring–summer daily 8am–12:30pm and 3:30–7pm (autumn–winter to 6pm). Metro: Colosseo or Cavour, then cross the blvd. and walk up the flight of stairs. Turn right, and you'll head into the piazza; the church will be on your left.

Santa Maria d'Aracoeli ★ On the Capitoline Hill, this landmark church was built for the Franciscans in the 13th century. According to legend, Augustus once ordered a temple erected on this spot, where a prophetic sibyl forecast the coming of Christ. In the interior are a coffered Renaissance ceiling and a mosaic of the Virgin over the altar in the Byzantine style. If you're enough of a sleuth, you'll find a tombstone carved by the great Renaissance sculptor Donatello. The church is known for its **Bufalini Chapel,** a masterpiece by Pinturicchio, who frescoed it with scenes illustrating the life and death of St. Bernardino of Siena. He also depicted St. Francis receiving the stigmata. These frescoes are a high point in early Renaissance Roman painting. You have to climb a long flight of steep steps to reach the church, unless you're already on neighboring Piazza del Campidoglio, in which case you can cross the piazza and climb the steps on the far side of the Museo Capitolino (earlier in this chapter).

Scala dell'Arce Capitolina 14. ✆ **06-69763839.** Free admission. Daily 9am–12:30pm and 3–6:30pm. Bus: 44, 46, 60, or 75.

Santa Maria in Cosmedin This little church was begun in the 6th century but was subsequently rebuilt. A Romanesque campanile (bell tower) was added at the end of the 11th century, although its origins go back to the 3rd century. The church was destroyed several times by earthquakes or by foreign invasions, but it has always been rebuilt.

People come not for great art treasures, but to see the **"Mouth of Truth,"** a large disk under the portico. As Gregory Peck demonstrated to Audrey Hepburn in the film *Roman Holiday,* the mouth is supposed to chomp down on the hands of liars who insert their paws. (According to local legend, a former priest used to keep a scorpion in back to bite the fingers of anyone he felt was lying.) The purpose of this disk (which is not of particular artistic interest) is unclear. One hypothesis says that it was used to collect the faithful's donations to God, which were introduced through the open mouth.

Piazza della Bocca della Verità 18. ✆ **06-6787759.** Free admission. Summer daily 9am–6pm; winter daily 9am–5pm. Metro: Circo Massimo. Bus: 30 or 170.

The Pantheon & Attractions near Piazza Navona & Campo de' Fiori

THE PANTHEON & NEARBY ATTRACTIONS

The Pantheon stands on **Piazza della Rotonda,** a lively square with cafes, vendors, and great people-watching.

Galleria Doria Pamphilj ★ This museum offers a look at what it was like to live in an 18th-century palace. It has been restored to its former splendor and expanded to include four rooms long closed to the public. It's partly leased to tenants (on the upper levels), and there are shops on the street level—but you'll overlook all this after entering the grand apartments of the Doria Pamphilj family, which traces its lineage to before the great 15th-century Genoese admiral Andrea Doria. The apartments surround the central court and gallery. The **ballroom, drawing rooms, dining rooms,** and **family chapel** are full of gilded furniture, crystal chandeliers, Renaissance tapestries, and family portraits. The **Green Room** is especially rich, with a 15th-century Tournay tapestry, paintings by Memling and Filippo Lippi, and a seminude portrait of Andrea Doria by Sebastiano del Piombo. The **Andrea Doria Room,** dedicated to the admiral and to the ship of the same name, contains a glass case with mementos of the great 1950s maritime disaster.

Skirting the central court is a **picture gallery** with a memorable collection of frescoes, paintings, and sculpture. Most important are the portrait of Innocent X, by Velázquez; *Salome,* by Titian; works by Rubens and Caravaggio; the *Bay of Naples,* by Pieter Bruegel the Elder; and a copy—not the original—of Raphael's portrait of Principessa Giovanna d'Aragóna de Colonna (who looks remarkably like Leonardo's *Mona Lisa*). Most of the sculpture came from the Doria country estates: marble busts of Roman emperors, bucolic nymphs, and satyrs.

Via del Corso 305. www.doriapamphilj.it. ✆ **06-6797323.** Admission 11€ adults, 7.50€ students/seniors. Daily 10am–5pm. Closed holidays. Private visits can be arranged. Metro: Barberini or Colosseo.

Sunlight streams through the dome of the Pantheon.

The Pantheon ★★★ Of all ancient Rome's great buildings, only the Pantheon ("All the Gods") remains intact. It was built in 27 B.C. by Marcus Agrippa and was reconstructed by Hadrian in the early 2nd century A.D. This remarkable building, 43m (142 ft.) wide and 43m (142 ft.) high (a perfect sphere resting in a cylinder) and once ringed with white marble statues of Roman gods in its niches, is among the architectural wonders of the world because of its dome and its concept of space. Hadrian himself is credited with the basic plan, an architectural design that was unique for the time. The once-gilded dome is merely show. A real dome, a perfect, massive hemisphere of cast concrete, is supported by a solid ring wall. Before the 20th century, the dome was the biggest pile of concrete ever constructed. The ribbed dome outside is a series of almost weightless cantilevered bricks. Animals were sacrificed and burned in the center, and the smoke escaped through the only means of light, the oculus, an opening at the top 5.5m (18 ft.) in diameter.

Michelangelo came here to study the dome before designing the cupola of St. Peter's (whose dome is .5m/2 ft. smaller than the Pantheon's). The walls are 7.5m (25 ft.) thick, and the bronze doors leading into the building weigh 20 tons each. About 125 years ago, Raphael's tomb was discovered here (fans still bring him flowers). Vittorio Emanuele II, king of Italy, and his successor, Umberto I, are interred here as well. Today it is a Catholic church (Chiesa di Santa Maria ad Martyres). Until the 5th century, it was a temple dedicated to all the Roman gods. In 609, Emperor Phocas gave it to Pope Boniface IV, who consecrated it, dedicated it to St. Mary and all the Christian martyrs, and renamed it Santa Maria ad Martyres.

Piazza della Rotonda. ✆ **06-68300230.** Free admission. Mon–Sat 8:30am–7:30pm; Sun 9am–1pm. Bus: 30, 40, 62, 64, 81, or 492 to Largo di Torre Argentina.

PIAZZA NAVONA & NEARBY ATTRACTIONS

Piazza Navona ★★★, one of the most beautifully baroque sites in all Rome, is an ocher-colored gem, unspoiled by new buildings or traffic. Its shape results from the ruins of the Stadium of Domitian that lie beneath it. Chariot races were once held here (some rather unusual, such as the one in which the head of the winning horse was lopped off as it crossed the finish line and was then carried by runners to be offered as a sacrifice by the Vestal Virgins atop the Capitoline). In medieval times, the popes used to flood the piazza to stage mock naval encounters. Today the piazza is packed with vendors and street performers, and lined with pricey cafes where you can enjoy a cappuccino or gelato and indulge in unparalleled people-watching.

Besides the twin-towered facade of 17th-century Santa Agnes, the piazza boasts several baroque masterpieces. The best known, in the center, is Bernini's **Fountain of the Four Rivers (Fontana dei Quattro Fiumi) ★★★**,

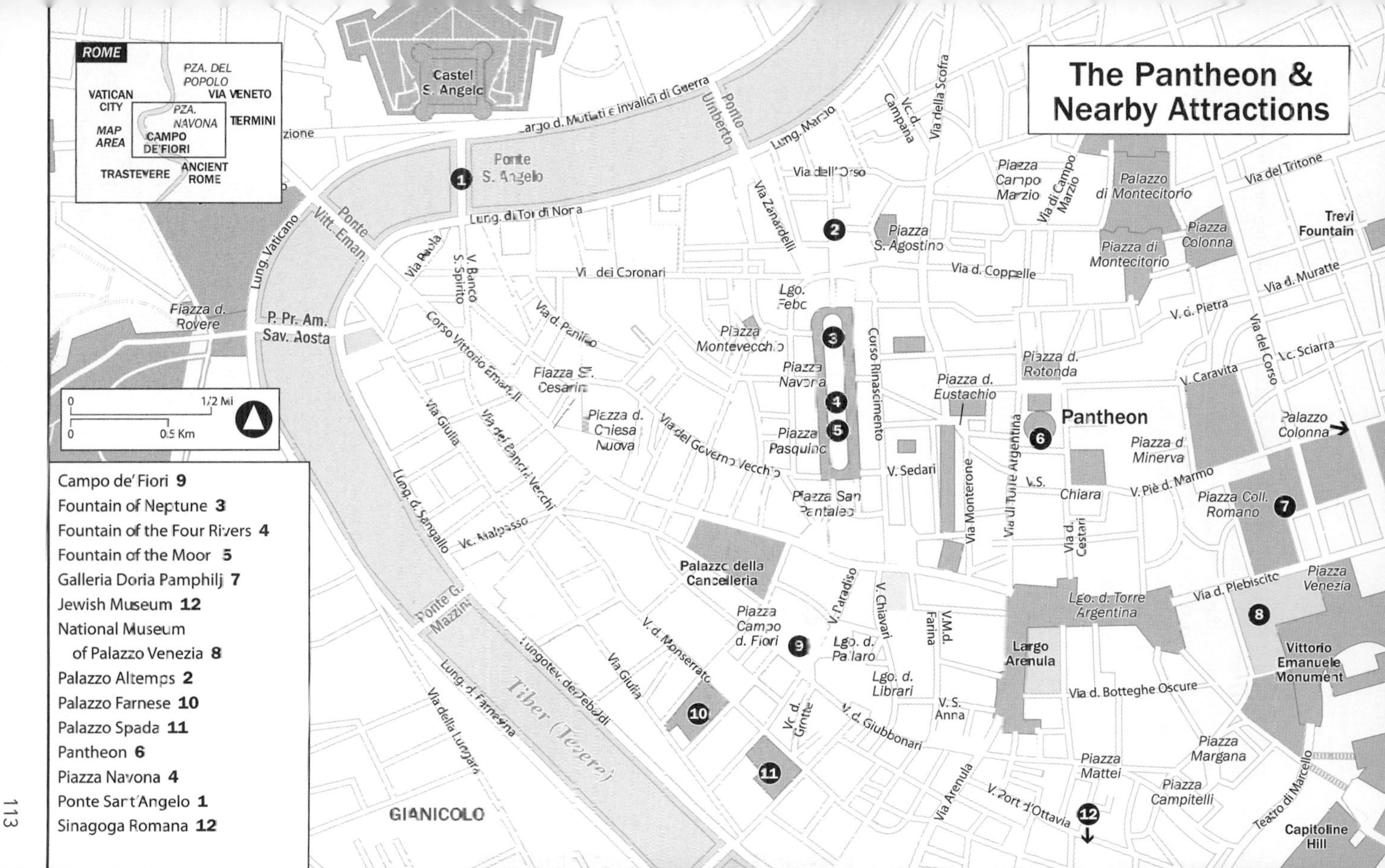

The Pantheon & Nearby Attractions
ROME
PZA. DEL POPOLO
VATICAN CITY
VIA VENETO
PZA. NAVONA
TERMINI
MAP AREA
CAMPO DE'FIORI
TRASTEVERE
ANCIENT ROME
0
1/2 Mi
0
0.5 Km
Campo de' Fiori 9
Fountain of Neptune 3
Fountain of the Four Rivers 4
Fountain of the Moor 5
Galleria Doria Pamphilj 7
Jewish Museum 12
National Museum of Palazzo Venezia 8
Palazzo Altemps 2
Palazzo Farnese 10
Palazzo Spada 11
Pantheon 6
Piazza Navona 4
Ponte Sant'Angelo 1
Sinagoga Romana 12
Castel S. Angelo
Ponte S. Angelo
Ponte Umberto
Ponte Vitt. Eman.
Ponte G. Mazzini
P. Pr. Am. Sav. Aosta
Piazza d. Rovere
Lung. Vaticano
Lung. di Tor di Nora
Lung. Marzio
Via Zanardelli
Via dell'Orso
Vc. d. Campana
Via della Scrofa
Piazza Campo Marzio
Via di Campo Marzio
Palazzo di Montecitorio
Piazza di Montecitorio
Piazza Colonna
Via del Tritone
Trevi Fountain
Via d. Muratte
Piazza S. Agostino
Via d. Coppelle
Vi. dei Coronari
V. Banco S. Spirito
Via Paola
Corso Vittorio Emanuele
Via d. Panico
Lgo. Febo
Piazza Montevecchio
Piazza Navona
Piazza Pasquino
Piazza San Pantaleo
Corso Rinascimento
Piazza d. Chiesa Nuova
Via del Governo Vecchio
Via dei Banchi Vecchi
Via Giulia
Lung. d. Sangallo
Vc. Malpasso
Piazza d. Eustachio
Piazza d. Rotonda
Pantheon
Piazza d. Minerva
V. Sedari
Via Monterone
Via di Torre Argentina
V. S. Chiara
Via d. Cestari
V. Piè d. Marmo
Piazza Coll. Romano
Via del Corso
V. d. Pietra
V. Caravita
Vc. Sciarra
Palazzo Colonna
Palazzo della Cancelleria
Piazza Campo d. Fiori
Lgo. d. Pallaro
Lgo. d. Librari
V. Chiavari
V. Paradiso
V.M.d. Farina
V. S. Anna
V. d. Giubbonari
Vc. d. Grotte
V. d. Monserrato
Lungotev. dei Tebaldi
Tiber (Tevere)
Lung. d. Farnesina
Via della Lungara
GIANICOLO
Lgo. d. Torre Argentina
Largo Arenula
Via d. Plebiscito
Piazza Venezia
Vittorio Emanuele Monument
Via d. Botteghe Oscure
Piazza Mattei
Piazza Margana
Piazza Campitelli
Via Arenula
V. Port. d'Ottavia
Teatro di Marcello
Capitoline Hill

whose four stone personifications symbolize the world's greatest rivers: the Ganges, Danube, della Plata, and Nile. It's fun to try to figure out which is which. (***Hint:*** The figure with the shroud on its head is the Nile, so represented because the river's source was unknown at the time.) At the south end is the **Fountain of the Moor (Fontana del Moro),** also by Bernini. The **Fountain of Neptune (Fontana di Nettuno),** which balances that of the Moor, is a 19th-century addition.

Palazzo Altemps ★ This branch of the National Roman Museum is housed in a 15th-century palace that was restored and opened to the public in 1997. It is home to the fabled Ludovisi Collection of Greek and Roman sculpture. Among the masterpieces of the Roman Renaissance, you'll find the *Ares Ludovisi,* a Roman copy of the original dated 330 B.C. and restored by Bernini during the 17th century. In the Sala delle Storie di Mosè is *Ludovisi's Throne,* representing the birth of Venus. The Sala delle Feste (the Celebrations' Hall) is dominated by a sarcophagus depicting the Romans fighting against the Ostrogoth barbarians; this masterpiece, carved from a single block, dates back to the 2nd century A.D. and nowadays is called *Grande Ludovisi (Great Ludovisi).* Other outstanding art from the collection includes a copy of Phidias's celebrated *Athena,* which once stood in the Parthenon in Athens. (The Roman copy here is from the 1st c. B.C. because the original *Athena* is lost to history.) The huge *Dionysus with Satyr* is from the 2nd century A.D.

Piazza San Apollinare 46, near the Piazza Navona. ✆ **06-39967700.** Admission 10€. Tues–Sun 9am–7:45pm. Last admission 1 hr. before closing. Bus: 70, 81, 87, or 116.

CAMPO DE' FIORI & THE JEWISH GHETTO

During the 1500s, **Campo de' Fiori ★** was the geographic and cultural center of secular Rome, site of dozens of inns. From its center rises a statue of the severe-looking monk Giordano Bruno, whose presence is a reminder that heretics were occasionally burned at the stake here. Today, circled by venerable houses, the campo is the site of an **open-air food market** held Monday through Saturday from early in the morning until around noon (or whenever the food runs out).

Built from 1514 to 1589, the **Palazzo Farnese ★**, on Piazza Farnese, was designed by Sangallo and Michelangelo, among others, and was an astronomically expensive project for the time. Its famous residents have included a 16th-century member of the Farnese family, plus Pope Paul III, Cardinal Richelieu, and the former Queen Christina of Sweden, who moved to Rome after abdicating. During the 1630s, when the heirs couldn't afford to maintain the *palazzo,* it became the site of the French Embassy, as it still is (it's closed to the public). For the best view of it, cut west from Via Giulia along any of the narrow streets (we recommend Via Mascherone or Via dei Farnesi).

Palazzo Spada ★, Piazza Capo di Ferro 13 (✆ **06-6861158**), was built around 1550 for Cardinal Gerolamo Capo di Ferro and later inhabited by the descendants of several other cardinals. It was sold to the Italian government in the 1920s. Its richly ornate facade, covered in high-relief stucco decorations in the Mannerist style, is the finest of any building from 16th-century Rome. The State Rooms are closed, but the richly decorated courtyard and a handful of galleries of paintings are open. Admission is 5€ Tuesday through Sunday from 8:30am to 7:30pm. To get there, take bus no. 46, 56, 62, 64, 70, 87, or 492.

Also in this neighborhood stands the **Sinagoga Romana Lungotevere Cenci** (✆ **06-6840061**), open only for services. Trying to avoid all resemblance to a Christian church, the building (1874–1904) evokes Babylonian and Persian

A Roman deli in the former ghetto.

details. The synagogue was attacked by terrorists in 1982 and since then has been heavily guarded by *carabinieri* (a division of the Italian army) armed with machine guns. On the premises is the **Jewish Museum of Rome** (**Museo Ebraico di Roma;** www.museoebraico.roma.it), Via Catalana (same phone), which displays the collections of the Jews of Rome, including the works of 17th- and 18th-century Roman silversmiths, precious textiles from all over Europe, parchments, and marble carvings saved when the ghetto synagogues were demolished. The restored museum now has six permanent exhibition rooms. Admission (including guided tour of the synagogue) is 10€ for adults, 4€ for students, with children 10 and under admitted free. From June 15 to September 15, hours are Sunday to Thursday 10am to 7pm, Friday 10am to 4pm. At other times, hours are Sunday to Thursday 10am to 5pm, Friday 9am to 2pm (bus: 30, 40, 46, 63, 271, 280, 630, or 780).

The Spanish Steps, the Trevi Fountain & Attractions Nearby

ON OR AROUND PIAZZA DI SPAGNA

The **Spanish Steps ★★** (**Scalinata di Spagna;** Metro: Piazza di Spagna) are alive with azaleas and other flowers in spring, and bustling with flower vendors, jewelry dealers, and photographers snapping pictures of visitors year-round. The steps and the square (Piazza di Spagna) take their names from the Spanish Embassy, which used to be headquartered here. Designed by Italian architect Francesco de Sanctis and built from 1723 to 1725, they were funded almost entirely by the French as a preface to Trinità dei Monti at the top.

The steps and the piazza below are always packed with a crowd: strolling, reading in the sun, browsing the vendors' carts, and people-watching. Near the steps, you'll also find an American Express office, public restrooms (near the Metro stop), and the most sumptuous McDonald's we've ever seen (cause for uproar among the Romans when it first opened).

Keats-Shelley House At the foot of the Spanish Steps is this 18th-century house where John Keats died of consumption on February 23, 1821, at age 25. Since 1909, when it was bought by well-intentioned English and American literary types, it has been a working library established in honor of Keats and Percy Bysshe Shelley, who drowned off the coast of Viareggio with a copy of Keats in his pocket. Mementos range from kitsch to the immortal. The apartment where Keats spent his last months, tended by his close friend Joseph Severn, shelters a death mask of Keats as well as the "deadly sweat" drawing by Severn.

Piazza di Spagna 26. www.keats-shelley-house.org. ✆ **06-6784235.** Admission 4.50€. Mon–Fri 10am–1pm and 2–6pm; Sat 11am–2pm and 3–6pm. Guided tours by appointment. Metro: Piazza di Spagna.

The crowds at the Spanish Steps.

Palazzo del Quirinale ★★ Until the end of World War II, this palace was the home of the king of Italy; before the crown resided here, it was the residence of the pope. Despite its Renaissance origins (nearly every important architect in Italy worked on some aspect of its sprawling premises), this *palazzo* is rich in associations with ancient emperors and deities. The colossal statues of the Dioscuri Castor and Pollux, which now form part of the fountain in the piazza, were found in the nearby great Baths of Constantine; in 1793 Pius VI had the ancient Egyptian obelisk moved here from the Mausoleum of Augustus. The sweeping view of Rome from the piazza, which crowns the highest of the seven ancient hills of Rome, is itself worth the trip. This palace houses the president of the republic.
Piazza del Quirinale. www.quirinale.it. ✆ **06-46991.** Admission 5€. Sun 8:30am–noon. Closed late June to early Sept. Metro: Barberini.

Trevi Fountain (Fontana di Trevi) ★★ As you elbow your way through the summertime crowds around the Trevi Fountain, you'll find it hard to believe that

Great Art in the Stables

Across from the Palazzo del Quirinale, the 18th-century Quirinale stables called the **Scuderie del Quirinale** or **Scuderie Papali,** Via XXIV Maggio 16 (www.scuderiequirinale.it; ✆ **06-39967500**), built for the pope's horses, have been transformed into an art gallery that hosts changing exhibitions. Exhibits have ranged from 100 masterpieces on loan from the Hermitage to Botticelli's illustrations for Dante's *Divine Comedy.* The stables were built on the site of the 3rd-century Temple of Serapis. (Some of the ruins can still be seen from the glass-enclosed stairs overlooking a private garden.) The galleries are open Sunday through Thursday 10am to 8pm, and Friday and Saturday 10am to 10:30pm. Admission is 10€.

this little piazza was nearly always deserted before the 1954 film *Three Coins in the Fountain* brought renewed interest to this lovely spot.

Supplied by water from the Acqua Vergine aqueduct and a triumph of the baroque style, it was based on the design of Nicola Salvi (who's said to have died of illness contracted during his supervision of the project) and was completed in 1762. The design centers on the triumphant figure of Neptunus Rex, standing on a shell chariot drawn by winged steeds and led by a pair of tritons. Two allegorical figures in the side niches represent good health and fertility.

On the southwestern corner of the piazza is a somber, not particularly spectacular-looking church, **SS. Vincenzo e Anastasio,** with a strange claim to fame. Within it survive the hearts and intestines of several centuries of popes. According to legend, the church was built on the site of a spring that burst from the earth after the beheading of St. Paul; the spring is one of the three sites where his head is said to have bounced off the ground.

Piazza di Trevi. Metro: Barberini.

AROUND VIA VENETO & PIAZZA BARBERINI

Piazza Barberini lies at the foot of several Roman streets, among them Via Barberini, Via Sistina, and Via Vittorio Veneto. It would be a far more pleasant spot were it not for the heavy traffic swarming around its principal feature, Bernini's **Fountain of the Triton (Fontana del Tritone)** ★. For more than 3 centuries, the strange figure sitting in a vast open clam has been blowing water from his triton. Off to one side of the piazza is the aristocratic side facade of the **Palazzo Barberini,** named for one of Rome's powerful families; inside is the **Galleria Nazionale d'Arte Antica** (see below). The Renaissance Barberini reached their peak when a son was elected pope as Urban VIII; he encouraged Bernini and gave him great patronage.

As you go up Via Vittorio Veneto, look for the small fountain on the right corner of Piazza Barberini—it's another Bernini, the **Fountain of the Bees (Fontana delle Api).** At first they look more like flies, but they're the bees of the

The Trevi Fountain at night.

Barberini, the crest of that powerful family complete with the crossed keys of St. Peter above them (the keys were always added to a family crest when a son was elected pope).

Monumental Cemetery of the Capuchin Brothers (Cimitero Monumentale dei Padri Cappuccini) One of the most mesmerizingly macabre sights in all Christendom, this is a series of chapels with thousands of skulls and bones woven into mosaic "works of art." To make this allegorical dance of death, the bones of more than 4,000 Capuchin brothers were used. Some of the skeletons are intact, draped with Franciscan habits. The creator of this chamber of horrors? The tradition of the friars is that it was the work of a French Capuchin. Their literature suggests that you should visit the cemetery while keeping in mind the historical moment of its origins, when Christians had a rich and creative cult for their dead and great spiritual masters meditated and preached with a skull in hand. Those who've lived through the days of crematoriums and other such massacres might view the graveyard differently, but to many who pause to think, this site has a message. The entrance is halfway up the first staircase on the right of the church.

Bone art at the Capuchin crypt.

Beside the Church of the Immaculate Conception, Via Vittorio Veneto 27. www.cappuccinivia veneto.it. ✆ **06-4871185.** Donation required. Fri–Wed 9am–noon and 3–6pm. Metro: Barberini.

National Gallery of Ancient Art (Galleria Nazionale d'Arte Antica) ★★ **Palazzo Barberini,** right off Piazza Barberini, is one of the most magnificent baroque palaces in Rome. It was begun by Carlo Maderno in 1627 and completed in 1633 by Bernini, whose lavishly decorated rococo apartments, the **Gallery of Decorative Art (Galleria d'Arte Decorativa),** are on view. This gallery is part of the **National Gallery of Ancient Art.**

The bedroom of Princess Cornelia Costanza Barberini and Prince Giulio Cesare Colonna di Sciarra stands just as it was on their wedding night, and many household objects are displayed in the decorative art gallery. In the chambers, which boast frescoes and hand-painted silk linings, you can see porcelain from Japan and Bavaria, canopied beds, and a wooden baby carriage.

On the first floor is a splendid array of paintings from the 13th to the 16th centuries, most notably *Mother and Child,* by Simone Martini, and works by Filippo Lippi, Andrea Solario, and Francesco Francia. Il Sodoma has some brilliant pictures here, including the *Rape of the Sabines* and the *Marriage of St. Catherine.* One of the best known is Raphael's *La Fornarina,* the baker's daughter who was his mistress and who posed for his Madonna portraits. Titian is represented by his *Venus and Adonis.* Also here are Tintorettos and El Grecos. Many visitors come just to see the magnificent Caravaggios, including *Narcissus.*

Via delle Quattro Fontane 13. http://galleriabarberini.beniculturali.it. ✆ **06-4824184.** Admission 5€. Tues–Sun 8:30am–6:30pm. Metro: Barberini.

PIAZZA DEL POPOLO

The restored **Piazza del Popolo ★★** is haunted with memories. According to legend, the ashes of Nero were enshrined here, until 11th-century residents began complaining to the pope about his imperial ghost. The **Egyptian obelisk** dates from the 13th century B.C.; it was removed from Heliopolis to Rome during Augustus's reign (it stood at the Circus Maximus). The piazza was designed in the early 19th century by Valadier, Napoleon's architect. The **Santa Maria del Popolo ★★**, with two Caravaggios, is at its northern curve, and opposite are almost-twin baroque churches, overseeing the never-ending traffic.

MAXXI (National Museum of the XXI Century Arts) ★ The city of Michelangelo has gone modern with the opening of this stunning building constructed on the site of former army barracks. The complex, costing 60 million euros, was the creation of an Iraqi-born architect, Zaha Hadid, who is known for her daring architecture. MAXXI (the first two letters stand for the Museum of Art, with the Roman numerals denoting the 21st century) houses Italy's growing national collection of contemporary art. In addition to its permanent collection, MAXXI will also host the most avant-garde exhibitions of modern art in Italy. The museum is divided into two sections—MAXXI art and MAXXI architecture. The museum lies north of Piazza del Popolo.

Via Guido Reni 4A, Flaminio. www.fondazionemaxxi.it. ✆ **06-39967350.** Admission 11€, free 13 and under. Tues–Fri and Sun 11am–7pm, Sat 11am–10pm. Closed Mon. Bus: 53, 217, 280, 910. Metro to Flaminio stop, then tram 2.

In the Villa Borghese

Villa Borghese ★★, in the heart of Rome, is 6km (3¾ miles) in circumference. One of Europe's most elegant parks, it was created by Cardinal Scipione Borghese in the 1600s. Umberto I, king of Italy, acquired it in 1902 and presented it to the city of Rome. With lovely landscaped vistas, the greenbelt is crisscrossed

The Villa Borghese.

by roads, but you can escape from the traffic and seek a shaded area under a tree to enjoy a picnic or relax. On a sunny weekend, it's a pleasure to stroll here and see Romans at play, relaxing or in-line skating. There are a few casual cafes and some food vendors; you can also rent bikes here. In the northeast of the park is a small zoo; the park is also home to a few outstanding museums.

Galleria Borghese ★★★ This legendary art gallery includes such masterpieces as Bernini's *Apollo and Daphne,* Titian's *Sacred and Profane Love,* Raphael's *Deposition,* and Caravaggio's *Jerome.* The collection began with the gallery's founder, Scipione Borghese, who, by the time of his death in 1633, had accumulated some of the greatest art of all time, even managing to acquire Bernini's early sculptures. Some paintings were spirited out of Vatican museums and even confiscated when their rightful owners were hauled off to prison until they became "reasonable" about turning over their art. The collection suffered at the hands of Napoleon's sister, Pauline, who married Prince Camillo Borghese in 1807 and sold most of the collection (many works are now in the Louvre in Paris). One of the most popular pieces of sculpture in the gallery, ironically, is Canova's sculpture of Pauline as *Venus Victorious.* (When Pauline was asked whether she felt uncomfortable posing in the nude, she replied, "Why should I? The studio was heated.")

Important information: No more than 360 visitors at a time are allowed on the ground floor, and no more than 90 are allowed on the upper floor. Reservations are essential, so call ✆ **06-32810** (Mon–Fri 9am–6pm; Sat 9am–1pm). However, the number always seems to be busy. You can also make reservations by calling ✆ **060608** or going online at www.ticketeria.it. If you'll be in Rome for a few days, try stopping by in person on your first day to reserve tickets for a later day. Better yet, before you leave home, contact **Select Italy** (www.selectitaly.com; ✆ **800/877-1755**).

Piazzale del Museo Borghese 5 (off Via Pinciana). www.galleriaborghese.it. ✆ **06-32810.** Admission 8.50€. Tues–Sun 9am–7pm. Bus: 5, 19, 52, 116, 204, 490, or 910.

Museo Carlo Bilotti ★ Who was this Carlo Bilotti, you ask? He was a retired Italian-American perfume executive from Palm Beach, Florida. He spent his life, when not hawking Old Spice, collecting one of the world's finest private collections of modern art. From Salvador Dalí to Andy Warhol, he knew all the "household names" in the art world—and was often their patron. At the end of his life in 2006, he donated his treasure-trove to the city of Rome, which restored a 16th-century palace in the Villa Borghese to house his collection. Bilotti was a friend of Giorgio de Chirico, and the permanent collection includes 22 canvases by that surrealist artist. De Chirico spent most of his life in Rome, dying here in 1978. Other works are by Larry Rivers, Dubuffet, and Giacomo Manzù, who is represented here by a large cardinal in bronze.

Villa Borghese, at Viale Fiorello La Guardia. www.museocarlobilotti.it. ✆ **060608.** Admission 5.50€ adults, 4.50€ children. Tues–Sun 9am–7pm. Metro: Flaminio.

National Etruscan Museum (Museo Nazionale Etrusco di Villa Giulia) ★★★ This 16th-century papal palace shelters a priceless collection of art and artifacts from the mysterious Etruscans, who predated the Romans. Known for their sophisticated art and design, they left a legacy of sarcophagi, bronze sculptures, terra-cotta vases, and jewelry, among other items. If you have time for only the masterpieces, head for Room 7, with a remarkable 6th-century-B.C. *Apollo from Veio* (clothed, for a change). The other two widely acclaimed statues here are *Dea con Bambino (Goddess with a Baby)* and a greatly mutilated but still powerful

Hercules with a stag. In Room 8, you'll see the lions' sarcophagus from the mid–6th century B.C., which was excavated at Cerveteri, north of Rome.

Finally, one of the world's most important Etruscan art treasures is the bride-and-bridegroom coffin from the 6th century B.C., also dug out of the tombs of Cerveteri (in Room 9). Near the end of your tour, another masterpiece of Etruscan art awaits you in Room 33: the *Cista Ficoroni,* a bronze urn with paw feet, mounted by three figures, dating from the 4th century B.C.

Piazzale di Villa Giulia 9. www.villagiulia.beniculturali.it. ✆ **06-3226571.** Admission 8€. Tues–Sun 8:30am–7:30pm. Bus: 926. Tram: 3, 19. Metro: Flaminio.

National Gallery of Modern Art (Galleria Nazionale d'Arte Moderna) ★ This gallery of modern art is a short walk from the Etruscan Museum (see above). With its neoclassical and Romantic paintings and sculpture, it makes a dramatic change from the glories of the Renaissance and ancient Rome. Its 75 rooms also house the largest collection in Italy of 19th- and 20th-century works by Balla, Boccioni, de Chirico, Morandi, Manzù, Burri, Capogrossi, and Fontana. Look for Modigliani's *La Signora dal Collaretto* and large *Nudo.* There are also many works of Italian optical and pop art and a good representation of foreign artists, including Degas, Cézanne, Monet, and van Gogh. Surrealism and expressionism are well represented by Klee, Ernst, Braque, Mirò, Kandinsky, Mondrian, and Pollock. You'll also find sculpture by Rodin. Several other important sculptures, including one by Canova, are on display in the museum's gardens.

Viale delle Belle Arti 131. www.gnam.beniculturali.it. ✆ **06-322981.** Admission 8€, free for children and seniors. Tues–Sun 8:30am–7:30pm. Bus: 2 or 926. Tram: 3 or 19.

The Appian Way & the Catacombs

Of all the roads that led to Rome, **Via Appia Antica** (built in 312 B.C.) was the most famous. It eventually stretched all the way from Rome to the seaport of Brindisi, through which trade with the colonies in Greece and the East was funneled. (According to Christian tradition, it was along the Appian Way that an escaping Peter encountered the vision of Christ, causing him to go back into the city to face subsequent martyrdom.) The road's initial stretch in Rome is lined with the great monuments and ancient tombs of patrician Roman families—burials were forbidden within the city walls as early as the 5th century B.C.—and, beneath the surface, miles of tunnels hewn out of the soft tufa stone.

These tunnels, or catacombs, were where early Christians buried their dead and, during the worst times of persecution, held church services discreetly out of the public eye. A few of them are open to the public, so you can wander through mile after mile of musty-smelling tunnels whose soft walls are gouged out with tens of thousands of burial niches (long shelves made for two to three bodies each). In some dank, dark grottoes (never stray too far from your party or one of the exposed light bulbs), you can still discover the remains of early Christian art. The requisite guided tours, hosted by priests and monks, feature a smidgen of extremely biased history and a large helping of sermonizing.

The Appia Antica has been a popular Sunday lunch picnic site for Roman families (following the half-forgotten pagan tradition of dining in the presence of one's ancestors on holy days). The Via Appia Antica is closed to cars on Sundays, open for the picnickers and bicyclists—along with in-line skaters and a Sunday-only bus route to get out here.

You can take bus no. 218 from the San Giovanni Metro stop, which follows the Appia Antica for a bit and then veers right on Via Ardeatina at Domine Quo Vadis Church. After another long block, the no. 218 stops at the square Largo M.F. Ardeatine, near the gate to the San Callisto Catacombs. From here, you can walk right on Via delle Sette Chiese to the San Domitilla Catacombs or walk left down Via d. Sette Chiese to the San Sebastiano Catacombs.

An alternative is to ride the Metro to the Colli Albani stop and catch bus no. 660, which wraps up the Appia Antica from the south, veering off it at the San Sebastiano Catacombs (if you're visiting all three, you can take bus 218 to the first two, walk to San Sebastiano, and then catch bus 660 back to the Metro).

Of the monuments on the Appian Way, the most impressive is the **Tomb of Cecilia Metella ★**, within walking distance of the catacombs. The cylindrical tomb honors the wife of one of Julius Caesar's military commanders from the republican era. Why such an elaborate tomb for such an unimportant person in history? Cecilia Metella was singled out for enduring fame simply because her tomb has remained and the others have decayed.

Catacombs of St. Callixtus (Catacombe di San Callisto) ★★ "The most venerable and most renowned of Rome," said Pope John XXIII of these funerary tunnels. The founder of Christian archaeology, Giovanni Battista de Rossi (1822–94), called them "catacombs par excellence." These catacombs are often packed with tour-bus groups, and they have perhaps the cheesiest tour, but the tunnels are simply phenomenal. They're the first cemetery of the Christian community of Rome, burial place of 16 popes in the 3rd century. They bear the name of St. Callixtus, the deacon whom Pope St. Zephyrinus put in charge of them and who was later elected pope (A.D. 217–22) in his own right. The complex is a network of galleries stretching for nearly 19km (12 miles), structured in five levels and reaching a depth of about 20m (65 ft.). There are many sepulchral chambers and almost half a million tombs of early Christians. Paintings, sculptures, and epigraphs (with symbols such as the fish, anchor, and dove) provide invaluable material for the study of the life and customs of the ancient Christians and the story of their persecutions.

Entering the catacombs, you see at once the most important crypt, that of nine popes. Some of the original marble tablets of their tombs are still preserved. The next crypt is that of St. Cecilia, the patron of sacred music. This early Christian martyr received three ax strokes on her neck, the maximum allowed by Roman law, which, unfortunately for her, failed to kill her outright. Farther on, you'll find the famous Cubicula of the Sacraments with its 3rd-century frescoes.

Via Appia Antica 110–126. www.catacombe.roma.it. ✆ **06-5130151.** Admission 8€ adults, 5€ children 6–15, free for children 5 and under. Thurs–Tues 9am–noon and 2–5pm. Bus: 118.

Catacombs of St. Domitilla (Catacombe di Domitilla) ★★★ This oldest of the catacombs is the hands-down winner for most enjoyable catacombs experience. Groups are small, most guides are genuinely entertaining and personable, and, depending on the mood of the group and your guide, the visit may last anywhere from 20 minutes to over an hour. You enter through a sunken 4th-century church. There are fewer "sights" than in the other catacombs—although the 2nd-century fresco of the *Last Supper* is impressive—but some of the guides actually hand you a few bones out of a tomb niche. (Incidentally, this is the only catacomb where you'll still see bones; the rest have emptied their tombs to rebury the remains in ossuaries on the inaccessible lower levels.)

Via d. Sette Chiese 280. www.domitilla.info. ✆ **06-5110342.** Admission 8€ adults, 5€ children 6–14. Wed–Mon 9am–noon and 2–5pm. Closed Jan.

Catacombs of St. Sebastian (Catacombe di San Sebastiano) Today the tomb of St. Sebastian is in the basilica, but his original resting place was in the catacombs underneath it. From the reign of Valerian to the reign of Constantine, the bodies of Sts. Peter and Paul were hidden in the catacombs, which were dug from tufa, a soft volcanic rock. The big church was built in the 4th century. The tunnels here, if stretched out, would reach a length of 11km (6¾ miles). In the tunnels and mausoleums are mosaics and graffiti, along with many other pagan and Christian objects from centuries even before the time of Constantine. Unfortunately, though the catacombs are spectacular, the tour here is very restricted, one of the shortest and least satisfying of all the catacombs visits.

Via Appia Antica 136. www.catacombe.org. ✆ **06-7850350.** Admission 8€ adults, 5€ children 6–15, free for children 5 and under. Mon–Sat 9am–noon and 2–5pm. Closed Nov 20–Dec 20.

More Attractions

AROUND STAZIONE TERMINI

Basilica di Santa Maria Maggiore ★ This great church, one of Rome's four major basilicas, was built by Pope Liberius in A.D. 358 and rebuilt by Pope Sixtus III from 432 to 440. Its 14th-century **campanile** is the city's loftiest. Much doctored in the 18th century, the church's facade isn't an accurate reflection of the treasures inside. The basilica is noted for the 5th-century Roman mosaics in its nave, and for its coffered ceiling, said to have been gilded with gold brought from the New World. In the 16th century, Domenico Fontana built a now-restored "Sistine Chapel." In the following century, Flaminio Ponzo designed the **Pauline (Borghese) Chapel** in the baroque style. The church also contains the **tomb of Bernini,** Italy's most important baroque sculptor/architect. Ironically, the man

Rome street scene.

who changed the face of Rome with his elaborate fountains is buried in a tomb so simple that it takes a sleuth to track it down (to the right, near the altar).

Piazza di Santa Maria Maggiore. ✆ **06-69886800.** Free admission. Daily 7am–7pm. Metro: Termini.

Museo Nazionale Romano

This museum is divided into four different sections: Palazzo Massimo alle Terme; the Diocletian Baths (Terme di Diocleziano), with the annex Octagonal Hall; and Palazzo Altemps (which is near Piazza Navona; see p. 135 for a complete listing).

Diocletian Baths (Terme di Diocleziano) and the Octagonal Hall (Aula Ottagona) ★ Near Piazza dei Cinquecento, which fronts the rail station, this museum occupies part of the 3rd-century-A.D. Baths of Diocletian and part of a convent that may have been designed by Michelangelo. The Diocletian Baths were the biggest thermal baths in the world. Nowadays they host a marvelous collection of funereal artworks, such as sarcophagi, and decorations dating from the Aurelian period. The baths also have a section reserved for temporary exhibitions.

The **Octagonal Hall** occupies the southwest corner of the central building of the Diocletian Baths. Here you can see the *Lyceum Apollo,* a copy of the 2nd-century-A.D. work inspired by the Prassitele. Also worthy of a note is the *Aphrodite of Cyrene,* a copy dating from the second half of the 2nd century A.D. and discovered in Cyrene, Libya.

Viale E. di Nicola 79. ✆ **06-39967700.** Admission 7€. Tues–Sun 9am–7:45pm. Last admission 1 hr. before closing. Metro: Termini.

Palazzo Massimo alle Terme ★ If you'd like to go wandering in a virtual garden of classical statues, head for this *palazzo,* built from 1883 to 1887 and opened as a museum in 1998. Much of the art here, including the frescoes, stuccoes, and mosaics, was discovered in excavations in the 1800s but has never been put on display before.

If you ever wanted to know what all those emperors from your history books looked like, this museum will make them live again, togas and all. In the central hall are works representing the political and social life of Rome at the time of Augustus. Note the statue of the emperor with a toga covering his head, symbolizing his role as the head priest of state. Other works include an altar from Ostia Antica, the ancient port of Rome, plus a statue of a wounded Niobid from 440 B.C. that is a masterwork of expression and character. Upstairs, stand in awe at all the traditional art from the 1st century B.C. to the Imperial Age. The most celebrated mosaic is of the *Four Charioteers.* In the basement are a rare numismatic collection and an extensive collection of Roman jewelry.

Largo di Villa Peretti. ✆ **06-39967700.** Admission 7€. Tues–Sun 9am–7:45pm. Last admission 1 hr. before closing. Admission includes entrance to Terme di Diocleziano (see above). Metro: Termini.

IN THE TESTACCIO AREA & SOUTH

St. Paul Outside the Walls (Basilica di San Paolo Fuori le Mura) ★

The Basilica of St. Paul, whose origins date from the time of Constantine, is Rome's fourth great patriarchal church. It was erected over the tomb of St. Paul, which was definitively identified in 2005 and can be visited. The basilica fell victim to fire in 1823 and was subsequently rebuilt. It is the second-largest church in Rome after St. Peter's. From the inside, its windows may appear to be stained glass, but they're actually translucent alabaster. With its forest of single-file columns and mosaic medallions (portraits of the various popes), this is one of the most streamlined and elegantly decorated churches in Rome. Its most important treasure is a 12th-century candelabrum by Vassalletto, who's also responsible for the remarkable cloisters containing twisted pairs of columns enclosing a rose garden. Of particular interest is the baldacchino (richly embroidered fabric of silk and gold, usually fixed or carried over an important person or sacred object) of Arnolf di Cambio, dated 1285, that miraculously wasn't damaged in the fire. The Benedictine monks and students sell a fine collection of souvenirs, rosaries, and bottles of Benedictine (a liqueur made by the monks) every day except Sunday and religious holidays.

Via Ostiense 190. www.annopaolino.org. ✆ **06-69880800.** Basilica free admission; cloisters admission 3€. Basilica daily 7am–7pm. Cloisters daily 9am–6pm. Metro: Basilica di San Paolo.

IN TRASTEVERE

From many vantage points in the Eternal City, the views are panoramic, but one of the best spots for a memorable vista is the **Janiculum Hill (Gianicolo) ★★**, across the Tiber. It's not one of the seven hills, but it's certainly one of the most visited (and a stop on many bus tours). The Janiculum was the site of a battle between Giuseppe Garibaldi and the forces of Pope Pius IX in 1870—an event commemorated with statuary. Take bus no. 41 from Ponte Sant'Angelo.

Galleria Nazionale d'Arte Antica a Palazzo Corsini ★ This palace was once the home of Napoleon's brother and, later, Christina, the exiled queen of Sweden. Today it houses one of Rome's greatest collections of Renaissance and baroque art. The palace from the 1400s houses the original half of Rome's National Gallery of paintings; the other half is in the Palazzo Barberini. Most of the paintings are from the European school of the 17th and 18th centuries. The collection, formed in the 18th century—often from possessions in the Corsini family—is unique in that it is still intact today. Search out such notable works as Murillo's *Madonna and Child*, Caravaggio's *St. John the Baptist*, a **triptych** by Fra Angelico, and Guido Reni's *Salome with the Head of St. John the Baptist*. Also be on the lookout for fine works by Andrea del Sarto, Rubens, van Dyck, Joos van Cleve, Guercino, and Luca Giordano.

Via della Lungara 10. ✆ **06-68802323.** Admission 4€, free for children 14 and under. Tues–Sun 8:30am–7:30pm. Bus: 23, 65, or 280.

Santa Cecilia in Trastevere ★ A cloistered and still-functioning convent with a fine garden, Santa Cecilia contains the *Last Judgment*, by Pietro Cavallini (ca. 1293), a masterpiece of Roman medieval painting. Another treasure is a late-13th-century baldacchino by Arnolfo di Cambio over the altar. The church is built on the reputed site of Cecilia's long-ago palace, and for a small fee you can descend under the church to inspect the ruins of some Roman houses, as well as peer through a gate at the stucco grotto beneath the altar.

Mosaics in St. Cecilia in Trastevere.

Piazza Santa Cecilia 22. ✆ **06-5899289.** Church free admission; Cavallini frescoes 2.50€; excavations 2.50€. Main church and excavations daily 9:30am–1pm and 4–6:30pm. Frescoes Tues and Thurs 10am–noon; Sun 11:30am–noon. Bus: 8, 44, 75, 170, or 181.

Santa Maria in Trastevere ★ This Romanesque church at the colorful center of Trastevere was built around A.D. 350 and is one of the oldest in Rome. The body was added around 1100, and the portico was added in the early 1700s. The restored mosaics on the apse date from around 1140, and below them are the 1293 mosaic scenes depicting the life of Mary done by Pietro Cavallini. The faded mosaics on the facade are from the 12th or 13th century, and the octagonal fountain in the piazza is an ancient Roman original that was restored and added to in the 17th century by Carlo Fontana.

Piazza Santa Maria in Trastevere. www.vicariatusurbis.org/Ente.asp?ID=2. ✆ **06-5814802.** Free admission. Daily 7:30am–8pm. Bus: 23, 280, or 780.

WHERE TO EAT

Rome remains one of the world's great capitals for dining, with even more diversity today than ever. Most of its *trattorie* haven't changed their menus in a quarter of a century (except to raise the prices, of course), but there's an increasing number of chic, upscale spots with chefs willing to experiment, as well as a growing handful of Chinese, Indian, and other ethnic spots for those days when you just can't face another plate of pasta. The great thing about Rome is that you don't have to spend a fortune to eat really well.

Rome's cooking isn't subtle, but its kitchens rival anything the chefs of Florence or Venice can turn out. The city's chefs borrow—and even improve on—the cuisine of other regions. One of its oldest neighborhoods, Trastevere, is a gold mine of colorful streets and restaurants with time-tested recipes.

See "All About Vino," in chapter 2, to learn about Roman wines. Most of the wines on the Roman table are from the Castelli Romani, the little hill towns surrounding Rome.

Restaurants generally serve lunch between 1 and 3pm, and dinner between about 8 and 10:30pm; at all other times, restaurants are closed. Dinner is taken late in Rome, so although a restaurant might open at 7:30pm, even if you get there at 8pm, you'll often be the only one in the place. A heavier meal is typically eaten at midday, and a lighter one is eaten in the evening.

What if you're hungry outside those hours? Well, if you don't take continental breakfast at your hotel, you can have coffee and a pastry at any **bar** (really a cafe, although there will be liquor bottles behind the counter) or a ***tavola calda*** (hot table). These are stand-up snack bar–type arrangements, open all day long and found all over the city.

A ***servizio*** (tip) of 10% to 15% is often added to your bill or included in the price, although patrons often leave an extra .50€ to 3€ as a token.

Near Stazione Termini

EXPENSIVE

Agata e Romeo ★★ NEW ROMAN One of the most charming places near the Vittorio Emanuele Monument is this striking duplex restaurant done up in turn-of-the-20th-century Liberty style. You'll enjoy the creative cuisine of Romeo Caraccio (who manages the dining room) and his wife, Agata Parisella (who prepares her own version of sophisticated Roman food). The pasta specialty is *paccheri all'amatriciana* (large macaroni tubes with pancetta and a savory tomato sauce topped with pecorino cheese). The chef is equally adept at fish or meat dishes, including braised beef cheeks laid on chestnut purée or swordfish rolls scented with orange and fennel cream. The starters are a feast for the eye and palate, especially wild salmon with sour cream, chives, and salmon eggs, or else scallops wrapped in a crispy pancetta with leek sauce. The most luscious dessert is Agata's *millefoglie,* puff pastry stuffed with almonds. The wine cellar offers a wide choice of international and domestic wines.

Via Carlo Alberto 45. www.agataeromeo.it. ✆ **06-4466115.** Reservations recommended. All pastas 30€; meat and fish 45€; fixed-price menus 110€–130€. AE, DC, MC, V. Mon–Fri 12:30–2:30pm and 8–10:30pm. Closed Aug 8–30. Metro: Vittorio Emanuele.

MODERATE

Il Quadrifoglio NEAPOLITAN Situated in a grandiose palace, this well-managed restaurant lets you sample the flavors and herbs of Naples and southern Italy. You'll find a tempting selection of antipasti, such as anchovies, peppers, capers, onions, and breaded and fried eggplant, all garnished with fresh herbs and virgin olive oil. The pastas are made daily, and the linguine with small squids is especially delectable, as is the spaghetti with sea urchins. Try a zesty rice dish (one of the best is *sartù di riso,* studded with vegetables, herbs, and meats), followed by anchovy pie. Dessert anyone? A longtime favorite is *torta caprese,* with hazelnuts and chocolate.

Via del Boschetto 19. ✆ **06-4826096.** Reservations recommended. Main courses 12€–20€. AE, DC, MC, V. Mon–Sat noon–3pm and 7pm–midnight. Closed Aug 5–25. Metro: Cavour.

INEXPENSIVE

Arancia Blu ★★ 🎁 VEGETARIAN/ITALIAN This rustic, out-of-the-way charmer offers Rome's best vegetarian cuisine. Under soft lighting and wood ceilings, surrounded by wine racks and university intellectuals, the friendly waiters will help you compile a menu to fit any dietary need. The dishes at this trendy spot are inspired by peasant cuisines from across Italy and beyond. The appetizers range from hummus and tabbouleh to zucchini-and-saffron quiche or salad with apples, Gorgonzola, and balsamic vinegar. The main courses change seasonally and may be lasagna with red onions, mushrooms, zucchini, and ginger; couscous *con verdure* (vegetable couscous); or *ravioli ripieni di patate e menta* (ravioli stuffed with potatoes and mint served under fresh tomatoes and Sardinian sheep's cheese). They offer 600 wines and inventive desserts, such as dark-chocolate cake with warm orange sauce.

Via Prenestina 396E. www.aranciabluroma.com. ✆ **06-4454105.** Reservations highly recommended. Main courses 10€–13€; 2 fixed-price menus 37€. No credit cards. Daily 8pm–midnight. Bus: 5, 14, or 19.

Monte Arci ROMAN/SARDINIAN On a cobblestone street near Piazza Indipendenza, this restaurant is set behind a sienna-colored facade. It features Sardinian specialties such as *nialoreddus* (a regional form of *gnocchetti*); pasta with clams, lobster, or the musky-earthy notes of porcini mushrooms; and lamb sausage flavored with herbs and pecorino cheese. The best pasta dish we've sampled is *paglia e fieno al Monte Arci* (homemade pasta with pancetta, spinach, cream, and Parmesan). It's all home cooking, hearty but not that creative.

Via Castelfirdardo 33. ✆ **06-4941347.** Reservations recommended. Main courses 10€–18€. AE, MC, V. Mon–Fri 12:30–3pm; Mon–Sat 7–11:30pm. Closed Aug. Metro: Stazione Termini or Repubblica.

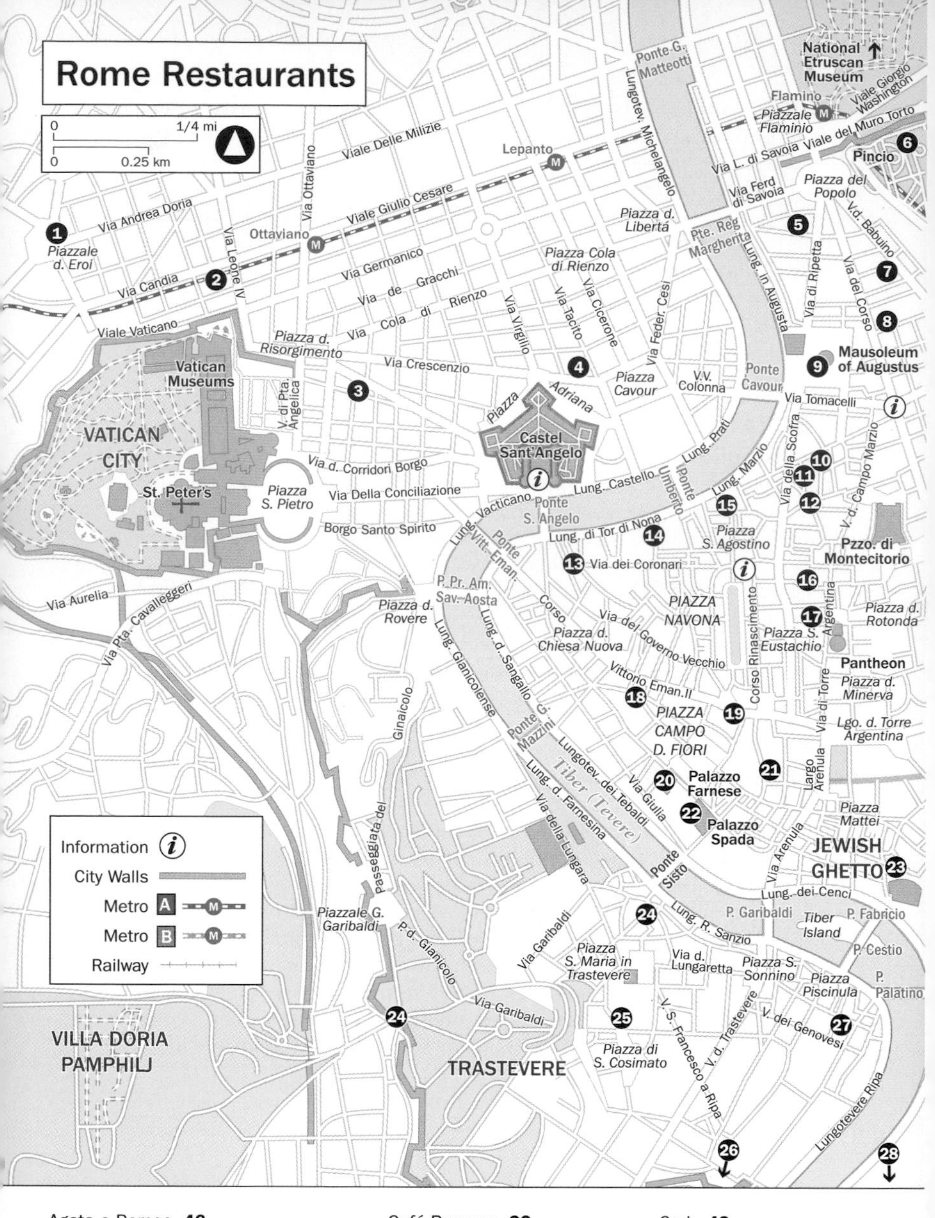

Agata e Romeo **46**
Al Ceppo **29**
Antico Arco **25**
Armando Al Pantheon **17**
Asinocotto **27**
Boccondivino **11**
Brunello Ristorante **34**
Café Mancini Ristorante dal 1905 **10**
Café Romano **32**
Caffetteria Canova Tadolini **7**
Camponeschi **20**
Casina Valadier **6**
Cesare **4**
Césarina **36**
Checchino dal 1887 **28**
Colline Emiliane **39**
Crab **43**
Dal Bolognese **5**
Di Fronte a… **8**
Glass **24**
Grappolo D'Oro Zampanò **18**
Hostaria dei Bastioni **2**
Hostaria Nerone **44**
Il Bacaro **12**

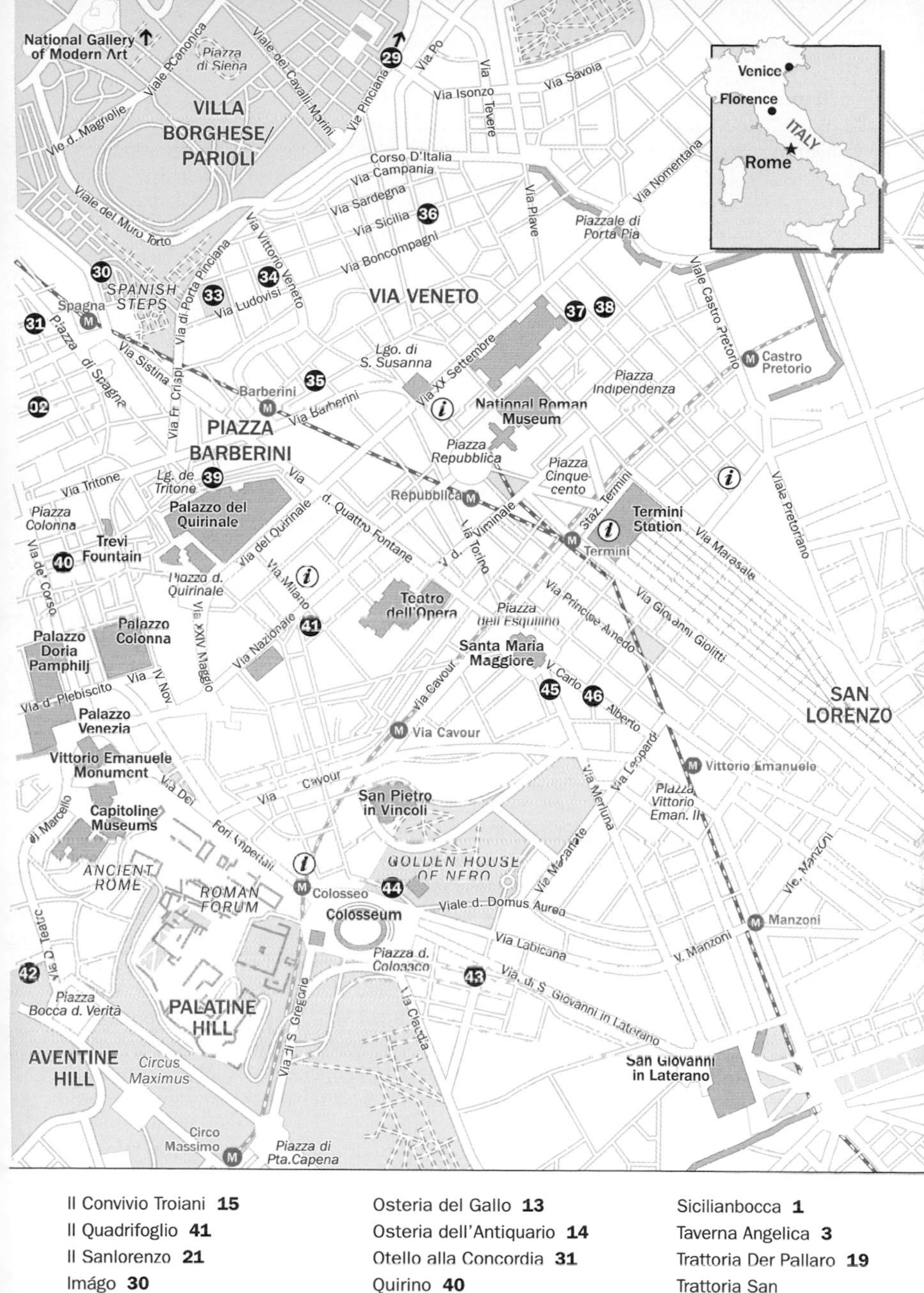

Il Convivio Troiani **15**
Il Quadrifoglio **41**
Il Sanlorenzo **21**
Imágo **30**
Ketumbar **26**
La Terrazza dell'Eden **33**
Maccheroni **16**
Monte Arci **38**
Osteria del Gallo **13**
Osteria dell'Antiquario **14**
Otello alla Concordia **31**
Quirino **40**
Rhome **9**
Ristorante da Pancrazio **22**
Scoglio di Frisio **45**
Sicilianbocca **1**
Taverna Angelica **3**
Trattoria Der Pallaro **19**
Trattoria San Teodoro **42**
Trimani Wine Bar **37**
Tuna **35**
Vecchia Roma **23**

Trimani Wine Bar ★ CONTINENTAL Opened as a tasting center for French and Italian wines, spumantes, and liqueurs, this is an elegant wine bar with a stylish but informal decor and comfortable seating. More than 30 wines are available by the glass. To accompany them, you can choose from a bistro-style menu, with dishes such as salade niçoise, vegetarian pastas, herb-laden bean soups *(fagioli)*, and quiche. Also available is a wider menu, including meat and fish courses. The specialty is the large range of little *bruschette* with cheese and radicchio—the chef orders every kind of prosciutto and cheese from all over Italy. The dishes are matched with the appropriate wines. The dessert specialty is cinnamon cake with apples and a flavor of fresh rosemary.

Trimani maintains a shop about 37m (120 ft.) from its wine bar, at V. Goito 20 (✆ **06-4469661**), where you can purchase an astonishing array of Italian wines.

Via Cernaia 37B. www.trimani.com. ✆ **06-4469630.** Reservations recommended. Main courses 10€–18€; glass of wine (depending on vintage) 3€–29€. AE, DC, MC, V. Daily 11:30am–3pm and 5:30pm–12:30am. Closed 2 weeks in Aug. Metro: Repubblica or Castro Pretorio.

Near Via Veneto & Piazza Barberini

VERY EXPENSIVE

La Terrazza dell'Eden ★★★ ITALIAN/INTERNATIONAL La Terrazza serves some of the city's finest cuisine; you get the added bonus of a sweeping view over St. Peter's. The service is formal and flawless, yet not intimidating. The chef prepares a seasonally changing menu that's among the most polished in Rome. You might start with braised artichokes with scallops, salted cod purée, and a basil-scented mousse, or else delectable zucchini blossoms stuffed with ricotta and Taleggio cheese, black olives, and cherry tomatoes. The pasta specialty is penne filled with ricotta cheese, plus mortadella, walnuts, and pecorino cheese, which might be followed by such dishes as grilled swordfish with sweet-and-sour spinach and a tomato fondue, oven-baked whole baby chicken with wild mushrooms, or grilled filet of beef with smoked pancetta and fresh thyme.

In the Hotel Eden, Via Ludovisi 49. ✆ **06-47812752.** Reservations recommended. Main courses 48€–60€; 6-course fixed-price menu, wines not included 110€. AE, DC, MC, V. Daily 12:30–2:30pm and 7:30–10:30pm. Metro: Barberini.

MODERATE

Cesarina ☺ EMILIANA-ROMAGNOLA/ROMAN This place has long been a favorite of Roman families. Specializing in the cuisines of Rome and the region around Bologna, it's named for Cesarina Masi, who opened it in 1960 (many old-timers fondly remember her strict supervision of the kitchen and how she lectured regulars who didn't finish their *tagliatelle*). Although Cesarina died in the 1980s, her traditions are kept by her family. The polite staff rolls a cart from table to table laden with an excellent *bollito misto* (an array of well-seasoned boiled meats) and often follows with *misto Cesarina*—four kinds of creamy, handmade pasta, each with a different sauce. Equally appealing are the *saltimbocca* (veal with ham) and the *cotoletta alla Bolognese* (tender veal cutlet baked with ham and cheese). A dessert specialty is *semifreddo Cesarina* (ice cream with whipped cream) with hot chocolate, so meltingly good that it's worth the 5 pounds you'll gain.

Via Piemonte 109. www.ristorantecesarinaroma.it. ✆ **06-4880828.** Reservations recommended. Main courses 13€–45€; tasting menu 40€. AE, DC, MC, V. Mon–Sat 12:30–3pm and 7:30–11pm. Metro: Barberini. Bus: 53 or 910.

Colline Emiliane ★★ EMILIANA-ROMAGNOLA Serving the *classica cucina Bolognese,* Colline Emiliane is a small, family-run place—the owner is the cook and his wife makes the pasta (about the best you'll find in Rome). The house specialty is an inspired *tortellini alla panna* (with cream sauce and truffles), but the less-expensive pastas, including *maccheroni al funghetto* (with mushrooms) and *tagliatelle alla Bolognese* (in meat sauce), are excellent, too. As an opener, we suggest *culatello di Zibello,* a delicacy from a small town near Parma that's known for having the world's finest prosciutto. Main courses include *braciola di maiale* (boneless rolled pork cutlets stuffed with ham and cheese, breaded, and sautéed) and an impressive *giambonnetto* (roast veal Emilian-style with roast potatoes).

Via degli Avignonesi 22 (off Piazza Barberini). ✆ **06-4817538.** Reservations highly recommended. Main courses 12€–22€. MC, V. Tues–Sun 12:45–2:45pm; Tues–Sat 7:45–10:45pm. Closed Aug. Metro: Barberini.

Tuna ★ SEAFOOD This seafood emporium in the center of Rome, overlooking the Via Veneto, is dedicated to serving some of the freshest fish in the capital. Not only is the fish fresh, but the chef also requires it to be of optimal quality. From crayfish to sea truffles, from oysters to sea urchins, the fish is turned into platters of delight with perfect seasonings and preparation. Start with the midget mussels or the octopus salad or else calamari and artichoke tempura. For a main course, the catch of the day is in general the best choice, or else you may order sliced sea bass with chives and fresh thyme.

Via Veneto 11. www.tunaroma.it. ✆ **06-4201-6531.** Reservations required. Main courses 15€–30€. AE, MC, V. Tues–Sun 12:30–3pm and 7:30pm–midnight. Closed 2 weeks in Aug. Metro: Barberini.

Near Ancient Rome

EXPENSIVE

Crab ★ SEAFOOD For Rome, this is an unusual name. Launched at the dawn of the 21st century, this trattoria is ideal after a visit to the nearby Basilica of San Giovanni. As you enter, you are greeted with a display of freshly harvested crustaceans and mollusks, which are what you can expect to headline the menu. The signature dish is king crab legs (hardly from the Mediterranean). Fish is shipped in "from everywhere," including oysters from France, lobster from the Mediterranean and the Atlantic, and some catches from the Adriatic. The antipasti is practically a meal in itself, including a savory sauté of mussels and clams, an octopus salad, and scallops gratin, which might be followed by a succulent lobster ravioli in *salsa vergine* (a lobster-based sauce). You can also order fresh sea urchins. For dessert, we recommend an arrangement of sliced tropical fruit that evokes the campy hat worn by Carmen Miranda in all those late-night movies. Most of the main courses, except for some very expensive shellfish and lobster platters, are closer to the lower end of the price scale.

Via Capo d'Africa 2. ✆ **06-7720-3636.** Reservations required. Main courses 22€–45€. AE, DC, MC, V. Mon 7:45–11:30pm; Tues–Sat 1–3:30pm and 8–11:30pm. Closed Aug. Metro: Colosseo. Tram: 3.

Trattoria San Teodoro ★ ☺ 🎁 ROMAN At last there's a good place to eat in the former gastronomic wasteland near the Roman Forum and Palatine Hill. The helpful staff welcomes you to a shady terrace or a dimly lit dining room resting under a vaulted brick ceiling and arched alcoves. The chef handles seafood exceedingly well (try the mini baby squid sautéed with Roman artichokes). His signature dish is seafood carpaccio made with tuna, turbot, or sea bass. Succulent meats, such as medallions of veal in a nutmeg-enhanced cream sauce, round out the menu at this family friendly place. All the pastas are homemade, including black *tagliolini* pasta with anchovy jus and crispy cuttlefish.

Via dei Fienili 49–51. www.st-teodoro.it. ✆ **06-6780933.** Reservations recommended. Main courses 23€–29€. MC, V. Mon–Sat 12:30–3:30pm and 7:30–11pm. Closed 2 weeks at Christmas. Metro: Circo Massimo.

MODERATE

Scoglio di Frisio NEAPOLITAN/PIZZA This trattoria, a longtime favorite, offers a great introduction to the Neapolitan kitchen. Here you can taste a genuine plate-size Neapolitan pizza (crunchy, oozy, and excellent) with clams and mussels. Or, you can start with a medley of savory stuffed vegetables and antipasti before moving on to chicken cacciatore or well-flavored tender veal

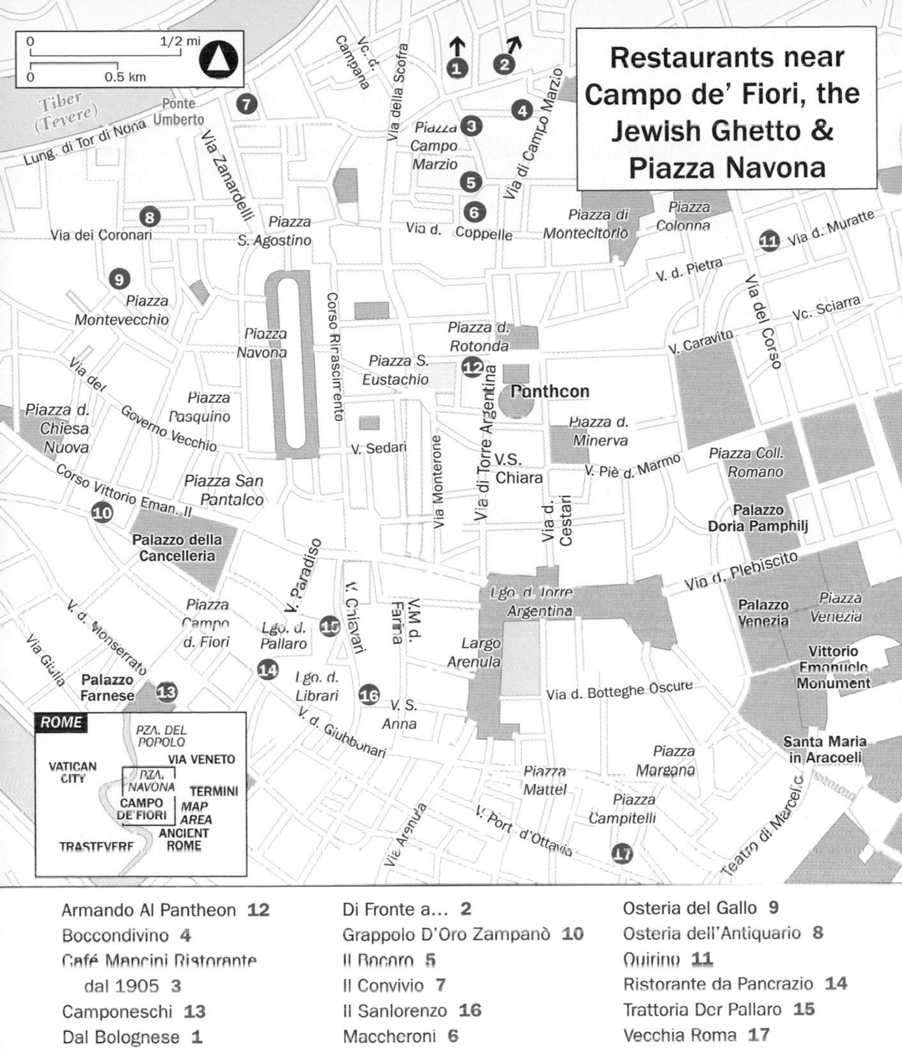

scaloppini. Scoglio di Frisio also makes for an inexpensive night of hokey but still charming entertainment, as cornball "O Sole Mio" renditions and other Neapolitan songs issue forth from a guitar, mandolin, and strolling tenor. The nautical decor (in honor of the top-notch fish dishes) is complete with a high-ceiling grotto of fishing nets, crustaceans, and a miniature three-masted schooner.

Via Merulana 256. www.scogliodifrisio.com. ✆ **06-4872765.** Reservations recommended. Main courses 13€–22€; set menu 30€. AE, DC, MC, V. Daily noon–11:30pm. Metro: Vittorio Emanuele. Bus: 16 or 714.

INEXPENSIVE

Hostaria Nerone ★ ROMAN/ITALIAN Built atop the ruins of the Golden House of Nero, this trattoria is run by the energetic de Santis family, which cooks, serves, and handles the crowds of hungry locals and visitors. Opened in 1929 at the edge of Colle Oppio Park, it contains two compact dining rooms and a flowering shrub–lined terrace that offers a view over the Colosseum and the Bath of Trajan. The copious antipasti buffet offers the bounty of Italy's fields and seas. The pastas include savory spaghetti with clams and our favorite, *pasta e fagioli* (with beans). There are also grilled crayfish and swordfish, and Italian sausages with polenta. Roman-style tripe is a favorite, but maybe you'll skip it for the *osso buco* (veal shank) with mashed potatoes and seasonal mushrooms. The list of some of the best Italian wines is reasonably priced.

Via Terme di Tito 96. ✆ **06-4817952.** Reservations recommended. Main courses 12€–15€. AE, DC, MC, V. Mon–Sat noon–3pm and 7–11pm. Metro: Colosseo. Bus: 75, 85, 87, 117, or 175.

Near Campo De' Fiori & the Jewish Ghetto

Vegetarians looking for monstrous salads (or anyone who just wants a break from all those heavy meats and starches) can find great food at the neighborhood branch of **Insalata Ricca,** Largo dei Chiavari 85 (www.linsalataricca.it; ✆ **06-68803656**). From Monday to Saturday there is a fixed-price lunch menu at 10€. It's open Monday to Saturday noon to 4pm and 7pm to midnight, and Sunday noon to midnight.

EXPENSIVE

Camponeschi ★ SEAFOOD/ROMAN The fish dishes served here are legendary, and so is the front-row view of the Piazza Farnese. The restaurant is elegance itself, with a two-to-one staff/diner ratio. The cuisine is creative, refined, and prepared with only the freshest of ingredients, with a superb wine list. The chefs work hard to make their reputation anew every night, and they succeed admirably with such dishes as lobster with black truffles and raspberry vinegar for an appetizer, or foie gras with port and sultana. We love their generous use of truffles, particularly in a masterpiece of a dish, *tagliolini* soufflé flavored with white truffles. Among the more succulent pastas is one made with a roe deer sauce. If the pope ever dined here, he would assuredly bestow papal blessings on such main courses as the rack of venison marinated with blueberries or a heavenly partridge in a brandy sauce with fresh mushrooms.

Piazza Farnese 50. www.ristorantecamponeschi.it. ✆ **06-6874927.** Reservations required. Main courses 20€–40€. MC, V. Mon–Sat 8pm–midnight. Closed 2 weeks in Aug. Metro: Piazza Argentina.

MODERATE

Ristorante da Pancrazio ROMAN This place is popular as much for its archaeological interest as for its good food. One of its two dining rooms is decorated in the style of an 18th-century tavern; the other occupies the premises of Pompey's ancient theater and is lined with carved capitals and bas-reliefs. In this historic setting, you can enjoy time-tested Roman food. Two particular classics are prepared with skill: saltimbocca and tender roast lamb with potatoes. Some superb main courses include beef rolls stuffed with ham, carrots, and celery in a tomato sauce; baby lamb's ribs fried with artichokes; and grouper in a zucchini flower sauce.

Piazza del Biscione 92. www.dapancrazio.it. ✆ **06-6861246.** Reservations recommended. Main courses 13€–25€. AE, DC, MC, V. Thurs–Tues noon–3pm and 7:30pm–midnight. Closed 3 weeks in Aug (dates vary). Bus: 46, 62, or 64.

Trattoria Der Pallaro ★★ 🎁 ROMAN The cheerful woman in white who emerges with clouds of steam from the bustling kitchen is owner Paola Fazi, who runs two dining rooms where value-conscious Romans go for good food at bargain prices. (She also claims—though others dispute it—that Julius Caesar was assassinated on this site.) The fixed-price menu is the only choice and has made the place famous. Ms. Fazi prepares everything with love, as if she were feeding her extended family. As you sit down, your antipasto, the first of eight courses, appears. Then comes the pasta of the day, followed by such main dishes as roast veal with broad beans and homemade potato chips, or roast pork cutlets, tender and flavorful. For your final courses, you're served mozzarella, cake with custard, and fruit in season.

Largo del Pallaro 15. www.trattoriaderpallaro.com. ✆ **06-68801488.** Reservations recommended. Fixed-price menu 25€. No credit cards. Tues–Sun noon–3:30pm and 7pm–12:30am. Closed Aug 12–25. Bus: 40, 46, 60, 62, or 64.

Vecchia Roma ROMAN/ITALIAN Vecchia Roma is a charming, moderately priced trattoria in the heart of the ghetto. Movie stars have frequented the place, sitting at the crowded tables in one of the four small dining rooms (the back room is the most popular). The owners are known for their *frutti di mare* (fruits of the sea), a selection of briny fresh seafood. A savory selection of antipasti, including salmon or vegetables, is always available. The pastas and risottos are savory, including spaghetti with baby octopus and black squid ink. The chef's specialties are lamb and *spigola* (a type of whitefish). Other signature dishes include veal kidneys in a sweet mustard sauce.

Piazza Campitelli 18. www.ristorantevecchiaroma.com. ✆ **06-6864604.** Reservations recommended. Main courses 16€–22€. AE, DC, MC, V. Thurs–Tues 1–3:30pm and 8–11pm. Closed 10 days in Aug. Bus: 46, 64, 84, or 916. Metro: Colosseo.

Near Piazza Navona & the Pantheon

EXPENSIVE

Il Convivio Troiani ★ ROMAN/INTERNATIONAL This is one of the most acclaimed restaurants in Rome, and one of the few to be granted a coveted Michelin star. Its 16th century building is a classic setting in pristine white with accents of wood. The Troiani brothers turn out an inspired cuisine based on the best and freshest ingredients at the market. Their menu is seasonally adjusted to take advantage of what's good during any month. Start with a tantalizing fish and shellfish soup with green tomatoes and sweet peppers, and follow with such pastas as homemade lasagna with red prawns, coconut milk, pine nuts, artichokes, and mozzarella. More imaginative is the homemade duck ravioli in a red chicory sauce. A main dish might be oxtail served with spicy "smashed" potatoes and black truffles.

Vicolo dei Soldati 31. www.ilconviviotroiani.com. ✆ **06-6869432.** Reservations required. All main courses 28€–44€; fixed-price menu 98€. AE, DC, MC, V. Mon–Sat 8–11pm. Bus: C3, 30, 70, or 81. Metro: Piazza di Spagna.

MODERATE

Cafè Mancini Ristorante dal 1905 ITALIAN/SEAFOOD Near the Pantheon and Piazza Navona, this restaurant was originally established in Naples in 1905—hence its name. Five generations of the Mancini family have since turned out a sublime cuisine based on regional fare and fish dishes from their native Campania. The chefs pay special attention to the products of the season. And somehow the family combines high-quality ingredients with moderate prices. We can make a meal out of the delectable appetizers, especially the *delizie di mare* with a tuna tartare and a skewer of prawns in a *tagliolini* pasta. It comes with a very soft sea bass carpaccio. Or else you might prefer *sfizi di cicci bacco,* with mozzarella, Parma ham, beef tartare, and zucchini flowers. All the pastas are homemade, including *tagliatelle* with prawns and almond pesto sauce. In-the-know locals favor such dishes as grilled squid with potatoes, zucchini, and a black-olive sauce. The setting is elegant and formal, the service top-notch.

Via Metastasio 21. ✆ **06-6872051.** Reservations recommended. Main courses 7€–25€. AE, DC, MC, V. Mon–Sat noon–3pm and 7–11:30pm. Metro: Piazza Navona.

Il Sanlorenzo MEDITERRANEAN/SEAFOOD Right off the Piazza Navona and all its tourist-trap restaurants is a bastion of good food and service, all at a moderate price. The decor is both sophisticated and contemporary, with antique wood furniture, plus modern art adorning the walls. Inspired by the bounty of the fields and streams of Latium, the chefs adroitly prepare a cuisine of both simplicity and elegance. Try the spaghetti with sea urchins, a real delicacy, or else the risotto with tiger prawns and black truffles. Paccheri is another homemade pasta dish, this one served with swordfish, eggplant, and smoked *provola* cheese. You might start with a savory seafood fish soup. Small calamari appear in a delectable fry, or else you can order grilled dentice (a white fish) with a seafood sauce. For dessert, why not the chocolate soup with vanilla ice cream and a raspberry meringue?

Via dei Chiavari 4–5. www.ilsanlorenzo.it. ✆ **06-686-5097.** Reservations required. Main courses 18€–37€; 7-course degustation menu 75€. AE, DC, MC, V. Tues–Fri 12:45–2:45pm and 7:30–11:45pm; Sat–Mon 7:30–11:45pm. Closed 3 weeks in Aug. Bus: 60 or 64.

Osteria dell'Antiquario ★ 🎁 INTERNATIONAL/ROMAN This virtually undiscovered *osteria* enjoys a location a few blocks down the Via dei Coronari as you leave the Piazza Navona and head toward St. Peter's. In a stone-built stable from the 1500s, this restaurant has three dining rooms used in winter. In nice weather, try to get an outdoor table on the terrace; shaded by umbrellas, they face a view of the Palazzo Lancillotti. Begin with a delectable appetizer of sautéed shellfish (usually mussels and clams). Some of the more savory offerings include potato gnocchi with clams and wild mushrooms, stewed scorpion fish with tomato sauce, swordfish steak with a parsley-laced white-wine sauce, or veal escalope with ham and sage.

Piazzetta di S. Simeone 26–27, Via dei Coronari. www.osteriadellantiquario.it. ✆ **06-6879694.** Reservations recommended. Main courses 12€–30€. AE, DC, MC, V. Thurs–Tues 7–11pm. Closed 15 days in mid-Aug, Christmas, and Jan 6–30. Bus: 70, 81, or 90.

INEXPENSIVE

Armando al Pantheon ★ ROMAN In business for half a century, this incredibly inviting oasis lies near the Pantheon and off one of the most trafficked squares in historic Rome. The aura is romantic and classic, with paintings adorning the walls. Claudio and Fabrizio invite you into their little joint for a special dinner. If you want the tried and true, there are plenty of traditional recipes. But if you want fancier fare such as duck with prunes, you'll find that, too. The most delightful dish is *tagliolini al tartufo,* a bowl of steaming hot pasta topped with rich black truffles uprooted in Umbria. Less grand is the spaghetti with fresh mushrooms and saffron. Spelt balls come in a truffle sauce, and guinea fowl is cooked in dark beer and served with fat porcini mushrooms.

Salita dei Crescenzi 31. www.armandoalpantheon.it. ✆ **06/688-03-034.** Reservations recommended. Main courses 10€–24€. AE, DC, MC, V. Mon–Fri 12:30–3pm and 7–11pm; Sat 12:30–3pm.

Grappolo d'Oro Zampanò ROMAN There's no need to pay a lot of money to eat very well near the tourist-clogged Piazza Navona. This trattoria offers good and filling Roman cuisine with most dishes given an inventive twist. The decor is simple, with walls adorned with modern art, but the food is not, and it's also market fresh. Appetizers are savory, especially the tart with anchovies and endive or the octopus salad in an olive sauce. A favorite of locals is the pecorino cheese flan with crispy bacon or a selection of antipasti. At least eight succulent pastas are served nightly, a specialty being pumpkin-filled fagottini with Gorgonzola sauce and fresh rosemary. A classic Roman dish main course is salt cod with raisins, pine nuts, and fresh tomatoes, or else you may prefer the tangy grilled lamb ribs.

Piazza Della Cancelleria 80–84. ✆ **06/689-7080.** Reservations recommended. Main courses 10€–20€. MC, V. Sat–Mon 12:30–2pm and 7–11pm. Closed 2 weeks in Aug. Bus: 64.

Osteria del Gallo ★ ROMAN You can escape the tourist traps of the Piazza Navona, such as Tre Scalini, by finding this place in a tiny little alley off the west-northwest side of the fabled square. It's very small, with a lovely area for outdoor seating, and is definitely off the beaten track. The chef/owner comes out to take your order personally. He is justly proud of his homemade pastas such as gnocchi with mussels and arugula, linguine with seafood, and a typical Roman recipe for *tagliolini cacio e pepe* (with cheese and pepper). Menu items include a variety of fresh fish dishes roasted in a salt crust to retain their juice and flavor. Other favorites include filet of beef cooked with green pepper. All desserts are homemade, including one of the best tiramisu turned out in the area.

Vicolo di Montevecchio 27. www.osteriadelgalloroma.it. ✆ **06-6873781.** Reservations highly recommended. Main courses 8€–14€. AE, DC, MC, V. Wed–Mon 11:30am–3pm and 6–11:30pm. Bus: 64.

Quirino ROMAN/ITALIAN/SICILIAN Quirino is a good place to dine after you've tossed your coin into the Trevi. The atmosphere is typical Italian, with hanging chianti bottles, a beamed ceiling, and muraled walls. We're fond of the mixed fry of tiny shrimp and squid rings, and the vegetarian pastas are prepared with only the freshest ingredients. The regular pasta dishes are fabulous, especially our favorite: *paccheri* (large pasta tubes) with swordfish, *bottarga* (tuna roe), and cherry tomatoes. A variety of fresh and tasty fish is always available and always grilled to perfection. For dessert, try the yummy chestnut ice cream with hot chocolate sauce or the homemade cannoli.

Via delle Muratte 84. ✆ **06-6794108.** Reservations recommended. Main courses 8€–18€; fish dishes 15€–20€. AE, MC, V. Mon–Sat noon–11:30pm. Closed 3 weeks in Aug. Metro: Barberini, Spagna, or Colosseo.

Near Piazza Del Popolo & the Spanish Steps

VERY EXPENSIVE

Imàgo ★★★ INTERNATIONAL/ITALIAN Great food and a sweeping panorama of ancient Rome lure patrons to the sixth floor of this deluxe hotel on the Spanish Steps. There's so much talk of the view that it is easy to overlook the superb traditional Italian cuisine. Chefs frequent the Roman markets early in the morning, securing the freshest products for their menu, which changes daily. The brilliant chef, Francesco Apreda, a Neapolitan, serves Italian food, but it's influenced by the rest of the world—for example, sea bass with a ginger sauce evocative of Thailand. The Kennedys and Princess Di used to dine here; now you are likely to see President Napolitano, feasting on pheasant ravioli with truffles. Apreda delights other guests with such delectable dishes as grilled veal shoulder with hazelnut oil, wild mushrooms, and persimmons, or roasted pigeon with black tea, artichokes, and a grape sauce.

In the Hotel Hassler, Piazza della Trinità dei Monti 6. www.imagorestaurant.com. ✆ **06-69934726.** Reservations required. Jacket and tie for men at dinner. Main courses 38€–45€; 7-course degustation menu 130€. AE, DC, MC, V. Daily 7:30–10:30pm. Metro: Piazza di Spagna.

EXPENSIVE

Brunello Ristorante ★★ ITALIAN This chicly modern bar, lounge, and restaurant is helping bring back the Via Veneto as an elegant rendezvous place. The days of *la dolce vita* live on here. Your martini will arrive with a few drops of Chanel No. 5 rubbed along its glass stalk. Earthy tones such as brown dominate among the wall coverings and the upholstered seating in autumnal shades, along with gilt sculptures. The menu is impressively innovative, with fresh ingredients that explode in your mouth. The chef likes to experiment. Starters might include black fried king prawns, shrimp, and artichokes in a creamy sweet pepper sauce, or else crispy radicchio pie with cream cheese. Among the more tempting mains are vodka- and honey-marinated salmon with a sea terrine and citrus petals or else turbot *escalopes* with fresh herbs and vanilla-scented fennel. The wine cellar boasts 500 labels from every region of Italy.

In the Regina Hotel Baglioni, Via Vittorio Veneto 70/A. www.brunellorestaurant.com. ✆ **06-48902867.** Reservations recommended. Main courses 21€–34€; fixed-price 3-course lunch menu 37€. AE, DC, MC, V. Restaurant Mon–Sat noon–3pm and 7:30–11pm. Lounge Mon–Sat 6pm–1am. Metro: Piazza di Spagna.

Rhome ★★ ITALIAN The name of the restaurant is a fusion of the words "Rome" and "home." The restaurant and its cuisine are modern and innovative, with a stunning interior design. A traditional Italian cuisine is based on the best of market-fresh ingredients obtained by shopping that morning. The chef cleverly selects appropriate herbs, spices, and fresh vegetables, which he transforms into classic dishes, such as fettuccine with artichokes and saffron; *tonnarelli* with goat cheese and sweet red peppers; or, simple but tasty, the veal meatballs with creamy mashed potatoes. The bean soup with field chicory is some of the best we've had, and in season you might delight in the deer medallions with chestnut honey. Later in the evening, diners enjoy music selected by a DJ, or, on occasion, live entertainment from international musicians.

Piazza Augusto Imperatore 46. www.rhomerestaurant.it. ✆ **06-68301430.** Reservations required. Main courses 10€–22€. AE, DC, MC, V. Mon–Fri noon–3pm and 8pm–12:30am; Sat 8pm–12:30am. Closed 2 weeks in Aug. Metro: Piazza di Spagna.

MODERATE

Boccondivino ★ ITALIAN Part of the fun of this restaurant involves wandering through historic Rome to reach it. Inside, you'll find delicious food and an engaging mix of the Italian Renaissance with imperial and ancient Rome, thanks to columns salvaged from ancient monuments by 16th-century builders. Modern art and a hip staff dressed in black and white serve as a tip-off, though, that the menu is completely up-to-date. Dishes vary with the seasons, but you might find linguine with lemon and cinnamon; carpaccio of beef; various risottos, including a version with black truffles; and grilled steaks and veal. Especially intriguing is duck breast with a fig sauce, red rice, and potato pie. If you're a seafood lover, look for either the marinated and grilled salmon or a particularly subtle blend of roasted turbot stuffed with foie gras. Desserts feature the fresh fruit of the season, perhaps marinated pineapple or fruit-studded house-made ice creams. The restaurant's name, incidentally, translates as "divine mouthful."

Piazza Campo di Marzio 6. www.boccondivino.it. ✆ **06-68308626.** Reservations required. Main courses 18€–28€. AE, DC, MC, V. Mon–Fri 12:30–3pm; Mon–Sat 7:30–11pm. Bus: 87 or 175.

Café Romano ★ INTERNATIONAL On the most exclusive "fashion street" of Rome, this stylish venue is neither restaurant nor brasserie. Annexed to the landmark Hotel d'Inghilterra, the cafe can serve you throughout the day, beginning with a late breakfast or concluding with a post-theater dinner well after midnight. Two salons are divided by an arch resting on two columns under a barrel-vaulted ceiling with padded settees. The atmosphere is cosmopolitan, with an eclectic, well chosen menu. You can taste dishes from around the world: from moussaka to fish couscous, from the Lebanese *mezze* (appetizers) to Chicago rib-eye steak, from the Thai-like green chicken curry to the Japanese-inspired salmon teriyaki. Flavors are beautifully blended in such starters as smoked goose breast with candied peaches or beef tartare with thyme-flavored mushrooms. Among the more appealing mains are homemade fusilli pasta with wild mushrooms, smoked bacon, and Parmesan, or sautéed roast tuna served with sweet peppers, olives, and capers. Everything is served on fine bone china with silver cutlery and crystal glassware.

In the Hotel d'Inghilterra, Via Borgognona 4. www.royaldemeure.com. ✆ **06-69981500.** Main courses 18€–35€. AE, DC, MC, V. Daily noon–midnight. Metro: Piazza di Spagna.

Caffetteria Canova Tadolini ROMAN *La roma bene* (the upper class) flock to this cafe at the museum dedicated to the famous neoclassical sculptor Antonio Canova and his talented pupil Adamo Tadolini. Museum cafes can be trite, but this one is literally in the museum, with its period-piece *ottocento*-style tables and chairs stationed beneath statues and plaster fragments. The cafe/museum has been a great hit since it opened with its 400-bottle all-Italian wine list and 25 varieties of tea. The bar and cafeteria are located on the ground floor; the more formal restaurant is one flight up. The chef's special dishes begin with such appetizers as salmon and Roman lettuce salad with *crostini* served with a yogurt-and-ginger sauce, and follow with sautéed tuna steak or spaghetti with shrimp, zucchini, and cherry tomatoes. The location is in the very heart of Rome.

Via del Babuino 150A–B. www.canovatadolini.com. ✆ **06-32110702.** Reservations recommended. Main courses 16€–24€. AE, DC, MC, V. Mon–Sat 8am–8pm. Metro: Piazza di Spagna.

Dal Bolognese ★ BOLOGNESE This is one of those rare dining spots that's chic but actually lives up to the hype with noteworthy food. Young actors, models, artists from nearby Via Margutta, and even corporate types on expense accounts show up, trying to land one of the few sidewalk tables. To begin, we suggest *misto di pasta:* four pastas, each with a different sauce, arranged on the same plate. Another good choice is thin slices of savory Parma ham or the delectable prosciutto and vine-ripened melon. For your main course, specialties that win hearts year after year are *lasagne verdi* and *tagliatelle alla Bolognese.* The chefs also turn out the town's most recommendable veal cutlets Bolognese topped with cheese. They're not inventive, but they're simply superb.

You might want to cap your evening by dropping into the **Rosati** cafe next door (or the **Canova,** across the street) to enjoy one of the tempting pastries.

Piazza del Popolo 1–2. ✆ **06-3611426.** Reservations required. Main courses 19€–30€. AE, DC, MC, V. Tues–Sun 12:30–3pm and 8–11pm. Closed 3 weeks in Aug. Metro: Flaminio.

Di Fronte a . . . ITALIAN After a hard morning's shopping in the Piazza di Spagna area, this is an ideal spot for a lunch break. Its name (which translates as "in front of . . .") comes from the fact that the restaurant lies right in front of a stationery shop (owned by the father of the restaurant's proprietor). We prefer the dining room in the rear, with its changing exhibitions of pictures. You'll be seated at a marble table on wrought-iron benches with leather cushions. The chef prepares a tasty cuisine that is simple but good—nothing creative, but a good boost of energy to hit the stores again. Salads are very large, as are the juicy half-pound burgers. You can also order more substantial food such as succulent pastas and tender steaks. The pizza isn't bad, either. For dessert, try the *pizza bianca,* which is a pizza crust topped with chocolate cream or seasonal fruit.

Via della Croce 38. ✆ **06-6780355.** Reservations recommended for dinner. Main courses 10€–19€. AE, DC, MC, V. Tues–Sun noon–3:30pm and 7–11pm. Metro: Piazza di Spagna.

Il Bacaro ★ ITALIAN Unpretentious and accommodating to foreigners, this restaurant contains about a half-dozen tables and operates from an ivy-edged hideaway alley near Piazza di Spagna. The restaurant is known for its fresh and tasty cheese. This was a *palazzo* in the 1600s, and some vestiges of the building's former grandeur remain, despite an impossibly cramped kitchen where the efforts of the staff to keep the show moving are nothing short of heroic. The offerings are time tested and flavorful: spaghetti with tuna roe and crispy artichokes; grilled beef steak with cheese fondue; warm beef carpaccio with radicchio, chicory, and truffles; swordfish roulades with shrimp and zucchini; and a savory pasta, *trofie,* with a white meat ragout, porcini mushrooms, and sun-dried tomatoes.

Via degli Spagnoli 27, near Piazza delle Coppelle. www.ilbacaro.com. ✆ **06-6872554.** Reservations recommended. Main courses 13€–22€. MC, V. Mon–Sat 8pm–2am. Metro: Piazza di Spagna.

INEXPENSIVE

Maccheroni ROMAN In a rustic tavern in the heart of Rome, you can savor food that you usually have to go to the countryside to enjoy. The decor is informal, with wood-paneled walls and pop art; and on a good night the place can seat 160 satisfied diners, both visitors and locals. The chef shops wisely for his bevy of regional dishes and backs up his menu with a well-chosen wine list that includes the house chianti. Pasta is the house specialty, and it's never better than in the spaghetti flavored with bacon and onion. You can also order fettuccine with black-truffle sauce or ravioli with pumpkin flowers. The menu features a traditional Roman cuisine, and everything is well prepared, including *maccheroni all'amatriciana* (either the red version with tomatoes and bacon along with pecorino cheese, or the white version without tomatoes). Tender, juicy beefsteaks are also served.

Piazza delle Copelle 44. www.ristorantemaccheroni.com. ✆ **06-68307895.** Reservations recommended. Main courses 8€–21€. AE, MC, V. Mon–Sat 1–3pm and 8pm–midnight. Metro: Piazza di Spagna. Bus: 64, 70, 87, or 116.

Otello alla Concordia ☺ ROMAN On a side street amid the glamorous boutiques near the northern edge of the Spanish Steps, this is one of Rome's most reliable restaurants. A stone corridor from the street leads into the dignified

Palazzo Povero. Choose a table in the arbor-covered courtyard or the cramped but convivial dining rooms. Displays of Italian bounty decorate the interior, where you're likely to rub elbows with the shopkeepers from the fashion district. The *spaghetti alle vongole veraci* (with clams) is excellent, as are Roman-style saltimbocca (veal with ham), *abbacchio arrosto* (roast lamb), eggplant parmigiana, a selection of grilled or sautéed fish dishes (including swordfish), and several preparations of veal.

Via della Croce 81. www.otello-alla-concordia.it. ✆ **06-6791178.** Reservations recommended. Main courses 8€–20€. AE, DC, MC, V. Mon–Sat 12:30–3pm and 7:30–11pm. Closed 2 weeks in Jan. Metro: Piazza di Spagna.

Near Vatican City

The no. 6 branch of **Insalata Ricca,** a salad-and-light-meals chain, is across from the Vatican walls at Piazza del Risorgimento 5 (www.linsalataricca.it; ✆ **06-39730387**).

MODERATE

Cesare ROMAN/TUSCAN The area around the Vatican is not the place to look for great restaurants. But Cesare is a fine old-world dining room known for its deft handling of fresh ingredients. You can select your fresh fish from the refrigerated glass case at the entrance. We come here for the fresh and tender seafood salad, brimming with cuttlefish, shrimp, squid, mussels, and octopus, and dressed with olive oil, fresh parsley, and lemon. Our table was blessed with an order of *spaghetti all'amatriciana* in a spicy tomato sauce flavored with hot peppers and bits of salt pork. The *saltimbocca alla romana,* that classic Roman dish, is a masterpiece as served here—butter-tender veal slices topped with prosciutto and fresh sage and sautéed in white wine. Another specialty is smoked swordfish; you can order fresh sardines and fresh anchovies if you want to go truly Roman. The cooks also keep the wood-fired pizza ovens hot.

Via Crescenzio 13, near Piazza Cavour. www.ristorantecesare.com. ✆ **06-6861227.** Reservations recommended. Main courses 10€–28€; fixed-price Tuscan menu 38€. AE, DC, MC, V. Daily 12:30–3pm; Mon–Sat 7:30pm–midnight. Closed in Aug. Bus: 23, 34, or 49. Metro: Lepanto or Ottaviano.

INEXPENSIVE

Hostaria dei Bastioni ROMAN/SEAFOOD This simple but well-managed restaurant is about a minute's walk from the entrance to the Vatican Museums and has been open since the 1960s. Although a warm-weather terrace doubles the size during summer, many diners prefer the inside room as an escape from the roaring traffic. The menu features the staples of Rome's culinary repertoire, including fisherman's risotto (a broth-simmered rice dish with fresh fish, usually shellfish), a vegetarian *fettuccine alla bastione* with orange-flavored creamy tomato sauce, and an array of grilled fresh fish. The food is first-rate—and a bargain at these prices.

Via Leone IV 29. ✆ **06-39723034.** Reservations recommended Fri–Sat. Main courses 8€–19€; fixed-price menus 10€–13€. AE, DC, MC, V. Mon–Sat noon–3pm and 7–11:30pm. Closed July 15–Aug 1. Metro: Ottaviano.

Siciliainbocca ★ SICILIAN The best Sicilian restaurant in Rome lies close to the Vatican, ideal for a lunch when visiting either St. Peter's or the papal museums. Natives of Sicily own and operate this place, and their specialties taste virtually the same as those encountered in Sicily itself. The menu features a large variety of delectable smoked fish, including salmon, swordfish, and tuna. The homemade pastas here are the best Sicilian versions in town, especially the classic *maccheroni alla Norma,* with ricotta, a savory tomato sauce, and sautéed eggplant. You might also opt for such dishes as linguine with sautéed scampi and cherry tomatoes, or a typical Palermitan pasta with sardines, wild fennel, and pine nuts. Other good-tasting and typical dishes include swordfish with capers, olives, tomatoes, and Parmesan cheese.

Via E. Faà di Bruno 26. www.siciliainboccaweb.com. ✆ **06-37358400.** Main courses 15€–25€. AE, DC, MC, V. Mon–Sat 1:30–3pm and 8–11:30pm. Closed 3 weeks in Aug. Metro: Ottaviano San Pietro.

Taverna Angelica SOUTHERN ITALIAN This tavern is not luxurious in any way, but it serves good affordable food in a position only 200m (656 ft.) from the Vatican. Even priests from St. Peter's come here to dine on such well-prepared dishes as potato ravioli with *guanciale,* an Italian specialty made from dry pig cheeks. One of the most imaginative pastas is spelt spaghetti with a pesto made with pistachios and walnuts, or else the fettuccine with clams and porcini mushrooms served with an arugula pesto. All the dishes are based on fresh regional produce, including breast of guinea fowl stuffed with dried tomatoes and mozzarella.

Piazza A. Capponi 6. www.tavernaangelica.it. ✆ **06-6874514.** Reservations required. Main courses 10€–23€; 2-course fixed-price lunch menu 20€, 3-course 25€. AE, MC, V. Daily 7pm–midnight; Sun noon–3pm. Closed 10 days in Aug. Metro: Ottaviano San Pietro.

In Trastevere

MODERATE

Antico Arco ★ 🎁 ITALIAN Named after one of the gates of early medieval Rome (Arco di San Pancrazio), which rises nearby, Antico Arco is on Janiculum Hill not far from Trastevere and the American Academy. It's a hip restaurant with a young, stylish clientele. Carefully crafted dishes with fresh ingredients include ravioli stuffed with beans in a seafood soup or green homemade *tagliolini* with red mullet and a saffron sauce. Other palate-pleasing dishes include crispy suckling pig in a sweet-and-sour sauce, with fennel and a citrus soufflé, or else crunchy shrimp with artichoke purée and an anise sauce. A white chocolate tiramisu is a heavenly concoction.

Piazzale Aurelio 7. www.anticoarco.it. ✆ **06-5815274.** Reservations recommended. Main courses 15€–32€; fixed-price menu 75€. AE, DC, MC, V. Daily 7pm–midnight. Bus: 115 or 870.

Asinocotto ITALIAN Within a pair of cramped dining rooms (one on street level, the other upstairs), you'll be served by a cheerful staff that's well practiced in hauling steaming platters of food up the steep flight of stairs. The simple white-painted walls accented by dark timbers and panels are a nice background to the flavorful dishes that stream from the busy kitchens of Giuliano Brenna. The menu is fairly sophisticated, thanks to the owner's stint as a chef at the Hotel Eden, one of Rome's more upscale hotels. Look for elaborate antipasti such as quail and watercress in a "Parmesan basket," or smoked sturgeon on a salad of Belgian endive with black olives. You might follow with handmade ravioli filled with sea bass, lettuce, and a sauvignon sauce, or a zesty oxtail soup with artichoke hearts au gratin. Other imaginative dishes include *orecchiette* pasta with eggplant, bacon, and smoked ricotta, or guinea fowl breast with a flavoring of orange and green tea. The restaurant's name, incidentally, translates as "cooked donkey meat," but don't look for that on the menu anytime soon.

Via dei Vascellari 48. www.asinocotto.com. ✆ **06-5898985.** Reservations recommended. Main courses 13€–23€. AE, DC, MC, V. Mon–Fri noon–2:30pm; Tues–Sun 7:30–11pm. Tram: 8.

Glass ★★ 🎁 ROMAN When this chic restaurant and wine bar opened, management claimed it was an "attempt to give Trastevere back to the Romans." Pretend you're a native and you should have a good time here on one of its two floors. Theatrical lighting and lots of glass (including the floors) give the place a modernist aura, rather rare for the district. Glass doubles as a wine bar. The cuisine is both innovative and traditional. Some of our favorite dishes are gnocchi with pancetta, chanterelle mushrooms, and almonds, and risotto with almond milk, zucchini flowers, and king crab. Other innovative dishes are a filet of tuna under a coffee flavored crust and pistachio-crusted scallops, fresh pork belly, and baby asparagus. One dessert is about as good as it gets: a caramelized banana tart with strawberry gelatin and peanut-butter ice cream.

Vicolo del Cinque 58. www.glass-restaurant.it. ✆ **06-58335903.** Reservations recommended. Main courses 18€–26€; fixed-price menus 60€–75€. AE, DC, MC, V. Restaurant daily 8–11:30pm. Wine bar daily 8pm–2am. Bus: 23 or 125.

Villa Borghese

EXPENSIVE

Casina Valadier ★ ROMAN Once one of the hottest dining tickets in Rome, this chic restaurant closed its doors seemingly forever. But once again, the glitterati of Rome are flocking here for the to-die-for cocktails, the superb cuisine, and the panoramic views of Rome itself. In the heart of Villa Borghese, the terrace of the restaurant is the most evocative in the city. Placed on the site of the ancient Collis Hortulorum, the highest point of the Pincio district, the original building dates from 1816 and was the creation of the famous architect Giuseppe Valadier. In its heyday, this restaurant was the most fashionable place in Rome, attracting people such as King Farouk of Egypt and Gandhi.

The best of the menu is a regionally based repertoire of savory dishes with imaginative, intelligent associations of flavors. Diners take delight in jazzed-up Roman classics such as rigatoni with bacon, onions, peppers, and pecorino, or a cherry- and sesame-encrusted pork filet. Start, perhaps, with a duck-breast carpaccio or a warm ricotta cheese round with an olive and pistachio pesto. For dessert, dare you try the fried zucchini flowers stuffed with rice and served with cinnamon ice cream?

Villa Borghese, Piazza Bucarest. www.casinavaladier.it. ✆ **06-69922090.** Reservations required. Main courses 15€–35€. AE, DC, MC, V. Daily 1–3pm and 8–11pm. Bus: 53.

A Romantic Picnic in the Borghese Gardens

Our favorite place for a picnic in all of Rome is in the Borghese Gardens, followed by a reserved visit to the Galleria Borghese. **Gina,** Via San Sebastianello 7A (www.ginaroma.com; ✆ **06-6780251**), has come up with a marvelous idea. This deli will provide you with a picnic basket complete with thermos, glasses, and linen for a picnic to be enjoyed in the fabled gardens. For 40€, two persons can enjoy panini (tomato, eggplant, and mozzarella on focaccia) along with a fresh fruit salad, dessert, and coffee.

In Testaccio

MODERATE

Checchino dal 1887 ★ ROMAN During the 1800s, a wine shop flourished here, selling drinks to the butchers working in the nearby slaughterhouses. In 1887, the ancestors of the restaurant's present owners began serving food, too. Slaughterhouse workers in those days were paid part of their meager salaries with the *quinto quarto* (fifth quarter) of each day's slaughter (the tail, feet, intestines, and other parts not for the squeamish). Following centuries of Roman tradition, Ferminia, the wine shop's cook, transformed these products into the tripe and oxtail dishes that form an integral part of the menu. Many Italian diners come here to relish the *rigatoni con pajata* (pasta with small intestines), *coda alla vaccinara* (oxtail stew), *fagioli e cotiche* (beans with intestinal fat), and other examples of *la cucina povera* (food of the poor). In winter, a succulent wild boar with dried prunes and red wine is served. Safer and possibly more appetizing is the array of salads, soups, pastas, steaks, cutlets, grills, and ice creams. The English-speaking staff is helpful, tactfully proposing alternatives if you're not ready for Roman soul food.

Via di Monte Testaccio 30. www.checchino-dal-1887.com. ✆ **06-5743816.** Reservations recommended. Main courses 10€–25€; fixed-price menu 46€–63€. AE, MC, V. Tues–Sat 12:30–3pm and 8pm–midnight (June–Sept closed Sun–Mon). Closed Aug and 1 week in Dec (dates vary). Metro: Piramide. Bus: 75 from Termini Station.

Ketumbar ★ 🎁 JAPANESE/ITALIAN How chic can Roma get? Ketumbar (Malay for coriander) has brought sophistication to Testaccio, once known as a *paisano* sector of Roma. Featured in several magazines devoted to the high life in Italy, the decor is sleek and minimalist, or, as one critic dubbed it, "Gothic-cum-Asia-fantasia." A young and hip crowd heads out of the center of Rome to this neighborhood to sample the truly excellent food, but also to see and be seen on the circuit. The decorator obviously went to Indonesia for much of the furnishings. But the potsherds (pieces of broken Roman amphora) remind us that we're still in an ancient part of Rome. Everything we've sampled here has been a delight.

Via Galvani 24. www.ketumbar.it. ✆ **06-57305338.** Reservations required. Main courses 10€–18€. AE, DC, MC, V. Daily 8pm–midnight. Closed Aug. Metro: Piramide. Bus: 3, 23, or 75.

In Parioli

MODERATE

Al Ceppo ★★ ROMAN Because the place is somewhat hidden (only 2 blocks from the Villa Borghese, near Piazza Ungheria), you're likely to rub elbows with more Romans than tourists. It's a longtime favorite, and the cuisine is as good as ever. "The Log" features an open wood-stoked fireplace on which the chef roasts lamb chops, liver, and bacon to perfection. The beefsteak, which comes from Tuscany, is succulent. Other dishes that we continue to delight in are *tagliatelle* with porcini mushrooms and roast sausage, cod ravioli with sautéed shrimp, braised beef with lemon meatballs, and baked scampi with cherry tomatoes and green olives.

Via Panama 2. www.ristorantealceppo.it. ✆ **06-8419696.** Reservations recommended. Main courses 17€–30€. AE, DC, MC, V. Tues–Sun 12:30–3pm and 8–11pm. Closed last 2 weeks of Aug. Bus: 52 or 910.

SHOPPING

Rome offers temptations of every kind. In our limited space below, we've summarized certain streets known throughout Italy for their shops. The monthly rent on these famous streets is very high, and those costs are passed on to you. Nonetheless, a stroll down some of these streets presents a cross section of the most desirable wares in Italy.

The Top Shopping Streets

VIA BORGOGNONA This street begins near Piazza di Spagna, and both the rents and the merchandise are chic and ultraexpensive. Like its neighbor, Via Condotti, Via Borgognona is a mecca for wealthy, well-dressed women and men from around the world. Its storefronts have retained their baroque or neoclassical facades.

VIA COLA DI RIENZO Bordering the Vatican, this long, straight street runs from the Tiber to Piazza Risorgimento. Because the street is wide and clogged with traffic, it's best to walk down one side and then up the other. Via Cola di Rienzo is known for stores selling a wide variety of merchandise at reasonable prices—from jewelry to fashionable clothes and shoes.

VIA CONDOTTI Easy to find because it begins at the base of the Spanish Steps, this is Rome's poshest shopping street. A few down-to-earth stores have opened recently, but it's largely a playground for the superrich. For us mere mortals, it's a great place for window-shopping and people-watching.

VIA DEL CORSO Not attempting the stratospheric image or prices of Via Condotti or Via Borgognona, Via del Corso boasts styles aimed at younger consumers. Some gems are scattered amid the shops selling jeans and sporting equipment. The most interesting are nearest the cafes of Piazza del Popolo.

VIA FRANCESCO CRISPI Most shoppers reach this street by following Via Sistina (see below) 1 long block from the top of the Spanish Steps. Near the intersection of these streets are several shops well suited for unusual and less expensive gifts.

VIA FRATTINA Running parallel to Via Condotti, it begins, like its more famous sibling, at Piazza di Spagna. Part of its length is closed to traffic. Here the concentration of shops is denser, although some aficionados claim that its image is less chic and prices are slightly lower than at its counterparts on Via Condotti. It's usually thronged with shoppers who appreciate the lack of motor traffic.

VIA NAZIONALE The layout recalls 19th-century grandeur, but the traffic is horrendous. It begins at Piazza della Repubblica and runs down almost to the 19th-century monuments of Piazza Venezia. You'll find an abundance of leather stores (more reasonable in price than those in many other parts of Rome) and a welcome handful of stylish boutiques.

VIA SISTINA Beginning at the top of the Spanish Steps, Via Sistina runs to Piazza Barberini.

A Pause Before Purchasing

Although Rome has many wonderful boutiques, you'll find better shopping in Florence and Venice. If you're continuing on to either of these cities, you may want to hold off a bit, as you're likely to find a better selection and better prices.

The shops are small, stylish, and based on the tastes of their owners. The pedestrian traffic is less dense than on other major streets.

VIA VITTORIO VENETO Via Veneto is filled these days with expensive hotels and cafes and an array of relatively expensive stores selling shoes, gloves, and leather goods.

Shopping A to Z

ANTIQUES Prices have risen to alarming levels as wealthy Europeans increasingly outbid one another in a frenzy. Any antiques dealer who risks the high rents of central Rome is acutely aware of valuations, so although you might find gorgeous pieces, you're not likely to find any bargains.

Beware of fakes, remember to insure anything that you have shipped home, and, for larger purchases—anything more than 156€ at any one store—keep your paperwork in order to obtain your tax refund (see chapter 17).

Via dei Coronari, in a colorful section of the Campus Martius, is lined with stores offering magnificent vases, urns, chandeliers, chaises, refectory tables, and candelabra. To find the street's entrance, turn left out of the north end of Piazza Navona and pass the ruins of Domitian's Stadium—it will be just ahead. There are more than 40 antiques stores in the next 4 blocks (most are closed 1–4pm).

A few minutes south of Piazza del Popolo, **Via Laurina** lies midway between Via del Corso and Via del Babuino. It is filled with beautiful stores where you can find anything from an antique print to a 17th-century chandelier.

BOOKSTORE The **Lion Bookshop,** Via dei Greci 36 (✆ **06-32654007;** Metro: Piazza di Spagna; bus: 116 or 117), is the oldest English-language bookshop in town, specializing in literature, both American and English. It also sells children's books and photographic volumes on both Rome and Italy. A vast choice of English-language videos is for sale or rent. It's closed in August.

COSMETICS & PERFUMES Since the 18th century, **Antica Erboristeria Romana,** Via di Torre Argentina 15 (www.anticaerboristeriaromana.it; ✆ **06-6879493;** Metro: Colosseo; bus: 40, 46, 62, or 64), has dispensed "wonders" from its tiny wooden drawers, some of which are labeled with skulls and crossbones. You'll find scented paper, licorice, and herbal remedies.

DEPARTMENT STORES In Piazza Colonna, **La Rinascente,** Via del Corso 189 (www.rinascente.it; ✆ **06-6784209;** Metro: Piazza Barberini, Piazza di Spagna, or Colosseo; bus: 117), is an upscale store offering clothing, hosiery, perfume, cosmetics, housewares, and furniture. It also has attractively priced clothing for men, women, and children. This is the largest of the Italian department-store chains, with another branch at Piazza Fiume.

FABRICS **Bassetti Tessuti ★★**, Corso Vittorio Emanuele II 73 (www.fratellibassetti.com; ✆ **06-6892326;** bus: 30, 40, 62, or 64), Rome's largest fabric store and a tradition since 1954, lies in a nondescript *palazzo* where many of Italy's top designers go for everything from lush silk from Lake Como to feather-soft wool from Piedmont. Seemingly endless aisles of fabric await you, and you are likely to rub elbows with some representatives from Italy's famed fashion houses, including such lines as Giorgio Armani. In all, there are some 200,000 fabrics sold here in every hue.

FASHION **Battistoni,** Via Condotti 61A (www.battistoni.com; ✆ **06-6976111;** Metro: Piazza di Spagna), is known for the world's finest men's shirts. It also hawks a cologne, Marte (Mars), for the "man who likes to conquer."

Emporio Armani ★★, Via del Babuino 140 (www.armani.com; ✆ **06-36002197;** Metro: Piazza di Spagna), stocks relatively affordable menswear crafted by the designer who has dressed perhaps more stage and screen stars than any other in Italy. If these prices aren't high enough for you, try the more expensive line a short walk away at **Giorgio Armani,** Via Condotti 77 (www.armani.com; ✆ **06-6991460;** Metro: Piazza di Spagna). The merchandise here is sold at sometimes staggering prices that are still often 30% less than what you'd pay elsewhere.

Blunauta, Piazza di Spagna 35 (www.blunauta.it; ✆ **06-6789806;** Metro: Piazza di Spagna), has made a name for itself with its easy-to-wear men's and women's clothing made in natural fibers. We made off with a man's zip cardigan in gray heather wool. Women will be drawn to the likes of a velvet-trimmed watermelon-pink cashmere twin set.

Dating to 1870, **Schostal,** Via del Corso 158 (www.schostalroma.com; ✆ **06-6791240;** bus: 117), is for men who like their garments (from underwear to cashmere overcoats) conservative and well crafted. The prices are more reasonable than you might think, and the staff is courteous and attentive.

Behind all the chrome mirrors is swank **Valentino ★★**, Via Condotti 13 (www.valentino.it; ✆ **06-6790479;** Metro: Piazza di Spagna), where you can become one of the most fashionable women in town—if you can afford to be. Valentino's men's haute couture is sold nearby at Via Bocca di Leone 15 (✆ **06-6787585;** Metro: Piazza di Spagna).

The prices at **Sisley,** Via Giolitti 9 (www.sisley.com; ✆ **06-47825258;** Metro: Termini), are more down to earth. It's famous for sweaters, tennis wear, blazers, and sportswear.

One of the hottest, hippest designer boutiques in Rome is **L'Anatra all'Arancia ★★**, Via Tiburtina 105–9 (✆ **06-4456293;** Metro: Piazza Vittorio). In addition to some big and up-and-coming names, the owner, Donatella Baroni, stocks her own labels.

Max Mara, Via Frattina 28 (www.maxmara.com; ✆ **06-6793638;** Metro: Piazza di Spagna), is one of the best outlets in Rome for chic women's wear. The fabrics are appealing and the alterations are free.

Rapidly approaching the stratospheric upper levels of Italian fashion is **Renato Balestra,** Via Abruzzi 3 (www.renatobalestra.it; ✆ **06-4821723;** Metro: Piazza di Spagna or Barberini), whose women's clothing attains standards of lighthearted elegance at its best. This branch carries a complete line of the latest ready-to-wear.

FLEA MARKETS On Sundays from 7am to 1pm, every peddler from Trastevere and the surrounding Castelli Romani sets up a temporary shop at the sprawling **Porta Portese open-air flea market,** near the end of Viale Trastevere (catch bus 75 to Porta Portese, then a short walk to Via Portuense). The vendors are likely to sell everything from secondhand paintings of Madonnas and bushels of rosaries to 1947 TVs and books printed in 1835. Serious shoppers can often ferret out a good buy. If you've ever been impressed with the bargaining power of the Spaniard, you haven't seen anything until you've bartered with an Italian. By 10:30am, the market is full of people. As at any street market, beware of pickpockets.

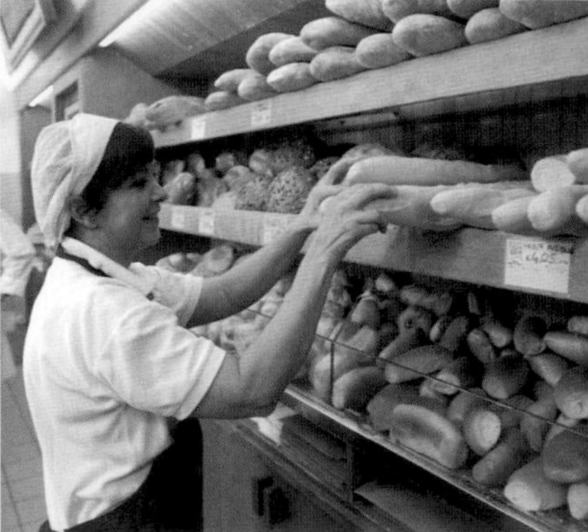

FROM LEFT: **Fresh produce for sale at Castroni; Antico Forno Campo de' Fiori.**

FOOD & FOOD MARKETS At old-fashioned **Castroni ★★**, Via Cola di Rienzo 196 (www.castronicoladirienzo.it; ✆ **06-6874383;** bus: 70 or 81), you'll find an array of unusual foodstuffs from around the Mediterranean. If you want herbs from Puglia, peperoncino oil, cheese from the Valle d'Aosta, or an obscure brand of balsamic vinegar, Castroni will have it. It also carries foods that are exotic in Italy but commonplace in North America, like taco shells and peanut butter.

Near Santa Maria Maggiore, Rome's largest market takes place Monday through Saturday from 7am to noon at **Nuovo Mercato dell'Esquilino** (www.nuovomercatoesquilino.it; Metro: Vittorio Emanuele). Most of the vendors at the gigantic market sell fresh fruit, vegetables, and other foodstuff, although some stalls are devoted to cutlery, clothing, and the like.

There's also a market Monday to Saturday 6am to noon at **Campo de' Fiori** (bus: 46, 62, or 64). It's Rome's most picturesque food market—but it's also the priciest. Things start bustling in the predawn as the florists arrange bouquets and fruit and vegetable vendors set up their stalls. After admiring the figs and peaches at the food market, stop for a delectable panino or *pizza Bianca* at **Antico Forno Campo de' Fiori,** Piazza Campo de' Fiori 22 (www.fornocampodefiori.com; ✆ **06-68806662**), and then make your way to **Marco Roscioli Salumeria,** Via del Giubbonari 21 (✆ **06-6864045**), right down the street. Here you can inhale the intoxicating, though expensive, aroma of truffles and some of Rome's best prosciutto.

GLOVES A real little discovery, **Sergio di Cori,** Piazza di Spagna 53 (www.dicorigloves.it; ✆ **06-6784439;** Metro: Piazza di Spagna), sells the most exquisite assortment of couture leather gloves in Rome. But the prices are reasonable, especially if you order the unlined gloves. Even if you don't, there are many bargains even in the silk-lined gloves.

HOUSEWARES **Spazio Sette,** hidden at Via d. Barberi 7, off Largo di Torre Argentina (www.spaziosette.it; ✆ **06-6869747;** Metro: Colosseo), is far and away Rome's best housewares emporium, a design boutique of department-store proportions. It goes way beyond Alessi teakettles to fill three huge floors with the greatest names, and latest word, in Italian and international design.

Another good bet is **Bagagli,** Via Campo Marzio 42 (www.bagagli vittorio.com; ✆ **06-6871406;** Metro: Piazza di Spagna), offering a good selection of Alessi, Rose & Tulipani, and Villeroy & Boch china in a pleasantly kitschy old Rome setting that comes complete with cobblestone floors.

If the big names don't do it for you, you may prefer **c.u.c.i.n.a.,** Via Mario de'Fiori 65 (www.cucinastore.com; ✆ **06-6791275;** bus: 80, 81, 117, or 119), a stainless-steel shrine to everything you need for a proper Italian kitchen, sporting designs that are as beautiful in their simplicity as they are utilitarian.

JEWELRY Rome's most prestigious jeweler for more than a century, **Bulgari ★★★**, Via Condotti 10 (www.bulgari.com; ✆ **06-6793876;** Metro: Piazza di Spagna), boasts a shop window that's a visual attraction in its own right. Bulgari designs combine classical Greek aesthetics with Italian taste, changing in style with the years yet clinging to tradition.

The fantastical gold and silver pieces made at **Fausto Maria Franchi ★★**, Via del Clementino 98 (www.fmfranchi.com; ✆ **06-687-1558;** bus: 115 or 913), fall somewhere between jewelry and sculpture. Franchi's designs have been hailed around the world. His artisan goldsmith and silversmith *bottega* lies in the heart of Rome on an ancient street commissioned by Sisto V. The art gallery displaying Franchi's wares stands alongside the vaulted workshop. Most of the jewelry designs incorporate precious stones; some of the jewelry is organic, even baroque.

One of the city's best gold- and silversmiths, **Federico Buccellati ★★★**, Via Condotti 31 (www.federicobuccellati.it; ✆ **06-6790329;** Metro: Piazza di Spagna), specializes in neo-Renaissance creations. The designs of the handmade jewelry and holloware recall those of Renaissance gold master Benvenuto Cellini.

Luogo Myriam B, Via dei Volsci 75 (www.myriamb.it; ✆ **06-44361305;** Metro: Termini), turns out a stunning array of extravagant bracelets and necklaces. Check out his earrings with latex, shells, tulle, rock crystal, and even industrial wire mesh.

Window-shopping at famed jeweler Bulgari.

LEATHER Italian leather is among the very best in the world; it can attain butter-soft textures more pliable than cloth. You'll find hundreds of leather stores in Rome, many of them excellent.

At **Alfieri,** Via del Corso 1–2 (✆ **06-3611976;** Metro: Piazza di Spagna; bus: 117), you'll find virtually any garment you can think of fashioned in leather. Opened in the 1960s with a funky counterculture slant, it prides itself on leather jackets, boots, bags, belts, shirts, hats, pants for men and women, short shorts, and skirts that come in at least 10 (sometimes neon) colors.

Although everything is made in Italy, the emphasis is on reasonable prices rather than ultrahigh quality, so check the stitching and workmanship before you invest.

If famous names in leather wear appeal to you, you'll find most of the biggies at **Casagrande,** Via Cola di Rienzo 206 (✆ **06-6874610;** Metro: Lepanto; bus: 32 or 81), such as Fendi and its youth-conscious offspring, Fendissime, plus Cerruti, Moschino, and Valentino. This well-managed store has developed an impressive reputation for quality and authenticity since the 1930s. The prices are more reasonable than those for equivalent merchandise in other parts of town.

Gucci, just one of the many Italian luxury brands with shops in Rome.

Fendi ★★★, Largo Goldoni (www.fendi.com; ✆ **06-334501;** Metro: Piazza di Spagna), is well known for its avant-garde leather goods, but it also has furs, stylish purses, ready-to-wear clothing, and a new line of men's clothing and accessories. Fendi also carries gift items, home furnishings, and sports accessories.

Of course, **Gucci ★★★**, Via Condotti 8 (www.gucci.com; ✆ **06-6790405;** Metro: Piazza di Spagna), has been a legend since 1900. Its merchandise consists of high-class leather goods, such as suitcases, handbags, wallets, shoes, and desk accessories. It also has elegant menswear and women's wear, including beautiful shirts, blouses, and dresses, as well as ties and neck scarves. Prices have never been higher.

MOSAICS Mosaics are an art form as old as the Roman Empire. **Maffettone Design,** Via di Panico 26 (www.maioliche-maffettone.it; ✆ **06-6832754;** Metro: Piazza Paoli; bus: 40, 46, 62, or 64), is the best place in Rome to go for decorative tiles and mosaics inspired by ancient Roman designs. The tables and furniture are handmade in little workshops spread in the countryside around Rome—real quality craftsmanship.

Many of the objects displayed at **Savelli ★**, Via Paolo VI 27 (www.savellireligious.com; ✆ **06-68307017;** Metro: Ottaviano), were inspired by ancient originals discovered in thousands of excavations, including those at Pompeii and Ostia. Others, especially the floral designs, depend on the whim and creativity of the artist. Objects include tabletops, boxes, and vases. The cheapest mosaic objects are unsigned products crafted by students at an art school partially funded by the Vatican. Objects made in the Savelli workshops that are signed by the individual artists tend to be larger and more elaborate. The outlet also contains a collection of small souvenir items such as key chains and carved statues.

PAPER The best selection of paper in Rome, really beautiful stationery, is found at **Fabriano,** Via del Babuino 173 (www.fabrianoboutique.com; ✆ **06-3260-0361;** Metro: Piazza di Spagna), a charming store found in the heart of Rome. Its motto is, "We sell everything you need to write on and with." The store also stocks photo albums and children's paper toys, and there are many lovely gift items to take home with you.

PRINTS & ENGRAVINGS At **Alberto di Castro,** Via del Babuino 71 (www.dicastro.com; ✆ **06-3613752;** Metro: Piazza di Spagna), you'll find Rome's largest collection of antique prints and engravings. In rack after rack are depictions of everything from the Colosseum to the Pantheon.

Alinari, Via Alibert 16A (www.alinari.com; ✆ **06-6792923;** Metro: Piazza di Spagna), takes its name from the famed 19th-century Florentine photographer. Original prints and photos of Alinari are almost as prized as paintings in national galleries, and you can pick up your own here.

Giovanni B. Panatta Fine Art Shop, Via Francesco Crispi 117 (✆ **06-6795948;** Metro: Piazza di Spagna, Barberini), sells excellent color and black-and-white prints covering a variety of subjects, from 18th-century Roman street scenes to astrological charts. There's also a selection of reproductions of medieval and Renaissance art that's attractive and reasonably priced.

SHOES **Ferragamo** ★★★, Via Condotti 66–73 (www.salvatoreferragamo.it; ✆ **06-6781130;** Metro: Piazza di Spagna), sells elegant footwear, plus women's clothing, accessories, and ties, in an atmosphere full of Italian style. There are always many customers waiting to enter the shop; management allows them to enter in small groups. Figure on a 30-minute wait.

WINE & LIQUOR At historic **Buccone,** Via Ripetta 19 (www.enotecabuccone.com; ✆ **06-3612154;** Metro: Piazzale Flaminio), the selection of wines is among the finest in Rome.

Opened in 1821, **Trimani,** Via Goito 20 (www.trimani.com; ✆ **06-4469661;** Metro: Castel Pretorio, Repubblica; bus: 86, 92, or 360), sells wines and spirits from Italy, among other offerings. Purchases can be shipped to your home.

Ai Monasteri, Corso Rinascimento 72 (www.monasteri.it; ✆ **06-68802783;** Metro: Piazza di Spagna; bus: 30, 64, or 116), is a treasure-trove of liquors (including liqueurs and wines), honey, and herbal teas made in Italian monasteries and convents. You can buy excellent chocolates and other candies as well. You make your selections in a quiet atmosphere reminiscent of a monastery, 2 blocks from Bernini's Fountain of the Four Rivers in Piazza Navona. The shop will ship some items for you.

ENTERTAINMENT & NIGHTLIFE

When the sun goes down, Rome's palaces, ruins, fountains, and monuments are bathed in a theatrical white light. Few evening occupations are quite as pleasurable as a stroll past the solemn pillars of old temples or the cascading torrents of Renaissance fountains glowing under the blue-black sky.

The Fountain of the Naiads (Fontana delle Naiadi) on Piazza della Repubblica, the Fountain of the Tortoises (Fontana della Tartarughe) on Piazza Mattei, and the Trevi Fountain are particularly beautiful at night. The Capitoline Hill (or Campidoglio) is magnificently lit after dark, with its measured Renaissance facades glowing like jewel boxes. The view of the Roman Forum seen from the rear of the trapezoidal Piazza del Campidoglio is the grandest in Rome, more so than even the Colosseum. Bus no. 84, 85, 87, 117, 175, 186, 271, 571, or 850 takes you here at night, or you can ask for a taxi. If you're across the Tiber, Piazza San Pietro (in front of St. Peter's) is impressive at night without the tour buses and crowds. And a combination of illuminated architecture, Renaissance fountains, and sidewalk shows and art expos enlivens Piazza Navona.

Even if you don't speak Italian, you can generally follow the listings of special events and evening entertainment featured in ***La Repubblica,*** a leading Italian newspaper. ***Wanted in Rome*** has listings of jazz, rock, and such and gives an interesting look at expatriate Rome. And ***Un Ospite a Roma,*** available free from the concierge desks of top hotels, is full of details on what's happening. Check **InRomeNow.com** online for monthly updates of current cultural events.

During the peak of summer, usually in August, all nightclub proprietors seem to lock their doors and head for the seashore, where they operate alternate clubs. Some close at different times each year, so it's hard to keep up-to-date. Always have your hotel check to see if a club is operating before you make a trek to it. (Dance clubs, in particular, open and close with freewheeling abandon.)

Be aware that there are no inexpensive nightclubs in Rome. Many of the legitimate nightclubs, besides being expensive, are frequented by prostitutes.

The Performing Arts

CLASSICAL MUSIC **Auditorium Parco della Musica ★**, Viale de Coubertin (www.auditorium.com; ✆ **06-80241281**), is the largest concert facility in Europe, an ultramodern, almost sci-fi building constructed in 2002 by Renzo Piano, a world-famous architect. It offers 40,000 sq. m (430,600 sq. ft.) of gardens and three separate concert halls, plus one massive open-air theater. The best time to attend is summer, when concerts are often staged outside, and you can listen to the strains of Brahms or Schumann under a star-studded sky. Tickets and prices depend on the event. The auditorium can be reached by taking bus no. 2, 53, 217, 231, or 910, Line M and Tram 2D.

Teatro Olimpico, Piazza Gentile da Fabriano 17 (www.teatroolimpico.it; ✆ **06-3265991;** Metro: Flaminio), hosts a wide range of performances, from pop to chamber music to foreign orchestras. ***Note:*** The theater box office is open daily 10am to 7pm.

Check the daily papers for **free church concerts** given around town, especially near Easter and Christmas.

OPERA If you're in the capital for the opera season, usually from late December to June, you might want to attend the historic **Teatro dell'Opera,** Piazza Beniamino Gigli 1, off Via Nazionale (www.operaroma.it; ✆ **06-481601;** Metro: Repubblica). Nothing is presented in July and August; in summer, the venue usually switches elsewhere. Call ahead or ask your concierge before you go. Tickets are 11€ to 130€.

The Teatro dell'Opera.

DANCE Performances of the Rome Opera Ballet are given at the **Teatro dell'Opera** (see above). The regular repertoire of classical ballet is supplemented by performances of internationally acclaimed guest artists, and Rome is on the major agenda for troupes from around the world. Watch for announcements in the weekly entertainment guides about other venues, including the Teatro Olimpico, or even open-air ballet performances.

Opera at the Baths of Caracalla

After a 10-year slumber, opera returned in 2003 to the ancient **Baths of Caracalla ★★★**, Via della Terme di Caracalla. Productions were shut down when it was feared that audiences of 5,000 were damaging the open-air ruins. Conservation-minded officials ordered that once-grandiose sets be scaled down and the stage moved to 39m (130 ft.) from the actual ruins, which are now a backdrop and not part of the scenery as before. Only 2,000 spots on the bleachers are now available. The season is a short one, lasting from July 1 to August 9, so tickets should be reserved as far in advance as possible. For tickets and information, call or go to the ticket office at Piazza Beniamino Gigli 1 (www.operaroma.it; ✆ **06-48160255**), open Tuesday to Saturday 9am to 5pm and Sunday 9am to 1:30pm. Ticket prices range from 25€ to 110€.

Bars & Cafes

Unless you're dead set on making the Roman nightclub circuit, try what might be a far livelier and less expensive scene—sitting late at night on **Via Veneto, Piazza della Rotonda, Piazza del Popolo**, or one of Rome's other piazzas, all for the cost of an espresso, a cappuccino, or a Campari.

If you're looking for some scrumptious **ice cream,** see the entries for Café Rosati and Giolitti, below.

ON VIA VENETO Back in the 1950s (a decade that *Time* magazine gave to Rome, in the same way it conceded the 1960s and later the 1990s to London), **Via Vittorio Veneto** was the chic heart of Rome, crowded with aspiring and actual movie stars, their directors, and a group of card-carrying members of the jet set. Today the beautiful people wouldn't be caught dead on Via Veneto—it has become touristy. But visitors flock here by the thousands every night for cafe sitting and people-watching.

Sophisticated **Harry's Bar ★**, Via Vittorio Veneto 150 (www.harrysbar.it; ✆ **06-4742103**; Metro: Piazza di Spagna or Barberini), is a perennial favorite for out-of-towners. Every Italian town seems to have a Harry's Bar, a name that seems tattooed into the collective memory of life in Italy during the era of *la dolce vita,* but each is independent, and not part of a chain. In summer, tables are placed outside. For those who want to dine outdoors but want to avoid the scorching sun, there's an air-conditioned sidewalk cafe open from May to November. Meals inside cost about double what you'd pay outside. In

Treat yourself to a Bellini at Harry's Bar.

back is a small dining room serving some of the finest (and priciest) food in central Rome. A piano bar features live music starting at 11pm.

NEAR THE TERMINI A century-old bar, **Bar Marani,** Via dei Volsci 57 (✆ **06-490016;** Metro: Termini), has been compared to an old Fellini movie set. By the marketplace, this is a coffee bar that attracts students, visitors, Japanese tourists, shopkeepers, artists, pickpockets, contessas, and rock stars, who come for espresso or delicious ice cream. Try to grab a table on the vine-covered terrace. It's closed on Monday and in August.

Rive Gauche, Via dei Sabelli 43 (www.rive-gauche.it; ✆ **06-4456722;** Metro: Termini), is a sleek bar that attracts Roman yuppies, who are deserting their traditional glass of wine to sample the dozens of whiskey- or rum-laced concoctions.

Tazio Wine Bar, Boscolo Hotel Exedra, Piazza della Repubblica 47 (www.boscolohotels.com; ✆ **06-489381;** Metro: Repubblica), lies near the rail terminal fronting the Baths of Diocletian and Michelangelo's Basilica degli Angeli. A trendy gathering spot at night, it serves reasonably priced Italian wines along with champagnes and tasty meat or fish platters. In summer, the Tazio bar moves to the terrace overlooking the square.

NEAR CAMPO DE' FIORI In the center of Rome, a block from the Tiber, **Roof Top Lounge Bar** at the St. George Hotel, Via Giulia 62 (www.stgeorgehotel.it; ✆ **06-686611;** bus: 46, 62, or 64), is a summer rendezvous spot, attracting a young crowd who likes to enjoy a panoramic sweep over the rooftops and domes of Rome at night. Waiters from the wine bar serve at least 120 vintages by the glass along with snacks.

For hip romantic ambience where young crowds chat, sprawled on plush sofas and armchairs, drinking their *aperitivo* in front of the blazing fireplace, head to **Etablí,** Vicolo delle Vacche 9 (off Via dei Coronari) (www.etabli.it; ✆ **06-97616694;** Bus: 30, 70, 87, 492, 628).

Société Lutèce, Piazza Montevecchio 17 (off Via dei Coronari) (✆ **06-68301472;** bus: 30, 70, 87, 492, 628), was one of the first bars to introduce the Northern Italian aperitivo phenomenon to Rome. This stylish, laid-back spot is great for drinking and snacking before, after, or instead of dinner.

ON PIAZZA DEL POPOLO **Café Rosati ★**, Piazza del Popolo 5A (www.rosatibar.it; ✆ **06-3225859;** Metro: Piazzale Flaminio; bus: 117), has been around since 1923 and attracts a crowd of all persuasions, both foreign and domestic, who drive up in Maseratis and Porsches. It's really a sidewalk cafe/ice-cream parlor/candy store/confectionery/restaurant that has been swept up in the fickle world of fashion. The later you go, the more interesting the action will be. It serves lunch and dinner daily from noon to 11pm.

The management of **Canova Café,** Piazza del Popolo 16 (www.canovapiazzadelpopolo.it; ✆ **06-3612231;** bus: 117), has filled this place with boutiques selling expensive gift items, such as luggage and cigarette lighters, yet many Romans still consider the Canova to be *the* place on the piazza. It has a sidewalk terrace for people-watching, plus a snack bar, a restaurant, and a wine shop. In summer, you can sit in a courtyard with ivy-covered walls and flowers growing in terra-cotta planters. Food is served daily from noon to 3:30pm and 7 to 11pm, but the bar is open from 8am to midnight or 1am, depending on the crowd. Main courses cost 5.50€ to 13€.

NEAR THE PANTHEON The **Piazza della Rotonda,** across from the Pantheon, is the hopping place to be after dark, especially in summer. Although it's one of the most touristy places in Rome, locals come here, too, because it's a dramatic place to be at night when the Pantheon is lit up. Most cafes here are open until midnight or 2am.

Di Rienzo, Piazza della Rotonda 8–9 (www.ristorantedirienzo.com; ✆ **06-6869097;** Metro: Piazza di Spagna; bus: 62 or 116), is the top cafe on this piazza. In fair weather, you can sit at one of the sidewalk tables (if you can find one free). There's a full menu, or you can just nurse a drink.

Salotto 42, Piazza di Pietra 2 (www.salotto42.it; ✆ **06-6785804;** bus: 175), stands close to the Pantheon. This is the creation of a Swedish model, who runs a coffee shop by day and a chic cocktail bar after dark. Big books line the walls. At night patrons sip cocktails while sitting in stylish armchairs, enjoying Scandinavian snacks.

Tazza d'Oro, Piazza della Rotonda, Via degli Orfani 84 (www.tazzadorocoffeeshop.com; ✆ **06-6789792;** Metro: Barberini; bus: 46, 62, or 116), is known for serving its own brand of espresso. Another specialty, ideal on a hot summer night, is *granita di caffè* (coffee that has been frozen, crushed into a velvety, slushlike ice, and placed in a glass between layers of whipped cream). Also tantalizing are chocolate-coated coffee beans and an aromatic coffee liqueur, Aroma di Roma.

Strongly brewed coffee is liquid fuel to Italians, and many Romans will walk blocks and blocks for what they consider a superior brew. **Caffè Sant'Eustachio ★**, Piazza Sant'Eustachio 82 (www.santeustachioilcaffe.it; ✆ **06-68802048;** bus: 116), is one of Rome's most celebrated espresso shops, where the water supply is funneled into the city by an aqueduct built in 19 B.C. Rome's most experienced espresso judges claim the water plays an important part in the coffee's flavor, although steam forced through ground Brazilian coffee roasted on the premises has a significant effect as well.

Riccioli Cafe, Piazza delle Coppelle 13 (www.ricciolicafe.com; ✆ **06-68210313;** Metro: Piazza di Spagna; bus: 70), is the best oyster and champagne bar in Rome. In elegant yet informal surroundings, you can order drinks and oysters on the half shell (or more substantial meals). Many come here to see and be seen. The loftlike wine cellar has an excellent selection.

NEAR THE SPANISH STEPS Since 1760, the **Antico Caffè Greco ★★**, Via Condotti 86 (www.anticocaffegreco.eu; ✆ **06-6791700;** Metro: Piazza di Spagna), has been Rome's poshest coffee bar. Stendhal, Goethe, Keats, and D'Annunzio have sipped coffee here before you. Today you're more likely to see Japanese tourists and ladies who lunch, but there's plenty of atmosphere. In front is a wooden bar, and beyond is a series of small salons. You sit at marble-topped tables of Napoleonic design, against a backdrop of gold or red damask, romantic paintings, and antique mirrors. The house specialty is Paradise, made with lemon and orange.

One of the best places to taste Italian wines, brandies, and grappa is at **Antica Enoteca,** Via della Croce 76B (www.anticaenoteca.com; ✆ **06-6790896;** Metro: Piazza di Spagna). A stand-up drink in its darkly antique confines is the perfect ending to a visit to the nearby Spanish Steps. You can opt for a postage-stamp table in back or stay at the bar.

Rome's chicest cafe continues to be **Caffetteria Canova Tadolini,** Via del Babuino, 150 A/B (www.museoateliercanovatadolini.it; ✆ **06-3211-0702**), part of a museum dedicated to Antonio Canova, the neoclassical sculptor, and his student Adamo Tadolini. Unlike most cafes at museums, the establishment here *is* the museum. You sit at *ottocentro*-style tables beneath statues and plaster fragments. The museum-cum-cafe serves drinks as well as full meals, including succulent pastas.

NEAR THE TREVI FOUNTAIN At night we'd recommend a stroll by the Trevi Fountain, beautifully lit, followed by a stopover at an elegant ice-cream shop, **San Crispino,** Via della Panetteria 42 (www.ilgelatodisancrispino.it; ✆ **06-6793924;** Metro: Barberini). White-jacketed scoopers will dish out freshly made ice creams and sorbets in such flavors as ginger and cinnamon, fresh walnut and dried fig, chestnut and rum, whiskey, and even "ricotta soft." Sorbets are especially delectable, ranging from melon to pear, from Seville orange to fresh strawberry. Prices go from 1.70€ to 8€, and the place is closed on Tuesdays.

NEAR PIAZZA COLONNA For gelato fans, **Giolitti,** Via Uffici del Vicario 40 (www.giolitti.it; ✆ **06-6991243;** Metro: Barberini; bus: 116), is one of the city's most popular nighttime gathering spots and the oldest ice-cream shop. Some of the sundaes look like Vesuvius about to erupt. Many people take gelato out to eat on the streets; others enjoy it in the post-Empire splendor of the salon inside.

NEAR PIAZZA NAVONA Head for the **Antico Caffè della Pace,** Via della Pace 3–5 (www.caffedellapace.it; ✆ **06-6861216;** bus: 30, 40, or 46), right off the heartbeat of Piazza Navona. In existence for more than a century, it attracts painters, musicians, writers, antique collectors, fashionistas, and politicians during the day. It's a wild scene on Saturday night, when it's packed with a gorgeous young crowd that comes to see and be seen.

Fluid, Via del Governo Vecchio 46–47 (www.fluideventi.com; ✆ **06-6832361;** bus: 64), lies only a short walk from the Piazza Navona. This supermodern bar has a liquid theme. Some of the seating is on plastic cubes evoking ice. Walls and ceiling are sculpted to give the impression of a

Desserts on display at Antico Caffè Greco.

A few of the many flavors of gelato available at Giolitti.

waterway grotto. Mostly it attracts patrons in the age range of 25 to 40, who enjoy an *aperitivo* buffet and a respectable wine *carte*.

IN TRASTEVERE Fans of *Fellini's Roma* know what **Piazza Santa Maria** in Trastevere looks like at night. The square, filled with milling throngs in summer, is graced with an octagonal fountain and a 12th-century church. Children run and play on the piazza, and occasional spontaneous guitar fests break out when the weather is good.

Birreria La Scala, Piazza della Scala 60 (✆ **06-5803763;** bus: 23 or 125), lies only 100m (328 ft.) from Piazza di Santa Maria in Trastevere, the heart of the district. Its selection of beer is the best in the area. There's live music Tuesday, Thursday, and Sunday nights, and the bar is open until 1am.

Freni e Frizioni ("Brakes and Clutches"), Via del Politeama 4–6 (near Piazza Trilussa; ✆ **06-58334210;** bus: 23, 271, or 280), is a mechanics-garage-turned-nighttime-hot spot, with an ethnic-inflected aperitivo spread (think curried risotto). On the adjacent square, an effervescent crowd lounges against stone walls and parked motorini.

NEAR TESTACCIO **Il Barone Rosso,** Via Libetta 13 (www.baronerosso.com; ✆ **06-57288961;** Metro: Garbatella), is the biggest and best German beer garden in Rome, and on a summer night this "Red Baron" can be a lot of fun. Opened in 1996, this 380-seat club is the largest in Rome, with a summer garden that always overflows in fair weather. The staff serves lots of beer and other drinks, along with Italian pizzas and German snacks, salads, and sandwiches. Hours are daily 7pm to 3am.

Live-Music Clubs

At **Alexanderplatz,** Via Ostia 9 (www.alexanderplatz.it; ✆ **06-58335781;** Metro: Ottaviano), you can hear jazz Monday through Saturday from 9pm to 2am, with live music beginning at 10pm. The good restaurant here serves everything from *gnocchi alla romana* to Japanese fare. There's no cover; instead you pay a 1-month membership fee of 10€.

Big Mama, Vicolo San Francesco a Ripa 18 (www.bigmama.it; ✆ **06-5812551;** Metro: Piramide; bus: H or 780), is a hangout for jazz and blues musicians where you're likely to meet the up-and-coming stars of tomorrow, and sometimes even the big names. For big acts, the cover is 12€ to 30€, plus 14€ for a seasonal membership fee.

Fonclea, Via Crescenzio 82A (www.fonclea.it; ✆ **06-6896302;** bus: 49, 492, or 982), offers live music every night: Dixieland, rock, and R&B. This is basically a cellar jazz place and crowded pub that attracts folks from all walks of Roman life. The music starts at 7pm and usually lasts until 2am. There's also a restaurant featuring grilled meats, salads, and crepes. A meal starts at 20€, but if you want dinner, it's best to reserve a table.

Arciliuto, Piazza Monte Vecchio 5 (www.arciliuto.it; ✆ **06-6879419;** bus: 46, 62, or 64), is a romantic candlelit spot that was reputedly once the studio of Raphael. Monday through Saturday from 10pm to 1:30am, you can enjoy a music-salon ambience, with a pianist, guitarist, and violinist. The presentation also includes live Neapolitan songs, new Italian madrigals, and even current hits from Broadway or London's West End. This place is hard to find, but it's within walking distance of Piazza Navona. There is no cover, but there's a one-drink minimum with beverages starting at 10€. It's closed from July 15 to September 5.

Nightclubs & Dance Clubs

In a high-tech, futuristic setting, **Boheme,** Via Velletri 13–19 (www.boeme.it; ✆ **06-8412212;** bus: 63, 86, or 92), provides two dance floors. The type of music played is house and pop music from the '80s, '90s, and today. It's open Friday to Sunday 11pm to 3:30am. Admission is 10€. It is closed in July and August.

Piper, Via Tagliamento 9 (www.piperclub.it; ✆ **06-8555398;** bus: 63), opened in 1965 in a former cinema and became the first modern disco of its kind in Italy. Many dances such as "the shake" were first introduced to Italy at this club. No longer what it was in those years of *la dolce vita,* the Piper is still going strong. Today it lures with fashion shows, screenings, some of the hottest parties in town, and various gigs, drawing a casual and mixed-age crowd. The pickup scene here is hot and heavy. The kind of music you'll hear depends on the night. It's open Tuesday to Sunday 11pm to 5am, charging a cover of 20€ to 26€, including one drink.

A Nightlife Note

A neighborhood with an edge, **Testaccio** is radical chic—in other words, don't wander around alone at night. Although the area has its charms, it still has a long way to go before it can be called regentrified.

Gilda, Via Mario de' Fiori 97 (www.midra.it; ✆ **06-6797396;** Metro: Piazza di Spagna), is an adventurous nightclub/disco/restaurant that attracts a post-35 set, most often couples. In the past, it has hosted Diana Ross and splashy Paris-type revues. Expect first-class shows, and disco music played between the live acts. The disco (midnight–4am) presents music of the 1960s plus more current tunes. The attractive piano bar, Swing, features Italian and Latin music. The cover ranges from 15€ to 30€ and includes the first drink. It's closed on Monday.

Don't be put off by the facade of **Locanda Atlantide,** Via dei Lucani 22B (www.locandatlantide.it; ✆ **06-44704540;** Metro: Porta Maggiore; bus: 71), thinking that you've arrived at a bunker for a Gestapo interrogation. This former warehouse in San Lorenzo is the setting of a nightclub, bar, concert hall, and theater. Every day there's something different—perhaps jazz on Tuesday, a play on Wednesday, or a concert on Thursday, giving way to dance-club action on Friday and Saturday with DJ music. The cover ranges from 3€ to 15€, depending on the evening; hours are Tuesday to Sunday from 8pm to 2am. It's closed June 15 to September 15.

Gay & Lesbian Clubs

L'Alibi, Via Monte Testaccio 44 (www.lalibi.it; ✆ **06-5743448;** bus: 95), in Testaccio, is a year-round stop on many gay men's agendas. The crowd, however, tends to be mixed, both Roman and international, straight and gay, male and female. One room is devoted to dancing. It's open Wednesday through Sunday from 11pm to 4am, and the cover is 10€ to 15€.

Skyline, Via Pontremoli 36 (www.skylineclub.it; ✆ **06-7009431;** Metro: San Giovanni), has moved to the San Giovanni district of Rome. It attracts a large number of gay men with a scattering of lesbians. It's amusing, fun, and often rowdy. Porn movies are shown every night. Conceived as an American bar on two levels, it offers two backrooms where the action is hot, hot, hot. Shows are presented weekly. It's open daily 10:30pm to 4am.

WHERE TO STAY

See the section "The Neighborhoods in Brief," earlier in this chapter, to get an idea of where you might want to base yourself.

If you like to gamble and arrive without a reservation, head quickly to the **airport information desk** or, once you get into town, to the offices of **Enjoy Rome** (see "Visitor Information," earlier in this chapter), where the staff can help you reserve a room, if any are available.

All the hotels listed serve breakfast (often a buffet with coffee, fruit, rolls, and cheese), but it's not always included in the rate, so check the listing carefully.

Nearly all hotels are heated in the cooler months, but not all are air-conditioned in summer, which can be vitally important during a stifling July or August. The deluxe and first-class ones are, but after that, it's a tossup. Be sure to check the listing carefully before you book a stay in the dog days of summer!

Near Stazione Termini

Despite a handful of pricey choices, this area is most notable for its concentration of cheap hotels. It's not the most picturesque location and parts of the neighborhood are still transitional, but it's certainly convenient in terms of transportation and easy access to many of Rome's top sights.

VERY EXPENSIVE

Exedra ★★ This neoclassical palace overlooking the Piazza della Repubblica at the rail terminal also fronts the Baths of Diocletian and Michelangelo's Basilica degli Angeli. The Exedra is a study in modern elegance combined with the romance of the past. It's luxury living on a grand scale, from the spacious standard double rooms to a variety of suites. Our favorite rooms are the top-floor accommodations in the Clementino Wing, each with bare brick walls and the original ceiling beams. Rooms feature such decorative notes as printed leather headboards and whorled silk wall coverings. You can take morning coffee on the rooftop garden terrace overlooking the Fountain of the Naiads. The spa is linked to the rooftop swimming pool by a glass elevator.

Piazza della Repubblica 47, 00187 Roma. www.exedra roma.boscolohotels.com ✆ **06-489381.** Fax 06-40938000. 240 units. 260€–700€ double; from 506€ junior suite; from 1,100€ suite. AE, DC, MC, V. Parking 35€. Metro: Repubblica. **Amenities:** 3 restaurants; 2 bars; babysitting; concierge; rooftop pool; room service; spa; Wi-Fi (20€ per 24 hr.). *In room:* A/C, TV, hair dryer, minibar.

St. Regis Grand ★★★ This restored landmark is more plush and upscale than any hotel in the area; for comparable digs, you'll have to cross town to check into the Excelsior or Eden. And for sheer opulence, not even those hotels equal it. Its drawback is its location at the dreary Stazione Termini, but once you're inside its splendid shell, all thoughts of railway stations vanish.

When César Ritz founded this outrageously expensive hotel in 1894, it was the first to offer a private bathroom and two electric lights in every room. Restored to its former glory, it is a magnificent Roman *palazzo* combining Italian and French styles in decoration and furnishings. Guest rooms, most of which are exceedingly spacious, are luxuriously furnished. Hand-painted frescoes are installed above each headboard. For the best rooms and the finest service, ask to be booked on the St. Regis floor.

Via Vittorio Emanuele Orlando 3, 00185 Roma. www.stregis.com/grandrome. ✆ **06-47091.** Fax 06-4747307. 161 units. 337€–1,030€ double; from 1,260€ junior suite; from 2,500€ suite. AE, DC,

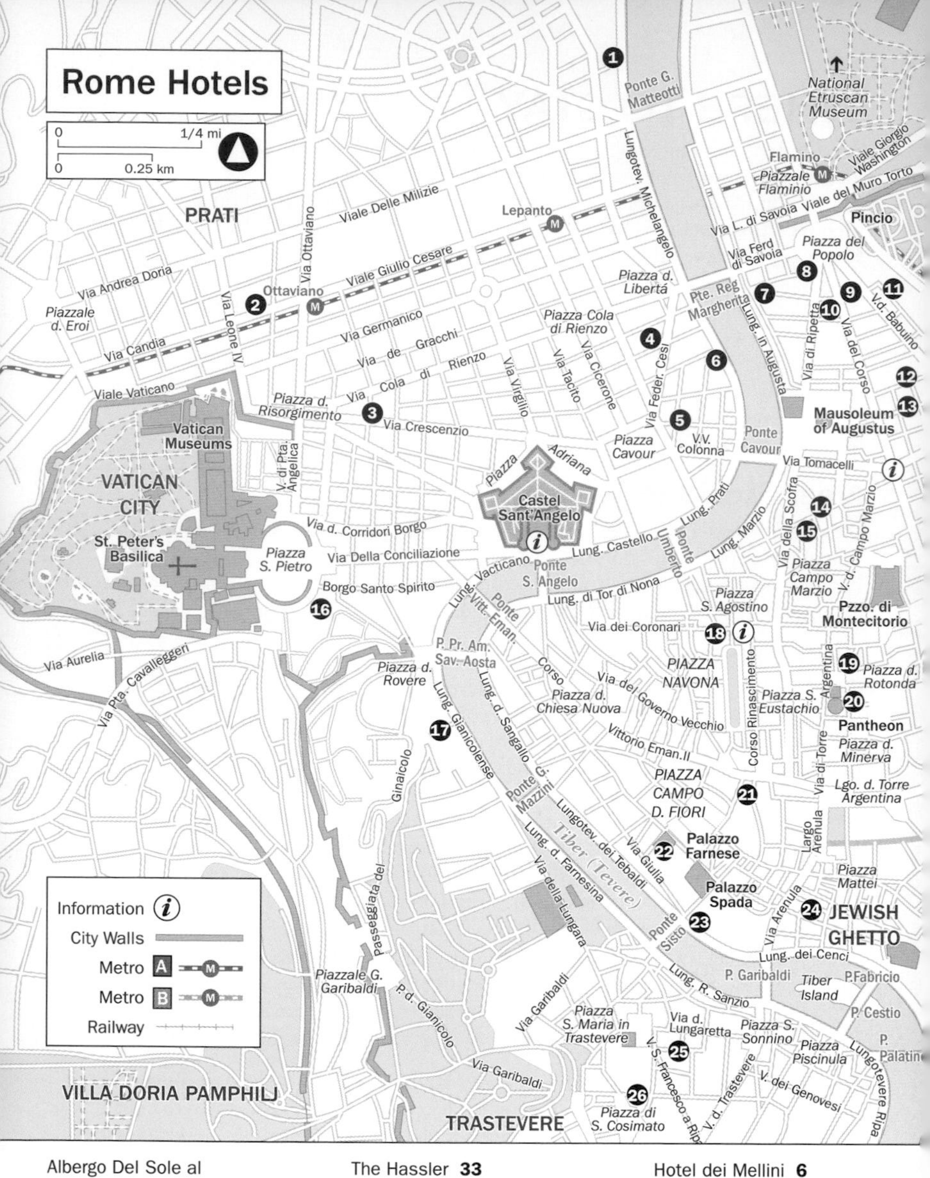

Albergo Del Sole al Pantheon **19**
Albergo Santa Chiara **20**
Babuino 181 **10**
Boscolo Hotel Aleph **41**
Capo d'Africa **59**
Casa Howard **39**
Colosseum Hotel **53**
Daphne Veneto **42**
Exedra **49**
Fontanella Borghese **15**
The Hassler **33**
Hotel Adriano **14**
Hotel Alexandra **40**
Hotel Aphrodite **48**
Hotel Arenula **24**
Hotel Art by the Spanish Steps **12**
Hotel Cisterna **25**
Hotel Condotti **29**
Hotel d'Inghilterra **30**
Hotel Dei Consoli **3**
Hotel dei Mellini **6**
Hotel de Russie **11**
Hotel Eden **35**
Hotel Fiamma **44**
Hotel Lancelot **58**
Hotel Locarno **7**
Hotel Morgana **56**
Hotel Panda **8**
Hotel Parlamento **32**
Hotel Piazza di Spagna **30**
Hotel Ponte Sisto **23**

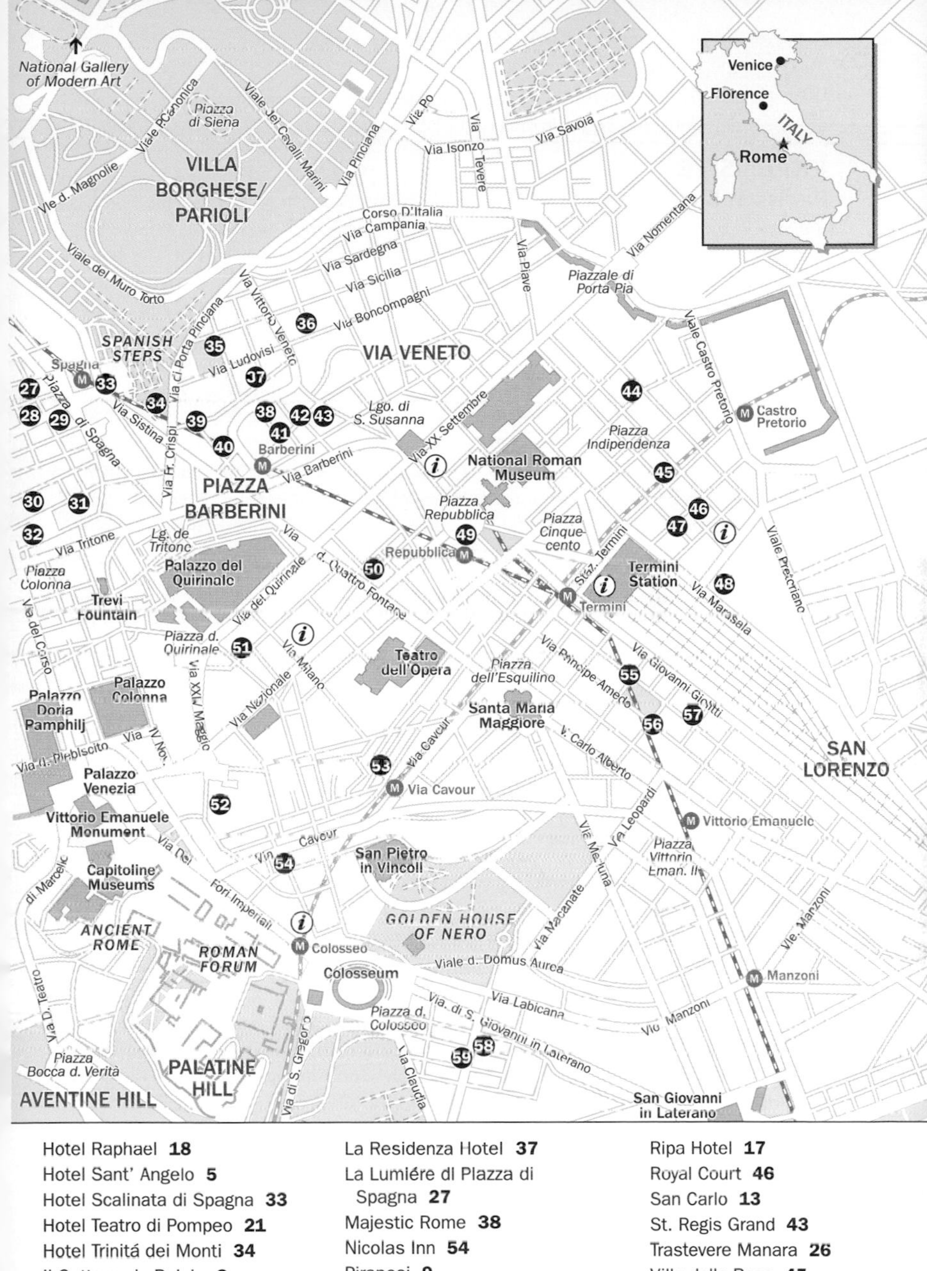

Hotel Raphael **18**
Hotel Sant' Angelo **5**
Hotel Scalinata di Spagna **33**
Hotel Teatro di Pompeo **21**
Hotel Trinitá dei Monti **34**
Il Gattopardo Relais **2**
The Inn at the Roman Forum **52**
The Inn at the Spanish Steps **28**
Kennedy Hotel **57**
La Residenza Hotel **37**
La Lumiére di Piazza di Spagna **27**
Majestic Rome **38**
Nicolas Inn **54**
Piranesi **9**
Portrait Suites **31**
Radisson Blu Es **55**
Residenza Cellini **50**
Residenza Farnese **22**
Residenza Paolo VI **16**
Ripa Hotel **17**
Royal Court **46**
San Carlo **13**
St. Regis Grand **43**
Trastevere Manara **26**
Villa delle Rose **45**
Villa Laetitia **1**
Villa Spalletti Trivelli **51**
Visconti Palace Hotel **4**
Westin Excelsior **36**
Yes Hotel **47**

MC, V. Parking 20€–30€. Metro: Repubblica. **Amenities:** Restaurant; bar; babysitting; concierge; exercise room; room service; spa. *In room:* A/C, TV, hair dryer, minibar, Wi-Fi (15€ per 24 hr.).

EXPENSIVE

Radisson Blu ES ★★ If you want a hypermodern atmosphere, this hotel is for you. This hotel is so dramatic, innovative, and high-tech that its opening sparked a bit of recovery in the old but decaying Esquilino quarter on the fringe of the Termini. A government-rated five-star luxe hotel, it is posh yet comfortably modern. It has everything from a Turkish bath to a business center. Don't judge the hotel by its rather dull seven-story exterior, which resembles an office building. Inside, the lobby showcases the ruins of a 2nd-century-A.D. Roman road. The midsize to spacious bedrooms emphasize minimalist Japanese designs, with wool rugs, glass desks, and plastic chairs in orange or pea green. Rooms are soundproof; some open onto balconies with city views.

Via Turati 171, 00185 Roma. www.eshotel.it. ✆ **06-444841.** Fax 06-44341396. 232 units. 199€–330€ double; from 299€ junior suite; from 349€ suite. AE, DC, MC, V. Parking 15€. Metro: Vittorio Emanuele. **Amenities:** 2 restaurants; bar; babysitting; exercise room; rooftop outdoor pool; room service; spa. *In room:* A/C, TV, hair dryer, minibar, Wi-Fi (free).

Residenza Cellini ★ 🎁 This undiscovered small hotel from the '30s is run by the English-speaking De Paolis family, who welcome you with warm hospitality. Gaetano, Donato, and Barbara have only a few rooms and they lavished attention on them, making them comfortable and stylish. Bedrooms are spacious and traditionally furnished, with polished wood pieces and Oriental carpets on the hardwood floors. The king-size beds have hypoallergenic orthopedic mattresses, and the bathrooms come with hydrojet shower or Jacuzzi.

Via Modena 5, 00184 Roma. www.residenzacellini.it. ✆ **06-47825204.** Fax 06-47881806. 6 units. 145€–240€ double; 170€–280€ junior suite. Rates include buffet breakfast. AE, DC, MC, V. Parking 35€. Metro: Repubblica. **Amenities:** Bar; airport transfer (55€); concierge; room service. *In room:* A/C, TV, hair dryer, minibar, Wi-Fi (free).

MODERATE

Hotel Morgana Between Santa Maria Maggiore and Stazione Termini, the completely up-to-date Morgana is a hotel of style and substance. Bedrooms are most comfortable and furnished in a sleek modern styling based on traditional designs. The rooms have all the modern amenities and a vaguely English-style decor. The English-speaking staff is pleasant and will help guide you to some of the city's most important attractions, many of which lie only a short walk from the hotel. Since this hotel lies in a noisy section of Rome, all of the bedrooms are soundproof.

Via F. Turati 33–37, 00185 Roma. www.hotelmorgana.com. ✆ **06-4467230.** Fax 06-4469142. 106 units. 100€–235€ double; 165€–250€ suite. Rates include buffet breakfast. AE, DC, MC, V. Parking 15€. Metro: Termini. **Amenities:** Bar; airport transfer (55€); babysitting; concierge; room service. *In room:* A/C, TV, hair dryer, minibar, Wi-Fi (10€ per 24 hr.).

Kennedy Hotel A 5-minute walk from the Termini Station, this completely restored hotel is one of the best bets for those who want to stay in the rail station area. The hotel, launched in 1963 when President Kennedy died, was named to honor his memory. The building itself is from the late 19th century, although it has been much restored and modernized over the years. The hotel is within an easy walk of many of the historical monuments of Rome, including the Basilica

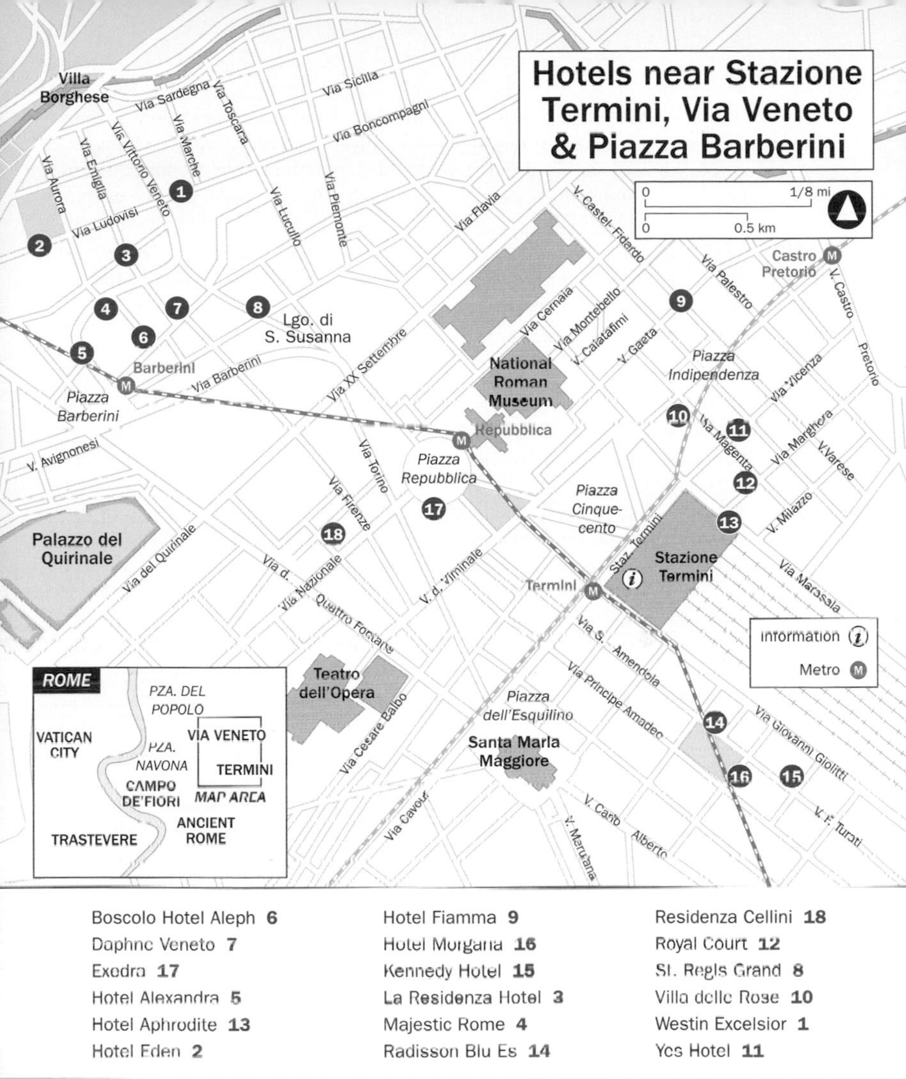

of S. Maria Maggiore, the Opera House, the Colosseum, and the Roman Forum. Bedrooms are renovated, with tasteful furnishings and double-glass soundproofing. Many rooms open to views of the antique Roman wall of Servio Tullio.

Via Filippo Turati 62–64, 00185 Roma. www.hotelkennedy.net. ✆ **06-4465373.** Fax 06-4465417. 52 units. 70€–159€ double; 120€–260€ suite. Rates include buffet breakfast. AE, DC, MC, V. Parking 15€. Metro: Termini. **Amenities:** Bar; exercise room; room service. *In room:* A/C, TV, hair dryer, Wi-Fi (18€ per 24 hr.).

Royal Court ★ 🎁 This winner lies in a restored Liberty-style palace a short walk from the Termini. The hotel evokes a tranquil, elegantly decorated private town house. Some of the superior rooms offer Jacuzzis in their bathrooms, but all units feature well-maintained-and-designed bathrooms with tub/shower combinations. The superior rooms also come with small balconies opening onto cityscapes. Even the standard doubles are comfortable, but if you're willing to pay the price, you can stay in the deluxe doubles, which are like junior suites in most Rome hotels. Some of the bedrooms are large enough to sleep three or four guests comfortably.

Via Marghera 51, 00185 Roma. www.morganaroyalcourt.com. ✆ **06-44340364.** Fax 06-4469121. 24 units. 130€–250€ double. Rates include buffet breakfast. AE, DC, MC, V. Parking 25€. Metro: Termini. **Amenities:** Bar; airport transfers (55€); babysitting; room service. *In room:* A/C, TV, hair dryer, minibar, Wi-Fi (10€ per 24 hr.).

Villa delle Rose ☺ Located less than 2 blocks north of the rail station, this hotel is an acceptable, if not exciting, choice. In the late 1800s, it was a villa with a dignified cut-stone facade inspired by the Renaissance. Despite many renovations, the ornate trappings of the original are still visible, including the lobby's Corinthian-capped marble columns and the flagstone-covered terrace that is part of the verdant back garden. The look is still one of faded grandeur. Much of the interior has been redecorated and upgraded with traditional wall coverings, carpets, and tiled bathrooms. Breakfasts in the garden do a lot to add country flavor to an otherwise very urban setting. Families often book here, asking for one of the three rooms with lofts that can sleep up to five.

Via Vicenza 5, 00185 Roma. www.villadellerose.it. ✆ **06-4451788.** Fax 06-4451639. 37 units, some with shower only. 72€–160€ double. Rates include buffet breakfast. AE, DC, MC, V. Free parking (only 4 cars). Metro: Termini or Castro Pretorio. **Amenities:** Bar; room service; free Wi-Fi (lobby). *In room:* A/C (in 30 rooms), TV, hair dryer, minibar (in some).

INEXPENSIVE

Hotel Aphrodite Completely renovated, this government-rated three-star hotel in the heart of Rome is a four-story hotel offering good value. Directly next to Stazione Termini, it is a reliable and well-run choice, although the surrounding area is a little seedy at night. For rail passengers who want quick check-ins and fast getaways, it's the most convenient choice. Bedrooms are attractively and comfortably furnished with modern pieces and parquet floors, along with marble bathrooms with shower and mosaic tiles. A special feature here is the sunny rooftop terrace. Ask at the desk about the possibility of taking walking tours through the historic districts.

Via Marsala 90, 00185 Roma. www.accommodationinrome.com. ✆ **06-491096.** Fax 06-491579. 50 units. 90€–120€ double; 110€–150€ triple. Rates include continental breakfast. AE, DC, MC, V. Parking 15€. Metro: Termini. *In room:* A/C, TV, hair dryer, minibar, Wi-Fi (in some; free).

Hotel Fiamma Near the Baths of Diocletian, the Fiamma is in a renovated building, with four floors of bedrooms and a ground floor faced with marble and plate-glass windows. It's an old favorite, if a bit past its prime. The lobby is long and bright, filled with a varied collection of furnishings, including overstuffed chairs and blue enamel railings. On the same floor is an austere marble breakfast room. The comfortably furnished guest rooms range from small to medium in size, and the small bathrooms are tiled, with adequate shelf space.

Via Gaeta 61, 00185 Roma. www.leonardihotels.com. ✆ **06-4818436.** Fax 06-4883511. 79 units, shower only. 72€–135€ double; 110€–180€ triple. Rates include buffet breakfast. AE, DC, MC, V. Parking 20€. Metro: Termini. **Amenities:** Room service. *In room:* A/C, TV, hair dryer, minibar, Wi-Fi (5€ per 2 hr.).

Yes Hotel We'd definitely say yes to this hotel, which lies only 100m (328 ft.) from Stazione Termini. Opened in 2007, it was quickly discovered by frugally minded travelers who want a good bed and comfortable surroundings for the night. It's a two-story hotel housed in a restored 19th-century building with simple, well-chosen furnishings resting on tiled floors. There is a sleek, modern look to both the bedrooms and public areas, and the staff is helpful but not effusive.

Via Magenta 15, 00185 Roma. www.yeshotelrome.com. ✆ **06-44363836.** Fax 06-44363829. 29 units. 95€–220€ double. DC, MC, V. Parking 17€. Metro: Termini. **Amenities:** Bar; babysitting; room service. *In room:* A/C, TV, hair dryer, Wi-Fi (5€ per 24 hr.).

Near Via Veneto & Piazza Barberini

If you stay in this area, you definitely won't be on the wrong side of the tracks. Unlike the area near the dreary rail station, this is a beautiful and upscale commercial neighborhood, near some of Rome's best shopping.

VERY EXPENSIVE

Hotel Eden ★★★ It's not as grand architecturally as the Westin Excelsior, nor does it have the views of the Hassler, and it's certainly not a summer resort like the Hilton. But the Eden is Rome's top choice for discerning travelers who like grand comfort but without all the ostentation.

For several generations after its 1889 opening, this hotel, about a 10-minute walk east of the Spanish Steps, reigned over one of the world's most stylish shopping neighborhoods. Recent guests have included Pierce Brosnan, Tom Cruise, Emma Thompson, and Nicole Kidman. The Eden's hilltop position guarantees a panoramic city view from most guest rooms; all are spacious and elegantly appointed with a decor harking back to the late 19th century, plus marble-sheathed bathrooms. Try to get one of the front rooms with a balcony boasting views over Rome.

Via Ludovisi 49, 00187 Roma. www.edenroma.com. ✆ **06-478121.** Fax 06-4821584. 121 units. 328€–840€ double; from 1,340€ suite. AE, DC, DISC, MC, V. Parking 60€. Metro: Piazza Barberini. **Amenities:** Restaurant, La Terrazza (review, p. 130); bar; airport transfers (85€); babysitting; concierge; exercise room; room service; sauna. *In room:* A/C, TV/DVD, CD player, hair dryer, mini bar, Wi-Fi (19€ per 24 hr.).

Majestic Rome ★★ Built in 1889 in the center of Rome, this government-rated five-star hotel is completely modernized and up-to-date, and one of the grandest addresses of Rome, standing on the street that enjoyed its *la dolce vita* heyday in the 1950s. The Majestic was the center of high society life in Rome in the 1920s, when movie stars and royalty paraded through its lobby. It's still a home for many celebrities and political figures, and much of the past splendor has been regained in a sensitive restoration. The spacious rooms are beautifully appointed—often filled with antiques, including tapestries and frescoes—and many accommodations open onto private balconies. The on-site restaurant Filippo La Mantia specializes in creative Sicilian cuisine.

Via Vittorio Veneto 50, 00187 Roma. www.rome-hotels-majestic.com. ✆ **06-421441.** Fax 06-4880984. 98 units. 335€–720€ double; from 1,200€ suite. AE, DC, MC, V. Parking 70€. Metro: Piazza Barberini. **Amenities:** Restaurant; bar; airport transfers (82€); babysitting; concierge; exercise room; room service. *In room:* A/C, TV/DVD, CD player, hair dryer, minibar, Wi-Fi (free).

Westin Excelsior ★ If money is no object, this is a good place to spend it. Architecturally more grandiose than either the Eden or the Hassler, the Excelsior is not as up-to-date or as beautifully renovated as either the Eden or the St. Regis Grand. The Excelsior has never moved into the 21st century the way some other grand hotels have. For our money today, we prefer the Hotel de Russie, and we've always gotten better service at the Hassler (see reviews for both later), but the Excelsior remains a favorite, especially among older visitors who remember it from decades past. The guest rooms come in two varieties: new (the result of a major renovation) and traditional. The older ones are a bit worn, while the newer ones have more imaginative color schemes and plush carpeting. All are spacious and elegantly furnished, always with antiques and silk curtains.

Via Vittorio Veneto 125, 00187 Roma. www.westin.com/excelsiorrome. ✆ **800/325-3589** in the U.S., or 06-47081. Fax 06-4826205. 316 units. 347€–550€ double; from 1,770€ suite. AE, DC, DISC, MC, V. Parking 43€–70€. Metro: Piazza Barberini. **Amenities:** Restaurant; bar; airport transfers (85€); babysitting; children's programs; concierge; exercise room; indoor heated pool; room service; spa. *In room:* A/C, TV, hair dryer, minibar, Wi-Fi (15€ per 24 hr.).

EXPENSIVE

Boscolo Hotel Aleph ★★ Called sexy and decadent by some hotel critics when it opened, this winning choice leads the pack among "new wave" Italian hotels. A luxury hotel in the center of Rome, Aleph was designed by Adam Tihany, who said he wanted to "humanize the rooms with indulgent details." Only a minute's walk from the Via Veneto, the hotel offers spacious guest rooms adorned with elegant Italian fabrics, a tasteful decor, and all the latest technology. Murano chandeliers, window blinds made of strings of metal beads, a dramatic roof terrace overlooking the heart of Rome, and an indoor swimming pool are just some of the features of this hotel. Tihany wanted something eccentric and intriguing, exclusive yet provocative—and his creation is all that and vastly comfortable as well, with a 1930s- and 1940s-inspired style.

Via San Basilio 15, 00187 Roma. www.aleph-roma.boscolohotels.com. ✆ **06-422901.** Fax 06-42290000. 96 units. 204€–380€ double; from 506€ junior suite; from 880€ suite. AE, DC, MC, V. Parking 35€. Metro: Barberini. **Amenities:** 2 restaurants; 2 bars; airport transfers (60€); babysitting; concierge; exercise room; indoor heated pool; room service; sauna; spa. *In room:* A/C, TV, hair dryer, minibar, Wi-Fi (20€ per 24 hr.).

Hotel Alexandra ★ 🎁 This is one of your few chances to stay on Via Veneto without going broke (although it's not exactly cheap). Set behind the stone facade of what was a 19th-century mansion, the Alexandra offers immaculate and soundproof guest rooms. The rooms range from cramped to midsize, but each has been redecorated, filled with antiques or tasteful contemporary pieces. They have extras such as swing-mirror vanities and brass or wooden bedsteads. The breakfast room is appealing: Inspired by an Italian garden, it was designed by noted architect Paolo Portoghesi.

Via Vittorio Veneto 18, 00187 Roma. www.hotelalexandraroma.com. ✆ **06-4881943.** Fax 06-4871804. 60 units, some with shower only. 280€ double; 390€ junior suite. Rates include buffet breakfast. AE, DC, MC, V. Parking 26€–36€. Metro: Piazza Barberini. **Amenities:** Babysitting; room service; Wi-Fi (4€ per hr.). *In room:* A/C, TV, hair dryer, minibar.

MODERATE

Daphne Veneto ★ 🎁 In a restored building from the 19th century deep in the heart of Rome, this is a top-notch B&B, just minutes on foot from the Trevi Fountain. The midsize guest rooms have an understated elegance with crisp linens and fluffy comforters on the beds. The public rooms contain sitting areas, cozy reading sections, a lending library, and high-speed Internet access. Floors are reached by elevator, and two of the units are two-bedroom, two-bathroom suites. Fresh fruit and freshly baked pastries are served with your morning coffee.

Via di San Basilio 55, 00187 Roma. www.daphne-rome.com. ✆ **06-87450086.** Fax 06-233240967. 8 units. 140€–220€ double; 320€–460€ suite. Rates include buffet breakfast. AE, MC, V. Nearby parking 30€. Metro: Piazza Barberini. **Amenities:** Airport transfers (55€). *In room:* A/C, hair dryer, Wi-Fi (free).

La Residenza Hotel ★★ In a superb but congested location, this little hotel successfully combines intimacy and elegance. A bit old-fashioned and homey, the converted villa has an ivy-covered courtyard and a series of public rooms with Empire divans, oil portraits, and rattan chairs. Terraces are scattered throughout. The guest rooms are generally spacious, containing bentwood chairs and built-in furniture, including beds. The dozen or so junior suites boast balconies. The bathrooms have robes, and rooms even come equipped with ice machines.

Via Emilia 22–24, 00187 Roma. www.hotel-la-residenza.com. ✆ **06-4880789.** Fax 06-485721. 29 units. 160€–280€ double; 230€–380€ suite. Rates include buffet breakfast. AE, MC, V. Parking (limited) 20€. Metro: Piazza Barberini. **Amenities:** Bar; babysitting; room service. *In room:* A/C, TV, hair dryer, minibar.

Near Ancient Rome

EXPENSIVE

Capo d'Africa ★ 🎁 Installed in a beautiful 19th-century building and boasting a strong colonial look, this hotel lies in the heart of Imperial Rome between the Forum and the Domus Aurea in the Celio district of Rome, a few steps from the Colosseum. Endowed with a "contemporary classic" look, it attracts visitors with its sophisticated interior design, works of art, high-tech facilities, and impeccable service. Best of all is a splendid rooftop terrace with a panoramic view over some of the dusty ruins of the world's most famous monuments. Rooms are midsize and furnished with good taste; they are spread across three floors.

Via Capo d'Africa 54, 00184 Roma. www.hotelcapodafrica.com. ✆ **06-772801.** Fax 06-77280801. 65 units. 380€–400€ double; 480€–540€ suite. Rates include buffet breakfast. AE, DC, MC, V. Parking 45€. Metro: Colosseo. **Amenities:** Restaurant; bar; babysitting; exercise room; room service. *In room:* A/C, TV, hair dryer, minibar.

The Inn at the Roman Forum ★ 🎁 This is one of the secret discoveries of Rome, with the Roman Forum itself as a neighbor. A restored 15th-century building dripping with antiquity, the inn even has a small section of Trajan's Marketplace on-site. You enter the front doorway like a resident Roman, greeting your host in the living room. Sleek, classically styled bedrooms are spread across three upper floors, opening onto views of the heart of Rome. Three back bedrooms open onto a walled-in garden complete with fig and palm trees. The most elegant and expensive double has a private patio with a designer bathroom.

Via degli Ibernesi 30, 00185 Roma. www.theinnattheromanforum.com. ✆ **06-69190970.** Fax 06-45438802. 12 units. 210€–960€ double; from 1,040€ suite. Rates include buffet breakfast. AE, DC, MC, V. Parking 30€. Bus: 64 or 117. **Amenities:** Bar; airport transfers (55€); babysitting; concierge; room service. *In room:* A/C, TV/DVD, hair dryer, minibar, MP3 docking station, Wi-Fi (10€ per day).

MODERATE

Hotel Adriano This hotel is housed within the original walls of a 15th-century *palazzo,* and it's been converted into a well-run and government-rated three-star hotel to welcome guests and house them comfortably. The location is close to some of the major landmarks, including Piazza di Spagna, Piazza Navona, and the Pantheon, as well as lying a few steps from the Parliament. You can find a well-upholstered armchair waiting for you under the vaulted ceilings of the public rooms, perhaps facing a reproduction of a Titian nude. Rooms are decorated in shades of gray, taupe, and white. You can enjoy breakfast on the hotel's roof terrace.

Via di Pallacorda 2, 00186 Roma. www.hoteladriano.com. ✆ **06-68802451.** Fax 06-68803926. 80 units. 142€–297€ double; 337€–500€ suite. Rates include buffet breakfast. AE, DC, MC, V. Parking 30€. Bus: 95 or 175. **Amenities:** Bar; airport transfers (55€); babysitting; concierge; room service; Wi-Fi (5€ per 24 hr., in lobby). *In room:* A/C, TV, minibar.

INEXPENSIVE

Colosseum Hotel Two short blocks southwest of Santa Maria Maggiore, this hotel offers affordable and small but comfortable rooms. Someone with flair and lots of money designed the public areas and upper halls, which hint at baronial grandeur. The drawing room, with its long refectory table, white walls, red tiles, and armchairs, invites lingering. The guest rooms are furnished with well-chosen antique reproductions (beds of heavy carved wood, dark-paneled wardrobes, and leatherwood chairs); all have stark white walls, and some have old-fashioned plumbing in the bathrooms.

Via Sforza 10, 00184 Roma. www.hotelcolosseum.com. ✆ **06-4827228.** Fax 06-4827285. 50 units. 88€–230€ double; 108€–285€ triple. Rates include buffet breakfast. AE, DC, MC, V. Parking 30€. Metro: Cavour. **Amenities:** Bar; babysitting; bikes; room service. *In room:* A/C, TV, hair dryer, Wi-Fi (10€ per 24 hr.).

Hotel Arenula ★ At last a hotel has opened in Rome's old Jewish ghetto, and it's a winner and quite affordable. It takes its name from Via Arenula, that timeworn street linking Largo Argentina to Ponte Garibaldi and the Trastevere area. The restored building is from the 19th century, and the Patta family turned it into this undiscovered and comfortable inn. Close at hand are such attractions as the Pantheon, the Colosseum, and the Piazza Navona. Rooms are furnished in a tasteful, traditional way. They are most inviting and comfortable, with pale-wood pieces and immaculate bathrooms. There's no elevator, so be prepared to climb some stairs.

Via Santa Maria de Calderari 47, 00186 Roma. www.hotelarenula.com. ✆ **06-6879454.** Fax 06-6896188. 50 units. 100€–133€ double. Rates include buffet breakfast. AE, DC, MC, V. Metro: Colosseo. Bus: 40. **Amenities:** Room service. *In room:* A/C, TV, hair dryer.

Hotel Lancelot ★ Close to the Colosseum, this hotel opened in 1953 but has been much renovated and altered ever since. Run by the Khan family, the hotel has been accurately hailed by *National Geographic Traveler* as one of Rome's best hotel values. Rooms range from midsize to spacious; all doubles have showers, and the lone suite comes with a bathtub. Bedrooms are comfortable and individually decorated, and some open onto private terraces. All the rooms at this hotel are soundproof. A charming on-site restaurant serves Roman specialties.

Via Capo d'Africa 47, 00184 Roma. www.lancelothotel.com. ✆ **06-70450615.** Fax 06-70450640. 60 units. 175€–210€ double; 300€ suite. Rates include buffet breakfast. AE, DC, MC, V. Parking 10€. Metro: Colosseo. **Amenities:** Bar; babysitting. *In room:* A/C, TV, hair dryer, Wi-Fi (free).

Nicolas Inn Only 4 blocks from the Colosseum, this small B&B is also convenient for exploring the Roman Forum. In a warm, cozy atmosphere, a few guests are housed on the second floor of an early-20th-century building. Rich fabrics and cherry-colored wood make this hotel a winner, that and its comfortably furnished midsize to spacious bedrooms. A major asset of the inn is the personal attention provided for each guest. Guests find a complimentary map of Rome in their bedrooms.

Via Cavour 295, 00184 Roma. www.nicolasinn.com. ✆ **06-97618483.** 4 units. 100€–180€ double. Rates include continental breakfast. No credit cards. Parking 30€. Metro: Cavour. **Amenities:** Airport transfers (50€). *In room:* A/C, TV, fridge, hair dryer, Wi-Fi (free).

Near Campo De' Fiori

EXPENSIVE

Residenza Farnese ★ Among the boutique hotels springing up around Campo de' Fiori, the new Farnese in a 15th-century mansion emerges near the top. Opt for one of the front rooms overlooking Palazzo Farnese, with Michelangelo's Renaissance cornice bathed in sunlight. Bedrooms are fresh and modernized, ranging in size from small to spacious, each with a freshly restored private bathroom with a shower. The location in the heart of ancient Rome puts you within walking distance of many of the major sights, particularly the Roman Forum or even St. Peter's. The owner, Signora Zema, is a gracious host who can provide much helpful advice. She has placed contemporary art throughout as a grace note, and she believes in a generous breakfast to fortify you for the day.

Via del Mascherone 59, 00186 Roma. www.residenzafarneseroma.it. ✆ **06-68210980.** Fax 06-80321049. 31 units. 145€–300€ double; 230€–500€ junior suite. Rates include buffet breakfast. MC, V. Bus: 64. **Amenities:** Bar; room service. *In room:* A/C, TV, hair dryer, minibar, Wi-Fi (free).

MODERATE

Hotel Teatro di Pompeo Built atop the ruins of the Theater of Pompey, this small charmer lies near the spot where Julius Caesar met his end on the Ides of March. Intimate and refined, it's on a quiet piazza near the Palazzo Farnese and Campo de' Fiori. The rooms are decorated in an old-fashioned Italian style with hand-painted tiles, and the beamed ceilings date from the days of Michelangelo. The guest rooms range from small to medium in size, each with a tidy but cramped bathroom.

Largo del Pallaro 8, 00186 Roma. www.hotelteatrodipompeo.it. ✆ **06-68300170.** Fax 06-68805531. 13 units, shower only. 180€–210€ double; 240€–270€ triple. Rates include buffet breakfast. AE, DC, MC, V. Bus: 46, 62, or 64. **Amenities:** Bar; babysitting; room service; Wi-Fi (3€ per hr., in lobby). *In room:* A/C, TV, hair dryer, minibar.

Near Piazza Navona & the Pantheon

Travelers who want to immerse themselves in the atmosphere of ancient Rome, or those looking for romance, will prefer staying in this area over the more commercial Via Veneto area. Transportation isn't the greatest and you'll do a lot of walking, but that's the reason many visitors come here in the first place—to wander and discover the glory that was Rome. You're also within walking distance of the Vatican and the ruins of classical Rome. Many bars and cafes are within an easy walk of all the hotels located here.

VERY EXPENSIVE

Hotel Raphael ★★ With a glorious location adjacent to Piazza Navona, the Raphael is within easy walking distance of many sights. The ivy-covered facade invites you to enter the lobby, which is decorated with antiques that rival the cache in local museums (there's even a Picasso ceramics collection). The guest rooms (some quite small) were refurbished with a Florentine touch. Some of the suites have private terraces. The deluxe rooms, the executive units, and the junior suites were conceived by Richard Meier, the famous architect who has designed buildings all over the world. Each of them is lined with oak and equipped in a modern high-tech style that includes a digital sound system. The Raphael is often the top choice of Italian politicos in town for the opening of Parliament. We love its rooftop restaurant with views of all of the city's prominent landmarks.

Largo Febo 2, 00186 Roma. www.raphaelhotel.com. ✆ **06-682831.** Fax 06-6878993. 50 units. 272€–600€ double; 442€–900€ suite. AE, DC, MC, V. Parking 40€. Bus: 70, 81, 87, or 115. **Amenities:** Restaurant; bar; babysitting; concierge; exercise room; room service; sauna; Wi-Fi (free, in lobby). *In room:* A/C, TV/DVD, hair dryer, minibar.

EXPENSIVE

Albergo Del Sole al Pantheon ★ You're obviously paying for the million-dollar view, but you might find that it's worth it to be across from the Pantheon. This building was constructed in 1450 as a home, and the first records of it as a hostelry appeared in 1467, making it one of the world's oldest hotels. The layout is amazingly eccentric—prepare to walk up and down a lot of three- or four-step staircases. The guest rooms vary greatly in decor, much of it hit-or-miss, with compact, tiled full bathrooms. The rooms opening onto the piazza still tend to be noisy at all hours. The quieter rooms overlook the courtyard, but we always prefer to put up with the noise just to enjoy one of the world's greatest views. For the grandest view of the Pantheon, ask for room no. 106 or 108.

Piazza della Rotonda 63, 00186 Roma. www.hotelsolealpantheon.com. ✆ **06-6780441.** Fax 06-69940689. 30 units. Summer 380€–500€ double, 530€–800€ suite; off season 230€–276€ double, from 372€ suite. Rates include buffet breakfast. AE, DC, MC, V. Bus: 64. **Amenities:** Bar; babysitting; Jacuzzi; room service. *In room:* A/C, TV, hair dryer, minibar.

MODERATE

Albergo Santa Chiara This is a family-run hotel near the Pantheon in the very inner core of historic Rome. Since 1838, the Corteggiani family has been welcoming sightseers to classic Rome. The white walls and marble columns here speak of former elegance, although the rooms today are simply furnished, functional, yet comfortable. The size? They range from the size of a broom closet to a suite large enough to be classified as a small Roman apartment. We go for those units facing the Piazza della Minerva, although you'll often have to listen to late-night revelers who don't know when to go home.

Via Santa Chiara 21, 00186 Roma. www.albergosantachiara.com. ✆ **06-6872979.** Fax 06-6873144. 96 units, half with shower only. 250€–310€ double; 460€–550€ suite. Rates include buffet breakfast. AE, DC, MC, V. Metro: Piazza di Spagna. **Amenities:** Bar; babysitting; room service. *In room:* A/C, TV, hair dryer, minibar.

Near Piazza Del Popolo & the Spanish Steps

This is a great place to stay if you're a serious shopper, but expect to part with a lot of extra euros for the privilege. This is a more elegant area than the Via Veneto—think Fifth Avenue all the way.

VERY EXPENSIVE

The Hassler ★★ The Westin Excelsior is a grander palace, and the Eden and the de Russie are more up-to-date, but the Hassler has something that no other hotel can boast—a coveted location at the top of the Spanish Steps. The Hassler, rebuilt in 1944 to replace the 1885 original, is not quite what it used to be. But because it's such a classic, and because of that incredible location, it gets away with charging astronomical rates. The lounges and the guest rooms, with their "Italian Park Avenue" trappings, strike a faded, if still glamorous, 1930s note. The guest rooms range from small singles to some of the most spacious suites in town. High ceilings make them appear larger than they are, and many of them open onto private balconies or terraces. The front rooms, dramatically overlooking the Spanish Steps, are often noisy at night, but the views are worth it.

Piazza Trinità dei Monti 6, 00187 Roma. www.hotelhasslerroma.com. ✆ **800/223-6800** in the U.S., or 06-699340. Fax 06-69941607. 95 units. 490€–780€ double; from 1,500€ suite. AE, DC, MC, V. Parking 30€. Metro: Piazza di Spagna. **Amenities:** 2 restaurants, including Imàgo (review, p. 137); bar; airport transfers (100€); babysitting; bikes; concierge; exercise room; room service; spa. *In room:* A/C, TV/DVD, hair dryer, minibar, Wi-Fi (20€ per 24 hr.).

Hotel Art by the Spanish Steps ★★ This discovery lies near the Spanish Steps on "the street of artists," as Via Margutta is called. A former college has been turned into a hotel in a modern, minimalist style. Of particular interest is the Hall. The lobby, once a chapel, sits under a frescoed vaulted ceiling, where works of contemporary artists abound. The corridors of the four floors housing the rooms are decorated in blue, orange, yellow, and green. Forming a border for the corridors are stretches of milky glass with verses from poets such as Federico García Lorca. High-tech furnishings and bright colors adorn the bedrooms, which make good use of wood and Florentine leather. The rooms also feature glass, metal, and mosaic tiles that pick up the colors of the corridor.

Via Margutta 56, 00187 Roma. www.hotelartrome.com. ✆ **06-328711.** Fax 06-36003995. 46 units. 250€–350€ double; from 500€ suite. AE, DC, MC, V. Parking 25€. Metro: Piazza di Spagna. **Amenities:** Bar; babysitting; bikes; exercise room; room service; sauna. *In room:* A/C, TV, minibar.

Hotel de Russie ★★★ ☺ This government-rated five-star hotel has raised the bar for every other hotel in the city. For service, style, and modern luxuries, it beats out the Eden, the Westin Excelsior, and the St. Regis Grand. Just off the Piazza del Popolo, it reopened in 2000 to media acclaim for its opulent furnishings and choice location. Public areas are glossy and contemporary. About 30% of the bedrooms are conservative, with traditional furniture, while the remaining 70% are more minimalist, with a stark and striking style.

Via del Babuino 9, 00187 Roma. www.hotelderussie.it. ✆ **888/667-9477** in North America, or 06-328881. Fax 06-3288888. 122 units. 680€–960€ double; from 1,430€ suite. AE, DC, MC, V. Parking 55€. Metro: Flaminia. **Amenities:** Restaurant; bar; airport transfers (85€); babysitting; children's programs; concierge; exercise room; room service; spa. *In room:* A/C, TV, fax, hair dryer, minibar, Wi-Fi (20€ per 24 hr.).

Hotel d'Inghilterra ★★ The Inghilterra holds on to its traditions and heritage, even though it has been renovated. Situated between Via Condotti and Via Borgogna, this hotel was the guesthouse of the 17th-century Torlonia princes. If you're willing to spend a king's ransom, Rome's most fashionable small hotel is comparable to the Hassler and the InterContinental. The rooms have mostly old pieces (gilt and lots of marble, mahogany chests, and glittery mirrors) complemented by modern conveniences. The preferred rooms are higher up, opening onto a tile terrace, with a balustrade and a railing covered with flowering vines and plants.

Via Bocca di Leone 14, 00187 Roma. http://hoteldinghilterra.warwickhotels.com. ✆ **06-699811.** Fax 06-69922243. 89 units. Summer 320€–580€ double, from 945€ suite; off season 225€–348€ double, from 630€ suite. AE, DC, MC, V. Parking 25€. Metro: Piazza di Spagna. **Amenities:** Restaurant, Café Romano (review, p. 139); bar; babysitting; room service. *In room:* A/C, TV/DVD, hair dryer, minibar.

The Inn at the Spanish Steps ★★★ This intimate, upscale inn was the first new hotel to open in this location in years. The people who run Rome's most famous cafe, Caffè Greco, created it where Hans Christian Andersen once lived.

Andersen praised the balcony roses and violets, and so can you. Every room is furnished in an authentic period decor, featuring antiques, elegant draperies, and parquet floors. The superior units come with a fireplace, a frescoed or beamed ceiling, and a balcony. The hotel is completely modern, from its hypoallergenic mattresses to its generous wardrobe space.

Via dei Condotti 85, 00187 Roma. www.atspanishsteps.com. ✆ **06-69925657.** Fax 06-6786470. 24 units. 230€–720€ double; from 680€ suite. Rates include buffet breakfast. AE, DC, MC, V. Metro: Piazza di Spagna. **Amenities:** Bar; babysitting; airport transfers (55€); concierge; room service. *In room:* A/C, TV, hair dryer, kitchenette (in some), minibar, MP3 docking station (in some).

Portrait Suites ★★ For those who don't want to stay at the Hassler but prefer the luxury of an intimate and deluxe boutique hotel, this all-suite inn is the answer. This six-story historic building is decorated in an elegant contemporary style, including walls lined with photographs and drawings by Salvatore Ferragamo. All accommodations are spacious, with such features as large marble bathrooms. On top of the building is a terrace opening onto a panoramic sweep of Rome.

Via Bocca di Leone 23, 00187 Roma. www.lungarnohotels.com. ✆ **06-69380742.** Fax 06-69190625. 14 units. 390€–780€ double; 680€–2,300€ suite. Rates include buffet breakfast. AE, DC, MC, V. Parking 25€. Metro: Piazza di Spagna. **Amenities:** Bar; babysitting; room service. *In room:* A/C, TV, hair dryer, kitchenette, minibar, Wi-Fi (free).

Villa Spalletti Trivelli ★★★ 🎁 On a side street on patrician Quirina Hill, this gem of a hotel offers a rare opportunity to experience home life as lived by a Roman nobleman and his family a century ago, in this case the Spalletti-Trivelli family, titled since 1667. A $4-million renovation has turned the early-20th-century neoclassical villa into a sumptuous address furnished with antiques, tapestries, and Italian art. Just steps from the Piazza del Quirinale and only a 5-minute walk from the Trevi Fountain, the villa opens onto a splendid Italian garden. The spacious bedrooms range from romantically decorated units to grand deluxe suites fit for a visiting president.

Via Piacenza 4, 00184 Roma. www.villaspalletti.it. ✆ **06-48907934.** Fax 06-4871409. 12 units. 360€–627€ double; from 770€ suite. AE, DC, MC, V. Metro: Barberini. **Amenities:** Restaurant; bar; exercise room; room service; sauna. *In room:* A/C, TV, minibar, Wi-Fi (free).

EXPENSIVE

Babuino 181 ★★ 🎁 Rome's newest boutique hotel is a welcome addition, especially to those who want to avoid cramped accommodations. The location is bull's-eye in the historic center a short stroll to the Piazza del Popolo, the Spanish Steps, art galleries, and smart cafes. Though Via del Babuino positively vibrates during the day, it settles down in the evening. The owners, the little hotel group Alberto Moncada di Paternò, specialize in transforming historical residences by filling them inside with modern art and design. Special touches include Frette linens and bathrobes, a Nespresso machine, and a wall-mounted flatscreen TV. Bathrooms are clad in yellow marble, with toilets and a bidet in a separate little room. Bedrooms are spacious and furnished in a sleek contemporary style with muted gray and beiges.

Via del Babuino 181, 00187 Roma. www.romeluxurysuites.com/babuino. ✆ **06/3229-5295.** 14 units. 305€–435€ double; 430€–700€ suite. AE, DC, MC, V. Metro: Flaminio. **Amenities:** Bar; airport transfers (65€); babysitting; concierge; room service. *In room:* A/C, TV, hair dryer, minibar, MP3 docking station, Wi-Fi (free).

Hotel Locarno If you'd like to experience Rome as visitors such as Mary Pickford and Douglas Fairbanks did in the 1920s, head for this monument to Art Deco. In the heart of Rome, near Piazza del Popolo, this hotel opened its doors in 1925 and it's been receiving visitors ever since, even through a world war. In fair weather, breakfast is served in the garden or on the roof garden; this is an experience worth savoring. Bedrooms in the older section are a bit chintzy, but the newer wing has fresher accommodations. All of the original floors, doors, and bathroom fixtures in this newer section were recently refurbished. Rooms are reached by taking a bird-cage elevator.

Via della Penna 22, 00186 Roma. www.hotellocarno.com. ✆ **06-3610841.** Fax 06-3215249. 66 units. 270€–465€ double; 395€–1,200€ suite. Rates include buffet breakfast. AE, DC, MC, V. Parking 25€. Metro: Flaminio. Bus: 116 or 117. **Amenities:** Bar; airport transfers (55€); bikes; room service. *In room:* A/C, TV, minibar, Wi-Fi (free).

Hotel Scalinata di Spagna ★★★ This is Rome's most famous boutique hotel. The deluxe Hassler is across the street but far removed in price and grandeur from this intimate, upscale B&B at the top of the Spanish Steps. Its delightful little building—only two floors are visible from the outside—is nestled between much larger structures, with four relief columns across the facade and window boxes with bright blossoms. The recently redecorated interior features small public rooms with bright print slipcovers, old clocks, and low ceilings. The decor varies radically from one guest room to the next. Some have low beamed ceilings and ancient-looking wood furniture; others have loftier ceilings and more run-of-the-mill furniture.

Piazza Trinità dei Monti 17, 00187 Roma. www.hotelscalinata.com. ✆ **06-69940896,** or booking 06-6793006. Fax 06-69940598. 16 units, tubs only. 130€–290€ double; 230€–350€ junior suite. Rates include buffet breakfast. AE, MC, V. Parking 40€. Metro: Piazza di Spagna. **Amenities:** Bar; airport transfers (75€); babysitting; room service. *In room:* A/C, TV, hair dryer, minibar, Wi-Fi (free).

La Lumière di Piazza di Spagna ★ We never thought another little inn would open near the Spanish Steps because real estate was no longer available. Wrong. Along comes this charmer in a five-story 18th-century building of great character (with an elevator). Rooms are spacious and exquisitely furnished in a classic style, with a panoramic view of the Spanish Steps. All of them have adjoining bathrooms with Jacuzzi spa showers. When you're served a breakfast buffet on the terrace, the sights of the city of Rome are at your feet. Outside your door you'll find the best and most exclusive shops in Rome.

Via Belsiana 72, 00187 Roma. www.lalumieredipiazzadispagna.com. ✆ **06-69380806.** Fax 06-69294231. 10 units. 120€–350€ double; 150€–410€ triple. Rates include buffet breakfast. AE, DC, MC, V. Parking 30€. **Amenities:** Airport transfers (65€); room service. *In room:* A/C, TV, hair dryer, minibar, Wi-Fi (free).

Piranesi ★★ Right off the Piazza del Popolo sits one of Rome's most select boutique hotels, boasting more affordable prices than you'll find at the Hotel de Russie, which fronts it. If you lodge here, you'll be staying in one of the most historic areas of Rome. Bedrooms are tranquil and decorated in a style evocative of the 18th-century Directoire. Bare pinewood floors and cherrywood furniture are grace notes, as are the immaculate bathrooms. The most dramatic aspect of the Piranesi is its panoramic rooftop terrace.

Via del Babuino 196, 00187 Roma. www.hotelpiranesi.com. ✆ **06-328041.** Fax 06-3610597. 32 units. 220€–350€ double; 298€–420€ suite. Rates include buffet breakfast. AE, MC, V. Parking

40€. Metro: Flaminio. Bus: 117. **Amenities:** Bar; exercise room; room service; sauna; Wi-Fi (12€ per 24 hr.) *In room:* A/C, TV, hair dryer, minibar.

MODERATE

Casa Howard ★ It's rare to make a discovery in the tourist-trodden Piazza di Spagna area. That's why Casa Howard comes as a pleasant surprise. The B&B occupies about two-thirds of the second floor of a historic structure. The welcoming family owners maintain beautifully furnished guest rooms, each with its own private bathroom (although some bathrooms lie outside the bedrooms in the hallway). The Green Room is the most spacious, with its own en suite bathroom.

Via Capo le Case 18, 00187 Roma. www.casahoward.com. ✆ **06-69924555.** Fax 06-6794644. 5 units. 170€–250€ double. MC, V. Parking 25€. Metro: Piazza di Spagna. **Amenities:** Babysitting; room service; sauna. *In room:* A/C, TV, hair dryer, Wi-Fi (free).

Fontanella Borghese ★ Close to the Spanish Steps in the exact heart of Rome, this hotel surprisingly remains relatively undiscovered. Much renovated and improved, it has been installed on the third and fourth floors of a palace dating from the end of the 18th century. The building once belonged to the princes of the Borghese family, and the little hotel looks out onto the Borghese Palace. It lies within walking distance of the Trevi Fountain, the Pantheon, and the Piazza Navona. The location is also close to Piazza Augusto and the Ara Pacis. In the midsize bedrooms, plain wooden furniture rests on parquet floors, and everything is in a classical tradition comfortably modernized for today's travelers. Half of the bathrooms come with tubs, the rest with showers. The staff of the front desk is one of the most helpful in central Rome.

Largo Fontanella Borghese 84, 00186 Roma. www.fontanellaborghese.com. ✆ **06 68809-504.** Fax 06-6861295. 29 units, half with shower only. 160€–230€ double; 230€–280€ triple. AE, DC, MC, V. Nearby parking 25€. Metro: Piazza di Spagna. **Amenities:** Room service. *In room:* A/C, TV, hair dryer, minibar.

Hotel Condotti The Condotti is small, choice, and terrific for shoppers intent on being near the tony boutiques. The born-to-shop crowd often thinks that the hotel is on Via Condotti because of its name—actually, it's 2 blocks to the north. The staff, nearly all of whom speak English, is cooperative and hardworking. The mostly modern rooms might not have much historical charm (they're furnished like nice motel units), but they're comfortable and soothing. Each room is decorated with traditional furnishings, including excellent beds (usually twins). Room no. 414 has a geranium-filled terrace.

Via Mario de' Fiori 37, 00187 Roma. www.hotelcondotti.com. ✆ **06-6794661.** Fax 06-6790457. 26 units, shower only. 94€–360€ double; 124€–390€ triple. Rates include buffet breakfast. AE, DC, MC, V. Parking 20€. Metro: Piazza di Spagna. **Amenities:** Airport transfers (60€); babysitting; bikes; room service. *In room:* A/C, TV, hair dryer, minibar, Wi-Fi (free).

Hotel Piazza di Spagna About a block from the downhill side of the Spanish Steps, this hotel is small but classic, with an inviting atmosphere made more gracious by the helpful manager, Elisabetta Giocondi. The guest rooms boast a functional streamlined decor; some even have Jacuzzis in the tiled bathrooms. Accommodations are spread across three floors, with very tidy bedrooms with high ceilings and cool terrazzo floors.

Via Mario de' Fiori 61, 00187 Roma. www.hotelpiazzadispagna.it. ✆ **06-6796412.** Fax 06-6790654. 17 units, some with shower only. 120€–250€ double; 160€–350€ triple. Rates include buffet breakfast. AE, DC, MC, V. Nearby parking 25€. Metro: Piazza di Spagna. Bus: 117. **Amenities:** Bar; airport transfers (65€); Internet (10€ per 24 hr., in lobby); room service. *In room:* A/C, TV, hair dryer, minibar.

Hotel Trinità dei Monti Between two of the most bustling piazzas in Rome (Barberini and Spagna), this is a friendly and well-maintained place. The hotel occupies the second and third floors of an antique building. Its guest rooms come with herringbone-pattern parquet floors and big windows, and are comfortable, if not flashy. Each has a tidy tiled bathroom. The hotel's social center is a simple coffee bar near the reception desk. Don't expect anything terribly fancy, but the welcome is warm and the location is ultraconvenient.

Via Sistina 91, 00187 Roma. www.hoteltrinitadeimonti.com. ✆ **06-6797206.** Fax 06-6990111. 24 units. 114€–220€ double; 150€–250€ triple. Rates include buffet breakfast. AE, DC, MC, V. Parking 35€. Metro: Barberini or Piazza di Spagna. **Amenities:** Bar; babysitting; room service. *In room:* A/C, TV, hair dryer, minibar, Wi-Fi (10€ per 24 hr.).

INEXPENSIVE

Hotel Panda This small hotel occupies two floors of a restored 19th-century building only 50m (160 ft.) from the Spanish Steps. Bedrooms are simply but adequately furnished, resting (for the most part) under vaulted wood-beamed ceilings on stone tiled floors. Some of the accommodations have 19th-century frescoes; others have hand-painted tiles in the bathrooms. This is one of the oldest hotels in the historical center of Rome, attracting patrons with its economical prices and its family-like atmosphere. Air-conditioning carries a daily supplement of 6€.

Via della Croce 35, 00187 Roma. www.hotelpanda.it. ✆ **06-6780179.** Fax 06-69942151. 20 units, 8 with bathroom. 78€ double without bathroom; 108€ double with bathroom; 140€ triple with bathroom. AE, MC, V. Parking 30€. Metro: Piazza di Spagna. *In room:* A/C on request (6€ per day), Wi-Fi (free).

Hotel Parlamento The hard-to-find Parlamento has a two-star government rating and moderate prices. Expect a friendly *pensione*-style reception. The furnishings are antiques or reproductions, and carved wood or wrought-iron headboards back the firm beds. The bathrooms were recently redone with heated towel racks, phones, and (in a few) even marble sinks. Rooms are different in style; the best are no. 82, with its original 1800s furniture, and nos. 104, 106, and 107, which open onto the roof garden. You can enjoy the chandeliered and *trompe l'oeil* breakfast room, or carry your cappuccino up to the small roof terrace with its view of San Silvestro's bell tower.

Via delle Convertite 5 (at the intersection with Via del Corso), 00187 Roma. www.hotelparlamento.it. ✆/fax **06-69921000.** 23 units. 90€–195€ double; 110€–205€ triple. Rates include buffet breakfast. AE, DC, MC, V. Parking 30€. Metro: Piazza di Spagna. **Amenities:** Bar; concierge; room service. *In room:* A/C on request (12€ per day), TV, hair dryer.

San Carlo Prices are surprisingly low for a building only 5 minutes on foot from the Spanish Steps and adjacent to the via Condotti with some of the best luxury shops and boutiques in Rome. The structure itself was meticulously renovated from a 19th-century mansion. Accommodations are spread across four floors. Equally desirable rooms lie in an annex with beamed ceilings, terra-cotta floors, and the occasional fresco. Accommodations are available as a single, double, triple, or quad. Superior rooms open onto a private terrace covered with an awning and containing outdoor furniture. Many of the bathrooms are clad in marble.

Via delle Carrozze 92/93, 00187 Roma. www.hotelsancarloroma.com. ✆ **06-6784548.** Fax 06-69941197. 50 units. 125€–210€ double. Rates include buffet breakfast. AE, DC, MC, V. Parking 30€. Metro: Piazza di Spagna. **Amenities:** Bar; babysitting; concierge; room service. *In room:* A/C, TV, minibar, Wi-Fi (in some; free).

Near Vatican City

For most visitors, this is a rather dull area to base yourself. It's well removed from the ancient sites, and not a great restaurant neighborhood. But if the main purpose of your visit centers on the Vatican, you'll be fine here, and you'll be joined by thousands of other pilgrims, nuns, and priests.

VERY EXPENSIVE

Visconti Palace Hotel ★★ Completely restructured and redesigned, this palatial hotel is graced with one of the most avant-garde contemporary designs in town. Stunningly modern, it uses color perhaps with more sophistication than any other hotel. The location is idyllic, lying in the Prati district between Piazza di Spagna and St. Peter's. The rooms and corridors are decorated with modern art, the bathrooms are in marble, and there are many floor-to-ceiling windows and private terraces. Taste and an understated elegance prevail in this bright, welcoming, and functional atmosphere.

Via Federico Cesi 37, 00193 Roma. www.viscontipalace.com. ✆ **06-3684.** Fax 06-3200551. 242 units. 350€–380€ double; 450€ junior suite; 650€ suite. AE, DC, MC, V. Parking 35€. Metro: Ottaviano. Bus: 30, 70, or 913. **Amenities:** Bar; exercise room; room service; Wi-Fi (7€ per hr) *In room:* A/C, TV, hair dryer, minibar.

EXPENSIVE

Hotel dei Consoli ★ 🎁 This rather elegant hotel in the Prati district is just a short stroll from the Vatican Museums. The hotel occupies three floors in a building restored in the imperial style, with cornices and columns. Stained glass and fine art create an inviting ambience. All of the bedrooms are handsomely furnished and decorated, but deluxe units have whirlpool tubs, as do the junior suites. Draperies and bedding are in elegant silks, and the bathrooms are adorned with the finest porcelain. A roof terrace with a panoramic view crowns the building.

Via Varrone 2 D, 00193 Roma. www.hoteldeiconsoli.com. ✆ **06-68892972.** Fax 06-68212274. 28 units. 280€–320€ double; from 360€ triple. Rates include buffet breakfast. AE, DC, MC, V. Parking 28€–33€. Metro: Ottaviano–San Pietro. **Amenities:** Bar; room service. *In room:* A/C, TV, minibar, Wi-Fi (15€ per 24 hr)

Hotel dei Mellini ★ On the right bank of the Tiber, this government-rated four-star hotel lies between St. Peter's Basilica and the Spanish Steps. There is much refined elegance here, and the public rooms evoke the setting of a privately owned manor house yet in the heart of Rome. Guest rooms are spacious and have a classic Art Deco styling in their choice of furnishings and fixtures. The roof terrace opens onto panoramic views.

Via Muzio Clementi 81, 00193 Roma. www.hotelmellini.com. ✆ **06-324771.** Fax 06-32477801. 80 units. 180€–295€ double; from 250€ suite. Rates include buffet breakfast. AE, DC, MC, V. Parking 30€. Metro: Lepanto. **Amenities:** Restaurant; bar; room service; Wi-Fi (25€ per 24 hr., in lobby). *In room:* A/C, TV, hair dryer, minibar.

Residenza Paolo VI ★★ 🎁 On the premises of a former monastery, this hotel opened in 2000. With its marvelous panorama of St. Peter's Square, it offers one of the great views in Rome. One reader wrote, "I felt I was at the gates of heaven sitting on the most beautiful square in the Western world." The hotel is filled with beautifully decorated and comfortable bedrooms, with modern bathrooms with tubs and showers in the junior suites, and showers only in the regular doubles. In spite of its reasonable prices, the inn is like a small luxury hotel.

Via Paolo VI 29, 00193 Roma. www.residenzapaolovi.com. ✆ **06-684870.** Fax 06-6867428. 35 units, some with shower only. 149€–367€ double; from 479€ junior suite. Rates include American buffet breakfast. AE, DC, MC, V. Metro: Ottaviano. Bus: 64, 91, or 916. **Amenities:** Bar; babysitting; room service. *In room:* A/C, TV, hair dryer, minibar, Wi-Fi (free).

MODERATE/INEXPENSIVE

Hotel Sant'Angelo This hotel, off Piazza Cavour (northeast of the Castel Sant'Angelo) and a 10-minute walk from St. Peter's, is in a relatively untouristy area. Operated by the Torre family, it occupies the second and third floors of an imposing 200-year-old building. The rooms are simple, modern, and clean, with wooden furniture and views of the street or a bleak but quiet courtyard. Rooms are small but not cramped, each with a comfortable bed, plus a tiled bathroom.

Via Marianna Dionigi 16, 00193 Roma. www.hotelsa.it. ✆ **06-3242000.** Fax 06-3204451. 31 units, shower only. 90€–300€ double; 120€–460€ triple. Rates include buffet breakfast. AE, DC, MC, V. Parking 25€–30€. Metro: Piazza di Spagna. **Amenities:** Bar; airport transfers (54€); babysitting; room service. *In room:* A/C, TV, hair dryer.

Il Gattopardo Relais Close to St. Peter's and the Vatican Museums, this family-run *pensione* is located in an elegantly restored building from the 19th century. In the historic Prati district, the Art Nouveau building is decorated in a romantic style with individually designed and soundproof rooms. Locals refer to it as a *hotel de charme*. A collection of antiques, tapestries, and Italian art is scattered throughout.

Viale Giulio Cesare 94, 00192 Roma. www.ilgattopardorelais.it. ✆ **06-37358480.** Fax 06-37501019. 6 units. 110€–220€ double; 150€–250€ triple; 130€–250€ junior suite. Rates include buffet breakfast. AE, DC, MC, V. Metro: Ottaviano. **Amenities:** Bar. *In room:* A/C, TV.

Villa Laetitia ★★★ Anna Fendi, of the fashion dynasty, has opened this stylish and superchic haven of elegance along the Tiber. With its private gardens, this Art Nouveau mansion lies between the Piazza del Popolo and the Prati quarter. The bedrooms are virtual works of art and are decorated with antique tiles gathered by Fendi on her world travels along with other objets d'art. For the smart, trendy, and well-heeled traveler, this is a choice address. Many of the rooms contain well-equipped kitchenettes. Accommodations are like small studios with terraces or gardens. Each rental unit has a different design and personality. Artists and designers in particular are attracted to this intimate, personalized hotel.

Lungotevere delle Armi 22–23, 00195 Roma. www.villalaetitia.com. ✆ **06-3226776.** Fax 06-3232720. 15 units. 190€–220€ double; 270€–350€ suite. AE, DC, MC, V. Metro: Lepanto. **Amenities:** Bar; airport transfers (55€); babysitting; room service; spa; Wi-Fi (free, in lobby). *In room:* A/C, TV/DVD, hair dryer, minibar.

In Trastevere

EXPENSIVE

Hotel Ponte Sisto ★ Steps from the River Tiber, this hotel lies on the most exclusive residential street in historic Rome at the gateway to Trastevere. The hotel is imbued with a bright, fresh look that contrasts with some of the timeworn buildings surrounding it. Windows look out on the core of Renaissance and baroque Rome. This 18th-century structure has been totally renovated with class and elegance. If you can live in the small bedrooms (the singles are really cramped), you'll enjoy this choice address with its cherrywood furnishings. Try for one of the upper-floor rooms for a better view; some come with their own terrace.

Via dei Pettinari 64, 00186 Roma. www.hotelpontesisto.it. ✆ **06-6863100.** Fax 06-68301712. 103 units. 200€–320€ double; 450€–550€ suite. Rates include buffet breakfast. AE, DC, MC, V. Parking 26€. Tram: 8. **Amenities:** Airport transfers (55€); concierge; room service. *In room:* A/C, TV, hair dryer, minibar.

Ripa Hotel ★ This government-rated four-star hotel provides an unusual opportunity to stay across the Tiber in Trastevere, one of the oldest districts of Rome. The neighborhood may be historic, but the structure itself dates from 1973, although it's been completely restored since that time. The building is in concrete and glass, with a lobby of wooden and marble floors, filled with 1970s-style armchairs. The midsize to large bedrooms are furnished in minimalist modern. The members of the Roscioli family, the owners, imbue both the public and private rooms of the hotel with a very contemporary look.

Via degli Orti di Trastevere 3, 00153 Roma. www.ripahotel.com. ✆ **06-58611.** Fax 06-5882523. 170 units. 130€–240€ double; 260€–440€ suite. Rates include buffet breakfast. AE, DC, MC, V. Parking 18€. Bus: H. **Amenities:** Restaurant; bar; babysitting; concierge; exercise room; room service. *In room:* A/C, TV, hair dryer, minibar, Wi-Fi (15€ per 24 hr.).

INEXPENSIVE

Hotel Cisterna Well into its second decade, this hotel is just being discovered. It lies in a restored 18th-century palace in the colorful and evocative neighborhood of Trastevere. The prices and the very aura of the district are untouristy, which is what an increasing number of discerning visitors are seeking. It's a well-run little hotel with decent prices. Most bedrooms are midsize; they are not overly decorated but are comfortably furnished. The furnishings, though simple, are classic in style.

Via della Cisterna 8, 00153 Roma. www.cisternahotel.it. ✆ **06-5817212.** Fax 06-5810091. 20 units. 140€ double; 165€ triple. Rates include buffet breakfast. AE, DC, MC, V. Bus: H. Closed Aug. **Amenities:** Room service. *In room:* A/C, TV, minibar, Wi-Fi (free).

Trastevere Manara ★ Manara opened its restored doors in 1998 to meet the demand for accommodations in Trastevere. This little gem has fresh, bright bedrooms with immaculate tiles. All of the bathrooms, which also have been renovated and contain showers, are small. The price is hard to beat for those who want to stay in one of the most atmospheric sections of Rome. Most of the rooms open onto the lively Piazza San Cosimato, and all of them have comfortable, albeit functional, furnishings. Breakfast is the only meal served, but many good restaurants lie just minutes away.

Via L. Manara 24a–25, 00153 Roma. www.hoteltrastevere.net. ✆ **06-5814713.** Fax 06-5881016. 18 units. 103€–105€ double. Rates include buffet breakfast. AE, DC, MC, V. Bus: H. Tram: 8. **Amenities:** Airport transfers 52€. *In room:* A/C, TV, hair dryer.

In Parioli

VERY EXPENSIVE

The Duke Hotel Roma ★★ This boutique hotel has burst into a renewed life, as celebrities are once again staying here. The Duke is nestled between the parks of Villa Borghese and Villa Glori. A free limo service links the hotel to the

Via Veneto. The elegant bedrooms and superior suites are distributed across six floors, with many opening onto private balconies. All the accommodations are different in size and shape. The interior design combines a classical Italian bourgeois style with the warmth of an English gentleman's club.

Via Archimede 69, 00197 Roma. www.thedukehotel.com. ✆ **800/223-5652** in the U.S. and Canada, or 06-367221. Fax 06-36004104. 78 units. 410€–515€ double; 920€–1,385€ suite. Rates include buffet breakfast. AE, DC, MC, V. Parking 25€. Metro: Piazza Euclide. **Amenities:** Restaurant; bar; airport transfers (65€); room service. *In room:* A/C, TV, hair dryer, minibar, Wi-Fi (6.50€ per hr.).

In Monte Mario

VERY EXPENSIVE

Cavalieri Hilton ★★ ☺ If you want resort-style accommodations and don't mind staying a 15-minute drive from the center of Rome (the hotel offers frequent, free shuttle service), consider the Hilton. With its pools and array of facilities, Cavalieri Hilton overlooks Rome and the Alban Hills from atop Monte Mario. It's set among 6 hectares (15 acres) of trees, flowering shrubs, and stonework. The guest rooms and suites, many with panoramic views, are contemporary and stylish. Soft furnishings in pastels are paired with Italian furniture in warm-toned woods, including beds with deluxe linen. Each unit has a spacious balcony.

Via Cadlolo 101, 00136 Roma. www.romecavalieri.com. ✆ **800/445-8667** in the U.S. and Canada, or 06-35091. Fax 06-35092241. 372 units. 310€–800€ double; from 650€ suite. AE, DC, DISC, MC, V. Parking 30€. **Amenities:** 2 restaurants; 3 bars; airport transfers (90€–380€); babysitting; concierge; exercise room; 2 pools (including 1 heated indoor pool); room service; spa; 2 outdoor tennis courts (lit). *In room:* A/C, TV/DVD, CD player (in suites), hair dryer, minibar, Wi-Fi (12€ per hr.).

At the Airport

Cancelli Rossi If you're nervous about making your flight, you could book into this very simple motel-style place, located 2.5km (1½ miles) from the airport. Two floors are served by an elevator, and the decor is minimal. Rooms range from small to medium and are functionally furnished but reasonably comfortable, with good beds and tiled bathrooms. The atmosphere is a bit antiseptic, but this place is geared more for business travelers than vacationers. A restaurant in an annex nearby serves Italian and international food.

Via Portuense 2443, 00054 Fiumicino. www.cancellirossi.it. ✆ **06-6507221.** Fax 06-65049168. 50 units. 113€–150€ double. Rates include buffet breakfast. AE, DC, DISC, MC, V. Free parking. **Amenities:** Restaurant; bar; airport shuttle (Mon–Sat 7–9:45am and 5:15–8:55pm every 20 min. 6€); babysitting; exercise room; room service. *In room:* A/C, TV, hair dryer, minibar.

Hilton Rome Airport Only 200m (656 ft.) from the air terminal, this first-class hotel is the closest to FCO. The Hilton doesn't pretend to be more than it is—a bedroom factory at the airport. Follow the broad hallways to one of the midsize to spacious "crash pads," each with deep carpeting, generous storage space, and large, full bathrooms. The best units are the executive suites with extra amenities such as separate check-in, trouser press, and voice mail.

Via Arturo Ferrarin 2, 00050 Fiumicino. www.hilton.com. ✆ **800/445-8667** in the U.S. and Canada, or 06-65258. Fax 06-65256525. 517 units. 170€–380€ double; 330€–455€ suite. AE, DC, MC, V. Parking 25€. Metro: Fiumicino Aeroporto. **Amenities:** 2 restaurants; bar; babysitting; children's center; exercise room; indoor pool (heated in winter); room service; sauna. *In room:* A/C, TV, hair dryer, minibar, Wi-Fi (27€ per 24 hr.).

SIDE TRIPS FROM ROME: TIVOLI, OSTIA ANTICA & MORE

Tivoli & the Villas

Tivoli, known as Tibur to the ancient Romans, is 32km (20 miles) east of Rome on Via Tiburtina, about an hour's drive with traffic. If you don't have a car, take Metro Line B to the end of the line, the Rebibbia station. After exiting the station, board a Cotral bus for the trip the rest of the way to Tivoli. Cotral buses to Tivoli depart from both Rebibbia and Ponte Mammolo Metro station (Line B). Generally, buses depart about every 20 minutes during the day.

EXPLORING THE VILLAS

Hadrian's Villa (Villa Adriana) ★★★ In the 2nd century A.D., the globe-trotting Hadrian spent the last 3 years of his life in the grandest style. Less than 6km (3¾ miles) from Tivoli, he built one of the greatest estates ever erected, and he filled acre after acre with some of the architectural wonders he'd seen on his many travels. Perhaps as a preview of what he envisioned in store for himself, the emperor even created a representation of Hades. Hadrian was a patron of the arts, a lover of beauty, and even something of an architect. He directed the staggering feat of building much more than a villa: It was a self-contained world for a vast royal entourage and the hundreds of servants and guards they required to protect them, feed them, bathe them, and satisfy their libidos.

Hadrian erected theaters, baths, temples, fountains, gardens, and canals bordered with statuary throughout his estate. He filled the palaces and temples with sculpture, some of which now rests in the museums of Rome. In later centuries, barbarians, popes, and cardinals, as well as anyone who needed a slab of marble, carted off much that made the villa so spectacular. But enough of the fragmented ruins remain for us to piece together the story. For a glimpse of what the villa used to be, see the plastic reconstruction at the entrance.

After all the centuries of plundering, there's still a bit left. The most outstanding remnant is the **Canopo,** or Canopus, a re-creation of the town of

The grounds at Hadrian's Villa.

Canope with its famous Temple of the Serapis. The ruins of a rectangular area, **Piazza d'Oro,** are still surrounded by a double portico. Likewise, the **Doric Pillared Hall** (or Sala dei Pilastri Dorici) remains to delight, with its pilasters with Doric bases and capitals holding up a Doric architrave. The ruins of the **Baths** remain, revealing rectangular rooms with concave walls. The apse and the ruins of some magnificent vaulting are found at the Great Baths. Only the north wall remains of the **Pecile,** otherwise known as the Stoa Poikile or "Painted Porch," which Hadrian discovered in Athens and had reproduced here. The best is saved for last—the **Teatro Marittimo,** a circular maritime theater in ruins with its central building enveloped by a canal spanned by small swing bridges. For a closer look at some of the items excavated, you can visit the museum on the premises and a visitor center near the villa parking area.

Largo Marguerite Yourcenar, Tivoli. www.beniculturali.it. ✆ **0774-530203.** Admission 6.50€. Daily 9am–sunset (about 7:30pm in summer, 5:30pm Nov–Mar). Closed New Year's Day and Christmas. Bus: 4 from Tivoli.

Villa d'Este ★★ Like Hadrian centuries before, Cardinal Ippolito d'Este of Ferrara believed in heaven on earth, and in the mid–16th century he ordered this villa built on a hillside. The dank Renaissance structure, with its second-rate paintings, is not that noteworthy; the big draw for visitors is the **spectacular gardens** below (designed by Pirro Ligorio).

You descend the cypress-studded slope to the bottom; on the way you're rewarded with everything from lilies to gargoyles spouting water, torrential streams, and waterfalls. The loveliest fountain is the Ovato Fountain (Fontana dell Ovato), by Ligorio. But nearby is the most spectacular achievement: the **Fountain of the Hydraulic Organ (Fontana dell'Organo Idraulico),** dazzling with its water jets in front of a baroque chapel, with four maidens who look tipsy. The work represents the genius of Frenchman Claude Veanard. The moss-covered **Fountain of the Dragons (Fontana dei Draghi),** also by Ligorio, and the so-called **Fountain of Glass (Fontana di Vetro),** by Bernini, are the most intriguing. The best walk is along the promenade, with 100 spraying fountains. The garden is worth hours of exploration, but it's a lot of walking, with some steep climbs.

Piazza Trento 5, Tivoli. www.villadestetivoli.info. ✆ **0774-332920.** Admission 8€. The bus from Rome stops near the entrance. Tues–Sun 8:30am to 1 hr. before sunset. Bus: Roma-Tivoli.

The gardens at Villa d'Este.

Villa Gregoriana ★ Villa d'Este dazzles with artificial glamour, but the Villa Gregoriana relies more on nature. The gardens were built by Pope Gregory XVI in the 19th century. At one point on the circuitous walk carved along a slope, you can stand and look out onto the most panoramic waterfall (Aniene) at Tivoli.

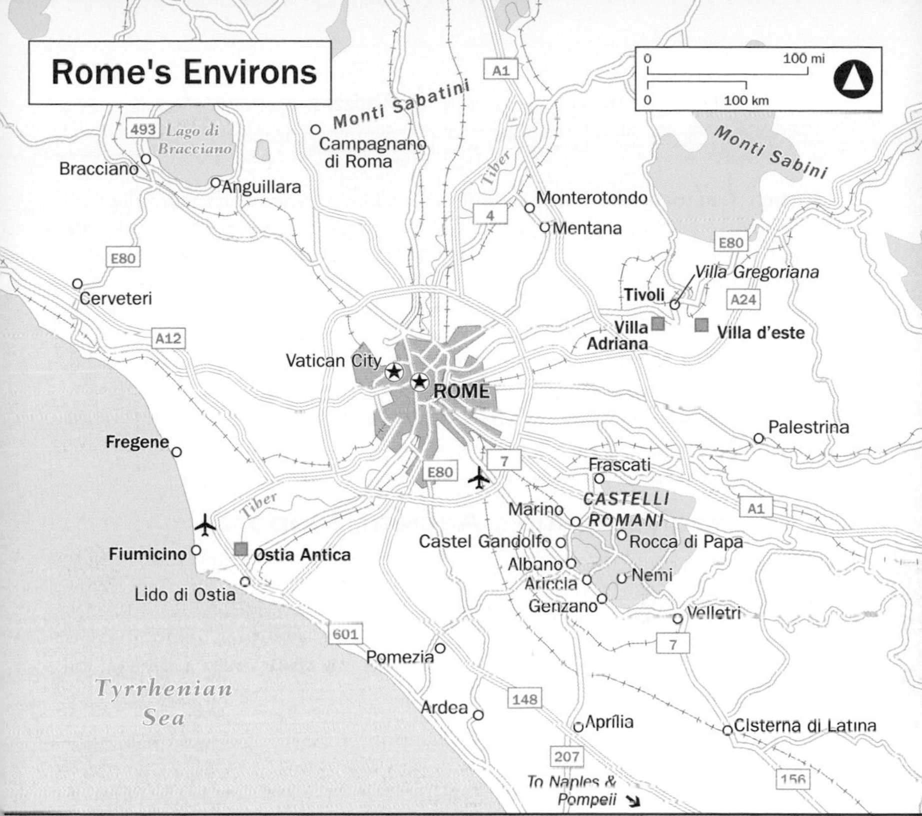

The trek to the bottom on the banks of the Anio is studded with grottoes and balconies that open onto the chasm. The only problem is that if you do make the full descent, you might need a helicopter to pull you up again (the climb back up is fierce). From one of the belvederes, there's a panoramic view of the Temple of Vesta on the hill. Following a $5.5-million restoration, the property has been much improved, and hikers can now explore the on-site grottoes. However, wear rubber-soled shoes, and remember to duck your head. A former school has been converted into a visitor center designed by architect Gae Aulenti.

Largo Sant'Angelo, Tivoli. www.villagregoriana.it. ✆ **06-39967701.** Admission 5€. Apr–Oct 15 Tues–Sun 10am–6:30pm; Mar and Oct 16–Nov Tues–Sat 10am–2:30pm, Sun 10am–4pm. The bus from Rome stops near the entrance.

WHERE TO EAT

Albergo Ristorante Adriano ITALIAN In a stucco-sided villa a few steps from the ticket office sits an idyllic stop for either before or after you visit Hadrian's Villa. It offers terrace dining under plane trees or indoor dining in a high-ceilinged room with terra-cotta walls, neoclassical moldings, and white Corinthian pilasters. The cooking is home style, and the menu includes roast lamb, grilled suckling pig with wild fennel, or ravioli stuffed with ricotta and spinach in a raw basil-laced tomato sauce. The best dish we've ever sampled here is the risotto with pumpkin flowers, although the quail with grape sauce ran a close second. Desserts include such delights as apple pie with a mascarpone sauce.

Largo M. Yourcenar 2. www.hoteladriano.it. ✆ **0774-382235.** Reservations recommended. Main courses 10€–30€. AE, DC, MC, V. Mon–Sat 2:30–4pm and 8–10pm; Sun 12:30–2:30pm and 8–10:30pm.

Antica Trattoria del Falcone ROMAN One of the town's more dependable choices lies in the historic core on the main artery leading off Largo Garibaldi. Because of its location, it attracts a lot of visitors, but that doesn't mean that it's a tourist trap. Far from it. The food is regionally inspired by a kitchen that specializes in market-fresh ingredients. Specialties include perfectly grilled fish as well as *saltimbocca alla romana* (a veal and ham dish). Mixed roast meats, done over the coals, are our favorites. Another dish we like is homemade *crespella,* which is like a rolled pancake. It's stuffed with ricotta, nuts, and fresh spinach.
Via del Trevio 34. www.ristoranteilfalcone.it. ✆ **0774-312358.** Reservations recommended. Main courses 6€–10€; fixed-price menus 13€–18€. AE, DC, MC, V. Daily 11:30am–4pm and 6:30–11:30pm.

Ostia Antica: Rome's Ancient Seaport

Ostia Antica is one of the area's major attractions, particularly interesting to those who can't make it to Pompeii. If you want to see both ancient and modern Rome, grab your swimsuit, towel, and sunblock and take the Metro Line B from Stazione Termini to the Magliana stop. Change here for the Lido train to Ostia Antica, about 26km (16 miles) from Rome. Departures are about every half-hour, and the trip takes only 20 minutes. The Metro lets you off across the highway that connects Rome with the coast. It's just a short walk to the excavations.

Later, board the Metro again to visit the **Lido di Ostia,** the beach. Italy might be a Catholic country, but you won't detect any religious conservatism in the skimpy bikinis on the beach here. There's a carnival atmosphere, with dance halls, cinemas, and pizzerias. The Lido is set off best at Castelfusano, against a backdrop of pine woods. This stretch of shore is referred to as the Roman Riviera.

Ostia Antica's Ruins ★★ Ostia, at the mouth of the Tiber, was the port of ancient Rome, serving as the gateway for all the riches from the far corners of the Empire. It was founded in the 4th century B.C. and became a major port and naval base primarily under two later emperors, Claudius and Trajan.

A prosperous city developed, full of temples, baths, theaters, and patrician homes. Ostia flourished for about 8 centuries before it began to wither away. Gradually it became little more than a malaria bed, a buried ghost city that faded into history. A papal-sponsored commission launched a series of digs in the 19th century; however, the major work of unearthing was carried out under Mussolini's orders from 1938 to 1942 (the work had to stop because of the war). The city is only partially dug out today, but it's believed that all the chief monuments have been uncovered. There are quite a few visible ruins unearthed, so this is no dusty field like the Circus Maximus.

These principal monuments are clearly labeled. The most important spot is **Piazzale delle Corporazioni,** an early version of Wall Street. Near the theater, this square contained nearly 75 corporations, the nature of their businesses identified by the patterns of preserved mosaics. Greek dramas were performed at the **ancient theater,** built in the early days of the Empire. The classics are still aired here in summer (check with the tourist office for specific listings), but the theater as it looks today is the result of much rebuilding. Every town the size of Ostia had a forum, and during the excavations a number of pillars of the ancient **Ostia**

Forum were uncovered. At one end is a 2nd-century-B.C. temple honoring a trio of gods, Minerva, Jupiter, and Juno (little more than the basic foundation remains). In addition, in the enclave is a well-lit **museum** displaying Roman statuary along with some Pompeii-like frescoes. Also of special interest are the ruins of **Thermopolium,** which was a bar; its name means "sale of hot drinks." The ruins of **Capitolium and Forum** remain; this was once the largest temple in Ostia, dating from the 2nd century A.D. A lot of the original brick remains, including a partial reconstruction of the altar. Of an *insula,* a block of apartments, **Casa Diana** remains, with its rooms arranged around an inner courtyard. There are perfect picnic spots beside fallen columns or near old temple walls.

Via dei Romagnoli 717. www.ostiaantica.net. ✆ **06-56352830.** Admission 6.50€. Nov–Feb Tues–Sun 8:30am–4pm, Mar Tues–Sun 8:30am–5pm; Apr–Oct Tues–Sun 8:30am–6pm. Metro: Ostia Antica Line Roma–Ostia–Lido.

The Roman Castles

For the Roman emperor and the wealthy cardinal in the heyday of the Renaissance, the Roman Castles (Castelli Romani) exerted a powerful lure, and they still do. The Castelli aren't castles, but hill towns— many of them with an ancient history. Several produce wines that are well regarded.

The ideal way to explore the hill towns is by car. But you can get a limited review by taking one of the buses that leaves every 20 minutes from Rome's Anagnina stop on Metro Line A.

NEMI

The Romans flock to Nemi in droves, particularly from April to June, for the succulent **wild strawberries** grown there, acclaimed by some gourmets as Europe's finest. In May, there's a strawberry festival. There are no direct buses from Rome to Nemi. To get to Nemi from Rome take the Cotral bus to Genzano from the Anagnina Metro stop in Rome. From Genzano take another bus to Nemi. The trip lasts 1 hour and 15 minutes.

Nemi was also known to the ancients. A temple to the hunter Diana was erected on **Lake Nemi,** which was said to be her "looking glass." In A.D. 37, Caligula built luxurious barges to float on the lake. Mussolini drained Nemi to find the barges, but it was a dangerous time to excavate them from the bottom. They were senselessly destroyed by the Nazis during the infamous retreat.

At the **Roman Ship Museum (Museo delle Navi)** ★, Via di Diana 13 (✆ **06-39967900**), you can see two scale models of the ships destroyed by the Nazis. The major artifacts on display are mainly copies because the originals now

Reserving Winery Tours

While exploring the Castelli Romani, the hill towns around Rome, you might want to visit some of the better-known wineries. The region's most famous producer of Frascati is **Fontana Candida,** Via di Fontana Candida, Monte Porzio Catone (www.fontanacandida.it; ✆ **06-9401881**), whose winery, 23km (14 miles) southwest of Rome, was built around 1900. To arrange visits, contact the **Gruppo Italiano Vini,** Villa Belvedere, 37010 Calmasino, Verona (www.gruppoitalianovini.com; ✆ **045-6269600**).

rest in world-class museums. Opening hours are all year-round Monday to Saturday 9am to 7pm, Sunday 9am to 1pm. Admission is 3€. To reach the museum, head from the center of Nemi toward the lake.

The 15th-century **Palazzo Ruspoli,** a private baronial estate, is the focal point of Nemi, but the town itself invites exploration—particularly the alleyways that the locals call streets and the houses with balconies jutting out over the slopes.

Where to Eat

Ristorante Il Castagnone ROMAN/SEAFOOD This well-managed dining room of the town's best hotel takes pride in its menu, with Roman-based cuisine that emphasizes seafood above meat. The attentive formal service is usually delivered with gentle humor. Amid neoclassical accessories and marble, you can order fine veal, chicken, beef, and fish dishes such as fried calamari, spaghetti with shellfish in garlicky tomato-based sauce, and roasted lamb with potatoes and Mediterranean herbs. The agricultural treasures of the region are on display in such dishes as *pappardelle* with cuttlefish and artichokes, sea bass crepes in orange sauce, *tagliolini* in green sauce with porcini mushrooms, and salmon carpaccio with ricotta. There's a sweeping lake view from the restaurant's windows.

In the Diana Park Hotel, Via Nemorense 56, Nemi. www.hoteldiana.com. ✆ **06-9364041.** Reservations recommended. Main courses 10€–22€. AE, DC, MC, V. Tues–Sun noon–3pm and 8–11pm. Closed Nov.

FRASCATI ★

About 21km (13 miles) from Rome on Via Tuscolana and 482m (1,581 ft.) above sea level, Frascati is one of the most beautiful hill towns. It's known for the wine to which it lends its name, as well as for its villas, which were restored after the severe destruction caused by World War II bombers. To get there, take one of the Cotral buses leaving from the Anagina stop of Metro Line A. From there, take the blue Cotral bus to Frascati. Again, the transportation situation in Italy is constantly in a state of flux, so check your route at the station.

Although Frascati wine is exported and served in many of Rome's restaurants and *trattorie,* tradition holds that it's best near the vineyards from which it came. Romans drive up on Sunday just to drink it.

Stand in the heart of Frascati, at Piazza Marconi, to see the most important of the estates: **Villa Aldobrandini ★**, Via Massaia. The finishing touches to this 16th-century villa were added by Maderno, who designed the facade of St. Peter's in Rome. While you can't visit the interior, the gardens, with grottoes, yew hedges, statuary, and fountains, make for a nice outing. It is necessary to book the visit by phone at ✆ **06-6833785.** The gardens are open Monday to Friday 9am to 1pm and 3 to 5pm (to 6pm in summer).

You also might want to visit the bombed-out **Villa Torlonia,** adjacent to Piazza Marconi. Its grounds have been converted into a public park whose chief treasure is the Theater of the Fountains, designed by Maderno.

A Rare View

If you have a car, you can continue about 5km (3 miles) past the Villa Aldobrandini in Frascati to **Tuscolo,** an ancient spot with the ruins of an amphitheater dating from about the 1st century B.C. It offers what may be one of Italy's most panoramic views.

Where to Eat

Cacciani Ristorante ROMAN Cacciani is the top restaurant in Frascati, where the competition has always been tough. It boasts a terrace commanding a view of the valley, and the kitchen is exposed to the public. To start, we recommend the pasta specialties, such as pasta *cacio e pepe* (pasta with *caciocavallo* cheese and black pepper), or the original spaghetti with seafood and lentils. For a main course, the grilled baby lamb with chicory is always fine. Of course, there is a large choice of wine.

Via Armando Diaz 13. www.cacciani.it. ✆ **06-9401991.** Reservations required. Main courses 14€–17€; fixed-price menus 25€–50€. AE, DC, MC, V. Tues–Sun 12:30–3pm and 7:30–10:30pm.

Etruscan Historical Sights

CERVETERI (CAERE)

As you walk through Rome's Etruscan Museum (Villa Giulia), you'll often see CAERE written under a figure vase or sarcophagus. This is a reference to the nearby town known today as Cerveteri, one of Italy's great Etruscan cities, whose origins could date from as far back as the 9th century B.C.

Of course, the Etruscan town has long since faded, but not the **Necropolis of Cerveteri ★★** (✆ **06-39967150**). Cerveteri is often called a "city of the dead," and the effect is eerie. When you go beneath some of the mounds, you'll discover the most striking feature: The tombs are like rooms in Etruscan homes. The main burial ground is the Necropolis of La Banditaccia. Of the graves thus far uncovered, none is finer than the **Reliefs' Tomb (Tomba Bella),** the burial ground of the Matuna family. Articles such as utensils and even house pets were painted in stucco relief. Presumably these paintings were representations of items that the dead family would need in the world beyond. The necropolis is open Tuesday to Sunday from 8:30am to 1 hour before sunset. Admission is 6€ for adults, 3€ for children.

Relics from the necropolis are displayed at the **Museo Nazionale Cerite,** Piazza Santa Maria Maggiore (✆ **06-9941354**). The museum, housed within the ancient walls and crenellations of Ruspoldi Castle, is open Tuesday through Sunday from 8:30am to 7:30pm. Admission to the museum is free.

You can reach Cerveteri by bus or car. If you're driving, head out Via Aurelia, northwest of Rome, for 45km (28 miles). By public transport, take Metro Line A in Rome to the Cornelia stop; from here you can catch a Cotral bus to Cerveteri. The trip takes about an hour and costs 3.50€. There is no number to call for information, but you can visit the Cotral website at **www.cotralspa.it**. Once you're at Cerveteri, it's a 2km (1¼-mile) walk to the necropolis; follow the signs pointing the way.

TARQUINIA ★

If you want to see tombs even more striking and more recently excavated than those at Cerveteri, go to Tarquinia, a town with medieval turrets and fortifications atop rocky cliffs overlooking the sea. It would seem unusual for a medieval town to have an Etruscan name, but actually, Tarquinia is the adopted name of the old medieval community of Corneto, in honor of the major Etruscan city that once stood nearby.

The main attraction in the town is the **Tarquinia National Museum ★**, Piazza Cavour (✆ **06-39967150**), devoted to Etruscan exhibits and sarcophagi excavated from the necropolis a few miles away. The museum is housed in the Palazzo Vitelleschi, a Gothic palace from the mid–15th century. Among the

Frescoes from the Etruscan Necropolis.

exhibits are gold jewelry, black vases with carved and painted bucolic scenes, and sarcophagi decorated with carvings of animals and relief figures of priests and military leaders. But the biggest attraction is in itself worth the ride from Rome: the almost life-size pair of **winged horses ★★** from the pediment of a Tarquinian temple. The finish is worn here and there, and the terra-cotta color shows through; but the relief stands as one of the greatest Etruscan masterpieces ever discovered. The museum is open Tuesday to Sunday 8:30am to 7:30pm, and charges 6€ admission adults, 3€ for those 18 to 25 years old. A combination ticket for the Tarquinia National Museum and the Etruscan Necropolis costs 8€. It's closed Christmas, January 1, and May 1.

A 6€ fee for adults, 3€ for those age 18 to 25, admits you to the **Etruscan Necropolis ★★** (✆ **06-39967150**), covering more than 4.5km (2¾ miles) of rough terrain near where the ancient Etruscan city once stood. Thousands of tombs have been discovered, some of which haven't been explored even today. Others, of course, were discovered by looters, but many treasures remain even though countless pieces were removed to museums and private collections. The **paintings** on the walls of the tombs have helped historians reconstruct the life of the Etruscans—a heretofore impossible feat without a written history. The paintings depict feasting couples in vivid colors mixed from iron oxide, lapis lazuli dust, and charcoal. One of the oldest tombs (from the 6th c. B.C.) depicts young men fishing while dolphins play and colorful birds fly high above. Many of the paintings convey an earthy, vigorous, sex-oriented life among the wealthy Etruscans. The tombs are generally open Tuesday through Sunday from 8:30am to 1 hour before sunset. You can reach the gravesites by taking a bus from the Barriera San Giusto to the Cimitero stop. Or try the 20-minute walk from the museum. Inquire at the museum for directions.

To reach Tarquinia by car, take Via Aurelia outside Rome and continue on the autostrada toward Civitavecchia. Bypass Civitavecchia and continue another 21km (13 miles) north until you see the exit signs for Tarquinia. As for public transport, a *diretto* train from the Roma Trastevere station takes 1 hour.

5

FLORENCE

Botticelli, Michelangelo, and Leonardo da Vinci all left their mark on Florence, the cradle of the Renaissance and Tuscany's alfresco museum. With Brunelleschi's dome as a backdrop, follow the River Arno to the Uffizi Gallery and soak in centuries of great painting. Wander across the Ponte Vecchio, taking in the tangle of Oltrarno's medieval streets. Then sample seasonal Tuscan cooking in a Left Bank trattoria. You've discovered the art of fine living in this masterpiece of a city.

SIGHTSEEING Michelangelo's *David* stands tall (literally) behind the doors of the **Accademia,** and nearby, the delicate painting of Fra' Angelico in the convent of **San Marco** enchants. Works by Florentines Donatello, Masaccio, and Ghiberti fill the city's churches and museums. Once home to the Medici, the **Palazzo Pitti** is stuffed with Raphaels and Titians, and backed by the fountains of the regal **Boboli Garden.** Climb the **Duomo's cupola** for views to the hills beyond.

SHOPPING Italy's leather capital strains at the seams with handmade gloves, belts, bags, and shoes sold from workshops, family-run boutiques, and high-toned stores, as well as at tourist-oriented **San Lorenzo Market.** Splurge on designer wear from glamorous fashion houses along **Via de' Tornabuoni** or Renaissance scents from the convent-turned-perfumery, **Officina Profumo-Farmaceutica Santa Maria Novella.** For authentic artisan goods, wander the alleyways of the **Oltrarno.**

RESTAURANTS & DINING Florentine eating is more cosmopolitan than in the countryside, but flavors still have Tuscany at their core. Even in the best restaurants, meals might kick off with peasant concoctions like ***ribollita*** (vegetable stew) before moving onto the chargrilled delights of a ***bistecca alla fiorentina*** (Florentine beefsteak on the bone)—all washed down with a fine **Chianti Classico.** At lunchtime order a plate of cold cuts, or if you're feeling adventurous ***lampredotto alla fiorentina*** (a sandwich of cow's stomach stewed in tomatoes and garlic).

NIGHTLIFE & ENTERTAINMENT Kick your evening off with *aperitivo* hour: Simple, tasty buffets are piled high for early evening drinkers to enjoy. When you've dined to your fill, retire to a wine bar in the **Oltrarno,** or to one of the edgier joints of **Santo Spirito** and **San Frediano,** where DJs play till the wee hours. If you're keen on opera, classical, theater, or jazz, you'll find it here, too.

ABOVE: **Biking the streets of Florence.**
PREVIOUS PAGE: **Michelangelo's *David* statue at the Accademia.**

The Duomo of Florence.

THE BEST TRAVEL EXPERIENCES IN FLORENCE

- **Drinking in the full 360 degrees of Piazza della Signoria, when it's deserted in the early morning:** Find a comfortable perch on Florence's marquee square—the site of Savonarola's infamous Bonfire of the Vanities—and take in Benvenuto Cellini's bronze *Perseus* holding aloft the head of Medusa, a replica of Michelangelo's *David,* the Uffizi, Giambologna's *Rape of the Sabines,* and the Palazzo Vecchio. It's the best free show in town. See p. 194.
- **Catching a glimpse of where Tuscan art was born:** In Room 2 of the Uffizi, the great Madonnas of Cimabue, Duccio di Buoninsegna, and Giotto di Bondone are displayed side by side. Between them, these three great painters of the 1200s and 1300s shaped Florentine and Sienese art for generations. See p. 206.
- **Eating some of Italy's best gelato:** You name the flavor, you're sure to find it somewhere. Everyone from Vespa-riding ravers to well-dressed contessas come for their daily fix. Our favorite spots are Vivoli and Carapina. See p. 234.
- **Basking in the lights of the Renaissance:** At dusk, make the stiff climb up to the ancient church of San Miniato al Monte. Sit down on the steps and watch the city begin its daily twinkle. See p. 224.
- **Hitting San Frediano after dark:** We love the buzz of this fashionable Left Bank neighborhood. Join young Florentines as they eat creative, contemporary Tuscan food at the likes of iO and Il Santo Bevitore, then round off the night with live music at Volume. See p. 237, 238, and 246.

ESSENTIALS

Arriving

BY PLANE Several European airlines service Florence's **Amerigo Vespucci Airport** (www.aeroporto.firenze.it; ✆ **055-306-1300** for the switchboard; 055-306-1700 or 055-306-1702 for flight info), also called **Peretola,** just 5km (3 miles) northwest of town. There are no direct flights to or from the United States, but you can make connections through London, Paris, Amsterdam, Frankfurt, and other major European cities. The half-hourly **SITA-ATAF "Vola in bus"** to and from downtown's bus station at Via Santa Caterina 15r (✆ **800-424-500**), beside the train station, costs 5€ one-way or 8€ round-trip. There's also a less frequent service operated by **Terravision** (www.terravision.eu; ✆ **050-26-080**). Metered **taxis** line up outside the airport's arrival terminal and charge a flat, official rate of 20€ to the city center (22€ on holidays, 23€ after 10pm).

The closest major international airport with direct flights to North America is Pisa's **Galileo Galilei Airport** (www.pisa-airport.com; ✆ 050 849300), 97km (60 miles) west of Florence. Two to three **trains** per hour leave the airport for Florence, most requiring a change at Pisa Centrale (60–90 min.; 5.80€). Early-morning flights or lots of bags might make train connections from Florence to the airport difficult; one solution is the regular train from Florence into Pisa Centrale, with a 10-minute taxi ride around 10€ from the train station to Pisa Airport. Alternatively, 10 daily buses operated by **Terravision** (www.terravision.eu; ✆ **050-26-080**) connect downtown Florence directly with Pisa Airport in 70 minutes. One-way ticket prices are 10€ adults, 4€ children ages 5 to 12; round-trip fares are 16€ and 8€, respectively.

BY TRAIN Florence is Tuscany's rail hub, with regular connections to all Italy's major cities. To get here from Rome, take high-speed Frecciarossa or Frecciargento trains (40 daily; 1½ hr.; make sure it's going to Santa Maria Novella station, not Campo di Marte; reserve tickets ahead). There are high-speed and IC trains to Milan (at least hourly; 1¾–3 hr.) via Bologna (37 min.–1 hr.). There's also a daily night-train sleeper service from Paris Bercy, operated by **Thello** (www.thello.com).

Most Florence-bound trains roll into **Stazione Santa Maria Novella,** Piazza della Stazione (www.trenitalia.it), which you'll see abbreviated as **S.M.N.** The station is an architectural masterpiece in its own right—albeit one dating to Italy's Fascist period, rather than the Renaissance—and lies on the northwestern edge of the city's compact historic center, a brisk 10-minute walk from the Duomo and a 15-minute walk from Piazza della Signoria and the Uffizi.

BY BUS Because Florence is such a well-connected train hub, there's little reason to take the longer, less comfortable intercity coaches (one exception is if you're arriving from **Siena;** see p. 281).

BY CAR The **A1 autostrada** runs north from Rome past Arezzo to Florence and continues to Bologna. The **A11** connects Florence with Lucca, and **unnumbered superhighways** run to Siena (the *SI-FI raccordo*) and Pisa (the so-called *FI-PI-LI*).

Florence's "City Code"

What used to be Florence's city code—**055**—is now an integral part of every phone number. Always dial it (including the initial zero, even from overseas), even when calling to another number from within Florence itself.

Driving to Florence is easy; the problems begin once you arrive. Almost all cars are banned from the historic center—only residents or merchants with special permits are allowed into this camera-patrolled *zona a trafico limitato* (the "ZTL"). You may be stopped at some point by the traffic police. Have the name and address of the hotel ready and they'll wave you through. You can drop off baggage there (the hotel will give you a temporary ZTL permit); then you must relocate to a parking lot. Ask your hotel which is most convenient: Special rates are available through most hotels.

Your best bet for overnight or longer-term parking is one of the city-run garages. The best deal if you're staying the night (better than many hotels' garage rates) is at the **Parterre parking lot** under Piazza Libertà, at Via Madonna delle Tosse 9 (✆ **055-550-1994**). It's open round the clock, costing 2€ per hour, or 20€ for 24 hours; it's 65€ for up to a week's parking. There's voluminous information on Florence's parking options at **www.firenzeparcheggi.it**.

Don't park your car overnight on the streets in Florence without local knowledge; if you're towed and ticketed, it will set you back substantially—and the headaches to retrieve your car are beyond description.

Visitor Information

TOURIST OFFICES The most convenient tourist office is at Via Cavour 1r (www.firenzeturismo.it; ✆ **055-290-832**), about 3 blocks north of the Duomo. The office is open Monday through Saturday from 8:30am to 6:30pm. Their free map is quite adequate for navigation purposes—there's no need to upgrade to a paid-for version.

The train station's nearest tourist office (✆ **055-212-245**) is opposite the terminus at Piazza della Stazione 4. With your back to the tracks, take the left exit, cross onto the concrete median, and bear right; it's across the road about 30m (100 ft.) ahead. The office is usually open Monday through Saturday from 8:30am to 7pm (sometimes to 2pm in winter) and Sunday 8:30am to 2pm. This office often gets crowded; unless you're really lost, press on to the Via Cavour office, above.

Another helpful office sits under the Loggia del Bigallo on the corner of Piazza del Duomo and Via dei Calzaiuoli, open Monday through Saturday from 9am to 7pm (5pm mid-Nov through Feb) and Sunday 9am to 2pm.

WEBSITES The official Florence information website, **www.firenzeturismo.it**, contains a wealth of up-to-date information on Florence and its province, including itineraries and a hotel search database. At **www.firenzeturismo.it/arte-musei-firenze.html** you'll find a downloadable PDF with the latest updated opening hours for all the major city sights. The best city blogs are generally written in Italian by locals: **Io Amo Firenze** (http://ioamofirenze.blogspot.com) is handy for reviews of the latest eating, drinking, and events in town. For regularly updated Florence information and ideas, also visit **www.frommers.com/destinations/florence**.

City Layout

Florence is a smallish city, sitting on the Arno River and petering out to olive-planted hills rather quickly to the north and south but extending farther west and, to a lesser extent, east along the Arno valley with suburbs and light industry. It has a compact center best negotiated on foot. No two major sights are more than a 20- or 25-minute walk apart, and most of the hotels and restaurants in this chapter are in the relatively small ***centro storico*** **(historic center),** a compact tangle of medieval streets and *piazze* (squares) where visitors spend most of their time. The bulk of Florence, including most of the tourist sights, lies north of the river, with the **Oltrarno,** an old artisans' working-class neighborhood, hemmed in between the Arno and the hills on the south side. The tourist offices hand out two versions of a Florence *pianta* (city plan) free: Ask for the one *con un stradario* (with a street index), which shows all the roads and is better for navigation.

THE NEIGHBORHOODS IN BRIEF

THE DUOMO The area surrounding Florence's gargantuan cathedral is about as central as you can get. The Duomo is halfway between the two great churches of Santa Maria Novella and Santa Croce as well as at the midpoint between the Uffizi Gallery and the Ponte Vecchio to the south and San Marco and the Accademia with Michelangelo's *David* to the north. The streets north of the Duomo are long and can be traffic-ridden, but those to the south make up a wonderful medieval tangle of alleys and tiny squares heading toward Piazza della Signoria.

This is one of the oldest parts of town, and the streets still vaguely follow the grid laid down when the city began as a Roman colony. Via degli Strozzi/Via degli Speziali/Via del Corso was the *decumanus maximus,* the main east-west axis; Via Roma/Via Calimala was the key north-south *cardo maximus.* The site of the Roman city's forum is today's **Piazza della Repubblica.** The area surrounding it is one of Florence's main shopping zones. The Duomo neighborhood is, understandably, one of the most hotel-heavy parts of town, offering a range from luxury inns to student dives and everything in between.

PIAZZA DELLA SIGNORIA This is the city's civic heart and perhaps the best base for museum hounds—the Uffizi Gallery, Bargello sculpture collection, and Ponte Vecchio leading toward the Pitti Palace are all nearby. It's a well-polished part of the tourist zone but still retains the narrow medieval streets

Address Finding: The Red & the Black

The address system in Florence and some other Tuscan cities has a split personality. Private homes, some offices, and hotels are numbered in black (or blue), while businesses, shops, and restaurants are numbered independently in red. (That's the theory anyway; in reality, the division between black and red numbers isn't always so clear-cut.) The result is that 1, 2, 3 (black) addresses march up the block numerically oblivious to their 1r, 2r, 3r (red) neighbors. You might find the doorways on one side of a street numbered: 1r, 2r, 3r, 1, 4r, 2, 3, 5r . . .

The color codes occur only in the *centro storico* and other older sections of town; outlying districts didn't bother with this rather confusing system.

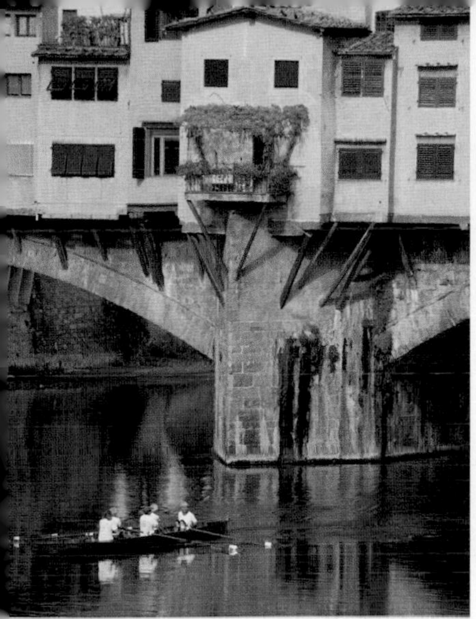

The Ponte Vecchio, which spans the Arno.

where Dante grew up. The few blocks just north of the **Ponte Vecchio** have reasonable shopping, but unappealing modern buildings were planted here to replace the district destroyed during World War II. The entire neighborhood can be stiflingly crowded in summer, but in those moments when you catch it empty of tour groups, it remains the most romantic heart of pre-Renaissance Florence.

SAN LORENZO & THE MERCATO CENTRALE This small wedge of streets between the train station and the Duomo, centered on the Medici's old family church of San Lorenzo and its Michelangelo-designed tombs, is market territory. The vast indoor food market is here, and many of the streets are filled daily with stalls hawking leather jackets and other tourist wares. It's a colorful neighborhood, blessed with a range of budget hotels, but not the quietest.

PIAZZA SANTA TRÍNITA This piazza sits just north of the river at the south end of Florence's shopping mecca, Via de' Tornabuoni, home to Gucci, Armani, Ferragamo, and more. It's a pleasant, well-to-do (but still medieval) neighborhood in which to stay, even if you don't care about haute couture. If you're an upscale shopping fiend, there's no better place to be.

SANTA MARIA NOVELLA This neighborhood, bounding the western edge of the *centro storico,* has two characters: the run-down unpleasant zone around the train station and the nicer area south of it between the church of Santa Maria Novella and the river.

In general, the train station area is the least attractive part of town in which to base yourself. The streets are mostly heavily trafficked and noisy, and you're a little removed from the action. This area does, however, have more good budget options than any other quarter, especially along **Via Faenza** and its tributaries. ***Tip:*** Try to avoid anything on busy Via Nazionale.

The situation improves dramatically as you move east into the San Lorenzo area or pass Santa Maria Novella church and head toward the river. **Piazza Santa Maria Novella** and its tributary streets have seen a few top-priced, stylish boutique hotels open in recent years, and are attracting something of a bohemian nightlife scene.

SAN MARCO & SANTISSIMA ANNUNZIATA These two churches are fronted by *piazze*—**Piazza San Marco,** now a busy transport hub, and **Piazza Santissima Annunziata,** the most architecturally unified square in the city—that together define the northern limits of the *centro storico.* The neighborhood is home to Florence's university, Michelangelo's *David* at the Accademia, the San Marco monastery, and long, quiet streets with some real hotel gems. The daily walk back from the heart of town up here may tire some, but others welcome being removed from the worst of the high-season crush.

SANTA CROCE The church at the eastern edge of the *centro storico* is also the focal point of one of the most genuine neighborhoods left in the old center. Few tourists roam too far off **Piazza Santa Croce,** so if you want to feel like a city resident, stay around here. The streets around the **Mercato di Sant'Ambrogio** and **Piazza de'Ciompi** have an especially appealing, local feel. The Santa Croce neighborhood also boasts some of the best restaurants and bars in the city—*aperitivo* hour is especially vibrant along **Via de' Benci.**

The quiet back streets of the Oltrarno.

THE OLTRARNO & SAN FREDIANO "Across the Arno" is the artisans' neighborhood, still packed with workshops where craftspeople hand-carve furniture and hand-stitch leather gloves. It began as a working-class neighborhood to catch the overflow from the expanding medieval city on the opposite bank, but it also became a rather chic area for aristocrats to build palaces on the edge of the countryside. The largest of these, the **Pitti Palace,** later became the home of the grand dukes and today houses a set of paintings second only to the Uffizi in scope. Behind it spreads the baroque fantasies of the Boboli Garden, Florence's best park. Masaccio's frescoes in Santa Maria della Carmine here were some of the most influential of the early Renaissance.

It has always attracted a slightly bohemian crowd—poets Robert and Elizabeth Barrett Browning lived here from just after their secret marriage in 1847 until Elizabeth died in 1861. The Oltrarno's lively tree-shaded center, **Piazza Santo Spirito,** is a world unto itself, lined with bars and close to some great restaurants (and lively nightlife, too). West of here, the neighborhood of **San Frediano,** around the Porta Pisana, is becoming ever more fashionable for hip locals and visitors, and **San Niccolò** at the foot of Florence's southern hills is a buzzing nightlife spot.

IN THE HILLS From just about any vantage point in the center of Florence, you can see that the city ends abruptly to the north and south, replaced by green hills spotted with villas. To the north is the Etruscan-founded village of **Fiesole,** which was here long before the Romans built Florence below.

South of the Arno, the hills hemming in the Oltrarno—with such names as Bellosguardo (Beautiful Glimpse) and Monte Uliveto (Olive Grove Hill)—are blanketed in farmland. With panoramic lookouts like Piazzale Michelangiolo and the Romanesque church of San Miniato al Monte, these hills offer some of the best walks around the city, as Elizabeth Browning, Henry James, and Florence Nightingale could tell you.

Owing to the distance from the city's key sights, first-time visitors probably will not want to choose accommodations in the hills. But for those who don't need to be in town every day and want a cooler, calmer, and altogether more relaxing vacation, the hills can be heaven. Bus links with the center are fairly good, too.

Getting Around

Florence is a **walking** city. You can leisurely stroll between the two top sights, the Duomo and the Uffizi, in less than 5 minutes. The hike from the most northerly sights, San Marco with its Fra' Angelico frescoes and the Accademia with Michelangelo's *David,* to the most southerly, the Pitti Palace across the Arno, should take no more than 30 minutes. From Santa Maria Novella across town to Santa Croce is an easy 20- to 30-minute walk.

Most of the streets, however, were designed to handle the moderate pedestrian traffic and occasional horse-drawn cart of a medieval city. Sidewalks, where they exist, are narrow—often less than .5m (2 ft.) wide. Although the *centro storico* is increasingly being closed to traffic, this doesn't always include taxis, residents with parking permits, people without permits who drive there anyway, and the endless swarm of noisy Vespas and *motorini* (scooters). However, since the election of center-left Mayor Matteo Renzi in 2009, the city has become noticeably more pedestrian friendly, a trend that is likely to continue while he is in office.

BY BUS You'll rarely need to use Florence's efficient **ATAF bus system** (www.ataf.net; ✆ **800/424-500** in Italy) since the city is so compact. The cathedral is a mere 5- to 7-minute walk from the train station. Bus tickets cost 1.20€ and are good for 90 minutes. A four-pack (*biglietto multiplo*) is 4.70€, a 24-hour pass 5€, a 3-day pass 12€, and a 7-day pass 18€. Tickets are sold at *tabacchi* (tobacconists), bars, and most newsstands. ***Note:*** Once on board, validate your ticket in the box near the rear door to avoid a steep fine. Since traffic is limited in most of the historic center, buses make runs on principal streets only, save four tiny electric buses (*bussini* services C1, C2, C3, and D) that trundle about the *centro storico*. The most useful lines to outlying areas are no. 7 (for Fiesole) and nos. 12 and 13 (for Piazzale Michelangiolo).

BY TAXI Taxis aren't cheap, and with the city so small and the one-way system forcing drivers to take convoluted routes, they aren't an economical way to get about town. They are most useful to get you and your bags between the train station and your hotel in the virtually busless *centro storico*. The standard rate is .90€ per kilometer (slightly more than a half-mile), with a whopping minimum fare of 3.30€ to start the meter (that rises to 5.30€ on Sun; 6.60€ 10pm–6am), plus 1€ per bag. There's a taxi stand outside the train station; otherwise, call **Radio Taxi** at ✆ **055-4242** or 055-4390. For the latest taxi information, see **www.socota.it**.

BY BICYCLE & SCOOTER Many of the bike-rental shops in town are located just north of Piazza San Marco, such as **Alinari,** Via San Zanobi 38r (www.alinarirental.com; ✆ **055-280-500**), which rents bikes (2.50€ per hour; 12€ per day) and mountain bikes (3€ per hour; 18€ per day). It also rents 50cc and 100cc scooters (10€ or 15€ per hour; 30€ or 55€ per day). Another renter with similar prices is **Florence by Bike,** Via San Zanobi 120–122r (www.florencebybike.it; ✆ **055-488-992**).

BY CAR Trying to drive in the *centro storico* is a frustrating, useless exercise, and moreover, unauthorized traffic is not allowed past signs marked ZTL. As of press time, there was talk of introducing a city charge (1€ per day or thereabouts) even to drive into the center to park. Florence is a maze of one-way streets and pedestrian zones, and it takes an old hand to know which laws to break in order to get where you need to go—plus you need a permit to do anything beyond dropping off and picking up bags at your hotel. Park your vehicle in one of the huge underground lots on the center's periphery and pound the pavement. (See "By Car" under "Getting There," earlier in this chapter.)

[Fast FACTS] FLORENCE

Business Hours Hours mainly follow the Italian norm (see chapter 17). In Florence, however, many of the larger and more central shops stay open through the midday *riposo* or nap (note the sign *ORARIO NONSTOP*).

Consulates See "Embassies & Consulates," in chapter 17.

Doctors There's a walk-in **Tourist Medical Service,** Via Lorenzo il Magnifico 59, north of the city center between the Fortezza del Basso and Piazza della Libertà (✆ **055-475-411**), open Monday to Friday 11am to noon and 5 to 6pm, Saturday 11am to noon only; take bus no. 8 or 20 to Viale Lavagnini, or bus no. 12 to Via Poliziano. English-speaking **Dr. Stephen Kerr** keeps an office at Piazza Mercato Nuovo 1 (www.dr-kerr.com; ✆ **335-836-1682** or 055-288-055), with office hours Monday through Friday from 3 to 5pm without an appointment (appointments are available 9am–3pm). The consultation fee is 50€ to 60€; it's slightly cheaper if you show a student ID card.

Hospitals The most central hospital is **Santa Maria Nuova,** a block northeast of the Duomo on Piazza Santa Maria Nuova (✆ **055-27-581**), open 24 hours. For a **free translator** to help you describe your symptoms, explain the doctor's instructions, and aid in medical issues in general, call the volunteers at the **Associazione Volontari Ospedalieri** (**AVO;** www.federavo.it; ✆ **055-234-4567**) Monday, Wednesday, and Friday from 4 to 6pm and Tuesday and Thursday from 10am to noon.

Internet Access Most hotels in the city center now offer wireless Internet, for free or a small fee. Otherwise, head to the chain **Internet Train** (www.internettrain.it), with six locations in Florence, including their very first shop at Via dell'Oriuolo 40r, a few blocks from the Duomo (✆ **055-263-8968**); Via Guelfa 54r, near the train station (✆ **055-214-794**); Borgo San Jacopo 30r, in the Oltrarno (✆ **055-265-7935**); and Via de' Benci 36r (no phone). The magnetic access card you buy is good at any Internet Train store nationwide. They also provide printing, scanning, webcam, and fax services, plus other services (bike rental, international shipping, 24-hr. film developing) at some offices. Open hours vary, but generally run at least daily from 9am to 8:30pm, often later. Alternatively, if you have your own laptop or smartphone, buy a time-limited pass from **www.wifipass.it**, a network of Wi-Fi hotspots.

Laundry & Dry Cleaning Although there are several coin-op shops—including several in the **Wash & Dry** chain (www.washedry.it)—instead visit a pay-by-weight *lavanderia,* so you don't have to waste a morning sitting there watching it go in circles. The cheapest are around the university (east of San Marco), and one of the best is a nameless joint at **Via degli Alfani 44r** (✆ **055-247-9313**), where they'll do a load overnight for around 6€. It's closed Saturday afternoon and all day Sunday. Always check the price *before* leaving your clothes—some places charge by the item. Dry cleaning *(lavasecco)* is much more costly and available at *lavanderie* throughout the city (ask your hotel for the closest).

Pharmacies There are 24-hour pharmacies (also open Sun and state holidays) in **Stazione Santa Maria Novella** (✆ **055-216-761**; ring the bell btw. 1 and 4am); at **Piazza San Giovanni 20r,** just behind the Baptistery at the corner of Borgo San Lorenzo (✆ **055-211-343**); and at **Via dei Calzaiuoli 7r,** just off Piazza della Signoria (✆ **055-289-490**). On holidays and at night, look for the sign in any pharmacy window telling you which ones are open.

Police To report lost property or passport problems, call the *questura* (urban police headquarters) at ✆ **055-49-771. *Note:*** It is illegal to knowingly buy fake goods anywhere in the city (and, yes, a "Rolex" watch at 20€ counts as *knowingly*). You may be served a hefty on-the-spot fine if caught.

Post Offices Florence's **main post office** (✆ **055-273-6481**) is at Via Pellicceria 3, off the southwest corner of Piazza della Repubblica. It is open Monday through Saturday from 8:15am to 7pm. You can also send packages via **UPS,** Via di Pratignone 56a in Calenzano (✆ **02-3030-3039**).

To receive mail at the central post office, have it sent to [your name], Fermo Posta Centrale, 50103 Firenze, Italia/ITALY. They'll charge you a nominal sum when you come to pick it up; bring your passport for ID. They hold mail for 30 days.

Safety As in any city, plenty of pickpockets are out to ruin your vacation, and in Florence you'll find light-fingered youngsters (especially around the train station), but otherwise you're safe. Do steer clear of the Cascine Park after dark, when it becomes somewhat seedy and you may run the risk of being mugged; and you probably won't want to hang out with the late-night heroin addicts shooting up on the Arno mud flats below the Lungarno embankments on the edges of town. See chapter 17 for more safety tips.

EXPLORING FLORENCE

On Piazza Del Duomo

The cathedral square is filled with tourists and caricature artists during the day, strolling crowds in the early evening, and knots of students strumming guitars on the Duomo's steps at night. Though it's always crowded, the piazza's vivacity and the glittering facades of the cathedral and the Baptistery doors keep it an eternal Florentine sight. The square's closure to traffic in 2009 has made it a more welcoming space than ever for strolling.

Battistero (Baptistery) ★★★ RELIGIOUS SITE In choosing a date to mark the beginning of the Renaissance, art historians often seize on 1401, the year Florence's powerful wool merchants' guild held a contest to decide who would receive the commission to design the **North Doors** ★★ of the Baptistery to match the Gothic **South Doors,** cast 65 years earlier by Andrea Pisano. The era's foremost Tuscan sculptors each cast a bas-relief bronze panel depicting his own vision of the *Sacrifice of Isaac*. Twenty-two-year-old Lorenzo Ghiberti, competing against the likes of Donatello, Jacopo della Quercia, and Filippo Brunelleschi, won. He spent the next 21 years casting 28 bronze panels and building his doors.

Battistero (Baptistery) **28**
Campanile di Giotto **30**
Cappelle Medicee **2**
Casa Buonarroti **41**
Casa di Dante **35**
Casa Guidi **13**
Cenacolo di Sant'Apollonia **18**
Duomo (Cathedral of Santa Maria del Fiore) **31**
Fontana del Nettuno **38**
Forte di Belvedere **17**
Galleria degli Uffizi **42**
Galleria dell'Accademia *(David)* **24**
Giardino di Boboli **16**
Loggia dei Lanzi **39**
Loggia del Bigallo **29**
Museo Archeologico **21**
Museo dell'Opera del Duomo **32**
Museo di Mineralogia e Litologia **20**
Museo di Santa Maria Novella **4**
Museo Galileo **43**
Museo Horne **45**
Museo Nazionale del Bargello **37**
Museo Opificio delle Pietre Dure **25**
Museo Stibbert **1**
Museo Zoologia "La Specola" **15**
Ognissanti **5**
Orsanmichele **36**
Palazzo Medici-Riccardi **26**
Palazzo Pitti **12**
Palazzo Vecchio **40**
Parco delle Cascine **6**
Piazzale Michelangiolo **46**
Ponte Vecchio **8**
San Felice **14**
San Lorenzo **27**
San Marco **19**
San Miniato al Monte **47**
Santa Croce **44**
Santa Felícita **11**
Santa Maria del Carmine **9**
Santa Maria Maddalena dei Pazzi **33**
Santa Maria Novella **3**
Santa Trínita **7**
Santissima Annunziata **22**
Santo Spirito **10**
Sinagoga & Jewish Museum **34**
Spedale degli Innocenti **23**

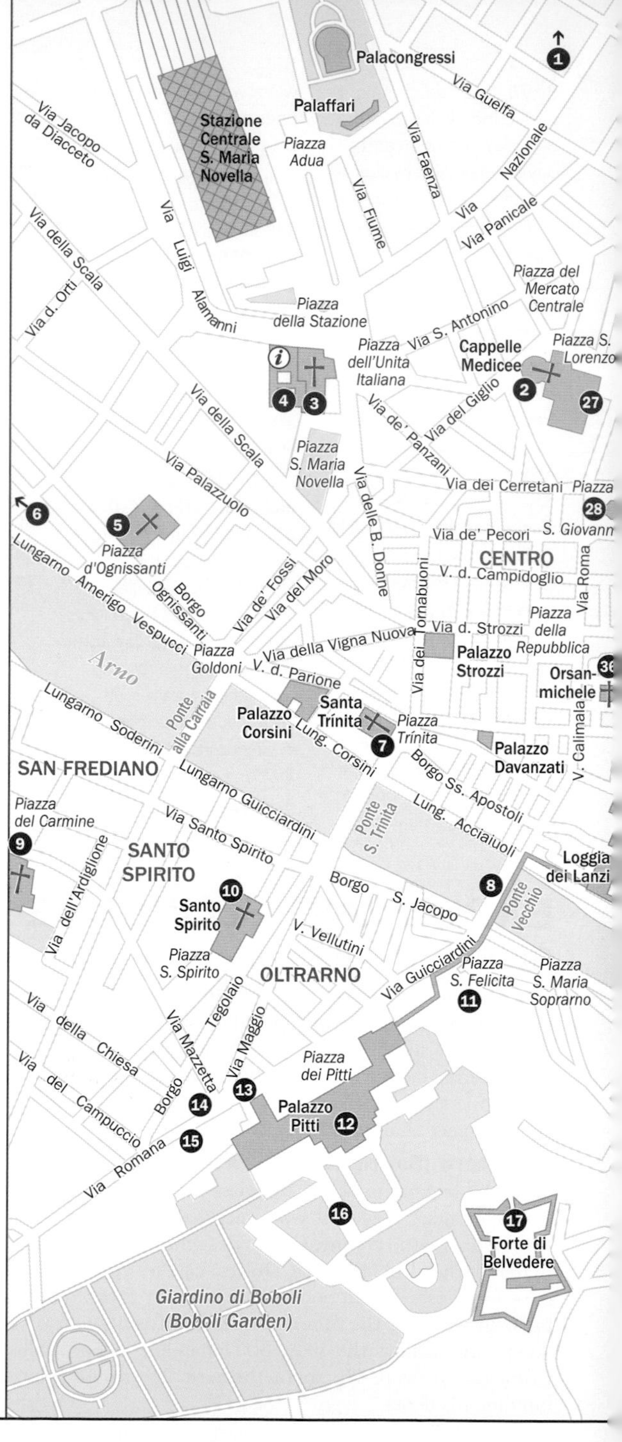

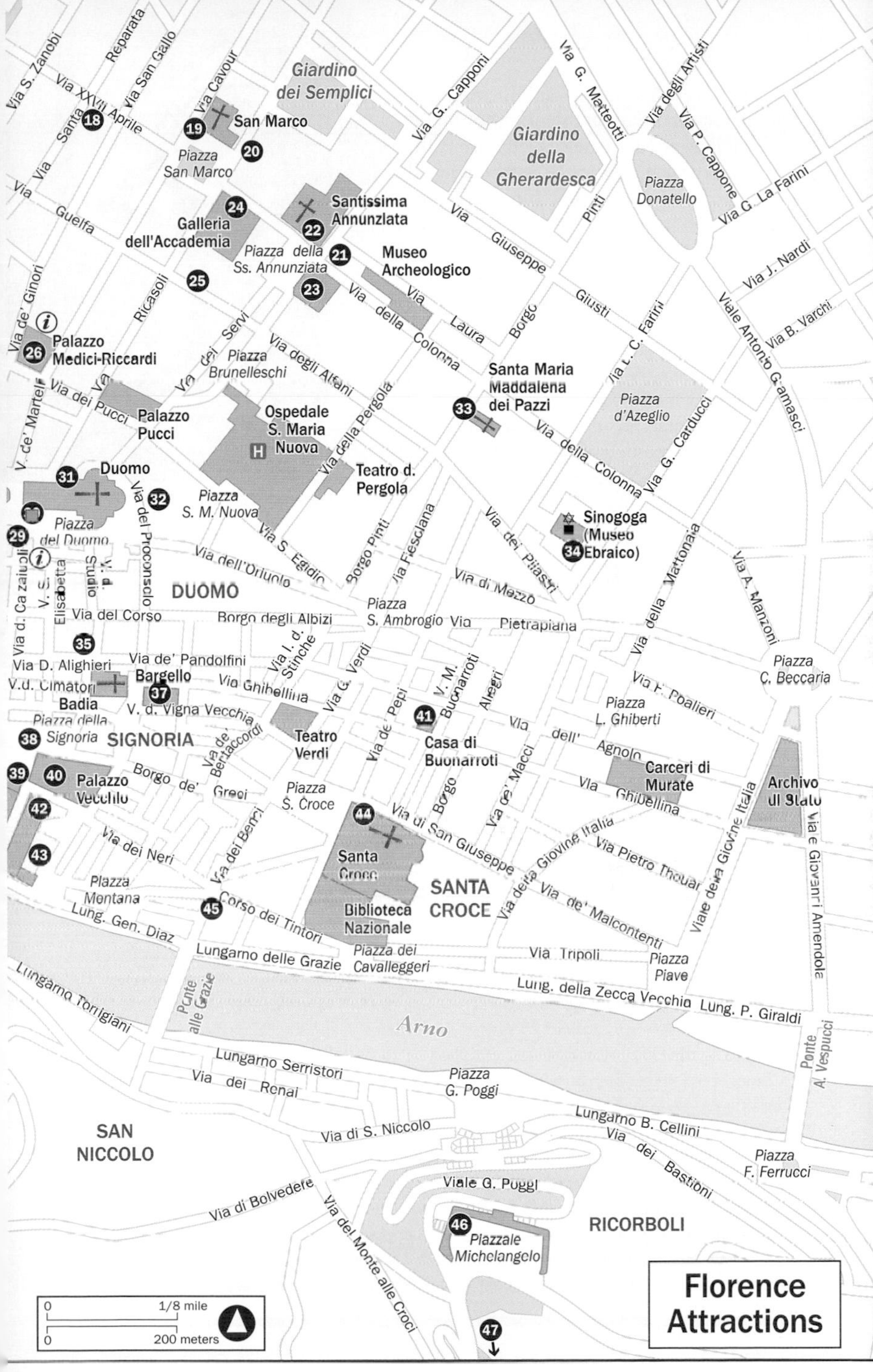
Florence Attractions
Giardino dei Semplici
San Marco
Piazza San Marco
Giardino della Gherardesca
Piazza Donatello
Santissima Annunziata
Galleria dell'Accademia
Piazza della Ss. Annunziata
Museo Archeologico
Palazzo Medici-Riccardi
Piazza Brunelleschi
Santa Maria Maddalena dei Pazzi
Piazza d'Azeglio
Palazzo Pucci
Ospedale S. Maria Nuova
Teatro d. Pergola
Duomo
Piazza S. M. Nuova
Piazza del Duomo
Sinogoga (Museo Ebraico)
DUOMO
Piazza S. Ambrogio
Piazza C. Beccaria
Bargello
Badia
Piazza L. Ghiberti
SIGNORIA
Teatro Verdi
Casa di Buonarroti
Carceri di Murate
Archivio di Stato
Palazzo Vecchio
Piazza S. Croce
Santa Croce
Biblioteca Nazionale
SANTA CROCE
Piazza Montana
Piazza dei Cavalleggeri
Piazza Piave
Arno
Piazza G. Poggi
SAN NICCOLO
Piazza F. Ferrucci
RICORBOLI
Piazzale Michelangelo
0 1/8 mile
0 200 meters

A street musician.

The result so impressed the merchants' guild—not to mention the public and Ghiberti's fellow artists—they asked him in 1425 to do the **East Doors ★★★**, facing the Duomo, this time giving him the artistic freedom to realize his Renaissance ambitions. Twenty-seven years later, just before his death, Ghiberti finished 10 dramatic lifelike Old Testament scenes in gilded bronze, each a masterpiece of Renaissance sculpture and some of the finest examples of low-relief perspective in Italian art. The panels now mounted here are excellent copies; the originals are in the Museo dell'Opera del Duomo (see below). Years later, Michelangelo was standing before these doors and someone asked his opinion. His response sums up Ghiberti's accomplishment as no art historian could: "They are so beautiful that they would grace the entrance to Paradise." They've been called the Gates of Paradise ever since.

The interior is ringed with columns pilfered from ancient Roman buildings and is a spectacle of mosaics above and below. The floor was inlaid in 1209, and the ceiling was covered between 1225 and the early 1300s with glittering **mosaics ★★**. Most were crafted by Venetian or Byzantine-style workshops, which worked off designs drawn by the era's best artists. Coppo di Marcovaldo drew sketches for the over 7.8m-high (26-ft.), ape-toed *Christ in Judgment* and the *Last Judgment* that fills over a third of the ceiling.

Piazza San Giovanni. www.operaduomo.firenze.it. ✆ **055-230-2885.** Admission 4€. Mon–Sat 12:15–7pm; Sun and 1st Sat of month 8:30am–2pm. Bus: C2, 14, 23, or 71.

DISCOUNT tickets FOR THE CITY

Launched in 2011, the **Firenze Card** (www.firenzecard.it) is valid for 72 hours, includes bus transport, costs 50€, and buys you entrance to around 25 sites, including the Uffizi, Accademia, Cappella Brancacci, Palazzo Pitti, and San Marco. It also gets you into shorter lines, making prebooking tickets for the major sites unnecessary. Any E.U. citizen 17 and under enters free with a cardholder.

Amici degli Uffizi membership (www.amicidegliuffizi.it) costs 60€ for adults, 40€ anyone 25 and under, 100€ for a family, and is valid for a calendar year (Jan–Dec). It secures admission (without queuing) into 15 or so state museums, including the Uffizi, Accademia, San Marco, Cappelle Medicee, and Palazzo Pitti. Two children go free with a family ticket, and membership permits multiple visits (useful for the Uffizi). Join Tuesday through Saturday inside Uffizi entrance no. 2; take photo ID. The **Opera del Duomo** sells a number of *cumulativi*, including one that covers Brunelleschi's cupola and the Museo dell'Opera for 11€. Inquire at the ticket office almost opposite the Baptistery.

Campanile di Giotto (Giotto's Bell Tower) ★★ HISTORIC SITE In 1334, Giotto started the cathedral bell tower but completed only the first two levels before his death in 1337. He was out of his league with the engineering aspects of architecture, and the tower was saved from falling by Andrea Pisano, who doubled the thickness of the walls. Andrea, a master sculptor of the Pisan Gothic school, also changed the design to add statue niches—he even carved a few of the statues himself—before quitting the project in 1348. Francesco Talenti finished the job between 1350 and 1359.

The **reliefs** and **statues** in the lower levels—by Andrea Pisano, Donatello, and others—are all copies; the weatherworn originals are now housed in the Museo dell'Opera del Duomo (see below). You can climb the 414 steps to the top of the tower. What makes this 84m-high (276-ft.) **view ★★** memorable are great views of the Baptistery as you ascend, and the best close-up shot in the entire city of Brunelleschi's dome.

Piazza del Duomo. www.operaduomo.firenze.it. ✆ **055-230-2885.** Admission 6€. Daily 8:30am–6:50pm. Bus: C2, 14, 23, or 71.

Duomo (Cattedrale di Santa Maria del Fiore) ★★ CATHEDRAL By the late 13th century, Florence was feeling peevish: Its archrivals Siena and Pisa sported huge new Duomos filled with art while it was saddled with the tiny 5th- or 6th-century Santa Reparata as a cathedral. So, in 1296, the city hired Arnolfo di Cambio to design a new Duomo, and he raised the facade and the first few bays before his death in 1302. Work continued under the auspices of the Wool Guild and architects Giotto di Bondone (who concentrated on the bell tower) and Francesco Talenti (who finished up to the drum of the dome). The facade we see today is a neo-Gothic composite designed by Emilio de Fabris and built from 1871 to 1887 (for its story, see "Museo dell'Opera del Duomo," below).

The baptistery, with its glittering bronze doors by Lorenzo Ghiberti.

The Duomo's most distinctive feature is its enormous **dome ★★★**, which dominates the skyline and is a symbol of Florence itself. The raising of this dome, the largest in the world in its time, was no mean architectural feat, tackled admirably by Filippo Brunelleschi between 1420 and 1436 (see "One Man & His Dome," below). You can climb up between the two shells of the cupola for one of the classic panoramas across the city (not recommended for claustrophobes or anyone lacking a head for heights). At the base of the dome, just above the drum, Baccio d'Agnolo began adding a balcony in 1507. One of the eight sides was finished by 1515, when someone asked Michelangelo—whose artistic opinion was by this time taken as cardinal law—what he thought of it. The master reportedly scoffed, "It looks like a cricket cage." Work was halted, and to this day the other seven sides remain rough brick.

Piazza del Duomo. www.operaduomo.firenze.it. ✆ **055-230-2885.** Admission to church free; Santa Reparata excavations 3€; cupola 8€. Church Mon–Wed and Fri 10am–5pm; Thurs 10am–4:30pm (July–Sept till 5pm, May and Oct till 3:30pm); Sat 10am–4:45pm; Sun 1:30–4:45pm. Free tours every 40 min. daily; times vary. Cupola Mon–Fri 8:30am–7pm; Sat 8:30am–5:40pm. Bus: C1, C2, 14, 23, or 71.

The Duomo, featuring Brunelleschi's dome.

Museo dell'Opera del Duomo (Duomo Works Museum) ★ MUSEUM This museum exists mainly to house the sculptures removed from the niches and doors of the Duomo group for restoration and preservation from the elements.

The courtyard is enclosed to show off—under natural daylight—Lorenzo Ghiberti's original gilded bronze panels from the Baptistery's ***Gates of Paradise*** ★★★, which are displayed on rotation as they're restored. Ghiberti devoted 27 years to this project (1425–52), and you can admire up close his masterpiece of *schiacciato* (squished) relief—using the Donatello technique of almost sketching in perspective to create the illusion of depth in low relief.

Also here is **Michelangelo's *Pietà*** ★ (1548–55), his second and penultimate take on the subject, which the sculptor probably had in mind for his own tomb. The face of Nicodemus is a self-portrait, and Michelangelo most likely intended to leave much of the statue group only roughly carved, just as we see it. The museum also houses the **Prophets** carved for the bell tower, the most noted

A detail from the della Robbia marble choirs at the Duomo Museum.

ONE MAN & HIS dome

Filippo Brunelleschi, a diminutive man whose ego was as big as his talent, managed in his arrogant, quixotic, suspicious, and brilliant way to invent Renaissance architecture. Having been beaten by Lorenzo Ghiberti in the contest to cast the Baptistery doors (see above), Brunelleschi resolved he'd rather be the top architect than the second-best sculptor and took off for Rome to study the buildings of the ancients. On returning to Florence, he combined subdued gray *pietra serena* stone with smooth white plaster to create airy arches, vaults, and arcades of classically perfect proportions in his own variant on the ancient Roman orders of architecture. He designed San Lorenzo, Santo Spirito, and the elegant Ospedale degli Innocenti, but his greatest achievement was erecting the dome over Florence's cathedral.

The Duomo, then the world's largest church, had already been built, but nobody had been able to figure out how to cover the daunting space over its center without spending a fortune and without filling the church with the necessary scaffolding—plus no one was sure whether he could create a dome that would hold up under its own weight. Brunelleschi insisted he knew how, and once granted the commission, revealed his ingenious plan—which may have been inspired by close study of Rome's Pantheon.

He built the dome in two shells, the inner one thicker than the outer, both shells thinning as they neared the top, thus leaving the center hollow and removing a good deal of the weight. He also planned to construct the dome of giant vaults with ribs crossing over them, with each of the stones making up the actual fabric of the dome being dovetailed. In this way, the walls of the dome would support themselves as they were erected. In the process of building, Brunelleschi found himself as much an engineer as architect, constantly designing winches, cranes, and hoists to carry the materials faster and more efficiently up to the level of the workmen.

His finished work speaks for itself, 45m (148 ft.) wide at the base and 90m (295 ft.) high from drum to lantern. For his achievement, Brunelleschi was accorded a singular honor: He's the only person ever buried in Florence's cathedral.

of which are the remarkably expressive figures carved by Donatello: the drooping, aged face of the *Beardless Prophet;* the sad, fixed gaze of *Jeremiah;* and the misshapen ferocity of the bald ***Habakkuk*** ★ (known to Florentines as *Lo Zuccone*—"Pumpkin Head"). Mounted on the walls above are two putty-encrusted marble ***cantorie*** **(choir lofts).** The slightly earlier one (1431) on the entrance wall is by Luca della Robbia. Across the room, Donatello's ***cantoria*** ★ (1433–38) takes off in a new artistic direction as his singing cherubs literally break through the boundaries of the "panels" to leap and race around the entire *cantoria* behind the mosaicked columns.

Piazza del Duomo 9 (behind the back of the cathedral). www.operaduomo.firenze.it. ✆ **055-230-2885.** Admission 6€. Mon–Sat 9am–7:30pm; Sun 9am–1:45pm. Last admission 40 min. before close. Bus: C1, C2, 14, 23, or 71.

PIAZZA DELLA signoria

When the medieval Guelph party finally came out on top after their political struggle with the Ghibellines, they razed part of the old city center to build a new palace for civic government. It's said the Guelphs ordered architect Arnolfo di Cambio to build what we now call the Palazzo Vecchio in the corner of this space, but to be careful that not 1 inch of the building sat on the cursed former Ghibelline land. This odd legend was probably fabricated to explain Arnolfo's quirky off-center architecture.

The space around the *palazzo* became the new civic center of town, L-shaped **Piazza della Signoria ★★**, named after the oligarchic ruling body of the medieval city. Today, it's an outdoor sculpture gallery, teeming with tourists, postcard stands, horses and buggies, and very expensive cafes.

The statuary on the piazza is particularly beautiful, starting on the far left (as you're facing the Palazzo Vecchio) with Giambologna's equestrian statue of *Grand Duke Cosimo I* (1594). To its right is one of Florence's favorite sculptures to hate, the ***Fontana del Nettuno*** (*Neptune Fountain;* 1560–75), created by Bartolomeo Ammannati as a tribute to Cosimo I's naval ambitions but nicknamed by the Florentines *Il Biancone,* "Big Whitey." Note the **porphyry plaque** set in the ground in front of the fountain. This marks the site where puritanical monk Savonarola held the Bonfire of the Vanities: With his fiery apocalyptic preaching, he whipped the Florentines into a reformist frenzy, and hundreds filed into this piazza, arms loaded with paintings, clothing, and other effects that represented their "decadence." They consigned it all to the flames. However, after a few years the pope (not amused by Savonarola's criticisms) excommunicated first the monk and then the entire city for supporting him. On May 23, 1498, Florentines decided they'd had enough of the rabid-dog monk, dragged him and two followers to the torture chamber, pronounced them heretics, and led them into the piazza for one last day of fire and brimstone. In the very spot where

5

Around Piazza della Signoria & Santa Trínita

Galleria degli Uffizi (Uffizi Gallery) ★★★ ART MUSEUM The Uffizi is one of the world's great museums, and the single best introduction to Renaissance painting, with works by Giotto, Masaccio, Paolo Uccello, Sandro Botticelli, Leonardo da Vinci, Perugino, Michelangelo, Raphael Sanzio, Titian, Caravaggio . . . and the list goes on. The painting gallery is housed in the structure built to serve as the offices (*uffizi* is Florentine dialect for *uffici,* or "offices")

they once burned their luxurious belongings, they put the torch to Savonarola himself. The event is commemorated by an anonymous painting kept in Savonarola's old cell in San Marco (p. 217) and by the plaque here.

To the right of the *Neptune Fountain* (pictured above) is a long, raised platform fronting the Palazzo Vecchio known as the *arringheria,* from which soapbox speakers would lecture to crowds before them (we get our word "harangue" from this). On its far left corner is a copy (original in the Bargello) of Donatello's ***Marzocco,*** symbol of the city, with a Florentine lion resting his raised paw on a shield emblazoned with the city's emblem, the *giglio* (lily). To its right is another Donatello replica, ***Judith Beheading Holofernes.*** Farther down is a man who needs little introduction, Michelangelo's ***David,*** a 19th-century copy of the original now in the Accademia. Near enough to David to look truly ugly in comparison is Baccio Bandinelli's ***Heracles*** (1534). Poor Bandinelli was trying to copy Michelangelo's muscular male form but ended up making his Heracles merely lumpy.

At the piazza's south end is one of the square's earliest and prettiest embellishments, the **Loggia dei Lanzi ★★** (1376–82), named after the Swiss guard of lancers *(lanzi)* Cosimo de' Medici stationed here. The airy loggia was probably built on a design by Andrea Orcagna—spawning another of its many names, the Loggia di Orcagna (another is the Loggia della Signoria). At the front left corner stands Benvenuto Cellini's masterpiece in bronze, ***Perseus*** **★★★** (1545), holding out the severed Medusa's head before him. On the far right of the loggia is Giambologna's ***Rape of the Sabines*** **★★**, one of the most successful Mannerist sculptures in existence, and a piece you must walk all the way around to appreciate, catching the action and artistry from different angles. Talk about moving it indoors, away from the elements, continues . . . but for now, it's still here.

of the Medici, commissioned by Cosimo I from Giorgio Vasari in 1560—perhaps his greatest architectural work. The painting gallery was started by Cosimo I as well and is now housed mostly in the second-floor rooms that open off a long hall lined with ancient statues and frescoed with grotesques.

The first room off to your left after you climb Vasari's monumental stairs (**Room 2;** Room 1 houses Roman reliefs) presents you with a crash course in the Renaissance's roots. On the right is Cimabue's *Santa Trínita Maestà* (1280), still rooted in the Byzantine traditions that governed painting in the early Middle

Ages. On the left is Duccio's ***Rucellai Maestà*** ★★ (1285), painted by the master who founded the Sienese school of painting. The style is still medieval but introduces innovations into the rigid traditions.

In the center of the room is Giotto's incredible ***Ognissanti Maestà*** ★★★ (1310), by the man who's generally credited as the founding father of Renaissance painting. His innovations are mainly in the very simple details, the sorts of things we take for granted in art today, such as the force of gravity, the display of basic emotions, the individual facial expressions, and the figures that look like they have an actual bulky body under their clothes.

Room 3 pays homage to the 14th-century Sienese school with delicately crafted works by Simone Martini and the Lorenzetti brothers, including Martini's ***Annunciation*** ★★★ (1333). Pietro and Ambrogio Lorenzetti helped revolutionize Sienese art and the Sienese school before succumbing to the Black Death in 1348. Of their work here, Ambrogio's 1342 ***Presentation at the Temple*** ★ is the finest, with a rich use of color and a vast architectural space painted with some understanding of perspective.

Rooms 5 and 6 represent the flourishing of International Gothic; Gentile da Fabriano's ***Procession of the Magi*** ★ (1423) is especially resplendent, and loaded with detail and caricature.

In the center of **Room 8** is Piero della Francesca's ***Portrait of Federico da Montefeltro and Battista Sforza*** ★★, painted around 1465 or 1470 and the only work by this remarkable Sansepolcran to survive in Florence. The rest of the room is devoted to Filippo Lippi. His most exquisite Madonna is the ***Madonna and Child with Two Angels*** ★★ (1455–66)—also a tender portrait of his mistress, Lucrezia Buti.

The walls separating **Rooms 10 to 14** were knocked down in the 20th century to accommodate the resurgent popularity of Sandro Filipepi—better known by his nickname, Botticelli ("little barrels"). Fourteen of his paintings line the walls, along with works by his pupil (and son of his former teacher) Filippino Lippi, and by Domenico Ghirlandaio, Michelangelo's first artistic master. In the ***Birth of Venus*** ★★, the love goddess is born of the sea on a half shell, blown to shore by the Zephyrs. Ores, a goddess of the seasons, rushes to clothe her. Some say the long-legged goddess was modeled on Simonetta Vespucci, a renowned Florentine beauty, cousin to Amerigo (the naval explorer after whom America is named) and not-so-secret lover of Giuliano de' Medici, Lorenzo the Magnificent's brother. ***Primavera: Allegory of Spring*** ★★ is harder to evaluate, since contemporary research indicates it may not actually be an allegory of spring influenced by the humanist poetry of Poliziano but rather a celebration of Venus, who stands in the center, surrounded by various complicated references to Virtues through mythological characters.

Room 15 boasts Leonardo da Vinci's ***Annunciation*** ★★★, which the young artist painted in 1472 or 1475 while still in the workshop of his master, Andrea del Verrocchio. The ***Adoration of the Magi*** ★★, on which Leonardo didn't get much beyond the sketching stage, shows how he could retain powerful compositions even when creating a fantasy landscape.

Room 19 is devoted to both Perugino, who did the luminous *Portrait of Francesco delle Opere* (1494), and Luca Signorelli, whose *Holy Family* (1490–95) was painted as a tondo set in a rectangle, with allegorical figures in the background and a torsion of the figures that were to influence Michelangelo's version (in a later room). **Room 23** contains Andrea Mantegna's triptych of the ***Adoration of the Magi, Circumcision, and Ascension*** ★ (1463–70), showing his excellent draftsmanship and fascination with classical architecture. **Room 25** is overpowered by Michelangelo's ***Holy Family*** ★★ (1506–08), one of the few panel paintings by the master. The glowing colors and shocking nudes in the background seem to pop off the surface, and the torsion of the figures was to be taken up as the banner of the Mannerist movement.

Michelangelo's *Holy Family* at the Uffizi Gallery.

Room 26 is devoted largely to High Renaissance darling Raphael. His ***Madonna of the Goldfinch*** ★ (1505) was painted in a Leonardesque style for a friend's wedding, and is more vivid than ever after a 2009 restoration. Also here are important portraits including ***Pope Leo X with Cardinals Giulio de' Medici and Luigi de' Rossi*** ★★ and *Pope Julius II,* as well as a famous *Self-Portrait.*

Room 27 covers Florentine Mannerism, especially Andrea Del Sarto's pupils Rosso Fiorentino and Pontormo. Fiorentino's ***Moses Defends the Daughters of Jethro*** ★ (1523) owes much to Michelangesque nudes.

Room 28 honors the great Venetian Titian, of whose works you'll see include a warm full-bodied ***Flora*** ★★ and a poetic, somewhat suggestive ***Venus of Urbino*** ★ languishing on her bed.

Pay your respects to Dutch master Rembrandt in **Room 44,** where he immortalized himself in two *Self-Portraits,* one done as a youth and the other as an old man. If you need to pause for breath, prices at the Uffizi's terrace **cafe** are no worse than in the piazza below. It's a nice spot to catch a new angle on the Palazzo Vecchio's facade.

Downstairs is a space used to house temporary exhibitions that, at their best, provide some added context to the permanent collection, but at worst are just a way to slap a few more euros onto your entrance fee. However, it's certainly worth visiting the space devoted to Caravaggio and the Caravaggeschi. Caravaggio was the baroque master of chiaroscuro—painting with extreme harsh light and deep shadows. The Uffizi preserves his painting of the severed head of *Medusa,* a *Sacrifice of Isaac,* and his famous ***Bacchus*** ★. The Caravaggeschi (painters who followed his style) included Artemisia Gentileschi, the only female painter to make a name for herself in the early baroque. Artemisia was the victim in a sensational rape trial: It evidently affected her professional life; the violent ***Judith Slaying Holofernes*** ★ is featured here, in all its gruesome detail.

Piazzale degli Uffizi 6 (off Piazza della Signoria). www.uffizi.firenze.it. ✆ **055-238-8651.** (Reserve tickets at www.firenzemusei.it or ✆ 055-294-883.) Admission 6.50€ (10€–11€ with compulsory temporary exhibition). Tues–Sat 8:15am–6:50pm; also same hours 1st, 3rd, and 5th Sun of month. Ticket window closes 45 min. before museum. Bus: C1 or C2.

Museo Galileo ★ ☺ MUSEUM The laptop computer and smartphone don't hold a candle to the beautifully engraved intricate mechanical instruments from Florence's history of science museum. Galileo and his peers practiced a science

Reserving Tickets for the Uffizi & Other Museums

If you're not buying a cumulative ticket (see "Discount Tickets for the City," above), you should bypass the hours-long line at the Uffizi by reserving a ticket and an entry time in advance by calling **Firenze Musei** at ✆ **055-294-883** (Mon–Fri 8:30am–6:30pm; Sat until 12:30pm) or visiting **www.firenzemusei.it** (you may need to have patience with their website, however). You can also reserve for the Accademia Gallery (another interminable line, to see *David*), as well as the Galleria Palatina in the Pitti Palace, the Bargello, and several others. There is a 3€ fee (4€ for the Uffizi or Accademia, where a reservation is very strongly advised); you can pay by credit card.

that was an art form of the highest aesthetic order. The cases display such beauties from the original Medici collections (begun by Cosimo I) as a mechanical calculator from 1664—a gleaming bronze sandwich of engraved disks and dials—and an architect's compass and plumb disguised as a dagger, complete with sheath. In the field of astronomy, the museum has the lens with which Galileo discovered four of the moons of Jupiter (which he prudently named after his Medici patrons).

Piazza dei Giudici 1 (just east of the Uffizi along the riverside). www.museogalileo.it. ✆ **055-265-311.** Admission 8€ adults, 5€ for ages 7–18 and 65 and over. Mon and Wed–Sun 9:30am–5pm; Tues 9:30am–1pm. Bus: C1.

Museo Nazionale del Bargello (Bargello Museum) ★★ MUSEUM Inside this 1255 Gothic *palazzo* is Florence's premier sculpture museum, with works by Michelangelo, the della Robbias, and Donatello.

In the *palazzo*'s old **armory** are 16th-century works, including some of Michelangelo's earliest sculptures. Carved by a 22-year-old Michelangelo while he was visiting Rome, ***Bacchus*** ★ (1497) was obviously inspired by the classical antiquities he studied there but is also imbued with his own irrepressible Renaissance realism—here is a (young) God of Wine who's actually drunk, reeling back on unsteady knees and holding the cup aloft with a distinctly tipsy wobble. The *palazzo*'s inner **courtyard**—one of the few medieval *cortile* in Florence to survive in more-or-less its original shape—is studded with the coats of arms of past *podestà* (mayors) and other notables. The grand stairwell leads up to the old **Salone del Consiglio Generale (General Council Room) ★★**, a vast space with a high ceiling filled with glazed terra-cotta Madonnas by Luca della Robbia and his clan, and some of the most important sculptures of the early Renaissance.

Donatello dominates the room, starting with a mischievously smiling *Cupid* (ca. 1430–40). He sculpted the *Marzocco,* lion symbol of the Florentine Republic, out of *pietra serena* between 1418 and 1420. The marble *David* (1408) is an early Donatello, but the bronze ***David*** ★★ (1440–50)—or perhaps *Mercury,* opinion is divided—is a much more mature piece, the first freestanding nude since antiquity. Against the far wall is ***St. George*** ★, carved in 1416 for a niche of Orsanmichele. The relief below it of the saint slaying his dragon is the first example of the sculptor's patented *schiacciato* technique.

In the back right corner of this room are two bronze relief panels by Brunelleschi and Ghiberti of the *Sacrifice of Isaac,* finalists in the famous 1401 competition for the commission to cast the Baptistery's doors (p. 199). Ghiberti's panel won.

Donatello's bronze *David* at the Bargello.

Via del Proconsolo 4. ✆ **055-238-8606.** Admission 4€. Daily 8:15am–1:50pm. Closed 2nd and 4th Mon and 1st, 3rd, and 5th Sun of each month. Bus: C1 or C2.

Orsanmichele ★★ RELIGIOUS SITE This bulky structure halfway down Via dei Calzaiuoli looks more like a Gothic warehouse than a church—which is exactly what it was, built as a granary and grain market in 1337. After a miraculous image of the Madonna appeared on a column inside, however, the lower level was turned into a chapel. The city's merchant guilds each undertook the task of decorating one of the outside nichelike Gothic tabernacles around the lower level with a statue of their guild's patron saint. Masters such as Ghiberti, Donatello, Verrocchio, and Giambologna all cast or carved masterpieces to set here (those remaining are mostly copies).

In the chapel's dark interior, the elaborate Gothic ***Tabernacle*** **★** (1349–59) by Andrea Orcagna protects a luminous 1348 *Madonna and Child* painted by Giotto's student Bernardo Daddi, to which miracles were ascribed during the Black Death of 1348–50.

Across Via dell'Arte della Lana from the Orsanmichele's main entrance is the 1308 Palazzo dell'Arte della Lana, now the entrance to the upstairs **museum of the statues ★** that once surrounded the exterior. Many of the original sculptures are here, well labeled, including Donatello's marble *St. Mark* (1411–13); Ghiberti's bronze *St. John the Baptist* (1413–16), the first life-size bronze of the Renaissance; and Verrocchio's *Incredulity of St. Thomas* (1473–83). Alas, the room is rarely open—Monday is the day you'll most likely get lucky.

Via Arte della Lana 1. ✆ **055-210-305.** Free admission. Daily 10am–5pm. Bus: C2.

Palazzo Vecchio ★ PALACE Florence's fortresslike town hall was built from 1299 to 1302 on the designs of Arnolfo di Cambio, Gothic master builder of the city. The palace was once home to the various Florentine republican governments (and today to the municipal government). Cosimo I and his ducal Medici family moved to the *palazzo* in 1540 and engaged in massive redecoration. Michelozzo's 1453 **courtyard ★**, just through the door, was left architecturally intact but frescoed by Vasari with scenes of Austrian cities to celebrate the 1565 marriage of Francesco de' Medici and Joanna of Austria.

The grand staircase leads up to the **Sala dei Cinquecento,** named for the 500-man assembly that met here in the pre-Medici days of the Florentine Republic and site of the greatest fresco cycle that ever wasn't. Leonardo da Vinci was commissioned in 1503 to paint one long wall with a battle scene celebrating a famous Florentine victory. He was always trying new methods and materials and decided to

The Palazzo Vecchio, in the Piazza della Signoria.

mix wax into his pigments. Leonardo had finished painting part of the wall, but it wasn't drying fast enough, so he brought in braziers stoked with hot coals to try to hurry the process. As others watched in horror, the wax in the fresco melted under the intense heat and the colors ran down the walls to puddle on the floor. The search for whatever remains of his work continues to this day. Michelangelo never even got past making the preparatory drawings for the fresco he was supposed to paint on the opposite wall—Pope Julius II called him to Rome to paint the Sistine Chapel. Eventually, the bare walls were covered by Vasari and assistants from 1563 to 1565 with blatantly subservient frescoes exalting Cosimo I and his dynasty. Against the wall, opposite the door you enter, is Michelangelo's statue of ***Victory*** ★, carved from 1533 to 1534 for the Julius II tomb but later donated to the Medici.

The first series of rooms on the second floor is the **Quartiere degli Elementi,** again frescoed by Vasari. Crossing the balcony overlooking the Sala dei Cinquecento, you enter the **Apartments of Eleonora di Toledo,** decorated for Cosimo's Spanish wife. Her small private chapel is a masterpiece of mid-16th-century painting by Bronzino. Farther on, under the coffered ceiling of the **Sala dei Gigli,** are Domenico Ghirlandaio's fresco of *St. Zenobius Enthroned* with ancient Roman heroes and Donatello's original ***Judith and Holofernes*** ★ bronze (1455), one of his last works.

Piazza della Signoria. ✆ **055-276-8325.** Admission 6€. Fri–Wed 9am–7pm; Thurs and public holidays 9am–2pm. Bus: C1 or C2.

Ponte Vecchio (Old Bridge) ★ ARCHITECTURE The oldest and most famous bridge across the Arno, the Ponte Vecchio was built in 1345 by Taddeo Gaddi to replace an earlier version. The characteristic overhanging shops have lined the bridge since at least the 12th century. In the 16th century, it was home to butchers until Cosimo I moved into the Palazzo Pitti across the river. He couldn't stand the stench as he crossed the bridge from on high in the Corridoio Vasariano every day, so he evicted the meat cutters and moved in the classier gold- and silversmiths, tradesmen who occupy it to this day.

The Ponte Vecchio's fame saved it in 1944 from the Nazis, who had orders to blow up all the bridges before retreating out of Florence as Allied forces advanced. They couldn't bring themselves to reduce this span to rubble—so they blew up the ancient buildings on either end instead to block it off. The Great Arno Flood of 1966 wasn't so discriminating, however, and severely damaged the shops. Apparently, a private night watchman saw the waters rising alarmingly and called many of the goldsmiths at home, who rushed to remove their valuable stock before it was washed away.

Via Por Santa Maria/Via Guicciardini. Bus: C3 or D.

Santa Trínita ★★ CHURCH Beyond Bernardo Buontalenti's late-16th-century **facade** lies a dark church, rebuilt in the 14th century but founded by the Vallombrosans before 1177. The third chapel on the right has what remains of the detached frescoes by Spinello Aretino, which were found under Lorenzo Monaco's excellent 1422 frescoes covering the next chapel down.

In the right transept, Domenico Ghirlandaio frescoed the **Cappella Sassetti ★** in 1483 with a cycle on the *Life of St. Francis,* but true to form he set all the scenes against Florentine backdrops and peopled them with portraits of contemporary notables. The most famous is *Francis Receiving the Order from Pope Honorius,* which in this version takes place under an arcade on the north side of Piazza della Signoria—the Loggia dei Lanzi is featured in the middle, and on the left is the Palazzo Vecchio. (The Uffizi btw. them hadn't been built yet.) In the little group on the far right, the unhandsome man with the red cloak is Lorenzo the Magnificent.

The south end of the piazza leads to the **Ponte Santa Trínita ★**, Florence's most graceful bridge. In 1567, Ammannati built a span here that was set with four 16th-century statues of the seasons in honor of the marriage of Cosimo II. After the Nazis blew up the bridge in 1944, it was rebuilt, and all was set into place again—save the head on the statue of Spring, which remained lost until a team dredging the river in 1961 found it by accident.

Piazza Santa Trínita. ✆ **055-216-912.** Free admission. Mon–Sat 8am–noon and 4–6pm; Sun 4–6pm. Bus: C3, 6, 11, 36, or 37.

Around San Lorenzo & the Mercato Centrale

The church of San Lorenzo is practically lost behind the leather stalls and souvenir carts of Florence's vast **San Lorenzo street market** (see "Shopping," later

Vasari's Corridor

The enclosed passageway that runs along the top of Ponte Vecchio is part of the **Corridoio Vasariano (Vasari Corridor) ★**, a private elevated link between the Palazzo Vecchio and Palazzo Pitti, and now hung with the world's best collection of artists' self-portraits. Duke Cosimo I found the idea of mixing with the hoi polloi on the way to work rather distressing, and so commissioned Vasari to design his VIP route in 1565. It's often possible to walk the corridor, although closures for restoration work are common. Inquire at the tourist office. **Context Travel** (p. 226) operates an excellent guided walk through the corridor, costing 100€ per person.

Catching an Exhibition at the Strozzi

The two spaces inside the Renaissance **Palazzo Strozzi ★★**, Piazza Strozzi—known as the **Piano Nobile**—and the basement **Strozzina,** are Florence's major spaces for temporary and contemporary art shows, and have been experiencing a 21st-century renaissance of their own under new and energetic directorship. Major hits of recent years have included the likes of 2011's Picasso, Miró, Dalí. There's always lots going on around the shows, too, including talks, late-night events, and even discovery trails aimed at 5- to 9-year-olds. Check **www.palazzostrozzi.org** for the latest exhibition news.

in this chapter). In fact, the hawking of wares and bustle of commerce characterize all the streets of this neighborhood, centered on both the church and the nearby **Mercato Centrale food market.** This is a colorful scene, but one of the most pickpocket-happy in the city, so be wary. ***Note:*** You are liable for a fine if you knowingly buy counterfeit goods in the city.

Cappelle Medicee (Medici Chapels) ★★ MONUMENT/MEMORIAL When Michelangelo built the New Sacristy between 1520 and 1533 (finished by Vasari in 1556), it was to be a tasteful monument to Lorenzo the Magnificent and his generation of fairly pleasant Medici. When work got underway on the Chapel of the Princes in 1604, it was to become one of the world's most god-awful and arrogant memorials, dedicated to the grand dukes, some of Florence's most decrepit tyrants. The **Cappella dei Principi (Chapel of the Princes)** is an exercise in bad taste, a mountain of cut marbles and semiprecious stones—jasper, alabaster, mother-of-pearl, agate, and the like—slathered onto the walls and ceiling with no regard for composition and still less for chromatic unity. The pouring of ducal funds into this monstrosity began in 1604 and lasted until the rarely conscious Gian Gastone de' Medici drank himself to death in 1737 without an heir—but teams kept doggedly at the thing, and they were still finishing the floor in 1962.

Michelangelo's **Sagrestia Nuova (New Sacristy) ★★**, built to jibe with Brunelleschi's Old Sacristy in San Lorenzo proper, is much calmer. (An architectural tidbit: The windows in the dome taper as they get near the top to fool you into thinking the dome is higher.) Michelangelo was supposed to produce three tombs here (perhaps four) but ironically got only the two less important ones done. So Lorenzo de' Medici the Magnificent—wise ruler of his city, poet of note, grand patron of the arts, and moneybags behind much of the Renaissance—ended up with a mere inscription of his name next to his brother Giuliano's on a plain marble slab against the entrance wall. Admittedly, they did get one genuine Michelangelo sculpture to decorate their slab, a *Madonna and Child* that's perhaps the master's most beautiful version of the theme.

On the left wall of the sacristy is Michelangelo's ***Tomb of Lorenzo ★***, duke of Urbino (and Lorenzo the Magnificent's grandson), whose seated statue symbolizes the contemplative life. Below him on the elongated curves of the tomb stretch *Dawn* (female) and *Dusk* (male), a pair of Michelangelo's most famous sculptures. This pair mirrors the similarly fashioned and equally important *Day* (male) and *Night* (female) across the way. One additional point *Dawn* and *Night* brings out is that Michelangelo really wasn't too adept at the female body.

The Medici Chapels.

Piazza Madonna degli Aldobrandini (behind San Lorenzo, where Via Faenza and Via del Giglio meet). ✆ **055-238-8602.** Admission 6€. Daily 8:15am–4:50pm. Closed 1st, 3rd, and 5th Mon, and 2nd and 4th Sun of each month. Bus: C1, C2, 6, 11, 14, 22, 23, 36, or 37.

Palazzo Medici-Riccardi ★ PALACE The Palazzo Medici Riccardi was built by Michelozzo in 1444 for Cosimo de' Medici il Vecchio; it's the prototype Florentine *palazzo,* on which the more overbearing Strozzi and Pitti palaces were later modeled. It remained the Medici private home until Cosimo I officially declared his power as duke by moving to the city's traditional civic brain center, the Palazzo Vecchio. A door off the right of the entrance courtyard leads up a staircase to the **Cappella dei Magi,** the oldest chapel to survive from a private Florentine palace; its walls are covered with gorgeously dense and colorful Benozzo Gozzoli **frescoes** ★★ (1459–63). Rich as tapestries, the walls depict an extended *Journey of the Magi* to see the Christ child, who's being adored by Mary in the altarpiece.

Via Cavour 3. www.palazzo-medici.it. ✆ **055-276-0340.** Admission 7€ adults, 4€ ages 6–12. Thurs–Tues 9am–7pm. Bus: C1, 14, or 23.

San Lorenzo ★ CHURCH A rough brick anti-facade and the undistinguished stony bulk of a building surrounded by market stalls hide what is most likely the oldest church in Florence, founded in A.D. 393. It was later the Medici family's parish church, and Cosimo il Vecchio, whose wise behind-the-scenes rule made him popular with the Florentines, is buried in front of the high altar. The plaque marking the spot is inscribed PATER PATRIE—"Father of His Homeland."

Off the left transept is the **Sagrestia Vecchia (Old Sacristy)** ★, one of Brunelleschi's purest pieces of early Renaissance architecture. The focal sarcophagus contains Cosimo il Vecchio's parents, Giovanni di Bicci de' Medici and his wife, Piccarda Bueri, and a side chapel is decorated with an early star map that shows the night sky above the city in the 1440s.

On the wall of the left aisle is Bronzino's huge fresco of the ***Martyrdom of San Lorenzo*** ★ (the poor soul was roasted on a grill).

Left of the church's main door is an entrance to the cloister and inside it a stairwell leading up to the **Biblioteca Laurenziana (Laurentian Library)** ★★.

Michelangelo designed this library in 1524 to house the Medici's manuscript collection, and it stands as one of the most brilliant works of Mannerist architecture.

Piazza San Lorenzo. ✆ **055-214-042.** Admission to church 3.50€; admission to library 3€; combined admission 6€. Church Mon–Sat 10am–5:30pm; Sun Mar–Oct 1:30–5:30pm. Laurentian Library Mon–Sat 9:30am–1pm. Bus: C1, 14, or 23.

On or Near Piazza Santa Maria Novella

Piazza Santa Maria Novella boasts patches of grass and a central fountain. The two squat obelisks, resting on the backs of Giambologna tortoises, once served as the turning posts for the "chariot" races held here from the 16th to the mid–19th century. Once a depressed and down-at-heel part of the center, the area now hosts some of Florence's most fashionable hotels.

Museo di Santa Maria Novella ★ ART MUSEUM The cloisters of Santa Maria Novella's convent are open to the public as a museum. The **Chiostro Verde,** with a cypress-surrounded fountain and chirping birds, is named for the greenish tint in the pigment used by Paolo Uccello in his **frescoes ★★**. His works line the right wall as you enter. The **Cappella degli Spagnoli (Spanish Chapel) ★**, off the cloister, got its name when it became the private chapel of Eleonora of Toledo, recently arrived in Florence to be Cosimo de' Medici's bride. The chapel was frescoed by Andrea di Bonaiuto and his assistants with allegories on the preaching of the Dominicans, whose Florence base this was.

Piazza Santa Maria Novella (entrance behind gate left of the church facade). www.museicivicifiorentini.it/en/smn. ✆ **055-282-187.** Admission 2.70€ adults, 1€ ages 4–17. Fri–Mon 10am–4pm. Bus: C2, 6, 11, 22, 36, or 37.

Santa Maria Novella ★★ CHURCH Of all Florence's major churches, the home of the Dominicans is the only one with an original **facade ★** that matches its era of greatest importance. The lower Romanesque half was started in the 14th century by architect Fra' Jacopo Talenti, who had just finished building the church itself (started in 1246). Leon Battista Alberti finished the facade, adding a classically inspired Renaissance top that not only went seamlessly with the lower half but also created a Cartesian plane of perfect geometry.

Inside, on the left wall, is **Masaccio's *Trinità* ★★★** (ca. 1428), the first painting ever to use perfect linear mathematical perspective. Florentine citizens and artists flooded in to see the fresco when it was unveiled, many remarking in awe that it seemed to punch a hole back into space, creating a chapel out of a flat wall. The **transept** is filled with spectacularly frescoed chapels. The **sanctuary ★** behind the main altar was frescoed after

Santa Maria Novella.

A view of the city, dominated by Brunelleschi's dome.

1485 by Domenico Ghirlandaio with the help of his assistants and apprentices, probably including a young Michelangelo. The left wall is covered with a cycle on the *Life of the Virgin* and the right wall with a *Life of St. John the Baptist.* The works are less biblical stories than snapshots of the era's fashions and personages, full of portraits of the Tornabuoni family who commissioned them.

The **Cappella Gondi** to the left of the high altar contains a *Crucifix* carved by Brunelleschi.

Piazza Santa Maria Novella. ✆ **055 219-257.** Admission 3.50€. Mon–Thurs 9am–5:30pm; Fri 11am–5:30pm; Sat 9am–5pm; Sun noon–5pm. Bus: C2, 6, 11, 22, 36, or 37.

Near San Marco & Santissima Annunziata

Cenacolo di Sant'Apollonia ★ ART MUSEUM There are no lines at this former convent and no crowds: Few people even know it's here. What they're missing is one vast wall covered with the vibrant colors of Andrea del Castagno's masterful *Last Supper* (ca. 1450). Castagno used his paint to create the rich marble panels that checkerboard the *trompe l'oeil* walls and broke up the long white tablecloth with the dark figure of Judas the Betrayer, whose face is painted to resemble a satyr, an ancient symbol of evil.

Via XXVII Aprile 1. ✆ **055-238-8607.** Free admission. Daily 8:15am–1:50pm. Closed 1st, 3rd, and 5th Sun and 2nd and 4th Mon of each month. Bus: 1, 6, 11, 14, 17, or 23.

Galleria dell'Accademia ★★ ART MUSEUM The first long hall here is devoted to Michelangelo and, although you pass his *Slaves,* most visitors are immediately drawn down to the far end, a tribune dominated by the most famous sculpture in the world: **Michelangelo's *David* ★★★**. A hot young sculptor fresh from his success with a *Pietà* in Rome (p. 93), Michelangelo took on in 1501 a huge slab of marble that had been lying around the Duomo's work yards so long it earned a nickname, Il Gigante (the Giant). It was with a twist of humor that Michelangelo, only 29 years old, finished in 1504 a Goliath-size David for his city.

There was originally a spot reserved for it high on the left flank of the Duomo, but Florence's republican government soon wheeled it down to stand on Piazza della Signoria in front of the Palazzo Vecchio to symbolize the defeated tyranny of the Medici, who had been ousted a decade before (but would return with a vengeance). The sculpture was moved to the Accademia in 1873 and a copy took its place in the piazza.

The hall leading up to *David* is lined with perhaps Michelangelo's most fascinating works, the four famous *nonfiniti* (unfinished) ***Slaves,*** or ***Prisoners*** ★★★. Like no others, these statues symbolize Michelangelo's theory that sculpture is an "art that takes away superfluous material." The great master saw a true sculpture as something that was inherent in the stone, and all it needed was a skilled chisel to free it from the extraneous rock.

Seeing *David* Without a Reservation

The wait to get in to see *David* can be an hour or more if you didn't reserve ahead (see details on how to make reservations below). Try getting there before the museum opens in the morning or an hour or two before closing time.

Nearby, in a similar mode, is a statue of ***St. Matthew*** ★★ (1504–08), which Michelangelo began carving as part of a series of Apostles he was at one point going to complete for the Duomo. (The *Pietà* at the end of the corridor on the right is by one of Michelangelo's students, not by the master as was once thought.)

Off this hall of *Slaves* is the first wing of the painting gallery, which includes a panel, possibly from a wedding chest, known as the ***Cassone Adimari*** ★, painted by Lo Scheggia in the 1440s. It shows the happy couple's promenade to the Duomo, with the green-and-white marbles of the Baptistery prominent in the background. Other rooms house a fine collection of pre-Renaissance panels dating to the 1200s and 1300s.

Via Ricasoli 60. www.polomuseale.firenze.it. ✆ **055-238-8609.** (Reserve tickets at www.firenzemusei.it or ✆ 055-294-883; booking fee 4€). Admission 6.50€; 11€ with temporary exhibition. Tues–Sun 8:15am–6:50pm. Last admission 30 min. before close. Bus: C1, 6, 7, 11, 14, 23, 31, or 32.

Museo Archeologico (Archaeological Museum) ★ MUSEUM This embarrassingly rich collection, in an apparently permanent state of reorganization, is often overlooked by visitors in full-throttle Renaissance mode. It conserves Egyptian sarcophagi and hieroglyphs, Roman remains, and an important Etruscan *bucchero* pottery collection. The relics to be on the lookout for include an early-4th-century-B.C. bronze ***Chimera*** ★★, a mythical beast with a lion's body and head, a goat head sprouting from its back, and a serpent for a tail. (The tail was incorrectly restored in 1785.) The beast was found near Arezzo in 1553 and probably made in a Chiusi or an Orvieto workshop as a votive offering.

Such is the chaos that it's impossible to predict what you'll find next, but do track down an extraordinarily rare **Hittite wood-and-bone chariot** from the 14th century B.C. Room XVI upstairs had at the time of writing a 1st-century-B.C. cast bronze ***Arringatore*** (*Orator*) found near Perugia. The focus of the top floor is the ***Idolino*** ★. The history of this nude bronze lad with his outstretched hand is long, complicated, and in the end a bit mysterious. The current theory is that he's a Roman statue of the Augustan period (around the time of Christ).

Piazza Santissma Annunziata 9b. www.firenzemusei.it. ✆ **055-23-575.** Admission 4€. Tues–Sun 8:15am–6:50pm. Bus: C1, 6, 14, 23, 31, or 32.

San Marco ★★★ ART MUSEUM In 1437, Cosimo de' Medici il Vecchio, grandfather of Lorenzo the Magnificent, had Michelozzo convert a medieval monastery here into a new home for the Dominicans, in which Cosimo also founded Europe's first public library. The monastery's most talented friar was International Gothic painter Fra' Angelico, and he left many of his finest works, devotional images painted with the technical skill and minute detail of a miniaturist or an illuminator but on altarpiece scale.

The old **Pilgrim's Hospice ★★** is full of his altarpieces and painted panels, notably an exquisite ***Deposition*** **★**, the 2011-restored *Tabernacolo dei Linaioli* (1435) whose predella scenes are especially enchanting, and the 1443 ***San Marco Altarpiece*** **★★**, with Medici saints Cosmas and Damian. Also off the cloister is the **Sala del Capitolo (Chapter House),** frescoed from 1441 to 1442 with a huge *Crucifixion* by Fra' Angelico and his assistants. The door next to this leads past the staircase up to the Dormitory (see below) to the **Sala del Cenacolo (Small Refectory),** now the gift shop, with a *Last Supper* frescoed by Domenico Ghirlandaio.

The **Dormitorio (Dormitory) ★★** of cells where the monks lived is one of Fra' Angelico's masterpieces and his most famous cycle of frescoes. In addition to the renowned ***Annunciation*** **★★** at the top of the stairs to the monks' rooms, Angelico painted the cells themselves with simple works to aid his fellow friars in their meditations.

Piazza San Marco 1. ✆ **055-238-8608.** Admission 4€. Mon–Fri 8:30am–1:50pm; Sat–Sun 8:15am–4:50pm. Closed 2nd and 4th Mon of each month. Bus: C1, 1, 6, 7, 10, 11, 14, 17, 20, 25, 31, 32, or 33.

Santissima Annunziata ★ CHURCH In 1230, seven Florentine nobles had a spiritual crisis, gave away all their possessions, and retired to the forests to contemplate divinity. They returned to what were then fields outside the city walls and founded a small oratory, proclaiming they were Servants of Mary, or the Servite Order. The oratory was enlarged by Michelozzo (1444–81) and later redesigned in the baroque. The main art interest is in the **Chiostro dei Voti (Votive Cloister),** designed by Michelozzo with Corinthian capitaled columns and decorated with some of the city's finest Mannerist **frescoes ★★** (1465–1515). Rosso Fiorentino provided an *Assumption* (1513) and Pontormo a *Visitation* (1515) just to the right of the door, but the main works are by their master, Andrea del Sarto, whose *Birth of the Virgin* (1513), in the far right corner, is one of his finest works. To the right of the door into the church is a damaged but still fascinating *Coming of the Magi* (1514) by del Sarto, who included a self-portrait at the far right, looking out at us from under his blue hat.

The **interior** is excessively baroque. Just to the left as you enter is a huge tabernacle hidden under a mountain of *ex votos* (votive offerings). It was designed by Michelozzo to house a small painting of the *Annunciation.* Legend holds that this painting was started by a friar who, vexed that he couldn't paint the Madonna's face as beautifully as it should be, gave it up and took a nap. When he awoke, he found an angel had filled in the face for him. Newlywed brides in Florence don't toss their bouquets—they head here after the ceremony to leave their flowers at the shrine for good luck.

On the **piazza ★★** outside, flanked by elegant porticos (see Spedale degli Innocenti, below), is an equestrian statue of *Grand Duke Ferdinando I,* Giambologna's last work; it was cast in 1608 after his death by his student Pietro Tacca, who also did the two little fountains of fantastic mermonkey-monsters.

Piazza Santissima Annunziata. ✆ **055-266-181.** Free admission. Daily 7:30am–12:30pm and 4–6:30pm. Bus: C1, 6, 14, 23, 31, or 32.

Spedale degli Innocenti ARCHITECTURE Europe's oldest foundling hospital, opened in 1445, is still going strong as a convent orphanage, though times have changed a bit. The Lazy Susan set into the wall on the left end of the arcade—where once people left unwanted babies, swiveled it around, rang the bell, and ran—has since been blocked up. The colonnaded **portico** ★ (built 1419–26) was designed by Filippo Brunelleschi when he was still an active goldsmith. It was his first great achievement as an architect and helped define the new Renaissance style he was developing. Its repetition by later artists in front of other buildings on the piazza makes it one of the most exquisite squares in Tuscany. The spandrels between the arches of Brunelleschi's portico are set with glazed **terra-cotta reliefs** of swaddled babes against rounded blue backgrounds—hands-down the masterpieces of Andrea della Robbia.

Piazza Santissima Annunziata 12. ✆ **055-203-7308.** Admission 5€. Daily 10am–7pm. Bus: C1, 6, 14, 23, 31, or 32.

Around Piazza Santa Croce

Piazza Santa Croce is pretty much like any grand Florentine square—a nice bit of open space ringed with souvenir and leather shops and thronged with tourists. Its unique feature (aside from the one time a year it's covered with dirt and violent, Renaissance-style soccer is played on it) is **Palazzo Antellesi** on the south side. This well-preserved, 16th-century patrician house is owned by a contessa who rents out her apartments (p. 261).

Casa Buonarroti ★ MUSEUM Although Michelangelo never actually lived in this modest *palazzo,* he did own the property and left it to his nephew Lionardo. Lionardo named his own son after his famous uncle, and this younger Michelangelo became devoted to the memory of his namesake, converting the house into a museum and hiring artists to fill the place with frescoes honoring the genius of his great uncle.

The good stuff is upstairs, starting with a display rotating pages from the museum's collection of original drawings. In the first room off the landing are Michelangelo's earliest sculptures: the Donatello-esque *Madonna of the Steps,* carved before 1492 when he was a 15- or 16-year-old student in the Medici school. A few months later, the prodigy was already finished carving another marble, a confused, almost Pisano-like tangle of bodies known as the *Battle of the Centaurs and Lapiths.*

Via Ghibellina 70. www.casabuonarroti.it. ✆ **055-241-752.** Admission 6.50€; combined ticket with Santa Croce 8€. Wed–Mon 9:30am–2pm. Bus: C2, C3, 14, or 23.

Santa Croce ★★ CHURCH The center of the Florentine Franciscan universe was begun in 1294 by Gothic master Arnolfo di Cambio in order to rival the church of Santa Maria Novella being raised by the Dominicans across the city. The church wasn't consecrated until 1442, and even then it remained faceless until the neo-Gothic **facade** was added in 1857. It's a vast complex that demands 2 hours of your time, at least, to see properly.

The Gothic **interior** is vast, and populated with the tombs of rich and famous Florentines. Starting from the main door, immediately on the right is the

Inside Santa Croce.

first tomb of note, a mad Vasari contraption containing the bones of the most venerated Renaissance master, **Michelangelo Buonarroti,** who died of a fever in Rome in 1564 at the ripe age of 89. The pope wanted him buried in the Eternal City, but Florentines managed to sneak his body back to Florence. Close to Michelangelo's monument is a pompous 19th-century cenotaph to Florentine **Dante Alighieri,** one of history's great poets, whose *Divine Comedy* codified the Italian language. Elsewhere seek out monuments to philosopher **Niccolò Machiavelli, Gioacchino Rossini** (1792–1868), composer of the *Barber of Seville,* architect **Lorenzo Ghiberti,** and **Galileo Galilei** (1564–1642).

The right transept is richly decorated with frescoes. The **Cappella Castellani** was frescoed by Agnolo Gaddi, with a tabernacle by Mino da Fiesole and a *Crucifix* by Niccolò Gerini. Agnolo's father, Taddeo Gaddi, was one of Giotto's closest followers, and the senior Gaddi is the one who undertook painting the **Cappella Baroncelli** ★ (1332–38) at the transept's end. The frescoes depict scenes from the *Life of the Virgin,* and include an *Angel Appearing to the Shepherds* that constitutes the first night scene in Italian fresco.

Giotto himself frescoed the two chapels to the right of the high altar. The frescoes were whitewashed over during the 17th century but uncovered from 1841 to 1852 and inexpertly restored. The **Cappella Peruzzi** ★★, on the right, is a late work and not in the best shape. The many references to antiquity in the styling and architecture of the frescoes reflect Giotto's trip to Rome and its ruins. Even more famous, including as the setting for a scene in the film *A Room with a View,* is the **Cappella Bardi** ★★. Key panels here include the *Trial by Fire Before the Sultan of Egypt* on the right wall, full of telling subtlety in the expressions and poses of the figures. In one of Giotto's most well-known works, the *Death of St. Francis,* monks weep and wail with convincing pathos.

Outside in the cloister is the **Cappella Pazzi** ★, one of Filippo Brunelleschi's architectural masterpieces (faithfully finished after his death in 1446). Giuliano da Maiano probably designed the porch that now precedes the chapel, set with glazed terra-cottas by Luca della Robbia. The rectangular chapel is one of Brunelleschi's signature pieces and a defining example of (and model for) early Renaissance architecture.

From back in the cloister enter the **Museo dell'Opera** where, in the long hall of the former refectory, hangs Cimabue's ***Crucifix*** ★, by the artist who began bridging the gap between Byzantine tradition and Renaissance innovation, not least by teaching Giotto to paint.

Piazza Santa Croce. www.santacroceopera.it. ✆ **055-246-6105.** Admission 5€ adults, 3€ ages 11–17; combined ticket with Casa Buonarotti 8€. Mon–Sat 9:30am–5pm; Sun 1–5pm. Bus: C1, 3, or 23.

The Oltrarno, San Niccolò & San Frediano

Museo Zoologia "La Specola" ★ ☺ MUSEUM Italy has few zoos, but this is its largest zoological collection, with rooms full of insects, crustaceans, and stuffed birds and mammals—everything from ostriches and apes to a rhinoceros. The museum was founded here in 1775, and the collections are still displayed in the style of an old-fashioned natural sciences museum, with specimens crowded into beautiful old wood-and-glass cases. The last 10 rooms contain an important collection of **human anatomical wax models ★** crafted between 1775 and 1814 by Clemente Susini for medical students. The life-size figures are flayed, dissected, and disemboweled to varying degrees and are truly disgusting, but fascinating

Via Romana 17. www.msn.unifi.it. ✆ **055-234-6760.** Admission 6€ adults, 3€ children 6–14 and seniors 65 and over. Tues–Sun 10:30am–5:30pm. Bus: C3, D, 11, 36, or 37.

Palazzo Pitti & Giardino di Boboli (Pitti Palace & Boboli Garden) ★★ ART MUSEUM Although the original, much smaller Pitti Palace was a Renaissance affair probably designed by Filippo Brunelleschi, that *palazzo* is completely hidden by the enormous Mannerist mass we see today, designed largely by Bartolomeo Ammannati. Inside is Florence's most extensive set of museums, including the Galleria Palatina, a huge painting gallery second in scope only to the Uffizi, with works by Raphael, Titian, and Rubens.

The painting gallery—the main, and for many visitors, most interesting of the Pitti museums—is off Ammannati's **interior courtyard ★** of gold-tinged rusticated rock grafted onto the three classical orders. The ticket office is outside the main gate, on the far right as you face it from the piazza.

Galleria Palatina ★★★ If the Uffizi represents mainly the earlier masterpieces collected by the Medici, the Pitti Palace's painting gallery continues the story with the High Renaissance and later eras, a collection gathered by the Medici, and later the Grand Dukes of Lorraine. The works are still displayed in the old-world fashion, which hung paintings according to aesthetics—how well, say, the Raphael matched the drapes—rather than academic chronological order.

While the first batch of rooms have decorative interest, the art-historical meat starts later: Filippo Lippi's 1452 *Madonna and Child* and a minor Botticelli in the **Sala di Prometeo (Room of Prometheus)** are a mere appetizer for the **Sala dell'Educazione di Giove (Room of Jupiter's Education).** Here you'll find a 1608 ***Sleeping Cupid*** **★★** that Caravaggio painted while living in exile from Rome (avoiding murder charges) on the island of Malta.

The opulence of the Galleria Palatina at the Pitti Palace.

The **Sala dell'Iliade (Iliad Room)** has Raphael's portrait of a ***Pregnant Woman*** ★, along with some Titian masterpieces and *Mary Magdalene* and ***Judith*** ★, two paintings by one of the only female artists of the early baroque, Artemisia Gentileschi, who often turned to themes of strong biblical women. Raphael is also the focus of the **Sala di Saturno (Saturn Room)** ★★, where the transparent colors of his *Madonnas* and probing portraits show the strong influence of both Leonardo da Vinci and Raphael's old master Perugino, whose *Deposition* and a *Mary Magdalene* hang here as well.

The star of the **Sala di Giove (Jupiter Room)** is Raphael's ***La Velata*** ★★, one of the crowning achievements of his short career and a summation of what he had learned about color, light, naturalism, and mood. The **Sala di Marte (Mars Room)** is dominated by Rubens, including the enormous ***Consequences of War*** ★★, which an aged Rubens painted for his friend Sustermans at a time when both were worried that their Dutch homeland was on the brink of battle.

The **Sala di Apollo (Apollo Room)** has a masterful early *Portrait of an Unknown Gentleman* by famed early-16th-century Venetian painter Titian as well as his sensual, luminously gold ***Mary Magdalene*** ★, the first in a number of takes on the subject the painter was to make throughout his career. There are several works by Andrea del Sarto, whose late *Holy Family* and especially *Deposition* display the daring chromatic experiments and highly refined spatial compositions that were to influence his students Pontormo and Rosso Fiorentino as they went about mastering Mannerism.

Appartamenti Reali The other wing of the *piano nobile* is taken up with the Medici's private apartments, which have been restored to their late 19th-century appearance when the kings of the House of Savoy, first rulers of the unified Italy, used the suites as their Florentine home. The over-the-top sumptuous fabrics, decorative arts furnishings, stuccoes, and frescoes reflect the neo-baroque tastes of the Savoy kings.

Galleria d'Arte Moderna ★ Modern art isn't what draws most people to the capital of the Renaissance, but the Pitti's collection includes some important works by the 19th-century Tuscan school of art known as the Macchiaioli, who painted a kind of Tuscan Impressionism, concerned with the *macchie* (marks of color on the canvas and the play of light on the eye). Some of the movement's great talents are here, including Silvestro Lega, Telemaco Signorini, and Giovanni Fattori, the genius of the group.

Galleria del Costume & Museo degli Argenti These aren't the most popular of the Pitti's museums, and the **Museo degli Argenti** has what seem like miles of the most extravagant and often hideous objets d'art and housewares the Medici and Lorraines could put their hands on. The **Costume Gallery** is marginally more interesting. The collections concentrate on the 18th to 20th centuries but also display outfits from back to the 16th century.

Giardino di Boboli (Boboli Garden) ★★ The statue-filled park behind the Pitti Palace is one of the earliest and finest Renaissance gardens, laid out mostly between 1549 and 1656 with box hedges in geometric patterns, groves of ilex, dozens of statues, and rows of cypress. Just above the entrance through the courtyard of the Palazzo Pitti is an oblong **amphitheater** modeled on Roman circuses, with a **granite basin** from Rome's Baths of Caracalla and an **Egyptian obelisk** of Ramses II, but in 1589 this was the setting for the wedding reception of Ferdinando de' Medici's marriage to Christine of Lorraine. For the occasion, the Medici commissioned entertainment from Jacopo Peri and Ottavio

Rinuccini, who decided to set a classical story entirely to music and called it *Dafne*—the world's first opera. (Later, they wrote a follow-up hit *Erudice,* performed here in 1600; it's the first opera whose score has survived.)

Around the park, don't miss the rococo **Kaffehaus,** with bar service in summer, and, near the high point, the **Giardino del Cavaliere ★**, the Boboli's prettiest hidden corner—a tiny walled garden of box hedges with private views over the hills of Florence's outskirts. Toward the south end of the park is the **Isolotto ★**, a dreamy island marooned in a pond full of huge goldfish, with Giambologna's *L'Oceano* composition at its center. At the north end, down around the end of the Pitti Palace, are some fake caverns filled with statuary, attempting to invoke a classical sacred grotto. The most famous, the **Grotta Grande,** was designed by Giorgio Vasari, Bartolomeo Ammannati, and Bernardo Buontalenti between 1557 and 1593, dripping with phony stalactites and set with replicas of Michelangelo's unfinished *Slave* statues. You can usually get inside on the hour (but not every hour) for 15 minutes.

Piazza de' Pitti. **Galleria Palatina and Apartamenti Reali: ✆ 055-238-8614;** reserve tickets at www.firenzemusei.it or ✆ 055-294-883. Admission (with Galleria d'Arte Moderna) 8.50€; 13€ with temporary exhibition. Tues–Sun 8:15am–6:50pm. **Galleria d'Arte Moderna: ✆ 055-238-8616.** Admission (with Galleria Palatina) 8.50€. Tues–Sun 8:15am–6:50pm. **Museo degli Argenti and Galleria del Costume: ✆ 055-238-8709.** Admission (with Giardino di Boboli) 7€; 9€ with temporary exhibition. Nov–Feb daily 8:15am–4:30pm; Mar and Oct daily 8:15am–5:30pm; Apr–May and Sept daily 8:15am–6:30pm; June–Aug daily 8:15am–6:50pm. Closed 1st and last Mon of month. **Giardino di Boboli: ✆ 055-238-8791.** Admission (with Museo degli Argenti) 7€. Nov–Feb daily 8:15am–4:30pm; Mar and Oct daily 8:15am–5:30pm; Apr–May and Sept daily 8:15am–6:30pm; June–Aug daily 8:15am–7:30pm. Closed 1st and last Mon of month. Cumulative ticket for everything, valid 3 days, 12€. E.U. citizens ages 18 and under or 65 and over enter free. Bus: C3, D, 11, 36, or 37.

Piazzale Michelangiolo SQUARE This panoramic piazza is a required stop for every tour bus. The balustraded terrace was laid out in 1885 to give a sweeping **vista ★★** of the entire city, spread out in the valley below and backed by the green hills of Fiesole beyond. The bronze replica of *David* here points right at his original home, outside the Palazzo Vecchio.

Viale Michelangelo. Bus: 12 or 13.

San Miniato al Monte ★★ CHURCH High atop a hill, its gleaming white-and-green facade visible from the valley below, San Miniato is one of the few ancient churches of Florence to survive the centuries virtually intact. The current building began to take shape in 1013, under the auspices of the powerful Arte di Calimala guild, whose symbol, a bronze eagle clutching a bale of wool, perches atop the **facade ★★**. This Romanesque facade is a particularly gorgeous bit of white Carrara and green Prato marble inlay. Above the central window is a 13th-century mosaic of *Christ Between the Madonna and St. Miniato* (a theme repeated in the apse).

The **interior** has a few Renaissance additions, but they blend in well with the overall medieval aspect—an airy, stony space with a raised choir at one end, painted wooden trusses on the ceiling, and tombs interspersed with inlaid marble symbols of the zodiac paving the floor.

Below the choir is an 11th-century **crypt** with small frescoes by Taddeo Gaddi. Off to the right of the raised choir is the **sacristy,** which Spinello Aretino covered in 1387 with cartoonish yet elegant frescoes depicting the ***Life of St. Benedict* ★**. Off the left aisle of the nave is 15th-century **Cappella del**

Cardinale del Portogallo ★★, a collaborative effort by Renaissance artists built to honor young Portuguese humanist Cardinal Jacopo di Lusitania, who was sent to study in Perugia but died an untimely death at age 25 in Florence. Around the back of the church is San Miniato's **monumental cemetery ★**, one enormous "city of the dead," whose streets are lined with tombs and mausoleums built in elaborate pastiches of every generation of Florentine architecture (with a marked preference for the Gothic and the Romanesque). It's a peaceful spot soundtracked only by birdsong and the occasional tolling of the church bells.

Via Monte alle Croci/Viale Galileo Galilei (behind Piazzale Michelangiolo). ✆ **055-234-2731.** Free admission. Daily 8am–12:30pm and 3–5:30pm (closed some Sun afternoons); sometimes open through *riposo* in summer. Bus: 12 or 13.

Santa Felícita ★ CHURCH The 2nd-century Greek sailors who lived in this neighborhood brought Christianity to Florence with them, and this little church was probably the second to be established in the city, the first edition of it rising in the late 4th century. The current version was built in the 1730s. The star works are in the first chapel on your right—paintings by Mannerist master Pontormo (1525–27). His ***Deposition* ★★** and frescoed *Annunciation* are rife with his garish color palette of oranges, pinks, golds, lime greens, and sky blues, and exhibit his trademark surreal sense of figure.

Piazza Santa Felícita (2nd left off Via Guicciardini across the Ponte Vecchio). ✆ **055-213-018.** Free admission. Daily 8am–noon and 3:30–6:30pm. Bus: C3 or D.

Santa Maria del Carmine ★★★ CHURCH Following a 1771 fire that destroyed everything but the transept chapels and sacristy, this Carmelite church was almost entirely reconstructed in high baroque style. To see the famous **Cappella Brancacci ★★★** in the right transept, you have to enter through the cloisters (doorway to the right of the church facade) and pay admission. The frescoes here were commissioned by an enemy of the Medici, Felice Brancacci, who in 1424 hired Masolino and his student Masaccio to decorate it with a cycle on the *Life of St. Peter.* Masolino probably worked out the cycle's scheme and painted a few scenes along with his pupil before taking off for 3 years to serve as court painter in Budapest, during which time Masaccio kept painting, quietly creating the early Renaissance's greatest frescoes. Masaccio left for Rome in 1428, where he died at age 27. The cycle was completed between 1480 and 1485 by Filippino Lippi.

Masolino was responsible for the *St. Peter Preaching,* the upper panel to the left of the altar, and the two top scenes on the right wall, which shows his fastidiously decorative style in a long panel of *St. Peter Healing the Cripple* and *Raising Tabitha,* and his *Adam and Eve.* Contrast this first man and woman, about to take the bait offered by the snake, with the ***Expulsion from the Garden* ★★**, opposite it, painted by Masaccio. Masolino's figures are highly posed, expressionless models. Masaccio's Adam and Eve, on the other hand, burst with intense emotion. The top scene on the left wall, the ***Tribute Money* ★★**, is also by Masaccio, and it showcases another of his innovations, linear perspective. The two scenes to the right of the altar are Masaccio's as well, with the ***Baptism of the Neophytes* ★★** taking its place among his masterpieces.

Piazza del Carmine. ✆ **055-276-8224.** Free admission to church; Brancacci Chapel 4€; cumulative ticket with Palazzo Vecchio 8€. Wed–Sat and Mon 10am–5pm; Sun 1–5pm. Bus: D, 6, 11, 36, or 37.

Santo Spirito ★ CHURCH One of Filippo Brunelleschi's masterpieces of architecture, this 15th-century church doesn't look like much from the outside (no true facade was ever built), but the **interior ★** is a marvelous High Renaissance space—an expansive landscape of proportion and mathematics worked out in classic Brunelleschi style, with coffered vaulting, tall columns, and the stacked perspective of arched arcading. Good late-Renaissance and baroque paintings are scattered throughout, but the best stuff lies up in the transepts and in the east end, surrounding the extravagant **baroque altar** with a ciborium inlaid in *pietre dure* around 1607.

The famed **piazza** outside is one of the focal points of the Oltrarno, shaded by trees and lined with trendy cafes that see some bar action in the evenings.

Piazza Santo Spirito. ✆ **055-210-030.** Free admission. Mon–Tues and Thurs–Sat 10am–12:30pm and 4–5:30pm; Sun 4–5:30pm. Bus: C3, D, 11, 36, or 37.

Organized Tours

If you want to get under the surface of the city, **Context Travel ★** (www.contexttravel.com; ✆ **800-691-6036** in the U.S. or 06-976-25-204 in Italy), offers insightful tours led by academics and other experts in their field in a variety of specialties, from the gastronomic to the archaeological. Tours are limited to six people and cost between 40€ and 75€ per person. Context also conducts a guided walk through the Vasari Corridor (subject to availability; see p. 213). **CAF Tours,** Via Roma 4 (www.caftours.com; ✆ **055-283-200**), offers two half-day bus tours of town (47€), including visits to the Uffizi, the Accademia, and Piazzale Michelangiolo, as well as several walking tours and cooking classes from 25€ to 80€. **ArtViva** (www.italy.artviva.com; ✆ **055-264-5033**) has a huge array of walking tours and museum guides for every budget, starting at 25€. Websites such as **Viator.com, GetYourGuide.com,** and **Isango.com** have a vast range of locally organized tours and activities, reviewed and rated by users.

Call **I Bike Italy** (www.ibikeitaly.com; ✆ **055-012-3994**) to sign up for 1-day rides through Chianti for 80€, or 2 days to Siena for 329€.

Outdoor Activities

Florence's best park is the Medici grand dukes' old backyard to the Pitti Palace, the **Giardino di Boboli** (p. 222). Less scenic, but free and more jogger-friendly, is the **Parco delle Cascine** along the Arno at the west end of the historic center. Originally a wild delta of land where the Arno and Mugnone rivers met, the area later became a Medici hunting reserve and eventually a pasture for the grand duke's milk cows. Today, the Cascine is home to tennis courts, pools, a horse racetrack, and some odd late-18th- and early-19th-century features like an incongruous pyramid and funky neoclassical fountains. There's a flea market here every Tuesday morning. Although perfectly safe in the daylight, this park becomes a hangout for drug addicts after dark, as do many sections of the Arno's banks away from the center, so steer clear.

For **bike rental** information, see p. 197.

WHERE TO EAT

Florence is awash with restaurants, though many in the most touristy areas (around the Duomo and Piazza della Signoria) are of low quality, charge high prices, or both. We'll point out the few that are worth a visit. The highest concentrations of excellent *ristoranti* and *trattorie* are around Santa Croce and across the

> **It's All Tripe**
>
> New York has the hot dog. London has pie and mash. Florence has . . . cow's intestine in a sandwich. The city's traditional street food, *lampredotto* (the cow's fourth stomach) stewed with tomatoes, has made a big comeback over the last decade, including on the menus of some fine-dining establishments. However, the best places to sample it are still the city's *trippai,* tripe vendors who sell it from takeaway vans around the center, alongside other, more "regular" sandwiches. The most convenient are in **Piazza de' Cimatori** and on **Via de' Macci** at the corner of Piazza Sant'Ambrogio. A hearty, nutritious lunch should come to around 4€. Most are open Monday through Saturday, but close in August, when Florentines flee their city.

river in the Oltrarno. Bear in mind that menus at restaurants in Tuscany can change weekly or even (at the best places) daily.

Near the Duomo

MODERATE

Paoli TUSCAN Paoli has one of the most *suggestivo* (oft used Italian word for "evocative") settings in town, with tables under a 14th-century vaulted ceiling whose ribs and lunettes are covered with fading 18th-century frescoes. The *ravioli con burro e salvia* (with butter and sage) may not be especially creative, but it's freshly made and tasty. In mushroom season you can order *risotto ai funghi,* and a year-round offering is the scrumptious *secondo, entrecôte di manzo arlecchino* (a thick steak in cognac-spiked cream sauce with peppercorns and sided with mashed potatoes).

Giant wine casks at Cantinetta dei Verrazzano.

Via dei Tavolini 12r. www.casatrattoria.com. ✆ **055-216-215.** Reservations recommended. Main courses 14€–22€. AE, DC, MC, V. Daily noon–3:15pm and 7–11pm. Bus: C1 or C2.

INEXPENSIVE

Cantinetta dei Verrazzano ★ WINE BAR Owned by the Castello di Verrazzano, one of Chianti's best-known wine-producing estates (p. 272), this wood-paneled *cantinetta* with a full-service bar/*pasticceria* and seating area helped spawn a revival of stylish wine bars as convenient spots for fast-food breaks. It promises a delicious self-service lunch or snack of focaccia, plain or studded with rosemary, onions, or olives; buy it hot by the slice or as *farcite* (sandwiches filled with prosciutto, arugula, cheese, or tuna). Platters of Tuscan cold cuts and aged cheeses are also available.

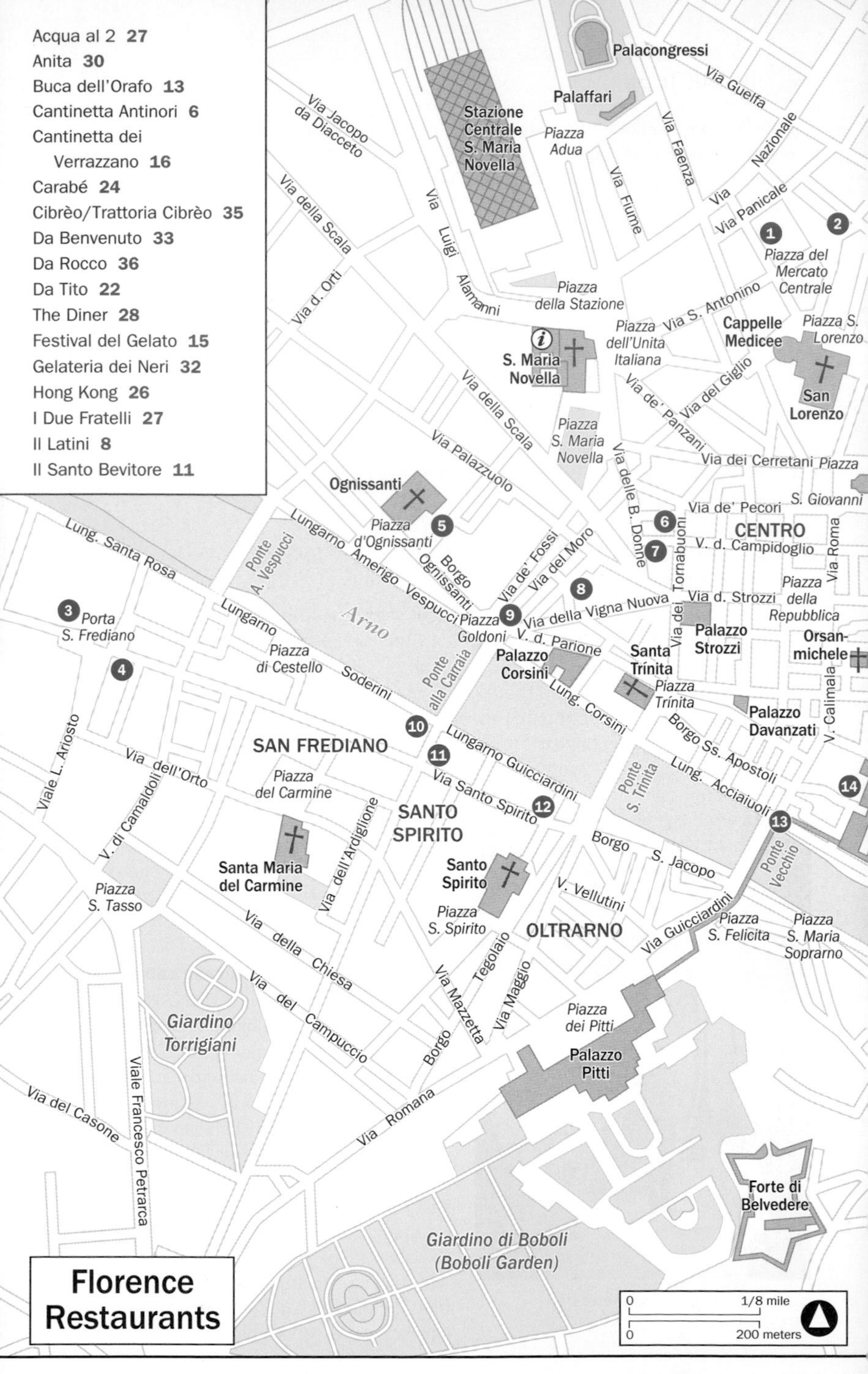
Acqua al 2 27
Anita 30
Buca dell'Orafo 13
Cantinetta Antinori 6
Cantinetta dei Verrazzano 16
Carabé 24
Cibrèo/Trattoria Cibrèo 35
Da Benvenuto 33
Da Rocco 36
Da Tito 22
The Diner 28
Festival del Gelato 15
Gelateria dei Neri 32
Hong Kong 26
I Due Fratelli 27
Il Latini 8
Il Santo Bevitore 11
Florence Restaurants
Palacongressi
Palaffari
Stazione Centrale S. Maria Novella
Piazza Adua
Via Guelfa
Via Nazionale
Via Faenza
Via Fiume
Via Panicale
Piazza del Mercato Centrale
Via Jacopo da Diacceto
Via della Scala
Via Luigi Alamanni
Via d. Orti
Piazza della Stazione
Via S. Antonino
Cappelle Medicee
Piazza S. Lorenzo
San Lorenzo
Piazza dell'Unita Italiana
S. Maria Novella
Via del Giglio
Via de' Panzani
Piazza S. Maria Novella
Via Palazzuolo
Via dei Cerretani
Piazza S. Giovanni
Ognissanti
Piazza d'Ognissanti
Via delle B. Donne
Via de' Pecori
CENTRO
Via Roma
V. d. Campidoglio
Lung. Santa Rosa
Lungarno Amerigo Vespucci
Borgo Ognissanti
Ponte A. Vespucci
Via de' Fossi
Via del Moro
Via dei Tornabuoni
Piazza della Repubblica
Via d. Strozzi
Arno
Piazza Goldoni
Via della Vigna Nuova
Porta S. Frediano
Lungarno Soderini
Piazza di Cestello
V. d. Parione
Palazzo Strozzi
Orsanmichele
Palazzo Corsini
Santa Trínita
Piazza Trínita
Ponte alla Carraia
Lung. Corsini
Palazzo Davanzati
V. Calimala
Viale L. Ariosto
Via dell'Orto
SAN FREDIANO
Lungarno Guicciardini
Borgo Ss. Apostoli
Ponte S. Trínita
Lung. Acciaiuoli
Via Santo Spirito
V. di Camaldoli
Piazza del Carmine
Via dell'Ardiglione
SANTO SPIRITO
Borgo S. Jacopo
Ponte Vecchio
Santa Maria del Carmine
Santo Spirito
V. Vellutini
Piazza S. Tasso
Piazza S. Spirito
OLTRARNO
Via Guicciardini
Piazza S. Felicita
Piazza S. Maria Soprarno
Via della Chiesa
Tegolaio
Via Mazzetta
Via Maggio
Via del Campuccio
Piazza dei Pitti
Giardino Torrigiani
Borgo
Palazzo Pitti
Viale Francesco Petrarca
Via del Casone
Via Romana
Forte di Belvedere
Giardino di Boboli (Boboli Garden)
0 1/8 mile
0 200 meters

Giardino dei Semplici
San Marco
Piazza San Marco
Giardino della Gherardesca
Piazza Donatello
Santissima Annunziata
Galleria dell'Accademia
Piazza della Ss. Annunziata
Museo Archeologico
Ospedale d. Innocenti
Palazzo Medici-Riccardi
Piazza Brunelleschi
Santa Maria Maddalena dei Pazzi
Piazza d'Azeglio
Palazzo Pucci
Ospedale S. Maria Nuova
Duomo
Teatro d. Pergola
Campanile
Piazza del Duomo
Piazza S. M. Nuova
Sinogoga (Museo Ebraico)
DUOMO
Piazza S. Ambrogio
Bargello
Badia
Piazza della Signoria
SIGNORIA
Teatro Verdi
Casa di Buonarroti
Piazza L. Ghiberti
Piazza C. Beccaria
Carceri di Murate
Archivo di Stato
Palazzo Vecchio
Piazza S. Croce
Uffizi
Santa Croce
SANTA CROCE
Piazza Mentana
Biblioteca Nazionale
Piazza dei Cavalleggeri
Piazza Piave
Arno
Ponte alle Grazie
Ponte A. Vespucci
Piazza G. Poggi
SAN NICCOLO
Il Vegetariano 21
iO; Osteria Personale 4
Kome 31
La Carraia 10
La Giostra 34
La Mescita 25
Le Mossacce 20
L'Osteria di Giovanni 9
Mario 2
Nerbone 1
Olio e Convivium 12
Ora d'Aria 14
Osteria delle Belle Donne 7
Paoli 17
Pugi 23
Sabatino 3
Sostanza 5
Vini e Vecchi Sapori 19
Vivoli 29

Dining in Florence.

Via dei Tavolini 18r (off Via dei Calzaiuoli). www.verrazzano.com. ✆ **055-268-590.** Tasting plates 4.50€–8€; glass of wine 4€–8€. AE, DC, MC, V. Mon–Sat 8am–9pm. Bus: C1 or C2.

I Due Fratellini ★ WINE BAR Just off the busiest tourist thoroughfare lies one of the last of a dying breed: a *fiaschetteria* (derived from the word for a flask of wine). It's the proverbial hole in the wall, a doorway about 1.5m (5 ft.) deep with rows of wine bottles against the back wall and the cheapest tasty lunch in town. You stand, munching and sipping, on the cobblestones of the narrow street surrounded by Florentines on their lunch break and a few bemused tourists. The *cinghiale piccante con caprino* (spicy cured wild boar sausage with creamy goat cheese) is excellent.

Via dei Cimatori 38r (2 blocks from Piazza della Signoria, off Via Calzaiuoli). www.iduefratellini.com. ✆ **055-239-6096.** Sandwiches from 2.50€; wine from 2€ a "shot." No credit cards. Daily 9am–8pm (July–Aug closed Sat–Sun). Closed 2 weeks in mid-Aug. Bus: C1 or C2.

Le Mossacce ★ FLORENTINE Delicious, cheap, abundant, fast home cooking: This tiny *osteria,* filled with lunching businesspeople, farmers in from the hills, locals who've been coming since 1942, and a few knowledgeable tourists, is authentic to the bone. The waiters hate breaking out the printed menu, preferring to rattle off a list of Florentine faves like *ribollita, crespelle,* and *lasagne al forno.* Unlike in many cheap joints catering to locals, the *secondi* are pretty good. You could try the *spezzatino* (goulashy veal stew) or a well-cooked, reasonably priced *bistecca alla fiorentina,* but I put my money on the excellent *involtini* (thin slices of beef wrapped tightly around a bread stuffing and artichoke hearts, then cooked to juiciness in tomato sauce).

Via del Proconsolo 55r (a block south of the Duomo). www.trattorialemossacce.it. ✆ **055-294-361.** Reservations recommended for dinner. Main courses 9€–11€. AE, MC, V. Mon–Fri noon–2:30pm and 7–9:30pm. Bus: C1 or C2.

Near Piazza della Signoria

VERY EXPENSIVE

Ora d'Aria ★★★ CONTEMPORARY TUSCAN Marco Stabile is a celebrated young Tuscan chef at the very height of his creative powers, and the 2010 relocation of his signature restaurant right into the heart of the *centro storico* has only seen his fame grow. Seasonality and a modern interpretation of Tuscan food traditions are the overarching themes of his cooking. You'll need to book ahead (and save up) to enjoy the delights of *gnocchetti di patate con pomodorini confit e guancia affumicata* (gnocchi with confit tomatoes and smoked pig's cheek) or *maialino con sottobosco, aglio e lavanda* (piglet with berries, garlic, and lavender).

Via dei Georgofili 11r (off Via Lambertesca). www.oradariaristorante.com. ✆ **055-200-1699.** Main courses 32€–34€. AE, MC, V. Tues–Sat 12:30–2:30pm; Mon–Sat 7:30–10:30pm. Closed Aug. Bus: C1 or C2.

MODERATE

Acqua al 2 ★ ITALIAN Under a barrel-vaulted ceiling and dim sconce lights, diners sit elbow-to-elbow at tightly packed tables to sample this innovative restaurant's *assaggi* (tastings) courses. Acqua al 2 is proud of its almost cultish status, attained through the success of its *assaggio di primi,* which offers you a sampling of five flavorful pastas or *risotti.* If you order the *assaggio* for two, you both just may have room left over for a grilled portobello mushroom "steak," one of the many veal dishes, or something more cross-cultural, like *couscous d'agnello* (lamb). They also offer *assaggi* of salads, cheese, and desserts. Tour companies have started bringing in tourists by the busload on occasion, but the crowd still remains a good mix of locals and travelers.

Via della Vigna Vecchia 40r (at Via dell'Acqua). www.acquaal2.it. ✆ **055-284-170.** Reservations recommended. Main courses 9€–18€; *assaggio* 10€ for pasta, 5.50€ for dessert. AE, MC, V. Daily 7pm–1am. Closed 1 week in Aug. Bus: C1 or C2.

Buca dell'Orafo FLORENTINE A *buca* is a cellar joint with half a dozen crowded tables serving good, seasonal Florentine fare. A few locals come here every night, but Orafo's years in the guidebooks have made Americans its primary customers—Florentines aren't willing to give this place up yet, though, and you can still find a smattering of locals if you reserve a late seating. Alas, the heavy tourism has jacked its prices substantially above what you'd expect for peasant food. That food is still very well prepared, however, and the location can't be beat. If it's on the menu, go for the *paglia e fieno alla boscaiola* (a "hay and straw" mix of both egg and spinach fettuccine in mushroom-meat sauce). Orafo's best *secondo* is *arista di maiale con patate* (roast pork loin with potatoes), while candied stewed pears round out the meal nicely.

Volta dei Girolami 28r (under the arched alley left of the Ponte Vecchio). www.bucadellorafo.com. ✆ **055-213-619.** Reservations strongly recommended. Main courses 16€–22€. No credit cards. Tues–Sat noon–2:30pm and 7:30–9.45pm. Bus: C1, 3, 6, 11, 36, 37, or 68.

Vini e Vecchi Sapori FLORENTINE/TUSCAN Within sight of the Palazzo Vecchio is this authentic *osteria* with a wood-beamed ceiling, brick floor, the end

family-friendly **EATING**

It'd be a sin for any family to visit Florence and not drop by one of its premier **gelato** parlors to sample the rich Italian equivalent of ice cream. (See "A Big Step Up from Ice Cream: Florentine Gelato," on p. 234.) If the kids mutiny and absolutely insist on a hamburger, head to the **Diner** (p. 232). **Il Latini** (p. 234) can be one of the most fun places to eat in Florence with kids—you're seated at communal tables under battalions of hanging ham hocks and treated to huge portions of the Tuscan bounty. No food is too fancy or oddball to offend suspicious young palates, the waiters love to ham it up, and a festive atmosphere prevails. It's much lower-key at **Da Benvenuto** (p. 232): The dishes are simple and homey, and they're sure to have a plate of plain spaghetti and tomato sauce to please finicky youngsters. If your little ones like Chinese food, **Hong Kong,** Via dei Servi 35r (www.ristorantehongkong.com; ✆ **055-239-8235**) is a reliable central choice for Cantonese staples like sizzling stir-fry platters.

of a giant chianti barrel embedded in one wall, and a handwritten menu that starts *"Oggi C'è . . ."* ("Today we got . . ."). As the sign proudly proclaims, this buzzing one-room joint is devoted to "wine and old flavors," which means lunch could consist of anything from a rib-sticking stewlike *ribollita* and a *frittata rustica* (a darkly fried omelet thick with potatoes and vegetables) to an excellent crostini assortment and *scamorza e speck al forno* (smoked mozzarella melted with ham in a bowl, to scoop out and slather onto bread). The owner will continue pacing back and forth, passing around the lone menu, and welcoming people in off the street until he feels like going home.

Via dei Magazzini 3r (the alley off the northeast corner of Piazza della Signoria). ✆ **055-293-045.** Main courses 10€–14€. No credit cards. Tues–Sat 9am–11pm; Sun noon–2:30pm. Bus: C1 or C2.

INEXPENSIVE

Da Benvenuto ★ ☺ TUSCAN/ITALIAN This is a no-nonsense trattoria, simple and good, a neighborhood hangout that somehow found its way into many a guidebook over the years. Yet it continues to serve good helpings of tasty Florentine home cooking to travelers and locals seated together in two brightly lit rooms. This is often our first stop on any trip to Florence, where we usually order ravioli or *gnocchi*—both served in tomato sauce—and follow with a *scaloppa di vitello al vino bianco* (veal escalope cooked in white wine).

Via della Mosca 16r (at the corner of Via dei Neri). ✆ **055-214-833.** Main courses 6€–18€. AE, MC, V. Daily 12:30–3pm and 7–10:30pm. Bus: C1, 3, 13, 23, or 71.

The Diner ☺ AMERICAN/FAST FOOD If you or the kids are craving something familiar, then roll up for breakfast, lunch, or dinner at this tiny American-style diner between Santa Croce and Piazza della Signoria. Squeeze into fun, informal booth seating for Californian eggs Benedict (with avocado and tomato) or a pancake stack at breakfast, omelets anyway you like them at lunch, and a fine array of burgers with fries—go for the Pica Burger, served with a spicy pesto for a (small) concession to your Italian hosts. If you like your burger well cooked *(ben cotto)* be sure to ask: They usually arrive pink. There's free Wi-Fi, too.

Via dell'Acqua 2 (behind the Bargello). www.theflorencediner.com. ✆ **055-290-748.** Breakfast 6€–7€; lunch 6€–8€; burgers 7€–10€. AE, DC, MC, V. Daily 8am–10:30pm. Bus: C1 or C2.

Near San Lorenzo & the Mercato Centrale

INEXPENSIVE

Mario ★ FLORENTINE This is down-and-dirty Florentine lunchtime at its best, a trattoria so basic the little stools don't have backs and a communal spirit so entrenched the waitresses will scold you if you try to take a table all to yourself. Since 1953, their stock in trade has been feeding market workers, and you can watch the kitchen through the glass as they whip out a wipe-board menu of simple dishes at lightning speed. Hearty *primi* include *tortelli di patate al ragù* (ravioli stuffed with potato in meat *ragù*), *minestra di farro e riso* (emmer-and-rice soup), and *penne al pomodoro* (pasta quills in fresh tomato sauce). The *secondi* are basic but good; try the *coniglio arrosto* (roast rabbit) or go straight for the *fiorentina* steak, often priced to be the best deal in town.

Via Rosina 2r (north corner of Piazza Mercato Centrale). www.trattoria-mario.com. ✆ **055-218-550.** Reservations not accepted. Main courses 7.50€–11€. No credit cards. Mon–Sat noon–3:30pm. Closed Aug. Bus: C1.

Nerbone ★ FLORENTINE Nerbone has been stuffing stall owners and market patrons with excellent Florentine *cucina povera* (poor people's food) since the Mercato Centrale opened in 1874. You can try *trippa alla fiorentina, pappa al pomodoro,* or a plate piled with boiled potatoes and a single fat sausage. But the mainstay here is a *panino con bollito,* a boiled beef sandwich that's *bagnato* (dipped in the meat juices). Eat standing with the crowd of old men at the side counter, sipping glasses of wine or beer, or arrive early to fight for one of the few tables.

In the Mercato Centrale, entrance on Via dell'Ariento, stand no. 292 (ground floor). ✆ **055-219-949.** All dishes 4€–7€. No credit cards. Mon–Sat 7am–2pm. Bus: C1.

Near Piazza Santa Trinita

EXPENSIVE

Cantinetta Antinori TUSCAN The Antinori *marchesi* started their wine empire 26 generations ago, and, taking their cue from an ancient vintner tradition, installed a wine bar in their 15th-century *palazzo* 30 years ago. Most ingredients come fresh from the Antinori farms, as does all the fine wine. Start with the *fettuccine all'anatra* (noodles in duck sauce) and round out the meal with the mighty *gran pezzo* (a thick slab of oven-roasted Chianina beef). If you choose this worthy splurge as a *secondo,* skip the first course and instead follow your steak with *formaggi misti,* which may include pecorino made fresh that morning. Their *cantucci* (Pratese biscotti) come from Tuscany's premier producer.

Palazzo Antinori, Piazza Antinori 3 (at the top of Via Tornabuoni). www.cantinetta-antinori.com. ✆ **055-292-234.** Reservations recommended. Main courses 24€–30€. AE, DC, MC, V. Mon–Fri noon–2:30pm and 7–10:30pm. Closed Aug and Dec 24–Jan 6. Bus: C1, 6, 11, 22, 36, 37, or 68

L'Osteria di Giovanni ★★ TUSCAN Giovanni Latini comes from one of Florence's best-known culinary clans, whose eponymous eatery on Via del Palchetti is a household name in Florence, but he and his daughters Caterina and Chiara have made quite a name for themselves in the same neighborhood. Their *osteria* features a sophisticated but social atmosphere, with well-dressed Italians and tourists sharing either the quiet front room or the more communal back room. If they are in season, you may be offered some fresh, garden-raised fava beans with pecorino, followed by sautéed squid with asparagus and cherry tomatoes. Don't miss the *involtini di vitello con pecorino fresco, melanzane e funghi* (sliced veal wrapped around fresh pecorino, eggplant, and mushrooms). Save room for chocolate mousse.

Via del Moro 22 (near the Ponte alla Carraia). www.osteriadigiovanni.com. ✆ **055-284-897.** Reservations recommended. Main courses 19€–26€. AE, MC, V. Tues–Sat noon–2:30pm and 7–11pm; Mon 7–11pm. Closed Aug. Bus: C3, 6, 11, 36, 37, or 68.

Osteria delle Belle Donne ★ TUSCAN Tucked away on a narrow street (whose name refers to the women of the night who once worked this then-shady neighborhood) parallel to exclusive Via de' Tornabuoni, this packed-to-the-gills lunch spot immediately drew the area's chic boutique owners and sales staff. It now tries to accommodate them and countless others in a rather brusque style—no lingering over lunch; dinner isn't as rushed. Tuscan cuisine gets reinterpreted and updated by the talented chef, who placates the local palate without alienating it: Traditional dishes appear in the company of innovative specials such as cream of zucchini and chestnut soup or lemon-flavored chicken.

A BIG STEP UP FROM ICE CREAM: FLORENTINE gelato

Gelato is a Florentine institution—a creamy, sweet, flavorful food item on a different level entirely from what the English-speaking world calls "ice cream." Making fine Florentine gelato is a craft taken seriously by all except the tourist-pandering spots around major attractions that serve air-fluffed bland "vanilla" and nuclear-waste pistachio so artificially green it glows.

Festival del Gelato, Via del Corso 75r, just off Via dei Calzaiuoli (www.festivaldelgelato.com; ✆ **055-239-4386**), is one of the few serious contenders right in the center, offering about 50 flavors along with pounding pop music and colorful neon. It's open daily, but closed all January.

Vivoli ★★, Via Isole delle Stinche 7r, a block west of Piazza Santa Croce (www.vivoli.it; ✆ **055-239-2334**), is still the city's institution. Exactly how renowned is this bright *gelateria?* Taped to the wall is a postcard bearing only "Vivoli, Europa" for the address, yet it was successfully delivered to this world capital of ice cream. It's open all day Tuesday through Sunday. Nearby **Gelateria dei Neri ★★**, Via dei Neri 20–22r (✆ **055-210-034**) gets less acclaim, but plenty of locals think this is up there with Vivoli. Their ricotta and fig gelato is divine. It's open daily. Best of the "new breed" of Florentine *gelateria* is **Carapina ★★**, Via Lambertesca 18R (www.carapina.it; ✆ **055-291-128**), where a serious commitment to sourcing and seasonality is rewarded with some sensational fruit flavors. It's also open daily.

A block south of the Accademia (pick up a cone after you've gazed upon *David*'s glory) is **Carabé,** Via Ricasoli 60r (www.gelatocarabe.com; ✆ **055-289-476**). It offers genuine Sicilian gelato in the heart of Florence, with ingredients shipped in from Sicily by the Sicilian owners. May 16 through September, it's open daily; February 15 through May 15 and October through November 15, it's open Tuesday through Sunday only.

South of the Arno, Florentines crowd into unassuming **La Carraia ★**, Piazza N. Sauro 25r (✆ **055-280-695**). It's open daily.

Via delle Belle Donne 16r. www.casatrattoria.com. ✆ **055-238-2609.** Reservations recommended. Main courses 12€–18€. DC, MC, V. Daily noon–3pm and 7pm–midnight. Closed most of Aug. Bus: C1, 6, 11, 22, 36, 37, or 68.

Near Santa Maria Novella

MODERATE

Il Latini ★ ☺ FLORENTINE Arrive here at 7:30pm to join the crowd massed at the door, for even with a reservation you'll have to wait as they skillfully fit parties together at the communal tables. In fact, sharing a common meal with complete strangers is part of the fun here. Under hundreds of hanging prosciutto ham hocks, the waiters try their hardest to keep a menu away from you and suggest something themselves. This usually kicks off with *ribollita* and *pappa al pomodoro* or *penne strascicate* (in a *ragù* mixed with cream). If everyone agrees on the *arrosto misto,* you can get a table-filling platter heaped high with assorted roast meats. Finish off with a round of *cantucci con vin santo* for all the adults.

Via del Palchetti 6r (off Via della Vigna Nuova). www.illatini.com. ✆ **055-210-916.** Reservations strongly recommended. Main courses 14€–22€. AE, DC, MC, V. Tues–Sun 12:30–2:30pm and 7:30–10:30pm. Closed 15 days in Aug and Dec 24–Jan 6. Bus: 1, 6, 36, 37, or 68.

Sostanza FLORENTINE This trattoria is popularly called Il Troia (the Trough) because people have been lining up at the long communal tables since 1869 to enjoy huge amounts of some of the best traditional food in the city. The *primi* are very simple: pasta in sauce, *tortellini in brodo* (meat-stuffed pasta in chicken broth), and *zuppa alla paesana* (peasant soup *ribollita*). The *secondi* don't steer far from Florentine traditions either, with *trippa alla fiorentina* or their mighty specialty *petti di pollo al burro* (thick chicken breasts fried in butter). We've never seen an empty seat in the place while walking by at dinnertime, so it's certainly worth calling ahead.

Via Porcellana 25r (near the Borgo Ognissanti end). ✆ **055-212-691.** Reservations strongly recommended. Main courses 10€–16€. No credit cards. Mon–Fri noon–2:15pm and 7:30–9:45pm. Closed Aug. Bus: 11, 36, 37, or 68.

Near San Marco & Santissima Annunziata

If you're staying north of San Marco and don't fancy the walk into the center, locals swear by **Da Tito ★**, Via San Gallo 112r (www.trattoriadatito.it; ✆ **055-472-475**), where you'll find traditional Florentine cooking, fresh pasta handmade daily, and a friendly welcome. It's popular, so book ahead. San Marco is also the place to head for *schiacciata alla fiorentina,* sweetish olive-oil flatbread loaded with savory toppings. You'll find the best in the city at **Pugi ★**, Piazza San Marco 9b (www.focacceria-pugi.it; ✆ **055-280-981**), open 7:45am (8:30am Sat) to 8pm Monday to Saturday, but closed most of August.

INEXPENSIVE

Il Vegetariano VEGETARIAN Come early to one of Florence's best vegetarian restaurants and use your coat to save a spot at one of the communal wood tables before heading to the back to get your food. The self-service menu changes constantly but uses only fresh produce in such dishes as risotto with yellow squash and black cabbage; a quichelike *pizza rustica* of ricotta, olives, tomatoes, and mushrooms; and a plate with *farro* (emmer) and a hot salad of spinach, onions, sprouts, and bean-curd chunks sautéed in soy sauce. There's a nice patio in back.

Via delle Ruote 30r (off Via Santa Reparata). www.il-vegetariano.it. ✆ **055-475-030.** Reservations not accepted. Main courses 7.50€–9€. No credit cards. Tues–Fri 12:30–3:30pm; Tues–Sun 7:30pm–midnight. Closed 3 weeks in Aug and Dec 24–Jan 2. Bus: C1 or anything to San Marco.

La Mescita LIGHT FARE This tiny *fiaschetteria* is immensely popular with local businesspeople and students from the nearby university. Lunch can be a crushing affair, and they have signs admonishing you to eat quickly to give others a chance to sit. You'll be eating with Italians, and it's not for the timid because you have to take charge yourself: securing a seat, collecting your own place setting, and getting someone's attention to give your order before going to sit down. They offer mainly sandwiches, though there are always a few simple meat and pasta dishes ready as well. *Melanzana* (eggplant) is overwhelmingly the side dish of choice, and you can look to the cardboard lists behind the counter to select your wine, although the house wine is very good, and a quarter liter of it is cheaper than a can of soda.

Via degli Alfani 70r (near the corner of Via dei Servi). ✆ **347-795-1604.** Sandwiches and simple dishes 4€–7€. No credit cards. Mon–Sat 11am–4pm. Closed Aug. Bus: C1.

Near Santa Croce

VERY EXPENSIVE

Cibrèo ★★ TUSCAN There's no pasta and no grilled meat—can this be Tuscany? Rest assured that while Fabio Picchi's culinary creations are a bit out of the ordinary, most are based on antique recipes. Picchi's fan-cooled main restaurant room, full of intellectual babble, is where the elegance is in the substance of the food and the service, not in surface appearances. Waiters pull up a chair to explain the list of daily specials, and those garlands of hot peppers hanging in the kitchen window are a hint at the chef's favorite spice. All the food is spectacular, and dishes change regularly, but if they're available try the yellow pepper soup drizzled with olive oil; the soufflé of potatoes and ricotta spiced and served with pecorino shavings and *ragù;* or the roasted duck stuffed with minced beef, raisins, and *pinoli.*

Via Andrea del Verrocchio 8r (next to Sant'Ambrogio Market). www.edizioniteatrodelsalecibreofirenze.it. ✆ **055-234-1100.** Reservations required. Main courses 36€. AE, DC, MC, V. Tues–Sat 1–2:30pm and 7:30–11:15pm. Closed July 26–Sept 6. Bus: C2, C3, 14, or 71.

EXPENSIVE

Kome ★ 🎁 JAPANESE/SUSHI There's something refreshingly cosmopolitan about perching in a *kaiten,* grazing on *hosomaki* made by a skilled Japanese chef right in front of you. Florence's best sushi joint gets the formula about right: Nigiri with octopus, cuttlefish, prawn, or tuna are light and fresh straight from the conveyor. An excellent mixed tempura of seasonal vegetables, prawn, and anchovy is the best among five or six hot dishes cooked to order. Keep track of your total as you eat, however: The check soon mounts up, especially if you wash it all down with a Kirin or two. They also offer delivery via **www.thefood.it**.

Via de' Benci 41r. ✆ **055-200-8009.** Reservations not accepted. Sushi 3.50€–8€. AE, MC, V. Mon–Sat noon–3pm; daily 7–11pm. Bus: C3 or 23.

La Giostra ★ TUSCAN The chef/owner is Dimitri d'Asburgo Lorena, a Habsburg prince (with some local Medici blood for good measure) who opened this restaurant merely to indulge his love of cooking. They start you off with a complimentary flute of spumante before you plunge into the tasty *crostini misti* and exquisite *primi.* Among the more enlightened are *ravioli di brie con carciofini Morelli* (ravioli stuffed with brie and dressed with artichokes), and homemade *taglierini* with white truffles. For an encore, try the *nodino di vitella ai tartufi bianchi* (veal slathered in eggy white truffle sauce with fresh truffle grated on top) or the lighter *spianata alle erbe aromatiche di Maremma* (a huge platter of spiced beef pounded flat and piled with a salad of rosemary sprigs, sage, and other herbs). Don't leave without sampling the sinfully rich Viennese Sacher torte, made from an old Habsburg family recipe.

Borgo Pinti 12r (off Piazza Salvemini). www.ristorantelagiostra.com. ✆ **055-241-341.** Reservations recommended. Main courses 16€–24€. AE, DC, MC, V. Daily noon–2:30pm and 7pm–midnight. Bus: C1, 14, 23, or 71.

MODERATE

Trattoria Cibrèo ★★ 🏷 FLORENTINE This is the casual trattoria of celebrated chef-owner Fabio Picchi; its limited menu comes from the same creative kitchen that put on the map his premier and more than twice as expensive *ristorante* next door. Picchi takes his inspiration from traditional Tuscan recipes, and the first thing you'll note is the absence of pasta. After you taste the velvety *passata di peperoni gialli* (yellow bell-pepper soup), you won't care much. The stuffed roast rabbit demands the same admiration.

Via de' Macci 122r. ✆ **055-234-1100.** Main courses 14€. AE, DC, MC, V. Tues–Sat 1–2:30pm and 7–11:15pm. Closed July 26–Sept 6. Bus: C2, C3, 14, or 71.

INEXPENSIVE

Anita FLORENTINE You're unlikely to find too many surprises on the menu at this backstreet trattoria; what you will find, however, is proper Florentine cooking with friendly service just a stone's throw from the city's marquee monuments. A typical trip through the courses might start with Tuscan *crostini* with chicken livers and pecorino cheese, followed by *pici al cinghiale* (hand-rolled, thick pasta with boar sauce), then *lombatino di vitello all'aceto balsamico* (thick veal steak with a creamy balsamic vinegar sauce). It's hearty and delicious local cooking at fair prices.

Via del Parlascio 2r (corner of Via Vinegia). ✆ **055-218-698.** Reservations recommended for dinner. Main courses 8€–14€. MC, V. Mon–Sat noon–2:30pm and 7–10:15pm. Bus: C1, C2, C3, 23.

Da Rocco FLORENTINE This tiny trattoria, one of the best bargains in the city, is tucked away inside Sant'Ambrogio Market. It's a great place to get acquainted with a proper local eating experience, with simple food served to hungry workers without any show. Behind the takeaway counter is an enclosed seating area with booths big enough for four. Staff is friendly, but also rushed off their feet, so don't expect any special treatment (there is a menu in English, if you're struggling). Hearty dishes of lasagna, various other pasta dishes, or roast meats such as *coniglio* (rabbit) straight from the market rarely cost more than 5€. Get here by 1pm if you want a table.

Mercato di Sant'Ambrogio. No phone. Reservations not accepted. Main courses 5€. MC, V. Mon–Sat noon–2:30pm. Bus: C2, C3, or 14.

In the Oltrarno & San Frediano

Dining right in the deli is hot in foodie Tuscany right now, and you'll find Florence's best spots south of the Arno. As well as **Olio e Convivium,** below, we love **Zeb ★★**, Via San Miniato 2r (www.zebgastronomia.com; ✆ **055-234-2864**), where an all-chalkboard menu features creative dishes such as ravioli stuffed with pear and pecorino cheese in a pear sauce. It's all about the ingredients in all their dishes, which range from 8€ to 15€. Zeb serves lunch Thursday through Tuesday and dinner Thursday to Saturday.

EXPENSIVE

iO: Osteria Personale ★★★ CONTEMPORARY TUSCAN The stripped brick and sleek banquette seating wouldn't be out of place in Brooklyn or Shoreditch, but the exceptional food here is resolutely Tuscan. Not Tuscan like you've tasted before, though: There's no pasta on a modular dinner menu that's divided into seafood, meat, and vegetarian dishes—a "renewal" of Tuscan food tradition, is how proprietor Matteo Fantini describes it. You buy by the dish, in any sequence you fancy, or go for a multidish tasting menu. The likes of raw squid ribbons served with sage-infused garbanzo cream or spelt with artichoke, cocoa beans, and *robiola* cheese deliver traditional flavors, but are served up in a clean, deconstructed style. There's even a chalkboard on the wall with diagrams showing how some of the dishes are built—Fantini's equivalent of the football coach's playbook.

Borgo San Frediano 167r. www.io-osteriapersonale.it. ✆ **055-933-1341.** Reservations highly recommended. Main courses 14€–20€; tasting menus 40€ 4 dishes, 55€ 6 dishes. AE, DC, MC, V. Mon–Sat 8–10:45pm; also open for *aperitivo* from 7pm. Closed first 10 days in Jan and all Aug. Bus: 6 and D.

Olio e Convivium ★★ CONTEMPORARY ITALIAN This slightly fussy, but nevertheless thoroughly satisfying little restaurant is set in tiled surrounds inside one of the Oltrarno's best delicatessens. Its menu eschews the style and content of "typical Florence." You can choose one of their creative, skillfully presented pasta combinations like *tagliolini con capesante, carciofi e calamari* (thin pasta with scallops, artichokes, and squid). Or order one of their "gastronomy tasting plates," built straight from the deli counter. The wines-by-the-glass list is short, creative, and a little pricey; the soft classical music soundtrack makes for a refined atmosphere.

Via Santo Spirito 6. www.conviviumfirenze.it. ✆ **055-265-8198.** Main courses 14€–28€. MC, V. Mon–Sat noon–2:30pm; Tues–Sat 7–10:30pm. Closed 3 weeks in Aug. Bus: C3, D, 6, 11, 36, 37, or 68.

MODERATE

Il Santo Bevitore ★★ CONTEMPORARY ITALIAN Encapsulating all that's best about the new generation of Florentine eateries, this restaurant-enoteca (wine cellar) takes the best of Tuscan tradition and sprinkles it with some contemporary fairy dust. A buzzing, candlelit interior is the setting for clever combinations presented with style—and a smile. Best of the antipasti are the tasting platters, including cured meats sliced right at the bar and an *assaggio di sott'olio* (a trio of preserved vegetables in olive oil). Pastas skew to the unusual, pulling in influences from across Italy, such as in the *tortelloni* filled with *cavolo nero* cabbage and pancetta served with a pecorino cream sauce. Seasonal mains might include a tartare of Chianina beef or roast *baccalà* (salt cod) with late-harvest radicchio. The wine list is similarly intriguing. Lunch is a daily menu only.

Via Santo Spirito 66r (corner of Piazza N. Sauro). www.ilsantobevitore.com. ✆ **055-211-264.** Reservations highly recommended. Main courses 8.50€–25€. MC, V. Mon–Sat 12:30–3pm; daily 7–11pm. Closed 10 days in Aug. Bus: C3, D, 6, 11, 36, 37, or 68.

INEXPENSIVE

Sabatino ★ FLORENTINE It feels a long way off the tourist trail—and, in a way, it is—but a mere 10-minute walk from the Cappella Brancacci and you're eating in Florence before the arrival of mass tourism. Sabatino is the kind of San Frediano trattoria where local families and work colleagues meet to eat good food in simple surrounds, for a modest outlay. Dishes are straightforward and Florentine: *tortellini in brodo* (meat-filled pasta parcels in a clear broth), a selection of pasta dishes for around 4€, and a daily-changing roster of roasts such as *pollo ripieno* (herb-stuffed chicken), *faraona* (guinea hen), or *vitello* (veal). Whitewashed walls hung with farming implements remind you that it's all about the produce.

Via Pisana 2r (just outside the Porta Pisana). ✆ **055-225-955.** Main courses 5€–7€. AE, MC, V. Mon–Fri noon–2:30pm and 7:15–10pm. Bus: 6 and D.

In the Hills

MODERATE

Le Cave di Maiano ★ TUSCAN This converted farmhouse is the countryside trattoria of choice for Florentines wishing to escape the city heat on a summer Sunday afternoon. You can enjoy warm-weather lunches on the tree-shaded stone terrace with a bucolic view. In cooler weather, you can dine inside rustic rooms with haphazard paintings scattered on the walls. The *antipasto caldo* of varied *crostini* and fried polenta is a good way to kick off a meal, followed by a *misto della casa* that gives you a sampling of *primi*. This may include *penne strascicate* (stubby pasta in cream sauce and tomato *ragù*) or *riso allo spazzacamino* (rice with beans and black cabbage). The best *secondo* is the *pollastro al mattone* (chicken roasted under a brick with pepper) or the *lombatina di vitello alla griglia* (grilled veal chop).

Via Cave di Maiano 16 (in Maiano, halfway btw. Florence and Fiesole east of the main road). www.trattoriacavedimaiano.it. ✆ **055-59-133.** Reservations recommended. Main courses 10€–18€. AE, DC, MC, V. Daily 12:30–3pm and 7:30pm–midnight. Bus: 7 (get off at Villa San Michele, then turn around and take the road branching to the left of the winding one your bus took; continue on about 1.2km/¾ mile up this side road, past the Pensione Bencistà); a taxi is a better idea.

SHOPPING

The cream of the crop of Florentine shopping lines both sides of elegant **Via de' Tornabuoni,** with an extension along **Via della Vigna Nuova** and other surrounding streets. Here you'll find big names like Gucci, Armani, and Ferragamo ensconced in old palaces or modern minimalist boutiques.

On the other end of the shopping spectrum is the haggling and general fun of the colorful and noisy **San Lorenzo street market.** Antiques gather dust by the truckload along **Via Maggio** and other Oltrarno streets. Another main corridor of stores somewhat less glitzy than those on Via de' Tornabuoni begins at **Via Cerretani** and runs down **Via Roma** through the Piazza della Repubblica area; it keeps going down **Via Por Santa Maria,** across the **Ponte Vecchio** with its gold jewelry, and up **Via Guicciardini** on the other side. Store laden side tributaries off this main stretch include **Via della Terme, Borgo Santissimi Apostoli,** and **Borgo San Jacopo** (which becomes **Via Santo Spirito** as it heads west). Over in the east of the center, **Borgo degli Albizi** has seen a flourishing of one-off stores, with an emphasis on young, independent fashions.

Shopping along Via dei Tornabuoni.

General Florentine **shopping hours** are Monday through Saturday from 9:30am to noon or 1pm and 3 or 3:30 to 7:30pm, although increasingly, many shops are staying open on Sunday and through that midafternoon *riposo* or nap (especially the larger stores and those around tourist sights).

Shopping A to Z

Here's **what to buy in Florence:** leather, fashion, shoes, marbleized paper, hand-embroidered linens, artisan craft goods, Tuscan wines, handmade jewelry, *pietre dure* (known also as "Florentine mosaic," inlaid semiprecious stones), and antiques.

ART & ANTIQUES

The antiques business is clustered where the artisans have always lived and worked: the Oltrarno. Dealers' shops line Via Maggio, but the entire district is packed with venerable chunks of the past. On "this side" of the river, Borgo Ognissanti has the highest concentration of aging furniture and art collectibles.

The large showrooms of **Gallori-Turchi,** Via Maggio 14r (✆ **055-282-279**), specialize in furnishings, paintings, and weaponry (swords, lances, and pistols) from the 16th to 18th centuries. They also offer majolica and ceramic pieces and scads of hand-carved and inlaid wood. Nearby you'll find **Guido Bartolozzi Antichità,** Via Maggio 18r (✆ **055-215-602**), under family management since 1887. This old-fashioned store concentrates on the 16th to 19th centuries. They might be offering a 17th-century Gobelin tapestry, an inlaid stone tabletop, or wood intarsia dressers from the 1700s. The quality is impeccable. For the serious collector who wants his or her own piece of Florence's cultural heritage, the refined showroom at **Gianfranco Luzzetti,** Borgo San Jacopo 28A (✆ **055-211-232**), offers artwork and furniture from the 1400s to 1600s. They have a gorgeous collection of 16th-century Deruta ceramics and majolica, canvases by the likes of Vignale and Bilivert, and even a glazed terracotta altarpiece from the hand of Andrea della Robbia. Bring sacks of money.

BEAUTY PRODUCTS

You may never in your life have been inside anywhere quite like the **Officina Profumo-Farmaceutica Santa Maria Novella ★★**, Via della Scala 16 (✆ **055-216-276**), an old-style pharmacy, herbalist, bookstore, and even museum, opened in 1612 and still part of the Dominican convent attached to the church. In an atmosphere of subdued reverence, choose your favorite scents, soaps, remedies, and essences for your body, mind, child, or even pet dog.

BOOKS

Even the smaller bookshops in Florence these days have at least a few shelves devoted to English-language books. **Feltrinelli International,** Via Cavour 12 (www.lafeltrinelli.it; ✆ **055-219-524**), is one of the few of any size. For English-only reading, hit **Paperback Exchange,** Via delle Oche 4r (www.papex.it; ✆ **055-293-460**), the best for books in English, specializing in titles relating in some way to Florence and Italy. Much of their stock is used, and you can't beat the prices locally—Italy is generally an expensive place to buy books.

CERAMICS

La Botteghina del Ceramista, Via Guelfa 5r (✆ **055-287-367**), is about the most reasonably priced city outlet for artisan ceramics. Daniela Viegi del Fiume deals in hand-painted ceramics from the best traditional artisans working in nearby Montelupo and the famed Umbrian ceramics center of Deruta.

If you can't make it to the Chianti workshop of **Giuseppe Rampini ★** (p. 276 in chapter 6), visit his classy showroom at Borgo Ognissanti 32–34 (right at Piazza Ognissanti; www.rampiniceramics.com; ✆ **055-219-720**).

CRAFTS

Florentine traditional "mosaics" are actually works of inlaid semiprecious stone called *pietre dure*. The creations of Ilio de Filippis and his army of apprentices at **Pitti Mosaici ★**, Piazza Pitti 23–24r (www.pittimosaici.com; ✆ **055-282-127**), reflect traditional techniques and artistry. Ilio's father was a *pietre dure* artist, and his grandfather was a sculptor. (The family workshop was founded in 1900.) There's another store at Via Guicciardini 80r.

Professore Agostino Dessi and his daughter Alice preside over the traditional Venetian Carnevale and commedia dell'arte–style mask-making at **Alice Atelier ★**, Via Faenza 72r (www.alicemasks.com; ✆ **055-287-370**). All masks are made using papier-mâché, leather, and ceramics according to 17th-century techniques, hand-painted with tempera, touched up with gold and silver leaf, and polished with French lacquer.

DEPARTMENT STORES

Florence's central branch of the national chain **Coin,** Via Calzaiuoli 56r (www.coin.it; ✆ **055-280-531**), is a stylish multifloored display case for upper-middle-class fashions—a vaguely chic Macy's. **La Rinascente,** Piazza della Repubblica 2 (www.rinascente.it; ✆ **055-219-113**), is another of Italy's finer department stores. This six-floor store serves as an outlet for top designers (Versace, Zegna, Ferré, and so on). It also has areas set up to sell traditional Tuscan goods (terra-cotta, alabaster, olive oils, and wrought iron).

FASHION & CLOTHING

Although Italian fashion reached its pinnacle in the 1950s and 1960s, the country has remained at the forefront of both high (Armani, Gucci, Pucci, Ferragamo, just to name a few) and popular (evidenced by the spectacular success of Benetton in the 1980s) fashion. Florence plays second fiddle to Milan in today's Italian fashion scene, but the city has its own cadre of well respected names, plus, of course, outlet shops of all the hot designers. The epicenter of the city's high fashion is **Via de' Tornabuoni.** Serious clothes shoppers should also consider visiting one of the outlet malls clustered around the city. Best of the bunch is the **Mall** (www.themall.it), a half-hour south-east of Florence in Leccio Reggello. Units include Bottega Veneta, Stella McCartney, Gucci, Armani, Dior, and about 20 others—with steep discounts off last season's threads for women, men, and kids. With 1 day's notice, you can prebook a shuttle bus to collect you from any Florence hotel (✆ **055-865-7775;** or e-mail info@themall.it; 25€ per person), or take the train from Santa Maria Novella to Rignano sull'Arno and then a short cab ride.

FOR MEN & WOMEN Marchese **Emilio Pucci**'s ancestors have been a powerful banking and mercantile family since the Renaissance, and in 1950 Marchese suddenly turned designer and shocked the fashion world with his flowing silks in outlandish colors. His women's silk clothing remained the rage into the early 1970s and had a renaissance in the 1990s club scene. Drop by the flagship store at Via dei Tornabuoni 20–22r (www.pucci.com; ✆ **055-265-8082**).

Then there's **Giorgio Armani,** Via Tornabuoni 48r (www.giorgioarmani.com; ✆ **055-219-041**), Florence's outlet for Italy's top fashion guru. The service and store are surprisingly not stratospherically chilly. The **Emporio Armani** branch at Piazza Strozzi 16r (www.emporioarmani.com; ✆ **055-284-315**) is the outlet for the more affordable designs. The merchandise is slightly inferior in workmanship and quality but considerably less expensive. The rest of the Via dei' Tornabuoni is fleshed out with the mainstays of Italian style, notably **Salvatore Ferragamo** (www.salvatoreferragamo.it; ✆ **055-292-123**) at 4r.

But the biggest name to walk out of Florence onto the international catwalk has to be **Gucci ★**, with the world flagship store at Via de' Tornabuoni 73r (www.gucci.com; ✆ **055-264-011**). This is where this Florentine fashion empire was started by saddle-maker Guccio Gucci in 1904. You enter through a phalanx of their trademark purses and bags.

Florence has caught the vintage fashion bug, and on the two floors of **Pitti Vintage ★**, Borgo degli Albizi 72r (www.pittivintage.com; ✆ **055-234-4115**), you'll find classic threads, stylish men's shirts and ties, and accessories for women such as silk scarves, 1980s bags, and haute couture dresses. Prices are fair and the welcome is friendly.

FOR WOMEN **Loretta Caponi,** Piazza Antinori 4r (www.lorettacaponi.com; ✆ **055-213-668**), is world famous for her high-quality intimates and embroidered linens made the old-fashioned way. Under Belle Epoque ceilings are nightgowns of all types, as well as underwear, bed, and bath linens of the highest caliber. There's also a section for the little ones in the back. There's another branch at Via delle Belle Donne 28r (✆ **055-211-074**).

JEWELRY

If you've got the financial clout of a small country, the place to buy your baubles is the Ponte Vecchio, famous for its gold- and silversmiths since the 16th century. The craftsmanship at the stalls is usually of a decent quality, and so they seem to compete instead over who can charge the highest prices. **Aprosio ★**, Via Santo Spirito 11 (www.aprosio.it; ✆ **055-290-534**), is a glass and crystal jewelry designer without equal in the city. The store is arranged like a temple to creativity. Semiprecious stones are crafted into elaborate necklaces, classy earrings, and simple brooches at **Tharros Bijoux,** Via Condotta 2r (at corner of Via de' Cerchi; www.tharros.com; ✆ **055-284-126**).

Florence is also a good place to root around for interesting costume jewelry. The audacious bijoux at **Angela Caputi,** Via Santo Spirito 58r (www.angelacaputi.com; ✆ **055-212-972**), aren't for the timid. Much of Angela's costume jewelry is at least oversize and bold and often pushes the flamboyance envelope. Tradition goes out the window at **Falsi Gioelli ★**, Via dei Tavolini 5r (✆ **055-293-296**). Prepare to be assaulted by primary colors the minute you step into this funky "false" jeweler, where everything from hair bands and bracelets to necklaces and earrings in bright shades of acrylic is handmade on the premises. Items are inexpensive. There's another branch at Via de' Ginori 34r (✆ **055-287-237**).

LEATHER, ACCESSORIES & SHOES

It has always been a buyers' market for leather in Florence, but these days it's tricky to sort out the jackets mass-produced for tourists from the high-quality artisan work. The most fun you'll have leather shopping, without a doubt, is at the outdoor stalls of the **San Lorenzo** market, even if the market is rife with mediocre goods (see "Florence's Famous Street Market," below). Never accept the first price they throw at you; sometimes you can bargain them down to almost half the original asking price.

Shoes and bags are among the big draws at Salvatore Ferragamo.

Our favorite spot, where we get to watch the artisans at work before buying, is at the **Scuola del Cuoio (Leather School) of Santa Croce ★**. It's around the back of the church: Enter through Santa Croce itself (right transept) or on Via San Giuseppe 5r (www.scuoladelcuoio.com; ✆ **055-244-533**). The very-fine-quality soft-leather merchandise isn't cheap.

In the imposing 13th-century Palazzo Spini-Feroni lording over Piazza Santa Trínita are the flagship store, museum, and home of **Ferragamo,** Via de' Tornabuoni 4–14r (www.ferragamo.it; ✆ **055-292-123**). Salvatore Ferragamo was the man who shod Hollywood in its most glamorous age and raised footwear to an art form. View some of Ferragamo's funkier shoes in the second-floor museum or slip on a pair yourself in the showrooms downstairs—if you think your wallet can take the shock.

For more made-in-Florence accessorizing, head to **Madova Gloves,** Via Guicciardini 1r (www.madova.com; ✆ **055-239-6526**). Gloves are all they sell in this tiny shop, and they do them well. The grandchildren of the workshop's founders do a brisk business in brightly colored, supple leather gloves lined with cashmere and silk.

MARKETS

Somewhere in the center of the mercantile whirlwind of Florence hides the indoor **Mercato Centrale food market ★** (btw. Via dell'Ariento and Piazza del Mercato Centrale). Downstairs you'll find meat, cheese, dry goods, tripe, *baccalà* (dried salt cod), and a good cheap eatery, **Nerbone** (p. 233). The upstairs is devoted to fruits and veggies—a cornucopia of fat eggplants, long yellow peppers, artichokes, and peperoncini bunched into brilliant red bursts. In all, you couldn't ask for better picnic pickings. The market is open Monday through Saturday from 7am to 2pm (until 5pm Sat Sept–June).

Florence's Famous Street Market

The queen of Florentine markets is the daily **San Lorenzo market,** filling Piazza San Lorenzo, Via del Canto de' Nelli, Via dell'Ariento, and other side streets around the basilica. It's a wildly chaotic and colorful array of hundreds of stands hawking T-shirts, silk scarves, marbleized paper, souvenirs, and lots and lots of leather. However, almost all of the buyers here are tourists, and you'll find plenty of lemons among the occasional deals on quality goods. By all means have a browse—San Lorenzo in full swing is quite a sight—but it's not worth committing to half a day of picking through it all and fending off sales pitches. ***Note:*** Haggling is accepted, and even expected, at most of Florence's outdoor markets (but don't try it in stores). It's also an offense (punishable with a hefty fine) to knowingly buy counterfeit goods. And, yes, buying a "Rolex" for 20€ does count as *knowingly.*

As if two names weren't enough, the **Mercato Nuovo,** or **della Paglia (Straw Market),** is also known as Mercato del Porcellino or Mercato del Cinghiale because of the bronze wild boar statue at one end, cast by Pietro Tacca in the 17th century after an antique original now in the Uffizi. Pet the well-polished *porcellino*'s snout to ensure a return trip to Florence. Most of the straw stalls disappeared by the 1960s. These days, the loggia hawks mainly tourist trinkets. Beware of pickpockets. It's open daily.

For more of a local flavor, head east beyond Santa Croce to find the daily flea market, the **Mercato delle Pulci ★**, in Piazza de' Ciompi, which specializes in a bit of everything, from costume jewelry, ornaments, and vintage buttons to silver, antique bric-a-brac, and yesteryear postcards. The nearby food market where Florentines shop (Mon–Sat), the **Mercato di Sant'Ambrogio,** is also home to one of the city's best cheap lunch spots, **Da Rocco** (p. 237).

PAPER & JOURNALS

Il Papiro, Via dei Tavolini 13r (www.ilpapirofirenze.it; ✆ **055-213-823**), is a small Tuscan chain of jewel box–size shops specializing in marbled and patterned paper, as plain gift-wrap sheets or as a covering for everything from pens and journals to letter openers or full desk sets. There are further branches at Via Cavour 49r (✆ **055-215-262**), Piazza del Duomo 24r (✆ **055-281-628**), Lungarno Acciaiuoli 42r (✆ **055-264-5613**), and Via Porta Rossa 76r (✆ **055-216-593**).

Scriptorium, Via dei Servi 5–7r (✆ **055-211-804**), is our favorite journal supplier, and one of the few fine stationery stores in Florence with little marbleized paper. Come here for hand-sewn notebooks, journals, and photo albums made of thick paper—all bound in soft leather covers. With classical music or Gregorian chant playing in the background, you can also shop for calligraphy and signet wax sealing tools.

TOYS

Since 1977, Florence's branch of national chain **La Città del Sole,** Via dello Studio 23r (www.cittadelsole.it; ✆ **055-277-6372**), has sold old-fashioned wooden brain teasers, construction kits, hand puppets, 3-D puzzles, science kits, and books. There's nary a video game in sight. **La Tartaruga,** Borgo degli Albizi 60r (✆ **055-234-0845**), is an enchanting, old-fashioned toy store stuffed with handmade wooden toys, stuffed dolls, and wrapping paper.

ENTERTAINMENT & NIGHTLIFE

Florence has bundles of excellent, mostly free, listings publications. At the tourist offices, pick up the free monthly ***Informacittà*** (www.informacitta.net), which is strong on theater and other arts events, as well as markets. Younger and hipper, pocket-size monthly ***Zero*** (http://firenze.zero.eu) is hot on the latest eating, drinking, and nightlife. It's available free from trendy cafe-bars, shops, and usually the tourist office, too. ***Firenze Spettacolo,*** a 1.80€ Italian-language monthly sold at most newsstands, is the most detailed and up-to-date listing of nightlife, arts, and entertainment. Free monthly ***iOVO*** (www.iovo.it) is good on contemporary arts and cultural goings-on in the city.

The Performing Arts

Florence doesn't have the musical cachet or grand opera houses of Milan, Venice, or Rome, but there are two symphony orchestras and a fine music school in

Fiesole. The city's public theaters are certainly respectable, and most major touring companies stop in town on their way through Italy. Get tickets to all cultural and musical events online (they'll send an e-mail with collection instructions) or in person at **Box Office,** Via delle Carceri 1 (www.boxol.it; ✆ **055-210-804**).

Many concerts and recitals staged in major halls and private spaces are sponsored by the **Amici della Musica** (www.amicimusica.fi.it; ✆ **055-607-440**), so check their website to see what "hidden" concert might be on while you're here.

CHURCH CONCERTS Many Florentine churches fill the autumn with organ, choir, and chamber orchestra concerts, mainly of classical music. The tiny **Santa Maria de' Ricci** (✆ **055-215-044**) on Via del Corso has a free organ concert most nights, starting at 7 or 9:15pm (pass by during the day to check). Technically it's free, but contributions to the church's upkeep, as well as that of the nearby Chiesa di Dante, are appreciated. The **Orchestra da Camera Fiorentina (Florentine Chamber Orchestra;** www.orcafi.it; ✆ **055-783-374**) also runs a season at historic sites around the city; tickets are available from Box Office. **St. Mark's,** Via Maggio 18 (www.concertoclassico.info; ✆ **340-811-9192**), hosts regular, often nightly, operas and operatic music concerts inside its church in the Oltrarno. Tickets cost 15€ to 30€.

CONCERT HALLS & OPERA One of Italy's busiest stages, Florence's contemporary **Teatro Comunale,** Corso Italia 12 (www.maggiofiorentino.com; ✆ **055-277-9350**), offers everything from symphonies to ballet to plays, opera, and concerts. The main theater seats 2,000, with orchestra rows topped by horseshoe-shaped first and second galleries. Its smaller Piccolo Teatro, seating 500, is rectangular, offering good sightlines from most any seat. The Teatro Comunale is the seat of the prestigious annual Maggio Musicale Fiorentino.

The **Teatro Verdi,** Via Ghibellina 99r (www.teatroverdionline.it; ✆ **055-212-320**), is Florence's opera and ballet house, with the nice ritual of staging Sunday-afternoon shows during the January-through-April season. The **Orchestra della Toscana** (www.orchestradellatoscana.it) plays classical concerts here November through May, and occasionally plays cheap Saturday afternoon shows aimed at children.

Enjoy an evening at a cafe in Florence.

THEATER The biggest national and international touring companies stop in Florence's major playhouse, the **Teatro della Pergola,** Via della Pergola 12 (www.teatrodellapergola.com; ✆ **055-226-4353**). La Pergola is the city's chief purveyor of classical and classic plays from the Greeks and Shakespeare through Pirandello, Samuel Beckett, and Italian modern playwrights. Performances are professional and of high quality—and, of course, in Italian.

cafe CULTURE

Florence no longer has a glitterati or intellectuals' cafe scene, and when it did—from the late-19th-century Italian Risorgimento era through *la dolce vita* of the 1950s—it was basically copying the idea from Paris. Although they're often overpriced tourist spots today, Florence's high-toned cafes are fine if you want designer pastries served to you while you sit on a piazza and people-watch.

At the refined, wood-paneled, stucco-ceilinged, and very expensive 1733 cafe **Gilli,** Via Roma 1r (www.gilli.it; ✆ **055-213-896**), tourists gather to sit with the ghosts of Italy's Risorgimento, when the cafe became a meeting place of the heroes and thinkers of the unification movement from the 1850s to the 1870s. The red-jacketed waiters at **Giubbe Rosse,** Piazza della Repubblica 13–14r (www.giubberosse.it; ✆ **055-212-280**), must have been popular during the 19th-century glory days of Garibaldi's red-shirt soldiers. This was once a meeting place of the Futurists, but today it, too, is mainly a tourists' cafe with ridiculous prices.

Once full of history and now mainly full of tourists, **Rivoire,** Piazza della Signoria/Via Vacchereccia 4r (www.rivoire.it; ✆ **055-214-412**), has a chunk of prime real estate on Piazza della Signoria. Smartly dressed waiters serve adventurously priced sandwiches to cappuccino-sipping patrons.

The Club & Music Scenes

Italian clubs are rather cliquey—people usually go in groups to hang out and dance only with one another. There's plenty of flesh showing, but no meat market. Singles hoping to find random dance partners will often be disappointed.

LIVE MUSIC Florence's best jazz venue is the aptly named **Jazz Club,** Via Nuova de' Caccini 3 (www.jazzclubfirenze.com; ✆ **055-247-9700**). You need to join, online or at the venue, which costs 8€ for the year and entitles you to free entry to all concerts. It's closed Sunday, Monday, and all summer. The forthcoming program is posted on their website. New kid on the block is **Volume ★**, Piazza Santo Spirito 5r (www.volume.fi.it; ✆ **055-2381-460**), which opened in 2010; it's an artsy cafe-cum-creperie-cum-*gelateria* by day, with contemporary art hanging on the walls. When night falls, Left Bank revelers stop in for cocktails (around 6€), followed by live acoustic music 4 or 5 nights a week (Thurs night is a blues jam).

DANCE BARS & NIGHTCLUBS Any guide to nightclubbing should come with a health warning: What's hot (and what's not) can change from month to month. If you're clubbing at the cutting edge, we suggest you consult the listings magazines recommended above, or check the websites for **Zero** (http://firenze.zero.eu) and **Firenze Spettacolo** (www.firenzespettacolo.it).

It's not exactly cutting edge, but the most centrally located nightclub is **Yab,** Via Sassetti 5r (www.yab.it; ✆ **055-215-160**), just behind the post office on Piazza della Repubblica. This dance club for 20-somethings is a perennial favorite, an archetypal 1980s disco complete with velvet rope, bouncers, and an eclectic, upbeat music policy.

Much more fashionable is **Dolce Vita,** Piazza del Carmine (www.dolcevitaflorence.com; ✆ **055-284-595**), still going strong after 3 decades leading Florence's nightlife scene, and these days attracting clued-up 30-somethings who have grown up with the city's iconic DJ bar.

Bars, Pubs & Wine Bars

BARS & PUBS **Via dei Benci ★**, which runs south from Piazza Santa Croce toward the Arno, is the *centro storico*'s cool-bar central, and a great place to kick off a night with *aperitivo* hour. (Wander in from around 7pm, buy a drink, and help yourself to any of the food laid out buffet style.) **Moyo,** at no. 23r (www.moyo.it; ✆ **055-247-9738**), does some of the best *aperitivo* in Florence, and is frequented by beautiful people drinking cocktails. **Oibò,** up the road at Borgo de' Greci 1A (corner of Via dei Benci; www.oibo.net; ✆ **055-263-8611**), is also popular with fashionable 20- and 30-somethings. They mix a decent cocktail and after 10pm DJs spin house and dance sounds.

At **Sei Divino ★**, Borgo Ognissanti 42r (✆ **055-217-791**), you'll find artisan beers, Tuscan wines by the glass, and some interesting cocktails, as well as *aperitivo* plates piled high from 7pm every night. **Caffe Sant'Ambrogio,** Piazza Sant'Ambrogio 7 (www.caffesantambrogio.it; ✆ **055-247-7277**), is a funky cafe-bar by day and a popular wine bar after dark. South of the river, neighbors **Zoe,** Via dei Renai 13 (✆ **055-243-111**), and **Negroni** (at no. 17r, ✆ **055-243-647**) are buzzing on a weekend, pumping out music and fashionable chatter until late.

If it's a pub you're seeking, try **Kikuya,** Via dei Benci 43r (www.kikuya pub.it; ✆ **055-234-4879**), where you'll find draft ales and soccer on the screens.

For a swanky cocktail with a panoramic view of the city, check out the rooftop **Sky Lounge** of the Hotel Continentale, Vicolo dell'Oro 6r (next to Ponte Vecchio; www.lungarnohotels.com, ✆ **055-2726-4000;** Apr–Oct). Sunset is the best time to visit. The million-dollar view is amortized by the steep price of a martini.

WINE BARS The best wine lists focusing on handpicked labels, most offered with plates of cheese and other snacks, tend to be in the Oltrarno. **Il Volpe e L'Uva ★**, Piazza de' Rossi, by Santa Felícita (www.levolpieluva.com; ✆ **055-239-8132**), is popular with visitors and locals, and has a compelling by-the-glass list. Nearby, a great little wine bar right across from the Pitti Palace called **Pitti Gola e Cantina,** Piazza de' Pitti 16 (✆ **055-212-704**), sells glasses of fine wine from 7€ to 12€. The kitchen also serves light dishes for 8€ to 15€. We also love the buzzy little corner of the Oltrarno known as San Niccolò, a 10-minute walk from the Ponte Vecchio, where the wine bars serve substantial Tuscan dishes alongside antipasti platters to share. Our favorite well-stocked cantinas are at **Bevo Vino ★**, Via San Niccolò 59r (✆ **055-200-1709**); **Il Rifrullo,** Via San Niccolò 57r (www.ilrifrullo.com; ✆ **055-234-2621**); and **Fuori Porta ★**, Via Monte alle Croci 10 (✆ **055-234-2483**). Partying goes on here till late.

The LGBT Scene

The gay nightlife scene in Florence is gradually growing, but for lesbians it's still fairly limited. The best place for a predisco drink in the company of a young and friendly gay, lesbian, bisexual, and trans crowd is **YAG Bar ★**, Via de' Macci 8r (www.yagbar.com; ✆ **055-246-9022**). It's open nightly from 9pm all year.

One of Florence's dark rooms is the **Crisco Club,** Via Sant'Egidio 43r, east of the Duomo (www.criscoclub.it; ✆ **055-248-0580**), for men only. Its 18th-century building contains a bar and a dance floor open Tuesday through Saturday from 9pm to 3am (until 5am weekends). Check the website for one-off events and performances.

The city's major gay dance floor is **Tabasco,** Piazza Santa Cecilia 3r (www.tabascogay.it; ✆ **055-213-000**). Italy's first gay disco attracts crowds of men (mostly in their 20s and 30s) from all over the country. The music is generally techno, disco, and retro rock, but entertainment offerings also include cabaret, art shows, and the occasional transvestite comedy. In summer, foreigners arrive in droves.

Spectator Sports

There's only really one game in town when it comes to spectator sports: *calcio*. To Italians, soccer/football is something akin to a second religion, and an afternoon at the stadium can offer you as much insight (if not more) into local culture as a day in the Uffizi. The local team, **Fiorentina** (nicknamed *i viola,* "the purples"), plays in Italy's top league, Serie A. You can usually catch them alternate Sundays from September through May at the Stadio Comunale Artemio Franchi, Via Manfredo Fanti 4 (www.violachannel.tv). Tickets are best bought ahead of time from **Chiosco degli Sportivi,** Via degli Anselmi 1 (an alley off Piazza della Repubblica; ✆ **055-292-363**). To reach the stadium from the center, take a train from Santa Maria Novella to Campo di Marte (5 min.) or bus no. 10 from San Marco.

WHERE TO STAY

In the past few years, thanks to growing competition, the recent financial crises, and unfavorable euro-dollar and euro-pound exchange rates, the trusty forces of supply and demand have brought hotel prices in Florence down for the first time in memory, but it is still difficult to find a high-season double you'd want to stay in for much less than 100€. In addition, some of the price drops have been added back in taxes: Since July 2011, Florence's city government levies an extra 1€ per person per night per government-rated hotel star, for the first 5 nights of any stay. The tax is payable on arrival.

For help finding a room, inquire at the tourist office (see above) or see the subsection on accommodations at **www.firenzeturismo.it**, a site sponsored by the province that lists virtually every hotel and other type of accommodation in town.

Peak hotel season is mid-March through early July, September through early November, and December 23 through January 6. May, June, and September are particularly popular; January, February, and August are the months to grab a bargain—never be shy to haggle if you're coming in these months.

To help you decide which area you'd like to base yourself in, consult "The Neighborhoods in Brief," earlier in this chapter. Note that we've included parking information only for those places that offer it. As indicated below, many hotels offer babysitting services; note, however, these are generally "on request." A couple of days' notice is advisable.

Near the Duomo

The city's best located, quality B&B, **La Dimora degli Angeli ★**, Via Brunelleschi 4 (www.ladimoradegliangeli.it; ✆ **055-288-478**), has six rooms that combine contemporary and 19th-century styling in midsize units ideally suited to a romantic getaway. Doubles range 110€ to 155€ including breakfast.

VERY EXPENSIVE

Savoy ★★ This 1893 hotel underwent a complete transformation by Sir Rocco Forte and his sister, who designed the warm, stylishly minimalist modern interiors. Rooms are standardized, with walk-in closets, marble bathrooms, and mosaics over the tubs. The different room "styles"—classic, executive, and deluxe—really refer to size. Among the four suites (two rooms, two TVs, leather easy chairs, white marble bathrooms), two include a Turkish bath. Rooms on the fifth floor, added in 1958, just peep over the surrounding buildings for spectacular views, especially those on the Duomo (back) side. You're just a few steps from all the city's sights and shopping.

Piazza della Repubblica 7, 50123 Firenze. www.hotelsavoy.it. ✆ **800/223-6800** in the U.S., or 055-27-351 in Italy. Fax 055-273-5888. 102 units. 530€ double; 620€ executive double; 830€ studio; 1,250€–2,700€ suite. Breakfast 32€. AE, DC, MC, V. Valet garage parking 29€. Bus: C2, 6, 11, 22, 36, or 37. **Amenities:** Restaurant; bar; babysitting; concierge; gym; room service; Wi-Fi (free). *In room:* A/C, TV, fax (on request), hair dryer, minibar.

EXPENSIVE

Calzaiuoli ★ As central as you can get, the Calzaiuoli offers comfortable, well-appointed rooms on the main strolling drag halfway between the Uffizi and the Duomo. The halls' rich runners lead up a *pietra serena* staircase to the midsize and largish rooms decorated with painted friezes and framed etchings. The firm beds rest on patterned carpets; the bathrooms range from huge to cramped, but all have fluffy towels (and a few have Jacuzzis). The rooms overlook the street, with its pedestrian carnival and some of the associated noise, or out the back—either over the rooftops to the Bargello and Badia towers or up to the Duomo's cupola.

Via Calzaiuoli 6 (near Orsanmichele), 50122 Firenze. www.calzaiuoli.it. ✆ **055 212 456.** Fax 055 268-310. 53 units. 120€–490€ double. Rates include breakfast. AE, DC, MC, V. Valet garage parking 26€. Bus: C2. **Amenities:** Bar; babysitting; concierge. *In room:* A/C, TV, hair dryer, minibar, Wi-Fi (free).

MODERATE

Bigallo In the competition for best location, the Bigallo is hard to beat, sitting on the corner of Piazza del Duomo. Request one of the few rooms facing the Duomo to guarantee a view like no other, within poking distance of Giotto's bell tower, although the decor is a little bland. Suites all have the Duomo view as well as a mezzanine space—well worth the extra 30€ to 40€. The traffic-free zone doesn't mean you won't have significant pedestrian noise that drifts up from the cobbled street below, as this is the city's most tourist-trammeled intersection.

Vicolo degli Adimari 2 (off Via Calzaiuoli by Piazza del Duomo), 50122 Firenze. www.hotelbigallo.it. ✆/fax **055-216-086.** 17 units. 104€–199€ double; 133€–271€ suite. Rates include breakfast. AE, DC, MC, V. Garage valet parking 21€. Bus: C2. **Amenities:** Concierge. *In room:* A/C, TV, hair dryer, minibar, Wi-Fi (5€ per day).

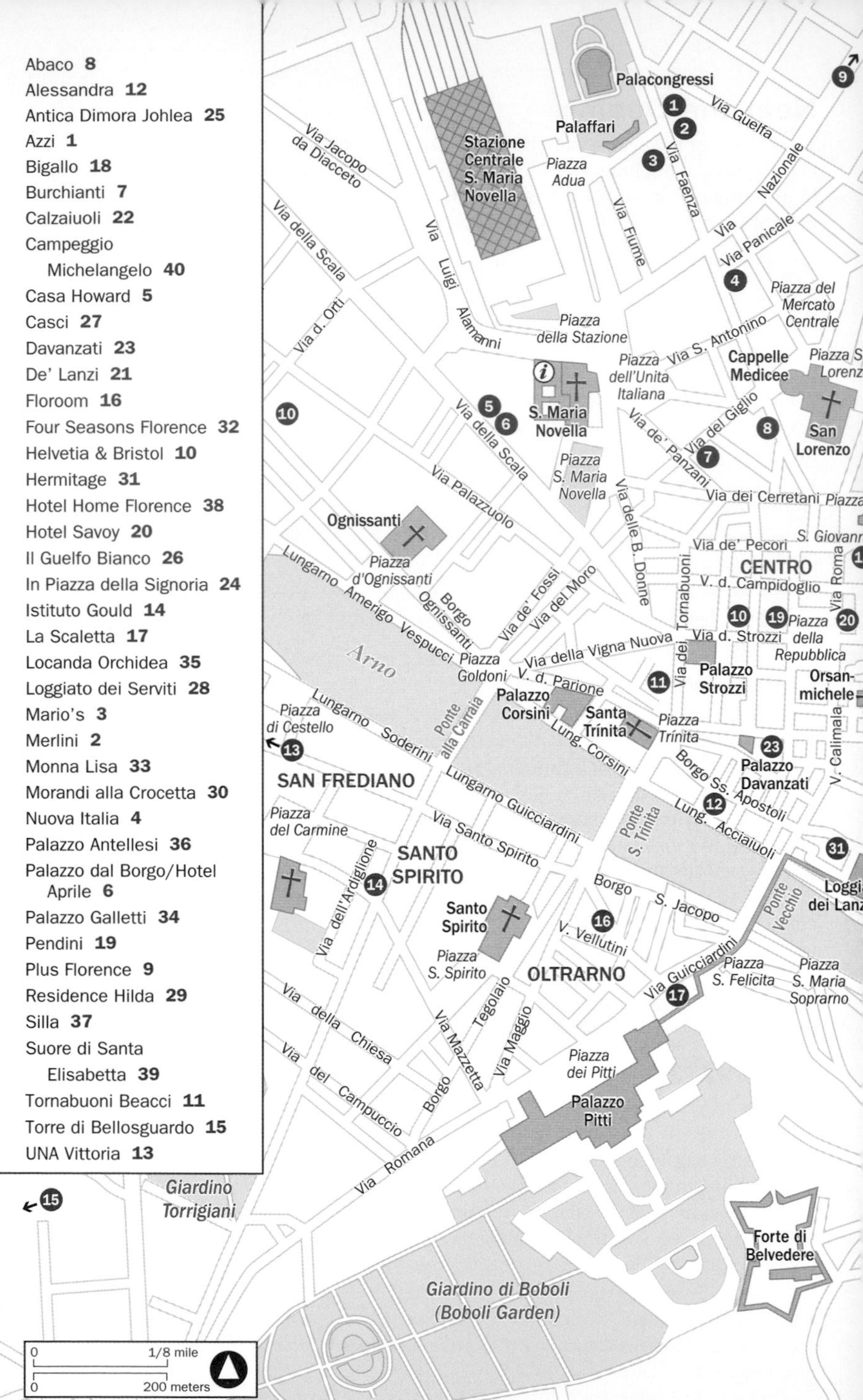
Abaco 8
Alessandra 12
Antica Dimora Johlea 25
Azzi 1
Bigallo 18
Burchianti 7
Calzaiuoli 22
Campeggio Michelangelo 40
Casa Howard 5
Casci 27
Davanzati 23
De' Lanzi 21
Floroom 16
Four Seasons Florence 32
Helvetia & Bristol 10
Hermitage 31
Hotel Home Florence 38
Hotel Savoy 20
Il Guelfo Bianco 26
In Piazza della Signoria 24
Istituto Gould 14
La Scaletta 17
Locanda Orchidea 35
Loggiato dei Serviti 28
Mario's 3
Merlini 2
Monna Lisa 33
Morandi alla Crocetta 30
Nuova Italia 4
Palazzo Antellesi 36
Palazzo dal Borgo/Hotel Aprile 6
Palazzo Galletti 34
Pendini 19
Plus Florence 9
Residence Hilda 29
Silla 37
Suore di Santa Elisabetta 39
Tornabuoni Beacci 11
Torre di Bellosguardo 15
UNA Vittoria 13
Palacongressi
Palaffari
Stazione Centrale S. Maria Novella
Piazza Adua
Via Guelfa
Via Nazionale
Via Faenza
Via Fiume
Via Jacopo da Diacceto
Via della Scala
Via Luigi Alamanni
Via Panicale
Piazza del Mercato Centrale
Piazza della Stazione
Via d. Orti
Piazza dell'Unita Italiana
Via S. Antonino
Cappelle Medicee
Piazza S. Lorenzo
S. Maria Novella
Via del Giglio
Via de' Panzani
San Lorenzo
Piazza S. Maria Novella
Via Palazzuolo
Via delle B. Donne
Via dei Cerretani
Ognissanti
Piazza d'Ognissanti
Via de' Pecori
S. Giovanni
CENTRO
V. d. Campidoglio
Via Roma
Lungarno Amerigo Vespucci
Borgo Ognissanti
Via de' Fossi
Via del Moro
Via dei Tornabuoni
Via d. Strozzi
Piazza della Repubblica
Arno
Piazza Goldoni
Via della Vigna Nuova
V. d. Parione
Palazzo Strozzi
Orsanmichele
Palazzo Corsini
Santa Trínita
Piazza Trínita
Piazza di Cestello
Lungarno Soderini
Ponte alla Carraia
Lung. Corsini
V. Calimala
Palazzo Davanzati
SAN FREDIANO
Lungarno Guicciardini
Borgo Ss. Apostoli
Ponte S. Trinita
Lung. Acciaiuoli
Piazza del Carmine
Via Santo Spirito
SANTO SPIRITO
Via dell'Ardiglione
Borgo S. Jacopo
Ponte Vecchio
Loggia dei Lanzi
Santo Spirito
V. Vellutini
Piazza S. Spirito
OLTRARNO
Via Guicciardini
Piazza S. Felicita
Piazza S. Maria Soprarno
Via della Chiesa
Via Mazzetta
Borgo Tegolaio
Via Maggio
Via del Campuccio
Piazza dei Pitti
Palazzo Pitti
Via Romana
Giardino Torrigiani
Forte di Belvedere
Giardino di Boboli (Boboli Garden)
0 1/8 mile
0 200 meters

Florence Hotels

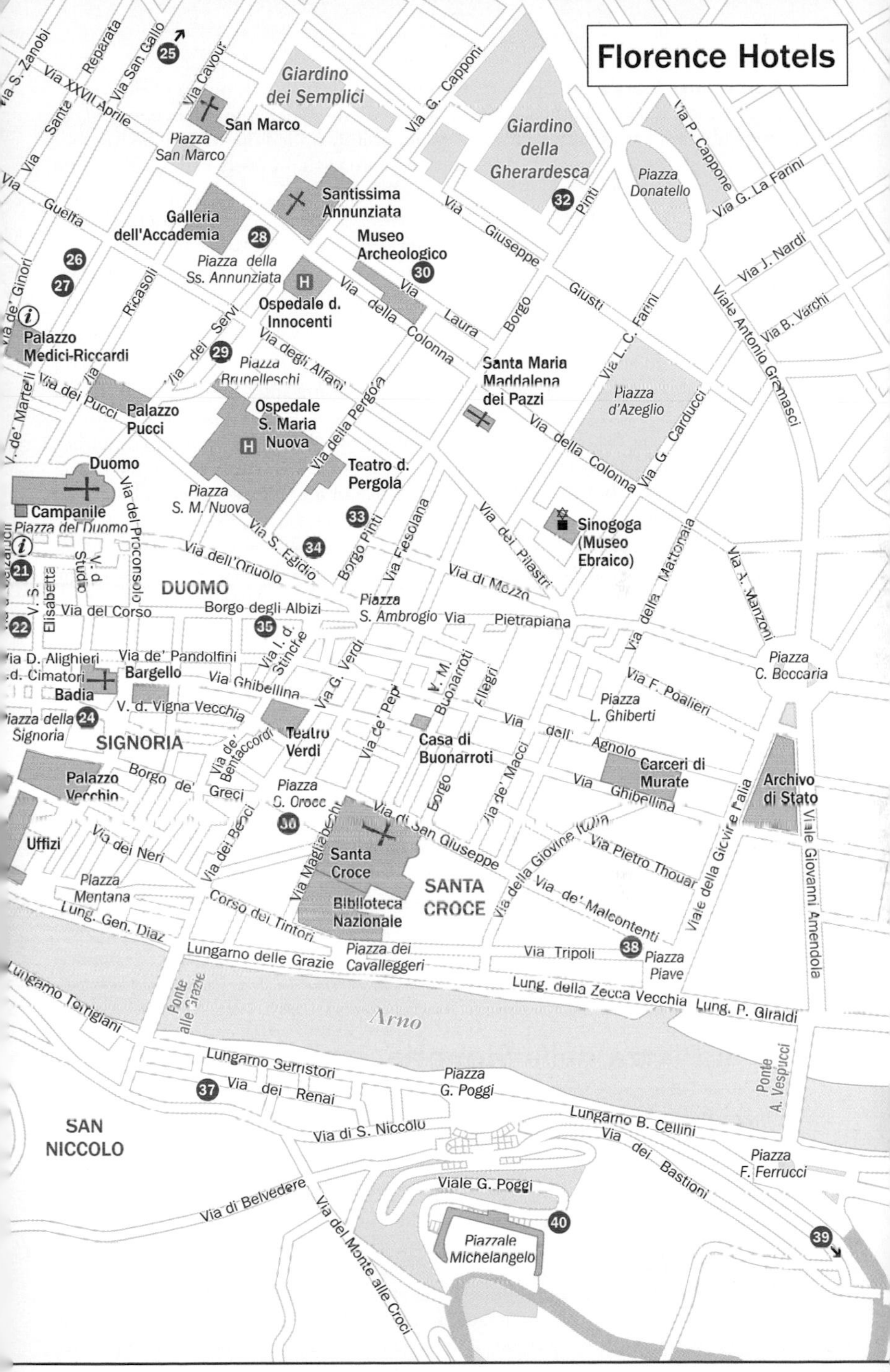

Burchianti ★★ 🎁 In 2002, rising rents forced the kindly owner of this venerable inn (established in the 19th c.) to move up the block into the *piano nobile* of a neighboring 15th-century *palazzo*. She definitely traded up. Incredible frescoes dating from the 17th century and later decorate virtually every ceiling. This little gem fills up quickly, so be sure to book well in advance.

Via del Giglio 8 (off Via Panzani), 50123 Firenze. www.hotelburchianti.it. ✆ **055-212-796.** Fax 055-272-9727. 12 units. 100€–130€ double; 115€–155€ triple; 140€–170€ junior suite. Rates include breakfast. AE, DC, MC, V. Garage parking 25€. Bus: C2, 6, 14, 22, 36, or 37. **Amenities:** Concierge. *In room:* A/C, TV, hair dryer, minibar, Wi-Fi (free).

Pendini ☺ Built during the heyday of the 1880s, when Florence was briefly the capital of the newly unified Italy, the Pendini rises above the arcades of Piazza della Repubblica. The entrance is not very welcoming and the furniture has seen better days, but it is clean and a great value for the location, poised next to the top shops in the city, and it retains a certain old-fashioned charm. The rather large accommodations on the piazza have the best views, over the bustle of the cafe-lined square, but they also pose a real risk of a noisy night. One child stays free in a parent's room.

Via Strozzi 2 (on Piazza della Repubblica), 50123 Firenze. www.hotelpendini.it. ✆ **055-211-170.** Fax 055-281-807. 42 units. 90€–189€ double; 120€–240€ triple. 1 child stays free in parent's room. Rates include breakfast. AE, MC, V. Bus: C2, 6, 11, 22, 36, or 37. **Amenities:** Bar; concierge. *In room:* A/C, TV, hair dryer (on request), Wi-Fi (free).

INEXPENSIVE

Abaco ★ Owner Bruno continues to please his guests with a clean, efficient little hotel in a prime location, albeit short on creature comforts. The Abaco has inherited a few nice touches from its 15th-century *palazzo,* including high wood ceilings, stone floors (some parquet), and even a carved *pietra serena* fireplace. Each room is themed after a Renaissance artist, with framed reproductions of the painter's works; this hotel is more beatnik, less Bulgari, and has been done up with quirky antique-style pieces such as gilded frame mirrors and rich half-testers over the beds. It's at a busy intersection, but the double-paned windows help. Those who are not okay with lugging suitcases up stairs should look elsewhere.

Via dei Banchi 1 (off Via de' Panzani), 50123 Firenze. www.abaco-hotel.it. ✆ **055-238-1919.** Fax 055-282-289. 7 units. 45€–75€ double without bathroom; 60€–90€ double with bathroom; extra 20€ per person to make a triple or quad. Rates include breakfast. AE, MC, V. Garage parking 24€. Bus: C2, 6, 14, 22, 36, or 37. **Amenities:** Bar; concierge. *In room:* A/C, TV, hair dryer, Wi-Fi (free).

Near Piazza della Signoria

The best B&B close to this bustling civic heart of the city is aptly named **In Piazza della Signoria ★**, Via dei Magazzini 2, 50122 Firenze (www.inpiazza dellasignoria.com; ✆ **055-239-9546**). The 10 refined rooms, named after famous Florentines through the ages and embellished in the *residenza d'epoca* style with antique furnishings, cost between 160€ and 220€ without a view; it's an extra 30€ to 40€ per night for one of the best views in Florence.

EXPENSIVE

Hermitage ★ This ever-popular hotel is located right at the foot of the Ponte Vecchio. The rooms are of moderate size, occasionally a bit dark, but they're full of 17th- to 19th-century antiques and boast double-glazed windows to cut down on noise. Rooms have either wood floors or thick rugs, and superior room bathrooms have Jacuzzis; those that don't face the Ponte Vecchio are on side alleys and quieter. Their famous roof terrace is covered in bright flowers that frame postcard views of the Arno, Duomo, and Palazzo Vecchio. The charming breakfast room full of picture windows gets the full effect of the morning sun. The owners and staff excel in doing the little things that help make your vacation go smoothly—but prices are a bit inflated.

Vicolo Marzio 1/Piazza del Pesce (to the left of the Ponte Vecchio as you're facing it), 50122 Firenze. www.hermitagehotel.com. ✆ **055-287-216.** Fax 055-212-208. 28 units. 120€–220€ double; 160€–250€ triple. Rates include breakfast. AE, MC, V. Valet garage parking 25€. Bus: C1, 3, 12, 13, or 23. **Amenities:** Bar; babysitting; concierge; Wi-Fi (2€ per hour). *In room:* A/C, TV, hair dryer.

Near San Lorenzo & the Mercato Centrale

MODERATE

Il Guelfo Bianco ★★ Once you enter this refined hotel you'll forget it's on busy Via Cavour. Its windows are triple-paned, blocking out nearly all traffic noise, and many rooms overlook quiet courtyards and gardens out back. The interior successfully combines modern comforts with antique details. Some rooms have retained such 17th-century features as frescoed or painted wood ceilings, carved wooden doorways, and the occasional parquet floor—deluxe rooms 101, 118, 228, and 338 have a separate seating area. The friendly staff is full of advice.

Via Cavour 29 (near the corner of Via Guelfa), 50129 Firenze. www.ilguelfobianco.it. ✆ **055-288-330.** Fax 055-295-203. 40 units. 99€–250€ double, 133€–300€ triple. Rates include breakfast. AE, DC, MC, V. Valet garage parking 26€–32€. Bus: C1, 14, or 23. **Amenities:** Restaurant; bar; babysitting; concierge; room service. *In room:* A/C, TV, hair dryer, minibar, Wi-Fi (free).

INEXPENSIVE

Casci ★ ☺ 💰 This clean hotel in a 15th-century *palazzo* is run by the Lombardis, one of Florence's most accommodating families. It's patronized by a host of regulars who know a good value when they find it. The frescoed bar room was, from 1851 to 1855, part of an apartment inhabited by Gioachino Rossini, composer of the *Barber of Seville* and *William Tell Overture*. The rooms ramble on toward the back forever, overlooking the gardens and Florentine rooftops, and are mouse-quiet except for the birdsong. Ask for a double with a bath and shower, as those units are the most recently updated. A few family suites in back sleep four to five. The central location means some rooms (with double-paned windows) overlook busy Via Cavour, so if you're seeking quiet ask for a room facing the inner courtyard.

Via Cavour 13 (btw. Via dei Ginori and Via Guelfa), 50129 Firenze. www.hotelcasci.com. ✆ **055-211-686.** Fax 055-239-6461. 25 units. 80€–150€ double; 100€–190€ triple; 120€–230€ quad. Rates include buffet breakfast. 10% discount for cash payment; check website for offers, including 1 free museum ticket per guest Nov–Feb. AE, DC, MC, V. Garage parking 15€–23€. Bus: C1, 14, or 23. Closed 2 weeks in Dec and 3 weeks in Jan. **Amenities:** Bar; babysitting; concierge. *In room:* A/C, TV/DVD, DVD library, fridge, hair dryer, Wi-Fi (free)

Near Piazza Santa Trínita

VERY EXPENSIVE

Helvetia & Bristol ★★ This classy Belle Epoque hotel is the most central of the top luxury properties in town, host in the past to the Tuscan Macchiaioli painters as well as De Chirico, playwright Pirandello, and atom-splitting Enrico Fermi.

The attentive staff oversees the rather cushy accommodations outfitted with marble bathrooms, large, firm beds, and heavy curtains. Most rooms have at least one antique work of art on the fabric-covered walls, and all are well insulated from the sounds of the outside world. The large 17th-century canvases add an air of dignity.

Via dei Pescioni 2 (opposite Palazzo Strozzi), 50123 Firenze. www.royaldemeure.com. ✆ **055-26-651.** Fax 055-288-353. 67 units. 285€–475€ classic double; 325€–540€ executive double; 396€–660€ deluxe double. AE, DC, MC, V. Valet garage parking 45€. Bus: C2, 6, 11, 22, 36, 37, or 68. **Amenities:** Restaurant; bar; babysitting; bikes; concierge; room service. *In room:* A/C, TV, hair dryer, minibar, Wi-Fi (18€ per day).

MODERATE

Alessandra ★ This old-fashioned *pensione* in a 1507 *palazzo* just off the river charges little for its simple comfort and kind hospitality. The rooms differ greatly in size and style, and while they won't win any awards from *Architectural Digest,* there are a few antique pieces and parquet floors to add to the charm. The bathrooms are outfitted with fluffy white towels, and the shared bathrooms are ample, clean, and numerous enough that you won't have to wait in line in the morning.

Borgo SS. Apostoli 17 (btw. Via dei Tornabuoni and Via Por Santa Maria), 50123 Firenze. www.hotelalessandra.com. ✆ **055-283-438.** Fax 055-210-619. 27 units, 20 with private bathroom. 110€ double without bathroom; 150€–175€ double with bathroom; 150€ triple without bathroom; 195€ triple with bathroom; 160€ quad without bathroom; 215€ quad with bathroom. Rates include buffet breakfast. AE, MC, V. Valet garage parking 22€–27€. Bus: 6, 11, 36, 37, or 68. **Amenities:** Bar; concierge. *In room:* A/C, TV, hair dryer, minibar (in some), Wi-Fi (free).

Davanzati ★★ ☺ A dizzying array of recently renovated rooms, each equipped to a high specification, plus a great location at an unbeatable value make this one of our favorite moderately priced hotels in the *centro storico.* No two units in the sympathetically converted, 15th-century *palazzo* are the same: Your best bet is to tell the friendly staff your party size and requirements, and let them advise. Our personal favorite is no. 100, in light wood with cream fabrics and multiple split levels that have private sleeping areas, ideal if you're traveling with kids (who will also like the laptop and PlayStation that are standard in every room).

Via Porta Rossa 5 (on Piazza Davanzati), 50123 Firenze. www.hoteldavanzati.it. ✆ **055-286-666.** Fax 055-265-8252. 21 units. 120€–188€ double; 150€–312€ superior sleeping up to 4; 190€–352€ suite. Rates include breakfast. Valet garage parking 26€. AE, MC, V. Bus: C2, 6, 11, 22, 36, 37, or 68. **Amenities:** Bar; babysitting; concierge. *In room:* A/C, TV, hair dryer, minibar, Wi-Fi (free).

Near Santa Maria Novella

EXPENSIVE

Montebello Splendid ★★ For charm and grace—as well as realistically priced luxury—this boutique hotel just west of the center is a hit. Enter a splendid garden in front of this restored palace, with a columned Tuscan-style *loggia,* and be ushered into a regal palace with Italian marble, stuccowork, and luminous niches. Each of the midsize to spacious bedrooms is individually decorated and soundproof—with a lavish use of parquet, marble, soft carpeting, and elegant fabrics—and deluxe beds and first-class bathrooms are clad in marble and equipped with hydromassages, among other features.

Via Garibaldi 14, 50123 Firenze. www.montebellosplendid.com. ✆ **055-27471.** Fax 055-2747700. 60 units. 199€–369€ double. AE, DC, MC, V. Parking 30€. Bus: C2, C3, or D. **Amenities:** Restaurant; bar; concierge; gym and spa; room service. *In room:* A/C, TV, hair dryer, Wi-Fi (free).

MODERATE

Casa Howard ★★ Quirky, midsize, individual rooms in this *palazzo* turned chic, contemporary guesthouse come with stylized themes: If you're the intellectual type, you'll enjoy the Library Room, which is filled with wall-to-wall reading. Our other favorite rooms include the Fireplace Room, with two picture windows. The three different rooms that comprise the Oriental Room are filled with objects collected by the owners in Asia, including a gigantic lacquer red shower. The Black and White Room lives up to its name, right down to a zebra armchair, and the small, cozy Hidden Room is dressed in sensual red. ***Note:*** The surroundings are plush and refined, and the welcome is friendly, but this is *not* a hotel. If you require hotel-type services to enjoy a stay, look elsewhere.

Via della Scala 18, 50123 Firenze. www.casahoward.com. ✆ **0669-924-555.** Fax 0667-94-644. 13 units. 120€–240€ double. Rates include breakfast. AE, MC, V. Bus: 11, 36, 37, or 68. **Amenities:** Concierge. *In room:* A/C, TV, hair dryer, minibar, no phone, Wi-Fi (free).

Between Santa Maria Novella & the Mercato Centrale

MODERATE

Mario's ★★ In a traditional Old Florence atmosphere, the Masieri and Benelli families run a first-rate ship. Your room might have a wrought-iron headboard and massive reproduction antique armoire, and look out onto a peaceful garden. The beamed ceilings in the common areas date from the 17th century, although the building became a hotel only in 1872. The only major drawback is its location—it's a bit far from the Duomo nerve center. Hefty discounts during off-season months "de-splurge" this lovely choice.

Via Faenza 89 (1st floor; near Via Cennini), 50123 Firenze. www.hotelmarios.com. ✆ **055-216-801.** Fax 055-212-039. 16 units. 80€–150€ double; 110€–185€ triple. Rates include breakfast. AE, DC, MC, V. Bus: 1, 2, 12, 13, 28, 29, 30, 35, 57, or 70. **Amenities:** Bar, babysitting, concierge. *In room:* A/C, TV/DVD, hair dryer, Wi-Fi (free).

INEXPENSIVE

Azzi ★ Musicians Sandro and Valentino, the owners of this former *pensione* (also known as the Locanda degli Artisti/Artists' Inn), have created here a haven for artists, artist *manqués,* and students. It exudes a relaxed bohemian feel—not all the doors hang straight and not all the bedspreads match, though strides are being made (and they've even discovered some old frescoes in a couple of the rooms). You'll love the open terrace with a view where breakfast is served in warm weather, as well as the small library of art books and guidebooks. Only two rooms face the noisy street out front—you don't want either of those.

Via Faenza 88r (1st floor), 50123 Firenze. www.hotelazzi.com. ✆ **055-213-806.** Fax 055-239-8322. 16 units. 80€–130€ double; 85€–140€ triple. Rates include breakfast. AE, DC, MC, V. Garage parking 16€. Bus: 1, 2, 12, 13, 28, 29, 30, 35, 57, or 70. **Amenities:** Bar; concierge; Wi-Fi (free). *In room:* A/C, TV, hair dryer, no phone.

Merlini ★ Run by the Sicilian Gabriella family, this cozy third-floor walk-up renovated in 2010 is a notch above your average budget place, the best in a building full of tiny *pensioni.* The optional breakfast is served on a sunny glassed-in terrace decorated in the 1960s with frescoes by talented American art students and overlooking a leafy large courtyard. Room nos. 1, 4 (with a balcony), 6 through 8, and 11 all have views of the domes topping the Duomo and the Medici Chapels across the city's terra-cotta roofscape.

Via Faenza 56 (3rd floor), 50123 Firenze. www.hotelmerlini.it. ✆ **055-212-848.** 10 units. 50€–80€ double without bathroom; 50€–100€ double with bathroom. Garage parking 20€. AE, DC, MC, V. Bus: 1, 2, 12, 13, 28, 29, 30, 35, 57, or 70. **Amenities:** Bar. *In room:* A/C, TV, hair dryer, no phone, Wi-Fi (free).

Nuova Italia A Frommer's fairy tale: With her trusty Arthur Frommer's *Europe on $5 a Day* in hand, the fair Eileen left the kingdom of Canada on a journey to faraway Florence. At her hotel, Eileen met Luciano, her baggage boy in shining armor. They fell in love, got married, bought a castle (er, hotel) of their own called the Nuova Italia, and their clients live happily ever after . . . The rooms are medium to small, and a little characterless, but the attention to detail and impeccable service makes the Nuova Italia stand out. Every room has triple-paned windows, though some morning rumble from the San Lorenzo market still gets through. The family's love of art is manifested in framed posters and paintings, and staff here really puts itself out for guests, recommending restaurants, shops, and day trips.

Via Faenza 26 (off Via Nazionale), 50123 Firenze. www.hotel-nuovaitalia.com. ✆ **055-287-508.** Fax 055-210-941. 20 units. 54€–139€ double; 74€–149€ triple. Rates include breakfast. AE, MC, V. Garage parking 24€. Bus: 1, 2, 12, 13, 28, 29, 30, 35, 57, or 70. **Amenities:** Bar; concierge. *In room:* A/C, TV, hair dryer, Wi-Fi (free).

Near San Marco & Santissima Annunziata

VERY EXPENSIVE

Four Seasons Florence ★★★ If the Medici should miraculously return to Florence, surely the clan would move in here. Installed in the overhauled historic Palazzo della Gherardesca and a former convent, this spa hotel offers spectacular frescoes, museum-worthy sculptures, and Florentine artisanal works, with its oldest wing dating from the 1440s. Its grounds are on one of the largest private gardens in the city. Damask draperies, regal appointments in all the bedrooms, fabric-trimmed walls, ceramic floors, an elegant spa, rich marble bathrooms, and luxurious beds and furnishings are just some of the features that make this perhaps the finest Four Seasons in Europe.

Borgo Pinti 99, 50121 Firenze. www.fourseasons.com/florence. ✆ **055-2626-250.** Fax 055-2626-500. 116 units. 550€–850€ double. AE, DC, MC, V. Free valet parking. Bus: 8 or 70. **Amenities:** 4 restaurants; 2 bars; concierge; gym; outdoor pool; room service; spa. *In room:* TV/DVD, CD player, fax (on request), fridge (on request), hair dryer, MP3 docking station, Wi-Fi (free).

MODERATE

Antica Dimora Johlea ★★ 🎁 A *dimora* is a refined residence, and that's exactly what this boho B&B feels like—a regal, but still homey and comfortable Florentine home. Rooms are midsize with parquet floors and four-poster beds, and come embellished with rich fabrics; the interior decor draws inspiration from East and West. Space throughout is at a premium, but that just makes it all the cozier. We're docking one star for a rather bland location 15 minutes' walk north of Piazza della Signoria, but adding it right back on again for Florence's best roof terrace in this price category—a little aerie that looks right at Brunelleschi's dome.

Antica Dimora Johlea is part of a mini *residenza* empire that's grown up in the surrounding streets. All offer a similar take on a Florence city break—see the website for details of four more comfortable, character-filled *dimore* if this place is full.

Via San Gallo 80, 50129 Firenze. www.johanna.it. ✆ **055-463-3292.** Fax 055-463-4552. 6 units. 100€–170€ double. Rates include buffet breakfast. No credit cards. Bus: C1, 1, 7, 20, or 25. **Amenities:** Honesty bar. *In room:* A/C, TV/DVD, DVD library, hair dryer, Wi-Fi (free).

Loggiato dei Serviti ★ There's no mistaking the Renaissance aura: The Loggiato is installed in the building designed by Antonio da Sangallo the Elder in 1527 to mirror the Ospedale degli Innocenti across the piazza, forming part of one of Italy's most beautiful squares. High vaulted ceilings in soft creams abound throughout and are supported by the gray columns of the bar/lounge. The wood or brick-tiled floors in the rooms are covered with rugs, and most of the beds have wood frames and fabric canopies for an antique feel. The rooms along the front can be a bit noisy in the evenings because traffic is routed through the edges of the piazza, but we usually reserve one anyway, just for the magical view.

Piazza Santissima Annunziata 3, 50122 Firenze. www.loggiatodeiservitihotel.it. ✆ **055-289-592.** Fax 055-289-595. 38 units. 120€–205€ double. Rates include breakfast. AE, DC, MC, V. Valet garage parking 20€. Bus: C1, 6, 14, 23, 31, 32, or 71. **Amenities:** Babysitting; concierge; Wi-Fi (free). *In room:* A/C, TV, hair dryer, minibar.

Morandi alla Crocetta ★ This subtly elegant hotel belongs to a different era, when travelers stayed in private homes filled with family heirlooms and well-kept antiques. Although the setting is indeed historic (it was a 1511 Dominican nuns' convent), many of the old-fashioned effects, such as the wood-beam ceilings, 1500s artwork, and antique furnishings, are the result of a redecoration. It has all been done in good taste, however, and there are still plenty of echoes of the original structure, from exposed brick arches to one room's 16th-century fresco fragments.

Via Laura 50 (a block east of Piazza Santissima Annunziata), 50121 Firenze. www.hotelmorandi.it. ✆ **055-234-4747.** Fax 055-248-0954. 10 units. 100€–150€ double; 150€–180€ triple. Rates include breakfast. AE, DC, MC, V. Garage parking 20€. Bus: 6, 14, 23, 31, 32, or 71. **Amenities:** Bar, babysitting; concierge. *In room:* A/C, TV, hair dryer, minibar, Wi-Fi (8€ per day; free in low season).

Near Santa Croce

EXPENSIVE

Hotel Home Florence ★★ Minimalist chic meets dazzling bright-white (like an ultrafashionable ski resort) at this 2009 addition to Florence's crop of design hotels. A harmonious colonial villa on the eastern fringe of the *centro storico* was transformed in 2009 into the ultimate city bolt-hole for anyone seeking sleek design at a reasonably sensible price. Rooms are kitted out to a top contemporary spec: All-white home wares and furnishings are by the Cyrus Company (which owns the hotel); there are Nespresso machines and iPods in all the rooms and a free bar (alcoholic drinks extra) throughout. If money is no object, the suite has a terrace that surveys the city skyline, and there's an unforgettable rooftop Jacuzzi rentable by the night (250€) with a 360-degree panorama of Florence.

Piazza Piave 3, 50122 Firenze. www.hhflorence.it. ✆ **055-243-668.** Fax 055-200-9852. 38 units. 150€–300€ double; 300€–450€ suite. Rates include breakfast. AE, DC, MC, V. Garage parking 30€. Bus: 8, 12, 13, 14, 23, 31, 32, 33, 70, or 71. **Amenities:** Bar; airport transfer (free); babysitting; bikes; concierge; gym; Jacuzzi; room service. *In room:* A/C, TV, hair dryer, minibar (free), Wi-Fi (free).

Monna Lisa ★★ There's a certain old-world elegance, reminiscent of an English country manor, to the richly decorated common rooms and the gravel-strewn garden of this 14th-century *palazzo.* Among the potted plants and framed oils, the hotel has Giambologna's original rough competition piece for the *Rape of the Sabines,* along with many pieces by neoclassical sculptor Giovanni Duprè, whose family's descendants own the hotel. They try their best to keep the entire place looking like a private home, and many rooms have the original painted wood ceilings, as well as antique furniture and richly textured wallpaper and fabrics, although the Jacuzzi tubs in superior units are very much 21st-century additions. Outbuildings known as La Scudera and La Limonaia overlook a peaceful garden.

Borgo Pinti 27, 50121 Firenze. www.monnalisa.it. ✆ **055-247-9751.** Fax 055-247-9755. 45 units. 139€–289€ double. Rates include buffet breakfast. AE, DC, MC, V. Garage parking 20€. Bus: C1, C2, 14, 23, or 71. **Amenities:** Bar; babysitting; concierge; small gym. *In room:* A/C, TV, hair dryer, minibar, Wi-Fi (5€ per 30 min.).

MODERATE

Palazzo Galletti ★★ Palazzo living doesn't come much more refined than in the restored 18th-century surrounds of this *residenza d'epoca* B&B. Elegant rooms are arranged around a tranquil atrium, and named after the planets (which themselves are named after Roman gods). Doubles are on the big side for Florence, with tall ceilings, but if you can stretch to a suite such as Giove or Cerere, you'll have a memorable stay surrounded by original 18th-century frescoes restored by the owners. Breakfast is served in a vaulted former kitchen that predates the *palazzo*—it originally belonged to a building that stood here in the 1500s.

Via Sant'Egidio 12, 50122 Firenze. www.palazzogalletti.it. ✆ **055-390-5750.** Fax 055-390-5752. 11 units. 100€–160€ double; 170€–240€ suite. Rates include breakfast. MC, V. Bus: C1, C2, 14, 23, or 71. **Amenities:** Concierge. *In room:* A/C, TV, hair dryer, Internet (free).

INEXPENSIVE

Locanda Orchidea ★ ☺ If you need to flop on a tight budget, but don't want to compromise on location, there's nowhere cleaner or friendlier at the price. Units are compact, but plenty big enough if you're here to see the city, not your bedroom, and arranged around a communal sitting area with free tea and coffee. Rooms at the back are the most desirable, as they overlook a peaceful courtyard. Bathrooms are shared, but each room has a sink. The large family room with its own shower is a great deal.

Borgo degli Albizi 11 (close to Piazza San Pier Maggiore), 50122 Firenze. www.hotelorchidea florence.it. ✆/fax **055-248-0346.** 7 units. 50€–80€ double; 65€–100€ triple; 75€–120€ quad. No credit cards. Bus: C1, C2, 14, 23, or 71. **Amenities:** Wi-Fi (free).

A Soothing Central Spa

If you can't stretch to one of Florence's upscale spa hotels, book a session at **Soulspace,** Via Sant'Egidio 12 (www.soulspace.it; ✆ **055-200-1794**). This calm, contemporary spot has a heated pool and hammam (Turkish bath), and a range of modern spa treatments for women and men, including aromatherapy massages. Day spa packages cost from 50€ upward.

In the Oltrarno & San Frediano

EXPENSIVE

Palazzo Magnani Feroni ★★ A luxurious Renaissance palace from the 16th century, and a 5-minute walk from the Ponte Vecchio, this place has been converted from a nobleman's residence to boutique accommodations with a dozen suites in six grades. Painstaking attention has been paid to the restoration and conversion of each one, and the palace houses extensive period furnishings and packs bags of character. The suites themselves combine luxury and charm with modern conveniences. At dusk each evening you can enjoy a drink on a panoramic terrace watching the sun set over Florence's rooftops.

Borgo San Frediano 5, 50124 Firenze. www.palazzomagnaniferoni.com. ✆ **055-239-9544.** Fax 055-260-8908. 12 units. 180€–490€ suite. Rates include breakfast. Parking 12€. Bus: C3, D, 6, 11, 36, 37, or 68. **Amenities:** Bar; concierge; gym; room service. *In room:* A/C, TV/DVD, CD player, minibar, Wi-Fi (free).

MODERATE

Floroom ★ This hybrid between boutique hotel and contemporary premium B&B, overlooking a tiny Oltrarno piazza, is aimed squarely at a new, younger generation of visitor to the city. Rooms are small and monochrome, with privacy screens separating the sleeping and bathroom areas, and hung with striking black-and-white photography. Clever use of reclaimed materials, occasional exposed wood beams, and furniture in a 1950s style custom built for the space, ensure the design never veers to the cold. There's a small communal mezzanine where you can help yourself to drinks and snacks. Travel light, bring an iPad, and settle in.

Opened in 2010 by the same owners, four-room **Floroom 2 ★**, Via del Sole 2 (www.floroom.com; ✆ **055-216-674**), provides equally chic, stripped-down neoclassical style in the *centro storico*, just off Via de' Tornabuoni.

Via del Pavone 7 (behind Piazza della Passera), 50125 Firenze. www.floroom.com. ✆/fax **055-230-2462.** 4 units. 120€–160€ double. Rates include Italian breakfast. MC, V. Minimum stay 2 nights. Bus: C3, D, 11, 36, 37, or 68. No children 14 and under. **Amenities:** Honesty bar. *In room:* A/C, TV, Wi-Fi (free).

La Scaletta Three partners, Andrea, Paolo, and Fabrizi, took over this well-worn old shoe of a place in 2005, one of the only remaining *palazzo* on this block between the Pitti Palace and Ponte Vecchio. The inn's star is the flower-bedecked, sun-kissed terrace offering a 360-degree vista over the Boboli Garden, the Oltrarno rooftops, and (beyond a sea of antennas) the monumental heart of Florence. Return visitors book months in advance for the homey rooms that have tiny bathrooms and old tiled floors. Street-side accommodations have double-paned windows that really do block the noise, and the worn, dark wood lacquer furniture is pleasantly unassuming.

Via Guicciardini 13 (2nd floor; near Piazza de' Pitti), 50125 Firenze. www.hotellascaletta.it. ✆ **055-283-028.** Fax 055-283-013. 13 units. 75€–140€ double; 90€–165€ triple. AE, MC, V. Bus: C3 or D. **Amenities:** Restaurant (May–Oct); bar (May–Oct); concierge. *In room:* A/C, TV, hair dryer, minibar, Wi-Fi (free).

UNA Vittoria ★★ Is this a boutique hotel or a disco? Either way, this outpost of the small Italian chain UNA is in a class of its own when it comes to contemporary styling at an affordable price. The second you step into the floor-to-ceiling mosaic in the reception area, you realize this is no ordinary Florentine inn. Midsize rooms are bold and contemporary (quite unchainlike), and all come equipped with modern amenities like 32-inch plasma TVs. A rolling program of renovations ensures interiors never grow tired. Executive rooms come with supersexy all-in-one rainfall shower/tub combos.

Via Pisana 59 (at Piazza Pier Vettori), 50143 Firenze. www.unahotels.it. ✆ **055-22-771.** Fax 055-22-772. 84 units. 109€–306€ double. Rates include breakfast. MC, V. Garage parking 20€. Bus: 6. **Amenities:** Restaurant; bar; bikes; concierge. *In room:* TV, hair dryer, Wi-Fi (free).

In the Hills

EXPENSIVE

Torre di Bellosguardo ★★★ This castle was built around a 13th-century tower sprouting from a hillside on the southern edge of Florence. Spend a few days here above the city heat and noise, lounging by the pool, hiking the olive groves, or sitting on a garden bench to enjoy the intimate close-range vista of the city. Don't come expecting a climate-controlled and carpeted bastion of luxury, however. With its echoey halls, airy loggias, and imposing stone staircases, the Bellosguardo feels just a few flickering torches shy of the Middle Ages—exactly its attraction. It's packed with antiques, and the beds from various eras are particularly gorgeous. Some rooms have intricately carved wood ceilings, others sport fading frescoes, and many have views, including a 360-degree panorama in the romantic tower suite.

Via Roti Michelozzi 2, 50124 Firenze. www.torrebellosguardo.com. ✆ **055-229-8145.** Fax 055-229-008. 16 units. 250€–290€ double; 290€–340€ suite. AE, MC, V. Free parking. Bus: D, 12, or 13 to Piazza Tasso (then taxi up hill). **Amenities:** Bar; airport transfer (free); babysitting; concierge; exercise room; Jacuzzi; outdoor pool (June–Sept) and small indoor pool; room service; sauna; Wi-Fi (free). *In room:* A/C (in some), TV, hair dryer, minibar.

MODERATE

Pensione Bencistà ★ ☺ This comfortable and quiet family-run *pensione* in a rambling 14th-century villa gets you the same drop-dead view and escape from the city as the local celeb hangout, Villa San Michele, at one-fifth the price—plus owners who are friendly and truly consider you a guest in their home. Antiques abound in aging, elegantly cluttered salons that are straight out of an E. M. Forster novel. Many accommodations have big old chests of drawers, and some open onto the pretty little garden. If the budget will stretch, go for a superior with a balcony and much more space. Some rooms, bathrooms especially, are getting a little tired for this price category, but that million-dollar view is irreplaceable.

Via Benedetto da Maiano 4 (just below Fiesole off the main rd.), 50014 Fiesole (FI). www.bencista.com. ✆/fax **055-59-163.** 40 units. 143€–158€ double; 160€–178€ double with view; 180€–192€ triple. Half board 13€ per person. MC, V. Free parking. Bus: 7. **Amenities:** Restaurant; bar; airport transfer (free); babysitting; concierge; Internet (free). *In room:* Hair dryer.

Apartments

Many of the agencies listed under "Tips on Accommodations," in chapter 17, also handle villas in Florence's hills and apartments in town. One of the most reputable city specialists is **Florence and Abroad,** Via San Zanobi 58 (www.florenceandabroad.com; ✆ **055-487-004**), which matches different tastes and budgets to a wide range of apartments. Another reputable agency for short-term apartment and house rentals (weekly and monthly) is **Windows on Tuscany,** Via de' Serragli 6r (www.windowsontuscany.com; ✆ **055-268-510**). Online agencies **Cross Pollinate** (www.cross-pollinate.com) and **RentXpress** (www.rentxpress.com; ✆ **02-8734-4500** in Italy) also have good apartment portfolios covering Florence.

For basic grocery shopping, try **Conad City,** Via dei Servi 56r (✆ **055-280-110**), or any central branch of **Supermercato il Centro:** There's a map at **www.ilcentro.biz**.

Palazzo Antellesi ★ Many people passing through Piazza Santa Croce notice Giovanni di Ser Giovanni's 1620 graffiti frescoes on the overhanging facade of no. 21, but few realize they can actually stay there (week-long bookings only). The 16th-century *palazzo* is owned by Signora Piccolomini, who rents them out to anyone who has dreamed of lying in bed next to a roaring fire under a 17th-century frescoed ceiling, or sipping tea in a living room surrounded by *trompe l'oeil* Roman ruins with a 16th-century wood ceiling above (the Donatello, which sleeps six to seven). Even in the more standard units the furnishings are tasteful, with wicker, wood, or wrought-iron bed frames; potted plants; and the occasional 18th-century inlaid wood dresser to go with the plush couches. Author R. W. B. Lewis wrote about the Antellesi in the final chapter of *City of Florence*.

Piazza Santa Croce 21, 50122 Firenze. www.palazzoantellesi.com. ✆ **845/704-2426** in the U.S., or 055-244-456. Fax 055-234-5552. 13 units, sleeping 2–7. $2,100–$5,500 per week (all priced in U.S. dollars). Final cleaning and utilities extra. No credit cards. Garage parking 16€. Bus: C1, 3, or 23. **Amenities:** Babysitting; exercise room. *In room:* A/C, TV/DVD, CD player, hair dryer, kitchen, Wi-Fi (free).

Residence Hilda ★★★ ☺ This is the best place in the city to combine apartment convenience with hotel services. What these elegant apartments lack in period charm they comfortably make up for with space, crisp, contemporary design, and modern facilities—and the fact that they are available from a single night upward. All units have large living areas, with a double or twin sofa-bed, big bathrooms, well-equipped kitchens, and a double bedroom; family suites are big enough to set up home in. The airy, cool design includes stripped and polished floors, cream walls, and sliding divider doors. The location, between the Duomo and Santissima Annunziata, is ideal. Child equipment like highchairs and cots are included in the price.

Via dei Servi 40 (2 blocks north of the Duomo), 50122 Firenze. www.residencehilda.it. ✆ **055-288-021.** Fax 055-287-664. 12 units. 150€–450€ per night for apt sleeping 2–5. Breakfast 7.50€ (served next door). AE, MC, V. Valet garage parking 30€. Bus: C1, 6, 14, 23, 31, 32, or 71. **Amenities:** Airport transfer (free); babysitting; concierge; room service. *In room:* A/C, TV, DVD player (on request), CD player (on request), hair dryer, kitchen, Wi-Fi (free).

Hostels, Camping & Convents

Florence's central hostels are immensely popular, especially in summer. If you aren't able to e-mail or call to reserve a space—months ahead, if possible—show up when they open with your fingers crossed.

An alternative budget option is to stay in a religious house. A few monasteries and convents in the Florence area are happy to receive guests for a modest fee. The **Suore di Santa Elisabetta,** Viale Michelangiolo 46, 50125 Firenze (close to Piazza Ferrucci; www.csse-roma.eu; ✆/fax **055-681-1884**), occupies a colonial villa a short walk south of Ponte San Niccolò. Simple en suite singles (for either sex), doubles, and family rooms are on offer; there's no need for you to be religious, merely respectful. Bus nos. 12, 13, and 39 drop you almost at the door, and the sisters also have a small, free, locked car park. The easiest way to build a monastery and convent itinerary in the city and beyond is via agent **MonasteryStays.com**. Note that most religious houses have a curfew, generally 11pm or midnight.

Campeggio Michelangelo ☺ Here you can sleep with a select 1,000 of your fellow campers and have almost the same vista that the tour buses get up above on Piazzale Michelangiolo. (Sadly, a stand of trees blocks the Duomo.) Of course, you're packed in like sardines on this small plateau with very little shade (in Aug, arrive early to fight for a spot along the tree-lined fringe), but you get a bar, a minimart, a laundromat, cheap prices, and that killer view.

Viale Michelangelo 80 (just east of Piazzale Michelangiolo), 50125 Firenze. www.ecvacanze.it/en/campingmichelangelo. ✆ **055-681-1977.** Fax 055-689-348. Open camping (sleeps 1,000). 9.50€–12€ per adult, plus 12€–14€ per pitch. Campers 13€–15€. Rented tents (sleep 2) 36€. MC, V. Free parking. Bus: 12 or 13. **Amenities:** Restaurant; bar.

Plus Florence ☺ It's an ugly, functional building, and a 10-minute walk in the wrong direction from San Lorenzo, but the services and facilities at Florence's newest "flashpacking" hostel put hotels that cost five times the price to shame. Rooms are ample in size and clean, and come with hotel-style accoutrements (towels, linen, small private shower room). Triples have a three-berth bunk (double down, single up) if you're traveling as a small family; there are also female-only accommodations. If you're a light sleeper, avoid rooms that face the busy street out front. The phenomenal services beat those at most hotels in town: There's an indoor pool, a Turkish bath, a minispa and salon, and free Wi-Fi throughout. There's no curfew.

Via Santa Caterina d'Alessandria 15, Firenze. www.plusflorence.com. ✆ **055-462-8934.** 110 units. Dorm room from 19€ per person; 55€–65€ double; 75€–85€ triple. Breakfast 6€. MC, V. Bus: 8, 20, or 70. **Amenities:** Restaurant; bar; concierge; gym; indoor pool; sauna; small spa. *In room:* A/C (in some), TV, no phone, Wi-Fi (free).

A SIDE TRIP TO FIESOLE

Although it's only a city bus ride away from Florence, Fiesole is very proud of its status as an independent municipality. In fact, this hilltop village high in the wash of green above Florence predates that city in the valley by centuries.

An Etruscan colony from Arezzo probably founded a town here in the 6th century B.C. on the site of a Bronze Age settlement. By the time Caesar set up a Roman retirement colony on the banks of the Arno below, Faesulae was the most important Etruscan center in the region. It butted heads with the upstart Fiorenza in the valley almost right from the start. Although it eventually became a Roman town, building a theater and adopting Roman customs, it always retained a bit of the Etruscan otherness that has kept it different from Florence throughout the ages. Following the barbarian invasions, it became part of Florence's administrative district in the 9th century, yet continued to struggle for self-government. Medieval Florence put an end to it all in 1125 when it attacked and razed the entire city, save the cathedral and bishop's palace.

Becoming an irrelevant footnote to Florentine history has actually aided Fiesole in the end. Modern upper middle-class Florentines have decided it's posh to buy an old villa on the hillside leading up to the town and maintain the villa's extensive gardens. This means that the oasis of cultivated greenery separating Florence from Fiesole has remained. Even with Florence so close by, Fiesole endures as a Tuscan small town to this day, entirely removed from the city at its feet and hence the perfect escape from summertime crowds. It stays relatively cool all summer long, and while you sit at a cafe on Piazza Mino, sipping an iced cappuccino, it might seem as though the lines at the Uffizi and pedestrian traffic around the Duomo are very distant indeed.

Essentials

GETTING THERE Take bus no. 7 from Florence, from the station or down the right flank of San Marco, on Via La Pira. A scenic 25-minute ride through the greenery above Florence, takes you to Fiesole's main square, Piazza Mino.

VISITOR INFORMATION The **tourist office** is at Via Portigiani 3, 50014 Fiesole (www.comune.fiesole.fi.it; ✆ **055-596-1323;** daily 10:30am–1pm and 1:30–5pm).

Exploring Fiesole

Fiesole's two museums and its Teatro Romano archaeological site keep the same hours and use a single admission ticket, costing 10€ adults, 6€ students age 7 to 25 and seniors 65 and over, and free for children 6 and under. A family ticket costs 20€. They are all open April through September daily from 10am to 7pm, March and October daily from 10am to 6pm, and in winter Wednesday through Monday from 10am to 2pm. For more information, visit www.museidifiesole.it or call ✆ **055-596-1293.**

Cattedrale di San Romolo CATHEDRAL The cathedral's 13th century **bell tower,** with its comically oversize crenellations added in the 18th century, can be spotted for miles around. The cathedral is a pleasingly bare-walled medieval

The Cattedrale di San Romolo (Duomo) in Fiesole.

church, built in 1028 using columns from nearby Roman buildings. The **crypt** is supported by slender columns with primitive carvings on the capitals. The remains of St. Romolo, Fiesole's patron, reside under the altar, and 15th-century lunette frescoes tell his story.

Piazzetta della Cattedrale. ✆ **055-599-566.** Free admission. Daily 8am–noon and 3–6pm (2–5pm in autumn and winter). Bus: 7.

Museo Bandini ART MUSEUM Newly restructured, this modest museum to the left of the Roman Theater entrance has a small collection of 13th- to 15th-century Florentine paintings by the likes of Bernardo Daddi, Taddeo and Agnolo Gaddi, Nardo di Cione, Bicci di Lorenzo, Sandro Botticelli, and Neri di Bicci, plus a couple of ringers by the likes of Umbrian Luca Signorelli.

Via Duprè 1. ✆ **055-59-118.** For admission and hours, see the section intro above.

San Francesco CHURCH Up a sharp hill with sublime city views, the ancient focal point of the Etruscan and Roman town are this church and convent. The 14th-century church has been largely overhauled, but at the end of a small nave hung with devotional works—Piero di Cosimo and Cenni di Francesco are both represented—is a fine *Crucifixion and Saints* altarpiece by Neri di Bicci. Off the cloisters is a quirky but interesting little ethnographic museum.

Via San Francesco (off Piazza Mino). ✆ **055-59-175.** Free admission. Daily 9am–noon and 3–5pm (7pm in summer). Bus: 7.

Teatro Romano (Roman Theater & Archaeological Museum) ★ MUSEUM Fiesole's archaeological area is romantically overgrown with grasses, amid which sit sections of column, broken friezes, and other remnants of architectural elements. Beyond the **Roman Theater** to the right, recognizable by its three rebuilt arches, are the remains of the 1st-century-A.D. **baths.** Near the arches is a little cement balcony over the far edge of the archaeological park. From it, you get a good look at the best stretch that remains of the 4th-century-B.C. **Etruscan city walls.** At the other end of the park from the baths are the floor and steps of a 1st-century-B.C. **Roman Temple** built on top of a 4th-century-B.C. Etruscan one. To the left are some oblong **Lombard tombs** from the 7th century A.D., when this was a necropolis.

Among the collections in the modest **Museum** are the bronze "she-wolf," a fragment of the back of what was probably a statue of a lion, lots of Etruscan urns and Roman architectural fragments, and Bronze Age remains found atop the hill now occupied by San Francesco.

Via Portigiani 1. ✆ **055-59-118.** For admission and hours, see the section intro above.

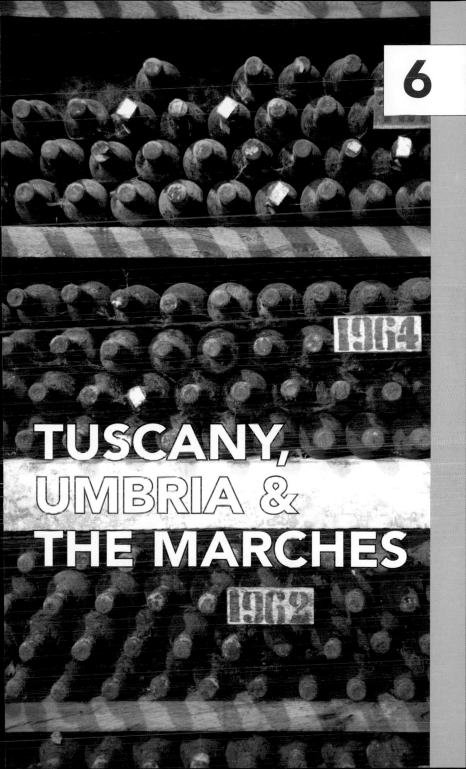

6

TUSCANY, UMBRIA & THE MARCHES

As the cradle of the Renaissance, Tuscany, Umbria, and the Marches boast some of the world's most mesmerizing art and architecture, from the sublime work of Piero della Francesca in Arezzo, to preserved Renaissance towns like Urbino, to the Gothic *palazzi* of Siena. Yet the region isn't all churches and museums: This is a land of lush, fertile landscapes, snowcapped Apennine mountains, and olive groves and vineyards that produce rich oils and world-famous wines.

SIGHTSEEING The narrow, stone streets of **Siena** and **San Gimignano** drip with medieval atmosphere, while **Pisa's Leaning Tower** is a mind-blowing sight. Don't overlook Umbria, with the **Basilica di San Francesco** in Assisi and **Galleria Nazionale** in cosmopolitan Perugia. Farther south, soak up the exuberant facade of **Orvieto's cathedral.**

EATING & DRINKING Eating here is a real joy, whether you dine in a fine Tuscan ***osteria,*** grab a crisp, fatty ***porchetta*** **sandwich** at an Umbrian market, or just snack on Ascoli Piceno's stuffed olives. Sample the rich **gelato** of Siena, **Baci chocolates** in Perugia, and Lucca's **olive oil**—it's like sipping liquidized olives straight off the tree. Then there's the wine: not just the **chianti,** but the delicate **Vino Nobile** of Montepulciano and the subtle whites of **Orvieto.**

HISTORY Central Italy's complex recorded history begins with the Etruscans, a heritage best explored today at exceptional museums in **Volterra** and **Orvieto.** The Romans have left a less visible legacy, so it's in towns that thrived during the **Renaissance** that you really feel like you've stepped back in time. **Urbino** and **Gubbio** have museums stuffed with important artifacts from the region's turbulent past.

ARTS & CULTURE While the art of Florence often dominates Tuscan itineraries, make time for the preserved medieval center of Siena, especially its Gothic **Palazzo Pubblico** and artisans that work along **Via Stalloreggi.** The genius of Giotto is on full display in the basilica at **Assisi,** while the legacy of Piero della Francesca is preserved in **Arezzo's San Francesco.** Music festivals in Spoleto, Lucca, and Perugia are giant outdoor parties.

THE BEST TRAVEL EXPERIENCES IN TUSCANY, UMBRIA & THE MARCHES

- **Wandering San Gimignano's center at dusk:** The popular town's skyline pierced by 14 towers (sometimes nicknamed "skyscrapers") secures it the number-one spot on the hill-town trail. However, when the tour buses have left, the quiet streets exude a haunted, medieval air unlike anywhere else in Italy. See p. 295.

PREVIOUS PAGE: **Wine bottles in Chianti, Tuscany.**

Poppy fields outside San Gimignano.

- **Tasting the wine in chianti country:** The vine-studded hills between Florence and Siena nurture one of Italy's most famous exports. Against a backdrop of ancient villages and crenellated castles, you can sample *vino* direct from the cantinas around Castellina, Greve, and Radda. See p. 272.
- **Biking the walls of Lucca:** Kids and octogenarians alike peddle Tuscany's greatest cycle track, 5km (2¾ miles) in length. Lucca's 16th-century ramparts are so thick they now serve as a promenade and public park lined with chestnut and ilex trees planted by Marie-Louise of Bourbon. See p. 306.
- **Rising early to gaze in wonder at Assisi's Basilica:** Great artists Simone Martini, Pietro Lorenzetti, and Giotto told their stories in paint on the walls of this great church dedicated to Italy's patron, St. Francis. Assisi's holiest site is at its most serene early in the morning. See p. 338.
- **Following in the footsteps of Raphael:** Raphael was born in the ravishing Renaissance city of Urbino, high in the hills of Le Marche. Visit his birthplace before soaking up some of the art he and his contemporaries created in the Palazzo Ducale. See p. 363.

THE CHIANTI ★★

You can find many people's idea of earthly paradise in the 167 sq. km (64 sq. miles) of land between Florence and Siena, known as the Chianti. This is the world's definitive wine region, in both history and spirit; these hills have been an oenological center for several thousand years. Indeed, one local grape, the canaiolo nero—one of the varietals that traditionally goes into Chianti Classico—was known to the ancients as the "Etruscan grape." The name Chianti, probably derived from that of the local noble Etruscan family Clantes, has been used to describe the hills between Florence and Siena for centuries, but it wasn't until the mid–13th century that Florence created the **Lega del Chianti** to unite the region's three most important centers—Castellina, Radda, and Gaiole—and chose the black rooster as their symbol. By 1404, the red wine long produced here was being called chianti as well, and in 1716 a grand ducal decree defined

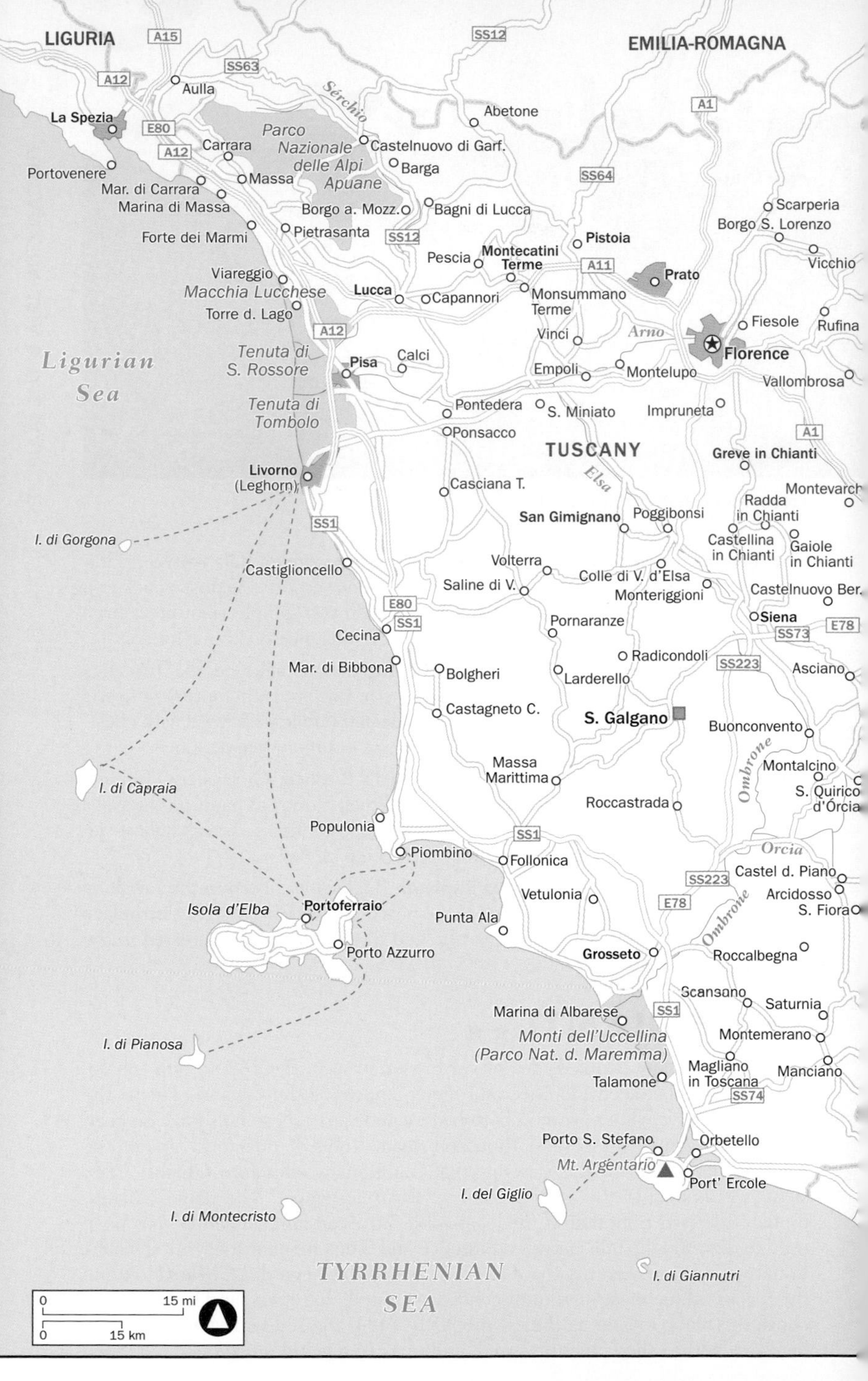

LIGURIA
EMILIA-ROMAGNA
TUSCANY
Ligurian Sea
TYRRHENIAN SEA
La Spezia
Portovenere
Aulla
Carrara
Massa
Mar. di Carrara
Marina di Massa
Forte dei Marmi
Pietrasanta
Viareggio
Macchia Lucchese
Torre d. Lago
Parco Nazionale delle Alpi Apuane
Abetone
Castelnuovo di Garf.
Barga
Borgo a. Mozz.
Bagni di Lucca
Pistoia
Scarperia
Borgo S. Lorenzo
Vicchio
Pescia
Montecatini Terme
Prato
Lucca
Capannori
Monsummano Terme
Fiesole
Rufina
Vinci
Arno
Florence
Tenuta di S. Rossore
Pisa
Calci
Empoli
Montelupo
Vallombrosa
Tenuta di Tombolo
Pontedera
S. Miniato
Impruneta
Ponsacco
Livorno (Leghorn)
Greve in Chianti
Casciana T.
Elsa
Montevarchi
San Gimignano
Poggibonsi
Radda in Chianti
Castellina in Chianti
Gaiole in Chianti
I. di Gorgona
Castiglioncello
Volterra
Saline di V.
Colle di V. d'Elsa
Monteriggioni
Castelnuovo Ber.
Siena
Pornaranze
Cecina
Radicondoli
Mar. di Bibbona
Bolgheri
Larderello
Asciano
Castagneto C.
S. Galgano
Buonconvento
Ombrone
Montalcino
S. Quirico d'Orcia
Massa Marittima
I. di Capraia
Roccastrada
Populonia
Orcia
Piombino
Follonica
Castel d. Piano
Arcidosso
S. Fiora
Vetulonia
Isola d'Elba
Portoferraio
Punta Ala
Porto Azzurro
Grosseto
Roccalbegna
Scansano
Saturnia
Marina di Albarese
Monti dell'Uccellina (Parco Nat. d. Maremma)
Montemerano
I. di Pianosa
Magliano in Toscana
Manciano
Talamone
Porto S. Stefano
Orbetello
Mt. Argentario
Port' Ercole
I. del Giglio
I. di Montecristo
I. di Giannutri
A15
A12
SS63
SS12
E80
A1
SS64
A11
SS1
E78
SS73
SS223
SS74
0
15 mi
15 km

Tuscany & Umbria
ADRIATIC SEA
Venice
Tuscany
Umbria
Rome
Forli
Rimini
Riccione
SAN MARINO
San Marino
Pesaro
Fano
Urbino
Ancona
LE MARCHE
Monte Falterona, Campigna, e Foreste Casentinesi
Camaldoli
Stia
Poppi
Bibbiena
La Verna
Caprese Mich.
Sansepolcro
Arno
Arezzo
Monterchi
Cittá di Castello
Mt. Cucco
Gubbio
Macerata
Tolentino
Mte. S. Savino
Castiglion Fio.
Lucignano
Cortona
Umbertide
Tevere
Gualdo-Tadino
Sinalunga
Castiglione del Lago
Lago Trasimeno
Perugia
Camerino
Nocera Umbra
Assisi
Mt. Subasio
Montepulciano
Pienza
Chianciano Terme
UMBRIA
Torgiano
Spello
Chiusi
Sarteano
Cetona
Cittá d. Pieve
Deruta
Foligno
Radicofani
Marsciano
Montefalco
Trevi
Parco dei Monti Sibillini
Piano Grande
Abbadia S. Salvatore
Nera
Parco Naturale Regionale
Castell'Azzara
Paglia
Todi
Spoleto
Acquapendente
Orvieto
Cascia
Parco Nazionale del Gran Sasso
Sovana
Sorano
Bolsena
Pitigliano
Bagnoregio
Lago di Bolsena
Fiora
Amelia
Lugnano
Terni
Piediluco
Montefiascone
Narni
Parco Nazional del Gran Sasso e Monti della Laga
Orte
Rieti
Vulci
Viterbo
LAZIO
L'Aquila
Tarquinia
ABRUZZI
To Rome
SS16
A14
SS9
SS67
E45
E78
SS71
A1
SS76
SS326
SS77
SS78
SS75
SS3
SS2
SS448
SS4
SS74
SS1
SS1B

the boundaries of the Chianti and laid down rules for its wine production, making it the world's first officially designated wine-producing area.

By the 19th century, the title "chianti" was being used by hundreds of poor-quality, *vino*-producing hacks, both within the region and from far-flung areas, diminishing the reputation of the wine. To fight against this, Greve and Castelnuovo Berardenga joined the original Lega cities and formed the **Consorzio del Gallo Nero** in 1924, reviving the black rooster as their seal. The *consorzio* (still active—their members produce about 80% of the Chianti Classico that's bottled) pressed for laws regulating the quality of chianti wines and restricting the Chianti Classico name to their production zone. When Italy devised its DOC and DOCG laws in the 1960s, chianti was one of the first to be defined as DOCG, guaranteeing its quality as one of the top wines in Italy.

Essentials

GETTING AROUND The only way to explore the Chianti effectively is by **car.** But know that many of the roads off the major SS222 (known as the Chiantigiana) are unpaved and sometimes heavily potholed (so-called *strade bianche,* or "white roads"). More importantly, wine tasting presents its own obstacles to driving, and so oenophiles might consider joining a wine tour. Local tourist offices, especially in Siena, have a number of them from which to choose. One wine tour guide in particular is memorable: **Dario Castagno,** who wrote a well-received book called *Too Much Tuscan Sun,* in response to Frances Mayes's bestseller of a similar name. Track him down at **www.dariocastagno.com**.

On the other hand, **biking** through the Chianti can be one of Tuscany's most rewarding and scenic workouts. Rent a bike in central Greve at **Ramuzzi,** Via Italo Stecchi 23 (www.ramuzzi.com; ✆ **055-853-037**); the cost is 20€ per day for a road bike or mountain bike, and 55€ a day for a scooter. There are discounts for multiple days.

You can visit the major towns by **bus,** but be prepared to wait awhile until the next ride comes along. **SITA** (www.sitabus.it; ✆ **055-214-721**) from Florence services Strada (40 min. from Florence), Greve (1 hr.), Panzano (65–80 min.), Radda or Castellina (95 min.), and Gaiole (2 hr.); it leaves approximately hourly for stops up through Greve and Panzano and between one to three times a day all the way to Gaiole. Monday through Saturday, different lines of **TRA-IN** buses (www.trainspa.it; ✆ **0577-204-111**) from Siena hit Radda (55 min. from Siena), Gaiole (50 min.–1 hr.), and Castellina (35 min.).

VISITOR INFORMATION You can pick up information on the Chianti at a **Florence tourist office** (see "Essentials," in chapter 5, for details) or the **Siena tourist office** (see "Siena," later in this chapter). The unofficial capital is **Greve in Chianti,** and its tourist office (✆ **055-854-6299**) is on the main square, at Piazza Matteotti 11. From Easter to October, it's open daily from 10am to 1pm and 2 to 7pm, but out of season you may find it closed. In **Castellina,** the tourist office, at Via Ferruccio 40 (✆ **0577-741-392**), is usually open Monday through Saturday 9am to 1pm and each of those afternoons except Wednesday 2 to 6pm. **Radda**'s tourist office, Piazza del Castello (✆ **0577-738-494**), is open Monday to Saturday 10:30am to 12:30pm and 3:15 to 6pm between November and Easter; in high season, hours are

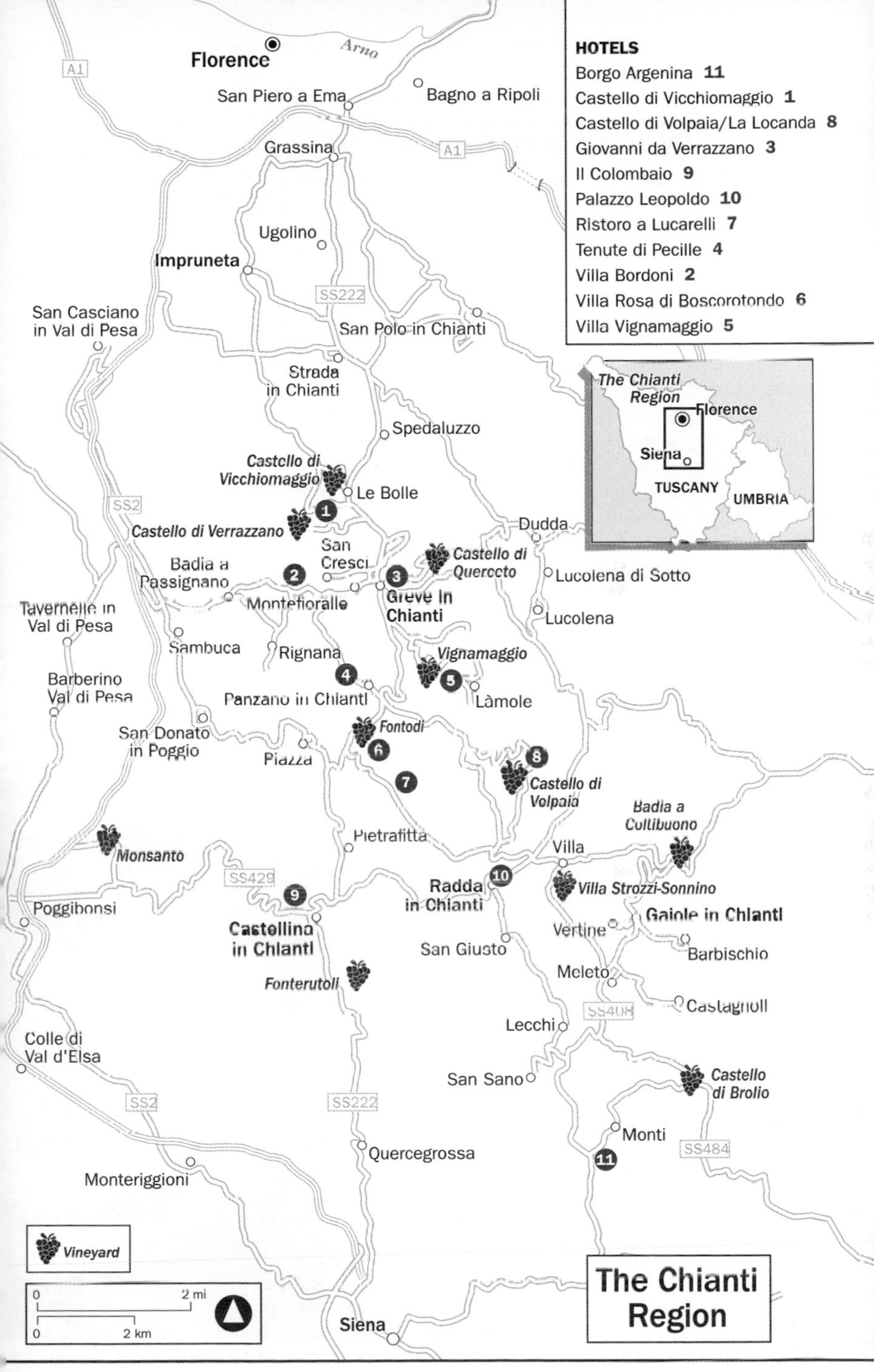

HOTELS
Borgo Argenina 11
Castello di Vicchiomaggio 1
Castello di Volpaia/La Locanda 8
Giovanni da Verrazzano 3
Il Colombaio 9
Palazzo Leopoldo 10
Ristoro a Lucarelli 7
Tenute di Pecille 4
Villa Bordoni 2
Villa Rosa di Boscorotondo 6
Villa Vignamaggio 5
The Chianti Region
Florence
Siena
TUSCANY
UMBRIA
Florence
Arno
A1
San Piero a Ema
Bagno a Ripoli
Grassina
Ugolino
Impruneta
SS222
San Casciano in Val di Pesa
San Polo in Chianti
Strada in Chianti
Spedaluzzo
Castello di Vicchiomaggio
Le Bolle
SS2
Castello di Verrazzano
Dudda
San Cresci
Castello di Querceto
Badia a Passignano
Lucolena di Sotto
Montefioralle
Greve in Chianti
Tavernelle in Val di Pesa
Lucolena
Sambuca
Rignana
Vignamaggio
Barberino Val di Pesa
Panzano in Chianti
Làmole
Fontodi
San Donato in Poggio
Piazza
Castello di Volpaia
Badia a Coltibuono
Monsanto
Pietrafitta
Villa
SS429
Radda in Chianti
Villa Strozzi-Sonnino
Poggibonsi
Gaiole in Chianti
Castellina in Chianti
Vertine
San Giusto
Barbischio
Fonterutoli
Meleto
SS408
Castagnoli
Lecchi
Colle di Val d'Elsa
San Sano
Castello di Brolio
SS2
SS222
Monti
Quercegrossa
SS484
Monteriggioni
Vineyard
0 2 mi
0 2 km
Siena
The Chianti Region

slightly longer and it's open Sunday morning. In **Gaiole,** the tourist office is beside the main road, at Via Galileo Galilei 1 (✆ **0577-749-411;** daily in season 10am–1pm and 3–6pm).

WINE FESTIVALS The second weekend in September, Greve in Chianti hosts the annual **Rassegna del Chianti Classico,** a bacchanalian festival of food and dancing that showcases wine from all the region's producers. **Radda** sponsors its own wine festival, **Radda nel Bicchiere,** in early June, where buying the commemorative glass lets you sample 50 to 60 wines for free.

Exploring the Chianti & Its Wineries

The main artery, leading south from Florence and linking many great wine towns and producers, is the SS222, the so-called Chiantigiana. At the bend in the road called Le Bolle beyond Strada is a right turnoff for the **Castello di Vicchiomaggio** ★ (www.vicchiomaggio.it; ✆ **055-854-079**). This A.D. 957 Lombard fortress was modified in the 15th century and is today one of the best preserved of the typical Chianti castles. Its estate produces well-regarded wines, including Ripa delle More, a sangiovese/cabernet sauvignon. You can taste for free at the roadside Cantinetta San Jacopo wine shop (on the SS222 right at the turnoff for the castle) daily from 10am to 6pm. One-hour tours of the cellars, parts of which date to the 10th century, depart at 11:30am and 4:30pm daily between March and October, costing 8€ per person. Booking is essential. They also offer cooking courses (anywhere from 1–2 hr. to several days) and rent rooms (see "Where to Stay in the Chianti," below).

A bit farther along on the right is the turnoff for the **Castello di Verrazzano** ★★ (www.verrazzano.com; ✆ **055-854-243** or 055-290-684), the 12th-century seat of the Verrazzano family. Young Giovanni Verrazzano, born here in 1485, sailed out of the Chianti to discover New York. The estate has been making wine at least since 1170, and you can sample it daily from 10am to 1pm and 2 to 7pm at the roadside shop; tasting is free. Their "jewel" is a 100% sangiovese called Sasello, while the Bottiglia Particolare (Particular [Special] Bottle) is in the Super Tuscan style, at 70% sangiovese and 30% cab. Four daily tours of the gardens and cellars run Monday through Friday starting at 10am (last one goes at 3pm); book ahead at least a day in advance, a week or more in advance in high season. Each is different, and prices range from 14€ for a tour and tasting of three wines to 48€ for a tour, wine tasting, and a four-course lunch (you'll get a few more wines, too) and 85€ to 110€ depending on group size to include transportation to and from Florence. Booking is essential for all tours.

The Castello di Verrazzano winery in Chiar

Throughout the Middle Ages, the Chianti princelings and their heavily fortified castles ruled the patchwork of fiefdoms that made up this area. As alliances sweetened castle-to-castle relations in the later Middle Ages, trade began flowing. Valley crossroads became market towns,

The gardens at Villa Vignamaggio.

and one such town began growing along the tiny river Greve in the 13th or 14th century. As trade became increasingly important, so did that market town. Today, as **Greve in Chianti ★**, the oversize village is the center of the wine trade and the unofficial capital of Chianti.

The central **Piazza Matteotti** is a rough triangle surrounded by a mismatched patchwork arcade—each merchant had to build the stretch in front of his own shop. The statue in the center is of the intrepid explorer **Giovanni Verrazzano** (for whom the bridge in New York is named), and the narrow end of the piazza spills into the tiny **Piazzetta Santa Croce,** whose pretty little church houses an *Annunciation* by Bicci di Lorenzo and a 13th-century triptych.

Greve is the host of Chianti's annual September wine fair, and there are, naturally, dozens of wine shops in town. The best is the **Enoteca del Chianti Classico,** Piazzetta Santa Croce 8 (✆ **055-853-297**). At Piazza Matteotti 69–71 is one of Italy's most famous butchers, **Macelleria Falorni** (www.falorni.it; ✆ **055-854-363**), established in 1700 and still containing a cornucopia of hanging *prosciutti* and dozens of other cured meats, along with a decent wine selection. It's open daily. For **visitor information,** see the beginning of this chapter.

South of Greve, the SS222 takes you past the left turn for Lamole. Along that road you'll find **Villa Vignamaggio ★★** (www.vignamaggio.com; ✆ **055-854-661**), a russet-orange villa surrounded by cypress and elegant gardens that might seem suspiciously similar to Signor Leonato's home in the 1993 movie *Much Ado About Nothing.* Kenneth Branagh's choice of movie sets wasn't the first time this 14th- or 15th-century villa garnered fame. Lisa Gherardini, who grew up to pose for Leonardo da Vinci's *Mona Lisa,* was born here in 1479. The estate's wine was famous in the past and in 1404 became the first red wine of these hills to be referred to as "chianti" in written record. Long derelict in reputation, Vignamaggio wines have been stunningly revived in recent years, and it has become one of the top local vineyards. Book ahead at least a week in advance and you can tour the cellar and ornate gardens and sample the wines; the tasting tour with simple snacks costs 25€, with lunch priced at 50€, and with dinner priced at 58€. They also rent rooms (see "Where to Stay in the Chianti," below).

The Chiantigiana next cuts through the town of **Panzano in Chianti ★**. The town is known for its embroidery and for another famed butcher, **Antica Macelleria Cecchini ★**, Via XX Luglio 11 (✆ **055-852-020**), where Dario Cecchini loves to entertain visitors with classical music and tastes of his products, while he recites the entirety of Dante's *Inferno* from memory. (A local character, Dario is fast becoming one of the most famous butchers in the world.) There's clearly something in Panzano's water supply, because the proprietor of the Old Town's exceptional enoteca (wine cellar), **Accademia del Buon Gusto ★**, Piazza Ricasoli 11 (www.accademiadelbuongusto.com; ✆ **055-856-0159**), is also something of a philosopher. An hour with Stefano Salvadori provides a unique wine education, and a particular insight into the smaller Chianti estates—which produce tiny quantities "for love, not money." Tasting is "without obligation," but we guarantee you'll end up buying something special.

The Chianti is known for its wine and its scenery.

Just south of town is the turnoff for the Romanesque **Pieve di San Leolino.** Beyond the 16th-century portico, this simple, atmospheric church conserves several 14th- and 15th-century Sienese altarpieces, plus on the left aisle a *Madonna with Sts. Peter and Paul* (1260–80), attributed to Meliore di Jacopo. The SS222 continues south toward Castellina.

An Etruscan center later fortified by the Florentines as an outpost against rival Siena, **Castellina in Chianti ★** is one of the more medieval-feeling hill towns of the region and a triumvirate member of the old Lega del Chianti. Castellina's medieval walls survive almost intact, and central Piazza del Comune is dominated by the imposing crenellated **Rocca** fortress, which now houses the **Museo Archeologico del Chianti Senese** (www.museoarcheologicochianti.it; ✆ **0577-742-090**). Inside is a modest collection of finds from nearby Etruscan tombs and displays on Etruscan wine culture, as well as access to the *torre* (tower) for views over the surrounding woods and vineyards. Admission costs 5€ adults, 3€ for children 7 to 14, students, and seniors 65 and over; it's open 11am to 7pm daily April through October and 11am to 5pm on weekends only November to March. The nearby **Via delle Volte** is an evocative tunnel street with open windows facing out to the valley—it's a soldiers' walk from the town's days as a Florentine bastion. You can taste a few drops of *vino* at **La Castellina**'s enoteca in the ground floor of the family *palazzo* at Via Ferruccio 26 (✆ **0577-740-454**). The **Bottega del Vino,** Via della Rocca 13 (www.enobottega.it; ✆ **0577-741-110**), is another good wine outlet. Castellina's gelateria, **L'Antica Delizia ★**, Via Fiorentina 4 (by the SS222; www.anticadelizia.it; ✆ **0577-741-337**), sells the best ice cream within a day's cycle in any direction. It's closed Tuesday.

Just outside town (follow signs marked TOMBE ETRUSCHE on the SS222 just north of the Castellina junction) is a 6th-century-B.C. Etruscan tomb, the

Ipogeo Etrusco di Montecalvario ★. It's a perfect example of its type, a little green beanie of a hill surrounded by pines, topped with a pair of cypress, and slashed with stone-walled tunnels leading to the burial chambers beneath. You're free to wander.

From Castellina, you can take a long but rewarding detour on the road toward Poggibonsi into the Val d'Elsa to visit the vineyards of **Monsanto ★★** (www.castellodimonsanto.it; ✆ **055-805-9000**), which produces one of our favorite chianti wines. (Their Classico Riserva 1995 is among the best we've ever tasted.) At this medieval estate, Dr. Laura Bianchi carries on her father Fabrizio's iconoclastic oenological traditions—after buying Monsanto in 1961, he was among the first to produce a 100% sangiovese chianti, and using only *sangiovese grosso* grapes at that. (Because this was illegal back in 1974, they still listed all the unused grapes on the labels.) Aside from an exquisite "chardonnay" (aged half in steel and half in wood, so that its fruitiness isn't overpowered with oak but still has its body and longevity), they use native grapes as much as possible. The result is a suite of remarkable and singular wines. They do tastings and direct sales Monday through Friday from 9am to 5pm (until 6pm in summer); or, reserve a 1-hour tasting tour of the cellars for 18€ per person a few days in advance, which you can extend with outstanding vintages and add a plate of local salami and cheese to accompany the wine for 35€ a head. Visits don't run in December or January.

If you're tired of these wine-sodden hills, you can shoot down the Chiantigiana from here to Siena, an 18km (11-mile) trip. It takes you past the medieval hamlet of **Fonterutoli ★** (www.fonterutoli.com; ✆ **0577-741-385**), a working *borgo* (village) that has been supporting the winemaking business of the Mazzei Marquis since 1435. Fonterutoli produces some of the most highly regarded wines in the region, including an excellent Chianti Classico and Chianti Classico Riserva, Supertuscans Siepi and Brancaia (the latter a sangiovese and merlot cru), and the superb fruity ICT Badiola, a sangiovese wine (with 3% each of merlot and cabernet) that's among Tuscany's best 10€ bottles. The roadside enoteca is open Monday to Saturday 10am to 7pm and Sunday 10am to 1pm and 3 to 7pm.

Radda in Chianti ★, one of the three players in the original Lega del Chianti and still an important wine center, retains its medieval street plan and a bit of its walls. The center of town is the 15th-century **Palazzo del Podestà,** studded with the mayoral coats of arms of past *podestà;* there's an information board explaining who's who outside **San Niccolò** opposite. The local butcher here is a true artisan; **Porciatti** will give you a taste of traditional salami and cheeses at their *alimentari* on Piazza IV Novembre 1 at the gate into town (www.casaporciatti.it; ✆ **0577-738-055**). They also sell local products, from wines to pasta.

Seven kilometers (4⅓ miles) north of Radda on a secondary road is the **Castello di Volpaia ★★** (www.volpaia.com; ✆ **0577-738-066**), a first-rank wine estate with a medieval stone heart. The castle here was a Florentine holding buffeted by Sienese attacks and sieges from the 10th to 16th centuries. The still-impressive central keep is all that remains, but it's surrounded by an evocative 13th-century *borgo* (village) containing the Renaissance La Commenda church. You can tour the winery daily at 11am and 3pm—installed in a series of buildings throughout the little village (with an eye to preserving its medieval visual charm; there is nonetheless high-tech plumbing, through which the wine flows, buried seamlessly inside the stone walls)—for 16€ per person; the tour includes a tasting of the wines and their fantastic olive oil. Call ahead, preferably a week in advance. The central tower has an enoteca (daily 10am–1pm and 4–7pm) for drop-in tastings (5€ for three wines) and direct sales of some of the wines that helped found the Chianti Consorzio in 1924, plus award-winning (and scrumptious) olive oils and farm-produced white and red vinegars. They also rent accommodations (see "Where to Stay in the Chianti," below).

Beside a side-road to just east of Radda, you'll see the workshop and showroom of **Ceramiche Rampini ★★**, Casa Beretone di Vistarenni (www.rampiniceramics.com; ✆ **0577-738-043**). The artisan family originates in Gubbio, in Umbria, and here creates spectacular hand-painted ceramics based on antique Florentine motifs or inspired by the Renaissance art of Venetian painter Arcimboldo.

From Radda, an 8km (5-mile) eastward trip brings you to the beautifully isolated **Badia a Coltibuono ★** (www.coltibuono.com; ✆ **0577-74-481**). The abbey's core was founded in A.D. 770, but the monastery was owned and expanded by the Vallombrosan Order from the 12th century to 1810, when the Napoleonic suppressions passed it into private hands and it became an agricultural estate. You can visit the 11th-century San Lorenzo church, but the rest is via a 45-minute guided tour only (afternoons only May–Oct; 5€). The wine estate is owned by the Stucchi-Prinetti family; Chianti Classico comes in a light style here, but the Riserva is a mouth-filling delight. The family's most famous member, international cookbook maven Lorenza de' Medici, started a famed (and egregiously overpriced) culinary school here in summers, though it's now run by an acolyte, and her son, Paolo, runs the acclaimed on-site **Ristorante Badia a Coltibuono** (✆ **0577-749-424;** closed Nov–Feb; main courses 18€). There's a direct-sales office for their products called the **Osteria** (✆ **0577-749-479**) down at the main road. March through December, it's open daily 10am to 7pm. Tasting is free, but in the friendly proprietor's words, "It's not a bar!"

Heading south directly from Badia a Coltibuono on the SS408 will take you through **Gaiole in Chianti,** the third member of the Lega del Chianti. An ancient market town like Greve, Gaiole is now basically modernized without much to see, aside from the wine shops: the **Cantina Enoteca Montagnani,** Via B. Bandinelli 13–17 (✆ **0577-749-517**), and **La Cantinetta del Chianti,** Via Ricasoli 33 (www.lacantinettadelchianti.it; ✆ **0577-749-125**).

A side road here leads west past the 12th-century Castello di Spaltenna (now a hotel) 3km (1¾ miles) to the 13th-century **Castello di Vertine,** an imposing castle surrounded by a 9th-century village.

East of Gaiole, an unfinished road winds up to the fortified medieval hamlet of **Barbischio.** For more castle viewing, head south of Gaiole to the turnoff for Meleto and Castagnoli. **Castello di Meleto**'s twin circular towers stand mighty at either expanse of a long blank wall to watch over the estate's vineyards. The poor castle-cum-villa was built in the 1100s, partially dismantled by the Sienese in the 15th century, rebuilt by the Florentines, and then smashed by the Sienese again in the 16th century before a 1700s restoration transformed it into the villa we see today.

Farther south of Gaiole, the SS484 branches east toward Castelnuovo Berardenga and the famous **Castello di Brolio ★★** (www.ricasoli.it; ✆ **0577-749-066**). The Chianti as a region may date to the 1200s, but Chianti Classico as a wine was born here in the mid–19th century. The Brolio castle has been in the Ricasoli family since 1141, though its vineyards date from at least 1007; the current fortress was rebuilt in 1484. "Iron Baron" Bettino Ricasoli inherited it in 1829 at age 20 and, before he went off in 1848 to help found a unified Italy and become its second prime minister, spent his days here, teaching—really, dictating—scientific farming methods to his workers. He also whiled away the time tinkering with grape varietals. By the mid–19th century, he'd arrived at a quaffable formula balancing sangiovese, canaiolo, trebbiano, and malvasia grapes that was used when Italy's wine-governing DOC and DOCG laws were written in the 1960s. You can visit the castle grounds, including the small chapel (Bettino rests in peace in the family crypt) and the gardens, and walk along the wall for a view of the lower Chianti valleys. Admission is 5€, and includes a taste of the estate wine on departure. Between March and November, the gardens are open daily 10am to 6pm, or dusk if it falls earlier.

After years of being passed to larger corporate ownership, Brolio declined as a winery; then in 1993 the Baron Francesco Ricasoli brought it back into the family. He effected a drastic turnaround, investing, replanting vines, and rigorously revising the philosophy to rocket Brolio back to respect on the Italian wine scene, winning acclaim and awards once again. They now produce several wines, including the newest—a single Castello di Brolio, 100% sangiovese Chianti Classico. To buy their award-winning wines, visit the wine shop (✆ **0577-730-220**) between April and October from Monday to Friday 9am to 7:30pm, Saturday and Sunday from 11am to 7pm. They offer a range of tours (advance booking obligatory) with a wine tasting at the end.

Where to Eat

Albergaccio di Castellina ★★ CONTEMPORARY TUSCAN This renowned place offers an excellent mix of fine cuisine and rustic timbered atmosphere with valley views, and a changing roster of dishes steeped in local traditions but enlivened by the creativity of chef Sonia Visman. Strict seasonality is the key to the cooking, but among the tasty combinations we've sampled, we heartily recommend the *bavette con timo e pecorino di fossa* (thin noodles with tomatoes, thyme, and aged pecorino cheese) and *gnocchi di ricotta con tartufo marzolo* (dollops of ricotta with shaved truffles and thyme leaves). The *rollé di maiale con cavolo nero* (pork *involtini* made with black cabbage, tomatoes, and wild fennel) and *piccione sfumato al marsala con fichi caramellati* (Marsala-perfumed pigeon with caramelized figs) are fine *secondi*.

Via Fiorentina 63, Castellina in Chianti (beside the road toward San Donato). www.albergacciocast.com. ✆ **0577-741-042.** Reservations highly recommended. 1/2/3/4 courses 26€/42€/54€/64€; tasting menus 58€ and 65€. MC, V. Mon–Sat 12:30–2pm and 7:30–9:30pm (lunch only Wed–Thurs). Closed last 2 weeks of Nov and 1st week of Dec; call ahead in winter.

La Cantinetta di Rignana ★★ TUSCAN A medieval ramble of stone houses at the end of a long dirt road hides La Cantinetta, one of the Chianti's most refined countryside *trattorie*. The outdoor tables take in a sweeping view, and the staff is given to warbling snatches of folk songs and opera as they prepare handmade pasta (ravioli, gnocchi, or *tagliolini*) with your pick of rich sauces—the thick, pasty *noci* (nut) sauce is excellent. In season, be sure to start with the artichokes from their garden, soaked all day outside and then served roasted with olive oil. Grilled meats top the main courses (try the pheasant if it's on). The white-chocolate mousse is legendary.

Loc. Rignana, Greve in Chianti. www.lacantinettadirignana.it. ✆ **055-852-601.** Reservations strongly recommended. Main courses 9€–18€. AE, DC, MC, V. Wed–Mon noon–3:30pm and 6:30–11pm (daily in summer).

DINING WITH dario

Panzano's famous opera-singing butcher, Dario Cecchini, brings his own meat, love of conviviality (large, shared tables are a feature), and Dante-esque sense of humor to three celebrated (m)eateries in the village—any of which is worth the trip here on its own. **Solociccia ★★** opened in 2007 right across from his butcher shop, at Via XX Luglio 11. As the name ("only flesh") suggests, this is not a place for vegetarians: Among the six meat courses, look out for *ramarino in culo,* "rosemary up the you-know-what," which are little peach-shaped balls of tartare impaled with a sprig of rosemary. The menu is fixed (30€) and sitting times are 7 and 9pm Thursday through Saturday and 1pm Sunday.

Above the shop itself, the **Officina della Bistecca ★** is Dario's multicourse homage to all-things-cow, including the sacred *bistecca alla fiorentina,* of course. The fixed menu costs 50€, including house wine, and sittings are Tuesday, Friday, and Saturday at 8pm and Sunday at 1pm. The same space at lunchtimes Monday through Saturday hosts **Dario DOC ★★**, offering fast food, Tuscan-style. For 10€, McDonald's-starved children (and adults) can feast on a fresh, bread-crumbed beef burger, oven-cooked "fries," sides of pickles and shredded red onion, and two great relishes. The atmosphere is communal and fun, but the quality of the food is as serious as his two "grown-up" restaurants. For information and to reserve (advisable at Solociccia and the Officina), call ✆ **055-852-727** (for Soliciccia) or ✆ **055-852-176** (for the Officina), or see www.dariocecchini.com.

Le Vigne TUSCAN The aptly named Le Vigne is tucked between the rows of vines covering the slopes southeast of Radda. You can watch vintners working the vines as you sip your wine and sample such well-turned dishes as *pici all'aglione* (hand-rolled spaghetti with tomatoes, leeks, and a dab of pancetta), bready *ribollita,* boned duck stuffed with *porchetta,* and excellent *arrosto misto,* a mixed roast which might include a trio like pigeon, chicken, and pork, served with seasonal vegetables.

Podere Le Vigne (off SS408 to Villa just east of Radda in Chianti). www.ristorantepoderelevigne.com. ✆ **0577-738-301.** Reservations recommended. Main courses 10€–18€. AE, MC, V. Wed–Mon noon–2:30pm and 7:15–9:30pm (daily in summer). Closed Nov 15–Mar 15.

Nerbone di Greve ★ FLORENTINE/TUSCAN You don't expect traditional cuisine served right on the piazza of a busy wine and tourism town to taste this good—but then, this is the Chianti outpost of Nerbone, the legendary lunch joint in Florence's Mercato Centrale. The stripped brick vault decorated with simple wooden furniture is surprisingly stylish. The menu cleaves to the ultratraditional, kicking off with pasta staples and *crostini* topped with pork cheek (*guancia*). Nerbone's real strength, however, is its meat *secondi:* steak tartare is constructed at your table, to taste; a simple *arista di maiale con mele* (sliced pork with rosemary and a caramelized apple) is overflowing with succulent flavor; and of course, there's a proper Florentine selection of offal, such as *collo ripieno* (stuffed chicken neck) and *lingua bollita* (boiled ox tongue). It's Tuscan fare done properly.

Piazza Matteotti 22, Greve in Chianti. www.nerbonedigreve.it. ✆ **055-853-308.** Reservations recommended. Main courses 12€–16€. MC, V. Wed–Mon 11:30am–3:30pm and 7:30–10:30pm.

Where to Stay in the Chianti

Besides the choices below, the medieval **Castello di Volpaia** (www.volpaia.com; ✆ **0577-738-066**), recommended above for its wine, rents out apartments with kitchenettes and TVs and, in a few, working fireplaces in the stony buildings of its 13th-century village for 95€ to 150€ per night for two people (plus a sofa bed for children if required), or 180€ to 340€ per night for one that sleeps seven. Guests can take part in various programs, from self-guided hikes to cooking lessons and, of course, tastings. They also rent lovely villas (sleeping up to 8 or 11) with private gardens and pools with views (Sat–Sat rental only), and lease a *casa colonica* on a nearby hillock amid the estate's vineyards to a hotelier who operates it as an exquisite rustic-chic hotel, **La Locanda** ★ (www.lalocanda.it; ✆ **0577-738-832**), with 220€ to 290€ double rooms.

Borgo Argenina ★★ From the flagstone terrace of Elena Nappa's hilltop B&B (she bought the whole medieval hamlet), you can see the farmhouse where Bertolucci filmed *Stealing Beauty* in 1996. Against remarkable odds (she'll regale you with the anecdotes), Elena has created the rural retreat of your dreams. Since the place isn't easy to find, English-speaking Elena will send you directions when you reserve. In addition to four doubles, she offers accommodations in two suites, two small houses (for two or three people), and the Villa Oliviera (for four). When faced with all the questions guests often inundate her with when booking (Do you have air-conditioning? Is there parking? How much of a deposit do I need to make?), Elena replies, "Don't worry. Just come!" Great advice.

Loc. Argenina (near San Marcollino Monti), 53013 Gaiole in Chianti. www.borgoargenina.it. ✆ **0577-747-117.** Fax 0577-747-228. 10 units. 170€ double, 200€–240€ suite; 240€–300€ house. 3-night minimum stay. Rates include breakfast. DC, MC, V. Free parking. Closed Nov–Feb. **Amenities:** Restaurant (3 days per week); smoke-free rooms. *In room:* Hair dryer, minibar, Wi-Fi (free).

Castello di Vicchiomaggio ★★ This fine wine estate (see above) has always had a few recommendable apartments, but the conversion in 2007 of the old priest's house into 10 bed-and-breakfast units upped the quality ante considerably. Quarters each comprise two large (for Tuscany) rooms with cool tile floors, decorated in antique creams for a clean, modern take on country styling. The sitting area can be converted to sleep one extra child or adult; two units have small outdoor spaces. The outdoor pool is terraced into the hill with sensational views over the vineyards, and the tiny adjacent chapel hosts occasional recitals in summer.

Via Vicchiomaggio 4, 50022 Greve in Chianti (FI). www.vicchiomaggio.it. ✆ **055-854-079.** Fax 055-853-911. 16 units, 10 rooms and 6 apts. 120€–158€ double; apts from 118€ per night. Rates include breakfast (rooms only). AE, MC, V. Free parking. **Amenities:** Restaurant (lunch daily; dinner 3 days per week); babysitting; outdoor pool (June–Sept); smoke-free rooms. *In room:* A/C (rooms only), TV, hair dryer, Wi-Fi (free; rooms only).

Il Colombaio ★ This modest, excellently priced hotel sits in a 16th-century stone house at the edge of Castellina (near the Etruscan tomb and a 5-min. walk into town) and once housed shepherds who spent the night after selling their sheep at market. The good-size rooms with their sloping beam-and-tile ceilings, terra-cotta floors, and iron bed frames seem to belong to a well-to-do 19th-century farming family. Upstairs accommodations are lighter and airier than the ground-floor rooms (formerly stalls) and enjoy better views over the vineyards (a few overlook the road). You breakfast in winter under stone vaults and in summer on a terrace sharing its countryside vistas with the pool.

tuscan tours: **BIKING, HORSEBACK RIDING & MORE**

Florence-based **I Bike Italy ★** (www.ibikeitaly.com; ✆ **055-0123994**) offers guided single-day rides in the Tuscan countryside, past olive groves, vineyards, castles, and vine-covered estates. Tours begin daily in Florence at 9:30am in front of the agency office on Via de'Lamberti 1. The company provides a shuttle service to carry you in and out of the city and also provides 21-speed bicycles, helmets, water bottles, and a bilingual guide to show you the way, fix flats, and so on. Tours cover a scenic 24 to 48km (15- to 30-mile) stretch, at an average speed of 5 kmph (3¼ mph), and return to Florence around 5pm. The cost is 80€ per person, with lunch included.

Cilium Classico (www.ciclismoclassico.com; ✆ **800/866-7314** in the U.S.) has more than a decade of experience leading biking tours in Italy. From April to October, the outfit runs guided rides through Tuscany, always van supported, or will help you arrange a do-it-yourself bike trip. Trips sometimes include Italian and cooking lessons, along with wine tasting and cultural itineraries. Groups average 10 to 18 people, with all ages and ability levels welcome.

U.S.-based **Custom Tours in Tuscany** (www.customtoursintuscany.com; ✆ **847/432-1814** in the U.S.) can customize a daylong tour around your personal interests. Its staff can help you visit Florence's monuments, guide you through its "secret" alleyways, and show you where to buy antiques, gold, leather, extra-virgin olive oil, or linens at the best possible prices. Its Tuscan day tours outside Florence include visits to Lucca, Siena, San Gimignano, and Cortona.

Only 20km (12 miles) from Florence in Pontassieve is the **Vallebona Ranch** (www.vallebona.it; ✆ **055-8397246**), where Western riding is the tradition. You can choose from individual, hour-long lessons; full-day horseback rides returning daily to the guest rooms at the centuries-old farmhouse (1-week package with full board and 12 hours' riding time from 610€ per person); or weeklong inn-to-inn treks that begin and end at Vallebona (from 840€ per person).

Via Chiantigiana 29, 53011 Castellina in Chianti (SI). www.albergoilcolombaio.it. ✆ **0577-740-444.** Fax 0577-740-402. 13 units. 85€–100€ double. Rates include breakfast. AE, MC, V. Free parking. **Amenities:** Babysitting; concierge; outdoor pool (June–Sept); smoke-free rooms. *In room:* TV, hair dryer, minibar, Wi-Fi (free).

Villa Bordoni ★★★ Our favorite luxury hotel along the Chianti Road is this restored wisteria-smothered inn and restaurant, marooned in the vines west of Greve and run by two Scottish expats. A stay in one of its rustic, chic bedrooms and a gourmet dinner at its intimate restaurant is one of the highlights of the wine country. Originally a 16th-century villa with an olive mill and chapel, today this vineyard-ringed hotel evokes an English country house with beautifully furnished bedrooms, filled with original Italian antiques and beamed ceilings.

Via San Cresci, 31–32 Loc. Mezzuola, 50022 Greve in Chianti (FI). www.villabordoni.com. ✆ **055-854-6230.** Fax 055-851-9114. 11 units. 170€–310€ double; 260€–340€ junior suite. Rates include breakfast. AE, MC, V. Free parking. Closed Jan–Feb. **Amenities:** Restaurant (daily mid-Apr to Oct, closed Mon otherwise); bar; babysitting; bikes (free); concierge; outdoor pool (Apr–Oct); smoke-free rooms. *In room:* A/C, TV/DVD, hair dryer, minibar, MP3 docking station (in suites), Wi-Fi (free).

Villa Vignamagglo ★ You can't actually stay in the room where Mona Lisa grew up, but you can certainly make do with the apartments and suites here, many with a tiny kitchenette and complimentary bottle of the estate's award-winning chianti. This is one of the most hotel-like *agriturismi* in the area, offering amenities such as daily maid service. The heavy wood-beam ceilings and the comfortable rustic furnishings mesh well with the contemporary designer lights and cast-iron bed frames; five units even have Jacuzzi tubs and air-conditioning. You can stay in one of several suites in the villa, rent the small cottage next door, or shack out in a suite in one of the old stone peasant houses dotting the property on either side of the road.

Villa Vignamaggio (5km/3 miles southeast of Greve), 50022 Greve in Chianti (FI). www.vignamaggio.com. ✆ **055-854-661.** Fax 055-854-4468. 26 units, 14 apts and 12 rooms. 150€ double; 200€–275€ apt. Minimum 2-night stay; 10% discount for stays of a week or longer. DC, MC, V. Free parking. Closed mid-Dec to mid-Mar. Turn off the SS222 just south of Greve onto the Lamole road, then follow the signs. **Amenities:** Restaurant (closed Tues and Sun); babysitting; bikes (free); concierge; small exercise room; 2 outdoor pools (1 heated); outdoor tennis court; Wi-Fi (free). *In room:* A/C, TV, hair dryer, kitchenette (in apts), minibar.

SIENA ★★★

70km (43 miles) S of Florence, 232km (144 miles) N of Rome

Siena is a medieval city of brick. Viewed from the summit of the Palazzo Pubblico's tower, its sea of roof tiles blends into a landscape of steep, twisting stone alleys. This cityscape hides dozens of Gothic palaces and pastry shops galore, unseen neighborhood rivalries, and painted altarpieces of unsurpassed elegance.

Siena is proud of its past. It trumpets the she-wolf as its emblem, a holdover from its days as Saena Julia, the Roman colony founded by Augustus about 2,000 years ago (though the official Sienese myth has the town founded by the sons of Remus, younger brother of Rome's legendary forefather). Siena still parcels out the rhythms of life, its rites of passage and communal responsibilities, to the 17 *contrade* (neighborhood wards) formed in the 14th century. Compared with its old medieval rival, Siena is as inscrutable in its culture, decorous in its art, and festive in its life attitude as Florence is forthright, precise, and serious on all counts. Where Florence produced hard-nosed mystics such as Savonarola, Siena gave forth saintly scholars like St. Catherine (1347–80) and St. Bernardino (1380–1444).

The city's heyday was in the 13th and 14th centuries; Sienese merchants established in 1270 the Council of Nine, an oligarchy that ruled over Siena's greatest republican era, when civic projects and artistic prowess reached their greatest heights. Artists like Duccio, Simone Martini, and the Lorenzetti brothers invented a distinctive Sienese art style, a highly developed Gothicism that was an artistic foil to the emerging Florentine Renaissance. Then, in 1348, the Black Death hit the city, killing perhaps three-quarters of the population, decimating the social fabric, and devastating the economy. Siena never recovered, and much of it has barely changed since. As a result, it offers your best chance in Italy to slip into the rhythms and atmosphere of the Middle Ages.

Essentials

GETTING THERE The bus is often more convenient than the train, because Siena's **rail** station is outside town. Some 19 trains daily connect Siena with **Florence** (usually 90 min.), via Empoli. Siena's **train station** is at Piazza

Roselli, about 3km (1¾ miles) north of town. Take the no. 9 or 10 bus to Piazza Gramsci in Terza di Camollia or a taxi.

Buses are faster and let you off right in town: TRA-IN and SITA (www.sitabus.it) codeshare express (*corse rapide;* around 25 daily; 75 min.) and slower buses (*corse ordinarie;* 14 daily; 95 min.) from **Florence**'s main bus station to Siena's Piazza Gramsci. Siena is also connected with **San Gimignano** (at least hourly Mon–Sat; 10 direct, rest change in Poggibonsi; 65–80 min. not including layover), **Perugia** (two to four daily; 90 min.), **Arezzo** (eight daily; 90 min.), and **Rome**'s Tiburtina station (five to nine daily; 3 hr.).

There's a fast **road** direct from **Florence** (it has no route number; follow the green signs toward Siena), or take the more scenic route, down the Chiantigiana SS222 (see "The Chianti," earlier in this chapter). From **Rome** get off the A1 north at the Val di Chiana exit and follow the SS326 west for 50km (31 miles). From **Pisa** take the highway toward Florence and exit onto the SS429 south just before Empoli (100km/62 miles total). The easiest way into the center is from the Siena Ovest highway exit.

Siena **parking** (www.sienaparcheggi.com; ✆ **0577-228-711**) is now coordinated, and lots charge between .50€ and 1.60€ per hour (most at the top end of that scale). Luckily, many hotels have a discount deal with the nearest lot; around 15€ per day is standard. All lots are well signposted, with locations just inside city gates.

GETTING AROUND There is no efficient public transport system in the center, so it's up to your feet to cover the steep ups and downs that characterize the center. The city does run **minibuses,** called *pollicini* (www.sienamobilita.it; ✆ **0577-204-246**), which run quarter-hourly (every half-hour Sat afternoon and all day Sun) from the main gates into the city center from 6:30am to 8:30pm.

You can call for a radio **taxi** at ✆ **0577-49-222** (7am–9pm only); they also queue at the train station and in town at Piazza Matteotti.

VISITOR INFORMATION The **tourist office,** where you can get a useless free map or pay .50€ for a useful one, is at Piazza del Campo 56, 53100 Siena (www.terresiena.it; ✆ **0577-280-551**). It's open daily 9am to 7pm.

Piazza del Campo.

Exploring Siena

Several tunnel-like stepped alleys lead down into **Piazza del Campo (Il Campo) ★★★**, arguably the most beautiful piazza in Italy. Crafted like a sloping scallop shell, the Campo was first laid out in the 1100s on the site of the Roman forum. The herringbone brick pavement is divided by white marble lines into nine sections representing the city's medieval ruling body, the Council of Nine. At the top of the Campo is a poor 19th-century replica of Jacopo della Quercia's

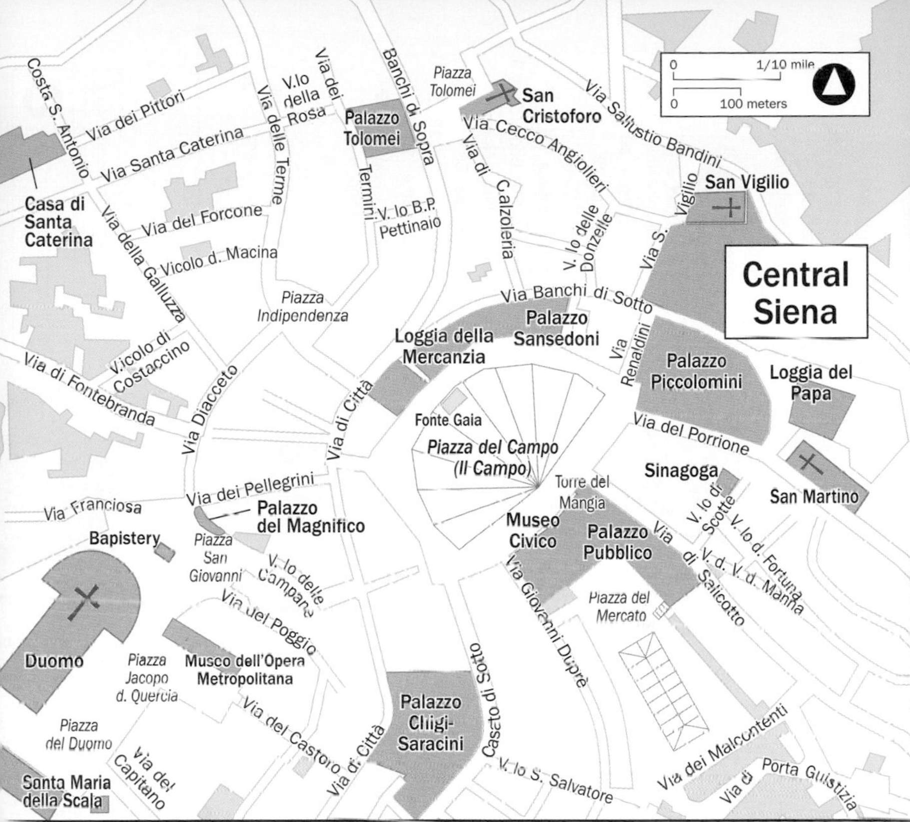

14th-century fountain, the **Fonte Gaia ★★**. Some of the restored, but badly eroded, original panels are in Santa Maria della Scala (see below).

The crenellated town hall, the **Palazzo Pubblico ★★** (1297–1310) is the city's finest Gothic palace, and the Museo Civico inside is home to Siena's best artworks (see below). When the Black Death finally abated in 1348, the citizens built a loggia chapel, the **Cappella della Piazza,** at the left end of the *palazzo*'s base to give thanks that at least parts of the city had been spared. Rising above it is the slender 100m-tall (328-ft.) brick **Torre del Mangia ★** (1338–48), crowned with a Lippo Memmi–designed cresting in white travertine. It was the second-tallest tower in medieval Italy and was named after a slothful bell ringer nicknamed Mangiaguadagni, or "profit eater." (There's an armless statue of him in the courtyard.)

If you fancy climbing 503 steps and aren't particularly claustrophobic, the tower is a great place to check out the unforgettable view across Siena's cityscape and the rolling countryside beyond. Admission is 8€. The tower (entrance in the courtyard) is open from October 16 through February from 10am to 4pm, otherwise from 10am to 7pm.

Archivio di Stato ★ MUSEUM The 1469 **Palazzo Piccolomini** is a touch of Florence peeking into the southeast corner of the Campo. It was designed by Bernardo Rossellino in the Florentine Renaissance style and is now home to the Archivio di Stato (head down the corridor off the left of the courtyard to grab the elevator to the fourth floor). The State Archive preserves, among other notable

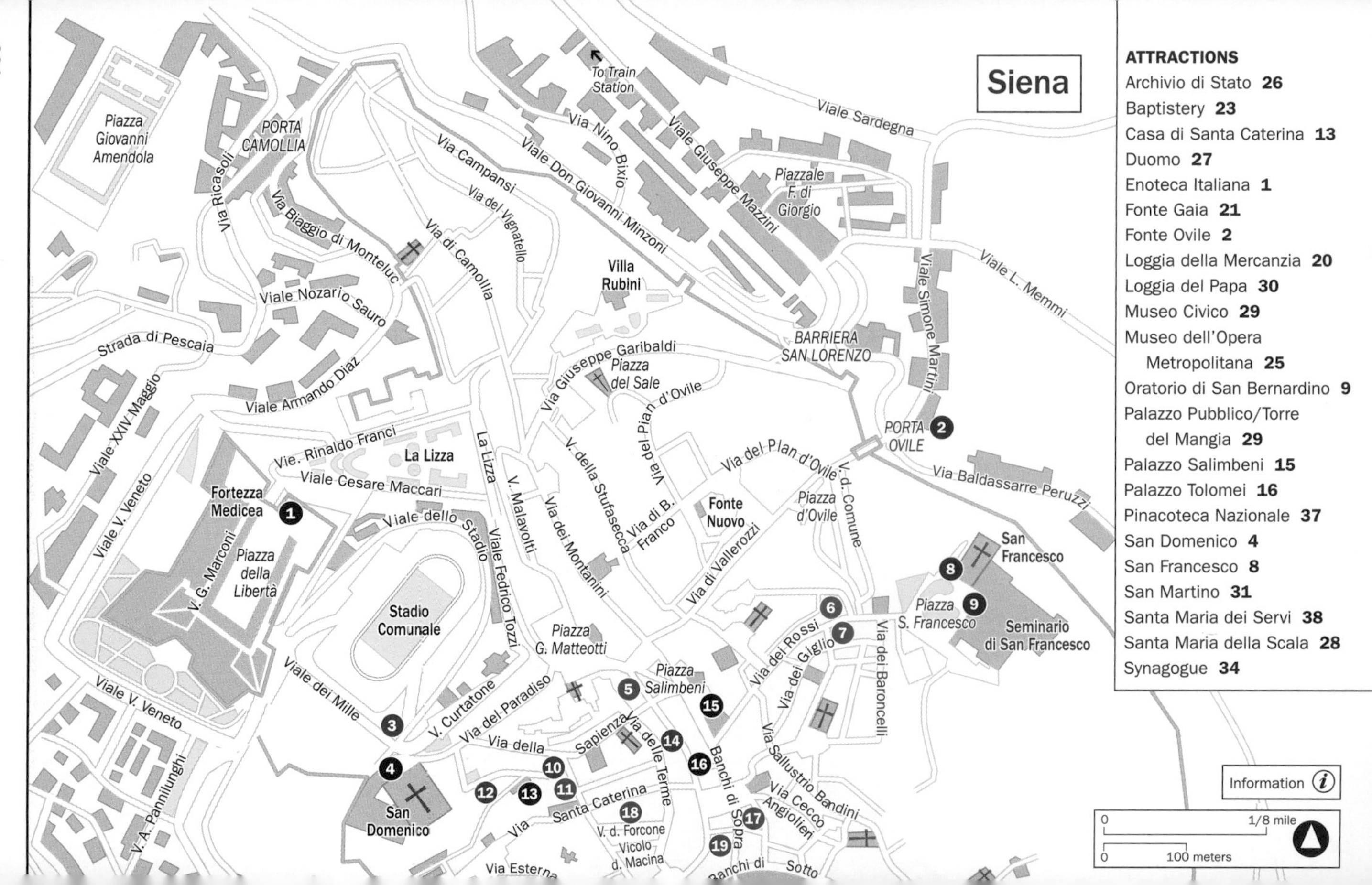
Siena
ATTRACTIONS
Archivio di Stato 26
Baptistery 23
Casa di Santa Caterina 13
Duomo 27
Enoteca Italiana 1
Fonte Gaia 21
Fonte Ovile 2
Loggia della Mercanzia 20
Loggia del Papa 30
Museo Civico 29
Museo dell'Opera Metropolitana 25
Oratorio di San Bernardino 9
Palazzo Pubblico/Torre del Mangia 29
Palazzo Salimbeni 15
Palazzo Tolomei 16
Pinacoteca Nazionale 37
San Domenico 4
San Francesco 8
San Martino 31
Santa Maria dei Servi 38
Santa Maria della Scala 28
Synagogue 34
Information
0 1/8 mile
0 100 meters
To Train Station
Viale Sardegna
Piazza Giovanni Amendola
PORTA CAMOLLIA
Via Ricasoli
Via Campansi
Via Nino Bixio
Viale Don Giovanni Minzoni
Viale Giuseppe Mazzini
Piazzale F. di Giorgio
Via del Vignatello
Via Biaggio di Monteluc
Via di Camollia
Villa Rubini
Viale Simone Martini
Viale L. Memmi
Viale Nozario Sauro
Strada di Pescaia
BARRIERA SAN LORENZO
Via Giuseppe Garibaldi
Piazza del Sale
Via del Pian d'Ovile
Viale Armando Diaz
Viale XXIV Maggio
PORTA OVILE
Vle. Rinaldo Franci
La Lizza
V. della Stufasecca
Via del Plan d'Ovile
V. d. Comune
Via Baldassarre Peruzzi
Viale Cesare Maccari
V. Malavolti
Fortezza Medicea
Viale V. Veneto
Viale dello Stadio
Via dei Montanini
Via di B. Franco
Fonte Nuovo
Piazza d'Ovile
San Francesco
Piazza della Libertà
V. G. Marconi
Stadio Comunale
Viale Fedrico Tozzi
Via di Vallerozzi
Piazza S. Francesco
Seminario di San Francesco
Piazza G. Matteotti
Via dei Rossi
Via del Giglio
Via dei Baroncelli
Viale dei Mille
V. Curtatone
Via del Paradiso
Piazza Salimbeni
Sapienza
Via delle Terme
Via della
Banchi di Sopra
Via Sallustrio Bandini
Via Cecco Angiolieri
San Domenico
Via Santa Caterina
V. d. Forcone
Vicolo d. Macina
Via Esterna
Banchi di Sotto
V. A. Pannilunghi

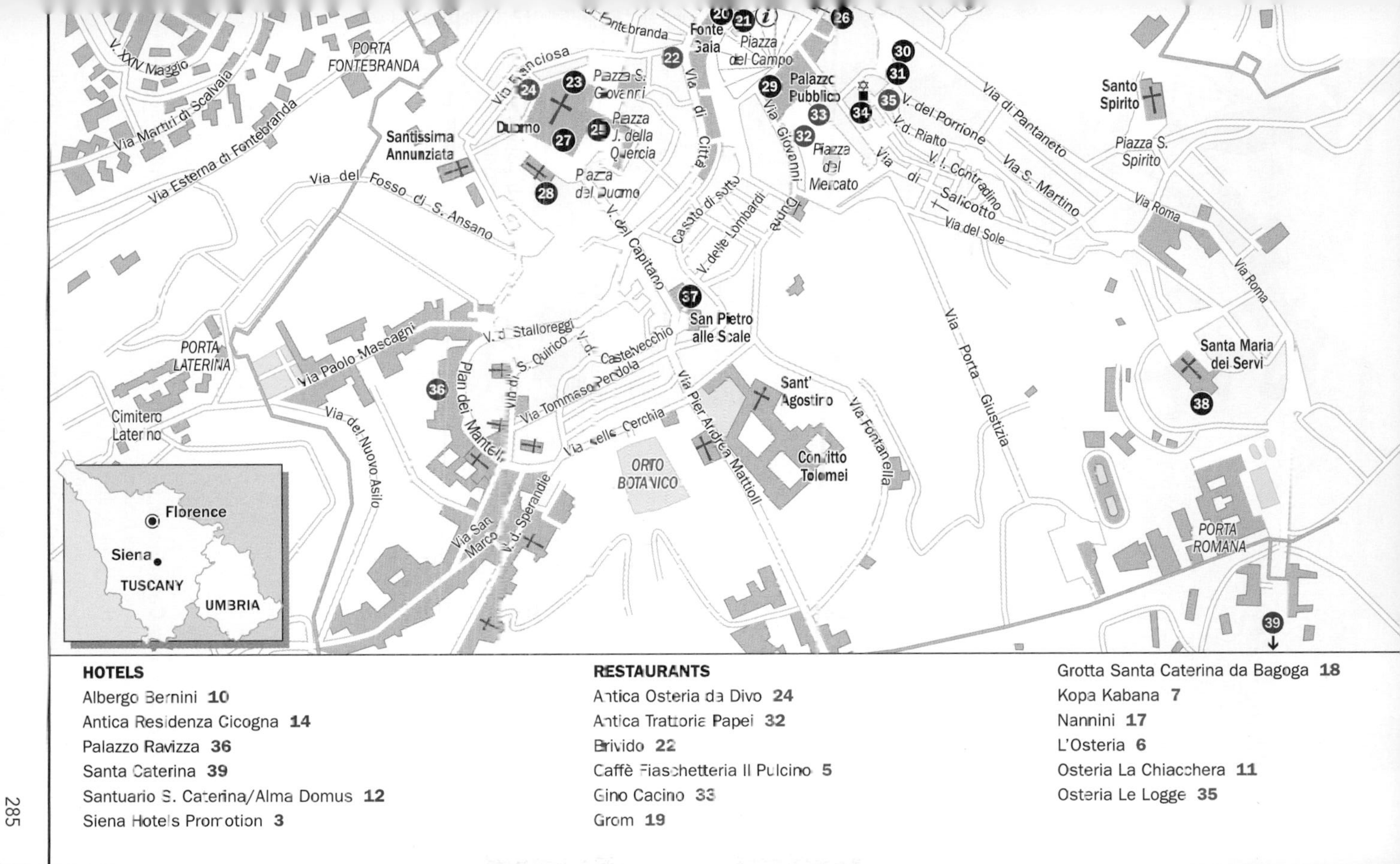

HOTELS

Albergo Bernini 10
Antica Residenza Cicogna 14
Palazzo Ravizza 36
Santa Caterina 39
Santuario S. Caterina/Alma Domus 12
Siena Hotels Promotion 3

RESTAURANTS

Antica Osteria da Divo 24
Antica Trattoria Papei 32
Brivido 22
Caffè Fiaschetteria Il Pulcino 5
Gino Cacino 33
Grom 19
Grotta Santa Caterina da Bagoga 18
Kopa Kabana 7
Nannini 17
L'Osteria 6
Osteria La Chiacchera 11
Osteria Le Logge 35

documents, Boccaccio's will and Jacopo della Quercia's contract for the Fonte Gaia. But the main thing to see is a remarkable set of wooden covers dating back to 1258 and made for the city's account books, called the ***Tavolette di Biccherna*** ★, painted from the 13th to 17th centuries with religious scenes, daily working life in the civic offices, and important events in Siena's history—Sano di Pietro, Vecchietta, and Ambrogio Lorenzetti even did a few.

Via Banchi di Sotto 52 (facing Loggia del Papa). ✆ **0577-241-745.** Free admission. Mon–Sat hourly viewings at 9:30, 10:30, and 11:30am. Bus: A (pink) or B.

TOP: **Horses race through Siena during the Palio;** ABOVE: **A fountain in Il Campo in Siena.**

Baptistery ★ CHURCH The Duomo's baptistery was built between 1355 and 1382 beneath the cathedral's choir and supports a Gothic facade left unfinished by Domenico di Agostino. The upper walls and vaulted ceilings inside were **frescoed by Vecchietta** and his school in the late 1440s (look for the alligator) but "touched up" in the 19th century. What you're principally here to see, though, is the **baptismal font** ★★ (1417–30). The frames are basically Gothic, but the gilded brass panels were cast by the foremost Sienese and Florentine sculptors of the early Renaissance, including Jacopo della Quercia, Lorenzo Ghiberti, and Donatello, whose *Feast of Herod* is a masterful early study of precise perspective and profound depth.

Piazza San Giovanni (down the stairs around the rear right flank of the Duomo). ✆ **0577-283-048.** Admission on cumulative ticket, or 3€. Mid-June to mid-Sept daily 9:30am–8pm; mid-Sept to Oct and Mar to mid-June daily 9:30am–7pm; Nov–Feb daily 10am–5pm.

Casa di Santa Caterina ★ HISTORIC HOME The remarkable Caterina Benincasa, daughter of a rich Sienese dyer, took a nun's veil (but never an order's vows) in 1355 at the age of 8 after her first of many visions of Christ. Her name and reputation for devout wisdom and saintly life spread, and in 1378 she was chosen as Siena's ambassador to Pope Gregory XI in Avignon. Caterina died in

Rome in 1380, at age 33, and was canonized 80 years later. In 1939, she was declared patron saint of Italy, and in 1970, together with St. Teresa of Avila, was elevated to a Doctor of the Church.

The house where she was born was converted into a sanctuary in 1466, and it remains a peaceful, reflective spot. To the left is the old family kitchen transformed into an **oratory** and decorated in the 16th and 19th centuries with paintings by Il Pomarancio, Il Riccio, Francesco Vanni, and others. The majolica-tiled floor is 16th century.

At the bottom of Via Santa Caterina below, nestled amid the remaining green of the narrow valley between San Domenico and the Duomo, is the brick 1246 **Fonte Branda,** a public wash house battlemented like a tiny fortress.

Costa di San Antonio (btw. Via della Sapienza and Via Santa Caterina). www.caterinati.org. ✆ **0577-280-801.** Free admission. Easter–Oct daily 9am–12:30pm and 3–6pm; winter daily 9am–12:30pm and 3:30–6pm. Bus: A (red).

Cripta ★ CHURCH Beneath Siena's cathedral is the city's latest major artistic discovery, in a room widely referred to as the "crypt," although no bodies have been found here. In fact, this subterranean room is part of the pre-14th-century Romanesque church. What the 21st-century restoration workers scraped up was a cycle of frescoes painted between 1270 and 1275, shedding some light on the early development of the Sienese school. The crypt has only been viewable since 2004, and scholars have yet to attribute the cycle to a particular artist (some have speculated it may be the work of Duccio). What is more or less certain is that the style and composition, such as the way Christ's feet are oddly crossed on the crucifix, have been mirrored—almost copied—by later painters.

Piazza del Duomo. ✆ **0577-283-048.** Admission on cumulative ticket, or 6€. Mid-June to mid-Sept daily 9:30am–8pm; mid Sept to Oct and Mar to mid-June daily 9:30am–7pm; Nov–Feb daily 10am–5pm.

Duomo ★★★ CATHEDRAL Siena's cathedral is a rich treasure house of Tuscan art. Despite being an overwhelmingly Gothic building, the Duomo has one eye-popping Romanesque holdover: its 1313 **campanile** with its black-and-white banding. The Duomo was built from around 1215 to 1263, involving Gothic master Nicola Pisano as architect at some point. His son, Giovanni, drew up the plans for the lower half of the **facade,** begun in 1285. Giovanni Pisano, along with his studio, also carved many of the statues adorning it (most of the originals are now in the Museo dell'Opera Metropolitana; see below).

Siena's Cumulative Tickets

Siena has a bewildering range of **reduced-price cumulative ticket** combos you can pick up at any of the participating museums or sites. The **Musei Comunali** pass, valid for 2 days, covers civic museums—Museo Civico and Santa Maria della Scala—for 11€. The **S.I.A.,** valid for 7 days and available March 15 through October only, gives you access to those sites plus the Museo dell' Opera Metropolitana, Baptistery, Sant'Agostino, and Museo Diocesano for 17€. In winter months, it's 3€ cheaper, but excludes the last two. The **OPA Pass** costs 10€ and offers entry to the Duomo, Museo dell'Opera Metropolitana, Baptistery, Cripta, and Oratorio di San Bernardino.

By 1339, having defeated Florence 80 years earlier, Siena was its rival's equal. It began its most ambitious project yet: to turn the already huge Duomo into merely the transept of a new cathedral, one that would dwarf St. Peter's in Rome and trumpet Siena's political power, spiritual devotion, and artistic prowess. The city started the new nave off the Duomo's right transept but completed only the fabric of the walls when the Black Death hit in 1348, decimating the population and halting building plans forever. The **half-finished walls** remain—a monument to Siena's ambition and one-time wealth.

You could wander inside for hours, just staring at the **flooring ★★★**, a mosaic of 59 etched and inlaid marble panels (1372–1547). The top artists working in Siena lent their talents, including Domenico di Bartolo, Matteo di Giovanni, Pinturicchio, and, especially, Beccafumi, who designed 35 scenes (1517–47)—his original cartoons are in the Pinacoteca Nazionale (see below). The ones in the nave and aisles are usually uncovered, including the *Sibyls,* mythical Greek prophetesses, but the most precious ones under the apse and in the transepts are protected by cardboard flooring and uncovered from mid–August to early October in honor of the Palio.

At the entrance to the right transept, the small octagonal **Cappella Chigi ★** was designed by Roman baroque master Gian Lorenzo Bernini in 1659. It houses the *Madonna del Voto,* a fragmentary late-13th-century painting by a follower of Guido da Siena. The work fulfilled a vow the Sienese made on the eve of the Montaperti battle that they would devote their city to the Madonna should they win the fight against Florence (they did). At the entry to the left transept is Nicola Pisano's masterpiece **pulpit ★★** (1265–68), on which he was assisted by

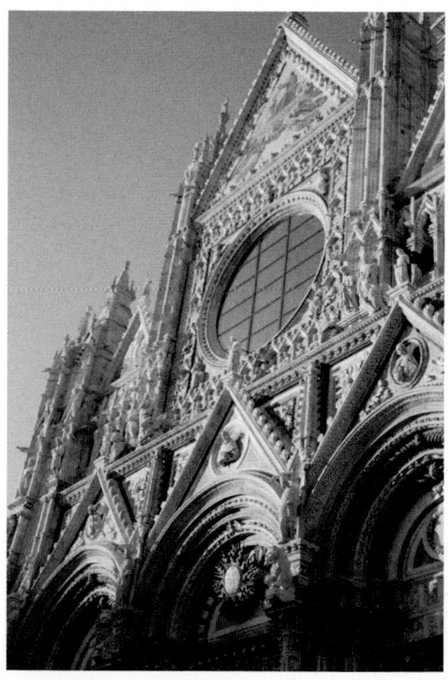

Siena's masterpiece, the Duomo.

Inside the Duomo.

his son, Giovanni, and Arnolfo di Cambio. The elegantly Gothic panels depict the life of Christ in crowded, detailed turmoil, divided by figures in flowing robes.

Umbrian master Pinturicchio is the star in the **Libreria Piccolomini ★★★**, built in 1485 by Cardinal Francesco Piccolomini (later Pope Pius III—for all of 18 days before he died in office) to house the library of his famous uncle, Pope Pius II. Pinturicchio and his assistants covered the ceiling and walls with 10 giant frescoes (1507) displaying rich colors and a fascination with mathematically precise, but somewhat cold, architectural space. The frescoes celebrate the life of Aeneas Silvio Piccolomini, better known as the humanist Pope Pius II.

Piazza del Duomo. ✆ **0577-283-048.** Admission on cumulative ticket, or 3€, except when floor uncovered 6€. Mar–May and Sept–Oct Mon–Sat 10:30am–7:30pm, Sun 1:30–5:30pm; Nov–Feb Mon–Sat 10:30am–6:30pm, Sun 1:30–5:30pm; June–Aug Mon–Sat 10:30am–8pm, Sun 1:30–6pm.

Enoteca Italiana ★ WINERY The 16th-century Fortezza Medicea di Santa Barbara has been turned into a (slightly untidy) public park. Its courtyard is an open-air theater, its ramparts are a place for a stroll and a view, and its vaults are filled with Italy's **national wine museum.** Here you can sample a choice selection of Italian wines by the glass or go all out on an entire bottle from their extensive cantina (around 1,600 labels cool their heels here), or just roam the vaulted basement armed with a barcode reader that can access information on all the bottles.

Fortezza Medicea. www.enoteca-italiana.it. ✆ **0577-228-843.** Free admission; glass of wine 3€–6.50€; cold plate of typical regional foods 8€–10€. Mon noon–8pm; Tues–Sat noon–1am.

Museo Civico ★★★ ART MUSEUM There are a number of wonderful frescoed rooms here, but the museum's pride comes with the masterpieces of Sienese painting giants Simone Martini and Ambrogio Lorenzetti. The **Sala del Mappamondo**—named after a now lost Ambrogio Lorenzetti painting of the world—contains two of Simone Martini's greatest works. On the left is his masterpiece, a ***Maestà* ★★★**. Incredibly, this was his very first painting, finished in 1315 (he went over it again in 1321). It's the next generation's answer to Duccio's groundbreaking work on the same theme painted just 4 years earlier and now in the Museo dell'Opera Metropolitana (see below).

Those fabrics can be seen again across this great hall in Simone Martini's other masterwork, the fresco of ***Guidoriccio da Fogliano* ★★**, where the captain of the Sienese army rides his charger across the territory he has just conquered (Montemassi, in 1328). Recently, iconoclastic U.S. art historians have disputed the attribution of this work to Martini, claiming that it was either a slightly later work or even a 16th-century fake.

The adjacent **Sala della Pace** was where the Council of Nine met, and to keep them mindful of how well they needed to govern, the city commissioned Ambrogio Lorenzetti (1338) to fresco the walls with the single most important piece of secular art to survive from medieval Europe, the ***Allegory of Good and Bad Government and Their Effects on the Town and Countryside* ★★★**. Good government is represented by a bearded old man surrounded by virtues. A prosperous 14th-century Siena is pictured here—recognizable by its towers, battlemented houses, and the Duomo squeezed into the corner. The *Bad Government* frescoes are, perhaps appropriately, in a high state of ruin. Monstrous Tyranny reigns with the help of such henchmen as Cruelty, Fraud, and the creaturelike Deceit. Unfortunately, in the aftermath of the Black Death of 1348, *Bad Government* pretty much came to pass.

Palazzo Pubblico, Piazza del Campo. ✆ **0577-292-226.** Admission on cumulative ticket with Torre del Mangia 13€; or 7.50€ adults with reservation, 8€ adults without reservation; 4€ students and seniors 65 and over with reservation, 3.50€ students and seniors without reservation; free for ages 11 and under. Nov–Mar 15 daily 10am–6pm; Mar 16–Oct daily 10am–7pm. Bus: A (pink), B.

Museo dell'Opera Metropolitana ★★ MUSEUM Housed in the walled-up right aisle of the Duomo's abortive new nave, Siena's outstanding Duomo museum contains all the works removed from the facade for conservation as well as disused altarpieces, including Duccio's masterpiece. It also offers one of the city's best views. The **ground floor** has the fascinating but weather-beaten facade **statues by Giovanni Pisano** and his school (1284–96), remarkable for their Gothic plasticity. The focus of the room, however, is Duccio's restored 30 sq. m (323 sq. ft.) **stained glass window ★★** made in the late 1280s for the window above the cathedral's apse. Nine panels depict the Virgin Mary, Siena's four patron saints, and the four Biblical Evangelists.

Upstairs is the museum's (indeed, the city's) masterpiece, **Duccio's *Maestà* ★★★**. It's impossible to overstate the importance of this double-sided altarpiece: Not only did it virtually found the Sienese school of painting, but it has also been considered one of the most important medieval paintings in Europe since the day it was unveiled. When Duccio finished the work on June 9, 1311, it was reportedly carried in procession from the painter's workshop on Via Stalloreggi to the Duomo's altar by the clergy, government officials, and every last citizen in Siena. The central scene of the *Maestà,* or Virgin Mary in Majesty enthroned and surrounded by saints, became the archetypal grand subject for a Sienese painter.

Almost overlooked on a side wall is Pietro Lorenzetti's incredible ***Birth of the Virgin* ★★**. Instead of painting a triptych with a central main scene and two unrelated side panels, as was the norm, Lorenzetti created a single continuous space by painting vaulted ceilings that seem to grow back from the pointed arches of the triptych's frame. This is the last work Pietro painted before succumbing to the plague.

If you take the stairs (past rooms of baroque canvases and a couple of Matteo di Giovanni altarpieces) that lead up to the walkway atop the would-be facade of the "New Duomo," the **Facciatone ★★**, you get the best visualization of how the enlarged Duomo would have looked as well as sweeping views across the city's rooftops with the Torre del Mangia towering over the Campo.

Piazza del Duomo 8. www.operaduomo.siena.it. ✆ **0577-283-048.** Admission on cumulative ticket, or 6€. Mid-June to mid-Sept daily 9:30am–8pm; mid-Sept to Oct and Mar to mid-June daily 9:30am–7pm; Nov–Feb daily 10am–5pm.

Pinacoteca Nazionale ★ ART MUSEUM Siena's painting gallery houses the most representative collection of the Sienese school of art. It wouldn't be fair to label it a museum of second-rate paintings by first-rate artists, but the supreme masterpieces of Siena do lie elsewhere. It's laid out more or less chronologically starting on the second floor, though the museum is constantly rearranging (especially the last bits).

Rooms 3 and 4 have works by the first great Sienese master, Duccio, including an early masterpiece showing Cimabue's influence, the tiny 1285 *Madonna dei Francescani* (in poor condition, it's kept under glass). Rooms 5 to 8 pay homage to the three great early-14th-century painters, Simone Martini and the brothers Pietro and Ambrogio Lorenzetti. Of Martini, be sure to look at the four charming narrative panels from the *Altar of Beato Agostino Novello.* The best

Lorenzetti works are in the small side rooms off Room 7, including a *Madonna Enthroned* and a *Madonna of the Carmelites* by Pietro; also look for Ambrogio's tiny landscapes in Room 12, an expressive but much deteriorated *Crucifixion,* and his last dated work, a 1343 *Annunciation.* On the first floor, look for Domenico Beccafumi's huge **cartoons ★★**, from which many of the panels in the Duomo floor were made.

Via San Pietro 29. ✆ **0577-286-143.** Admission 4€. Sun–Mon 9am–1pm; Tues–Sat 8:15am–7:15pm.

San Domenico ★ CHURCH The Dominican's Siena home is an enormous, severe, and vaguely unattractive pile of bricks (1226), jutting above a modern section of town. The **Cappella di Santa Caterina (Chapel of St. Catherine)** halfway down the right wall was frescoed with scenes from the saint's life. All except the right wall (where in 1593 Francesco Vanni painted Catherine performing an exorcism) were frescoed by Sodoma in 1526. The focal point of the chapel, however, is Catherine's venerated head, in a gilt reliquary case, on the altar.

At the end of the nave, on the right, is an ***Adoration of the Shepherds* ★** by Francesco di Giorgio Martini, dominated by a crumbling Roman triumphal arch in the background and a *Pietà* above.

Piazza San Domenico. No phone. Free admission. Daily 7am–12:55pm and 3–6:30pm. Bus: A (red).

Santa Maria della Scala ★★ ☺ MUSEUM The hospital across from the Duomo entrance cared for the infirm from the 800s up until the 1990s, when its wards, halls, and chapels began to be restructured as a diverse and constantly changing museum complex and exhibition space. The original decorations of the hospital itself, inside, also merit a visit on their own.

The **Sala del Pellegrinaio ★★**, which held hospital beds until just a few years ago, has walls frescoed in the 1440s with scenes from the history of the hospital and its good works (all well labeled). Most are vivid works by Domenico di Bartolo, richly colored and full of amusing details of hospital life in the 1400s. An adjacent hall houses **Bambimus,** Siena's Museum of Children's Art, where paintings are hung at tot-friendly heights and there's usually something crafty for them to explore themselves. Elsewhere on the ground floor, the recently restored **Sagrestia Vecchia (Old Sacristy) ★** has a damaged and complex fresco cycle completed by Vecchietta in 1449, and the adjacent **Cappella della Madonna** a surreal and rather gruesome ***Massacre of the Innocents* ★** (1482), by (of course) Matteo di Giovanni.

Downstairs are Jacopo della Quercia's original **Fonte Gaia ★** alongside plaster casts and explanations of its 20-year restoration process, and the **Oratorio di Santa Caterina della Notte ★**, where St. Catherine prayed at night.

Piazza del Duomo 2. www.santamariadellascala.com. ✆ **0577-534-571.** Admission on cumulative ticket, or 5.50€ with reservations, 6€ without reservations, free for ages 11 and under. Mar 17–Oct 15 daily 10:30am–6:30pm; Oct 16–Mar 16 daily 10:30am–4:30pm.

Where to Eat

Antica Osteria da Divo ★★ CONTEMPORARY SIENESE This former trattoria has thrived since it went midscale and greatly improved its menu to offer excellent innovative dishes rooted in Sienese traditions in a classy, but not frosty, atmosphere of soft jazz. The main dining room is a crazy medieval mélange of stone, brick, wood supports, and naked rock, while the rooms in back and in the basement

The Perfect Sienese Gelato

Superstar high-quality chain *gelateria* **Grom** hit Siena in 2010, grabbing a prime site at Via Banchi di Sopra 11–13 (www.grom.it; ✆ **0577-289-303**). Queues are long and the cold stuff is tasty. However, we still make the short detour down Via de' Rossi to **Kopa Kabana ★**, at no. 52–54 (✆ **0577-223-744**), for a daily changing range of flavors, including *panpepato,* based on the peppery Sienese cake.

are actually Etruscan tombs carved from the tufa. *Pici al ragout di lepre* (thick hand-rolled pasta in hare *ragù*) and *gnocchetti di patate con erbe cipollina e pecorino di fossa* (gnocchi with chives swimming in melted pecorino cheese) are palate-pleasing *primi.* For the main course, they ascribe to the growing school of Italian cooking wherein a side dish is included with each *secondo* (making a meal here less costly than the prices below would suggest).

Via Franciosa 25–29 (2 streets down from the left flank of the Duomo). www.osteriadadivo.it. ✆ **0577-284-381.** Reservations recommended. Main courses 20€–24€. MC, V. Wed–Mon noon–2:30pm and 7–10:30pm. Closed 2 weeks Jan–Feb. Bus: A (green, yellow).

Grotta Santa Caterina da Bagoga ★★ SIENESE This tiny, brick-vaulted dining room in a quiet corner of the center is run by former Palio-winning jockey "Bagoga"—check out the race memorabilia hung on the walls. There's plenty of classic Southern Tuscan grills, but the kitchen is especially strong on stews, such as *coniglio alla Senese* (rabbit stewed on the bone with capers, tomatoes, and herbs), *peposo* (spicy beef stew), and even unusual dishes like *filetto alla birra scura* (beef in dark beer). There is a spectacular selection of desserts, and each is paired with an appropriate sweet wine, including *Panpepato* (sticky Sienese cake dusted with pepper) with *vinpepato* (fortified chianti with herbs and spices). The romantically inclined should book ahead to secure one of four snug outdoor tables.

Via della Galluzza 26. www.bagoga.it. ✆ **0577-282-208.** Reservations recommended. Main courses 7€–15€. AE, MC, V. Tues–Sun 12:30–2:30pm and 7:30–10:30pm. Bus: A (pink).

La Chiacchera SIENESE This is a tiny joint with worn wooden tables, terra-cotta floors, and barrel ends embedded everywhere. Young couples come here to save money on the date (not only is it cheap, but there's no cover charge or service fee—though tips are greatly appreciated). A choice first course is the *pici boscaiola* (long strands of fat, hand-rolled pasta in tomato-and-mushroom sauce), though the *penne arrabbiata* (in piquant tomato sauce) goes pretty quickly, too. *Secondi* are simple peasant dishes such as *salsicce e fagioli.*

Costa di Sant'Antonio 4 (near San Domenico, off Via della Sapienza under the Albergo Bernini). ✆ **0577-280-631.** Reservations recommended. Main courses 7€–8€. MC, V. Daily noon–3pm and 7pm–midnight. Bus: A (red).

L'Osteria ★★ TUSCAN/GRILL The mission at this boisterous grill is straightforward: to turn out tasty cooking using local ingredients whenever possible. The menu is short and focused, emphasizing simple, ingredient-led dishes. *Primi* include the classic *pici cacio e pepe* (hand-rolled pasta with pecorino cheese and black pepper), but the grill is the star with flavor packed into seared beef, wild boar, *bistecca di vitello* (veal steak), and (our favorite) a succulent *tagliata* of the local Cinta Senese breed of pig. Pair any of the above with a simple side of *patate fritte* (fries) or garbanzo beans dressed with olive oil and you have yourself a Tuscan taste sensation.

Via de' Rossi 79–81. ✆ **0577-287-592.** Reservations highly recommended. Main courses 7.50€–18€. AE, MC, V. Mon–Sat 12:30–2:30pm and 7:30–10:30pm.

Shopping

Artisan crafts and food are the best buys in town. The most authentic Sienese ceramics feature only black, white, and—surprise—the reddish-brown Crayola color of "burnt sienna," or *terra di Siena*. **Ceramiche Artistiche Santa Caterina,** with showrooms at Via di Città 74–76 (✆ **0577-283-098**) and a workshop outside town at Via Mattioli 12 (✆ **0577-45-006**), sells high-quality ceramics, courtesy of Maestro Marcello Neri, who trained at Siena's premier art and ceramics institutions, and his son, Fabio. **Sator Print ★**, Via Stalloreggi 70 (www.satorprint.com; ✆ **0577-247-478**), sells hand-decorated prints and original art and calligraphy based on historic Sienese designs. Nothing inside is cheap, but you'll find an affordable, authentic gift or souvenir with little trouble.

At **Vetrate Artistiche Toscane,** Via della Galluzza 5 (www.glassisland.com; ✆ **0577-48-033;** closed Sat), everything from souvenir trinkets to photo frames and simple jewelry is handmade on the premises. Prices are reasonable.

The **Antica Drogheria Manganelli,** Via di Città 71–73 (✆ **0577-280-002**), is an upscale deli that has made its own *panforte* and soft *ricciarelli* almond cookies since the 19th century. Our favorite food stop is more proletarian, however: **Gino Cacino ★**, Piazza del Mercato 31 (www.ginocacinosiena.it; ✆ **0577-223-076;** closed Wed afternoon), sells all manner of fresh and preserved delights, and will even load you a sandwich with pecorino aged in olive oil, Tuscan salami, anchovies, or anything else you fancy from his top-quality deli counter.

Entertainment & Nightlife

If the sheer spectacle of an evening lounging in the Campo isn't enough, the **Enoteca Italiana** (p. 289) is the only state-sponsored wine bar in Italy, in vaults that were built for Cosimo de' Medici in 1560. Drink by the glass or buy one of 1,600 bottles on sale. **Enoteca I Terzi,** Via dei Termini 7 (www.enotecaiterzi.it; ✆ **0577-44-329**), is under the vaulted ceiling of a 12th-century tower, and sells fine wine by the glass. For something younger and more local, head down **Via Pantaneto ★** toward the university buildings. Names may change, but bars down here go on till late.

Where to Stay

For help finding a room, stop by the **Siena Hotels Promotion** booth on Piazza San Domenico (www.hotelsiena.com; ✆ **0577-288-084**), where for 1.50€ to 4€, depending on the category of hotel, they'll find you a room and reserve it. The booth is open Monday through Saturday from 9am to 7pm (until 8pm in summer). The city **tourist office** (p. 282) also books accommodations.

Aia Mattonata ★★ 🎁 This tiny, tranquil boutique inn, crafted from an old stone farmhouse renovated in 2009, is enveloped by the gently rolling Tuscan hills just a 10-minute ride from central Siena. Both the midsize guest rooms and the classy common areas (where you'll find an honesty snack bar) remain true to their Tuscan roots, but have an added touch of rustic refinement. Two rooms have romantic *baldacchino* (canopy) beds, but the smallest (not by much) shares with the garden a sublime view toward the Torre del Mangia and Siena's ochre rooftops.

Strada del Ceraiolo 1, 53100 Siena. www.aiamattonata.it. ✆ **0577-592-677.** Fax 0577-392-073. 6 units. 155€–240€ double. Rates include breakfast. AE, MC, V. Free parking. Closed Nov–Feb. Bus: 31. From Siena Ovest junction, head toward Roccastrada, then after 1km/½ mile follow SS46 left toward Casciano di Murlo; after 2km/1¼ miles Strada del Ceraiolo is on left. No children 11 and under. **Amenities:** Bar; bikes (free); concierge; exercise room; outdoor pool; room service; smoke-free rooms; small spa. *In room:* A/C, TV, hair dryer, Wi-Fi (free).

Antica Residenza Cicogna ★★ This friendly, family-run B&B has established itself as one of the most desirable pads in the center of town—and you'll need to book ahead in peak season to secure one of the handful of rooms. Units are compact, but the place is dripping with character, and its location (a 5-min. walk from the Campo) could hardly be better. Among the neat doubles, all of which come with textured wallpaper and carefully matched fabrics, our favorite is "Liberty," which comes with slightly more space (including for an extra bed if necessary) and a *baldacchino* (canopy) bed.

Via dei Termini 67, 53100 Siena. www.anticaresidenzacicogna.com. ✆ **0577-285-613.** 7 units. 80€–100€ double; 110€–150€ suite. Rates include buffet breakfast. MC, V. Garage parking 18€. **Amenities:** Smoke-free rooms. *In room:* A/C, TV, hair dryer, Wi-Fi (free).

Palazzo Ravizza ★ The Santi-Ravizza family has run this hotel in a 17th-century Renaissance *palazzo* since the 1920s. The rooms tend to be large, with high ceilings—some gorgeously frescoed, a few with painted details around the wood beams. Those on the front catch some traffic noise, but on the back you'll hear only birdsong and the splashing fountain in the garden with sublime countryside vistas. The Ravizza is just outside the center of Siena, but still inside the city walls, offering a good Sienese neighborhood experience away from the tourist bustle.

Pian dei Mantellini 34 (near Piazza San Marco), 53100 Siena. www.palazzoravizza.it. ✆ **0577-280-462.** Fax 0577-221-597. 35 units. 90€–150€ double. Rates include breakfast. AE, DC, MC, V. Free parking. Closed early Jan to early Feb. Bus: A (green, yellow). **Amenities:** Bar; babysitting; concierge; room service; smoke-free rooms; Wi-Fi (free). *In room:* A/C, TV, hair dryer, minibar.

Santa Caterina ★ You'll find some of the friendliest hoteliers in Siena here, and they've been slowly reinvesting in the place. The character-filled rooms have tile floors (antique terra-cotta flooring in some), soft beds, and chunky furniture made of old wood. Ask for a room with a view down a verdant, unspoiled valley south of Siena. In summer you can breakfast in the pretty little garden; a glassed-in breakfast veranda is used for winter dining.

Via Enea Silvio Piccolomini 7 (just outside the Porta Romana), 53100 Siena. www.hscsiena.it. ✆ **0577-221-105.** Fax 0577-271-087. 22 units. 85€–195€ double. Rates include buffet breakfast. AE, DC, MC, V. Free parking along street or 10€–15€ in rear lot. Bus: A (pink) or 2. **Amenities:** Babysitting; bikes; concierge; smoke-free rooms. *In room:* A/C, TV, hair dryer, minibar, Wi-Fi (free).

Santuario S. Caterina/Alma Domus ☺ Terraced into the hill below San Domenico church in a relatively untouristy part of Siena, this simple, cheap hotel is run by the nuns of St. Catherine, so there's a certain monastic quality—but also a kindly hospitality and meditative calm. Many of the midsize rooms have tiny balconies with great views of the Duomo. The furnishings are a mix of modular and old-fashioned, with a few wrought-iron bed frames (but soft mattresses), giving some rooms a slightly institutional feel—units modernized in 2011 are of a higher standard.

Via Camporegio 37 (the steep street down off Piazza San Domenico), 53100 Siena. www.hotelalmadomus.it. ✆ **0577-44-177.** Fax 0577-47-601. 28 units. 65€–75€ double; 80€–95€ triple; 95€–110€ quad. Rates include breakfast. MC, V. Bus: A (red). **Amenities:** Smoke-free rooms. *In room:* A/C, TV (some), hair dryer on request, Wi-Fi (8€ per 6 hr.).

SAN GIMIGNANO ★★

42km (26 miles) NW of Siena, 52km (32 miles) SW of Florence

The scene that hits you when you pass through the Porta San Giovanni gate, inside the walls of **San Gimignano,** and walk the narrow flagstone Via San Giovanni is thoroughly medieval. The center is peppered with the tall towers that have made this "city of the beautiful towers" the poster child for Italian hill towns everywhere. There were at one time around 70 of the things spiking the sky above this little village, although only a dozen or so remain. The spires started rising in the bad old days of the 1200s, partly to defend against outside invaders but mostly as command centers for San Gimignano's warring families. Several successive waves of the plague that swept through (1348, 1464, and 1631 were especially bad) caused an economy based on textiles and hosting passing pilgrims to crumble, and San Gimignano became a provincial backwater. By the time tourism began picking up in the 19th century, visitors found a preserved medieval village of decaying towers.

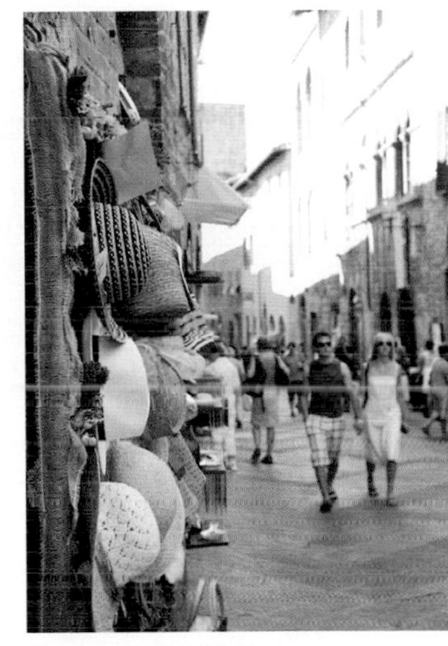

Shopping in San Gimignano.

San Gimignano is by far the most popular Tuscan hill town, a day-trip destination for masses of tour buses coming from Siena and Florence. Therefore, the town is best enjoyed in the evening, after the tour buses leave, especially in the off season and on spring nights: The alleyways are empty, and you can wander in the yellow light of street lamps.

Essentials

GETTING THERE The approximately 30 daily **trains** on the line between **Siena** (trip time: 25–40 min.) and Empoli, where you can connect from **Florence** (1 hr.), stop at Poggibonsi. From **Poggibonsi,** over 30 buses make the 25-minute run to San Gimignano Monday through Saturday, but only six buses run on Sunday.

SITA (www.sitabus.it; ✆ **055-47-821**) and TRA-IN (www.trainspa.it; ✆ **0577-204-111**) codeshare hourly (at least, fewer on Sun) **buses** for most of the day from both **Florence** (50 min.) and **Siena** (45 min.) to Poggibonsi, many of which meet right up with the connection to San Gimignano (a further 20–25 min.). From **Siena** there are also 10 direct buses (1¼ hr.) Monday through Saturday.

Arriving by **car,** take the Poggibonsi Nord exit off the **Florence-Siena** highway or the SS2. San Gimignano is 12km (7½ miles) from Poggibonsi.

VISITOR INFORMATION The **tourist office** is at Piazza Duomo 1 (www.sangimignano.com; ✆ **0577-940-008**). It's open daily March through October from 9am to 1pm and 3 to 7pm, and November through February from 9am to 1pm and 2 to 6pm.

Exploring San Gimignano

Anchoring the town, at the top of Via San Giovanni, are its two interlocking triangular *piazze:* **Piazza della Cisterna ★★**, centered on a 1237 well, and **Piazza del Duomo,** flanked by the city's main church and civic palace. The town also has some fascinating outdoor frescoes that you can view for free. The archway to the left of the Collegiata's facade leads to a pretty brick courtyard called Piazza Pecori. On the right, under brick vaulting, is a fresco of the *Annunciation* painted in 1482 by either Domenico Ghirlandaio or his brother-in-law and pupil, Sebastiano Mainardi. The door to the right of the tourist office leads into a courtyard of the Palazzo del Comune, where Taddeo di Bartolo's 14th-century *Madonna and Child* is flanked by two works on the theme of justice by Sodoma, including his near-monochrome *St. Ivo.*

Collegiata ★★ CHURCH The main church in town—it no longer has a bishop, so it's no longer officially a *duomo* (cathedral)—was started in the 11th century and took its present form in the 15th century. It's not much from the outside, but the interior is smothered in 14th-century frescoes, making it one of Tuscany's most densely decorated churches.

The right wall was frescoed from 1333 to 1341—most likely by Lippo Memmi—with three levels of **New Testament scenes** (22 in all) on the life and Passion of Christ along with a magnificent *Crucifixion.* In 1367, Bartolo di Fredi frescoed the left wall with 26 scenes out of the **Old Testament,** and Taddeo di Bartolo provided the gruesome ***Last Judgment*** frescoes around the main door in 1410.

In 1468, Giuliano da Maiano built the **Cappella di Santa Fina ★★** off the right aisle, and his brother Benedetto carved the relief panels for the altar. Florentine Renaissance master Domenico Ghirlandaio decorated the tiny chapel's walls with some of his finest, airiest works: In 1475 he frescoed two scenes summing up the life of Santa Fina, a local girl who, though never officially canonized, is one of San Gimignano's patron saints. Little Fina, who was very devout and wracked with guilt for having committed the sin of accepting an orange from a boy, fell down ill on a board one day and didn't move for 5 years, praying the entire time. Eventually, St. Gregory appeared to her and foretold her death, whereupon the board on which she lay miraculously produced flowers. The town still celebrates their child saint every year on March 12.

A Great Point of View

Behind the Collegiata, the remains of the city's 14th-century fortress, the **Rocca,** are now a public park. Climb atop the crumbling ramparts for a view of the surrounding farmland and the best panorama of San Gimignano's towers. There's also a little **Museo del Vino** (✆ **0577-941-267**) inside, where you can taste Tuscany's only DOCG white wine, Vernaccia di San Gimignano (3.50€–5€ a glass).

Piazza del Duomo. ✆ **0577-940-316.** Admission 3.50€ adults, 1.50€ ages 6–18. Nov–Mar Mon–Sat 10am–4:40pm, Sun 12:30–4:40pm; Apr–Oct Mon–Fri 10am–7:10pm, Sat 10am–5:10pm, Sun 12:30–7:10pm. Closed 1st Sun in Aug, Mar 12, Nov 16–30, and Jan 16–31.

Museo Civico & Torre Grossa ★★ ART MUSEUM In the late 13th century, the city government moved from the Palazzo del Podestà, across from the Collegiata, to the brand new **Palazzo del Comune** (or del Popolo). You can climb its **Torre Grossa (Big Tower) ★★**, finished in 1311, for one of the best tower-top views of the cityscape and rolling countryside in Tuscany.

The small museum was built around a large fresco in the Sala del Consiglio of the ***Maestà*** **★★** (1317) by the Sienese Lippo Memmi. Up the stairs is the **Pinacoteca (Civic Painting Gallery),** but before entering it, duck through the

Two of San Gimignano's towers.

door to the Camera del Podestà to see perhaps San Gimignano's most famous **frescoes** ★. Painted in the 14th century by Memmo di Filippuccio, they narrate a rather racy story of courtship and love in quite a departure from the usual religious themes of the era.

The first major work in a painting gallery that's especially strong on pre-Renaissance works is a Coppo di Marcovaldo Crucifix, immediately on the right, surrounded by Passion scenes, one of the masterpieces of 13th-century Tuscan art. Benozzo Gozzoli's *Madonna and Child with Saints* (1466) has an almost surreal *Pietà* with a delicate landscape running the length of the predella. A 25-year-old Filippino Lippi painted the matching tondi of the *Annunciation* in 1482, and the huge early-16th-century *Madonna in Glory with Sts. Gregory and Benedict,* with its wild Umbrian landscape, is a late work by Pinturicchio.

Two works in the rooms to the right tell the stories of the city's most popular patron saints. Lorenzo di Niccolò Gerini did a passable job in 1402 on the *Tabernacle of Santa Fina,* built to house the teen saint's head and painted with scenes of the four most important miracles of her brief life. In the late 14th century, Taddeo di Bartolo painted the *Life of St. Gimignano* as an altarpiece for the Collegiata; the saint himself sits in the middle, holding in his lap the town he was constantly invoked to protect.

Piazza del Duomo. ✆ **0577-990-312.** Admission 5€ adults, 4€ ages 6–18 and 65 and over. Apr–Sept daily 9:30am–7pm; Oct–Mar daily 10am–5:30pm.

Museo della Tortura (Torture Museum) ☺ MUSEUM The Torture Museum (the original one in town, not to be mistaken with poorer imitations) is serendipitously installed in the medieval **Torre del Diavolo (Devil's Tower).** Its iron maidens, racks—both the spiked and unspiked varieties—chastity belts, various bone-crunching manacles, breast-rippers, and other medieval party favors are accompanied by engrossingly dispassionate descriptions of their uses and history. If nothing else, older kids might think it's cool (though the historical etchings and watercolors showing the torture instruments at work are potentially upsetting).

Via del Castello 1 (just off Piazza della Cisterna). ✆ **0577-942-243.** Admission 8€ adults, 5.50€ students. Mar daily 10am–5pm; Apr–Oct daily 10am–7pm; Nov–Feb Mon–Fri 10:30am–4:30pm, Sat–Sun 10am–6pm.

San Gimignano 1300 ★ ☺ MUSEUM It took a team of five skilled craftsmen (two named Michelangelo and Raffaello, honestly) 3 years and a ton of clay to build the 800 structures that make up this 1:100 scale model of San Gimignano around 1300, with its 72 towers intact. It's not just a child-size model of this enchanting place; serious historical archive research by the universities at Florence and Pisa contributed to what is a unique reproduction of a medieval walled town, by digging up details of buildings long lost to history. Make sure to stick around long enough until an "artificial night" falls over the model, too.

Via Berignano 23. www.sangimignano1300.com. ✆ **0577-941-078.** Admission 5€ adults, 3€ children. June–Aug daily 8am–11pm; Sept–May daily 8am–8pm.

Sant'Agostino ★ CHURCH This 13th-century church at the north end of town is full of accomplished 15th-century frescoes. In 1464, a plague swept the town and the citizens prayed to their patron saint to end it. When the sickness passed, they dutifully hired Benozzo Gozzoli to paint a thankful scene, on the nave's left wall, showing St. Sebastian and his cloak full of angels stopping and breaking the plague arrows being thrown down by a vengeful God and his angelic hosts. The city liked the results, so they commissioned Gozzoli to spend the next 2 years frescoing the choir behind the main altar floor-to-ceiling with scenes rich in architectural detail from the ***Life of St. Augustine*** ★★.

Piazza Sant'Agostino. ✆ **0577-907-012.** Free admission. Daily 7am–noon and 3–7pm (Nov–Apr closes at 6pm, and Jan to mid-Apr closed Mon mornings).

Where to Eat & Stay

Few of San Gimignano's restaurants are outstanding, but its white wine certainly is. **Vernaccia di San Gimignano,** the only DOCG white wine in Tuscany, is a slightly peppery, dry wine old enough to have been cited in Dante's *Divine Comedy.* Our favorite place to sip a glass or two is on the couple of panoramic tables at **diVinorum** ★, Via degli Innocenti 5 (www.divinorumwinebar.com; ✆ **0577-907-192**). There are over 20 wines by the glass, and *bruschettone* (large bruschetta) to accompany them cost around 8€. The town's essential foodie stop is **Gelateria di Piazza** ★★, Piazza della Cisterna 4 (✆ **0577-942-244**), for creative combinations like raspberry and rosemary (it works) and the signature *crema di Santa Fina,* made with saffron.

Hotels here aren't cheap, nor are they by any measure the finest lodgings in Italy. However, there is a special ambience about the center of San Gimignano at dusk, when the tour groups are gone, so below we recommend our favorites in the town itself. If you prefer to find a farmhouse bed-and-breakfast or *agriturismo* nearby, of which there are dozens, the San Gimignano tourist office (see above) has an extensive selection and can book on your behalf.

Chiribiri ☺ ITALIAN This cramped, eight-table trattoria in a tiny cellar at the southern tip of town is an oasis of value among some distinctly overpriced competition. The food is straight-up Italian classics with a Tuscan twist: lasagna or spaghetti with a choice of sauces to start; beef in chianti, *cinghiale in umido* (wild boar stew), and *osso buco* are among the well-executed mains. Handily for families, it's also open all day, so kids can eat when they want.

Piazzetta della Madonna 1. ✆ **0577-941-948.** Reservations recommended. Main courses 8€–12€. No credit cards. Daily 11am–11pm.

Dorandò ★★ TUSCAN Dorandò is an elegant splurge tucked away just off Piazza Duomo, where the stone-walled rooms, alabaster platters, and knowledgeable waiters create a backdrop for San Gimignano's best fine dining. The chef attempts to keep the oldest traditions of Sangimignanese cooking alive—many of the recipes purport to be medieval, some even Etruscan, in origin—while balancing Slow Food philosophy with hearty home-cooking quality. The menu varies with the season and market, but if the excellent *cibrèo* (chicken livers and giblets scented with ginger and lemon) is offered, by all means order it. Desserts are excellent, too. Vicolo dell'Oro 2. www.ristorantedorando.it. ✆ **0577-941-862.** Reservations highly recommended. Main courses 20€–24€; tasting menu 50€. AE, MC, V. Tues–Sun noon–2:30pm and 7–9:30pm (daily Easter–Sept). Closed Dec 10–Jan 31.

L'Antico Pozzo ★ L'Antico Pozzo is the choicest inn within the walls, a 15th-century *palazzo* converted to a hotel in 1990 with careful attention to preserving the structural antiquity without sacrificing convenience. Over the building's colorful history it has hosted Dante, the Inquisition trials, a religious community, and an 18th-century salon. Accommodations vary in size and decor, but none is small, and the large junior suites have wood ceilings and spumante waiting for you. "Superior" doubles have 17th-century ceiling frescoes and the smaller "standard" rooms on the third floor have wood floors and a view of the Rocca and a few towers. Via San Matteo 87, 53037 San Gimignano. www.anticopozzo.com. ✆ **0577-942-014.** Fax 0577-942-117. 18 units. 110€–140€ double; 165€–180€ superior double. Rates include breakfast. DC, MC, V. Garage parking 20€. Closed for 20 days Jan–Feb. **Amenities:** Bar; babysitting; bikes; concierge; smoke-free rooms. *In room:* A/C, TV, hair dryer, minibar, Wi-Fi (1 hr. daily free).

Leon Bianco ★ Typical of a 500-year-old building turned hotel, the rooms here can't seem to agree on a style or decor scheme, but most retain some element from the 14th-century *palazzo*—a painted wood-beam ceiling here, an old stone wall in a bathroom there, or a brick barrel vault filling one room. Accommodations overlook the pretty well of the tower-lined piazza out front or across rooftops to the countryside. (A few, however, overlook the partially glassed-in courtyard of the lobby.) "Superior" rooms are larger and come with minibars. Piazza della Cisterna, 53037 San Gimignano. www.leonbianco.com. ✆ **0577-941-294.** Fax 0577-942-123. 26 units. 85€–118€ standard double; 115€–138€ superior double. Rates include breakfast. AE, DC, MC, V. Closed Nov 10 until just before Christmas and Jan 10 to early Feb. **Amenities:** Bar; concierge; exercise room; Jacuzzi; room service; smoke-free rooms. *In room:* A/C, TV, hair dryer, minibar, Wi-Fi (.50€ per hour).

VOLTERRA ★

29km (18 miles) SW of San Gimignano, 50km (31 miles) W of Siena, 72km (45 miles) SW of Florence, 300km (186 miles) NW of Rome

Volterra is, in the words of the writer D. H. Lawrence, "on a towering great bluff that gets all the winds and sees all the world." The city seems to rear higher than any other in Tuscany, rising a precipitous 540m (1,772 ft.) above the valley below. It's a fortresslike town, drawn out thinly along a narrow ridge with a warren of medieval alleys falling steeply off the main piazza.

Lawrence came here to study the Etruscans, who took the 9th-century-B.C. town established by the Villanovan culture and by the 4th century B.C. had turned it into Velathri, one of the largest centers in Etruria's 12-city confederation. The Etruscans left some haunting bronzes and a stupefying collection of alabaster

IN SEARCH OF craftsmanship

Volterrans have been working the watery, translucent calcium sulfate stone found around their mountain for almost 3,000 years. The Etruscans turned the **alabaster** into the sarcophagi that fill the Guarnacci museum; the industry revived in the late 19th century, mainly to crank out lampshades for the exploding market in electric lights. The working of alabaster is taken very seriously in town, and you can major in it at the local art school.

The *comune* has put Plexiglas plaques at the workshops of some of the best traditional artisans, who still handwork every stage. The large **Rossi Alabastri** (✆ **0588-86-133**) outfit works out of a shop at Piazzetta della Pescheria, at one end of the Roman theater panoramic walk. At **alab'Arte ★**, Via Orti S. Agostino 28 (www.alabarte.com; ✆ **0588-87-968**), you can roam the open sculptural workshop and buy any finished pieces that catch your eye. Via Porta all'Arco has several fine shops, including the town's top artiste, **Paolo Sabatini ★**, at no. 45 (✆ **0588-87-594**). For some of the better craft objects, the **Società Cooperativa Artieri Alabastro,** Piazza dei Priori 4–5 (✆ **0588-87-590**), has since 1895 been a cooperative showroom and sales outlet for artisans who don't have big enough operations to open their own.

The town's rep for workmanship goes beyond alabaster, too. **Fabula Etrusca,** Via Lunga le Mura del Mandorlo 10 (www.fabulaetrusca.it; ✆ **0588-87-401**), sells exquisite (but expensive) handcrafted jewelry, much of it made to Etruscan-influenced designs. Prints and lithographs created from hand-engraved zinc plates are another specialty. Our two favorite workshops, where everything is created on-site, are **L'Istrice ★**, Via Porta all'Arco 23 (www.laboistrice.it; ✆ **0588-85-422**), and **Bubo Bubo ★**, Via Roma 24 (✆ **0588-80-307**).

funerary urns. The art of carving the translucent white alabaster still flourishes today in artisan workshops scattered throughout the city, but modern Volterra has only recently moved beyond the shrunken womb of its medieval inner circle of walls to fill in the abandoned extent of Velathri's 4th-century B.C. defensive belt. These days it's as likely to be known as the fictional home of the Volturi, from Stephanie Meyer's teen vampire trilogy, *Twilight.*

Essentials

GETTING THERE Driving by **car** is comfortably the simplest option for getting there: Volterra is on the SS68 about 30km (19 miles) from where it branches off the Colle di Val d'Elsa exit on the Florence-Siena highway. From San Gimignano, head southwest on the secondary road to Castel di San Gimignano, which is on the SS68.

From **Siena,** there are 16 daily TRA-IN **buses** (www.trainspa.it) that make the 20- to 30-minute trip to **Colle di Val d'Elsa,** from which there are four daily buses to Volterra (50 min.). From **San Gimignano,** you have to first take a bus to Poggibonsi (20 min.), four of which daily link up with buses to Colle di Val d'Elsa for the final transfer. From **Florence,** take one of five daily buses (three on Sun) to Colle di Val d'Elsa and transfer there (2½–3 hr. total). Six to 10 **CPT** (www.cpt.pisa.it) buses run there Monday through Saturday from **Pisa** (change in Pontedera; 2–2½ hr. total).

VISITOR INFORMATION Volterra's helpful **tourist office,** Piazza dei Priori 19–20, 56048 Volterra (www.volterratur.it; ✆ **0588-87-257**), offers both tourist information and free hotel reservations. It's open daily from 9:30am to 1pm and 2 to 6pm.

Exploring Volterra

One **cumulative admission ticket** covers all three major museums—the Museo Etrusco Guarnacci, Museo Diocesano d'Arte Sacra, and Pinacoteca e Museo Civico. It costs 10€ adults, 6€ students and seniors 60 and over, 20€ family of five (children 5 and under are admitted free). All museums' summer hours run March 16 through November 1.

Baptistery CHURCH The baptistery drum, with its one side of distinctive black-and-white marble bands, was built in 1283, but the dome was added in the 16th century. Just inside the door is an Etruscan funerary urn recycled as a holy water stoup, and in the center is an 18th-century font. This polychrome affair replaced the smaller, more elegant **marble font** Andrea Sansovino carved with simple reliefs in 1502, now against the right wall.

Piazza San Giovanni. No phone. Free admission. Summer daily 7am–7pm; winter daily 8am–12:30pm and 3–6pm.

Duomo ★ CATHEDRAL Beyond the 13th-century Pisan-style facade, the first thing that strikes you in this 12th-century church is its coffered **ceiling.** It was carved and embossed with gold and azure in 1580 and is filled with portraits of Volterran saints, including St. Linus, a venerable native son who became the second pope, filling St. Peter's shoes in A.D. 67.

In the right transept is a life-size sculpted wood group of the ***Deposition*** **★**, painted in bright primaries and heavy gold. It looks vaguely mid-20th-century but was actually carved around 1228 by anonymous Pisan masters, artists who were bridging the gap between stiff Byzantine traditions and the more fluid, emotional art of the Romanesque era. In the left aisle of the church is a **pulpit** assembled from 13th-century Pisan relief panels in the 16th century; the *Last Supper* facing the nave is particularly arresting for its visual style and whimsical detail. Next up the left aisle is a magnificently restored 1497 ***Annunciation*** **★** by Fra' Bartolomeo.

In the **Cappella dell'Addolorata (Lady Chapel) ★**, off the end of the left aisle, in the niche housing the *Nativity* terra-cottas, Benozzo Gozzoli frescoed an intimate backdrop for the scene, placing it in a rocky pass bursting with foliage and the horse train of the Magi riding in from the distance.

Piazza San Giovanni. No phone. Free admission. Summer daily 8am–12:30pm and 3–6pm; winter daily 8am–12:30pm and 3–5pm.

Museo Diocesano d'Arte Sacra ART MUSEUM The medieval and early Renaissance fragments salvaged from an older version of the cathedral and other Volterran churches, along with a few good paintings, make this small museum a good half-hour bonus if you've bought the town's cumulative admission ticket (see above). Among the sculptural pieces are some works by Tino di Camaino and Romanesque elements fitted with Roman friezes. Of the paintings, keep an eye out for Rosso Fiorentino's Mannerist *Madonna of Villamagna* (1521) and a *Madonna of Ulignano* (1545) by Daniele "da Volterra" Ricciarelli.

Palazzo Vescovile, Via Roma 13. ✆ **0588-86-290.** Admission by cumulative ticket. Daily 9am–1pm (summer also 3–6pm).

A Cappuccino, a Gelato & a Glass of Wine

Right on the main square, with a few tables outside, sits the very friendly little **Bar Priori,** Piazza Priori 2 (no phone), our regular coffee-break stop. There's nowhere better than **L'Incontro** ★, Via Matteoti 18 (✆ **0588-80-500**), for a gelato or relaxed pit stop, with home-made pastries. Their artisan chocolate is also pretty good. Our favorite enoteca in town is grottolike **La Vena di Vino,** Via Don Minzoni 30 (www.lavenadivino.com; ✆ **0588-81-491**), which has an especially good range of reds plus cheese platters to accompany them. Glasses range from 2€ to 6€.

Museo Etrusco Guarnacci ★★ MUSEUM Volterra has managed to hold on to a horde of valuable remains from its rich past: Presentation at this museum is a little dry, but this is without doubt one of the world's leading Etruscan collections. Besides the prehistoric section with its Villanovan tombs and some Roman busts and mosaic floors, the lion's share of this three-floor museum is taken up with more than 600 **Etruscan funerary urns** ★. Most of these date from the 3rd century B.C., but there are some entire tomb finds gathered from as early as the 9th century B.C. The effect of room after room lined with these intricate studies on the Etruscans' views of life and death is fascinating. One of the finest, the **Urna degli Sposi** ★ is a striking bit of portraiture: an early-1st-century-B.C. sarcophagus lid carved with the figures of a husband and wife, both very old, somewhat dour-faced and full of wrinkles, but staying together even in death.

Also here, among the bronzes, is an early-3rd-century-B.C. votive figure of an exceedingly elongated young boy known as the ***Ombra della Sera (Shadow of the Evening)*** ★★.

Via Don Minzoni 15. ✆ **0588-86-347.** Admission by cumulative ticket, or 8€. Summer daily 9am–7pm, winter daily 8:30am–1:45pm.

Palazzo dei Priori PALACE The Palazzo dei Priori (1208–57) is the oldest building of its kind in Tuscany, the Gothic town hall on which Florence's Palazzo Vecchio and many other civic buildings in the region were modeled. Walk up to the first floor to see the town council chamber, which aside from getting a new vaulted ceiling in 1516 has pretty much looked the same over its 740 years of continuous use. The end wall was frescoed with an *Annunciation* by Jacopo di Cione or his brother Orcagna in 1383.

Volterra's civic palace sits on a medieval rectangle of a piazza. The **Piazza dei Priori** ★ is laid with mason-cut stone and surrounded on all sides with 13th- and 14th-century buildings, some crenellated, some with Gothic two-light windows, and some just implacably old and stony. It's particularly evocative under the moonlight. Across from the Palazzo dei Priori is the **Palazzo Pretorio,** sprouting the rough old **Torre del Porcellino**—a tower named after the weather-beaten little sculpted boar jutting out near the top window.

Piazza dei Priori. ✆ **0588-86-050.** Admission 1.50€. Mid-Mar to Oct daily 10:30am–5:30pm; Nov to mid-Mar Sat–Sun 10am–5pm.

Pinacoteca e Museo Civico ★ ART MUSEUM Volterra's worthy painting gallery contains some pick-of-the-litter works by artists working in Volterra between the 12th and 17th centuries, as well as a coin collection stretching back to the 7th century. Room 4 has a remarkably intact polyptych of the ***Madonna with Saints*** ★ (1411), complete with pinnacles, predella, and all, signed by Taddeo di Bartolo; the guy in the red cape and beard in the tiny left tondo is Santa Claus (that is, St. Nicholas of Bari). In Room 11 is a *Christ in Glory with Saints* (1492), the last great work from the brush of Florentine Domenico Ghirlandaio. The figures create a perfectly oval architectural frame for the Flemish-inspired landscape detailing of the background—if you look hard, you can spot a giraffe, recently acquired by the Medici for their menagerie, being led along the road.

Room 12 pulls out all the stops and hits you with two large 1491 Luca Signorelli paintings, including a remarkably colored ***Annunciation*** ★, and an early masterpiece by Rosso Fiorentino, who painted the ***Deposition*** ★★★ here (1521). The late Renaissance instruction of his teacher Andrea del Sarto shows through in the young artist's work, as do the influences of other contemporary masters, like Filippino Lippi, from whom Rosso lifted the basic composition, and Michelangelo, from whom he copied the pose of the mourning St. John on the right. (It's Eve expelled from the garden on the Sistine Chapel ceiling.) Try to picture it hanging amid the bright Cenni frescoes in San Francesco church, where it originally sat atop the altar.

Via dei Sarti 1. ✆ **0588-87-580.** Admission by cumulative ticket, or 6€ adults, 4€ students and seniors 60 and over. Summer daily 9am–7pm; winter daily 8:30am–1:45pm.

Porta all'Arco ★ ARCHITECTURE At the end of Via Porta all'Arco stands the main gateway to Etruscan Volterra, a huge arch of a gate that has survived since the 4th century B.C.—with a bit of Roman-era rebuilding in the 1st century B.C. On the outside of the arch are mounted three basalt heads—worn by well over 2,000 years of wind and rain to featurelessness—said to represent the Etruscan gods Tinia (Jupiter), Uni (Juno), and Menrva (Minerva). In 1944, just before intense fighting began against the Germans laying siege to the city, Volterran partisans saved the gate from destruction by filling it overnight with stones—both for structural support and to keep it from being a focus of attack.

No phone. Free admission.

San Francesco CHURCH Just inside the 14th-century Porta San Francesco, Volterra's 13th-century Franciscan church has one overwhelming reason to visit: Halfway up the right aisle is the **Cappella Croce del Giorno** ★★, frescoed with the *Legend of the True Cross* in medieval Technicolor by Cenni di Francesco. (The light switch is outside the chapel entrance.) Cenni painted this story in 1410, creating an unmatched example of early-15th-century narrative art. His vivid and unusual color palette, eye for detail, and painterly tailoring have also left us a valuable record of the dress and architecture of his era.

Piazza San Francesco (off Via San Lino). No phone. Free admission. Daily 8:30am–6:30pm.

Teatro Romano (Roman Theater & Baths) RUINS A left turn off Via Guarnacci as you head steeply down toward Porta Fiorentina takes you to a walkway atop the medieval ramparts overlooking the impressive remains of Volterra's Roman theater and baths. These are some of the best-preserved Roman remains in Tuscany, dating back to the 1st century B.C. The view from up here is the best way to see it all, but there's an entrance down on Viale Francesco Ferrucci if you want to wander among the stones.

Viale Francesco Ferrucci. ✆ **0588-86-050.** Admission 3.50€ adults, 2.50€ students. Summer daily 10:30am–5:30pm; winter Sat–Sun 10am–4pm.

Where to Eat & Stay

A budget alternative to our favorite places to stay, listed below, is the **Foresteria Volterra,** Borgo San Lazzero (www.foresteriavolterra.it; ✆ **0588-80-050**), in a quiet wood about 1km (⅔ mile) east of the center. Rooms are slightly institutional, but spotless, cheery, and well-equipped, and come in all configurations from single up to quad. A double room costs between 62€ and 82€ depending on the season.

As for dining, tiny **Bada Ganzo,** Via dei Marchesi 13 (✆ **0588-80-508**), offers a contemporary take on Volterran cuisine. *Primi* such as ravioli with *pecorino Volterrano e noci* (local sheep's milk cheese and hazelnuts) range from 7€ to 8.50€; *secondi* such as *pollo arrosto al vino e uvetta* (chicken roasted with wine and raisins) cost between 8€ and 12€.

Da Badò ★ TUSCAN The small and simple Badò is loved and respected by locals for its unwavering commitment to Volterran cuisine—though popularity and plaudits have pushed prices a couple of euros per dish beyond the norm. The thick-sliced prosciutto in the *antipasto* of local meat is gorgeously soft and salty (note, some cuts come with plenty of fat attached). There's a selection of delicious meat and *baccalà* (salt cod) dishes for the main, but Badò's specialty *secondo*, for those who can stomach tripe, is *trippa alla Volterrana*, stewed with tomatoes and herbs.

Borgo San Lazzero 9 (just east of the walls). www.trattoriadabado.com. ✆ **0588-86-477.** Reservations recommended. Main courses 13€–16€. MC, V. Thurs–Tues 12:30–2pm and 7–9:30pm. Closed Feb 10–28 and Nov 15–30.

Il Sacco Fiorentino TUSCAN This inventive establishment features a Tuscan menu with international touches while remaining a moderately priced and friendly neighborhood hangout. The traditional *pappardelle* (wide pasta) with wild boar and porcini *ragù* is excellent, as is the odd *tagliatelle con pollo, peperoni e curry,* pasta enveloped in curry-chicken sauce with fresh peppers. For a *secondo,* try *piccione al forno con radicchio e vin santo* (roast pigeon with bitter leaves and sweet wine).

Piazza XX Settembre 18. ✆ **0588-88-537.** Reservations recommended. Main courses 11€–16€. AE, DC, MC, V. Thurs–Tues noon–3pm and 7–10pm. Closed Jan.

Lo Sgherro ★ TUSCAN There's no ceremony at this neighborhood trattoria—just solid, regional cooking at prices that have gone out of fashion elsewhere in Tuscany—where your order is hollered through a hole in the wall to *mamma* in the kitchen. Pasta staples are all present—*lepre* (hare) and *cinghiale* (boar)—but the house special *penne allo sgherro* (with minced pork, mushrooms, and artichokes) tops them all. A long list of tasty *secondi* might include *coniglio alla Vernaccia con olive* (rabbit cooked in Vernaccia wine with olives). The dining room could use a lick of paint, and if you know Tuscan food there are few surprises, but you won't find a more authentic eating experience this close to the lair of the Volturi.

Borgo San Giusto 74 (a 10-min. downhill walk from Porta San Francesco). ✆ **0588-86-473.** Main courses 7.50€–17€. MC, V. Tues–Sun noon–2pm and 7–10pm.

Podere Marcampo ★★ This restored brick-and-stone *agriturismo,* opened in 2010, commands unmatched 360-degree views of Volterra, Le Balze, and the enveloping silence of the Valdicecina. After a 5-year conversion, the place has retained its traditional farmhouse feel, with terra-cotta flooring, exposed beams, and dark-wood fittings keeping the large, fully equipped apartments and hotel-style doubles firmly rooted in their Tuscan heritage. Of the rooms, La Ginestraia is our favorite, with a large bathroom and double shower.

The same family owners run the Ristorante Del Duca in Volterra, and can build half-board packages on request. Apartments must be booked by the week in summer, at a small discount on the daily rate.

Signposted by road, 1.5km (1 mile) northwest of Volterra. www.agriturismo-marcampo.com. ✆ **0588-85-393.** 6 units. 80€—118€ double; 105€–160€ apt. Rates include breakfast (rooms only). AE, MC, V. Free parking. **Amenities:** Outdoor pool; smoke-free rooms. *In room:* A/C, TV/ DVD, hair dryer, minibar, Wi-Fi (free).

San Lino ★ Volterra isn't blessed with a dazzling range of hotels within the historic center, but the San Lino is probably the best, a 13th-century *palazzo* 5 minutes' downhill walk from Piazza dei Priori that until 1978 was a cloistered convent. The standard rooms on the first floor, reserved mainly for students and groups, have functional furniture and subcompact bathrooms: It's well worth upgrading to a superior room on the second floor, for more space, more character, and the choice of a view of the large rear sun terrace with a small pool or the atmospheric street outside.

Via San Lino 26 (near Porta San Francesco), 56048 Volterra (Pisa). www.hotelsanlino.com. ✆ **0588-85-250.** Fax 0588-80-620. 44 units. 90€–105€ double; 110€–125€ triple; 125€–140€ quad. Rates include breakfast. AE, DC, MC, V. Garage parking 11€. Closed Dec–Feb. **Amenities:** Restaurant; bar; outdoor pool; smoke-free rooms. *In room:* A/C, TV, hair dryer, minibar, Wi-Fi (free).

LUCCA ★

72km (45 miles) W of Florence, 335km (208 miles) NW of Rome

Lucca is apparently the most civilized of Tuscany's small cities, a stately grid of Roman roads snug behind a mammoth belt of tree-topped battlements. It's home to Puccini and soft pastel plasters, an elegant landscape of churches and palaces, delicate facades, and Art Nouveau shop fronts. The sure lines of the churches here inspired John Ruskin to study architecture, and everyone from rebellious teens to fruit-shopping grandmothers tools around this town by bicycle.

Lucca's greatest cultural contribution has been musical. The city had a "singing school" as early as A.D. 787, and this crucible of musical prodigies gave the world Luigi Boccherini (1743–1805), the composer who revitalized chamber music in the 18th century with such compositions as his *Minuet no. 13,* and most famously the operatic genius Giacomo Puccini (1858–1924), whose *Tosca, Madame Butterfly, Turandot,* and *La Bohème* have become some of the world's favorite operas.

Essentials

GETTING THERE Lucca is on the Florence-Viareggio **train** line, with about 30 trains daily (fewer on Sun) connecting with **Florence** (trip time: 75–90 min.), **Pistoia** (40 min.–1 hr.), and **Montecatini Terme** (25–40 min.). A similar number of trains make the short hop to/from **Pisa** (30 min.). The **station** is a short walk south of Porta San Pietro.

By **car,** the A11 runs from Florence past Prato, Pistoia, and Montecatini before hitting Lucca. Inside the walls, you'll usually find a pay-parking space underground at **Mazzini** (enter from the east, through the Porta Elisa, and take an immediate right).

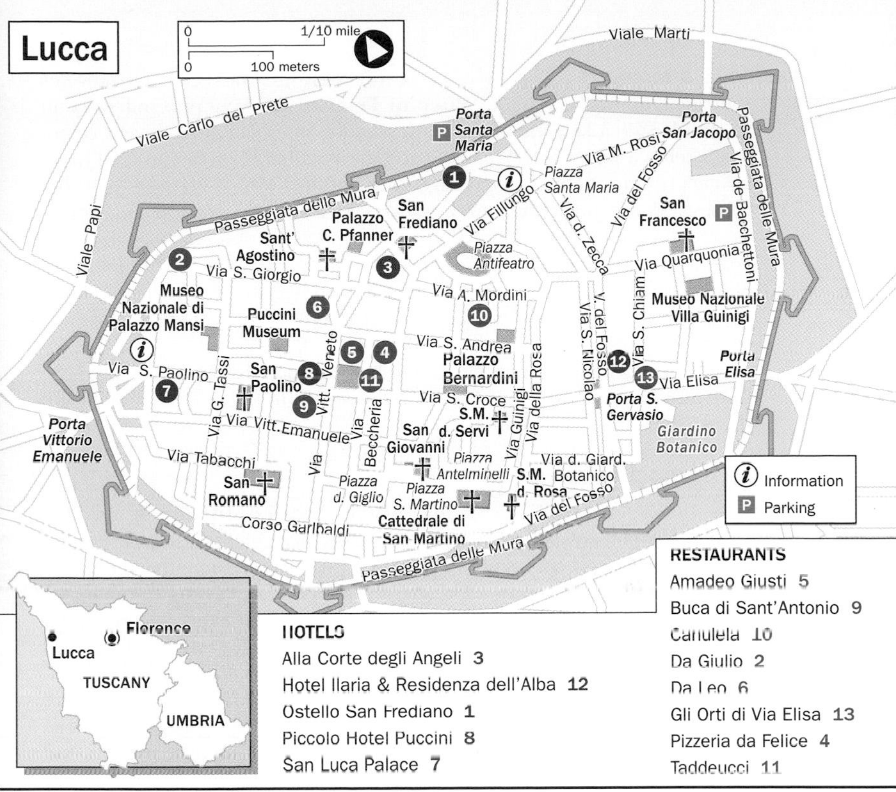

A **VaiBus** (www.vaibus.it) service runs hourly from Florence (70 min.) and from Pisa (50 min.) to Lucca's Piazzale Verdi.

GETTING AROUND A set of *navette* (electric **minibuses**) whiz down the city's peripheral streets, but the flat center is easily traversable on foot.

To really get around like a Lucchese, though, you need to **rent a bike.** You can try **Antonio Poli,** Piazza Santa Maria 42 (www.biciclettepoli.com; ✆ **0583-493-787;** daily 8:30am–7:30pm, closed Sun mid-Nov to Feb and Mon mornings year-round), and **Cicli Bizzarri,** next door at Piazza Santa Maria 32 (www.ciclibizzarri.net; ✆ **0583-496-031;** Mon–Sat 8:30am–1pm and 2:30–7:30pm, and same hours Sun Mar to mid-Sept). The going rates are 3€ an hour for a regular bike, 4€ to 4.50€ for a mountain bike, and 6.50€ for a tandem.

Taxis line up at the train station (✆ **0583-494-989**), Piazza Napoleone (✆ **0583-491-646**), and Piazzale Verdi (✆ **0583-581-305**).

VISITOR INFORMATION The main **tourist office** is inside the north side of the walls at Piazza Santa Maria 35, 55100 Lucca (www.luccaturismo.it; ✆ **0583-919-931;** daily 9am–7pm, sometimes later in summer). The *comune* also has a small **local info office** on Piazzale Verdi (✆ **0583-442-944**), which keeps similar hours.

For **events** and theater, pick up the English-language monthly ***Grapevine*** for 2€ at most newsstands.

FESTIVALS & MARKETS The shore of nearby Lago di Massaciuccoli provides the backdrop to the summer **Puccini Festival ★** (www.puccinifestival.it; ✆ **0584-359-322**), the biggest annual date in a local opera lover's calendar. There's a seasonal ticket office at Viale Puccini 257a, in Torre del Lago, or book tickets online. Prices range from 35€ to 125€. With every year that passes, Lucca's July **Summer Festival** (www.summer-festival.com) grows in size and profile. Recent headline acts to grace the outdoor stage in Piazza Napoleone have included Grammy winners Arcade Fire and Elton John. On September 13, an 8pm candlelit procession from San Frediano to the Duomo honors the **Volto Santo,** a statue of Christ that tradition holds was carved by Nicodemus himself.

A huge **antiques market,** one of Italy's most important, is held the third Sunday (and preceding Sat) of every month in Piazza Antelminelli and the streets around the Duomo.

Exploring Lucca

The most curious feature of Lucca's street plan is **Piazza Anfiteatro ★**, near the north end of Via Fillungo, where a series of houses were built during the Middle Ages into the remains of a 1st- or 2nd-century-A.D. Roman amphitheater, which had been used for centuries as a quarry for raw materials to raise the city's churches and palaces. The most resplendent of those churches is **San Frediano ★**, Piazza San Frediano (✆ **0583-493-627**), whose **facade** sports a glittering 13th-century mosaic two stories high. Berlinghiero Berlinghieri designed it in a Byzantine/medieval style and threw just enough color into the Apostles and ascending Christ to balance the tens of thousands of gold-leaf tiles for a truly eye-popping effect. The interior highlight is a Romanesque **baptismal font** in the right aisle from around the 12th century, dismantled and squirreled away in the 18th century and reassembled only a few decades ago. A Lombard sculptor gave us the stories of Moses on the large lower basin, and one Maestro Roberto signed the last two panels of the Good Shepherd and six prophets. The church is open Monday to Saturday 8:30am to noon and 3 to 5:30pm, Sunday 9 to 11:30am and 3 to 5:30pm.

Cattedrale di San Martino ★★ CATHEDRAL The **facade ★** of Lucca's Duomo is an eye-catching example of the Pisan–Lucchese Romanesque school of architecture. Long lines of baby columns—every variety imaginable—backed by discreet green-and-white Romanesque banding are stacked into three tiers of arcaded loggias. The 13th-century **reliefs under the portico ★★** are beautiful examples of medieval stonework, a few of them carved by Guido da Como. Around the central door are the months of the year and stories from the life of St. Martin of Tours.

Biking Lucca's city walls.

Detail from the mosaics at San Frediano in Lucca.

In the 14th- to 15th-century **interior,** talented local sculptor Matteo Civitali designed the **pavement** as well as the holy-water stoups and the **pulpit.** Halfway down the left aisle is Civitali's octagonal **Tempietto** (1482), built of white Carrara and red porphyry marble, with a St. Sebastian on the backside. It houses Lucca's most holy relic, the ***Volto Santo*** ★. This thick-featured, bug-eyed, time-blackened wooden statue of Jesus crucified was reputed to have been started by Nicodemus.

To access the area beyond the crossing, you must pay an admission fee (see below). On the right aisle just past a few steps is the entrance to the former sacristy, containing a 1479 altarpiece of the ***Madonna Enthroned with Saints*** by Domenico Ghirlandaio over a predella by his pupil Bartolomeo di Giovanni. The sacristy is also home to the Duomo's masterpiece, Jacopo della Quercia's **Tomb of Ilaria Carretto Guinigi** ★★. Married in 1403 to Paolo Guinigi and dead 2 years later at age 26, Ilaria had only been in the limelight for a brief moment. But her rich husband also happened to be the town boss, so she was guaranteed everlasting fame as the subject of Jacopo della Quercia's International Gothic masterpiece in marble.

Piazza San Martino. ✆ **0583-957-068.** Admission to church free; transepts and Ilaria tomb 2€ adults, 1.50€ children 6–14. Cumulative ticket for tomb, Museo, and San Giovanni 6€ adults, 4€ children 6–14. Mon–Fri 9:30am–5:45pm (closes 4:45pm Nov–Mar), Sat 9:30am–6:45pm, Sun 9:30–10:45am and noon–6pm.

Chiesa e Battistero di San Giovanni e Santa Reparata ★ CHURCH The Duomo's Romanesque neighbor has a 16th-century facade and a 12th-century body, but excavations have revealed the structure is actually five layers (and several more centuries) deep. It sits atop a much older Lombard church that served until the early 700s as Lucca's cathedral, which in turn was built atop a 5th-century-A.D. Paleo-Christian church and 6th-century cemetery, which took the place of a Roman temple built atop Roman houses (from which some mosaic fragments survive). In the 9th century, a crypt was added. In all, 12 centuries of

CIRCUMNAVIGATING LUCCA'S walls

The walls are Lucca's defining characteristic, and they make up a city park more than 4km (2½ miles) long but in parts only about 18m (59 ft.) wide, filled with avenues of plane, chestnut, and ilex trees planted by Marie Louise Bourbon in the 19th century. The shady, paved paths of Lucca's formidable bastions are busy year-round with couples walking hand in hand, tables of old men playing unfathomable card games, families strolling, children playing, and hundreds of people on bicycles, from tykes to octogenarians. **Rent a bike ★★** (see "Getting Around," above) and take a spin, peering across Lucca's rooftops and down into its palace gardens and narrow alleys, gazing toward the hazy mountains across the plane, and checking out the 11 bastions and six gates.

The defensive walls you see today—a complete kidney-shaped circuit built from 1544 to 1654—are Lucca's fourth and most impressive set and perhaps the best preserved in Italy. About 12m (39 ft.) high and 30m (98 ft.) wide at their base, the walls were never put to the test against an enemy army, though it turned out they made excellent dikes—there's no doubt they saved the city in 1812 when a massive flood of the Serchio River inundated the valley.

history jumble together in a confusing but interesting mélange beneath the pavement inside. You're free to wander a well-signed route in the church's bowels.

Piazza San Giovanni. ✆ **0583-490-530.** Admission 2.50€ adults, 1.50€ children 6–14. Cumulative ticket for Ilaria tomb, Museo, and San Giovanni 6€ adults, 4€ children 6–14. Apr—Oct daily 10am–6pm. Nov–Mar Mon–Fri 10am–2pm, Sat 10am–6pm, Sun 10am–5pm.

San Michele in Foro ★ CHURCH The exterior of this church is as beautiful as a 12th-century Romanesque church can get. It boasts a Pisan-inspired **facade ★★** of blind arches with lozenges and colonnaded arcades stacked even higher than San Martino's, and it's smack in the center of town—on top of the ancient Roman forum, in fact, hence the name. Past the marvelous facade, with its orderly rows of doggedly unique columns topped by a Romanesquely flattened St. Michael, however, the **interior** is a little disappointing. The church's best art hangs on the far wall of the right transept, a painting of ***Sts. Roch, Sebastian, Jerome, and Helen*** ★ by Filippino Lippi, whose figures are more humanly morose but every bit as graceful as those of his famous teacher Sandro Botticelli. As you leave, check out the **medieval graffiti drawings** scratched on the columns of the left aisle (especially the third and fourth from the door).

Piazza San Michele. ✆ **0583-48-459.** Free admission. Summer daily 7:40am–noon and 3–6pm; winter daily 9am–noon and 3–5pm.

Torre Guinigi ★ HISTORIC SITE Only one of the two towers sprouting from the top of the 14th-century palace, home of Lucca's iron-fisted ruling family, still stands, but it certainly grabs your attention. Historians tell us that many of Lucca's towers once had little gardens like this on top—the city was civilized even in its defenses—but that doesn't diminish the delight at your first glance at this stack of bricks 44m (144 ft.) high with a tiny forest of holm oaks overflowing the summit. For a closer look, climb the 230 steps for a spectacular **view ★★** of Lucca's skyline with the snowcapped Apuan Alps and the Garfagnana in the distance.

Via Sant'Andrea 14 (at Via Chiavi d'Oro). ✆ **347-627-0423.** Admission 3.50€ adults, 2.50€ children 6–12 and seniors 65 and over. Cumulative ticket with Torre delle Ore, on Via Fillungo, 5€ adults, 4€ children and seniors. Apr–May daily 9am–7:30pm; June–Sept daily 9am–6:30pm; Oct and Mar daily 9:30am–5:30pm; Nov–Feb daily 9:30am–4:30pm.

Where to Eat

Gastronomically, Lucca is famous for its extra-virgin olive oil, a light-green elixir that's drizzled on just about every dish in these parts. The most typically Luccan dish is the creamy, filling *zuppa di farro,* a soup made with spelt, an emmer- or barleylike grain cooked al dente. Accompany any dish with Lucca's excellent yet little-known DOC **wines,** Rosso delle Colline Lucchesi and Montecarlo. *Buccellato,* a dense, sweet bread flavored with raisins and fennel seeds, is equally in demand at bakery **Taddeucci,** Piazza San Michele 34 (www.taddeucci.com; ✆ **0583-494-933**).

Buca di Sant'Antonio ★ LUCCHESE Since before 1782, this has been the premier gastronomic pit stop inside Lucca's walls. The menu changes regularly, but expect exciting lineups like *sella di coniglio lardellata su radicchietti di campo* (a cold rabbit salad), followed by ravioli filled with ricotta and lightly sautéed in butter and zucchini, and then move to one of their signature dishes, *capretto allo spiedo con patate arrosto e sformato di carciofi* (tender spit-roasted kid with roast potatoes and artichoke pudding). Finish it off with a green apple sorbet and smile the rest of the day.

Via della Cervia 3 (a side alley just west of Piazza San Michele). ✆ **0583-55-881.** Reservations highly recommended. Main courses 15€. AE, DC, MC, V. Tues–Sat 12:30–3pm and 7:30–10:30pm; Sun 12:30–3pm.

Canuleia ★ MODERN ITALIAN This little restaurant may only carry the humble TRATTORIA sign above its door, but the kitchen can justly claim to be among Lucca's most creative. You will find traditional Lucchese items on the menu, but Canuleia's strength lies in taking the best of the Italian peninsula—and beyond—and combining it in creative ways. Start, perhaps, with *sformatino di pecorino con salsa di pere* (pecorino cheese soufflé with pear salsa), followed by a risotto *alla pernice* (with partridge) and *petto d'anatra salsa teriyaki* (duck breast with teriyaki sauce). The informal shaded garden is a delightful spot in warmer months.

Via Canuleia 14. www.ristorantecanuleia.it. ✆ **0583-467-470.** Reservations recommended. Main courses 12€–20€. AE, MC, V. Mon–Sat 12:30–2pm and 7:30–10pm.

Da Leo ★★ LUCCHESE/TUSCAN This authentic Lucchese dining spot run by the amiable Buralli family has the best value meals in the center—locals swear you can pay twice as much for inferior food at many of Lucca's other popular spots, and it has retained a devoted following. The food isn't fancy, but they execute traditional dishes well: *minestra di farro, ravioli alla crema di spinaci* (with spinach cream), *arrosto di maialino con patate* (roast piglet and potatoes), and the excellent *zuppa ai cinque ceriali* (a soup with emmer, red and green lentils, barley, and cannellini beans).

Via Tegrimi 1 (just north of Piazza San Salvatore). www.trattoriadaleo.it. ✆ **0583-492-236.** Reservations recommended. Main courses 9€–16€. No credit cards. Daily noon–2:30pm and 7:30–10:30pm.

NORTH OF THE CITY

Antica Locanda di Sesto ★★★ LUCCHESE There's been a roadside restaurant here serving the finest Lucchese dishes since the 1300s—and it's still going strong under family ownership. Local and seasonal specialties permeate the menu, which is delivered in a relaxed country dining room where friendly staff nevertheless preserve a welcome nod to old-fashioned restaurant formalities. Among the *primi,* Lucchese soups like *farro* (spelt wheat) and *garmugia* (spring vegetables and ground meat) stand out. For *secondi,* there are plenty of choices from the grill (Cinta Senese pork, cuts of beef) or oven (piglet, rabbit, kid), as well as *gran fritto toscano* (deep-fried mixed meats on the bone and seasonal vegetables). Unusually for Tuscany, there's also fare for vegetarians beyond the usual pastas, with dishes like grilled Tomino cheese drizzled in balsamic vinegar and served with shredded radicchio and pine nuts. The fine house wines and olive oil hail from the family estate.

Via Ludovica 1660, Sesto di Moriano (signposted off SS12, 11km/7 miles north of Lucca; or take Garfagnana bus from Lucca, journey time 30 min.). www.anticalocandadisesto.it. ✆ **0583-578-181.** Reservations highly recommended. Main courses 12€–18€. MC, V. Sun–Fri 12:30–2:30pm and 8–10pm.

Shopping

Lucca's main shopping promenades are the elite **Via Fillungo ★** and more proletarian **Via Santa Lucia,** both epicenters of the evening *passeggiata.* Cross-street **Via Buia** also has a number of chic boutiques. Since 1965, the best wine cellar in town has been **Enoteca Vanni ★**, Piazza San Salvatore 7 (www.enotecavanni.com; ✆ **0583-491-902**), with hundreds of bottles lining the cryptlike rooms under the tiny storefront. Lucca has lots of jewelry stores but none more gorgeous than **Carli,** Via Fillungo 95 (✆ **0583-491-119**), specializing in antique jewelry, watches, and silver from its high-vaulted room frescoed in 1800.

Entertainment & Nightlife

The **Teatro del Giglio,** Piazza del Giglio 13–15 (www.teatrodelgiglio.it; ✆ **0583-465-320**), presents opera, plays, and ballet in the fall, winter, and spring months, and concerts in the summer, with a rare orchestral performance in the winter as well. Tickets cost from 14€ to 65€. Every evening at 7pm, the Chiesa di San Giovanni hosts an opera recital or orchestral concert dedicated to hometown composer Giacomo Puccini, in a series called **Puccini e la sua Lucca** (www.puccinielasualucca.com). Tickets are 17€ (13€ for those 22 and under) and can be purchased all day inside San Giovanni.

If you're seeking somewhere livelier than the street cafes that line every piazza, DJ bar **Zero,** Via San Paolino 58 (no phone), is where Lucca's 20-somethings gather for evening *aperitivi* and to drink cocktails and socialize until late.

Where to Stay

An economical alternative to our favorite hotels below is the delightful **Ostello San Frediano,** Via della Cavallerizza (www.ostellolucca.it; ✆ **0583-469-957**), which has 140 beds in multibed rooms, standard doubles, and family rooms sleeping six. The cost is 19€ to 22€ per day for a bunk in a multibed room. Private units cost 60€ for two people, 78€ for three, and 100€ for four.

Alla Corte degli Angeli ★★ This welcoming, warrenlike *palazzo* just off Via Fillungo is blessed with the most romantic rooms in town. The individually restored bedrooms are well proportioned, although not enormous, and simply kitted out with Italian antique furniture. The design flourish is provided by a unique, hand-painted fresco adorning the walls and ceiling of each, carefully coordinated with the room's fabrics and moniker: Each unit is named after a flower and our favorites include Orchidea and Ortensia, both of which come with large hydromassage tubs.

Via degli Angeli 23 (off Via Fillungo), 55100 Lucca. www.allacortedegliangeli.com. ✆ **0583-469-204.** Fax 0583-991-989. 10 units. 130€–210€ double. Rates include buffet breakfast. AE, DC, MC, V. Garage parking 15€. Closed 2 weeks in Jan. **Amenities:** Bikes; concierge. *In room:* A/C, TV, minibar, MP3 docking station, Wi-Fi (free).

Hotel Ilaria & Residenza dell'Alba ★ The former stables in the gardens of the Villa Bottini these days provide deluxe, businesslike accommodations with modern rooms, where all guests enjoy such complimentary perks as a snack bar and free use of bikes. The rooms are fitted simply but stylishly with cherry veneer built-in units and double-paned windows—though you don't need them on this quiet street—and standard rooms had new parquet flooring added in 2011. The rooms opening onto the little canal out front are nice, but even better views are over the rear terrace dotted with potted camellias and shaded by a sycamore. The same group owns three restaurants in town, including Buca di Sant'Antonio (see above), and you can work out a pension deal for 30€ to 40€ per person extra.

Via del Fosso 26, 55100 Lucca. www.hotelilaria.com. ✆ **0583-47-615**. Fax 0583-991 961. 41 units. 110€–260€ double. Rates include buffet breakfast. AE, DC, MC, V. Garage parking 10€. **Amenities:** Bar; babysitting; bikes (free); concierge; Jacuzzi (outdoor). *In room:* A/C, TV, hair dryer, minibar, Wi-Fi (free).

Piccolo Hotel Puccini This tiny hotel boasts Lucca's best location, just off the central piazza of San Michele. Your neighbor is the ghost of Puccini, who grew up across the street. The prices are fantastic for the location and comfort. Most of the rooms are smallish, but they have firm beds, compact bathrooms, carpeting, and reproduction opera playbills framed on the walls. Be sure to request one of the lighter rooms along the front (this street sees little traffic), from where you can lean out and see a sliver of the fabulous San Michele facade. The Puccini fills quickly, so book ahead.

Via di Poggio 9 (off Piazza San Michele), 55100 Lucca. www.hotelpuccini.com. ✆ **0583-55-421.** Fax 0583-53-487. 14 units. 95€ double. AE, MC, V. Garage parking 15€. **Amenities:** Bar; babysitting; bikes; concierge. *In room:* TV, hair dryer, Wi-Fi (1.50€ per day).

PISA ★★

76km (47 miles) W of Florence, 333km (206 miles) NW of Rome

Nothing says Pisa more than its Leaning Tower, keystone of the Romanesque Campo dei Miracoli, but this city of ancient architectural wonders also has a young and upbeat feel. Native son Galileo may be long gone but students still come here to study at the prestigious university where he taught, and to enjoy the city's vibrancy. It is probably Tuscany's liveliest city when night falls: Locals and students while away their evenings in the bars and nightclubs around Piazza Garibaldi, and along Borgo Stretto and the banks of the Arno.

The city began as a seaside settlement around 1000 B.C. and was expanded into a naval trading port by the Romans in the 2nd century B.C. By the 11th century, Pisa had grown into one of the peninsula's most powerful maritime republics. Its extensive trading in the Middle East helped import Arabic ideas (decorative and scientific), and its wars with the Saracens led it to create an offshore empire. In 1284, Pisa's battle fleet was destroyed by Genoa at Meloria (off Livorno), a staggering defeat allowing the Genoese to take control of the Tyrrhenian Sea and forcing Pisa's long slide into twilight. Its Ghibelline nature gave Florence the excuse it needed to take control in 1406. Despite a few small rebellions, Florence stayed in charge until Italian unification in the 1860s.

Essentials

GETTING THERE There are around 20 direct **trains** daily from **Rome** (2¾–4 hr.). From **Florence,** 50 daily trains make the trip (60–90 min.). **Lucca** offers over 25 runs here every day (25–35 min.). On the Lucca line, day-trippers (and anyone staying in either of the hotels recommended below) should get off at **San Rossore station,** a few blocks west of Piazza del Duomo and the Leaning Tower. All other trains—and eventually the Lucca one—pull into **Pisa Centrale** station. From here, bus no. 4 or the **LAM Rossa** bus will take you close to Piazza del Duomo.

There's a Florence-Pisa fast **highway** (the so-called FI.PI.LI) along the Arno valley. Take the SS12 or SS12r from Lucca. For details on parking locations and charges, see **www.pisamo.it**.

Tuscany's main international **airport, Galileo Galilei** (www.pisa-airport.com), is just 3km (2 miles) south of the center. Trains zip you from the airport to Centrale station in 5 minutes; the LAM Rossa bus departs every 9 minutes for Centrale station and then the Campo. A metered taxi ride will cost 10€ to 15€ (drivers accept credit cards).

GETTING AROUND **CPT** (www.cpt.pisa.it; ✆ **050-505-511** or 800-012-773 in Italy) runs the city's **buses.** Bus no. 4 and the LAM Rossa bus run to near the Campo dei Miracoli.

Taxis can be found on Piazza della Stazione and Piazza del Duomo. Call a radio taxi at ✆ **050-541-600** or 055-555-330.

VISITOR INFORMATION The main **tourist office** is at Piazza Vittorio Emanuele II 16, Pisa (www.pisaunicaterra.it; ✆ **050-42-291;** Mon–Sat 9am–7pm, Sun 9am–4pm). There's also a desk inside the arrivals hall at the airport (✆ **055-502-518;** daily 9:30am–11:30pm).

To find out what's going on in town, pick up a copy of the monthly ***ToDo*** (often in bars and cafes), or check it online at **www.todomagazine.it**.

FESTIVALS & MARKETS Since the 1400s, teams from the north and south sides of the Arno have dressed in Renaissance costumes and tried their darnedest to run one another over with a giant 7-ton (14,000-lb.) decorated cart on the Ponte di Mezzo. This inverse tug-of-war, the **Gioco del Ponte ★**, is held on the last Sunday in June. Also in June is the **Festa di San Ranieri,** when Pisans honor their patron saint by lining the Arno with torches on the 16th, then running a boat race on the 17th. There's an excellent **food market** Monday through Saturday on and around Piazza delle Vettovaglie.

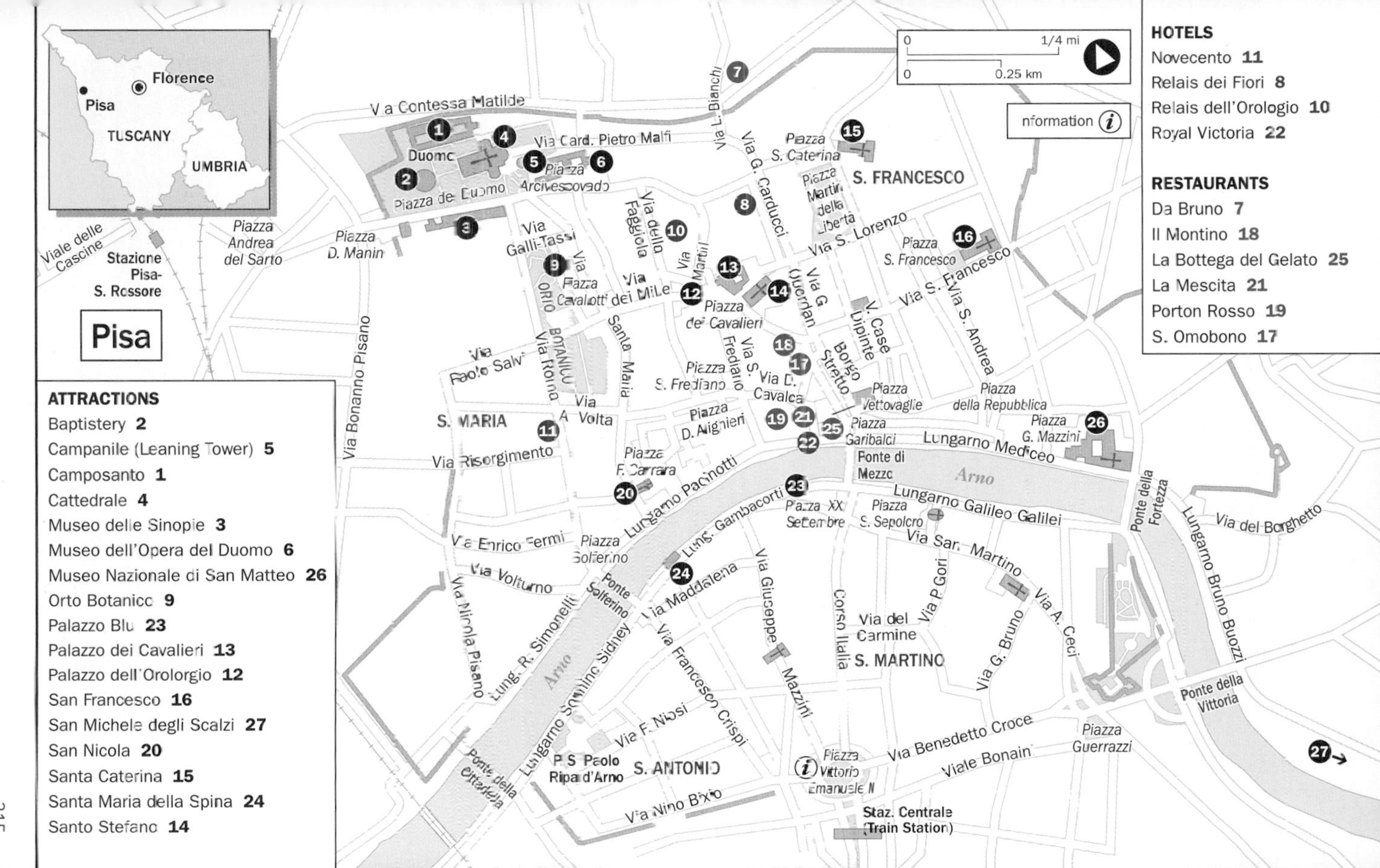

Pisa
ATTRACTIONS
Baptistery 2
Campanile (Leaning Tower) 5
Camposanto 1
Cattedrale 4
Museo delle Sinopie 3
Museo dell'Opera del Duomo 6
Museo Nazionale di San Matteo 26
Orto Botanico 9
Palazzo Blu 23
Palazzo dei Cavalieri 13
Palazzo dell'Orolorgio 12
San Francesco 16
San Michele degli Scalzi 27
San Nicola 20
Santa Caterina 15
Santa Maria della Spina 24
Santo Stefano 14
HOTELS
Novecento 11
Relais dei Fiori 8
Relais dell'Orologio 10
Royal Victoria 22
RESTAURANTS
Da Bruno 7
Il Montino 18
La Bottega del Gelato 25
La Mescita 21
Porton Rosso 19
S. Omobono 17
0 1/4 mi
0 0.25 km
information
Florence
Pisa
TUSCANY
UMBRIA
Viale delle Cascine
Stazione Pisa-S. Rossore
Piazza Andrea del Sarto
Piazza D. Manin
Via Bonanno Pisano
Via Contessa Matilde
Duomo
Piazza del Duomo
Via Card. Pietro Maffi
Piazza Arcivescovado
Via L. Bianchi
Via G. Carducci
Piazza S. Caterina
S. FRANCESCO
Piazza Martiri della Libertà
Via S. Lorenzo
Piazza S. Francesco
Via S. Francesco
Via S. Andrea
Via della Faggiola
Via Martiri
Via Galli-Tassi
Piazza Cavalotti
Via dei Mille
Piazza dei Cavalieri
Via G. Oberdan
V. Case Dipinte
Borgo Stretto
Piazza Vettovaglie
Piazza della Repubblica
Piazza G. Mazzini
Lungarno Mediceo
ORTO BOTANICO
Via Roma
Santa Maria
Via Paolo Salvi
Via S. Frediano
Piazza S. Frediano
Via D. Cavalca
Piazza D. Alighieri
Piazza Garibaldi
Ponte di Mezzo
Arno
S. MARIA
Via A. Volta
Via Risorgimento
Piazza F. Carrara
Lungarno Pacinotti
Piazza XX Settembre
Piazza S. Sepolcro
Lungarno Galileo Galilei
Ponte della Fortezza
Lungarno Bruno Buozzi
Via del Borghetto
Via Enrico Fermi
Piazza Solferino
Lung. Gambacorti
Via Volturno
Ponte Solferino
Via Maddalena
Via Giuseppe Mazzini
Corso Italia
Via San Martino
Via P. Gori
Via del Carmine
Via G. Bruno
Via A. Ceci
S. MARTINO
Via Nicola Pisano
Lung. R. Simonelli
Lungarno Sonnino Sidney
Via Francesco Crispi
Via F. Niosi
P. S. Paolo Ripa d'Arno
S. ANTONIO
Piazza Vittorio Emanuele II
Via Benedetto Croce
Viale Bonaini
Piazza Guerrazzi
Ponte della Vittoria
Ponte della Cittadella
Via Nino Bixio
Staz. Centrale (Train Station)

Exploring Pisa

On a grassy lawn wedged into the northwest corner of the city walls, medieval Pisans created one of the most dramatic squares in the world. Dubbed the **Campo dei Miracoli (Field of Miracles) ★★★**, Piazza del Duomo contains an array of elegant buildings that heralded the Pisan-Romanesque style. A hidden part of its appeal, aside from the beauty of the buildings, is its spatial geometry. If you take an aerial photo of the square and draw connect-the-dot lines between the centers, doors, and other focal points, you'll come up with all sorts of perfect triangles and tangential lines of mathematical grace.

Admission charges for the monuments and museums of the Campo are tied together in a complicated way. The Cattedrale alone costs 2€ (though it's free Nov–Feb). Any other single sight is 5€; any two sites cost 6€. To access everything except the Leaning Tower costs 8€ between November and February and 10€ otherwise. Children 9 and under enter free. For more information, visit their website at **www.opapisa.it**. Admission to the Leaning Tower is separate (see below).

Baptistery ★★ CHURCH Italy's biggest baptistery (104m/341 ft. in circumference) was begun in 1153 by Diotisalvi, who gave it its lower Romanesque drum. Nicola and Giovanni Pisano "Gothicized" the upper part from 1277 to 1297 and Cellino di Nese capped it with a Gothic dome in the 1300s.

The **pulpit ★★** by Nicola Pisano (1255–60) is perhaps his masterpiece and the prototype for a series he and his son Giovanni carried out over the years (the last is in Pisa's Duomo; the other two are in Pistoia and Siena). Heavily influenced by classical works—including the Roman sarcophagi and Greek vase now in the Camposanto—Nicola's high-relief panels (a synopsis of Christ's life) include pagan gods converted to Christianity as Madonnas and saints. The other main attraction of the baptistery is its renowned **acoustics.**

Piazza del Duomo. www.opapisa.it. ✆ **050-835-011.** For prices, see above. Apr–Sept daily 8am–8pm; Mar daily 9am–6pm; Oct daily 9am–7pm; Nov and Feb daily 9am–5pm; Dec–Jan daily 9:30am–4:30pm. Bus: E, 4, LAM Rossa.

The interior of Pisa's Baptistery.

Pisa's sprawling Duomo.

Camposanto CEMETERY Begun in 1278 by Giovanni di Simone to house the shiploads of holy Golgotha dirt (the mount where Christ was crucified) brought back by an archbishop from the Crusades, the Camposanto has been burial ground for Pisan bigwigs ever since.

The walls were once covered with important 14th- and 15th-century frescoes by Taddeo Gaddi, Spinello Aretino, and Benozzo Gozzoli, among others. On July 27, 1944, however, American warplanes launched an attack against the city (which was still in German hands) and the cemetery was bombed. The wooden roof caught fire, and its lead panels melted, destroying many of the wall paintings and severely damaging the few that remained—some have been returned, however. The most fascinating panel to survive the bombing is the 1341 ***Triumph of Death*** ★, attributed to Florentine Buonamico Buffalmacco.

Piazza del Duomo. www.opapisa.it. ✆ **050-835-011.** For prices, see above. Same hours as the Baptistery; see above. Bus: E, 4, LAM Rossa.

Cattedrale ★★ CATHEDRAL Buscheto, the architect who laid the cathedral's first stone in 1063, kicked off a new era in art by building what was to become the model for the Pisan-Romanesque style. All the key elements are here on the **facade** ★, designed and built by Buscheto's successor, Rainaldo: alternating light and dark banding, rounded blind arches with Moorish-inspired lozenges at the top and colored marble inlay designs, and Lombard-style open galleries of tiny mismatched columns stacked to make the facade much higher than the church roof.

The **main door** is one of three cast by students of Giambologna after a 1595 fire destroyed the originals. On the back of the right transept, across from the bell tower, is a 2008 cast of the bronze **Door of San Ranieri** ★★★; the only original door survives in the Museo dell'Opera (see below) and was cast by Bonnano Pisano in 1180 while he was working on the bell tower.

On the north side of the nave is Giovanni Pisano's masterpiece **pulpit** ★★ (1302–11)—it's the last of the famed Pisano pulpits and, along with the one in Pistoia, the greatest. Hanging low near the pulpit is a large **bronze lamp** that, according to legend, a bored Galileo was staring at one day during Mass, watching it sway gently back and forth, when his law of pendulum motion suddenly hit him. In the apse is the last of the major survivors of the fire, an enormous

13th-century mosaic ***Christ Pancrator,*** completed in 1302 by Cimabue, who added the St. John the Evangelist on the right.

Piazza del Duomo. www.opapisa.it. ✆ **050-835-011.** For prices, see above. Apr–Sept Mon–Sat 10am–8pm, Sun 1–8pm; Mar Mon–Sat 10am–5:30pm, Sun 1–5:30pm; Oct Mon–Sat 10am–6:30pm, Sun 1–6:30pm; Nov–Feb Mon–Sat 10am–12:45pm and 2–4:30pm, Sun 2–4:30pm. Bus: E, 4, LAM Rossa.

Leaning Tower of Pisa ★★★ ICON The problem with Pisa's Torre Pendente—and the bane of local engineers for 8 centuries—is that you can't stack that much heavy marble on shifting subsoil and keep it all upright. It was started in 1173 by Guglielmo and Bonnano Pisano, who also cast the Duomo's original doors. They reached the third level in 1185 when they noticed a lean, at that point about 3.8cm (1½ in.). Work stopped and wasn't resumed until 1275 under Giovanni di Simone. He tried to correct the tilt by curving the structure back toward the perpendicular, giving the tower its slight banana shape. In 1284, work stopped yet again. In 1360, Tommaso di Andrea da Pontedera capped it off at about 51m (167 ft.) with a vaguely Gothic belfry.

Excavations around the base in the early 19th century caused the tower to start falling faster than ever (about 1mm/.04 in. a year), and by 1990 the lean was about 4.6m (15 ft.), so Pisa's mayor closed the tower. Stabilization work continued until December 2001 when, righted to its lean of 1838 (when it was a mere 4m/13 ft. off), the tower reopened. Now the number of visitors is controlled via 30-minute slots—and a massive admission charge.

Piazza del Duomo. www.opapisa.it. ✆ **050-835-011.** Admission 15€, or 17€ if you reserve a timed slot (essential in peak periods). Apr–Sept daily 8:30am–8pm (sometimes until 10:30pm June–Aug); Mar daily 9am–5:30pm; Oct daily 9am–7pm; Nov and Feb daily 9:30am–5pm; Dec–Jan daily 10am–4:30pm. Children 7 and under not permitted. Bus: E, 4, LAM Rossa.

The Leaning Tower of Pisa.

THE BEST OF THE REST OF pisa

If you go down Via Santa Maria from Piazza del Duomo and take a left on Via dei Mille, you'll come out into **Piazza Cavalieri,** possibly the site of the Roman town's forum and later the square where citizens of the medieval city-state met to discuss political issues. Giorgio Vasari remodeled the **Palazzo dei Cavalieri** in 1562 and decorated it with recently restored and very detailed graffiti; it now houses the renowned Scuola Normale Superiore.

East along the Arno near Ponte Fortezza is Pisa's only significant painting collection, the **Museo Nazionale di San Matteo ★★**, Piazza San Matteo in Soarta 1 (✆ **050-541-865**). Pride of the collection is the Sienese master Simone Martini's polyptych of the ***Virgin and Child with Saints*** ★. Other star works are a *St. Paul* by Masaccio (the only part of his lost *Pisa Altarpiece* still in Pisa), the greenishly aged *Madonna dell'Umiltà* by Gentile da Fabriano, and a Donatello gilded bronze reliquary *Bust of St. Rossore* (1427). It's open Tuesday through Saturday from 8:30am to 7pm and Sunday from 9am to 1:30pm; admission is 5€, free for children 18 and under and seniors 65 and over. In 2009, the city opened a collection of art by painters who have worked in Pisa over the centuries, displayed at the renovated **Palazzo Blu ★**, Lungarno Gambacorti 9 (www.palazzoblu.org; ✆ **050-916-950**), the striking blue palace on the banks of the Arno. It houses some perhaps lesser-known Tuscan artists, such as Giovan Battista Tempesti, who often chose the city as a backdrop for their paintings, and stages contemporary shows, too. Admission is free, and it's open Tuesday to Sunday 10am to 1pm and 4 to 10pm.

Museo dell'Opera del Duomo ★ MUSEUM The old Chapter-House-cum-convent has been transformed into a storehouse for sculptures, paintings, and other works from the ecclesiastical buildings on Piazza del Duomo. Room 2 is, since 2008, the home of the cathedral's last remaining 12th-century original portal, the **Door of San Ranieri ★★★**. Elsewhere, seek out the Islamic 11th-century bronze **griffin ★**, war booty from the Crusades, which long decorated the Duomo's cupola before it was replaced by a copy.

Upstairs, the last few rooms house the precious legacy of Carlo Lasinio, who restored the Camposanto frescoes in the early 19th century and, fortunately for posterity, made a series of **etchings ★★** of each fresco. Not only did the original publication of these prints have an important influence on the developing pre-Raphaelite movement at the time, but they're the best record we have of the paintings that went up in flames when the Camposanto was bombed in 1944.

Piazza Arcivescovado 6. www.opapisa.it. ✆ **050-835-011**. For prices, see above. Same hours as Baptistery; see above. Bus: E, 4, LAM Rossa.

Entertainment & Nightlife

The bar of the minute waxes and wanes, but **Bazeel,** Lungarno Pacinotti 1 (at Piazza Garibaldi; www.bazeel.it; ✆ **340-2881-113**), is ever popular for an *aperitivo,* live big-screen sports, cocktails, and DJ sets till late on weekends. At **Orzo Bruno ★**, Via Case Dipinte 6 (www.orzobruno.it; ✆ **050-578-802**), 20-somethings gather in animated groups to enjoy the place's artisan beer, brewed out back. Glasses cost 3€ and 4€ (slightly less 7–8:30pm). ***Note:*** The city is *very* quiet in August, and many places close for almost the whole month.

Where to Eat & Stay

Pisa is such a major day-trip site that few people stay here overnight, which helps keep hotel prices down but also limits quality options in the center. The low season for most hotels in Pisa is August.

Happily, there are plenty of good restaurant options. For pizza or *cecina* (a garbanzo-bean flour flatbread served warm), stop in at **Il Montino,** Vicolo del Monte (✆ **050-598-695**), a favorite slice stop for Pisans. There's much good dining in and around Pisa's produce market: In addition to our favorites below, you could try **Porton Rosso ★**, Via Porton Rosso 11 (www.osteriadelportonrosso.com; ✆ **050-580-566**), where seafood is the house specialty. Main courses cost up to 16€; it's closed Sunday and most of August.

La Mescita ★ PISAN/WINE BAR The marketplace location and simple decor of this popular spot belie its reputation for skillful cooking. The menu changes each month, but often includes the delicious likes of a *sformatino di melanzane* (eggplant soufflé in tomato sauce), to be followed perhaps by *ravioli di ceci con salsa di gamberetti e pomodoro fresco* (ravioli stuffed with a garbanzo bean pâté and served in shrimp-and-tomato sauce) or *strozzapreti al trevisano e Gorgonzola* (pasta curlicues in a cheesy sauce topped with shredded bitter radicchio). You can stick to tradition with your *secondo* by ordering the *acciughe ripieni* (stuffed anchovies). Because the place operates as an enoteca (wine cellar) after hours, the wine list is long and detailed.

Via Cavalca 2 (just off the market square). www.osterialamescitapisa.it. ✆ **050-957-019.** Reservations recommended. Main courses 15€. AE, DC, MC, V. Tues–Sun 7:45–11pm; Sat–Sun 1–2:30pm. Closed 20 days in Aug. Bus: 4, E, Lam Rossa, or LAM Verde.

Novecento ★ Opened in late 2006, this immaculately converted colonial villa set around a courtyard garden is Pisa's best affordable boutique hotel. Rooms are small, certainly—none has a bath, for example, nor are there family-size units—but decor is refreshingly contemporary, with muted colors, the occasional flash of exuberance, and not an antique armoire in sight. Most peaceful and most comfortable of the rooms is the Garden Room, a self-contained unit with a small "antechamber" standing alone amid the lush subtropical greenery.

Via Roma 37, 56100 Pisa. www.hotelnovecento.pisa.it. ✆ **050-500-323.** Fax 050-220-9163. 14 units. 80€–120€ double; 90€–170€ Garden Room. Rates include breakfast. AE, MC, V. Parking on street (10€ per day). Bus: E or 4. **Amenities:** Babysitting; concierge. *In room:* A/C, TV, hair dryer, minibar, Wi-Fi (free).

Relais dell'Orologio ★★ These are the best lodgings in central Pisa, a hotel of charm and grace worthy of Pisa's status as a major tourist destination. It's also one of the most tranquil hotels in the center, despite a location just yards from the city's heartbeat, Piazza dei Cavalieri. This former historic mansion was constructed as a fortified tower in the 13th century, and great respect was shown for the style of the original building in its modernization. Small to midsize bedrooms are furnished with Italian flair and style, and many retain their wooden beams. You'll pay a little extra for a room overlooking the courtyard garden, perhaps the quietest spot in the city within 5 minutes' walk of the Campo. For tighter budgets, the same owners run the 12-room B&B **Relais dei Fiori,** Via Carducci 35 (www.relaisdeifiori.com; ✆ **050-556-054**), where doubles cost between 75€ and 175€.

Via della Faggiola Ugiccione 12–14, 56126 Pisa. www.hotelrelaisorologio.com. ✆ **050-830-361.** Fax 050-551-869. 21 units. 135€–375€ double; 225€–685€ suite. Rates include buffet breakfast.

AE, DC, MC, V. Garage parking 30€. Bus: E or 4. **Amenities:** Restaurant, bar, babysitting; room service; Wi-Fi (free, in lobby). *In room:* A/C, TV, hair dryer, minibar.

S. Omobono ★ PISAN Around a column surviving from the medieval church that once stood here, locals gather at this trattoria to enjoy authentic Pisan home cooking. Open with something like *brachette alla renaiaola* (an antique Pisan dish consisting of large pasta squares in a purée of turnip greens and smoked fish) or *tagliatelle alla scarpara* (in a sausage *ragù*). The *secondi* are simple and straightforward: *baccalà alla livornese* (salt cod stewed with tomatoes) or *maiale arrosto* (thinly sliced roast pork), with which you can order fried polenta slices or ultra-Pisan *ceci* (garbanzo) beans.

Piazza S. Omobono 6 (next to the market square). ✆ **050-540-847.** Reservations recommended. Main courses 8.50€–10€. DC, MC, V. Mon–Sat 7:30–10pm. Closed Aug 8–20. Bus: 4, E, Lam Rossa, or LAM Verde.

AREZZO

85km (53 miles) SE of Florence, 246km (153 miles) N of Rome

Arezzo is a medium-size Tuscan city, an agricultural center clambering up a low hill, best known for its artistic masterpieces by **Piero della Francesca,** and stained-glass marvels by **Guillaume de Marcillat.** As Arretium, Arezzo was an important member of the 12-city Etruscan confederation, and it was famous in Roman times for its mass-produced *corallino* ceramics. The Ghibelline medieval *comune* ran afoul of Florence's Guelphs, and the city's armies were soundly trounced by Florence in the 1289 Battle of Campaldino. (The Florentine forces counted a young Dante Alighieri among its foot soldiers.) More recently, the city's gotten some international face time as the setting for Roberto Benigni's 1999 Oscar winning film *La Vita è Bella (Life Is Beautiful).*

A market along Arezzo's streets.

Another towering Aretine was Giorgio Vasari (1512–74), a mediocre painter, a much more talented architect, and, with his book *Lives of the Artists*—a collection of biographies of masters from Cimabue and Giotto through Michelangelo—the unwitting author of the first art history text.

Essentials

GETTING THERE The main **rail** line between **Rome** (hourly; 2 hr.–2 hr., 55 min.) and **Florence** (45 trains daily; 40–90 min.) also passes **Orvieto** (15 trains daily; 1 hr.–1 hr., 50 min.) on its way to Arezzo. The station is at Piazza della Repubblica just southwest of the walls. From Siena take the LFI **bus** (www.lfi.it; ✆ **0575-324-294**).

The quickest route by **car** from Florence or Rome is the **A1 autostrada.**

VISITOR INFORMATION The tourist information desk is inside the Palazzo Comunale, Piazza Libertà 1 (http://turismo.provincia.arezzo.it; ✆ **0575-401-945;** Mon–Fri 11am–1pm and 2–4pm, Sat–Sun 11am–4pm).

FESTIVALS & MARKETS On the third Sunday in June and the first Sunday in September, Arezzo pulls out the stops for a full-fledged medieval jousting tournament, the **Giostra del Saracino ★★**, dating from at least the 16th century. After an afternoon of flag-tossing and pageantry, mounted, armored riders thunder across dirt-lined Piazza Grande with their lances aimed at the effigy of a Saracen warrior.

On the first Sunday and the prior Saturday of every month, Piazza Grande is filled with more than 500 dealers in one of Italy's leading **antiques fairs ★**. See **www.arezzofieraantiquaria.org**.

Exploring Arezzo

Arezzo's main square, **Piazza Grande ★**, is charmingly off-kilter. Since 1200, it has listed alarmingly to one side, creating a slope crowned with the graceful **Logge Vasari ★** designed in 1573 by Giorgio Vasari.

Casa di Vasari (Vasari's House) HISTORIC HOME The first art historian—who chronicled the lives of Michelangelo, da Vinci, Masaccio, and others—Vasari (1511–74) bought this house in 1540. He decorated it with Mannerist artworks, often by his students, but executed the allegorical frescoes in the **Sala del Trionfo della Virtù** himself. Clearly he was a much better architect than he was painter, but they do provide a fascinating window into High Renaissance mores and the influence of classical ideas on 16th-century Tuscan elites.

Via XX Settembre 55. ✆ **0575-409-040.** Admission 2€ adults, 1€ ages 18–25, free 17 and under. Wed–Sat and Mon 9am–7pm; Sun 9am–1pm.

Cattedrale di Arezzo CATHEDRAL Arezzo's cathedral was slowly agglomerated between 1278 and 1510, though it took until 1859 to raise the neo-Gothic bell tower and until 1935 to finish the simple facade. Among the masterpieces inside, the greatest may be the seven **stained-glass windows ★** (1516–24) by the undisputed master of the form, the French immigrant **Guillaume de Marcillat.** This is one of the few complete cycles of his work in Italy that hasn't been destroyed, and it includes the *Pentecost* rose window in the facade; the *Calling of St. Matthew,* the *Baptism of Christ,* the *Expulsion of Merchants from the Temple,* the *Adulteress,* and the *Raising of Lazarus* along the right wall; and *Saints Silvester and Lucy* in the chapel to the left of the apse.

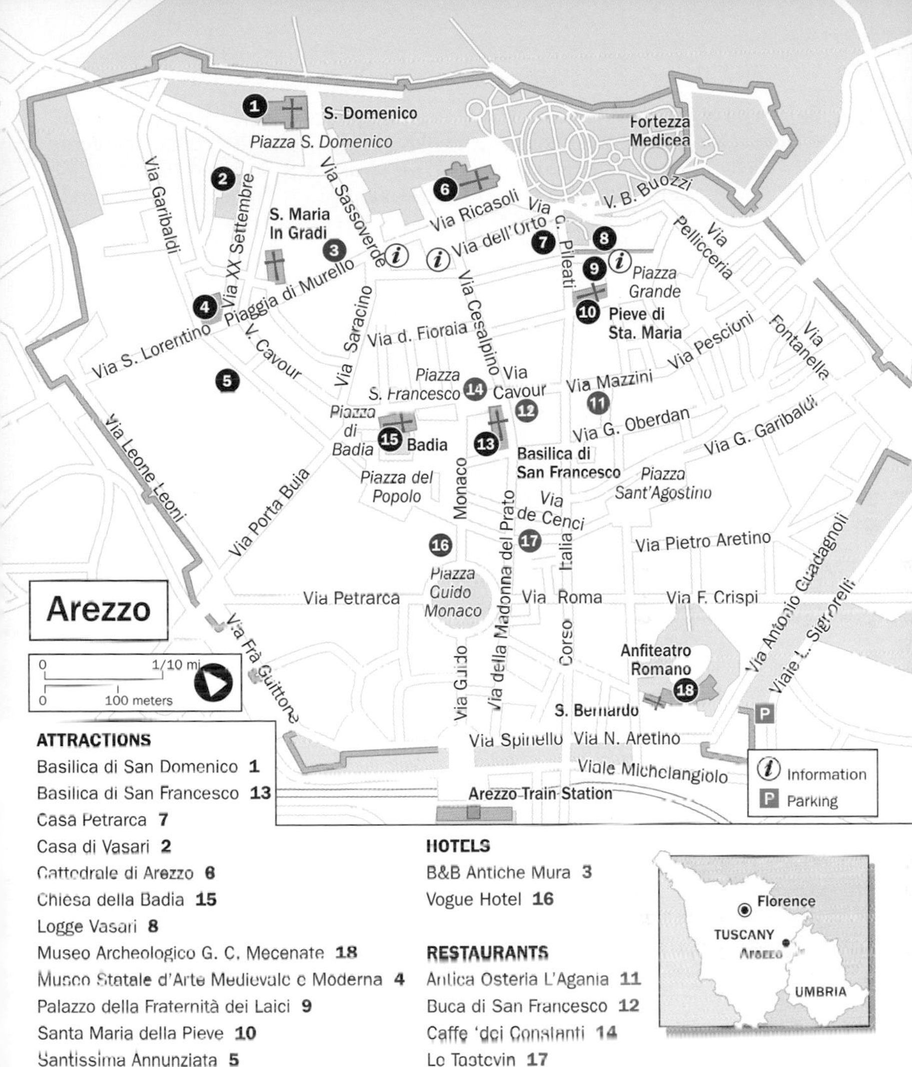

At the end of the left aisle, on the wall next to the sacristy door, is a scraggly haired but still magnificent ***Mary Magdalene*** frescoed by Piero della Francesca in around 1459.

Piazza del Duomo. ✆ **0575-23-991.** Free admission. Daily 7am–12:30pm and 3–6:30pm.

San Domenico CHURCH The interior of this 13th-century church contains several engaging 14th-century **fresco fragments** and one real gem. Over the high altar is a justly lauded ***Crucifix*** ★, painted by Cimabue in the 1260s, then brilliantly restored and returned to this place of honor in early 2003. The chapel to the right of the high altar contains a 14th-century stone *Madonna and Child* and a delicate fresco of the *Annunciation* by Spinello Aretino.

Piazza San Domenico. ✆ **0575-22-906.** Free admission. Nov–Mar daily 9am–6:30pm; Apr–Oct daily 9am–7pm.

San Francesco ★★ CHURCH One of the greatest fresco cycles by one of the greatest artists of the Renaissance holds court in this 14th-century church. Piero della Francesca's ***Legend of the True Cross* ★★★**, completed in 1466 inside the **Capella Bacci,** has drawn art-loving pilgrims from around the world for centuries. Piero's work features perfect perspective and hauntingly ethereal figures that nonetheless convey untold depths of emotion. You can see most of them from the ropes at the base of the altar steps, about 10m (33 ft.) away, but it is well worth paying for a ticket to get up close.

Spend some time admiring the rest of the church, though the remaining frescoes are a lot more faded and damaged than Piero's masterpiece. French master Guillaume de Marcillat added the **rose window** in 1520.

Piazza San Francesco. ✆ **0575-20-630.** Required reservation for Piero cycle tickets at www.pierodellafrancesca.it or ✆ **0575-352-727.** Admission to church free; Piero cycle 6€ including booking fee. Church Mon–Sat 8:30am–noon and 2:30–6:30pm, Sun 9:45–10:45am and 1–5pm. Piero cycle by 30-min. slot only, on the half-hour Nov–Mar Mon–Fri 9am–5:30pm, Sat 9am–5pm, Sun 1–5pm; Apr–Oct Mon–Fri 9am–6:30pm, Sat 9am–5:30pm, Sun 1–5:30pm.

Santa Maria della Pieve ★ CHURCH This 12th-century church is Lombard Romanesque architecture at its most beautiful, with a craggy, eroded **facade ★** of stacked arcades in luminous beige stone. The fat 36m (118-ft.) **bell tower** "of the hundred holes," with its bifore windows (mullioned windows with two lights), is a 1330 addition. Inside, on the high altar above the raised crypt, is a 1320 **polyptych of the *Madonna and Child with Saints* ★**—all wearing gorgeously worked fabrics—by Sienese master Pietro Lorenzetti.

Corso Italia 7. ✆ **0575-22-629.** Free admission. May–Sept daily 8am–7pm; Oct–Apr daily 8am–noon and 3–6pm.

Where to Eat & Stay

Arezzo is a great place to eat, with plenty of *osterie* and bars offering relatively cheap eats compared to other Tuscan towns. Be sure to grab a coffee and pastry at the venerable **Caffè dei Constanti ★** (✆ **0575-182-4075;** Wed–Sun 7:30am–2am, also open Mon Apr–Sept), Piazza San Francesco 19 (opposite San Francesco), which was featured in Roberto Benigni's *Life Is Beautiful* (there's a small still from the movie at the door). Founded in 1805, the cafe is also the best place in town for an *aperitivo* (from 6pm). Excellent deli **Gastronomia Il Cervo ★★**, Via Cavour 38–40 (✆ **0575-20-872**), also has an interesting a la carte menu. Better still, pick from the downstairs deli bar, loaded with dishes prepared that morning. Filling, creative salads like pasta with zucchini, Speck, and Parmesan or squid with potato and celery always hit the mark. Dishes range 8€ to 10€.

Hotels in Arezzo cater mainly to businesspeople passing through, though the handful of smaller B&Bs and guesthouses are more appealing for travelers.

B&B Antiche Mura ★★ This remarkable guesthouse is plugged into the old city walls in rooms that date back to the 1200s—much of it feels like a plush museum, with walkways over glass-covered foundations and baroque furnishings. Each room is named and styled after a famous woman in literature or the movies, from Madame Bovary's period decor to the sensual reds used in the Marilyn Monroe room; all are comfy and feature exposed brick walls and wood-beam ceilings.

Piaggia di Murello 35, 52100 Arezzo. www.antichemura.info. ✆ **0575-20-410.** Fax 0575-016-2231. 6 units. 75€ double. Rates include breakfast vouchers for use in nearby cafes. AE, DC, MC, V. Free parking nearby. **Amenities:** Concierge. *In room:* A/C, TV, Wi-Fi (free).

L'Agania ★ TUSCAN This small joint doesn't bother with a wine list; a staff member plunks down a bottle of the eminently quaffable house chianti (just 5€). The locals pack into this long, wood-paneled room especially for the thick rib-sticking *ribollita* (minestrone with bread chunks), but you can also mix and match gnocchi, *tagliatelle,* and creamy polenta with the basic Tuscan sauces. The trattoria proudly offers the lovely "local dishes" foreign visitors rarely order, such as tripe *(trippa)* and the very fatty *grifi e polenta* (chunks of veal stomach in polenta).

Via Mazzini 10. www.agania.com. ✆ **0575-295-381.** Reservations recommended for dinner in high season. Main courses 7€–10€. AE, DC, MC, V. Tues–Sun noon–3pm and 7–10:30pm. Closed last 2 weeks of June.

MONTEPULCIANO ★

67km (41 miles) SE of Siena, 124km (77 miles) SE of Florence, 186km (116 miles) N of Rome

The biggest and highest of southern Tuscany's hill towns, steeply graded Montepulciano, with its medieval alleyways and plethora of Renaissance palaces and churches, has just enough tourist infrastructure to make it the best base for visiting the Tuscan south. The fields around the town produce a violet-scented, orange speckled ruby wine called **Vino Nobile di Montepulciano:** This area has been known since at least the 8th century for its superior wine. The locals call themselves Poliziani after the Roman name for the town, and Poliziano is also the name that the local classical scholar/humanist Angelo Ambrogini took when he went to Florence to hold discourses with Lorenzo de' Medici, tutor Lorenzo's sons, and write some of the most finely crafted Renaissance poetry of the era—some say his *Stanze per la Giostra* inspired Botticelli's mythological paintings, such as the *Birth of Venus* and *Allegory of Spring*.

The steep, winding streets of Montepulciano.

Essentials

GETTING THERE **Car** is the best method: From Siena, the most scenic route is south on the SS2 to San Quirico d'Orcia, where you get the SS146 eastbound through Pienza to Montepulciano. From Florence, take the A1 south to the Chianciano Terme exit, and then take SS146 (direction Chianciano) for 18km (11 miles).

Six TRA-IN **buses** (www.trainspa.it; ✆ **0577-204-111**) run daily from Siena (1½ hr.), most coming through Pienza (20 min.) en route. **LFI** (✆ **0578-31-174**) buses run three times daily (none on Sun) from Florence to Bettolle, where you transfer for the bus to Montepulciano (2¼ hr. total).

VISITOR INFORMATION Montepulciano's pro-loco **tourist office** is in the little parking lot just below Porta al Prato (www.prolocomontepulciano.it; ✆ **0578-757-341**). It's open daily from 9:30am to 12:30pm and

3 to 6pm (until 8pm in summer); it's closed Sunday afternoons, but not for *riposo* in August.

FESTIVALS & MARKETS Poliziani also used to gallop horses pell-mell through the streets in an annual Palio, but for safety reasons this has been reduced in modern times to the **Bravio delle Botti ★★**. In this only slightly less perilous race, the locals don 14th-century costumes as teams from the traditional *contrade* (neighborhoods) roll barrels weighing more than 79kg (175 lb.) toward the finish line. (Oh, yeah: It's uphill.) To witness the hernias and join in the pageantry before the race and the feast after, drop by town on the last Sunday in August.

Exploring Montepulciano

Outside the city walls below Porta al Prato squats the church of **Sant' Agnese,** with a striped 1935 facade surrounding a 14th-century portal. Inside, the first chapel on the right has a frescoed *Madonna* by Simone Martini.

You'll see architecture by Antonio Sangallo the Elder before you even get inside the walls. **Porta al Prato** was reconstructed in the 1500s on his designs, and the Medici balls above the gate hint at Montepulciano's long association with Florence. One block up Via Gracciano nel Corso, a Florentine Marzocco lion reigns from atop a **column.** (It's a copy of a 1511 original, now in the town museum.) To the right (no. 91) is the massive **Palazzo Avignonesi,** with grinning lions' heads, and across the street is the **Palazzo Tarugi** (no. 82). Both are by Vignola, the late Renaissance architect who designed Rome's Villa Giulia. In lieu of an Etruscan museum, Montepulciano has the **Palazzo Bucelli** (no. 73), the sort of place that makes archaeologists grimace—the lower level of the facade is embedded with a patchwork of Etruscan reliefs and funerary urns. Most probably came from the Chiusi area, and they represent the collection of 18th-century antiquarian scholar and former resident Pietro Bucelli.

Take the Bus

Montepulciano's Corso is *very steep indeed.* If you are unfit, or suffer from health problems, **take the bus.** Little orange *pollicini* connect the junction just below the Porta al Prato and Piazza Grande in about 8 minutes. The official point of origin is "the fifth tree on the right above the junction." Tickets cost 1€ each way for all passengers above 1m (3⅓ ft.) tall. Buses run every 20 minutes.

Next on the right is **Sant'Agostino ★**, with a facade by Michelozzo in a style mixing late Gothic with early Renaissance. Over the high altar is a wooden crucifix by Donatello, and, behind it, the entrance to the choir of an older church on this spot, with frescoes and an Antonio del Pollaiolo crucifix. On Piazza Michelozzo in front of the church stands the **Torre di Pulcinella,** a short clock tower capped with a life-size Pulcinella, the black-and-white clown from Naples, who strikes the hours. It was left by a philandering Neapolitan bishop who was exiled here for his dalliances.

Montepulciano's historic and civic heart, the highest point in town, is **Piazza Grande ★**. Its **Palazzo Comunale ★** was designed by Michelozzo as a late-14th-century homage in travertine to Florence's Palazzo Vecchio. (Teens may recognize it from the 2009 vampire movie *Twilight: New Moon*—filmed here, despite being set in Volterra.) Daily from 10am to 6pm, you can wander through civic offices to climb the tower for a great view of the surrounding countryside. (It's 2€ to climb,

UNDERGROUND tunnels & NOBLE WINE

The local wine consortium, the **Consorzio del Vino Nobile di Montepulciano** (www.consorziovinonobile.it), has a **showroom and tasting center** in the basement of the Palazzo del Capitano on Piazza Grande where you can sample the wares of every member (which means most Vino Nobile vineyards) Monday through Friday from 10am to 1pm and 3 to 6pm, Saturday from 10am to 3pm. Hours can be erratic out of season.

In town itself, the **Gattavecchi ★** *cantine*, Via di Collazzi 74 (www.gattavecchi.it; ✆ **0578-757-110**), burrow under Santa Maria dei Servi, with moldy tunnels and a staircase leading down to an even moldier chapel-like structure carved out of the rock—no one knows when it dates from or what it was, but it's intriguingly and suggestively located directly below the altar of the church. Bottles such as their Riserva dei Padri Serviti and 100% sangiovese Parceto have been well received worldwide. Tasting is free, and a few euros gets you a tasting plate of meats and cheeses to accompany the superlative wine. At Piazza Grande, the **Contucci** winery (www.contucci.it; ✆ **0578-757-006**), presided over by knowledgeable, gregarious winemaker Adamo, occupies the 13th-century cellars of the Palazzo Contucci.

free for children 12 and under; watch your head.) Back on terra firma, to your left is the **Palazzo Nobili-Tarugi,** with an arcaded loggia on the corner facing a **well** topped by the Medici arms flanked by two Florentine lions and two Poliziani griffins. Both the palace and well are the design of Antonio Sangallo the Elder, as is the **Palazzo Contucci** across from the Palazzo Comunale.

The last side of Piazza Grande is taken up by the rambling brick nonfacade (the real facade was never added) of the 17th-century **Cattedrale di Santa Maria Assunta ★**. The gold-heavy triptych on the high altar is by Taddeo di Bartolo (1401) and depicts the *Assumption of the Virgin with Saints* topped by *Annunciation* and *Crowning of the Virgin* pinnacles, and is banded with a *Passion* cycle in the predella. Bartolo was one of the Sienese artists of the generation after the 1348 Black Death, and this is one of his greatest works.

Outside the walls is Antonio da Sangallo the Elder's **Tempio di San Biagio ★★** (1518–34), one of the undisputed masterpieces of High Renaissance architecture. It became fashionable in the High Renaissance to build a church, usually on a Greek cross plan, just outside a city so that the classically inspired architecture would be unimpaired by surrounding buildings and the church could be appreciated from all angles. The interior, while as peaceful and elegantly restrained as the overall structure, has nothing to hold you.

An alternative to our lodging choices below, **La Dimora nel Corso ★**, Via Gracciano nel Corso (www.trattoriadicagnano.it; ✆ **0575-758-757**), features a harmonious mix of wood-beam ceilings, terra cotta tiles, and fresh, modern tones (and occasionally furniture). Rooms and miniapartments at this converted *palazzo* on the Corso were completely refitted in 2011 and offer plenty of space for families. Doubles range 85€ to 120€.

Where to Eat & Stay

Acquacheta ★★★ SOUTHERN TUSCAN/GRILL This outstanding cellar eatery is strictly for carnivores: *"bistecca numero uno"* is how Adamo, the winemaker at Contucci, describes it. The style is informal and rustic, fussily so—they insist you drink water and wine from the same beaker—but they take produce very seriously: Meat is sold by weight and brought to your table by a cleaver-wielding chef for your approval before it goes onto the flame-grill (only briefly . . . if you like your steak anything but rare, holler). Pair their excellent beef with a side like baked pecorino cheese served with a cold, sliced pear. If a plate of cow isn't for you, there's a lengthy specials list, too, plus three pastas and five sauces to combine any way you please.

Via del Teatro 22 (down right side of Palazzo Contucci from Piazza Grande). www.acquacheta.eu. ✆ **0578-717-086.** Reservations essential. Main courses 7€–18€. MC, V. Wed–Mon noon–3pm and 7:30–10:30pm. Closed mid-Jan to mid-Mar.

Duomo ★ This friendly, family-run joint is the most pleasant full-service hotel in the center. The very firm beds have thick floral-print quilts and pleasingly simple cast-iron frames, and the furniture, while mostly unobtrusively modern, includes a few writing tables and fat armoires made of old wood. There's a sitting area with a fireplace and a cozy TV room that opens onto a small terra-cotta-tiled courtyard where you can take your coffee and rolls in the morning.

Via San Donato 14 (next to the Duomo), 53045 Montepulciano (SI). www.albergoduomomontepulciano.it. ✆/fax **0578-757-473.** 13 units. 75€–95€ double; 115€ triple. Rates include breakfast. AE, MC, V. Free parking. Closed 2 weeks in Jan or Feb. **Amenities:** Bar. *In room:* A/C (in some), TV, hair dryer, minibar, Wi-Fi (free).

Fattoria Pulcino ★ TUSCAN/GRILL If you could mark a spot for a perfect panorama of Montepulciano, your *X* would come down somewhere near the terrace at Pulcino. The large, informal restaurant's cooking is almost beside the point, but a menu of pasta and grilled meats is perfectly executed, if limited. The "local" choice is *pici di Montepulciano,* a thick, hand-rolled spaghetti. Ordering from the grill (the free-range chicken half and veal steak are especially succulent) means a longer wait; everything here is cooked to order from scratch.

Via SS146 per Chianciano 35 (3km/2 miles SE of town). www.pulcino.com. ✆ **0578-758-711.** Main courses 10€–16€. AE, MC, V. Daily noon–10pm; winter hours vary, so call ahead.

Meublé Il Riccio This hotel's name comes from the *ricci* (hedgehogs) that were carved on the wooden supports once adorning the outside of this 13th-century house. They now decorate the rooms, which are comfortable with functionally modern furniture and whitewashed walls. Guests share the pretty sitting room and a rooftop terrace where the views stretch over the Valdichiana and even get in the top of the Palazzo Comunale's tower. It's a two-story walk-up with no elevator.

Via Talosa 21 (a few steps off Piazza Grande), 53045 Montepulciano (SI). www.ilriccio.net. ✆/fax **0578-757-713.** 6 units. 100€ double; 116€ triple. Breakfast 8€. MC, V. Free parking. **Amenities:** Bar; bike rental. *In room:* A/C, TV, hair dryer, minibar.

A Side Trip to Pienza ★

Just 13km (8 miles) west of Montepulciano, Pienza owes its existence to the ambitions and ego of a quintessential Renaissance man. Pope Pius II (of Siena's illustrious Piccolomini family) was born here in 1405 when the town was called Corsignano, and in 1459 (a year after he was elected pope), he commissioned Florentine architect Bernardo Rossellino to level the medieval core of the town and create the first stage of what would be the model High Renaissance city. He renamed it Pienza, in his own honor.

A farm on the outskirts of Pienza.

The grand scheme didn't get very far (the pope died in 1464), but what has remained is perfectly preserved and has become a UNESCO-protected site. The graceful **Piazza Pio II ★★★** is the architectural set-piece. Tour its **Palazzo Piccolomini** (www.palazzopiccolominipienza.it; ✆ **0578-748-503**), the pope's residence, lived in by descendants of the Piccolomini family until 1968, and the **Duomo ★**. Unusually for Tuscany, the **five altarpieces ★** painted specifically for the cathedral by Sienese masters (1460–62) are still *in situ;* they make a good study of how the mid-15th century artists worked a theme. Four of the five paintings are *Madonna and Child with Saints* (the other is an *Assumption*). Afterwards, walk behind the Duomo for views of Monte Amiata and the sweeping Val d'Orcia. The **tourist office** is inside the Palazzo Vescovile on Piazza Pio II, Corso Rossellino 30, 53026 Pienza (✆ **0578-749-905**). Between mid-March and October, it's open Wednesday through Monday 10am to 1pm and 3 to 6pm; through the rest of the year, it's weekends only.

You can see most of the town in half a day. It takes about 5 minutes to cover Pienza's main drag, **Corso Rossellino,** whose food stores specialize in the products from this bountiful corner of Tuscany, namely wines, honey, and pecorino cheese (also known as *cacio*). Cheese tasting is more popular than wine tasting here, and stores offer their varieties of *fresco* (fresh), *semistagionato* (partially aged), *pepperocinato* (dusted with hot peppers), or *tartufato* (truffled). Taste as much cheese as you will, but by all means save room for lunch at the reasonably priced **Latte di Luna,** Via San Carlo 2–4 (✆ **0578-748606;** closed Tues). A meal of homemade *pici* pasta and a savory grilled meat will cost around 20€, main courses range 7€ to 16€.

PERUGIA ★★

164km (102 miles) SE of Florence, 176km (109 miles) N of Rome

Perugia is a capital city in a medieval hill town's clothing—a warren of Gothic palaces and jazz cafes, where ancient alleys of stone drop precipitously off a 19th-century shopping promenade. It produced and trained some of Umbria's finest artists, including Gentile da Fabriano and Perugino (born Pietro Vannucci in nearby Città della Pieve), from whose workshop emerged Pinturicchio, Lo Spagna, and Raphael. In addition to one the finest art galleries in Italy, there are several important churches and smaller museums to see, but it's this combination of shops, bars, and sights—the juxtaposition of medieval and contemporary Umbria—that makes the city so appealing. Perugia is also a respected university town, whose student population ensures a lively cultural calendar.

Essentials

GETTING THERE Two **rail** lines serve Perugia. The state railway connects with **Rome** (2–3 hr.; most trains require a change at Foligno) and **Florence** (2¼ hr.; most trains require a change at Terontola) every couple of hours. There are also hourly trains to **Assisi** (20–30 min.) and **Spoleto** (1¼ hr.). The station is a few kilometers southwest of the center at Piazza Vittorio Veneto (✆ **147-888-088**), but well connected with buses to/from Piazza Italia (1€). The station for the **Umbria Mobilità–operated regional railway** (✆ **800/512-141**), Sant'Anna, is closer, in Piazzale Bellucci (near the bus station). These tiny trains serve **Todi** every couple of hours.

Perugia is connected by three fast, and free, **roads.** The Raccordo Perugia-A1 runs east-west between the A1, Lago Trasimeno, and Perugia, bypassing the city to link with the E45 (aka SS3bis). The E45 runs south to Todi and Terni (for Rome). Heading southeast, the SS75bis connects the E45 at Perugia with Assisi and Spoleto.

Parking is fairly abundant, with the most convenient being the underground pay lot at Piazza Partigiani. For information about parking in Perugia, visit www.sipaonline.it.

SULGA lines (www.sulga.it; ✆ **075-500-9641**) also has one **bus** (Mon and Fri) from Florence (6pm; 2 hr.), six or seven daily from Assisi (30 min.) and Todi (40 min.), and around six a day from Rome (2½ hr.); the morning buses usually stop at the airport. **Umbria Mobilità** (www.umbriamobilita.it; ✆ **800/512-141**) buses connect Perugia with Assisi (six buses daily; 50 min.), Gubbio (six buses daily; 1 hr., 10 min.), and Todi (six buses daily; 1 hr., 15 min.).

The Arco di Augusto.

There's also a regional **airport:** Six weekly **Ryanair** (www.ryanair.com; ✆ **0871/246-0000**) flights connect London Stansted with Perugia's **Aeroporto Internazionale dell'Umbria** (www.airport.umbria.it; ✆ **075-592141**), 10km (6 miles) east of the city at San Egidio. Flights are usually met by a minibus outside the terminal, taking you to Perugia train station and Piazza Italia (30–40 min.; 3.50€), but heading back there are just three buses per day, so check times in advance (just one Sat–Sun). Taxis cost around 25€.

VISITOR INFORMATION The **tourist office** is at Piazza Matteotti 18 (www.regioneumbria.eu; ✆ **075-573-6458**). It's open daily from 8:30am to 6:30pm. You can also pick up a copy of ***Viva Perugia*** (1€) at newsstands to find out what's going on around town. The **Città Museo** (www.perugiacittamuseo.it; ✆ **075-577-2805**) pass covers 12 of Perugia's cultural attractions, and gives discounts at shops and the Partigiani car park. Visiting any five within a 48-hour period costs 10€ (plus free entry for one child 17 and under).

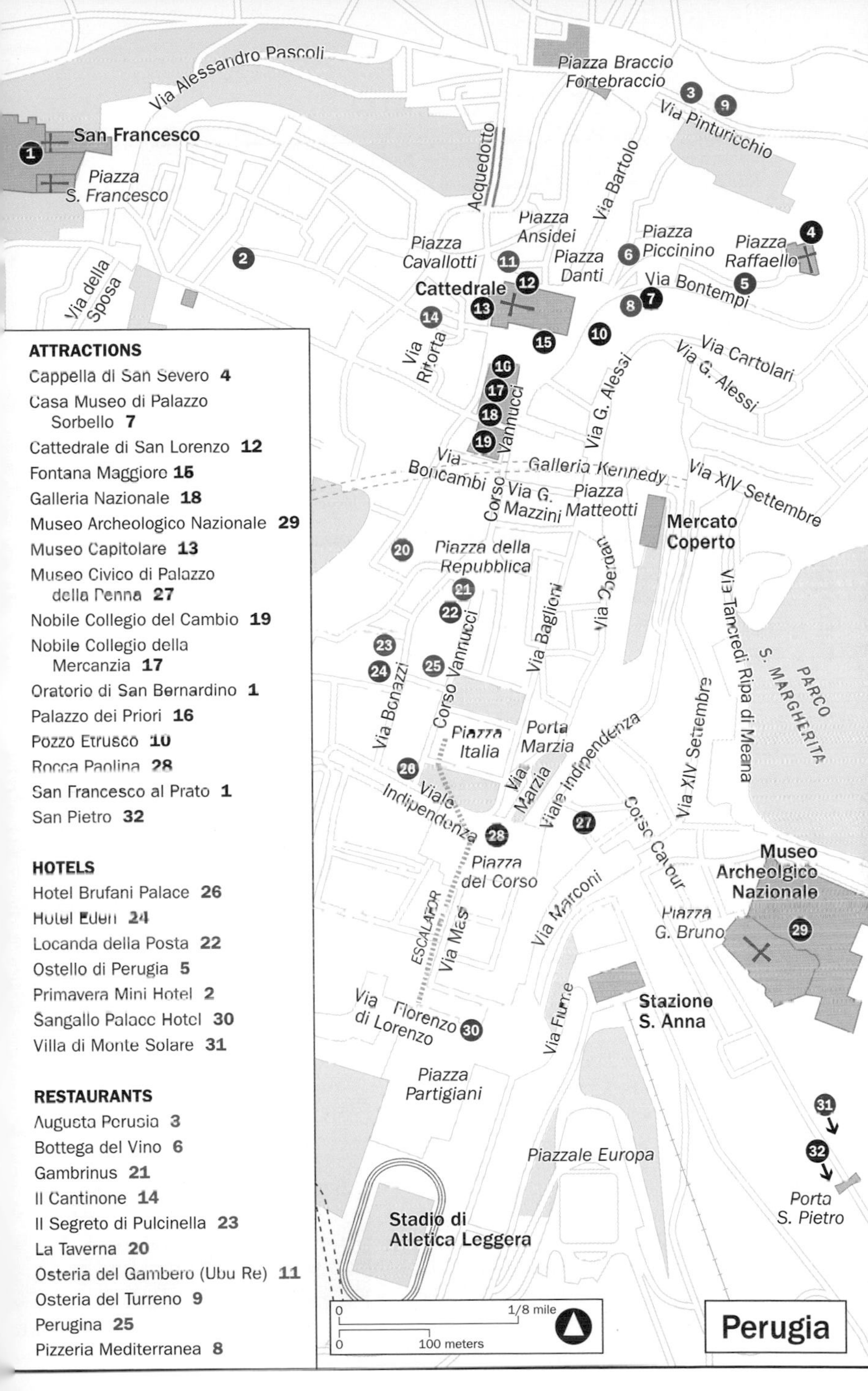
Via Alessandro Pascoli
Piazza Braccio Fortebraccio
Via Pinturicchio
San Francesco
Piazza S. Francesco
Acquedotto
Via Bartolo
Piazza Ansidei
Piazza Piccinino
Piazza Raffaello
Piazza Cavallotti
Piazza Danti
Via Bontempi
Via della Sposa
Cattedrale
Via Ritorta
Via Cartolari
Via G. Alessi
Corso Vannucci
Via Boncambi
Galleria Kennedy
Via XIV Settembre
Via G. Mazzini
Piazza Matteotti
Mercato Coperto
Piazza della Repubblica
Via Oberdan
Via Baglioni
Via Tancredi Ripa di Meana
Parco S. Margherita
Via Bonazzi
Piazza Italia
Porta Marzia
Viale Indipendenza
Via Marzia
Corso Cavour
Piazza del Corso
Escalator
Via Masi
Via Marconi
Museo Archeolgico Nazionale
Piazza G. Bruno
Stazione S. Anna
Via Fiume
Via Florenzo di Lorenzo
Piazza Partigiani
Piazzale Europa
Porta S. Pietro
Stadio di Atletica Leggera
1/8 mile
100 meters
Perugia
ATTRACTIONS
Cappella di San Severo 4
Casa Museo di Palazzo Sorbello 7
Cattedrale di San Lorenzo 12
Fontana Maggiore 15
Galleria Nazionale 18
Museo Archeologico Nazionale 29
Museo Capitolare 13
Museo Civico di Palazzo della Penna 27
Nobile Collegio del Cambio 19
Nobile Collegio della Mercanzia 17
Oratorio di San Bernardino 1
Palazzo dei Priori 16
Pozzo Etrusco 10
Rocca Paolina 28
San Francesco al Prato 1
San Pietro 32
HOTELS
Hotel Brufani Palace 26
Hotel Eden 24
Locanda della Posta 22
Ostello di Perugia 5
Primavera Mini Hotel 2
Sangallo Palace Hotel 30
Villa di Monte Solare 31
RESTAURANTS
Augusta Perusia 3
Bottega del Vino 6
Gambrinus 21
Il Cantinone 14
Il Segreto di Pulcinella 23
La Taverna 20
Osteria del Gambero (Ubu Re) 11
Osteria del Turreno 9
Perugina 25
Pizzeria Mediterranea 8

THE CITY OF *CIOCCOLATO*

Perugia is a chocoholic's paradise, with the **Baci** brand of chocs made here and a weeklong **Eurochocolate Festival** (www.eurochocolate.com) held annually from mid- to late October. Hour-by-hour festivities are held throughout town, staged by chocolate manufacturers from all over the world. You can witness a chocolate-carving contest, when the scraps of 1,000-kg (455-lb.) blocks are yours for sampling, and entire multiple-course menus are created around the chocolate theme.

All year, **Perugina ★** (✆ **075-573-4760;** Mon 2:30–7:45pm, Tues–Sat 9:30am–7:45pm, Sun 9:30am–1:30pm and 3–7:45pm) has a shop selling all the major chocolate products at Corso Vannucci 101, but you shouldn't miss the handmade chocolates and sensational gelato (1.80€–2.80€) at **Augusta Perusia ★★**, Via Pinturicchio 2 (www.cioccolatoaugustaperusia.it; ✆ **075-573-4577;** Mon–Sat 10:30am–8:30pm, Sun 10:30am–1pm and 4–8pm). More convenient is **Gambrinus** at Via Luigi Bonazzi 3 (just off the Corso), with tempting gelato flavors for 1.70€ to 4.20€. It's open daily from 11am to 1am.

FESTIVALS & MARKETS One of Europe's most important jazz festivals, **Umbria Jazz ★★** (www.umbriajazz.com) usually runs for 2 weeks in mid-July. Established in 1973, it draws top international names to town for concerts, and instructors from Boston's prestigious Berklee College of Music hold seminars and workshops.

Exploring Perugia

Perugia's public living room is **Corso Vannucci ★**, a wide promenade that's the stage for one of Italy's most lively and decorous evening *passeggiate*. One end of Corso Vannucci is anchored by the 19th-century **Piazza Italia** (see "Perugia's 'Medieval Pompeii,'" below), while another end cuts into Perugia's superb main square, **Piazza IV Novembre.** The centerpiece of the piazza is the **Fontana Maggiore ★★**, one of Italy's most photogenic public fountains, with panels and figures carved between 1278 and 1280 by Gothic master sculptors Nicola Pisano and his son Giovanni.

The escalator from the lower part of Perugia to older section of the city.

Cappella di San Severo ★ CHURCH Before he set off for Florence and Rome, a young Perugino protégé named Raphael Sanzio made his first attempt at fresco in this 14th-century chapel in 1505. Though damaged, the upper half of this work, with the *Holy Trinity* surrounded by saints seated on clouds, shows the germ of Raphael's budding genius and his eye for composition and naturalism. By 1521, Raphael had died young, and his now-septuagenarian teacher, Perugino—just 2 years from the grave himself, with his talent fading—finished the scene with six posed saints along the bottom.

Piazza Raffaello. ✆ **075-573-3864.** Admission 3€ adults, 2€ seniors 65 and over, 1€ children 7–14, free for children 6 and under; includes admission to Pozzo Etrusco, valid 1 week. May–July and Sept–Oct Tues–Sun 10am–1:30pm and 2:30–6pm; Nov–Mar Tues–Sun 11am–1:30pm and 2:30–5pm; Apr and Aug daily 10am–1:30pm and 2:30–6pm.

Galleria Nazionale ★★★ ART MUSEUM One of central Italy's top museums, Perugia's National Gallery houses the largest and finest collection of Umbrian art in the world, including plenty of Perugino paintings.

Rooms 2 and 3 show the development of 13th-century Perugian painting. It was heavily influenced by the artists working on Assisi's Basilica di San Francesco and therefore torn between the local traditional eastern influences and the classicism of the new Florentine masters, Cimabue and Giotto. The highlight in Room 2 is a *Madonna* by Sienese master **Duccio di Buoninsegna,** painted for Perugia's San Domenico church around 1310.

Rooms 5 to 7 are devoted to early-15th-century altarpieces from the brushes of Bartolo di Fredi, Ottaviano Nelli, and Bicci di Lorenzo. Among them, in Room 6, is Gentile da Fabriano's tiny gemlike ***Madonna and Child*** ★ (1405), an International Gothic masterpiece. Look out also for **Taddeo di Bartolo**'s *Pentecost* ★ of 1403 (Room 5) and **Iacopo Salimbeni**'s monochrome *Crucifixion* ★ of 1420 (Room 6), the first for its radical composition, the second for a display of facial emotion that wouldn't become the norm for decades.

Room 8 is entirely dedicated to the finely detailed ***Guidalotti Polyptych*** crafted by Beato Angelo around 1448, while **Room 11** contains the museum's greatest masterpiece, Piero della Francesca's ***Polyptych of Sant'Antonio*** ★★★. The most arresting portion is the pinnacle's *Annunciation* scene, worked with a delicacy and sense of perspective unheard of at the time.

Rooms 22 to 26 contain what many visitors come here for—the 15th- and 16th-century art starring large **altarpieces by Perugino** ★. He may have been assisted on the 1505 *Monteripido Altarpiece* background by his young pupil Raphael (Room 23). His later works here, especially the *Polyptych of St. Augustine* (which he worked on for 20 years and was still unfinished at his death), show how he eventually developed a more transparent, spatially spare style with delicate landscapes and crafted pastel figures.

Palazzo dei Priori, Corso Vannucci 19. www.gallerianazionaleumbria.it. ✆ **075-574-1247.** Admission 6.50€ adults, 3.25€ ages 18–25 (E.U. citizens only), free for children 17 and under and seniors 65 and over (E.U. citizens only). Mon 9:30am–7:30pm; Tues–Sun 8:30am–7:30pm.

Nobile Collegio del Cambio ★★ ART MUSEUM The meeting rooms of Perugia's Moneychanger's Guild, just to the left of the National Gallery, make up one of the best-preserved "office suites" of the Renaissance. Perugino was hired in 1496 to fresco their **Sala dell' Udienza** with a style and scenery illustrating the humanist marriage of Christianity and classicism. It's perhaps his masterpiece in the medium, replete with a studied naturalism and precise portraiture, and a virtual catwalk of late-15th-century fashion. Perugino's less-talented student Giannicola di Paolo frescoed the adjacent **Capella di San Giovanni Battista** from 1509 to 1529.

Palazzo dei Priori, Corso Vannucci 25. ✆ **075-572-8599.** Admission 4.50€ adults, 2.50€ seniors 65 and over, free for children 12 and under. Dec 20–Jan 6 Tues–Sat 9am–12:30pm and 2:30–5:30pm, Sun 9am–1pm; Mar 1–Oct 31 Mon–Sat 9am–12:30pm and 2:30–5:30pm, Sun 9am–1pm; Nov 1–Dec 19 and Jan 7–Feb 28 Tues–Sat 8am–2pm, Sun 9am–12:30pm.

Where to Eat

Dining in Perugia is polarized: There are several worthy fine restaurants and plenty of cheap *pizzerie* supported by the student population, but few *trattorie* in between. Of the *pizzerie,* the best is **Il Segreto di Pulcinella,** Via Larga 8, off Via Bonazzi and a short walk from Piazza della Repubblica (✆ **075-573-6284**). Pizzas cost 4€ to 7€. It's open Tuesday through Sunday from 12:10 to 2:30pm and 8:30pm to midnight.

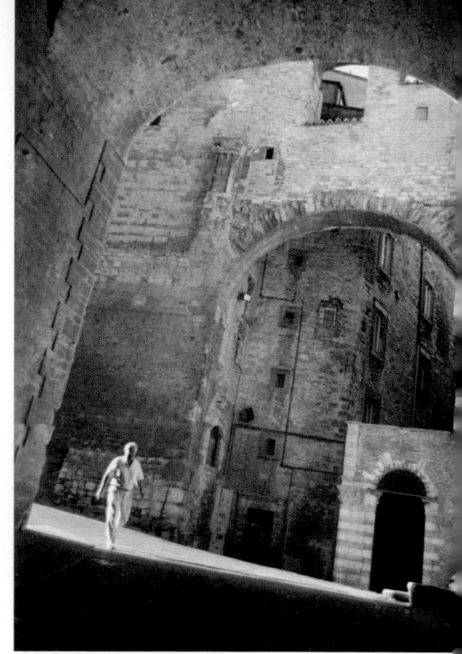

Perugia's ancient streets.

Bottega del Vino ★ UMBRIAN Bottega del Vino is one of Perugia's most popular dining spots. The focus here is fresh produce from the farms around Perugia, with homemade Umbrian pastas, cured ham, and even beef angus steaks. The melted cheese appetizers are addictive treats, and there's a huge choice of local wine—no surprise, given that the restaurant also doubles as a wine bar. The terrace is one of the best places in town for evening *aperitivo.*

Via del Sole 1. ✆ **075-571-6181.** Reservations recommended. Main courses 13€. DC, MC, V. Tues–Sun noon–3pm and 7pm–midnight. Closed Jan.

La Taverna ★★ UMBRIAN The best restaurant in town, candlelit La Taverna is removed from the hubbub (but still central; just follow the signs). Couples meet for a romantic meal and families celebrate special occasions under the brick barreled vaults or outside in the tiny courtyard. If they're available and you have an appetite, go for the *caramelle rosse al Gorgonzola,* a 'zola-soaked plate of homemade ravioli filled with juicy beets. Follow that up with *medaglioni alle punte di asparagi,* which are cuts of filet, smothered in a creamy asparagus sauce and scalloped potatoes. Outdoor seating is limited, so call ahead for one of the tables.

Via delle Streghe 8 (near Corso Vannucci's Piazza Repubblica). ✆ **075-572-4128.** Reservations recommended. Main courses 9€–16€. AE, DC, MC, V. Tues–Sun 12:30–2:30pm and 7:30–11pm.

Osteria del Gambero (Ubu Re) ★ UMBRIAN/SEAFOOD Ubu Re feels a bit like a posh private home, with modern art prints, soft jazz, and a small, intimate dining room well off the main drag. This has become one of the best restaurants in Perugia, with contemporary riffs on local cuisine—it can be a little heavy for lunch, unless you plan to doze for a couple of hours. The tasty breads, pasta, and desserts are made on-site, and seasonal dishes grace the menu, anything

PERUGIA'S "MEDIEVAL POMPEII"

To cow the insurgent Perugini into submission after he put down their rebellion against his salt tax, Pope Paul III demolished more than one-quarter of the city in 1530, pointedly including the palaces of the fractious former leaders, the Baglioni family. He then ordered Antonio da Sangallo the Younger to build him a fortress, the **Rocca Paolina ★**, in the gaping empty space. By 1543, the massive bastion was complete, and it helped uphold papal domination over Perugia for more than 300 years. At the Italian unification in 1860, when Perugia was finally freed from the pope's yoke, workers came to dismantle the fortress. They found themselves outnumbered, however, as almost every man, woman, and child in the city descended with grim faces on the hated *rocca* and began to tear it apart stone by stone with pickaxes, shovels, and their bare hands.

In the building process, a whole neighborhood of the medieval town was preserved, intact but eerily silent and still, buried beneath the newer streets above. The vaults of the *rocca* now serve as a **public exhibition space**, and stretches of the subterranean streets are interspersed with the escalators that connect Piazza Italia, which partially takes up the space the dismantled fortress left, with the parking lots below. An underground "Via Baglioni" leads through a section of this almost-forgotten city, with dozens of houses and churches abandoned for hundreds of years. You can clamber through doorless entrances, climb the remains of stairways, walk through empty rooms, and wander at will through the maze of mute walls. Enter the underground city daily (no admission fee) from the escalators at Piazza Italia (daily 6:15am–1:45am), through the Porta Marzia on Via Marzia, or by riding the escalators up from Piazza Partigiani.

from *mousse tepida di piccione* (pigeon soufflé in black truffle sauce) to lamb and potato pudding—their pastas with squid or Sagrantino are always sensational. They offer a good value fixed-price menu for 30€, and a seafood menu for 32€.
Via Baldeschi 8/a (behind the Duomo). ✆ **075-573-5461.** Reservations recommended. Main courses 14€. MC, V. Tues–Sun 7:30–11:30pm. Closed 2 weeks in Jan, 2 weeks in July.

Osteria del Turreno ★ UMBRIAN/ITALIAN This *tavola calda* diner opposite the cathedral has been serving basic lunches with a Perugian twist for decades. The day's dishes are displayed canteen-style; pick what you fancy, pay at the till, and take it to your table, inside or out. Options always include simple pasta (such as lasagna, 4.10€), grilled meats, and plenty of salad and veg. Desserts are a bit scarce—but beer and wine (3€ for a quarter liter) aren't!
Piazza Danti 16. ✆ **075-572-1976.** Main courses 6€–7€. Sun–Fri 9am–3pm.

Where to Stay

Most Perugian hotels are flexible about rates, which dive 40% to 50% below posted prices in the off season, so it always pays to ask. If you have a car, there are plenty of romantic and historic *agriturismi* and rental apartments in the surrounding countryside; the best of the latter is the **Villa Nuba Apartments ★★**, just 1.5km (1 mile) outside town (Eugubina 70, Collegiorgio II; www.villanuba.com; ✆ **075-572-5765**), with rates as low as 50€ per night.

Brufani Palace ★ Where the bastions of the papal Rocca Paolina once glowered, Perugia's bastion of luxury now rises, built in 1883 by a Grand Tour guide as an inn for his English clients. It offers standardized comforts and (from most rooms) spectacular views. Most accommodations are done in a modernized classic style—or, in the newer ones, a gilded 18th-century decor to match the original marble statues in the public areas—all with fresh carpets and wall fabrics, heavy curtains, and sparkling bathrooms with marble sinks; some have Jacuzzi tubs. The first-floor rooms are older and grander—a few even have high, frescoed ceilings and the original furnishings.

Piazza Italia 12, 06100 Perugia. www.brufanipalace.com. ✆ **075-573-2541.** Fax 075-572-0210. 94 units. 325€ double; 460€ junior suite; 850€–980€ suite. AE, DC, MC, V. Garage parking 31€. **Amenities:** Restaurant/American bar (tables on the piazza in summer); babysitting; concierge; small exercise room; indoor pool; room service. *In room:* A/C, TV, VCR and fax (in suites), hair dryer, minibar, Wi-Fi (6€ per hour).

Eden ★ This cozy three-star property, in a completely renovated building dating back to the 13th century, is a great deal considering the central location, especially out of season. Most rooms come with stupendous views over the countryside and the old town—compact but stylish, the furnishings are simple and contemporary, with not a medieval antique in sight. Even the art on the walls is modern. Expect exceptionally friendly staff and attentive service.

Via Cesare Caporali 9, 06123 Perugia. www.hoteleden.perugia.it. ✆ **075-572-8102.** Fax 075-572-0342. 12 units. 65€–95€ double. Rates include breakfast. MC, V. Garage parking 25€. **Amenities:** Bar. *In room:* A/C, TV, hair dryer, Wi-Fi (free).

Sangallo Palace ☺ Ranking just under Brufani Palace (see above), this palace is right below the historic center—it sits atop the Partigiani garage, so it's just a 10-minute walk and a few escalator rides from Corso Vannucci. The hotel is modern, elegant, and preferred by business types in town for conferences. Over each bed is a framed reproduction of a Perugino or Pinturicchio. The medium-size to spacious guest rooms come with amenities like private safes, an interactive television, and wide beds with firm mattresses, and they often open onto panoramic countryside views. In summer, breakfast is served on the (noisy) terrace.

Via Masi 9, 06121 Perugia. www.sangallo.it. ✆ **075-573-0202.** Fax 075-573-0068. 93 units. 126€–178€ double; 169€–222€ suite. Rates include breakfast. AE, DC, MC, V. Garage parking 15€ per day. **Amenities:** Restaurant; babysitting; small children's center; small exercise room; Internet (2.50€ per hour); Jacuzzi; small indoor heated pool; room service; tennis courts (1km/⅔ mile away). *In room:* A/C, TV, hair dryer, minibar.

Villa di Monte Solare ★★ This gorgeous luxury hotel lies 25 minutes outside Perugia, up in the hills. There are nightly classical music concerts in the villa's frescoed chapel, a huge range of spa treatments in a converted *limonaia,* and Michelin-worthy dinners in a jacket-and-tie restaurant led by local chef Nicola Fanfano. The main house is impeccably furnished in period chairs and paintings with ancient terra-cotta floors, while the surrounding farm buildings where most of the guests stay are fitted with ultramodern furnishings. The hotel offers walking tours of the historic property and of the surrounding towns, as well as cycling tours and cooking classes.

Via Montali, 7 Colle San Paolo (near Panicale). www.villamontesolare.com. ✆ **075-832-376.** Fax 075-835-5462. 21 units. 200€–240€ double; 240€–280€ superior double; 300€–350€ suite. Rates include breakfast. AE, DC, MC, V. Free parking. **Amenities:** Formal restaurant; bar; concierge; pool; spa. *In room:* A/C, TV, hair dryer, minibar, Wi-Fi (10€ per day).

ASSISI ★★★

27km (17 miles) E of Perugia, 190km (118 miles) SE of Florence, 175km (109 miles) N of Rome

Arrive early in the morning, before the first tour buses, and you'll soon see that Assisi is a special place—the rising sun behind Monte Subasio, often shrouded in mist, cuts massive silhouettes behind this medieval city of miracles. A peculiar blend of romance, architecture, and devotion make it the quintessential Umbrian hill town—the absolutely essential stop on any Umbrian tour. For Christian pilgrims the magic is all about **St. Francis,** patron saint of Italy, founder of one of the world's largest monastic orders, and generally considered just about the holiest person to walk the earth since Jesus. The biggest draw is the giant **Basilica di San Francesco,** built to honor the saint but now almost as much a temple to pre-Renaissance painter **Giotto.** The rest is an ideally sited hill town, hardly spoiled by its pesky traffic and tat shops, and absorbing its millions of annual tourists and pilgrims with a quiet ease. Though inevitably commercial, Assisi has avoided an invasion of tack that's all too apparent in parts of Tuscany, and it's not hard to find a back street all to yourself.

Essentials

GETTING THERE From **Perugia,** there are about 20 **trains** daily (25–30 min.). From **Florence** (2–3 hr.), there are trains every 2 hours or so, though some require a transfer at Terontola. The station is in the modern valley town of Santa Maria degli Angeli, about 5km (3 miles) from Assisi, with bus connections to Assisi every 20 minutes (1€), or you can take a **taxi** for about 15€ to 20€.

By **car,** Assisi is 18km (11 miles) east of Perugia, off the SS75bis. Driving the center's steep streets is forbidden for tourists. The best strategy is to **park** in Piazza Matteotti (1.15€ per hour), keep walking west, and finish at the basilica; it's all downhill.

Socializing on the Corso Vannucci.

Basilica di San Francesco.

Eight Umbria Mobilità **buses** (www.umbriamobilita.it; ✆ **800/512-141**) run seven times daily (Mon–Fri) between **Perugia** and Assisi's Piazza Matteotti (50 min.; 3.20€; 4€ if you pay on the bus). They also run about five buses from **Gubbio** (1¾ hr.). **SULGA** (www.sulga.it; ✆ **075-500-9641**) runs two buses daily from **Rome**'s Tiburtina station, taking about 3 hours, and one daily trip from Piazza Adua in **Florence,** which takes about 2½ hours.

VISITOR INFORMATION The **tourist office** (www.comune.assisi.pg.it; ✆ **075-812-534**) is in the Palazzo S. Nicola on Piazza del Comune, 06081 Assisi. It's open summer daily from 8am to 6:30pm, winter Monday through Saturday from 8am to 2pm and 3 to 6pm, Sunday from 9am to 1pm. The private websites **www.assisionline.com** and **www.assisiweb.com** also have good info.

FESTIVALS & MARKETS In the city of St. Francis, all **church holidays** are pilgrim-ridden, solemn religious rites. But for the **Calendimaggio ★★** spring celebration, the first weekend (starting Thurs) after May 1, Assisi goes totally pagan. The town divides itself into "upper" and "lower" factions that date to the 1300s. The festivities, with processions, medieval contests of strength and skill, and late-night partying—all in 14th-century costume, of course—go back much further to the pre-Roman rites of spring. Call ✆ **075-812-534** for info.

Exploring Assisi

The main square in town is **Piazza del Comune.** The medieval edition of what may have been the old Roman forum (see below) is most famous for the six gleaming white Corinthian columns and tympanum of the **Tempio di Minerva** a 1st-century-B.C. Roman temple the Assisians sensibly recycled into the church of **Santa Maria sopra Minerva** (daily 6:45am–8pm; free), with a thoroughly uninteresting baroque interior.

Basilica di San Francesco ★★★ ICON Although Assisi's basilica is first and foremost a site of Christian pilgrimage, it's also a masterpiece of medieval architecture and the home of some exuberant medieval art. The almost simultaneous construction of huge Lower (1228) and Upper (1230) churches in contrasting Romanesque and Gothic styles had no peer or precedent. Franciscan Brother Elias, the probable architect, built the basilica to house Francis's recently

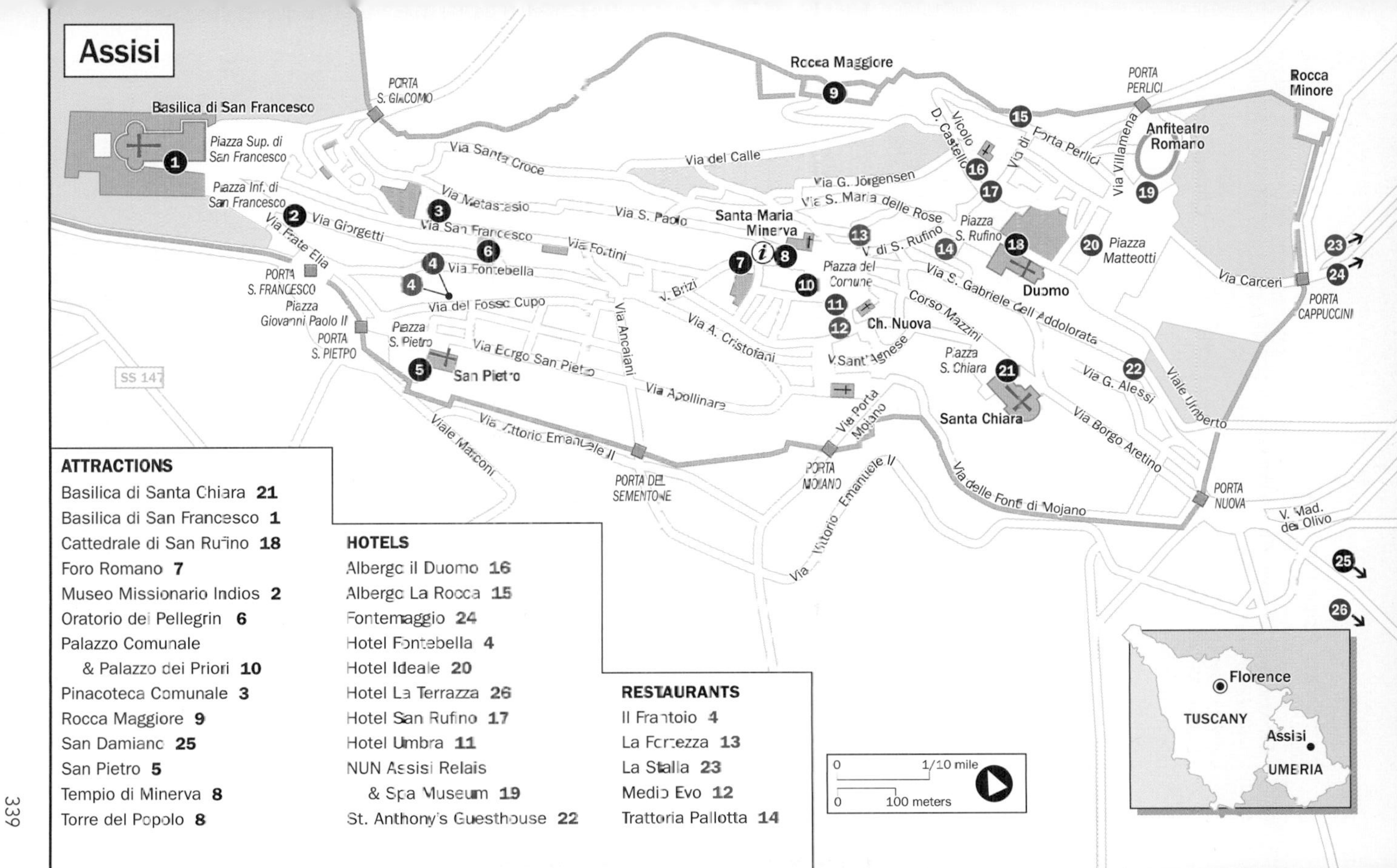

Assisi
ATTRACTIONS
Basilica di Santa Chiara 21
Basilica di San Francesco 1
Cattedrale di San Rufino 18
Foro Romano 7
Museo Missionario Indios 2
Oratorio dei Pellegrin 6
Palazzo Comunale & Palazzo dei Priori 10
Pinacoteca Comunale 3
Rocca Maggiore 9
San Damiano 25
San Pietro 5
Tempio di Minerva 8
Torre del Popolo 8
HOTELS
Albergo il Duomo 16
Albergo La Rocca 15
Fontemaggio 24
Hotel Fontebella 4
Hotel Ideale 20
Hotel La Terrazza 26
Hotel San Rufino 17
Hotel Umbra 11
NUN Assisi Relais & Spa Museum 19
St. Anthony's Guesthouse 22
RESTAURANTS
Il Frantoio 4
La Fortezza 13
La Stalla 23
Medio Evo 12
Trattoria Pallotta 14
Basilica di San Francesco
Piazza Sup. di San Francesco
Piazza Inf. di San Francesco
PORTA S. GIACOMO
Via Santa Croce
Via Metastasio
Via San Francesco
Via Giorgetti
Via Frate Elia
PORTA S. FRANCESCO
Piazza Giovanni Paolo II
PORTA S. PIETRO
Via Fontebella
Via del Fosso Cupo
Piazza S. Pietro
San Pietro
Via Borgo San Pietro
SS 147
Viale Marconi
Via Vittorio Emanuele II
PORTA DEL SEMENTONE
Via Ancaiani
Via Apollinare
Via A. Cristofani
V. Brizi
Via Fortini
Via S. Paolo
Via del Calle
Rocca Maggiore
Santa Maria Minerva
Piazza del Comune
Ch. Nuova
V. Sant'Agnese
Via Porta Mojano
PORTA MOJANO
Via G. Jörgensen
Via S. Maria delle Rose
V. di S. Rufino
Piazza S. Rufino
Via S. Gabriele dell'Addolorata
Corso Mazzini
Piazza S. Chiara
Santa Chiara
Duomo
Vicolo D. Castello
Via di Porta Perlici
PORTA PERLICI
Via Villamena
Anfiteatro Romano
Piazza Matteotti
Rocca Minore
Via Carceri
PORTA CAPPUCCINI
Via G. Alessi
Viale Umberto
Via Borgo Aretino
Via delle Fonti di Mojano
PORTA NUOVA
V. Mad. del Olivo
Florence
TUSCANY
Assisi
UMBRIA
0 1/10 mile
0 100 meters

Dress Appropriately

San Francesco and Santa Chiara, like many other churches throughout Italy, have a strict **dress code:** Entrance to the basilica is *forbidden* to those wearing shorts or miniskirts or showing bare shoulders. You also must remain silent and cannot take photographs in the Upper Church of San Francesco.

sanctified bones. Today it still moves the devout to tears and art lovers to fits of near-religious ecstasy.

The Lower Church Entered through a Gothic portal under a Renaissance porch on Piazza Inferiore di San Francesco (the lower of the two squares abutting the church), the basilica's bottom half is a low-ceilinged, extremely dim cryptlike church. The first chapel on the left is the **Cappella di San Martino ★★**, frescoed with that saint's life by the Sienese genius Simone Martini (1312–15). Martini amply displays both his penchant for boldly patterned fabrics—not unusual in an artist from a textile center—and his mastery of the medieval forms and themes of late Gothic Sienese painting.

Halfway up the nave on either side are stairs descending to the **crypt** containing the venerated **stone coffin of St. Francis** surrounded by the graves of four of his followers—for pilgrims this is the most sacred part of the church, despite the endless stream of tourists filing up and down the steps.

Up the nave again, the **Cappella della Santa Maria Maddalena ★**, the last chapel on the right, was frescoed with the *Life of St. Mary Magdalene* by Giotto and his assistants (1303–09). For two of the more dramatic scenes—the *Raising of Lazarus* and a *Noli Me Tangere*—Giotto borrowed the compositions from the same scenes he'd recently finished in his fresco cycle for Padua's Scrovegni Chapel (p. 511).

In the **left transept's barrel vault** and on its walls, early Sienese master Pietro Lorenzetti left one of his masterpieces. A 1320 cycle of *Christ's Passion* ends with a huge and colorful, but sadly damaged, ***Crucifixion* ★★**, and on the wall is a touching and dynamic *Deposition,* featuring a gaunt Christ and whimpering Mary.

The **barrel vault of the right transept ★** was originally frescoed in 1280 by Giotto's master, Cimabue, but only his *Madonna Enthroned with Four Angels and St. Francis* survives, containing what has become the most popular portrait of the saint.

The Upper Church The tall, light-filled Gothic interior of the Upper Church is a striking contrast to its downstairs neighbor. Assuming you're coming up from the Lower Church you'll begin with the oldest frescoes in the Upper Church, those in the **transept.** As with most of the frescoes in this church, no one can agree on the attribution of these works. Some hold the opinion that Cimabue did them all (with the help of assistants) in 1277; others allow him only the masterful and dramatic composition of the ***Crucifixion* ★** and pin the rest on his Roman assistants (Jacopo Torriti, Rustici, and possibly Pietro Cavallini).

The lower register of the nave, with 28 scenes of the ***Life of St. Francis* ★★★**, is what most art aficionados have traveled here to see: the frescoes of Giotto. These frescoes were fully restored in 2002, 5 years after the earthquake that shattered them. Again, there were probably assistants at work here, and there's strong evidence that one pupil, the anonymous Maestro di Santa Cecilia, finished the final four compositionally crowded scenes and may have touched up the first. But most of the attempts to find some additional unknown master can perhaps be written off as iconoclasm—everyone from

Frescoes of St. Francis in Assisi.

Giotto's contemporaries to Vasari to many modern-day art historians accepts Giotto as the primary author of the cycle.

The frescoes pick up the story (at the transept end of the right aisle) as Francesco's initial glimmers of saintliness begin to appear, running through all the most famous incidents of his life, from renouncing his father's inheritance (and taking off all his clothes), to the appearance of stigmata in 1472. On the entrance wall is perhaps the most famous and charming of the scenes, where Francis preaches to the birds.

Piazza Superiore di San Francesco. www.sanfrancescoassisi.org. ✆ **075-819-001.** Free admission. Lower Church daily 6am–6:45pm; Upper Church daily 8:30am–6:45pm. You may visit church for Mass on Sun (before 2pm), but purely touristic visits at this time are frowned on.

Basilica di Santa Chiara ★ CHURCH The vast interior of this 1260, early Gothic church is dark and perennially crowded with people filing down into the neo-Gothic crypt to see the original stone **tomb of St. Clare.** Born to a local minor noble family in 1193, Chiara (anglicized to Clare) was a friend of Francis who followed the mystic's example against her parents' wishes. In 1211, she abandoned her parental household and ran off to meet Francis, who clothed her in sackcloth after his own fashion and hacked off her hair, signaling Clare's renunciation of earthly goods and the beginning of her quest for spiritual enlightenment. She soon gathered a large enough female following at San Damiano that Francis urged her to set up a convent there, and she became abbess. (The order she founded, the Poor Clares, didn't move into town until after her death.)

Off the right wall of the church built to house her tomb is the **Oratorio del Crocifisso,** preserving the venerated 12th-century crucifix that spoke to St. Francis at San Damiano and set him on his holy path.

Piazza Santa Chiara. ✆ **075-812-282.** Free admission. Daily 6:30am–noon and 2–7pm (6pm in winter).

Cattedrale di San Rufino CATHEDRAL Assisi's cathedral is off a quiet walled piazza that receives some historians' votes as the true site of Assisi's Roman forum. The first church on this spot may have been raised as early as the 5th century.

The current incarnation dates from 1134, and the interior was remodeled in 1571, following structural damage, and deserves your attention only if you're interested in the font in which St. Francis, St. Clare, and Emperor Frederick II were baptized (to the right as you enter), and the newer memorials to Pope John Paul II. You can enter the **Museo Diocesano e Cripta di San Rufino** (✆ **075-812-712**), from the entrance outside the church; the crypt's rough vaulting and Ionic columns are, along with the bell tower, the only surviving bits of the 11th-century cathedral. The beautifully presented museum section preserves detached frescoes by Puccio Capanna, more works by Dono Doni, and triptychs by L'Alunno and Matteo da Gualdo.

Piazza San Rufino. www.assisimuseodiocesano.com. ✆ **075-812-283.** Free admission to the church; Museo Diocesano e Cripta 3€ adults, 2.50€ children 12–18 and seniors, 1.50€ children 8–11, free for children 7 and under. Church Mon–Fri 7:30am–12:30pm and 2:30–7pm; Sat–Sun and Aug daily 7am–7pm. Museo Diocesano e Cripta Mar 16–Oct 15 Thurs–Tues 10am–1pm and 3–6pm (Aug 10am–6pm); Oct 16–Mar 15 Thurs–Tues 10am–1pm and 2:30–5:30pm.

Foro Romano ★ RUINS Assisi's secular highlight is a little underwhelming for non–history buffs, but the remnants of this Roman Forum can still hold some magic. An entrance room (the old crypt of San Nicolò Church) houses inscribed tablets and headless statues, but the main passage leading off from here preserves a tiny piece of 2nd-century-B.C. Asisium—a slice of the old forum some 3.9m (13 ft.) below 21st-century Piazza del Comune.

Via Portica 2 (on the edge of Piazza del Comune). ✆ **075-815-5077.** Admission 4€ adults; 2.50€ students, children 8–17, and seniors 65 and over; free for children 7 and under; joint ticket with Rocca Maggiore and Pinacoteca Comunale 8€ and 5€. June–Aug daily 10am–1pm and 2:30–7pm; Mar–May and Sept–Oct daily 10am–1pm and 2:30–6pm; Nov–Feb daily 10:30am–1pm and 2–5pm.

Museo Missionario Indios MUSEUM Assisi's newest museum is also the most atypical, though it still retains a religious link, this time via the Capuchin religious order (an offshoot of the Franciscans). The museum is testimony to the order's missionary work with the native tribes of Amazonia (along the upper Solimões River, Brazil), displaying photos, instruments, masks, and handicrafts from the region. This isn't what most visitors associate with Assisi, but it makes an intriguing break from all things St. Francis.

Via San Francesco 19. www.mumamuseo.it. ✆ **075-812-480.** Free admission. Tues–Sat 10am–6:30pm; Sun 3–6:30pm.

Rocca Maggiore ★★ CASTLE The bleached yellow bones of this fortress glower high above the city, a reminder of the hated Cardinal Albornoz, who built the 14th-century version we see today to establish papal authority over Assisi. Beyond the circular rampart added in the 16th century by Pope Paul III, you can enter the outer walls to visit the restored keep and soldiers' quarters. From the top of the keep is a stunning view to Assisi below—indeed, the best part of a visit here is the walk up the hill through ever narrowing streets.

Piazzale delle Libertà Comunali, at the top of town, at the ends of Via della Rocca, Via del Colle, and the stepped Vicolo San Lorenzo off Via Porta Perlici. ✆ **075-815-292.** Admission 5€ adults; 3.50€ students, children 8–18, and seniors 65 and over; free for children 7 and under; joint ticket with Foro Romano and Pinacoteca Comunale 8€ and 5€. June–Aug daily 9am–8pm; Apr–May and Sept–Oct daily 10am–6:30pm; Nov–Feb daily 10am–4:30pm; Mar 10am–5:30pm.

Where to Eat

Several of Assisi's restaurants serve a local flatbread called ***torta al testa,*** usually split and stuffed with cheeses, sausages, and vegetables (spinach is popular). The breads make good snacks and appetizers, and are best at La Stalla (see below). For a posh picnic, visit **La Bottega dei Sapori,** Piazza del Comune 34 (www.labottegadeisapori.com; ✆ **075-812-294**), a family business selling delicious truffle spreads, vinegars, and panini.

La Fortezza ★★ UMBRIAN This is one of Assisi's great hidden treasures. Since 1960, the Chiocchetti family has offered refined *ristorante* service and inspired cuisine at trattoria prices, and all just a few steps above the main piazza. The *cannelloni all'Assisiana* are scrumptious (fresh pasta sheets wrapped around a veal *ragù,* all baked under parmigiana), as is the *gnocchi alla Fortezza* (homemade gnocchi tossed with a garden of chopped vegetables: tomatoes, mushrooms, zucchini, peas, onions, and more). For a *secondo,* try the *coniglio in salsa di mele* (rabbit in a sort of curry of white wine, saffron, and apples) or marinated wild boar in sweet and sour sauce.

Vicolo della Fortezza/Piazza del Comune (up the stairs near the Via San Rufino end). www.lafortezzahotel.com. ✆ **075-812-993.** Reservations recommended. Main courses 10€–13€. MC, V. Fri–Wed 12:30–2:30pm and 7:30–9:30pm. Closed Feb and 1 week in July.

La Stalla ★★ GRILL/UMBRIAN This is about as rustic as it gets, a series of former livestock stalls made of stone walls and low-beamed ceilings thoroughly blackened by smoke. It's noisy and chaotic (there's also a sunny terrace if you crave more air), but it just may be one of your most memorable Umbrian meals. Start with the *assaggini di torta al testo,* small samplers of Assisian flatbread, split and stuffed with prosciutto and cheese or spinach and sausage. Next up, the *tris tico,* a scooped-out wooden platter laden with a trio of the house specialty *primi,* usually *strangozzi, gnocchi* (both in tomato sauce), and *bigoli* (a ricotta-and-spinach log dusted with Parmesan). For *secondi,* you have a wide range of choices, all barbecued on the grill, from *bistecca di vitello* (grilled veal) to *spiedino di cacciagione* (grilled game). The *salsicce* (sausages) are out of this world.

Via Eremo delle Carceri 24 (1.6km/1 mile east of town). www.fontemaggio.it. ✆ **075-812-317.** Reservations strongly recommended (but not always accepted). Main courses 7€–12€. MC, V. Tues–Sun 12:30–2:30pm and 7:30–10pm. Head out Porta Cappuccini; the turnoff is about 1km/⅔ mile along on the right (follow the signs for the Fontemaggio campground/hostel complex).

Medio Evo ★ ITALIAN/UMBRIAN Down a steep S-curve from the center of town, Medio Evo offers well-spaced tables set with flowers beneath magnificent stone-vaulted ceilings that truly deserve the title of medieval. Meat is sourced exclusively from Umbrian and Tuscan farms, olive oil is 100% Umbrian, and the pasta is made fresh daily; try the *tortellini* stuffed with pheasant. Menus are seasonal, but in summer *secondi* might include roast lamb chops with cheese and mushrooms, or rabbit stewed in Montefalco red wine. Don't overlook the desserts, with a fabulous chocolate mousse and classic tiramisu on offer.

Via Arco dei Priori 4B (a dogleg down from Piazza del Comune). www.ristorantemedioevoassisi.it. ✆ **075-813-068.** Reservations strongly recommended. Main courses 10€–18€. AE, DC, MC, V. Tues–Sun 12:30–3pm and 7:30–10:45pm.

Where to Stay

Book ahead, book ahead, book ahead. Never show up in Assisi, especially from Easter to fall, without a reservation. If you do, you'll spend half your morning at the tourist office calling hotels, only to find yourself stuck overnight in one of the hideous large constructions 4km (2½ miles) away in Santa Maria degli Angeli. The official central booking office is **Consorzio Albergatori ed Operatori Turistici di Assisi,** Via A. Cristofani 22a (www.visitassisi.com; ✆ **075-816-566**).

Brigolante Guest Apartments ★ ☺ If you have a car, skip Assisi's expensive central hotels in preference for this rural gem—still only 5 minutes' drive from town in the foothills of Monte Subasio. The 16th-century *agriturismo,* once part of a castle, offers three self-catering apartments featuring terra-cotta floors, hand-painted tiles, antiques, and period furniture. Host Rebecca and her family are especially welcoming and the apartments are perfect for families, with a large outdoor space, sandpit, and playground.

Via Costa di Trex 31, 06081 Assisi (6km/4 miles east of Assisi). www.brigolante.com. ✆ **075-802-250.** 3 units. 370€–550€ per week; daily rates available Nov–Mar (except mid-Dec to early Jan). AE, MC, V. Free parking. **Amenities:** Bikes. *In room:* A/C, TV, full kitchen.

NUN Assisi Relais & Spa Museum ★★ This slick boutique hotel offers an elegant blend of medieval Italy and contemporary style, with rooms decked out in crisp white designer furniture. The renovated building once formed part of St. Catherine's 13th-century nunnery, with original vaulted ceilings and frescoes sprinkled throughout the rooms. The "museum" is actually a posh spa set atmospherically among Roman foundations. The breakfast buffets are delicious minibanquets. Note that some rooms have problems receiving reliable Wi-Fi.

Eremo delle Carceri 1A, 06081 Assisi. www.nunassisi.com. ✆ **075-815-5150.** Fax 075-816-580. 8 units. 260€ double. Rate includes breakfast. AE, DC, MC, V. Garage parking 25€ per day. **Amenities:** Restaurant; bar; concierge; indoor pool; room service; spa (free). *In room:* A/C, TV, minibar, Wi-Fi (free).

Umbra ★★ Antiques buffs will feel right at home in the collection of 13th-century houses from which the Umbra was converted, thanks to agreeable old furniture like 19th-century dressers, 18th-century desks, and 17th-century armoires. Many rooms have views over the rooftops and valley, some have balconies, and the hotel is graced with little hidden panoramic terraces. Ask to see the basement kitchen and laundry rooms, where the town's Roman walls make up part of the foundations.

Via Delgli Archi 6 (off the west end of Piazza del Comune), 06081 Assisi. www.hotelumbra.it. ✆ **075-812-240.** Fax 075-813-653. 24 units. 110€ standard double; 125€ superior double. Rates include breakfast. AE, DC, MC, V. Garage parking 10€ per day. Closed mid-Jan to Easter. **Amenities:** Restaurant; bar; babysitting; bikes; concierge; room service. *In room:* A/C, TV, hair dryer, minibar, Wi-Fi (free).

GUBBIO ★

39km (24 miles) NE of Perugia, 170km (106 miles) SE of Florence, 200km (124 miles) N of Rome

Gubbio is the classic Umbrian hill town, a magical, medieval city of sharp-edged fortresslike buildings, stacked at the base of a monumental tree-covered pyramid of a mountain. Gubbio is proud of its patron saint, medieval palaces, and homespun school of painting. And its hill-town cocoon of Gothic silence occasionally

Gubbio.

bursts open with the spectacular color and noise of some of the region's most deeply ingrained traditional **festivals.**

In the Dark Ages Gubbio suffered its share of Gothic sacking, but by the 11th century it emerged as a bustling trade center. The smooth talking of its incorruptible and wise bishop **Ubaldo** is said to have saved the town from Barbarossa in the 1150s, and after dutifully sanctifying the man soon after his death (he was canonized in 1192), the medieval city went about building walls and attacking its neighbors in grand Umbrian style.

During its peak, Gubbio became widely known for the high-quality glazed ceramics and majolica that came out of its workshops, especially that of Maestro **Giorgio Andreoli** (ca. 1472–1554), an innovator and one of the world's greatest masters of the craft.

Essentials

GETTING THERE The closest **train** station is at Fossato di Vico (✆ **075-919-230**), 19km (12 miles) away on the Rome-Ancona line. Ten trains run daily from **Rome** (2¼ hr; 11€), and nine daily from **Spoleto** (45–60 min; 4.80€). Nine daily buses (six on Sun) connect the train station with Gubbio (30 min.) for around 2€.

There are eight or nine daily **Umbria Mobilità buses** (www.umbriamobilita.it; ✆ **800/512-141**) from **Perugia** (4.60€; 5.50€ if you pay on board) to Piazza 40 Martiri (1 hr., 10 min.).

By **car,** the SS298 branches north from Perugia, off the E45, through rugged scenery.

VISITOR INFORMATION The **tourist office** is at Via della Repubblica 15, 06024 Gubbio (www.comune.gubbio.pg.it; ✆ **075-922-0693** or 075-922-0790). It's open Monday through Friday from 8:30am to 1:45pm and 3:30 to 6:30pm, Saturday from 9am to 1pm and 3:30 to 6:30pm, and Sunday from 9:30am to 1pm and 3 to 6pm; October through March, all afternoon hours are 3 to 6pm.

FESTIVALS & MARKETS Gubbio's biggest annual bash, the **Corso dei Ceri ★★★**, is held on May 15 to honor St. Ubaldo. Three teams of burly young men in colorful silk shirts carry 15-foot-long wooden battering ram–like objects called *ceri,* or "candles." After an enormous banquet and a procession of the relics of St. Ubaldo and the *ceri,* the day ends with a race between the candle-carrying teams—the finish lies more than 300m (984 ft.) of vertical elevation along a switchbacked road at the mountainside basilica of Sant'Ubaldo. The contest is to see how many times the runners let their candles fall.

Exploring Gubbio

Gubbio's main square is the brick-paved terrace of **Piazza Grande,** a medieval minimalist space open on the south side to a panoramic sweep over the lower part of town and across the wide valley beyond. If you want to avoid the climb, take the free elevator at the junction of Via Repubblica and Via Baldassini (daily 7:45am–7pm).

Outside Porta Romana, a left up Via San Gerolamo leads to the base of the *funivia,* a ski-lift contraption that dangles you in a little blue cage as you ride up the side of **Monte Ingino** (you can also walk up steep Via San Ubaldo from behind the Duomo, a vertical elevation of 300m/984 ft.). It lets you off just below the **Basilica di Sant'Ubaldo.** The current structure is a 16th-century incarnation over whose high altar the withered corpse of the local patron saint, Ubaldo, is preserved in a glass casket. Usually stored in the aisle are the three giant wooden *ceri* used during the annual **Corso dei Ceri** (see "Festivals & Markets," above). The **Funivia Colle Eletto** (✆ **075-927-3881**) runs daily, but with excruciatingly complex hours: check locally. Round-trip tickets are 5€ adults, 4€ children 4 to 13; one-way tickets are 4€ adults, 3€ children.

Duomo CATHEDRAL The interior of the 13th-century **cathedral** (aka Basilica dei Santi Mariano e Giacomo Martiri) is striking for its "wagon vaulting," a receding series of pointed arches defining the graceful bulk and space of the single central nave. Most of the art on the nave altars is by local talent, including multiple works by Virgilio Nucci, Benedetto Nucci, Sinibaldo Ibi, and Antonio Gherardi. The fourth niche on the right opens up to the florid baroque **Capella San Sacramento** (1644–72) by Francesco Allegrini and Gherardi.

Via Montefeltro. ✆ **075-922-0904.** Free admission. Oct–Mar daily 10am–4:30pm; Apr–Sept daily 10am–5pm.

Museo d'Arte Palazzo Ducale PALACE While Renaissance-era Gubbio was under the fairly benevolent ducal rule of nearby Urbino, Duke Federico da Montefeltro commissioned Francesco di Giorgio Martini to build him this palace in the 1470s. Although the sumptuous decorations have mostly been stripped away—the entire studio of *intarsia* wood paneling was moved to New York's Metropolitan Museum of Art—a few furnishings, painted ceilings, and simple terracotta flooring survive. You enter through a stunning Renaissance courtyard of pink brick accented in gray *pietra serena.* Past the ticket booth, a spiral staircase leads down to **foundations** of the structures that stood on this site as long ago as the 10th century, along with countless ceramic shards.

Via Montefeltro. ✆ **075-927-5872.** Admission 5€ adults, 2.50€ ages 18–25, free for children 17 and under and seniors 65 and over. Tues–Sun 8:30am–7:30pm. Ticket office closes 30 min. before museum. Closed Dec 25–Jan 1.

Museo della Ceramica-Torre di Porta Romana MUSEUM The 13th-century Porta Romana is the only survivor of six identical defensive towers that guarded Gubbio's entrances. Its private owners are serious history buffs who have restored the gate tower and set up an eclectic but worthy ceramics museum inside. The museum's most valuable installation is a collection of more than 250 **majolica** pieces spanning local production from 1500 to 1950. In the central display case are two **Maestro Giorgio** plates signed and dated 1530, another one attributed to him, and eight pieces by his son and workshop. (The city itself owns only one of Maestro Giorgio's works.)

Porta Romana (Via Dante 24). www.museoportaromana.it. © **075-922-1199.** Free admission. Daily 9am–1pm and 3:30–7:30pm (until 8pm in summer).

Museo del Palazzo dei Consoli ★★ MUSEUM Facing Piazza Grande is Gubbio's imposing Palazzo dei Consoli, whose square Guelph crenellations and off-center 91m (299-ft.) bell tower dominate Gubbio from afar. The tongue of a staircase sprouting from the raised central door to the piazza below adds a touch of delicate grace to the Gothic solidity. Eugubine master architect Gattapone designed the *palazzo* in 1332.

Inside the vast and poorly lit barrel vault of the main hall, used for public assemblies of the medieval commune, is the town museum, with the largest collection of Roman materials in Umbria. The real prize here is in a back room, the seven **Eugubine Tables ★**—the only existing record of the Umbri language transposed in Etruscan and Latin letters (ancient Umbria's **Rosetta Stone**). The tablets were inscribed on bronze from 200 to 70 B.C., and mainly detail the finer points of religious divination—they're thought to be priestly textbooks to help find the will of the gods through animal sacrifice and watching the flight patterns of birds. A local farmer turned up the tablets while he was plowing his fields in 1444, and the city convinced him to sell them for 2 years' worth of grazing rights.

Upstairs is a small **majolica and porcelain collection,** including plates painted by Maestro Giorgio in the 16th century. Take the narrow "secret corridor" from here, past a row of medieval toilets, and up another stair to the small **pinacoteca** gallery of minor paintings, mainly 13th- to 16th-century Eugubine works.

Piazza Grande. © **075-927-4298.** Admission 5€ adults, 2.50€ children 7–25, free for children 7 and under and seniors. Apr–Sept daily 10am–1pm and 3–6pm; Oct–Mar daily 10am–1pm and 2–5pm.

Sant'Agostino ★ CHURCH The entire interior of this 13th-century church was once covered with frescoes. Remaining today are the exquisitely detailed and colored **cycle of the *Life of St. Augustine*,** covering the walls and vaulting in the apse, and a *Last Judgment* on the arch outside it. The work was carried out by Eugubine master Ottaviano Nelli and his assistants in the 1420s. Nelli's brush also whipped up the *St. Ubaldo and Two Saints* fresco on the fifth altar of the right aisle, while Felice Damiani took care of *St. Ambrogio Baptizing St. Augustine* at the third altar.

Via Dante 24 (just outside Porta Romana). Free admission. Daily 7:30am–noon and 4–7pm.

Where to Eat & Stay

Gubbio is especially known for its white and black truffles, served in a variety of ways throughout the town. To buy them fresh (or arrange a delivery), visit **La Grotta del Tartufo** (www.papatartufi.it; © **347-230-5452**) at Via Picardi 1, just off Piazza 40 Martiri.

Gubbio contains some decent hotels, but if you have a car, you'll find much better accommodations in the surrounding countryside. Romantic and tranquil, **La Cuccagna,** Fraz. S. Cristina 22 (www.lacuccagna.com; © **075-920-317**), is a justly popular B&B in the hills south of Gubbio (doubles 70€–90€).

Bosone Palace ★★ This property occupies the 14th-century Palazzo Raffaelli, once the home of the influential Bosone Raffaelli (to whom Petrarch dedicated a sonnet, "Spirito Gentil"). Splurge on one of the Renaissance suites, which have 17th-century frescoes. (Try for no. 212, which has the larger bathroom and frescoes in both rooms.) Even if you opt for the standard doubles, you aren't sacrificing.

Via XX Settembre 22 (near Piazza Grande), 06024 Gubbio (PG). www.hotelbosone.com. ✆ **075-922-0688.** Fax 075-922-0552. 30 units. 80€ double; 130€ 4-person junior suite; 155€ 4-person Renaissance suite. Rates include breakfast. AE, DC, MC, V. Free parking nearby. **Amenities:** Concierge; room service; Wi-Fi (free; in public areas). *In room:* TV, hair dryer, minibar.

Grotta dell'Angelo ★ ITALIAN/UMBRIAN This cavernous space of tunnels and wine caves has been a thriving *osteria* for about 700 years, but the best place to sit in spring and summer is the vine-shaded terrace outside (in the winter time, grab a seat in the long, barrel-vaulted dining room and ask for a tour of the cellar). Local meats are grilled on a wood fire, such as *anatra e porchetta,* a goose and pork combination served with fennel. The homemade gnocchi is the house specialty.

Via Gioia 47. www.grottadellangelo.it. ✆ **075-927-3438.** Main courses 9€–14€. AE, DC, MC, V. Wed–Mon 12:30–2:30pm and 7:30–11pm. Closed Jan 7–Feb 7.

Relais Ducale ★★ You simply can't get more central than the 14th-century and Renaissance guest quarters of Federico da Montefeltro's palace. The mansard rooms, with their sloping ceilings, are a bit cheaper, but spring for a room on the upper floors with a panorama over the jumble of rooftops and Piazza Grande, to the stitched-together fields of the green valley beyond. But even Foresteria rooms on the first and second floors are memorable—a pair inhabits long barrel-vaulted rooms of rough ancient stone.

Via Galeotti 19/Viale Ducale 2, 06024 Gubbio. www.relaisducale.com. ✆ **075-922-0157.** Fax 075-922-0159. 32 units. 85€ double; 115€ deluxe double. Rates include breakfast. AE, DC, MC, V. Free parking in public lots nearby. **Amenities:** Restaurants (family owns 3 nearby, including Taverna del Lupo, recommended below, for which pension plans are available); babysitting; bikes; concierge; room service; Wi-Fi (free, in public areas). *In room:* A/C, TV, VCR on request, hair dryer, minibar.

Taverna del Lupo ★ UMBRIAN Each of the five tunnels of vaulted stonework that make up this 30-year-old Eugubine culinary landmark feels like a little medieval trattoria. This is the home of the truffle, black and white, and storied chef Claudio Ramacci blends the delicacy into a variety of dishes—it's not cheap, and is probably best as a dinner venue for most budgets. The *sfogliatina del Lupo con tartufo* (a light lasagna made with cheese, bits of ham and mushrooms, and white truffle shavings) is excellent. To stay with the precious white mushroom, you can order as a *secondo* the *scallopina affogato di tartufo* (a tender veal scallop "drowning" in truffles).

Via Ansidei 21 (on the corner of Via Repubblica, a few blocks uphill from Piazza 40 Martiri). www.tavernadellupo.it. ✆ **075-927-4368.** Reservations strongly recommended. Main courses 7€–25€; tasting menus without wine 20€–46€. AE, DC, MC, V. Tues–Sun noon–3pm and 7pm–midnight (July–Aug open daily).

SPOLETO ★

63km (39 miles) SE of Perugia, 212km (132 miles) SE of Florence, 126km (78 miles) N of Rome

A sleepy repository of Roman ruins and medieval buildings, **Spoleto** is terraced up a high hill backed by the deep-green forested slopes of a sacred mountain. Dreamed up in 1958 by the Italian-American composer Gian Carlo Menotti, the **Festival dei Due Mondi** (aka **Spoleto Festival**) brings heavy-duty culture to Spoleto every June, in the form of music, dance, and theater showcased by premier Italian and international performers. Though an ongoing legal dispute between the old and new organizers (the government took the festival away from the Menotti family in 2008) has marred the festivities somewhat, the event still attracts high-quality artists.

Essentials

GETTING THERE Spoleto is a main **rail** station on the Rome-Ancona line, and all 16 daily trains from **Rome** stop here (about 1½ hr.). From **Perugia,** take one of the 20 daily trains to Foligno (25 min.) to transfer to this line for the final 20-minute leg. From outside the station, take bus A, B, or C to Piazza Carducci on the edge of the old town.

By **car,** the town sits on the old Roman Via Flaminia, now the SS3. There's usually plenty of parking, but the easiest option is to make for the Spoletosfera parking garage, signposted from the SS3's Spoleto Sud exit (1€ per hour).

VISITOR INFORMATION The **information center** at Piazza della Libertà 7 (www.visitspoleto.it; ✆ **0743-220-773**) hands out heaps of info and an excellent map. It's open Monday to Friday from 9am to 1:30pm and 2 to 7pm, Saturday 9am to 1pm, and Sunday 10am to 1pm and 3:30 to 6:30pm.

FESTIVALS & MARKETS Spoleto's be-all and end-all annual event bridges the end of June and early July. The **Spoleto Festival ★★** (www.festivaldi spoleto.it) offers 3 weeks of world-class drama, music, and dance held in evocative spaces like an open-air restored Roman theater and the pretty

Spoleto.

piazza fronting the Duomo. A secondary **Spoleto Estate** season of music, art, and theater runs from just after the festival ends through September. (Contact the tourist office for info.)

Exploring Spoleto

The Duomo and the Ponte delle Torri are Spoleto's real attention-grabbers, so if you're pressed for time, head straight for the highlights of upper Spoleto. Highlight of the **Lower Town** is the 11th-century Romanesque **San Gregorio di Maggiore,** Piazza della Vittoria (✆ **0743-44-140**), which replaced an earlier oratory here in a cemetery of Christian martyrs. The church's namesake saint was killed in a spectacle at the nearby amphitheater in A.D. 304, as were a supposed 10,000 lesser-known martyrs whose bones symbolically reside beneath the altar. Passing under the portico (a 16th-c. addition), you'll see how a 1950s restoration carefully returned the interior to its medieval state, removing most baroque additions to reveal the Romanesque architecture and 14th-century frescoes. It opens daily from 8am to noon and 4 to 6pm, and admission is free.

Piazza del Mercato, the probable site of the old Roman forum, is a bustling spot lined with grocers and fruit vendors' shops. A walk along Via del Ponte brings you to the **Ponte delle Torri** ★★, with nine towering pylons separating stately arches. The bridge is 80m (264 ft.) high and 232m (760 ft.) long, spanning a gorge. It's believed to date from the 13th century and is one of the most photographed sights in Spoleto. Goethe praised it when he passed this way in 1786.

Spoleto Gastro-Shopping

For an excellent selection of olive oil and local wines, visit **Bartolomei Orvieto** at 97 Corso Cavour (www.oleificiobartolomei.it; ✆ **0763 344550**), where you can taste and drink the products before buying.

Casa Romana HISTORIC HOME Under Spoleto's Palazzo Comunale lies the Casa Romana, a 1st-century-A.D. patrician house that supposedly belonged to Vespasia Polla, the mother of the Emperor Vespasian. The intricate monochromatic patterns in the mosaic floors are well preserved, and you can also see the marble well cap and the bases of a few carved columns supporting the display cases of smaller excavated materials.

Via di Visiale. ✆ **0743-234-350.** Admission 2.50€ adults, 2€ ages 15–25 and seniors 65 and over, 1€ children 7–14, free for children 6 and under. Daily 10:30am–5:30pm.

Cattedrale di Santa Maria dell'Assunta ★★ CATHEDRAL Toward the top end of Via Saffi, the low graded steps of Via dell'Arringo flow down to the left into **Piazza del Duomo,** the most beautiful main square in Spoleto, with the cathedral backed by a *rocca*-crowned green hill. The main attraction is the dazzling facade of the 12th-century Duomo, with a 1207 mosaic by Solsterno surrounded by eight rose windows. The bell tower was pieced together using stone looted from Roman temples, and the porch is a 1492 addition.

The Duomo's interior retains its original pavement, but the rest was redecorated in a lavish baroque style in the 17th century for Pope Urban VII, who's commemorated with a Gian Lorenzo Bernini bust high above the central door inside. The first chapel on the right, **Cappella di San Leonardo,** has a not-quite-finished **fresco** (1497) by a 17-year-old Pinturicchio.

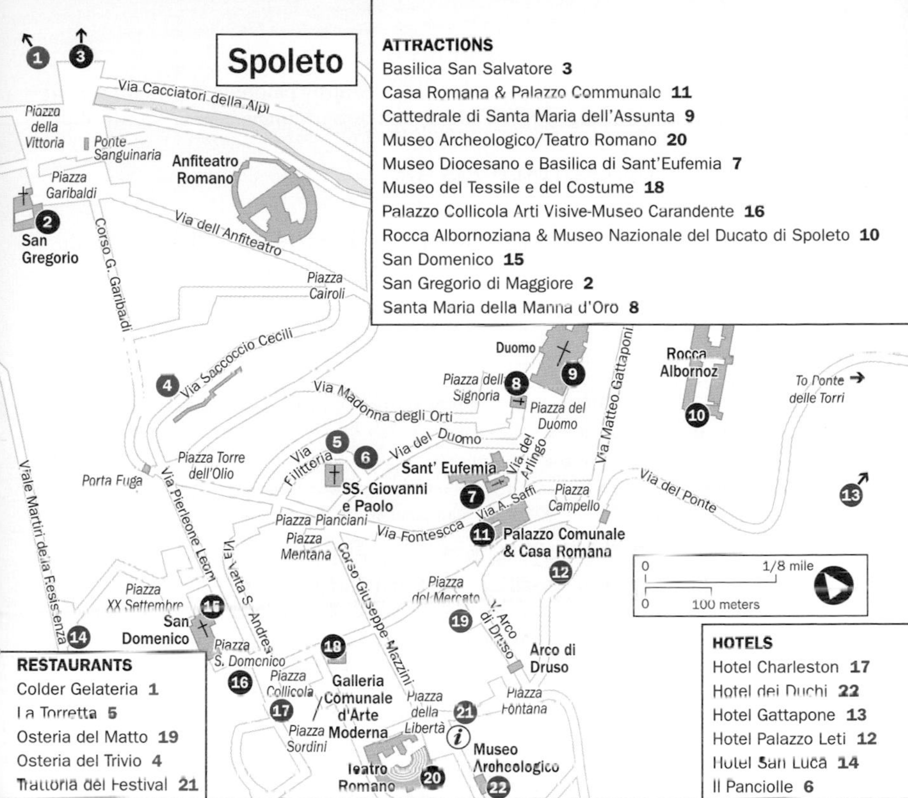

The right transept is home to a *Madonna and Child with Saints* (1599) by baroque master Annibale Carracci as well as a monument to Filippo Lippi, designed by his son, Filippino, at the request of Lorenzo de' Medici. According to Vasari, Lorenzo couldn't convince the Spoletcans to return the body to Florence when the irascible painter died just before completing his fresco cycle here. Though a monk, Filippo was quite the womanizer, and when he died, rumors ran wild that he'd been poisoned by the enraged family of a local girl whose honor he had compromised.

Lippi's ***Life of the Virgin*** ★ fresco cycle covers the **apse.** Begun in 1467, the frescoes were almost finished by 1469 when the master suddenly died, at the height of his powers. The cycle was finished by his assistants, Fra' Diamante and Pier Matteo d'Amelia. The first scene on the left, the *Annunciation,* is believed to be almost entirely from the master's hand, as is the magnificently colored *Incoronation of the Virgin* in the curving space above, with God taking the place of Jesus and a rainbow of saints and Old Testament figures surrounding Mary's richly patterned gown. The central panel, the *Dormition of the Virgin,* is also mainly from Lippi's brush and contains on the right several portraits by way of signature. Filippo is the man in the black hat, turned toward us and wearing for the last time the white monk's habit that seemed so inappropriate throughout his philandering life.

As you leave the Duomo, you'll pass the entrance to the **Cappella delle Reliquie (Reliquary Chapel)** on the left aisle, restored in 1993. They include

16th-century intarsia wood cupboards, a 14th-century painted wooden *Madonna and Child,* and a rare letter written and signed by St. Francis. (Assisi has the only other bona fide signature.)

Piazza del Duomo. ✆ **0743-231-063.** Free admission. Daily 8:30am–12:30pm and 3:30–5:30pm (until 7pm Apr–Oct).

Museo Archeologico/Teatro Romano ★ MUSEUM/RUINS At the edge of Piazza della Libertà, Via Apollinare leads down to the entrance of Spoleto's 1st-century-A.D. Roman theater. Partly destroyed and buried over the ages, it was all but forgotten until 1891, when local archaeologist Giuseppe Sordini began excavating. Extensively restored in the 1950s, it now serves as an evocative venue for the Spoleto Festival.

The attached Museo Archeologico (which can be visited using the same admission ticket) preserves relics from a 7th-century-B.C. warrior's tomb and materials recovered from the theater area, including the torso of a young boy and 1st-century-A.D. portrait busts of Julius and Augustus Caesar.

Via di Sant'Agata 18A. ✆ **0743-223-277.** Admission 4€ adults, 2€ ages 18–25, free for children 17and under and seniors 65 and over. Daily 8:30am–7:30pm.

Museo Diocesano e Basilica di Sant'Eufemia ★ MUSEUM This museum and old church lies within the **Palazzo Arcivescovado,** built atop the 8th-century palace of the Lombard dukes. The palace courtyard incorporates the facade of the 12th-century Basilica di Sant'Eufemia. The simple Romanesque stone interior has a second-story *matroneum* (women's gallery), 15th-century frescoes on some of the columns, and a 1200s Cosmatesque altar, inherited from the Duomo. The double stairs in the courtyard lead up to the Museo Diocesano. In Room 2 is the Sienese Domenico Beccafumi's 16th-century baroque *Adoration of the Child,* and among the sculptures in Room 3 is a 14th-century *Madonna del Cholera.*

Via A. Saffi 13. ✆ **0743-231-022.** Admission 3€ adults, 2.50€ ages 15–25 and seniors 65 and over, 2€ children 7–14, free for children 6 and under. Wed–Fri 11am–1pm and 2:30–5:30pm (to 6pm Apr–Oct); Sat–Sun 11am–5pm.

Rocca Albornoziana ★★ ☺ CASTLE The Rocca is a fierce-looking castle built from 1359 to 1362 by Gubbio's master architect, Gattapone, for the papal watchdog, Cardinal Albornoz. It rests atop the site of the oldest prehistoric settlement in Spoleto and was used as a prison until 1982—inmates included members of the Red Brigades terrorist organization and Mehmet Ali Agca, who tried to assassinate Pope John Paul II in 1981.

Much of the interior is now occupied by the **Museo Nazionale del Ducato di Spoleto** (✆ **0743-223-055**), which chronicles the history of the city from Roman times to the Renaissance, with an ensemble of richly inscribed sarcophagi, mosaics, and plenty of religious art and statuary.

Piazza Campello. ✆ **0743-224-952.** Admission 7.50€ adults, 6.50€ ages 15–25, 3.50€ children 7–14, free for children 6 and under. Tues–Sun 8:30am–7:30pm (last ticket 6:45pm).

San Domenico CHURCH Straight up Via Leone Pierleone from Piazza Torre dell'Olio is the pink- and white-banded 13th-century San Domenico. The first altar on the right preserves an early-15th-century fresco of the *Triumph of St. Thomas Aquinas,* with tiny monks, prelates, and scholars discussing the theologian's writings. There are more 15th-century frescoes in the presbytery and transept chapels, plus a painted crucifix from the 1300s above the main altar.

Piazza San Domenico, Via Leone Pierleone. ✆ **0743-223-240.** Free admission. Daily 9:30am–noon and 3:30–5pm (until 6pm Apr–Oct).

Where to Eat & Stay

Its location at the Piazza Vittoria end of Viale Trento e Trieste (no. 29) isn't exactly convenient, but **Colder Gelateria ★★** (✆ **0743-235-015**) serves some of the best gelato (notably the "bread and chocolate" flavor) in Umbria, created by local artisans Crispini. Its open daily from 12:30pm to midnight.

Accommodations are tight during the Spoleto Festival; reserve by March if you want to find a good, central room. One of the most appealing options outside town is the **Le Logge di Silvignano,** Frazione Silvignano 14 (www.leloggedisilvignano.it; ✆ **0743-274-098**), a gorgeous palace complex in the hills southeast of Spoleto. Rentals are usually by the week only, starting at 500€ to 700€ for a two-person suite.

La Torretta ★★ UMBRIAN This historic wine cellar oozes charm and excels at what the Italians call *"rustico chic."* Run by the indefatigable Salvucci brothers, most of the menu is sourced locally and Umbrian dishes (and truffles) are the focus—highlights from the kitchen include the *sformatino di riso tartufato* (baked rice cooked in a broth, with a butter, onion, and truffle sauce), and the *strangozzi alla Spoletina* (traditional homemade pasta, with tomato, garlic, red pepper, and parsley sauce). Outdoor seating is available in summer.

Via Filitteria 43. www.trattorialatorretta.com. ✆ **0743-44-954.** Reservations recommended. Main courses 9€–16€. AE, DC, MC, V. Wed–Mon 12:30–2:30pm and 7:45–10:45pm (closed Sun evening).

Osteria del Matto ★ UMBRIAN Eating here is certainly an interesting experience, though perhaps not for everyone. There's no menu to choose from, just a blackboard telling you what you're going to eat, and waiters telling you when you're going to eat it—dinners often last 3 to 4 hours. Your host-cum-entertainer-in-chief is the gregarious Filippo Matto (a former butler to composer Gian Carlo Menotti), who carves meats, welcomes guests, and generally goofs around. Load up on the small plates of meats, onion frittata wedges, artichokes, and *crostini,* usually followed by a single pasta dish.

Vicolo del Mercato 3 (under the big arch on the south side of Piazza del Mercato). ✆ **0743-225-506.** Reservations not necessary. Full meal 18€ without wine. MC, V. Wed–Mon 11am–3pm and 5pm–2am.

Palazzo Leti ★★ Staying in this elegant and artfully restored hotel really is like being in a palace. It was built by the noble Letti family in the late 13th century, and has been enlarged many times since. All rooms have a view of the Monteluco hills, and even the cheapest standard doubles come with antique beds, rugs, and closets. The classical art and style is ramped up in the deluxe rooms, where you'll find more space, and wood-beam or beautifully engraved ceilings. Breakfasts are truly lavish.

Via degli Eremiti 10, 06049 Spoleto. www.palazzoleti.com. ✆ **0743-224-930.** Fax 0743-202-623. 12 units. 130€–200€ double. Rates include breakfast. AE, DC, MC, V. Free parking. **Amenities:** Bar; babysitting; bikes; concierge; room service; spa. *In room:* TV, hair dryer, minibar, Wi-Fi (free).

San Luca ★★ ☺ This is a wonderful, family-friendly hotel, and just a short walk from the historic center. The building dates back to the mid–19th century, when it was used as a tannery. The tranquil courtyard, replete with fountain and tables, is a pleasant place to relax, while the lounge features real log fires in winter. The spacious rooms are well-equipped with all the extras, including heated bathrooms finished in Carrara marble and—unusual in this part of the world—real soundproofing.

Via Interna delle Mura 21, 06049 Spoleto. www.hotelsanluca.com. ✆ **0743-223-399.** Fax 0743-223-800. 35 units. 100€–150€ standard double; 195€–240€ superior double. Rates include buffet breakfast. AE, DC, MC, V. Garage parking (13€ per day). **Amenities:** Restaurant (groups only); bar; babysitting; bikes; concierge; room service (bar). *In room:* A/C, TV, hair dryer, minibar, Wi-Fi (2€ per hour).

Trattoria del Festival ☺ UMBRIAN The cavernous pair of vaulted brick rooms here are large enough to host the festival hordes yet still leave room for die-hard locals who come for the best fixed-priced menus in town. The two more "expensive" of these are the ones to order, because they let you sample a pair of *primi* (the chef's surprise, but one is assured to involve truffles) and include all the incidentals, save wine.

Via Filippo Brignone 8 (near Piazza della Libertà). www.trattoriadelfestival.com. ✆ **0743-220-993.** Reservations recommended. Main courses 7€–10€; fixed-price menu without wine 17€. AE, DC, MC, V. Thurs–Tues noon–3pm and 7pm–midnight. Closed Feb.

A Side Trip to Todi ★

Taking S418 out of Spoleto for 45km (28 miles) northwest will lead you toward what is reputedly "the most livable town in the world." At Acquasparta, get on A3 northwest. Soon you'll come to this well-preserved medieval town, today a retreat for wealthy artists and diplomats. The setting is simply lovely. The central **tourist office** is under the arches at Palazzo del Popolo 38/39, 06059 Todi (www.comune.todi.pg.it/fap; ✆ **075-894-2526**). It's open Monday through Saturday from 9:30am to 1pm and 3:30 to 7pm, Sunday 10am to 1pm and 3:30 to 7pm (in winter it closes at 6pm, and is not open Sun afternoons).

Todi's cathedral.

The central square, **Piazza del Popolo ★★**, was built over the Roman forum. It contains three beautiful palaces: the **Palazzo del Popolo,** built in 1213; the **Palazzo del Capitano,** dating from 1292; and the 14th-century **Palazzo dei Priori,** with a trapezoidal tower. At the north end of the piazza rises the **Duomo's facade ★**, which ran the stylistic gamut from Romanesque through the

Renaissance but still came out blessedly simple in the end. Inside on the entrance wall, framing a gorgeous rose window, is a ***Last Judgment*** ★ frescoed by Ferraù di Faenza in 1596 that owes about 80% of its figures and design directly to Michelangelo's *Last Judgment* in Rome's Sistine Chapel.

Also here are **Santa Maria della Consolazione** ★★, standing guard over Todi with its domes and exquisite stained glass, and 13th-century **San Fortunato,** in Piazza della Repubblica, burial site of the town's most famous citizen, the monk/medieval poet Fra' Jacopone. To the right of the church, a path leads uphill to the ruins of a 14th-century **Rocca.** From here, a walk up the Viale della Serpentina will reward you with a bird's-eye view of the surrounding valley. If the climb seems a bit much, check the view from Piazza Garibaldi.

Our favorite place to stay is **San Lorenzo Tre** ★★, Via San Lorenzo 3 (www.sanlorenzo3.it; ✆ **075-894-4555**), a simple, historic guesthouse that drips with character and doesn't break the bank. Decked out in the style of a late-19th-century middle-class family (only the bathrooms are modern), rooms feature period furniture, linens, and wood-beam ceilings. Doubles range from 75€ to 100€. At **Pane e Vino** ★★, Via Ciuffelli 33 (www.panevinotodi.com; ✆ **075-894-5448;** closed Wed), the specialty is black Noria truffles: thick, Umbrian *strangozzi* pasta with truffles, and beef or spiced lamb with truffles are our favorites. Dishes range from 10€ to 16€.

ORVIETO ★★

87km (54 miles) W of Spoleto, 86km (53 miles) SW of Perugia, 152km (95 miles) S of Florence, 121km (75 miles) N of Rome

The defining feature of southern Umbria's most touristy town is its cathedral, with its dazzling facade: day-trippers come to Orvieto from as far as Florence and Rome to see it. The rest of town looks much as it did 500 years ago—a preserved medieval center stuck high on a volcanic plug some 315m (1,033 ft.) above the plain, visible for miles in every direction. This impenetrable perch ensured that Etruscan "Velzna" was among the most powerful members of the *dodecapoli* (Etruscan confederation of 12 cities); its Etruscan heritage has left an underground world that's just as much fun.

The city seems not so much to rise as to grow out of the flat top of its butte. The buildings are made from blocks of the same ***tufo*** volcanic rock (tufa, or more accurately, tuff, in English), on which Orvieto rests, giving the disquieting feeling that the town evolved here of its own volition.

Essentials

GETTING THERE Fourteen **trains** on the main **Rome-Florence** line stop at Orvieto daily (1 hr., 45 min. from Florence; 1 hr., 20 min. from Rome). From **Perugia,** take the train to Terontola (16 trains daily) for this line heading south toward Rome (1¼ hr. total train time).

Orvieto's **station** is in the dreary new town of Orvieto Scalo in the valley. To reach the city, cross the street and take the **funicular** (www.atcterni.it; every 10 min. 7:20am–8:30pm), a modern version of the steep cog railway that ran on hydraulic power in the 19th century.

Orvieto is straightforward to reach by **car,** especially from southern Tuscany: It's right by the A1. The main link to the rest of Umbria is the SS448 to Todi (40 min.).

VISITOR INFORMATION The **tourist office** is opposite the Duomo at Piazza Duomo 24, 05018 Orvieto (www.comune.orvieto.tr.it; ✆ **0763-341-772**). It's open Monday through Friday from 8:15am to 1:50pm and 4 to 7pm, Saturday from 10am to 1pm and 3:30 to 7pm, and Sunday from 10am to noon and 4 to 6pm.

Exploring Orvieto

Duomo ★★ CATHEDRAL Orvieto's mesmerizing (or gaudy, or both) Duomo was ordered built in 1290 by Pope Nicholas IV to celebrate the miracle that had occurred 27 years earlier at nearby Bolsena. The structure ran through its share of architects over its first few hundred years—including Florentine Andrea Orcagna; a couple of Pisanos; and, most significantly, Sienese Lorenzo Maitani (1310–30). Maitani left his Gothic stamp on the building, especially the facade. Here he executed, with the help of his son, Vitale, and Niccolò and Meo Nuti, the excellent carved marble **relief panels ★★** in the lower register (protected by Plexiglas after many vandalism incidents). The far right panels are a *Last Judgment* preamble for the Signorelli frescoes inside. The most striking is the lower-right panel, a jumble of the wailing faces of the damned and the leering grins of the demonic tormentors dragging them to eternal torture.

Capella del Corporale Inside, the left transept houses the Cappella del Corporale (1357–64), frescoed by Ugolino di Prete Ilario. Its right-hand wall highlights **the Miracle of Bolsena:** In 1263, a young priest who doubted the miracle of transubstantiation—the transformation of the communion wafer and wine into the actual body and blood of Christ—was saying Mass at Bolsena. As he raised the Host toward the heavens, it began dripping blood onto the *corporale* (altar cloth).

Cappella San Brizio To the right of the high altar is the Cappella San Brizio, containing one of the Renaissance's greatest **fresco cycles ★★★**. Fra' Angelico started the job in 1447 but finished only two of the vault triangles: *Christ as Judge* and a gold-backed stack of *Prophets*. It wasn't until 1499 that Cortonan Luca Signorelli strode into town, with the council hailing him as Italy's most famous painter and practically throwing at him the contract to finish the paintings. After completing the ceiling vaults to Fra' Angelico's designs, Signorelli went into hyperdrive with his own style on the walls. By 1504, the Duomo had some of the most intense studies ever seen of the naked human body, plus a horrifically realistic and fascinating rendition of the ***Last Judgment.*** Michelangelo, master of the male nude, who was most impressed, made many sketches of the figures, and found a prime inspiration for his own *Last Judgment* in the Sistine Chapel.

The Orvieto All-in-One Card

The useful ***Carta Unica*** cumulative ticket (www.cartaunica.it) costing 18€ adults and 15€ students and seniors 60 and over gets you into everything we recommend below (and more)—plus either one funicular plus one bus ride *or* 5 hours in the ex–Campo della Fiera parking lot.

Buy the ticket from the funicular car park (✆ **0763-302-378**) in Orvieto Scalo, any participating sight, or the Carta Unica office (10am–6pm daily in summer, shorter hours in winter) next to Orvieto's tourist office at Piazza Duomo 23. It's valid for a year.

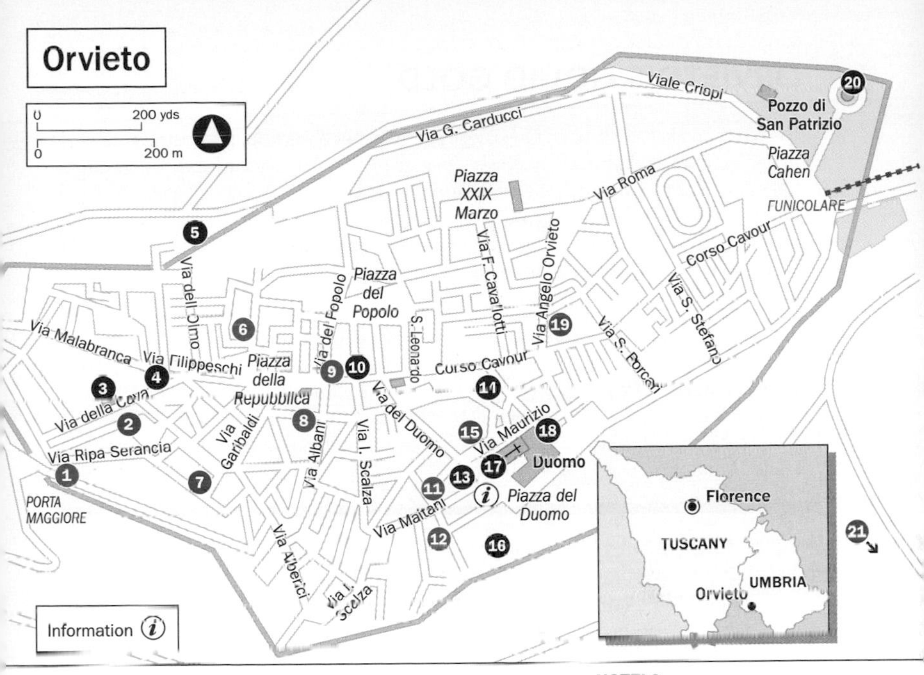

ATTRACTIONS

Duomo **18**

Grotte della Rupe
(Etruscan Orvieto Underground) **16**

Museo Archeologico Nazionale **18**

Museo Claudio Faina e Civico **13**

Museo delle Maioliche Medievali **4**

Museo dell'Opera del Duomo
& Museo Emilio Greco **17**

Necropoli Etrusca di Crocifisso del Tufo **5**

Pozzo della Cava **3**

Pozzo di San Patrizio **20**

Teatro Mancinelli **14**

Torre del Moro **10**

HOTELS

Casa Flavia **19**

Hotel Duomo **15**

Hotel La Badia **21**

Palazzo Piccolomini **2**

Ripa Medici Bed & Breakfast **7**

RESTAURANTS

Al San Francesco **12**

Caffè Montanucci **9**

La Palomba **8**

Le Grotte del Funaro **1**

Tipica Trattoria Etrusca **11**

Trattoria dell'Orso **6**

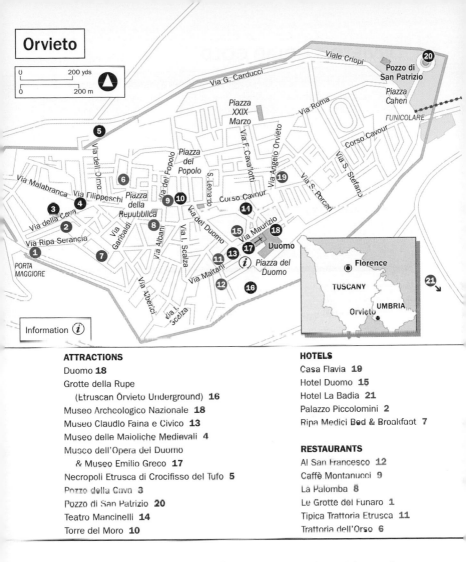

The most famous fresco, on the left wall, is *The Preaching of the Antichrist,* a highly unusual subject in Italian art. The prominent prostitute in the foreground reaching back to accept money for her services is a bit of painterly revenge—it's a portrait of a girlfriend who had recently dumped Signorelli. On the far left is Signorelli's "signature": two black-robed figures bearing portraits of Signorelli and his skull-capped predecessor Fra' Angelico standing behind.

To the right of the altar is *The Entrance to Hell,* filled with Dantean details such as a group of the indolent being led off by a devil bearing a white banner, and a man raising his fists to curse God as he sees Charon rowing across the Styx for him. This fresco sets you up for the last scene: the writhing, twisting, sickly colored mass of bodies, demons, and horror of *The Damned in Hell.* Signorelli

ORVIETO'S LIQUID GOLD

The plains and low hills around Orvieto grow the grapes—verdello, grechetto, and Tuscan varietals trebbiano and malvasia—that go into one of Italy's great wines, a pale straw-colored DOC white called simply **Orvieto Classico.** A well-rounded and judiciously juicy white (often with a hint of crushed almonds), it goes great with lunch. Most Orvieto Classico you'll run across is *secco* (dry), but you can also find bottles of the more traditional *abboccato* (semidry/semisweet), *amabile* (medium sweet), and *dolce* (sweet) varieties.

To sample a glass (or buy a bottle) with a pastry or *panino*, drop by the **Cantina Foresi,** Piazza Duomo 2 (✆ **0763-341-611**). Ask to see the small, moldy cellar carved directly into the *tufo*. To **visit a vineyard,** pick up a copy of the Strada dei Vini brochure at the tourist office or at the **Enoteca Barberani** at Via Maitani 1 (www.barberani.it; ✆ **0763-341-532**); it lists the wineries along with the hours of tours and contact numbers.

didn't pull any punches here. One winged devil is making off with a familiar blonde on his back—the jilted artist's ex-mistress again.

Piazza del Duomo. www.museomodo.it. ✆ **0763-341-167.** Admission 3€ including Cappella di San Brizio, free for children 10 and under. Apr–Oct Mon–Sat 9:30am–7pm, Sun 1–5:30pm (to 6:30pm July–Sept); Nov–Mar Mon–Sat 9:30am–1pm and 2:30–5pm (Sun to 5:30pm).

Grotte della Rupe (Etruscan Orvieto Underground) ★★ HISTORIC SITE The Orvieto *comune* has opened some of the tunnels under the city, with guided tours providing a taster of the vast network honeycombing the *tufo* subsoil (15m/45 ft. below the surface). The visit can be overly didactic, but you do get to see an underground 14th-century olive press (the constant temperature of 14°C /58°F was great for oil making). You can also peer down a few claustrophobically narrow Etruscan-era wells, wander around a subterranean quarry for *pozzolano* (a volcanic stone powdered to make cement mix) in use as late as the 19th century, and tour a series of Etruscan pigeon coops (no, seriously) carved out of the cliffside rock. Note that the tour involves a steep climb up and down 55 steps, along a narrow rock-hewn passage.

Piazza Duomo 23 (next to the tourist info office; daily 10:30am–5:30pm). www.orvietounderground.it. ✆ **0763-344-891.** Admission (by guided tour only, 45 min.–1 hr.) 6€ adults, 5€ students and seniors. Tours daily at 11am and 12:15, 3, 4, and 5:15pm (other times can be arranged); tours only Sat–Sun in Feb. English tours usually at 11:15am, but check in advance.

Museo Claudio Faina e Civico ★ MUSEUM The core of this Etruscan museum dates from a private collection started in 1864 and contains almost as much material from Chiusi and the Perugia area as it does from Orvieto area tombs. The highlights include an intriguing collection of **Etruscan black *bucchero* ware** from the 6th and the 5th century B.C., and some **Attic black-figure** (6th-c.-B.C.) and **red-figure** (5th-c.-B.C.) vases and amphorae that originated in Athenian workshops and were bought by discriminating Etruscan collectors. The museum even has three black-figure **amphorae by Greek master Exekias** (540 B.C.) that were fished out of the nearby Crocifisso del Tufo necropolis.

Piazza del Duomo 29. www.museofaina.it. ✆ **0763-341-511** or 0763-341-216. Admission 4.50€ adults; 3€ ages 7–12, seniors 65 and over, and families of 4 or more. MC, V. Apr–Sept daily 9:30am–6pm; Oct–Mar daily 10am–5pm (closed Mon Nov–Mar).

Pozzo di San Patrizio (St. Patrick's Well) ★ ☺ HISTORIC SITE Orvieto's main military problem throughout history has been a lack of water. Fleeing Emperor Charles V's army in 1527, Pope Clement VII took shelter in the city. He hired Antonio Sangallo the Younger to dig a new well that would ensure an abundant supply in case the pope should have to ride out another siege. Sangallo set about sinking a shaft into the tufa at the lowest end of town. His design (which you can climb down through) was unique: He equipped the well with a pair of wide spiral staircases, lit by 72 internal windows, forming a double helix so that mule-drawn carts could descend on one ramp and come back up the other without colliding. Eventually, workers did strike water—almost 10 years later, at which point Clement was dead and the purpose moot.

Viale San Gallo (near the funicular stop on Piazza Cahen). ✆ **0763-343-768.** Admission 5€ adults, 3.50€ students. May–Aug daily 9am–7:45pm; Mar–Apr and Sept–Oct daily 9am–6:45pm; Nov–Feb daily 10am–4:45pm.

Shopping

You'll see the Michelangeli clan's **wood sculptures,** puppets, and stacked-contour reliefs all over town, while their showroom (www.michelangeli.it; ✆ **0763-342-660**) is at Via Gualverio Michelangeli 3, just off the Corso. One of the top **antiques shops** in town is **Carlo & Cesare Bianchini,** Via Duomo 37 (✆ **0763-344-626**), which is filled with gorgeous *pietra dure* tabletops inlaid with semiprecious stones and marbles. The wares here don't come cheap. **Duranti Profumerie,** Via del Duomo 13–15 (✆ **0763-344-606**), sells local perfumes and beauty products for men and women. For **wine shops,** see "Orvieto's Liquid Gold," above.

Where to Eat & Stay

Orvieto's unofficial pasta is *umbrichelli,* simple flour-and-water spaghetti rolled out unevenly by hand and somewhat chewy—similar to the *pici* of southern Tuscany, but not as thick. For a cappuccino and a cake, try **Caffè Montanucci,** Corso Cavour 21–23 (✆ **0763-341-261**), which has sold excellent local marmalades and a vast assortment of chocolate against a backdrop of Michelangeli wood reliefs since 1913. It's open Thursday through Tuesday from 6:30am to midnight and has public computers for Internet access. Sit in the garden at the back for maximum tranquillity.

The hotel situation in Orvieto is fairly uninspiring. Most inns are of a consistently bland modern motel style, and the price doesn't come close to matching the standard of the accommodations. If you have a car, consider **Inncasa** ★★, Località San Giorgio 6 (www.inncasa.eu; ✆ **0763-393-682**), 5km (3 miles) or so north of Orvieto on SR79bis, one of the best hotels in the region. Lavish rooms ("junior penthouses") start at 183€ in high season.

Le Grotte del Funaro ★ UMBRIAN Dating from at least the 1100s, when the eponymous *funaro* (rope maker) had his workshop here, these grottoes carved into the tufa draw Italians and tourists alike. The *bruschette miste Umbre* give their Tuscan *crostini* cousins a run for the money, but save room for the *ombrichelli* *del Funaro* (in a heavy sauce of tomatoes, sausage, artichokes, and mushrooms). For a sampling platter of the best grilled meats, order the *grigliata mista* (suckling pig, lamb, sausage, and yellow peppers). After 10pm, the restaurant transforms into a piano bar.

Via Ripa Serancia 41 (at the west end of town near Porta Maggiore; well signposted). www.grottedelfunaro.it. ✆ **0763-343-276.** Reservations recommended. Main courses 10€–13€; pizza 5.50€–8.50€; fish-tasting menu without wine 32€, minimum 2 people. AE, DC, MC, V. Tues–Sun noon–3pm and 7pm–midnight. Closed 1 week in July.

Palazzo Piccolomini ★★ Converted from a 16th-century *palazzo,* the family-run Piccolomini is the most inviting hotel in the center of town. It retains some palatial grandeur in echoey salons and the remnants of decorative frescoes, but the rooms tend toward the elegantly simple, with missionary-style wood furnishings, compact bathrooms, and modernized comforts (some suites have plush touches like heated towel racks and canopied beds). The ground-floor rooms have high vaulted ceilings, while those on the upper floors often have views across lichen-splayed roof tiles to the countryside.

Piazza Ranieri 36 (2 blocks down from Piazza della Repubblica), 05018 Orvieto. www.hotelpiccolomini.it. ✆ **0763-341-743.** Fax 0763-391-046. 32 units. 154€ double; 196€ triple; 244€ suite. AE, MC, V. Rates include breakfast. Parking 15€ in main public lot next door. **Amenities:** Restaurant; babysitting; concierge; room service; Wi-Fi (free, in public areas). *In room:* A/C, TV, hair dryer, minibar.

Ripa Medici Bed & Breakfast ★★★ This gem of a B&B is an incredibly good value, right in the heart of town—there are just two rooms, though (it's more like an apartment rental), with a shared living room, two modern bathrooms, and a shared kitchen. The whole property is decked out in period furnishings, wood floors, and rugs. The views across the old town are fabulous and your host, Sabrina, is a font of local knowledge. Her mother also offers Italian home-cooking lessons.

Vicolo Ripa Medici 14, 05018 Orvieto. www.ripamedici.it. ✆ **0763-341-343.** 2 units. 65€ double. AE, DC, MC, V. Rates include breakfast. Free parking. *In room:* A/C, TV, hair dryer, Wi-Fi (free).

Trattoria dell'Orso ★★ UMBRIAN Chef Gabriele di Giandomenico uses the freshest local ingredients and traditions (mixed with those of his native Abruzzo) to create memorable dishes that change daily, which is why his Neapolitan partner, Ciro Cristiano, prefers to recite them to you in delectable detail rather than break out the printed menu. In the tiny rooms surrounded by Michelangeli wood sculptures—including a remarkably realistic "lacy" curtain—you can sample fresh homemade *tagliatelle,* served perhaps with mushrooms and truffles, with broccoli, or with baby tomatoes, basil, and shredded *scamorza* cheese. The local specialty *secondo* is chicken with olives, or try Gabriele's *faraona* (game hen) stuffed with truffles.

Via della Misericordia 18–20. ✆ **0763-341-642.** Reservations recommended. Main courses 8€–16€. AE, DC, MC. Wed–Sun noon–2pm and 7:30–10pm. Closed Feb, July, and Nov.

LE MARCHE ★

The region of Le Marche (pronounced *Mark*-eh) takes its name from the medieval Marches of Camerino, Fermo, and Ancona, nominally part of the Papal States but with a rich history that goes back thousands of years. Today the

Adriatic coastline of Le Marche is riddled with umbrella-laden sandy beaches that attract thousands of tourists in the summer, but it's the history and the art that provide the appeal inland. With a pastoral hinterland of craggy hills as the landscape moves toward the Apennine Mountains, Le Marche is home to Raphael's enticing Renaissance city of Urbino, as well as the lesser known gem of Ascoli Piceno, a medieval city built almost entirely of *travertino* marble.

The countryside of Le Marche is sparsely inhabited, and you'll need a car to get about freely as public transportation, including rail lines, is severely limited beyond the coast.

Urbino ★★

101km (63 miles) NE of Perugia, 107km (66 miles) NE of Arezzo, 35km (22 miles) W of Pesaro, 70km (43 miles) S of Rimini

Locals are not modest—but are somewhat accurate—in hailing Urbino as "the ideal Renaissance city." This mellow, medieval artistic center is on the UNESCO list of World Heritage Sites for good reason, with a gorgeous historic core virtually unchanged from the 15th century, a cache of tantalizing artwork, and one of the nation's finest medieval fortresses looming above it all.

The fortress—and indeed the flowering of Urbino—owes its existence to Federico da Montefeltro (1444–82), a powerful duke but also a great patron of arts and letters. Under his leadership, Urbino reached the zenith of its power and

Urbino's Piazza della Repubblica.

influence, almost without rival in western Europe. His son, Guidobaldo, continued in his father's footsteps. Urbino's most celebrated artists grew up in this era. Raffaello Sanzio (1483–1520), more popularly known as Raphael, was born here; and the designer of St. Peter's Basilica in Rome, Donato Bramante (1444–1514), was born in a village nearby.

Founded in 1506 by Duke Guidobaldo, the Università di Urbino is one of the oldest in the world, and today its student population and never-ending stream of art-conscious international travelers lend the city a surprisingly cosmopolitan air.

ESSENTIALS

GETTING THERE From just outside the Pesaro train station (p. 366), hourly **buses** operated by **Adriabus** (www.amibus.it; ✆ **0722-376711**) run to Urbino, taking 45 to 55 minutes and costing 3.20€ one-way. You can buy tickets from machines on board (exact change only), or from the cafe opposite the bus stop. Buses arrive at Piazza Borgo Mercatale just below Urbino's Old Town—walk up or take the **elevator** from here (daily 6:30am–8:30pm; .50€).

By **car,** the main gateway to Urbino is also Pesaro via the SS423, a well-maintained two-lane highway (it's around 35km/22 miles from the A14 autostrada to Urbino). There's plenty of parking at Piazza Borgo Mercatale (1.20€ per hour).

VISITOR INFORMATION Across from Palazzo Ducale, the **tourist office** at Piazza Rinascimento 1 (www.turismo.pesarourbino.it; ✆ **0722-26-13**) is open daily 9am to 1:30pm and 2:30 to 6pm, but the elevator office near the bus station in Piazza Borgo Mercatale also supplies maps and information.

EXPLORING URBINO

In a secluded mountain setting, the hub of Urbino is the animated triangle of **Piazza della Repubblica,** lying in a dip between the twin humps of a hill. A walking tour of the city center with some major stopovers (see below) will take at least 5 to 6 hours, not counting time out for lunch, although much of the pleasure here comes from aimlessly wandering the narrow streets. Reniassance fans often overlook the city cathedral, the **Basilica Cattedrale di Santa Maria**

Assunta, a neoclassical pile built between 1789 and 1801, but its bright interior contains a couple of gems painted by local boy Federico Barocci. His *Ultima Cena (Last Supper)* painted in the 1590s, stands in the Capella del Ss. Sacramento to the left of the altar, while his first major work, *Martiri di San Sebastian* (1557) lies in the third chapel on the right.

Casa Natale di Raffaello HISTORIC HOME Raphael was born in this comfortable town house in 1483 and lived here with his father, Giovanni Santi, until he turned 14. The two-story museum is sparsely furnished but filled with mementos, including coins, books, paintings from Giovanni Santi, copies of Raphael's work, and local ceramics. In the room where the painter was born, a genuine fresco by the young artist, a *Madonna and Child,* has been preserved, though some art critics attribute this painting to Raphael's father (who was court painter to the Duke of Urbino).

Via Raffaello 57. ✆ **0722-320105.** Admission 3€. Mar–Oct Mon–Sat 9am–1pm and 3–7pm, Sun 10am–1pm; Nov–Feb Mon–Sat 9am–2pm, Sun 10am–1pm.

Oratorio di San Giovanni Battista & Oratorio di San Giuseppe CHURCH These two adjacent churches are manned by the same volunteers—if San Giuseppe looks closed, ask someone at San Giovanni to let you in. The chief treasures of the **Oratorio di San Giovanni Battista**—dating from 1416—are its brilliantly colored **frescoes** ★ by the Salimbene brothers, who depicted delicate scenes from the life of St. John the Baptist as well as a *Crucifixion.* The painters allegedly created their sketches from the blood of a freshly killed lamb.

Completed in 1515 and renovated in the 17th century, the **Oratorio di San Giuseppe** contains a nave with a colossal statue of St. Joseph, completed in 1732. The very beautiful **stucco nativity scene** ★ in the grottolike Capella del Presepe is a life-size work that was the masterpiece of the artist Federico Brandani, created around 1550.

Via Barocci 31. ✆ **347-6711181. Oratorio di San Giovanni Battista:** Admission 2.50€. Mon–Sat 10am–12:30pm and 3–5:30pm; Sun 10am–12:30pm (Oct–Mar daily 10am–12:30pm). **Oratorio di San Giuseppe:** Admission 2€. Daily 10am–12:30pm.

Palazzo Ducale ★★★ & Galleria Nazionale delle Marche ★★ PALACE/ART MUSEUM The greatest palace ever built in Le Marche, this imposing monument looms over the entire city, a vision of harmonious design and elegance by the Dalmatian architect Luciano Laurana. The palace was constructed between 1465 and 1482 for the formidable Federico da Montefeltro, lord of Urbino, and now serves principally as the home of the **Galleria Nazionale delle Marche.** Though you can wander rooms in the basement and ground floors (where there's a fairly dry collection of ancient marble tombstones), the art gallery is located on the first and second floors, and here's where you'll find the best rooms in the palace.

The collection begins in the **Iole Apartments,** where Federico first lived before his ducal apartments were completed in 1474. The early Renaissance work on display here is outshined by the **Alcova del Duca** (Hall 3), the duke's wooden bed chamber (or "recess"), a rare piece of medieval furniture made around 1460. Look out also for the "Hall of the King of England" in the guest apartments (Hall 13), where labels inform that "James III" stayed here in 1700; the son of deposed Stuart king James II was never crowned however, and lived a life of exile in Italy and France (his mother was Mary of Modena).

The Palazzo Ducale.

The highlights of the collection lie in the grand ducal apartments, where the **Hall of Hearings** (Hall 16) contains two paintings by the great **Piero della Francesca,** a somber *Madonna with Child and Angel* and a *Flagellation of Christ.* Beyond here is the most awe-inspiring room in the palace, Frederico's tiny **Studiolo** (Ducal Study), decorated with stunning inlays often attributed to Botticelli from around 1476. Just van Gand, who painted the gallery's *Gathering of the Apostles,* also painted some of the portraits here. Botticelli is also thought to have decorated the inlaid doors of the duke's bedroom (Hall 20) and the **Sala degli Angeli** (Hall 21). In the latter you'll find the *Ideal City,* a masterpiece of perspectivist wizardry, usually credited to Laurana, and Uccello's long and thin *Profanation of the Host* of 1465, a detailed work that frequents the pages of art history books. Cortona master-painter Luca Signorelli has a couple of works in the Sala delle Veglie (Hall 23), along with Raphael's father, Giovanni Santi. **Raphael** himself holds court in the duchjess's drawing room (Hall 25), where his enigmatic *La Muta (The Mute One),* the portrait of a gentlewoman, is the most important painting in the collection thanks to her Mona Lisa–like smile. Painted in 1507, the picture now resides behind Plexiglas, having been stolen in 1975 and returned to Urbino in good condition 2 years later in one of the country's most sensational art thefts.

The second floor **Rovere apartments** are not quite as enticing, containing work from the 16th to 18th centuries from the likes of Urbino artists Federico Barocci and Federico Brandani, and baroque master Gaetano Lapis.

Piazza Duca Federico 107. www.palazzoducaleurbino.it. ✆ **0722-322625.** Admission 5€ adults, 2.50€ E.U. citizens ages 18–25, free ages 17 and under. Mon 8:30am–2pm; Tues–Sun 8:30am–7:15pm. Last ticket sold 1 hr. before closing.

WHERE TO EAT & STAY

Be sure to visit **Raffaello Degusteria,** Via Donato Bramante 6, to stock up on traditional Urbino foods (www.raffaellodegusteria.it; ✆ **0722-329546;** Mon–Sat 9am–1pm and 4–8pm).

Albergo San Domenico ★ One of the most prestigious addresses in le Marches, this simple, captivating *albergo* abuts the 14th-century Church of San Domenicot, its rooms converted from a 16th-century convent. A 4-minute walk from the main square of town, the hotel is the most convenient in Urbino, located across from the Ducal Palace (the views tend to be of the parking lot on the other side of the building, however). Bedrooms are spacious but relatively spartan, and breakfasts are generous.

Piazza Rinascimento 3, 61029 Urbino. www.viphotels.it. ✆ **0722-26-26.** Fax 0722-2727. 31 units. 123€–215€ double; 205€–235€ suite. AE, DC, MC, V. Parking 9€ per day. **Amenities:** Restaurant; bar; babysitting; bikes; exercise room; room service. *In room:* A/C, TV, hair dryer, minibar, Wi-Fi (5€ per hour)

Antica Osteria "da la Stella" ★★ MARCHIGIANI/ROMAGNOLI This is the most popular restaurant in town for good reason; the menu is incredibly inventive, the service is top-notch, and the food is always seasonal and fresh. Specializing in local "Montefeltro" cuisine, and the traditions of Le Marche and Romagna, dishes might include grilled lasagna with asparagus, *tagliatelle* with white truffle, or lamb cutlets with sesame seeds, all served with distinctive homemade breads. The elegant but rustic wood interior enhances the experience. It's conveniently located just steps away from the Casa Natale di Raffaello.

Via Santa Margherita 1. www.anticaosteriadalastella.com. ✆ **0722-320-228.** Reservations recommended. Main courses 15€–23€. AE, DC, MC, V. Tues–Sun 12:30–2:30pm and 7:30–10:30pm.

Hotel Mamiani Urbino ★★ Although this luxurious, modern hotel lies in the hills outside the center, it's worth the 10-minute bus ride (the bus stops just outside, every 20 min. or so). All the rooms are contemporary and stylish, with all the usual amenities and complimentary breakfast, though deluxe rooms and suites also come with spellbinding views of the city.

Via Bernini 6, 61029 Urbino. www.hotelmamiani.it. ✆ **0722-322-309.** Fax 0722-329-055. 72 units. 85€–95€ double; 125€ suite. AE, DC, MC, V. Free parking. **Amenities:** Restaurant; bar. *In room:* A/C, TV, hair dryer, minibar, Wi-Fi (free).

Trattoria del Leone ★ MARCHIGIANI Centrally located del Leone is an excellent cheaper option, with 7€ to 8€ buying you a decent lunch with good, local wine. The folks here take pride in their traditional Le Marche dishes like mushroom frittata (omelet) and rabbit stuffed with *porchetta* (roast pork). The specialty of the house, *passatelli vegetariani,* is a delicious Emilian pasta made from bread crumbs, eggs, Parmesan cheese, and nutmeg, but despite the vegetarian label, note that it's cooked in chicken broth.

Via Cesare Battisti 5. www.latrattoriadelleone.it. ✆ **0722-329-894.** Reservations recommended for dinner. Main courses 10€–12€. AE, DC, MC, V. Mon–Fri 7:30–10:30pm; Sat–Sun 12:30–2:30pm and 7:30–10:30pm.

Pesaro

216km (134 miles) NE of Perugia, 148km (92 miles) S of Ravenna, 122km (76 miles) N of Ancona, 315km (196 miles) E of Florence

During the late Roman and Byzantine periods, Pesaro formed part of the Duchy of the Pentapolis, one of the five major seaports of the Adriatic. Those glory days are over, but Pesaro is still thriving—a more minor port today, and a laid-back seaside resort with a small but attractive historic center known as the birthplace of Gioacchino Rossini.

In early August, Pesaro's annual **Rossini Opera Festival** (www.rossiniop-erafestival.it; ✆ **0721-38-001**), featuring the composer's large repertoire of bel canto operas, draws music lovers from around the world.

ESSENTIALS

GETTING THERE If you're approaching Pesaro from the north, you can take one of 35 **trains** per day from the seaside resort of Rimini. Travel time is half an hour, and the train costs 3.60€ one-way. From the west, 26 trains arrive daily from Bologna, taking 2 hours and costing 10€ one-way. **Adriabus** (www.amibus.it; ✆ **0722-376-711**) runs hourly **buses** (no. 46) from Urbino to just outside Pesaro train station; 3.20€ buys you a one-way ticket for the trip, which takes 45 minutes on the fast bus.

VISITOR INFORMATION Near the seafront, the **tourist office,** Via Trieste 164 (www.turismopesaro.it; ✆ **0721-69-341**), is open Monday and Saturday 9am to 1pm, and Tuesday to Friday 9am to 1pm and 3 to 6pm.

EXPLORING PESARO

The wide main square, **Piazza del Popolo,** occupies the heart of Pesaro. Cafes and the massive **Palazzo Ducale**—built in the 15th century by Alessandro Sforza—flank the piazza, which is dominated by a landmark fountain adorned with tritons and sea horses. Try to make time for the 19th-century **cathedral** (daily 9am–noon and 4–6pm; ✆ **0721-30-043**), Via Rossini 56, where a series of huge, stunning **Roman and Byzantine mosaics ★★** have been uncovered in the basement, visible through glass panels in the nave. Turn on the lights, left of the entrance (1€ for 7 min.).

Casa Rossini HISTORIC HOME Opera devotees flock to **Casa Rossini,** the town house where the great Rossini was born in 1792. This is a modest shrine to the *"cigno pesarese"* ("swan of Pesaro"), composer of *The Barber of Seville* and three dozen or so other works, and really of interest to fans only. The museum displays photographs, signed opera scores, theatrical memorabilia, even Rossini's small piano, but is mostly a series of fairly dry portraits used to commemorate various periods in the composer's life (labeled in Italian only). Universally honored, Rossini died in Paris in 1868, but was reinterred in Florence's Santa Croce (p. 220) in 1887.

Via Rossini 34. ✆ **0721-387357.** Admission 4€ adults, 2€ ages 15–26, free for children 14 and under. June to mid-Sept Wed and Fri–Sun 9:30am–12:30pm and 4–7pm, Tues and Thurs 9:30am–12:30pm and 4–10:30pm; mid-Sept to May Tues and Fri–Sat 10am–1pm and 3:30–7pm, Wed–Thurs and Sun 10am–1pm.

Musei Civici ★ MUSEUM Pesaro's art museum contains one of Italy's finest collections of **Renaissance and baroque ceramics ★**, much of it striking for its spontaneous, almost modern, use of color and design, though the main highlight inside is Giovanni Bellini's huge and splendid ***Coronation of the Virgin* ★** polyptych. The altarpiece was completed in 1475 and dominates all of the other art in the Sala Bellini, even the fiery *Fall of the Giants* by Guido Reni and Marco Zoppo's sensuous *Pietà*. In the adjacent Sala Hercolani Rossini you'll find Bellini's *Padre Eterna,* Tintoretto's stern portrait of Domenico Robusti, and work from the Bolognese school by the likes of Michele di Matteo and Ludovico Carracci.

Via Toschi Mosca 29. www.museicivicipesaro.it. ✆ **0721-387-474.** Admission 4€ adults (7€ with Casa Rossini), 2€ ages 15–25 (3€ with Casa Rossini), free for children 14 and under. Audio guides 4€. June–Sept Tues and Thurs–Sun 10am–1pm and 4–7:30pm, Wed 10am–1pm; Oct–May Tues–Thurs 10am–1pm, Fri–Sat 10am–1pm and 3:30–7pm.

Pesaro's harbor.

WHERE TO EAT & STAY

The most atmospheric place to grab a cake and cappuccino in Pesaro is the **Caffe Ducale** (daily 7am–2am; ✆ **0721-34-279**), Piazza del Popolo 21.

Da Alceo ★★ SEAFOOD On the ground floor of the Hotel Le Terrazze, Da Alceo stands 5km (3 miles) east of the center of Pesaro. The fish is the freshest around, and the varied menu boasts first-rate ingredients prepared with both skill and flair. Try such delights as baked "peter fish" with fresh vegetables, or scampi in a champagne sauce. The homemade pasta *(passatelli)* is served with scampi and monkfish. Monkfish, one of the most popular kinds of seafood in Le Marche, is also served with potatoes and black olives. Always ask about what was "just caught"—the fresh fish can be prepared either grilled or sautéed, as you like it.

Strada Panoramica Ardizio 119. www.ristorantealceo.it. ✆ **0721-51-360.** Reservations recommended. Main courses 12€–32€, fixed price menu 70€, 2 courses 35€–40€. AE, DC, MC, V. Tues–Sat 12:30–2pm and 8–11pm; Sun 12:30–2pm.

Hotel Excelsior ★★ The town's top luxury hotel is a five-star beauty overlooking the Adriatic, with it's own private beach (though this is a hefty 40€–50€ per day extra in summer) and lavish spa and pool facilities. The spacious rooms feature an all-white retro 1950s theme and wood floors, blended with contemporary style and amenities; opt for superior rooms with ocean-facing balconies if you can. The restaurant serves excellent Italian seafood if you want to lounge all day, though the hotel is within walking distance of the historic center.

Lungomare Nazario Sauro, 61121 Pesaro. www.excelsiorpesaro.it. ✆ **0721-630-011.** Fax 0721-35502. 49 units. 175€–225€ double; 377€–395€ suite. AE, DC, MC, V. Parking 20€ per day. **Amenities:** Restaurant, bar, free bikes; gym; indoor heated pool; room service; sauna; spa. *In room:* A/C, TV, hair dryer, minibar, Wi-Fi (free).

Ancona

139km (87 miles) NE of Perugia, 87km (54 miles) SE of Urbino, 76km (46 miles) S of Pesaro

The capital of Le Marche juts out into the Adriatic, an ancient port that still acts as a gateway for thousands of visitors passing through to Greece, Slovenia, and Croatia.

Founded by Greek settlers in around 387 B.C., Ancona was built in the form of an amphitheater on the slopes of a rocky promontory, thriving during the

Roman and medieval periods. The port has always been a strategic target for invaders: It was bombarded by the Austrians in 1915 and then by Allied forces in 1944. An earthquake leveled part of the old town in 1972. Throw in a major New Orleans–caliber flood or two, and you wonder how all the monuments have remained standing.

The World War II memorial at Passetto Beach in Ancona.

In spite of its past adversity, today's Ancona is prospering as more than just a stopover between ferry boats. Many travelers spend their layover in Ancona at the sparkling **Passetto Beach,** with its blue waters and family-friendly sands (but not *the* sandiest along the east coast), although enough history and art has survived in the city center to take up a full day.

ESSENTIALS

GETTING THERE Ancona is a major transportation hub for Le Marche, with frequent **rail** links to both Milan (4–5 hr.; 39€–52€) and Rome (3–4 hr.; 15€–33€). Many visitors approach Ancona on a train from Pesaro. Trains run every half an hour to make the 30- to 50-minute run that costs 3.40€ to 11€ one-way. The train from Venice takes 4 to 5 hours, costing 34€ to 59€ one-way. **Motorists** heading south along the Adriatic coast approach Ancona from Pesaro, on the A14 autostrada.

VISITOR INFORMATION Offering good maps, the **tourist office** at Via Gramsci 2A (www.comune.ancona.it/turismo/en; ✆ **320-0196321**) is open April to December daily 10am to 1pm and 4 to 8pm.

EXPLORING ANCONA

As a remnant of Ancona's illustrious past, the **Arco di Traiano** ★, built to honor the emperor Trajan, who constructed the port in A.D. 115, still stands at the northern end of Lungomare Vanvitelli. The sculptural reliefs have gone with the wind, but the arch is still one of the best preserved along the Adriatic.

Duomo ★ CATHEDRAL Dedicated to St. Cyriacus (San Ciriaco), the 4th-century martyr and patron saint of Ancona, this cathedral is Romanesque with both Byzantine and Lombard architectural features. The cathedral is reached by climbing a steep garden staircase, *Scalone Nappi* (you can also take bus 11 from Piazza Cavour). Inside, the marble columns were actually those that once held up a Roman Temple of Venus. However, the glory of the church is not inside, but on its facade, which is fronted by a majestic Gothic porch made of pink stone and held up by two fierce lions.

Piazzale del Duomo. ✆ **071-52688.** Free admission. Mon–Sat 8am–noon and 3–7pm (closes 6pm in winter).

Museo Archeologico Nazionale delle Marche MUSEUM Installed in the Palazzo Ferretti, this museum, one of the major repositories of art in Le Marche, is stuffed with prehistoric and archaeological relics of the region. Look for exceptional Greek vases, sculpture, and metalwork left by Greek traders. Greek jewelry was unearthed early in the 20th century, and the collection includes bronze incense-burning pots, the most famous of which, the Ionian Dinos of Amandola, date from the 5th century B.C.

Palazzo Ferretti, Via Ferretti 6. www.archeomarche.it. ✆ **071-202-602.** Admission 4€ adults, 2€ ages 18–25, free for those 17 and under. Tues–Sun 8:30am–7:30pm. Bus: 11.

Museo della Città di Ancona MUSEUM This small but illuminating museum tells the story of Ancona from prehistory to the 1960s, through archaeological finds, old photos, original prints, paintings, and models. The building itself is part of the attraction, housed in the 13th-century **Hospital of St. Thomas of Canterbury** and the former fish market dating back to 1817.

Piazza del Plebiscito. ✆ **071-222-5045.** Admission 3.10€ adults, 1.80€ ages 16–25, free for those 15 and under. Mid-June to mid-Sept Tues–Fri 5–8pm, Sat–Sun 10am–1pm and 5–8pm; mid-Sept to mid-June Tues–Fri 10am–1pm, Sat–Sun 10am–1pm and 4–7pm.

Pinacoteca Civica "Francesco Podesti" ★ ART MUSEUM This is one of the finest art galleries in Le Marche, established by a donation from local painter Francesco Podesti in the 1880s. We come here mainly to see the works of Carlo Crivelli, who has the dubious distinction of being called "one of the tidiest of all Renaissance artists." In his *Madonna col Bambino,* look for his trademark: a depiction of apples and cucumbers hanging overhead. The collection includes minor works by big names such as Titian's *L'Apparizione della Vergine (Apparition of the Virgin)* and Lorenzo Lotto's *Sacra Conversazione (Holy Conversation)*, both of whom are also represented by their own versions of the Madonna. There is even a modest collection of Italian art from the 20th century.

Palazzo Bosdari, Via Ciriaco Pizzecolli 17. ✆ **071-222-5045.** Admission 4.70€ adults, 3.60€ ages 16–25, free for those 15 and under. Tues–Sat 9am–7pm; Sun 10am–1pm and 4–7pm.

WHERE TO EAT & STAY

Boccon Divino ★ SEAFOOD/MARCHIGIANI Housed in 18th-century vaulted palace stables in the historic center (near Piazza del Plebiscito), this fine restaurant consistently knocks out high-quality meals with seasonal, fresh ingredients. Expect local specialties with a contemporary inventive twist, and excellent wines from across Le Marche. The chef's tasting menu is especially recommended, where you choose a meat (typically lamb) or fish-based menu (such as *stoccafisso all'anconetana,* salted cod), and let the chef create. Enjoy the courtyard tables in summer.

Via Matteotti 13. ✆ **071-57-269.** Reservations recommended. Main courses 15€–26€; tasting menu from 55€. AE, DC, MC, V. Mon–Fri 12:15–3pm and 5:30–11pm; Sat 5:30–11pm.

Grand Hotel Palace The town's most convenient hotel for the port area (and ferries) opened in 1968 and is showing its age, but remains a good value considering the location—there are better hotels in the Ancona area, but all of them lie inland on the fringes of town. Fronting the harbor in the city center, the Grand offers a roof garden terrace where breakfast is served—guests take in the view from the best vantage point in Ancona. Classic decor fills its public and private rooms, often enhanced with antiques and luxurious touches like beds dressed in damask. Try, if possible, for a room with a view of the port. Bedrooms are midsize, each with a small bathroom (half with showers, the others with tubs).

Lungomare Vanvitelli 24, 60121 Ancona. www.hotelancona.it. ✆ **071-201-813.** Fax 071-2074832. 40 units. 150€ double; 300€ suite. Rates include buffet breakfast. AE, DC, MC, V. Parking 20€. Closed Dec 23–Jan 1. **Amenities:** Bar; babysitting; room service. *In room:* A/C, TV, hair dryer, minibar, Wi-Fi (free).

La Moretta 1897 ★ SEAFOOD/MARCHIGIANI This classic trattoria offers fine dining against a background of wood-paneled walls and top notch service. The menu always features fresh fish from the Adriatic and the agricultural bounty of the local countryside. We always gravitate here just to devour its *brodetto all'anconetana*, which is the typical local fish soup. This might be followed with *maccheroncino in salsa righera* (homemade long pasta with fresh fish and a "fruits of the sea" sauce). Another local favorite is *racchiusi di mare* (a kind of ravioli stuffed with fish). Piazza Plebiscito 52. www.trattoriamoretta.com. ✆ **071-202-317.** Reservations recommended. Main courses 10€–22€. AE, DC, MC, V. Mon–Sat 12:15–3pm and 5:30–11pm. Closed Jan 1–8.

Ascoli Piceno

175km (109 miles) SE of Perugia, 122km (76 miles) S of Ancona

One of the architectural treasures of Le Marche, Ascoli Piceno is known as "the city of travertine," a type of marble used harmoniously throughout its medieval and Renaissance buildings, and its hundred towers. Ringed by steep hills, the city lies in a valley where the Castellano and Tronto rivers meet. Ascoli was the metropolis of the Piceni, a Bronze Age tribe that once controlled the region bordering the Adriatic, and was fought over through much of the Middle Ages before reverting to a beautifully preserved backwater.

Allow at least a full day to explore the town, much of which can be appreciated from the outside, even if you never duck into a church or a museum (although there are plenty of those, too).

ESSENTIALS

GETTING THERE Most travelers by **train** go through the gateway of San Benedetto del Tronto, 39km (24 miles) to the east of Ascoli on the coast. At San Benedetto, trains arrive from Ancona frequently, a one-way fare costing 4.70€. The trip takes around 1 hour. From San Benedetto, trains run every half-hour for the 45-minute trip to Ascoli Piceno, costing 2.60€. The Ascoli train station lies on Piazzale della Stazione in the new part of town, east of the Castellano River.

Buses from San Benedetto are more crowded than trains and passage takes an hour; we do not recommend them. From Rome, however, it's convenient to take the **Start** bus (www.startspa.it; ✆ **800-443-040**) that runs eight times a day from Fiumicino airport and Stazione Termini, and takes around 3 hours to Ascoli train station; the cost is 15€.

For **motorists,** Ascoli Piceno is usually approached by drivers heading down the Adriatic coast, perhaps after a stopover in Ancona (see above). Once you reach San Benedetto del Tronto, cut inland along S4 for the final run into Ascoli.

VISITOR INFORMATION In the heart of town, the **tourist office** is situated in the Palazzo Comunale at Piazza Arringo 7 (www.comune.ascolipiceno.it; ✆ **0736-253-045**), open Monday to Friday 9:30am to 6:30pm, Saturday 9am to 1pm and 3 to 6pm, and Sunday 10am to 7pm.

EXPLORING ASCOLI PECINO

Start at **Piazza del Popolo ★★**, the main square in the heart of the *centro storico,* and one of the most ravishing public spaces in Italy. Elongated and beautifully proportioned, it's surrounded by elegant Gothic and Renaissance mansions and riddled with imposing arcades. To get your bearings, stop for a coffee or a drink at

Caffè Meletti ★, Piazza del Popolo 20 (www.caffemeletti.com; ✆ **0736-255-559**); founded in 1904, it remains the most famous watering hole in Le Marche. Silvio Meletti first served his now-famous anisette liqueur at this cafe, and it was introduced to the world in the classic 1960 film *I delfini* by Citto Maselli. In summer, the cafe is open daily from 7am to midnight (closed Mon in winter).

Dominating the square is **Palazzo dei Capitani ★** (✆ **0736-244975**), the former town hall, erected in the 13th century. Visitors can walk inside for a look at its 16th-century arcaded courtyard. At the narrow end of the square, the handsome Romanesque-Gothic **Chiesa di San Francesco ★** is open daily from 8am to noon and 3:30 to 7:30pm. Admission is free. The church was founded to commemorate the visit of St. Francis to Ascoli in 1215, though it wasn't formally consecrated until 1371. The church has several Lombard architectural features and a wood crucifix rescued from a 1535 fire.

Duomo CATHEDRAL The austere cathedral combines classical, Romanesque, and baroque architectural features. The facade is from the 1530s, built to the design of Cola dell'Amatrice, but the transept was once a Roman basilica. The octagonal dome actually was first constructed in the 8th century. The interior is richly decorated; Carlo Crivelli's magnificent *Polittico,* a polyptych completed in 1473, sits in the Cappella del Sacramento. Stairs lead down into the Cripta di Sant'Emidio, which houses mosaics and the tomb of the city's patron saint. Adjacent to the cathedral stands the squat **baptistery** from the 12th century.

Piazza Arringo. ✆ **0736-259-774.** Free admission. Daily 7am–12.30pm and 5:30–7:30pm.

Musei Civici MUSEUM Under the umbrella of the **Musei Civici,** the city runs three absorbing museums in the center of Ascoli, all within easy walking distance of each other.

Housed in the massive Palazzo Arringo, facing Piazza Arringo, is the **Pinacoteca Civica,** home to some of the most famous paintings in Le Marche. Highlights include two 15th century triptychs by Carlo Crivelli, who married the solidity of Renaissance geometry with late Gothic decorative opulence, and *La salita al Calvario* by Cola dell'Amatrice, who designed the facade of the Duomo.

The **Galleria d'Arte Contemporanea,** in the former convent of St. Augustine, Corso Mazzini 90, contains numerous paintings by artists like Lucio Fontana, Sebastian Matta, Filippo de Pisis, and Gino Severini, and 40 paintings and 38 drawings by abstract master Osvaldo Licini.

The **Museo della Ceramica** on the Piazza San Tommaso is the newest addition, opened in 2007 next to the Romanesque church of San Tommaso. The museum is divided into five sections that chronicle the history of ceramic production in Ascoli Piceno, from majolica of the 15th century, to 19th- and 20th-century artists such as local boy Emidio Paci.

Piazza San Tommaso. www.ascolimusei.it ✆ **0736-298-213.** Admission to all 3 museums 8€ adults, 5€ students. Oct–Mar 15 Tues–Fri 10am–5pm, Sat–Sun 10am–7pm; Mar 16–Sept daily 10am–7pm.

Museo Archeologico Statale di Ascoli MUSEUM Housed in the 16th-century Palazzo Panichi, this museum, a storehouse of archaeological finds from all over the Ascoli region, will primarily appeal to history buffs. Inside, three sections cover prehistory, the history of the Piceni Bronze Age tribe to the early Roman era, and the Roman period itself.

There are rare artifacts uncovered from the nearby necropolis at Salino and at Monteprandone, a special room dedicated to Piceni artifacts going back to the 6th century B.C., and a detailed Roman polychrome mosaic.

Piazza Arringo 28. ✆ **0736-253-562.** Admission 2€ adults, 1€ ages 18–25, free 17 and under. Tues–Sun 8:30am–7:30pm.

WHERE TO EAT & STAY

When in Ascoli be sure to try the **olive all'Ascolana** (stuffed olives Ascolana style), and the wines of the **Rosso Piceno** (Rosso Piceno Superiore is one of 11 DOC wines made in the Le Marche region).

Albergo Piceno ★★ This is a small but beautifully designed hotel set in an 18th-century building in the heart of town, and artfully restored in 2007. The luxurious rooms and chic bathrooms are decorated with bold, colorful paintings by local artists, and the breakfast buffet is generous (the fresh pastries are delicious). You can walk to the hotel from the train and bus station, but there's no dedicated parking; you'll have to find a space at the public lot nearby.

Via Minucia 10, 63100 Ascoli Piceno. www.albergopiceno.it. ✆ **0736-253-017.** Fax 0736-251803. 20 units. 110€ double; 135€ triple. Rates include buffet breakfast. AE, DC, MC, V. **Amenities:** Bar; exercise room; room service. *In room:* A/C, TV, hair dryer, minibar, Wi-Fi (free).

Residenza 100 Torri ★★ This exclusive hotel was created from the stables of a patrician *palazzo* dating from the 13th century. The hotel lies in the ancient core of town, within walking distance of Piazza del Popolo. All of the individually designed bedrooms have been furnished with sophisticated designer taste, and the latest in modern accessories installed. From the parquet floors to the soft upholstery to the romantic canopied beds, this is a pocket of posh. Breakfast is served in the winter garden under a pyramidal glass roof.

Via Mazzoni 6, 63100 Ascoli Piceno. www.centotorri.com. ✆ **0736-255-123.** Fax 0736-251646. 14 units. 128€–180€ double; 190€–360€ suite. Rates include buffet breakfast. AE, DC, MC, V. Parking 15€ per day. **Amenities:** Bar; babysitting; room service; spa. *In room:* A/C, TV, hair dryer, Internet (free), minibar.

Ristorante Piccolo Teatro ★ ITALIAN/ASCOLANA Conveniently located in an 18th-century *palazzo* in the historic center, this tiny culinary gem is very popular with locals, so reserve ahead. Service is top-notch and the food is superb, with appetizers such as black bean soup with bacon and local specialties such *frittura di pesce* (fried fish) and *orata con finocchietto selvatico e limone* (sea bream with fennel and lemon).

Via Goldoni 2, at Via Trieste. www.alpiccoloteatro.it. ✆ **0736-261-574.** Reservations recommended. Main courses 8€–18€. AE, DC, MC, V. Tues–Sun 11am–11:30pm.

Rua dei Notari ★★ ITALIAN/ASCOLANA A short walk from the central Piazza del Popolo in the Palazzo Guiderocchi, this restaurant is the top choice for dinner. Exquisite main courses include *filetto di maiale bardato al guanciale* (pork filet wrapped with bacon), while local pastas such as *maccheroncini di campofilone in salsa rossa alla moda marchigiana* (Le Marche–style macaroni with red sauce) are equally tasty. It's also the best place to try the local *olive all'Ascolana* (6€) and bottles of Rosso Piceno.

Via Cesare Battisti 3. www.ruadeinotari.it. ✆ **0736-258-393.** Reservations recommended. Main courses 10€–18€; fixed menu 30€. AE, DC, MC, V. Wed–Mon 7:30–10:30pm.

7

BOLOGNA & EMILIA-ROMAGNA

In the northern reaches of central Italy, the region of Emilia-Romagna is renowned for its cuisine and for its ravishing art cities: learned Bologna, Byzantine Ravenna, and Renaissance Modena. Here, such families as the dukes of Ferrara rose in power and influence in the Middle Ages, creating courts that attracted talented painters and poets.

Yet it's the region's culinary heritage that is likely to leave the greatest impression. Emilia-Romagna is one of Italy's most bountiful farming districts, and many Italians consider it to be the gastronomic center of the entire nation. Traditional dishes like *tortelloni, tagliatelle al ragù,* and *passatelli,* not to mention Bolognese sauce, have spread across the world. Visitors also come to sample the Prosciutto di Parma, Modena's balsamic vinegar, and the king of cheese, Parmigiano-Reggiano.

Bologna, the region's booming capital, stands at the crossroads between Venice and Florence and is linked by express highways to Milan and Tuscany. It makes an excellent base for Emilia-Romagna, with all the major cities in the region an easy train ride away.

THE BEST TRAVEL EXPERIENCES IN BOLOGNA & EMILIA-ROMAGNA

- **Dining in Bologna:** Bologna (and the Emilia-Romagna region in general) has given the world not only Bolognese sauce, but also the pasta shapes of tortellini and *tagliatelle.* See p. 384.
- **Viewing the Byzantine mosaics of Ravenna:** Take a break from the Italian Renaissance at Ravenna, one time Byzantine capital and crammed with astonishing mosaic art. See p. 400.
- **Visiting the "land of engines":** Modena makes the world's fastest and most desired sports cars; visit Ferrari, Maserati, and Lamborghini to find out what makes them so special. See p. 408.
- **Taking the food tours of Parma:** Parmesan cheese, prosciutto ham, fine wine, and really, really expensive balsamic vinegar await on gastronomic food tours of the Parma area. See p. 415.
- **Touring the world's smallest republic:** It's true—you are not in Italy anymore when you visit tiny San Marino, a totally independent nation with a gasp-inducing setting, high above the Adriatic coastal plain. See p. 422.

BOLOGNA ★★

52km (32 miles) S of Ferrara, 151km (94 miles) SW of Venice, 378km (234 miles) N of Rome

Home to the world's oldest continually operating university, Bologna or *La Dotta* (the Learned), is a dynamic city of redbrick towers and stately colonnades. Its well-preserved historic center, all pink and red stone, is one of the largest in Italy,

PREVIOUS PAGE: **Bologna's Baptistery.**

Bologna's Palazzo Communale

but this is no museum: Bologna is a big, working city of one million inhabitants. It's also one of the richest cities in Italy, often ranking at the top in terms of quality of life, and one of the most cosmopolitan, attracting the flagship stores of major U.S. brands such as Disney, Apple, and Nike, and even—gasp—McDonald's. Not to say that Bologna is lacking on the gastronomic front—quite the opposite. The city is also nicknamed *La Grassa* (the Fat), and is generally considered Italy's gourmet capital.

Founded as the Roman *colonia* of Bononia in 189 B.C., Bologna boomed in the Middle Ages thanks to its extensive trade links, and the university dates its foundation to 1088. In 1401 the art-loving Bentivoglio family began running the city, and remained in charge until 1506, when Bologna became one of the Papal States. In World War II, 44% of the city was either destroyed or severely damaged by Allied bombing, but there have been more recent tragedies: On August 2, 1980, a bomb exploded at a Bologna train station killing 85 people and wounding 200 (neo-fascists were responsible).

Today Bologna is thriving again, with a vast legacy of historic architecture, monuments, and art preserved within its medieval core, easily tackled on foot. The city's famed towers—Le Due Torri—dominate the center, but learned Bologna is above all a city of museums, with everything from 16th-century waxworks to reminders of Jewish Italy on display.

Essentials

GETTING THERE **By Plane** The international **Aeroporto Guglielmo Marconi** (www.bologna-airport.it; ✆ **051-6479615**) is 6km (3¾ miles) north of the city center and served by such domestic carriers as Alitalia and Meridiana; all the main European airlines also fly to this airport, including Ryanair (London-Stansted), EasyJet, and British Airways (both London-Gatwick), making flights from the U.K. especially competitive. A **bus** (marked AEROBUS) runs daily (6am–12:15am) every 15 to 30 minutes from

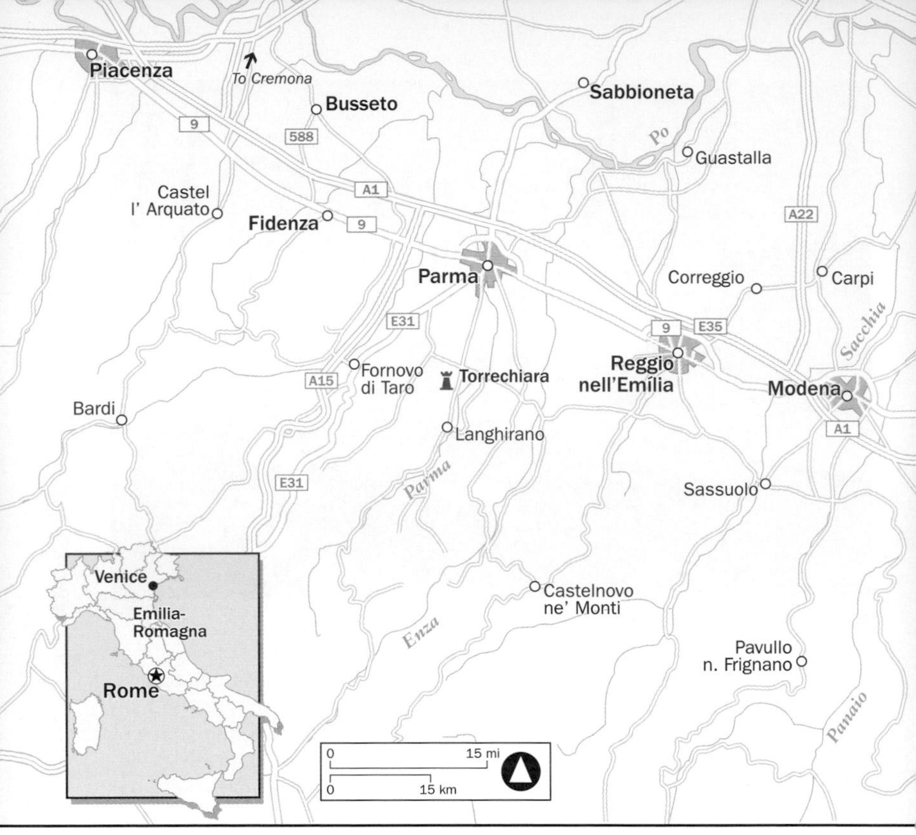

the airport to Bologna's rail station (Stazione Centrale). A one-way ticket costs 6€, and the trip usually takes 20 minutes.

By Train Bologna's **Stazione Centrale** is at Piazza Medaglie d'Oro 2 (✆ **892021**). Trains arrive hourly from Rome (trip time: 3½ hr.). There are also high-speed trains from Rome to Bologna (trip time 2 hr.–2 hr., 20 min.). A second-class one-way fare costs 39€ to 59€. From Milan, trip times range from just over 1 hour to 2 hours, 50 minutes, costing 15€ to 42€ one-way. Bus nos. A, 25, and 30 run between the station and the historic core of Bologna, Piazza Maggiore. Taxis use the meter, which starts at 3.15€—expect to pay around 6€ for trips into the center.

By Car If you are driving in from Florence, continue north along A1 until reaching the outskirts of Bologna, where signs direct you to the city center. From Milan, take A1 southeast along the Apennines. From Venice or Ferrara, follow A13 southwest. From Rimini, Ravenna, and the towns along the Adriatic, cut west on A14.

VISITOR INFORMATION The main **tourist office** (✆ **051-239660**) is at Piazza Maggiore in the Palazzo del Podestà, open daily 9am to 7pm. There is another office at the airport (in the arrivals hall; ✆ **051-6472113**), open Monday to Saturday 9am to 7pm, and on Sunday and holidays 9am to 4pm. The tourism website is www.bolognaturismo.info.

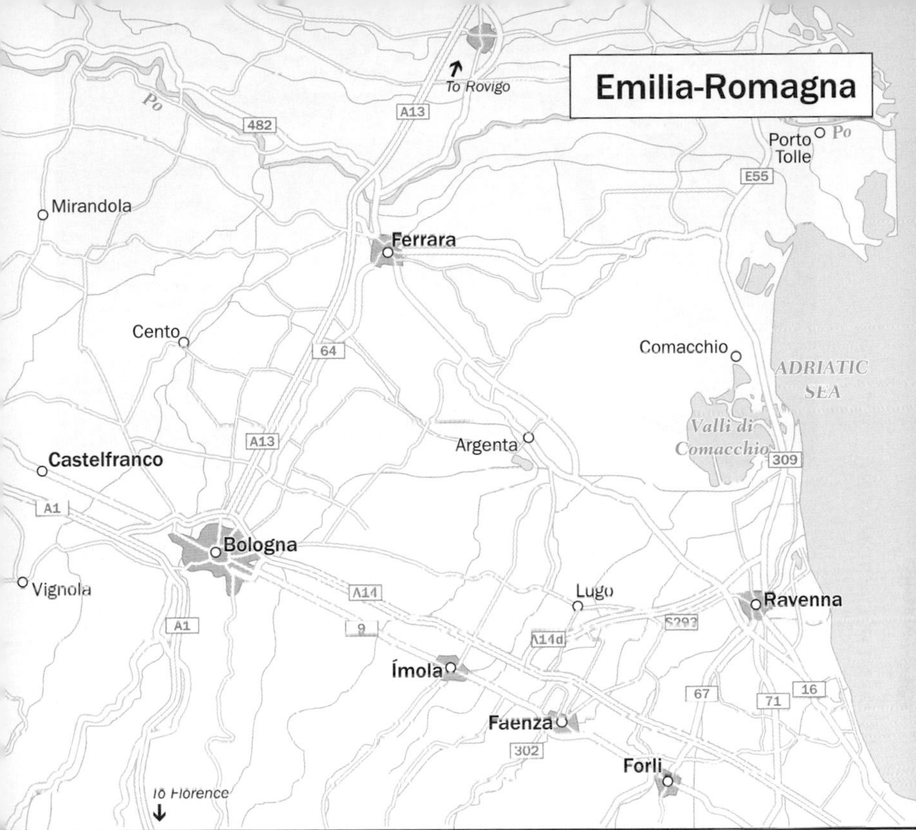

GETTING AROUND Central Bologna is easy to cover on foot; most of the major sights are in and around Piazza Maggiore. If, however, you don't want to walk, **city buses** leave for most points from Piazza Nettuno or Piazza Maggiore, and the train station. Free maps are available at the storefront office of the **ATC** (Azienda Trasporti Comunali) at Piazza XX Settembre (www.atc.bo.it; ✆ **051-290290**). You can buy tickets at one of many booths and *tabacchi* in Bologna, or just pay on the bus. Tickets cost 1.50€ on the bus (no change), or 1.20€ if you buy in advance from a *tabacchi,* and are valid for 1 hour. A **citypass**—a single ticket which allows 10 rides—costs just 11€. Once on board, you must have your ticket validated or you'll be fined up to 150€.

Taxis are on 24-hour radio call at ✆ **051-372727** (Cooperativa Taxisti Bolognesiare) or ✆ **051-4590** (Consorzio Autonomo Taxisti). The meter starts at 3.10€ and goes up 1.05€ to 1.15€ per kilometer.

Exploring Bologna

At the heart of Bologna lies the monumental space of **Piazza Maggiore,** dominated by the central Palazzo del Podestà (built around 1200 and home to the visitor information center), Palazzo Communale, and the Basilica di San Petronio. The adjacent **Piazza Nettuno** contains the **Fontana di Nettuno** (Neptune Fountain) ★★, which has gradually become a symbol of the city, although it was designed in 1566 by a Frenchman named Giambologna (the Italians altered his

Detail from the tomb of St. Domenico.

name). Viewed as irreverent by some, "indecent" by the Catholic Church, and magnificent by those with more liberal tastes, this 16th-century fountain depicts Neptune with rippling muscles, a trident in one arm, and a heavy foot on the head of a dolphin. The church forced Giambologna to manipulate Neptune's left arm to cover his monumental endowment. Around his feet are four highly erotic cherubs, also with dolphins. At the base of the fountain, four very sensual sirens spout streams of water from their breasts.

On the wall near the fountain lies the **Shrine for the Fallen of the Liberation,** a collection of hundreds of black-and-white photos of World War II partisans killed by the Nazis. Next to it is a simpler glass memorial to those killed by the terrorist bomb attack on Bologna station in 1980.

Basilica di San Domenico ★ CHURCH This grand church was consecrated in 1251 but has undergone many restorations since then, notably from 1728 to 1732, when the interior was completely remodeled in an elegant baroque style. The highlight inside is the beautifully crafted **tomb of St. Dominic.** You'll find it in the awe-inspiring **Cappella di San Domenico,** a large chapel on the right side of the nave, smothered in frescoes by Guido Reni and other Bolognese painters from the early 1600s. The sculptured tomb itself is a Renaissance masterpiece, a joint enterprise of Niccolò Pisano, Guglielmo (a friar), Niccolò dell'Arca, Alfonso Lombardi, and the young Michelangelo. Observe the gaze and stance of Michelangelo's *San Procolo,* which appears to be the "rehearsal" for his later *David* (this time fully clothed). To get a closer look at the church cloisters and exquisite **choir stalls ★**, carved by Damiano da Bergamo, another friar, in the 16th century, walk to the back (right) of the church and pay .50€.

Piazza San Domenico 13. ✆ **051-6400411.** Free admission. Mon–Sat 9am–noon and 3:30–6pm; Sun 3:30–5pm. Bus: A, 16, 30, 38, 39, or 59.

Basilica di San Petronio ★★ CHURCH Looming over Piazza Maggiore, this enormous Gothic basilica honors the patron saint of Bologna, bishop of the city from 431 to 450 (his remains were reinterred here in 2000). Although work started in 1390, the church took until 1663 to complete, and even then the facade was still not finished—legend has it that the construction was curtailed by Pope Pius IV when the Vatican learned that the basilica was to be larger than St. Peter's. Between 1425 and 1438, Jacopo della Quercia of Siena graced the

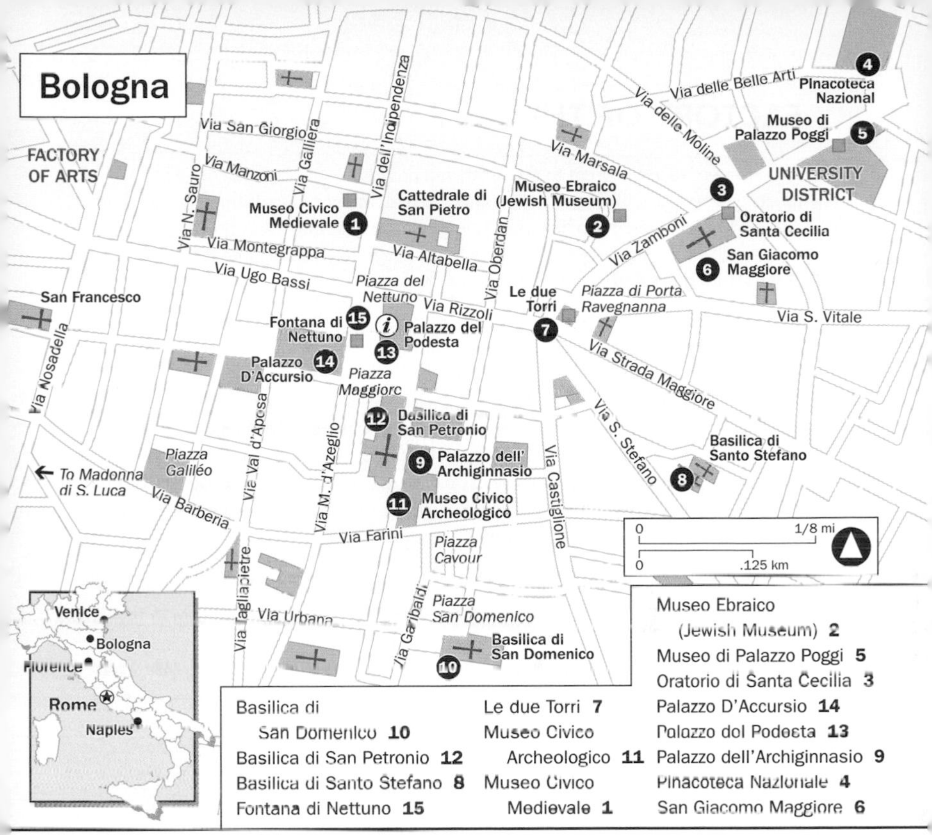

Bologna
FACTORY OF ARTS
Via San Giorgio
Via Manzoni
Via Galliera
Via dell'Indipendenza
Via N. Sauro
Museo Civico Medievale 1
Cattedrale di San Pietro
Museo Ebraico (Jewish Museum) 2
Via Marsala
Via delle Moline
Via delle Belle Arti
Pinacoteca Nazional 4
Museo di Palazzo Poggi 5
UNIVERSITY DISTRICT
3
Oratorio di Santa Cecilia
Via Zamboni
San Giacomo Maggiore 6
Via Montegrappa
Via Altabella
Via Oberdan
Via Ugo Bassi
Piazza del Nettuno
Via Rizzoli
Le due Torri 7
Piazza di Porta Ravegnanna
Via S. Vitale
San Francesco
Fontana di Nettuno 15
Palazzo del Podesta 13
Palazzo D'Accursio 14
Piazza Maggiore
Via Strada Maggiore
Via Nosadella
Basilica di San Petronio 12
Via S. Stefano
Basilica di Santo Stefano 8
Piazza Galiléo
Via Val d'Aposa
Via M. d'Azeglio
Palazzo dell' Archiginnasio 9
Via Castiglione
To Madonna di S. Luca
Via Barberia
Museo Civico Archeologico 11
Via Farini
Piazza Cavour
0 1/8 mi
0 .125 km
Via Tagliapietre
Via Urbana
Via Garibaldi
Piazza San Domenico
Basilica di San Domenico 10
Venice
Bologna
Florence
Rome
Naples
Basilica di San Domenico 10
Basilica di San Petronio 12
Basilica di Santo Stefano 8
Fontana di Nettuno 15
Le due Torri 7
Museo Civico Archeologico 11
Museo Civico Medievale 1
Museo Ebraico (Jewish Museum) 2
Museo di Palazzo Poggi 5
Oratorio di Santa Cecilia 3
Palazzo D'Accursio 14
Palazzo del Podesta 13
Palazzo dell'Archiginnasio 9
Pinacoteca Nazionale 4
San Giacomo Maggiore 6

central door with a masterpiece Renaissance sculpture. Of the 22 art-filled chapels inside, the most jaw-dropping is the **Cappella Bolognini**, the fourth on the left as you enter; it's embellished with frescoes painted by Giovanni da Modena between 1408 and 1420, representing scenes from the life of San Petronio, the three kings of the nativity, and heaven and hell (you'll need .20€ to turn on the chapel lights). The tiny **Museo di San Petronio** (at the back, to the left) houses church relics and precious illuminated manuscripts. Note that parts of the church are likely to be covered up or closed during a major **restoration project** through September 2013.

Piazza Maggiore. www.basilicadisanpetronio.it. ✆ **051-225442.** Free admission. Daily 7:45am–1pm and 3–6pm. Bus: A, 11, 13, 14, 17, 18, 19, 20, or 25.

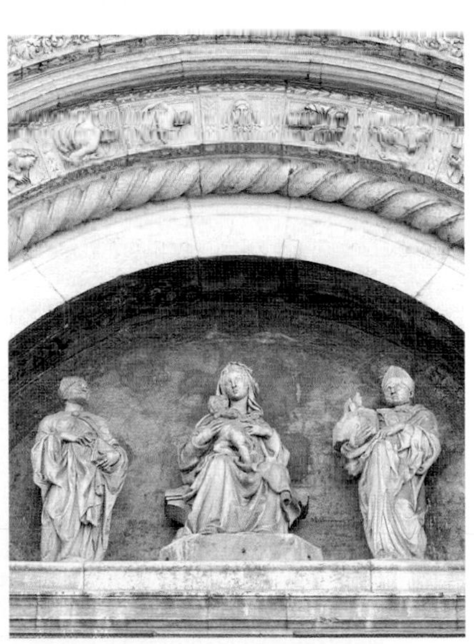

The main doorway to the Basilica di San Petronio.

FACTORY OF THE arts

For decades, no visitor went to the northwest corridor of old Bologna, home to tobacco factories, saltworks, and slaughterhouses. Today, only a 15-minute walk from the heart of Bologna, it has become a center of art, boutiques, and chic restaurants and cafes. The district between Via Don Minzoni and Via Riva di Reno is now called **Manifattura della Arti,** or Factory of the Arts.

At its core is the **Museo d'Arte Moderna di Bologna** (aka MAMbo), Via Don Minzoni 14 (www.mambo-bologna.org; ✆ **051-649-6611**), hailed as the Bologna version of London's Tate Modern. Admission is 6€ for adults, 4€ for ages 6 to 17, and free for children 5 and under. Hours are Tuesday, Wednesday, and Friday noon to 6pm; Thursday noon to 10pm; Saturday and Sunday noon to 8pm. The museum showcases a permanent collection of modern Italian art, but is also home to traveling exhibitions of the avant-garde. On-site is **L'Ex Forno** (www.mambo-bologna.org; ✆ **051-649-3896**), one of the best places in Bologna for a light lunch, featuring such dishes as salade niçoise or *risotto al funghi* (mushroom risotto), costing from around 12€ per platter. It's open Tuesday to Sunday from 11:30am to 2am.

Experimental music and dance performances are showcased at the theater of the **Centro di Musica e Spettacolo** (CIMES) at Via Azzo Gardino 65A (www.muspe.unibo.it/cimes; ✆ **051-209-2400**), sponsored by the University of Bologna.

Near MAMbo and CIMES at Via Azzo Gardino 65 is a striking red stucco silo housing a library and the **Cinema Lumière,** part of the **Cineteca di Bologna** (www.cinetecadibologna.it; ✆ **051-219-5311**), an art and film organization with two theaters. Festivals are devoted to a range of artists, from actor Sean Penn to the notorious director Pier Paolo Pasolini, who was killed in Rome by a male hustler.

Basilica di Santo Stefano ★ CHURCH A cluster of churches, chapels, and cloisters make up what is collectively known as the **Basilica di Santo Stefano,** a primarily Romanesque complex that includes some of the oldest places of worship in the city. A church has stood on this site since the 5th century, converted from a much older Roman Temple of Isis.

The first church you enter is the **Chiesa del Crocifisso** (Church of the Crucifix), a relatively plain space that has been altered many times over the centuries, with an 11th-century crypt and an altar that contains the remains of saints Vitale and Agricola (martyred in 304). To the left is the entrance to the **Basilica del Santo Sepolcro,** a polygonal brick church dating principally from the 12th century and built directly over the Roman temple. In the center is a small marble chapel modeled after the Holy Sepulcher in Jerusalem and adorned with bas-reliefs, containing the former tomb of San Petronio, who was reinterred in the Basilica di San Petronio in 2000. Continuing left, you enter the spacious but humble church of **Santi Vitale e Agricola.** The present Lombard Romanesque building dates from the 11th century. Reenter Santo Sepolcro and head into the **Cortile di Pilato** (Courtyard of Pilate), onto which several tiny chapels open, including the **Chiesa del Martyrium** at the far end. Legend has it that the marble basin in the courtyard was the one in which Pontius Pilate washed his hands after condemning Christ to death. (Actually, it's a Lombard bathtub from the 8th c.) Through the courtyard to the right, proceed into the **Chiostro,** a pretty two-tier Romanesque cloister from the 11th and 12th centuries. Beyond here is a gift shop and the **Museo di San Stefano,** housed in the old **Capella della Benda** and containing church reliquaries, chalices, and artwork from Michele di Matteo and Jacopo di Paolo.

Via Santo Stefano 24. www.abbaziasantostefano.it. ✆ **051-223256.** Free admission. Daily 9am–noon and 3:30–6:30pm. Bus: 11, 13, 90, or 96.

Le due Torri ★★ MONUMENT/MEMORIAL Built by city patricians in the 12th century, these leaning towers, the virtual symbol of Bologna, keep defying gravity year after year. In the Middle Ages, Bologna contained dozens of these brick skyscrapers. The towers were status symbols: The more powerful the family was, the taller its tower was. The smaller one, the **Garisenda,** is only 49m (162 ft.) tall, but because the Garisendas didn't prepare a solid foundation, it sways tipsily to the south, about 3m (11 ft.) from perpendicular. In 1360, part of the tower was lopped off because it was viewed as a threat to public safety. Access to the Garisenda still isn't allowed. The taller one, the **Asinelli** (102m/334 ft. tall, a walk-up of nearly 500 steps), inclines almost 2.5m (7½ ft.). The reward for scaling the Asinelli is a panoramic view of the red-tile roofs of Bologna and the green hills beyond.

Piazza di Porta Ravegnana. Admission 3€. Daily 9am–6pm (to 5pm in winter). Last entry 20 min. before close. Bus: 11, 13, 14, 19, 25, or 27.

Museo Civico Archeologico ★ MUSEUM This museum houses one of Italy's major Ancient Egyptian collections, as well as important discoveries dug up in Emilia. One floor below street level, the Egyptian section presents a notable array of mummies and sarcophagi, while the ground floor contains a gallery of casts, displaying copies of famous Greek and Roman sculptures. On the first floor are two exceptional burial items from Verrucchio (Rimini). Note the wood furnishings, footrests, and throne of tomb 89, decorated with scenes from everyday life and ceremonial parades.

Upstairs the Etruscan relics constitute the best part of the museum, especially the highly stylized *Askos Benacci,* depicting a man on a horse that's perched on yet another animal. Also displayed are terra-cotta urns, a vase depicting fighting Greeks and Amazons, and a bronze Certosa jar from the 6th century B.C. The museum's greatest treasure is Phidias's head of Athena Lemnia, a copy of the 5th-century-B.C. Greek work.

Palazzo Galvani, Via dell'Archiginnasio 2. www.comune.bologna.it/museoarcheologico. ✆ **051-2757211.** Admission 4€ adults, 2€ students and children 15–17, free for children 14 and under. Tues–Fri 9am–3pm; Sat–Sun 10am–6:30pm. Bus: A or 29B.

Le due Torri: the Asinelli Tower and the Garisenda Tower.

Museo Civico Medievale ★ MUSEUM This carefully curated art museum is crammed with treasures from Bologna's medieval golden age, though not much is labeled in English and the bulk of the collection comprises carved tombs, sarcophagi, and assorted statuary. It does, however, contain a remarkable selection of ivory carvings, and a bizarre copper statue of Pope Boniface VIII dating from 1301, looking a bit like an alien (room 7). Room 16 contains rare *codici miniati* (illuminated manuscripts), while delicate gold crosses are displayed in room 5.

Palazzo Ghisilardi, Via Manzoni 4. ✆ **051-2193930.** Admission 4€ adults, 2€ students and children 15–17, free for children 14 and under. Tues–Fri 10am–3pm; Sat–Sun and holidays 10am–6:30pm. Bus: A, 11, 20, 27, or 28.

Museo Ebraico (Jewish Museum) ★ MUSEUM This museum is a thoughtful monument to Bologna's Jewish community, in the heart of what was once the Jewish ghetto. Exhibits cover the history of the Jews up to 1948 (the creation of modern Israel), the Shoah (the Holocaust), and the Jews in Emilia-Romagna and specifically Bologna itself, where there was a thriving Jewish community of merchants and moneylenders in the medieval period—Jews were only forced into the ghetto in 1555, by order of the Pope, and were expelled from the city entirely in 1593. Jews were finally emancipated in Italy in 1860. Visits include free radio headsets that automatically switch to commentary (alternating between Italian and English) in each room.

Via Valdonica 1/5. www.museoebraicobo.it. ✆ **051-2911280.** Admission 4€ adults, 2€ students 25 and under. Sun–Thurs 10am–6pm; Fri 10am–4pm. Bus: C, 14, 19, 25, or 27.

Musei di Palazzo Poggi ★ MUSEUM The first floor of this gorgeous palace is home to an eclectic series of science-related collections assembled by the Instituto delle Scienze, which was founded back in 1711 (and is now part of the university). Though the beautifully decorated rooms themselves are a key part of the attraction, the old-fashioned collections and curios on display more than justify a couple of hours. Note that the popular **Museo della Specola** (Observatory Museum, dating from 1726) will be closed until the end of 2012.

Other highlights include 18th-century anatomical waxwork models—from babies in the womb to the controversial "La Venerina," a wax model of a dead woman that can be taken apart to reveal internal organs. The rooms date back to the 16th century, with the Sala di Davide and Sala di Mosé featuring the most vivid murals, most by local boy Prospero Fontana (1512–1597).

Palazzo Poggi, Via Zamboni 33. www.museopalazzopoggi.unibo.it. ✆ **051-2099398.** Admission 3€ adults, 1€ students. Summer Tues–Sun 10am–1pm; winter Tues–Fri 10am–1pm and 2–4pm, Sat–Sun 10:30am–1:30pm and 2:30–5:30pm. Bus: C.

Palazzo D'Accursio ★ MUSEUM Built in the 14th century, the ornate Palazzo D'Accursio (or Palazzo Comunale) served as the Bologna city hall till 2008. Enter through the courtyard, then proceed up the steps (or elevator) to the first floor, where you can view the relatively modest **Sala d'Ercole** (often host to temporary exhibitions), and the far grander **Sala del Consiglio Comunale** or City Council Hall (Tues–Sun 10am–1pm; free admission). This richly frescoed gallery was the work of baroque masters Angelo Michele Colonna and Gioacchino Pizzoli (1675–1677).

Continue up to the second floor and the **Sala Farnese,** once known as the Royal Hall and rebuilt in 1665 by Cardinal Girolamo Farnese. The adjacent **Capella Farnese** has fragments of exuberant mannerist frescoes painted by Prospero Fontana in 1562.

From the Sala Farnese you can visit two museums, for which you have to pay (the rest of the *palazzo* is free). The **Museo di Giorgio Morandi** is devoted to the works of the eponymous Bolognese painter (1890–1964). His subject matter (a vase of flowers or a box) might have been mundane, but he transformed these objects into works of art of startling intensity and perception. Some of his finest works are landscapes of Grizzana, a village where he spent many lazy summers working and drawing. There's also a reconstruction of his studio.

The second museum is the **Collezioni Comunali d'Arte,** an art gallery housed in the former winter apartments of the papal legates, containing paintings from the 14th- to 19th-century. The best works here are the neoclassical canvases from the likes of Bologna-native Pelagio Palagi (1775–1860), and Cincinnato Baruzzi (1796–1878), but there's also a strong lineup of Emilian painters from the baroque and less fashionable rococo periods such as Donato Creti (1671–1749).

Piazza Maggiore 6. Free admission to the *palazzo*. **Collezioni Comunali d'Arte:** www.comune.bologna.it/iperbole/MuseiCivici. ✆ **051-2193998.** Admission 4€ adults, 2€ students and children 15–17, free for children 14 and under. Tues–Fri 9am–6:30pm; Sat–Sun 10am–6:30pm. **Museo di Giorgio Morandi:** www.museomorandi.it. ✆ **051-2031111.** Admission 6€ adults, 4€ students and children 6–18, free for children 5 and under; free on Wed. Tues–Fri 11am–6pm; Sat–Sun 11am–8pm. Bus: A, 11, 13, 14, 17, 18, 19, 20, or 25.

Palazzo dell'Archiginnasio ★★ HISTORIC SITE From 1563 to 1803 this stately building was the home of **Bologna University (UNIBO),** and today it functions primarily as an academic library (closed to visitors). You can, however, wander the ground floor courtyard and first floor corridors, richly decorated in murals and ancient family crests, and visit the spellbinding first-floor **Teatro Anatomico.** This venerable lecture hall—built in 1637 and dressed entirely in cedar wood— is where dissections of dead bodies were held in the name of medical science. Tiered wooden benches surround a central marble-topped table, while the canopy above the lecturer's chair is supported by two slightly macabre skinless statues. Ask the guardians on duty for a peek inside the **Stabat Mater Hall,** where Rossini's opera *Stabat Mater* was performed for the first time in 1842.

Piazza Galvani. www.archiginnasio.it. ✆ **051-276811.** Free admission. Mon–Fri 9am–6:45pm; Sat 9am–1:45pm. Bus: A or 29B.

Pinacoteca Nazionale di Bologna ★★ ART MUSEUM The most significant works of Emilian and Bolognese painting from the 14th century to the heyday of the baroque have been assembled under one roof in this huge art museum, the former St. Ignatius Monastery, dating back to 1728. The galleries are beautifully curated and laid out chronologically, beginning with rare works from the 14th and 15th centuries, such as Vitale de Bologna's (1330–59) rendition of St. George slaying the dragon in Gallery 1. Giotto (who was actually from Florence) dominates Gallery 3 with his five-paneled *Polittico di Bologna* (1330), while the work of early Bologna Renaissance artists—Jacopo di Paolo, Giovanni da Bologna, and Michele di Matteo—are also featured. Frescoes salvaged from the **Church of the Madonna di Mezzaratta** fill Galleries 7 and 8, while local boys of the High Renaissance—Francesco Raibolini, aka Francia; Lorenzo Costa; and Amico Aspertini among them—fill Galleries 9 through 20. Don't miss **Raphael**'s *St. Cecilia in Estasi,* tucked away in Gallery 15, and **El Greco**'s diminutive *Last Supper* in Gallery 19.

Bologna was also a major center for mannerist and baroque painting in the 16th and 17th centuries, with giant canvases from Ludovico, Annibale, and

Agostino **Carracci** in Gallery 23, and especially **Guido Reni** (1575–1642) in Gallery 24. Reni steals the show with his *St. Sebastian* and massive *Pietà,* along with his penetrating *St. Andrea Corsini, The Slaying of the Innocents,* and his masterpiece, *Ritratto della Madre* (a revealing portrait of his mother). The later baroque efforts in Galleries 25 to 29 are far less appealing in comparison.

Via delle Belle Arti 56. www.pinacotecabologna.beniculturali.it. ✆ **051-4209411.** Admission 4€ adults, 2€ ages 18–25, free for children 17 and under. Tues–Sun 9am–7pm. Closed holidays. Bus: 20, 28, 36, 37, 89, 93, 94, or 99 (to Porta San Donato).

San Giacomo Maggiore (Church of St. James) ★ CHURCH This treasure-filled church was a Gothic structure built between 1267 and 1315 by the Augustinians, and restored at the end of the 15th century. Dedicated to the medieval rulers of Bologna, the **Cappella Bentivoglio** (behind the altar to the left) is the most sacred haunt, although time has dimmed the luster of its late-15th-century frescoes by **Lorenzo Costa:** *Triumph of Fame, Triumph of Death* and *Madonna Enthroned* (painted with members of the Bentivoglio family). It's still worth coughing up .50€ to turn on the lights. Opposite is the tomb of Anton Galeazzo Bentivoglio, designed by Jacopo della Quercia in 1438, who labored so long over the doors to the Basilica of San Petronio (p. 378).

In the 13th century **Oratorio di Santa Cecilia ★★** (next door to the church, a few steps farther along at Via Zamboni 15), you'll discover more enchanting frescoes by Bologna Renaissance heavyweights Amico Aspertini, Francesco Raibolini, and Lorenzo Costa. It's open daily 10am to 1pm and 3 to 7pm (2–6pm in winter). Admission is free.

Piazza Rossini, Via Zamboni. ✆ **051-225970.** Free admission. Daily 7am–noon and 3:30–6:30pm. Bus: C.

Where to Eat

Bologna is one of the best places to eat in Italy, from Michelin-starred haute cuisine to neighborhood *osterie* that serve up hearty Emilian dishes and desserts for a handful of euros. Bolognese sauce did originate here, but if you order "spaghetti alla Bolognese" expect pained looks from your waiter—the sauce (typically just called *ragù*) is served here exclusively with *tagliatelle.*

After dinner, many restaurant patrons skip the dessert course and head for high-quality ice-cream vendor **Gelatauro,** Via San Vitale 98 (www.gelatauro.com; ✆ **051-230049;** Mon 9am–8pm, Tues–Thurs 8:30am–11pm, Fri–Sat 8:30am–midnight, Sun 9:30am–11pm), run by three brothers and known for its organic gelato, including one divine concoction made from Sicilian oranges and such fresh herbs as jasmine and bergamot (and hot chocolate in winter).

EXPENSIVE

Bitone ★ EMILIAN When this long-revered restaurant opened in 1834, it was a stop for stagecoaches en route to Florence. Today it's the best place to splurge on an expensive dinner, with fine food invariably cooked to perfection in an elegant Art Deco dining room. The antipasti selections are among the best in Bologna, including a mousse made with mortadella and ricotta. The pasta selections are sublime, including various versions of tortellini. A classic veal cutlet Bolognese always appears on the menu, as do succulent lamb cutlets. The restaurant is outside the city center, so you'll need to take a taxi or a bus.

Via Emilia Levante 111. www.ristorantebitone.it. ✆ **051-546110.** Main courses 25€–30€; fixed-price menu 65€. AE, DC, MC, V. Wed–Sun noon–2pm and 8–11pm. Closed Aug. Bus: 19, 27, or 94.

Da Cesari ★ BOLOGNESE In business for more than a century, this rustic, two-floor restaurant stands in the heart of the historic district. The dishes overflow with fresh, seasonal ingredients, deftly handled by the kitchen staff. I could order the pumpkin-stuffed ravioli with butter and Parmesan once a week. Prepared with equal skill are such pasta dishes as homemade *tortelloni* stuffed with ricotta cheese and white truffle, or appetizers such as salmon-and-sea-bass carpaccio with an orange vinaigrette. Main courses are hearty, including beef filet with Parmesan, white truffle, and polenta; and sea bass filet with potatoes, olives, and tomatoes.

Via de' Carbonesi 8 (south of Piazza Maggiore). www.da-cesari.it. ✆ **051-237710.** Reservations required. Main courses 9.50€–18€; degustation menu 40€–50€. DC, MC, V. Mon–Sat 12:30–2:30pm and 7:30–11pm. Closed 3 weeks in Aug and Jan 1–7. Bus: 11, 13, 20, 29B, 30, 38, or 39.

MODERATE

Drogheria della Rosa ★ BOLOGNESE/ITALIAN Some of the best homemade pastas, for which Bologna is famous, are served here. A mixed clientele of all ages patronizes the premises of chef/owner Emanuele Addone, who installed his restaurant in a former pharmacy, the original doors and window frames still intact. The produce is market fresh, the cooking superb, and the wine cellar has several hundred choices. Start perhaps with *culatello,* a prized cured ham, or a classic *tortelli,* which is stuffed with zucchini blossoms. An eggplant ravioli comes with fresh tomatoes and basil, and vegetable pie is laced with a Parmesan cream sauce. Sautéed lamb with fresh rosemary is given extra flavor by the balsamic vinegar of Modena, while the roast breast of guinea fowl is served with spicy honey.

Via Cartoleria 10. www.drogheriadellarosa.it. ✆ **051-222529.** Reservations recommended. Main courses 9€–10€. MC, V. Mon–Sat 12:30–3pm and 8–10:30pm. Closed Aug 10–27 and 1st week of Jan. Bus: C, 11, or 13.

Marco Fadiga Bistrot ★★ 🎁 CONTEMPORARY ITALIAN Not all chefs in Bologna specialize in the classic recipes of yesterday. Marco Fadiga is the most acclaimed chef in the city, and he's known for inventive dishes with unusual flavor combinations. Fadiga operates a casually chic bistro decorated with Tintin pictures and old champagne crates, along with a scattering of graffiti. Look for his daily specials posted on a chalkboard menu. I am dazzled by his appetizers (9€)—perhaps prawns in a vinaigrette of mango, dried tomatoes, or fresh basil; or else an artichoke-and-squid salad with a nutty vinaigrette. Main course creations could include tandoori chicken with prawns, or scrumptious gnocchi in broth with mussels.

Via Rialto 23C. ✆ **051-220118.** Reservations required. Main courses 14€; pasta 12€. AE, MC, V. Tues–Sat 7:30pm–midnight. Bus: C, 11, or 13.

Montegrappa da Nello ★ 🎁 BOLOGNESE This wonderful trattoria is one of the few restaurants still doing classic Bolognese cuisine. The menu's signature dish is *tortellini Montegrappa,* a pasta favorite served in a cream-and-meat sauce. The restaurant is also known for its fresh white truffles and porcini mushrooms. A good example is the *graminia,* a very fine white spaghetti presented with mushrooms, cream, and pepper. Real risotto is also a specialty—simply prepared with thick-grain rice, tongue-tingling sauces that might included sangiovese wine and artichokes, and none of that gloopy cheese.

Via Montegrappa 2. www.ristorantedanello.com. ✆ **051-236331.** Reservations recommended for dinner. Main courses 10€–17€. AE, DC, MC, V. Tues–Sun noon–3pm and 7–11:30pm. Closed 1 week in Jan and all of Aug. Bus: A, 11, 20, 27, or 28.

Osteria Satyricon ★★ BOLOGNESE Foodies might disagree on which is the very best restaurant in Bologna, but this upscale *osteria* is always at or near the top of everyone's list. Inside the cozy cellarlike interior, local food of the highest quality is served: All the classics are here, beginning with an exceptional plate of cold cuts and including *tagliatelle al ragù,* Bolognese-style cutlets, and *gramigna* (thin, short, curled pasta) with artisanal sausages. More creative dishes can range from sea urchin risotto to filet-mignon hamburgers. Save room for the incredible soufflé, and wash it all down with a local licorice *digestif.* The restaurant is outside the center, so you'll need to take a taxi or a bus.

Via delle Armi 3. www.osteriasatyricon.com. ✆ **051-444320.** Reservations recommended. Main courses 7€–15€. AE, DC, MC, V. Wed–Mon 7:30–10:30pm. Taxi around 12€ from center. Bus: 13 or 96.

Vicolo Colombina ★★ BOLOGNESE If you don't want to go far, this hip, contemporary restaurant lies just off the Piazza Maggiore, decorated by the work of local artists and the black-and-white 1930s-style photos of Eric Serafini. Culinary wizard Massimiliano Poggi takes a fresh approach to classic dishes such as *gramigna alla salsiccia* (pasta with sausage) and *tagliatelle al ragù,* but also comes up with more inventive fare—think filet of beef au gratin with Bolognese-style pesto sauce. The really adventurous should try the notorious *bollito,* a traditional Bolognese combo that includes *doppione* (breast of beef), *lingua* (tongue), *testina* (calf's head), and *zampone* (stuffed pig's trotters, like a sausage).

Vicolo Colombina 5/B. www.vicolocolombina.it. ✆ **051-233919.** Main courses 11€–18€; fixed-price menu 30€. AE, DC, MC, V. Tues 7:30–10:30pm; Wed–Sun 12:30–2:30pm and 7:30–10:30pm. Bus: 17, 18, or 86.

INEXPENSIVE

On a stroll along **Via Pescherie Vecchie** and the adjacent streets, the city's traditional salumeria area between Piazza Maggiore and the Due Torri, you can assemble a high-quality picnic (see "Shopping," below). The stalls of Bologna's central food market, the **Mercato delle Erbe,** Via Ugo Bassi 25 (www.mercatodelleerbe.it), are open Monday to Wednesday 7am to 1:15pm and 5:30 to 7:30pm, Thursday and Saturday 7am to 1:15pm, and Friday 7am to 1:15pm and 4:30 to 7:30pm.

Enoteca Italiana, Via Marsala 2/B (www.enotecaitaliana.it; ✆ **051-235989**), is an inviting and aromatic shop-cum-wine-bar on a side street just north of Piazza Maggiore. You can stand at the bar and sip a local wine while enjoying a sandwich. For a movable feast, you can stock up on ham, salami, and cheese at the deli counter. It's open Monday to Saturday from 7:30am to 9:30pm (also Sun in Nov–Dec).

Osteria dell'Orsa ITALIAN This restaurant, which offers some of the best *ragù alla bolognese* in town, occupies a 15th-century building near the university. Most diners—there are as many locals as students and tourists—opt for the high-ceilinged, medieval-looking main floor, though there's also an informal cantina-like cellar room with communal wood tables, friendly service, and a warm atmosphere. You won't go wrong if you preface a meal with any kind of pasta labeled *bolognese.* Other options are homemade *tagliolini,* veal cutlet *fiorentina,* and tortellini with cheese, ham, and mushroom sauce. If you feel adventurous, you can always try grilled donkey meat *(somarello)*.

Via Mentana 1F. www.osteriadellorsa.com. ✆ **051-231576.** Reservations recommended. Main courses 6€–15€. AE, DC, MC, V. Daily noon–3pm and 7pm–12:30am (closes 1 hr. earlier Sat–Sun). Bus: C.

Shopping

Note that most shops in Bologna close all day on Sunday, and again on Thursday afternoons—most also close for a 2- to 3-hour lunch break every day.

Galleria Marescalchi, Via Mascarella 116B (✆ **051-245710;** daily 10am–1pm and 4–8pm), features traditional art, offering paintings and prints for view or sale by native son Morandi and Italian modern master De Chirico, as well as Chagall and Magritte.

An array of traditional breads, pasta, and pastries makes **Atti ★**, Via Caprarie 7 (www.paoloatti.com; ✆ **051-220425;** Mon–Wed 10am–7:15pm, Thurs 10am–4pm, Fri–Sat 10am–7:30pm, Sun 10:30am–1:30pm), tempting whether you're hungry or not. If you crave chocolate, head to **Majani,** Via de' Carbonesi 5 (✆ **051-234302;** Mon–Sat 9am–1pm and 3–7:30pm; closed Thurs afternoon), which claims to be Italy's oldest sweets shop, having made and sold confections since 1796. **Roccati,** Via Clavature 17A (www.roccaticioccolato.com; ✆ **051-261-964;** Mon–Sat 9am–1pm and 3:30–8pm, Sun 10am–1pm and 3:30–8pm), is run by a husband-and-wife team that is still celebrated for the *gianduja* chocolate their ancestors made for the princes of Savoy starting in 1909. When you bite into their cognac-filled chocolates, you'll think you've entered paradise. At **Tamburini ★**, Via Caprarie 1 (www.tamburini.com; ✆ **051-234726;** Mon–Fri 8:30am–7pm, Sat 8:30am–7:30pm, Sun 10am–6:30pm), one of Italy's most lavish food shops, you can choose from an impressive array of meats and fish, soups and salads, vegetables, and sweets, as well as fresh pasta to prepare at home.

If you have hard-to-fit feet, walk to **Piero,** Via delle Lame 56 (www.pierocalzature.it; ✆ **051-558680;** Mon–Fri 9am–1pm and 3:30–7:30pm, Sat 9am–7:30pm; closed Thurs afternoon), for attractive footwear for men and women in large sizes, ranging up to European size 53 for men (American size 20) and size 46 for women (American size 14). Bruno Magli quickly made a name for himself after opening a small shoe business in Bologna in 1936. Today Bologna's stylish **Galleria Cavour** shopping arcade (www.galleriacavour.net), off Via Farini a short walk from Piazza Maggiore, features a posh **Bruno Magli** shop selling leather bags, jackets, and coats for men and women—in addition to shoes (www.brunomagli.it; ✆ **051-266915;** Mon–Fri 10am–1pm and 3:30–7:30pm, Sat 10am–7:30pm).

Pastries at Atti.

The Veronesi family has been closely tied to the jewelry trade in Bologna since the 1890s. Now split up and competing among themselves, the various factions are represented by **F. Veronesi & Figli,** Piazza Maggiore 4 (www.veronesi1893.it; ✆ **051-224835;** Mon–Sat 9am–12:30pm and 3:30–7:30pm), which offers contemporary jewelry, watches, and silver using ancient designs, and **Giulio Veronesi** (www.giulioveronesi.it), with locations at Piazza Re Enzo 1H (✆ **051-234237;** Tues–Sun 9:30am–1pm and 3:30–7:30pm) and Galleria Cavour 1E (✆ **051-234196;** daily 9:30am–12:50pm and 3:30–7:30pm, closed Thurs afternoon), which sells modern jewelry and Rolex watches.

Entertainment & Nightlife

Thanks in part to a huge population of students, Bologna has a vibrant, diverse nightlife scene. Via Zamboni, Via delle Belle Arti, and the surrounding area (known as Piccola Pigalle or **"Little Pigalle,"** after the raunchy Parisian district), are the usual haunts of night owls. You can usually find a place for a drink, a shot of espresso, or a light meal as late as 3am. ***Aperitivo,*** where a glass of wine and as many snacks as you like costs just 5€ in local cafes and bars, usually starts around 6pm and runs for a couple of hours.

CAFES & BARS

Camera a Sud ★, Via Valdonica 5 (www.cameraasud.net; ✆ **051-0951448;** Mon–Sat noon–1am, Sun 5pm–1am) is a supercool student hangout in the old Jewish quarter (near the Jewish museum). The cozy interior is perfect for sipping coffee or wine, reading, and just lounging away the afternoon.

Café de Paris, Piazza del Francia 1C (www.cafedeparisbologna.org; ✆ **051-234980;** Mon–Sat 8am–3am, Sun 4pm–3am), is another hot spot, attracting a young crowd with its sleek, modern white couches and elegant interior. It serves light, tasty, and market-fresh platters of food throughout the day and night, costing from 15€ to 20€. *Aperitivo* runs daily 6 to 10pm.

Facing the Duomo beneath the arcades on Piazza Maggiore is **Bar Giuseppe,** Piazza Maggiore 1 (✆ **051-264444;** daily 5:30am–3am), serving some of the best espresso and gelato in the city since 1804. The tastiest dry martinis in Bologna are served at **Nu Lounge Bar,** Via dei Musei 6 (www.nu-lounge.com; ✆ **051-222532;** daily noon–2:30am), attracting a post-30 crowd of fashionistas last seen munching on those addictive Calabrian green olives.

At 10:30pm, make your way to the cellars of a 16th-century *palazzo* near the university at **Cantina Bentivoglio ★★**, Via Mascarella 4B (www.cantinabentivoglio.it; ✆ **051-265416**). That's when you'll hear some of the best jazz in Bologna. It is open daily from 8pm to 2am. It is also open for lunch Monday to Friday from 12:15 to 2:45pm.

Osteria de Poeti ★, Via Poeti 1 (www.osteriadepoeti.com; ✆ **051-236166;** Tues–Fri 12:30–2:30pm and 7:30pm–2:30am, Sat–Sun 7:30pm–2:30am), is Bologna's oldest *osteria* and has been in operation since around 1600. The brick-vaulted ceilings, stone walls, and ancient wine barrels provide just the sort of ambience you would expect to find in such a historic establishment. Stop in to enjoy the live jazz and folk music that's on tap most nights. Main dishes such as fried rabbit with artichokes cost 15€, while pastas such as tortellini in meat broth are 9€ to 12€.

CLUBS

As you might expect, Bologna boasts a lively club scene, and you'll find somewhere to dance most nights of the week. It was Bologna—not Rome or Milan—where **Italian hip-hop** developed in the 1990s, with the likes of Sangue Misto and Camelz in Effect, and the genre still drives much of the local club culture.

Le Stanze, Via del Borgo di San Pietro (www.lestanzecafe.com; ✆ **051-273602**), is more of a trendy lounge-come-restaurant than club, but at the weekends DJs and cocktails rule. The 17th-century ex-chapel interior makes it one the most atmospheric places in town to boogie.

For international guest DJs and a big club atmosphere visit **Link,** Via Fantoni 21 (www.link.bo.it; ✆ **051-370971**), on the outskirts of the city, or **La Scuderia,** Piazza Verdi 2 (www.lascuderia.bo.it; ✆ **051-229189**), in the university district. Check websites like **www.bologna.2night.it** for the latest information.

Cassero, Via Don Minzoni 18 (www.cassero.it; ✆ **051-6494416**), is Bologna's most popular gay bar and club, with a noisy, discolike atmosphere and floor shows. The biggest attraction here is the setting—the club occupies one of Bologna's medieval gates, the top of which serves as a roof garden and open-air dance floor in good weather. Cassero is also the Bologna headquarters of Arcigay and Arcilesbiche, a gay and lesbian center organizing cultural meetings and entertainment.

THEATERS

The 18th-century **Teatro Comunale,** Largo Respighi 1 (www.tcbo.it; ✆ **051-529958**), is the venue for major cultural presentations, including opera, ballet, and orchestral presentations.

Music lovers flock to the Sala Mozart at the **Accademia Filarmonica di Bologna,** Via Guerrazzi 13 (www.accademiafilarmonica.it; ✆ **051-222997**), to hear performances by Haydn, Brahms, Vivaldi, and, of course, Mozart himself. The boy genius was only 14 years old when he earned a diploma in composition at this academy in 1770.

Bologna Rental Apartments

If you aim to stay for a week or longer, or have a large group, renting an apartment in Bologna could save you a lot of money—studios for two people in the center, with full kitchen, start at around 450€ per week. Websites such as **www.homeaway.com** are a good place to start, but you can also contact owners directly. Operated by the Hotel Metropolitan (www.hotelmetropolitan.com; ✆ **051-229393**), the modern and well-equipped **Met's Apartments ★★** are the plushest options in the city, only 150m (492 ft.) from Piazza Maggiore. Rates range from 100€ to 400€ per day depending on the size of the apartment and time of year. **Il Nespolo ★**, Via Lodovico Varthema 18 (just outside the center), is a fabulous apartment in an elegant neighborhood, and can accommodate up to six guests in two bedrooms. Weekly rates range from 550€ to 850€. The best way to book it is through www.flipkey.com. Those on a budget should consider **Pietro's, the Studio Flat ★★**, Via Broccaindosso 61 (www.pietros.it; ✆ **389-5162090**), a compact but cute studio in an old building with a tiny shower and kitchen. Rates start at just 420€ per week.

Where to Stay

Bologna hosts four to six trade fairs a year, during which hotel room rates rise dramatically. Some hotels announce their prices in advance; others wait to see what the market will bear. At trade fair times (dates vary yearly; check with the tourist office), business clients from throughout Europe book the best rooms, and you'll be paying a lot of money to visit Bologna.

An important note on parking: Much of central Bologna is closed to cars without special permits from 7am to 8pm daily (including Sun and holidays). When booking a room, be prepared to present your car registration number, which the hotel will then provide to the police to ensure that you are not fined for driving in a restricted area. Also, ask about parking facilities as well as the most efficient route to take to reach your hotel, because many streets in central Bologna are permanently closed to traffic. A permit is required to park in the center; hotel guests can purchase one through their hotel, if offered.

VERY EXPENSIVE

Grand Hotel Majestic ★★★ The Majestic boasts a location near Bologna's main square and is a superb atmospheric choice. Its four-story facade is crafted of the same reddish brick that distinguishes many of the city's older buildings, and the interior is noted for its wall and ceiling frescoes. In fact, the restaurant frescoes were painted by the Carracci brothers in the 16th century, and part of an old Roman road can be seen on the way to the breakfast room. The rooms are elegantly appointed featuring Venetian-style furniture and a Murano glass chandelier. All are generally spacious, with the fourth-floor units being the largest. The latter feature a new range of junior suites and deluxe rooms sporting 18th-century French-style interiors.

Via dell'Indipendenza 8, 40121 Bologna. www.duetorrihotels.com. ✆ **051-225445.** Fax 051-234840. 109 units. 270€–440€ double; from 550€ suite. Rates include buffet breakfast. AE, DC, MC, V. Parking 35€ per day. Bus: A, 11, 20, 27, or 28. **Amenities:** Restaurant; bar; airport transfers (30€); babysitting; bikes; exercise room; room service; spa. *In room:* A/C, TV, hair dryer, minibar, Wi-Fi (free).

EXPENSIVE

Art Hotel Novecento ★ The design of this inn evokes Europe of the 1930s, the Art Deco heyday of elegant travel. Although it turns to the past for its inspiration, it is completely up-to-date in its amenities. Ideal for a romantic weekend, the hotel lies in the very heart of Bologna. The building itself is in the so-called Viennese Secession style, taking inspiration from flower motifs and the works of the painter Gustav Klimt. Each of the midsize bedrooms is decorated in an individual style. Regardless of your room assignment, you can count on a great bed and a beautiful bathroom—you even get a leopard-print bathrobe. The hotel's breakfast is the best in town.

Piazza Galileo 4/3, 40126 Bologna. www.art-hotel-novecento.it. ✆ **051-7457311.** Fax 051-7457322. 25 units. 183€–253€ double; 356€ suite. Rates include buffet breakfast. AE, DC, MC, V. Parking 26€. Bus: 11, 13, 20, or 30. **Amenities:** Bar; bikes (free); room service. *In room:* A/C, TV, hair dryer, minibar, Wi-Fi (free).

Art Hotel Orologio ★ This charming small hotel faces the *orologio* (clock) on the civic center in the heart of medieval Bologna, with a view of Piazza Maggiore and the Podestà Palace. The guest rooms all have modern furnishings with wrought-iron bed frames. Most are small but provide reasonable comfort, including tidy bathrooms. This is the ideal place for those who want a historical atmosphere without forfeiting modern comforts.

Via IV Novembre 10, 40123 Bologna. www.art-hotel-orologio.it. ✆ **051-7457411.** Fax 051-7457422. 35 units, some with shower only. 200€–243€ double; from 346€ suite. Rates include buffet breakfast. AE, DC, DISC, MC, V. Parking 26€ per day. Bus: 11, 13, 20, or 30. **Amenities:** Bar; airport transfers (20€); babysitting; bikes; room service. *In room:* A/C, TV, hair dryer, minibar, Wi-Fi (free).

Hotel Metropolitan ★★ This plush hotel features a simple, minimalist design ethic inspired by East Asia, with clean, modern rooms and superb levels of service. Expect plenty of candles, drapes, Chinese teas, and contemporary Asian art on the walls to enhance the experience. The peaceful rooftop garden is a good place to relax, and you can enjoy drinks on the hotel terrace. There's no pool or spa, but the hotel offers special rates at the Prime Fitness Club and the Beauty Spa, both nearby, which offer a huge range of facilities. It's a 5- to 10-minute walk from the train station, and just 5 minutes from Piazza Maggiore.

Via Dell'Orso 6, 40121 Bologna. www.hotelmetropolitan.com. ✆ **051-229393.** Fax 051-224602. 50 units. 150€–170€ double; from 300€ suite. Free parking. AE, DC, MC, V. Bus: A, 11, 20, 27, or 28. **Amenities:** Restaurant; bar; babysitting; room service. *In room:* A/C, TV, hair dryer, minibar, Wi-Fi (free).

Il Convento dei Fiori di Seta ★★ This small 15th-century convent is now one of the most enticing hotels in Bologna, following an artful restoration. The original brick walls and painted, vault ceilings have been preserved, but modern conveniences have been installed throughout. The bedrooms are comfortably and stylishly decked out in a contemporary, minimalist style; four have been carved out of the old church apse, while six lie on the upper floor.

Via Orfeo 34-4, 40124 Bologna. www.ilconventodeifioridiseta.com. ✆ **051-272039.** Fax 051-2750001. 10 units. 160€–190€ double; 220€–270€ suite. Rates include continental breakfast. AE, DC, MC, V. Parking 25€. Bus: 11, 13, 32, or 33. **Amenities:** Bar; concierge; Jacuzzi; room service; sauna. *In room:* A/C, TV, Wi-Fi (free).

MODERATE

Albergo Al Cappello Rosso If you need a break from rustic charm, this is the hotel for you, dating from 1375 and located just 50m (164 ft.) from Piazza Maggiore. In the 14th century, the "Red Hat" in the hotel's name referred to the preferred headgear of the privileged tradesmen who stayed here. Now the hotel has been revamped into an ultramodern place with no hint of its past. The guest rooms tend to be modular, small to medium in size, and have good beds. Breakfast is the only meal served.

Via dei Fusari 9, 40123 Bologna. www.alcappellorosso.it. ✆ **051-261891.** Fax 051-227179. 32 units. 140€ double. AE, DC, MC, V. Parking 25€. Bus: 11, 13, 20, or 30. **Amenities:** Babysitting; bikes; room service; Wi-Fi (free, in lobby). *In room:* A/C, TV, hair dryer, minibar.

Antica Residenza d'Azeglio ★★ Genial hosts Roberto and Agostino have created one of Bologna's most appealing B&Bs, just 5 minutes walk from Piazza Maggiore. Each room has a different color-coded theme, though they all feature rich, 19th-century furnishings and artwork. Your hosts can provide valuable assistance on where to go and how to make bookings, and will serve coffee, fruit, water, and other drinks throughout the day at no extra charge. The continental breakfast can be served in your room.

THE WORLD'S GREATEST china SHOP

Faenza, 58km (36 miles) southeast of Bologna, has lent its name to a form of fine tin-glazed ceramics called faience, also known as *maiolica* (majolica). Thought to be of Moorish and Spanish origin, Italian production began in the 14th century, and designs are characterized by brilliant colors and floral decorations. The art reached its pinnacle in the 16th century, when the "hot-fire" process was perfected, during which ceramics were baked at a temperature of 950°C (1,742°F).

The legacy of this fabled industry is preserved at the **Museo Internazionale delle Ceramiche,** Viale Baccarini 19 (www.micfaenza.org; ✆ **0546-697311**), called "the world's greatest china shop." Housed here are works from the artisans of Faenza as well as from around the world, including pre-Columbian pottery from Peru. Of exceptional interest are Etruscan and Egyptian ceramics and a wide-ranging collection from the Orient, dating from the Roman Empire.

Also on display are Picasso vases and a platter with his dove of peace, a platter in rich colors by Chagall, a "surprise" from Matisse, and a framed ceramic plaque of the *Crucifixion* by Georges Rouault.

It's open from October to March, Tuesday to Friday 10am to 1:30pm, and Saturday and Sunday from 10am to 5:30pm; April to September, hours are Tuesday to Sunday 10am to 7pm. Admission is 8€ (5€ for children 12–16, free for children 11 and under). It's closed New Year's Day, May 1, August 15, and Christmas.

Via Massimo d'Azeglio 64, 40013 Bologna. www.anticaresidenzadazeglio.it. ✆ **051-6447389.** Fax 051-3393354. 5 units. 120€ double; 140€ suite. Rates include buffet breakfast. AE, DC, MC, V. Parking 20€ per day. Bus: 29B or 52. **Amenities:** Babysitting; bikes (free); room service (snacks and drinks). *In room:* A/C, TV, hair dryer, minibar, Wi-Fi (free).

Hotel Commercianti ★ 🎁 The location of this historic hotel, right beside San Petronio in the pedestrian area of Piazza Maggiore, is hard to beat. Recent restorations have uncovered original wooden features, which you can see in the hall and the rooms in the old tower. Despite the centuries-old history, the atmosphere is bright, and all modern luxuries are offered. The guest rooms, most small or medium in size, are decorated with antique furniture.

Via de' Pignattari 11, 40124 Bologna. www.art-hotel-commercianti.it. ✆ **051-7457511.** Fax 051-7457522. 34 units, half with shower only. 136€–179€ double; from 282€ suite. Rates include buffet breakfast. AE, DC, DISC, MC, V. Parking 28€ per day. Bus: 11, 13, 20, or 30. **Amenities:** Bar; babysitting; bikes (free); room service. *In room:* A/C, TV, hair dryer, minibar, Wi-Fi (free).

Hotel Porta San Mamolo ★★ In the heart of Bologna, this justly popular hotel has some bedrooms that date back 3 centuries. But everything is up-to-date and modern today in this restored building that lies only a 10-minute walk from Piazza Maggiore. Our favorite spot here is a traditional courtyard and winter garden where breakfast is served. Bedrooms are midsize, streamlined, and modern, with a slightly romantic aura. Refined fabrics and the latest technology are set off by the delicate pastel colors of the walls. Best are the rooms on the top floor with a terrace opening onto panoramic views of Bologna.

Vicolo del Falconi 6–8, 40124 Bologna. www.hotel-portasanmamolo.it. ✆ **051-583056.** Fax 051-3311739. 43 units. 100€–172€ double; 220€–252€ suite. AE, DC, MC, V. Parking 20€ per day. Bus: 29B or 52. **Amenities:** Bikes; room service; Wi-Fi (free, in lobby). *In room:* A/C, TV, fridge, hair dryer.

INEXPENSIVE

Albergo delle Drapperie ★ In the oldest part of the city, the Albergo is the latest version of the long-standing Hotel Apollo. Completely restored since its use as a traditional guesthouse in 1800, it's been given a new lease on life as a no-frills B&B. The hotel is ideal for sightseeing, located only 100m (328 ft.) from the landmark Piazza Maggiore. The style, as is to be expected, is traditional with much use of wood and Italian tiles, even frescoes on the ceilings. Bedrooms are comfortably appointed, often featuring exposed wooden beams.

Via della Drapperie 5, 40124 Bologna. www.albergodrapperie.com. ✆ **051-223955.** Fax 051-238732. 21 units. 75€–85€ double; 100€–110€ triple. AE, MC, V. Bus: A, 11, 20, 27, or 28. **Amenities:** Wi-Fi (free, in lobby). *In room:* A/C, TV, minibar.

FERRARA ★

417km (259 miles) N of Rome, 52km (32 miles) N of Bologna, 100km (62 miles) SW of Venice

Ferrara is still relatively undiscovered by tourists, but it's richly blessed, with much of its artistic and historic legacy intact. Among its treasures are a gorgeous cathedral and the formidable Castello Estense, along with an extraordinary ensemble of Renaissance palaces. Though these palaces, for the most part, have long been robbed of their furnishings, the faded frescoes, the paintings that weren't carted off, and the palatial rooms are reminders of the vicissitudes of power.

Ferrara was founded back in the Italian Dark Ages, but its Golden Age began when Azzo VII of Este was nominated perpetual *podestà* (mayor) in 1242—the Este family ruled the city and a sizeable slice of northern Italy for another 350 years. When Papa Borgia (Pope Alexander VI) was shopping for a third husband for the apple of his eye, darling Lucrezia, his gaze fell on Alfonso d'Este, son of the shrewd but villainous Ercole I, the ruling duke of Ferrara. As the duchess of Ferrara, a position she held until her death, Lucrezia bore seven children (she died in 1519 giving birth to an eighth, who also died soon after). But one of her grandchildren, Alfonso II, wasn't as prolific and left the family without a direct heir. The greedy eye of Pope Clement VIII took quick action, gobbling up the city as his personal fiefdom in 1598. Ferrara slid into a long and slow decline under papal control, but Cesare d'Este, Alfonso's cousin and official heir, fled to Modena where the Este family continued to rule.

Essentials

GETTING THERE **By Train** Getting to Ferrara by **train** is fast and efficient because it's on the main line between Bologna and Venice. Around two trains an hour depart both cities for Ferrara. Trip time is 30 to 45 minutes from Bologna, and the fare starts at 4.40€ one-way. Trip time from Venice is 1 hour to 1½ hours and the fare costs 7.30€ to 31€, depending on the train and the class of service. Ravenna is an hour away, with hourly departures all day (6.20€). From the train station it's a 20- to 30-minute walk to the

Duomo, but you can also take the frequent no. 2 bus to Piazza Travaglio (1.50€; pay on board with correct change). For more information, call ✆ **0532 599 411** (www.atc.bo.it).

By Car If you have a **car** and are coming from Bologna, take A13 north. From Venice, take A4 southwest to Padua and continue on A13 south to Ferrara.

VISITOR INFORMATION The helpful **tourist office** is inside the Castello Estense, Piazza del Castello (www.ferrarateraeacqua.it; ✆ **0532-299303**). It's open Monday to Saturday from 9am to 1pm and 2 to 6pm, Sunday 9:30am to 1pm and 2 to 5pm.

SPECIAL EVENTS The center of Ferrara is taken over by a twice weekly market (mostly clothes) Wednesday and Friday (mornings only). Not quite as dramatic as its counterpart in Siena, Ferrara's **Palio di San Giorgio** is a popular event held in the Piazza Ariostea the last Sunday of May. Two-legged creatures run first, in races for young men and young women. They are followed by donkeys and, in the main event, horses ridden bareback by jockeys representing Ferrara's eight traditional districts.

Some excellent jazz and classical concerts are the main events of **Estate a Ferrara,** an outdoor festival that begins in early July and runs until late August, when the festivities are augmented by street musicians, mimes, and orators, who partake in the **Busker's Festival.**

Exploring Ferrara

Ferrara's **medieval walls,** massive enough to be topped with trees and lawns, encircle the city with an aerie of greenery. The wide paths on top of the walls are ideal for biking, jogging, and strolling; they provide wonderful views of the city and surrounding farmland. Bikes are useful in Ferrara as the sights are spread out. Many hotels offer guests free use of bikes, or you can rent them from the lot outside the train station.

The **Corso Ercole I d'Este** is one of the two main streets in the historic center, flanked by beautiful *palazzi*. To the south lies the heart of the old city, the area around the Castello Estense and the Piazza Cattedrale. Much of the historic district southwest of here, riddled with narrow medieval streets, is home to the **University of Ferrara,** founded in 1391, with some 12,000 students enrolled today.

Casa Romei ★ HISTORIC HOME This lavish mansion was built between 1440 and 1450 for Giovanni Romei, a once lowly administrator who married into the family of the fleshy Borso d'Este (1413–71), first duke of Ferrara. Its elegant furnishings were carted off by the Este clan in 1598, but many of the wonderfully vibrant frescoes that smothered the chambers remain. The **Sala delle Sibille,** with its original terra-cotta fireplace, is the best example, richly painted with images of the sibyls (classical Greek prophetesses). Beyond the courtyard, the **Lapidario** contains a mixed bag of historic artifacts saved from churches in the area (as well as the original house baths), and you can view more frescoes by Sebastiano Filippi (aka Bastianino) in the rooms upstairs.

Via Savonarola 30. ✆ **0532-234130.** Admission 3€ adults, 1.50€ students 18–25, free for children 17 and under. Tues–Sun 8:30am–7:30pm. Bus: 1, 7, 9, or 21 from the train station.

Castello Estense ★ CASTLE This dazzling moated castle dominates the center of Ferrara, its hefty walls and drawbridges softened somewhat by elegant

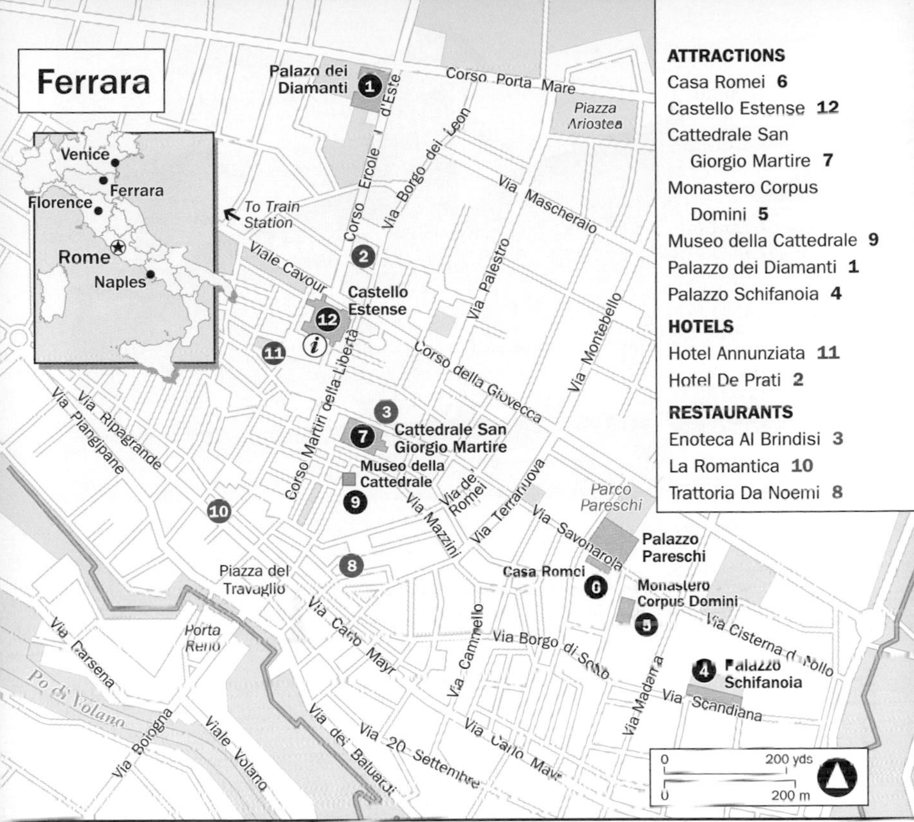

terraces and four, soaring Renaissance towers, remodeled in the 16th century. The castle began as a bricklayer's dream in 1385, when Niccolò II d'Este (1338–88) ordered its construction after a local revolt, although its face has been lifted and wrenched about for centuries. It was home to the powerful Este family until 1598, and then served as the offices of the papal legate until Italian reunification in 1860. Today you can view many of its once-lavish rooms on a clearly marked tourist route (all labeled in English), enhanced with displays that introduce the history of the city, beginning with the arrival of the Estes in Ferrara in 1264. Visits begin on the lower levels and include a peek into the dank **dungeons** where Parisina d'Este, wife of Duke Niccolò d'Este III, was murdered with her lover, Ugolino (the duke's illegitimate son), in 1425, creating the inspiration for Browning's "My Last Duchess." From here you walk up to the ducal apartments beginning with the tiny **Ducal Chapel,** thought to have been completed around 1591 for Renata di Francia, daughter of Louis XII, wife of Ercole II d'Este, and Calvinist sympathizer. Highlights beyond here include frescoes and painted ceilings of the 16th-century **Salone dell'Aurora** (the Salon of Dawn) and especially the **Salone dei Giochi** (the Salon of Games), mostly the work of Leonardo da Brescia and Bastianino. From the smaller Salleta dei Giochi you can access the **Torre dei Leoni** (Lions Tower; extra 2€; Tues–Sat 10am–4:30pm), a breezy viewpoint over the city 122 steps up. Further along you can view the **Sala di Governa,** Ercole II's seat of power 1534 to 1559, and the **Sala degli Stemmi,** smothered in coats of arms and the seat of power during the days of the papal legates.

Castello Estense.

Largo Castello. www.castelloestense.it. ✆ **0532-299233.** Admission 8€ adults, 6.50€ children ages 11–18, free for ages 10 and under. June–Feb Tues–Sun 9:30am–5:30pm; Mar–May daily 9:30am–5:30pm. Bus: 1, 7, 9, 11, or 21 from the train station.

Cattedrale San Giorgio Martire ★★ CATHEDRAL A short stroll from the Este Castle, the 12th-century cathedral of St. George weds the delicate Gothic with a more virile Romanesque. Its outstanding feature is its **triple facade ★★** with a magnificent porch. Over the tympanum, the Last Judgment is depicted in stone in a style evocative of a French Gothic cathedral. Never finished, the stunning pink-and-white marble **bell tower** (campanile) was built to the designs of Leon Battista Alberti.

The interior of this massive structure is heavily baroque, festooned with *trompe l'oeil* frescoes. In the third chapel on the right are 16th-century frescoes of the *Virgin in Glory with St. Barbara and St. Catherine,* by Bastianino (2€ to turn on the lights). The latter also painted a fresco of the *Last Judgment* in the apse, above the choir, inspired by Michelangelo's Sistine Chapel (but not quite as good).

Piazza della Cattedrale. ✆ **0532-207449.** Free admission. Mon–Sat 7:30am–noon and 3–6:30pm; Sun 7:30am–12:30pm and 3:30–7:30pm. Bus: 11 from the train station.

Monastero Corpus Domini MONASTERY Founded in 1406, this cloistered monastery is best known for containing the marble tombs of the House of Este, lords of Ferrara. Here lie Alfonso I, Alfonso II, Ercole I, and Ercole II, but also Lucrezia Borgia (wife of Alfonso I), who is far better remembered today than her husband and his family. Much of the church interior was decorated in the baroque style, with a huge fresco by G. Ghedini covering the ceiling.

Via Pergolato 4. ✆ **0532-207825.** Free admission. Mon–Fri 9:30–11:30am and 3:30–5:30pm. Bus: 1, 7, 9, or 21 from the train station.

Museo della Cattedrale ★ MUSEUM The cathedral museum, housed in the former San Romano church and monastery opposite the cathedral, is especially well endowed with works by Ferrara's most outstanding 15th-century painter, **Cosmé Tura,** with excellent English labeling. Visits begin with a room of rare 15th-century illuminated manuscripts, while the old sacristy contains various relics and vestments—look out for reliquaries containing (allegedly) fragments of St. George's skull, and parts of his arm.

The main attractions lie in the old church itself, beginning with the four great canvases created by Tura in the 1460s to cover the cathedral organ. Aesthetically controversial, the most intriguing image is Tura's St. George slaying the dragon to save a red-stockinged damsel in distress. Nearby is the outstanding Jacopo della Quercia *Madonna della Melagrane,* a perfectly carved statue of a sweet, regal Madonna with a pomegranate in one hand and a baby Christ in the other, dating from 1406. Also from the Renaissance heyday of Ferrara are some huge 16th-century *arazzi* (tapestries).

Via San Romano 1–9. ✆ **0532-244949.** Admission 6€ adults, 3€ for students, children 17 and under free; 7€ joint admission with Palazzo Schifanoia. Tues–Sun 9am–1pm and 3–6pm. Bus: 11 from the train station.

Palazzo dei Diamanti ★ MUSEUM Another jewel of Este splendor (it belonged to the duke's brother Sigismondo d'Este), this *palazzo* gets its name from the 9,000 diamond-shaped stones on its facade. Inside, on the first floor, the spacious **Pinacoteca Nazionale** houses the works of all the major Ferrarese artists—notably the trio of old masters, Tura, del Cossa, and Roberti—in roughly chronological order. There are some other gems on display—an *Adoration of the Magi* by the Bellini brothers and a tiny *Cristo con l'animula della Vergine* by Mantegna join paintings by local boy Ercole Roberti in early galleries, while the work of Tura is shown with Bologna artist Amico Aspertini. The work of Sebastiano Filippi (Bastianino) is well-represented in the giant Salone d'Onore, with its 16th-century wood ceiling, and there is a huge ensemble of vivid Il Garofalo oil paintings displayed in the old apartments of Virginia dei Medici and Cesare d'Este. The galleries end with Garofalo's epic *Polittico Costabili,* covering a whole wall.

Corso Ercole d'Este 21. ✆ **0532-205844** or 0532-244949. www.palazzodiamanti.it. Admission to Pinacoteca 4€ adults, 2€ E.U. citizens 18–25, free for children 17 and under. Free audio guides. Tues–Sun 9am–2pm (to 7pm Thurs). Bus: 3C, or 4C from the train station.

Palazzo Schifanoia ★★★ HISTORIC HOME The fortresslike Schifanoia Palace was begun in 1385 for Alberto V d'Este and was enlarged by his ancestor Duke Borso d'Este between 1450 and 1471. Used variously as a warehouse and factory in later years, its frescoes were only rediscovered in the 1820s and, as a result, much of the incredibly lavish work inside was lost forever. You can imagine what it would have looked like by wandering through the first section, where parts of complex frescoes have been preserved *in situ*—a raised walkway takes you up closer. Though nothing remains of the original furnishings, the rooms have been enhanced by displays of archaeological finds, antique bronzes, Renaissance plates, and pottery.

A detail from the Salon of Months' astrological wall cycle in the Palazzo Schifanoia.

The real showstopper here is upstairs, where the **Salone dei Mesi (Salon of the Months) ★★★** is one

7

BOLOGNA & EMILIA-ROMAGNA | Ferrara

of the most important art works in Italy. Even with half the frescoes faded away, this is a mesmerizing and complex vision, an astrological wall cycle representing the 12 months, created by all the top Ferrara painters of the 15th century: Francesco del Cossa, Ercole de' Roberti (who both painted the Mar, Apr, and May scenes), and others. Each month is subdivided into three horizontal bands: The lower band shows scenes from the daily life of courtiers and people, the middle shows the relative sign of the zodiac, and the upper depicts the triumph of the classical divinity for that myth. Humanist Pellegrino Prisciani conceived the subjects of the cycle, although Cosmé Tura, the official court painter, was probably the organizer of the works, which were created to celebrate the investiture of Borso d'Este as duke of Ferrara in 1471 by Pope Paul II.

Via Scandiana 23. ✆ **0532-244949.** Admission 6€ adults, 3€ for students, free for 17 and under; 7€ joint admission with Museo della Cattedrale. Tues–Sun 9am–6pm. Closed Mon and major holidays. Bus: 1, 7, 9, or 21 from the train station.

Where to Eat

On a sunny day, you might put together a picnic to enjoy atop Ferrara's medieval walls. Buy what you need on the **Via Cortevecchia,** a narrow brick street near the cathedral lined with traditional salumerias such as **Marchetti** at no. 35 (✆ **0532-204800;** Mon–Sat 8am–1pm and 4:30–7pm, Sun 9:30am–1pm; closed Wed afternoon). The nearby **Mercato Comunale,** at the corner of Via Santo Stefano and Via del Mercato, is crowded with food stalls and open until 1pm Monday to Saturday, and 3:30 to 7:30pm Friday.

Enoteca Al Brindisi ★ FERRARESE This small, atmospheric place claims, with some justification, to be the oldest wine bar in the world, with a tradition of uncorking bottles dating from 1435—Titian was a regular, and Copernicus is said to have lived upstairs while studying for his degree in 1503. Squeeze into one of the small, wooden booths and admire the ancient bottles of booze all around you, gathering dust. Lunch menus are simple but thoughtfully put together tasters of local specialties; *cappellacci di zucca* (squash ravioli) and the macaroni pie, a crusty delight, are favorites, but the plates of cold cuts and cheese are also a good bet. Pair your meal with one of their excellent wines.

Via Adelardi 11. www.albrindisi.net. ✆ **0532-471225.** Main courses 7€–10€; tasting menu 13€–50€. AE, DC, MC, V. Daily 11am–1am. Bus: 11 from the train station.

La Romantica ★ 🎁 FERRARESE/SEAFOOD One of the city's most delightful dining experiences is in what used to be the stables of a 17th-century merchant's house. In a bright, fashionable space, the well-trained chefs dazzle your palate with one taste sensation after another. Here is a chance to dine on several rare regional recipes, including pumpkin/squash ravioli in a tomato-cream sauce (*cappellacci di zucca*), given added flavor by walnuts and Parmesan cheese. Seafood is another specialty, with salmon, salt cod, and dishes such as baked grouper in potato crust on the menu.

Wine bottles at Enoteca Al Brindisi.

Via Ripagrande 36. www.trattorialaromantica.com. ✆ **0532-765975.** Reservations recommended. Main courses 13€–18€; tourist menu 15€. MC, V. Thurs–Tues 12:30–2:30pm and 7:30–10:30pm; Mon 7:30–10:30pm. Bus: 2 from the train station.

Trattoria Da Noemi ★ FERRARESE/ITALIAN This first-rate restaurant offers a more creative, contemporary approach to local cuisine in a house that dates back to 1400. Stick with classics such as fried zucchini flower and pumpkin ravioli, served with Bolognese sauce, cooked to perfection; order the grilled meats if you fancy something more substantial. The local pastas—such as *pasticcio di maccheroni ferrarese*—are also worth trying. Service here is always friendly, even if the restaurant is full (which it normally is).

Via Ragno 31. www.trattoriadanoemi.it. ✆ **0532-769070.** Reservations recommended. Main courses 8€–24€. AE, DC, MC, V. Wed–Mon 12:15–2:30pm and 7–11pm. Bus: 11 or 2 from the train station.

Shopping

Ferrara has a rich tradition of artisanship dating from the Renaissance. You can find some of the best, albeit expensive, products in the dozen or so antiques stores in the historic center.

You find beautifully designed, colorful ceramics at **La Marchesana,** Via Cortevecchia 38A (www.lamarchesana.it; ✆ **0532-240535**). It's open Monday to Saturday 9:30am to 12:30pm and 3:30 to 7:30pm (Sun mornings only). Every month Tuesday through Sunday 9am to 1pm, the **open-air antiques and handicraft markets** feature lots of junk amid the increasingly rare treasures. The markets are conducted in Piazza Municipale (mostly antiques and bric-a-brac) and Piazza Savonarola (mainly handicrafts and bric-a-brac).

Chocolate addicts should make a pilgrimage to **La Bottega del Cioccolato,** Via San Romano 23 (www.rizzati.it; ✆ **0532-711504**), which sells local Rizzati chocolates of every description, including their famed "beer chocolate" and La Tenerina, a moist chocolate cake.

Entertainment & Nightlife

During July and August, concerts and temporary art exhibits are offered as part of the **Estate a Ferrara** program. The tourist office can provide a schedule of events and dates, which vary from year to year. During the rest of the year, you can rub elbows with fellow drinkers, and usually lots of students, at a refreshingly diverse collection of bars, pubs, and discos, including **Enoteca Al Brindisi** (p. 398) and **Il Bistrot** (www.ildongiovanni.com; ✆ **0532-243363**), in the old stock exchange at Corso Ercole I D'Este 1, offering more than 40 wines by the glass.

For more earthy, late-night drinking make for **Bar Settimo,** Via Cortevecchia 49 (✆ **0532-205145**), often frequented by performers at the nearby Teatro Communale, or hip lounge cafe **Tsunami,** Via Savanarola 2 (www.tsunami-cafe.it; ✆ **0532-211103**), popular with local students for its free Wi-Fi, cheap buffet, and cocktails.

Where to Stay

Hotel Annunziata ★★★ This slick, fashionable design hotel in the heart of the city offers incredible value. Spacious rooms feature crisp, contemporary Italian design (Tisettanta furnishings, Pozzi-Ginori fittings); shiny metallic bathrooms; and a simple, minimalist color scheme that contrasts bright reds with whites and grays. iPads are available for guests to play with on request, and the buffet breakfast will keep you full all day. Six rooms (including cool loft suites) are located at the enticing **Prisciani** annex at Via Garibaldi 70, a small residence dating back to the 14th century (book through the hotel website).

Piazza Repubblica 5, 44121 Ferrara. www.annunziata.it. ✆ **0532-201111.** Fax 0532-203233. 27 units. 89€–109€ double; from 119€ suite. Rates include buffet breakfast. AE, DC, MC, V. Bus: 1, 7, 9, 11, or 21. **Amenities:** Restaurant; bar; babysitting; bikes (free); room service. *In room:* A/C, TV, hair dryer, minibar, Wi-Fi (free).

Hotel De Prati ★ Set in the heart of the old city, this tranquil little family-run hotel dates back to the early 1900s, and offers cozy, spotless rooms and a tasty continental breakfast. Rooms are adorned with the modern work of local artists, but some Edwardian elements have been retained in the antique beds and fittings. The helpful English-speaking staff will accommodate just about any request, and parking is a bargain. They also rent the spacious **De Prati Apartments** in an 18th-century *palazzo,* perfect for families.

Via Padiglioni 5, 44100 Ferrara. www.hoteldeprati.com. ✆ **0532-241905.** Fax 0532-241966. 16 units. 95€ double. AE, DC, MC, V. Public parking 3€ per day. Bus: 1, 7, 9, 11, or 21. **Amenities:** Babysitting; bikes; room service. *In room:* A/C, TV, hair dryer, minibar, Wi-Fi (free).

Piazza Nova Guest House ★ Close to the Palazzo dei Diamanti, this gorgeous apartment complex set in a 19th-century building features antique furniture, Persian rugs, and oak-beamed ceilings. Each suite is decked out with a blend of period and modern furnishings, and all come with a full kitchen, DVD player, and PlayStation 2. The breakfast is top-notch, with especially good homemade bread and cakes.

Corso Porta Mare 133, 44100 Ferrara. www.piazzanova.com. ✆ **0532-757614.** Fax 0532-750292. 6 suites. 70€–100€ double suite; 90€–120€ triple suite. Rates include buffet breakfast. AE, DC, MC, V. Free public parking. Bus: 4C or 7. **Amenities:** Bikes (free). *In room:* A/C, TV/DVD, hair dryer, kitchen, Wi-Fi (free).

RAVENNA ★★★

74km (46 miles) E of Bologna, 145km (90 miles) S of Venice, 130km (81 miles) NE of Florence, 365km (226 miles) N of Rome

Ravenna, Italy's city of mosaics, is one of the most beguiling destinations in Emilia-Romagna. As the capital of the Western Roman Empire (from A.D. 402) and the Visigoth Empire (from A.D. 476), and then the seat of the Byzantine governor of Italy (A.D. 540–752), Ravenna became one of the greatest cities on the Mediterranean. It is best known today for the many exquisite mosaics created during that time—the finest in all Western art and the most splendid outside Istanbul. Although it now looks much like any other small Italian city, the low Byzantine domes of its churches still evoke its Eastern past.

Essentials

GETTING THERE With hourly **trains** that take only 1 hour, 20 minutes from Bologna, Ravenna can easily be visited on a day trip; one-way fare is 6.80€. There's also frequent service from Ferrara (1 hr., 15 min.), which has connections to Venice; the one-way fare from Ferrara is 6.20€. The train station is a 10-minute walk from the center at Piazza Fernini (✆ **892021**). The tourist

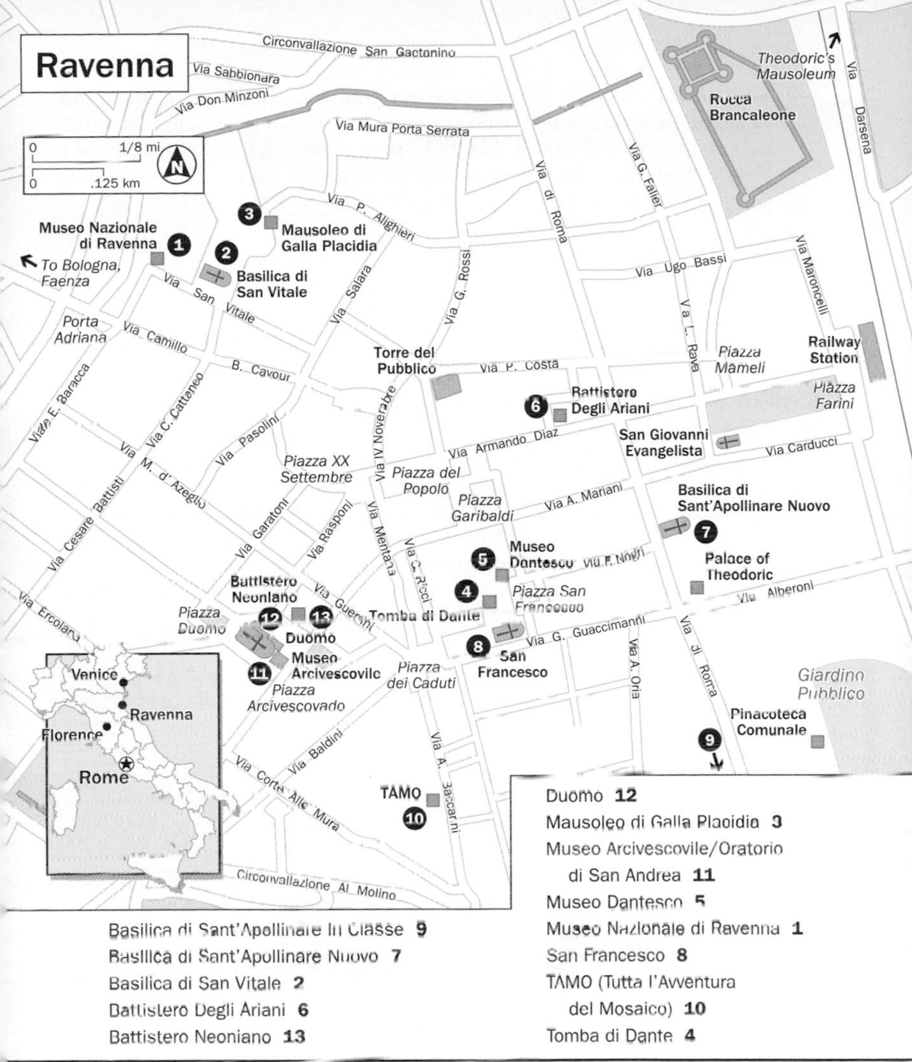

office (below) has rail schedules and more details. If you have a **car** and are coming from Bologna, head east along A14. From Ferrara, take the SS16.

GETTING AROUND Ravenna operates a useful bicycle rental scheme; get keys from the tourist office that provide unlimited access to bikes all over the city. Rates are 9.50€ per day for adults and 8.50€ for students (free for children 10 and under).

To visit the Basilica di Sant'Apollinare in Classe from central Ravenna, take bus no. 4—buy tickets (1.20€) in advance from any bar or *tabacchi*.

VISITOR INFORMATION The helpful **tourist office** is at Via Salara 8 (www.turismo.ravenna.it; ✆ **0544-35404**). It's open Monday to Saturday 8:30am to 7pm, and Sunday from 10am to 6pm. Stop in here for a good map, bicycle rental, and a combination ticket to the city's attractions.

SPECIAL EVENTS If you're here in June and July, you can enjoy the **Ravenna Festival Internazionale.** Tickets begin at 10€, but go much higher. For information, call ✆ **0544-249211;** for tickets, call ✆ **0544-249244** (Teatro Alighieri). A **Dante Festival** is held the second week in September, sponsored by the church of San Francesco.

Exploring Ravenna

At the center of Ravenna is the elegant **Piazza del Popolo,** from which all the major sights are within easy walking distance. You can see all of them in a fairly rushed day, but you really need 2 days to get the best out of the city—and those mosaics.

Basilica di Sant'Apollinare in Classe ★★ CHURCH About 6km (3¾ miles) and 15 minutes by bus south of the city, this huge, incongruous church of glittering mosaics dates from the 6th century. Dedicated to St. Apollinare, the early bishop of Ravenna, the original basilica stands side by side with a 10th-century campanile, symbols of faded glory now resting in a lonely low-lying area. Inside is a cavernous central nave flanked by two aisles and 24 columns of veined Greek marble, but the mosaic-smothered apse provides the major reason for visiting. These **mosaics** are extraordinary, rich in gold and turquoise, set against a pastoral background of top-heavy birds nesting in shrubbery. St. Apollinare stands in the center, with a row of lambs on either side lined up as in a processional; the 12 lambs symbolize the Apostles.

Via Romea Sud 224, Classe. www.soprintendenzaravenna.beniculturali.it. ✆ **0544-473569.** Admission 5€ adults, 2.50€ ages 18–25, free for children 17 and under. Daily 8:30am–7:30pm. Bus: 4 from rail station or Piazza Caduti (1.20€).

Basilica di Sant'Apollinare Nuovo ★★ CHURCH Once again mosaics take center stage at this 6th-century basilica, originally Ostrogoth King Theodoric's palatinate church but featuring a blend of styles from subsequent restorations.

The Basilica di Sant'Apollinare in Classe.

Ravenna Combo Tickets

If you're planning on seeing more than one sight in Ravenna, the most economical choice is to buy a **combination ticket.** The combo ticket for sights managed by the provincial authorities—the Museo Nazionale di Ravenna, Mausoleo di Teoderico, and Basilica di Sant'Apollinare in Classe—costs 10€. Buy tickets at any of the respective sights. To see any of the sights managed by the Diocese of Ravenna works department—Battistero Neoniano, San Vitale, Mausoleo di Galla Placidia, Museo Arcivescovile, and Basilica di Sant'Apollinare—you automatically receive a combo ticket for all of them (9.50€), as there is no single entry ticket (see www.ravennamosaici.it).

The arches on both sides of the spacious nave are lined with dazzling mosaics: 22 holy virgins (female saints and martyrs) line up on the left, led by the Three Kings and ending with Mary and the baby Jesus, while 26 male martyrs, led by St. Martin, stand at the right, ending with the adult Jesus.

Via di Roma (btw. Via Carducci and Via Alberoni). www.ravennamosaici.it. ✆ **0544-541688.** Admission 9.50€ adults, 8.50€ students, free for children 10 and under. Apr–Sept daily 9am–7pm; Mar and Oct daily 9:30am–5:30pm; Nov–Feb daily 10am–5pm.

Basilica di San Vitale ★★★ CHURCH This richly ornamented octagonal church dates from the mid–6th century, part of the complex containing the Mausoleo di Galla Placidia (see below). The huge **mosaics** inside—intense greens and golds, lit by light from translucent panels—are among the most celebrated in the Western world, a blend of Roman and Byzantine styles. Covering the apse is a mosaic of a clean shaven Christ astride the world, flanked by saints and angels. To the right is a mosaic of Empress Theodora and her court, while to the left is the world-famous image of the man who married this courtesan/actress in 525, **Emperor Justinian** (who never actually visited Ravenna).

Via San Vitale 17. www.ravennamosaici.it. ✆ **0544-215193.** Admission 9.50€ adults, 8.50€ students, free for children 10 and under. Apr–Sept daily 9am–7pm; Mar and Oct daily 9am–5:30pm; Nov–Feb daily 9:30am–5pm.

Battistero Degli Ariani (Arian Baptistery) CHURCH This tiny gem of a chapel offers a free taste of Ravenna's artistic heritage with a gorgeous mosaic ceiling under its octagonal dome. Another relic of the 6th century and the rule of Theodoric, the mosaics depict the baptism of Christ and the 12 Apostles.

Vicolo Degli Ariani (btw. Via Diaz and Via Paolo Costa). www.soprintendenzaravenna.beniculturali.it. ✆ **0544-543711.** Free admission. Mar–Oct daily 8:30am–7:30pm; Nov–Feb daily 8:30am–4:30pm.

Battistero Neoniano ★ (Neonian Baptistery) CHURCH This octagonal baptistery was completed in the 5th century by Bishop Neone on the site of an ancient Roman bath. The mesmerizing ceiling is adorned with mosaics showing John the Baptist baptizing Christ, surrounded by a spectacular representation of 12 crown-carrying Apostles in deep violet-blues and sparkling golds. The baptistery originally served a cathedral that no longer stands. The present-day **Duomo** (daily 7am–noon and 2:30–5pm; free admission), next to the baptistery, was built in the mid–18th century and is of little interest except for some unusual pews, and frescoes by Domenico and Andrea Barbiani (1751).

Detail from mosaics in the Mausoleum of Galla Placidia.

Piazza del Duomo. www.ravennamosaici.it. ✆ **0544-215201.** Admission 9.50€ adults, 8.50€ students, free for children 10 and under. Apr–Sept daily 9am–7pm; Mar and Oct daily 9:30am–5:30pm; Nov–Feb daily 10am–5pm. Closed Christmas and New Year's Day.

Mausoleo di Galla Placidia ★★ MONUMENT/MEMORIAL This 5th-century mausoleum (part of the San Vitale complex), looks deceptively plain from the outside, but the dimly lit interior contains some eye-popping mosaics. Translucent panels bring the mosaics alive in all their grace and harmony, vivid with hues of peacock blue, moss green, Roman gold, eggplant, and burnt orange. The mosaics in the cupola glitter with 570 tiny gold stars. Popular tradition claims that the cross-shaped structure houses the tomb of Galla Placidia (386–452), daughter of Theodosius I, last emperor to rule over both the eastern and the western halves of the Roman Empire. Galla, who actually died in Rome (and is probably buried there), is one of history's most powerful women. She became virtual ruler of the Western Roman Empire after her second husband, Constantius III, died and she was named regent for her son Valentinian III, who was only 6 at the time of his father's death; Galla held the position for 12 years.

Via Fiandrini Benedetto. www.ravennamosaici.it. ✆ **0544-541688.** Admission 9.50€ adults, 8.50€ students (Mar to mid-June 2€ discount), free for children 10 and under. Apr–Sept daily 9am–7pm; Mar and Oct daily 9am–5:30pm; Nov–Feb daily 9:30am–5pm.

Museo Arcivescovile—Oratorio di San Andrea ★ MUSEUM This twofold attraction is housed in the 6th-century Archbishop's Palace (*arcivescovile*). In the museum, the major showstoppers are the huge embossed silver cross of Bishop Agnellus (487–570), a rare calendar showing the dates for Easter between 532 and 626, and an exquisite ivory throne carved for Archbishop Maximian from around the mid–6th century.

In the tiny 6th-century chapel (oratory) dedicated to St. Andrea are yet more brilliant mosaics. Pause in the antechamber to look at an intriguing mosaic above the entrance, an unusual representation of Christ as a warrior, stepping on the head of a lion and a snake; tough but haloed, he wears partial armor. The chapel, built in the shape of a Greek cross, contains other mosaics that are "angelic," both figuratively and literally. Busts of saints and apostles stare down at you with the ox-eyed look of Byzantine art.

Piazza Arcivescovado. www.ravennamosaici.it. ✆ **0544-541688.** Admission 9.50€ adults, 8.50€ students, free for children 10 and under. Apr–Sept daily 9am–7pm; Mar and Oct daily 9:30am–5:30pm; Nov–Feb daily 10am–5pm.

A Day at the Beach

Take bus no. 70 or 80 (www.atm.ra.it; ✆ **199-199-558;** 2€; every 30 min.) from the Ravenna train station, and in 20 minutes you can enjoy white-sand beaches set against a backdrop of pine forests. Lined with beach clubs, snack shops, and ice-cream stands, these beaches are extremely crowded during the summer. The most beautiful beaches are found along a stretch called the **Punta Marina di Ravenna.** The Marina di Ravenna is also lively at night, with pubs and discos open until the wee hours.

Museo Nazionale di Ravenna MUSEUM Housed in the cloisters of the former Benedictine Monastery next to San Vitale, this museum contains archaeological objects from the early Christian and Byzantine periods: icons, fragments of tapestries, medieval armaments and armory, sarcophagi, ivories, ceramics, and bits of broken pieces from the stained-glass windows of San Vitale. It also contains the 14th-century cycle of frescoes of Santa Chiara that once adorned the church of Clarisse di Ravenna, today the Teatro Luigi Rasi.

Via Fiandrini Benedetto (adjacent to Via San Vitale). ✆ **0544-543711.** Admission 5€ adults, 2.50€ ages 18–25. Tues–Sun 8:30am–7:30pm.

TAMO (Tutta l'Avventura del Mosaico) MUSEUM This new permanent exhibition of mosaics is housed in the pretty 14th-century church of San Nicolò. The mosaics on display here are mostly post-Byzantine, but there are rare medieval pieces retrieved from churches and houses in the surrounding area, as well as the work of contemporary artists, and multimedia exhibits charting the history of the technique.

Via Rondinelli Nicolo' 2. www.tamoravenna.it. ✆ **0544-213371.** Admission 4€. Mar–Oct daily 10am–6.30pm; Nov–Feb Tues–Fri 10am–5pm, Sat–Sun 10am–6pm.

Tomba di Dante (Dante's Tomb) MONUMENT/MEMORIAL Just off Piazza Garibaldi, the humble temple containing the remains of Dante Alighieri,

The beach outside Ravenna.

"the divine poet," was built in 1780 and graced with a simple marble bas-relief. The author of the *Divine Comedy,* in exile from his hometown of Florence, died in Ravenna on September 14, 1321. To the right of the tomb in the church graveyard is a mound of earth in which Dante's urn went "underground" from March 1944 to December 1945 because it was feared that his grave might suffer from Allied bombings. Near the tomb is the 5th-century church of **San Francesco** ★ (Mon–Sat 7am–noon and 3–6pm, Sun 7:45am–12:30pm; free), the site of the poet's funeral and worth a look for the beautiful mosaics in the crypt under the altar, now half underwater and filled with goldfish (.50€ to turn on the lights). Note also that the **Museo Dantesco,** housed in the nearby Franciscan cloisters (Via Dante Alighieri 2A), should be open by the end of 2012, displaying artwork inspired by the poet.

Via Dante Alighieri. ✆ **0544-33662.** Free admission. Daily 10am–6:30pm (Oct–Mar closes 4pm).

Where to Eat

A walk through Ravenna's lively food market, the **Mercato Coperto,** will introduce you to the bounty of Emilia-Romagna. It's near the center of town on Piazza Andrea Costa and is open Monday to Saturday 7am to 2pm, and on Friday also 4:30 to 7:30pm. Inside you'll find the no-frills self-service canteen **Bizantino,** where the *menù turistico* is just 7.90€ and plates of pasta run 3.40€ to 4.70€. It's open for lunch only, Monday to Friday 11:45am to 2:45pm.

Cinema Alexander ★ ITALIAN/SEAFOOD This intriguing restaurant was a former cinema dating back to 1924, which explains the striking (and very un-Byzantine) decor of vintage black-and-white film posters. Sometimes old movies are projected onto the walls while you eat. The slick menu is divided into "Terre" (land) and "Mare" (sea) options, and though they knock out a mean steak, it's the latter where the chefs excel, with an exceptional cod dish, and delicious calamari couscous gracing a seasonal menu.

Via Bassa del Pignataro 8. www.ristorantealexander.it. ✆ **0544-212967.** Reservations recommended. Main courses 15€–28€. AE, DC, MC, V. Tues–Sun 12:30–2:30pm and 7:30–11:30pm (closed Sun in summer).

La Gardèla ★ ROMAGNOLA A few steps from the 12th-century Torre Pubblica (Ravenna's very own leaning tower), La Gardèla is spread out over two levels, with paneled walls lined with racks of wine bottles and a small street terrace. The waiters bring out an array of typical but savory dishes, including spinach ravioli with poppy seeds, and *spezzatino alla contadina* (roast veal with potatoes, tomatoes, and herbs). Ravioli is stuffed with truffles, and one of the best pasta dishes, *tagliatelle,* is offered with porcini mushrooms. The Piatti del Giorno menu is printed up every day for lunch, a popular choice with locals; pastas run 6€ to 7€, with mains 9€ to 10€. Figure on 3.50€ for a quarter liter of wine.

Via Ponte Marino 3. www.ristorantelagardela.com. ✆ **0544-217147.** Reservations recommended. Fixed-price menus 18€–30€. AE, DC, MC, V. Fri–Wed noon–2:30pm and 7–10pm. Closed Jan 25–31.

Locanda del Melarancio ★★ ROMAGNOLA Housed in the wonderfully atmospheric 16th-century Casa Succi, this local favorite focuses on highly creative seasonal specialties and regional dishes. Begin with a typical plate of cold cuts and *squaquerone,* a delicate soft cheese popular in these parts, before moving on to the exquisite potato spaghetti with pistachio pesto. Main courses feature duck breast with port, cherries, and fresh spinach, and steaks drizzled with inventive toppings: zucchini jam, strawberry sauce, onion and chili jam, and Parmesan and truffle oil. Save room for the magical *crema cotta,* served with strawberries. The tavern in the basement offers cheaper meals and a publike atmosphere in the evenings.

Via Mentana 33. www.ilmelarancio.it. ✆ **0544-215258.** Reservations recommended. Main courses 8€–20€. AE, DC, MC, V. Thurs–Tues noon–2:30pm and 7:30–11pm.

Shopping

One of the best places to admire (and buy) mosaics is **Akomena Spazio Mosaico,** Via Chartres 3 (www.akomena.com; ✆ **0544-554700;** Mon–Fri 8:30am–12:30pm), a gallery where replicas of Christ, the Madonna, the saints, and penitent sinners appear in all their majesty amid more secular forms. Virtually anything can be shipped. Artists Enzo Scianna and Valeria Mazzarol's private gallery, **Laboratorio di Mosaico,** Via di Roma 34A (ring the bell, hours are informal; www.ravennamosaic.it; ✆ **0544-37556**), is a worthy competitor.

Entertainment & Nightlife

One of the best enotecas in town is **Ca' De Ven,** Via Corrado Ricci 24 (www.cadeven.it; ✆ **0544-30163**), open Tuesday to Sunday 11am to 2:15pm and 6 to 10pm (Sun evenings 5:30–9:30pm). Enjoy top regional wines with a fine selection of seasonal Romagna food (mains 7.50€–9€), such as sausages and potatoes, and rabbit in pickled onion sauce.

Further entertainment is offered by the **Teatro Alighieri,** Via Mariani 2 (www.teatroalighieri.org; ✆ **0544-249244**), which sponsors free summer concerts in the various squares and churches around town.

Beside the **Marina di Ravenna** (the beach), you'll find a handful of pubs and dance clubs. Our favorite is **BBK,** Lungomare Cristoforo Colombo 171 (www.bbkbeach.com; ✆ **0544-438494**), an open-air dance club featuring top DJs: It attracts a crowd that's mainly in their 20s and early 30s. BBK is open only in June, July, and August.

Where to Stay

Albergo Cappello ★ This is Ravenna's most charming boutique hotel. It's small but choice, housed in a meticulously restored palace from the 1300s, with 15th-century frescoes gracing the corridor. Even though it's old, the hotel boasts up-to-date amenities, although the wine cellar and the architectural style of the splendid rooms have been retained. The various color schemes inspired the names of the rooms: Yellow Gem, Green Gold, Rose and Roses. Painted beamed ceilings and terra-cotta floors are grace notes from another time, but the furnishings are modern, either contemporary in style or else reproductions of antiques.

Via IV Novembre 41, 48100 Ravenna. www.albergocappello.it. ✆ **0544-219813.** Fax 0544-219814. 7 units. 160€–200€ double. Rates include buffet breakfast. AE, MC, V. Parking 13€. **Amenities:** Restaurant; wine bar; room service. *In room:* A/C, TV, hair dryer, Wi-Fi (free).

Hotel Centrale Byron This Art Deco–inspired hotel is a few steps from Piazza del Popolo and is named for Lord Byron, who shared a nearby palace with his mistress (and her husband!) in the 1820s. The small guest rooms are simply but comfortably furnished, and the bathrooms are a bit cramped. Overall, though, this is a great deal, especially for singles (rooms from 45€) and families (quadruples from 110€), with a great location, convenient to the train station.

Via IV Novembre 14, 48100 Ravenna. www.hotelsravenna.it. ✆ **0544-212225.** Fax 0544-34114. 54 units, shower only. 70€–110€ double. Rates include buffet breakfast. AE, DC, MC, V. Parking 15€. **Amenities:** Bar; room service. *In room:* A/C, TV, hair dryer, minibar, Wi-Fi (free).

M club ★★ 🎁 This small B&B is a real gem, with just six color-themed rooms littered with antiques and paintings. Much of the historic interior has been preserved—note the original timber beams in the ceiling—but every room has been equipped with modern amenities and the bathrooms are spanking new. Our favorite is the Green Room, with its elegant 18th-century wrought-iron canopy bed, but all represent excellent value.

Piazza Baracca 26, 48121 Ravenna. www.m-club.it. ✆ **333-9556466.** Fax 0544-215250. 6 units. 80€–100€ double; 130€ suite. Rates include buffet breakfast. AE, DC, MC, V. Parking 10€. **Amenities:** Bikes (free). *In room:* A/C, TV, hair dryer, fridge, Wi-Fi (free).

MODENA ★

40km (25 miles) NW of Bologna, 403km (250 miles) NW of Rome, 130km (81 miles) N of Florence

Though the careers of Enzo Ferrari (1898–1988) and Luciano Pavarotti (1935–2007) might seem world's apart, they had one thing in common: Both grew up in Modena. Pavarotti was no doubt inspired by Modena's rich cultural legacy, which includes one of the most enchanting cathedrals in Italy. On the food front, Modena's chefs enjoy an outstanding reputation in hard-to-please gastronomic circles—Lambrusco wine and especially balsamic vinegar are specialties around here. Yet Modena is first and foremost a dynamic industrial center: Ferrari went on to establish one of the world's most exclusive sports car manufacturers, and Modena is still "the capital of motors," also home to De Tomaso, Lamborghini, Pagani, and Maserati.

Modena was ruled by the Estes of Ferrara from the 13th century, but after Ferrara fell to Pope Clement VIII in 1598, the Este family made Modena their main base, ruling the city as dukes until Italian reunification in 1860. Today Modena is an industrial zone blessed with Italy's highest per-capita income, and it can seem as sleek as the sports cars it produces. This is partially because of its 20th-century face-lift—the city was largely rebuilt following World War II bombings.

Essentials

GETTING THERE There are good **train** connections to and from Bologna (one train every 30 min.); trip time is 20 to 30 minutes, and a one-way fare is 3.60€. Trains arrive from Parma once every 30 minutes (trip time: 30 min.); the one-way fare is 5€. For information and schedules, call ✆ **892021.** If you have a **car** and are coming from Bologna, take A1 northeast until you see the turnoff for Modena.

VISITOR INFORMATION The **tourist office** is on Via Scudari 8 (http://turismo.comune.modena.it; ✆ **059-2032660**). It's open Monday 3 to 6pm, Tuesday to Saturday 9:30am to 12:30pm and 3 to 6pm, and Sunday 9:30am to 12:30pm.

SPECIAL EVENTS All of Modena seems to be a stage during 1 week each year at the end of June or beginning of July, when vendors, artists, mimes, and other performers take to the streets for the **Settimana Estense;** festivities culminate in a parade in which the town turns out in Renaissance attire.

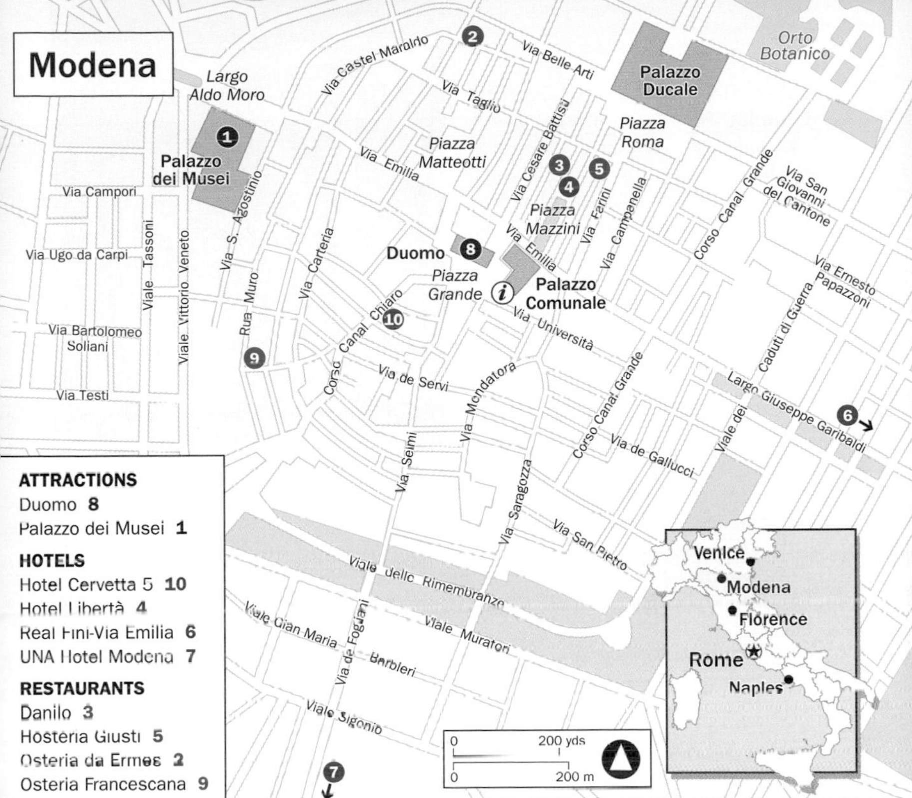

Exploring Modena

Central Modena is easy to navigate on foot, with most of the sights close to Piazza Grande and the medieval cathedral.

Duomo ★★ CATHEDRAL One of the glories of the Romanesque in northern Italy, Modena's cathedral was founded in 1099. Consecrated in 1184, it was dedicated to St. Geminiano, the patron saint of Modena and the bishop of the city in the 4th century. Legend has it that only his intervention convinced Attila the Hun to spare the city. Towering from the rear is the **Ghirlandina,** a 12th- to 14th-century campanile, 87m (285 ft.) tall. Leaning slightly, the bell tower guards the replica of the Secchia Rapita (stolen bucket), garnered as booty from the defeated Bolognese.

The facade of the Duomo features a 13th-century rose window by Anselmo da Campione. It also boasts Wiligelmo's main entrance, with pillars supported by lions, as well as Wiligelmo bas-reliefs depicting scenes from Genesis. The south door, the "Princes' Door," was designed by Wiligelmo in the 12th century and is framed by bas-reliefs illustrating scenes in the saga of the patron saint.

Inside, there's a dimly lit vaulted ceiling, and the overall effect is gravely impressive. The Modenese restored the cathedral during the first part of the 20th century, so its present look resembles the original design. The marble gallery above the crypt is an outstanding piece of sculpture by Anselmo da Campione, supported by four lions. Two hunchbacks hold up the pulpit, by Arrigo da

A detail from the Duomo of Modena.

Campione. And the crypt, now the **Capella SS Sacramento,** where the body of the patron saint was finally taken, is a forest of columns; here you'll find Guido Mazzoni's *Holy Family* group in terra-cotta (aka *Madonna della Pappa*), completed in 1480. Back in the nave lies Antonio Begarelli's delicate version of the same subject, completed in 1527. The left hand apse contains a magnificent polyptych, *l'Incoronazione della Vergine,* by Serafino dei Serafini (1385), but the lavish gold-leaf mosaics beyond here are actually 19th-century imitations, not Byzantine originals.

The adjacent **Museo del Duomo** and **Museo Lapidario** display various cathedral treasures, from ancient stonework and medieval vestments, to precious Flemish tapestries donated to the cathedral in 1598 by noblemen fleeing Ferrara.

Corso Duomo. www.duomodimodena.it. ✆ **059-216078.** Free admission; museums 3€. Daily 7:30am–12:30pm and 3:30–7pm. Museums Tues–Sun 9:30am–12:30am and 3:30–6:30pm. Bus: 6 or 11.

Palazzo dei Musei ★ MUSEUM This sprawling complex of museums occupies an austere palace built between 1764 and 1771 for Francesco III d'Este. Several museums call the palace home, beginning with the **Lapidario Estense** (mostly old tombs) on the ground floor, open daily 8:30am to 7:30pm (free). If short of time, focus on the more rewarding Galleria Estense on the top floor, though you might also take a peek inside the **Biblioteca Estense** (www.cedoc.mo.it; ✆ **059-222248**), one of the greatest libraries in southern Europe. The library contains around 500,000 printed works, and an assortment of the most interesting volumes is kept under glass for visitors to inspect. Of these, the most celebrated is the 1,200-page *Bible of Borso d'Este,* bordered with stunning miniatures.

The **Galleria Estense** is most noted for its paintings from the Emilian and Bolognese schools from the 14th to the 18th centuries, but there are plenty of beauties from other schools to make this a worthy visit. The nucleus of the collection was acquired by the Este family during the heyday of their duchies in Ferrara and then Modena.

Gianlorenzo Bernini's bust of Francesco I kicks off the collection, which is laid out chronologically. Wander through the galleries and you'll spy two paintings of *Madonna and Child* by Botticelli; Correggio tackles the same subject nearby. There's a vivid fresco cycle from Nicolò dell'Abate, and in a gallery full of portraits, an image of *Francesco I d'Este* by Spanish master Velázquez. Raphael's dainty *Testa di Madonna* is encased in glass, and beyond here are large galleries dedicated to Tintoretto, and a tiny, gorgeous portable altar painted by El Greco. The final galleries feature huge Veronese canvases and paintings by the great Emilian artists of the 16th and 17th centuries, Guido Reni and Ludovico Carracci.

An illuminated manuscript at the Biblioteca Estense.

Largo Porta Sant' Agostino 337 (off Via Emilia). www.spsae-mo.beniculturali.it. ✆ **059-4395711.** Gallery admission 4€ adults, 2€ ages 18–25, free for children 17 and under. Library free admission. Gallery Mon 8:30am–2pm; Tues–Sat 8:30am–7:30pm; Sun 2–7:30pm. Library Mon–Thurs 8:30am–7:15pm; Fri 8:30am–6:45pm; Sat 8:30am–1:45pm.

Where to Eat

Eating in Modena restaurants is a real treat, but if you want to put together a wonderful picnic, pick your way through the food stalls of the outdoor market on **Via Albinelli,** open weekdays from 6:30am to 2pm and Saturday afternoons in summer from 5 to 7pm; if you miss it there's not much else to buy in the center.

Danilo ★★ MODENSE This restaurant has been justly popular with locals (Pavarotti was a regular) since it opened in 1934. Modena specialties dominate the menu: *tortelloni di zucca* (pumpkin tortelloni), *lasagne al forno* (baked lasagna), sausages and dumplings, and the classic/notorious *carrello dei bolliti,* a spread of various boiled meats. In fact, there's always lots of more familiar beef on offer, from a wonderfully light carpaccio to more substantial *osso buco* and steaks.

Via Coltellini 31. ✆ **059-225498.** Reservations recommended. Main courses 8€–16€. AE, MC, V. Mon–Sat 12:30–2pm and 7:30–10:30pm.

Hosteria Giusti ★★★ MODENSE This gastronomic treasure is one of celebrity chef's Mario Batali's favorites, for good reason. Adriano Morandi's exclusive restaurant has just four tables, and is open only at noon for lunch, while evenings are reserved for groups of between 16 and 24. The interior is designed to resemble a family home, all exposed beams and terra-cotta floors. Morandi's menu is constantly changing, but might include zucchini blossoms stuffed with risotto, thick cut pasta with cured pig's cheek, and homemade sausage *(zampone)* served with *zabaglione* (light custard made with Lambrusco).

The entrance is hidden within the main anchor of the Giusti empire, the equally enticing **Salumeria Giusti ★★** (Tues–Sat 9:30am–1pm and 5:15–7:30pm), where you can stock up on all manner of Modena specialties. Documents dated 1598 suggest this is Europe's oldest delicatessen. If the restaurant is

THE LAND OF motors

Modena lies at the heart of what is known as La Terra dei Motori, the "Land of Motors," home to all of Italy's famed sports car manufacturers. Many of the factories are accessible by public transport, but fans who intend to do the full pilgrimage really need a car. For hassle-free touring, contact **Motorstars** (www.motorstars.org; ✆ **059-921667**).

Ferrari was founded by Enzo Ferrari in 1929, going on to make some of the world's most sought-after sports cars: In 2009 a 1957 Testa Rossa was auctioned for $12.1 million, a world record at the time. Fans can visit the **Museo Ferrari** ★, Via Dino Ferrari 43 (www.ferrari.com; ✆ **0536-943204**), in Maranello (a suburb some 18km/11 miles from central Modena), which displays engines, trophies, and both antique and the latest Ferrari cars. You can also tour the Pista di Fiorano (the test track) and the Viale Enzo Ferrari (the factory itself). Admission is 13€ and opening hours are May to September daily 9:30am to 7pm, and October to April daily 9:30am to 6pm. Tours run daily at 12:30pm and 1:30pm, but you need to buy tickets in advance on the website.

Maserati was founded in Bologna in 1914, but is now based in Modena. You can view over 20 vintage Maserati cars at the **Museo Panini** (www.paninimotormuseum.it), the de facto Maserati museum in the Modena suburb of Cittanova (on the SS9). Highlights include a rare Maserati Tipo 6CM from the 1930s and a Maserati A6G/54 from the 1950s. You must make an appointment to visit: The museum is open March to October (closed Aug), Monday to Friday from 9:30am to 12:30pm and from 3:30 to 6:30pm, and Saturday from 9:30am to 12:30pm. Admission is free.

Comparative newcomer **Lamborghini** was founded by Ferruccio Lamborghini in 1963. The **Museo Lamborghini** (www.visit-lamborghini.com; ✆ **051-9597008**), Via Modena 12, opened in 2001 in the company's hometown of Sant' Agata Bolognese, halfway between Bologna and Modena. Admission is 13€ (students 10€), with a highly recommended tour of the actual factory 40€ (students 30€). The museum is usually open Monday to Friday 10am to 12:30pm and 1:30 to 5pm, but call ahead to confirm.

Finally, motorcycle manufacturer **Ducati** dates back to 1926. If you call in advance, you can visit the factory and the **Museo Ducati,** Via Cavalieri Ducati 3, in the Bologna suburb of Borgo Panigale (www.ducati.com; ✆ **051-6413111**). The museum and factory are open Monday to Friday 9:30am to 12:45pm and 2:30 to 5:15pm. On Saturdays you can visit the museum only, 10am to noon. Admission is 10€. From Bologna Central Station, take a taxi (15€–20€, around 20 min.).

not open, grab a coffee or *aperitivo* (5€ plus snacks) in the refined **Caffetteria Drogheria Giusti** ★ next door. The Hosteria's back entrance deposits you on narrow Vicolo Squallore, where you'll find the well-stocked Giusti **Bottiglieria** (wine cellar).

Via Farini 75/Vicolo Squallore 46. www.hosteriagiusti.it. ✆ **059-222533.** Main courses 12€–20€. AE, DC, MC, V. Tues–Sat noon–3pm. Closed Aug.

Osteria da Ermes ★★ MODENSE This Modena lunch-only institution is a real experience and very popular—get there early to avoid the long lines. Eccentric owner Ermes and his wife have been cooking up fresh food from the market for over 40 years here, chatting and offering advice and tips as they serve. There's no menu—Ermes will just tell you what they have that day. Dishes might include fried cod, stuffed bell peppers, and simple *tagliatelle* with mushrooms or *ragù*. Help yourself to some Lambrusco from the fridge.

Via Ganaceto 89. ✆ **059-238065.** No reservations. Fixed menu 20€–25€. No credit cards. Mon–Sat noon–3pm.

Osteria Francescana ★★★ INTERNATIONAL/VEGETARIAN In a city known for having some of the most demanding palates in Italy, chef Massimo Bottura satisfies, serving his contemporary, stylish cuisine on mismatched plates purchased in New York. Bottura has taken all he learned from a decade of work with Alain Ducasse, and has used it to forge his own style and unique dishes. One reviewer called his cream sauce "edible gold." He still makes his heavenly *Modenese tortellini* based on his grandmother's recipe, but every other dish is his own invention. Creations might include "razor clams," where the "clam" is made of seaweed and stuffed with real clams, scallops, and oysters; or an intense "rice surf and turf," sea urchin topped with rice in veal juice, black truffle, and pomegranate.

Via Stella 22. www.osteriafrancescana.it. ✆ **059-210118.** Reservations required. Main courses 18€–30€; fixed-price menu 90€–160€. AE, DC, MC, V. Mon–Fri 12:30–2pm and 8–10:30pm; Sat 8–10:30pm. Closed Jan and Aug.

Shopping

While in Modena consider picking up a bottle or two of the item that changed salad forever: **balsamic vinegar.** A short walk from the Duomo, **Fini,** Corso Canalchiaro 139 (www.store.hotelrealfini.it; ✆ **059-223320;** Mon–Sat 9am–1:30pm and 5–7:45pm, Sun 11:30am–1pm, closed Wed afternoon), sells bottles of Modena's aromatic variety, plus other fabulous food products. The really good stuff is made by **Acetaia Bompana di Vecchi ★★**, Via Vignolese 1704, in San Donnino, 10km (6¼ miles) south of the center near the Modena Sud exit of the A1 autostrada (www.bompana.com; ✆ **059-469008**). Their shop is open Monday to Saturday 8:30am to 12:30pm and 2 to 7pm. You can taste before you buy.

Balsamic vinegar for sale in Modena.

Entertainment & Nightlife

With fine wines, coffee, snacks, and live music, **Caffè Concerto ★**, Piazza Grande 26 (www.caffeconcertomodena.com; ✆ **059-222232**), is always a great place to start or end an evening. It's open daily 8am to 3am. Opera arrives in winter at the **Teatro Comunale,** Corso Canal Grande 85 (www.teatrocomunalemodena.it; ✆ **059-2033010** for reservations), and the summer brings a major opera festival.

Where to Stay

Hotel Cervetta 5 ★ With a perfect location in an old town house near Piazza Grande, this outstanding hotel is an incredible deal. Rooms are simple but elegant, with modern amenities and a stylish all-white color scheme, giving it a boutique feel. The healthy breakfast buffet is small but beautifully presented. As an added bonus for drivers, secure parking is right next door. Note that there is no elevator, so ask for a low floor if climbing stairs is an issue, and also that you'll only get local TV in the rooms.

Via Cervetta, 5, 41100 Modena. www.hotelcervetta5.com. ✆ **059-238447.** Fax 059-237209. 22 units. 85€–120€ double; 155€ triple. Breakfast 10€. AE, DC, MC, V. Parking 15€. **Amenities:** Bar. *In room:* A/C, TV, hair dryer, minibar, Wi-Fi (free).

Hotel Libertà A modern hotel wrapped in an aged exterior, this Best Western lodge is steps from the cathedral and the Palazzo Ducale. Marble and terra-cotta floors run throughout. The guest rooms favor floral wallpapers and blond-wood furniture; some top-floor rooms are made cozy by sloping ceilings with skylights. Each room provides a good night's sleep. Several restaurants are close, and the staff will make recommendations.

Via Blasia 10, 41100 Modena. www.hotelliberta.it. ✆ **059-222365.** Fax 059-222502. 51 units, shower only. 119€–190€ double; 149€–260€ triple. Rates include buffet breakfast. AE, DC, DISC, MC, V. Parking 20€. **Amenities:** Bar; concierge; room service. *In room:* A/C, TV, hair dryer, minibar, Wi-Fi (free).

Real Fini-Via Emilia ★ Real Fini is the top choice for most visiting businesspeople, as it offers the largest and best-accessorized rooms in town, though it lies just outside the historic center (10–15 min. walk). The hotel is imbued with sleek modern Italian styling, but the luxurious rooms feature all-wood paneling and Art Deco touches that hark back to a more glamorous era of travel. Free limos are on offer to whisk you to their feted sister restaurant, Baia del Re.

Via Emilia Est 441, 41100 Modena. www.hotelviaemilia.it. ✆ **059-2051511.** Fax 059-364804. 90 units. 110€–195€ double; 160€–288€ suite. AE, DC, MC, V. Parking 15€. **Amenities:** Bar; babysitting; exercise room; room service; sauna. *In room:* A/C, TV, hair dryer, minibar, Wi-Fi (3€ per hour).

UNA Hotel Modena ★★ Drivers should consider this superb hotel, located around 7km (4⅓ miles) from the historic center (9km/5½ miles from A1 exit Modena Nord), but offering the best accommodations in Modena. Nondrivers take heart; the hotel is just 495m (550 yards) from the Baggiovara train station, which has hourly connections to central Modena (20 min.). Renaissance it is not: The theme here is 100% contemporary Italian style, with modern, elegant rooms tricked out with flatscreen TVs, trendy reading lamps, and sleek bathrooms.

Via Luigi Settembrini 10, 41126 Modena. www.unahotels.it. ✆ **059-5139595.** Fax 059-5139577. 95 units. 109€ double; 189€ suite. Rates include buffet breakfast. AE, DC, MC, V. Free parking. **Amenities:** Restaurant; bar; exercise room; room service; sauna; spa. *In room:* A/C, TV, hair dryer, minibar, Wi-Fi (free).

PARMA ★

457km (283 miles) NW of Rome, 97km (60 miles) NW of Bologna, 121km (75 miles) SE of Milan

Parma was the home of Correggio, Il Parmigianino, Bodoni (of typeface fame), and Toscanini, and has also given us prosciutto (Parma ham) and of course, parmigiano (Parmesan) cheese. Parma rose in influence and power in the 16th century as the seat of the Farnese duchy, and is still one of the most prosperous cities in Italy.

Upon the extinction of the male Farnese line, Parma came under the control of the French Bourbons. Its most beloved ruler, Marie-Louise, widow of Napoleon and niece of Marie Antoinette, arrived in 1815 after the Congress of Vienna awarded her the city. Marie-Louise became a great patron of the arts, and much of the collection she acquired is on display at the Galleria Nazionale (see "Exploring Parma," below). Rising unrest in 1859 forced her abdication, and, in 1860, following a plebiscite, Parma was incorporated into the kingdom of Italy.

The city has also been a mecca for opera lovers such as Verdi, the great Italian composer whose works include *Il Trovatore* and *Aïda*. He was born in the small village of Roncole, north of Parma, in 1813. In time, his operas echoed through the Teatro Regio, the opera house that was built under the orders of Marie-Louise. Because of Verdi, Parma became a center of music, and even today the opera house is jampacked in season.

Essentials

GETTING THERE **By Train** Parma is served by the Milan Bologna **rail** line, with hourly trains arriving from Milan (trip time: 1½ hr.); the one-way fare starts at 9.75€. From Bologna, trains depart for Parma every 30 minutes or so (around 1 hr.), the one-way fare starts at 6.80€. There are only two or three direct trains a day from Florence (2 hr.); most journeys will require a change in Bologna. The one-way fare begins at 20€. For information and schedules, call ✆ **892021**.

By Car If you have a **car** and are starting out in Bologna, head northwest along A1. Don't drive into the old town without first contacting your hotel—without a special pass you'll be fined 90€. You can park on the street, outside the restricted area, where you see blue lines (not blue and white lines), or aim for the official parking lots: Goito, Toschi, Duc, Dus, and Via Abbeveratoia (around 1€–1.70€ per hour).

VISITOR INFORMATION The **tourist office** at Via Melloni 1A (http://turismo.comune.parma.it; ✆ **0521-218889**) is open Monday 9am to 1pm and 3 to 7pm, Tuesday to Saturday 9am to 7pm, and Sunday 9am to 1pm.

Exploring Parma

The compact center of Parma is easily explored on foot, with most of the sights within walking distance of the central Piazza Duomo and Palazzo della Pilotta. A short stroll across the Ponte Verdi and the Parma River lies the grassy expanse of the tranquil Parco Ducale.

Basilica di Santa Maria della Steccata ★ CHURCH This ornate 16th-century church is worth a peek for the impressive fresco cycle painted by Parmigianino between 1530 and 1539, on the arch above the presbytery. It depicts the Biblical parable of the wise and foolish virgins, enhanced with animal and plant motifs set against a red background. Later frescoes were completed by Michelangelo Anselmi (east apse, 1540s) and Barnardino Gatti (the dome, 1560).

Piazza della Steccata 9. ✆ **0521-234937.** Free admission. Daily 9am–noon and 3–6:30pm.

Battistero (Baptistery) ★★★ CHURCH Among the greatest Romanesque buildings in northern Italy, the baptistery was primarily the work of Benedetto Antelami. The project was begun in 1196, although it was only completed between 1302 and 1307. Made of salmon-colored Verona marble, it's spanned by four open tiers (the fifth is closed off). Inside, the baptistery is stunning, richly frescoed with biblical scenes: a *Madonna Enthroned* and a *Crucifixion.* Note also the touching image of Our Lady of Compassion, her long robe appearing to shield the children huddled below her.

Piazza del Duomo 7. www.cattedrale.parma.it. ✆ **0521-235886.** Admission 6€ adults, 7€ with Museo Diocesano; 4€ students, 5€ with Museo Diocesano. Daily 9am–12:30pm and 3–6:45pm.

Camera di San Paolo Correggio (1494–1534), one of Italy's greatest painters of the High Renaissance, frescoed this tiny chamber with vivid mythological scenes, cherubs, and Greek gods—including one of Diana over the fireplace, around 1519. The chamber forms part of the **Appartamento della Badessa,** a series of apartments that were once occupied by the abbesses of the former Benedictine Convento di San Paolo, though only the richly frescoed Stanza dell' Araldi—painted by local boy Alessandro Araldi in 1514—compares with Correggio's work.

Via Melloni 3 (off Strada Garibaldi). ✆ **0521-533221.** Admission 2€ adults, 1€ ages 18–25, children 17 and under free. Tues–Sun 8:30am–noon and 2–6pm.

Duomo ★★ CATHEDRAL Built in the Romanesque style in the 11th century, with 13th-century Lombard lions guarding its main porch, the dusty pink Duomo stands side by side with a campanile constructed in the Gothic-Romanesque style and completed in 1281. Inside, almost every inch is smothered in frescoes—the effect is utterly spellbinding. The octagonal cupola (bring 2€ to turn on the lights) was frescoed in the 1520s by that master of light and color, Correggio. His magnificent fresco, *Assumption of the Virgin,* foreshadows the baroque. In the transept to the right (on floor level) is a somber Romanesque bas-relief, *The Deposition from the Cross,* by Benedetto Antelami, each face bathed in sadness. Made in 1178, the bas-relief is the best-known work of the 12th-century artist, who was the most important sculptor of the Romanesque in northern Italy.

The **Museo Diocesano,** on the other side of the piazza, is a modern, well-presented collection of artifacts from the cathedral, and mosaics from the Palazzo Vescovile (bishop's palace), through the ages—highlights include a series of Antelami's sculptures from

Detail from the exterior of the Baptistery.

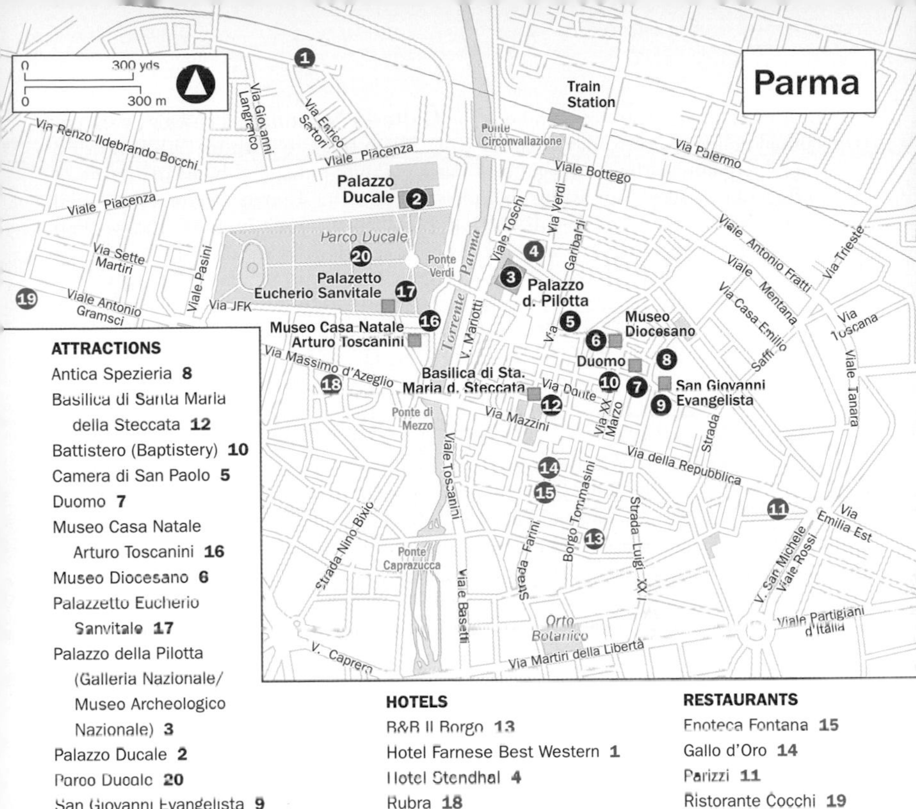

the Baptistery (p. 416), removed here for preservation—but you'll need to read Italian to make the most of this.

Piazza del Duomo 1. www.cattedrale.parma.it. ✆ **0521-235886.** Free admission. Daily 7:30am–12:30pm and 3–7pm. **Museo Diocesano:** Admission 5€ adults, 7€ with Battistero; 3€ students, 5€ with Battistero. Daily 9am–12:30pm and 3–6:30pm.

Museo Casa Natale Arturo Toscanini MUSEUM Toscanini was the greatest orchestral conductor of the first half of the 20th century. This is the house where the maestro was born in 1867, and where he spent his childhood. Today it's crammed with interesting mementos: his famous portrait by Giacomo Grosso (1916), his poncho, desk, and family portraits. One room is dedicated to the composers he worked with most closely: Puccini, Verdi, and Wagner. Upstairs it's the enigmatic black-and-white photographs capturing Toscanini in action, and a video of one of his performances, that really bring home his talent.

Via Rodolfo Tanzi 13. www.museotoscanini.it. ✆ **0521-285499.** Admission 2€ adults, 1€ students. Wed–Sat 9am–1pm and 2–6pm; Sun 2–6pm.

Palazzo della Pilotta: Galleria Nazionale and Museo Archeologico Nazionale ★★ MUSEUM Built in the 1580s, the fortresslike Palazzo della Pilotta housed the ruling Farnese family during Parma's Golden Age. Badly damaged by bombs in World War II, it has been restored and turned into a complex of museums.

The premier attraction here is the **Galleria Nazionale,** boasting an exceptional collection of work by Parma artists from the late 15th to 19th centuries, notably paintings by Correggio and Parmigianino, enhanced by a smattering of other old masters. Admission includes entry to the **Teatro Farnese,** a virtual jewel box, evocative of Palladio's theater at Vicenza. Built in 1618, the wooden structure was bombed in 1944 and has been wonderfully restored. If you want to visit only the theater, it costs 2€, and is open Tuesday to Sunday 8:30am to 2pm.

Beyond the theater, a carefully planned route takes in all the major galleries, a blend of medieval stone halls and modern spaces crafted from scaffolding, arranged chronologically from the early Renaissance on.

In Gallery 9 don't miss *La Scapigliata* ★★ (aka the "Female Head"), one of the most celebrated paintings by the Italian master of the Renaissance, **Leonardo da Vinci.** In Gallery 11 you'll find the work of Benedetto Antelami and the *Portrait of Erasmus of Rotterdam* (1530) by Hans Holbein, while Gallery 12 contains portraits by Bedoli, Caracci, and *Healing of the Blind Man* by El Greco.

Canaletto holds court in Gallery 13, but the rest of the collection comprises fairly mediocre baroque and mannerist work until the special section devoted to **Correggio** (Gallery 18). Here is Correggio's *Coronation,* a golden fresco that's a work of great beauty, and his *Madonna della Scodella* (with a bowl), with its agonized faces. Correggio's *Madonna della Scala* (of the stairs), the remains of a fresco, is also displayed. But his masterpiece here is *St. Jerome with the Madonna and Child.* Imbued with delicacy, it represents age, youth, and love—a gentle ode to tenderness. Look out also for one of Parmigianino's best-known paintings, *Turkish Slave,* the alluring portrait of a young woman.

Also in the *palazzo* is the **Museo Archeologico Nazionale.** It houses Egyptian sarcophagi; Etruscan vases; Roman- and Greek-inspired torsos; Bronze Age relics; and its best-known exhibit, the Tabula Alimentaria, a bronze-engraved tablet dating from the reign of Trajan and excavated at Velleia in Piacenza.

Piazzale della Pilotta 15. www.gallerianazionaleparma.it. ✆ **0521-233309** (Galleria Nazionale) or 0521-233718 (Museo Archeologico). Galleria Nazionale admission 6€ adults, 3€ ages 18–25, free for children 17 and under. Museo Archeologico admission 4€ adults, 2€ E.U. citizens 18–25, free for children 17 and under. Galleria Nazionale Tues–Sun 8:30am–2pm. Museo Archeologico Nov–May Tues–Fri 9am–5pm, Sat 9am–3pm, Sun 12:30–7:30pm; June–Oct Tues–Sun 9am–2pm.

Parco Ducale and the Palazzo Ducale ★★ PARK/PALACE The gravel paths, wide lawns, and splashing fountains of the **Parco Ducale,** across the river from the Palazzo Pilotta, provide a tranquil retreat from Parma's more crowded areas. The main attraction here is the stately **Palazzo Ducale,** which was transformed into a posh residence by Ottavio Farnese in the 16th century (it had previously been a medieval castle). Inside are some original frescoes in the Sala dell'Amore by Agostino Carracci, and later 18th century work by Benigno Bossi in the extraordinary Sala degli Uccelli. The palace was partially destroyed during World War II and later rebuilt.

On the south side of the park the far humbler **Palazzetto Eucherio Sanvitale** (✆ **0521-230267;** Jan–Feb and Nov–Dec 10am–1pm and 2–4pm, Mar–Apr and Oct 10am–1pm and 2–5pm, May–Sept 10am–1pm and 2–6pm; free admission) built around 1520, contains frescoes by Parmigianino depicting a *Madonna and Child,* recently restored, though most of the murals in other rooms are extremely faded.

Parco Ducale (Via dei Farnese). www.servizi.comune.parma.it. ✆ **0521-235311.** Park free admission. Palazzo Ducale admission 3€ adults, 1.50€ ages 24 and under. Palazzo Ducale Mon–Sat 9am–noon. Parco Ducale Apr–Oct daily 6am–midnight; Nov–Mar daily 7am–8pm.

San Giovanni Evangelista ★ CHURCH Behind the Duomo is this dimly lit, atmospheric church with a soaring campanile. After admiring the baroque facade, pass into the interior to see yet another cupola by Correggio. From 1520 to 1524, the High Renaissance master depicted the *Vision of San Giovanni*. Vasari, author of *Lives of the Artists* and a contemporary of Correggio, liked it so much that he became completely carried away in his praise, suggesting the "impossibility" of an artist conjuring up such a divine work and marveling that it could actually have been painted "with human hands." Correggio also painted a St. John with pen in hand, in the transept (over the door to the left of the cuploa). Il Parmigianino, the second Parmesan master, did some frescoes in the chapel at the left of the entrance.

To the left of the main church entrance is the unassuming gateway to the **Monastero San Giovanni Evangelista** (Mon–Sat 8:30am–noon and 3–6pm, Sun 10am–1pm and 3:30–6pm; free admission), containing three serene 16th-century cloisters. You can also visit the Monumental Library of 1523, richly frescoed with giant maps of Italy, the Holy Land, and Greece, and the Refectory containing Bedoli's *Last Supper*.

Around the corner at Borgo Pipa 1, the **Antica Spezieria,** or "Old Pharmacy" (✆ **0521-233309;** 2€ adults, 1€ ages 18–25, free for children 17 and under; Tues–Sun 8:30am–2pm), is where monks made potions for some 6 centuries, a practice that lasted until the closing years of the 19th century. Mortars and jars, some as old as the Middle Ages, line the shelves.

Piazzale San Giovanni 1. ✆ **0521-235311.** Free admission to church and monastery. Church Mon–Sat 8–11:45am and 3–7pm; Sun 8am–12:30pm and 3–7:45pm.

Where to Eat

The chefs of Parma are acclaimed throughout Italy. Of course, Parmigiano-Reggiano has added just the right touch to millions of Italian meals, and the word *parmigiana* or Parmesan is quite familiar to English-speaking diners. Try to take a food tour of the region if you can (see "The Land of Cured Meats and the King of Cheese," below).

Gallo d'Oro ★ PARMIGIANA This is our favorite trattoria. It has an unpretentious decor with flea-market items such as antique cinema posters and old-fashioned toys. Downstairs is a bodega where locals pile in to taste the wine of the region, especially Lambrusco, which seems to go with anything served in Parma. Start with *salumi misti*, a variety of locally cured hams. All the pasta dishes are homemade, including *tortelli ripieni* (pasta stuffed with cottage cheese and fresh spinach) and the ubiquitous pumpkin ravioli. For a main course, I recommend the tender roasted lamb stuffed with bread, cheese, and eggs; or the aubergine casserole.

Borgo della Salina 3. ✆ **0521-208846.** Reservations recommended. Main courses 8.50€–11€. AE, DC, MC, V. Mon–Sat noon–3pm and 7–midnight; Sun noon–3pm.

Parizzi ★ PARMIGIANA/ITALIAN The building that houses Parizzi dates from 1551, when it first opened as an inn; the current restaurant was opened in 1958 by the father of the present owner. Seated under the skylit patio, you'll

The Land of Cured Meats and the King of Cheese

Parma is the home of Parmigiano-Reggiano cheese, Prosciutto di Parma ham, fine wine, and balsamic vinegar. Taking a **guided tour** is the best way to appreciate not only the quality and varieties of what's produced here, but also the great skill and effort required to make it. **Food Valley** (www.foodvalleytravel.com; ✆ **0521-798515**), Viale Fratti 38D in Parma, offers a range of tours from 1 to several days. The 1-day Food Valley Gourmet Tour takes in a Parmesan dairy, prosciutto factory, Torrechiara castle, Colli di Parma wine tasting, and a visit to a balsamic vinegar producer. Prices start at 110€ per person. Friendly competition is provided by the equally qualified **Parma Golosa Gourmet Tours** (www.parmagolosa.it; ✆ **0521-1910007**), with a range of shorter, specialized food tours. For more information about Parma cheeses, contact the **Consorzio del Parmigiano Reggiano,** Via dei Mercati 9 (www.parmigiano-reggiano.it; ✆ **0521-292700**). For insights into the dressing and curing of Parma hams, contact the **Consorzio del Prosciutto di Parma,** Via dell'Arpa 8B (www.prosciuttodiparma.com; ✆ **0521-246211**).

enjoy rich cuisine that's among the best in town. After you're shown to a table, a cart filled with antipasti is wheeled before you, containing shellfish, stuffed vegetables, and marinated salmon. Then you might be tempted by *culatello,* cured ham made from sliced haunch of wild boar; a pasta served with a sauce of herbs and Parmigiano-Reggiano; a parmigiano soufflé with white truffles; or pheasant ravioli with black truffles.

Strada della Repubblica 71. www.ristoranteparizzi.it. ✆ **0521-285952.** Reservations required. Main courses 18€–28€; 6-course degustation menu 70€. AE, DC, MC, V. Tues–Sun noon–2:30pm and 7:30–10:30pm. Closed 3 weeks in Aug and Jan 8–15.

Parma Rotta ★ 🎁 PARMIGIANA If you don't mind driving 1.6km (1 mile) out of town along the road to Langhirano, this is a Parma classic. It's the best neighborhood trattoria I know for sampling some of the hearty and flavor-filled dishes of the region, such as sautéed duck breast—slightly rare—served with a combination fruit-and-vegetable flavoring. No one knows for sure how old the building housing the restaurant is, but everything has had a century or so to mellow out. The spit-roasted lamb or the roast smoked pork is reason enough to come out here, although I'm also fond of the grilled beef cooked in a wood-stoked oven. For a first course, many locals prefer *tortelli di erbetta,* pasta stuffed with fresh greens.

Via Langhirano 158. www.parmarotta.com. ✆ **0521-966738.** Reservations recommended. Main courses 15€–25€. AE, DC, MC, V. Tues–Sat noon–2:30pm and 8–10:30pm.

Ristorante Cocchi ★★ 🎁 PARMIGIANA This is the local foodies choice for best cuisine in town. Don't be put off by the unlikely location inside a hotel on the far side of the ring road enveloping the city. When you arrive, you may think you're at the wrong address, but press on for an amazing culinary discovery.

Start with *strolghino,* a thin salami made from lean leg meat. It's carved tableside and is delectable. The rice dishes are without equal in town. Savarin is Parmesan- and risotto-filled "envelopes" of cooked ham, veal *polpettini,* and a porcini ragout. The *bomba di riso* is marinated pigeon that has been braised and deboned. These ingredients are layered inside a rice-lined dome and baked. Save room for the delectable *amaretti* (macaroons) for dessert.

16A Viale Gramsci. www.hoteldaniel.biz. ✆ **0521-995147.** Reservations required. Main courses 9€–24€. AE, DC, MC, V. Sun–Fri noon–2:30pm and 7:30–10pm. Closed Sat.

Shopping

Parma's most famous food product—parmigiano (Parmesan) cheese, the best being Parmigiano-Reggiano—is savored all over the world. Virtually every corner market sells thick wedges of the stuff, but if you're looking to buy your cheese in a special setting, head for the **Salumeria Garibaldi,** Via Garibaldi 42 (www.specialitadiparma.it; ✆ **0521-235606**), open Monday to Saturday 8am to 8pm. You might also take a walk through the city's **food market** at Piazza Ghiaia, near the Palazzo della Pilotta; it's open Monday through Saturday 8am to 1pm and 3 to 7pm.

Enoteca Fontana, Strada Farini 24A, sells bottles from virtually every vineyard in the region, and the staff is extremely knowledgeable (see "Entertainment & Nightlife" below).

Entertainment & Nightlife

If you'd like to sample a glass or two of great wine, head for atmospheric **Enoteca Fontana ★**, Strada Farini 24A (✆ **0521-286037**), open Tuesday to Thursday 9am to 3pm and 5 to 10pm, and Friday and Saturday 9am to 3pm and 5 to 10:30pm (closed Aug). You can stand at the ancient old bar or take a seat at one of the long communal tables. Sample from a list of hundreds of wines from Emilia-Romagna, many of them from the immediate region. You might decide to order a light meal, too, from the short menu of panini, ham-and-cheese platters, and pastas.

At **Bacco Verde,** Via Cavallotti 33 (✆ **0521-230487**), sandwiches, glasses of beer, and a wide selection of Italian wines are dispensed in a cramped but convivial setting ringed with antique masonry. It's open Monday to Thursday noon to 2pm and 7pm to 1am, and Saturday to Sunday 7pm to 1am.

Cheese and sausages for sale at Salumeria Garibaldi.

SAN MARINO: THE WORLD'S smallest REPUBLIC

With an area of just 62 sq. km (24 sq. miles) and an estimated population of around 30,000, **San Marino** is the world's smallest republic and an essential day trip from the Adriatic coast (San Marino is the third smallest country in Europe, with only Vatican City and Monaco being smaller).

Though it really is an independent, sovereign nation, you'd never guess it: San Marino is completely encircled by Italy, everyone speaks Italian, and there are no customs or border controls. Apart from the sheer novelty of a visit, the old capital (aka **Città di San Marino**), with its narrow, cobbled streets, occupies a dramatic perch high above the plain—make sure you go on a clear day. Perhaps the most revealing sign that you've left Italy is the profusion of duty-free shops, many sporting Cyrillic billboards to attract the hordes of Russian tourists that seem to love coming here.

Make sure you visit the **Museo di Stato,** Piazzetta del Titano 1 (www.museidistato.sm; ✆ **0549-883835;** Sept–May daily 9am–5pm, June–Aug daily 8am–8pm; free admission), with its mixture of art and historical exhibits gathered from all over this tiny nation. The **Museo di San Francesco,** Via Basilicius (Apr–Sept daily 8am–8pm, Oct–Mar daily 9am–5pm; 3€), houses minor works of art saved from San Marino's churches in a pretty 14th-century cloister. Finally, be sure to clamber up to the two towers high above the city, the **Castello della Guaita** and the **Castello della Cesta** (both Apr–Sept daily 8am–8pm, Oct–Mar daily 8:50am–5pm; 3€, or 4.50€ for joint admission), some 750m (2,460 ft.) above sea level. A **Funivia** (cable car) connects the Old Town every 15 minutes with the less touristy **Borgo Maggiore** down the mountain (2.80€, or 4.50€ round-trip), where you can pick up the buses back to Rimini.

Getting there: The seaside resort of **Rimini** is the main gateway to San Marino, easily accessible by train from Bologna and Pesaro. **Buses** depart the Rimini train station every hour (Mon–Sat 8:10am–7:25pm), less frequently on Sundays, for the 45-minute trip to San Marino—don't get off the bus till the last stop, just outside the Old Town. One-way fares are 4€. Call ✆ **0541-662069** to confirm times.

Life in Parma extends beyond munching on strips of salty ham and cheese. The **Teatro Regio,** Via Garibaldi 16, near Piazza della Pace (www.teatroregioparma.org; ✆ **0521-039399**), is the site of concerts throughout the year.

In the mood for dancing? Head for **Dadaumpa,** Via Emilio Lepido 48 (www.dadaumpa.com; ✆ **0521-483813**), a stylish and lighthearted venue for dance tunes on the eastern outskirts of town (take a taxi).

Where to Stay

B&B Il Borgo ★ This is actually a renovated two-story apartment in an old town house, perfect for experiencing the city like a local for a few days. The location is central, within walking distance of everything, and the apartment is fully equipped: Upstairs is the bed and bathroom, while downstairs is the kitchen with microwave and washer/dryer. A desktop computer and printer is available to surf the Internet. There's no breakfast as such, but owner Enza

Borelli makes sure the fridge is stocked with fresh fruit and yogurt, and there's coffee for the espresso maker.

Borgo Claudio Merulo 12, 43100 Parma. www.ilborgobb.it. ✆ **0521-639554.** Fax 0521-639554. 1 unit. 70€–90€ double. AE, DC, MC, V. Parking 10€. *In room:* A/C, TV, hair dryer, minibar, Wi-Fi (free).

Hotel Farnese Best Western This chain hotel is in a quiet area convenient to the town center (around 1.6km/1 mile/5 min. by taxi), but also the autostrada, airport, and fairs. The guest rooms, ranging from small to medium, are fairly standard chain fare, but modern and cozy. There is free parking outside the hotel, but you have to pay for the covered parking underneath it. Service is always good, and the swimming pool is a nice extra (it's the only hotel with a pool close to the city center).

Via Reggio 51A, 43100 Parma. www.farnesehotel.it. ✆ **800/780-7234** in the U.S. and Canada, 800-820080 toll-free in Italy, or 0521-994247. Fax 0521-992317. 76 units. 124€–140€ double. Rates include buffet breakfast. AE, DC, MC, V. Free parking outdoors; 8€ indoors. **Amenities:** Restaurant; bar; babysitting; bikes; exercise room; pool; room service. *In room:* A/C, TV, hair dryer, minibar, Wi-Fi (free).

Hotel Stendhal This is all about location and value for money: The Stendhal sits on a square near the opera house, a few minutes' walk from all the important sights and 6 blocks south of the train station. The guest rooms are well maintained and furnished with contemporary pieces that are reproductions of various styles, ranging from rococo to provincial. Try for one of the traditional-looking rooms with classic furnishings.

Via Bodoni 3, 43100 Parma. www.hotelstendhal.it. ✆ **0521 208057.** Fax 0521-285655. 62 units, 23 with shower only. 99€–130€ double. Rates include continental breakfast. AE, DC, MC, V. Parking 14€. **Amenities:** Restaurant; bar; babysitting; room service; Wi-Fi (free, in lobby). *In room:* A/C, TV, hair dryer, minibar.

Rubra ★ Another cozy complex of apartments worthy of consideration that is just a 5-minute walk from all the main sights in the city center. Housed in a building dating back to the 15th century, the apartments are clean, comfortable, and come with access to a tranquil garden (and even bikes and laptops if you ask). All have full kitchens (free coffee, tea, and water) and washing machines, and the upstairs apartments have outdoor terraces. Ask the owners about hooking you up with tours of the local cheese and ham makers.

Strada Massimo d'Azeglio 48, 43100 Parma. www.bbrubra.com. ✆/fax **0521-289140.** 5 units. 80€ double. Breakfast 5€. No credit cards. Parking 10€. **Amenities:** Bikes. *In room:* A/C, TV/DVD, hair dryer, kitchen, minibar, Wi-Fi (free).

8

VENICE

Few cities in the world are one of a kind, and in that tight fraternity several stand out, perhaps none more than Venice, formerly the Most Serene Republic of Venice. To see for the first time this most improbable cityscape of canals, bridges, gondolas, and stone palaces that seem to float on water is to experience one of life's great pleasures. To see it a second, third, and fourth time is to appreciate Venice's greatness. Tucked away in Italy's northeastern corner at the upper reaches of the Adriatic Sea, it is hard to imagine how Venice parlayed its position into becoming a great maritime power. But then again, this city is full of surprises—from the grandeur of Piazza San Marco, to the splendid solitude of Cannaregio's canal-side quays and Rialto's vibrant fish market.

Things to Do After studying **Piazza San Marco,** unquestionably one of the world's great squares both for its beauty and pageantry, see the breathtaking mosaics in **St. Mark's Basilica** and ride the elevator to the top of the **bell tower** for a commanding view of the city. Titian, Giorgione, and Tintoretto feature prominently in the **Accademia Gallery** and in numerous churches, while a rich collection of 20th-century paintings and sculptures can be seen at the **Peggy Guggenheim Collection.** A visit to the outer reaches of Castello, Dorsoduro, and Cannaregio gives you a peek at what it's really like to live in this unique city. A **gondola ride** is, perhaps, cliché, but it is also likely to be one of your best Venetian memories.

Relaxation Put on your walking shoes and get lost along the back *calli* (streets), uncrowded *campi* (squares), and hidden *canali* (canals); turn left when the signs to the sights say to go right and in a flash you will encounter the true, living, breathing side of Venice. With nary a car in sight, getting lost has never been this relaxing. Consider coming in winter; while often cold and damp, it just might afford you the memorable experience of walking on planks above the *acqua alta* (high water).

Restaurants & Dining While Venetians, like all Italians, love to linger over a proper meal of *primo* and *secondo* (most likely one or both made with fish), this city has garnered fame with its *cicchetti,* tapaslike snacks that are eaten standing at *bacari* (wine bars) and washed down with a glass of *ombra* (wine). *Bacari* are everywhere, but one of the best spots to find them is on the **San Polo** side of the Rialto bridge, where they are frequented by those working in the nearby fish market.

Nightlife & Entertainment There are a few pubs around town and even a dance club, but for the best nightlife, grab a gelato (or a bottle of wine and a few glasses) and head to Piazza San Marco, where you can listen to the music

PREVIOUS PAGE: **The Bridge of Sighs (Ponte dei Sospiri).**

Boats tied along one of Venice's canals.

emanating from the cafes for free. Or better yet, seek out one of the numerous *campi* (squares) sprinkled around the city. Alternatively, dress up for an opera at **La Fenice.**

THE BEST TRAVEL EXPERIENCES IN VENICE

- **Picnicking at the Punta della Dogana:** Eating in Venice can get expensive, something that will make your cheap picnic here at the point where the Grand Canal meets the Venetian lagoon that much more perfect. Nearby Campo San Vio offers a valid alternative. See p. 454.
- **Viewing Venice from the top of the Campanile di San Marco:** While you think you may know Venice after having cruised the canals and traipsed through the alleys, the view from the top of the city's tallest and most famous bell tower will give you a new perspective you won't easily forget. See p. 446.
- **Peeking inside Venice's royal palace:** With so much to see outside, you may be tempted to skip the Itinerari Segreti guided tour of the Palazzo Ducale. Fight that temptation. The tour gives intriguing insight into how the doges ruled Venice through the centuries. Secret passageways and torture chambers will provide fun for the whole family. See p. 447.
- **Exploring the city during Carnevale:** For a taste of what Venice might have been like during the glory days of La Serenissima Republic, don a mask and walk through town during the final days (and nights) of Carnevale. Take time to listen to some of the concerts that reverberate through many of the city's *campi* well into the evenings. See p. 464.
- **Celebrating the end of the plague at the Festa del Redentore:** For more than 400 years, Venetians have been taking time out of their busy July schedules to celebrate the end of the 1577 plague. Walking across the wide Giudecca canal on a temporary bridge made of boats and seeing Venice under a barrage of fireworks is unforgettable. See p. 465.

ESSENTIALS

Getting There

BY PLANE You can fly into Venice from North America via Rome or Milan with **Alitalia** or a number of other airlines, or by connecting through a major European city with European carriers. No-frills carrier **easyJet** (www.easyjet.com) flies direct from London much cheaper than the major airlines, as does **Ryanair** (www.ryanair.com), though the latter sometimes uses the airport in nearby Treviso (a 1-hr. bus ride to Venice).

Flights land at the **Aeroporto Marco Polo,** 7km (4¼ miles) north of the city on the mainland (www.veniceairport.it; ✆ **041-260-9260**). There are two bus alternatives: The **ATVO airport shuttle bus** (www.atvo.it; ✆ **0421-594-671**) connects with Piazzale Roma not far from Venice's Santa Lucia train station (and the closest point to Venice's attractions accessible by car or bus). Buses leave for/from the airport about every 30 minutes, cost 5€, and make the trip in about 20 minutes. The less expensive local public **ACTV bus no. 5** (✆ **041-2424**) costs 2€, takes 30 to 45 minutes, and runs between two and four times an hour depending on the time of day. Buy tickets for either at the newsstand just inside the terminal from the signposted bus stop. With either bus, you'll have to walk to or from the final stop at Piazzale Roma to the nearby ***vaporetto*** (water bus) stop for the final connection to your hotel. It's rare to see porters around who'll help with luggage, so pack light.

A **land taxi** from the airport to the Piazzale Roma (where you get the *vaporetto*) will run about 40€.

The most fashionable and traditional way to arrive in Piazza San Marco is by sea. For 15€, 13€ if you buy online, the **Cooperative San Marco/ Alilaguna** (www.alilaguna.it; ✆ **041-240-1701**) operates a large *motoscafo* (shuttle boat) service from the airport with stops at Murano and the Lido before arriving after about 1 hour and 15 minutes in Piazza San Marco. This *Linea Blu* (the blue line) runs almost every 30 minutes from about 6am to midnight. The *Linea Arancio* (orange line) has the same frequency, costs the same, and takes the same amount of time to arrive at San Marco, but gets there through the Grand Canal (Canal Grande), which is much more spectacular and offers the possibility to get off at one of the stops along the Grand Canal. This might be convenient to your hotel and could save you having to take another means of transportation. If you arrive at Piazza San Marco and your hotel isn't in the area, you'll have to make a connection at the *vaporetto* launches. (Your hotel can help you with the specifics if you booked before you left home.)

A **private water taxi** (20–30 min. to/from the airport) is convenient but costly—there is a fixed 100€ fee to arrive in the city, for up to four passengers with one bag each (10€ more for each extra person up to a maximum of 12). It's worth considering if you're pressed for time, have an early flight, are carrying a lot of luggage (a Venice no-no), or can split the cost with a friend or two. It may be able to drop you off at the front (or side) door of your hotel or as close as it can maneuver given your hotel's location (check with the hotel before arriving). Your taxi captain should be able to tell you before boarding just how close he can get you. Try the **Corsorzio Motoscafi Venezia** (www.motoscafivenezia.it; ✆ **041-522-2303**) or **Venezia Taxi** (www.veneziataxi.it; ✆ **041-723-112**).

BY TRAIN Trains from Rome (3¾ hr.), Milan (2½ hr.), Florence (2 hr.), and all over Europe arrive at the **Stazione Venezia Santa Lucia.** To get there, all must pass through (though not necessarily stop at) a station marked Venezia-Mestre. Don't be confused: Mestre is a charmless industrial city that's the last stop on the mainland. Occasionally trains end in Mestre, in which case you have to catch one of the frequent 10-minute shuttles connecting with Venice; it's inconvenient, so when you book your ticket, confirm that the final destination is Venezia Santa Lucia.

On exiting, you'll find the Grand Canal immediately in front of you, a sight that makes for a heart-stopping first impression. You'll find the docks for a number of *vaporetti* lines (the city's public ferries or "water buses") to your left and right. Head to the booths to your left, near the bridge, to catch either of the two lines plying the Grand Canal: the no. 2 express, which stops only at the San Marcuola, Rialto Bridge, San Tomà, San Samuele, and Accademia before hitting San Marco (26 min. total); and the no. 1, which makes 13 stops before arriving at San Marco (a 33-min. trip). Both leave every 10 minutes or so, but in the mornings before 9am and the evenings after 8pm the no. 2 sometimes stops short at Rialto, meaning you'll have to disembark and hop on the next no. 1 or 2 that comes along to continue to San Marco.

Note: The *vaporetti* go in two directions from the train station: left down the Grand Canal toward San Marco—which is the (relatively) fast and scenic way—and right, which also eventually gets you to San Marco (at the San Zaccaria stop) if you are on the 2, but takes more than twice as long because it goes the long way around Dorsoduro (and serves mainly commuters). If you get the no. 1 going to the right from the train station, it will go only one more stop before it hits its terminus at Piazzale Roma.

BY BUS Though rail travel is more convenient and commonplace, Venice is serviced by long-distance buses from all over mainland Italy and some international cities. The final destination is Piazzale Roma, where you'll need to pick up *vaporetto* no. 1 or no. 2 (as described above) to connect you with stops in the heart of Venice and along the Grand Canal.

BY CAR The only wheels you'll see in Venice are those attached to luggage. Venice is a city of canals and narrow alleys. **No cars are allowed,** or more to the point, no cars could drive through the narrow streets and over the footbridges—even the police, fire department, and ambulance services use boats. Arriving in Venice by car is problematic and expensive—and downright exasperating if it's high season and the parking facilities are full (they often are). You can drive across the Ponte della Libertà from Mestre to Venice, but you can go no farther than Piazzale Roma at the Venice end, where many garages eagerly await your euros. The rates vary with, for example, the public **ASM garage** (www.asmvenezia.it; ✆ **041-272-7111**) charging 25€ for a 24-hour period, while private outfit **Garage San Marco** (www.garagesanmarco.it; ✆ **041-523-2213**) costs 30€ for 24 hours. Some garages also have hourly rates.

Vaporetti lines 1 and 2, described above, both stop at Piazzale Roma before continuing down the Grand Canal to the train station and, eventually, Piazza San Marco.

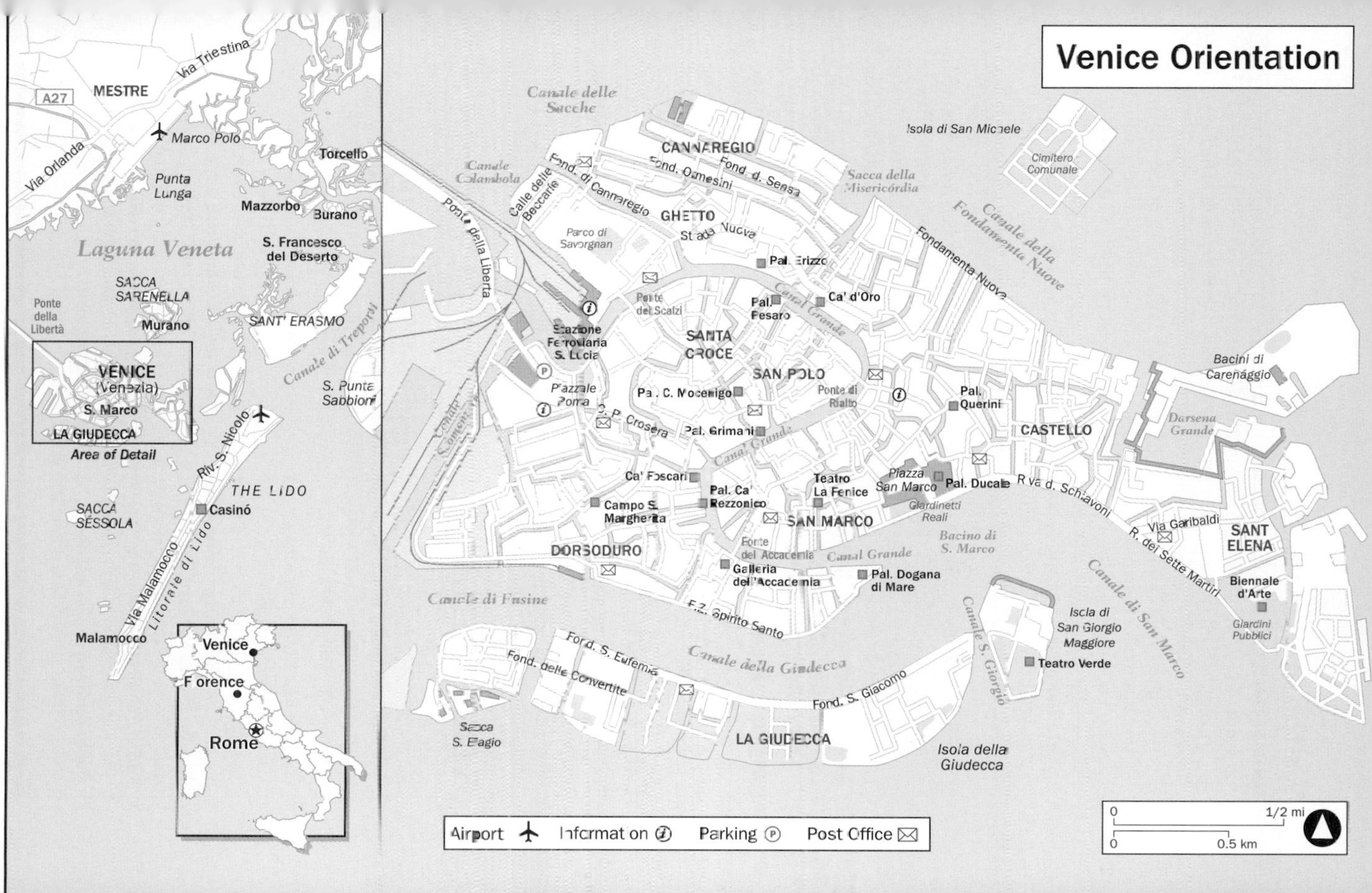

Venice Orientation
MESTRE
A27
Via Triestina
Via Orlanda
Marco Polo
Torcello
Punta Lunga
Mazzorbo
Burano
Laguna Veneta
S. Francesco del Deserto
SACCA SARENELLA
Ponte della Libertà
Murano
SANT' ERASMO
Canale di Treporti
VENICE (Venezia)
S. Marco
LA GIUDECCA
Area of Detail
S. Punta Sabbioni
Riv. S. Nicolo
THE LIDO
SACCA SESSOLA
Casinó
Via Malamocco
Litorale di Lido
Malamocco
Venice
Florence
Rome
Canale delle Sacche
Canale Colombola
Calle delle Beccarie
Fond. di Cannaregio
CANNAREGIO
Fond. Ormesini
Fond. d. Sensa
GHETTO
Strada Nuova
Parco di Savorgnan
Ponte della Libertà
Sacca della Misericordia
Isola di San Michele
Cimitero Comunale
Canale della Fondamenta Nuove
Fondamenta Nuova
Pal. Erizzo
Ca' d'Oro
Pal. Fesaro
Ponte dei Scalzi
Canal Grande
Stazione Ferroviaria S. Lucia
SANTA CROCE
SAN POLO
Piazzale Roma
Pal. C. Mocenigo
Ponte di Rialto
Pal. Querini
Bacini di Carenaggio
Darsena Grande
CASTELLO
S. P. Crosera
Pal. Grimani
Ca' Foscari
Pal. Ca' Rezzonico
Teatro La Fenice
Piazza San Marco
Pal. Ducale
R. va d. Schiavoni
Giardinetti Reali
Campo S. Margherita
SAN MARCO
Via Garibaldi
SANT ELENA
Bacino di S. Marco
R. dei Sette Martiri
DORSODURO
Ponte del Accademia
Canal Grande
Galleria dell'Accademia
Pal. Dogana di Mare
Biennale d'Arte
Canale di San Marco
Canale di Fusine
Isola di San Giorgio Maggiore
Giardini Pubblici
F.Z. Spirito Santo
Canale S. Giorgio
Fond. S. Eufemia
Fond. delle Convertite
Canale della Giudecca
Teatro Verde
Fond. S. Giacomo
Sacca S. Biagio
LA GIUDECCA
Isola della Giudecca
Airport
Information
Parking
Post Office
0 1/2 mi
0 0.5 km

Visitor Information

TOURIST OFFICES The main office is on Fondamenta San Lorenzo, 5 minutes from Piazza San Marco (www.turismovenezia.it; © **041-529-8711;** *vaporetto:* San Zaccaria). It's open daily from 10am to 6pm. During peak season, a small info booth with erratic hours operates in the arrivals hall at the Marco Polo Airport. You might be better off going to private agencies that often offer help more willingly than the official tourist offices, including with booking hotels for a small fee. **Venezia Si** (© **041-522-2264**) has a few offices around town, including one inside the train station on your left just before you exit. It is open Monday to Friday 8am to 7pm, and Saturday and Sunday 9am to 1pm and 2 to 5:30pm.

The tourist office's *LEO Bussola* brochure is useful for museum hours and events, but their map helps you find only *vaporetto* lines and stops. (It's well worth buying a street map at a news kiosk; see "Getting Around," below.) More useful is the info-packed monthly *Un Ospite di Venezia* (www.unospitedivenezia.it); most hotels have copies. Also keep an eye out for the ubiquitous posters around town with exhibit and concert schedules. The classical concerts held mostly in churches are touristy but fun and are advertised by an army of costumed touts handing out leaflets on highly trafficked streets.

WEBSITES The city's official tourist-board site is **www.turismovenezia.it**; the official site of the city government (also full of good resources) is **www.comune.venezia.it**. A good privately maintained site is **www.meetingvenice.it**.

City Layout

Keep in mind as you wander seemingly hopelessly among the *calli* (streets) and *campi* (squares) that the city wasn't built to make sense to those on foot but rather to those plying its canals. No matter how good your map and sense of

VENICE BY THE numbers

Central Venice is divided by the city's longest (4km/2½ miles) and widest (30–70m/98–230 ft.) waterway, the Grand Canal. Its 118 islands are separated by approximately 170 canals and connected by some 430 footbridges, mostly stone with iron balustrades added in the 19th century.

Only four bridges cross the Grand Canal: the **Ponte degli Scalzi,** just outside and to the left of the train station; the elegant white marble **Ponte Rialto** (the most recognizable bridge in Venice and, for centuries, the only one over the Grand Canal), connecting the districts of San Marco and San Polo; the wooden **Ponte Accademia,** connecting the Campo Santo Stefano area of the San Marco neighborhood with the Accademia museum across the way in Dorsoduro; and, since late 2008, the futuristic **Ponte della Costituzione** (a.k.a. the Calatrava bridge, after famed Spanish architect Santiago Calatrava, who designed it), which you will see around the corner to your right when you exit the train station.

The Scope of Venice

Central Venice refers to the built-up block of islands in the lagoon's center, including St. Mark's, the train station, and everything else in the six main *sestieri* (districts) that make up the bulk of the tourist city. Greater Venice includes all the inhabited islands of the lagoon—central Venice plus Murano, Burano, Torcello, and the Lido. The lagoon comprises everything, from the city to the mud flats to the fish farms to the dozens of abandoned or uninhabited islets.

direction, time after time you'll get lost. Just view it as an opportunity to stumble across Venice's most intriguing corners and vignettes.

Venice lies 4km (2½ miles) from terra firma, connected to the mainland burg of Mestre by the Ponte della Libertà, which leads to Piazzale Roma. Snaking through the city like an inverted S is the **Grand Canal,** the wide main artery of aquatic Venice.

The city is divided into six *sestieri* ("sixths," or districts or wards): **Cannaregio, Castello, San Marco, San Polo, Santa Croce,** and **Dorsoduro.** In addition to the six *sestieri* that cluster around the Grand Canal there are a host of other islands in the Venice lagoon. Opposite Piazza San Marco and Dorsoduro is **La Giudecca,** a tranquil, mostly residential and working-class place that is administratively part of Dorsoduro and offers great views of Piazza San Marco.

The **Lido di Venezia** is the city's sandy beach; it's a popular summer destination and holds a concentration of seasonal hotels. **San Michele,** located just off of the Cannaregio and Castello *sestieri*, is the cemetery island where such celebrities as Stravinsky and Diaghilev are buried.

Murano, Burano, and **Torcello** are popular destinations northeast of the city and easily accessible by *vaporetto*. Since the 13th century, Murano has exported its glass products worldwide; it's an interesting trip, but if your scope is a glass chandelier or something similar, you can do just as well in "downtown" Venice's myriad glass stores. Fishing village Burano is dotted with colorful houses and is famous for its lace, an art now practiced by very few island women. Torcello is the most remote and least populated. The 40-minute boat ride is worthwhile for history and art buffs, who'll be awestruck by the Byzantine mosaics of the cathedral (some of Europe's finest outside Ravenna). The cathedral's foundation dates to the 7th century, making this the oldest Venetian monument in existence.

The industrial city of **Mestre,** on the mainland, is the gateway to Venice, and while it holds no reason for exploration, in a pinch its host of inexpensive hotels is worth consideration when Venice's are full.

Neighborhoods in Brief

Based on a tradition dating from the 12th century, for tax-related purposes, the city has officially been divided into six *sestieri* that have basically been the same since 1711. The Grand Canal neatly divides them into three on each bank.

SAN MARCO The central *sestiere* shares the side of the Grand Canal with Castello and Cannaregio, anchored by the magnificent Piazza San Marco and St. Mark's Basilica to the south and the Rialto Bridge to the north; it's the most visited (and, as a result, the most expensive) of the *sestieri*. It's the commercial, religious, and political heart of the city and has been for more than a millennium. It is also its musical heart, home to the legendary La

A Note on Addresses

Within each *sestiere* is a most original system of numbering the *palazzi,* using one continuous string of 6,000 or so numbers. The format for addresses in this chapter is the official mailing address: the *sestiere* name followed by the building number in that district, followed by the name of the street or *campo* on which you'll find that address—for example, San Marco 1471 (Salizada San Moisè) means the mailing address is San Marco 1471, and you'll find it in the San Marco district on Salizada San Moisè. Be aware that San Marco 1471 may not necessarily be found close to San Marco 1475 and that many buildings aren't numbered at all.

Fenice Opera House; devastated by a fire in 1996, it was reopened in 2005 after an extensive restoration. Although you'll find glimpses and snippets of the real Venice here, ever-rising rents have nudged resident Venetians to look for housing in the outer neighborhoods: You'll be hard-pressed to find a grocery store or dry cleaner here. But if you're looking for Murano glass trinkets and mediocre restaurants, you'll find an embarrassment of choices. This area is a mecca of first-class hotels—but I'll give you some suggestions for staying here in the heart of Venice without going broke.

CASTELLO This quarter, whose tony canal-side esplanade Riva degli Schiavoni follows the Bacino di San Marco (St. Mark's Basin), is lined with deluxe hotels. It begins just east of Piazza San Marco, skirting Venice's most congested area north and east of Piazza San Marco (Riva degli Schiavoni can sometimes get so busy as to seem like Times Square on New Year's Eve), but if you head farther east in the direction of the Arsenale or inland away from

Venice's Castello neighborhood.

A cafe on Campo Santa Margherita in the Dorsoduro Section.

the *bacino,* the people traffic thins out, despite the presence of such major sights as Campo SS. Giovanni e Paolo and the Scuola di San Giorgio.

CANNAREGIO Sharing the same side of the Grand Canal with San Marco and Castello, Cannaregio stretches north and east from the train station to include the Jewish Ghetto and into the canal-hugging vicinity of the Ca' d'Oro and the Rialto Bridge. Its outer reaches are quiet, unspoiled, and residential ("*What* high-season tourist crowds?" you may wonder); one-quarter of Venice's ever-shrinking population of 65,000 lives here. Most of the city's one star hotels are clustered about the train station—not a dangerous neighborhood but not one known for its charm, either. The tourist shop-lined Lista di Spagna, which starts just to the left as you leave the train station, morphs into Strada Nova and provides an uninterrupted thoroughfare to the Rialto bridge.

SAN POLO This mixed-bag *sestiere* of residential corners and tourist sights stretches northwest of the Rialto Bridge to the church of Santa Maria dei Frari, which houses one of Titian's masterpieces, and the Scuola di San Rocco. The hub of activity at the foot of the bridge is due in large part to the Rialto market that has taken place here for centuries—some of the city's best restaurants have flourished in the area for generations, alongside some of its worst tourist traps. The spacious Campo San Polo is the main piazza of Venice's smallest *sestiere.*

SANTA CROCE North and northwest of the San Polo district and across the Grand Canal from the train station, Santa Croce stretches all the way to Piazzale Roma. Its eastern section is generally one of the least-visited areas of Venice— making it all the more desirable for curious visitors. Less lively than San Polo, it is as authentic and feels light-years away from San Marco. The quiet and lovely Campo San Giacomo dell'Orio is its heart.

DORSODURO You'll find the residential area of Dorsoduro on the opposite side of the Accademia Bridge from San Marco. Known for the Accademia and Peggy Guggenheim museums, it is the largest of the *sestieri* and has been known as an artists' haven (hence the tireless comparison with New York's

Greenwich Village—a far cry) until recent escalations of rents forced much of the community to relocate elsewhere. Good neighborhood restaurants, a charming gondola boatyard, the lively Campo Santa Margherita, and the sunny quay called le Zattere (a favorite promenade and gelato stop) all add to the character and color that make this one of the city's most-visited areas.

LA GIUDECCA Located opposite the Piazza San Marco and Dorsoduro, La Giudecca is a tranquil working-class residential area where you'll find a youth hostel and a handful of hotels (including the deluxe Cipriani, one of Europe's finest).

LIDO DI VENEZIA This slim, 11km-long (6¾-mile) island, the only spot in the Venetian lagoon where cars circulate, is the city's beach and separates the lagoon from the open sea. The landmark hotels here serve as a base for the annual Venice Film Festival.

Getting Around

Aside from on boats, the only way to explore Venice is by walking—and by getting lost repeatedly. You'll navigate many twisting streets whose names change constantly and don't appear on any map, and streets that may very well simply end in a blind alley or spill abruptly into a canal. You'll also cross dozens of footbridges. Treat getting bewilderingly lost in Venice as part of the fun, and budget more time than you'd think necessary to get wherever you're going.

STREET MAPS & SIGNAGE The free map offered by the tourist office and most hotels has good intentions, but it doesn't even show—much less name or index—all the *calli* (streets) and pathways of Venice. For that, pick up a more detailed map (ask for a *pianta della città* at news kiosks—especially those at the train station and around San Marco) or most bookstores. The best (and most expensive) is the highly detailed Touring Club Italiano map, available in a variety of forms (folding or spiral-bound) and scales. Almost as good, and easier to carry, is the simple and cheap 1:6,500 folding map put out by Storti Edizioni (its cover is white-edged with pink, which fades to blue at the bottom).

Still, Venice's confusing layout confounds even the best maps and navigators. You're often better off just stopping every couple of blocks and asking a local to point you in the right direction (always know the name of the *campo*/square or major sight closest to the address you're looking for, and ask for that).

As you wander, look for the ubiquitous yellow signs (well, *usually* yellow) whose destinations and arrows direct you toward five major landmarks: **Ferrovia** (the train station), **Piazzale Roma** (the parking garage), **Rialto** (one of the four bridges over the Grand Canal), **San Marco** (the city's main square), and the **Accademia** (the southernmost Grand Canal bridge).

BY BOAT The various *sestieri* are linked by a comprehensive *vaporetto* (water bus/ferry) system of about a dozen lines operated by the **Azienda del Consorzio Trasporti Veneziano (ACTV),** Calle Fuseri 1810, near the northwest corner of Piazza San Marco (www.actv.it; ✆ **041-528-7886**). Transit maps are available at the tourist office and most ACTV stations. It's easier to get around on foot, as the *vaporetti* principally serve the Grand Canal, the outskirts, and the outer islands. The crisscross network of small canals is the province of delivery vessels, gondolas, and private boats.

CRUISING THE canals

A leisurely cruise along the **Grand Canal ★★★** (p. 447) from Piazza San Marco to the Ferrovia—or the reverse—is one of Venice's must-dos. It's the world's most unusual Main Street, a watery boulevard whose *palazzi* have been converted into condos. Lower water-lapped floors are now deserted, but the higher floors are still coveted by the city's titled families, who have inhabited these glorious residences for centuries; others have become the summertime dream homes of privileged expats, drawn here as irresistibly as the romantic Venetians-by-adoption who preceded them—Richard Wagner, Robert Browning, Lord Byron, and (more recently) Woody Allen.

As much a symbol of Venice as the winged lion, the **gondola ★★★** is one of Europe's great traditions, incredibly and inexplicably expensive but truly as romantic as it looks (detractors who write it off as too touristy have most likely never tried it). The official, fixed rate is 80€ for a 40-minute tour (100€ 7pm–8am), with up to six passengers, and 40€ for every additional 20 minutes (50€ at night). That's not a typo: 150€ an hour for an evening cruise. ***Note:*** Though the price is fixed by the city, a good negotiator at the right time of day (when there is not too much business) can sometimes grab a small discount. And at these ridiculously inflated prices, there is no need to tip the gondolier.

Aim for late afternoon before sundown, when the light does its magic on the canal reflections (and bring a bottle of prosecco and glasses). If the gondola price is too high, ask visitors at your hotel or others lingering about at the gondola stations if they'd like to share it. Though the price is "fixed," before setting off establish with the gondolier the cost, time, and route (back canals are preferable to the trafficked and often choppy Grand Canal). They're regulated by the **Ente Gondola** (www.gondolavenezia.it; ✆ **041-528-5075**), so call if you have any questions or complaints.

And what of the serenading gondolier immortalized in film? Frankly, you're better off without. But if warbling is de rigueur for you, here's the scoop. An ensemble of accordion player and tenor is so expensive that it's shared among several gondolas traveling together. A number of travel agents around town book the evening serenades for around 35€ per person.

There are 12 gondola stations around Venice, including Piazzale Roma, the train station, the Rialto Bridge, and Piazza San Marco. There are also a number of smaller stations, with *gondolieri* in striped shirts standing alongside their sleek 11m (36-ft.) black wonders looking for passengers. They all speak enough English to communicate the necessary details.

A ticket valid for 1 hour of travel on a *vaporetto* is a steep 6.50€, while the 24-hour ticket is 18€. Most lines run every 10 to 15 minutes from 7am to midnight, and then hourly until morning. Most *vaporetto* docks (the only place you can buy tickets) have timetables posted. Note that not all docks sell tickets after dark. If you haven't bought a pass or extra tickets beforehand, you'll have to settle up with the conductor onboard (you'll have to find him—he won't come looking for you) for an extra .50€ per ticket or risk a stiff fine, no excuses accepted. Also available are 48-hour tickets (28€) and 72-hour tickets (33€). If you're planning to stay in Venice a while, it makes sense to pick up a Venice Card (see "Venice Discounts," on p. 442), with

VENETIAN dialect

If, after a few days in Rome and Florence, you were just getting the hang of matching your map with the reality of your new surroundings, you can put aside any short-term success upon your arrival in Venice. Even the Italians (non-Venetian ones) look befuddled when trying to decipher street names and signs (given that you can ever find any).

Venice's colorful thousand-year history as a once-powerful maritime republic helped mold the local dialect, which absorbed nuances and vocabulary from far-flung outposts in the East and from the flourishing communities of foreign merchants who, for centuries, lived and traded in the city. Venetian dialect has in turn left its mark on the vernacular of many languages, including English that has inherited such Venetian words as *gondola* (naturally), *ciao, ghetto, lido,* and *arsenal.*

Venetian dialect is still widely used among the locals and its sing-song tone can be a joy to listen to. For those who know some Italian, try following the conversation between two *gondolieri* to get an idea of how difficult Venetian can be to understand. For the Venice-bound traveler just trying to make sense of Venetian addresses, the following will give you the basics. (***Note:*** Spellings can vary slight in Venetian so, for example, *salizada* is sometimes spelled *salizzada.*)

ca' The abbreviated use of the word *casa* is used for the noble *palazzi,* once private residences and now museums, lining the Grand Canal: Ca' d'Oro, Ca' Pesaro, and Ca' Rezzonico. There is only one *palazzo,* the Palazzo Ducale, the former doge's residence. (The doge, or "duke," was elected for life.) However, as time went on, some great houses gradually also began to be called *palazzi,* so today you'll also encounter the Palazzo Grassi or the Palazzo Labia.

calle Taken from the Spanish (though pronounced as if Italian, *ca*-lay), this is the most commonplace word for "street," known as *via* or *strada* elsewhere in Italy. There are numerous variations. ***Ruga,*** from the French word *rue,* is the name given to a few important *calle* near San Marco and the Rialto bridge that are flanked with stores. A ***ramo*** (literally "branch") is the offshoot of a street and is often used interchangeably with *calle.* ***Salizada*** (the Venetian dialect equivalent of the Italian word for paved, *selciato*) once meant a street paved in stone, implying that all other, less important *calli* were just dirt-packed or brick-paved alleyways. A ***stretto*** is a narrow passageway.

campo Elsewhere in Italy, it's *piazza.* In Venice, the only piazza is the Piazza San Marco (and its two bordering *piazzette*); all other squares are *campi* or the diminutive, *campielli.* Translated as "field" or "meadow," these were once small, unpaved grazing spots for the odd chicken or cow. Almost every one of Venice's *campi* carries the name of the church that dominates it (or once did), and most have wells, no longer used, in the center.

canale There are three wide, principal canals: the Canal Grande (affectionately called "il Canalazzo," the Canal), the Canale della Giudecca, and the Canale di Cannaregio. Each of the other 160-odd smaller canals is called a *rio.* A *rio terrà* is a filled-in canal—wide and straight—now used as a street. A *piscina* is a filled-in basin, now acting as a *campo* or piazza.

fondamenta Referring to the foundations of the houses lining a canal, this is a walkway along the side of a *rio* (small canal). Promenades along the Grand Canal near the Piazza San Marco and the Rialto are called *riva,* as in the Riva del Vin or Riva del Carbon, where cargo such as wine and coal were once unloaded.

sottoportego An alley that ducks under a building.

which you can buy 1-hour *vaporetto* tickets for 1.20€. Tickets must be validated in the yellow machines before getting on the *vaporetto*.

Just three bridges spanned the Grand Canal until 2008 when a fourth was added connecting the train station with Piazzale Roma. To fill in the gaps, *traghetti* skiffs (oversize gondolas rowed by two standing *gondolieri*) cross the Grand Canal at eight intermediate points. You'll find a station at the end of any street named Calle del Traghetto on your map and indicated by a yellow sign with the black gondola symbol. The fare is .50€, which you hand to the gondolier when boarding. Most Venetians cross standing up. For the experience, try the Santa Sofia crossing that connects the Ca' d'Oro and the Pescheria fish market, opposite each other on the Grand Canal just north of the Rialto Bridge—the gondoliers expertly dodge water traffic at this point of the canal, where it's the busiest and most heart-stopping.

BY WATER TAXI *Taxi acquei* (water taxis) charge high prices and aren't for visitors watching their euros. The meter starts at a hefty 15€ and clicks at 2€ per minute. Each bag over 50cm long (20 in.) costs 3€, plus there's a 10€ supplement for service from 10pm to 7am and a 10€ surcharge on Sundays and holidays (these last two charges, however, can't be applied simultaneously). If they have to come get you, tack on another 8€. Those rates cover up to two people; if any more squeeze in, it's another 1.50€ per extra passenger (maximum 20 people). Taking a taxi from the train station to Piazza San Marco or any of the hotels in the area will put you back about 65€ for two people, while there is a fixed 100€ fee (for up to four people) to go or come from the airport. Note that only taxi boats with a yellow strip are the official taxis sanctioned by the city.

Six water-taxi stations serve key points in the city: the **Ferrovia, Piazzale Roma,** the **Rialto Bridge, Piazza San Marco,** the **Lido,** and **Marco Polo Airport. Radio Taxi** (**© 041-723-112** or 041-522-2303) will come pick you up anywhere in the city.

BY GONDOLA If you come all the way to Venice and don't indulge in a gondola ride you might still be kicking yourself long after you have returned home. Yes, it's touristy, and, yes, it's expensive (see the "Cruising the Canals" box, on p. 435), but only those with a heart of stone will be unmoved by the quintessential Venetian experience. Do not initiate your trip, however, until you have agreed upon a price and synchronized watches. Oh, and don't ask them to sing.

[FastFACTS] VENICE

Acqua Alta During the tidal *acqua alta* (high water) floods, the lagoon rises until it engulfs the city, leaving up to 1.5 to 1.8m (5–6 ft.) of water in the lowest-lying streets (Piazza San Marco, as the lowest point in the city, goes first). Significant *acqua alta* can begin as early as late September or October, but usually takes place November to March. As many as 50 a year have been recorded since they first started in the late 1700s. The waters usually recede after just a few hours. Walkways are set up around town, but wet feet are a given. The complex system of hydraulic dams being constructed out in the lagoon to cut off the highest of these high tides (a controversial project due to its environmental impact) is well underway but won't be operational for years. ***Tip:*** If you are curious to see *acqua alta* (and it is indeed a wonderful spectacle), but aren't in Venice at the right time, you can still get lucky as very minor occurrences can happen all year-round. So if you happen to see big puddles forming in Piazza San Marco in the middle of a dry July day, you'll know what's up.

American Express Unfortunately, American Express closed its Venice office in 2009, leaving offices only in Milan and Rome.

Business Hours Standard hours for shops are Monday to Saturday 9am to 12:30pm and 3 to 7:30pm. In winter, shops are closed on Monday morning, while in summer it's usually Saturday afternoon. Most grocers are closed on Wednesday afternoon year-round. In Venice, just about everything is closed on Sunday, though tourist shops in the tourist spots such as the San Marco area are permitted to stay open during high season.

Climate May, June, September, and early October are the best months to visit with respect to weather (but also the most crowded). July and August are hot—at times, unbearably so. April and late October/early November are hit-or-miss; it can be glorious, rainy, cool, or damp, and only marginally less crowded. Also see *"Acqua Alta,"* above.

Consulates The **U.K. Consulate** in Venice is on the mainland in Mestre, at Piazzale Donatori di Sangue 2 (✆ **041-505-5990**); it's open Monday to Friday 10am to 1pm. The **U.S., Australia, Canada,** and **New Zealand** have consulates in Milan (p. 567); all also maintain embassies in Rome.

Crime Be aware of petty crime like pickpocketing on the crowded *vaporetti,* particularly the tourist routes, where passengers are more intent on the passing scenery than on watching their bags. Venice's deserted back streets are virtually crime-free, though occasional tales of theft have circulated. Generally speaking, Venice is one of Italy's safest cities.

Drugstores Venice's pharmacies take turns staying open all night. To find out which one is on call in your area, ask at your hotel or check the rotational duty signs posted outside all pharmacies.

Emergencies The best number to call in Italy (and the rest of Europe) with a **general emergency** is ✆ **112;** this connects you to the military-trained **Carabinieri** who will transfer your call as needed. For the **police,** dial ✆ **113;** for a medical emergency and to call an **ambulance,** the number is ✆ **118;** for the **fire department,** call ✆ **115.** All are free calls.

Holidays Venice's patron saint, San Marco (St. Mark), is honored on April 25, which also happens to be a national holiday, Liberation Day, celebrating the end of World War II. For a list of official state holidays, see the "Public Holidays" section on p. 45.

Hospitals The **Ospedale Civile Santi Giovanni e Paolo** (✆ **041-529-4111**), on Campo Santi Giovanni e Paolo, has English-speaking staff and provides emergency service 24 hours a day (*vaporetto:* San Toma).

Internet **Sala Giochi SS. Apostoli** (✆ **041-099-3684**), which is open daily 9:30am to 11pm, is in Campo SS. Apostoli, right at the base of the bridge that leads toward Rialto and San Marco. Checking Facebook, e-mail, or sending a few tweets costs 3€ for 30 minutes and 5€ for an hour, though from 9:30 to 10:30am and 6 to 7pm you can surf for free, if you buy a drink. You can also pay for Wi-Fi access (1.50€ for half an hour and 2.50€ for an hour) and there are phones for making cheap international calls.

Laundry The laundry service most convenient to San Marco is **Gabriella** (✆ **041-522-1758**), San Marco 985 on Rio Terrà Colonne (off Calle dei Fabbri), where they wash and dry your clothes within an hour or two for 15€ per load. They are open Monday to Friday 8am to 12:30pm.

Lost & Found The central **Ufficio Oggetti Rinvenuti** (✆ **041-274-8225**) is in the annex to the City Hall (Municipio), at San Marco 4134, on Calle Piscopia o Loredan, just off Riva del Carbon on the Grand Canal, near the Rialto Bridge (on the same side of the canal as the Rialto *vaporetto* station). The office is ostensibly open Monday to Friday from 9am to 1pm. There's also an **Ufficio Oggetti Smarriti** at the airport (✆ **041-260-9260**). The train station no longer has a lost-and-found, so if you lose something on the train or in the station, definitely talk to the police (they have a small office next to Track 1), but they are likely to direct you to the central Ufficio Oggetti Rinvenuti in the city hall annex.

Luggage Storage The *deposito bagagli* in the train station (✆ **041-785-531**) is located to the left of the station as you disembark from your train and head toward the exit. It's open daily from 6am to 11:50pm and charges 4€ for each bag for the first 5 hours, and then .60€ for each additional hour through the 12th hour. Then it's .20€ an hour.

Post Office Venice's **Posta Centrale** is at San Marco 5554, 30124 Venezia, on the San Marco side of the Rialto Bridge at Rialto Fontego dei Tedeschi (✆ **041-271-7111** or 041-528-5813; *vaporetto:* Rialto). This office sells *francobolli* (stamps) at Window 12 Monday to Saturday 8:30am to 6:30pm (for parcels, 8:10am–1:30pm).

Telephones See "Fast Facts: Italy," p. 933. The area code for Venice is ✆ **041.**

EXPLORING VENICE

Venice is notorious for changing and extending the opening hours of its museums and, to a lesser degree, its churches. Before you begin your exploration of Venice's sights, ask at the tourist office for the season's list of museum and church hours. During the peak months, you can enjoy extended museum hours—some places stay open until 7 or even 10pm. Unfortunately, these hours are not released until approximately Easter of every year. Even then, little is done to publicize the information, so you'll have to do your own research.

Piazza San Marco

Basilica di San Marco (St. Mark's Basilica) ★★★ CATHEDRAL With Venice's wealth growing in the 9th century thanks to its central role in world trade, the city decided that if it wanted to continue its march toward becoming a power to be reckoned with it needed a more important patron saint than the Greek St. Theodore that had been adopted. The city's rise had been rather recent and it had no connection to any of the big saints, so

Piazza San Marco and the Campanile.

Basilica di San Marco (St. Mark's Basilica) **14**
Ca' d'Oro **23**
Campanile di San Marco (Bell Tower) **13**
Chiesa di San Giorgio Maggiore **18**
Chiesa Santa Maria dei Miracoli **22**
Collezione Peggy Guggenheim (Peggy Guggenheim Collection) **6**
Dogana da Mar **9**
Galleria dell'Accademia (Accademia Gallery) **5**
I Gesuati (Santa Maria del Rosario) **4**
Il Ghetto (the Jewish Ghetto) **24**
Il Redentore **7**
Museo Comunità Ebraica (Jewish Museum of Venice) **24**
Museo Storico Navale e Arsenale (Navale History Museum and the Arsenal) **19**
Palazzo Ducale (Ducal Palace) **16**
Piazza San Marco **11**
Piazzetta San Marco **15**
Ponte dei Sospiri (Bridge of Sighs) **17**
Punta della Dogana (Customs House) **10**
Rialto **20**
Santa Maria della Salute **8**
Santa Maria Gloriosa dei Frari **1**
Scuola Grande di San Rocco **2**
Squero di San Trovaso **3**
SS. Giovanni e Paolo **21**
Torre dell'Orologio (Clock Tower) **12**

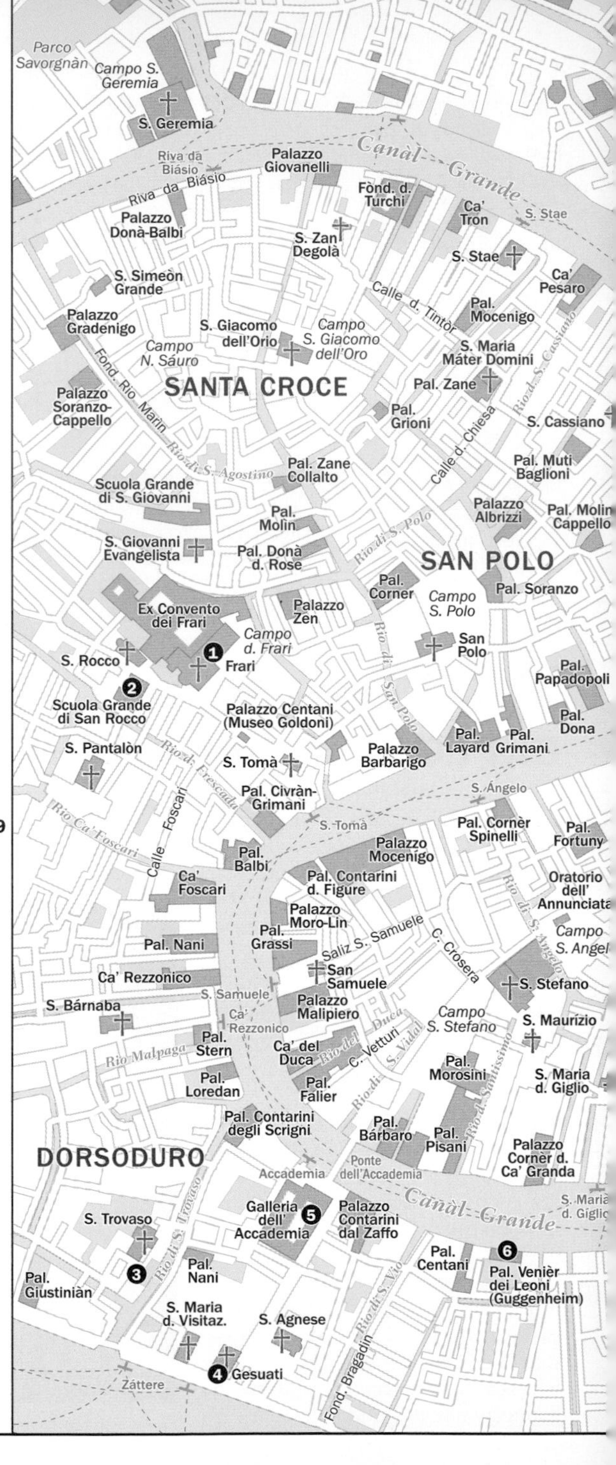

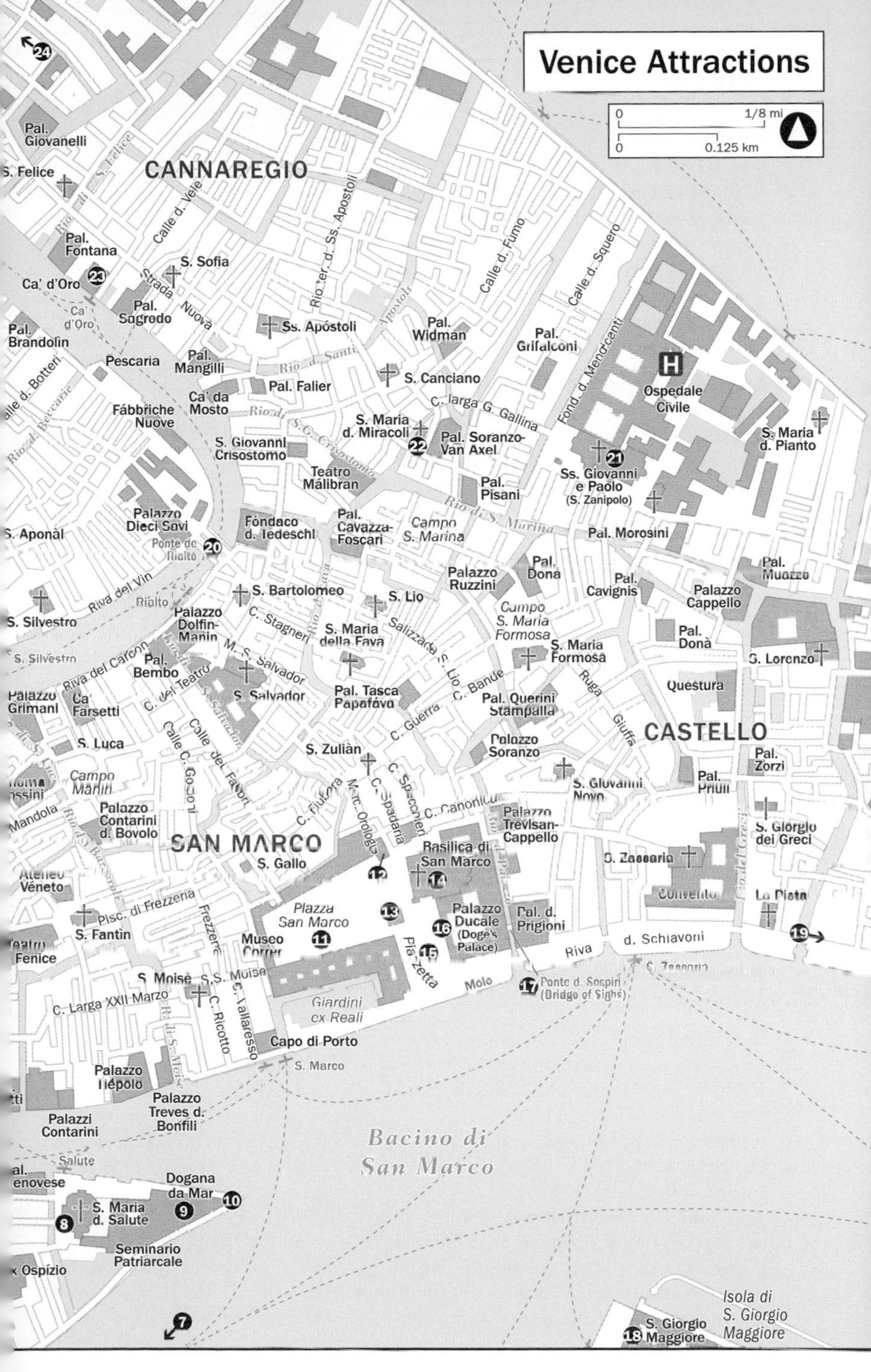
Venice Attractions
CANNAREGIO
SAN MARCO
CASTELLO
Bacino di San Marco
Ospedale Civile
Ss. Giovanni e Paolo (S. Zanipolo)
Basilica di San Marco
Palazzo Ducale (Doge's Palace)
Piazza San Marco
Museo Correr
Ponte d. Sospiri (Bridge of Sighs)
Ponte de Rialto
S. Maria d. Salute
Dogana da Mar
Isola di S. Giorgio Maggiore
S. Giorgio Maggiore
Giardini ex Reali
Teatro Fenice
Fondaco d. Tedeschi
Ca' d'Oro
Riva d. Schiavoni

VENICE discounts

The **Museum Pass** grants one admission to all the city-run museums over a 6-month period. That includes the museums of St. Mark's Square—Palazzo Ducale, Museo Correr, Museo Archeologico Nazionale, and the Biblioteca Nazionale Marciana—as well as the Museo di Palazzo Mocenigo (Costume Museum), the Ca' Rezzonico, the Ca' Pesaro, the Museo del Vetro (Glass Museum) on Murano, and the Museo del Merletto (Lace Museum) on Burano. The Museum Pass is available at any of the participating museums and costs 18€ for adults, 12€ for students under 29. There is also a **San Marco Museum Pass** that lets you into the museums of St. Mark's plus one of the other museums. It costs 14€, and 8€ for students.

The **Venice Card** is the Museum Pass on steroids, with a juiced up price to match: 40€, 30€ for those 6 to 29. It includes, among other things and in addition to everything the Museum Pass offers, discounts on temporary exhibits, more museums and (no kidding) two entrances to the municipal public toilets. You can pick one up at any of the Hellovenezia (www.hellovenezia.com) offices around town (there's one in the train station as well as at the Rialto and Santa Zaccaria *vaporetto* stops) or at the tourist information offices.

Venice, so delicate it cannot handle the hordes of visitors it receives every year, has been toying with the idea of charging admission to get into the very city itself. Slightly calmer heads seem to have prevailed, though, and instead we have **Venice Connected** (www.veniceconnected.it), which started in 2009 and gives discounts if you buy tickets through the website before arriving. You can get tickets for everything from transportation to museums, but you must do it for a particular day that is at least 4 days in the future. In return, the city gets, at least in theory, a better idea of how many people will be in town on a given day.

Also, for tourists between the ages of 14 and 29, there is the **Rolling Venice** card, which is something akin to the Venice Connected discounts for students. It's valid until the end of the year in which you buy it, costs just 4€, and entitles the bearer to significant (20%–30%) discounts at participating restaurants, and a similar discount on *traghetto* tickets. Holders of the Rolling Venice card also get discounts in museums, stores, language courses, hotels, and bars across the city (it comes with a thick booklet listing everywhere that you're entitled to get discounts). The card can be acquired at the same places as the Venice Card (see

two enterprising Venetian merchants created one. Legend has it that in 828 these two merchants smuggled the remains of St. Mark the Evangelist from Egypt by packing them in pickled pork to bypass the scrutiny of Muslim guards. With the saint's relics in hand, Venice had the link it needed and St. Mark quickly replaced St. Theodore as the city's patron saint. The Venetians built a small chapel to house the relics, one thing led to another, and pretty soon there was the cathedral that you see today.

Venice for centuries was Europe's principal gateway between the East and the West, so not surprisingly the architectural style for the sumptuous Byzantine Basilica di San Marco, replete with five mosquelike bulbed domes, was borrowed from Constantinople. Through the centuries (the original church was consecrated in the 9th c. though much of what you see was constructed in the 11th c.),

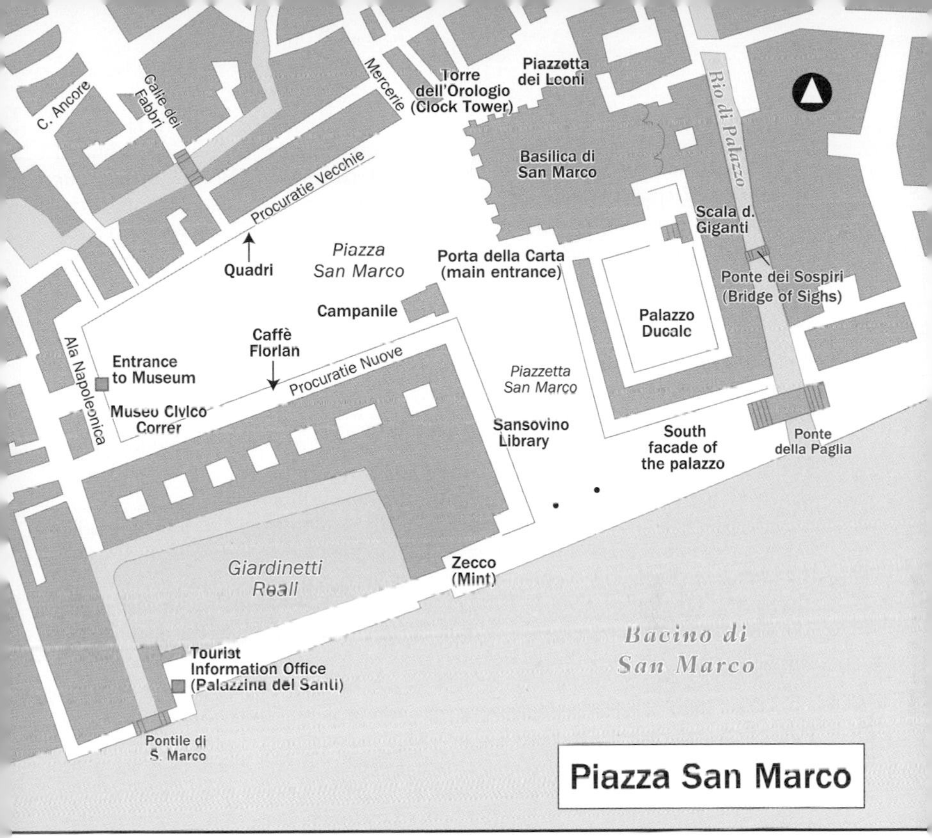

C. Ancore
Calle dei Fabbri
Mercerie
Torre dell'Orologio (Clock Tower)
Piazzetta dei Leoni
Rio di Palazzo
Procuratie Vecchie
Basilica di San Marco
Scala d. Giganti
Quadri
Piazza San Marco
Porta della Carta (main entrance)
Ponte dei Sospiri (Bridge of Sighs)
Campanile
Palazzo Ducale
Caffè Florian
Ala Napoleonica
Entrance to Museum
Procuratie Nuove
Piazzetta San Marco
Museo Civico Correr
Sansovino Library
South facade of the palazzo
Ponte della Paglia
Giardinetti Reali
Zecca (Mint)
Bacino di San Marco
Tourist Information Office (Palazzina del Santi)
Pontile di S. Marco

Piazza San Marco

wealthy Venetian merchants and politicians alike vied with one another in donating gifts to expand and embellish this church, the saint's final resting place and, with the adjacent Palazzo Ducale, a symbol of Venetian wealth and power. Exotic and mysterious, it is unlike any other Roman Catholic church.

Pigeons flock to Piazza San Marco.

And so it is that the Basilica di San Marco earned its name as the Chiesa d'Oro (Golden Church), with a cavernous interior exquisitely gilded with Byzantine mosaics added over some 7 centuries and covering every inch of both ceiling and pavement. For a closer look at many of the most remarkable ceiling mosaics and a better view of the Oriental carpet–like patterns of the pavement mosaics, pay the admission to go upstairs to the **Galleria** (the entrance to this and the Museo Marciano is in the atrium at the principal entrance); this was originally the women's gallery, or *matroneum*. It is also the only way to access the outside Loggia

Church Tours

Check with a tourist office for free tours being offered (erratically and usually during high season) in some of the churches, particularly the Basilica di San Marco and the Frari.

dei Cavalli (see below). Here you can mingle with the celebrated ***Triumphal Quadriga*** of four gilded bronze horses dating from the 2nd or 3rd century A.D.; the restored originals have been moved inside to the small museum. (The word *quadriga* actually refers to a car or chariot pulled by four horses though in this case there are only the horses.) The horses were brought to Venice from Constantinople in 1204 along with lots of other booty from the Fourth Crusade. For centuries these were symbols of the unrivaled Serene Republic and are the only quadriga to have survived from the classical era. Not to be outdone by looting-prone Venetians, Napoleon carted the horses off to Paris in 1798, though they were returned to Venice in 1815 after the fall of the French Empire.

A visit to the outdoor **Loggia dei Cavalli** is an unexpected highlight, providing a panoramic view of the piazza and what Napoleon called "the most beautiful salon in the world" upon his arrival in Venice in 1797. The 500-year-old **Torre dell'Orologio (Clock Tower)** stands to your right; to your left is the **Campanile (Bell Tower)** and, beyond, the glistening waters of the open lagoon and Palladio's **Chiesa di San Giorgio** on its own island. It is any amateur photographer's dream.

The church's greatest treasure is the magnificent altarpiece known as the **Pala d'Oro (Golden Altarpiece),** a Gothic masterpiece encrusted with close to 2,000 precious gems and 255 enameled panels. It was created in the 10th century and embellished by master Venetian and Byzantine artisans between the 12th and 14th centuries. It is located behind the main altar, whose green marble canopy on alabaster columns covers the tomb of St. Mark (skeptics contend that

A detail from the mosaics in St. Mark's Basilica.

Basilica di San Marco

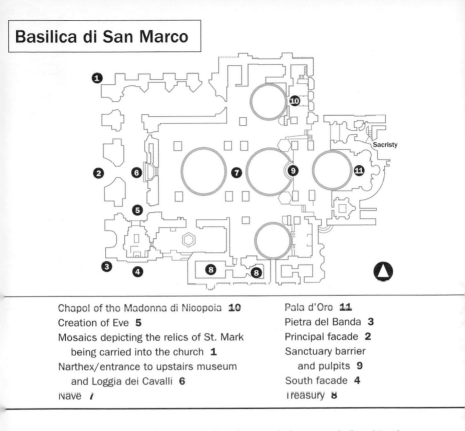

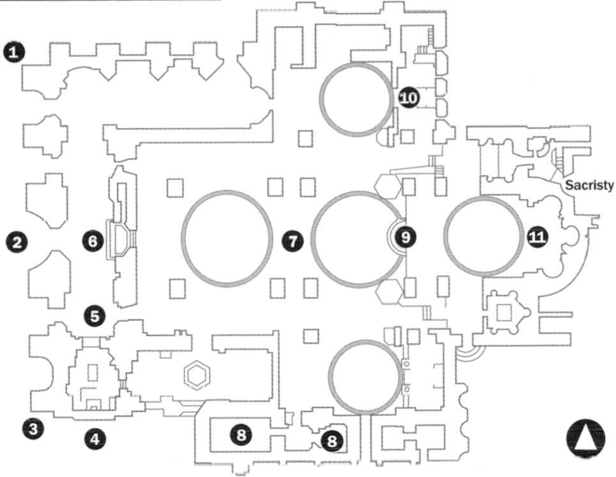

Chapel of the Madonna di Nicopeia **10**
Creation of Eve **5**
Mosaics depicting the relics of St. Mark being carried into the church **1**
Narthex/entrance to upstairs museum and Loggia dei Cavalli **6**
Nave **7**
Pala d'Oro **11**
Pietra del Banda **3**
Principal facade **2**
Sanctuary barrier and pulpits **9**
South facade **4**
Treasury **8**

his remains burned in a fire in 976 that destroyed the original church). Also worth a visit is the **Tesoro (Treasury),** with a collection of the crusaders' plunder from Constantinople and other icons and relics amassed by the church over the years. Much of the Venetian booty has been incorporated into the interior and exterior of the basilica in the form of marble, columns, capitals, and statuary. Second to the Pala d'Oro in importance is the 10th-century ***Madonna di Nicopeia,*** a bejeweled icon taken from Constantinople and exhibited in its own chapel to the left of the main altar.

In July and August (with much less certainty the rest of the year), church-affiliated volunteers give free tours Monday to Saturday, leaving four or five times

Know Before You Go . . .

The guards at the cathedral's entrance are serious about forbidding entry to anyone in inappropriate attire—shorts, sleeveless shirts (and shirts too short to hide your bellybutton), and skirts above the knee. With masses of people descending on the cathedral every day, your best bet for avoiding the long lines is to come early in the morning. Although the basilica is open Sunday morning for anyone wishing to attend Mass, you cannot enter merely to gawk as a tourist.

daily (not all tours are in English), beginning at 10:30am; groups gather in the atrium, where you'll find posters with schedules.

San Marco, Piazza San Marco. www.basilicasanmarco.it. ✆ **041-522-5697.** Basilica, free admission; Museo Marciano (St. Mark's Museum, also called La Galleria, includes Loggia dei Cavalli) 4€, Pala d'Oro 2€, Tesoro (Treasury) 3€. Basilica, Tesoro, and Pala d'Oro summer Mon–Sat 9:45am–5pm, Sun 2–4pm; winter closes an hour earlier. Museo Marciano summer daily 9:45am–4:45pm. *Vaporetto:* San Marco.

A bronze horse on the loggia of St. Mark's Basilica.

Campanile di San Marco (Bell Tower) ★★★ ICON An elevator will whisk you to the top of this 97m (318-ft.) bell tower where you get a breathtaking view of St. Mark's cupolas. It is the highest structure in the city, offering a pigeon's-eye view that includes the lagoon, its neighboring islands, and the red rooftops and church domes and bell towers of Venice—and, oddly, not a single canal. On a clear day, you may even see the outline of the distant snowcapped Dolomite Mountains. Originally built in the 9th century, the bell tower was then rebuilt in the 12th, 14th, and 16th centuries, when the pretty marble loggia at its base was added by Jacopo Sansovino. It collapsed unexpectedly in 1902, miraculously hurting no one except a cat. It was rebuilt exactly as before, using most of the same materials, even rescuing one of the five historical bells that it still uses today (each bell was rung for a different purpose, such as war, the death of a doge, religious holidays, and so on).

San Marco, Piazza San Marco. ✆ **041-522-4064.** Admission 8€. Easter to June daily 9am–5pm; July–Sept daily 9am–9pm; Oct daily 9am–7pm; Nov–Easter daily 9:30am–3:45pm. *Vaporetto:* San Marco.

Venice's Newest Bridge

After years of disputes about its utility and design, the **Ponte della Costituzione,** the fourth bridge spanning the Grand Canal, opened for business in 2008. Venice's newest bridge is an impressive sight. To visit it, come out of the Santa Lucia train station and turn right at the Grand Canal, where you'll encounter this futuristic creation of famed Spanish architect Santiago Calatrava. The bridge connects the train station with the Piazzale Roma parking lot, so it's probably not of much use to you if you have arrived by train, but that doesn't mean you can't cross it in awe anyway.

Boats make their way along the Grand Canal.

Canal Grande (Grand Canal) ★★★ NATURAL ATTRACTION A leisurely cruise along the "Canalazzo" from Piazza San Marco to the Ferrovia (train station), or the reverse, is one of Venice's (and life's) must-do experiences. Hop on the **no. 1** ***vaporetto*** in the late afternoon (try to get one of the coveted outdoor seats in the prow), when the weather-worn colors of the former homes of Venice's merchant elite are warmed by the soft light and reflected in the canal's rippling waters, and the busy traffic of delivery boats, *vaporetti*, and gondolas that fills the city's main thoroughfare has eased somewhat. The sheer number and opulence of the 200-odd *palazzi*, churches, and imposing republican buildings dating from the 14th to the 18th centuries is enough to make any boat-going visitor's head swim. Many of the largest canal-side buildings are now converted into imposing international banks, government or university buildings, art galleries, and consulates. The *vaporetto*'s Ferrovia (train station) stop is the obvious place to start or conclude a Grand Canal tour (the other being Piazza San Marco) though if you go one stop farther up the canal away from San Marco to Piazzale Roma you get to pass under the Ponte della Costituzione (see "Venice's Newest Bridge," below).

Best stations to start/end a tour of the Grand Canal are Ferrovia (train station) or Piazzale Roma on the northwest side of the canal and Piazza San Marco in the southeast. Tickets 6.50€.

Palazzo Ducale and Ponte dei Sospiri (Ducal Palace and Bridge of Sighs) ★★★ PALACE The pink-and-white marble Gothic-Renaissance Palazzo Ducale, residence and government center of the doges who ruled Venice for more than 1,000 years, stands between the Basilica di San Marco and St. Mark's Basin. A symbol of prosperity and power, it was destroyed by a succession of fires and was built and rebuilt in 1340 and 1424 in its present form. Forever being expanded, it slowly grew to be one of Italy's greatest civic structures. A 15th-century **Porta della Carta (Paper Gate),** the entrance adjacent to the basilica where the doges' official proclamations and decrees were posted, opens onto a splendid inner courtyard with a double row of Renaissance arches.

Ahead you'll see Jacopo Sansovino's enormous **Scala dei Giganti (Stairway of the Giants),** scene of the doges' lavish inaugurations and never used by mere mortals, which leads to the wood-paneled courts and elaborate meeting rooms of the interior. The walls and ceilings of the principal rooms were richly decorated by the Venetian masters, including Veronese, Titian, Carpaccio, and Tintoretto, to illustrate the history of the puissant Venetian Republic while at the same time impressing visiting diplomats and emissaries from the far-flung corners of the maritime republic with the uncontested prosperity and power it had attained.

If you want to understand something of this magnificent palace, the fascinating history of the 1,000-year-old maritime republic, and the intrigue of the government that ruled it, take the **Secret Itineraries tour ★★★** (see "An Insider's Look at the Palazzo Ducale," below). Failing that, at least shell out for the infrared audio-guide tour (at entrance: 6€) to help make sense of it all. Unless you can tag along with an English-speaking tour group, you may otherwise miss out on the importance of much of what you're seeing.

The first room you'll come to is the spacious **Sala delle Quattro Porte (Hall of the Four Doors),** whose ceiling is by Tintoretto. The **Sala del Anticollegio** (adjacent to the College Chamber and with a ceiling by Tintoretto), the next main room, is where foreign ambassadors waited to be received by this committee of 25 members. It is covered in works by Tintoretto, and Veronese's *Rape of Europe,* considered one of the *palazzo*'s finest. It steals some of the thunder of Tintoretto's *Three Graces* and *Bacchus and Ariadne*—the latter considered one of his best by some critics. A right turn from this room leads into one of the most impressive of the spectacular interior rooms, the richly adorned **Sala del Senato (Senate Chamber),** with Tintoretto's ceiling painting, *The Triumph of Venice.* Here laws were passed by the Senate, a select group of 200 chosen from the Great Council. The latter was originally an elected body, but in the 13th century it became an aristocratic stronghold that could number as many as 1,700. After passing again through the Sala delle Quattro Porte, you'll come to the Veronese-decorated **Stanza del Consiglio dei Dieci (Room of the Council of Ten,** the Republic's dreaded security police), of particular historical interest. It was in this room that justice was dispensed and decapitations ordered. Formed in the 14th century to deal with emergency situations, the Ten were considered more powerful than the Senate and feared by all. Just outside the adjacent chamber, in the **Sala della Bussola (the Compass Chamber),** notice the **Bocca dei Leoni (Lion's Mouth),** a slit in the wall into which secret denunciations and accusations of enemies of the state were placed for quick action by the much-feared Council.

The main sight on the next level down—indeed, in the entire palace—is the **Sala del Maggior Consiglio (Great Council Hall).** This enormous space is animated by Tintoretto's huge *Paradiso* at the far end of the hall above the doge's seat (the painter was in his 70s when he undertook the project with the help of his son). Measuring 7×23m (23×75 ft.), it is said to be the world's largest oil painting; together with Veronese's gorgeous *Il Trionfo di Venezia (The Triumph of Venice)* in the oval panel on the ceiling, it affirms the power emanating from the council sessions held here. Tintoretto also did the portraits of the 76 doges encircling the top of this chamber; note that the picture of the Doge Marin Falier, who was convicted of treason and beheaded in 1355, has been blacked out—Venice has never forgiven him. Although elected for life since sometime in the 7th century, over time *il doge* became nothing but a figurehead (they were never allowed to meet with foreign ambassadors alone); the power rested in the Great Council. Exit the

AN insider's LOOK AT THE PALAZZO DUCALE

The **Itinerari Segreti (Secret Itineraries)** ★★★ guided tours of the Palazzo Ducale is a must-see for any visit to Venice lasting more than a day. The tours offer an unparalleled look into the world of Venetian politics over the centuries and are the only way to access the otherwise restricted quarters and hidden passageways of this enormous palace, such as the doges' private chambers and the torture chambers where prisoners were interrogated. The story of Giacomo Casanova's imprisonment in, and famous escape from, the palace's prisons is the tour highlight (though a few of the less-inspired guides harp on this aspect a bit too much). It is highly advisable to reserve in advance, by phone (toll-free within Italy ✆ **848-082-000,** or from abroad 041-4273-0892) or in person at the ticket desk. Tours often sell out at least a few days ahead, especially from spring through fall. Tours in English are daily at 9:55, 10:45, and 11:35am and cost 18€ for adults, 12€ for children ages 6 to 14 and students ages 15 to 29. There are also tours in Italian at 9:30 and 11:10am and French at 10:20am and noon. The tour lasts about 75 minutes.

Great Council Hall via the tiny doorway on the opposite side of Tintoretto's *Paradiso* to find the enclosed **Ponte dei Sospiri (Bridge of Sighs),** which connects the Ducal Palace with the grim **Palazzo delle Prigioni (Prisons).** The bridge took its current name only in the 19th century, when visiting northern European poets romantically envisioned the prisoners' final breath of resignation upon viewing the outside world one last time before being locked in their fetid cells awaiting the quick justice of the Council of Ten. Some attribute the name to Casanova, who, following his arrest in 1755 (he was accused of being a Freemason and spreading antireligious propaganda), crossed this very bridge. One of the rare few to escape, something he achieved 15 months after his imprisonment began, he returned to Venice 20 years later. Some of the stone cells still have the original graffiti of past prisoners, many of them locked up interminably for petty crimes.

San Marco, Piazza San Marco. ✆ **041-271-5911.** Admission only on San Marco cumulative ticket (see "Venice Discounts," p. 442). For Itinerari Segreti guided tour in English, see "An Insider's Look at the Palazzo Ducale" box, below. Daily 8:30am–7pm (Nov–Mar until 5pm). *Vaporetto:* San Marco.

Rialto Bridge ★★ ARCHITECTURE This graceful arch over the Grand Canal is lined with overpriced boutiques and is teeming with tourists and overflow from the daily market along Riga degli Orefici on the San Polo side. Until the 19th century, it was the only bridge across the Grand Canal, originally built as a pontoon bridge at the canal's narrowest point. Wooden versions of the bridge followed; the 1444 one was the first to include shops, interrupted by a drawbridge in the center. In 1592, this graceful stone span was finished to the designs of Antonio da Ponte (whose last name fittingly enough means bridge), who beat out Sansovino, Palladio, and Michelangelo, with his plans that called for a single, vast, 28m-wide (92-ft.) arch in the center to allow trading ships to pass.

Ponte del Rialto.

Torre dell'Orologio (Clock Tower) ARCHITECTURE As you enter the magnificent Piazza San Marco, it is one of the first things you see, standing on the north side, next to and towering above the Procuratie Vecchie (the ancient administration buildings for the Republic). The Renaissance tower was built in 1496, and the clock mechanism of that same period still keeps perfect time. A lengthy restoration that finished in 2005 has helped keep the rest of the structure in top shape. The two bronze figures, known as "Moors" because of the dark color of the bronze, pivot to strike the hour. The tower is the entryway to the ancient Mercerie (from the word for "merchandise"), the principal souklike retail street of both high-end boutiques and trinket shops that zigzags its way to the Rialto Bridge. Guided tours are required and are included in the price of entrance.

San Marco, Piazza San Marco. Admission 12€, 7€ for children ages 6–14 and students ages 15–29; the ticket also gets you into the Museo Correr, the Museo Archeologico Nazionale, and the Biblioteca Nazionale Marciana (but not Palazzo Ducale, as you get with the San Marco Museum Pass, see "Venice Discounts," p. 442). Daily 10am–3:30pm; tours in English Mon–Wed 10 and 11am, Thurs–Sun 2 and 3pm. There are also tours in Italian and French. *Vaporetto:* San Marco.

Castello

Museo Storico Navale and Arsenale (Naval History Museum and the Arsenal) ★★ MUSEUM The Naval History Museum's most fascinating exhibit is its collection of model ships. It was once common practice for vessels to be built not from blueprints, but from the precise scale models that you see here. The prize of the collection is a model of the legendary *Bucintoro,* the lavish ceremonial barge of the doges. Another section of the museum contains an array of historic vessels. Walk along the canal as it branches off from the museum to the Ships' Pavilion, where the historic vessels are displayed.

A lion, the symbol of Venice, guards the Arsenale.

Verrochio's statue of Bartolomeo Colleoni, in the Castello

Occupying one-fifth of the city's total acreage, the arsenal was once the very source of the Republic's maritime power. It is now used as a military zone and is closed to the curious. The marble-columned Renaissance gate, with the Republic's winged lion above, is flanked by four ancient lions, booty brought at various times from Greece and points farther east. It was founded in 1104, and at the height of Venice's power in the 15th century, it employed 16,000 workers who turned out merchant and wartime galley after galley on an early version of massive assembly lines at speeds and in volume unknown until modern times.
Castello 2148 (Campo San Biasio). ✆ **041-520-0276.** Admission 3€. Mon–Fri 8:45am–1:30pm; Sat closes at 1pm. *Vaporetto:* Arsenale.

SS. Giovanni e Paolo ★ CHURCH This massive Gothic church was built by the Dominican order from the 13th to the 15th century and, together with the Frari Church in San Polo, is second in size only to the Basilica di San Marco. An unofficial Pantheon where 25 doges are buried (a number of tombs are part of the unfinished facade), the church, commonly known as Zanipolo in Venetian dialect, is also home to a number of artistic treasures.

Back to Scuola

Founded in the Middle Ages, the Venetian *scuole* (schools) were guilds that brought together merchants and craftspeople from certain trades (for example, the dyers of Scuola dei Carmini), as well as those who shared similar religious devotions (Scuola Grande di San Rocco). The guilds were social clubs, credit unions, and sources of spiritual guidance. Many commissioned elaborate headquarters and hired the best artists of the day to decorate them. The *scuole* that remain in Venice today house some of the city's finest art treasures.

The sculpture garden at the Peggy Guggenheim Collection.

Visit the **Cappella del Rosario ★** through a glass door off the left transept to see the three restored ceiling canvases by Paolo Veronese, particularly *The Assumption of the Madonna.* The brilliantly colored *Polyptych of St. Vincent Ferrer* (ca. 1465), attributed to a young Giovanni Bellini, is in the right aisle. You'll also see the foot of St. Catherine of Siena encased in glass.

Anchoring the large and impressive *campo,* a popular crossroads for this area of Castello, is the **statue of Bartolomeo Colleoni ★★**, the Renaissance condottiere who defended Venice's interests at the height of its power and until his death in 1475. The 15th-century work is by the Florentine Andrea Verrocchio; it is considered one of the world's great equestrian monuments and Verrocchio's best.

Castello 6363 (on Campo Santi Giovanni e Paolo). ✆ **041-523-7510** or 041-235-5913. Admission 3€. Mon–Sat 8:30am–12:30pm and 3:30–7pm. *Vaporetto:* Rialto.

Dorsoduro

Collezione Peggy Guggenheim (Peggy Guggenheim Collection) ★★★
MUSEUM The eccentric and eclectic American expatriate Peggy Guggenheim assembled this compilation of painting and sculpture, considered to be one of the most comprehensive and important collections of modern art in the world. She did an excellent job of it, with particular strengths in cubism, European abstraction, surrealism, and abstract expressionism since about 1910. Max Ernst was one of her early favorites (she even married him), as was Jackson Pollock.

Among the major works here are Magritte's *Empire of Light,* Picasso's *La Baignade,* Kandinsky's *Landscape with Church (with Red Spot),* and Pollock's *Alchemy.* The museum, one of Venice's most-visited attractions, is also home to Ernst's disturbing *The Antipope* and *Attirement of the Bride,* Giacometti's unique figures, Brancusi's fluid sculptures, and numerous works by Braque, Dalí, Léger, Mondrian, Chagall, and Miró.

Directly on the Grand Canal, the elegant 18th-century Palazzo Venier dei Leoni was purchased by Peggy Guggenheim in 1949 and was her home in Venice until her death in 1979. The graves of her canine companions share the lovely interior garden with several prominent works of the Nasher Sculpture Garden, while the canal-side patio watched over by Marino Marini's *Angel of the City* invites you to linger and watch the canal life. An interesting book shop and a cafe/bistro are located in a separate wing across the inside courtyard where temporary exhibits are often housed.

Don't be shy about speaking English with the young staff working here on internship; most of them are American. Sunday from 3 to 4pm is "Kids Day" with children between 4 and 10 given the chance to take part in a workshop where they create artworks inspired by the museum's collection (make sure your kid doesn't draw inspiration from one of the aforementioned Ernst paintings).

Dorsoduro 701 (on Calle San Cristoforo). www.guggenheim-venice.it. ✆ **041-240-5411.** Admission 12€ adults, 10€ 65 and over and those who present a train ticket to Venice on one of Italy's fast trains (Frecciarossa, Frecciargento, or Frecciabianca) dated no more than 3 days previous, 7€ students 26 and under and children ages 10–18. Wed–Mon 10am–6pm. *Vaporetto:* Accademia (walk around left side of Accademia, take 1st left, and walk straight ahead following signs—you'll cross a canal and then walk alongside another, until turning left to the museum).

Galleria dell'Accademia (Academy Gallery) ★★★ MUSEUM The glory that was Venice lives on in the Accademia, the definitive treasure house of Venetian painting and one of Europe's great museums. Exhibited chronologically from the 13th through the 18th centuries, the collection features

THE ART OF THE gondola

Putting together one of the sleek black boats is a fascinatingly exact science that is still done in the revered traditional manner at boatyards such as the **Squero di San Trovaso** (p. 455). The boats have been painted black since a 16th-century sumptuary law—one of many passed by the local legislators as excess and extravagance spiraled out of control. Whether regarding boats or baubles, laws were passed to restrict the gaudy outlandishness that, at the time, was commonly used to "outdo the Joneses."

Propelled by the strength of a single *gondoliere*, these boats, unique to Venice, have no modern equipment. They move with no great speed but with unrivaled grace. The right side of the gondola is lower because the *gondoliere* always stands in the back of the boat on the left. Although the San Trovaso *squero*, or boatyard, is the city's oldest and one of only three remaining (the other two are immeasurably more difficult to find), its predominant focus is on maintenance and repair. They will occasionally build a new gondola (which takes some 40–45 working days), carefully crafting it from the seven types of wood—mahogany, cherry, fir, walnut, oak, elm, and lime—necessary to give the shallow and asymmetrical boat its various characteristics. After all the pieces are put together, the painting, the *ferro* (the iron symbol of the city affixed to the bow), and the wood-carving that secures the oar are commissioned out to various local artisans.

Although some 10,000 of these elegant boats floated on the canals of Venice in the 16th century, today there are only 350. But the job of *gondoliere* remains a coveted profession, passed down from father to son over the centuries.

no one hallmark masterpiece in this collection; rather, this is an outstanding and comprehensive showcase of works by all the great master painters of Venice, the largest such collection in the world.

It includes Paolo and Lorenzo Veneziano from the 14th century; Gentile and Giovanni Bellini (and Giovanni's brother-in-law Andrea Mantegna from Padua) and Vittore Carpaccio from the 15th century; Giorgione (whose *Tempest* is one of the gallery's most famous highlights), Tintoretto, Veronese (see his *Feast in the House of Levi* here), and Titian from the 16th century; and, from the 17th and 18th centuries, Canaletto, Piazzetta, Longhi, and Tiepolo, among others.

Most of all, the works open a window to the Venice of 500 years ago. Indeed, the canvases reveal how little Venice has changed over the centuries. Housed in a deconsecrated church and its adjoining *scuola,* the church's confraternity hall, it is Venice's principal picture gallery, and one of the most important in Italy. Because of fire regulations, admission is limited, and lines can be daunting (check for extended evening hours in peak months), but put up with the wait and don't miss it.

Dorsoduro, at foot of Accademia Bridge. www.gallerieaccademia.org. ✆ **041-520-0345.** Admission 6.50€ adults, 3.25€ E.U. citizens 19–25 and free for E.U. citizens 18 and under, free for children 12 and under. Paying 1€ more a ticket, you can reserve tickets by phone or online, thereby saving yourself from potential lines. Daily 8:15am–7:15pm (Mon until 2pm). *Vaporetto:* Accademia.

I Gesuati (Santa Maria del Rosario) ★ CHURCH Built from 1724 to 1736 to mirror the Redentore across the wide Canale della Giudecca, the Jesuits' church counters the Palladian sobriety of the Redentore with rococo flair. The interior is graced by airy 1737–39 ceiling frescoes (some of the first in Venice) by Giambattista Tiepolo. Tiepolo also did the *Virgin in Glory with Saints Rosa, Catherine of Siena,* and *Agnes of Montepulciano* on the first altar on the right. The third altar has a Tintoretto *Crucifixion.*

Fondamenta Zattere ai Gesuati. ✆ **041-275-0462.** Admission 3€ adults, free for children 5 and under. Mon–Sat 10am–5pm; Sun 1–5pm. *Vaporetto:* Zattere.

Punta della Dogana ★★★ 📷 ARCHITECTURE The eastern tip (*punta*) of Dorsoduro is covered by the triangular 15th-century (restructured with a new facade in 1676–82) customs house that once controlled all boats entering the Grand Canal. It's topped by a statue of Fortune holding aloft a golden ball. Now it makes for remarkable, sweeping views across the *bacino* San Marco, from the last leg of the Grand Canal past Piazzetta San Marco and the Ducal Palace, over the nearby isle of San Giorgio Maggiore, La Giudecca, and out into the lagoon itself.

Fondamenta Dogana alla Salute. *Vaporetto:* Salute.

Santa Maria della Salute (Church of the Virgin Mary of Good Health) ★ CHURCH Generally referred to as "La Salute," this crown jewel of 17th-century baroque architecture proudly reigns at a commercially and aesthetically

Santa Maria della Salute, more commonly called the Salute.

important point, almost directly across from the Piazza San Marco, where the Grand Canal empties into the lagoon.

The first stone was laid in 1631 after the Senate decided to honor the Virgin Mary of Good Health for delivering Venice from a plague. They accepted the revolutionary plans of a young, relatively unknown architect, Baldassare Longhena (who would go on to design, among other projects, the Ca' Rezzonico). He dedicated the next 50 years of his life to overseeing its progress (he would die 1 year after its inauguration but 5 years before its completion).

The octagonal Salute is recognized for its exuberant exterior of volutes, scrolls, and more than 125 statues and its rather sober interior that is livened up in the sacristy where you will find a number of important ceiling paintings and portraits of the Evangelists and church doctors by Titian. On the right wall of the sacristy, which you have to pay to enter, is Tintoretto's *Marriage at Cana,* often considered one of his best paintings.

Dorsoduro (on Campo della Salute). ✆ **041-522-5558.** Free admission to church; sacristy 2.50€. Daily 9am–noon and 3–5:30pm. *Vaporetto:* Salute.

Squero di San Trovaso ★★ 🎁 HISTORIC SITE One of the most interesting (and photographed) sights you'll see in Venice is this small *squero* (boatyard), which first opened in the 17th century. Just north of the Zattere (the wide, sunny walkway that runs alongside the Giudecca Canal in Dorsoduro), the boatyard lies next to the Church of San Trovaso on the narrow Rio San Trovaso (not far from the Accademia Bridge). It is surrounded by Tyrolean-looking wooden structures (a true rarity in this city of stone built on water) that are home to the multigenerational owners and original workshops for traditional Venetian boats (see "The Art of the Gondola," above). Aware that they have become a tourist site themselves, the gondoliers don't mind if you watch them at work from across the narrow Rio di San Trovaso, but don't try to invite yourself in. ***Tip:*** It's the perfect midway photo op after a visit to the Gallerie dell'Accademia and a trip to Gelateria Nico (Zattere 922), whose chocolate *gianduiotto* is every bit as decadent as Venice just before the fall of the Republic.

Dorsoduro 1097 (on the Rio San Trovaso, southwest of the Accademia Gallery). No phone. Free admission. *Vaporetto:* Zattere.

The Frari (Santa Maria Gloriosa dei Frari).

San Polo & Santa Croce

Santa Maria Gloriosa dei Frari (Church of the Frari) ★★ CHURCH Known simply as "i Frari," this immense 13th- to 14th-century Gothic church is easily found around the corner from the Scuola Grande di San Rocco—make sure you visit both when you're in this area. Built by the Franciscans (*frari* is a dialectal distortion of *frati,* or "brothers"), it is the largest church in Venice after the San Marco. The Frari has long been considered something of a memorial to the ancient glories of Venice. Since St. Francis and the order he founded emphasized prayer and poverty, it is not surprising that the church is austere both inside and out. Yet it houses a number of important works, including two Titian masterpieces. The more striking is his *Assumption of the Virgin* over the main altar, painted when the artist was only in his late 20s. His *Virgin of the Pesaro Family* is in the left nave; for this work commissioned by one of Venice's most powerful families, Titian's wife posed for the figure of Mary (and then died soon afterward in childbirth).

San Polo 3072 (on Campo dei Frari). ✆ **041-522-2637.** Admission 3€ Mon–Sat 9am–6pm; Sun 1–6pm. *Vaporetto:* San Tomà (walk straight ahead on Calle del Traghetto; then turn right and left across Campo San Tomà; walk as straight ahead as you can, on Ramo Mandoler, then Calle Larga Prima, and turn right when you reach beginning of Salizada San Rocco).

Scuola Grande di San Rocco (Confraternity of St. Roch) ★★★ MUSEUM Jacopo Robusti (1518–94), called Tintoretto because his father was a dyer (his name being the diminutive of *tintore,* which means dyer), was a devout, unworldly man who traveled only once beyond Venice. His epic canvases are filled with phantasmagoric light and intense, mystical spirituality. This museum is a dazzling monument to his work—it holds the largest collection of his images anywhere. The series of the more than 50 dark and dramatic works took the artist more than 20 years to complete, making this the richest of the many confraternity guilds or *scuole* that once flourished in Venice.

Begin upstairs in the Sala dell'Albergo, where the most notable of the enormous, powerful canvases is the moving *La Crocifissione (The Crucifixion).* In the center of the gilt ceiling of the great hall, also upstairs, is *Il Serpente di Bronzo*

Tintoretto's paintings adorn the ceiling of San Rocco.

(*The Bronze Snake*). Among the eight huge, sweeping paintings downstairs—each depicting a scene from the New Testament—*La Strage degli Innocenti* (*The Slaughter of the Innocents*) is the most noteworthy, so full of dramatic urgency and energy that the figures seem almost to tumble out of the frame. As you enter the room, it's on the opposite wall at the far end of the room.

There's a useful guide to the paintings posted inside on the wall just before the entrance to the museum. There are a few Tiepolos among the paintings, as well as a solitary work by Titian. The works on or near the staircase are not by Tintoretto.

San Polo 3058 (on Campo San Rocco adjacent to Campo dei Frari). www.scuolagrandesanrocco.it. ✆ **041-523-4864.** Admission 8€ adults (price includes audio guide), 6€ ages 18–26, 18 and under free. Daily 9:30am–5:30pm. *Vaporetto:* San Tomà (walk straight ahead on Calle del Traghetto and turn right and immediately left across Campo San Tomà; walk as straight ahead as you can, on Ramo Mandoler, Calle Larga Prima, and Salizada San Rocco, which leads into the *campo* of the same name—look for crimson sign behind Frari Church).

Cannaregio

Ca' d'Oro (Galleria Giorgio Franchetti) ★★ MUSEUM The 15th-century Ca' d'Oro is one of the best preserved and most impressive of the hundreds of *palazzi* lining the Grand Canal. After the Palazzo Ducale, it's the city's finest example of Venetian Gothic architecture. Its name, the Golden Palace, refers to the gilt-covered facade that faded long ago and is now pink and white. Inside, the beam ceilings and ornate trappings provide a backdrop for the collection of former owner Baron Franchetti, who bequeathed his home and artworks to the city during World War I.

The core collection, expanded over the years, now includes sculptures, furniture, 16th-century Flemish tapestries, an impressive collection of bronzes (12th–16th c.), and a gallery whose most important canvases are Andrea Mantegna's *San Sebastiano* and Titian's *Venus at the Mirror*, as well as lesser paintings by Tintoretto, Carpaccio, Van Dyck, Giorgione, and Jan Steen. For a delightful break, step out onto the *palazzo*'s loggia, overlooking the Grand Canal, for a view up and down the waterway and across to the Pescheria, a timeless vignette of an unchanged city. Off the loggia is a small but worthy ceramics collection, open daily 10am to noon.

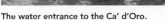

The water entrance to the Ca' d'Oro.

Cannaregio btw. 3931 and 3932 (on Calle Ca' d'Oro north of Rialto Bridge). www.cadoro.org. ✆ **041-520-0345.** Admission 6.50€, 6€ for ages 6–14 and students 30 and under. Mon 8:15am–2pm; Tues–Sun 8:15am–7:15pm. *Vaporetto:* Ca' d'Oro.

Chiesa Santa Maria dei Miracoli ★ CHURCH Hidden in a quiet corner of the residential section of

The Jews of Venice

Jews began settling in Venice in great numbers in the 16th century, and the Republic soon came to value their services as moneylenders, physicians, and traders. For centuries, the Jewish population was forced to live on an island that now encompasses the Campo Ghetto Nuovo, and drawbridges were raised to enforce a nighttime curfew. By the end of the 17th century, as many as 5,000 Jews lived in the Ghetto's cramped confines. Today the city's Jewish population is comprised of only about 500 people, few of whom live in the Ghetto.

Cannaregio northeast of the Rialto Bridge, the small and exceedingly attractive 15th-century Miracoli has one side of its precious polychrome-marbled facade running alongside a canal, creating colorful and shimmering reflections. The architect, Pietro Lombardo, a local artisan whose background in monuments and tombs is obvious, would go on to become one of the founding fathers of the Venetian Renaissance.

The less romantic are inclined to compare it to a large tomb with a dome, but the untold couples who have made this perfectly proportioned jewel-like church their choice for weddings will dispel such insensitivity. The small square in front is the perfect place for gondolas to drop off and pick up the newly betrothed. The inside is intricately decorated with early Renaissance marble reliefs, its pastel palette of pink, gray, and white marble making an elegant venue for all those weddings. In the 1470s, an image of the Virgin Mary was responsible for a series of miracles (including bringing back to life someone who spent half an hour at the bottom of the Giudecca Canal) that led pilgrims to leave gifts and, eventually, enough donations to have this church built. Look for the icon now displayed over the main altar.

Cannaregio, Rio d. Miracoli. No phone. Admission 3€. Mon–Sat 10am–5pm; Sun 3–5pm. *Vaporetto:* Rialto (located midway btw. the Rialto Bridge and the Campo SS. Giovanni e Paolo).

Il Ghetto (The Jewish Ghetto) ★★ HISTORIC SITE Venice's relationship with its longtime Jewish community fluctuated over time from acceptance to borderline tolerance, attitudes often influenced by the fear that Jewish moneylenders and merchants would infiltrate other sectors of the Republic's commerce under a government that thrived on secrecy and control. In 1516, 700 Jews were forced to move to this then-remote northwestern corner of Venice, to an abandoned site of a 14th-century foundry (*ghetto* is old Venetian dialect for "foundry," a word that would soon be used throughout Europe and the world to depict an area where isolated minority groups lived).

This *ghetto* neighborhood was totally surrounded by water. Its two access points were controlled at night and early morning by heavy gates manned by Christian guards (paid for by the Jews), both protecting and segregating its inhabitants. Within a century, the community grew to more than 5,000, representing many languages and cultures. Although the original Ghetto Nuovo (New Ghetto) was expanded to include the Ghetto Vecchio (Old Ghetto) and later the Ghetto Nuovissimo (Newest Ghetto), land was limited and quarters always cramped. The fact that the "New Ghetto" preceded the "Old Ghetto," which in turn was followed by the "Newest Ghetto" can be confusing, but remember that *ghetto* meant "foundry," and when the Jews moved into the area occupied by its ruins, they first occupied the newer part of the former foundry and then the older part and then still later the newest part. In 1797, when Napoleon rolled into town, the *ghetto* as an institution was disbanded and Jews were free to move elsewhere. Still, it remains the center of Venice's ever-diminishing community of Jewish families; although accounts vary widely, it's said that anywhere from 500 to 2,000 Jews live in all of Venice and Mestre.

Aside from its historic interest, this is also one of the less touristy neighborhoods in Venice (though it has become something of a nightspot) and makes for a pleasant and scenic place to stroll.

Venice's first kosher restaurant, **Gam Gam,** opened in 1996 on Fondamenta di Cannaregio 1122 (✆ **041-523-1495**), near the entrance to the Jewish Ghetto and close to the Guglie *vaporetto* stop. Owned and run by Orthodox Jews from New York, it serves lunch and dinner Sunday through Friday, with an early Friday closing after lunch.

Cannaregio (Campo del Ghetto Nuovo). *Vaporetto:* Guglie or San Marcuola (from either of the 2 *vaporetto* stops, or if walking from the train station, locate the Ponte delle Guglie; walking away from the Grand Canal along the Fondamenta di Cannaregio, take the 2nd right at the corner where Gam Gam is located; this is the entrance to the Calle del Ghetto Vecchio that leads to the Campo del Ghetto Nuovo).

Museo Communità Ebraica (Jewish Museum of Venice) ★ MUSEUM/SYNAGOGUE The only way to visit any of the area's five 16th-century synagogues is through one of the Museo Communità Ebraica's frequent organized tours conducted in English. Your guide will elaborate on the commercial and political climate of those times, the unique "skyscraper" architecture (overcrowding resulted in many buildings having as many as seven low-ceiling stories, several more than most Venetian buildings), and the daily lifestyle of the Jewish community until the arrival of Napoleon in 1797. You'll get to visit historic temples dedicated to the rites of all three major Jewish groups who called Venice home: Italian (Scola Italiana), Sephardic (Scola Levantina), and Ashkenazi (Scola Canton).

Cannaregio 2902B (on Campo del Ghetto Nuovo). www.museoebraico.it. ✆ **041-715-359.** Museum 3€ adults, 2€ children; museum and synagogue tour 8.50€ adults, 7€ children. Museum Sun–Fri 10am–7pm (Oct–May until 6pm); synagogue tours hourly 10:30am–5:30pm (Oct–May last tour 4:30). Closed on Jewish holidays. *Vaporetto:* Guglie.

A gondola on the Grand Canal, passing by San Giorgio Maggiore.

Giudecca & San Giorgio

Chiesa di San Giorgio Maggiore ★★ CHURCH This church sits on the little island of San Giorgio Maggiore across from Piazza San Marco. It is one of the masterpieces of Andrea Palladio, the great Renaissance architect from nearby

Il Redentore.

Vicenza. Most known for his country villas built for Venice's wealthy merchant families, Palladio was commissioned to build two churches (the other is the Redentore on the neighboring Giudecca island), beginning with San Giorgio, designed in 1565 and completed in 1610. To impose a classical facade on the traditional church structure, Palladio designed two interlocking facades, with repeating triangles, rectangles, and columns that are harmoniously proportioned. Founded as early as the 10th century, the interior of the church was reinterpreted by Palladio with whitewashed surfaces, stark but majestic, and unadorned but harmonious space. The main altar is flanked by two epic paintings by an elderly Tintoretto, *The Fall of Manna,* to the left, and the more noteworthy *Last Supper,* to the right, famous for its chiaroscuro. Through the doorway to the right of the choir leading to the Cappella dei Morti (Chapel of the Dead), you will find Tintoretto's *Deposition.*

To the left of the choir is an elevator that you can take to the top of the campanile—for a charge of 3€—to experience an unforgettable view of the island, the lagoon, and the Palazzo Ducale and Piazza San Marco across the way.

A handful of remaining Benedictine monks gather for Sunday Mass at 11am, sung in Gregorian chant.

On the island of San Giorgio Maggiore, across St. Mark's Basin from Piazzetta San Marco. ✆ **041-522-7827.** Free admission. Mon–Sat 9:30am–12:30pm; daily 2–6pm. *Vaporetto:* Take the Giudecca-bound *vaporetto* (82) on Riva degli Schiavoni and get off at the 1st stop, the island of San Giorgio Maggiore.

Il Redentore ★ CHURCH Perhaps the masterpiece among Palladio's churches, Il Redentore was commissioned by Venice to give thanks for being delivered from the great plague (1575–77), which claimed over a quarter of the population (some 46,000 people). The doge established a tradition of visiting this church by crossing a long pontoon bridge made up of boats from the Dorsoduro's Zattere on the third Sunday of each July, a tradition that survived the demise of the doges and remains one of Venice's most popular festivals (p. 464).

The interior is done in grand, austere, painstakingly classical Palladian style. The artworks tend to be workshop pieces (from the studios or schools, but not the actual brushes, of Tintoretto and Veronese), but there is a fine *Baptism of Christ* by Veronese himself in the sacristy, which also contains Alvise Vivarini's *Adoration* and *Angels* alongside works by Jacopo da Bassano and Palma il Giovane, who also did the *Deposition* over the right aisle's third chapel.

Campo del Redentore, La Giudecca. ✆ **041-523-1415.** Admission 3€. Mon–Sat 10am–5pm; Sun 1–5pm. *Vaporetto:* Redentore.

EXPLORING VENICE'S ISLANDS

Venice shares its lagoon with three other principal islands: Murano, Burano, and Torcello. Guided tours of the three are operated by a dozen agencies with docks on Riva degli Schiavoni/Piazzetta San Marco (all interchangeable). The 3- and 4-hour tours run 20€ to 35€, usually include a visit to a Murano glass factory (you can easily do that on your own, with less of a hard sell), and leave daily around 9:30am and 2:30pm (times change; check in advance).

You can also visit the islands on your own conveniently and easily using the *vaporetti*. Line nos. 5, 13, 18, 41, 42, A, B, and LN make the journey to Murano from Fondamente Nove (on the north side of Castello), and line LN continues on to Burano from where there is a boat that makes the short trip to Torcello. The islands are small and easy to navigate, but check the schedule for the next island-to-island departure (usually hourly) and your return so that you don't spend most of your day waiting for connections.

Murano & Its Glass

The island of **Murano ★★** has long been famous throughout the world for the products of its glass factories, but there's little here in variety or prices that you won't find in Venice. A visit to the **Museo del Vetro (Museum of Glass),** Fondamenta Giustinian 8 (✆ **041-739-586**), will put the island's centuries-old

Murano glass.

legacy into perspective and is recommended for those considering major buys. Hours are Thursday to Tuesday 10am to 6pm (Nov–Mar to 5pm), and admission is 6€ for adults and 3.50€ children 6 to 14 and students 30 and under, or free with the cumulative Museum Pass (see "Venice Discounts," on p. 442).

Dozens of *fornaci* (kilns) offer free shows of mouth-blown glassmaking almost invariably hitched to a hard-sell ("No obligation! Really!") tour of the factory outlet. These retail showrooms of delicate glassware can be enlightening or boring, depending on your frame of mind. Almost all the places will ship their goods, but that often doubles the price. On the other hand, these pieces are instant heirlooms.

Murano also has two worthy churches: **San Pietro Martire ★**, with its altarpieces by Tintoretto, Veronese, and Giovanni Bellini, and the ancient **Santa Maria e Donato ★**, with an intricate Byzantine exterior apse and a 6th-century pulpit and columns inside resting on a fantastic 12th-century inlaid floor.

Burano & Its Lace

Lace is the claim to fame of tiny, colorful **Burano ★★★**, a craft kept alive for centuries by the wives of fishermen waiting for their husbands to return from sea. It's worth a trip if you have time to stroll the back streets of the island, whose canals are lined with the brightly colored simple homes of the Buranesi fishermen. The local government continues its attempt to keep its centuries-old lace legacy alive with subsidized classes.

Visit the **Museo del Merletto (Museum of Lace Making),** Piazza Galuppi (✆ **041-730-034**), to understand why something so exquisite should not be left to fade into extinction. It's open Tuesday to Sunday 10am to 6pm (Nov–Mar to 5pm), and admission is 5€ adults and 3.50€ children 6 to 14 and students 29 and under, or free with the cumulative Museum Pass (see "Venice Discounts," on p. 442).

Street painters capture the colors on Burano.

Torcello & Its Cathedral

Nearby **Torcello ★★** is perhaps the most charming of the islands. It was the first of the lagoon islands to be called home by the mainland population fleeing Attila and his Huns (from here they eventually moved to join the growing area around where there is now the Rialto Bridge), but today it consists of little more than one long canal leading from the *vaporetto* landing past sad-sack vineyards to a clump of buildings at its center.

Torcello boasts the oldest Venetian monument, the **Cattedrale di Torcello (Santa Maria Assunta) ★★★**, whose foundation dates from the 7th century (**✆ 041-270-2464**). It's famous for its outstanding 11th- to 12-century Byzantine mosaics—a *Madonna and Child* in the apse and *Last Judgment* on the west wall—rivaling those of Ravenna's and St. Mark's basilicas. The cathedral is open daily 10:30am to 6pm (Nov–Feb to 5pm), and admission is 5€. You can climb the bell tower for a panorama for 3€. Also of interest is the adjacent **11th-century church** dedicated to St. Fosca and a **small archaeological museum;** the church's hours are the same as the cathedral's, and the museum is open Tuesday to Sunday 10am to 5:30pm (Nov–Feb to 5pm). Museum admission is 3€. A combined ticket for all three sights is 8€.

Peaceful Torcello is uninhabited except for a handful of families and is a favorite picnic spot (you'll have to bring the food from Venice—there are no stores on the island; there is a bar/trattoria and one rather expensive restaurant, the Cipriani, of Hemingway fame, which is worth a splurge). Once the tour groups have left, it offers a very special moment of solitude and escape when St. Mark's bottleneck becomes oppressive.

The Lido & Its Beaches

Although a convenient 15-minute *vaporetto* ride away from San Marco, Venice's **Lido beaches** are not much to write home about. For bathing and sun-worshipping there are much nicer beaches nearby—in Jesolo, to the north, for example. But the parade of wealthy Italian and foreign tourists (plus a good number of Venetian families with children) who frequent this coastal area throughout summer is an interesting sight indeed, although you'll find many of them at the elitist beaches affiliated with such deluxe hotels as the legendary Excelsior and the Des Bains.

There are two beach areas at the Lido. **Bucintoro** is at the opposite end of Gran Viale Santa Maria Elisabetta (referred to as the Gran Viale) from the *vaporetto* station Santa Elisabetta. It's a 10-minute stroll; walk straight ahead along Gran Viale to reach the beach. **San Nicolò,** about 1.5km (1 mile) away, can be reached by bus B. You'll have to pay 1€ per person (standard procedure at Italy's beaches) for use of the cabins and umbrella rental. Alternatively, you can patronize the more crowded and noisier **public beach,** Zona A at the end of Gran Viale. Keep in mind that if you stay at any of the hotels on the Lido, most of them have some kind of agreement with the different *bagni* (beach establishments).

The Lido's limited sports amenities, such as golf and tennis, are affiliated with its deluxe five-star hotels. Although there is car traffic, the Lido's wide, shaded boulevards are your best bet for jogging while you're visiting Venice. A number of bike-rental places along the Gran Viale rent bicycles for 5€ to 10€ an hour. *Vaporetto* line nos. 1, 2, 51, 52, and LN cross the lagoon to the Lido from the San Zaccaria–Danieli stop near San Marco.

carnevale A VENEZIA

Venetians once more are taking to the open *piazze* and streets for the pre-Lenten holiday of Carnevale. The festival traditionally was the celebration preceding Lent, the period of penitence and abstinence prior to Easter; its name is derived from the Latin *carnem levare,* meaning "to take meat away."

Today Carnevale lasts no more than 5 to 10 days and culminates in the Friday to Tuesday before Ash Wednesday. In the 18th-century heyday of Carnevale in La Serenissima Republic, well-heeled revelers came from all over Europe to take part in festivities that began months prior to Lent and reached a raucous climax at midnight on Shrove Tuesday. As the Venetian economy declined and its colonies and trading posts fell to other powers, the Republic of Venice in its swan song turned to fantasy and escapism. The faster its decline, the longer, and more licentious, became its anything-goes merrymaking. Masks became ubiquitous, affording anonymity and the pardoning of a thousand sins. Masks permitted the fishmonger to attend the ball and dance with the baroness, the properly married to carry on as if they were not. The doges condemned it and the popes denounced it, but nothing could dampen the Venetian Carnevale spirit until Napoleon arrived in 1797 and put an end to the festivities.

Resuscitated in 1980 by local tourism powers to fill the empty winter months when tourism comes to a screeching halt, Carnevale is calmer nowadays, though just barely. The born-again festival got off to a shaky start, met at first with indifference and skepticism, but in the years since has grown in popularity and been embraced by the locals. In the 1980s, Carnevale attracted an onslaught of what was seemingly the entire student population of Europe, backpacking young people who slept in the *piazze* and train station. Politicians and city officials adopted a middle-of-the-road policy that helped establish Carnevale's image as neither a backpacker's free-for-all outdoor party nor a continuation of the exclusive private balls in the Grand Canal *palazzi* available to a very few.

Carnevale is now a harlequin patchwork of musical and cultural events, many of them free of charge, which

Festivals & Special Events

Venice's most special event is the yearly pre-Lenten **Carnevale ★★★**, a 2-week theatrical resuscitation of the 18th-century bacchanalia that drew tourists during the final heyday of the Most Serene Republic. Most of today's Carnevale-related events, masked balls, and costumes evoke that time. Many of the concerts around town are free, when baroque to samba to gospel to Dixieland jazz music fills the *campi* and byways; check with the tourist office for a list of events. Carnevale builds for 10 days until the big blowout, **Shrove Tuesday** (Fat Tues), when fireworks illuminate the Grand Canal, and Piazza San Marco is turned into a giant open-air ballroom for the masses. Book your hotel months ahead, especially for the 2 weekends prior to Shrove Tuesday. See "Carnevale a Venezia," above, for more info.

The **Voga Longa ★★** (literally "long row"), a 30km (20-mile) rowing "race" from San Marco to Burano and back again, has been enthusiastically embraced since its inception in 1975, following the city's effort to keep alive the centuries-old appeals to all ages, tastes, nationalities, and budgets. Musical events are staged in some of the city's dozens of *piazze*—from reggae and zydeco to jazz and baroque. Special art exhibits are mounted at museums and galleries.

The city is the perfect venue; Hollywood could not create a more evocative location. This is a celebration of history, art, theater, and drama that one would expect to find in Italy, the land that gave us the Renaissance and Zeffirelli—and Venice, an ancient and wealthy republic that gave us Casanova and Vivaldi. Venice and Carnevale were made for each other.

heritage of the regatta. It takes place on a Sunday in mid- to late May; for exact dates, consult the tourist office or www.vogalonga.com. It's a colorful event and a great excuse to party, plus every local seems to have a relative or next-door neighbor competing.

Stupendous fireworks light the night sky during the **Festa del Redentore ★**, on the third Saturday and Sunday in July. This celebration, which marks the July 1577 lifting of a plague that had killed more than a quarter of the city's population, including the great painter Titian, is centered on the Palladio-designed Chiesa del Redentore (Church of the Redeemer) on the island of Giudecca. For the occasion, a bridge of boats across the Giudecca Canal links the church with the banks of Le Zattere in Dorsoduro, and hundreds of boats of all shapes and sizes fill the area. It's one big, floating *festa* until night descends and an awesome half-hour *spettacolo* of fireworks fills the sky.

The **Venice International Film Festival ★**, in late August and early September, is the most respected celebration of celluloid in Europe after Cannes. Films from all over the world are shown in the Palazzo del Cinema on the Lido as well as at various venues—and occasionally in some of the *campi*. Ticket prices vary, but those for the less-sought-after films are usually modest.

Venice hosts the latest in modern and contemporary painting and sculpture from dozens of countries during the prestigious **Biennale d'Arte ★★★** (www.labiennale.org; ✆ **041-521-8711**), one of the world's top international modern art shows. It fills the pavilions of the public gardens at the east end of Castello and in the Arsenale as well as in other spaces around the city from late May to October every odd-numbered year. In the past, awards have gone to Jackson Pollock, Henri Matisse, Alexander Calder, and Federico Fellini, among others. Tickets cost 20€, 16€ for those 65 and over, and 12€ for students and all those 26 and under.

The **Regata Storica ★★** that takes place on the Grand Canal on the first Sunday in September is an extravagant seagoing parade in historic costume as well as a genuine regatta. Just about every seaworthy gondola, richly decked out for the occasion and piloted by *gondolieri* in colorful livery, participates in the opening cavalcade. The aquatic parade is followed by three regattas along the Grand Canal. You can buy grandstand tickets through the tourist office or come early, very early, and find a piece of embankment near the Rialto Bridge for the best seats in town.

Other notable events include **Festa della Salute ★** on November 21, when a pontoon bridge is erected across the Grand Canal to connect the churches of La Salute and Santa Maria del Giglio, commemorating delivery from another plague in 1630. The **Festa della Sensa,** on the Sunday following Ascension Day in May, reenacts the ancient ceremony when the doge would wed Venice to the sea. April 25 is a local holiday, the **feast day of Saint Mark,** beloved patron saint of Venice and of the ancient republic. A special High Mass is celebrated in the Basilica of San Marco, and Venetians exchange roses with those they love.

Especially for Kids

It goes without saying that a **gondola ride** will be the thrill of a lifetime for any child or adult. If that's too expensive, consider the convenient and far less expensive alternative: a **ride on the no. 1 *vaporetto*.** They offer two entirely different experiences: The gondola gives you the chance to see Venice through the back door (and ride past Marco Polo's house); the *vaporetto* provides a utilitarian—but no less gorgeous—journey down Venice's aquatic Main Street, the Grand Canal. Look for the ambulance boat, the garbage boat, the firefighters' boat, the funeral boat, even the Coca-Cola delivery boat. Best sightings are the special gondolas filled with flowers and rowed by *gondolieri* in livery delivering a happy bride and groom from the church.

Judging from the squeals of delight, **feeding the pigeons in Piazza San Marco** (purchase a bag of corn and you'll be draped in pigeons in a nanosecond) could be the epitome of your child's visit to Venice, and it's the ultimate photo op. Be sure your child won't be startled by all the fluttering and flapping.

A jaunt to the neighboring **island of Murano** can be as educational as it is recreational—follow the signs to any *fornace* (kiln), where a glass-blowing performance of the island's thousand-year-old art is free entertainment. But be ready for the guaranteed sales pitch that follows.

Before you leave town, take the elevator to the **top of the Campanile di San Marco** (the highest structure in the city) for a pigeon's-eye view of Venice's rooftops and church cupolas, or get up close and personal with the four bronze horses on the facade of the Basilica San Marco. The view from its **outdoor loggia** is something you and your children won't forget.

Some children enjoy the **Museo Storico Navale (Naval History Museum)** and **Arsenale (Arsenal)** with its ship models and old vessels, and the many historic artifacts in the **Museo Civico Correr (Correr Civic Museum),** tangible vestiges of a time when Venice was a world unto itself.

The **winged lion,** said to have been a kind of good luck mascot to St. Mark, patron saint of Venice, was the very symbol of the Serene Republic and to this day appears on everything from cafe napkins to T-shirts. Who can spot the most flying lions? They appear on facades, atop columns, over doorways, as pavement mosaics, on government stamps, and on the local flag.

WHERE TO EAT

Eating cheaply in Venice is not easy, though it's by no means impossible. So plan well and don't rely on the serendipity that may serve you in other cities. If you've bought a Rolling Venice card, ask for the guide listing dozens of restaurants offering 10% to 30% discounts for cardholders. Bear in mind that, compared with Rome and other points south, Venice is a city of early meals: You should be seated by 7:30 to 8:30pm. Most kitchens close at 10 or 10:30pm, even though the restaurant may stay open until 11:30pm or midnight.

While most restaurants in Italy include a cover charge (*coperto*) that usually runs 1.50€ to 3€, in Venice they tend to instead tack on 10% to 12% to the bill for "taxes and service." Some places in Venice will very annoyingly charge you the cover and still add on 12%. A menu should state clearly what extras the restaurant charges (sometimes you'll find it in miniscule print at the bottom) and if it doesn't, take your business elsewhere.

BUDGET DINING Pizza is the fuel of Naples while bruschetta and *crostini* (small, open-face sandwiches) are the rustic soul food of Florence. In Venice it's *tramezzini* (small, triangular white bread half-sandwiches filled with everything from thinly sliced meats and tuna salad to cheeses and vegetables) and *cicchetti* (tapaslike finger foods, such as calamari rings, speared fried olives, potato croquettes, or grilled polenta squares), traditionally washed down with a small glass of wine, or *ombra*. Venice offers countless neighborhood bars called *bacari* and cafes where you can stand or sit with a *tramezzino,* a selection of *cicchetti,* a *panino,* or a *toast* (grilled ham and cheese sandwich). All of the above will cost approximately 3€ to 6€ if you stand at the bar, as much as double when seated. Bar food is displayed on the countertop or in glass counters and usually sells out by late afternoon, so though it can make a great lunch, don't rely on it for a light dinner. A concentration of popular, well stocked bars can be found along the Mercerie shopping strip that connects Piazza San Marco with the Rialto Bridge, the always lively Campo San Luca (look for **Bar Torino, Bar Black Jack,** or the character-filled **Leon Bianco** wine bar), and Campo Santa Margherita. Avoid the tired-looking pizza (revitalized only marginally by microwaves) you'll find in most bars; informal sit down neighborhood pizzerias everywhere offer savory and far fresher renditions for a minimum of 6€, plus your drink and cover charge—the perfect lunch or light dinner.

CULINARY DELIGHTS Venice has a distinguished culinary history, much of it based on its geographical position on the sea and, to a lesser degree, its

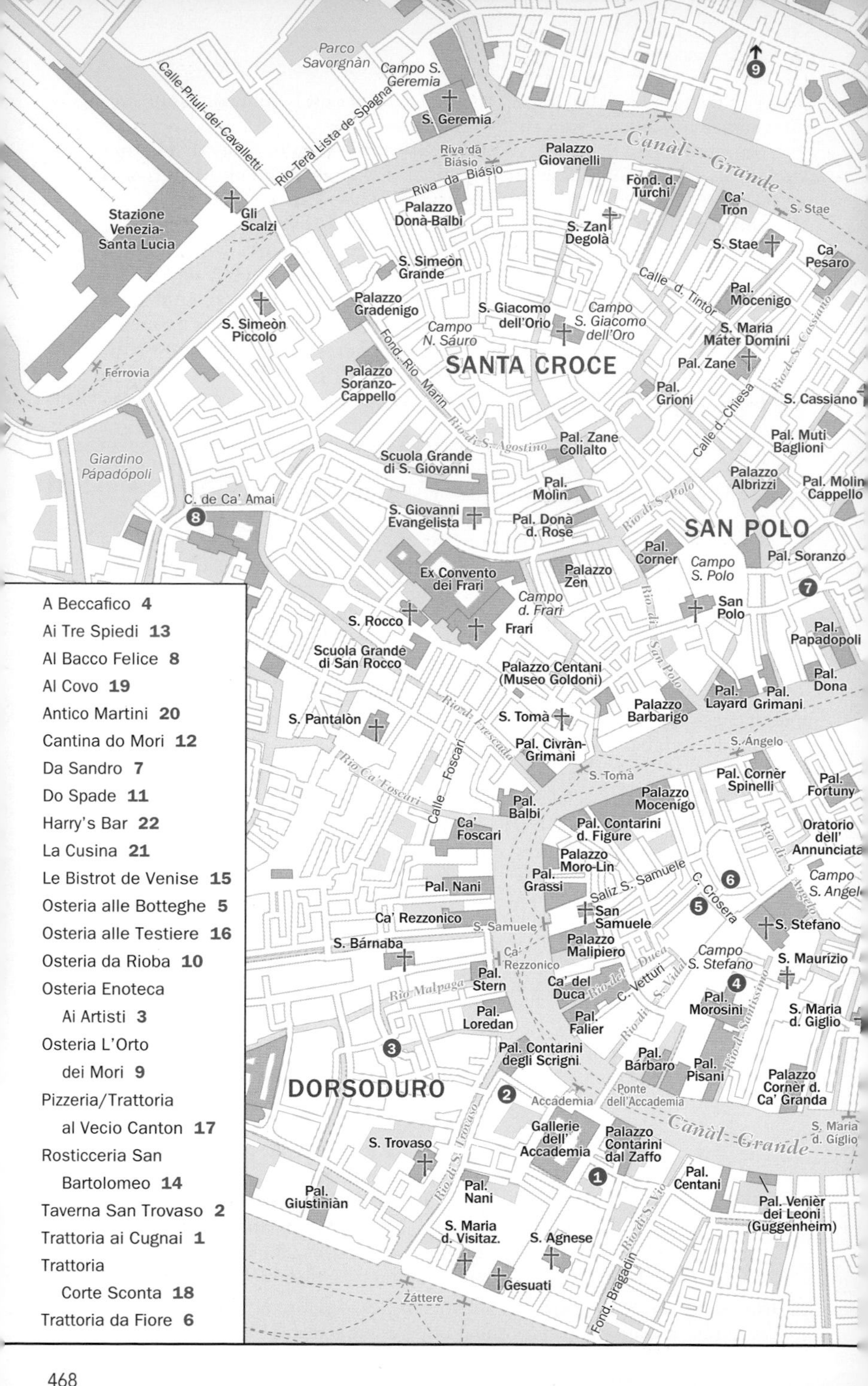

Parco Savorgnàn
Campo S. Geremia
S. Geremia
Calle Priuli dei Cavalletti
Rio Terà Lista de Spagna
Riva da Biásio
Riva da Biásio
Palazzo Giovanelli
Canàl Grande
Fond. d. Turchi
Ca' Tron
S. Stae
Stazione Venezia-Santa Lucia
Gli Scalzi
Palazzo Donà-Balbi
S. Zan Degolà
S. Stae
Ca' Pesaro
S. Simeòn Grande
Calle d. Tintor
Pal. Mocenigo
Palazzo Gradenigo
S. Giacomo dell'Orio
Campo S. Giacomo dell'Oro
S. Simeòn Piccolo
Campo N. Sáuro
S. Maria Mater Domini
Fond. Rio Marin
SANTA CROCE
Pal. Zane
Ferrovia
Palazzo Soranzo-Cappello
Pal. Grioni
S. Cassiano
Calle d. Chiesa
Rio di S. Agostino
Pal. Zane Collalto
Pal. Muti Baglioni
Giardino Pápadópoli
Scuola Grande di S. Giovanni
Palazzo Albrizzi
Pal. Molin Cappello
Pal. Molin
C. de Ca' Amai
8
S. Giovanni Evangelista
Pal. Donà d. Rose
Rio di S. Polo
SAN POLO
Pal. Corner
Campo S. Polo
Pal. Soranzo
Ex Convento dei Frari
Palazzo Zen
7
Campo d. Frari
San Polo
S. Rocco
Frari
Pal. Papadopoli
Scuola Grande di San Rocco
Palazzo Centani (Museo Goldoni)
Rio di San Polo
Pal. Dona
Pal. Layard
Pal. Grimani
Palazzo Barbarigo
S. Pantalòn
Rio d. Frescada
S. Tomà
Pal. Civràn-Grimani
S. Ángelo
Rio Ca' Foscari
Calle Foscari
S. Tomà
Pal. Cornèr Spinelli
Pal. Fortuny
Palazzo Mocenigo
Pal. Balbi
Ca' Foscari
Pal. Contarini d. Figure
Oratorio dell' Annunciata
Palazzo Moro-Lin
Pal. Grassi
Rio di S. Angelo
Campo S. Angelo
Pal. Nani
Saliz S. Samuele
C. Crosera
6
5
Ca' Rezzonico
S. Samuele
San Samuele
S. Stefano
S. Bárnaba
Palazzo Malipiero
Campo S. Stefano
S. Maurízio
Ca' Rezzonico
Rio Malpaga
Pal. Stern
Ca' del Duca
Rio del Duca
C. Vetturi
Rio di S. Vidal
4
Pal. Morosini
Rio d. Santissimo
S. Maria d. Giglio
Pal. Loredan
Pal. Falier
3
Pal. Contarini degli Scrigni
Pal. Bárbaro
Pal. Pisani
Palazzo Cornèr d. Ca' Granda
DORSODURO
2
Accademia
Ponte dell'Accademia
Canàl Grande
S. Maria d. Giglio
S. Trovaso
Rio di S. Trovaso
Gallerie dell' Accademia
Palazzo Contarini dal Zaffo
1
Pal. Centani
Pal. Giustiniàn
Pal. Nani
Rio di S. Vio
Pal. Venièr dei Leoni (Guggenheim)
S. Maria d. Visitaz.
S. Agnese
Fond. Bragadin
Gesuati
Záttere
9
A Beccafico 4
Ai Tre Spiedi 13
Al Bacco Felice 8
Al Covo 19
Antico Martini 20
Cantina do Mori 12
Da Sandro 7
Do Spade 11
Harry's Bar 22
La Cusina 21
Le Bistrot de Venise 15
Osteria alle Botteghe 5
Osteria alle Testiere 16
Osteria da Rioba 10
Osteria Enoteca Ai Artisti 3
Osteria L'Orto dei Mori 9
Pizzeria/Trattoria al Vecio Canton 17
Rosticceria San Bartolomeo 14
Taverna San Trovaso 2
Trattoria ai Cugnai 1
Trattoria Corte Sconta 18
Trattoria da Fiore 6

Venice Restaurants
0
1/8 mi
0
0.125 km
CANNAREGIO
SAN MARCO
CASTELLO
Bacino di San Marco
Isola di S. Giorgio Maggiore
Pal. Giovanelli
S. Felice
Pal. Fontana
S. Sofia
Ca' d'Oro
Pal. Sagredo
Pal. Brandolin
Pescaria
Pal. Mangilli
Ss. Apóstoli
Pal. Widman
Pal. Grifalconi
Ospedale Civile
Pal. Falier
S. Canciano
Ca' da Mosto
Fábbriche Nuove
S. Maria d. Miracoli
Pal. Soranzo-Van Axel
S. Maria d. Pianto
S. Giovanni Crisostomo
Teatro Málibran
Pal. Pisani
Ss. Giovanni e Paolo (S. Zanipolo)
Palazzo Dieci Savi
Fóndaco d. Tedeschi
Pal. Cavazza-Foscari
Campo S. Marina
Pal. Morosini
S. Aponal
Ponte de Rialto
Pal. Donà
Pal. Muazzo
Palazzo Ruzzini
Pal. Cavignis
Palazzo Cappello
S. Bartolomeo
S. Lio
Campo S. Maria Formosa
S. Silvestro
Rialto
Palazzo Dolfin-Manin
S. Maria della Fava
Pal. Donà
S. Maria Formosa
S. Lorenzo
Pal. Bembo
S. Salvador
Pal. Tasca Papafáva
Pal. Querini Stampalia
Questura
Palazzo Grimani
Ca' Farcotti
S. Luca
S. Zuliàn
Palazzo Soranzo
Pal. Zorzi
Campo Manin
Cinema Rossini
Palazzo Contarini d. Bovolo
S. Giovanni Novo
Pal. Priuli
Palazzo Trevisan Cappello
S. Giorgio dei Greci
S. Gallo
Basilica di San Marco
S. Zaccaria
Ateneo Veneto
Torre dell' Orologio
Convento
La Pietà
Campanile
Piazza San Marco
Palazzo Ducale (Doge's Palace)
Pal. d. Prigioni
S. Fantìn
Teatro La Fenice
Museo Correr
Piazzetta
Riva d. Schiavoni
S. Zaccaria
S. Moisè
Molo
Ponte d. Sospiri (Bridge of Sighs)
Giardini ex Reali
Capo di Porto
S. Marco
Palazzo Tiépolo
Palazzo Treves d. Bonfili
Palazzi Contarini
Salute
Pal. Genovese
Punta d. Dogana
S. Maria d. Salute
Dogana da Mar
Seminario Patriarcale
Ex Ospízio
S. Giorgio Maggiore
Calle d. Vele
Strada Nuova
Rio ter. d. Ss. Apóstoli
Calle d. Fumo
Calle d. Squero
Fond. d. Mendicanti
Rio d. Santi
Calle d. Botteri
Rio d. Beccarie
C. larga G. Gallina
Rio di S. Marina
Riva del Vin
Riva del Carbon
C. Stagneri
M. S. Salvador
Salizzada S. Lio
C. Bande
C. Guerra
Ruga Giuffa
C. del Teatro
Calle C. Goldoni
Calle dei Fabbri
C. Mandola
C. Canonica
Rio del Greci
C. Larga XXII Marzo
C. Vallaresso
C. Ricotto
Frezzeria
10
11
12
13
14
15
16
17
18
19
20
21
22
24

fishy BUSINESS

Eating a meal based on the day's catch (restaurants are legally bound to print on the menu when the fish is frozen) will be a treat but never inexpensive. Keep in mind that the price indicated on the menu sometimes refers to *l'etto* (per 100g), a fraction of the full cost (have the waiter estimate the full cost before ordering); larger fish are intended to feed two. Also, avoid splurging on fish or seafood on Mondays, when the Fish Market is closed (as are most good fish-serving restaurants). Restaurants open on Mondays will be serving you fish bought on Saturday.

historical ties with the Far East. You'll see things on Venetian menus you won't see elsewhere, together with local versions of time-tested Italian favorites. For first courses, both pasta and risotto (more watery in Veneto than usual) are commonly prepared with fish or seafood: Risotto *al nero di seppia* or *alle seppioline* (tinted black by the ink of cuttlefish, also called *risotto nero* or black risotto) or *spaghetti alle vongole* (with clams; clams without their shells are not a good sign) are two commonly found specialties. Both appear with *frutti di mare,* "fruit of the sea," which is mixed shellfish. *Bigoli,* a sort of thick spaghetti that's perfect for catching lots of sauce, is a Venetian staple as is creamy polenta, often served with *gamberetti* (small shrimp) or tiny shrimp called *schie,* or as an accompaniment to *fegato alla veneziana* (calf's liver cooked with onions and white wine). Some of the fish and seafood dishes they do particularly well include *branzino* (a kind of sea bass), *rombo* (turbot or brill), *moeche* (small soft-shelled crab) or *granseola* (crab), and *sarde in saor* (sardines in a sauce of onion, vinegar, pine nuts, and raisins).

From a host of good local wines, try the dry white Tocai and pinot from the Friuli region to the northeast of Venice and the light, sparkling prosecco that Venetians consume almost like a soft drink (it is the base of Venice's famous Bellini drink made with white peach purée). Popular local red wines include Bardolino, Valpolicella, and Soave, all of which come from Veneto, the region of which Venice is the capital. International grapes, above all cabernet franc and merlot, are also grown extensively in Veneto and make their way into many local wines. Grappa, the local firewater, is an acquired taste and is often offered in many variations. Neighborhood *bacari* wine bars provide the chance to taste the fruits of leading wine producers in the grape-rich regions of Veneto and neighboring Friuli.

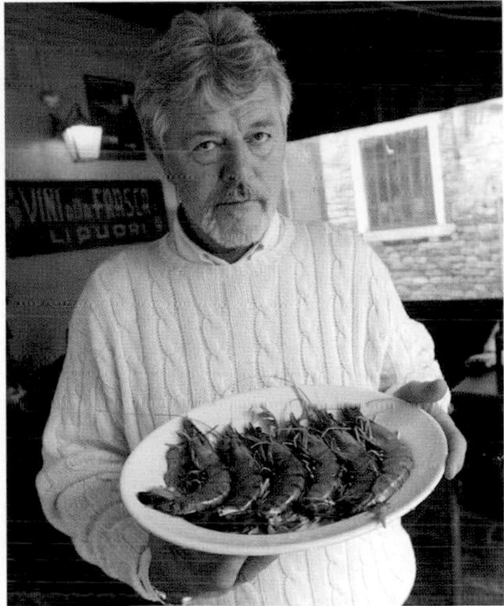

Seafood, a Venice specialty.

In San Marco

VERY EXPENSIVE

Antico Martini ★★ INTERNATIONAL/VENETIAN One of Venice's top restaurants started out in 1720 as a cafe, and the Baldi family, since 1921, has retained its airy, clubby atmosphere, especially at the outdoor tables in summertime. Venetian specialties such as *risotto di frutti di mare* and *fegato alla Veneziana* are prepared perfectly here, but the food, reputation, and location across from the opera house all come at a stiff price. If you want to dine as if you were at a classic Italian wedding, then try the tasting menu, which comes with both a fish and meat *secondo* broken up by a lemon sorbet. The price of the tasting menu might not even seem that expensive when you consider you probably won't have to dine for the next 24 hours.

Campo San Fantin (on the square occupied by La Fenice opera house). www.anticomartini.com **© 041-522-4121.** Reservations required. Main courses 25€–45€; fixed-price tasting menu 115€. AE, DC, MC, V. Daily noon–midnight. *Vaporetto:* Santa Maria del Giglio (walk straight up from the *vaporetto* stop and turn right out of the *campo,* cross the bridge, follow the street that goes to the left and then the right before opening onto the broad Calle Larga XXII Marzo; turn left up Calle delle Veste into Campo San Fantin).

La Cusina ★★ MODERN VENETIAN Excepting the Cipriani, La Cusina is the only hotel restaurant in Venice that deserves singling out on its own. The service is stellar, and the seating is in that most sought-after of spots: a terrace right on the Grand Canal overlooking floodlit Santa Maria della Salute across the water. On the often changed menu you may find ravioli stuffed with sea bass in a light cream sauce with wild fennel, *maltalgiati* noodles in a duck and truffle *ragù,* or rabbit saddle with sun-dried tomatoes and grilled leeks.

San Marco 2159 (in the Westin Hotel Europa & Regina off Calle Larga XXII Marzo). **© 041-240-0001.** Reservations highly recommended. Main courses 38€–46€. AE, DC, MC, V. Daily 7–10:30am, 12–2:30pm, and 7:30–10pm. *Vaporetto:* San Marco (head out of the southwest corner of Piazza San Marco down Salizada San Moisè; cross the bridge to continue straight on Calle XXII Marzo; you'll see hotel signs directing you down the alleyways to the left).

Le Bistrot de Venise ★★ FRENCH/VENETIAN At this popular meeting spot for Venetians, you can enjoy a simple and reasonably priced steak and salad, or you can go all out for a five-course dinner that, with a decent wine and the taxes, will cost about 120€ a person. Eel flourish in the rivers that empty into the Venetian lagoon and they are often on the Bistrot's ever-changing menu, including roasted with bay leaves, bread crumbs, cinnamon, and black pepper. If that is not enough to get your mouth watering (or perhaps slimy fish are not your thing), you can pick one of the other unique dishes made from historic 15th-century Venetian recipes. The faint of heart can always fall back on more typical Venetian favorites.

San Marco 4687 (on Calle dei Fabbri), below the Albergo al Gambero. www.bistrotdevenise.com. ✆ **041-523-6651.** Reservations not necessary. Main courses 28€–38€; classic Venetian tasting menu 48€; historical 5-course Venetian menu 80€. AE, MC, V. Daily noon–1am. Usually closes Dec 21–25. *Vaporetto:* Rialto (turn right along canal, cross small footbridge over Rio San Salvador, turn left onto Calle Bembo, which becomes Calle dei Fabbri; Bistrot is about 5 blocks ahead).

EXPENSIVE

A Beccafico ★★★ SICILIAN You might wonder why you should have Sicilian food in the heart of Venice . . . until you take your first bite of eggplant-laced *pasta alla norma* at this pleasant restaurant on Campo Santo Stefano. If eggplant is your thing, don't miss the *caponata,* a sort of thick vegetable spread of fried eggplant, pine nuts, and raisins that is served warm and spread over a piece of bread. The portions are not huge, in fact the signature dish, *sarde a beccafico,* comes with just two large, rolled sardines stuffed with bread crumbs, pine nuts, and currants. But they are superb and, anyway, you'll want room to try a dessert (special mention goes to the tiramisu and the lemon sorbet served in a carved-out half lemon). As an added bonus, the waiters are all smiles, something of a rarity in Venice, and the limoncello is on the house.

San Marco 2801 (in Campo Santo Stefano). www.abeccafico.com. ✆ **041-527-4879.** Reservations recommended. Main courses 20€–22€. AE, MC, V. Daily noon–3:30pm and 7–11pm. *Vaporetto:* Accademia (cross bridge to San Marco side and walk straight ahead to Campo Santo Stefano; the restaurant is on your right and toward the back end of the *campo*).

Trattoria da Fiore ★★ TRATTORIA/VENETIAN Don't confuse this laid-back trattoria with the expensive Osteria da Fiore near the Frari church. Start with the house specialty, the *pennette alla Fiore* for two (with olive oil, garlic, and seven in-season vegetables), and you may be happy to call it a night. Or try the *frittura mista,* over a dozen varieties of fresh fish and seafood. The Bar Fiore next door is a great place to snack or make a light lunch out of *cicchetti* (Wed–Mon 10:30am–10:30pm).

San Marco 3461 (on Calle delle Botteghe, off Campo Santo Stefano). ✆ **041-523-5310.** Reservations recommended. Main courses 14€–25€. AE, MC, V. Wed–Mon noon–3pm and 7–10pm. Closed 2 weeks in Jan and 2 weeks in Aug. *Vaporetto:* Accademia (cross bridge to San Marco side and walk straight ahead to Campo Santo Stefano; as you are about to exit the *campo* at northern end, take a left at Bar/Gelateria Paolin onto Calle delle Botteghe; also close to Sant'Angelo *vaporetto* stop).

MODERATE

Osteria alle Botteghe ITALIAN Casual, easy on the palate, not too hard on the wallet (by Venetian standards), and even easy to find (again, for Venice), this is a decent choice for pizza, a light snack, or an elaborate meal. You can have

FAMILY-friendly RESTAURANTS

Ai Tre Spiedi (p. 476) There's nothing in particular that flags this as kid-friendly, but its genial atmosphere, friendly service, and good cooking make it welcoming for families. Admittedly, most tables are taken by couples.

Da Sandro (p. 476) This place offers good pizza and pasta, seating outdoors, and low prices. They're happy, you're happy.

Pizzeria/Trattoria al Vecio Canton (p. 475) This spot offers plenty of seating, a good location near San Marco, low prices, and an extensive menu of pastas and some of the best pizzas in Venice.

Rosticceria San Bartolomeo (below) There's not much that isn't served at this big, efficient, and bustling fast-food *emporio* in the Rialto Bridge area. Much of it is displayed in glass cases to pique the fussy appetite, and you won't raise any eyebrows if you eat too little, too much, or at hours when the natives have either finished or haven't yet started.

Taverna San Trovaso (p. 478) Here you'll find a bustling atmosphere, good-natured waiters, and a lengthy menu that covers all sorts of dishes and pizzas to please finicky youngsters and more adventurous palates alike. Good value-priced menus, too.

stand-up *cicchetti* and sandwiches at the bar or window-side counter, while more serious diners head to the tables in back to enjoy the pizzas, pastas, or the glass counter–enclosed buffet of prepared dishes like eggplant *parmigiana,* lasagna, and fresh-cooked vegetables in season, reheated when you order.

San Marco 3454 (on Calle delle Botteghe, off Campo Santo Stefano). ✆ **041-522-8181.** Reservations not necessary. Main courses 10€–24€; *menù turistico* 17€. DC, MC, V. Mon–Sat 11am–11pm (and Sun in high season). *Vaporetto:* Accademia (cross bridge to San Marco side and walk straight ahead to Campo Santo Stefano; as you are about to exit the *campo* at northern end, take a left at Bar/Gelateria Paolin onto Calle delle Botteghe; also close to Sant'Angelo *vaporetto* stop).

INEXPENSIVE

Rosticceria San Bartolomeo ★ ☺ DELI/ITALIAN With long hours and a central location, this refurbished old-timer is Venice's most popular *rosticceria,* so the continuous turnover guarantees fresh food. With a dozen pasta dishes and as many fish, seafood, and meat entrees, this place can satisfy most any culinary desire. Because the ready-made food is displayed under a glass counter, you (and the kids) will know exactly what you're ordering, and that is sure to help avoid long, little faces. There's no *coperto* (cover charge) if you take your meal standing up or seated at the stools in the aroma-filled ground-floor eating area. If you prefer to linger, head to the dining hall upstairs, though it costs more and, frankly, for the money you can do much better elsewhere than this institutional setting.

San Marco 5424 (on Calle della Bissa). ✆ **041-522-3569.** Main courses 10€–18€. Prices are about 20%–30% higher upstairs, and there is a discount if you order to take away. AE, MC, V. Daily 9:30am–10pm (Mon until 3:30pm). *Vaporetto:* Rialto (with bridge at your back on San Marco side of canal, walk straight ahead to Campo San Bartolomeo; take underpass slightly to your left marked SOTTOPORTEGO DELLA BISSA; you'll come across the *rosticceria* at 1st corner on your right; look for GISLON [its old name] above the entrance).

In Castello

VERY EXPENSIVE

Al Covo ★★★ SEAFOOD/VENETIAN For years, this lovely restaurant has been deservingly popular with American food writers, putting it on the short list of every food-loving American tourist. There are nights when you hear nothing but English spoken here. But this slightly unpleasant fact has never compromised the dining at this warm and welcoming spot, where the preparation of superfresh fish and a wide selection of moderately priced wines is as commendable today—perhaps more so—as it was in its days of pretrendiness. Much of the tourist-friendly atmosphere can be credited to Diane Rankin, the co-owner and dessert whiz who hails from Texas. She will eagerly talk you through a wondrous fish-studded menu. Her husband, Cesare Benelli, is known for his infallible talent in the kitchen. Together they share an admirable dedication to their charming gem of a restaurant—the quality of an evening here is tough to top in this town.

Castello 3968 (Campiello della Pescheria, east of Chiesa della Pietà in the Arsenale neighborhood). www.ristorantealcovo.com. ✆ **041-522-3812.** Reservations required. Main courses 28€–36€; menu with choice of any combination of 1 *primo,* 1 *secondo,* and 1 dessert 54€. MC, V. Fri–Tues 12:45–2pm and 7:30–11pm (closed Mon–Tues at lunch). Closed usually 1 week in Jan and 1 week in Aug. *Vaporetto:* Arsenale (walk a short way back in the direction of Piazza San Marco, crossing over the 1st bridge and taking the 2nd right onto Calle della Pescheria; otherwise, it is an enjoyable 20-min. stroll along the waterfront Riva degli Schiavoni from Piazza San Marco, past the Chiesa della Pietà; take the 3rd left after the Hotel Metropole).

EXPENSIVE

Osteria alle Testiere ★★ ITALIAN/VENETIAN The limited seating for just 24 savvy (and lucky) patrons at butcher paper–covered tables, the relaxed young staff, and the upbeat tavernlike atmosphere belie the seriousness of this informal *osteria.* This is a guaranteed choice if you are a foodie curious to experience the increasingly interesting Venetian culinary scene without going broke. Start with the carefully chosen wine list; any of the 90 labels can be ordered by the half-bottle. The delicious homemade *gnocchetti ai calamaretti* (with baby squid) makes a frequent appearance, as does the traditional specialty *scampi alla busara,* in a "secret" recipe some of whose identifiable ingredients include tomato, cinnamon, and a dash of hot pepper. Cheese is not a fundamental part of Venetian cuisine, but Alle Testiere has an exceptional cheese platter.

Castello 5801 (on Calle del Mondo Novo off Salizada San Lio). www.osterialletestiere.it. ✆ **041-522-7220.** Reservations required for each of 2 seatings. Main courses 25€, and many types of fish sold by weight. MC, V. Mon–Sat 2 seatings at 7 and 9:15pm. *Vaporetto:* Equidistant from either the Rialto or San Marco stops. Find the store-lined Salizada San Lio (west of the Campo Santa Maria Formosa), and from there ask for the Calle del Mondo Novo).

Trattoria Corte Sconta ★★ SEAFOOD/VENETIAN The bare, simple decor doesn't hint at the trendiness of this out-of-the-way trattoria, nor at the high quality of its strictly seafood cuisine. The emphasis is on freshness here; they put the shrimp live on the grill. Seafood fans will want to make reservations here on their very first night to hang with the foodies, artists, and writers who patronize this hidden jewel. There's seafood-studded spaghetti, risotti with scampi, and a great *frittura mista all'Adriatico* (mixed Adriatic seafood fry). In nice weather, you can dine under a canopy of grapevines in the courtyard.

Castello 3886 (Calle del Pestrin). ✆ **041-522-7024.** Reservations recommended. Main courses 22€–28€. MC, V. Tues–Sat 11:30am–3:30pm and 7–11:30pm. Closed Jan 7–Feb 7 and July 15–Aug 15. *Vaporetto:* Arsenale (walk west along Riva degli Schiavoni and over the footbridge; turn right up Calle del Forno, and then as it crosses Calle Crosera, veer right up Calle del Pestrin).

MODERATE

Pizzeria/Trattoria al Vecio Canton ☺ ITALIAN/PIZZA Good pizza can be hard to find in Venice, quite literally. Tucked away in a northeast corner behind Piazza San Marco on a well-trafficked route connecting it with Campo Santa Maria Formosa, the Canton's wood-paneled taverna-like atmosphere and great pizzas are worth the time you'll spend looking for the place. There is a full trattoria menu as well, with a number of pasta and *contorni* (side dishes) of vegetables providing a palatable alternative.

Castello 4738a (at the corner of Ruga Giuffa). ✆ **041-528-5176.** Reservations not accepted. Main courses 12€–20€. AE, DC, MC. Wed–Mon noon–2:30pm and 7–10:30pm. *Vaporetto:* San Zaccaria (head down the road that flanks the left side of the Hotel Savoia e Jolanda until you reach Campo San Provolo; follow Salizada San Provolo out of the north side of the *campo*, cross the 1st footbridge on your left, and you'll find the pizzeria on the 1st corner on the left).

In Cannaregio

MODERATE

Ostaria da Rioba ★★ VENETIAN Located along a pleasant canal, this place oozes Venice. It offers various local favorites on the menu, such as numerous preparations of cod with polenta and fresh squid ink pasta. Weather permitting, insist on sitting outside, if at all possible, though the simple yet classic decor inside the restaurant will make for a pleasant dining experience as well. If you are outside, beware that about 30m (90 ft.) away there is a bar that often features loud live music.

Cannaregio 2553 (Fondamenta della Misericordia). ✆ **041-524-4379.** Reservations highly recommended. Main courses 19€–25€. MC, V. Tues–Sun 11am–3pm and 6–10pm. *Vaporetto:* San Marcuola (go around the church that's right at the stop, then go straight about 5 blocks until you get to the 1st bridge; cross and turn right on Fondamenta della Misericordia).

Osteria L'Orto dei Mori ★★ VENETIAN In this wonderful corner of Venice where the tourists thin out to the point that you can almost forget you are in a sort of Disneyland, you can sample a cuisine that perfectly blends Sicily and Venice while sitting at a table in a splendid, intimate *campo*. The simple, modern decor almost seems a gambit by the two owners, one Venetian and one Sicilian, to get you to concentrate on the food. For those in need of a break from pasta and rice, there are the scrumptious crepe filled with scampi, radicchio, and ricotta held together by a thin piece of bacon. The turbot cooked in foil is moist and light, a good thing as you must save space for dessert; the ricotta-and-pear mousse mixed with a hint of red wine will have you calculating if you can manage another meal here before you go back to the mainland.

Cannaregio 3386 (Fondamenta dei Mori at Campo dei Mori). www.osteriaortodeimori.com. ✆ **041-524-3677.** Reservations recommended. Main courses 18€–23€. AE, MC, V. Wed–Mon 12:30–3:30pm and 7–midnight (July–Aug closed for lunch Mon–Fri). *Vaporetto:* Madonna dell'Orto (from the *vaporetto* launch, walk through the *campo* to the canal and turn right; take the 1st bridge to your left, walk down the street and turn left at the canal onto Fondamenta dei Mori; go straight until you hit Campo dei Mori).

INEXPENSIVE

Ai Tre Spiedi ★★ ☺ VENETIAN Once upon a time, Venetians brought their visiting friends here to make a *bella figura* (good impression) without breaking the bank, and then swore them to secrecy. Well, the secret is out, and the prices have surely crept up, roughly coinciding with a change in ownership in 2006. Still, it is a very pleasant setting and the meal is just as appetizing as ever in this small, casually elegant trattoria with great, fresh fish. (When a restaurant is filled exclusively with French tourists, you know the cuisine can't be bad.) Try the traditional *bisato in umido con polenta* (braised eel), or, for a less daring but excellent choice, you can't go wrong with the grilled *orata* (John Dory). This is going to be one of the most reasonable choices for an authentic Venetian dinner of fresh fish; careful ordering needn't mean much of a splurge, either.

Cannaregio 5906 (on Salizada San Cazian). ✆ **041-520-8035.** Reservations not accepted. Main courses 11€–20€. AE, MC, V. Tues–Sat noon–3pm and 7–10pm; Sun 7–10pm. Closed July 20–Aug 10. *Vaporetto:* Rialto (on San Marco side of bridge, walk straight ahead to Campo San Bartolomeo and take a left, passing a post office, Coin department store, and the San Crisostomo church; cross 1st bridge after church, turn right at shoe store onto Salizada San Cazian).

In San Polo

MODERATE

Da Sandro ★ ☺ ITALIAN/PIZZERIA Sandro offers dozens of varieties of pizza (his specialty), as well as a full trattoria menu of simple pastas and entrees that will appeal to the kids if they can't stomach another pizza (as unlikely as that is). If you're looking for a 15€ pizza-and-beer meal where you can sit outside, this is a reliably good spot on the main drag linking the Rialto to Campo San Polo. Although Italians consider it sacrilegious, you won't raise any eyebrows if you order a pasta and pizza and pass on the meat or fish: This city has seen it all. There's communal seating at a few wooden picnic tables placed outdoors, with just a handful of small tables stuffed into the two dining rooms—which, unusually, are on opposite sides of the street. You can also get a takeaway pizza and have it in nearby Campo San Polo.

San Polo 1473 (Campiello dei Meloni). ✆ **041-523-4894.** Reservations not necessary. Main courses 11€–22€. AE, MC, V. Sat–Thurs 11:30am–11:30pm. *Vaporetto:* San Silvestro (with your back to Grand Canal, walk straight to store-lined Ruga Vecchia San Giovanni and take a left; head toward Campo San Polo until you come on Campiello dei Meloni).

Do Spade ★ VENETIAN From 1415 until just a few years ago, workers, fishmongers, and shoppers from the nearby Mercato della Pescheria flocked to this spot, once a colorful wine bar, with bonhomie galore. After a change of ownership in 2007 it became an upscale restaurant, but the rich and elaborate menu was out of place in this spot in Venice, and in 2008 there was another change in management and a return to the place's modest roots, with it being reborn as a friendly place to get exceptional renditions of local favorites at a fair price. The *cicchetti* are tasty and loads can be piled onto a single plate to make a full meal.

San Polo 860 (on Sottoportego do Spade). ✆ **041-521-0574.** Reservations not necessary. Main courses 11€–18€. No credit cards. Daily 10am–3pm and 6–10pm. *Vaporetto:* Rialto or San Silvestro (at San Polo side of Rialto Bridge, walk away from bridge and through open-air market until you come to an intersection with a pharmacy and Cassa di Risparmio di Venezia bank on 2 corners; take a left here and then take 2nd right onto Sottoportego do Spade).

INEXPENSIVE

Cantina do Mori ★★★ WINE BAR Since 1462, this has been the local watering hole of choice in the market area; legend even pegs Casanova as a habitué. *Tramezzini* (sandwiches; the roast pork with radicchio is incredible) and *cicchetti* (side dishes) take center stage here at what is one of the best of the few remaining old-time *bacari*. For the *ombra,* you've got an embarrassment of choice. Venetians stop in to snack and socialize before and after meals, but if you don't mind standing (there are no tables), this is the perfect choice for a light lunch. Though the *cicchetti* are cheap at about 1.50€ a pop, you are going to need quite a few to fill up, so beware that the cost can add up quickly. The best value are the small, 1€ *tramezzini;* four of these plus two *cicchetti* and a glass of wine will leave you satisfied and only about 12€ will be missing from your wallet as you head out the door.

San Polo 429 (entrances on Calle Galiazza and Calle Do Mori). ✆ **041-522-5401.** *Tramezzini* and *cicchetti* 1€–1.50€ per piece. No credit cards. Mon–Sat 8:30am–8pm (Wed until 2pm; June–Aug closed daily 2–4:30pm). *Vaporetto:* Rialto (cross Rialto Bridge to San Polo side, walk to end of market stalls, turn left on Ruga Vecchia San Giovanni and then immediately right, and look for small wooden cantina sign on right).

In Santa Croce

INEXPENSIVE

Al Bacco Felice ★★ ITALIAN This is the place in town if you are looking for great Italian standbys like *spaghetti alla carbonara* or *spaghetti all'amatriciana.* While not incredible, the food is very good, and you'll be hard pressed to find a better price-to-quality ratio in town. There is also fresh fish, including a mixed grill; and for those in need of a pizza, you won't be disappointed by the more than 50 choices. While Al Bacco Felice is just steps from the train station and Piazzale Roma, in this wonderfully quiet corner of town you will feel miles from the hustle and bustle.

Santa Croce 197E (on Corte dei Amai). ✆ **041-528-7794.** Main courses 8€–20€. MC, V. Daily noon–3:30pm and 6:15–11pm. *Vaporetto:* Piazzale Roma (you can walk here in 10 min. from the train station; otherwise, from the Piazzale Roma *vaporetto* stop keep the Grand Canal on your left and head toward the train station, passing a park on your right; cross the small canal at the end of the park and immediately turn right onto Fondamenta Tolentini; when you get to Campo Tolentini turn left onto Corte dei Amai).

In Dorsoduro

EXPENSIVE

Osteria Enoteca Ai Artisti ★★ VENETIAN Adding a touch of Trentino and Naples to traditional Venetian cuisine, Chef Francesca, who shops herself for the raw materials that end up on your plate, turns out memorable dishes that are always fresh and never disappoint. The *tagliatelle* with zucchini flowers and small prawns reaches near perfection as do most of the fish dishes, including the grilled sea bass and the John Dory with tomatoes and pine nuts. In nice weather, ask for a seat outside on the lovely canal that's a 5-minute walk from the Accademia bridge.

Dorsoduro 1169A (on Fondamenta della Toletta). www.enotecaartisti.com. ✆ **041-523-8944.** Reservations recommended. Main courses 19€–22€. AE, DC, MC, V. Mon–Sat noon–4pm and 7–10pm. *Vaporetto:* Accademia (walk to right around Accademia and take a right onto Calle Gambara; when this street ends at small Rio di San Trovaso, turn left onto Fondamenta Priuli; take the 1st bridge over the canal and onto a road that will quickly lead into Fondamenta della Toletta).

MODERATE

Taverna San Trovaso ★ ☺ VENETIAN Wine bottles line the wood-paneled walls, and low vaulted brick ceilings augment the sense of character in this canal-side tavern, always packed with locals and visitors. The *menù turistico* (a fixed-priced tourist menu that's usually a good deal) includes wine, a *frittura mista* (assortment of fried seafood), and dessert. The gnocchi are homemade, the local specialty of calf's liver and onions is great, and the simply grilled fish is the taverna's claim to fame. There is also a variety of pizzas as well as a few very recognizable Italian dishes, such as lasagna Bolognese, that will appeal to the younger members of your dinner party.

Dorsoduro 1016 (on Fondamenta Priuli). www.tavernasantrovaso.it. ✆ **041-520-3703.** Reservations recommended. Main courses 9.50€–18€. AE, DC, MC, V. Tues–Sun noon–2:45pm and 7pm–midnight. *Vaporetto:* Accademia (walk to right around Accademia and take a right onto Calle Gambara; when this street ends at small Rio di San Trovaso, turn left onto Fondamenta Priuli).

Trattoria ai Cugnai ★★ VENETIAN The unassuming storefront of this longtime favorite does little to announce that herein lies some of the neighborhood's best dining. The owners serve classic *cucina veneziana,* like the reliably good *spaghetti alle vongole veraci* (with clams) or *fegato alla veneziana* (liver). The homemade gnocchi and lasagna would meet most any Italian grandmother's approval (you won't go wrong with any of the menu's *fatta in casa* choices of daily homemade specialties, either). Equidistant from the Accademia and the Guggenheim, Ai Cugnai is the perfect place to recharge after an art overload.

Dorsoduro 857 (on Calle Nuova Sant'Agnese). ✆ **041-528-9238.** Reservations not necessary. Main courses 14€–20€. AE, MC, V. Tues–Sun 12:30–3pm and 7–10:30pm. *Vaporetto:* Accademia (head east of bridge and Accademia in direction of Guggenheim Collection; restaurant will be on your right, off the straight street connecting the 2 museums).

Picnicking

You don't have to eat in a fancy restaurant to enjoy good food in Venice. Prepare a picnic, and while you eat alfresco, you can observe the life in the city's *campi* or the aquatic parade on its main thoroughfare, the Grand Canal. Plus, shopping for your food can be an interesting experience as you will probably have to do it in the small *alimentari* (food shops), as supermarkets are scarce.

MERCATO RIALTO Venice's principal open-air market is a sight to see, even for nonshoppers. It has two parts, beginning with the produce section, whose many stalls, alternating with those of souvenir vendors, unfold north on the San Polo side of the Rialto Bridge (behind these stalls are a few permanent food stores that sell delicious cheese, cold cuts, and bread selections). The vendors are here Monday to Saturday 7am to 1pm, with some staying on in the afternoon.

At the market's farthest point, you'll find the covered **fish market,** with its carnival atmosphere, picturesquely located on the Grand Canal opposite the magnificent Ca' d'Oro and still redolent of the days when it was one of the Mediterranean's great fish bazaars. The area is filled with a number of small *bacari* bars frequented by market vendors and shoppers, where you can join in and ask for your morning's first glass of prosecco with a *cicchetto* pick-me-up. The fish merchants take Monday off and work mornings only.

CAMPO SANTA MARGHERITA On this spacious *campo,* Tuesday through Saturday from 8:30am to 1pm, a number of open-air stalls set up shop, selling fresh fruit and vegetables. This market, coupled with several shops around the *campo,* should ensure you meet all your picnic needs. There's even a conventional supermarket, one of the few in all of Venice, just off the *campo* in the direction of the quasi-adjacent *campo* San Barnaba, at no. 3019. San Barnaba is where you'll find Venice's heavily photographed **floating market** operating from a boat moored just off San Barnaba at the Ponte dei Pugni. This market is open daily from 8am to 1pm and 3:30 to 7:30pm, except Wednesday afternoon and Sunday. If you can't be bothered piecing together the picnic, you can also pick up panini, *tramezzini,* and drinks at any number of nearby bars.

THE BEST PICNIC SPOTS Alas, to picnic in Venice means you won't have much in the way of green space (if you are really desperate for green, you can walk half an hour past San Marco along the water, or take a *vaporetto,* to the Giardini Pubblici, Venice's only green park, but don't expect anything great). A much more enjoyable alternative is to find some of the larger *campi* that have park benches, and in some cases even a tree or two to shade them, such as Campo San Giacomo dell'Orio (in the quiet *sestiere* of Santa Croce). The two most central are **Campo Santa Margherita** (*sestiere* of Dorsoduro) and **Campo San Polo** (*sestiere* of San Polo).

For a picnic with a view, scout out the **Punta della Dogana (Customs House)** near La Salute Church for a prime viewing site at the mouth of the Grand Canal. It's located almost directly across from the Piazza San Marco and the Palazzo Ducale. Pull up on a piece of the embankment here and watch the flutter of water activity against a canvaslike backdrop deserving of the Accademia Museum. In this same area, another superb spot is the small **Campo San Vio** near the Guggenheim, which is directly on the Grand Canal (not many *campi* are) and even boasts two benches as well as the possibility to sit on an untrafficked small bridge. ***Note:*** It is not by accident that benches in Venice are about as hard to find as that perfect plate of *bigoli*—cafe and bar owners regularly petition the city to limit the number of benches, thereby obligating more tourists to stop in for an overpriced cold drink.

In the **patch of sun on the marble steps** leading down to the water of the Grand Canal, at the southern foot of the Rialto Bridge on the San Polo side, you won't find a bench, but there is no better ringside seat for viewing the Canalazzo's passing parade. If you don't mind sitting on the ground and the tide is not too high, this spot will afford you a memorable picnic.

To go a bit farther afield, you can take the LN *vaporetto* out to Burano and then the T for the 5-minute ride to the near-deserted island of **Torcello.** If you bring a basketful of bread, cheese, and wine, you can do your best to reenact the romantic scene between Katharine Hepburn and Rossano Brazzi from the 1955 film *Summertime.*

SHOPPING

A mix of low-end trinket stores and middle-market-to-upscale boutiques line the narrow zigzagging **Mercerie** running north between Piazza San Marco and the Rialto Bridge. More expensive clothing and gift boutiques make for great

Venice Shopping Strategies

There are two rules of thumb for shopping in Venice: If you have the good fortune of continuing on to Florence or Rome, shop for clothing, leather goods, and accessories with prudence in Venice, because most items are more expensive here. If, however, you happen on something that strikes you, consider it twice on the spot (not back at your hotel), and then buy it. In this web of alleys, you may never find that shop again.

window-shopping on **Calle Larga XXII Marzo,** the wide street that begins west of Piazza San Marco and wends its way to the expansive Campo Santo Stefano near the Accademia. The narrow **Frezzaria,** just west of Piazza San Marco and running north-south, offers a grab bag of bars, souvenir shops, and tony clothing stores.

In a city that for centuries has thrived almost exclusively on tourism, remember this: **Where you buy cheap, you get cheap.** There are few bargains to be had; the nonproduce part of the Rialto Market is as good as it gets, where you'll find cheap T-shirts, glow-in-the-dark plastic gondolas, and tawdry glass trinkets. Venetians, centuries-old merchants, aren't known for bargaining. You'll stand a better chance of getting a bargain if you pay in cash or buy more than one item.

Venice is uniquely famous for local crafts that have been produced here for centuries and are hard to get elsewhere: the **glassware** from Murano, the **delicate lace** from Burano, and the ***cartapesta*** **(papier-mâché) Carnevale masks** you'll find in endless *botteghe* (shops), where you can watch artisans paint amid their wares.

Now here's the bad news: There's such an overwhelming sea of cheap glass gewgaws that buying Venetian glass can become something of a turnoff (shipping and insurance costs make most things unaffordable; the alternative is to hand-carry anything fragile). There are so few women left on Burano willing to spend countless tedious hours keeping alive the art of lace-making that the few pieces you'll see not produced by machine in Hong Kong are sold at stratospheric prices; ditto the truly high-quality glass (though trinkets can be cheap and fun). Still, exceptions are to be found in all of the above, and when you find them you'll know. A discerning eye can cut through the dreck to find some lovely mementos.

Crafts

The **Murano Art Shop,** at San Marco 1232 (on the store-lined Frezzaria, parallel to the western border of, and close to, the Piazza San Marco; ✆ **041-523-3851**), is a cultural experience. At this small shop, every inch of wall space is draped with the whimsical crafts of the city's most creative artisans. Fusing the timeless with the contemporary—with a nod to the magic and romance of Venice's past—the store offers a dramatic, evolving, and expensive collection of masks, puppets, music boxes, and costume jewelry.

When it seems as if every gift-store window is awash with collectible bisque-faced dolls in elaborate pinafores and headdresses, head to **Bambole di Trilly,** at Castello 4974 (Fondamenta dell'Osmarin, off the Campo San Provolo on your way east out of Piazza San Marco in the direction of the Church of San Zaccaria; ✆ **041-521-2579**), where the hand-sewn wardrobes of rich Venetian fabrics and painstakingly painted faces are particularly exquisite. The perfect souvenir

Art glass for sale at Venini.

starts at about 20€ in this well-stocked workspace north of Campo San Zaccaria.

Glass

If you're going to go all out, look no further than **Venini,** Piazzetta dei Leoni 314 near the base of the clock tower in Piazza San Marco (✆ **041-522-4045**), since 1921 one of the most respected and innovative glassmakers in all of Venice. Their products are more works of art than merely blown glass. So renowned are they for their quality, Versace's own line of glass objects d'art are done by Venini. Their **workshop** on Murano is at Fondamenta Vetrai 50 (✆ **041-273-7211**). Cheap they are not, but no one else has such a lovely or original representation of hand blown Murano glassware.

For the glass-inclined, there is also the spacious emporium of items at **Marco Polo** (San Marco 1644; ✆ **041-522-9295**), just west of the Piazza San Marco on the Frezzaria. The front half of the first floor offers a variety of small gift ideas (candy dishes, glass-topped medicine boxes, paperweights).

Glass beads are called "Venetian pearls," and an abundance of exquisite antique and reproduced baubles are the draw at **Anticlea,** at Castello 4719A (a bit off Campo San Provolo going north on Calle San Provolo; ✆ **041-528-6946**). Once used for trading in Venice's far-flung colonies, they now fill the coffers of this small shop east of Piazza San Marco, sold singly or already strung. The open air stall of **Susie and Andrea** (Riva degli Schiavoni, near Pensione Wildner, just east of the Danieli) has handcrafted beads that are new, well made and strung, and moderately priced. The stall operates from February through November.

Leather & Shoes

One usually thinks of Florence when thinking of Italian leather goods. But the plethora of mediocre-to-refined shoe stores in Venice is testimony to the tradition of small shoe factories along the nearby Brenta canal that supply most of Italy, and much of the world, with made-in-Italy footwear. Venice has plenty of fine shoe stores (doesn't every Italian city?), but one original shop that deserves singling out for sheer oddness is **Atelier Segalin di Daniela Ghezzo,** San Marco 4365 (Calle dei Fuseri a few bridges away from the northwest corner of Piazza San Marco; ✆ **041-522-2115**). The fantastical footwear in an acid trip of colors and shapes, some of which are intended for Carnevale costumes, makes it worth stopping by even if you aren't in the market for a 1,000€ pair of curly toe shoes.

Linens & Lace

For hand-tatted lace from the only school still teaching it in Venice, ride out to Burano to visit the **Scuola dei Merletti,** Piazza B. Galuppi (✆ **041-730-034**), founded in 1872, closed in 1972, and reopened in 1981. (The Scuola dei

Making a Carnevale mask.

Merletti and its accompanying museum reopened in 2011 following a complete overhaul of the exhibition space.)

Masks

A shortage of mask *botteghe* (shops) in Venice is not a problem; the challenge is ferreting out the few exceptionally talented artists producing one-of-a-kind theatrical pieces. You will certainly get original at the tiny **La Bottega dei Mascareri,** San Polo 80 (with the Rialto Bridge at your back, it's quickly on your right amid the tourist booths pushed up against the church; ✆ **041-522-3857**), where the charming Boldrin brothers' least elaborate masks begin at about 15€, though you can quickly get up toward 100€. Anyone who thinks a mask is a mask is a mask should come here first for a look-see.

Not only does **Il Canovaccio,** Castello 5369–70 (Calle delle Bande near Campo Santa Maria Formosa; ✆ **041-521-0393**), produce high-quality artisan work, but it's undeniably cool. Rolling Stone guitarist Ron Wood has shopped here, and the shop provided the masks and costumes for the orgy scene in Stanley Kubrick's *Eyes Wide Shut.*

At **Rugadoro,** San Polo 1062 (Ruga Vecchia San Giovanni near the Rialto markets; ✆ **041-520-5487**), Sarah Zanarella takes a new twist by covering parts of her masks with antique fabrics. If your Venetian shopping list includes a mask, it's worth coming by here to see these creations, which start at 22€.

Paper Products

Biblos, San Marco 2087 (Calle Larga XXII Marzo; ✆ **041-521-0714**), carries leather-bound blank books and journals, marbleized paper, enamel pill boxes, watercolor etchings, and fountain pens. At nearby **Il Prato,** San Marco 2456 (Calle delle Ostreghe, the continuation of Calle Larga XXII Marzo;

(✆ **041-523-1148**), you'll find top end examples of photo albums, pencil holders, and many other handmade items covered in the typical Venetian paper.

ENTERTAINMENT & NIGHTLIFE

Visit one of the tourist information centers for current English-language schedules of the month's special events. The monthly *Ospite di Venezia* is distributed free or online at **www.unospitedivenezia.it** and is extremely helpful but usually available only in the more expensive hotels. If you're looking for serious nocturnal action, you're in the wrong town. Your best bet is to sit in the moonlit Piazza San Marco and listen to the cafes' outdoor orchestras, with the illuminated basilica before you—the perfect opera set.

For just plain hanging out at most any time of day, popular spots that serve as meeting points include **Campo San Bartolomeo,** at the foot of the Rialto Bridge (though it is a zoo here in high season), and nearby **Campo San Luca.** In less busy times you'll see Venetians of all ages milling about engaged in animated conversation, particularly from 5pm until dinnertime. In late-night hours, for low prices and low pretension, the absolute best place to go is **Campo Santa Margherita,** a huge open *campo* about halfway between the train station and the Accademia bridge.

The Performing Arts

Venice has a long and rich tradition of classical music, and there's always a concert going on somewhere. Several churches regularly host classical music concerts (with an emphasis on the baroque) by local and international artists. This was, after all, the home of Vivaldi. One of the more popular spots to hear the

The interior of Teatro La Fenice.

music of Vivaldi and his contemporaries is **Chiesa Santa Maria della Pietà** (the "Vivaldi Church"; www.vivaldichurch.it), between Campo Santo Stefano and the Accademia bridge. Concerts are held on weekends at 8:30pm; check the website for specific dates and tickets. A number of other churches and confraternities (such as San Stae, the Scuola di San Giovanni Evangelista, and the Scuola di San Rocco) host concerts. People dressed in period costumes stand around in heavily trafficked spots near San Marco and Rialto passing out brochures advertising the classical music concerts, so you'll have no trouble finding up-to-date information.

The city still remembers well when the famous **Teatro La Fenice ★★★** (San Marco 1965, on Campo San Fantin; www.teatrolafenice.it; ✆ **041-2424** or 041-786-511) went up in flames in January 1996. Carpenters and artisans rebuilt the theater, which originally opened in 1836, according to archival designs, and in December 2003 La Fenice (which appropriately means "the Phoenix") arose from the ashes as Ricardo Muti conducted the Orchestra and Chorus of La Fenice in an inaugural concert in a completely renovated hall. Its performances now follow a regular schedule.

Cafes

For tourists and locals alike, Venetian nightlife mainly centers on the many cafe/bars in one of the world's most remarkable *piazze:* Piazza San Marco. It is also the most expensive and touristed place to linger over a Campari or anything else for that matter, but it's a splurge that should not be dismissed too readily. For those on a particularly tight budget, you can hang out near the cafes and listen to the sometimes quite surprisingly good live classical music (you won't be alone).

The nostalgic 18th-century **Caffè Florian ★★** (San Marco 56A–59A; ✆ **041-241-7286;** closed Wed in winter), on the south side of the piazza, is the most famous and most theatrical inside. Have a Bellini (prosecco and fresh peach nectar) at the bar for half what you'd pay at an indoor table; alfresco seating is even more expensive when the band plays, but it's worth every cent. It's said that when Casanova escaped from the prisons in the Doge's Palace, he stopped here for a coffee before fleeing Venice.

On the opposite side of the square at San Marco 133–134 is the old-world **Caffè Lavena** (✆ **041-522-4070;** closed Tues in winter), and at no. 120 is **Caffè Quadri ★** (www.caffequadri.it; ✆ **041-522-2105;** closed Mon in winter), the first to introduce coffee to Venice, with a restaurant upstairs that sports Piazza San Marco views. At all spots, a cappuccino, tea, or Coca-Cola at a table will set you back about 8€. But no one will rush you, and if the sun is warm and the orchestras are playing, there's no more beautiful public open-air salon in the world. Around the corner (no. 11) and in front of the pink-and-white marble Palazzo Ducale is the best deal, **Caffè Chioggia ★★★** (✆ **041-528-5011;** closed Sun). Come here at midnight and watch the Moors strike the hour atop the Clock Tower from your outside table, while the quartet or pianist plays everything from quality jazz to pop until the wee hours.

If the weather is chilly or inclement, or for no other reason than to revel in the history and drama of Venice's grand-dame hotel, dress up and stroll into the landmark lobby of the Danieli hotel and **Bar Dandolo** (Castello 4196 on Riva degli Schiavoni, east of Piazza San Marco; ✆ **041-522-6480**). Tea or coffee costs 8€, a lot, perhaps, if you consider that for the same price you can buy eight coffees at a bar, but for this fee you can sit forever while enjoying the former

Musicians play at Quadri on Piazza San Marco.

residential *palazzo* of a 15th-century doge. A pianist plays from 7 to 9pm and from 10pm to 12:30am. Drinks are far more expensive; ask for the price list before ordering.

Birrerie & Gelaterie

Although Venice boasts an old and prominent university, dance clubs barely enjoy their 15 minutes of popularity before changing hands or closing down (some are open only in the summer months). Young Venetians tend to go to the Lido or mainland Mestre. Evenings are better spent lingering over a late dinner, having a pint in a *birrerie,* or nursing a glass of prosecco in one of Piazza San Marco's or Campo Santa Margherita's overpriced outdoor cafes. (***Note:*** Most bars are open Mon–Sat 8pm–midnight.)

As if Campo Santa Margherita didn't already have enough going for it, it is also home to **Il Doge** (no. 3058, at the end of the *campo* going toward San Barnaba), one of the city's best **gelato** sources. Not to be outdone, Campo Santo Stefano has excellent gelato at **Bar/Gelateria Paolin** (no. 2962; closed Fri). Another good choice is **Gelateria Nico** on the Zattere in Dorsoduro 922, and then there is always **Grom** in Campo San Barnaba and on the Strada Nova near Ca' d'Oro.

The **Devil's Forest Pub ★**, San Marco 5185, on Calle Stagneri (www.devilsforest.com; ✆ **041-520-0623**), offers the outsider an authentic chance to take in the convivial atmosphere and find out where Venetians hang out—despite the fact that the atmosphere is more British than Italian. It's popular for lunch with the neighborhood merchants and shop owners, and ideal for relaxed socializing over a beer and a host of games like backgammon, chess, and Trivial Pursuit. It is open daily 10am to 1am.

With its walls full of Irish paraphernalia confirming its credentials as the only real Irish pub in town, the **Inishark Irish Pub ★**, at Castello 5787 (Calle Mondo Novo just off Salizada San Lio, near Santa Maria Formosa; ✆ **041-523-5300;** closed Mon), is a big draw for young locals as well as tourists. There is an enormous flatscreen television where they show soccer matches and other sporting events, and they throw in free Wi-Fi. A Guinness and some Web surfing, anyone?

The party spills well out from the plate-glass windows of **Bar Torino,** San Marco 459 (Campo San Luca; ✆ **041-522-3914**), a bar that has brought this square to life after dark with live jazz many nights, unusual beer from Lapland, and good panini. It's open Tuesday to Sunday 7am to 2am.

In 1931, famed restaurateur and hotelier Giuseppe Cipriani opened **Harry's Bar ★★** right at the San Marco–Vallaresso *vaporetto* stop, San Marco 1323 (Calle Vallaresso; ✆ **041-528-5777**). This has been a preferred retreat for everyone from Hemingway—when he didn't want a bloody mary, he mixed his own drink: 15 parts gin, 1 part dry vermouth—to Woody Allen. Harry's is most famous for inventing the Bellini, a mix of champagne and peach purée. Prices—for both drinks and the fancy cuisine—are rather extravagant.

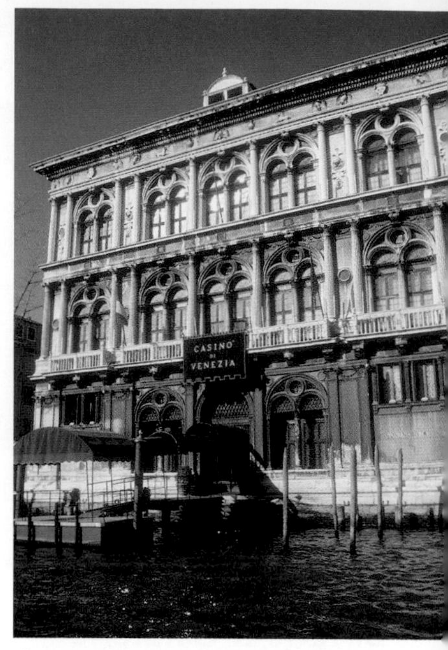

The water entrance to the Casino Municipale di Venezia.

The Casino

From May to October, **Casino Municipale di Venezia,** located at Palazzo Vendramin Calergi, Cannaregio 2040 (Fondamenta Vendramin; www.casinovenezia.it; ✆ **041-529-7111**), moves to its nondescript summer location on the Lido, where a visit is not as strongly recommended as during the winter months, when it is housed in this handsome 15th-century *palazzo* on the Grand Canal. Venice's tradition of gambling goes back to the glory days of the Republic and lives on in this august Renaissance palace built by Mauro Codussi. This is one of only four casinos on Italian territory. Though not of the caliber of Monte Carlo, what a remarkable setting it is! Richard Wagner lived and died in a wing of this *palazzo* in 1883.

Check with your hotel before setting forth; some offer free passes for their guests. Otherwise, if you're not a gambler or a curiosity seeker, it may not be worth the admission of 5€ to get in. ***Tip:*** If you pay a higher 10€ admission fee, the casino will provide you with a 10€ credit for gambling, so your admission could actually be free—and perhaps, if you're lucky, better than free. ***Note:*** A passport and jacket are required for entrance (you can rent the jacket there, the passport you have to bring yourself), and the casino is open daily from 3:30pm (11am for the slots) to 2:30am (Fri–Sat until 3am).

WHERE TO STAY

Few cities boast as long a high season as that of Venice, beginning with the Easter period. May, June, and September are the best months weather-wise and, therefore, the most crowded. July and August are hot (few of the one- and two-star hotels offer air-conditioning; when they do it usually costs extra). Like everything else, hotels are more expensive here than in any other Italian city, with no apparent upgrade in amenities. The least special of those below are clean and functional; at best, they're charming and thoroughly enjoyable, with the serenade of a passing gondolier thrown in for good measure. Some may even provide you with your best stay in all of Europe.

It's highly advisable to reserve in advance, even in the off season. If you haven't booked, come as early as you can on your arrival day, definitely before noon. There is a **travel agency in the train station** that will book rooms for you, but the lines are often long, especially in the morning.

Another alternative to reserve upon your arrival is through the **A.V.A.** (Venetian Hoteliers Association), online at www.veneziasi.it or ✆ **041-522-2264.** Simply state the price range you want to book, and they'll confirm a hotel while you wait. There are offices at the train station, in Piazzale Roma garages, and in the airport.

The rates below were compiled in late 2011. You can expect an annual increase of anywhere from 2% to 10%, depending on the category, but you might be hit with an increase of as much as 20% if the hotel you pick has been redone recently.

Elevators, light, and space are often in short supply in Venice hotels, characteristics that are a little easier to accept when you remember this is a city built on water. Venice hotels often have tiny bathrooms and the rooms themselves are generally dark and smaller than you'd expect to find in a similar hotel in another city. And that's not all . . . canal views aren't half as prevalent as they should be—and when you have them there's a chance you'll open the window onto a view of a nearby building you could almost touch. This doesn't mean that a welcoming family run hotel in an atmospheric neighborhood can't offer a memorable stay—just don't expect the amenities of the Danieli or Grand Canal vistas.

SEASONAL CONSIDERATIONS Most hotels observe high- and low-season rates and the high end hotels generally adapt their prices to availability. In the prices listed below, **single figures represent rack rates,** because the price varies too widely depending on availability, and you can usually get a room for much less, even in high season.

In San Marco

VERY EXPENSIVE

Hotel Gritti Palace ★★★ Although there are arguably more chichi hotels along the *bacino* off St. Mark's Square, if you're going for luxury status and the classiest hotel on the Grand Canal, the Gritti has been *it* for decades. It was the 16th-century palace of Doge Andrea Gritti, whose portrait graces one of the antiques-filled lounges, and everyone who is anyone has stayed here over the centuries, from international royalty to captains of industry, literary giants, and rock stars. Rooms have inlaid antique furnishings, gilt mirrors, ornate built-in dressers hand-painted in 18th-century Venetian style, tented curtains over the tall windows, and real box-spring beds set into curtained nooks. Many rooms have connecting doors so that families can share. Three of the suites on the *piano nobile* overlook the Grand Canal from small stone balconies; three more suites overlook the *campo*. Three junior suites open onto a side canal, with walk-in closets and one-and-a-half bathrooms.

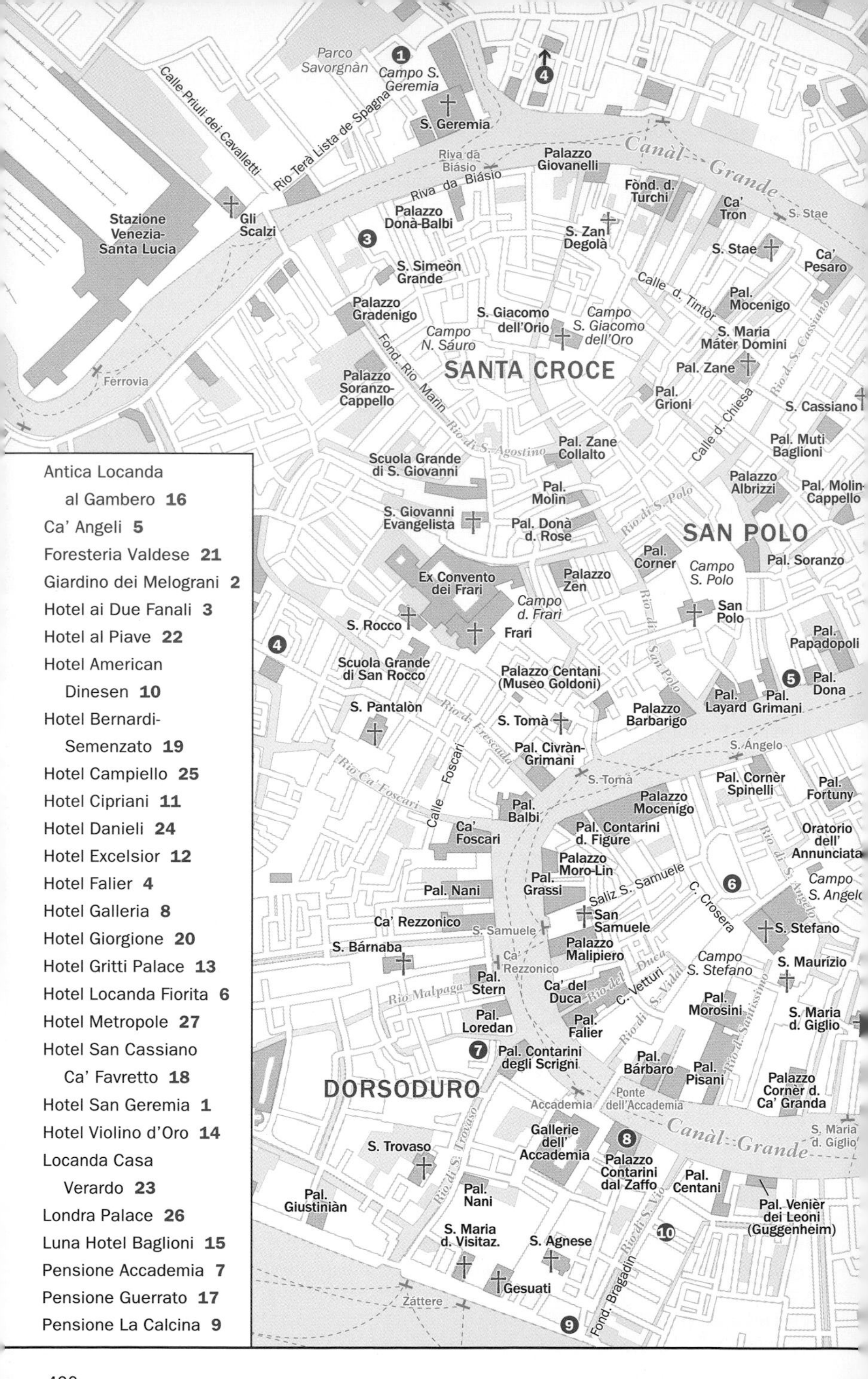

Antica Locanda al Gambero 16
Ca' Angeli 5
Foresteria Valdese 21
Giardino dei Melograni 2
Hotel ai Due Fanali 3
Hotel al Piave 22
Hotel American Dinesen 10
Hotel Bernardi-Semenzato 19
Hotel Campiello 25
Hotel Cipriani 11
Hotel Danieli 24
Hotel Excelsior 12
Hotel Falier 4
Hotel Galleria 8
Hotel Giorgione 20
Hotel Gritti Palace 13
Hotel Locanda Fiorita 6
Hotel Metropole 27
Hotel San Cassiano Ca' Favretto 18
Hotel San Geremia 1
Hotel Violino d'Oro 14
Locanda Casa Verardo 23
Londra Palace 26
Luna Hotel Baglioni 15
Pensione Accademia 7
Pensione Guerrato 17
Pensione La Calcina 9
Parco Savorgnàn
Campo S. Geremia
S. Geremia
Calle Priuli dei Cavalletti
Rio Terà Lista de Spagna
Riva da Biásio
Palazzo Giovanelli
Canàl Grande
Fond. d. Turchi
Ca' Tron
S. Stae
Ca' Pesaro
Stazione Venezia-Santa Lucia
Gli Scalzi
Palazzo Donà-Balbi
S. Zan Degolà
S. Simeòn Grande
Calle d. Tintor
Pal. Mocenigo
Palazzo Gradenigo
S. Giacomo dell'Orio
Campo S. Giacomo dell'Orio
Campo N. Sáuro
S. Maria Máter Domini
Fond. Rio Marin
SANTA CROCE
Pal. Zane
Rio d. S. Cassiano
Palazzo Soranzo-Cappello
Ferrovia
Pal. Grioni
S. Cassiano
Calle d. Chiesa
Rio di S. Agostino
Pal. Zane Collalto
Pal. Muti Baglioni
Scuola Grande di S. Giovanni
Palazzo Albrizzi
Pal. Molin-Cappello
Pal. Molin
Rio di S. Polo
S. Giovanni Evangelista
Pal. Donà d. Rose
SAN POLO
Pal. Corner
Campo S. Polo
Pal. Soranzo
Ex Convento dei Frari
Palazzo Zen
Campo d. Frari
Rio di San Polo
San Polo
S. Rocco
Frari
Pal. Papadopoli
Scuola Grande di San Rocco
Palazzo Centani (Museo Goldoni)
Pal. Dona
Pal. Layard
Pal. Grimani
S. Pantalòn
Rio d. Frescada
S. Tomà
Palazzo Barbarigo
Pal. Civràn-Grimani
S. Ángelo
Rio Ca' Foscari
Calle Foscari
S. Tomà
Pal. Cornèr Spinelli
Pal. Fortuny
Palazzo Mocenigo
Pal. Balbi
Ca' Foscari
Pal. Contarini d. Figure
Oratorio dell' Annunciata
Rio di S. Angelo
Palazzo Moro-Lin
Pal. Grassi
Saliz S. Samuele
C. Crosera
Campo S. Angelo
Pal. Nani
San Samuele
Ca' Rezzonico
S. Samuele
S. Stefano
S. Bárnaba
Palazzo Malipiero
Campo S. Stefano
S. Maurízio
Ca' Rezzonico
Pal. Stern
Ca' del Duca
Rio del Duca
C. Vetturi
Rio d. S. Vidal
Rio Malpaga
Pal. Morosini
Rio d. Santissimo
S. Maria d. Giglio
Pal. Loredan
Pal. Falier
Pal. Contarini degli Scrigni
Pal. Bárbaro
Pal. Pisani
Palazzo Cornèr d. Ca' Granda
DORSODURO
Ponte dell'Accademia
Accademia
Rio di S. Trovaso
S. Trovaso
Gallerie dell' Accademia
Palazzo Contarini dal Zaffo
S. Maria d. Giglio
Pal. Centani
Pal. Giustiniàn
Pal. Nani
Pal. Venièr dei Leoni (Guggenheim)
Rio di S. Vio
S. Maria d. Visitaz.
S. Agnese
Gesuati
Zàttere
Fond. Bragadin

Venice Hotels
CANNAREGIO
SAN MARCO
CASTELLO
Bacino di San Marco

Gritti Palace.

San Marco 2467 (Campo del Traghetto/Campo Santa Maria del Giglio), 30124 Venezia. www.hotelgrittipalacevenice.com. ✆ **041-794-611.** Fax 041-520-0942. 90 units. 950€ double deluxe; 1,295€ double with Grand Canal view; 2,300€ junior suite; 2,950€ suite with *campo* (square) view; 4,500€ presidential suite with canal view. AE, DC, MC, V. *Vaporetto:* Santa Maria del Giglio (the hotel is right there). **Amenities:** Venetian/Mediterranean/international restaurant; bar; babysitting; concierge; room service; smoke-free rooms; Wi-Fi. *In room:* A/C, TV w/pay movies, VCR (in suites), fax (in suites), hair dryer, minibar.

EXPENSIVE

Luna Hotel Baglioni ★★ Just off Piazza San Marco on the street leading down to Harry's Bar, this luxury hotel may be Venice's oldest inn, converted into a hotel from a convent in the 1200s. "Superior" rooms are situated on dreary airshafts but are otherwise very nice, midsize, and with more modern styling than the pricier-category rooms. The "deluxe" rooms are richly carpeted, with ornate stucco around the wall fabrics, Murano chandeliers and sconces, watercolors and prints, and double sinks with golden fixtures set in the marble bathrooms. Many sprout small balconies with a partial view of the little Royal Gardens at the Grand Canal. Junior suites are very large, with huge bathrooms, though only no. 505 has the views of the Bacino San Marco (into which the Grand Canal empties). The elegant breakfast room is covered with remarkable 18th-century frescoes and gilt-edged paintings.

San Marco 1243 (Calle di Ca' Vallaresso), 30124 Venezia. www.baglionihotels.com. ✆ **041-528-9840.** Fax 041-528-7160. 115 units. 651€ superior double; 690€ superior double with view; 735€ deluxe double; 870€ junior suite; 1,470€ suite; 1,600€ suite with lagoon view; 1,750€ Gran Lagoon suite; 2,050 Giorgione suite on 2 floors. Buffet breakfast 40€ (sometimes included in room rate). AE, DC, MC, V. *Vaporetto:* San Marco–Vallaresso (it's on the street leading straight up from the *vaporetto* stop). **Amenities:** Italian/international restaurant; piano bar (music 2–3 times a week); babysitting; concierge; room service; smoke-free rooms. *In room:* A/C, TV, fax (in suites), hair dryer, minibar, Wi-Fi.

MODERATE

Antica Locanda al Gambero ★★ Midway along a main strip connecting Piazza San Marco and the Rialto bridge, this was once a budget hotel, but after a full renovation, it now caters to a slightly better-heeled crowd. Surrounded by striped bedspreads and curtains, you can slumber in one of the 14 canal-side rooms (no. 203 also has a small balcony). Rooms on the first two floors have higher ceilings, though upstairs rooms are more newly renovated. The entire hotel is nonsmoking. By Venice standards, Gambero has all the comforts of a midscale hotel at moderate prices. Guests receive a 10% discount in the lively ground-floor Le Bistrot de Venise (p. 472).

San Marco 4687 (on Calle dei Fabbri), 30124 Venezia. www.locandaalgambero.com. ✆ **041-522-4384** or 041-520-1420. Fax 041-520-0431. 30 units. 250€ double, 275€ triple. Rates include continental breakfast. MC, V. *Vaporetto:* Rialto (turn right along canal, cross small footbridge over Rio San Salvador, and turn left onto Calle Bembo, which becomes Calle dei Fabbri; hotel is about 5 blocks ahead on left). **Amenities:** Restaurant, Le Bistrot de Venise (p. 472); bar (in restaurant); concierge. *In room:* A/C, TV, hair dryer, minibar, Wi-Fi.

Hotel Violino d'Oro ★★ This small boutique hotel at a tiny *campiello* with a marble fountainhead on the main shopping drag from San Marco to the Accademia may be relatively new, but the style is ever-popular 18th-century Venetian. The rooms, bathed in rich colors, are compact but graced with nice touches such as gold finishings on the marble-top desks, modest stuccoes and Murano chandeliers on the ceilings, and very firm beds. Six doubles even overlook Rio San Moisè canal, but you'll pay extra for the privilege. The low-season rates are incredible, and even high-season rates are (for Venice) not too bad for this location, level of comfort, and style. The entire hotel is nonsmoking.

San Marco 2091 (Calle Larga XXII Marzo), 30124 Venezia. www.violinodoro.com. ✆ **041-277-0841**. Fax 041-277-1001. 26 units. 300€ double; 325€ deluxe double; 410€ deluxe double with view. Ask about bargain rates during low season. Rates include buffet breakfast. AE, DC, MC, V. *Vaporetto:* San Marco–Vallaresso (walk straight up Calle di Ca' Vallaresso, left on Salizada San Moisè; cross the wide footbridge; the hotel is just across the little *campiello* on the left). **Amenities:** Bar; concierge; room service. *In room:* A/C, TV, hair dryer, minibar, Wi-Fi.

INEXPENSIVE

Hotel Locanda Fiorita ★★ This pretty little hotel is located in a red *palazzo* that retains the flair of its renovation in 18th-century Venetian style. The wisteria vine partially covering the facade is at its glorious best in May and June, but the Fiorita is appealing year-round, as much for its simply furnished rooms boasting new bathrooms as for its location on a *campiello* off the grand Campo Santo Stefano. Rooms 1 and 10 have little terraces beneath the wisteria pergola and overlook the *campiello;* they can't be guaranteed on reserving, so ask when you arrive. Right next door is **Bloom B&B** (✆ **340-149-8872;** fax 041-522-8043; www.bloom-venice.com), the Fiorita's more modern, and more expensive (250€ double) annex.

San Marco 3457a (on Campiello Novo), 30124 Venezia. www.locandafiorita.com. ✆ **041-523-4754.** Fax 041-522-8043. 10 units. 170€ double. Rates include continental breakfast. AE, DC, MC, V. *Vaporetto:* Sant'Angelo (walk to the tall brick building, and turn right around its side; cross a small bridge as you turn left down Calle del Pestrin; a bit farther down on your right is a small square 8 stairs above street level; hotel is in the *campiello*). **Amenities:** Babysitting; concierge; room service; smoke-free rooms. *In room:* A/C, TV, hair dryer, Wi-Fi.

In Castello

VERY EXPENSIVE

Hotel Danieli ★★★ Doge Dandolo built his glorious Venetian Gothic palace three doors down from the Palazzo Ducale in the 14th century, and it's been one of the most sumptuous hotels in Venice since 1822. Like the Gritti Palace (both hotels are owned by Starwood, as is the Westin Hotel Europa & Regina), it has been host to innumerable kings, celebrities, and other noted guests as far back as Dickens. The tone of this palatial hotel is set by the astounding four-story lobby of balustraded open balconies and stairwells, Venice's Oriental-tinged Gothic arches, and palm fronds. It's ornate throughout, and the rooms vary in decor, size, and style but are all opulently done. Rooms in the original structure have the most atmosphere but are smaller than the accommodations in the 19th-century wing. Either is far preferable to the 1940s wing next door where the rooms lack that genteel, vintage touch.

Castello 4196 (Riva degli Schiavoni), 30122 Venezia. www.danielihotelvenice.com. ✆ **041-522-6480.** Fax 041-520-0208. 231 units. 300€–870€ double; 505€–1,105€ double with lagoon view; 1,800€–3,090€ suite with lagoon view. Buffet breakfast 52€. AE, DC, MC, V. *Vaporetto:* San Zaccaria (the hotel's right at the *vaporetto* launch). **Amenities:** Roof terrace Italian restaurant; 2 bars (1 w/piano music); babysitting; bikes; children's center; concierge; golf course; exercise room; room service; sauna; smoke-free rooms; tennis court; watersports equipment/rentals. *In room:* A/C, TV w/pay movies, fax (in suite), hair dryer (in most), minibar, Wi-Fi.

EXPENSIVE

Hotel Metropole ★★ Vivaldi lived here from 1704 to 1738, when it was the chapter house of the La Pietà church next door, and he was its violin and concert master. The owner has tried to outfit his hotel as a Victorian-style home, packed with quirky collections of curios (fans, purses, bottle openers, crucifixes, cigarette cases), and its public salons are tucked with cozy bars and sitting niches. Accommodations vary widely in true Romantic style; you may find such details as Murano glass lamps and chandeliers, inlaid wood furnishings, and Romantic-era watercolors and prints. Rooms overlook the Bacino San Marco, the side canal where water taxis pull up, or the courtyard housing the lovely garden restaurant enlivened by nightly keyboard music. You get free car parking if you let them know you need it before 8pm the day you arrive.

Castello 4149 (Riva degli Schiavoni), 30122 Venezia. www.hotelmetropole.com. ✆ **041-520-5044.** Fax 041-522-3679. 67 units. 225€–500€ double; 338€–750€ junior suite; 383€–1,150€ suite. Buffet breakfast 20€ (sometimes included). AE, DC, MC, V. *Vaporetto:* San Zaccaria (walk right along Riva degli Schiavoni over 2 footbridges; the hotel is next to La Pietà church). **Amenities:** Venetian/Italian restaurant; bar; babysitting; concierge; room service; smoke-free rooms. *In room:* A/C, TV, hair dryer, minibar, Wi-Fi.

Londra Palace ★★ This 19th-century neo-Gothic palace is one of the best values on the prime real estate of the Riva degli Schiavoni. Tchaikovsky wrote his Fourth Symphony in room no. 108. With 100 windows overlooking the San Marco basin, from the "deluxe" rooms you can enjoy people-watching as well as distant vistas of the lagoon. Quieter, cheaper "superior" rooms look out on the inner courtyard. The restaurant, Do Leoni, is one of the best hotel dining rooms in town. The lobby and ground-floor salons were redesigned by the same architect who does Versace boutiques.

Castello 4171 (Riva degli Schiavoni), 30122 Venezia. www.londrapalace.com. ✆ **041-520-0533.** Fax 041-522-5032. 53 units. 230€–450€ standard double; 320€–560€ deluxe double with lagoon view; 410€–670€ junior suite. Rates include buffet breakfast. Extra bed 65€. AE, DC, MC, V. *Vaporetto:* San Zaccaria (on the canal right at the San Zaccaria *vaporetto* stop). **Amenities:** Venetian/international restaurant; bar; babysitting; concierge; golf (on Lido, special rate); room service; tennis (on Lido, special rate). *In room:* A/C, TV, hair dryer, minibar, Wi-Fi.

MODERATE

Hotel Al Piave ★★ The Puppin family's tasteful hotel is a steal: This level of attention, coupled with the sophisticated *buon gusto* in decor and spirit, is rare in this price category. You'll find orthopedic mattresses under ribbon candy–print or floral spreads, immaculate white-lace curtains, stained-glass windows, new bathrooms, and even (in a few rooms) tiny terraces. The family suites—with two bedrooms, minibars, and shared bathrooms—are particularly good deals, as are the small but stylishly rustic apartments with kitchenettes and washing machines (in the two smaller ones). Reserve far in advance.

Castello 4838–40 (on Ruga Giuffa), 30122 Venezia. www.hotelalpiave.com. ✆ **041-528-5174.** Fax 041-523-8512. 13 units. 125€–180€ double; 145€–235€ superior double; 190€–300€ family suite for 3; 260€–390€ family suite for 4 or 5. Rates include continental breakfast. AE, DC, MC, V. Closed Jan 7 to Carnevale. *Vaporetto:* Rialto (head southeast to the Campo Santa Maria Formosa, which is equidistant from Piazza San Marco and the Rialto Bridge; Ruga Giuffa is the road leaving the southeast corner of the *campo*). **Amenities:** Babysitting; concierge; smoke-free rooms; Wi-Fi. *In room:* A/C, TV, fridge (family suite), hair dryer, minibar.

Hotel Campiello ★ At this gem on a tiny *campiello,* the atmosphere is airy and bright, and the relaxed hospitality and quality service are provided by the Bianchini sisters, Monica and Nicoletta. Most rooms are done in authentic 18th-century and Art Nouveau antiques with inlaid armoires and bas-reliefs on the headboards. The building's original 15th-century marble-mosaic pavement is still evident, a vestige of the days when the hotel was a convent under the patronage of the nearby San Zaccaria.

Castello 4647 (on Campiello del Vin), 30122 Venezia. www.hcampiello.it. ✆ **041-520-5764.** Fax 041-520-5798. 16 units. 100€–250€ double; 120€–270€ triple; 140€–300€ quad; 170€–350€ suite. Ask about discounts in off season. Rates include buffet breakfast. AE, DC, MC, V. *Vaporetto:* San Zaccaria (head down the road that flanks the left side of the Hotel Savoia e Jolanda). **Amenities:** Bar; babysitting; concierge; room service; smoke-free rooms. *In room:* A/C, TV, hair dryer.

Locanda Casa Verardo ★★★ In 2000, Daniela and Francesco took over this one-star *pensione* and transformed it into a fine three-star hotel (and more than doubled its size), while still maintaining the feel of a Venetian *palazzo* romantically faded by time. The wood-paneled lobby is anchored by an ancient stone well. The rooms are done in chipped-stone floors, Murano chandeliers, and eclectic furnishings, from imposing armoires and 17th-century reproductions to pseudo Deco and modern functional; three have small terraces. The best accommodations come with stucco wall decorations and scraps of old ceiling frescoes—and tops are the six overlooking a little canal. The airy main hall doubles as a breakfast room.

Castello 4765 (at foot of Ponte Storto), 30122 Venezia. www.casaverardo.it. ✆ **041-528-6138** or 041-528-6127. Fax 041-523-2765. 23 units. 90€–250€ double; 125€–340€ deluxe double; 150€–390€ junior suite for 3–4. Rates include buffet breakfast. AE, MC, V. *Vaporetto:* San Zaccaria (walk straight ahead on Calle delle Rasse to Campo SS. Filippo e Giacomo; continue straight through the small *campo* to take Calle Chiesa to cross the 1st small bridge, Ponte Storto, to find the hotel on the left). **Amenities:** Bar; babysitting; concierge; room service; smoke-free rooms. *In room:* A/C, TV, hair dryer (on request), minibar, Wi-Fi.

INEXPENSIVE

Foresteria Valdese (Palazzo Cavagnis) ★★ Those lucky enough to get a room at this weathered, though elegant, 16th-century *palazzo* will find simple yet charming accommodations. Affiliated with Italy's Waldensian and Methodist churches, the *palazzo* often fills the large dormitory-style rooms with visiting church groups, though everyone is warmly welcomed, and you'll find an international and inter-religious mix here. Most of the plainly furnished rooms in this once-noble residence open onto a balcony overlooking a quiet canal. The 18th-century frescoes that grace the high ceilings in some doubles (including corner room no. 10) and two of the dorms are by the same artist who worked on the Correr Civic Museum. The reception is open daily from 9am to 1pm and 6 to 8pm. The hotel is nonsmoking. Sheets and towels are provided, but you have to make your own bed. You get the lower end of the price range listed below if you stay more than 1 night.

Castello 5170 (at the end of Calle Lunga Santa Maria Formosa), 30122 Venezia. www.foresteriavenezia.it. ✆ **041-528-6797.** Fax 041-241-6238. 6 units with private bathroom and TV (2–4 beds); 3 dorms (with 8, 11, or 16 beds), all with shared bathroom; 2 mini-apts (sleeping 2) with minikitchen and private bathroom. 95€–115€ double; 120€–140€ double with canal view; 25€–33€ dorm bed. Rates include buffet breakfast. DC, MC, V (but pay 3.5% more to use credit cards). Closed 2 weeks in Nov. *Vaporetto:* Rialto (head southeast to the Campo Santa Maria Formosa, which is equidistant from Piazza San Marco and the Rialto Bridge; look for the Bar all'Orologio where Calle Lunga Santa Maria Formosa begins). *In room:* TV (except in dorms), kitchenette (in apts), no phone.

In Cannaregio

Expect most (but not all) of the least expensive suggestions to be in or near the train-station neighborhood, an area full of trinket shops and budget hotels. It's comparatively charmless (though safe), and in the high season it's wall-to-wall with tourists who window-shop their way to Piazza San Marco, a half-hour to 45-minute stroll away. *Vaporetto* connections from the train station are convenient.

MODERATE

Giardino dei Melograni ★★★ In a building once used as a rest home for Venice's elderly Jews, the city's Jewish community offers you simple, spotless accommodations, a welcoming staff, and a perfect setting right on Campo del Ghetto Nuovo. Rooms in this nonsmoking, kosher building, where gentiles are just as warmly greeted as Jews, face either the *campo,* where you can watch the kids play in the afternoon, or a pleasant canal. The kosher breakfast is served in a room overlooking the *campo* and there is a private tree-shaded courtyard that invites relaxation; or if you are not the relaxing type and have to catch up on e-mail, the free Wi-Fi reaches out here. ***Note:*** For religious reasons, payment cannot be made on Saturday, so if that is your checkout day, be sure to settle accounts early.

Cannaregio 4587 (Campo del Ghetto Nuovo), 30131 Venezia. www.pardesrimonim.net. ✆/fax **041-822-6131.** 14 units. 120€–140€ standard double; 180€–210€ larger rooms that sleep 4.

Rates include kosher breakfast. AE, MC, V. *Vaporetto:* Guglie or San Marcuola (from either of the 2 *vaporetto* stops, or if walking from the train station, locate the Ponte delle Guglie; walking away from the Grand Canal along the Fondamenta di Cannaregio, take the 2nd right at the corner where the Gam Gam restaurant is located; this is the entrance to the Calle del Ghetto Vecchio that leads to the Campo del Ghetto Nuovo). **Amenities:** Wi Fi (free). *In room:* A/C, TV, hair dryer (on request), minibar.

Hotel Giorgione ★★ Original columns, huge wood beams, and prints of Giorgione's most famous paintings decorate the salons off the reception area of this 16th-century *palazzo,* which is minutes away from the Rialto bridge. The best rooms overlook the private brick courtyard, a shaded breakfast nook with a small, decorative pool, a hushed oasis save for the splashing of the fountain. "Standard" rooms are carpeted, with an early-19th-century style. In "superior" rooms, some beds have a small canopy curtain at the head, others are slightly lofted above the sitting area and flanked by twisting columns; some furnishings are 18th-century Venetian reproductions refreshingly done in brighter modern hues (in fact, each room follows its own, overwhelmingly strict, color scheme). Suites, with midsize sitting rooms and bedrooms, are done in a vaguely romantic style—matching embroidered fabrics, half-testers, and the like. No. 105 has a great private flower-fringed terrace.

Cannaregio 4587 (Campo SS. Apostoli), 30131 Venezia. ✆ **041-522-5810.** Fax 041-523-9092. 76 units. 170€–285€ standard double; 190€–340€ superior double; 245€–370€ junior suite; 250€–390€ suite. Rates include buffet breakfast. AE, DC, MC, V. *Vaporetto:* Ca' d'Oro (walk straight up Calle Ca' d'Oro and turn right onto broad Strada Nuova, which ends in Campo SS. Apostoli). **Amenities:** Bar (from 6pm); babysitting; concierge; room service; smoke-free rooms; Wi-Fi. *In room:* A/C, TV, hair dryer, minibar.

INEXPENSIVE

Hotel Bernardi-Semenzato ★★★ Don't be misled by the weather-worn exterior of this *palazzo;* inside, there are exposed hand-hewn ceiling beams, air-conditioned rooms outfitted with antique-style headboard/spread sets, and bright modern bathrooms. The enthusiastic, young English-speaking owners, Maria Teresa and Leonardo Pepoli, offer three-star style at one-star rates. The *dépendance* (annex), 3 blocks away, offers you the chance to feel as if you've rented an aristocratic apartment, with parquet floors and Murano chandeliers—room no. 5 is on a corner with a beam ceiling and fireplace, no. 6 (a family-perfect two-room suite) looks out on the confluence of two canals, and no. 2 overlooks the lovely garden of a *palazzo* next door. The Pepolis also opened yet another annex nearby consisting of just four rooms, all done in Venetian style, including one large family suite (two guest rooms, one of which can sleep four, with a common bathroom).

Cannaregio 4366 (on Calle de l'Oca), 30121 Venezia. www.hotelbernardi.com. ✆ **041-522-7257.** Fax 041-522-2424. Hotel 18 units, 11 with private bathroom. Main annex 7 units (www.locandaleo.it). New annex 6 units. *Frommer's* readers take 8% off these official rates: 75€ double with shared bathroom; 110€ double with private bathroom; 95€ triple with shared bathroom; 125€ triple with private bathroom; 110€ quad with shared bathroom; 155€ quad with private bathroom. Rates include breakfast. AE, DC, MC, V. *Vaporetto:* Ca' d'Oro (walk straight ahead to Strada Nova, turn right toward Campo SS. Apostoli; in the *campo,* turn to your left and take the 1st side street on your left, which is Calle de l'Oca). **Amenities:** Babysitting (on request); concierge; room service; Wi-Fi. *In room:* A/C, TV, hair dryer.

Hotel San Geremia ★★ If this gem of a two-star hotel had an elevator and was in San Marco, it would cost twice as much and still be worth it. Consider yourself lucky to get one of the tastefully renovated rooms—ideally, one of the seven overlooking the *campo* (better yet, one of three top-floor rooms with small terraces). The rooms have blond-wood paneling with built-in headboards and closets, or whitewashed walls with deep-green or burnished rattan headboards and matching chairs. The small bathrooms offer hair dryers and heated towel racks, and rooms with shared bathrooms have been renovated. Everything is overseen by an English-speaking staff and the owner/manager Claudio, who'll give you helpful tips and free passes to the casino.

Cannaregio 290A (on Campo San Geremia), 30121 Venezia. www.hotelsangeremia.com. ✆ **041-716-245.** Fax 041-524-2342. 20 units, 14 with private bathroom. 60€–75€ double with shared bathroom; 80€–100€ double with private bathroom. Rates do not include breakfast. AE, DC, MC, V. Closed the week of Christmas. *Vaporetto:* Ferrovia (exit the train station, turn left onto Lista di Spagna, and continue for a few minutes to Campo San Geremia). **Amenities:** Babysitting; concierge; room service. *In room:* TV, hair dryer, Wi-Fi.

In San Polo

MODERATE

Ca' Angeli ★★★ Brothers Giorgio and Matteo Wulten, from Dutch stock that came to Venice many generations ago, run this little gem right on the Grand Canal with a care and tenderness that is hard to find in Venice. The doubles are reasonably sized and most allow plenty of light to shine in on the paisley bedspreads and curtains. The bathrooms are modern, but everything else in this nonsmoking hotel is antique. Room 5 is the smallest double, but it more than makes up for it with a phenomenal terrace. Room 1, the junior suite, is the only one with a view of the Grand Canal, but everybody else can enjoy the view at breakfast while eating organic products in a wonderfully cheerful room with red carpets, chairs, and curtains that will get your day off in splendid fashion. The apartment sleeps five and is ideal for a family.

San Polo 1434 (on Calle del Traghetto della Madoneta), 30125 Venezia. www.caangeli.it. ✆ **041-523-2480.** Fax 041-241-7077. 7 units. 85€–195€ double; 95€–245€ small double with big terrace; 195–395€ junior suite with Grand Canal view; 215€–395€ apt for up to 5. Rates include buffet breakfast with certified organic products. MC, V. *Vaporetto:* San Silvestro (leaving the stop at your back go straight ahead to Campo Sant'Aponal; take the middle left, Calle di Mezzo, and follow it for a few minutes to Calle de Forno [if you end up in Campo San Polo you have gone too far], which turns into Calle del Traghetto della Madoneta; the building is at the end on your right). *In room:* A/C, TV, hair dryer, minibar, Wi-Fi.

INEXPENSIVE

Pensione Guerrato ★★★ The Guerrato is as reliable and clean a budget hotel as you're likely to find at these rates. Brothers-in-law Roberto and Piero own this former *pensione* in a 13th-century convent and manage to keep it almost always booked (mostly with Americans). The firm mattresses, good modern bathrooms, and flea-market finds (hand-carved antique or Deco headboards and armoires) show their determination to run a top-notch budget hotel in pricey Venice. The Guerrato is in the Rialto's heart, so think of 7am noise before requesting a room overlooking the marketplace (with a peek down the block to the Grand Canal and Ca' d'Oro). Piero and Roberto have also renovated the building's top floor (great views; no elevator, 70 steps) to create five more rooms—with air-conditioning (for which you will pay 10€).

San Polo 240A (on Calle Drio or Dietro la Scimia, near the Rialto Market), 30125 Venezia. www.pensioneguerrato.it. ✆ **041-522-7131.** Fax 041-528-5927. 20 units. 95€ double with shared bathroom; 140€ double with private bathroom; 120€ triple with shared bathroom; 155€ triple with private bathroom; 185€ quad with private bathroom. Pay in cash, get 10% off. Rates include buffet breakfast. AE, MC, V. Closed Dec 22–26 and Jan 8–early Feb. *Vaporetto:* Rialto (from the north side of the Ponte Rialto, walk straight ahead through the stalls and market vendors until the corner with the UniCredit Banca; go 1 more short block and turn right; the hotel is halfway down the narrow street). **Amenities:** Babysitting; concierge; smoke-free rooms; Wi-Fi. *In room:* A/C (top floor only), hair dryer.

In Santa Croce

EXPENSIVE

Hotel San Cassiano Ca' Favretto ★★ Call this place a moderate splurge choice, which gets two stars for its location and views. About half the rooms look across the Grand Canal to the gorgeous Ca' d'Oro (accounting for the highest rates listed below) and tend to be larger than the others, most of which open onto a side canal. Built into a 16th-century palace, the hotel is steeped in dusty old-world elegance, with Murano chandeliers (but no elevator). The rooms are outfitted in modest, dark-wood 1970s style faux antiques. The breakfast room is done in 18th-century-style pastels and stuccoes—get to breakfast early to snag one of the two tiny tables on the wide balcony overlooking the Grand Canal. There's also a wood-beam bar and TV lounge with a canal-view window and a few small tables on the private boat launch where you can sip an *aperitivo* in the evening.

Santa Croce 2232 (Calle della Rosa), 30135 Venezia. www.sancassiano.it. ✆ **041-524-1768.** Fax 041-721-033. 35 units. 310€ double; 335€ superior double; 400 double with Grand Canal view. Rates include breakfast. AE, DC, MC, V. *Vaporetto:* San Stae (turn left to cross in front of the church, take the bridge over the side canal and turn right; then turn left, cross another canal, turn right, and then left again; cross yet another canal and turn right, then immediately left and then left again toward the Grand Canal and the hotel). **Amenities:** Bar; babysitting; concierge; room service; smoke-free rooms. *In room:* A/C, TV, hair dryer, minibar, Wi-Fi.

MODERATE

Hotel Ai Due Fanali ★★ Ai Due Fanali's 16th-century altar-turned-reception-desk is an immediate clue to this hotel's impeccable taste and pursuit of aesthetic perfection. In a quiet square that's a 10-minute walk from the train station, Signora Marina Stae and her daughter Stefania have turned a part of the 14th-century *scuola* of the San Simeon Profeta church into this lovely hotel. Guest rooms boast headboards painted by local artisans, high-quality bed linens, chrome and gold bathroom fixtures, and good, fluffy towels. Breakfast is served on a panoramic terrace. Prices drop considerably from November 8 through March 30 with the exception of Christmas week and Carnevale. Ask about the four classy waterfront apartments with views (and kitchenettes), near Vivaldi's Church (La Pietà) east of Piazza San Marco, which sleep four to five people.

Santa Croce 946 (Campo San Simeon Profeta), 30125 Venezia. www.aiduefanali.com. ✆ **041-718-490.** Fax 041-718-344. 20 units. 95€–230€ double; 185€–380€ apt (minimum 3-day stay). Rates include breakfast, though not at apts. AE, MC, V. Closed most of Jan. *Vaporetto:* Ferrovia (cross the bridge over the Grand Canal; once you are to the other side of the canal, continue straight taking the 2nd left, which will have you cross a bridge before coming to Campo San Simeon Profeta). **Amenities** (at hotel only): Bar; concierge; room service. *In room:* A/C, TV, hair dryer, minibar, Wi-Fi.

INEXPENSIVE

Hotel Falier ★ Owned by the same fellow who put the lovely Hotel American Dinesen (see below) on Venice's map of moderately priced lodgings, the Falier is his savvy interpretation of less expensive accommodations, particularly worth booking when half-price low-season rates apply. With standard-size rooms (and modern bathrooms) attractively decorated with white lace curtains and flowered bedspreads, this is a reliable value even toward the upper part of the price range. The old-world lobby has potted ferns, Doric columns, and marble floors. While some may feel the need to be closer to Piazza San Marco, the Falier is much closer to the real Venice. The hotel is in a lively area lined with stores and bars between the large Campo Santa Margherita, one of the city's most character-filled *piazze,* and the much-visited Frari Church.

Santa Croce 130 (Salizada San Pantalon), 30135 Venezia. www.hotelfalier.com. ✆ **041-710-882** or 041-711-005. Fax 041-520-6554. 19 units. 50€–210€ double. Rates include continental breakfast. AE, MC, V. *Vaporetto:* Ferrovia. (If you've packed lightly, the walk from the train station is easy, easier yet from the Piazzale Roma. From the train station, cross the Scalzi Bridge, turn right along the Grand Canal until you get to the first footbridge, then left before crossing the bridge and continue along the little canal until you turn left on Fondamenta Minotti, which becomes Salizada San Pantalon.) **Amenities:** Concierge. *In room:* A/C, TV, hair dryer, Wi-Fi.

In Dorsoduro

MODERATE

Hotel American Dinesen ★★ Despite its decidedly unromantic name (did you travel transatlantic for this?), this hotel has both style and substance. One of the nicest of Venice's moderate hotels, it has the perfect combination of old-fashioned charm and utility. This three-story hotel located near the Peggy Guggenheim Collection offers a dignified lobby and breakfast room dressed with lovely Oriental carpets and marble floors, polished woods, leaded-glass windows, and French doors. The best choices are the larger corner rooms and those overlooking a quiet canal; some have small terraces. Every room is outfitted with traditional Venetian-style furnishings that usually include hand-painted furniture and Murano glass chandeliers. If it's late spring, don't miss a drink on the second-floor terrace beneath a wisteria arbor dripping with plump violet blossoms.

San Vio 628 (on Fondamenta Bragadin), 30123 Venezia. www.hotelamerican.com. ✆ **041-520-4733.** Fax 041-520-4048. 30 units. 80€–310€ double; 100€–370€ double with canal view; 140€–460€ junior suite. Rates include buffet breakfast. AE, MC, V. *Vaporetto:* Accademia (veer left around the Galleria dell'Accademia museum, taking the 1st left turn, and walk straight ahead until you cross the 1st small footbridge; turn right to follow the Fondamenta Bragadin that runs alongside the Rio di San Vio canal; the hotel is on your left). **Amenities:** Bar; babysitting; concierge; room service; smoke-free rooms. *In room:* A/C, TV, hair dryer, minibar, Wi-Fi.

Pensione Accademia ★★ The outdoor landscaping (a flowering patio on the small Rio San Trovaso and a grassy formal rose garden behind) and interior details (original pavement, wood-beam and decoratively painted ceilings) of this *pensione* create the impression that you're a guest in an aristocratic Venetian home from another era. The 17th-century villa is fitted with period antiques in first-floor "superior" rooms, and the atmosphere is decidedly old-fashioned and elegant (Katharine Hepburn's character lived here in the 1955 classic *Summertime*). Formally and appropriately called the Villa Maravege (Villa of Wonders), it was built as a patrician villa in the 1600s and used as the Russian consulate until the 1930s. The best rooms overlook the breakfast garden, which is snuggled into the confluence of two canals. In good weather, breakfast is served in the front garden.

Dorsoduro 1058 (Fondamenta Bollani, west of the Accademia Bridge), 30123 Venezia. www.pensioneaccademia.it. ✆ **041-521-0188.** Fax 041-523-9152. 27 units. 135€–260€ double; 170€–320€ superior double; 200€–350€ junior suite. Rates include buffet breakfast. AE, DC, MC, V. *Vaporetto:* Accademia (step off the *vaporetto* and turn right down Calle Gambara, which doglegs 1st left and then right; it becomes Calle Corfu, which ends at a side canal; walk left for a few meters to cross over the bridge, and then head to the right back up toward the Grand Canal and the hotel). **Amenities:** Bar; babysitting; concierge; room service; Wi-Fi. *In room:* A/C, TV, hair dryer, minibar.

Pensione La Calcina ★ British author John Ruskin stayed here in 1877 (you can request his room, no. 2, but good luck getting it), and this hotel on the sunny Zattere in the southern Dorsoduro has remained close to the heart of writers, artists, and assorted bohemians. Half the unfussy but luminous rooms overlook the Giudecca Canal in the direction of Palladio's 16th-century Redentore. Do your best to avoid the side rooms that overlook a very narrow canal and feel a bit claustrophobic. The outdoor floating terrace and the rooftop terrace are glorious places to begin or end the day. There are also three suites and two apartments.

Dorsoduro 780 (on Zattere ai Gesuati), 30123 Venezia. www.lacalcina.com. ✆ **041-520-6466.** Fax 041-522-7045. 29 units. 110€–240€ double without view; 150€–310€ double with Giudecca canal view. Rates include buffet breakfast. AE, DC, MC, V. *Vaporetto:* Zattere (follow le Zattere east; hotel is on water before 1st bridge). **Amenities:** Restaurant, bar; concierge; room service. *In room:* A/C, TV, hair dryer, minibar, Wi-Fi.

INEXPENSIVE

Hotel Galleria ★★ If you've always dreamed of reconciling your somewhat limited resources with a burning desire to fling open your hotel window and find the Grand Canal in front of you, this 17th-century *palazzo* is for you. But reserve way in advance because this quality-to-price ratio is extremely difficult to find on the canal. Owners Luciano Benedetti and Stefano Franceschini overhauled the hotel in 2004, keeping a sumptuous, 18th-century look in public spaces while giving a cozier feel to the new bedrooms. Six guest rooms overlook the canal; others have views that include the Ponte Accademia over an open-air bar/cafe (which can be annoying to anyone hoping to sleep before the bar closes). Breakfast, with oven-fresh bread, is served in your room.

Dorsoduro 878A (at foot of Accademia Bridge), 30123 Venezia. www.hotelgalleria.it. ✆ **041-523-2489.** Fax 041-520-4172. 9 units, 6 with bathroom. 80€–125€ double with shared bathroom; 90€–155€ double with private bathroom; 150€–235€ triple. Rates include continental breakfast. AE, DC, MC, V. *Vaporetto:* Accademia (with Accademia Bridge behind you, hotel is just to your left, next to Totem Il Canale gallery). **Amenities:** Babysitting; concierge; room service. *In room:* Hair dryer.

On Giudecca

You don't stay on Giudecca—the only one of Venice's main islands you must access by boat—for the atmosphere, the sights, or the hotel scene (though it does host the official IYH Hostel, an utterly average hostel that's terribly inconvenient, especially with its curfew). You come for the Cipriani.

VERY EXPENSIVE

Hotel Cipriani ★★★ Long regarded as Venice's top hotel, the elegant Cipriani is set into a string of Renaissance-era buildings on 1.2 hectares (3 acres) at the tip of Giudecca. Although by staying here you give up a central location and easy access to central Venice's sights, shops, and restaurants (it's a 10-min. boat ride to Piazza San Marco), that's the whole point. The hotel was opened in 1959 by Giuseppe Cipriani, who founded Harry's Bar and Torcello's Locanda Cipriani, and was such a good buddy to Ernest Hemingway that he appeared in one of the master's novels (*Across the River and into the Trees*). Room decor varies greatly, from full-bore 18th-century Venetian to discreetly contemporary, but all are among Venice's most stylish accommodations. The 15th-century Palazzo Vendramin annex, connected via a garden, is for guests who desire more privacy (not unusual, given their celebrity guest list) and a private butler.

Giudecca 10, 30133 Venezia. www.hotelcipriani.com. ✆ **041-520-7744.** Fax 041-520-3930. 95 units. 930€ double with garden view; 1,100€ double with lagoon view; 1,350€ double with lagoon view and balcony; 2,150€ junior suite with lagoon view and balcony; 2,840€ suite with lagoon view. Rates include American breakfast. AE, DC, MC, V. Closed Nov 2–Apr 11. *Vaporetto:* Zitelle. **Amenities:** 3 restaurants (excellent Italian Cipriani w/lagoon views, bar eatery, poolside lunch); 3 bars; babysitting; concierge; golf course; exercise room; Olympic-size outdoor pool; room service; sauna; spa; indoor tennis courts. *In room:* A/C, TV/VCR (free movies), fax (on request), hair dryer, kitchenette (only in junior suites and suites of the Palazzo Vendramin), minibar, Wi-Fi.

On the Lido

The Lido offers an entirely different Venice experience. The city is relatively close at hand, but you're really here to stay at an Italian beach resort and day-trip into the city for sightseeing. Although there are a few lower-end, moderately priced hotels here, they are entirely beside the point of the Lido and its jet-set reputation.

If you are looking for a more reasonable option—and one that's open year-round—check out the **Hotel Belvedere,** Piazzale Santa Maria Elisabetta 4 (www.belvedere-venezia.com; ✆ **041-526-0115;** fax 041-526-1486). It's right across from the *vaporetto* stop, has been in the same family for nearly 150 years, and sports a pretty good restaurant and a free beach cabana. It charges 80€ to 319€ for a double.

VERY EXPENSIVE

Hotel Excelsior ★★★ The Excelsior is the first place most celebs phone for film festival or Biennale accommodations. The hotel was the first successful attempt to turn the grassy wilds between the Lido's fishing villages into a bathing resort. Its core was built a century ago in a faux-Moorish style, with horseshoe arches peeking out all over; lots of huge, ornate salons and banquet halls; and a fountain-studded Arabian-style garden. As a purpose-built hotel, the rooms were cut quite large, with nice big bathrooms. Standard rooms keep the Moorish look going, with latticework doors, richly patterned wall fabrics, flamboyant bentwood headboards, and tented ceilings. Even if you don't have a sea view from your balcony, you might overlook the gorgeous garden or the private boat launch. A modern bar spills onto a large terrace overlooking the beach.

Lungarno Marconi 41, 30126 Venezia Lido. www.hotelexcelsiorvenezia.com. ✆ **041-526-0201.** Fax 041-526-7276. 197 units. 920€ double; 1,020€ double with sea or lagoon view; 2,100€ junior suite; 3,500€ sea-view suite. Rates include buffet breakfast. AE, DC, MC, V. Closed mid-Oct to mid-Mar. *Vaporetto:* Lido, then bus A. **Amenities:** 3 restaurants (Venetian/international terrace restaurant for dinner, lunch restaurants poolside and at beach); 2 bars; babysitting; bikes; courtesy boat from airport; children's program; concierge; executive-level rooms; special rates at nearby golf course; exercise room; outdoor pool; room service; smoke-free rooms; outdoor lighted tennis courts; watersports equipment/rentals. *In room:* A/C, TV w/pay movies, hair dryer, minibar, Wi-Fi.

9

THE VENETO & THE DOLOMITES

Shakespeare may have never set foot in these parts, but "fair Verona" and the surrounding area so fascinated him that he chose to set some of his best works (among them, *Romeo and Juliet, Two Gentlemen of Verona, The Taming of the Shrew*) in the Veneto. The backdrops to all of these plays showcase the rich history, art, and architecture that this extraordinary corner of Europe has to offer.

The Veneto's three major cities, **Padua, Vicenza,** and **Verona,** hold the most historical and artistic interest in the region, and they are all accessible by public transportation. Trains between these cities run on the Milan-Venice line and, hence, are inexpensive, frequent, and user-friendly. In fact, the distances between the cities are so small that you could very well stay put in Venice and tool into Verona—the most distant of the three—for an easy day trip. But this would be a great shame, since each of the cities warrants a slow exploration.

Verona was the home of the eternal lovers Romeo and Juliet; **Padua**, the city of Mantegna, contains frescoes by Giotto, and **Vicenza**, the city of Palladio, offers streets of Renaissance *palazzi* and hills studded with villas.

If time remains, you can also explore the **Riviera del Brenta,** with its Venetian *palazzi,* and such historic old cities as **Treviso** and **Bassano del Grappa.** Adventurers should roam farther afield to the limestone **Dolomites (Dolomiti),** one of Europe's greatest natural attractions. Some of these peaks in the northeastern Italian Alps soar to 3,200m (10,500 ft.). The Dolomiti are a year-round destination, with two high seasons: midsummer, when the hiking is great, and winter, when the skiers slide in. In places, the Dolomiti form fantastic shapes, combining to create a primordial landscape, with mountain chains resembling the teeth of a giant dragon. Clefts descend precipitously along jagged rocky walls; at other points a vast, flat tableland, spared nature's fury, emerges.

Travelers with an extra day or so to spare might first want to postpone their Dolomite adventure for a detour to **Trieste,** the unofficial capital of **Friuli–Venezia Giulia.** It was Venice's main rival in the Adriatic from the 9th century to the 15th century. Even though Trieste doesn't boast Venice's charm, it is still one of Italy's most interesting ports, with Habsburg monuments at its core and the world's largest accessible cave on its outskirts.

THE BEST VENETO & THE DOLOMITES TRAVEL EXPERIENCES

- **Descending the granddaddy of all grottoes:** Just outside Trieste, pack your courage and descend 500 steps into the largest underground cave open to the public. The Grotta Gigante is a 114m-high (374-ft.), 924m long (3,031-ft.) cavern carved out of the area's limestone *karst.* There is a tramway leading to its entrance from one of Trieste's major squares. See p. 543.

PREVIOUS PAGE: **View of the Dolomites.**

- **Enjoying opera under the stars in Verona:** Northern Italy is the home to some of opera's greatest composers, and there is no better place to experience one of their works than under the stars in summertime, in Verona's first-century coliseum, the Arena. See p. 524.
- **Driving the Great Dolomite Road:** This is easily among the most scenic drives in Europe. Twist and turn your way through majestic peaks and dramatic limestone cliffs between Bolzano and Cortina d'Ampezzo. See p. 550.
- **Sipping hot chocolate in Cortina d'Ampezzo:** There are plenty of ski resorts in Northern Italy with skiing that is just as good, but few can hold a candle to Cortina's glamour and charm. Skiers and nonskiers alike will be dazzled by views from the cable cars and the people-watching at the cafes below. See p. 546.
- **Cruising the Brenta Canal:** This waterway between Padua and Venice is studded with breathtaking villas. Visit Venice's version of Beverly Hills as it was meant to be seen—cruising on a riverboat. See p. 507.

THE RIVIERA DEL BRENTA ★★

The **Brenta Canal ★★**, running from Fusina to Padua, functioned as a mainland extension of Venice during the Renaissance, when wealthy merchants began using the area as a retreat from the city's summer heat. Ambitiously called "the Forgotten Riviera" because of the dozens of historic summertime villas built here by Venice's aristocracy and wealthy merchants, it can be visited by car or by boat—you can even stay in a few of the villas. Only one was designed by 16th-century master architect Palladio (the Villa Foscari), but many are Palladian-inspired (see "Palladio's Vicenza," later in this chapter). The best way to see the villas is on a cruise down the Brenta (see below). Call the **Brenta Canal tourist office** at ✆ **041-424-973** for more information.

The Villa Pisani.

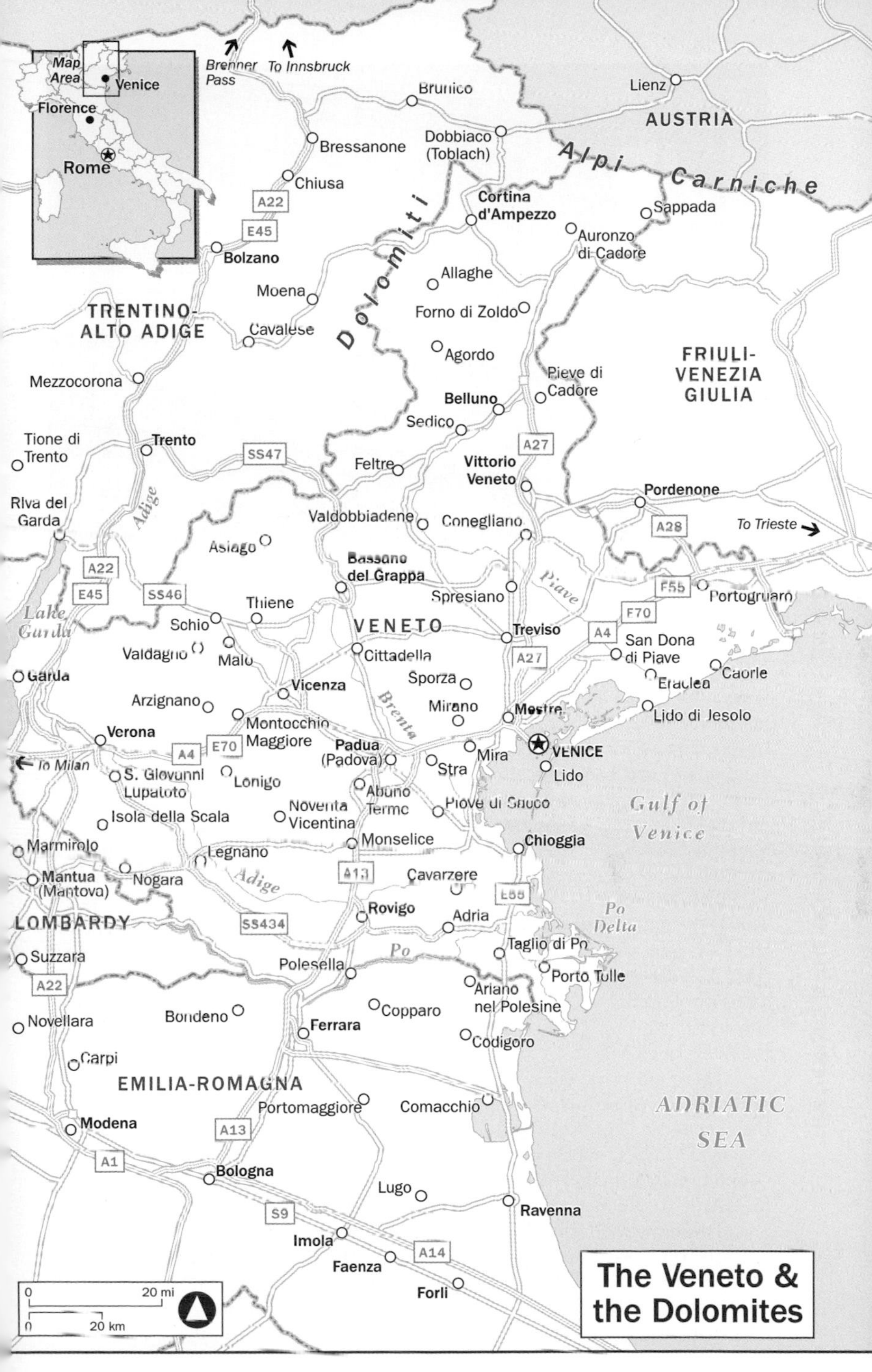
The Veneto & the Dolomites
Map Area
Venice
Florence
Rome
Brenner Pass
To Innsbruck
Brunico
Lienz
AUSTRIA
Dobbiaco (Toblach)
Bressanone
Alpi Carniche
Chiusa
Cortina d'Ampezzo
Sappada
Auronzo di Cadore
Dolomiti
Bolzano
Allaghe
Moena
Forno di Zoldo
TRENTINO-ALTO ADIGE
Cavalese
Agordo
FRIULI-VENEZIA GIULIA
Mezzocorona
Pieve di Cadore
Belluno
Sedico
Tione di Trento
Trento
Feltre
Vittorio Veneto
Pordenone
Riva del Garda
Adige
Valdobbiadene
Conegliano
To Trieste
Asiago
Bassano del Grappa
Piave
Spresiano
Portogruaro
Thiene
Lake Garda
Schio
VENETO
Treviso
San Dona di Piave
Valdagno
Malo
Cittadella
Garda
Sporza
Caorle
Eraclea
Vicenza
Brenta
Arzignano
Mirano
Mestre
Lido di Jesolo
Montocchio Maggiore
Verona
Padua (Padova)
Mira
VENICE
To Milan
Stra
Lido
S. Giovanni Lupatoto
Lonigo
Abano Terme
Piove di Sacco
Gulf of Venice
Noventa Vicentina
Isola della Scala
Monselice
Chioggia
Marmirolo
Legnano
Mantua (Mantova)
Nogara
Cavarzere
Po Delta
Rovigo
Adria
LOMBARDY
Taglio di Po
Suzzara
Po
Polesella
Porto Tolle
Ariano nel Polesine
Copparo
Bondeno
Novellara
Ferrara
Codigoro
Carpi
EMILIA-ROMAGNA
Portomaggiore
Comacchio
ADRIATIC SEA
Modena
Bologna
Lugo
Ravenna
Imola
Faenza
Forli
A22
E45
SS47
A27
A28
A22
E45
SS46
E55
E70
A4
A27
A4
E70
A13
E55
SS434
A22
A13
A1
S9
A14
0
20 mi
0
20 km

One of the rooms in the Villa Foscari.

More than 30 villas can be viewed from the boats but only three are visited. The important 18th-century **Villa Pisani ★★** (www.villapisani.com; ✆ **0425-920-016**) in Stra was commissioned by the family of a Venetian doge and is famous for its ballroom frescoes by Tiepolo and its extensive gardens. The hedge maze here—something to engage youngsters bored with having to tour all these frescoed mansions—sprouts a tower at the center so that you can get a bird's-eye view of the trip back out; during the crowded summer season, a young man stands up here calling out instructions to mazegoers to hurry them along so the next group can get in. The villa is open Easter to September, Tuesday to Sunday 9am to noon and 1:30 to 6pm (to 4pm in winter). Admission is 10€ for the villa, park, and gardens. It's free for seniors older than 60 and children younger than18.

The other two biggies are in Mira, and fair warning: Both keep erratic hours. The 18th-century **Villa Valmarana ★★** (✆ **044-321-803**) is dramatically set amid weeping willows; it's open Tuesday to Sunday from March to November (Dec–Feb open only on weekends) and costs 8€, free for children younger than 12. The **Villa Foscari** (also known as Villa Malcontenta, "the Unhappy Woman"; www.lamalcontenta.com; ✆ **041-547-0012** or 041-520-3966) is one of Palladio's finest works. It's open May to October Tuesday to Saturday 9am to noon and costs 10€.

There are other villas you can visit along the Riviera, each with a stately private home whose owners appreciate and fiercely protect the unique nature of their property. These structures don't follow the gracefully symmetrical rhythms of Palladio: Each appears to be a larger version of the *palazzi* lining Venice's Grand Canal. Although most villas welcome the occasional appropriately respectful visitor, do call in advance before you drop in.

These include the **Villa Sagredo,** Via Sagredo (www.villasagredo.it; ✆ **049-503174**), 1km (½ mile) northwest of the hamlet of Vigonovo. In a suitably gnarled garden, it was built on ancient Roman foundations, and the form it has today dates from around 1700, the result of frequent rebuilding. You must reserve in advance, and the owners prefer scheduled visits Tuesday to Friday 5 to

10pm or Saturday and Sunday 2 to around 8pm. A restaurant and a bar serve simple food and drink. Admission is free.

Essentials

GETTING THERE You can tour the Brenta Riviera by **buses** leaving from Venice headed for Padua. The buses, operated by the **ACTV** line (www.actv.it; ✆ **041-2424**), depart from the Venetian company's ticket office in Piazzale Roma daily every 15 to 30 minutes starting at 6:10am. A one-way ticket to Villa Foscari is 5€ and a one-way fare to the Villa Pisani is 5.20€.

If traveling by **car,** note that all villas open to the public are on the north bank of the canal along S11 headed west out of Venice toward Padua. At the APT in Venice, you can pick up the guide *Riviera del Brenta Venezia,* offering information on the villas and a map of their locations between Malcontenta and Stra.

VISITOR INFORMATION Contact the **APT tourist office** of Villa Widmann, Via Nazionale 420, Mira (✆ **041-424973**). From May to September, it's open Tuesday to Sunday 10am to 6pm; April and October Tuesday to Sunday 10am to 5pm; and November to March only Saturday and Sunday 10am to 5pm.

Touring the Canal

There are a number of companies willing to take you up the river for anywhere between 50€ and 95€. The tourism office promotes two of them: **I Battelli del Brenta,** Via Porciglia 34 (www.battellidelbrenta.it; ✆ **049-876-0233;** fax 049-876-3410), and **Delta Tour,** Via Toscana 2 (www.deltatour.it; ✆ **049-870 0232**). Other companies come in and out of the market. For more info on plying the rivers, canals, and other watery byways of the region, check out the local river-craft consortium's website at www.padovanavigazione.it.

I Battelli del Brenta embarks in Padua from the Scalinata del Portello at 8:30am on Wednesday, Friday, Saturday, and Sunday, arriving in Venice at 7pm; from Venice's Zattere ai Gesuati, they leave Tuesday, Thursday, and Saturday at 8:30am, finishing in Padua at 7pm. Full-day cruises cost about 85€, including lunch and entrance to all of the above-mentioned villas, while half-day cruises, at 51€, include a visit to the Villa Pasani.

Delta Tour greets passengers at the Villa Pisani at 8:30am (Tues–Fri), visits each of the estates, along with a tour guide, and finishes up at Fusina on the coast south of Venice. The 70€ fee includes a fish lunch, the tour guide's services, and entrance to the villas.

If you want to do the tour yourself, the largest concentration of country villas can be found between Stra and Mira. Bus schedules make that option nearly impossible, and a car tour does require some planning, since visiting hours and days differ from villa to villa and season to season. See the tourist office about a map.

Where to Eat

Trattoria Nalin VENETIAN/SEAFOOD Most of the Riviera del Brenta's restaurants focus on seafood, and this one is no exception. In a century-old building, the restaurant has flourished as a family-run enterprise since the 1960s. It's adjacent to the canal near the town center, and you'll probably gravitate to the terrace, where potted shrubs and flowers bloom in summer. The specialties vary with whatever happens to be in season but are likely to include *tagliatelle con salsa di calamaretti* (with squid sauce), *spaghetti al nero* (with octopus ink), crabs from the Venetian lagoon, and variations on polenta and risotto.

Via Nuovissimo 29, Mira. www.trattorianalin.it. ✆ **041-420083.** Reservations recommended. Main courses 16€–24€. AE, DC, MC, V. Tues–Sun noon–2:30pm; Tues–Sat 7:30–10pm. Closed Aug and Dec 25–Jan 10.

Where to Stay

Villa Ducale ★★ This hotel occupies an 1884 villa built atop an older structure amid a lovely park of gravel paths, fountains, and flowering bushes under the shade of exotic palms, magnolias, and pines. Rooms feature marvelous inlaid wood floors, Persian rugs, and Murano chandeliers hanging from high, frescoed ceilings. Wrought-iron bedsteads are surrounded by (mostly) antiques, and the marble bathrooms feature antique brass fittings. "Standard" rooms are smaller (some almost cramped—but those cost less), with simpler parquet floors and smaller bathrooms. "King" rooms are larger and overlook the park from balconies or a small terrace. The breakfast room/restaurant is intimate—in fact, the Ducale has a generally classier setting in its public areas than the Margherita (see below), but the Margherita tends to have classier rooms.

Riviera Martiri della Libertà 75, 30031 Dolo (Venezia). www.villaducale.it. ✆/fax **041-560-8020.** 11 units. 90€–180€ standard double; 125€–210€ "king" double with park view. Rates include breakfast. AE, DC, MC, V. Free parking. Pets welcome for 30€. **Amenities:** Seafood restaurant; bar; babysitting; bikes; concierge; Internet 8€ per hour; room service. *In room:* A/C, TV, hair dryer, minibar.

Villa Margherita ★★★ This 17th-century villa, expanded in the 19th century, once served as guest quarters for the noble Contarini family of Venice. Today it is run with refined gusto by the Dal Corso family, who provide fresh fruit and flowers in your room and a highly polished professional courtesy. All rooms overlook the large, pine-shaded lawn and are soundproofed against the noise of passing cars. "Standard" rooms, on the smaller side of medium size, have rugs scattered over wood floors. "Deluxe" rooms are larger (except for no. 218, which is a cozy lovers' nook with a spacious terrace), with more interesting antiques and richer fabrics, and are more frequently blessed with balconies. "Junior suites" are larger still. The salons downstairs are appropriately furnished in the manner of a rich country villa, with chessboards fronting fireplaces and plush armchairs. There is a frescoed Venetian/fish restaurant across the street.

Via Nazionale 416–417 (on the Venice side of Mira), 30034 Mira (Venezia). www.villa-margherita.com. ✆/fax **041-426-5838.** 19 units. 220€ standard double; 240€ deluxe double; 258€ junior suite. Rates often discounted in slower periods and off season. Rates include breakfast. AE, DC, MC, V. Parking free. Public bus stop, with half-hourly service to Venice, 15km (9¼ miles) away, is a 5-min. walk. **Amenities:** Bar; bikes; concierge; room service; smoke-free rooms. *In room:* A/C, TV, hair dryer, minibar.

PADUA ★

40km (25 miles) W of Venice, 81km (50 miles) E of Verona, 233km (144 miles) E of Milan

The University of Bologna had already grown to 10,000 students by the time Padua (Padova) founded its university in 1222. Padua was long the academic heartbeat of the powerful Venetian Republic—and far before that, an ancient

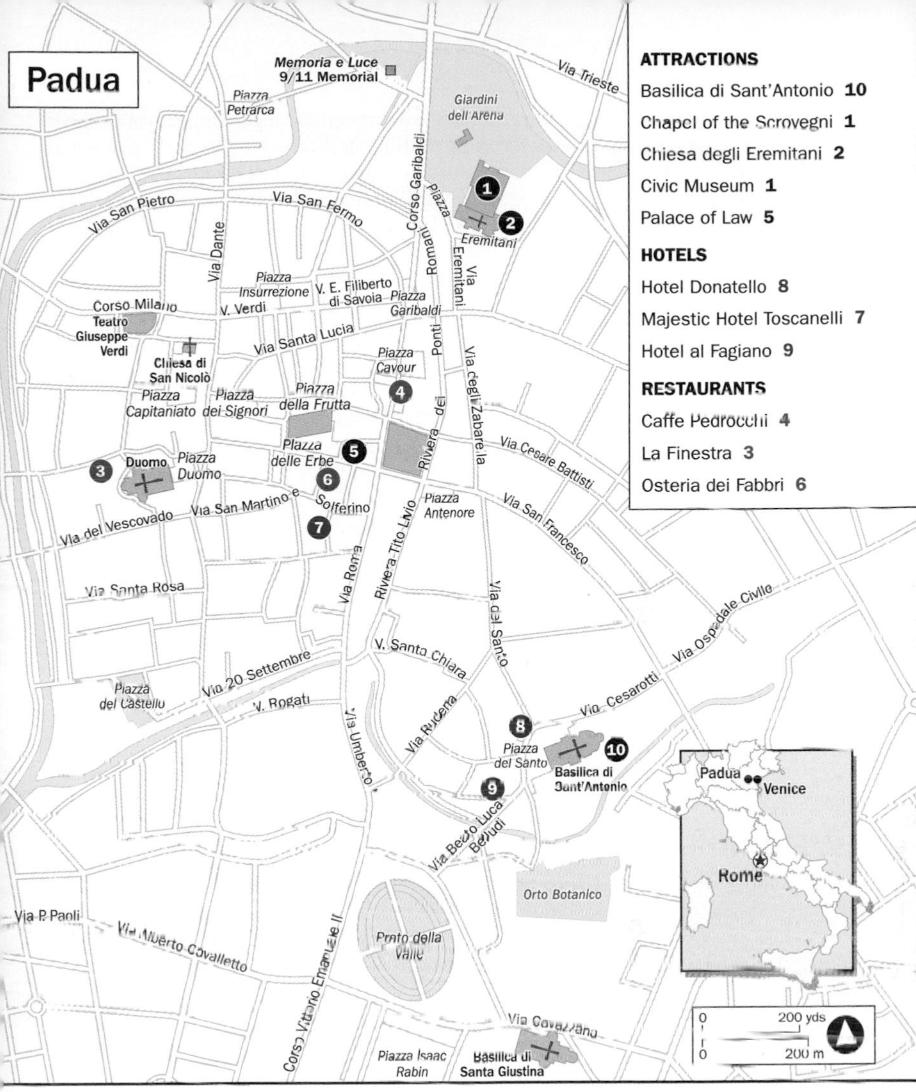

Roman stronghold—and for this reason one of the most important medieval and Renaissance cities in Italy. Dante and Copernicus studied here, and Petrarch and Galileo taught here. When you wander the narrow, cobbled, arcaded side streets in the timeless neighborhoods surrounding the "Bo" (named after a 15th-c. inn that once stood on the present-day site of the university), you are transported back to those earlier times.

Padua is a vital city, with a young university population that gets about by bicycle and keeps the city's piazzas and cafes alive. The historic hub of town still evokes the days in the late Middle Ages and the Renaissance when the city and its university flourished as a center of learning and art, although you'll have to visit during the scholastic year to witness it: Padua in summer is something of a ghost town.

You can spend a few hours or a few days in Padua, depending on your schedule. Its most important sights for those with limited time are Giotto's magnificent **frescoes** in the Scrovegni Chapel (fully restored btw. 1999 and 2001) and the revered pilgrimage site of the eight-domed **Basilica of Sant'Antonio di Padova,** whose important **equestrian statue** by Donatello stands in the piazza before it.

Essentials

GETTING THERE The **train** is best if you're coming from Venice, Milan, or Bologna. Trains depart for and arrive from Venice once every 30 minutes (trip time: 30 min.). Trains to and from Milan run every hour (trip time: 2½ hr.). Trains from Venice to Padua cost 2.90€ to 18€, depending on the train. Trains from Milan to Padua cost 13€ to 40€, depending on the train. For information and schedules, call © **892021** in Italy. Padua's main rail terminus is at Piazza Stazione, north of the historic core and outside the 16th-century walls. A bus will connect you to the center.

Buses from Venice arrive every 30 minutes (trip time: 45 min.), costing 4.30€ one-way. There are also connections from Vicenza every 30 minutes (trip time: 30 min.) at 3.60€ one-way. Padua's bus station is at Via Trieste 42 (www.sitabus.it; © **049-8206844**), near Piazza Boschetti (buses depart from Piazza Boschetti), 5 minutes from the rail station.

By **car,** take A4 west from Venice.

VISITOR INFORMATION The **tourist office** is at Galleria Pedrocchi (www.turismopadova.it; © **049-8767927**). It's open Monday to Saturday 9am to 12:30pm and 3 to 7pm. There's another tourist office at the train station (© **049-8752077**), open Monday to Saturday 9am to 7pm and Sunday 9:15am to 12:30pm.

Exploring the City

Basilica di Sant'Antonio ★★ CHURCH This enormous basilica's imposing interior is richly decorated, filled with tombs, works of art, and inlaid checkerboard marble flooring. It's all there to honor one man, Padua's patron Saint Anthony. Simply and commonly referred to as "Il Santo," Anthony was born in Lisbon in 1195 and died just outside of Padua in 1231. Work began on the church almost immediately but was not completed until 1307. Its eight domes bring to mind the Byzantine influence found in Venice's St. Mark's Basilica. A pair of octagonal, minaret-like bell towers enhances its Eastern appearance. Donatello's seven **bronze statues ★** and towering central ***Crucifixion*** (1444–48) that adorn the main altar are the basilica's artistic highlights.

The faithful could care less about the architecture and art; they flock here year-round to caress the **tomb ★** holding the saint's body (off the left aisle) and pray for his help in finding what they've lost. The tomb is always covered with flowers, photographs, and handwritten personal petitions left by devout pilgrims from every corner of the globe. The series of nine bronze bas-reliefs of scenes from the saint's life are some of the finest works by 16th-century northern Italian sculptors.

In his lifetime, St. Anthony was known for his eloquent preaching, so interpret as you will the saint's perfectly (some say miraculously) preserved **tongue, vocal chords,** and **jawbone** on display in the Cappella del Tesoro in the back of the church, directly behind the main altar. These treasured relics are carried through town in a traditional procession every June 13 to celebrate the feast day of Il Santo. You'll also see one of his original tattered tunics dating from 1231.

In front of the basilica across the large piazza, standing out amid the smattering of stalls selling St. Anthony–emblazoned everything, is Donatello's famous ***Gattamelata* equestrian statue ★★**. The first of its size to be cast in Italy since Roman antiquity, it is important for its detail, proportion, and powerful contrast between rider (the inconsequential Venetian condottiere Erasmo da Narni, nicknamed the "Spotted Cat") and horse. It was a seminal work that influenced Renaissance sculpture and casting and restored the lost art of equestrian statuary.

Piazza del Santo 11. www.basilicadelsanto.org. ✆ **049-8242811.** Free admission. Daily 6:30am–6:30pm. Bus: 3, 8, 12, or 18.

Chapel of the Scrovegni (Cappella degli Scrovegni) ★★★ CHURCH
This is the one uncontested must-see during your stay in Padua, so be prepared for lengthy lines in high season, a wait made even longer by the small numbers of controlled groups (25 people maximum) allowed to enter the chapel at any one time. Scandalously brief 15-minute visits are the limit imposed during peak periods; check when buying your ticket so you can plan accordingly. Another 15 minutes are spent in a separate room beforehand, watching a mandatory but decent documentary on the frescoes, in order to give the air temperature in the chapel a chance to stabilize in between visits. Art lovers armed with binoculars behold the scene in awe—the recently renovated cycle of **vibrant frescoes** by Giotto that revolutionized 14th-century painting is considered among the most important art leading up to the Renaissance.

Giotto worked from 1303 to 1306 to completely cover the ceiling and walls with 38 scenes illustrating the lives of the Virgin and of Christ from floor to ceiling. With your back to the front door, the three bands that cover the walls are: top right, *Life of Joachim;* top left, *Life of the Virgin;* right center, *The Childhood of Christ;* left center, *Christ's Public Life;* right bottom, *The Passion of Christ* (the third panel of Judas kissing Christ is the best known of the entire cycle); left bottom, *Christ's Death and Resurrection.* Above the entrance is the fresco of the *Last Judgment:* Christ, as judge, sits in the center, surrounded by the angels and apostles. Below him, to the right, are the blessed, while to the left, Giotto created a terrible hell in which devils and humans are condemned to eternal punishment.

Note: If you want to be assured that you will have more time in the chapel, consider visiting between 7 and 9:30pm on the 11€ "Double Turn" ticket, which allows you 30 minutes in the chapel.

Piazza Eremitani 8 (off Corso Garibaldi). www.cappelladegliscrovegni.it. For reservations: musei.comune@padovanet.it. ✆ **049-201-0020** for required reservations (call center lines Mon–Fri 9am–7pm, Sat 9am–6pm). Admission, which includes entrance to the Museo Civico Eremitani and others in the civic museum complex (see below), 13€ adults

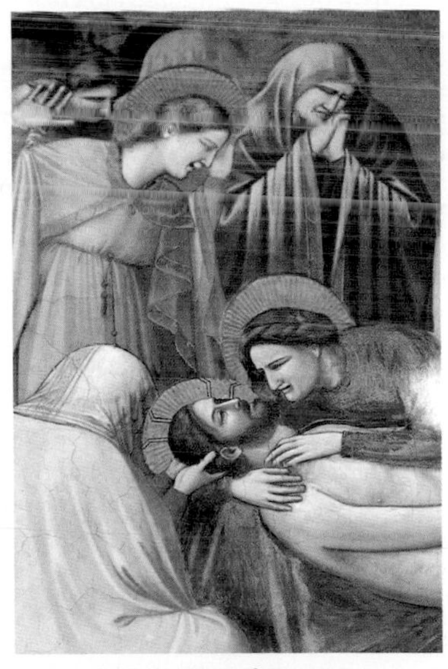

A detail from the Giotto frescoes.

Cumulative Tickets

If you plan on taking in all the sights of Padua during a short visit—or even if you plan on visiting the Scrovegni Chapel and only one other sight—a **PadovaCard** is a worthwhile investment. In addition to free use of the city's buses and free parking in some areas, the 15€ card gets you admission to the Cappella degli Scrovegni (you must call to make reservations), Musei Civici Eremitani, the Palazzo della Ragione, and other sites in Padua and the province as well as a seat in Caffè Pedrocchi. The card is valid for 48 hours and can be shared by both an adult and a child younger than 12. You'll find the card for sale at tourist offices and at sites at which you can use the card. A 72-hour card costs 20€. See www.padovacard.it.

(includes a 1€ reservation fee), or only 8€ on Mon as the Museo Eremitani is closed, 6€ ages 6–17, free for children 5 and younger (although admission still requires a reservation); free with purchase of PadovaCard (see "Cumulative Tickets," below). Daily 9am–7pm (until 10pm Mar–Nov). Entrance through the Museo Eremitani. Bus: 3, 8, 10, 12, 32, or 42.

Chiesa degli Eremitani ★ CHURCH One of Padua's tragedies occurred when this church was bombed by the Allies on March 11, 1944. Before that, it housed one of the greatest treasures in Italy, the **Ovetari Chapel (Cappella Ovetari),** with the first significant cycle of **frescoes** ★ by Andrea Mantegna (1431–1506). The church was rebuilt, but alas, you can't resurrect 15th-century frescoes. To the right of the main altar are the fragments left after the bombing. The best fresco saved is a panel depicting the dragging of St. Christopher's body through the streets. Note also the *Assumption of the Virgin.* Like Leonardo da Vinci, the artist had a keen eye for architectural detail. In the chancel chapel are some magnificent **frescoes** ★★ attributed to Guarineto, a Venetian student of Giotto.

Piazza Eremitani 9. ✆ **049-8756410.** Free admission (donations accepted). Mon–Sat 8am–6pm; Sun and religious holidays 10am–1pm and 4–7pm. Bus: 3, 8, 12, or 18.

Civic Museum (Musei Civici Eremitani) ★ MUSEUM These centuries-old cloisters that were once home to the monks (*eremitani* means "hermits") who officiated in the adjacent Scrovegni Chapel have been renovated to provide an airy display space as the city's civic museum. Its collection begins on the ground floor with the Archaeological Museum's division of Egyptian, Roman, and Etruscan artifacts. The upstairs collection represents an impressive panorama of minor works from major Venetian artists from the early 15th century to the 19th century: You'll find works by Titian, Tiepolo, and Tintoretto, whose *Crucifixion* is the museum's finest work. Special mention is given to Giotto's unusual wooden crucifix and Bellini's *Portrait of a Young Senator.*

Piazza Eremitani 8 (off Corso Garibaldi and adjacent to the Cappella Scrovegni). http://padovacultura.padovanet.it/musei. ✆ **049-820-4551**. Admission is a joint ticket with the Cappella Scrovegni 13€ adults, 8€ ages 6–17, free for children 5 and under (although admission to the Scrovegni Chapel still requires a reservation); free with purchase of PadovaCard (see "Cumulative Tickets," above). Tues–Sun 9am–7pm. Bus: 3, 8, 10, 11, 12, 32, or 42.

Palace of Law (Palazzo della Ragione) ★ ARCHITECTURE Located just south of the historic Caffè Pedrocchi, the picturesque open-air markets of **Piazza delle Erbe (Square of the Herbs)** ★★ and **Piazza della Frutta**

(Square of Fruit) frame this 13th-century *palazzo* and have stood as the town's political and commercial nucleus for centuries.

Considered a masterpiece of civil medieval architecture, it was heavily damaged by a fire in 1420 that destroyed, among other things, an elaborate cycle of frescoes by Giotto and his students that adorned **Il Salone (the Great Hall).** The hall was almost immediately rebuilt and today is the prime draw, for both its floor-to-ceiling 15th-century frescoes—commissioned immediately after the fire—and a large wooden sculpture of a horse attributed to Donatello (although many art historians don't agree). The 15th-century frescoes are similar in style and astrological theme to those that had been painted by Giotto, and comprise one of the very few complete zodiac cycles to survive until modern times. In 2011, the building was completely reopened to the public after a 10 year, 1-million-euro restoration. On the far (west) side of the adjoining piazzas' canvas-topped stalls is the **Piazza dei Signori,** most noteworthy for the 15th-century clock tower that dominates it, the first of its kind in Italy.

Piazza delle Erbe/Piazza della Frutta. http://padovacultura.padovanet.it/musei. ✆ **049-820-5006.** Admission to *palazzo* 4€ adults, 2€ children (8€ adults and 5€ children when there are exhibitions in the *palazzo*). Tues–Sun 9am–7pm (until 6pm in winter). Bus: 3, 5, 6, 8, 9, 10, 11, 12, 13, 15, 18, 22, or 42.

Where to Eat

Hailed as Europe's most elegant coffeehouse when it opened in 1831, **Caffè Pedrocchi ★★**, Via 8 Febbraio 15 (www.caffepedrocchi.it; ✆ **049-8781231**), off Piazza Cavour, is a neoclassical landmark. On sunny days, you might want to sit on one of the two stone porches; in winter, you'll have plenty to distract you inside. The sprawling bathtub-shaped travertine bar has a brass top and brass lion's feet; the velvet banquettes have maroon upholstery, red-veined marble tables, and Egyptian Revival chairs. It's open Tuesday to Sunday 8am to midnight.

La Finestra ★★ ITALIAN A very creative take on regional staples, you can begin with such delights as crispy prawns with spicy peanuts or sea scallops with a pumpkin puree. Five pastas always appear on the menu but each comes with unusual ingredients, perhaps chickpeas or caviar. For your main, select such inventive creations as monkfish in garlic broth, or seared tuna with saffron and braised onions.

Via dei Tadi 15. www.ristorantefinestra.it. ✆ **049-650313.** Reservations recommended. *Primi* 9€–15€; main courses 18€–20€. AE, MC, V. Tues–Thurs 7–11pm; Fri–Sat 12:30–3pm and 7–11pm; Sun 12:30–3pm. Closed Jan 1–7 and Aug 8–29.

Osteria Dei Fabbri ★ PADOVAN Simple, well-prepared food is the draw here. This rustic, old-fashioned tavern, or *osteria,* is a lively spot where intellectual types share tables with Zegna-suited bankers, and students stop by for a tipple or to find a quiet corner in which to pore over the newspaper (a pastime not encouraged during hours when meals are served). There's always at least one homemade pasta choice to start with, and *osso buco,* the specialty of the house, is especially memorable when accompanied by any of the local (and excellent) Venetian wines available by the bottle or glass. The *seppia al nero* (squid in its own ink) served on polenta is faithful to its Veneto roots but maybe just a little too rich for the uninitiated. If you don't come here for dinner, consider stopping by for the *dopo cena* (after-dinner drink) to top off your day in Padua.

Shopping on the Piazza delle Erbe.

Via dei Fabbri 13 (on a side street south of Piazza delle Erbe). www.osteriadeifabbri.it. ✆ **049-650-336.** Reservations recommended. *Primi* 8.50€–11€; *secondi* 12€–17€. AE, DC, MC, V. Mon–Sat 12:30–3pm and 7:30–10:30pm. Closed Dec 25–Jan 4.

Shopping

Padua is an elegant town where you'll find a wide roster of upscale consumer goods and luxury items, and less emphasis on souvenirs and handicrafts. For insights into the good life *alla Padovese,* trek through the neighborhood around the landmark **Piazza Insurrezione,** especially the **Galleria Borghese,** a conglomeration of shops off Via San Fermo.

Droves of shoppers head to the **Prato delle Valle** on the third Sunday of every month, when more than 200 antiques and collectibles vendors set up shop for the day. The square, one of the largest in all Europe, also hosts a smaller **weekly market** on Saturday. Shoes from nearby Brenta factories are the prevalent product, but the range of goods offered remains eclectic.

The outdoor markets (Mon–Sat) in the twin **Piazza delle Erbe** (for fresh produce) and **Piazza della Frutta** (dry goods), flanking the enormous Palazzo della Ragione, are some of Italy's best.

Specialty shops include **Roberto Callegari,** Via Davila 8 (www.robertocallegari.com; ✆ **049-8763131**), Padua's leading jewelry store, and **L'Antiquario Gemmologo,** Via Davila 6 (www.lantiquariogemmologo.eu; ✆ **049-664195**), run by Callegari's brother. He sells antique silver and also has an outstanding collection of jewelry next door. If you found the designer shops of Venice too pricey, you'll encounter the same merchandise by walking along **Via San Fermo,** where you'll find Prada, Armani, Gucci, Hermès, Max Mara, and the like.

Entertainment & Nightlife

The classical music season usually runs from October to April at different venues around town. The historic **Teatro Verdi,** at Via dei Livello 32 (www.teatrostabileveneto.it; ✆ **049-877-7011** or 049-8777-0213), is the most impressive location. Programs are available at the tourist office. Look for posters advertising performances by the world-class Solisti Veneti, who are Padovans but spend most of the year traveling abroad.

As a university city, Padua has a large, very visible student population. You can network with the student crowd at any of the popular cafes along Via Cavour, or in the *osterie,* wine bars, and beer dives in the porticoed medieval side streets encircling the Palazzo della Ragione (the area around the Bo) and its bookends Piazza delle Erbe and Piazza della Frutta. In the summer, the toned-down nightlife is to be found mostly around Prato della Valle.

Spend an evening in Padua at one of the city's wine bars or *enoteches.* **La Corte dei Leoni,** Via Pietro d'Abano 1 (✆ **049-8750083**), is more of a restaurant, but it offers live music on weekends.

For dancing in Padua, try **Disco Extra Extra,** Via Ciamician Giacomo 5 (✆ **049-620044**).

Where to Stay

Hotel al Fagiano ★ Although small, this family-run hotel is a great value for your money. Located just a few steps off the expansive Piazza del Santo (its most appealing asset), it doesn't exactly ooze coziness and charm, but given the less-than-encouraging hotel situation in town, the Fagiano's clean, bright, eclectic-styled rooms are still a standout choice. Bathrooms have been updated and include such niceties as hair dryers and bright lighting. Also, you rarely find air-conditioning and TVs at these rates. Don't confuse this Fagiano with the Hotel Buenos Aires, formerly known as the Fagiano and just a block away.

Via Locatelli 45 (west of Piazza del Santo), 35123 Padova. www.alfagiano.com. ✆ **049 875-0073.** Fax 049-875-3396. 40 units. 90€ double. AE, DC, MC, V. Private parking 10€. From train station, bus: 8, 12, 18, or 22. Pets stay free. **Amenities:** 24-hr. bar service; bikes; concierge; Wi-Fi (free). *In room:* A/C, TV.

Hotel Donatello This is a modern hotel in an old building, flush with amenities and enjoying a great location right at the Basilica di Sant'Antonio. More than half the rooms overlook the basilica, though those on the inner courtyard are quieter. Some rooms feature plush modular furnishings, some retro-Empire style. The older bathrooms have tubs with hand-held shower nozzles, but most are modernized. Apartments sleeping three to four come with two bedrooms and a common bathroom.

Via del Santo 102–104, 35123 Padova. www.hoteldonatello.net. ✆ **049-875-0634.** Fax 049-875-0829. 44 units. 198€ double; 231€ triple; 312€ apt for 4. Breakfast 13€. AE, DC, MC, V. Free parking in garage by reservation. Small pets accepted. **Amenities:** International restaurant; bar; concierge; room service. *In room:* A/C, satellite TV w/pay movies, minibar.

Hotel Majestic Toscanelli ★★ A four-star hotel this nice would cost a great deal more in nearby Venice, which is why the Toscanelli often finds itself with guests who make this their home base while they visit neighboring cities and the surrounding area. The hotel has old-world charm, with rooms tastefully done in classic decor with coordinated pastel themes, burnished cherrywood furniture, and large, bright bathrooms with white ceramic and marble tiles. Off the lobby, a bright and attractive breakfast room serves a good buffet breakfast. This quiet, historic neighborhood, with porticoed alleyways lined with antiques shops and wine bars, is entirely closed to traffic. From here it's an easy walk to Piazza delle Erbe.

Via dell'Arco 2 (2 blocks west of Via Roma and south of the Piazza delle Erbe), 35122 Padova. www.toscanelli.com. ✆ **049-663-244.** Fax 049-876-0025. 34 units. 139€–192€ double; 169€–227€ junior suite; 189€–290€ suite. Rates include buffet breakfast. Rates discounted mid-July to Aug. AE, DC, MC, V. Valet garage parking 19€. Pets 10€. **Amenities:** Bar; babysitting; concierge; room service; on-site spa. *In room:* A/C, satellite TV, hair dryer, kitchenette (in 2 units), minibar, Wi-Fi (free).

PALLADIO'S VICENZA ★★

203km (126 miles) E of Milan, 68km (42 miles) W of Venice, 52km (32 miles) NE of Verona

In the 16th century, Vicenza was transformed into a virtual laboratory for the architectural experiments of Andrea di Pietro, known as **Palladio** (1508–80). One of the greatest architects of the High Renaissance, he was inspired by the classical art and architecture of ancient Greece and Rome. Palladio peppered the city with *palazzi* and basilicas, and the surrounding hills with villas for patrician families.

The architect was particularly important to England and America. In the 18th century, Robert Adam was inspired by him, as is reflected by many country homes in England. Then, through the influence of Adam and others even earlier, the spirit of Palladio was brought to America (examples are Jefferson's Monticello and plantation homes in the antebellum South). Palladio even lent his name to this architectural style, Palladianism, which is identified by regularity of form, imposing size, and an adherence to lines established in the ancient world. Visitors arrive in Vicenza today principally to see the works left by Palladio; for this reason, the city was designated a UNESCO World Heritage Site in 1994.

Federico Faggin, inventor of the silicon chip, was born here, and many local computer-component industries now prosper on Vicenza's outskirts; its citizens earn one of the highest average incomes in the country.

Essentials

GETTING THERE From Padua (our last stopover), trains are frequent (trip time: 25 min.), a one-way fare costing 3€ to 17€, depending on the train. There are also frequent connections from Milan (trip time: 2½ hr.), at 11€ to 32€ one-way. For information and schedules, call ✆ **892021** in Italy. Vicenza's rail station is at Piazza Stazione (Campo Marzio), at the southern edge of Viale Roma.

By **car,** take A4 west from Venice toward Verona, bypassing Padua.

VISITOR INFORMATION The **tourist office,** at Piazza Matteotti 12 (www.vicenzae.org; ✆ **0444-320854**), is open daily 9am to 1pm and 2 to 6pm.

Exploring the World of Palladio

Basilica Palladiana ★★ CHURCH The magnificent bigger-than-life **Basilica Palladiana ★★** is not a church at all and was only partially designed by Palladio. Beneath it stood the Gothic-style Palazzo della Ragione (Law Courts and Assembly Hall) that Palladio was commissioned to convert to a High Renaissance style befitting a flourishing late-16th-century city under Venice's benevolent patronage. It was Palladio's first public work and secured his favor and reputation with the local authorities. He created two superimposed galleries, the lower with Doric pillars, and the upper with Ionic. The roof was destroyed by World War II bombing but has since been rebuilt in its original style. ***Note:*** *As of this writing, the Basilica Palladiana is in the final stages of a massive 15-million-euro overhaul to its roof and other structures, which is slated to be finished by 2012—art exhibits and other cultural events will celebrate the grand reopening throughout the fall and into the winter of 2013.*

Beside the basilica is the 13th-century **Torre Bissara ★**, soaring almost 82m (270 ft.). Across from the basilica is the **Loggia del Capitanio (Captain of the Guard) ★**, designed by Palladio in his waning years.

The Basilica Palladiana.

Piazza dei Signori. ✆ **0444-323681.** Free admission. Closed at press time, but it was previously open from Easter to Sept Tues–Sat from 9:30am–noon and 2–7pm; Sun 9:30–12:30pm and 2–7pm. Off season, it was closed Sun afternoon.

Civic Museum (Museo Civico) ★★ MUSEUM Looking more like one of the country villas for which Palladio was equally famous, this major work is considered one of his finest and is visited as much for its two-tiered, statue-topped facade as for the collection of Venetian paintings it houses on the first floor. Venetian masters you'll recognize include Tiepolo, Tintoretto, and Veronese, while the lesser known include works from the Vicenzan (founded by Bartolomeo Montagna) and Bassano schools of painting.

Piazza Matteotti (at Corso Palladio). www.museicivicivicenza.it. ✆ **0444-222-800.** Admission 8€ with cumulative ticket; it is not possible to buy a ticket just for the Teatro Olimpico or Palazzo Chiericati. Apr–Sept Tues–Sun 9am–7pm; Oct–Mar Tues–Sun 9am–5pm.

The stage of the Olympic Theater.

STROLL THROUGH palladio's WORKS

A walk along the Corso Palladio is one of the most memorable in Italy. This is Vicenza's main street, and what a grand one it is, lined with the magnificent *palazzi* of Palladio and his students (and *their* students, who, centuries later, were still influenced by Palladio's work), today converted into cafes, swank shops, and imposing banks. The first one of note, starting from its southwest cap near the Piazza Castello, is the **Palazzo Valmarana,** at no. 16, begun by Palladio in 1566. On the right (behind which stands the Piazza dei Signori and the Basilica Palladiana) is the **Palazzo del Comunale,** the Town Hall built in 1592 by Scamozzi (1552–1616), a native of Vicenza and Palladio's protégé and star pupil. This is said to be Scamozzi's greatest work.

Heading northeast from the Corso Palladio, take a left onto the Contrà Porti, the second most important street for its Palladian and Gothic *palazzi.* The two designed by Palladio are the **Palazzo Barbarano Porto,** at no. 11, and (opposite) **Palazzo Thiene,** at no.12 (now the headquarters of a bank); **Gothic *palazzi*** of particular note can be found at nos. 6 to 10, 14, 16, 17, and 19. Parallel, on Corso Fogazzaro, look for no. 16, **Palazzo Valmarana,** perhaps the most eccentric of Palladio's works.

Returning to Corso Palladio, look for no. 145/147, the pre-Palladian **Ca d'Oro (Golden Palace),** named for the gold leaf used in the frescoes that once covered its facade. The simple **16th-century *palazzo*** at no. 163 was Palladio's home.

Before reaching the Piazza Matteotti and the end of the Corso Palladio, you'll see signs for the **Church of Santa Corona ★**, set back on the left on the Via Santa Corona 2 (daily 8:30am–noon and 2:30–6pm). An unremarkable 13th-century Gothic church, it shelters two masterpieces (and Vicenza's most important church paintings) that make this worth a visit: Giovanni Bellini's *Baptism of Christ* (fifth altar on left) and Veronese's *Adoration of the Magi* (third chapel on right). This is Vicenza's most interesting church, far more so than the cavernous Duomo southwest of the Piazza dei Signori, but worth seeking out only if you've got the extra time.

Olympic Theater (Teatro Olimpico) ★★ ARCHITECTURE Palladio's masterpiece and last work—ideal for performances of classical plays—is one of the world's greatest theaters still in use. It was completed in 1585, 5 years after Palladio's death, by Vincenzo Scamozzi, and the curtain went up on the Vicenza premiere of Sophocles's *Oedipus Rex.* The arena seating area, in the shape of a half-moon, is encircled by Corinthian columns and balustrades. The simple proscenium abuts the arena. What's ordinarily the curtain in a conventional theater is here a permanent facade, U shaped, with a large central arch and a pair of smaller ones flanking it. The permanent stage set represents the ancient streets of Thebes, combining architectural detail with *trompe l'oeil.* Above the arches (to the left and right) are rows of additional classic statuary on pedestals and in niches. Over the area is a dome, with *trompe l'oeil* clouds and sky, giving the illusion of an outdoor Roman amphitheater.

Piazza Matteotti 11. www.teatrolimpicovicenza.it. ✆ **0444-222-800.** Admission 8€ with cumulative ticket; it is not possible to buy a ticket just for the Teatro Olimpico or Palazzo Chiericati. Apr–Sept Tues–Sun 9am–7pm; Oct–Mar Tues–Sun 9am–5pm.

Where to Eat

Antica Casa della Malvasia ★ VENETO This ever-lively, taverna-like *osteria* sits on a quiet, characteristic side street that links the principal Corso Palladio with the Piazza dei Signori. Service comes with a smile and is informal, the cooking is homemade and regional. The food is reliably good, but it's just an excuse to accompany the selection of wines (80), whiskeys (100), grappas (150), and teas (over 150). No wonder this place always buzzes. Even if you don't eat here, at least stop in for a late-night toddy, Vicentino style—it's a favorite spot for locals and visitors alike, and there's often live music on Tuesday and Thursday evenings.

Contrà delle Morette 5 (off Corso Palladio). ✆ **0444-543-704.** Reservations suggested during high season. *Primi* 5€–8€; *secondi* 7€–13€. Weekday lunch special: *primi* 4€; *secondi* 6€. AE, MC, V. Tues–Sun noon–3pm and 7pm–midnight (sometimes later).

Antica Trattoria Tre Visi ★★ VICENTINO Operating from the early 1600s until 1997 around the corner from the current address, this Vicentino institution is now located on an important *palazzo*-studded street in a setting somewhat less dramatic than the previous 15th-century *palazzo*. The menu has stayed unchanged, however, and this is good: Ignore items that concede to foreign requests and concentrate on the regional dishes they know how to prepare best. Almost all the pasta is made fresh daily, including the house specialty, *bigoli con anitra*, fat, spaghetti-like pasta served with duck ragout. The region's signature dish is *baccalà alla Vicentina*, a tender salt codfish simmered in a stew of onions, herbs, anchovies, garlic, and parmigiano for 8 hours before arriving at your table in perfection. Ask your waiter for help in selecting from Veneto's wide spectrum of very fine wines: It will enhance your bill but also the memories you'll bring home.

Corso Palladio 25 (near Piazza Castello). ✆ **0444-324-868.** Reservations suggested. *Primi* 10€–15€; *secondi* 16€–21€. AE, DC, MC, V. Tues–Sun 12:30–2:30pm; Tues–Sat 7:30–10pm. Closed July.

Entertainment & Nightlife

In Vicenza you can enjoy music presented in settings of architectural splendor. The outdoor **Teatro Olimpico,** Piazza Matteotti 3 (www.olimpico.vicenza.it; ✆ **0444-222800**), hosts cultural events from April to late September. For information about the actual programs being presented, call the theater. Look for a changing program of classic Greek tragedy (*Oedipus Rex* is an enduring favorite), Shakespearean plays (sometimes translated into Italian), chamber music concerts, and dance recitals. You can pick up schedules and buy tickets at the gate daily from 11am to 7pm. Tickets are 15€ to 40€ and can be bought at the gate Tuesday to Sunday 9am to 4:30pm.

More esoteric, and with a shorter season, is a series of concerts scheduled in June, the **Concerti in Villa.** Every year, it includes chamber music performed in or near villas (often privately owned) in the city's outskirts. Look for orchestras set up on loggias or under formal pediments, and audiences sitting on chairs in gardens or inside. Note that these depend on the whims of both local musicians and villa owners. Contact the tourist office (see "Essentials," above) for details.

Where to Stay

Due Mori ★ Due Mori's history as the oldest family-run hotel in Vicenza and its convenient location on a quiet side street just west of the sprawling Piazza dei

Signori make this the (deservedly) most popular spot in town for the budget-minded. Which is to say: Book early. In a modernized shell of a centuries-old *palazzo,* tasteful and authentic 19th-century pieces distinguish otherwise plain rooms whose amenities are kept at a minimum—but, then, so are the prices. This is as good as it gets in the very center of Palladio's hometown.

Via Do Rode 24 (1 block west of Piazza dei Signori), 36100 Vicenza. www.hotelduemori.com. ✆ **0444-321-886.** Fax 0444-326-127. 30 units, 27 with private bathroom. 60€ double with shared bathroom; 85€ double with private bathroom. Breakfast 7€. AE, MC, V. Free parking. Pets accepted. **Amenities:** Bar; Wi-Fi (3€/hr.). *In room:* Hair dryer (on request).

G. Boutique Tiozzo Revamped and renamed in 2011, this hotel still maintains the welcoming charm emblematic of Italian hospitality yet boasts a sleek, modern ambience that is tempting to international tourists and business travelers. What the rooms lack in spaciousness is compensated for by their clean, quiet, and stylish nature. The staff is attentive and friendly, adding a sense of warmth to elegant decor that can be experienced throughout the lobby, the communal areas, and all the guest rooms. In a location that can't be beat—situated in the center of the city—visitors can take advantage of the city's nightlife and retail.

Viale Giuriolo (next to Piazza Matteotti and the Teatro Olimpico), 36100 Vicenza. www.gboutiquehotel.com. ✆/fax **0444-326-458.** 18 units. 120€–180€ double; 130€–180€ suite. Breakfast included. AE, DC, MC, V. Parking 20€. Bus from station: 1, 2, 5, or 7. **Amenities:** Bar. *In room:* A/C, satellite TV, hair dryer, minibar.

VERONA ★★★

114km (71 miles) W of Venice, 502km (311 miles) NW of Rome, 81km (50 miles) W of Padua

Suspend all disbelief regarding the real-life existence of Romeo and Juliet, and your stay in Verona can be magical. After Venice, this is the Veneto's most-visited city. Verona reached a cultural and artistic zenith during the 13th and 14th centuries under the puissant, often cruel, and sometimes quirky della Scala, or Scaligeri, dynasty that took up rule in the late 1200s. In 1405 it surrendered to Venice, which remained in charge until the invasion of Napoleon in 1797.

During the time of Venetian rule, Verona became a prestigious urban capital and controlled much of the Veneto and as far south as Tuscany. You'll see the emblem of the *scala* (ladder) around town, heraldic symbol of the Scaligeri dynasty. The city has a locked-in-time character that recalls its medieval and Renaissance heyday, and the magnificent medieval *palazzi,* towers, churches, and stagelike piazzas you see today are picture-perfect testimony to its centuries-old influence and wealth.

For some reason, visitors spend remarkably little time in this beautiful medieval city. While it has a short list of attractions, it is a handsome town to stay in and visit at a leisurely pace. Statistics indicate that most tourists stop here for a night (or less)—I'd say try for at least 2 nights.

Essentials

GETTING THERE A total of 36 daily trains make the 2-hour run between Venice and Verona, costing 6.15€ to 28€ one-way, depending on the train. From Milan, there are even more connections, taking 2 hours to Verona, a one-way ticket costing 8€ to 24€. The trip from Rome on a high-speed train costs 64€ in second class, 87€ in first class. Rail arrivals are at Verona's

ATTRACTIONS

Arche Scaligere **12**

Arena di Verona **20**

Basilica de Sant'Anastasia **6**

Basilica San Zeno Maggiore **1**

Castelvecchio **2**

Duomo **3**

Giardino Giusti **5**

Juliet's House **15**

Juliet's Tomb **21**

Loggia del Consiglio **12**

Palazzo del Governo **12**

Roman Theater & Archaeological Museum **4**

Romeo's House **9**

San Fermo **23**

HOTELS

Colomba d'Oro **18**

Due Torri Hotel Baglioni **7**

Hotel Aurora **13**

Hotel Gabbia d'Oro **8**

Hotel Giulietta e Romeo **17**

Hotel Torcolo **19**

RESTAURANTS

Bottega dei Vino **22**

Osteria del Duca **11**

Ristorante 12 Apostoli **14**

Ristorante Il Desco **16**

Verona Antica **10**

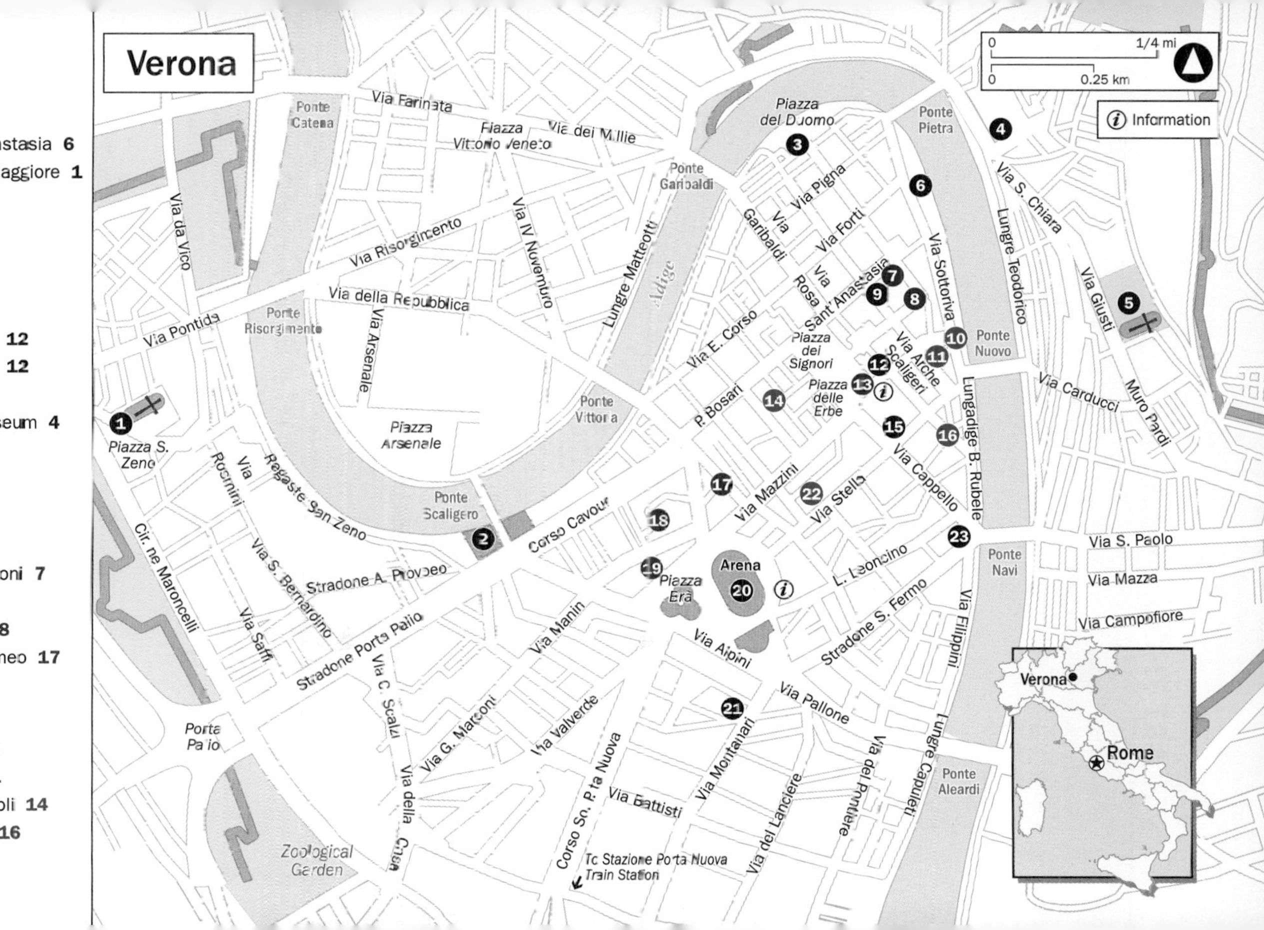

ART THOU, TRULY, romeo?

Though the city has plenty else to recommend it as a sightseeing capital of the Veneto, the local tourism economy is underpinned by hordes of bus groups, Shakespearian pilgrims, and hopeless romantics. They come to wander the streets where Capulets and Montagues once fought, Romeo pined, and Juliet sighed from her (completely false) balcony.

Wealthy Veronese families called Capuleti and Montecchi did exist. Did they feud? Probably. That often was the way with local clans vying for city power in the Middle Ages. But did their two houses, so alike in dignity, ever harbor secret, star-crossed lovers? Did Romeo and Juliet really exist?

The story is based in an ancient legend; the core tragic elements go back at least to the Greeks. To trace the Shakespeare version: The basic story was put into novella form (based on a medieval Sienese version) in 1476 and then subsequently retold in 1524 by Veneto-born Luigi da Porto. He chose to set it in Verona in the years 1302 to 1304 during the reign of the Scaligeri, and renamed the young couple Romeo and Giulietta. The popular *storia d'amore* was translated into English, at which point Shakespeare obviously got hold of it and worked his own magic.

With the genius of Shakespeare's pen, the story turned into theatrical gold. Translated into dozens of languages and performed around the world (check out the number of Asian and eastern European tourists who flock to Juliet's House), this universal and timeless tale of pure love has forever since been set in the tempestuous days of this medieval city—notwithstanding that version with Leo DiCaprio.

That said, Zeffirelli chose to film his classic 1968 interpretation in the tiny Tuscan town of Pienza, south of Siena. And, of course, the story emigrated to the New World and took up in the mean streets of New York as *West Side Story.*

Stazione Porta Nuova, Piazza XXV Aprile, south of the centrally located Arena and Piazza Brà; call © **892021** in Italy for information. At least six **bus** lines service the area, arriving at Piazza XXV (© **045-8057811**).

By **car,** take A4 west from Venice to the cutoff marked Verona Sud. From points north or south, take A22 and get off at the exit marked Verona Nord.

VISITOR INFORMATION The **main tourist office** is at Piazza Brà (www.tourism.verona.it; © **045-8068680**). Hours are Monday to Saturday 8:30am to 7pm and Sunday 9am to 1pm and 2 to 5pm.

SPECIAL EVENTS Opera festivals on a scale more human and accessible than those in cities such as Milan are presented in Verona annually between July and August. The setting is the ancient **Arena di Verona ★**, a site that's grand enough to accommodate as many elephants as might be needed for a performance of *Aïda.* Schedules change every year, so for more information and tickets, call © **045-8005151,** or go to www.arena.it. Prices of tickets vary with view lines and whatever is being staged, but usually they are 23€ to 198€.

Teatro Romano is known for its Shakespeare Festival in July. In recent years, it has included a week of English-language performances by the Royal Shakespeare Company. Festival performances begin in late May and June with jazz concerts. In July and August, there are also a number of ballets (such as Prokofiev's *Romeo and Juliet*) and modern dance performances. Check for a current schedule at ✆ **045-8077631** or with the tourist office. During Verona's summer-long festival of the arts, see what's happening in the Piazza dei Signori, where frequent **free concerts** (jazz, tango, classical) keep everyone out until the wee hours. And for something truly unique, check out **Sognando Shakespeare (Dreaming Shakespeare):** Follow this traveling theater of young, talented actors in costume as they wander the medieval corners of Verona, reciting *Romeo e Giulietta* (in Italian only) *in situ,* as Shakespeare would have loved it to be. For information, contact the tourist office. For information about performances July through September, call ✆ **045-800-0065.** Another important event is the 5-day **VinItaly wine fair** (that overlaps with the Olive Oil Fair) in mid-April.

Exploring the City

The city lies alongside the banks of an S-shaped curve in the Adige River. As far as the average visitor is concerned, everything of interest—with the exception of the Teatro Romano—is found in the *centro storico* on the south side of the river's loop; there's no site that cannot be easily and enjoyably reached by foot.

Opening onto **Piazza dei Signori ★★**, the handsomest in Verona, is the **Palazzo del Governo,** where Cangrande extended the shelter of his hearth and home to the fleeing Florentine Dante Alighieri. A marble statue of the "divine poet" stands in the center of the square, with an expression as cold as a Dolomite icicle, but unintimidated pigeons perch on his pious head. Facing Dante's back is the late-15th-century **Loggia del Consiglio,** frescoed and surmounted by five statues. Five arches lead into Piazza dei Signori.

The **Arche Scaligere** are outdoor tombs surrounded by wrought-iron gates that form a kind of open-air pantheon of the Scaligeri princes. One tomb, that of Cangrande della Scala, rests directly over the door of the 12th-century **Santa**

Piazza dei Signori.

Maria Antica. The mausoleum contains many Romanesque features and is crowned by a copy of an equestrian statue (the original is now at the Castelvecchio). The tomb nearest the door is that of Mastino II; the one behind it, and the most lavish of all, is that of Cansignorio.

Piazza delle Erbe (Square of the Herbs) ★★ is a lively square, flanked by palaces, that was formerly the Roman city's forum. Today, it's the fruit-and-vegetable market, milling with Veronese shoppers and vendors. In the center is a fountain dating from the 14th century and a Roman statue dubbed *The Virgin of Verona.* The pillar at one end of the square, crowned by a chimera, symbolizes the many years Verona was dominated by Venice. Important buildings include the early-14th-century **House of Merchants (Casa dei Mercanti);** the **Torre Gardello,** built by one of the Della Scala princes; the restored former **city hall** and the **Torre Lamberti,** soaring about 79m (260 ft.); the baroque **Palazzo Maffei;** and the **Casa Mazzanti.**

From the vegetable market, you can walk down **Via Mazzini,** the most fashionable street in Verona, to **Piazza Brà,** with its neoclassical town hall and Renaissance *palazzo,* the **Gran Guardia.**

Arena di Verona ★★ ICON The best-preserved Roman amphitheater in the world and the best known in Italy after Rome's Colosseum, the elliptical Arena was built in a slightly pinkish marble in the 1st century A.D. and stands in the very middle of town, with the Piazza Brà on its southern flank. Built to accommodate more than 20,000 people (outdone by Rome's contender that could seat more than twice that), it is in remarkable shape today (despite a 12th-c. earthquake that left only four arches of the outer ring standing), beloved testimony to the pride and wealth of Verona and its populace.

Piazza Brà. ✆ **045-800-3204.** Admission 6€, 4€ for students, and 1€ for children 8–14. Mon 1:30–7:30pm; Tues–Sun 8:30am–7:30pm (July–Aug summer opera season 9am–3:30pm or sometimes a little later). Last admission 45 min. before close.

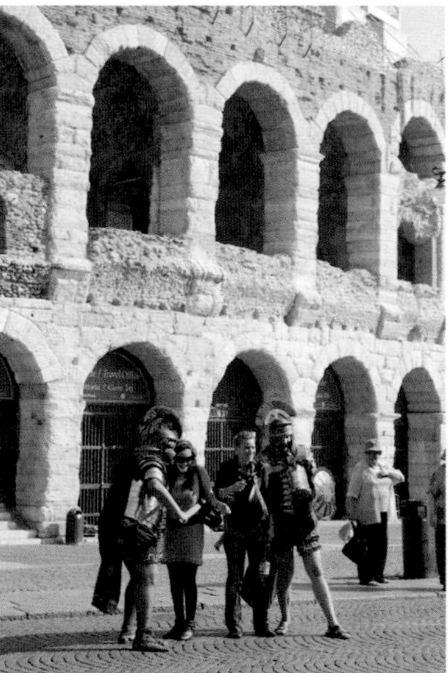

The Arena di Verona.

Basilica San Zeno Maggiore ★★ CHURCH This is one of the finest examples of Romanesque architecture in northern Italy, built between the 9th and 12th centuries. Slightly out of the old city's hub but still easily reached by foot, San Zeno (as it's often referred to), dedicated to the city's patron saint, is Verona's most visited church. Spend a moment outside to appreciate the fine, sober facade, highlighted by the immense 12th-century rose window, the **Ruota della Fortuna (Wheel of Fortune).**

This pales in importance compared to the **facade ★★** below—two pillars supported by marble lions and massive doors whose 48 bronze panels were sculpted from the 9th to the 11th centuries and are believed to have been some of the first castings in bronze since Roman antiquity. They are among the city's most cherished artistic treasures and are worth the trip here even if the church is closed. Not as sophisticated as those that would adorn the Baptistery doors of Florence's Duomo in the centuries to come, these are like a naive illustration from a children's book and were meant to educate the illiterate masses with scenes from the Old and New Testaments and the life of San Zeno. They are complemented by the stone bas-reliefs found on either side of the doors, the 12th-century work of Niccolo, who was also responsible for the Duomo's portal. The 14th-century **tower** on the left belonged to the former abbey, while the free-standing slender **campanile** on the right was begun in 1045.

The massive **interior ★** is filled with 12th- to 14th century frescoes and crowned by the nave's ceiling, designed as a wooden ship's keel. But the interior's singular highlight is the famous triptych of the ***Madonna and Child Enthroned with Saints,*** by Andrea Mantegna (1459), behind the main altar. Napoleon absconded with the beautiful centerpiece—a showcase for the Padua-born Mantegna's sophisticated sense of perspective and architectural detail—which was eventually returned to Verona, although two side panels stayed behind in the Louvre and in Tours. Look in the small apse to the left of the altar for the colored marble statue of a smiling San Zeno, much loved by the local Veronesi, in an act of blessing.

Piazza San Zeno. www.chieseverona.it. ✆ **045-592-813.** Admission 2.50€. Mar–Oct Mon–Sat 8am–6pm, Sun 1–6pm; Nov–Feb Tues–Sat 10am–1pm and 1:30–4pm, Sun 1–5pm.

Duomo ★ CATHEDRAL Begun in the 12th century and not finished until the 17th century, the city's main church still boasts its original main doors and portal, magnificently covered with low reliefs in the Lombard Romanesque style that are attributed to Niccolo, whose work can be seen at the Basilica of San Zeno Maggiore. The church was built upon the ruins of an even more ancient paleo-Christian church dating from the late Roman Empire. Visit the **Cappella Nichesola,** the first chapel on the left, where Titian's serene but boldly colorful *Assumption of the Virgin* is the cathedral's principal treasure, with an architectural frame by Sansovino (who also designed the choir). The excavations of Sant'Elena church, also in the Duomo complex, reveal a bit of 6th-century mosaic floor; the Baptistery contains a Romanesque font carved with scenes from the Nativity cycle.

Piazza Duomo (at Via del Duomo). www.chieseverona.it. ✆ **045-592-813.** Single admission 2.50€. Mar–Oct Mon–Sat 10am–5:30pm, Sun 1:30–5:30pm; Nov–Feb Tues–Sat 10am–1pm and 1:30–4pm, Sun 1–5pm.

Giardino Giusti ★ PARK/GARDEN One of Italy's oldest and most famous gardens, the Giardino Giusti was created at the end of the 14th century. These well-manicured Italian gardens, studded with cypress trees, form one of the most relaxing and coolest spots in Verona for strolls. You can climb up to the "monster balcony" for an incomparable view of the city.

The layout of the gardens was designed by Agostino Giusti. All its 16th-century characteristics—the grottoes, statues, fountains, box-enclosed flower garden, and maze—have remained intact. In addition to the flower displays, you can admire statues by Lorenzo Muttoni and Alessandro Vittoria, Roman remains, and the great cypress mentioned by Goethe. The gardens, with their adjacent 16th-century *palazzo,* form one of Italy's most interesting urban complexes. The maze of myrtle hedges reproduces the 1786 plan of the architect Trezza. Its complicated pattern and small size make it one of the most unusual in Europe. The gardens lie near the Roman Theater, a few minutes' walk from the heart of the city.

Via Giardino Giusti 2. ✆ **045-8034029.** Admission 5€. Apr–Sept daily 9am–7pm (to sunset off season).

Juliet's House (Casa di Giulietta) ★ MONUMENT/MEMORIAL There is no proof that a Capuleti (Capulet) family ever lived here (or, if they did, that a young girl named Juliet ever existed), and it wasn't until 1905 that the city bought what was an abandoned, overgrown garden and decided its future. Rumor is that this was once actually a whorehouse.

So powerful is the legend of Juliet that over half a million tourists flock here every year to visit the simple courtyard and home that are considerably less affluent-looking than the sumptuous Franco Zeffirelli version as you may remember it (the movie was filmed in Tuscany). Many are those who leave behind layer upon layer of graffiti along the lines of *"Valentina, ti amo!"* or who engage in the peculiar tradition (whose origin no one can seem to explain) of rubbing the right breast (now buffed to a bright gold) of the 20th-century bronze statue of a forever nubile Juliet.

The curious might want to fork over the entrance fee to see the spartan interior of the 13th-century home, restored in 1996. Ceramics and furniture on display are authentic to the era but did not belong to Juliet's family—if there ever was a Juliet at all. No one is willing to confirm (or deny) that the balcony was added to the *palazzo* as recently as 1928 (though that doesn't stop many a young lass from posing on it, staring dreamily at the sky).

La Tomba di Giulietta (**Juliet's Tomb; ✆ 045-800-0361**) is about a 15-minute walk south of here (near the Adige River on Via delle Pontiere 5; admission 4.50€ adults, 3€ students and those over 65, 1€ children 8–14, and free first Sun of each month; hours are Mon 1:30–7:30pm and Tues–Sun 9am–7pm; last admission is 45 min. before closing). The would-be site of the star-crossed lovers' suicide is found within the graceful medieval cloisters of the Capuchin monastery of San Francesco al Corso. Die-hard romantics may find this tomb, with its surely posed "sarcophagus," rather more evocative than the crowded scene at Juliet's House and worth the trip. Others will find it overrated and shouldn't bother. The adjacent church is where their secret marriage was said to have taken place. A small museum of frescoes is also adjacent.

Via Cappello 23 (southeast of Piazza delle Erbe). ✆ **045-803-4303.** Admission (to building only; courtyard is free) 6€ adults, 4.50€ children. Mon 1:30–7:30pm; Tues–Sun 8:30am–7:30pm. Last admission 45 min. before closing.

The balcony at Juliet's House (Casa di Giulietta).

Museo Castelvecchio ★★ MUSEUM Built on the order of Cangrande II in the 14th century, the Old Castle stands beside the Adige River (head out Via Roma) near the Ponte Scaligero, a bridge bombed by the Nazis and subsequently reconstructed. This former seat of the Della Scala family has been turned into an art museum, with important paintings from the Veronese school and other masters of northern Italy. Fourteenth- and 15th-century sculptures are on the ground floor, and on the upper floor you'll see masterpieces of painting from the 15th to the 18th centuries.

In the **Sala Monga** is Jacopo Bellini's *St. Jerome,* in the desert with his lion and crucifix. Two sisterlike portraits of Saint Catherina and Veneranda by Vittore Carpaccio grace the **Sala Rizzardi Allegri.** The Bellini family is also represented by a lyrical *Madonna con Bambino,* painted by Giovanni, a master of that subject.

Between the buildings is the most provocative equestrian statue we've ever seen, that of Cangrande I, grinning like a buffoon, with a dragon sticking out of his back. In the **Sala Murari della Corte Brà** is one of the most beguiling portraits in the castle—Giovanni Francesco Caroto's smiling red-haired boy. In the **Sala di Canossa** are Tintoretto's *Madonna Nursing the Child* and *Nativity,* and Veronese's *Deposition from the Cross* and *Pala Bevilacqua Lazise.*

In the **Sala Bolognese Trevenzuoli** is a rare self-portrait of Bernardo Strozzi, and in the **Sala Avena,** among paintings by the most famous Venetian masters, such as Gianbattista and Giandomenico Tiepolo and Guardi, hangs an almost satirical portrait of an 18th-century patrician family by Longhi.

Corso Castelvecchio 2. ✆ **045-8062611.** Admission 6€. Tues–Sun 8:30am–7:30pm; Mon 1:30–7:30pm. Last admission at 6:30pm. Bus: 21, 22, 23, 24, 31, or 32.

Roman Theater (Teatro Romano) & Archaeological Museum (Museo Archeologico) ★ THEATER/MUSEUM The Teatro Romano, built in the 1st century A.D., now stands in ruins at the foot of St. Peter's Hill. For nearly 25 years, a Shakespearean festival has been staged here in July and August; of course, a unique theatergoing experience is to see *Romeo and Juliet* or *Two Gentlemen of Verona* in this setting. The theater is across the Adige River (take the Ponte di Pietra). After seeing the remains of the theater, you can take a rickety elevator to the 10th-century Santi Siro e Libera church towering over it. In the cloister of St. Jerome is the Archaeological Museum, with interesting mosaics and Etruscan bronzes.

Via Rigaste Redentore (over the Ponte Pietra bridge behind the Duomo). www.estateteatraleveronese.it. ✆ **045-800-0360.** Admission 4€; free 1st Sun of each month. Mon 1:30–6:45pm; Tues–Sun 8:30am–6:45pm (during theater season 9am–3pm). Bus: 31, 32, 33, or 73.

Where to Eat

EXPENSIVE

Ristorante Il Desco ★★ VERONESE Il Desco offers highly creative cuisine made with a variety of the best ingredients the Veneto has to offer, with warm fresh-baked rolls and odd *amuse-bouches* such as olive-oil gelato with a tomato coulis. They tend to serve all meat dishes—from venison with pearl onions to salmon on a bed of lentils—extremely rare, so order it *ben cotto* (well done) if you want it cooked beyond merely flame-kissed. Some examples of the kitchen's rich creations include *papardelle* with sea snails, pork ravioli soup with shrimp, and stuffed pigeon and salt cod. Desserts are stupendous.

Via Dietro San Sebastiano 7. www.ildesco.com. ✆ **045-595-358.** Reservations highly recommended. *Primi* 26€–32€; *secondi* 40€–45€. AE, DC, MC, V. Tues–Sat 12:40–2pm and 7:40–10:30pm (open Mon in July, Aug, and Dec). Closed 15 days in June and 15 days btw. Dec and Jan.

Moderate

Bottega del Vino ★★ VERONESE/WINE BAR Oenophiles can push an evening's meal here into the stratosphere if they succumb to the wine cellar's unmatched 80,000-bottle selection, the largest in Verona. This atmospheric *bottega* first opened in 1890, and the old-timers who spend hours in animated conversation seem to have been here since then. The ambience and conviviality are reason enough to come by for a tipple at the well-known bar, where five dozen good-to-excellent wines are for sale by the glass for 3.50€ to 12€. There's no mistaking Verona's prominence in the wine industry here. At mealtimes the regulars head home and the next shift arrives: Journalists and local merchants fill the few wooden tables ordering simple but excellent dishes where the Veneto's wines have infiltrated the kitchen, such as the *risotto al Amarone,* sauced with Verona's most dignified red.

Via Scudo di Francia 3 (off Via Mazzini), Verona. www.bottegavini.it. ✆ **045-800-4535.** Reservations necessary for dinner. *Primi* 11€–15€; *secondi* 16€–28€. AE, DC, MC, V. Wed–Mon noon–3pm and 7pm–midnight. Bar Wed–Mon 10:30am–3pm and 6pm–midnight.

Osteria dela Duca ★ VERONESE There are no written records to confirm that this 13th-century *palazzo* was once owned by the Montecchi (Montague) family, and, thankfully, the discreet management never considered calling it the Ristorante Romeo. But here you are, nonetheless, dining in what is believed to be Romeo's house, enjoying one of the nicest meals in town amid a spirited and friendly neighborhood ambience. You might find *penne con pomodoro e melanzane* (fresh tomato sauce with eggplant) or a perfectly grilled chop or filet with rosemary-roasted potatoes. It will be simple, it will be delicious, you'll probably make friends with those sitting next to you, and you will remember your meal. If you don't have an adventurous palate, avoid anything on the menu that has *cavallo* or *asino* in it, unless you want to sample horsemeat, a local specialty, or donkey.

Via Arche Scaligeri 2 (east of Piazza dei Signori). ✆ **045-594-474.** Reservations not accepted. *Primi* 5€–7€; *secondi* 9€–12€; *menù turistico* 15€. MC, V. Mon–Sat 12:30–2:30pm and 7–10:30pm.

Ristorante 12 Apostoli ★★ REGIONAL/ITALIAN Operated by the two Gioco brothers, this is Verona's oldest restaurant, in business for 250 years. It's a festive place, steeped in tradition, with frescoed walls and two dining rooms separated by brick arches. Giorgio, the artist of the kitchen, changes his menu daily, while Franco directs the dining room. To begin, we recommend the tempting *antipasti alla Scaligera.* Along with considering the tantalizing meat courses, you might also try one of the pasta dishes, especially the ravioli that comes stuffed with fresh pumpkin or else ricotta cheese and fresh truffles. For dessert, try the homemade cake.

Vicolo Corticella San Marco 3. www.12apostoli.it. ✆ **045-596999.** Reservations recommended. Main courses 12€–28€. AE, DC, MC, V. Tues–Sun 12:30–2:30pm; Tues–Sat 7–10pm. Closed 1st week in Jan and June 15–July 5.

INEXPENSIVE

Veronica Antica VERONESE This is a local restaurant on the ground floor of a town house a short block from the river, across from a cobblestone arcade similar to the ones used in Zeffirelli's *Romeo and Juliet.* This place attracts locals, not just tourists. It's made even more romantic at night by a hanging lantern that dimly illuminates the street. Their dishes are hearty and robust, and specialties include *tagliatelle* with wild boar sauce; *cappellacci* (a kind of ravioli) with porcini mushrooms; or a delectable array of cold meats served with polenta.

Via Sottoriva 10. www.osteriaveronaantica.it. ✆ **045-8004124.** Reservations recommended. Main courses 7.50€–16€; fixed-price menu 10€. MC, V. Daily noon–2:30pm and 7–11pm.

The market at Piazza dell Erbe.

Shopping

The byword for shopping in Verona is *elegance*, and shops feature the fashions being touted in Milan and Rome. Don't look for touristy products or rustic crafts and souvenirs; instead, look for more upscale versions of all-Italian fashion and accessories. A worthwhile shop for men is **Class Uomo,** Via San Rocchetto 13B (www.classuomo.it; ✆ **045-595775**), and, for both genders, there's the classic **Armani,** Via Cappello 25 (www.armanijeans.com; ✆ **045-594727**).

You'll find a concentration of vendors selling antiques or old bric a brac in the streets around **Sant'Anastasia,** or head to **Piazza delle Erbe** for a more-or-less constant roster of merchants in flea market–style kiosks selling dusty and often junkier, collectibles of yesteryear, along with herbs, fruits, and vegetables.

Verona Nightlife: Wine Bars

Oenophiles will be in their element in Verona, the epicenter of the region's important viticulture, but the old-time wine bars are decreasing in number and atmosphere. After the obligatory pilgrimage to **Bottega del Vino** (see "Where to Eat," above) recapture the spirit of yesteryear at **Carro Armato,** in a 14th-century *palazzo* at Vicolo Gatto 2A/Vicolo San Piero Martire (1 block south of Piazza Sant'Anastasia; ✆ **045-803-0175**), a great choice when you want to sit and sample some of 30 or so regional wines by the glass (2€–5€) and make an informal meal out of fresh, inexpensive bar food. Oldsters linger during the day playing cards or reading the paper at long wooden tables, while a younger crowd fills the place in the evening. A small but good selection of cheeses and cold cuts or sausages might be enough to take the edge off, but there is always an entree or two and a fresh vegetable side dish. It's open Monday to Friday from 10am to 2pm and 5pm to 2am, Saturday and Sunday 10am to 2am without a lunch break.

The wonderful old wine bar **Enoteca dal Zovo,** on Vicolo San Marco in Foro 7/5 (off Corso Porta Borsari near Caffè Tubino; ✆ **045-803-4369**), is run by Oreste, who knows everyone in town, and they all stop by for his excellent selection of Veneto wines averaging 2€ a glass, or you can go for broke and start with the very best at 4€. Oreste's *simpatica* American-born wife, Beverly, can give you a crash course. Salami, olives, and finger foods will help keep you vertical, since the few stools are always occupied by senior gentlemen who are as much a part of the fixtures as the hundreds of dusty bottles of wines and grappa that line the walls. It's open Tuesday to Sunday from 9am to 8pm.

Where to Stay

Hotel rooms tend to be scarce during the County Fair in March and during the opera and theater season in July and August.

EXPENSIVE

Due Torri Hotel ★★★ Verona's choicest hotel occupies a 14th-century *palazzo* that was reopened in the 1950s. It's where rock stars and opera singers stay when they play in town, picking up where Mozart, Goethe, and Garibaldi left off—perhaps because they're among the few who can afford it. The airy lobby looks like a stage set, with original 1370s columns and carvings and contemporary frescoes of medieval scenes, the ceilings set with oil paintings. The room furnishings range from Louis XIV to Biedermeier, and even standard rooms are luxurious, with patterned wall coverings, Murano chandeliers, and large, marble-sheathed bathrooms with double sinks. Windows are double-paned, so even on the piazza things are quiet. The hotel is in the narrow end of Verona formed by the tight river bend, so many rooms on the upper floors and rooftop terrace have great views to the hills beyond.

Piazza Sant'Anastasia 4, 37121 Verona. www.duetorrihotels.com. ✆ **045-595-044.** Fax 045-800-4130. 90 units. 280€–595€ double; 535€–900€ junior suite. Discounts with online booking. Rates include breakfast. AE, DC, MC, V. Valet parking 30€. Small pets accepted. **Amenities:** Veronese/international restaurant; bar; babysitting; concierge; Wi-Fi (5€/hr.). *In room:* A/C, TV, hair dryer, Internet, minibar.

Hotel Gabbia d'Oro ★★ One wall dates to 1320 at this cozy hotel of stone-trimmed doorways, rustic beams, and smart liveried service around the corner from the main piazza, but most of the *palazzo* is 18th century. The atmosphere hovers between medieval and eclectic, vaguely 19th-century Victorian romantic. It's all a bit put on—falsified fresco fragments, half-testers, and collectibles in little glass cases on wall brackets—but the result is more or less effective. Most rooms are terribly snug, but artfully placed mirrors help open up the space. Careful touches abound, from comfy couches in the sitting areas to extra-large shower heads and stone reliefs set in the tubs. A few rooms have small "Romeo-o-Romeo" balconies. The lovely winter garden is half-enclosed and half-open for nice weather.

Corso Porta Borsari 4A, 37121 Verona. www.hotelgabbiadoro.it. ✆ **045-800-3060.** Fax 045-590-293. 27 units. 220€–380€ double; 285€–530€ junior suite. Breakfast included, except during opera season (June 29–Sept 2), when it's 23€. AE, DC, MC, V. Valet parking 30€. Bus: 72 or 73. Pets accepted for a fee. **Amenities:** Bar; babysitting; bikes; concierge; Inernet; room service. *In room:* A/C, TV, hair dryer, Internet, minibar.

MODERATE

Colomba d'Oro ★ A few steps from the Arena, Colomba d'Oro was built as a villa in the 1600s and later transformed into a monastery. During the 18th and

19th centuries, it served as an inn for travelers and employees of the postal service, and eventually grew into this large hotel. The building is efficiently organized and has an atmosphere somewhere between traditional and contemporary. Behind soundproof windows, the guest rooms are nicely appointed with matching fabrics and comfortable furniture. Some bathrooms are clad in marble.

Via C. Cattaneo 10, 37121 Verona. www.colombahotel.com. ✆ **045-595300.** Fax 045-594974. 51 units, 11 with shower only. 136€–248€ double; 180€–298€ suite. Rates include continental breakfast. AE, DC, MC, V. Parking 23€. **Amenities:** Room service. *In room:* A/C, TV, hair dryer, minibar, Wi-Fi (1€ per hour).

Hotel Giulietta e Romeo ★ A block from the Arena is this handsomely refurbished *palazzo*-hotel recommended for its upscale ambience, cordial can-do staff, and location in the heart of the *centro storico*. Brightly lit rooms are warmed by burnished cherrywood furnishings, and the large marble-tiled bathrooms are those you imagine finding in tony first-class hotels. The hotel takes its name seriously; there are two small marble balconies a la Juliet on the facade, but their view is unremarkable. The hotel is located on a narrow side street that is quiet and convenient to everything.

Vicolo Tre Marchetti 3 (south of Via Mazzini, 1 block east of the Arena), 37121 Verona. www.giuliettaeromeo.com. ✆ **045-800-3554.** Fax 045-801-0862. 30 units. 98€–290€ double; 168€–258€ triple. Rates include buffet breakfast. Mention Frommer's when booking and show book upon arrival for a 10% discount. Add approx. 30% to all above rates during the opera season and major trade fairs. AE, DC, MC, V. Parking 19€. From train station: buses going to Piazza Brà. Pets accepted by request. **Amenities:** Bar; babysitting; bikes; concierge; room service. *In room:* A/C, satellite TV, hair dryer, minibar, Wi-Fi (free).

INEXPENSIVE

Hotel Aurora It used to be location, location, location that had loyal guests returning to the Aurora. But after a refurbishing of all guest rooms and en suite bathrooms, it is the decor that brings them in as well. Six doubles are blessed with views of one of the world's great squares, the Piazza delle Erbe, and the white-umbrella stalls that make up the daily marketplace. Consider yourself lucky if you snag the top-floor double (there is an elevator!) with a small balcony. There's another terrace, overlooking the *mercato* (market), for the guests' use on the second floor, just above the breakfast room where the hotel's free daily ample buffet is served.

Piazza delle Erbe 2 (southwest side of the piazza), 37121 Verona. www.hotelaurora.biz. ✆ **045-597-834.** Fax 045-801-0860. 19 units, 16 (including all doubles) with private bathroom. 160€ double. Rates include buffet breakfast. AE, DC, MC, V. Parking 10€. Bus: 72 or 73. **Amenities:** Bar; concierge; room service. *In room:* A/C, satellite TV, hair dryer.

Hotel Torcolo Lifelong friends Signoras Silvia and Diana are much of the reason behind the deserving success of this small, comfortable hotel just 1 block off the lively Piazza Brà. Each guest room is individually done. Room no. 31 is a country-style sunny top-floor room (the hotel has an elevator) with exposed ceiling beams; nos. 16 (a triple), 18, 21, and 34 are done with original Liberty-style furnishings. They truly care about your comfort here: Rooms are equipped with orthopedic mattresses on stiff springs, double-paned windows (though it's quiet already), extra air conditioners on the top floor, and extra-wide single beds. They even keep different typical national travel tastes in consideration: They accept pets in a nod to Swiss travel habits, have a few rooms with tubs for Japanese guests, and offer some softer beds for the French. You can take the rather expensive breakfast outdoors on the small patio if the weather is pleasant, in a breakfast nook, or in your room.

Vicolo Listone 3 (just 1 block off the Piazza Brà), 37121 Verona. www.hoteltorcolo.it. ✆ **045-800-7512.** Fax 045-800-4058. 19 units. 70€–132€ double; 155€ double during the opera season. Discounted pricing Apr–May. MC, V. Parking garage available for fee. Closed around Dec and Jan holidays. From train station: buses to Piazza Brà. **Amenities:** Babysitting; concierge; room service. *In room:* A/C, TV, hair dryer, minibar.

TREVISO ★

31km (19 miles) N of Venice

Treviso is a bustling, prosperous small city and center in the northern Veneto. It seems to have changed little from its early days as a medieval market town and staunch ally to Venice. Much of the city had to be rebuilt after severe World War II damage, but it was done well. Treviso's medieval *palazzi* and houses with painted facades, churches frescoed by Giotto's follower Tomaso da Modena (1325–79), and pleasant streets cut across by pretty canals together make for a lovely, genuine-Italy break from the tourist beat of Padua-Vicenza-Verona.

Essentials

GETTING THERE There are **trains** two to four times an hour from Venice (25–35 min.). Fifteen runs daily (10 on Sun) come from Vicenza (40–80 min.).

Ten **buses** (✆ **0422-577-311**) run daily from Asolo (55 min.).

If you want to **drive,** the quick way from Venice is Autostrada A27 to the Treviso Sud exit, but the more direct route is the SS13 (though that can be slow going at rush hour and midday). From Padua, take Autostrada A4 past Venice to the A27.

VISITOR INFORMATION The **tourist office** is just behind the main Piazza dei Signori at Piazza Monte di Pietà 8 (http://turismo.provincia.treviso.it; ✆ **0422-547-632;** fax 0422-419-092) and is open daily from 9am to 12:30pm, plus Tuesday to Friday 2:30 to 6:30pm and Saturday and Sunday 3:30 to 6pm. There's also a provincial **tourist office** at Via Turazza 7a (www.trevisotour.org; ✆ **0422-541-052;** fax 0422-540-366), though it's mostly administrative.

Exploring the Town

The center of town is **Piazza dei Signori,** lined with arcades that run under the retro-medieval **Palazzo del Podestà,** rebuilt in the 1870s with a tall clock tower, and spread into a loggia under the 13th-century brick council hall **Palazzo dei Trecento.**

Just beyond this square, on Piazza San Vito, sits a pair of medieval churches: **Santa Lucia,** with Tomaso da Modena frescoes in the first alcove on the right, and **San Vito,** with its rather faded Byzantine-style frescoes from the 12th or 13th century. Both are open daily 9am to noon and 4 to 6pm.

The facade of the **Duomo ★** is from 1836, but it's flanked by Romanesque lions that, coupled with the seven green copper domes, speak to the cathedral's 12th-century origins in the Venetian-Byzantine style. The second pilaster features

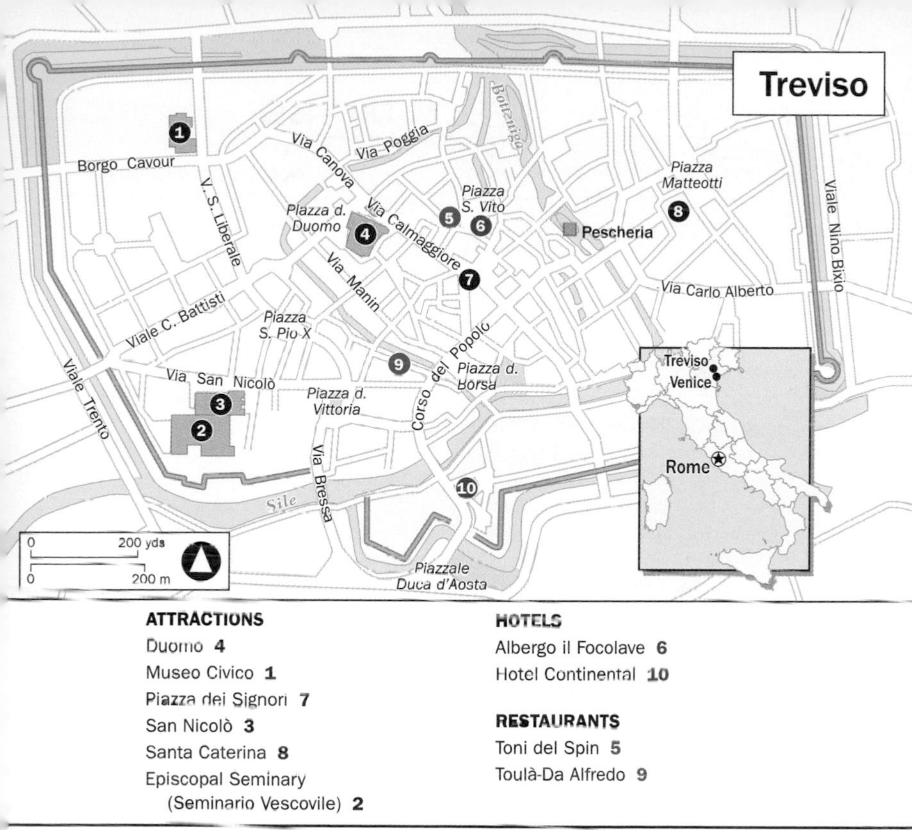

a late 1400s relief of the *Visitation,* by Lorenzo Bregno. The crypt contains a forest of columns and fragments of 14th-century fresco and mosaic. It's open Monday to Saturday 7:30am to noon and 3:30 to 7pm, Sunday 7:30am to 1pm and 3:30 to 8pm.

The **Museo Bailo,** Borgo Cavour 24 (✆ **0422-580-567**), previously the Museo Civico, holds the civic museum's remarkable collection of ancient bronze relics—including swords and ritualistic disks from the 5th century B.C., alongside Roman remains—as well as the city's collection of lesser-known works by the likes of Titian, Tiepolo, and Tintoretto. On the other side of town, across the wide Cagnan canals, whose islands host a daily fish market, stands a (deconsecrated) church that's now well worth seeking out. The highlight of **Santa Caterina** (✆ **0422-591-337**) is its frescoes by Tomaso da Modena, including a Madonna and (detached from a now-destroyed church and kept here) a series on the life of St. Ursula. Admission is 3€ for adults, 2€ for students, and 1€ for kids under 10; it's open every Tuesday to Sunday from 9am to 12:30pm and 2:30 to 6pm.

Down in the southwest corner of town, the big brick 13th- to 14th-century Dominican church of **San Nicolò ★** houses some good Gothic frescoes. Tomaso da Modena decorated the huge round columns with a series of saints, Antonio da Treviso painted the absolutely gargantuan St. Christopher—his .9m-long (3-ft.) feet strolling over biting fish—in 1410. San Nicolò is open daily 8am to 12:30pm and 3:30 to 7pm. Next door to the (unused) front door of the church is the

THE wine roads FROM TREVISO

The gently rolling foothills of the Dolomites around Treviso are known for producing fine wines. For a view of the ancient vines, take a drive along the two highways known as the **Strade dei Vini del Piave** in honor of the nearby Piave River. Both begin at the medieval town of **Conegliano,** where the tourist office is at Via XX Settembre 61 (www.turismo.provincia.treviso.it; ✆ **0438-21230**), open from Wednesday to Friday 9am to 12:30pm and 3 to 6pm, Saturday and Sunday 9am to 12:30pm.

You won't find route numbers associated with either of these wine roads, and each is badly signposted en route, beginning in central Conegliano. The less interesting is the **Strada del Vino Rosso (Red Wine Road),** running through 40km (25 miles) of humid flatlands southeast of Conegliano. Significant points en route include the scenic hamlets of Oderzo, Motta, and Ponte di Piave.

Much more scenic and evocative is the **Strada del Vino Bianco (White Wine Road),** or, more specifically, the **Strada del Prosecco,** meandering through the foothills of the Dolomites for about 39km (24 miles) northwest of Conegliano, ending at Valdobbiadene. It passes through particularly prestigious regions famous for their sparkling prosecco, a quality white meant to be drunk young, with the characteristic taste and smell of ripe apples, wisteria, and acacia honey. The most charming of the hamlets you'll encounter (blink an eye and you'll miss them) are San Pietro di Feletto, Follina, and Pieve di Soligno. Each is awash with family-run cantinas, kiosks, and roadside stands, all selling the fermented fruits of the local harvest and offering platters of prosciutto, local cheese, and crusty bread.

The best hotel for establishing a base here is in Conegliano. The **Canon d'Oro,** Via XX Settembre 131, 31015 Conegliano (www.hotelcanondoro.it; ✆ **0438-34246**), occupies a 15th-century building near the rail station and charges from

entrance to the adjoining seminary's **Sala del Capitolo,** Piazzetta Benedetto XI 2 (✆ **0422-3247**), frescoed in 1352 by Tomaso da Modena with 40 Dominicans busily studying and copying out manuscripts at their desks. It's open 8am to 6pm daily; admission is free (ring the bell if the door is shut).

Where to Eat

Toni del Spin ★ VENETIAN Blackboards with the daily list of dishes hang from the rough crossbeams beneath high, sloping wood ceilings of this legendary eatery. The kitchen prepares a carefully considered mix of simple but intriguing dishes such as *gazpacho andaluz* (cold tomato vegetable soup), *coniglio alle olive* (rabbit with olives), and of course, the ubiquitous *fegato alla veneziana* (Venetian-style liver).The house wine is good, and they charge

San Nicolò.

118€ for a double or 165€ for a junior suite, and 225€ for a suite.

If you're looking for a bite to eat in Conegliano, try our favorite restaurant, **Tre Panoce,** Via Vecchia Trevigiana 50 (www.trepanoce.it; ✆ **0438-60071**). Occupying a 16th-century stone building, it charges around 32€ for full meals that include a celebration of whatever is in season (wine not included). Your pasta could be flavored with radicchio, fresh mushrooms, wild herbs, or local cheese. Tre Panoce is in the hills above Conegliano, 1km (½ mile) from the town center. It's open from Tuesday to Saturday noon to 2:30pm and 8 to 10pm (closed Aug). The most formal restaurant in town is **Al Salisà,** Via XX Settembre 2 (www.ristorantealsalisa.com; ✆ **0438-24288**), in a stone building with 12th-century foundations. The excellent menu includes roasted veal with wild herbs, sea bass with seasonal vegetables and basil-flavored white-wine sauce, and fettuccine with wild duck. Expect to spend 28€ and up for a meal. It's open Thursday to Monday noon to 2:30pm and 7:30 to 10:30pm; Tuesday noon to 2:30pm.

decent prices on a select list of regional bottles—they even run a wine shop across the street.

Via Inferiore 7. www.ristorantetonidelspin.com. ✆ **0422-543829.** Reservations recommended. Main courses 8€–20€. AE, DC, MC, V. Tues–Sat 12:30–2:30pm; Mon–Sat 7:30–10:30pm.

Toulà Da Alfredo ★ NORTHERN ITALIAN/TREVISANO This chain of upmarket northern-cuisine restaurants, founded at the ski resort of Cortina about 2 hours north of Treviso in the Dolomites, is set in a modern series of rooms with odd murals and a ceiling *trompe l'oeil* frescoed with vines. The cuisine is refined yet traditional, and extremely pricey. The specialties often revolve around Treviso's signature roughage: a classic risotto with radicchio, for example, braised radicchio, or a radicchio *crespella* pastry.

Via Collalto 26. www.toula.it. ✆ **0422-540-275.** Reservations recommended. *Primi* 11€–26€; *secondi* 21€–34€. AE, DC, MC, V. Tues–Sun 12:30–2:30pm; Tues–Sat 7:30–11pm. Closed Aug 2–25. Bus: 1 or 7.

Shopping

The city is known for its production of wrought-iron and copper utensils, and the best place to find these goods is **Morandin,** Via Palestro 50 (www.morandinregali.com; ✆ **0422-543651**).

The cherries grown in the surrounding area ripen in June. At that time, you can buy them at all local markets, especially the **open-air market** on Tuesday and Saturday morning sprawling across Via Pescheria. Otherwise, one of the best selections is found at **Pam** supermarket, Piazza Borsa 18 (✆ **0422-583913**).

Porcini mushrooms with pasta.

Where to Stay

Albergo il Focolare ★ This simple hotel sits smack in the center of town, on a little street off the main drag a half-block from the Palazzo Podestà. Three of the largest rooms come with three beds: No. 29 has a small sitting area, no. 30 sits in the narrow end of the buildings with windows on three sides overlooking a canal, and the similar no. 34 lies directly above no. 30 on the top floor, so its windows have views over two canals. This won't be the quietest place you'll ever sleep, but it's clean.

Piazza Ancilotto 4, 31100 Treviso. www.albergoilfocolare.net. ✆/fax **0422-56-601.** 14 units. 100€–120€ double. Breakfast included. AE, DC, MC, V. Pets accepted. **Amenities:** Room service. *In room:* A/C, TV, hair dryer.

Hotel Continental The Continental is a large, well-worn hotel 3 blocks from the train station at the city walls, a 10-minute walk from the central piazza. The modular furnishings are a bit faded, but there are parquet floors and some nice old touches such as ornate wood entablatures, chandeliers, or mirrored closet doors silk-screened with Oriental prints. A few rooms have small vestibule sitting areas, and corner units are larger and tend to be more nicely furnished. There is, however, a bit of street noise from the busy road below, and while some bathrooms are new, others are aging, and many have shower nozzles you have to hold and no shower curtains.

Via Roma 16, 31100 Treviso. www.hcontinental.it. ✆ **0422-411-216.** Fax 0422-55-054. 80 units. 90€–205€ double; 115€–256€ triple. Rates include breakfast. AE, DC, MC, V. Parking 15€. Pets accepted. **Amenities:** Bar; babysitting; concierge; room service. *In room:* A/C, TV, hair dryer.

BASSANO DEL GRAPPA ★

37km (23 miles) N of Venice, 35km (22 miles) NE of Vicenza, 43km (27 miles) N of Padua, 16km (10 miles) W of Asolo, 47km (29 miles) W of Treviso

This picturesque town on the Brenta River is renowned for its centuries-old production of handcrafted ceramics and of grappa, Italy's national firewater of choice (see box, below). Its Palladian covered wooden bridge is a highlight of the small *centro storico.* The city's arcaded homes, whose facades are painted in the traditional manner, and small squares make this a lovely break from the larger towns described in this chapter.

Essentials

GETTING THERE To get here from Vicenza, you can take one of two dozen daily **FTV buses** (www.ftv.vi.it; ✆ **0424-30-850**) that make the 1-hour trip.

Frequent buses from Padua take half the time, making fewer stops. There are also a dozen **buses** (✆ **0423-493-464** or 0423-529-966) daily from nearby Asolo (25 min.).

By **car** from Asolo, take S248 for 11km (7 miles) west. From Padua, take the S47 north to Bassano. From Vicenza, take the S47 north and the S53 east. From Verona, take the S47 north and the A4 east.

VISITOR INFORMATION For information, call the **tourist office,** Lgo. Corona d'Italia 35 (www.comune.bassano.vi.it; ✆ **0424-524-351;** fax 0424-525-301). It's open daily from 9am to 1pm and Monday to Saturday from 2 to 6pm.

ITALIAN FIREWATER: grappa

As best as we can figure, grappa was invented by 11th-century Italian monks fiddling with the leftovers of the winemaking process: grape pulp, seeds, stems, and juices. Distilled and purified, the resulting after-dinner liqueur can range from clear to amber (which is usually aged), *morbido* ("soft" and smooth) to *duro* ("hard" and quite harsh to the uninitiated).

This Italian firewater was long known as *aqua vitae,* the "water of life," for its purported medicinal and restorative properties. Over the ages, it was believed to do everything from reviving the vital spirits, warming the belly (undoubtedly), relaxing the brain, sharpening the intellect, and clearing the vision to removing bodily impurities, repairing memory, prolonging life, and even curing the plague. The only benefit now touted—aside from inflicting raging intoxication—is its role as the ultimate *digestivo,* capable of helping settle your stomach after a huge Italian meal.

Nowadays, grappa is distilled from Piedmont in the west to Friuli in the east and as far south as Tuscany. You'll find bottles in all shapes and sizes; some seem to be sold more as works of glass-blowers' art than for the liqueur inside. There are labels hailing from renowned grappa distilleries, high-grade *aqua vitae* produced by vineyards (which have often raised the bar on grappa quality by forgoing the winemaking process entirely, distilling the stuff from whole grapes rather than just the scraps), and home-made hooch made in copper stills that are wheeled from farm to farm.

The most renowned producer in Bassano is **Nardini,** Ponte Vecchio 2 (www.nardini.it; ✆ **0424-227-741**), run by the same family since 1779. It is the leader in grappa production, responsible for 25% of the Italian market, and its wood-beam *taverna* at the base of the Ponte degli Alpini is on the register of Italy's Historic Locales. Most people order a Rosso, the house version of Campari and soda, using Nardini's own "Rosso" liquour. Walk out onto the bridge a bit to look back at the building's wall to see the bullet marks in the plaster from French rifles giving chase to the archduke of Austria on May 3, 1889.

Just up the street sits **Poli** (www.poligrappa.com; ✆ **0424-524-426**), founded in 1898 at nearby Schiavon, where its production is still centered. This Bassano sales outlet is a slick operation, with less atmosphere than Nardini, but it does incorporate a small but very informative grappa museum. It's all in Italian, but if you recall the basics of distillation from high-school science (or your college dorm), it all makes sense—and the elegant glass and copper machinery is beautiful in its own way. Plus, tastings here are free.

Exploring the Town

Bassano's historic center is just a half-dozen or so blocks in either direction; its medieval buildings and baroque *palazzi* snuggle along the Brenta River. Andrea Palladio designed Bassano's lovely symbol, the wooden **Ponte degli Alpini ★★** covered bridge, in 1569, and every time floods or disaster have struck, it has been rebuilt precisely along the original plan.

The stars of the **Museo Civico ★**, Piazza Garibaldi (✆ **0424-522-235** or 0424-523-336), are the Bassano family. Patriarch Jacopo was clearly the most talented, evident in his early *Flight into Egypt* and faded frescoes from local house facades to later works such as *St. John the Baptist* (1558) and *Pentecost* (1559), which are looser and show the influence of Titian. His sons Leandro and Francesco il Giovane (responsible for the nice *Lamentation*) had less success, as did their less talented sibling, Gerolano, who stayed in Bassano to run the family workshop. Admission—which also covers the ceramics museum (see below)—is 9€ for adults and 7€ for children under 18 or seniors older than 60. It's open Tuesday to Saturday from 9:30am to 6:30pm and Sunday from 3:30 to 6:30pm.

Palazzo Sturm (1765–66), overlooking the Brenta River on Via Schiavonetti, retains some original frescoes and stuccoes, and houses a ceramics museum heavy on 18th- and 19th-century porcelains, with a contemporary collection downstairs. Admission is 4€ adults, 3€ children, or else on the cumulative ticket with the Museo Civico, above. Its hours are also the same.

Where to Eat

Al Sole VENETIAN This is one of the more refined restaurants in town, serving elegant dishes of seasonal fresh ingredients such as *bigoli al sugo d'anatra* (thick homemade pasta in a duck *ragù*), *risotto agli asparagi bianchi* (risotto with the tender local white asparagus), or *baccalà con polenta* (salt cod served with creamy polenta). Your best luck with asparagus dishes will be in the spring while it's still in season.

Via Vittorelli 41–43. ✆ **0424-523-206.** Reservations recommended. *Primi* 6.50€–10€; *secondi* 10€–17€. AE, DC, MC, V. Tues–Sun noon–2:30pm and 7:30–10pm.

Birreria Ottone ★ AUSTRIAN/ITALIAN This popular 1870 beer hall inhabits a 13th-century *palazzo,* which lent its stone walls to the elegant dining room. Bassano friends and families gather here sometimes just to drink in good company, sometimes for a full meal of grub that runs the gamut from traditional Italian dishes and local Veneto specialties to the best of Tyrolean and Austrian cuisines.

Via Matteotti 48–50. ✆ **0424-522-206.** Reservations suggested on weekends. *Primi* 6€–7€; *secondi* 7.50€–15€. AE, DC, MC, V. Wed–Mon noon–3pm; Wed–Sun 7–11:30pm. Closed 2nd week of Aug.

Where to Stay

Bonotto Hotel Belvedere ★ It looks modern out front, but this has been Bassano's premier hotel since the 15th century. The Belvedere sits on the busy main road skirting the walls of the historic center, 4 blocks from the central Piazza Garibaldi, but the windows' double set of double panes cuts out most noise. Standard rooms in the 1985 wing have modular '80s-style units in baby blue or wood veneer and mirrors to make the midsize rooms feel larger. Superior accommodations are larger, with sturdy dark-wood furnishings and Jacuzzi tubs.

Junior suites are spruced up with 17th- and 18th-century Venetian-style antiques and double sinks, though some are done in a modern but still classy style, with embroidered sofas.

Should the Belvedere be full, they may put you up in their modern, 66-room **Hotel Palladio,** around the corner at Via Gramsci 2 (✆ **0424-523-777;** fax 0424-524-050). There a double runs from 138€ to 160€.

Piazzale Giardino 14, 36061 Bassano del Grappa (VI). www.bonotto.it. ✆ **0424-529-845.** Fax 0424-529-849. 87 units. 180€ standard ("Silver") double; 212€ superior ("Gold") double; 280€ junior suite. Rates include breakfast. AE, DC, MC, V. Parking 10€ in garage. **Amenities:** Excellent Veneto restaurant; bar; babysitting; free bikes; concierge; discount at golf course in nearby Asolo; exercise room and sauna at sister Hotel Palladio around the corner; room service. *In room:* A/C, TV w/pay movies, hair dryer, Internet, minibar.

Hotel Al Castello This is the best semibudget option in town, its rooms situated above a neighborhood bar in a goldenrod building against a tower of the half-ruined castle, just 3 blocks from the Ponte degli Alpini. Accommodations are medium to largish, with wood floors, box showers, thick beams, and a touch of class in the wood furnishings. Among the thoughtful touches are heated towel racks in the freshly tiled bathrooms. Room no. 10 is the best, with a small flower-bedecked balcony.

Piazza Terraglio 19, 36061 Bassano del Grappa (VI). www.hotelalcastello.it. ✆/fax **0424-228-665.** 11 units. 40€–60€ single; 70€–100€ double. Breakfast 6€. AE, DC, MC, V. Free parking. **Amenities:** Bar. *In room:* A/C, TV.

Villa Palma ★★ Don't be put off by the industrial zone you drive through to get to this 1680 countryside villa 5km (3 miles) outside Bassano. Once inside the gates, it's a quiet walled retreat of birdsong, manicured garden lawns, and pine trees onto which the marble-floor bar opens. Regular rooms are midsize with rattan furnishings, chipped stone floors, thick carpets, and doubled sinks (in most). Junior suites are larger, with elegant period-style furnishings, silk wall coverings, and Murano chandeliers. The most requested suite, no. 39, has a Jacuzzi; no. 53 lacks the Jacuzzi but enjoys long garden vistas. Even singles come with extra-wide *francesina* beds.

Via Chemin Palma 30, 36065 Mussolente (VI; 5km/3 miles from Bassano off the road to Asolo/Montebelluno). www.villapalma.it. ✆ **0424-577-407.** Fax 0424-87-687. 21 units. 100€ double; 180€ junior suite. Rates include breakfast. AE, DC, MC, V. Free parking. **Amenities:** Elegant Veneto restaurant; bar; concierge; heated indoor pool at nearby sports center; room service. *In room:* A/C, TV, hair dryer, minibar, Wi-Fi (free).

TRIESTE ★

116km (72 miles) NE of Venice, 667km (414 miles) NE of Rome, 407km (252 miles) E of Milan

Trieste faces west, toward the rest of Italy, to which it is connected only by a strip just a few miles wide of what might otherwise be Slovenian beachfront if either of the 20th century's world wars had ended differently. For many of its traditions—from the Slavic dialects you are likely to hear in the streets to the appearance of goulash and Viennese pastries on its menus—this handsome city of medieval, neoclassical, and modern buildings turns to other parts of Europe and is rightly considered a Habsburgian Adriatic port, tied more to Vienna than to Venice.

Piazza dell'Unità d'Italia.

Already a thriving port by the time it was absorbed into the Roman Empire in the 2nd century A.D., Trieste competed with Venice for control of the seas from the 9th through the 15th centuries. For several centuries it thrived under the Habsburgs; in the late 18th century, Maria Theresa, and later her heirs and successors, gave the city its grandiose neoclassical look. Trieste was the chief seaport of the Austro-Hungarian Empire until the conclusion of World War I, when Trieste became part of Italy. At the end of World War II, Allied forces and Yugoslavia jointly occupied Trieste, which became a free city issuing its own stamps and currency until 1954, when it was given back to Italy.

You're likely to notice that Trieste is still very much a seagoing city. The traditional *passeggiata* here means a stroll along the waterfront to enjoy a sea breeze and watch the sun set over the Adriatic.

In the cafes that remain (fewer now than before World War I), you can experience the city's history as one of Europe's intellectual centers. James Joyce arrived in 1904 and stayed for more than a decade, teaching English and writing *A Portrait of the Artist as a Young Man, Dubliners,* and at least part of *Ulysses;* the poet Rainer Maria Rilke lived nearby; Sigmund Freud spent time here; and the city was home to Italo Svevo, one of Italy's greatest 20th-century novelists.

Essentials

GETTING THERE Trieste is serviced by an **airport** at **Ronchi dei Legionari** (www.aeroporto.fvg.it; ✆ **0481-773224**), 35km (22 miles) northwest of the city. **Alitalia** (www.alitalia.com; ✆ **800/223-5730**) has daily flights to and from Rome. **Lufthansa** (✆ **800/645-3880** in the U.S., or 199-400-044 in Italy) offers daily flights from Trieste to Munich.

Trieste lies on a direct **rail** link from Venice. Trip time from Venice is 2½ hours, and a one-way ticket is 10€ to 24€. The station is on Piazza della Libertà (✆ **892021**), northwest of the historic center. It's better to fly, drive, or take the train to Trieste. Once here, you'll find a network of **local**

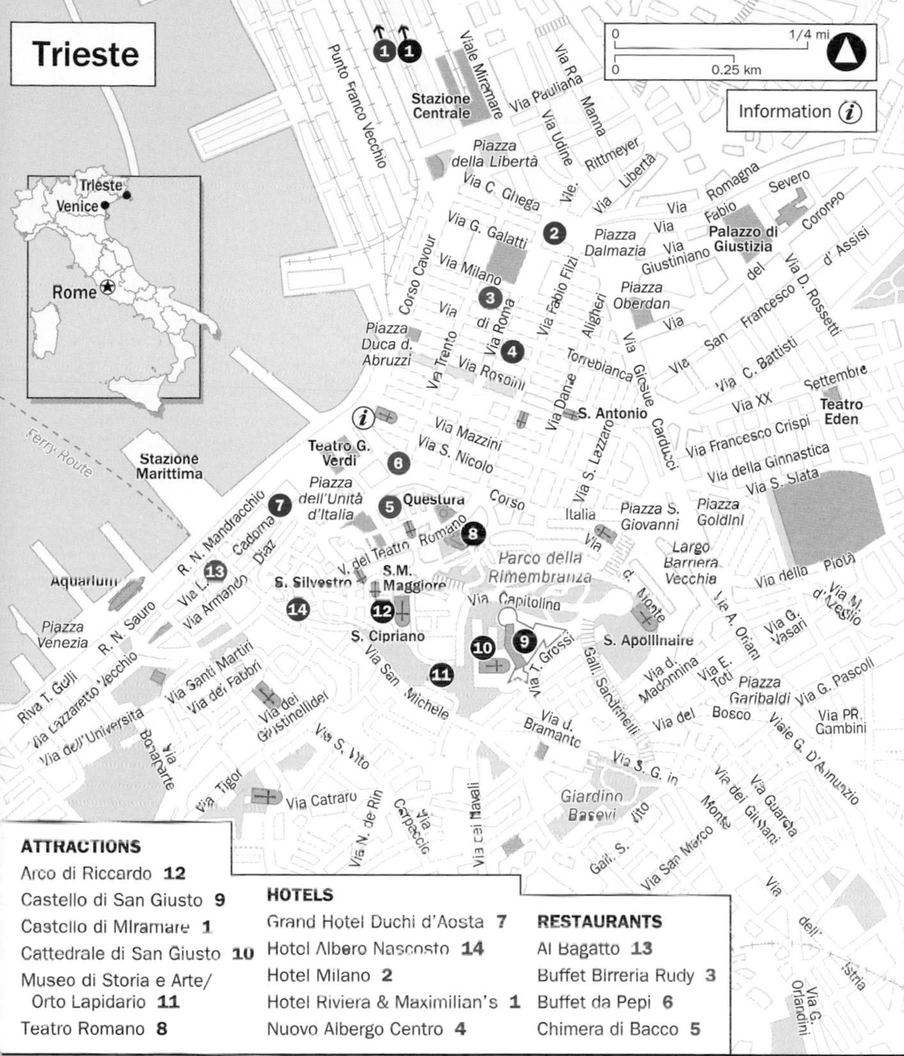

buses servicing the region from Corso Cavour (✆ **800-016675** toll-free in Italy).

By **car,** follow A4 northeast from Venice until you reach the end at Trieste.

VISITOR INFORMATION The **tourist office,** Piazza dell'Unità d'Italia (www.turismofvg.it; ✆ **040-3478312**), is open Monday to Saturday 9am to 6pm, and Sunday 9am to 1pm.

Exploring the City

The heart of Trieste is the neoclassical **Piazza dell'Unità d'Italia ★**, Italy's largest square that fronts the sea. Opening onto the square is the town hall with a clock tower, the Palace of the Government, and the main office of the Lloyd Triestino ship line. Flanking it are numerous cafes and restaurants, popular at night with locals who sip an aperitif and promenade along the seafront esplanade.

After visiting the main square, you might want to view Trieste from an even better vantage point. Head up the hill for another cluster of attractions—you can take an antiquated **tram** leaving from Piazza Oberdan and get off at Obelisco. At the **belvedere,** the city of the Adriatic will spread out before you.

Cathedral of St. Just (Cattedrale di San Giusto) CATHEDRAL This hilltop structure is one of several remarkable buildings atop the Capitoline Hill, which is littered with Roman ruins, evidence of the city's long history as an important port. In fact, the cathedral's squat, 14th-century **campanile** rises from the ruins of a 1st-century-A.D. Roman temple. Pleasingly asymmetrical, the cathedral is dedicated to Saint Just, Trieste's patron. It incorporates two 5th-century Romanesque basilicas, one already dedicated to San Giusto, the other to Santa Maria Assunta. You'll see what remains of both as you step inside: The two right aisles belong to the original San Giusto, the two left aisles to Santa Maria Assunta, and in the center is the 14th-century nave that was added to bring them together.

Piazza Cattedrale, Colle Capitolino. ✆ **040-302874.** Free admission. Daily 8:30am–noon and 4–7pm.

Miramare Castle (Castello di Miramare) ★ CASTLE Overlooking the Bay of Grignano, this castle was built by Archduke Maximilian, the brother of Franz Josef, the Habsburg emperor of Austria. Maximilian, who married Princess Charlotte of Belgium, was the commander of the Austrian navy in 1854. In an ill-conceived move, he and "Carlotta" sailed to Mexico in 1864, where he became the emperor in an unfortunate, brief reign. He was shot in 1867 in Querétaro, Mexico. His wife lived until 1927 in a château outside Brussels, driven insane by the Mexican episode. On the ground floor, you can visit Maximilian's bedroom

Miramare Castle (Castello di Miramare).

Going Underground

The Grotta Gigante, "Gigantic Cave" (www.grottagigante.it; ✆ **040-327-312**), lives up to its name: 114m high (374 ft.), 924m long (3,031 ft.), and 65m wide (213 ft.), this single-chamber cave is the world's largest underground cavern open to the public. The cave is about 15km (9¼ miles) north of the city near Opicina. An exciting way to get here is via the rickety tram that climbs into the hills from Piazza Oberdan (just west of the train station) and ends at Opicina, where you can catch the no. 42 bus to the cave. The tram runs every 20 minutes from 7:30am to 8pm, and the fare is 1.10€.

Admission is 11€ adults, 9€ students under 26 and seniors over 65, 8€ children ages 6 to 16. Tuesday to Sunday there are tours every hour November to February from 10am to noon and 2 to 4pm, March and October 10am to 4pm; tours are every half-hour April to September from 10am to 6pm. On the freeway, you can take the exit at Prosecco. By public transport, take the tram from Piazza Oberdan, and then bus no. 42 to Prosecco.

(built like a ship's cabin) and Charlotte's, as well as an impressive receiving room and more parlors, including a *chinoiserie* salon.

Enveloping the castle are magnificently designed grounds (the **Parco di Miramare**), ideal for pleasant strolls. In July and August, a **sound-and-light presentation** in the park depicts Maximilian's tragedy in Mexico. Tickets begin at 10€.

Viale Miramare. www.castello-miramare.it. ✆ **040-224220.** Castle admission 6€ adults, 4€ E.U. citizens ages 18–24, free for E.U. children 17 and under and seniors 66 and older; grounds free. English-language tours available for 21€ for 1–10 people. Castle daily 9am–7pm. Last admission 30 min. before closing. Grounds Apr–Sept daily 8am–7pm; Mar and Oct daily 8am–6pm; Nov–Feb daily 8am–5pm. Oct–Mar admission to the Castello after 5pm is from Viale dei Lecci only. Bus: 36.

St. Just Castle (Castello di San Giusto) CASTLE Constructed in the 15th century by the Venetians on the site of a Roman fort, this fortress maintained a sharp eye on the bay, watching for unfriendly visitors arriving by sea. From its bastions, panoramic views of Trieste unfold. Inside is a museum with a collection of arms and armor.

Piazza Cattedrale 3. ✆ **040-309362.** Castle 4€; museum 5€. Castle daily 9am–sunset. Museum Tues–Sun 9am–1pm.

Where to Eat

Buffet Birreria Rudy ★ TRIESTINO/AUSTRIAN Just because Trieste is currently part of Italy doesn't mean you can't indulge in the cuisines of its former identities. This small Austrian/Bavarian *Bierhalle* serves Spaten beer on tap and sausages, wurst, and goulash alongside pastas, soups, and boiled meats. If you can't choose between a *primo* or a *secondo,* get both at once; the gnocchi with goulash is memorable. Otherwise, stand at the bar and choose nibblers from behind the glass—roasted peppers, fried zucchini, rice croquettes, frankfurters in pastry—or grab a straw-bottomed chair at the little tables under Bavarian banners and pick from the chalkboard menu.

Via Valdirivo 32. www.buffetrudyspaten.it. ✆ **040-639-428.** *Primi* 4€–5€; *secondi* 9€–10€. AE, DC, MC, V. Mon–Sat 11am–midnight.

Sample the flavors of Central Europe

The region around Trieste has only been back in Italian hands since World War I, so the cuisine remains a buffet of Slovenian and Croatian flavors. Don't miss the *cevapcici* meatballs and *jota* soup, and pair them with one of the region's lovely Tocai wines, also borrowed from the Austro-Hungarians.

Buffet da Pepi ★ TRIESTINO Trieste has many such *tavola caldi* (hot-foods delis) like this one, though none compare to century-old Pepi, a much-beloved institution. You can get a panino of cold cuts or splurge on a 10€ platter of the house specialty, many varieties of pork: spicy *cotechini* (pork sausages), *porchetta* (roast pork), *bollito di maiale* (a Trieste dish of boiled pork), and prosciutto, all served with *crauti* (sauerkraut) and other vegetables.

Via della Cassa di Risparmio 3 (near Piazza della Borsa, 1 block from the water and 2 blocks north of Piazza dell'Unità d'Italia). ✆ **040-366-858.** Sandwiches and dishes 4€–11€. AE, DC, MC, V. Mon–Sat 9am–9pm. Closed July 15–Aug 7.

Chimera di Bacco ★ MODERN TRIESTINO Cuisine in Italy is changing to reflect more modern and refined tastes, and Chimera di Bacco leads that charge in Trieste on a little alleyway behind city hall. The clean and modern decor reflects the minimalist but elegant dishes, which range from Triestino favorites such as *la jota,* a stew of cabbage, potatoes, and beans, to a delicate boneless rabbit done with a Madeira sauce and Croatian prosciutto. You won't find a wide selection of fish dishes here, but rather a heavy emphasis on the best cuts of meat in an intricate presentation. A good selection of local wines pave the way to a romantic evening and a culinary treat.

Via del Pane 2. ✆ **040-364-023.** *Primi* 7€–9€; *secondi* 13€–19€. DC, MC, V. Mon–Sat noon–3pm and 6–11pm.

Candy on display at La Bomboniera.

Shopping

Trieste is a great place to shop for antiques. Look for examples of both Biedermeier and Liberty (Italian Art Nouveau) furniture and accessories, and wander at will through the city's densest collection of antiques dealers, the neighborhood around **Piazza dell'Unità d'Italia.** Dealers to look out for are **Davia,** Via dell'Annunziata 6 (✆ **040-304321**), specializing in antique engravings; and **Fulvio Rosso,** Via Armando Diaz 13 (✆ **040-306226**), specializing in crystal and porcelain from the turn of the 20th century.

Fine leather and suede goods fill **Christine Pelletterie,** Piazza della Borsa 15 (✆ **040-366212**), where women can find well-crafted shoes, bags, and pants.

Offering both casual and formal attire, **Max Mara,** Corso Italia 20 (www.maxmara.com; ✆ **040-636723**), features impeccable women's designs, plus shoes and bags.

The 130-year-old **La Bomboniera ★**, Via XXX Ottobre 3 (✆ **040-632752**), is a candy store as beautifully wrapped as the chocolates it sells, with etched glass, carved walnut shelves, and an elaborate glass chandelier. Besides fine chocolates, it offers traditional sweets and pastries of the region, as well as a few Austro-Hungarian specialties.

Entertainment & Nightlife

Trieste's most impressive theater, the **Teatro Verdi,** Corso Cavour via San Carlo (www.teatroverdi-trieste.com; ✆ **040-6722111**), has been compared to a blend of the Vienna State Opera and Milan's La Scala, presenting classical concerts and operas throughout the year. Tickets range from 22€ to 130€.

The town's loveliest cafe, almost adjacent to the above-mentioned theater, is the **Caffè Tommaseo,** Piazza Tommaseo 4-C (✆ **040-362666**). A younger crowd usually populates the Piazza dell'Unita at night, spilling out from the bars on its southeast corner.

Where to Stay

Grand Hotel Duchi d'Aosta ★ This is Trieste's best hotel, installed in one of the neoclassical buildings right on Piazza dell'Unità d'Italia. It is business oriented and modernized—with snappy service, a thermal pool, and Jacuzzi box showers in the marble bathrooms—but retains plenty of class in the stylish wood furnishings and old-world charm of its reception and Harry's Grill, which has tables on the square.

Piazza dell'Unità d'Italia 2, 34121 Trieste. www.grandhotelduchidaosta.com. ✆ **040-760-0011.** Fax 040-366-092. 53 units. 160€–330€ double. Breakfast 20€. AE, DC, MC, V. Parking 21€ in nearby garage. **Amenities:** International restaurant; bar; babysitting; concierge; indoor pool; room service; smoke-free rooms. *In room:* A/C, TV w/pay movies, hair dryer, minibar, Wi-Fi (free)

Hotel Albero Nascosto 🎁 The "hidden tree" hotel is a secluded gem in the historic center by the seafront. For the price, the rooms are very well equipped (compact apartments, really), with ample bathrooms and a kitchenette in most units. The recently restored rooms have a sleek but charming feel, with hardwood floors, exposed beams, and modern art gracing the walls, with sophisticated touches such as stocked bookshelves. Beyond its convenient but quiet location and excellent wine bar/tavern downstairs, the most compelling reason to stay at the Albero Nascosto may be the friendly and genteel staff.

Via Felice Venezian 18, 34124 Trieste. www.alberonascosto.it. ✆ **040-300-188.** Fax 040-303-733. 10 units. 75€–115€ single; 95€–165€ double; 115€–170€ triple. Rates include breakfast. AE, DC, MC, V. No parking. **Amenities:** Wine bar; concierge. *In room:* A/C (in some rooms), TV, hair dryer, kitchenette, minibar, Wi-Fi (free).

Hotel Riviera & Maximillian's ★★ This seaside retreat has been steadily expanded since it opened in 1910. Rooms in the older half have parquet floors, blue-tiled bathrooms, and carved wood furnishings with modern prints, and many neighboring doubles can be connected to make suites. Number 101 is a family suite, though it is one of only three rooms without a sea view. In the new half, rooms have balconies that are shaded by umbrella pines, cypress, and palms, and are cooled by Adriatic breezes. Rooms on the first floor have terraces opening directly onto the garden; those on the side have less of a sea view but more greenery.

Strada Costiera 22 (just north of Castello Miramare, 8km/5 miles from Trieste's center), 34010 Trieste. www.hotelrivieraemaximilian.com. ✆ **040-224-551.** Fax 040-224-300. 70 units. 140€–240€ double; 420€–1,250€ 1-room apt for 2 guests per week; 665€–2,100€ 2-room apt for 2 guests per week. Rates include breakfast. AE, DC, MC, V. Free parking. **Amenities:** International/Italian terrace restaurant; beach buffet in summer; bar; babysitting; children's center at beach; concierge; golf course; 2 outdoor pools (1 for adults, 1 for kids); room service; smoke-free rooms; nearby tennis courts; watersports equipment/rentals. *In room:* A/C, TV w/pay movies, hair dryer, kitchenette (in apts), minibar, Wi-Fi (5€/hr.).

CORTINA D'AMPEZZO: GATEWAY TO THE DOLOMITES ★★

161km (100 miles) N of Venice, 411km (255 miles) NE of Milan

Italy's best-known mountain resort, put on the international map when it hosted the 1956 Winter Olympics, is often associated with wealth and sophistication. Long before the Olympics, though, Cortina was attracting European Alpine enthusiasts, who began coming here for stays in the town's first hotels as early as the 1860s. In 1902, Cortina hosted its first ski competitions, and in 1909, the completion of the first road in and out of the town, the magnificent Strada di Dolomiti (built by the Austro-Hungarian military), opened the slopes to more skiers.

Even without its 145km (90 miles) of ski runs and 50 cable cars and chairlifts that make the slopes easily accessible, Cortina would be one of Europe's most appealing Alpine towns. The surrounding Dolomite peaks are simply stunning. Eighteen of them rise more than 3,000m (9,840 ft.), ringing Cortina in an amphitheater of craggy stone. In full light the peaks are a soft

The mountains surrounding Cortina.

bluish gray, and when they catch the rising and setting sun, they take on a welcoming rosy glow.

True to its reputation for glamour, Cortina can be expensive (especially in Aug and the high-ski-season months of Jan–Mar). Many well-to-do Italians have houses here, and a sense of privilege prevails. What's often forgotten, though, is that for all of the town's fame, strict zoning has put a damper on development; as a result, Cortina is still a mountain town of white timbered houses, built aside a rushing stream and surrounded by forests, meadows, and, of course, stunning Dolomite peaks.

Essentials

GETTING THERE The closest **train station** to Cortina is the one at **Calalzo di Cadore,** 30km (19 miles) south. From Calalzo, 30 daily buses connect with Cortina. There are 10 trains a day to Calalzo from Venice, but only two are direct (2½ hr; with connections, allow 3–4 hr.). There are also six daily direct runs from Padua (3 hr.).

Frequent **STI bus service** provides the only public transportation in and out of Cortina (www.sii.bz.it; ✆ **800-846-047** in Italy). There are two daily buses each from Bolzano (about 4 hr.), stopping in Bressanone (about 2¾ hr.), that head to Cortina, but with a change in Dobbiaco. There is also one daily bus to and from Venice (✆ **035-237-641;** 4½ hr.) and a daily bus to and from Milan (✆ **02-801-161;** 6½ hr.). The bus station in Cortina is located in the former train station on Via Marconi.

If you choose to come by **car,** the spectacularly scenic Grande Strada delle Dolomiti (p. 550) links Bolzano and Cortina, while S51 heads south toward Venice, connecting south of Belluno to Autostrada A27, for a total trip time of about 3 hours between Cortina and Venice.

VISITOR INFORMATION The **APT tourist office,** Piazetta San Franceesco 8 (www.cortina.dolomiti.com or www.dolomiti.com; ✆ **0436-3231;** fax 0436-3235), is open daily 9am to 12:30pm and 4 to 7pm. In addition to a list of accommodations, the English-speaking staff will provide a wealth of information on ski slopes, hiking trails, and bus schedules.

Exploring the Peaks of the Dolomites

Skiers and nonskiers alike will enjoy the eye-popping scenery on a trip up the surrounding mountainsides on the funicular systems that leave right from town. The most spectacular trip is the ascent on the **Freccia nel Cielo (Arrow in the Sky),** which departs from a terminus near the Stadio Olimpico del Ghiacchio (Olympic Ice-Skating Stadium), about a 10-minute walk north and west of the town center. It has three segments. The top station is at **Cima Tofana,** at 3,163m (10,375 ft.); the round-trip is 26€. It is a little less expensive (21€)—and just as satisfying, if mountain scenery and not high-Alpine skiing is your quest—to make the trip only as far as **Ra Valles,** the second stop, at 2,550m (8,364 ft.). The views over glaciers and the stony peaks are magnificent, and a bar serves sandwiches and other refreshments on an outdoor terrace. Or, for 12€, you could take the tramway as far as **Col Druscie,** whose views are still nothing to sneeze at, and there is a decent restaurant there as well. The funicular runs from mid-July to late September and mid-December to May 1, with departures every 20 minutes from 9am to 4 or 5pm, depending on the time of sunset; call ✆ **0436-5052** for information.

The **Funivia Faloria** (✆ **0436-2517**) arrives and departs from a terminus on the other side of town, about a 10-minute walk southeast of the town center. The ride is a little less dramatic than the one on the longer Freccia nel Cielo. Even so, the ascent over forests and meadows and then up a sheer cliff to the 2,100m-high (6,888-ft.) ski station at Faloria is not without thrills, and the view from the terrace bar at Faloria, down to Cortina and to the curtain of high peaks to the north, is one you won't soon forget. Like the Freccia nel Cielo, the Funivia Faloria runs from mid-July to late September and mid-December to May 1, with departures every 20 minutes from 9am to 4 or 5pm, depending on the time of sunset; round-trip fare is 16€.

Another trip for cable car enthusiasts is the one from the top of **Passo Falzarego,** 25km (16 miles) west of Cortina, to Lagazoul, a little skiing and hiking station at the 2,550m (8,364-ft.) level. In summer, you can follow a network of trails at the top and scamper for miles across the dramatic, rocky terrain, and as an eerie alternative to the funicular, you can make the climb up or down through a series of tunnels dug into the cliff during World War I battles. If you are not driving, five buses a day make the 35-minute trip between Cortina and the funicular stop at the top of the Passo Falzarego; the fare is 1.50€ each way. The *funivia* runs from mid-July to late September and mid-December to May 1, with departures every 30 minutes; round-trip fare is 12€. Call ✆ **0436-867-301** for information.

Skiing & Other Outdoor Pursuits

DOWNHILL SKIING

The **Faloria-Cristallo area** surrounding Cortina is known for its 30km (19 miles) of slopes and 16km (10 miles) of fresh-snow runs. At 1,223m (4,014 ft.) above sea level, Cortina's altitude isn't particularly forbidding (at least, compared with other European ski resorts), and though snowfall is *usually* abundant from late December to early March, a holiday in November or April might leave you

Cortina.

without adequate snow. Die-hard Cortina enthusiasts usually compensate for that, at least during the tail end of the season, by remaining only at the surrounding slopes' higher altitudes (there's lots of ski-ability at 2,743m/9,000 ft.) and traversing lower-altitude snowfields by cable car.

As Italy's premier ski resort, Cortina boasts more than 50 cable cars, and lifts spread out across the valley of the Boite River. The surrounding mountains contain about two dozen restaurants, about 145km (90 miles) of clearly designated ski trails, and a virtually unlimited number of off-piste trails for cross-country enthusiasts. Cortina boasts plenty of sunshine, a relative lack of crowds, and an array of slopes that will suit intermediate, advanced intermediate, and novice skiers alike. During winter, ski lifts are open daily 9am to between 4 and 5pm, depending on the time of sunset.

Cortina boasts eight distinct ski areas, each with its own challenges and charms. Regrettably, because they sprawl rather disjointedly across the terrain, they're not always easy to interconnect. The most appealing are the **Tofana-Promedes, Forcella Rossa,** and **Faloria-Tondi** complexes. The **Pocol, Mietres,** and **Socepres** areas are for novices; the **Cinque Torri** is good for intermediates; and the outlying **Falzarego** is a long, dramatic, and sometimes terrifying downhill jaunt not recommended for anyone except a very competent skier.

Despite the availability of dozens of cable cars originating outside the town center along the valley floor, Cortina's most dramatic cable cars are the **Freccia nel Cielo ("Arrow of the Sky"),** the region's longest and most panoramic (see above), and the **Funivia Faloria** (**Faloria chairlift;** www.funiviefaloria.com; ✆ **0436-2517**). It departs from Piazzale Marconi (bus station). Both of these cable cars are patronized even by visitors who'd never dream of skiing. A single round-trip ticket for the chairlift is 21€—although if you plan on spending time in Cortina, it's almost always more economical to buy a ski pass.

Ski passes are issued for from 1 to 21 days. They can include access to just the lifts around Cortina (about 50) or to all the ski lifts in the Dolomiti (around 464). By far the better value is the more comprehensive pass. This **Dolomiti Super Ski Pass** allows you unlimited access to a vast network of chairlifts and gondolas over Cortina and the mountains flanking at least 10 other resorts. The single-day pass is 37€ to 46€, but the daily cost goes down as you increase the days of the pass. For example, depending on the season, a 7-day pass is 198€ to 247€ and a 21-day pass is 496€ to 563€. The Cortina-only pass sells for about 10% less, but few people opt for it. Children 7 and under ski free.

Included in any pass is free transport on any of Cortina's bright-yellow ski buses that run the length of the valley in season, connecting the many cable cars. Depending on snowfall, the two ski lifts mentioned above, as well as most of the other lifts in Cortina, are closed from around April 25 to July 15 and September 15 to around December 1. For information, call ✆ **0436-862171.**

HIKING & ROCK CLIMBING

In this mountainous terrain, these two activities are often synonymous. The tourist office can provide maps of hiking trails throughout the surrounding region. For high-altitude hiking, canyoning, and rock climbing, you may want to join one of the excursions led by **Gruppo Guide Alpine Cortina,** Corso Italia 69A (www.guidecortina.com; ✆ **0463-868-505**), open daily 8am to noon and 4 to 8pm. A 3-day climbing course, for example, is 270€.

ICE-SKATING

At the **Stadio Olimpico del Ghiaccio,** just to the northwest of the town center on Via del Stadio (✆ **0436-866-342**), you can practice turns on the two recently refurbished rinks where Olympians tried for the gold in the 1956 games. Admission plus skate rental is 7€.

Where to Eat

Al Camin ALPINE If you follow the Via Alverà along the Ru Bigontina, a rushing mountain stream, about 10 minutes east from the center of town, you'll come to this charming, though rustic restaurant, where the cuisine is anything but unrefined. Next to a large stone fireplace you can enjoy *kenederli* (these dumplings flavored with liver are known as *canederli* outside Cortina) *in brodo* or *al formaggio,* as well as dishes that you may not encounter elsewhere, like *radicchio di prato,* a mountain green that appears in early spring and is served dressed with hot lard, and in winter, *formaggio fuso con funghi e polenta,* a lush combination of creamy melted mountain cheese and wild mushrooms served over polenta. The wine list is extensive.

Via Alverà 99. www.alcamincortina.dolomiti.org. ✆ **0436-862-01.** Reservations recommended. *Primi* 6€–9.50€; *secondi* 7€–18€. MC, V. Tues–Sun noon–3pm and 7–11:30pm.

Caffè Royal CAFE The Corso Italia, Cortina's pedestrians-only main street, is the center of the town's social life. This cafe is one of several that occupy the ground floors of large hotels along the street, and it is one of the more pleasant. As soon as it's even remotely possible to sit outdoors, tables are set out front on a sunny terrace. At other times, patrons are welcome to sit for hours over coffee, pastries, or light fare such as sandwiches in a pleasant room off the lobby of this hotel of the same name.

Corso Italia. ✆ **0436-867-045.** Sandwiches and snacks from about 2€. MC, V. Wed–Mon 8am–9pm.

La Tavernetta ALPINE A former barn, just steps from the Olympic ice-skating stadium, has been delightfully converted to a very stylish yet reasonably priced restaurant. The menu relies on local ingredients and typical dishes of the Alto Adige, and the rustic environs inspire you to eat heartily. You might want to begin with a dish of *gnocchi di spinachi* (filled with spinach and topped with a rich wild-game sauce), and then a robust *stinco di vitello con patate* (veal shank served with creamy potato) or *cervo in salsa di mirtilli* (venison with a sauce of myrtle berries with polenta).

Via del Stadio 27 a/b. ✆ **0436-867-494.** Reservations recommended. *Primi* 6.50€–12€; *secondi* 11€–20€. AE, MC, V. Thurs–Tues noon–2:30pm and 7:30–11pm.

The Great Dolomite Road ★★★

The **Grande Strada delle Dolomiti,** the scenic route between Bolzano (follow signs to Eggental/Val d'Ega) and Cortina going east, S241 and S48, is 110km (68 miles) of stunning views. The road curves around some of the highest peaks in the Dolomites, including 3,000m-tall (9,840-ft.) **Marmolda,** and goes through a scattering of mountain villages and ski resorts before dropping out of a high pass into Cortina. Some tour buses follow this route (the tourist offices in Bolzano and Cortina can provide a list of tour operators; check with the bus station in Bolzano), as do two daily buses of the **STI network** July through September (check with the bus station in Bolzano or www.sii.bz.it or ✆ **0471-450-111**). You may want to rent a car, if only for a day, to make the spectacular round-trip, one of Europe's most scenic drives (allow at least 2½ hr. each way over the twists and turns of the passes). Keep in mind that the Grande Strada delle Dolomiti is often closed to vehicles because of heavy snow in the winter months, and you will often need chains on your tires between November and April.

Where to Stay

Cortina is booked solid during the high season: August, Christmas, and late January through March. You should reserve well in advance. Rates are lowest in late spring and early fall. It's closed down tight in June. Keep in mind that many innkeepers prefer to give rooms to guests who will stay several days or longer and will take meals at the hotel.

Hotel Bellaria The Majoni family owns this pleasant hotel a short walk from the center on the northern edge of town, and they choose to keep prices down for the benefit of the patrons who come here year after year. (In ski season, the hotel generally rents out doubles by the week.) They provide some of Cortina's most reasonably priced accommodations, and they house their guests in handsome, sunny rooms that overlook the mountains and have fresh Alpine-style pine furnishings, firm new beds, and crisp fabrics. All of the bathrooms are fitted with heated towel racks. Downstairs there's a lovely paneled lounge, a dining room, a pleasant terrace in front of the house, and a lawn out back.

Corso Italia 266, 32043 Cortina d'Ampezzo. www.hbellaria.it. ✆ **0436-2505.** Fax 0436-5755. 22 units. 90€–160€ double; in winter, half board and long stays may be required: weekly rates 500€–610€. DC, MC, V. Free parking. Closed 1 month in fall or spring. **Amenities:** Tirolese/Italian restaurant; bar; babysitting; concierge; room service; smoke-free rooms. *In room:* TV, hair dryer.

Hotel Menardi ★ One of the oldest and most charming hostelries in Cortina successfully combines the luxury and service of a fine hotel with the homelike comfort of a mountain inn. The Menardi family, which converted its farmhouse into a guesthouse in the 1920s, has beautifully appointed the public rooms with antiques and comfortable furnishings. Rooms in the rear of the house are especially quiet and pleasant, looking across the hotel's spacious lawns to the forests and peaks; some newer (but still panel-and-pine Alpine) rooms are located in an annex next door, many have large balconies with picnic tables. Most guests take half board, but it is also possible to make bed-and-breakfast arrangements when the hotel is not fully booked. A pretty foot trail leads from the back lawn into town in 15 minutes.

Via Majon 110, 32043 Cortina d'Ampezzo. www.hotelmenardi.it. ✆ **0436-2400.** Fax 0436-862-183. 49 units. 100€–220€ double; 190€–260€ in winter, including requisite half board. Rates include breakfast. Add 20€–23€ per person for half board; add 30€–32€ per person for full board. DC, MC, V. Parking free or 8€ in garage. Closed Apr 10–June 15 and Sept 21–Dec 20. **Amenities:** International/Tirolese restaurant; bar; bikes; children's playground; concierge; golf course (9 holes, 3km/1¾ miles away); room service; smoke-free rooms. *In room:* TV, hair dryer, minibar, Wi-Fi.

Hotel Montana ★ Right in the center of town, this hotel occupies a tall, pretty Alpine-style house and is run by the amiable Adriano and Roberta Lorenzi, who provide some of the resort's nicest lodgings for the price. Guest rooms are pleasant and cozy, with old-style armoires, hardwood floors, and down quilts on the beds, and many open onto balconies overlooking the peaks. Most of the doubles are quite large, and many are beautifully paneled and have separate sitting areas. Half the rooms here are singles, making this an ideal spot for solo travelers. Breakfast is served in a pleasant room where guests tend to linger through much of the morning.

Corso Italia 94, 32043 Cortina d'Ampezzo. www.cortina-hotel.com. ✆ **0436-862-126.** Fax 0436-868-211. 30 units. Winter 620€–1,160€ double per week; summer 88€–175€ double per night. Rates include breakfast. AE, DC, MC, V. Free parking. Closed Nov and June. **Amenities:** Babysitting; bikes; concierge; room service. *In room:* Satellite TV, hair dryer, high-speed Internet connection.

Miramonti Majestic Grand Hotel The top deluxe spot in town since 1893, this enormous golden-age beauty of a hotel is set just outside and above the village, backed up against the pine forests with sweeping views of the cut-glass peaks. The decor, if uninspired, is perfectly pleasant, where 19th century meets modern, classy lines, and rooms contain a full complement of amenities. Public spaces devoted to après-ski fun include a piano bar, a billiards room, and even a small cinema, and it calls a (separately managed) golf course its next-door neighbor.

Loc. Peziè 103, 32043 Cortina d'Ampezzo. www.miramontimajestic.it. ✆ **0436-4201.** Fax 0436-867-019. 105 units. 255€–440€ superior double with half board. Even in off season, a 3-day minimum is often required. AE, DC, MC, V. Parking 43€ in garage. Closed Apr–June and Sept–Nov. **Amenities:** Regional/international restaurant; piano bar; babysitting; free bikes; children's center; golf course; exercise room; indoor heated pool; sauna; tennis courts (lighted at night). *In room:* TV, hair dryer, Internet.

Villa Nevada On a grassy hillside overlooking the town, valley, and mountains, the Villa Nevada is a low-slung Alpine building that has the appearance of a private home. The same ambience prevails inside, where an attractive paneled lounge is grouped around a hearth and opens to a sunny terrace. The guest rooms are bright and afford wonderful views over the Alpine landscape; they are rustically furnished with dark-stained pine pieces and thick rugs or carpeting, and all have large balconies. Located on the road to the outlying settlement of Ronco, the center of Cortina is a pleasant 20-minute walk downhill, but it could be a long uphill trek home.

Via Ronco 64, 32043 Cortina d'Ampezzo. www.villanevadacortina.com. ✆ **0436-4778.** Fax 0436-4853. 11 units. Winter 700€–1,000€ double per week; summer 560€–790€ double per week. Rates include buffet breakfast. No credit cards. Free parking. Closed first Sun in Oct to Dec 1 and after Easter to mid-June. **Amenities:** Bar; room service. *In room:* TV, hair dryer.

TRENT ★

232km (144 miles) NE of Milan, 101km (63 miles) N of Verona

Unlike other towns up here in the far north, which tend to lean heavily on their Austrian heritage, Trent is essentially Italian. The *piazze* are broad and sunny, the palaces are ocher-colored and tile-roofed, Italian is the lingua franca, and pasta is still a staple on menus. With its pleasant streets and the remnants of its most famous event, the 16th-century Council of Trent, Trent is a nice place to stay for a night or to visit en route to Bolzano and other places in the Trentino–Alto Adige.

Essentials

GETTING THERE Strategically located on a main north-south rail line between Italy and Austria, Trent is served by some 21 **trains** a day to and from Verona (55–69 min.), a major transfer point for trains to Milan, Florence,

Rome, Venice, Trieste, and all points south. There are about two dozen trains a day from Bolzano (32–49 min.). To reach the center of town from the train station, follow the Via Pozzo through several name changes until it reaches the Piazza del Duomo as Via Cavour.

If you wish to travel by **bus,** contact **Trentino Trasporti** (www.tteservizio.it; ✆ **0461-821-000**), which leaves from a terminal next to the train station, and is the major link to outlying mountain towns. There's also hourly service to and from Riva del Garda on Lago di Garda (1 hr., 40 min.; see chapter 10, "Milan, Lombardy & the Lakes").

By **car,** take A22 north from Verona or south from Bolzano.

VISITOR INFORMATION The **tourist office,** on Via Manci 2 (www.apt.trento.it; ✆ **0461-216000**), is open daily 9am to 7pm.

Exploring the City

Castello di Buonconsiglio ★★ CASTLE Many Council of Trent sessions were held in this bishop's palace/fortress on the north edge of town, which you can reach by walking north from the Duomo along Via Belenzani, and then east on Via Roma (though it's a bit of a trek from the rest of the center and the train station)—both streets, especially the former, are lined with the palaces, many with faded frescoes on their facades, built to house the church officials who came to Trent to attend the council sessions. The mazelike *castello* incorporates the 13th-century Castelvecchio, surrounded by medieval fortifications, and the elegant Magno Palazzo, a palace built for a prince-bishop in the 15th century.

Among the many small collections contained within the vast complex is the Museo Provincale d'Arte, where the pride of the collection is the ***Ciclo dei Mesi (Cycle of the Months)* ★★**, an enchanting fresco cycle painted around 1400. It presents a detailed look at life at court and in the countryside, showing amusements among the lords and ladies and much hard work among the peasants. It's housed in

The Fountain of Neptune (Fontana di Nettuno).

the Torre dell'Aquila, or Eagle's Tower; for admission, ask the guards at the Loggia del Romanino, an atrium named for the Renaissance artist who frescoed it.

Via Bernardo Clesio 3. www.buonconsiglio.it. ✆ **0461-233-770** or 0461-492-840. Admission 8€ adults, 5€ children. Apr–Sept Tues–Sun 10am–6pm; Oct–Mar Tues–Sun 9:30am–5pm. Bus: 5, 7, 10, or B.

Duomo CATHEDRAL The outcomes of many Council of Trent sessions were announced in this 13th- to 16th-century cathedral, delightfully situated on the wide expanse of the cafe-filled Piazza Duomo. This square, with a statue of Neptune at its center, is referred to as the city's *salotto* (sitting room), so popular is it as a place to pass the time. The decrees that came out of the council were read in the Duomo's Chapel of the Crucifix, beneath an enormous 15th-century cross. Beneath the altar of the main church is the crypt-cum-basilica Paleocristiana, a 6th-century church later used as a crypt for the city's powerful prince-bishops. A few scraps of mosaic and carvings remain.

Piazza Duomo. ✆ **0461-234-419.** Admission to the crypt 1€, or free with the Museo Diocesano ticket (see below). Mon–Sat 9:30am–12:30pm and 2:30–6pm. Crypt 10am–noon and 2:30–6pm. Bus: A.

Museo Diocesano MUSEUM The cathedral's museum is housed in the adjoining, heavily fortified palace of these bishops. The museum displays some fascinating paintings of council sessions that serve almost as news photos of the proceedings (one provides a seating plan for delegates), as well as 16th-century tapestries and statuary, objects from the Duomo's treasury, and a collection of medieval and Renaissance paintings. The latter often showcase local Saint Vigilio, Trent's 4th-century bishop and a literal iconoclast whose destruction of a Saturn idol earned him his martyrdom as enraged pagans beat him to death with their wooden shoes. By the Renaissance, these nail-studded sandals had inexplicably become the *zoccolo,* a silken slipper, which the hapless saint is always holding up in paintings as the symbol of his martyrdom.

Piazza Duomo 18. www.museodiocesanotridentino.it. ✆ **0461-234-419.** Admission (includes Duomo's crypt; see above) 4€ adults, 1€ ages 12–18, 8€ family. Wed–Mon 9:30am–12:30pm and 2:30–5:30pm (6pm June–Sept). Bus: A.

A Cable Car Ride and a Picnic

For a breezy view of Trent and a heart-thumping aerial ride as well, take the **cable car** from Ponte di San Lorenzo near the train station up to Sardagna, a village on one of the mountainsides that encloses the city. You may want to provision yourself at the market and enjoy a picnic on one of the grassy meadows nearby. The cable car (✆ **0461-822-075**) runs daily every 30 minutes from 7am to 10:30pm (7:30pm on weekends), and the fare is 1€ each way.

Where to Eat

It's almost a requirement to stroll down Trent's Renaissance streets with a gelato from **Gelateria Torre Verde di Zanella** on Via Suffragio 2 (✆ **0461-232039**). Many flavors are made from fresh local fruits in season.

Birreria Padevana BEER HALL/PIZZA This hip beer hall and cafe draws a big crowd for coffee and pastries in the morning and keeps serving a huge mix of pastas, *würstel,* and its own beer all day. You will probably be happiest if you order simply, maybe a plate of *würstel* (sausages) or goulash. Additionally, it keeps some of the latest hours in town, making Pedavena something of a late-evening spot in a town where the nightlife is scarce, especially as there is a separate room for smokers.

Piazza Fiera 13 at Via Santa Croce. www.birreriapedavena.com. ✆ **0461-986-255.** *Primi* 5€–7€; *secondi* 6€–12€; pizza 6€–8€. MC, V. Mon and Wed–Thurs 9am–12:30am; Fri–Sat 9am–1am; Sun 9am–midnight. Sometimes closed in July.

La Cantinota ITALIAN With its white tablecloths, excellent service, and reasonably priced menu, La Cantinota may be the most popular restaurant in Trent. The fare includes Italian and Tyrolean dishes and is truly inspired, making use of fresh local ingredients: wonderful homemade gnocchi, *strangola preti* (spinach dumplings coated in melted butter), rich risottos with porcini mushrooms, and venison with polenta. The adjoining piano bar is popular with local talent who tend to intersperse Frank Sinatra renditions with yodeling.

Via San Marco 24. www.cantinota.editarea.com. ✆ **0461-238-527.** Reservations recommended. *Primi* 6.50€–8€; *secondi* 11€–13€; tasting menus 25€–30€. AE, MC, V. Fri–Wed noon–3pm and 7–11pm. Piano bar 10:30pm–2am.

Scrigno del Duomo ★★ WINE BAR/ITALIAN This stylish wine bar and restaurant offers creative cooking in a stellar location. From the front courtyard, with tables set under the frescoed facade, you can peek through the gate at the fountain splashing away on Trent's main piazza while sipping on a glass from the huge wine list and nibbling on intricate twists on Northern Italian classics: a pigeon carpaccio, or sea bream in a wild thyme sauce. Dishes change constantly with the seasons and the chef's whims but usually include pasta or gnocchi with some combination of lake fish and zucchini, and its signature cheek of beef, stewed in merlot with cream of celery sauce and candied baby carrots.

Piazza Duomo 29. www.scrignodelduomo.com. ✆ **0461-220-030.** Reservations recommended. *Primi* 6€–8€; *secondi* 9€–15€; tasting menu 47€ without wine. MC, V. Daily 11am–2:30pm and 6pm–midnight.

Shopping

The most memorable food-and-wine shop in town is the **Enoteca del Corso,** Corso 3 Novembre 64 (✆ **0461-916424**), with wines from the region and everywhere else in Italy, as well as the salamis, olives, cheeses, and other salty tidbits that go well with them. Another outlet for the reds and whites produced throughout the Trentino and the rest of Italy is the **Grado 12,** Largo Carducci 12 (✆ **0461-982496**).

Where to Stay

Accademia Hotel ★ 🎁 This simple but nice hotel is the best choice in the center, though prices are a bit steep. It's set in a restored medieval house on an alley about a block from the Duomo and Piazza Santa Maria Maggiore (whose bell tower some rooms overlook). The reception area's whitewashed vaulted ceilings and stone doorjambs don't really carry over into the rooms, which are a bit spartan, if well equipped with modular or rattan furnishings, sometimes under nice sloping ceilings. The one drawback to its central location is its proximity to the church bells.

Vicolo Colico 4–6 (off Via Cavour), 38100 Trento. www.accademiahotel.it. ✆ **0461-233-600.** Fax 0461-230-174. 50 units. 150€–165€ double; 180€–195€ triple; 200€–220€ junior suite. Rates include buffet breakfast. AE, DC, MC, V. **Amenities:** Restaurant; woodsy enoteca (wine bar); bikes; concierge; room service; Wi-Fi (free). *In room:* A/C, TV, hair dryer, Internet, minibar.

Hotel Aquila D'Oro ★ This centuries-old *palazzo* has some of the nicest rooms in Trent, with a spalike focus on health and fitness in an ancient location right around the corner from Piazza Duomo. Each of the doubles has either a Roman sauna or a therapeutic shower known as a "water paradise," as well as either stationary bikes or treadmills. Decor throughout is stylishly contemporary, with a nice smattering of Oriental carpets, vaulted ceilings, and other interesting and cozy architectural touches in public rooms.

Via Belenzani 76, 38100 Trento. www.aquiladoro.it. ✆/fax **0461-986-282.** 19 units. 90€–250€ double. (Prices vary greatly depending on the individual room you choose.) Rates include buffet breakfast. AE, DC, MC, V. **Amenities:** Bar; concierge; room service; smoke-free rooms. *In room:* A/C, TV, hair dryer, minibar, Wi-Fi (free).

Hotel Garni (Hotel Venezia) This old hotel is very basic. It is rather less charming than its next-door neighbor, Aquila D'Oro (see above), and its "amenities" consist entirely of toilet paper and one towel, but it's cheap. Marked by 1950s-style furnishings, the simple, high-ceiling rooms are a bit dowdy but offer solid, old-fashioned comfort (unfortunately, some beds still bear the sags left by generations of travelers). Its selling point: Those rooms in the front come with stunning views over the Piazza Duomo. For the reception, walk around the corner to the "unofficial" entrance, on Piazza Duomo, to find someone to check you in. ***Note:*** Though the hotel's official name is now Hotel Garni, the name painted on the side of the building still says HOTEL VENEZIA (since it's a historic landmark, they can't change the outside!).

Via Belenzani 70/Piazza Duomo 45, 38100 Trento. www.hotelveneziatn.it. ✆/fax **0461-234-559.** 50 units, 28 with private bathroom. 59€ double without private bathroom; 76€ double with private bathroom; 92€ triple with private bathroom. Rates include continental breakfast. MC, V. Free parking 200m (656 ft.) from hotel. **Amenities:** Wi-Fi (free). *In room:* Hair dryer, no phone.

MILAN, LOMBARDY & THE LAKES

10

There's a lot more to Italy's most prosperous region than the factories that fuel its economy. Many of the attractions here are urban—in addition to Milan, a string of Renaissance cities dots the Lombardy plains, from Pavia to Mantua. To the north, the region bumps up against Switzerland, craggy mountains, and romantic lakes, and to the south, Lombardy spreads out across fertile farmland fed by the Po and other rivers.

The Lombards, originally one of the Germanic barbarian hordes who crossed the Alps during Rome's decline and ended up staying to settle down, have been ruled over the centuries by feudal dynasties, the Spanish, the Austrians, and the French. They tend to be more Continental than their neighbors to the south, faster talking, and more fast-paced as well.

THE BEST MILAN, LOMBARDY & THE LAKES EXPERIENCES

- **Spending a night out on the Navigli:** If you have 1 night out in Milan, this is where you should spend it (unless, of course, you have tickets for La Scala, but in that case you could always come to the Navigli for a nightcap). Locals and tourists mix in the bars and restaurants, most of which have tables out on the canals in good weather. See p. 566.
- **Strolling through the Viale Papiniano market:** Milan is shopping. Milan is Gucci, Prada, and Armani. Milan is also the Viale Papiniano market, a never-ending succession of stalls where you will find everything from 2€-a-pair underwear to designer clothing of dubious origin. See p. 561.
- **Seeing Lombardy and Emilia-Romagna collide in Mantua:** Lombardy has many merits, not the least of which is that it borders Emilia-Romagna. Come see the perfect collision of these two regions in wonderfully pleasant and evocative Mantua. If you can swing it, come in the fall when the local pumpkins and squash make it into every local recipe. See p. 597.
- **Relaxing on Lake Ledro:** Beautiful lake, pleasant towns, nice walks, stunning mountains . . . Lake Ledro, like its bigger cousins (Garda, Como, Maggiore), has it all, but its petite size and isolated location give it an added dimension that will make any stay here memorable. One caveat, you'll need a car to make it happen. See p. 602.
- **Hiking above Lake Como or Lake Maggiore:** The two most western of Italy's great lakes offer unlimited opportunities for some serious leg stretching (from 1 day on up). Many of the best hikes on Lake Como start either near the city of Como or farther up the lake at Menaggio. On Lake Maggiore, Stresa is a great jumping off point. See p. 609 and p. 620.

PREVIOUS PAGE: **Villas along Lake Como.**

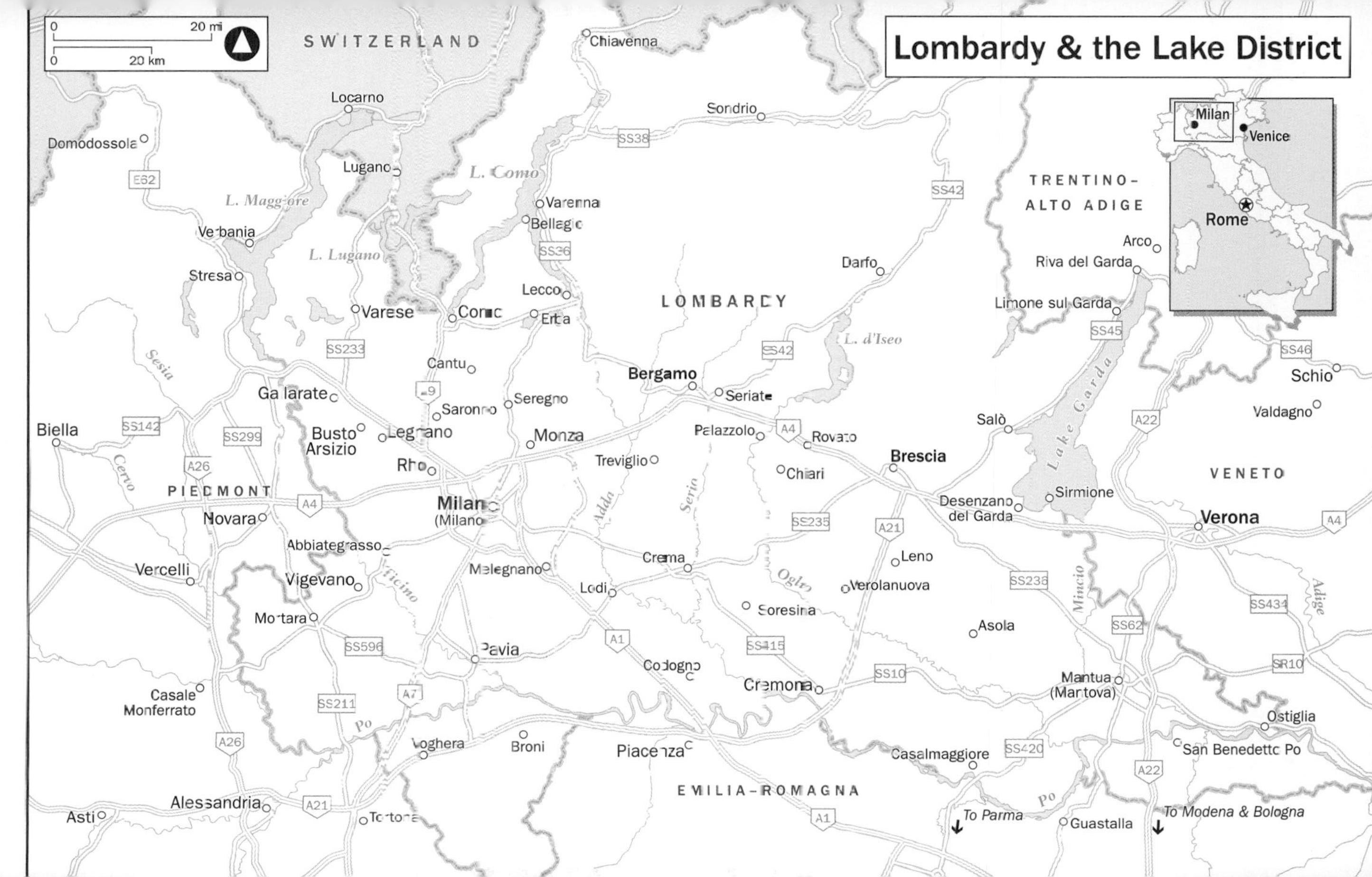
Lombardy & the Lake District
0
20 mi
20 km
SWITZERLAND
TRENTINO-ALTO ADIGE
VENETO
LOMBARDY
PIEDMONT
EMILIA-ROMAGNA
Milan
Venice
Rome
Domodossola
Locarno
Lugano
Chiavenna
Sondrio
Varenna
Bellagio
Lecco
Varese
Stresa
Verbania
Biella
Vercelli
Novara
Gallarate
Busto Arsizio
Legnano
Saronno
Cantu
Rho
Milan
(Milano)
Monza
Seregno
Bergamo
Treviglio
Crema
Pavia
Vigevano
Abbiategrasso
Casale Monferrato
Alessandria
Asti
Broni
Codogno
Soresina
Chiari
Rovato
Palazzolo
Brescia
Darfo
Leno
Verolanuova
Asola
Casalmaggiore
Guastalla
Mantua
Sirmione
Desenzano del Garda
Salò
Limone sul Garda
Riva del Garda
Arco
Verona
Valdagno
Schio
Ostiglia
L. Lugano
L. Como
L. d'Iseo
Lake Garda
Adige
Mincio
Po
Adda
Serio
Oglio
Sesia
Cervo
To Parma
To Modena & Bologna
A4
A1
A7
A21
A22
A26
E62
SS42
SS38
SS36
SS45
SS46
SS434
SR10
SS62
SS420
SS10
SS235
SS233
SS596
SS211
SS299
SS142

MILAN (MILANO)

552km (342 miles) NW of Rome, 288km (179 miles) NW of Florence, 257km (159 miles) W of Venice, 140km (87 miles) NE of Turin, 142km (88 miles) N of Genoa

While it's unlikely to knock you over with its beauty, Milan is a wonderful place to visit for both its big-ticket items—Leonardo's *The Last Supper,* Michelangelo's final sculpture, the Duomo—and its hidden treasures. That aloofness you feel when you enter Milan for the first time is a facade, and once you break through you'll realize a trip to northern Italy without a stop in Milan is like *risotto alla Milanese* without the saffron.

Things to Do The vastness of the Duomo and its *piazza* create a stunning contrast to the little, sinuous medieval streets that make navigating the center of Milan a constant challenge. A spin through town should include a stop at *The Last Supper,* the essence of Milan, but this famous work is just a smidgen of an art scene that is continually renewing itself, most recently with the opening of the Museo del Novecento dedicated to the 20th century.

Shopping A city that gave us Prada, Armani, and Versace could only be a shopper's paradise. But Milan is not only about the famous fashion brands that populate Via Montenapoleone and the surrounding streets; it is also a haven for fashionistas on a budget. And while you will find most Italian brands cost less in Milan than back home, you are also likely to notice subtle differences in styles and colors in the merchandise on the shelves.

Restaurants & Dining One of Milan's many contradictions is that it sets one of the finest (and most expensive) tables in Italy, yet you can also dine like a local for under 10€ during *aperitivo* hour. Pasta is everywhere here, just as it is in the rest of Italy, but your meal is just as likely to include polenta or risotto, both of which are served in variations that can sometimes stand in for an entire meal.

Nightlife & Entertainment Whether it's a beer and a stroll along the canals in the Navigli neighborhood or the pumping music of a dance club behind a nondescript door somewhere around town, Milan has it in spades. This is also home to La Scala, one of the world's premier opera houses.

Essentials

GETTING THERE **By Plane** Both of Milan's major airports are operated by **SEA** (www.seamilano.eu; ✆ **02-232-323**).

Milan Malpensa, 45km (28 miles) northwest of the center, is Milan's major international airport and an important hub for southern Europe. Conveniently, a 30-minute express train heads half-hourly to Cadorna train station, which is just as central as Stazione Centrale. There are also buses that will take you to Centrale in 50 minutes without traffic. The train, known as **Malpensa Express** (✆ **800-500-005**), costs 11€, while two bus companies run a combined five times per hour (**Malpensa Shuttle** at ✆ **02-6749-3083,** or **Autostradale** at ✆ **02-7200-1304**), and cost 7.50€ (see "Getting There," in the "Planning Your Trip to Italy" chapter, p. 930, for more information on the bus service). By taxi, the trip into town costs a wallet-stripping 85€, but it's the best choice when you are running late and it's not rush hour, or else after midnight, when it is indeed the only choice.

Milan Linate, only 8km (5 miles) east of the center, handles some European flights and many domestic flights. **Starfly** (✆ **02-5858-7237**)

FESTIVALS & markets IN MILAN

Though it's overshadowed by the goings-on in Venice, Milan's pre-Lenten **Carnevale** is a reasonably big deal in the city, with costumed parades and an easygoing good time, much of it focusing around Piazza del Duomo beginning a week or so before Ash Wednesday. Milan's biggest holiday, however, is December 7, the **feast of its patron saint,** Sant'Ambrogio (St. Ambrose). Those who don't leave the city for their sacrosanct day off can most likely be found milling about the *o bei o bei* **outdoor fair** (usually held in Piazza Castello or Piazza Sant'Ambrogio) that runs for several days around December 7.

Just before the city shuts down in August, the city council stages a series of June and July **dance, theater, and music events** in theaters and open-air venues around the city; call ✆ **02-7740-4343** for more information.

In a city as well dressed as Milan, it only stands to reason that some great-looking cast-offs are bound to turn up at **street markets**. Milan's largest street market is the one held on Viale Papiniano in the Ticinese/Navigli district (Metro: Sant'Agostino) on Tuesday mornings from 8am to 2pm and on Saturdays from 9am to 7:30pm; some stalls sell designer seconds as well as barely used high-fashion ware, though most offer basic staples like underwear and belts, usually cheaper than in department stores.

There's an **antiques market** on Via Fiori Chiari in the Brera district (Metro: Moscova) the third Saturday of each month, from 9am to about 7:30pm, but not in August, and another the last Sunday of each month on the quays along the Naviglio Grande in the Navigli district, from 9am to about 7:30pm (Metro: Porta Genova).

Each Saturday morning there's a large **flea market,** with everything from books to clothing to appliances, where Via Valenza meets Alzaia Naviglio Grande (when coming down Via Valenza, just before the bridge go down the driveway on the right and into the parking lot; Metro: Porta Genova). An even bigger flea market is held on Sundays at the San Donato Metro stop.

The city's largest **food market** is at Piazza Wagner, just outside the city center due west of the church of Santa Maria delle Grazie (follow Corso Magenta and its extension, Corso Vercelli, to Piazza Piemonte; the market is 1 block north; Metro: Piazza Wagner). It's held Monday through Saturday from 8am to 1pm and Tuesday through Saturday from 4 to 7:30pm; the displays of mouthwatering foodstuffs fill an indoor market space and stalls that surround it.

Stopping by **Eataly** in the Coin department store that dominates Piazza Cinque Giornate, a 15-minute walk east of the Duomo, is something of an obligation for all foodies. The **top floor of the Rinascente department store** in Piazza Duomo, with its mozzarella bar and fine selection of packaged Italian goodies, is another haven for food connoisseurs (as an added bonus, you get a close-up view of the Duomo).

makes the 30-minute trip by bus from 6am to midnight from Linate to Milan's Stazione Centrale for 4€. City bus no. 73 leaves every 10 minutes for the San Babila Metro stop downtown (1.50€ for a regular bus ticket bought from any newsagent inside the airport, 2€ onboard and you must have exact change) and takes about 25 minutes. The express no. 73X is faster though there is only one an hour. The trip into town by taxi costs about 15€.

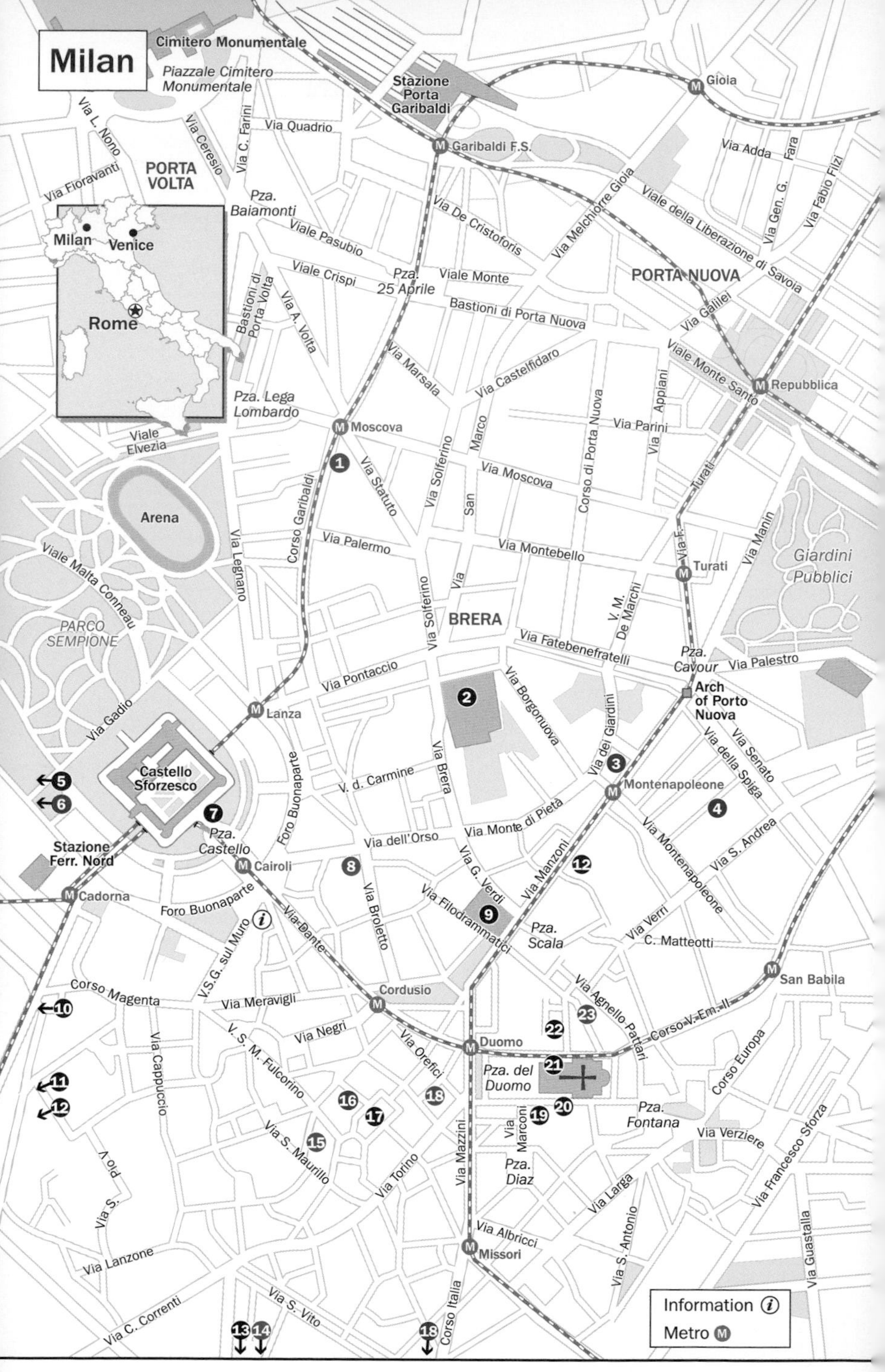
Milan
Cimitero Monumentale
Piazzale Cimitero Monumentale
Stazione Porta Garibaldi
Gioia
Garibaldi F.S.
PORTA VOLTA
PORTA NUOVA
Milan
Venice
Rome
Moscova
Arena
PARCO SEMPIONE
Giardini Pubblici
Turati
Repubblica
BRERA
Lanza
Castello Sforzesco
Stazione Ferr. Nord
Cadorna
Cairoli
Montenapoleone
Arch of Porto Nuova
Cordusio
Duomo
San Babila
Missori
Pza. del Duomo
Pza. Scala
Pza. Castello
Pza. Cavour
Pza. Fontana
Pza. Diaz
Pza. 25 Aprile
Pza. Baiamonti
Pza. Lega Lombardo
Information
Metro

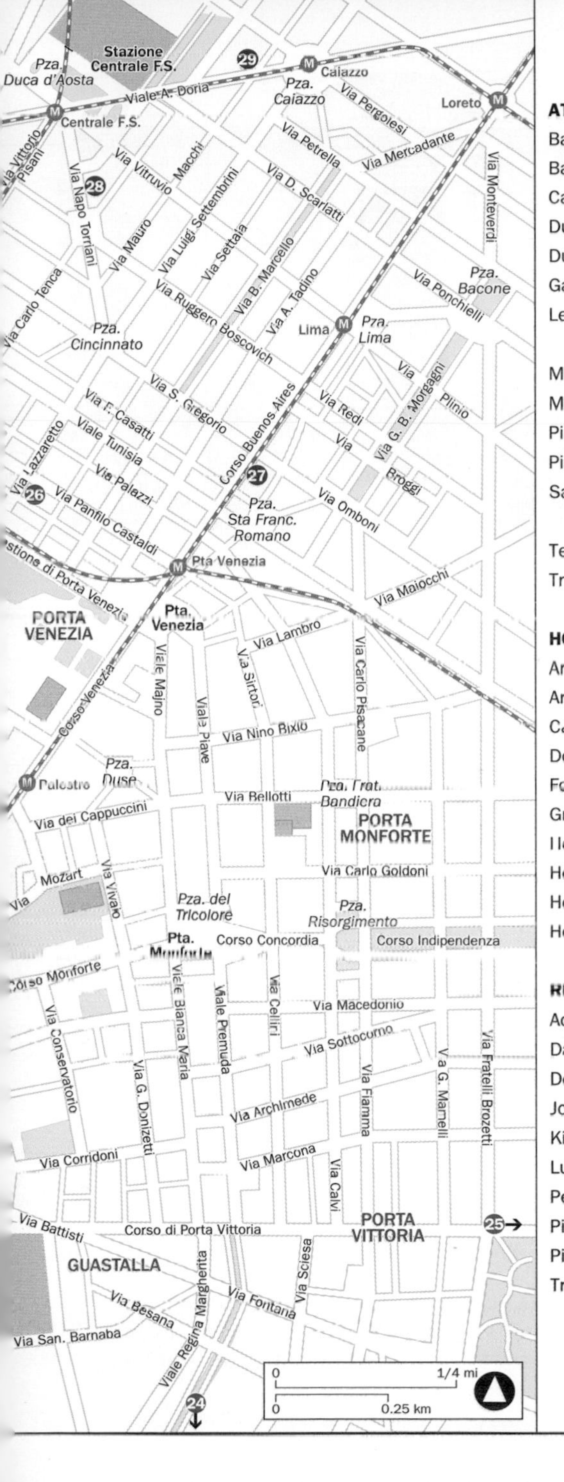

ATTRACTIONS

Basilica di San Lorenzo Maggiore **13**

Basilica di Sant'Ambrogio **11**

Castello Sforzesco **7**

Duomo & Baptistry **21**

Duomo Museum **20**

Galleria Vittorio Emanuele **22**

Leonardo da Vinci National Museum of Science and Technology **12**

Museo del Novecento **19**

Museo Teatrale alla Scala **9**

Pinacoteca Ambrosiana **17**

Pinacoteca di Brera **2**

Santa Maria delle Grazie/ The Last Supper **10**

Teatro alla Scala **9**

Triennale Design Museum **5**

HOTELS

Ariosto Hotel **6**

Art Hotel Navigli **18**

Carlyle Brera Hotel **1**

Doria Grand Hotel **29**

Four Seasons Hotel Milano **4**

Grand Hotel et de Milan **3**

Hotel Aurora **27**

Hotel Berna **28**

Hotel Gran Duca di York **16**

Hotel XXII Marzo **25**

RESTAURANTS

Acquasala **14**

Da Claudio **8**

Dongiò **24**

Joia **26**

Kiosk **14**

Luini Panzerotti **23**

Peck **18**

Piadineria Carletto **14**

Pizzeria Naturale **14**

Trattoria Milanese **15**

Crowds in the Piazza del Duomo.

Malpensa Shuttle buses also connect Malpensa and Linate about every 2 hours from 9:30am to 4:30pm daily. The trip takes 1 hour and costs 13€.

Budget-minded flyers should consider a third option, **Orio Al Serio** (www.sacbo.it) airport. Located just outside Bergamo and about an hour from Milan, Orio al Serio is a hub for discount airline Ryanair and a number of other budget airlines. Direct buses run to and from Stazione Centrale several times an hour.

By Train Milan is one of Europe's busiest rail hubs. Trains arrive and depart about every half-hour to and from Venice (2½ hr.), Florence (1¾ hr.), and Rome (3 hr.). **Stazione Centrale,** a vast structure of Fascist-era design, is about a half-hour walk northeast of the center, with easy connections to Piazza del Duomo by Metro, tram, and bus. The station stop on the Metro is Centrale F.S.; it is only 10 minutes (and 1.50€) away from the Duomo stop, in the heart of the city. If you want to see something of the city en route, take the no. 1 tram from the station to Piazza del Duomo. If you walk, follow Via Pisani through the district of high-rise office buildings to the equally cheerless Piazza della Repubblica, and from there continue south on the much more interesting Via Turati and Via Manzoni to Piazza del Duomo.

Chances are, you will arrive at Stazione Centrale, but some trains serve Milan's other train stations: **Cadorna** (with service to and from Como and Malpensa airport, for example), **Lambrate** (with service to and from Bergamo and other points east), and **Porta Garibaldi** (with service to and from Lecco and other points north). Conveniently, all three of these stations, along with Stazione Centrale, are on the same subway line: Linea 2, the green one.

A tip: Lines at Centrale's ticket windows can be epic, so save time and stress by using one of the many automatic ticket machines that take both cash and credit cards.

By Bus Given Milan's excellent rail links with other cities in Lombardy and throughout Italy, it's usually unnecessary to travel by long-distance buses, which tend to take longer, unless you are going to certain destinations such as the ski resorts in Valle d'Aosta. If you choose to travel by intercity bus, you'll likely arrive at and depart from the Lampugnano bus terminal (Metro: Lampugnano) though a few lines originate in Piazza Castello (Metro: Cairoli). **Autostradale** (www.autostradale.it; ✆ **02-7200-1304**), which operates many of the most popular bus lines, has ticket offices in front of the Castello Sforzesco on Piazza Castello, open daily 8:30am to 6pm, and on Via Paleocapa 1 flanking the Cadorna train station, open daily 7am to 7pm, where you are much more likely not to have to wait. **Savda** (www.savda.it; **0165-367-011**) runs three daily buses (more in the winter) to and from the hard-to-reach-by-train Aosta (2½ hr.).

By Car Milan is well served by Italy's superhighway (autostrada) system. The A1 links Milan with Florence and Rome (Florence is a little over 3 hr. away by car, Rome is a little under 6 hr.), and the A4 connects Milan with Verona and Venice to the east and Turin to the west (Venice is about 2½ hr. from Milan by car; Turin is a little over 1 hr.). Driving and parking in Milan are not experiences to be relished, and a fee must be paid to enter the central part of the city where you will find many one-way streets and others closed to all traffic except trams, buses, and taxis. Many hotels make parking arrangements for guests; ask when you reserve a room.

VISITOR INFORMATION The main **Azienda di Promozione Turistica (APT) tourist office** is at Piazza Castello 1, on the south side of the square where it meets via Beltrami (www.visitamilano.it; ✆ **02-7740-4343**). Hours are Monday to Friday from 9am to 6pm, Saturday 9am to 1:30pm and 2 to 6pm, Sunday from 9am to 1:30pm and 2 to 5pm. There is also an office in **Stazione Centrale** (✆ **02-7740-4318**), in front of tracks 13 and 14 with the same hours.

GETTING AROUND An extensive mix of **Metro, trams,** and **buses** makes it very easy to move around Milan on public transportation. The Metro closes at midnight (Sat at 1am), buses and trams run all night. Tickets good for a combination of Metro-trams-buses for 1¼ hours cost 1.50€. You can also purchase a carnet of 10 tickets for 14€ as well as a ticket good for unlimited travel for 1 day (4.50€) or 2 days (8.25€). Tickets are available at Metro stations and at newsstands. Stamp your ticket when you board a bus or tram—you can be slapped with a hefty fine if you don't. For information about Milan public transportation, visit the ATM information office in the Duomo Metro stop, open Monday through Saturday 7:45am to 7:15pm (www.atm.it; ✆ **800-808-181**).

CITY LAYOUT Milan is best imagined as a series of concentric circles radiating from the Piazza del Duomo at the center. Within the inner circle, once enclosed by the medieval city walls, are most of the churches, museums, and shops that will consume your visiting hours. Within the next circle, once enclosed by the so-called Spanish walls built in the 15th century, you will find some of the more outlying sites such as Parco Sempione and the church housing *The Last Supper.*

The city's major neighborhoods encircle the hub of all the circles, **Piazza del Duomo.** Looking west from the Duomo, you can see the

Cruising the Canals

Milan's *navigli,* or canals, are a focal point of the city's preparation for **Expo 2015,** but you can already start exploring them. **Navigli Lombardi** (www.naviglilombardi.it; ✆ **02-9227-3118**) has **canal tours** that bring visitors around Milan's historic canals and offer a new perspective on the historic Navigli neighborhood. Tour boats leave seven times a day from the top of the Naviglio Grande where it meets the Darsena, Milan's old port that connects the Naviglio Grande with the Naviglio Pavese. Cruises are 55 minutes long and cost 12€ for adults, 10€ for seniors 65 and over and children 12 and under; children 5 and under ride free. There are four departures Friday through Sunday between 3 and 6:10pm, and three morning departures Saturday and Sunday.

imposing **Castello Sforzesco** at one end of the well-heeled Magenta neighborhood. You can walk to the Castello in about 15 minutes by following first Piazza dei Mercanti or Via Orefici to Piazza Cordusio and, from there, Via Dante. The other major tourist draw in Magenta is the church of **Santa Maria delle Grazie;** to reach it, you'll leave Via Dante at Via Meravigli, which becomes Corso Magenta and leads to the church (total walking time from Piazza del Duomo to the church is about 30 min.).

Heading north from the Piazza del Duomo, walk through the glass-enclosed shopping center (the world's first), the **Galleria Vittorio Emanuele II.** As you emerge from the northern end of the Galleria, you'll find yourself in **Piazza della Scala** and in front of Milan's famous **opera house.** A 5-minute walk northeast along Via Manzoni takes you to Via Montenapoleone and the city's **high-fashion shopping district,** the epicenter of Italian design. A walk of about 10 minutes north of Piazza della Scala along Via Verdi, which then becomes Via Brera, brings you into the atmospheric **Brera neighborhood**—once home to the city's brothels, though it has gentrified over the last 3 or 4 decades—where cobblestone streets and old *palazzi* surround the city's major art collection, the **Pinacoteca di Brera.**

Another neighborhood to set your sights on is **Ticinese/Navigli,** usually referred to by the last word in that combination, which translates as "canals." Beyond the central city and due south of Piazza del Duomo, the Navigli's old quays follow what remains of an elaborate canal system, designed in part by Leonardo da Vinci, which once laced through the city. The charm of these waterways has not been lost on well-heeled young Milanese who have moved en masse into refurbished buildings that were once the haunts of the working classes. Bars, restaurants, shops, and galleries have populated the ground floors, making this a great neighborhood to head for at any time of day. Come to the Navigli for a stroll and a boat ride (see "Cruising the Canals" box) during the day, come back for an *aperitivo* and then stay for dinner and the nightlife (it's also the only bit of town that remains lively through Aug). You can walk to the Navigli in about 30 minutes from Piazza del Duomo by following Via Torino southwest to Corso di Porta Ticinese; alternatively, you can take any number of trams or hop on the Metro to Porta Genova.

[FastFACTS] MILAN

American Express The office is a few blocks from the Duomo, at Via Larga 4, on the corner with Via dell'Orso (✆ **02-721-041**), and is open Monday to Friday from 9am to 5:30pm (Metro: Duomo). Card members can arrange cash advances, receive mail (the postal code is 20121), and wire money.

Bookstores Milan has two English-language bookshops. The **American Bookstore,** between the Duomo and Castello Sforzesco at Via Camperio 16, at the corner with Via Dante (✆ **02-878-920**), is open Monday 1 to 7pm, Tuesday to Saturday 10am to 7pm (Metro: Cordusio). The **English Bookshop,** Via Ariosto at Via Mascheroni 12 (✆ **02-469-4468**), is open Monday to Saturday 9am to 8pm. **Rizzoli,** the glamorous outlet of one of Italy's leading publishers, in the Galleria Vittorio Emanuele (✆ **02-8646-1071**), also has some English-language titles, as well as a sumptuous collection of art and photo books; it's open daily 9am to 9pm (opens Sun at 10am, closes Sun–Mon at 8pm). There are several other big bookstores in and around Piazza del Duomo that also have a few English-language titles. English-language newspapers and magazines can be found at newsstands in Stazione Centrale and around Piazza del Duomo as well as at many other newsstands near tourist spots.

Consulates The **U.S. Consulate** is at Via Principe Amedeo 2/10 (✆ **02-2903-5333**); it's open Monday through Friday from 8:30am to noon for emergencies, otherwise only by appointment (Metro: Turati). The **Canadian Consulate** is at Via Vittor Pisani 19 (✆ **02-67-581**), open Monday through Friday from 8:30am to 12:30pm and 1:30 to 4pm. The **British Consulate,** Via San Paolo 7 (✆ **02-723-001**), is open Monday to Friday from 9:30am to 12:30pm and 2:30 to 4:30pm (Metro: Duomo). The **Australian Consulate,** at Via Borgogna 2 (✆ **02-777-041**), is open Monday to Thursday 9am to noon and 2 to 4pm (Metro: San Babila). And the **New Zealand Consulate,** at Via Terraggio 17 (✆ **02-7217-0001**), is open Monday to Friday from 8:30am to 12:30pm (Metro: Cadorna or Sant'Ambrogio).

Crime For police emergencies, dial ✆ **113** (a free call); you can reach the English-speaking staff of the tourist police at ✆ **02-863-701.** There is a police station in Stazione Centrale; and the main station, the **Questura,** is just west of the Giardini Pubblici, at Via Fatebenefratelli 11 (✆ **02-62-261;** Metro: Turati). Milan is generally safe, though public parks and the area in front of and to the west of Stazione Centrale are better avoided at night.

Drugstores Pharmacies rotate 24-hour shifts; dial ✆ **192** to find pharmacies that are open around the clock on a given day, or look for signs posted in most pharmacies announcing which shop is keeping a 24-hour schedule. The **Farmacia Stazione Centrale** (✆ **02-669-0735**), in the train station, is open 24 hours daily and some of the staff speak English.

Emergencies The best number to call in Italy with a **general emergency** is ✆ **112,** which connects you to the military-trained **Carabinieri** who will transfer your call as needed; for the **police,** dial ✆ **113;** for a **medical emergency** and to call an ambulance, the number is ✆ **118;** for the **fire department,** call ✆ **115.** All are free calls.

Holidays Milan's patron saint, Sant'Ambrogio (St. Ambrose), is honored on December 7. For a list of official state holidays, see the "Public Holidays" section on p. 45.

Hospitals The **Ospedale Maggiore Policlinico** (✆ **02-55-031**) is centrally located a 5-minute walk southeast of the Duomo at Via Francesco Sforza 35 (Metro: Duomo or Missori). Some of the medical personnel speak English.

Internet As you exit the front of the Centrale train station, on your left is **Grazia Internet Café** (Piazza

Shopping Binges & Soccer Pilgrimages

Bus trips organized by **Zani Viaggi** are tailored to all sorts of appetites, especially those that Milan cultivates so well, namely fashion and soccer. Excursions to the Serravalle outlet village (about 90 min. outside town); FoxTown (just across the border in Switzerland, about 1 hr. drive); and the Meazza stadium, also known as San Siro (home to Inter and AC Milan), leave from Foro Bonaparte 76, in front of the Castello. The shopping trip to Serravalle departs daily at 10am and costs 20€ round-trip, with return buses leaving Serravalle at 5pm. There is a daily bus to FoxTown (20€) at 2pm, with a return at 7pm. The 3-hour trip to Meazza stadium (28€) leaves Thursday at 10:30am, though it is sometimes cancelled if there are not enough people signed up. For more info, call ✆ **02-867-131** or visit www.zaniviaggi.it.

Duca D'Aosta 14; ✆ **02-670-0543**), with some 50 PCs and the possibility to pay for Wi-Fi access, open Monday to Friday 8am to midnight and Saturday and Sunday 9am to midnight. **Fnac** (✆ **02-869-541**), on Via Torino about a 10-minute walk south of the Duomo, is open Monday to Saturday 9:30am to 8pm and Sunday 11am to 8pm. **Secure Money Transfer** in the Duomo Metro station (✆ **02-3652-1721**) sells Internet access Monday to Friday 8am to 8pm, Saturday 9am to 7pm, and Sunday 9am to 5pm.

Laundry Self-service laundromats are sprinkled all over the city; one chain is **Lav@sciuga** (www.lavasciuga.net), which has several locations in Milan.

Lost & Found The lost-baggage number for **Malpensa** and **Linate** airports is ✆ **02-7485-2200.** The English-speaking staff at these offices handles luggage that has gone astray on most airlines serving the airports, though a few airlines maintain their own lost-baggage services. The **lost and found at Stazione Centrale** is open daily from 8am to 4pm.

Luggage Storage The luggage storage office in Stazione Centrale is on the ground floor near the ticket windows and is open daily from 6am to 11:50pm; the fee is 4€ per piece of baggage for the first 5 hours. It is an additional .60€ per hour for the next 7 hours and then an additional .20€ per hour after that.

Post Office The main post office, **Poste e Telecommunicazioni,** is just west of Piazza del Duomo at Via Cordusio 4 (✆ **02-7248-2126;** Metro: Cordusio). Windows are open Monday to Friday 8am to 7pm and Saturday 8:30am to 1:50pm. Most branch offices are open Monday to Saturday 8:30am to 1:30pm and some until 7pm. There is a post office in Stazione Centrale, open Monday through Friday 8am to 5:30pm and Saturday 8:15am to 3:30pm.

Taxis It is often difficult to flag down a taxi in Milan (though don't let that stop you from trying; if the light on the roof is on, it means the driver is free to pick up passengers), so your best bet is to go to the nearest taxi stand, usually located near major *piazze* and major Metro stops. There is a large taxi stand in Piazza del Duomo and another in Piazza della Scala. Or call a **radio taxi** at ✆ **02-4040,** 02-6767, 02-8585, 02-5353, or 02-8383 (the desk staff at many hotels will be happy to do this for you, even if you are not a guest). Cab meters start at 3.10€ and add a nighttime surcharge of 3.10€ and a Sunday surcharge of 1.55€. ***Note:*** When you call a taxi, the meter starts as soon as the car gets the call and sets off toward your pickup spot.

Telephones See "Fast Facts: Italy," p. 940. The area code for Milan is ✆ **02.**

Travel Services For budget travel options, including low-cost flights, contact **Zani Viaggi,** Foro

Bonaparte 76 near the castle (✆ **02-867-131**), open Monday through Friday from 9am to 7pm (Sat until 5pm). Students and those 25 and under should try **CTS (Centro Turistico Studentesco),** Corso di Porta Nuova 46 (✆ **02-2901-4553**), open Monday through Friday from 9am to 7pm and Saturday 10am to 1pm. This is the most centrally located CTS, but there are five others sprinkled around town, including one on Corso di Porta Ticinese 100 near the Navigli.

Exploring Milan

Basilica di San Lorenzo Maggiore ★ CHURCH The oldest church in Milan attests to the days when the city was the capital of the Western Roman Empire. This 4th-century, early-Christian structure has been rebuilt and altered many times over the centuries (its dome, the highest in Milan, is a 16th-c. embellishment and the facade is from the 19th c.), but it still retains the flavor of its roots in its octagonal floor plan and a few surviving remnants. These include 5th-century mosaics in the Cappella di Sant'Aquilino, which you enter from the atrium. You'll be rewarded with a glimpse of even earlier history if you follow the stairs from behind the altar to a cryptlike room that contains what remains of a Roman amphitheater.

In the piazza in front of the church you will find the **Columns of San Lorenzo ★★**, 16 monumental Corinthian columns that were part of a Roman temple that probably stood in what is now Piazza Santa Maria Beltrade near the top of Via Torino and were set up here in the 4th century when the San Lorenzo Maggiore was being built.

Corso di Porta Ticinese. www.sanlorenzomaggiore.com. ✆ **02-8940-4129.** Church: Free admission. Cappella di Sant'Aquilino: 2€ adults, 1€ children. Daily 7:30am–12:30pm and 2:30–6:30pm. Bus: 94. Metro: Missori. Tram: 3.

Basilica di Sant'Ambrogio ★★ CHURCH From the basilica that he constructed on this site in the 4th century A.D.—when he was bishop of Milan and the city, in turn, was briefly capital of the Western Roman Empire—Saint Ambrose had a profound effect on the development of the early church. Little remains of Ambrose's church, but the 11th-century structure built in its place, and renovated many times since, is remarkable. It has a striking atrium, lined with columned porticos and opening on the side to the brick facade, with two ranks of loggias and, on either side, a bell tower. This church set the standard for Lombard Romanesque architecture that you'll see imitated many times on your travels through Lombardy, and elsewhere as well; the imitation has continued

Milan on Two Wheels

The city began a bike-sharing program at the end of 2008 that, though directed at locals and commuters, is also a fun way for tourists to see more of the city. For 2.50€ a day and 6€ a week, you can buy a pass that gives you unlimited use of the bikes for 30-minute increments (then you pay .50€ for each half-hour after that, up to a maximum of 2 hr.). You pick up a bike in one of the many racks around town and leave it at another. Buy your pass online or at the **ATM offices** at the Centrale, Cadorna, Garibaldi, Duomo, Loreto, or Romolo Metro stops from 7:45am to 7:15pm (www.bikemi.com; ✆ **800-80-8181**).

through the centuries, including the University of California Los Angeles' Royce Hall built in the 1920s.

On your wanderings through the three-aisle nave you'll come upon a gold altar from Charlemagne's days in Milan, and, in the right aisle, the all-too-scant remains of a Tiepolo fresco cycle, most of it blown into oblivion by World War II bombs. The little that remains of the original church is the Sacello di San Vittore in Ciel d'Oro, a little chapel in which the cupola glows with 5th-century mosaics of saints (enter from the right aisle). The skeletal remains of Ambrose himself are on view in the crypt. As you leave the main church from the left aisle, you'll see another work of the great architect Bramante—his late-15th-century Portico della Canonica, lined with elegant columns, some of which are sculpted to resemble tree trunks.

Piazza Sant'Ambrogio 15. www.basilicasantambrogio.it. ✆ **02-8645-0895.** Church: Free admission. Sacello di San Vittore: 2€. Mon–Sat 10am–noon and 2:30–6pm; Sun 3–5pm. Bus: 50, 58, or 94. Metro: Sant'Ambrogio.

Castello Sforzesco ★★ CASTLE Though it's been clumsily restored many times, most recently at the end of the 19th century, this fortresslike castle continues to evoke Milan's two most powerful medieval and Renaissance families, the Visconti and the Sforza. The Visconti built the castle in the 14th century, and the Sforza, who married into the Visconti clan and eclipsed them in power, reconstructed it in 1450. The most influential residents were Ludovico il Moro and Beatrice d'Este (he of the Sforza and she of the famous Este family of Ferrara). After ill-advisedly calling the French into Italy at the end of the 15th century, Ludovico died in the dungeons of a château in the Loire valley—but not before the couple made the Castello and Milan one of Italy's great centers of the Renaissance. It was they who commissioned works by Bramante and Leonardo da Vinci, and these splendors can be viewed on a stroll through the miles of rooms that surround the Castello's enormous courtyards.

The rooms house a dozen city-administered museums known collectively as the Musei del Castello Sforzesco. They include a *pinacoteca* with works by Bellini, Correggio, and Magenta, and the extensive holdings of the Museo d'Arte Antica, filled with prehistoric finds from Lombardy, and the last work of 89-year-old Michelangelo, his unfinished ***Pietà Rondanini*** **★★**. There is also a small Egyptian museum (with the title being used a bit liberally by the city as there is really just one room).

Piazza Castello. ✆ **02-8846-3700.** Castle courtyards: Free admission. Daily 7am–6pm (summer until 7pm). Musei del Castello Sforzesco: Admission 6€ (there is some talk of reducing the entrance fee and cancelling the fee altogether for the *Pietà Rondanini*). Tues–Sun 9am–5:30pm. Metro: Cairoli, Cadorna, or Lanza.

Duomo ★★★ CATHEDRAL When Milanese think something is taking too long, they refer to it as *la fabbrica del duomo*—the making of the Duomo, a reference to the 6 centuries it took to complete the magnificent Gothic cathedral that rises from the center of the city (the final bronze door was put up only in 1960). The last of Italy's great Gothic structures—begun by the ruling Visconti family in 1386—the Duomo is one of the largest churches in the world (all agree that St. Peter's in Rome is the biggest, but after that there is some discussion, though it seems likely Milan's Duomo is in fifth place behind Seville's cathedral, Brazil's Basilica of the National Shrine of Our Lady of Aparecida, and New York's St. John the Divine). There are numerous flying buttresses, 135 marble spires, a stunning

Milan's Duomo.

triangular facade, and 2,000 statues adorning the massive but airy, almost fanciful exterior. Looking at the facade from directly in front of the Duomo can be overwhelming as you feel almost oppressed by the seemingly flat structure. To get a more telling perspective of both the facade and the entire church, view the Duomo from the far-end of the piazza where Via Mercanti starts. Another interesting perspective is from the courtyard in front of Palazzo Reale.

The cavernous **interior,** lit by brilliant stained-glass windows, seats 40,000 but is unusually spartan and serene, divided into five aisles by a sea of 52 columns. The poet Shelley used to sit and read Dante here amid monuments that include a gruesomely graphic statue of ***St. Bartholomew Flayed*** ★ and the tombs of Giacomo de Medici, two Visconti, and many cardinals and archbishops. Another British visitor, Alfred, Lord Tennyson, rhapsodized about the view of the Alps from the **roof** ★★★ (elevators on the church's exterior northeast corner; stairs on the exterior north side), where you get to wander amid the Gothic pinnacles, saintly statues, and flying buttresses. You are joined high above Milan by the spire-top gold statue of the *Madonnina* (the little Madonna), the city's beloved protectress.

Back on terra firma, the **crypt** contains the remains of San Carlo Borromeo, one of the early cardinals of Milan. A far more interesting descent is the one down the staircase to the right of the main entrance to the **Battistero Paleocristiano,** the ruins of a 4th-century baptistery believed to be where Saint Ambrose baptized Saint Augustine.

The Duomo houses many of its treasures across the piazza from the right transept in the ***Museo del Duomo***—closed for restoration in 2009 without a definite reopening date. Among the legions of statuary saints is a gem of a painting by Jacopo Tintoretto, *Christ at the Temple,* and some riveting displays chronicling the construction of the cathedral.

Though the scaffolding from its most recent restoration is down, visitors may still encounter some restoration work as the Duomo is always being touched

Temporary but Great

Milan gets many first-rate temporary exhibits on everything from contemporary Chinese art to retrospectives on Edward Hopper, the Impressionists, Caravaggio, and Canaletto. Most of these are held at the Palazzo Reale on the south side of Piazza Duomo. While hanging out in the piazza, mosey over to see if any of the exhibits suit your fancy, and if nothing else take a walk through the beautiful courtyard. Palazzo Reale, which dates back almost 1,000 years and housed first the city government in the Middle Ages and then various royals in the centuries that followed, suffered serious damage in an Allied bombardment in 1943 that partially destroyed the complex. Prices for the exhibits vary as do the opening hours, which are usually Monday 2:30 to 7:30pm and Tuesday through Sunday 9:30am to 7:30pm (Thurs and Sat until 10:30pm). For more information, call ✆ **02-8846-5236.**

up. The most recent restoration, completed in 2009, brought luster back to the church's white marble. Other restoration projects will continue on the sides and interior of the Duomo in a never-ending bid to keep the building looking its best.

Piazza del Duomo. ✆ **02-7202-2656.** Duomo: Free admission. Roof: 6€ by stairs, 10€ with elevator. Crypt: 2€. Baptistery: 4€. Museum: Before its closing, admission was 6€ adults, 3€ children 17 and under and seniors 65 and over. Duomo: Daily 8:30am–6:45pm. Roof: Daily 9am–5:45pm (Apr–Sept until 10pm). Crypt: Daily 9am–noon and 2:30–6pm. Baptistery: Tues–Sun 10am–noon and 3–5pm. Museum: Before its closing, Tues–Sun 9:30am–12:30pm and 3–6pm. Metro: Duomo.

Galleria Vittorio Emanuele II ★★★ ICON Milan's late-19th-century version of a mall is this wonderful steel-and-glass-covered, cross-shaped arcade. The elegant Galleria is the prototype of the enclosed shopping malls that were to become the hallmark of 20th-century consumerism. It's safe to say that none of the imitators have come close to matching the Galleria for style and flair. The designer of this urban marvel, Giuseppe Mengoni, didn't live to see the Milanese embrace his creation: He tripped and fell from a girder a few days before the Galleria opened in 1878. His shopping mall par excellence provides a lovely route between the Duomo and La Scala and is a fine locale for watching flocks of well-dressed Milanese—you'll understand why the Galleria is called *il salotto di Milano* (Milan's drawing room).

Just off Piazza del Duomo and Piazza della Scala. Metro: Duomo.

La Triennale di Milano Design Museum ★ MUSEUM Opened in 2007, this museum dedicated to design was long overdue for a city that has meant so much to the world of avant-garde chairs, couches, teapots, and lamps. There is a permanent collection (in name only as it is changed every year or two) dedicated to Italian industrial design that will interest even those convinced that a fork is a fork no matter how and by whom it is designed. There are also always temporary exhibits, sometimes as many as six on at the same time, which are usually dedicated to photography or some particular aspect of design such as the contribution of a particular country or person. To fuel up before or after a visit, there is a very pleasant cafe with a view onto Parco Sempione and an ever-changing selection of chairs that have made an impact on the design world through the ages.

Viale Alemagna 6. www.triennaledesignmuseum.it. ✆ **02-724-341.** Admission 8€ adults, 6.50€ students 25 and under and seniors 65 and over. Temporary exhibits range from free to 8€. Tues–Sun 10:30am–8:30pm (Thurs–Fri until 11pm). Bus: 61. Metro: Cadorna.

Museo del Novecento (Museum of 20th-Century Art) ★★ MUSEUM Milan's newest museum, which opened in late 2010, is proof that Italy's contribution to art did not stop in the 17th century and is worth a visit even for those who find 20th-century abstract paintings too much trouble to try to understand. You'll find a few pieces by some of the international greats, including Picasso and Kandinsky, but the focus here is on Italian artists and their effect on the artistic movements of the last century. Most interesting is futurism and the work of Umberto Boccioni, who dominates the first rooms. The futurists' manifesto said, "everything is in movement, everything runs, everything passes quickly" and nowhere is that philosophy more evident than in Boccioni's *Elasticity* and his sculpture *Unique Forms of Continuity in Space,* a preview of which you can get on the back of the Italian .20€ coin. There is a room farther along dedicated to De Chirico, but in general the museum peters out as you move up to the higher floors. From the top floor you get a commanding view of the Duomo and the piazza, and you can pull up a chair and enjoy a free hour of Wi-Fi if you have a smartphone or computer in tow. Watching the hundreds of people scurrying about in the piazza might be all you need to be sold on the futurist manifesto.

Tip: The undisputed star of the museum's collection is Giuseppe Pellizza da Volpedo's *The Fourth Estate,* which you can see for free. If you don't want to visit the rest of the museum, at least come for this massive homage to striking workers. When you enter the main door of the museum, rather than buy a ticket at the desk on the right, head straight up the circular staircase on the left and after a few curves you get to Volpedo's masterpiece, which was not well-received when unveiled 1901, but later became a symbol of oppressed workers around the world. Farther up the ramp is the entrance to the museum's collections.

Piazza Duomo 12 (*palazzo* dell'Argenario). www.museodelnovecento.org. ✆ **02-7634-0809.** Admission 5€ adults, 3€ students and seniors 65 and over, free for everybody Fri after 3:30pm. Tues–Sun 9:30am–7:30pm (Thurs and Sat until 10:30pm); Mon 2:30–7:30pm. Metro: Duomo.

Museo Nazionale della Scienza e della Tecnologia Leonardo da Vinci (Leonardo da Vinci National Museum of Science and Technology) ★ ☺ MUSEUM The heart and soul of this engaging museum are the **working scale models ★★** of Leonardo's submarines, airplanes, and other engineering feats that, for the most part, the master only ever invented on paper (each exhibit includes a reproduction of his drawings and a model of his creations). This former Benedictine monastery and its beautiful cloisters are also filled with planes, trains, carriages, sewing machines, typewriters, optical devices, and other exhibits, including some enchanting re-creations of workshops, all of which makes up one of the world's leading mechanical and scientific collections.

Via San Vittore 21. www.museoscienza.org. ✆ **02-485-551.** Admission 10€ adults, 7€ 25 and under and adults (up to 2 per group) accompanied by at least 2 children 14 and under, 4€ 65 and older. Tues–Sun 10am–5:30pm (Sat–Sun until 7pm). Metro: Sant'Ambrogio.

Pinacoteca Ambrosiana ★★ MUSEUM This exquisite collection focuses on treasures from the 15th through 17th centuries: An *Adoration* by Titian, Raphael's cartoon for his *School of Athens* in the Vatican, Botticelli's *Madonna and Angels,* Caravaggio's *Basket of Fruit* (his only still life), and other stunning works hang in a series of intimate rooms. Notable (or infamous) among the paintings is *Portrait of a Musician,* attributed to Leonardo but, according to many scholars, of dubious provenance; if it is indeed a Leonardo, it would be the only portrait of his to hang in an Italian museum. The adjoining Biblioteca Ambrosiana—open (except for special exhibitions) only to scholars—houses a wealth of Renaissance literaria, including the letters of Lucrezia Borgia and a strand of her hair. The most notable holdings, though, are Leonardo's *Codice Atlantico,* 1,750 drawings and jottings the master did between 1478 and 1519. These and the library's other volumes, including a rich collection of medieval manuscripts, are frequently put on view to the public; at these times, a fee of 10€ allows entrance to both the library and the art gallery.

Piazza Pio XI 2. www.ambrosiana.eu. ✆ **02-806-921.** Admission 8€ adults, 5€ children. Tues–Sun 10am–6pm. Metro: Cordusio or Duomo.

Pinacoteca di Brera ★★★ MUSEUM This 17th-century *palazzo* houses one of Italy's best collections of medieval and Renaissance art; and with its works spanning 6 centuries, it's inarguably the world's finest assembly of northern Italian painting. The concentration of so many masterpieces here is the work of Napoleon, who used the *palazzo* as the repository for the art he confiscated from public and private holdings throughout northern Italy; fittingly, a bronze likeness of the emperor greets you upon entering the courtyard. Upon entering the museum, be sure to look through the large glass door to the left that affords a wide open view of a room in the incredible Biblioteca Nazionale Braidense, one of Italy's largest public libraries. If you want to see more of this library, which looks like it belongs in a medieval monastery, before heading up the stairs to the museum, keep walking straight down a corridor until you see a staircase on the left that goes to the library (the librarians will usually let you have a look around even if you are not there to check out a book).

Three of Italy's greatest masterpieces hang in the Pinacoteca di Brera: Andrea Mantegna's amazingly foreshortened ***Dead Christ*** **★★★**, Raphael's ***Betrothal of the Virgin*** **★★★**, and Piero della Francesca's ***Madonna with Saints*** **★★** (the *Montefeltro Altarpiece*). It is an indication of this museum's ability to overwhelm visitors that the last two absolute masterpieces hang near each other in a room dedicated to works by Tuscan and Umbrian painters. Other pieces not to miss include Jacopo Tintoretto's ***Finding of the Body of St.***

A Last-Minute Invitation to *The Last Supper*

The Last Supper is seemingly on every tourist's itinerary of Milan, as well it should be. And with only 25 people allowed in at a time, not surprisingly it can be difficult to get a ticket if you don't book well in advance. If you can't get a reservation, in a pinch you can take an Autostradale (www.autostradale.it; ✆ **02-3391-0794**) guided 3-hour bus and walking tour of Milan's top attractions that guarantees admission to *The Last Supper* as part of the package. The tours cost 55€ and leave at 9:30am every day except Monday (also Wed 1pm and Fri–Sat 2:15pm) from near the taxi stand in Piazza Duomo. **Zani Viaggi** (www.zaniviaggi.it; ✆ **02-867-131**) has a similar tour with guaranteed admission to *The Last Supper* that costs 60€ and leaves from Foro Buonaparte in front of the castle Tuesday to Sunday at 9:30am and 2:30pm.

Mark* ★**, in which the dead saint eerily confronts appropriately startled grave robbers who come upon his corpse; Caravaggio's ***Supper at Emmaus* ★★**; and Francesco Hayez's ***The Kiss* ★★★**, probably Italy's most famous 19th-century painting, which, surprisingly enough, depicts a young couple kissing, though it actually represents the alliance between France (the woman dressed in blue) and Italy (the man in the red, white, and green of the Italian flag) that defeated the Austrians who at the time occupied a large swath of northern Italy. The final rooms include a few works by Canaletto, including his *View of the Grand Canal,* and several late-19th-century paintings by Giovanni Segantini. Before exiting into the gift shop you are met by the enormous ***Fiumana, Giuseppe Pellizza da Volpedo's preparatory work for his masterpiece *The Fourth Estate,* which hangs in the Museo del Novecento (p. 573).

Via Brera 28. www.brera.beniculturali.it. ✆ **02-7226-3264.** Admission 9€; 6.50€ E.U. citizens 18–25; free for E.U. citizens 17 and under and 65 and over; free after 7pm on the last Tues of every month when the museum closes at 11pm (this praxis has been renewed the last few years, but it is not a given it will continue). Tues–Sun 8:30am–7:15pm. Metro: Lanza or Montenapoleone. Tram: 1, 4, 8, 12, 14, or 27.

Santa Maria delle Grazie/*The Last Supper* ★★★ ICON The *Cenacolo Vinciano,* Leonardo da Vinci's *The Last Supper,* is perhaps Milan's biggest draw and one of the most famous pieces of art in the world. From 1495 to 1497, Leonardo painted this poignant portrayal of confusion and betrayal on the far wall of the refectory when this was a Dominican convent. Aldous Huxley called this fresco the "saddest work of art in the world," a comment in part on the deterioration that set in even before the paint had dried on the moisture-ridden walls. (It probably didn't help that the monks cooked their meals here.) The fresco got a lot of well-intentioned but poorly executed "touching up" in the 18th and 19th centuries, though a lengthy restoration completed in 1999 has done away with these centuries of overpainting, as well as tried to undo the damage wrought by the clumsy patching and damage inflicted when Napoleon's troops used the wall for target practice, and from when Allied bombing during World War II tore off the room's roof, leaving the fresco relatively untouched, but exposed to the elements for 3 years.

In short, *The Last Supper* is a mere shadow of the work the artist intended it to be, but the work, which captures the moment when Christ told his Apostles that one of them would betray him, remains amazingly powerful and evocative. Only 25 people are allowed to view the fresco at one time, and they must pass through a series of devices that remove pollutants from clothing. Accordingly, lines are long and tickets usually sell out days, if not weeks (and sometimes months), in advance so reserve early either online or over the phone (see below).

Often overlooked are the other treasures of the late-15th-century church itself, foremost among them the fine dome and other architectural innovations by one of the great architects of

***The Last Supper* by Leonardo da Vinci.**

the High Renaissance, Donato Bramante (one of the first architects of St. Peter's in Rome). To one side of the apse, decorated in marble and terra cotta, is a lovely cloister.

Piazza Santa Maria delle Grazie. *The Last Supper:* www.cenacolovinciano.org. ✆ **02-9280-0360.** Admission 6.50€ plus a booking fee of 1.50€; 3.25€ plus 1.50€ booking fee for E.U. citizens 18 to 25; E.U. citizens 17 and under and 65 and over pay only the booking fee. Tues–Sun 8:15am–6:30pm. Church: ✆ **02-467-6111.** Free admission. Mon–Sat 7:30am–noon and 3–7pm; Sun 7:20am–12:15pm and 3:30–9pm (may close earlier in winter). Metro: Cadorna or Conciliazione.

Where to Eat

Like all self-respecting Italians, the Milanese love their long, drawn-out sit-down meal, but this is also the financial capital with several large universities so in addition to the exceptional world-class dining options, you'll find many pizzerias and other low-cost eateries where you can grab a sandwich or other light fare on the run.

Tip: From late spring to late summer, Milan is home to legions of mosquitoes, particularly around the canals. Dusk is when they come to feed and unless you have something in your blood that keeps them away, make sure your dinner or *aperitivo all'aperto* in the Ticinese/Navigli neighborhood is accompanied by the proper precautions (bug spray or clothing that leaves no exposed skin).

VERY EXPENSIVE

Joia ★★ VEGETARIAN Some will no doubt welcome the respite from northern Italy's often heavy cuisine offered by Joia, which in 1996 became Europe's first vegetarian restaurant to be awarded a Michelin star. The refined atmosphere, created by the use of blond-wood and neutral tones, is the perfect setting for the innovative vegetarian creations of Swiss chef Pietro Leemann, a star in his profession. He uses only organic products and everything is always incredibly fresh, which you'd have to expect at these prices. The menu changes with the seasons and dishes come and go so a return visit always offers surprises. *Primi,* such as au gratin green ravioli filled with a mix of chickpeas and celery and served over a bed of string beans, can be ordered as a main course. There's an abundant assortment of cheeses and, as befits a place with a Michelin star, an impressive wine list.

Via P. Castaldi 18 (near Porta Venezia). www.joia.it. ✆ **02-2952-2124.** Reservations highly recommended. Main courses 30€; tasting menu 65€–80€. AE, DC, MC, V. Mon–Fri noon–2:30pm and 7:30–11:30pm. Closed Aug. Metro: Repubblica or Porta Venezia.

EXPENSIVE

Trattoria Milanese ★★★ MILANESE Giuseppe and Antonella Villa preside with a watchful eye over the centuries-old premises (a restaurant since 1933), tucked into a narrow lane in one of the oldest sections of Milan, just west of the Duomo. In the three-beamed dining room, Milanese families and other patrons share the long, crowded tables. Giuseppe, in the kitchen, prepares what many patrons consider to be some of the city's best traditional fare. The *risotto alla Milanese,* with saffron and beef marrow, is unforgettable, as is the minestrone that's served hot in the winter and at room temperature in the summer. The *costoletta alla Milanese,* breaded and fried in butter, is made with the choicest veal chops and is served with the bone. Polenta with rich Gorgonzola cheese is one of the few nonmeat second courses.

A TASTE OF bitter LOVE

For some people, the allure is the signature salt shaker–shaped, neon red bottle, often neatly lined up on windowsills in restaurants and bars. Others know it for its placement in vintage Art Deco posters. For many people, it's simply a bitter alcoholic concoction that tastes like cough medicine. But for many Milanese, it's the reward at the end of a hard day at work and the beginning of a night on the town.

Love it or hate it, **Campari** is the soul of Milan and is at the heart of all its signature cocktails. Campari is a bitter alcoholic drink that was invented in 1860 in Novara, a city in the Piedmont region. Today, Campari is manufactured in Piedmont at the home of its sweeter friend, Cinzano. (The vermouth company was purchased by Campari Group in the 1990s. The group is now headquartered just outside Milan in Sesto San Giovanni, though all the drinks are manufactured near Turin.)

Together, Campari, vermouth, and a splash of seltzer make up the ***americano,*** a drink that is usually served in street-side cafes with an orange slice on its rim. Its cousin, the ***negroni,*** skips the seltzer in favor of gin and is also usually served with orange garnishes though the fruit is often dropped at swankier night spots as the night goes on. A ***negroni sbagliato*** uses sparkling wine, often prosecco, instead of gin. A ***Campari orange,*** half Campari and half OJ, is a less-alcoholic option that will help you keep coherent later into the night.

What gives Campari its unique bitter and tangy essence? Local lore says that the secret blend of herbs is guarded by the manufacturing director and one other undisclosed custodian. One thing that is known, and frankly should have remained a secret, is the ingredient behind its almost fluorescent red hue: the squashed skeletons of South American insects. *Negroni*, anyone?

Via Santa Marta 11 (near Via Torino). ✆ **02-8645-1991.** Reservations required. Main courses 16€–25€. AE, DC, MC, V. Wed–Mon noon–3pm and 7–11:30pm. Metro: Cordusio.

MODERATE

Acquasala ★★★ 👪 PUGLIESE Southern Puglia in the far southeastern corner of Italy, in the heel of the boot, is home to a wonderful coastline, beautiful baroque buildings, and most importantly, mouthwatering food. Acquasala has brought one of that winning troika to the outer reaches of the string of bars and restaurants on the Naviglio Grande. In a break from the heavier Milanese food, here you'll find dishes that are lighter in everything but taste, including *orecchiette con cima di rape* (small ear-shaped pasta topped with rape) and *orecchiette con pomodorini freschi, rucola, e caciorìcotta* (with fresh tomatoes, arugula, and aged ricotta). The service is friendly and they start you off with some bruschetta and salami on the house. When they bring the paper bag, don't bring that home, it's filled with Pugliese bread and *taralli*, an addictive twisted cracker that's a local specialty.

Ripa di Porta Ticinese 71 (on Naviglio Grande). ✆ **02-8942-3983.** Reservations recommended. Main courses 9€–15€. Tues–Sun 12:30–2:30pm and 7:30–11:30pm. AE, MC, V. Metro: Porta Genova. Tram: 2.

Da Claudio ★★ RAW BAR One of Milan's idiosyncrasies is that it is a landlocked city, yet it has the freshest fish in the country. There is an explanation: The best catch is trucked up here from the shore every night to chase those bankers' euros. A fun place to enjoy Milan's maritime bounty without dispensing a fortune is at this Brera fish market, which becomes a popular raw bar at night. Almost everyone goes for the mixed plate, which includes some combination of raw tuna, sea bass, salmon, red snapper, sturgeon, shrimp, prawns, and cod. Order a plate and enjoy it while sitting on one of the bar stools next to young professionals who have just gotten off work. All plates come with a complimentary glass of prosecco and another dozen wines can be sampled by the glass (the Falanghina marries perfectly with the raw fish).

Via Cusani 1 (near castle). www.pescheriadaclaudio.it. ✆ **02-80-56-857.** Reservations not accepted. Mixed raw plate 11€–14€; 3 oysters 10€. AE, MC, V. Mon–Sat 11am–9:30pm (Mon until 8pm). Metro: Lanza or Cordusio.

Dongiò ★★ SOUTHERN ITALIAN The red-hot chili pepper is native to the Americas, but few places in the world have learned to work with the plant better than the Calabrians in the toe of the Italian boot; and few restaurants besides Dongiò have brought such wonderful Calabrian cuisine to northern Italy. All the pasta is made in-house and is coupled with Calabrian specialties, including sausage, sweet Tropea onions, pancetta, aged ricotta, and *n'duja,* a spicy, spreadable salami. For a mouthwatering taste of how these ingredients can be meshed into a *primo* approaching perfection, try the *spaghettoni alla Tamarro,* thick spaghetti topped with a red sauce that includes *n'duja* and a dash of the aged ricotta that has been worked into a cream. *N'duja* makes it onto the antipasto menu, and if you still haven't had enough of this most signature of Calabrian specialties, for your *secondo* you can get a large slice of grilled *Caciocavallo Silano* cheese filled with *n'duja.*

Via Bernardino Corio 3 (near Porta Romana). ✆ **02-551-1372.** Reservations highly recommended. Main courses 10€–18€. MC, V. Mon–Fri 12:30–3pm and 7:30–11pm; Sat 7:30–11pm. Metro: Porta Romana.

Peck ★★ ITALIAN Milan's most famous food emporium offers a wonderful selection of roast veal, risottos, *porchetta,* salads, cheeses, pastries, and other fare from its exquisite larder in this cafe upstairs from its **shop ★★★**, which is itself worth a visit. If you want the experience of consuming Peck food on the premises while keeping costs to a minimum, the cafe has sandwiches for 8.50€.

Via Spadari 9 (near Duomo). www.peck.it. ✆ **02-802-3161.** Reservations not accepted. Main courses 15€. AE, DC, MC, V. Mon–Sat 9:15am–7:30pm. Closed Jan 1–10 and July 1–20. Metro: Duomo.

Pizza Galore

In addition to Pizzeria Naturale, there are many other options for a terrific pizza that you will be talking about long after you've finished that last wedge. If you can accept a long wait (sometimes even if you have a reservation) and dodgy service, then **Da Maruzzella** (✆ **02-2952-5729**) at Piazza Oberdan 3, at the beginning of Corso Buenos Aires, is *the* spot for excellent pizza. **I Capatosta** (✆ **02-8941-5910**), on the Naviglio Grande at Alzaia Naviglio Grande 56 (not far from Pizzeria Naturale), also makes outstanding pizza (the Neapolitan variety with a slightly chewier crust that comes up higher on the edges). Two more options, **Fratelli la Bufala** and **Rossopomodoro,** are mentioned under "Pubs & Bars," below.

Pizzeria Naturale ★★ ☺ ITALIAN/PIZZA There are many good places in Milan to get a pizza (see "Pizza Galore," above), but this one combines a good location with a great space and efficient service. Some of the products used are organic (including the beers). The restaurant is located in a large open space flooded with light and decorated with tall columns of wine bottles. There is also seating out front and on a large terrace in the back. The pizzeria is located on the Naviglio Grande at the far end of the area where all the bars and restaurants are. There is **another Pizzeria Naturale**—the pizza is just as good, but the space much tighter and slightly less appealing—at Via De Amicis 24, about halfway between the canals and the Duomo.

Via Ripa di Porta Ticinese 79 (on Naviglio Grande). ✆ **02-8942-0299.** Reservations recommended Fri–Sat. Pizza 5€–12€. MC, V. Daily noon–3pm and 6–11pm. Metro: Porta Genova. Tram: 2.

INEXPENSIVE

Kiosk ★★ SEAFOOD This stand on Piazza XXIV Maggio offers wonderfully tasty fried fish that isn't greasy and won't make your stomach churn as you walk the nearby canals. You point, the guy weighs, you pay, and then you dig in either standing while watching the traffic, sitting at one of the few tables set up on the side of the stand, or, and this is the best option, you take your loot across the street where you eat while staring at the *darsena* (a bustling port until the 1960s). The fish on offer usually includes calamari (rings and tentacles are separated, convenient for those grossed out by the latter), shrimp, crab, and cod. There's also a bit of grilled fish available. The fresh fish on sale at the same stand will put to rest any questions you have regarding the quality of what you're eating.

Piazza XXIV Maggio (on the southwest side of the square close to the beginning of the Naviglio Pavese). ✆ **02-8940-2224.** Reservations not accepted. Main courses 5€–10€. Tues–Sat noon–7:30pm (summer Thurs–Sat until midnight, Sun until 9pm). Tram: 3 or 9.

Luini Panzerotti ★★ LIGHT FARE At this stand-up counter near the Galleria, a Milan institution since 1949, you'll find an ever-present line populated by a throng of well-dressed patrons all purchasing the house specialty: *panzerotto,* a pocket of pizza crust stuffed with all sorts of ingredients, including the basic cheese-and-tomato, that is either fried or baked. While your good sense may direct you toward the latter, the fried variety is the real deal and there really is no comparison.

Via Santa Radegonda 16 (near Duomo). www.luini.it. ✆ **02-8646-1917.** Reservations not accepted. Panzerotto 2.30€–2.50€. No credit cards. Mon 10am–5pm; Tues–Sat 10am–8pm. Closed Aug. Metro: Duomo.

Piadineria Carletto ★★ ITALIAN This small place right on busy Piazza XXIV Maggio, with no tables and only a few bar stools where you can sit, makes what are most probably Milan's best *piadine,* thin tortilla-like pieces of bread that get folded over and filled with anything you might find in a sandwich. The *piadina,* the actual bread, is made in front of you, standard practice in the Romagna region of central Italy from where the *piadina* hails, but all but impossible to find in Milan. The very friendly owners, Alessandro and his American wife, Laurie, are here on the weekends at lunch and can advise which of the many choices is right for you. The classic is *squacquerone* (a delicious, fresh creamy cheese) with arugula, but some of the inventive combinations are also terrific, such as one with sausage, *squacquerone,* and porcini mushrooms. Like the Italian panino, these are not drowned in sauce.

Piazza XXIV Maggio 1/10 (on the northeast side of the square just down the street from McDonald's). ✆ **02-8977-2938.** Reservations not accepted. *Piadina* 4€–8€. Mon–Fri noon–1am; Sat noon–2am; Sun 1–11pm. Tram: 3 or 9.

CAFES & GELATO

Bar Zucca/Caffè Miani, at the Duomo end of the Galleria Vittorio Emanuele II (www.caffemiani.it; ✆ **02-8646-4435;** Metro: Duomo), is a Milan institution that is said to have been a favorite watering hole of Giuseppe Verdi and Arturo Toscanini following performances at La Scala. While Milan does not have the same tradition of wonderful old cafes that you find seemingly on every street in the center of Turin, Bar Zucca, with its more than 140 years of history, does Milan proud. It was here that Campari (p. 577) was introduced to the world and it is here that you should find time to have a Campari drink while lingering at the tables in the Galleria or in one of the Art Nouveau rooms inside. After ponying up for the drink here, you can head out to cheaper haunts to continue your evening (see "Pubs & Bars," below).

For gelato, perhaps the best in the city can be found at **Grom,** Via Santa Margherita 16 (www.grom.it; ✆ **02-8058-1041**), right by La Scala; Corso di Porta Ticinese 51, near the San Lorenzo church; Corso Buenos Aires 13, perfectly placed for a break from your shopping spree; Corso XXII Marzo 5, a few steps from the Coin department store (see "Housewares," p. 584); and Via A. da Giussano 1, just off the line of stores on Corso Vercelli. Even the most ardent opponent of chain stores (Grom is selling its *fragola, nocciola,* and *cioccolato* all over Italy as well as in New York, Malibu, Paris, Tokyo, and Osaka) will be hard-pressed not to admit that Grom is the exception to the rule that teaches us to steer clear of standardization. If there is better gelato somewhere, please do let me know. The lines are often out the door, literally, and the price is slightly higher than most other gelato shops, but as you dig in it will become abundantly clear why. Look out for the flavor of the month, which is almost always worth a try.

Strollers in the atmospheric Brera neighborhood will want to make sure they pass by **Gelateria Toldo,** Via Ponte Vetero 9 (✆ **02-8646-0863;** Metro: Cordusio or Lanza), where the gelato is wonderfully creamy and many of the *sorbetto* selections are so fruity and fresh, they seem healthy. Going north on Via Ponte Vetero you get to Corso Garibaldi, one of the nicest streets in Milan to stroll, where at no. 55 you will find some more mouthwatering gelato at **Gelateria Garibaldi Créme,** run by a husband-and-wife team (he makes the gelato in the back and she mans the scooper), as well as surprisingly tasty soya-based sorbets, especially the cinnamon.

The **Pasticceria Confetteria Cova,** Via Montenapoleone 8 (✆ **02-600-0578;** Metro: Montenapoleone), is nearing its 200th year in refined surroundings near the similarly atmospheric Museo Poldi-Pezzoli. It's usually filled with shoppers making the rounds in this high-fashion district. You can enjoy a quick coffee and a brioche standing at the long bar, or take a seat in one of the elegant adjoining rooms as you dig into one of their many sweets. You can also buy goodies to bring home.

The **Pasticceria Marchesi,** Via Santa Maria alla Porta 13 (✆ **02-862-770;** Metro: Cordusio), is a historic pastry shop with an adjoining tearoom dating back to the first half of the 19th century. Because it's not far from Santa Maria delle Grazie, you can enjoy the old-world ambience and a cup of coffee (or one of the many teas and herbal infusions) as you dash off postcards of *The Last*

Supper. You'll want to accompany your beverage with elegant pastries, perhaps a slice of the *panettone* (cake with raisins and candied citron) that's a hallmark of Milan. No one prepares it better than Marchesi. If your budget is tight, it's still worth coming here for a coffee or cappuccino standing at the bar.

Shopping

The best fashion gazing is to be done along four adjoining streets north of the Duomo known collectively as the **Quadrilatero d'Oro (Golden Quadrilateral): Via Montenapoleone, Della Spiga, Via Borgospesso,** and **Via Sant'Andrea,** lined with Milan's most expensive high-fashion emporia. From Piazza della Scala, follow Via Manzoni a few blocks north or take the Metro to Via Montenapoleone. The main artery of this shopping heartland is Via Montenapoleone, lined with the most chichi boutiques and most elegant fashion outlets, with parallel Via della Spiga (the nicer of the two to walk down as it is closed to traffic) running a close second.

For more Milanese shopping, the less economically crippling type, cruise bustling **Corso Buenos Aires** (northeast of the center and just east of Stazione Centrale), home to a little bit of everything, from shops that hand-sew men's dress shirts to CD megastores. As it crosses Piazza Oberdan/Piazza Venezia heading south, it becomes Corso Venezia and the stores move up the scale very quickly. **Corso Vercelli** between the Wagner and Conciliazione Metro stops is another popular shopping street.

HIGH FASHION: CLOTHING, ACCESSORIES & SHOES

Milan is home to the flagship stores of a litany of designers: Armani, Prada, Krizia, Versace, Ermenegildo Zegna, Missoni, Moschino, Mila Schön, and Trussardi.

While high fashion, chillingly expensive boutiques, and designer labels all come down to personal taste, one store deserves a visit whether you're into his über-trendy designs or not: The Grand Central of Italian fashion is the flagship **Armani Megastore,** Via Manzoni 31, at the west end of Via Montenapoleone (✆ **02-7231-8600;** Metro: Montenapoleone). This flagship store (and offices) covers close to 1,000 sq. m (11,000 sq. ft.) and sells everything Giorgio Armani—high-fashion creations, Emporio Armani, Armani Jeans, the Armani Casa selection of home furnishings, and sparkling iPhone and iPad covers—and also houses flower, book, and art shops as well as a high-tech Sony electronics boutique/play center in the basement, an Emporio Café, and a branch of New York's Nobu sushi bar. The Armani Hotel, built on the top floors, opened in late 2011.

Milan is a shopper's paradise.

Of course, other major labels also have Milan addresses, most of which you will find on and around Via Montenapoleone.

Prada.

DESIGNER DISCOUNTS

If your fashion sense is greater than your credit line, don't despair: Even the most expensive clothing of the Armani ilk is usually less expensive in Italy than it is abroad, and citywide *saldi* (sales) run from early January into early February and again in late June and July.

Inspired by the window displays in the **Quadrilatero,** you can scour the racks of shops elsewhere for designer seconds, last year's fashions, imitations, and other bargains. The best place to begin is **Il Salvagente,** off Corso XXII Marzo at Via Fratelli Bronzetti 16 (✆ **02-7611-0328;** bus: 60 or 73, tram: 12 or 27), where you can browse through an enormous collection of designer clothing for men, women, and children (mostly smaller sizes) at wholesale prices. **DMagazine,** Via Montenapoleone 26 (✆ **02-7600-6027;** Metro: Montenapoleone), may sit on the boutique-lined main shopping drag, but its merchandise is pure discount overstock from big labels such as Armani, Prada, and Fendi.

Another haven for fashionistas looking for slightly eccentric designer clothes on a budget is the **Ticinese/Navigli** neighborhood. Women can shop at **Anna Fabiano,** on Corso di Porta Ticinese 40 (✆ **02-5811-2348** or 5830-6111; Metro: Sant'Ambrogio). Fabiano, who learned her tricks while designing for Fiorucci, favors linear cuts and mixing different types of fabrics to create an original style with a 1960s feel. Another Navigli stop is **Mauro Leone,** on Corso di Porta Ticinese 60 and 103 (www.mauroleone.com; ✆ **02-8942-9167**), where you will find all types of well-priced, Italian-made women's shoes. **Biffi,** on Corso Genova 5/6 (www.biffi.com; ✆ **02-831-1601;** bus: 94, Metro: Sant'Ambrogio), attracts fashion-conscious hordes of both sexes in search of designer labels and the store's own designs.

Some of the best Milanese fashion deals can be found in stores that are tucked into some of the less trodden and more atmospheric medieval alleys of the city center. On one of those streets, you will find **Donatella Pellini,** at Via Morigi 9 (✆ **02-7201-0199**), selling her own line of beautiful costume jewelry that looks like the real deal. In the Morigi shop, she sells her romantic and minimalist creations made with glass and synthetic resin; for more flamboyant costume jewelry, visit Pellini's shops on Via Manzoni 20 (✆ **02-7600-8084**) and on Corso Magenta 11 (✆ **02-7201-0569**).

MILAN IN style

Everyone knows Milan to be a fashion hub, with visitors flocking to Armani superstores and Dolce & Gabbana boutiques while ticking off the **fashion shows** (www.cameramoda.it) on their calendars: late September and late February for women's apparel, January and June for men's apparel.

What many foreigners forget, though, is that Milan does not just draw the line at clothing. It also dreams up some of the sexiest cars, couches, and kitchenware that Italy has to offer.

You'll know that **Alfa Romeo,** while built in Turin, is designed in Milan by just taking a look at the logo: It sports the city's red cross on the left, taken from its Crusaders' tunics, and the serpent favored by the ruling Visconti family on the right. The names of Alfa's models should also give some indication of which city rules the roost: the Milano, the Visconti, the Monza, and so forth. (Chevrolet and GM would later borrow some of these model names, though unfortunately not the designs themselves.)

For just about any other type of household mechanical device, if it looks good, chances are it was also designed in Lombardy or Piedmont. For example, **Pininfarina, Alessi,** and the **Memphis Group** are all in Turin, Milan, or somewhere in between.

Alessi, founded on the shores of Lake Orta, counted within its stable of architects such leading lights as Philippe Starck and Ettore Sottsass. But in 1980, the latter went on to form the Memphis Group, poaching some of the other top talent from his former employer as well. The event that launched the start-up group to fame was the 1981 edition of the Salone del Mobile, an annual furniture design show that draws industry leaders and tourists from around the globe.

The **Salone del Mobile** (www.cosmit.it) is nothing like what a casual customer would expect out of a furniture show. Held in mid-April, it features a lot more than just the latest designs in kitchens, living rooms, bathrooms, and lighting fixtures. It is essentially a contemporary art museum, complete with installation art and spectacles that fascinate even the least design-conscious observer. Most of all, it is the top excuse for Milan to throw parties that regular people actually have a chance of attending.

If you're not here in April, not to worry—the latest models tend to make their way into galleries and design stores around the city right away, making for a nice, city-wide tour of the latest living-room curves. Start off at **Galleria Post Design,** Via della Moscova 27 (www.memphis-milano.it; ✆ **02-655-4731**), which is the flagship store of the Memphis movement. Admire a multicolored bookshelf that could double as contemporary sculpture, and an assortment of rugs, lamps, and more. Even more avant-garde is **Dilmos,** Piazza San Marco 1 (www.dilmos.com; ✆ **02-2900-2437**) which almost crosses the line as a museum space rather than a retail store.

If, on the other hand, you're just looking to pick up a sleek, spider-shaped juicer or a stainless-steel toothpick holder, check out the flagship **Alessi** store, Via Manzoni 14/16 (www.alessi.com; ✆ **02-795-726**). If you happen to be driving around Lake Maggiore (or you're staying at Stresa and it's raining), it might be worth stopping in for a few bargains at Alessi's **factory outlet** in Crusinallo, Via Privata Alessi (✆ **0323-868-611**). Your kitchen counter will thank you.

If you are fond of colors and not afraid to wear them, visit the two tiny **Gallo** shops on Via Manzoni 16/b (✆ **02-783-602**) and Via Durini 26 (✆ **02-7600-2023**), where you'll find their signature multicolored striped socks, along with multicolored scarves, gloves, and T-shirts. The socks won't seem cheap compared with what you buy at Target, but a pair will give you an affordable piece of Milan fashion to bring home—even if you couldn't afford that Armani suit or Prada bag you had your eye on.

For designer shoes at a discount to go with the new socks, there is **Rufus,** Via Vitruvio 35 (✆ **02-204-9648;** Metro: Centrale or Lima), which carries men's and women's styles from lots of labels for under 100€.

HOUSEWARES

The top name in Italian houseware design since 1921 has been **Alessi,** which has hired the likes of Michael Graves, Philippe Starck, Frank Ghery, and Ettore Sottsass to design the latest in teakettles, bottle openers, and other housewares since the late 1980s. They maintain a main showroom at Corso Matteotti 9 (✆ **02-795-726;** Metro: San Babila) and a sales outlet at Via Montenapoleone 19 (www.alessi.com; ✆ **02-7602-1199;** Metro: Montenapoleone). You can also pick up Alessi stuff at the **Rinascente** department store next to the Duomo (✆ **02-88-521;** Metro: Duomo), Milan's less-over-the-top response to London's Harrods, or at **Coin,** a slightly lower-end department store at Piazza Cinque Giornate (✆ **02-5519-2083**).

The 1980s saw a renaissance of Italian industrial design when design team **Memphis,** led by Ettore Sottsass, virtually reinvented the art form, recruiting the best and brightest architects and designers to turn their talents to lighting fixtures, kitchen appliances, office supplies, even furnishings. Italian style has stayed at the very top of the designer housewares market (along with Scandinavian furniture) ever since. Part of the Memphis credo was to create the new modern and then bow out before it became establishment (the team self-destructed in 1988). You can still find their influential designs in many houseware shops and in the

The interior of La Scala.

showroom **Post Design,** at Via della Moscova 27 (✆ **02-655-4731;** Metro: Turati or Moscova).

Entertainment & Nightlife

On Wednesday and Thursday, Milan's newspapers tend to devote a lot of ink to club schedules and cultural events. If you don't trust your command of Italian to plan your nightlife, check out the tourist office in Piazza Castello—there are usually piles of fliers lying about that announce upcoming events. The tourist office also keeps visitors up-to-date with ***Milano Mese,*** a periodical it distributes for free with schedules of events, as well as listings of bars, clubs, and restaurants.

THE PERFORMING ARTS On the other side of the Galleria from the Duomo is Italy's premier opera house, **Teatro Alla Scala ★★**, Piazza Scala (✆ **02-887-91**), known to everyone as "La Scala." The calendar of events and online ticket office can be found at **www.teatroallascala.org**. Tickets go on sale about 3 months before a performance and sell out quickly for popular performances. Tickets can also be had the day of a performance; check the ticket office at the Duomo Metro stop for details on availability. Purchase tickets online (all major credit cards accepted) or at about a dozen travel agencies around the city, and at various travel agencies throughout the country. For a complete list, visit the website.

The adjacent museum, **Il Museo Teatrale Alla Scala** (✆ **02-8879-7473**), pays tribute to the leading Italian lights in opera and ballet, often hosting exhibits of costumes worn at La Scala performances long ago. Also of note for scholars is a library of more than 40,000 musical works. The museum and library are open daily from 9am to 12:30pm and from 1:30 to 5:30pm. Entrance is 5€.

MOVIES In Italy, English-language films are almost always dubbed into Italian, providing English speakers with an opportunity to bone up on their Italian but taking some of the fun out of a night at the movies. Fortunately, there are a

strolling THROUGH MILAN

The prime spot for a *passeggiata* (stroll) is the Piazza Duomo and the adjoining Galleria, Corso Vittorio Emanuele II, Via Mercanti, and Via Dante, but many of the neighborhoods that fan out from the center are ideal for wandering and looking into the life of the Milanese. The **Quadrilatero d'Oro** (the city's center for high fashion), just north of the Piazza Duomo on and around Via Montenapoleone, is known for window-shopping and trendy cafes and bars; **Magenta** is an old residential quarter, filled with some of the city's most venerable churches, west of Piazza Duomo (follow Via Orefici and its extension, Via Dante, toward the Castello Sforzesco); **Brera,** a once-seedy section that is now gentrified, is filled with bars and restaurants along the streets clustered around the Pinacoteca di Brera (follow Via Brera from the Teatro alla Scala and be sure to walk around pedestrian-only Via Fiori Chiari and then eventually head north on Corso Garibaldi); and Via Torino heads southwest from Piazza Duomo to Corso di Porta Ticinese and the popular **Navigli** neighborhood, where you can walk along the remaining *navigli* (canals) that once laced the city. The former warehouse entrances along them now house funky shops and galleries as well as hopping and unpretentious bars, *birrerie* (pubs), restaurants, and small clubs (to arrive directly at Navigli. Take the Metro to Porta Genova. **Parco Sempione,** the large park behind the castle, is another ideal spot for a stroll, and can provide respite on a hot day. A proper stroll in Milan is always accompanied by a stop at a cafe or *gelateria* (p. 580).

few theaters that screen English-language films in the original version 1 night a week. These three theaters take turns showing the same film on different nights of the week (the film changes every week): **Anteo,** Via Milazzo 9 (✆ **02-659-7732;** Metro: Moscova), on Monday; **Arcobaleno,** Viale Tunisia 11 (✆ **02-2940-6054;** Metro: Porta Venezia), on Tuesday; and **Mexico,** Via Savona 57 (✆ **02-4895-1802;** Metro: Porta Genova), on Thursday.

PUBS & BARS One of the most storied Brera hangouts is **Bar Jamaica,** Via Brera 32 (✆ **02-876723;** Metro: Lanza), an old-school bar where Mussolini once sat to work on his newspaper articles, and now arty locals and literati tolerate the company of better-heeled partygoers at the outdoor tables.

A publike atmosphere, induced in part by Guinness on tap and a very crowded *aperitivo* hour (see "How the Milanese Unwind," p. 588), prevails at Liberty-style **Bar Magenta,** Via Carducci 13, at Corso Magenta (✆ **02-805-3808;** Metro: Cadorna), in the neighborhood from which it takes its name; it's open Tuesday to Sunday 9am to 2am and has good panini.

En route to the Navigli, you can't help noticing the huge crowd of 20-somethings milling around outside the Basilica di San Lorenzo, maybe kicking around a soccer ball through the crowd, usually with cocktails and beers in hand. Chances are those drinks came from **Luca's Bar,** Corso Porta Ticinese 51 (✆ **02-5810-0405;** bus: 94; Metro: Sant'Ambrogio; tram: 3; just under the arch by the basilica), or **Martin Café** (✆ **02-837-3721**) next door, right on the piazza. Both places close at 2am and between them offer up a choice of about 15 beers on tap and in bottles costing 3€ to 5€ and cocktails at 4€ to 6€. Once you have a drink in hand, you can search for a place to sit on the benches in the piazza or take up a spot on the pavement. If your stomach starts growling after a few drinks, there are two good joints nearby that sell takeout pizza that you can bring back to the piazza: **Fratelli la Bufala** right on the square (✆ **02-837-6529**), and **Rossopomodoro** around the corner at Via Molino delle Armi 48 (✆ **02-8940-1333**).

The **Naviglio Pavese** also attracts a young crowd. Follow the left side of the canal as you leave the city center at your back and you will immediately come across a succession of bars, many of which have tables outside along the canal. The crowd that frequents the more picturesque **Naviglio Grande** is mixed and you'll find everybody from young revelers to families with young children. If you have only one night out in Milan, this is probably where you will want to spend it (you can always pop over to the Naviglio Pavese for a look). The left side of the canal as you leave the center is filled mostly with bars and in the summer months is closed to traffic. The right side, which is closed to traffic year-round, has mostly restaurants, all of which put tables out weather permitting. Several footbridges let you cross over. This is a great area for an evening stroll even if you don't plan to drink or eat.

JAZZ CLUBS While Milan's jazz-club scene is limited, there are two excellent options. **Le Scimmie,** which has its own bar-boat moored in the Naviglio Pavese canal, is on the canal at Via Ascanio Sforza 49 (www.scimmie.it; ✆ **02-8940-2874;** Metro: Porta Genova or Romolo; tram: 3) and operates Monday to Saturday, with shows starting between 10 and 10:30pm. **Blue Note,** an offshoot of the famous New York club, is at Via Borsieri 37 (www.bluenotemilano.com; ✆ **02-6901-6888;** Metro: Garibaldi or Zara), just north of the Porta Garibaldi train station, and gets the biggest names in jazz. Shows, which last about 75 minutes, are Monday through Saturday and usually start at 9pm and 11pm (June–Aug usually closed). You can buy tickets in person at the club, online, or by calling Monday through Friday 2 to 7pm.

MUSIC & DANCE CLUBS The dance scene changes all the time in Milan, but at whatever club is popular (or in business) at the moment, expect to pay a cover of 10€ to 15€—sometimes more for big-name live acts. **Tocqueville** (✆ **333-827-6676**), which is open Tuesday through Sunday, gets a young crowd moving to dance music. For something a little funkier, try **Plastic,** Viale Umbria 120 (✆ **02-733-996;** bus: 92; tram: 12, 27), where the people are a bit more colorful and the music more alternative. It's open Friday to Sunday.

Night Owls' Favorite Haunts

While Brera is always happening and the Navigli packs a crowd, another option for a night out is the San Lorenzo district in and around Piazza San Lorenzo (see "Pubs & Bars," below). Most of the action is right in the square, but on the side streets, especially in nearby Piazza della Vetra, you will find lots of life to keep you occupied deep into the night.

HOW THE MILANESE unwind

The Milanese begin to flood the bars around town about 6pm for the time-honored ***aperitivo.*** You pay for your drink and then get as many trips to the buffet table as your stomach can manage. The food on offer varies from a few sad pieces of dry sliced deli meats to extensive spreads of pasta, rice, vegetables, fruit, and everything else imaginable. Most places with a good spread charge about 8€ for a drink during the *aperitivo* time (the price drops once the food is taken away). Come by 7pm if you want to chow down because when the food runs out that's it. For a vast selection of *aperitivo* places, walk the left side of the Naviglio Grande until you find your favorite. **¡Mas!,** at no. 11, with a pseudo-Spanish theme, consistently has one of the best selections of food. Nurse your drink and you can have an abundant, and excellent, dinner for under 10€; by the third go at the buffet your stomach will be crying *no mas.*

Note: There are no specific club hours in Milan. Opening and closing times vary with the seasons and the crowds, with openings anywhere from 7 to 11pm and closings anywhere from 1am to dawn.

GAY CLUBS **Rhabar,** Via Alzaia Naviglio Grande 150 (✆ **393-904-5796** or 393-971-9561), caters to women and is open Wednesday to Sunday 7pm to 2am. Wednesday is singles night, Thursday karaoke. Big crowds come on the weekend. Take the no. 2 tram to the San Cristoforo stop, cross the footbridge and turn left keeping the canal on your left.

The two most popular bars in the center of town are the pseudo-1960s **Mono Bar,** Via Lecco 6 (✆ **339-481-0264**), open daily 6:30pm to 1am (Fri–Sat to 2am), and **Lelephant,** Via Melzo 22 (✆ **02-2951-8768**), which attracts a mostly young and gay-friendly crowd and is open Tuesday to Sunday 6:30pm to 2am. Both are near the Porta Venezia Metro stop.

Where to Stay

While you can pay more for a hotel room in Milan than you would almost anywhere else in Europe, there are also some decent accommodations at reasonable prices in good locations. It's difficult to find rooms in any price category when fashion shows and trade fairs are in full swing (the worst periods are the second half of Feb and Sept, when the woman's fashion shows are on, as well as mid-Apr, when the city is overrun by those attending the Salone del Mobile). All hotels (from the one-stars on up) raise their prices at these times and the upper end of the price range in the listings below is reserved for these periods. The lowest prices will be found in August, and to a lesser extent July, and the weekends tend to cost less than during the week. Remember that Milan is relatively small, so unless you chose a hotel way out in the boondocks you'll be reasonably close to everything.

VERY EXPENSIVE

Four Seasons Hotel Milano ★★★ Milan's top deluxe hotel, a converted 15th-century convent with a soothing courtyard, lies just off Via Montenapoleone, the city's swankiest shopping boulevard. Standard rooms, confusingly called "superior," are on the street (protected from noise by effective double-paned windows), with queen-size beds. Rooms are spacious, with thick rugs or parquet floors, designer chairs in comfy sitting areas, large marble-sheathed bathrooms with heated floors, and walk-in closets. "Executive" suites have a mid-size sitting area and can be connected to deluxe doubles to form a family suite. Five bilevel suites on the ground floor of the cloisters have vaulted ceilings and overlook a neighbor's quiet grassy garden.

Via Gesù 8, 20121 Milan. www.fourseasons.com/milan. ✆ **800-819-5053** in the U.S. and Canada, or 02-77-088 in Italy. Fax 02-7708-5000. 118 units. 520€–600€ superior double; 640€–710€ deluxe double; 640€–800€ junior suite; 1,350€–1,500€ executive suite; 9,300€ Royal Suite. (Prices do not include taxes and service charges.) AE, DC, MC, V. Valet parking 51€. Bus: 54, 64, 65, or 73. Metro: Montenapoleone. **Amenities:** 2 restaurants (elegant restaurant under celebrity chef, casual restaurant open lunch and dinner); bar; babysitting; bikes; children's program and kids' menu; concierge; executive-level rooms; small exercise room; room service; smoke-free rooms. *In room:* A/C, TV/VCR, hair dryer, kitchenette (in Royal suite), minibar, Wi-Fi.

Grand Hotel et de Milan ★★★ Perhaps Milan's most intimate luxury hotel, the Grand Hotel et de Milan balances family management with refined service in an 1863 building. It's positioned near La Scala (3 blocks away) with the shopping of Via Montenapoleone just across the street. The bathrooms are done in marble; rooms feature king size beds and heavy curtains, chipped stone floors, elegant upholstered furnishings, and muted skylight domes. "Deluxe" rooms are larger than "classic" ones and have genuine antiques. The suites genuinely feel like small apartments rather than hotel rooms, with their homelike arrangement of antiques and piped in opera (perhaps something by Maria Callas, once a regular guest). The presidential Giuseppe Verdi Suite is preserved with the same furnishings as when the composer spent his last 30 years here (he even died in this room), including the desk upon which he composed many operas.

Via Manzoni 29, 20121 Milan. www.grandhoteletdemilan.it. ✆ **02-723-141.** Fax 02-8646-0861. 95 units. 455€ classic double; 535€ deluxe double; 645€ junior suite; 900€–1,175€ suite. Breakfast 35€. AE, DC, MC, V. Garage parking 43€. Metro: Montenapoleone. **Amenities:** 2 Italian/Milanese restaurants; bar; babysitting; bikes; concierge; large exercise room; room service. *In room:* A/C, TV w/pay movies, hair dryer, minibar, Wi-Fi.

EXPENSIVE

Doria Grand Hotel ★ This luxury hotel offers enormously discounted prices on weekends, most of August, and the Christmas/New Year's holiday. Located about halfway between the main train station and Piazzale Loreto, it is far more comfortable and stylish than most hotels in its luxury class. The good-size rooms are exquisitely appointed with handsome woods, marble-topped furniture, and rich fabric wall coverings. The beautiful marble bathrooms are equipped with generous-size tubs, vanities, and a good selection of toiletries. A sumptuous buffet breakfast is served in a stylish room (where they also serve 30€ fixed-price menus at mealtimes), and Thursday and Friday evenings the piano bar becomes a jazz club.

Viale Andrea Doria 22, 20124 Milan. www.doriagrandhotel.it. ✆ **02-6741-1411.** Fax 02-669-6669. 124 units. 100€–300€ double. Rates include buffet breakfast. AE, DC, MC, V. Parking 30€ in garage. Bus: 90, 91, or 92. Metro: Loreto or Caiazzo. Tram: 1. **Amenities:** Restaurant; cafe; babysitting; concierge; room service; smoke-free rooms. *In room:* A/C, TV w/pay movies, hair dryer, minibar, Wi-Fi.

MODERATE

Ariosto Hotel ★★ Tucked away in a residential neighborhood of apartment houses and old villas near the Santa Maria delle Grazie church, the Ariosto is a refreshingly quiet retreat—all the more so because many of the newly refurbished rooms face a private garden, and some open onto balconies overlooking it. All rooms are decorated with wood-and-wicker furnishings, shiny parquet floors, and hand-painted wallpaper. Most of the doubles are decently sized (though singles tend to be narrow) with separate dressing areas off the tile or stone bathrooms, a few of which are equipped with Jacuzzis.

Via Ariosto 22, 20145 Milan. www.hotelariosto.com. ✆ **02-481-7844.** Fax 02-498-0516. 49 units. 85€–290€ double; 100€–310€ triple. Rates include breakfast. AE, DC, MC, V. Parking 25€ in garage. Closed 3 weeks in Aug. Metro: Conciliazione. Tram: 19. **Amenities:** Restaurant (Italian); bar; bikes; concierge; room service; smoke-free rooms. *In room:* A/C, TV w/pay movies, hair dryer, minibar, Wi-Fi.

Art Hotel Navigli ★ With its location just steps from the Naviglio Grande, this hotel is slightly removed from most of the tourist sites, but it more than makes up for that with its vicinity to the trendy shops and booming nightlife found up and down the canal. While the facade is shockingly nondescript, inside you will find a slightly artsy air (the hotel desperately tries to live up to its name) that includes fanciful carpets, modern art on the walls, and a minimalist edge to the furniture that rejuvenates without being overwhelming. Most of the rooms are large and come with marble-countered bathrooms, and a few also have a small terrace. There is a miniature garden with a few tables and umbrellas that offers a chance to unwind after running around town.

Via Angelo Fumagalli 4, 20143 Milan. www.arthotelnavigli.com. ✆ **02-8941-0530.** Fax 02-5811-5066. 103 units. 115€–215€ double. Rates include breakfast. AE, DC, MC, V. Parking 20€ in hotel garage or free on the street. Bus: 74. Metro: Porta Genova. Tram: 2. **Amenities:** Bar; smoke-free rooms. *In room:* A/C, TV w/pay movies, hair dryer, minibar, Wi-Fi.

Carlyle Brera Hotel ★ This sleek hotel located in the heart of Brera gives great value for what it costs. All rooms have parquet floors that, combined with the light-wood paneling found on some of the walls, create a minimalist look more common to hotels in a higher price range. Superior rooms are more spacious than a classic double, but other than that they are about the same. No matter what room you pick, you have a choice of eight types of pillows—no kidding.

Corso Garibaldi 84, 20121 Milan. www.hotelcarlyle.com. ✆ **02-2900-3888.** Fax 02-2900-3993. 97 units. 115€–305€ double. Rates include breakfast. AE, DC, MC, V. Parking 35€ in garage next to hotel. Bus: 94. Metro: Moscova. Tram: 2, 12, 14. **Amenities:** Restaurant (Italian); bar; room service; smoke-free rooms. *In room:* A/C, TV w/pay movies, hair dryer, minibar, Wi-Fi.

Hotel Berna ★★ The breakfast, which is up to the standards of most luxury hotels, coupled with friendly service and lots of little freebies such as hot and cold nonalcoholic drinks (both in the minibar and in the lobby) make staying here a very positive experience. Most standard doubles are small, but the furnishings are relatively new and the light pastel colors used for the curtains, walls, and bedding make the space seem airy enough. High ceilings also help.

Comfortable mattresses and good soundproofing ensure that you will get a good night's sleep here.

Via Napo Torriani 18, 20124 Milan. www.hotelberna.com. ✆ **02-6773-1800.** Fax 02-669-3892. 106 units and 16 across the street in Berna Tower. 109€–179€ double. Rates include breakfast. MC, V. Parking 18€ in hotel garage or free on street. Metro: Centrale. Tram: 1 or 5. **Amenities:** Bar. *In room:* A/C, TV, hair dryer, Wi-Fi.

Hotel Gran Duca di York ★ Scholars studying at the nearby Biblioteca Ambrosiana used this phenomenally placed *palazzo* in the 19th century. A restructuring completed in 2009 has greatly improved the hotel's look and the rooms are now sleek and simple yet inviting and comfortable. The windows on the rooms facing the street do not keep out all the traffic noise (which isn't constant, but is noticeable). The beds are hard, but if that takes away from your sleep you can always head to the minibar where the drinks are compliments of the hotel. The location, just off the main pedestrian drag leading from the Duomo to Castello Sforzesco, is tough to beat.

Via Moneta 1A, 20123 Milan. www.ducadiyork.com. ✆ **02-874-863.** Fax 02-869-0344. 33 units. 135€–240€ double. Rates include breakfast. AE, MC, V. Parking in nearby garage 30€. Metro: Cordusio. **Amenities:** Bar; babysitting; concierge; room service. *In room:* A/C, TV, hair dryer, minibar, Wi-Fi.

INEXPENSIVE

Hotel Aurora This 16-room hotel one flight up in a building on lively Corso Buenos Aires is clean, the rooms are decently sized, and though the bathrooms are small, they're in excellent condition. Rooms 110, 111, and 114 overlook the main street, yet the incredibly insulating windows block out just about all the noise, making these rooms desirable as they allow you to pop your head outside and watch the action down below. Donato Casella, the gregarious owner of the Hotel Aurora since 1987, lived for more than a decade in New York City and he's always ready to use his near-perfect English to tell you about his latest trip to the Big Apple. Sometimes a voucher for breakfast at a bar downstairs is thrown in with the room; if not, you're better off taking care of your hunger needs on your own rather than paying the 5€.

Corso Buenos Aires 18, 20124 Milan. www.hotelauroramilano.com. ✆ **02-204-7960.** Fax 02-204-9285. 16 units. 65€–150€ double. MC, V. Parking 24€ per day in nearby garage. Metro: Porta Venezia. Tram: 5 or 33. **Amenities:** Bar. *In room:* A/C, TV, hair dryer, Wi-Fi.

Hotel XXII Marzo ★★ This clean and friendly family-run hotel is a pleasant 20-minute walk (or 10-min. tram ride) from the Duomo along a bustling street, making it a good option if you don't have to be right in the center and you are okay with simplicity. The beds in the tile-floored rooms are old, though not overly soft, and the bathrooms tight, but if you are feeling cramped you can sit out in the little park in front of the hotel and watch the local fauna do their thing. If size is key and you want to be sure not to get one of the smaller rooms, you can pay 10€ more and book a triple for double occupancy.

Piazza Santa Maria del Suffragio 3 (just off Corso XXII Marzo near Piazza Cinque Giornate), 20129 Milan. www.hotel22marzo.com. ✆/fax **02-7010-7064.** 15 units. 65€–170€ double. Rates include breakfast. AE, MC, V. Bus: 73. Tram: 12 or 27. **Amenities:** Bar. *In room:* A/C, TV, Wi-Fi.

A Side Trip from Milan

PAVIA & THE CERTOSA

At one time, the quiet and remarkably well-preserved little city of **Pavia,** 35km (22 miles) south of Milan, was more powerful than Milan. It was the capital of the Lombard Kingdom in Italy (most of what is now modern-day Italy except for Sicily and Sardinia) in the 7th and 8th centuries, and by the early Renaissance, the Viscontis and later the Sforzas, the two families who so influenced the history of Milan and all of Lombardy, were wielding their power here. It was the Viscontis who made Pavia one of Europe's great centers of learning (when they founded the university) in 1361, built the city's imposing **Castello** in 1365, began construction on the **Duomo** (with the third-largest dome in Italy) in 1488, and founded the city's most important monument and the one that brings most visitors to Pavia, the Certosa.

The **Certosa ★★★** is 8km (5 miles) north of Pavia. One of the most unusual buildings in Lombardy, if not in all of Italy, this religious compound was commissioned by Gian Galeazzo Visconti in 1396 as a Carthusian monastery and a burial chapel for his family—officially as thanks for curing his second sickly wife (the first died) and granting him children and heirs. It was completed by the Sforzas in 1452. The facade of colored marble, the frescoed interior, and the riot of funerary sculpture is evidence that this brood of often-tyrannical despots were also dedicated builders with grand schemes and large coffers. The finest and most acclaimed statuary monument here, that of Ludovico il Moro (buried in France, where he died a prisoner of war) and Beatrice d'Este (buried in Milan's Santa Maria delle Grazie), sits in the left transept of the massive church, beneath lapis lazuli–rich frescoes by Bergognone. Its presence here is a twist of fate—the monks at Milan's Chiesa di Santa Maria delle Grazie (which houses *The Last Supper*) sold the tomb to the Certosa to raise funds. In the right transept is the 15th-century tomb of Gian Galeazzo Visconti.

Admission to the Certosa (✆ **0382-925-613**) is free; May to August, it's open Tuesday to Sunday 9 to 11:30am and 2:30 to 6pm (Nov–Feb to 4:30pm; Mar and Oct to 5pm; Apr and Sept to 5:30pm).

GETTING THERE Hourly trains from **Milan** stop at the station near the Certosa, just before the main Pavia station (30 min., 3.40€). ***Note:*** There are many trains that go to Pavia without stopping at the Certosa. To reach the Certosa from Pavia, take one of the half-hourly buses from the Autocorriere station (next to the train station); the trip takes about 15 minutes and costs 1€. By car, the Certosa is about half an hour south of Milan via Autostrada A7 (follow exit signs).

VISITOR INFORMATION The **tourist office** is near the main university building at Piazza Italia 5 (✆ **0382-596-022**); it's open Monday to Thursday from 9:15am to noon and 2:45 to 4:30pm, Friday 9:15am to noon.

BERGAMO

47km (29 miles) NE of Milan

Bergamo is two cities. **Città Bassa,** the lower, a mostly 19th- and 20th-century city, concerns itself with everyday business. **Città Alta,** a beautiful medieval/Renaissance town perched on a green hill, concerns itself these days with entertaining visitors who come to admire its *piazze, palazzi,* and churches; enjoy the

Bergamo's cable car.

lovely vistas from its belvederes; and soak in the hushed beauty that inspired Italian poet Gabriele d'Annunzio to call old Bergamo "a city of muteness." The distinct characters of the two parts of this city go back to its founding as a Roman settlement, when the town was set on the hill and farms and suburban villas dotted the plains below.

Essentials

GETTING THERE **By Train** Trains arrive from and depart for Milan hourly (50 min.; 5.15€). If you're coming from or going to nearby Lake Como, there's hourly service between Bergamo and Lecco, on the southeast end of the lake (40 min.; 3.40€).

By Bus An extensive bus network links Bergamo with many other towns in Lombardy. There are five to six buses a day to and from Como (2 hr.; 4.50€) run by **SPT** (www.sptlinea.it; ✆ **031-247-247**). Service to and from Milan is run by **Autostradale** (www.autostradale.it; ✆ **02-7200-1304**) and runs every half-hour (1 hr. trip time). The bus station is next to the train station on Piazza Marconi.

By Car Bergamo is linked directly to Milan via the A4, which continues east to Brescia, Verona, and Venice. The trip between Milan and Bergamo takes a little under an hour without traffic, but this is reputed to be the busiest stretch of autostrada in all of Italy so traffic is always a possibility. Parking in or near the Città Alta, most of which is closed to traffic, can be difficult. There is a parking lot on the northern end of the Città Alta near Porta Garibaldi (1.50€ per hour) and street parking along Viale delle Mura, which loops around the flanks of the walls of the Città Alta.

VISITOR INFORMATION The **Città Bassa tourist office** (www.turismo.provincia.bergamo.it; ✆ **035-210-204**) is right next to the train and bus stations at Viale Papa Giovanni XXIII 57; it's open daily 9am to 12:30pm and 2 to 5:30pm. The **Città Alta office** is at Via Gombito 13 (✆ **035-232-730**), right off Via Colleoni, and is open daily the same hours. If you are planning to travel farther afield and into the hills, ask either tourist office for the trail map of the Bergamo province.

GETTING AROUND Bergamo has an extensive **bus system** that runs through the Città Bassa and to points outside the walls of the Città Alta; tickets are 1€ and are available from newsstands and tobacco shops. With the exception of the trip from the train or bus stations up to the Città Alta, you probably won't have much need of public transit, as most of the sights are within an easy walk of one another.

To reach the Città Alta from the train station, take bus no. 1 or 1A and make the free transfer to the **Funicolare Bergamo Alta,** connecting the upper and lower cities and running every 7 minutes from 6:30am to 12:30am. You can make the walk to the funicular station in about 20 minutes (and see something of the new city en route) by following Viale Papa Giovanni XXIII and its continuations Viale Roma and Viale Vittorio Emanuele II.

If you're feeling hearty, a footpath next to the funicular winds up to Città Alta; the steep climb up (made easier by intermittent staircases) takes about 30 minutes. Bus no. 1A also continues up and around the Città Alta walls to end just outside Porta San Vigilio, and is more convenient to hotels San Lorenzo and Gourmet.

FESTIVALS & MARKETS Bergamo is a cultured city, and its celebrations include the May-to-June **Festival Pianistico** (which it shares with nearby Brescia), one of the world's major piano competitions. In September, the city celebrates its native composer, Gaetano Donizetti, with **performances of his works,** most of them at the Teatro Donizetti in the Città Bassa (see below).

CITY LAYOUT Piazza Vecchia, the Colleoni Chapel, and most of the other sights that bring visitors to Bergamo are in the **Città Alta**—the exception is the Accademia Carrara, which is in the Città Bassa but on the flanks of the hillside, so it's within easy walking distance of the upper-town sights. **Via Colleoni** cuts a swath through the medieval heart of the Città Alta, beginning at **Piazza Vecchia.** To reach this lovely square from the funicular station at **Piazza Mercato delle Scarpi,** walk along **Via Gombito** for about 5 minutes.

Exploring the Città Bassa

Most visitors scurry through Bergamo's lower, newer town on their way to the Città Alta, but you may want to pause long enough to enjoy a coffee along the **Sentierone,** the elongated piazza/street at the center of town. This spacious square graciously combines a mishmash of architectural styles (including 16th-c. porticos on one side, the Mussolini-era Palazzo di Giustizia and two imitation Doric temples on another). Locals sit in its gardens, lounge in its cafes, and attend classical concerts at the **Teatro Donizetti.** This 19th-century theater is the center of Bergamo's lively culture scene, with a fall opera season and a winter-to-spring season of dramatic performances; for details, check with the tourist office or call the theater at ✆ **035-416-0611** (http://teatro.gaetano-donizetti.com).

Exploring the Città Alta

The higher, older part of Bergamo owes its stone *palazzi,* proud monuments, and what remains of its extensive fortified walls to more than 3 centuries of Venetian rule, beginning in 1428, when soldiers of the Republic wrestled control of the city out of the hands of the Milan-based Visconti. The Venetians left their mark elegantly in the town's theatrically adjoining squares, **Piazza Vecchia** and **Piazza del Duomo,** which together create what French writer Stendhal went so far as to call the "most beautiful place on earth."

On Piazza Vecchia, you'll see traces of the Venetian presence in the 12th-century **Palazzo della Ragione (Courts of Justice),** which has been embellished with a graceful ground-floor arcade and the Lion of Saint Mark, symbol of the Venetian Republic, above a 16th-century balcony reached by a covered staircase (the bells atop its adjoining tower, the **Torre Civico,** sound the hours). The recently restored halls often host traveling art exhibits. Venice's Sansovino Library provided the inspiration for the **Biblioteca Civica (Public Library)** across the square. Piazza del Duomo, reached through one of the archways of the Palazzo della Ragione, is filled with an overpowering collection of religious structures that include the **Duomo** and the much more enticing **Cappella Colleoni** (see below), the **Baptistery,** and the **Basilica di Santa Maria Maggiore** (see below).

Bergamasco strongman Colleoni (see the Cappella Colleoni entry, below) lent his name to the upper town's delightful main street, cobblestoned and so narrow you can just about touch the buildings on either side when standing in the center. If you follow it to its far northwestern end, you'll emerge into **Largo Colle Aperto,** refreshingly green and open to the Città Bassa.

For better views and a short excursion into the countryside, board the **Funicolare San Vigilio** for the ascent up the San Vigilio hill; the funicular runs daily every 12 minutes or so between 7am and midnight and costs 1€. The strategic importance of these heights was not lost on Bergamo's medieval residents, who erected a summit-top **Castello** (✆ **035-236-284**), now mostly in ruin. Its keep, still surrounded by the old walls, is a park in which every bench affords a far-reaching view. It's open daily April to September 9am to 8pm, October and March 10am to 6pm, and November to February 10am to 4pm. When you head back down to the Città Alta, either by foot or with the funicular, instead of following Via Colleoni back into the center of the town, you can turn onto Viale delle Mura and follow the 16th-century bastions for about .8km (½ mile) to the Porta Sant'Agostino on the other side of the town.

Basilica di Santa Maria Maggiore ★ CHURCH Behind the plain marble facade and a portico whose columns rise out of the backs of lions lies an overly baroque gilt-covered interior hung with Renaissance tapestries. **Gaetano Donizetti,** the wildly popular composer of frothy operas, who was born in Bergamo in 1797 and returned here to die in 1848, is entombed in a **marble sarcophagus** that's as excessive as the rest of the church's decor. The finest works are the **choir stalls,** with rich wood inlays depicting landscapes and biblical scenes; they're the creation of Lorenzo Lotto. The stalls are usually kept under cloth to protect the sensitive hardwoods from light and pollutants, but they're unveiled for Lent. The octagonal **Baptistery** in the piazza outside the church was originally inside but removed, reconstructed, and much embellished in the 19th century.

Piazza del Duomo. ✆ **035-223-327.** Free admission. May–Sept Mon–Sat 9am–12:30pm and 2:30–6pm; Sun 9am–1pm and 3–6pm (Oct–Apr closed at 5pm).

Cappella Colleoni ★★★ CHURCH Bartolomeo Colleoni was a Bergamasco *condottiere* (captain) who fought for Venice to maintain the Venetian stronghold on the city. In return for his labors, the much-honored soldier was given Bergamo to rule for the Republic. If you've already visited Venice, you may have seen Signore Colleoni astride the Verrocchio equestrian bronze in Campo Santi Giovanni e Paolo. He rests for eternity here in Bergamo in this elaborate funerary chapel designed by Amadeo, the great sculptor from nearby Pavia (where he completed his most famous work, the Certosa; p. 592). The pink-and-white marble exterior, laced with finely sculpted columns and loggias, is airy and almost whimsical; inside, the soldier and his favorite daughter, Medea, lie beneath a ceiling frescoed by Tiepolo and are surrounded by reliefs and statuary. As in Venice, Colleoni appears on horseback atop his marble tomb.

Piazza del Duomo. ✆ **035-210-061.** Free admission. Apr–Oct daily 9:30am–12:30pm and 2–6pm; Nov–Mar Tues–Sun 9:30am–12:30pm and 2–4:30pm.

Where to Eat & Stay

The charms of staying in the Città Alta are no secret. Rooms tend to fill up quickly, especially in summer and on weekends. Reserve well in advance.

On the dining front, your gambols through the Città Alta can be nicely interspersed with fortifying stops at the city's many pastry shops and stand-up eateries. **Forno Tresoldi,** Via Colleoni 13, sells yummy pizzas and focaccia by the slice topped with cheese, salami, and vegetables (from 2€). It's open Tuesday to Sunday from 8am to 1:30pm and 4 to 10pm.

Agnello d'Oro ★★ In keeping with its location a few steps from Piazza Vecchia, the Agnello d'Oro looks like it's right out of an old tourist brochure extolling the quaint charms of Italy. The tall, narrow, ocher-colored building, with flower boxes in its tall windows, overlooks a small *piazzetta* where a fountain splashes next to potted greenery. The wood-paneled lounge and intimate dining room add to the charm quotient, which declines somewhat as you ascend in a tiny elevator to the rooms. These lean more toward serviceable comfort than to luxury, but warm color schemes and old prints compensate for the lack of space and amenities; the bathrooms are roomy and have been modernized. Front rooms have balconies overlooking the piazza. This is the most popular spot in the Città Alta (even though the friendliness level of the staff can vary wildly), so reserve early.

Via Gombito 22, 24129 Bergamo Alta. www.agnellodoro.it. ✆ **035-249-883.** Fax 035-235-612. 20 units. 93€ double. Continental breakfast 6€. AE, DC, MC, V. **Amenities:** Concierge; free Wi-Fi. *In room:* TV, hair dryer.

Antica Hosteria del Vino Buono ★★ NORTHERN ITALIAN The new ownership of this restaurant (formerly a wine bar) near the top of the funicular takes its food and wine seriously. It's a pleasure to dine in the handsome surroundings of brick, refinished in 2006 to give an older feel. For an introduction to food from the region, try one of the several tasting menus. Polenta figures prominently, including with wild mushrooms. Polenta *taragna* uses buckwheat and cornmeal as its base and here they fill it with Taleggio cheese. The main courses lean toward meat. A dish like roast quail or rabbit should be accompanied by a Valcalepio Rosso, a medium-strength red from local vineyards. The house wine, a local cabernet, is more economical, perhaps a little young but perfectly drinkable.

Piazza Mercato Delle Scarpe 25. ✆ **035-247-993.** Reservations recommended. *Primi* 8€; *secondi* 11€; *menù turistico* 23€, wine included. AE, DC, MC, V. Tues–Sun noon–2:30pm and 7–10:30pm (Tues closed for lunch).

Il Gourmet ★ This pleasant hotel offers the best of both worlds—it's only steps away from the Città Alta (a few hundred feet outside the Porta Sant'Agostino on the road leading up to the Castello) but on a rural hillside, giving it the air of a country retreat. The villa-style building is set behind walls in a lush garden and enjoys wonderful views. A wide terrace on two sides makes the most of these views. Many of the very large, bright rooms look across the hillside to the heavily developed valley. They have plain, wood-paneled furniture, a decor geared more to solid comfort than to style, and king-size beds. They also rent a large two-floor suite with a sitting area and kitchen downstairs. There's a very good restaurant on the premises—hence the name—with indoor and outdoor tables and midrange prices on Bergamasco and Lombard cuisine.

Via San Vigilio 1, 24129 Bergamo. www.gourmet-bg.it. ✆/fax **035-437-3004.** 11 units. 100€–130€ double; 110€–150€ triple; 180€–230€ apt with 2 double rooms. Continental breakfast 10€. AE, DC, MC, V. Closed Dec 27–Jan 7. **Amenities:** International/Bergamasco restaurant; bar; room service. *In room:* A/C, TV, hair dryer, minibar.

CAFES

Caffè del Tasso ★, Piazza Vecchia 3, is a prime piece of real estate on the main square of the Città Alta. It began life as a tailor's shop 500 years ago, but it's been a cafe and bar since 1581. Legend has it that Garibaldi's Red Shirts used to gather here (Bergamo was a stronghold of Italian independence, which explains why an edict from the 1850s on the wall of this cafe prohibits rebellion). The cafe is open daily from 8am to 8pm (until 1am in the summer).

While the location of **Caffè della Funicolare** in the Piazza Mercato delle Scarpe, in the upper terminal of the funicular that climbs the hill from the Città Bassa to the Città Alta, doesn't suggest a memorable dining experience, the station dates from 1887 and has enough Belle Epoque flourishes and curlicues to make the surroundings interesting. Plus, the dining room and terrace look straight down the hill to the town and valley, providing some of the best tables with a view (accompanied by low-cost fare) in the upper town. Stop in from 8am to 2am Wednesday to Monday for a coffee, one of the 50 kinds of beer on tap, a sandwich, or a salad.

MANTUA (MANTOVA)

158km (98 miles) E of Milan, 62km (38 miles) N of Parma, 150km (93 miles) SW of Venice

One of Lombardy's finest cities is in the farthest reaches of the region, making it a logical addition to a trip to Venice or Parma as well as to Milan. Like its neighboring cities in Emilia-Romagna, Mantua owes its past greatness and its beautiful Renaissance monuments to one family, in this case the Gonzagas, who rose from peasant origins to conquer the city in 1328 and ruled benevolently until 1707. The Gonzagas were avid collectors of art and ruled through the greatest centuries of Italian art, and you'll encounter the treasures they collected in the massive Palazzo Ducale that dominates much of the town center; in their refreshing suburban retreat, the Palazzo Te; and in the churches and *piazze* that grew up around their court.

One of Mantua's greatest charms is its location—on a meandering river, the Mincio, which widens here to envelop the city in a necklace of romantic lakes. Often shrouded in mist and surrounded by flat plains, Mantua, which has been recognized as a UNESCO World Heritage Site since 2008 for its excellence as an example of Renaissance town planning, can seem almost melancholy. But the Palazzo Ducale, the Galleria Museo Palazzo Valenti Gonzaga, and other monuments have been restored since the 1930s, and what will probably strike you more is what a remarkable gem of a city Mantua is.

Essentials

GETTING THERE **By Train** Ten trains daily arrive from Milan (2 hr.; 11€). There are hourly runs from Verona (30–40 min.; 3.30€), with connections to Venice.

By Car The speediest connections from Milan are via the autostrade, the A4 to Verona, and the A22 from Verona to Mantua (the trip takes about 2 hr.). From Mantua, it's an easy drive south to Parma on the SS420, or you can reach Modena on the A22 and then connect to the A1 to Bologna.

VISITOR INFORMATION The **tourist office** is at Piazza Mantegna 6 (www.turismo.mantova.it; ✆ **0376-432-432**), and is open daily from 9am to 5pm (Apr–Sept to 6pm).

FESTIVALS & MARKETS Mantua fights the postsummer blues with a **literature festival** the second weekend of September.

Year-round, Piazza delle Erbe is the scene of a bustling **food market** Monday through Saturday from 8am to 1pm. On Thursday mornings, a **bigger market,** filled with clothing, housewares, and more food, spills through Piazza Magenta and the adjoining streets.

CITY LAYOUT Mantua is tucked onto a point of land surrounded on three sides by the **Mincio River,** which widens here into a series of lakes, named prosaically **Lago Superiore, Lago di Mezzo,** and **Lago Inferiore.** Most of the sights are within an easy walk of one another within the compact center, which is only a 10-minute walk from the lakeside train station. Follow **Via Solferino e San Martino** to **Via Marangoni,** turn right, and follow that to **Piazza Cavallotti,** where a left turn on **Corso Umberto I** will bring you to **Piazza delle Erbe,** the first of the gracious *piazze* that flow through the city center to the palace of the Gonzagas. You can also make the trip on the no. 2 bus, which leaves from the front of the station.

Exploring Mantua

As you wander around, you'll notice that Mantua's squares are handsomely proportioned spaces surrounded by medieval and Renaissance churches and *palazzi.* The *piazze* open one into another, creating the wonderful illusion that walkers in the city are strolling through a series of opera sets.

The southernmost of these squares, and the place to begin your explorations, is **Piazza delle Erbe (Square of the Herbs) ★**, so named for the produce-and-food market that has been held here for centuries (see "Festivals & Markets," above). Mantua's civic might is clustered here in a series of late-medieval and early Renaissance structures that include the **Palazzo della Ragione (Courts of Justice)** and **Palazzo del Podestà (Mayor's Palace)** from the 12th and 13th centuries, and the **Torre dell'Orologio,** topped with a 14th-century astrological clock. Also on this square is Mantua's earliest religious structure, the **Rotunda di San Lorenzo ★**, a miniature round church from the 11th century (summer daily 10am–noon and 2:30–4:30pm, winter daily 11am–noon, though hours may vary; free admission). The city's Renaissance masterpiece, **Basilica di Sant'Andrea** (see below), is off to one side on Piazza Mantegna.

In the adjoining **Piazza Broletto** (just north as you work your way through the Old City), the statue of Virgil commemorates the poet who was born near here in 70 B.C. and celebrated Mantua's river Mincio in his *Bucolics.* The next square, **Piazza Sordello,** is huge, rectangular, and lined with well-restored medieval *palazzi.* Most notable, though, is the massive hulk of the **Palazzo Ducale** (see below) that forms one wall of the piazza. To enjoy Mantua's soulful lakeside vistas, follow Via Accademia through Piazza Arche and the Lungolago Gonzaga.

Basilica di Sant'Andrea ★ CHURCH A graceful Renaissance facade fronts this 15th-century church by Leon Battista Alberti, with an 18th-century dome by Juvarra. The simple arches seem to float beneath the classic pediment, and the unadorned elegance forms a sharp contrast to other Lombardy monuments, such as the Duomo in Milan, the Cappella Colleoni in Bergamo, and the Certosa in Pavia. Inside, the classically proportioned vast space is centered on a single aisle. The Gonzaga court painter Mantegna is buried in the first chapel on the left. The crypt houses a reliquary containing the blood of Christ (allegedly brought here by Longinus, the Roman soldier who thrust his spear into Jesus's side), which is carried through town on March 18, the feast of Mantua's patron, Sant'Anselmo. Piazza Mantegna. Free admission. Daily 7:30am–noon and 3–7pm.

Galleria Museo Palazzo Valenti Gonzaga MUSEUM After a restoration that lasted 2 decades, this 16th-century palace, which is still inhabited today, reopened its doors to visitors in 2008. The palace retains much of its former splendor, and visitors can wander through the public spaces, which are the *piano nobile* and the rooftop garden (the other floors are inhabited). This palace offers insight into how Mantuan noble families lived throughout the centuries; it is also home to a wonderfully restored cycle of 17th-century frescoes by Frans Geffels, which will appeal to fans of Flemish painting and subjects. Via Pietro Frattini 7. www.valentigonzaga.com. ✆ **0376-364-524** or 348-441-9954. Admission 8€ adults; 6€ seniors 65 and over; free for children 12 and under. Sat–Sun only with hourly guided tours 10am–noon and 3–6pm; Mon–Fri only with a previous reservation. Reservations and tickets at Piazza Mantegna 9/a right off Piazza Broletto.

Palazzo Ducale ★★ PALACE Behind the walls of this massive fortress/palace lies the history of the Gonzagas, Mantua's most powerful family, and what remains of the treasure trove they amassed in a rule that began in 1328 and lasted into the early 18th century. Between their skills as warriors and their penchant for marrying into wealthier and more cultured houses, they managed to acquire power, money, and the services of some of the top artists of the time including Pisanello, Titian, and, most notably, Andrea Mantegna, their court painter, who spent most of his career working for his Mantua patrons.

The most fortunate of these unions was that of Francesco Gonzaga to Isabelle d'Este in 1490. This well-bred daughter of Ferrara's Este clan commissioned many of the art-filled frescoed apartments you see today, including the Camera degli Sposi in Isabella's apartments—the masterpiece, and only remaining fresco cycle, of Mantegna. It took the artist 9 years to complete the cycle, and in it, he included many of the visitors to the court; it's a fascinating account of late-15th-century court life. Mantegna's *trompe l'oeil* oculus in the center of the ceiling is an icon of Renaissance art and a masterpiece of foreshortening.

Most of Mantegna's works for the palace, though, have been carted off to other collections; his famous *Parnassus,* which he painted for an intimate room known as the *studiolo,* is now in the Louvre, as are works that Perugino and Correggio painted for the same room.

The Gonzagas expanded their palace by incorporating any structure that lay within reach, including the Duomo and the Castello di San Giorgio (1396–1406). As a result, it's now a small city of 500 rooms connected by a labyrinth of corridors, ramps, courtyards, and staircases, filled with Renaissance frescoes and ancient Roman sculptures. The frescoes in the Sala del Pisanello feature Arthurian legends

The Hall of Mirrors in the Palazzo Ducale.

(mostly Tristan and Isolde) painted by Pisanello between 1436 and 1444. They were discovered beneath layers of plaster only in 1969. The Sale degli Arazzi (Tapestry Rooms) are hung with copies—woven at the same time but by a different Flemish workshop—of the Vatican's tapestries designed by Raphael and his students.

Other highlights include the Galleria degli Specchi (Hall of Mirrors); the low-ceiling Appartamento dei Nani (Apartments of the Dwarfs), where a replica of the Holy Staircase in the Vatican is built to miniature scale (in keeping with noble custom of the time, dwarfs were part of Isabella's court); and the Galleria dei Mesi (Hall of the Months). Some of the mostly delightful chambers in the vast complex make up the Appartamento Estivale (Summer Apartment), which looks over a courtyard where hanging gardens provide the greenery.

Piazza Sordello. www.mantovaducale.beniculturali.it. ✆ **0376-382-150.** Admission 6.50€, 3.25€ ages 18–25, free for ages 17 and under. Tues–Sun 8:15am–7:15pm. Last entrance at 6:20pm.

Palazzo Te ★ PALACE Federico Gonzaga, the pleasure-loving refined son of Isabella d'Este, built this splendid Mannerist palace as a retreat from court life. As you enter the courtyard, you'll see that the purpose of this palace was to amuse—the keystone of the monumental archway is designed to look like it's falling out of place. Throughout the whimsical interior, sexually frank frescoes by Giulio Romano (who left a scandal behind him in Rome over his licentious engravings) depict *Psyche* and other erotically charged subject matter and make unsubtle reference to one of Frederico's favorite pastimes (horses and astrology, Federico's other passions, also figure prominently). The greatest and most playful achievement here, though, has to do with power: In the **Sala dei Giganti (Room of the Giants)** ★★, Titan is overthrown by the gods in a dizzying play of architectural proportion that gives the illusion that the ceiling is falling. The Palazzo Te is the home of the Museo Civico, whose permanent collections on the upper floor include the Gonzaga family's coins, medallion, and other displays of its wealth and power, alongside more recently donated works of art.

The *palazzo* is a 20-minute walk from the center of town along Via Mazzini. En route, at Via Acerbi 47, sits **Casa di Mantegna,** the house and studio of Andrea Mantegna. Admission is free and it's open Tuesday to Sunday 10am to 12:30pm and 3 to 6pm (✆ **0376-360-506;** hours may vary).

Viale Te. www.palazzote.it. ✆ **0376-323-266.** Admission 8€ adults, 5€ seniors 60 and over, 2.50€ ages 12–18 and university students, and free for children 12 and under. Mon 1–6pm; Tues–Sun 9am–6pm.

Where to Eat & Stay

For accommodations, the tourist office can provide a complete list of what's available in the city and in farmhouses in the surrounding countryside, though they won't make the calls to reserve for you. Rates at the farmhouses tend to run about 35€ to 40€ per person. Because several of the properties are within a few kilometers of town, you can reach them without too much trouble by bike or combination bus ride and trek.

When it comes to dining, the local cuisine is quite refined—an array of pastas stuffed with pumpkin and squash, a fine selection of fish from the surrounding lakes and rivers, and exquisite risotto dishes (rice has been cultivated here since the early 1500s; the tourist office even promotes a *strada del riso,* or "rice road," through the region modeling the "wine roads" of other regions, and showing how important rice is to the area).

Broletto ★★ This atmospheric old hotel is in the center of the Old City, only a few steps from the lake, the *castello,* Piazza Sordello, and Piazza delle Erbe, making it the perfect base to start a late-night stroll. The rooms have contemporary furnishings that are vaguely rustic in design, with orthopedic bed frames. Bright corner room no. 16 has balconies and windows on two sides. The most alluring features of the decor, though, are the massive beams on the ceilings and other architectural details from the *palazzo*'s 16th-century origins

Via Accademia 1, 46100 Mantova. www.hotelbroletto.com. ✆ **0376-326-784.** Fax 0376-221-297. 16 units. 95€–130€ double. Rates include continental breakfast. AE, DC, MC, V. Closed Dec 23–28. **Amenities:** Babysitting; concierge. *In room:* A/C, TV, hair dryer, minibar, Wi-Fi.

Hotel ABC ★ Considering the pleasant surroundings and the amenities offered here, the prices are very low. A nice lounge area and breakfast room open onto a sunny terrace. Upstairs, the renovated rooms have bright tile floors, fresh plaster and paint, new modular furnishings, and modern bathrooms. Architectural details, such as stone walls and patches of old frescoes, have been uncovered to provide decorative touches. The management is extremely helpful, and their hospitality extends to lending out the three bikes they have on hand for free (first-come, first-served).

Piazza Don Leoni 25, 46100 Mantova. www.hotelabcmantova.it. ✆ **0376-322-329.** Fax 0376-310-303. 58 units. 74€–165€ double. Rates include buffet breakfast. MC, V. Parking 15€. **Amenities:** Restaurant (cafe); bar; free bikes; concierge. *In room:* TV, hair dryer, Wi-Fi.

Ochina Bianca ★★ NORTHERN ITALIAN Gilberto and Marcella Venturini serve distinctive variations on the local cuisine in these simple yet elegant dining rooms a few blocks north of the city center. Many of the dishes rely on fresh fish from the Mincio, which finds its way into such creations as *peperoni ripieni di pesce di fiume* (peppers filled with smoked fish and topped with a fresh tomato sauce) and many of the *risotti.* Grilled or sautéed freshwater fish is also often on the menu, as are traditional meat specialties such as *coniglio alla porchetta* (roasted rabbit with pork stuffing).

Via Finzi 2. ✆ **0376-323-700.** Reservations required. *Primi* 10€–11€; *secondi* 13€–15€. MC, V. Tues–Sun 12:45–2pm and 7:45–10pm. Closed Sun evening and last 3 weeks in Aug.

Trattoria due Cavallini ★ NORTHERN ITALIAN Your reward for the 10-minute walk south of the center (follow Via Trieste and its continuation, Corso Garibaldi, until you hit Via Salnitro) is a meal at one of Mantua's favorite informal *trattorie,* where, in good weather, you can eat in a shady courtyard. The menu is a festival of local favorites, with smooth *tortelli di zucca* and an aromatic *stinco di maiale* (roasted pork joint, infused with fresh herbs). The *torta sbrisolona*—a dry cornmeal, almonds, and butter cake—is served fresh from the oven.

Via Salnitro 5. ✆ **0376-322-084.** Reservations not necessary. *Primi* 6€–10€; *secondi* 8€–11€. AE, MC, V. Wed–Mon noon–3pm and 7:15pm–midnight.

LAKE GARDA (LAGO DI GARDA)

Sirmione: 130km (81 miles) E of Milan, 150km (93 miles) W of Venice; Riva del Garda: 170km (105 miles) NE of Milan, 199km (123 miles) NW of Venice, 43km (27 miles) S of Trent

Lake Garda ★★, the largest and easternmost of the lakes, laps against the flat plains of Lombardy and the Veneto at its southern extremes, and in the north becomes fiordlike, its deep waters backed by Alpine peaks. Garda's shores are green and fragrant with flowery gardens, groves of olives and lemons, and forests of pines and cypress.

Lemon groves are abundant around Lake Garda.

This pleasing, vaguely exotic landscape has attracted the likes of poet Gabriele d'Annunzio, whose villa near Gardone is one of the area's major attractions, and Benito Mussolini, whose Republic of Salò was headquartered here. Long before them, the Romans discovered the hot springs that still gush forth at Sirmione, the famed resort on a spit of land at the lake's southern reaches. Today's visitors come to swim (Garda is the cleanest of the major lakes), windsurf (Riva del Garda, at the northern end of the lake, is Europe's windsurfing capital), and enjoy the easygoing ambience of Garda's many pleasant lakeside resorts.

If you have a car, are set on spending a few days on a lake, and are willing to go slightly farther afield where there are still German and Dutch tourists, but English-speaking visitors are hard to come by, consider **Lake Ledro,** just 13km (8 miles) west of Riva del Garda on Lake Garda's northernmost shore. Lake Ledro is much smaller than its neighbor, but it offers many great opportunities for walks, has several good beaches, and generally has an intimate feel that is sometimes missing from the bigger lakes. Prices are also lower than on Garda

The thermal baths in Sirmione.

and the altitude at 670m (2,200 ft.) is considerably higher so you get relief from the sometimes-oppressive heat of Riva del Garda. Lake Ledro, which also makes for a nice day trip from Riva del Garda, has three main towns—Pieve di Ledro, Mezzolago, and Molina di Ledro—that fan out from west to east on the northern half of the lake. For more information, head online to **www.vallediledro.com**.

Sirmione

Garda's most popular resort juts several miles into the southern waters of the lake on a narrow peninsula of cypress and olive groves. Despite an onslaught of visitors, Sirmione manages to retain its charm. Vehicular traffic is kept to a minimum (the few motorists allowed onto the marble streets of the Old Town are required to switch off their cars' engines at traffic lights). The emphasis is on strolling, swimming in waters warmed in spots by underwater hot springs, and relaxing on sunny hotel terraces. ***One caveat:*** You may find Sirmione to be less than charming in July and August, when the crowds descend in full force.

10

ESSENTIALS

GETTING THERE **By Train** There are no direct trains, but you can ride the rails to nearby Desenzano del Garda (a 20-min. bus ride from Sirmione; buses half-hourly; 2€), which is on the trunk line from Milan to Venice. Trains run almost every half-hour in either direction, stopping in Venice (1½–2 hr.; 24€), Verona (25–35 min.; 11€), Brescia (25 min.; 9€), and Milan (1–1½ hr.; 18€).

By Bus Hourly bus service links Sirmione with Verona (1 hr.; 4€) and Brescia (1 hr.; 3.80€). For more information, contact **Trasporti Brescia** (✆ **030-44-061**) or **APT** (✆ **045-805-7811**) in Verona. In summer, a special bus makes a 35-minute run from Verona at 7pm on Monday, Wednesday, Friday, and Saturday.

By Boat Hydrofoils and ferries operated by **Navigazione Laghi** (www.navlaghi.it; ✆ **800-551-801** or 031-579-211) ply the waters of the lake. One to two hourly ferries and four daily hydrofoils connect Sirmione with Desenzano del Garda (20 min. by ferry, 3.80€; 10 min. by hydrofoil, 5.80€). Two daily ferries and three daily hydrofoils connect Sirmione with Gardone (1¼–2 hr. by ferry, 7.50€; 55 min. by hydrofoil, 11€), and Riva del Garda (almost 4 hr. by ferry, 11€; 2¼ hr. by hydrofoil, 14€). Service is curtailed October to April.

By Car Sirmione is just off the A4 between Milan and Venice. From Bologna, Florence, Rome, and other points south, take the A22 north from Modena to Verona, and from there the A4 west to Sirmione. From Venice the trip takes about 1½ hours, and from Milan a little over an hour. There's ample parking in the lakeside lots lining Viale Marconi, the broad avenue that runs down the peninsula to the entrance of the Old Town.

VISITOR INFORMATION The **tourist office** is outside the Old Town near the castle, at Viale Marconi 8 (© **030-916-245**). Easter to October, hours are daily 9am to 12:30pm and 3 to 6pm (though the hotel reservations people actually keep it open all day long, usually until 8pm); November to March, hours are Monday to Friday 9am to 12:30pm and 3 to 6pm, and Saturday 9am to 12:30pm.

EXPLORING THE TOWN

In addition to its attractive, albeit tourist-shop-ridden Old Town, Sirmione has many lakeside promenades, pleasant beaches, and even some open countryside where olive trees sway in the breeze. Anything you'll want to see can be reached easily on foot, though an open-air tram makes the short run out to the Roman ruins from the northern edge of the Old Town (but not btw. 12:30 and 2:30pm).

The moated and turreted **Castello Scaligero** (© **030-916-468**) marks the only landside entrance to the Old Town. Built in the 13th century by the della Scala family, who ruled Verona and many of the lands surrounding the lake, the castle warrants a visit mainly for the views from its towers. It's open Tuesday to Sunday 9am to 7pm. Admission is 4€.

From the castle, Via Vittorio Emanuele leads through the center of the town and emerges after a few blocks into the greener, garden-lined lanes that wind through the tip of the peninsula to the **Grotte di Catullo** (© **030-916-157**). Whether or not these extensive ruins at the northern tip of the peninsula were really, as they're alleged to have been, the villa and baths of the pleasure-loving Roman poet Catullus is open to debate. Even so, their presence here, on a hilltop fragrant with wild rosemary and pines, demonstrates that Sirmione has been a deservedly popular retreat for millennia, and you can wander through the evocative remains while enjoying wonderful lake views. March to October 14, the ruins are open Tuesday to Saturday 8:30am to 7pm and Sunday 9:30am to 6pm; admission is 4€ for adults, 2€ for those 18 to 25, and free for children 17 and under and seniors 65 and over.

If you want to enjoy the clean waters of the lake, the place to head is the small **Lido delle Bionde,** near the castle off Via Dante. In summer, the beach concession rents lounge chairs with umbrellas for 10€ per day, as well as kayaks and pedal boats for 8€ per hour.

WHERE TO EAT & STAY

Sirmione has many pleasant, moderately priced hotels, all of which book up quickly in July and August, when they also charge higher rates. You aren't allowed to drive into the Old Town until a guard at the entrance near the castle confirms that you have a hotel reservation. The tourist office will help you find a room in your price range on the day you arrive, but they won't book ahead of time.

In addition to the dining choices below, you can get a quick pizza with a lake view from the terrace at **L'Arcimboldo,** Via Vittorio Emanuele 71 (© **030-916-409;** closed Tues).

Eden ★ The American poet Ezra Pound once lived in this pink-stucco lakeside hotel, located on a quiet side street leading to the lake in the center of town. Despite its long history as a lakeside retreat, the Eden has been modernized with taste and an eye to comfort. You can see the lake from most of the attractive rooms, which are decorated with contemporary furnishings. The mirrored walls enhance the light and lake views. The bathrooms are large and many have big tubs. The marble lobby opens to a delightful shaded terrace and a swimming pier that juts into the lake.

Piazza Carducci 17/18, 25019 Sirmione (BS). www.hoteledenonline.it. ✆ **030-916-481.** Fax 030-916-483. 33 units. 100€–160€ double; 140€–190€ double with balcony and lake view. Rates include breakfast. AE, DC, MC, V. Free parking nearby or 10€ in garage. Closed Nov–Easter. **Amenities:** Bar; babysitting; concierge; room service; tennis courts nearby. *In room:* A/C, TV, hair dryer, minibar.

Hotel Speranza This modest hotel occupies the upper floors of an old building that arches across Sirmione's main street, providing a prime location near the castle and only a few steps in either direction from the lake. The emphasis here is on clean efficiency rather than luxury: Public rooms consist of a tiny lobby and breakfast room, and the bare-bones rooms are perfectly serviceable. In fact, the modern furnishings set against parquet floors and stark white walls make for a fairly chic look. Bathrooms are modernized (save for the flat waffle towels on heated racks) and have box showers.

Via Castello 6, 25019 Sirmione (BS). http://hotelsperanza.sitonline.it. ✆ **030-916-116.** Fax 030-916-403. 13 units. 90€–105€ double. Rates include breakfast. AE, DC, MC, V. Free parking in square with permit, available from hotel. Closed mid-Nov to late Feb. **Amenities:** Concierge. *In room:* A/C, TV.

Olivi ★★ This pleasant modern hotel offers the chance to live the high life at rates that won't break the bank. It's not directly on the lake, which you can see from most rooms and the sunny terrace, but instead commands a hilltop position near the Roman ruins amid pines and olive groves. The rooms are stunningly decorated in varying schemes of bold, handsome pastels and earth tones. There are separate dressing areas off the bathrooms, and most have balconies. There's a pool in the garden and an artificial river streams past the terrace and windows of the lobby and breakfast room.

Via San Pietro 5, 25019 Sirmione (BS). www.hotelolivi.it. ✆ **030-990-5365.** Fax 030-916-472. 58 units. 145€–202€ standard double; 173€–228€ "quality" double with balcony and lake view. Rates include breakfast. AE, MC, V. Free parking on grounds. Closed Jan. **Amenities:** 3 restaurants, 2 bars, babysitting; concierge; pool; room service. *In room:* A/C, TV, hair dryer, minibar, Wi-Fi.

Osteria Al Torcol ★★ ITALIAN Fresh food, well-priced wine, and good service come together in what is almost certain to be your best meal in the area. The menu changes with the seasons, though, thanks to its popularity, you're likely always to find the counterintuitive yet delicious *tagliolini* (fresh egg noodles) with pistachios and shrimp. Unless you have something particular against noodles, eggs, pistachios, or shrimp, this dish must be ordered by somebody in your group so everybody can have a taste. The fish, both from the lake and the Mediterranean, is always grilled just right and on nice days you can enjoy it out on the patio under the trees. You won't have the views available at so many of the other mediocre (at best) restaurants that populate the lake front, but you'll be glad you came all the same.

Via San Salvatore 30. ✆ **030-990-4605.** Reservations highly recommended. *Primi* 12€–15€; *secondi* 15€–25€. MC, V. May–Sept daily 12:30–3pm and 7:30–10:30pm; Oct–Jan open only Sat–Sun; Feb–Apr open only in evening.

Ristorante Pace ITALIAN For the total experience at this elegant and scrumptious restaurant you can arrive directly from the lake by boat. Once there, ask for, or better yet reserve, a table with a lake view from which you can see the sunset. The prices are a bit above the norm for Sirmione, but after your first spoonful of fish soup or the first bite of a perfectly grilled steak you will know the extra euros have been well spent. There is also seating in an inner area immersed in flowers and trees from where the adventurous can try the frog risotto.

Piazza Porto Valentino 5. ✆ **030-990-5877.** Reservations recommended. *Primi* 16€–24€; *secondi* 22€–26€. AE, MC, V. Daily 12:30–2:30pm and 7:30–10:30pm. In winter, closed 1 day a week, usually Mon.

Gardone Riviera

This little resort 47km (29 miles) south of Riva del Garda on the western shore of the lake offers visitors a pleasant place for a little relaxation as well as Il Vittoriale, one of Lake Garda's major sites and an interesting attraction that will appeal to 20th-century history buffs.

GETTING THERE For ferry connections with Riva del Garda and Sirmione, see those sections elsewhere in this chapter. You can also bus here from Riva del Garda in 65 minutes (3.70€). From Sirmione, you have to transfer at Desenzano del Garda for one of six daily runs (1 hr. total, 3.50€). Hourly buses also make the 1-hour trip to and from Brescia (3.80€), and two buses a day make the 3-hour trip to and from Milan (8.50€).

VISITOR INFORMATION Gardone's **tourist office** is at Corso Repubblica 8 (✆ **0365-20-347**). Hours are April to October daily 10am to 12:30pm and 3 to 6:30pm; November to March Monday to Wednesday and Friday 9am to 12:30pm and 3 to 6pm, and Thursday 9am to 12:30pm.

EXPLORING GARDONE RIVIERA

Gabriele d'Annunzio, once Italy's most famous soldier/poet, is remembered at the hillside estate **Il Vittoriale** (www.vittoriale.it; ✆ **0365-296-511**) not for his lackluster verse, but more for his adventures and grand lifestyle. He bought the estate in 1921 and died here in 1936. The claustrophobic rooms of this ornately and bizarrely decorated villa are filled with bric-a-brac and artifacts from the poet's colorful life, including many mementos of his long affair with actress Eleonora Duse. Elsewhere on the grounds, which cascade down the hillside in a series of luxuriant gardens, are the patrol boat D'Annunzio commanded in World War I, a museum containing his biplane and photos, and his pompous hilltop tomb.

Admission to the grounds only is 8€ for adults and 6€ for children ages 7 to 18 and seniors 65 and older; you pay 5€ adults, 3€ kids and seniors additional to tour the villa, which you can visit only via a 25-minute guided tour (in Italian; even if your Italian doesn't go much beyond pasta, pizza, and gelato, it's worth taking the tour to look inside the villa). April to September the grounds are open daily 8:30am to 8pm, and the villa is open Tuesday to Sunday 9:30am to 7pm; October to March the grounds are open daily 9am to 5pm, the villa Tuesday to Sunday 9am to 1pm and 2 to 5pm. The villa also hosts a July-to-August season of concerts and plays; call ✆ **0365-20-072** (www.teatrodelvittoriale.it) for more information.

WHERE TO STAY

Grand Hotel Fasano ★★ Terraces and balconies overlook a palm- and willow-shaded garden right on the lake, where guests can take breakfast or dinner and swim off the small pier. The terraces above the gardens host the awning-shaded, fan-cooled restaurant and bar, which feature live piano music several times a week. Rooms at either end of the villa are larger, those in the long connecting wing smaller but with larger terraces. "Classic" rooms are fitted with simple, homey furnishings but are very comfy, featuring modern bathrooms and paintings of *putti*. "Superior" rooms are larger, with small, curtained-off terrace/sitting areas. Accommodations in the separate Villa Principe, set amid the trees at one end of the property, are slightly more exclusive, with larger rooms but similar furnishings.

25083 Gardone Riviera (BS). www.ghf.it. ✆ **0365-290-220.** Fax 0365-290-221. 63 units in main hotel, 12 in Villa Principe. 110€–130€ standard double without lake view; 120€–145€ superior double without lake view; 130€–165€ standard double with lake view; 155€–205€ superior double with lake view; 185€–230€ deluxe double with lake view; 340€–435€ suite. Rates include breakfast. Half board available for stays of at least 3 nights. MC, V. Free parking. **Amenities:** 4 restaurants; bar; babysitting; bikes; concierge; nearby golf course; fitness center; outdoor heated pool; room service; outdoor tennis courts; watersports equipment/rentals. *In room:* A/C, TV, hair dryer, minibar, Wi-Fi (in some rooms).

Villa Fiordaliso ★★ This gorgeous villa, built in 1903, is a mix of neoclassical and Liberty style, and has hosted several famous guests, including poet Gabriele d'Annunzio, from 1921 to 1923, and Mussolini's mistress, Claretta Petacci, in 1944. The dictator visited his lover frequently at the villa, which has been a hotel since 1990. All rooms have lake views except the "Mimosa," which overlooks the garden from a small terrace. The "Gardenia" and the "Magnolia" below it have windows on three sides (lake view, garden view, and a view overlooking the road). The exquisite restaurant (closed Tues at lunch and Mon all day) has a Michelin star. In warm weather, meals are served on a broad terrace where the lake laps almost to the tables; in winter you dine in a series of rooms with inlaid wood floors and decorated ceilings.

Via Zanardelli 150, 25083 Gardone Riviera (BS). www.villafiordaliso.it. ✆ **0365-20-158.** Fax 0365-290-011. 7 units. 350€–500€ double; 700€ Claretta suite. Rates include continental breakfast. AE, DC, MC, V. Free parking. Closed Nov–Feb. Children 12 and under are not allowed. **Amenities:** Michelin star restaurant; bar; concierge; room service; watersports equipment/rentals. *In room:* A/C, TV, hair dryer, minibar, Wi-Fi.

Riva Del Garda

The northernmost town on the lake is not just a resort, but a real, prosperous Italian town, with medieval towers, a nice smattering of Renaissance churches and *palazzi*, and narrow cobblestone streets where everyday business proceeds in its alluring way.

ESSENTIALS

GETTING THERE **By Train** See "Getting There," under Sirmione, p. 603, for connections to Desenzano del Garda, from which you must take a bus (see below).

By Bus Six buses a day link Riva del Garda and Desenzano del Garda on the southern end of the lake, about a 2-hour trip (5.10€). You can also travel between Sirmione and Riva del Garda by bus, though except for a 4:30pm direct run, you must transfer at Peschiera (2 hr., 5€). Twenty-five daily buses connect Riva del Garda and Trent though you'll likely have to change in Rovereto (1⅔ hr.; 4€). From Verona there are 16 a day (2 hr.; 5€), and from Brescia five daily (2 hr., 5.65€).

By Boat Navigazione Laghi (see "Sirmione," p. 603, for more information) runs the boats. Two ferries and four hydrofoils per day connect Riva del Garda with Gardone (2¾ hr. by ferry, 9.20€; 1 hr., 20 min. by hydrofoil, 13€), Sirmione (almost 4 hr. by ferry, 11€; 2¼ hr. by hydrofoil, 19€), and Desenzano del Garda (4¼ hr. by ferry, 12€; 2½ hr. by hydrofoil, 16€). Schedules vary with the season, with very limited service in the winter.

By Car The fastest link between Riva del Garda and points north and south is via the A22, which shoots up the east side of the lake (exit at Mori, 13km/8 miles east of Riva del Garda). A far more scenic drive is along the western shore, on the beautiful corniche between Riva del Garda and Salò that hugs cliffs and passes through mile after mile of tunnel. Depending on the route, by car Riva del Garda is about an hour from Verona and about 45 minutes from Sirmione.

VISITOR INFORMATION The **tourist office,** which supplies information on hotels, restaurants, and activities in the area, is near the lakefront at Largo Medaglie d'Oro 5 (www.visittrentino.it; ✆ **0464-554-444**). Mid-April to mid-September, it's open daily 9am to 7pm; mid-September to mid-April, hours are daily 9am to 6pm, though they can vary.

FESTIVALS & MARKETS Riva del Garda becomes a cultural oasis in July, when the town hosts an **international festival of classical music.**

EXPLORING RIVA DEL GARDA

Riva del Garda's Old Town is pleasant enough, though the only historic attractions of note are the 13th-century **Torre d'Apponale** (a picturesque medieval tower on the main square, which is sometimes open for climbing) and, nearby, the moated lakeside castle, **La Rocca.** Part of the castle interior now houses an unassuming collection of local arts and crafts (✆ **0464-573-869**). It's open Tuesday to Sunday 10am to 12:30pm and 1:30 to 6pm; admission is 2€, free for children 12 and under and seniors 65 and over. The castle also occasionally hosts concerts and minor traveling exhibits.

The main attraction here is the **lake,** which Riva del Garda takes advantage of with a waterside promenade stretching for several miles past parks and pebbly beaches. The water is warm enough for swimming May to October, and air currents fanned by the mountains make Garda popular for windsurfing year-round.

WATER & LAND SPORTS

A convenient point of embarkation for a lake outing is the beach next to the castle, where you can rent rowboats or pedal boats for about 8.50€ per hour (buy 2 hr., get a third free); from March to October, the concession is open daily 8am to 8pm.

For a more adventurous outing, check out the **sailing** and **windsurfing** at **Sailing Du Lac,** Viale Rovereto 44 (www.sailingdulac.com; ✆ **0464-552-453**), where you can rent windsurf equipment for 45€ per day, 39€ for a half-day, or 19€ for an hour. Multiday and weekly packages, as well as lessons, are also available.

You can rent **bikes** from **Superbike Girelli,** Viale Damiano Chiesa 15 (✆ **0464-556-602**), for 12€ to 14€ per day for a mountain bike; or from **Cicli**

Pederzolli, Viale dei Tigli 24 (✆ **0464-551-830**), which charges 9€ per day for a city bike and 14€ for a mountain bike.

WHERE TO EAT & STAY

Birreria Spaten ITALIAN This noisy indoor beer garden occupies the ground floor of an old *palazzo* and features a wide-ranging mix of food from the surrounding regions (Trentino, Lombardy, or from the other side of the Alps). Many of the German and Austrian visitors who favor Riva del Garda opt for the schnitzel-sauerkraut-sauerbraten fare, but you can also enjoy decent pasta dishes, a pizza, or a simply grilled lake trout. If you can't decide, the *Piatto Spaten* is an ample 16€ sampler of their Tyrolean specialties, including *wurstel, canederli* (a giant bread dumpling), a ham steak, and sauerkraut. The restaurant will reopen in April 2012 following a complete internal renovation and though the cuisine will remain the same, expect prices to be a bit higher as the owners seek to earn back some of their investment.

Via Maffei 7. ✆ **0464-553-670.** Main courses 7.50€–16€. MC, V. Thurs–Tues noon–2:30pm and 6–11pm. Closed Nov–Mar.

Hotel Sole ★★ Despite the very reasonable prices, this is one of the finest places in town to lodge and offers a wonderful location right on the lake at the main square. The lobby is filled with rare Persian carpets and abstract art. The rooms, reached via a sweeping circular staircase, are warm and luxurious with tasteful furnishings and marble-trimmed bathrooms. The best rooms have balconies facing the lake. Lakeview rooms are outfitted in antique style while those overlooking the square and town are modern. The rooftop solarium and sauna are perfect for relaxing after a hard day on the lake.

Piazza III Novembre 35, 38066 Riva del Garda (TN). www.hotelsole.net. ✆ **0464-552-686.** Fax 0464-552-811. 81 units. 78€–150€ double without lake view; 102€–176€ double with lake view. Add 15€ per person for half board and 25€ for full board. AE, DC, MC, V. Parking on street 5€, in garage 10€. Closed Nov to 2 weeks before Easter (except at Christmastime and during frequent trade fairs). **Amenities:** International restaurant; bar; free bikes; concierge; small exercise room; room service; sauna. *In room:* A/C (in some rooms), TV, hair dryer, minibar, Wi-Fi.

LAKE COMO (LAGO DI COMO)

Como (town): 65km (40 miles) NE of Milan; Menaggio: 35km (22 miles) NE of Como and 85km (53 miles) N of Milan; Varenna: 50km (31 miles) NE of Como and 80km (50 miles) NE of Milan

The first sight of the dramatic expanse of azure-hued **Lake Como ★★★**, ringed by gardens and forests and backed by the snowcapped Alps, is likely to evoke strong emotions. Romance, soulfulness, even gentle melancholy—these are the stirrings that over the centuries the lake has inspired in poets (Lord Byron), novelists (Stendhal), composers (Verdi and Rossini), and plenty of other visitors, too—be they deposed queens, such as Caroline of Brunswick, whom George IV of England exiled here for her adulterous ways, well-heeled modern travelers who glide up and down these waters in the ubiquitous lake steamers, or, these days, the rich and über-famous (George Clooney owns a villa here).

Less than an hour from Milan by train or car, Como's verdant shores provide a wonderful respite from modern life. Tellingly, Lake Como served as a backdrop for the romantic scenes in *Star Wars II: Attack of the Clones*—one of the very few settings in the film that was *not* created entirely by computer programs. It

When 1 Day Is All You Have

With northern Italy offering so much for the visitor, you are likely to wish you had another day, week, or even month to do everything you have set your sights on. With that in mind, here is a suggestion for **the perfect day trip to Lake Como from Milan.** Get an early train to Como and spend a few hours taking in the city, including a lakeshore walk to Villa Olmo and perhaps a trip up to Brunate on the funicular, especially if it is a clear day. Then grab a ferry (only take the hydrofoil, in which you will be forced to be inside for the whole trip, if you are in a real rush) to Bellagio where you can stroll the town and enjoy a late lunch. As the afternoon fades into early evening, hop another ferry for the short trip to Varenna on the eastern shore. With gelato in hand, walk along Varenna's lovely lakeside before popping into a small trattoria for dinner (you are on vacation so gelato before dinner is allowed, but if you are a fundamentalist on these matters do dinner first then the walk/gelato). With appetite satiated and legs tired, head up the steps to Varenna's train station for the last run back to Milan (usually at 10:20pm, but be sure to check as schedules change).

seems even George Lucas realized Como is better than any digital creation he can come up with.

Como

The largest and southernmost town on the lake isn't likely to charm you immediately, but the historic center is lovely if you take the time to stroll it and pop into its little churches. Long a center of silk making, Como still bustles today with commerce and industry. You'll probably want to stay in one of the more peaceful settings farther up the lake, but Como amply rewards a day's visit with some fine Renaissance churches and palaces, a nice lakefront promenade, and the chance to take a funicular for a bird's-eye view of the lake.

ESSENTIALS

GETTING THERE **By Train** One to three trains hourly connect Milan and Como's Stazione San Giovanni on Piazzale San Gottardo (regional from Milan's Piazza Garibaldi station, 55–60 min., 4.45€; high-speed from Milan's Stazione Centrale station, 40 min., 12€). There are also twice-hourly trains from Milan's Cadorna station to the more convenient Como Lago station right on the shorefront at Piazza Giacomo Matteotti. These trains take an hour and cost 4.45€.

One of the many villas along Lake Como.

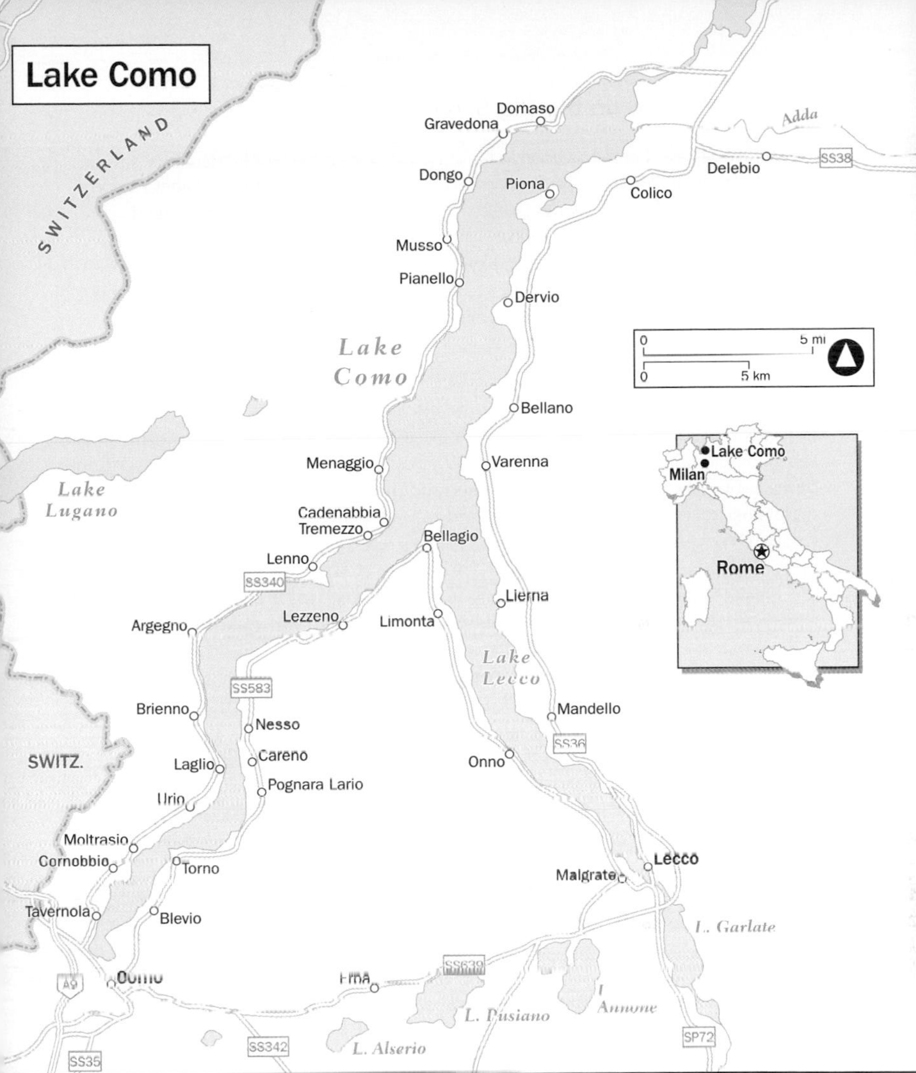

VISITOR INFORMATION The **regional tourist office** dispenses a wealth of information on hotels, restaurants, and campgrounds around the lake from its offices at Piazza Cavour 17 (www.lakecomo.org; ✆ **031-269-712**). It's open daily 9am to 1pm and 2 to 5pm. There is also a **city tourist office** in a little trailer along Via Maestri Comacini around the right side of the cathedral (✆ **031-264-215**). It's open Tuesday to Friday 10am to 12:30pm and 2:30 to 6pm, Saturday and Sunday 10am to 1pm and 2 to 6pm.

EXPLORING COMO

Part Gothic and part Renaissance, the **Piazza del Duomo,** in the center of town just off the lake, is festooned with exuberant masonry and sculpture. The main entrance is flanked by statues of Como natives Pliny the Elder and Pliny the

Lake Como on the Big Screen

Picturesque Lake Como has been featured in several films. Parts of *Star Wars Episode II: Attack of the Clones* (2002) were filmed at a villa in Lake Como, including the scene in which Anakin Skywalker and Padmé secretly marry. *Ocean's Twelve* (2004) also featured Lake Como as home to infamous thief and rival to Daniel Ocean, the Night Fox. In *Casino Royale* (2006), James Bond spends some time recuperating at a hospital in Lake Como after being tortured; this is also where he starts to fall in love with Vesper Lynd, a Bond girl.

Younger (the former wrote a 37-volume encyclopedia in the 1st century A.D. and the latter produced, among other things, a famous account of the eruption of Vesuvius that buried Pompeii in A.D. 79). Inside, beneath an 18th-century dome by Juvarra—the architect who designed much of Turin—is a lavish interior hung with mostly 16th-century paintings and tapestries, with lots of helpful leaflets in English to explain the major works of art. It's open daily 7:30am to noon and 3 to 7pm. The black-and-white-striped 13th-century **Broletto (Town Hall)** abuts the Duomo's left flank, and adjoining it is the **Torre del Comune.** As a study in contrasts, the starkly modernist and aptly named **Casa del Fascio,** built in 1936 as the seat of the region's Fascist government, rises just behind the Duomo.

Como's main street, **Corso Vittorio Emanuele II,** cuts through the medieval quarter, where wood-beamed houses line narrow streets. Just 2 blocks south of the Duomo, the five-sided, 12th-century **San Fedele** stands above a charming square of the same name; parts of the church, including the altar, date from the 6th century. It's open daily 8am to noon and 3:30 to 7pm.

For picturesque views of the lake, there is a **short, pleasant walk** up the western shore to the neoclassical Villa Olmo where interesting art exhibitions are often held.

For a quick retreat and stunning views of the lake, and on clear days the Alps, take the **funicular** (www.funicolarecomo.it; ✆ **031-303-608**) for a 7-minute ride up to Brunate (it leaves from the Lungo Lario Trieste every 15 min. or so, in summer every half-hour, and costs 2.80€ one-way or 5.10€ round-trip), a tiny town that sits right above Como. Brunate is the starting point for many hiking trails, including one that takes you all the way to Bellagio.

WHERE TO EAT

Ristorante Sociale ITALIAN/TRATTORIA This trattoria, located on an unassuming street behind the Duomo, is where locals go after a play or a concert at the nearby Teatro Sociale to enjoy one of the lake's best-priced meals. You'll find well-done standbys such as *risotto alla milanese* and beef stew with polenta, but also nice alternatives including stuffed vegetables; risotto with radicchio; and a refreshing chicken, tomato, basil, and pineapple salad that only appears on the menu in the summer months. You can choose between three distinct dining environments: The ground floor has vaulted brick ceilings that recall an *osteria* of yesteryear; one flight up is a more refined atmosphere with a painted frieze circling the room; and, weather permitting, you can dine in a pleasant, though cramped, courtyard that comes complete with a view of the lake (well, painted onto one of the walls).

Via Rodari 6. www.ristorantesociale.it. ✆ **031-264-042.** Reservations not necessary. Main courses 8.50€–19€. AE, MC, V. Wed–Mon noon–2pm and 7:30–10:30pm.

WHERE TO STAY

With Como's fame has come a paucity of decent moderately priced hotels. Fortunately, there are still a few options and for those ready to splash out, really splash out, nearby Cernobbio is home to one of the top hotels in Italy.

Hotel Metropole Suisse ★ This massive 1892 hotel occupies one side of Como's main square overlooking the lake. Accommodations vary; some rooms are carpeted and have nice contemporary furnishings; others are older, with wood floors, brass beds, and embroidered upholstery. Almost all rooms overlook the lake at least partially—some full-on (the best with small balconies), some obliquely over the cafes ringing the piazza, and others beyond the tree-lined promenade leading to the city park. The corner bar/lounge has picture windows for lake views, and the restaurant (under separate management) has tables out on the piazza.

Piazza Cavour 19, 22100 Como. www.hotelmetropolesuisse.com. ✆ **031-269-444.** Fax 031-300-808. 71 units. 128€–198€ double; 160€–246€ junior suite. Rates include buffet breakfast. AE, DC, MC, V. Parking 16€. **Amenities:** International restaurant; bar; babysitting; concierge; nearby golf course; room service; sauna; smoke free rooms; free Wi-Fi. *In room:* A/C, TV w/pay movies, hair dryer, minibar.

Le Stanze del Lago ★★ The *stanze* (rooms in Italian) are actually five small apartments that are in tiptop shape and kept immaculately clean. Opened in 2009 by Luca and his wife, Barbara, the apartments all have a bedroom with a double bed and a living room with a pullout couch, table, and a small kitchen area off to the side. La Stanza sui Tetti and La Stanza del Faro have sloped ceilings that give a cozy feel to the apartments while La Stanza dell'Elba and La Stanza del Duomo have exposed-brick walls for a more rustic setting. The location is as central as you can get, right above the Ristorante Sociale (see review above), which offers discounts to guests at Le Stanze, and a few steps from both the Duomo and the Como Lago train station.

Via Rodari 6, 22100 Como. www.lestanzedellago.com. ✆ **339-544-6515** or 339-837-4590. 5 units. 80€–100€ for 2 people; 90€–110€ for 3–4 people. AE, DC, MC, V. **Amenities:** Wi-Fi. *In room:* A/C, TV, kitchenette.

Villa d'Este ★★★ One of the most exclusive hotels in the world, this Renaissance villa in Cernobbio is set amid 4 hectares (10 acres) of meticulously landscaped lakeside gardens. It has hosted everyone from Mark Twain to Joseph Heller, Clark Gable to Brad Pitt, Carreras to Madonna. Guests can arrive by helicopter or private boat (something which, incidentally, you can rent for yourself when you arrive). No expense is spared, from the marble in the spacious bathrooms and the genuine antique prints and oil paintings lining the halls and rooms, to the Como silk brocades covering the antiques and the Empire furnishings that actually date back to Napoleon's stay here when it was still a private villa. No two rooms are alike, but all are fit for royalty. The main pool floats on the lake while indoors you'll find another pool as well as tennis and squash courts.

Via Regina 40, 22012 Cernobbio, Lago di Como. www.villadeste.it. ✆ **031-3481.** Fax 031-348-873. 152 units. 490€–810€ double; 835€–1,750€ junior suite. Rates include buffet breakfast (or continental breakfast served in your room). AE, DC, MC, V. Free parking. Closed mid-Nov to

Feb. **Amenities:** 3 restaurants (a formal, jacket-and-tie international restaurant; casual dinner-only grill in Queen's Pavilion; Japanese dinner restaurant); 2 bars (1 elegant w/music, the other poolside); babysitting; free bikes; concierge; 7 18-hole golf courses (14km/8¾ miles away); exercise room; Jacuzzi; 2 heated pools (indoor and outdoor); room service; sauna; spa; 2 tennis courts (indoor and lighted outdoor); watersports equipment/rentals. *In room:* A/C, TV w/pay movies and VCR (on request), hair dryer, minibar, Wi-Fi.

Bellagio & the Central Lake Region

By far the loveliest spot on the lake (and where travelers should definitely set their sights) is the section known as the Centro Lago. Three towns—**Bellagio, Varenna,** and **Menaggio**—sit across the water from one another on three different shorelines.

ESSENTIALS

GETTING THERE & GETTING AROUND **By Train** The closest train station to Bellagio is in Varenna, with trains hourly to and from Milan (about 70 min.; 6.25€). Alternatively you can ride the rails to Como (see above)—from where you can continue by bus or boat. If you're planning to leave the central part of the lake after dinner, the 10:20pm train from Varenna to Milan (with an hour stopover in Lecco) will be your last chance to do so. ***Tip:*** The ticket window at Varenna's station is rarely, if ever, open, and the automatic ticket machine has been broken for the better part of a decade. Get on without a ticket and find the ticket collector, who will have you pay a regular-price ticket without tacking on the large onboard acquisition fee.

By Boat From Como, boats arriving at the Centro Lago towns stop first at Bellagio: by ferry 2 hours (8.30€), by hydrofoil 35 to 45 minutes (12€). They continue on to Menaggio (by ferry another 15 min., 3.70€; by hydrofoil another 5 min., 5.70€). About half the boats then stop in Varenna as well (plus there are about two dozen short-haul ferries each from Bellagio and Menaggio to Varenna: by ferry 10 min., 3.70€; by hydrofoil 5 min., 5.70€). You can also get day passes good for just the central lake (12€) or for the whole lake (22€).

Many of the ferries carry cars for an additional fee. Schedules vary with the season, but from Easter through September a ferry or hydrofoil makes the trip from Como to Bellagio and other towns along the lake at least hourly. For more information, contact **Navigazione Laghi** (www.navlaghi.it; ✆ **800-551-801** or 031-579-211); the office is on the lakefront in Como on Lungo Lario Trieste.

By Bus One to three **SPT buses** (www.sptlinea.it; ✆ **031-247-247**) per hour travel from Como to Bellagio (a little more than 1 hr.; 3.10€). Hourly buses to Menaggio also take a little more than an hour (3.40€). Buses leave Como from the bus station in Piazza Matteotti next to the Como Lago train station. Buses to Menaggio and other towns on the western edge of the lake also stop at the San Giovanni train station; get bus tickets at the bar inside the train station.

By Car Bellagio is connected to Como by a picturesque lakeshore road, SS583, which can be very crowded in summer. The A9 links Como with Milan in about an hour. To reach Menaggio from Como, follow route SS340 along the western shore of the lake. For Varenna, follow SS342 from

Como to Nibionno, a speck of a town where you transfer to the SS36, which runs north through Lecco and then along the lake's eastern shore.

BELLAGIO

Bellagio ★★★ is at the tip of the peninsula at a point where the lake forks into three distinct basins: One long leg sweeps north into the Alps, Como is at the southern end of the western leg, and Lecco is at the southern end of the eastern leg. Boats from Bellagio make it easy to visit the nearby shores of the Centro Lago.

VISITOR INFORMATION The **IAT tourist office** is at Piazza Mazzini on the lakefront (✆ **031-950-204**). It's open April to October Monday to Saturday 9am to 12:30pm and 1 to 6pm, Sunday 10am to 2pm; November to March Monday, Tuesday, Thursday 9am to 12:30pm and 2:30 to 5pm, Wednesday 9am to 1pm, Friday and Saturday 9am to 7pm, Sunday 3 to 6pm. There is also a **Bellagio city tourist office** at Piazza della Chiesa 14 (www.bellagiolakecomo.com; ✆ **031-951-555**). Its hours are Monday 9:30am to 1pm, Tuesday to Sunday 9:30 to 11am and 2 to 4pm (Wed and Sun closed at 3:30pm).

FESTIVALS & MARKETS A pleasant way to spend a summer evening in Bellagio is at one of the concerts held in the Chiesa dei Cappuccini, on the grounds of the Rockefeller Foundation in June and July. Bellagio's outdoor market fills the waterfront every third Wednesday of the month.

The narrow streets of Bellagio.

Exploring Bellagio

Nestled amid cypress groves and verdant gardens, Bellagio features earth-toned old buildings climbing from the lakefront promenade along stepped cobbled lanes. While Bellagio is a popular retreat for everyone from Milanese out for a day of relaxation to British and Americans who come to relax for a week or two, the town has, for the most part, managed to keep its dignity despite the crush of tourists that arrive in the summer months.

One of Bellagio's famed gardens surrounds the **Villa Melzi** built by Francesco Melzi, a friend of Napoleon and an official of his Republic. The villa was the retreat of Franz Liszt and is now the home of a family that allows the public to stroll through their acres of manicured lawns and fountains and to visit a pavilion where a collection of Egyptian sculpture is on display. It's open from late March through October daily 9:30am to 6:30pm; admission is 6€ (for information on guided tours: ✆ **339-457-3838;** daniela@giardinidivillamelzi.it).

 Drinking with Dante

Bellagio has a great bar called **Divina Commedia ★★**, Salita Mella 43–45 (www.divinacommedia.com; ✆ **031-951-680**), modeled after Dante's epic poem. Upstairs, frescoes with puffy clouds and cherubs signify Paradise; the ground floor is Purgatory; and the tiny basement room is a fantastical black-lit Inferno cave of papier-mâché demons. There is a sister bar in Milan (Corso XXII Marzo 42), but it's outside of the city center, so if you're into Dante, get your fix here in Bellagio.

Where to Eat

La Grotta ★ ITALIAN/PIZZERIA Tucked away on a stepped street just off lakefront Piazza Mazzini, this cozy restaurant consists of a series of vaulted-ceiling dining rooms. The service is extremely friendly, and the wide-ranging menu includes the famous *pizzoccheri,* the sinfully rich buckwheat pasta with melted cheese, butter, and cabbage from Valtellina just north of here. For something lighter, you can't go wrong with the fish specials, especially the lake trout, or the delectable pizzas that are the best for miles around.

Salita Cernaia 14. ✆ **031-951-152.** Reservations not necessary. Pizza 6€–11€; main courses 7€–15€. AE, MC, V (credit cards accepted only for bills of more than 25€). Daily noon–3pm and 7–11:30pm (Oct–June closed Mon).

Ristorante Barchetta ★★ SEAFOOD One of Bellagio's best restaurants specializes in fresh lake fish and other seafood. In all but the coldest weather, food is served on a bamboo-enclosed heated terrace. There is also a bar on the terrace. Most of the pastas don't use seafood but are innovative variations on traditional recipes, such as *ravioli caprino* (filled with goat cheese, topped with pear sauce) and savory risotto with hazelnuts and pistachios. For a main course, however, you should try one of the delicious preparations of local perch or angler fish; the meat entrees, including baby lamb chops with rosemary, are also good. You can enjoy a pasta dish, as well as a meat and a fish dish, on one of the set menus.

Salita Mella 13. ✆ **031-951-389.** Reservations highly recommended. Main courses 16€–25€; tasting menu (for 2 only) 45€ per person, not including wine. AE, DC, MC, V. Thurs–Mon noon–2:30pm and 7–10:30pm. Closed Nov–Mar.

Where to Stay

For a wider selection of moderately priced hotels, you'd do best to head across the lake from Bellagio to Menaggio or Varenna (see below).

Giardinetto The best local lodging deal is at this little hotel at the top of town, reached from the lakefront by Bellagio's narrow-stepped streets. A snug lobby with a big fireplace opens onto a gravelly grapevine-covered terrace, where you're welcome to bring your own food for an alfresco meal. Most of the rooms are quite large and bright, with big windows (those on the upper floors provide nice views from balconies over the town and lake beyond, especially nos. 18–20) and furnishings like solid old armoires and, in the better rooms, box-spring-and-mattress beds rather than cots. Some rooms are on the airshaft, however, and others come with no window whatsoever so make sure you ask what you are getting. All in all, this hotel is basic but comfortable enough.

Piazza della Chiesa, 22021 Bellagio. giardinetto@aol.it. ✆ **031-950-168.** 13 units, 11 with private bathroom. 65€–70€ double. Breakfast 6€. No credit cards. Parking 10€ in nearby garage. Closed Nov–Apr. *In room:* Hair dryer.

Hotel Du Lac ★★ The Leoni family has been providing old-fashioned comfort at this 150-year-old hotel overlooking the lake from the main piazza for half a century. Downstairs, a bar spills onto the arcaded sidewalk in front and there are a series of pleasant sitting rooms. Meals are served in a nicely appointed dining room with panoramic views of the lake. In the guest rooms, each of which is unique, you'll find cushy armchairs and a nice smattering of antiques and reproductions that lend a great amount of charm. Many of the smallish rooms have balconies or terraces, and there's a rooftop sun terrace with sweeping lake views. Guests have free access to a sports center nearby with a pool, tennis courts, and children's play area.

Piazza Mazzini 32, 22021 Bellagio. www.bellagiohoteldulac.com. ✆ **031-950-320.** Fax 031-951-624. 39 units. 150€–200€ double; 210€–240€ superior double with lake view. Rates include buffet breakfast. Half board available. MC, V. Parking 10€ in nearby garage. Closed early Nov to Easter. **Amenities:** Restaurant (Italian/international); bar; babysitting; concierge. *In room:* A/C, TV, hair dryer, minibar, Wi-Fi.

VARENNA

You can happily spend some time clambering up and down the steep steps that substitute for streets in this charming village (on the eastern shore of the lake, about 10 min. by ferry from Bellagio) that, until not too long ago, made its living by fishing. The main attraction, though, is outside town.

In season, **ferries** make the 10 minute run between Bellagio and Varenna about every half-hour (see "By Boat," earlier). There's a tiny **tourist office** at Piazza Venini 1 (www.varennaitaly.com; ✆ **0341-830-367**), open Saturday and Sunday 10am to 12:30pm and 3:30 to 6:30pm (Aug also open Mon–Fri).

Exploring Varenna

The hilltop ruins of the **Castello di Vezio** (www.castellodivezio.it; ✆ **348-824-2504**) are about a 20-minute walk above the town on a gradually ascending path. The main reason for a visit is to enjoy the stunning views of the lake, its shoreline villages, and the backdrop of mountains at the northern end. The castle is open daily from 10am. April through June and September, it closes at 6pm (Sat–Sun at 7pm); July and August, it closes at 7pm (Sat–Sun at 8pm); March and October, it closes at 5pm (Sat–Sun at 6pm). The castle is closed November to February, and closes when there is bad weather. Admission is 1€.

Where to Eat & Stay

Albergo Milano ★★ A friendly Italian-Swiss couple took over this old house hanging over Varenna's lakefront in 2002 and turned it into one of the most pleasant retreats by the lake. All rooms are nonsmoking and have balconies or terraces from which to enjoy the views: nos. 1 and 2 open onto a wide terrace, and nos. 5 and 6 both have full-on lake vistas; the rest overlook the neighbor's pretty garden with partial lake views. In summer, breakfast is served on the outdoor terrace. There are also three nearby annexes that enjoy all the services of the main hotel, including breakfast. The **Casa Gialla** is a two-bedroom apartment with views of a quiet alley that accommodates up to five guests. The **Casa Rossa**

offers five rooms in an adjacent building with either a balcony or terrace and great lake views. **Casa 3Archi** can sleep up to four in a bedroom and large living room. Via XX Settembre 29, 23829 Varenna. www.varenna.net. ✆ **0341-830-298.** Fax 0341-830-061. 8 units. 115€–145€ double with lateral lake view and balcony; 150€–160€ double with full lake view and balcony; 160€–170€ double with full lake view and terrace. Rates include buffet breakfast. 3-course dinner 35€ upon request (restaurant closed Tues and Sun). MC, V. Free parking on the street or 14€ in nearby garage. Closed mid-Nov through Mar. **Amenities:** Restaurant; bar; concierge; room service; Wi-Fi. *In room:* Hair dryer (on request), Wi-Fi (Casa Gialla and Casa 3Archi don't have any Internet connection, but guests can connect in lobby of the hotel).

Cavatappi ★★ 🎁 ITALIAN With five tables placed in a rustic setting of stone walls and copper pots hanging over a fireplace, this is the type of simple, homey restaurant where you expect to eat well. And eat well you will whether it's the lake fish that has just been brought up from Varenna's tiny port, risotto cooked with smoked cheese and red wine, or the beef filet and lamb ribs that will remind you that when the raw materials are right the preparation is almost a formality. A place that calls itself *cavatappi* (corkscrews) is obliged to have an excellent wine list so no surprise there (a 2000 Sassicaia with the beef?). With space tight, the restaurant is not always child friendly, especially if you're expecting to have junior sleep in the stroller parked by your table while you eat.
Via XX Settembre 10. www.ilcavatappiwine-food.it. ✆ **0341-815-349.** Reservations highly recommended. Main courses 12€–20€. MC, V. Thurs–Tues 12:30–2:30pm and 7:30–10pm.

MENAGGIO

This lively resort town hugs the western shore of the lake, across from Bellagio on its peninsula and Varenna on the distant shore. Hikers should stop in at the **tourist office** on Piazza Garibaldi 8 (www.menaggio.com; ✆/fax **0344-32-924**), open daily 9am to 12:30pm and 2:30 to 6pm (Nov–Mar closed Wed and Sun). The very helpful staff distributes a booklet, ***Hiking in the Area around Menaggio,*** with descriptions of more than a dozen walks, with maps and instructions on what buses to take to trail heads. The town's **bus stop** is at Piazza Garibaldi (Sun on Via Mazzini); tickets are sold at Bar Centrale or the newsstand on Via Calvi at the piazza.

Exploring Around Menaggio

The major nearby attraction is **Villa Carlotta** (www.villacarlotta.it; ✆ **0344-40-405**), located about 2.5km (1½ miles) south of town. Begun in 1643, this is the most famous villa on the lake. After a succession of owners, including Prussian royalty who lavished their funds and attention on the gardens, the villa is now in the hands of the Italian government. It's filled with romantic paintings, statues by Canova and his imitators, and Empire furnishings, but the gardens are the main attraction, with azaleas, orchids, banana trees, cacti, palms, and forests of ferns spreading in all directions. You can take the no. C10 bus from Menaggio or walk along the lake (about 30–45 min.). The nearest ferry landing is at Cadenabbia. The villa and gardens are open daily April to October from 9am to 6:30pm, and in March from 9am to 4pm. Admission is 8.50€ for adults and 4.50€ for seniors 65 and over and students.

WATERSPORTS The lido, at the north end of town, has a good **beach,** as well as a **pool,** and is open late June to mid-September daily 9am to 7pm. The tourist office has information on water-skiing and other activities. Also ask

The gardens at the Villa Carlotta.

at the hostel (see below) about boat and bike rentals, which are available to nonguests during slow periods.

Where to Eat & Stay

Albergo-Ristorante Il Vapore ★ This very pleasant small restaurant/hotel faces a quiet square just off the lakefront. The rooms are comfortable, with rather nice modern furnishings (plus antiques in a few), though the bathrooms are cramped. Six rooms open onto partial lake views: nos. 21 and 22 from tall windows, nos. 25 and 26 from small terraces, and nos. 28 and 29 (the biggest room, with windows on two sides for a breeze) from tiny balconies. Meals of local specialties from the nearby mountain valleys are normally served beneath the wisteria-shaded arbor of the entryway or in an attractive pale-blue dining room with paintings by local artists. It's best to call ahead in winter to make sure they are open.

Piazza Grossi 3, 22017 Menaggio. www.hotelvapore.it. ✆ **0344-32-229.** Fax 0304-34-850. 10 units. 55€ double without lake view; 60€ double with lake view. Breakfast 7€. No credit cards. **Amenities:** Restaurant; bar. *In room:* No phone.

Menaggio Youth Hostel This youth hostel is easily accessible by boat from Bellagio and other towns on the Centro Lago and is frequented about evenly by frugal adults and backpacking students. The dorms are relatively cozy, with no more than six beds per room. Most of the rooms, admittedly a little rundown, have a view of the lake—nos. 3, 4, and 5 on the first floor even share a balcony. Everyone enjoys the view from the large, sunny communal terrace. The hostel serves a 12€ dinner that even attracts locals. (You're expected to set your own table on the porch, retrieve each course as it's called, and wash your own dishes.) Saturday night there is a barbecue with meat, polenta, and couscous.

Via IV Novembre 86 (on the south edge of town), 22017 Menaggio (CO). www.menaggiohostel.com. ✆/fax **0344-32-356.** 35 beds. 17€ per person in dorm; 68€ triple with bathroom; 74€ family room with private bathroom (up to 4 people). Rates include breakfast. No credit cards. Closed 1st weekend in Nov to Mar 15. Office open 8am–2pm and 5pm–midnight. **Amenities:** Restaurant; bar; bike, kayak, and rowboat rental. *In room:* No phone, Wi-Fi.

LAKE MAGGIORE (LAGO MAGGIORE) & THE BORROMEAN ISLANDS

Stresa: 90km (56 miles) NW of Milan

Anyone who reads Hemingway will know this lake, its views of the Alps, and its forested shores from *A Farewell to Arms.* That's just the sort of place Lake Maggiore ★★ is—a pleasure ground that's steeped in associations with famous figures (Flaubert, Wagner, Goethe, and many of Europe's other great minds seem to have been inspired by the deep, moody waters) and not-so-famous wealthy visitors. Fortunately, you need not be famous or wealthy to enjoy Maggiore, the top bit of which is in Switzerland.

The Alps rise above Lake Maggiore.

Stresa

The major town on the lake is a pretty, festive little place, with a long lakefront promenade, a lively and attractive commercial center, and a bevy of restaurants and hotels that range from the expensively splendid to the affordably comfortable.

ESSENTIALS

GETTING THERE **By Train** Stresa is linked with Milan by 20 trains a day (regional: 55 min.–75 min.; 7.40€).

By Boat Boats arrive and depart from Piazza Marconi, connecting Stresa with the Borromean Islands (Isole Borromee). It takes 5 minutes to move from island to island (3.50€ for one leg or 12€ for three-island pass). Many other lakeside spots can be reached, with most boats on the lake operated by **Navigazione Laghi** (www.navlaghi.it; ✆ **800-551-801** or 0322-233-200).

By Car A8 runs between Milan and Sesto Calende, near the southern end of the lake; from there, Route SS33 follows the western shore to Stresa. The trip takes a little over an hour.

VISITOR INFORMATION The **tourist office** is at the ferry dock (✆/fax **0323-31-308**) and is open daily 10am to 12:30pm and 3 to 6:30pm (Nov–Feb closed Sun). You can also get info from private websites (try www.lagomaggiore.it). For hiking information, ask for the booklet *Percorsi Verdi*.

FESTIVALS & MARKETS May to September, Stresa draws visitors from around the world for its **Settimane Musicali,** or Festival of Musical Weeks, a major gathering of classical musicians. The festival has an information office at Via Carducci 38 (www.stresafestival.eu; ✆ **0323-31-095**).

EXPLORING STRESA & THE ISLANDS

Stresa

Strolling and relaxing are the main activities in Stresa. The action (that is to say the strolling and relaxing) takes place mostly at the lakeside promenade, running from the center of town north past the grand lakeside hotels, including the Iles des Borromées, where Hemingway set *A Farewell to Arms*. Sooner or later, though, most visitors climb into a boat for the short ride to the Borromean Islands.

Borromean Islands (Isole Borromee)

These three islands, named for the Borromeo family that has owned them since the 12th century, float just off Stresa and entice visitors with their stunning beauty. Note that Isola Bella and Isola Superiore have villages you can hang out in for free while Isola Madre consists solely of the admission-charging gardens.

Public **ferries** leave for the islands every half-hour from Stresa's Piazza Marconi; a 12€ **three-island pass** is the most economical way to visit them. If you buy your admission tickets for the *isole* sights at the Stresa ferry office along with your ferry tickets, you'll save 1€ off each—though the ticket agents will not advise you of this; you have to ask. Buy tickets only from the public Navigazione Laghi (see "Getting There," above), in the big building with triple arches. Private boats also make the trip out to the island—at obscene rates; you'll see other ticket booths as well as hucksters dressed as sailors trying to lure you aboard (for large groups, the prices can be reasonable, but do your negotiating on the dock before you get on the boat). For more information, visit **www.borromeoturismo.it**.

The Borromeo Palazzo.

ISOLA BELLA Isola Bella (5 min. from Stresa) remains true to its name, with splendid 17th-century gardens that ascend from the shore in 10 luxuriantly planted terraces. The Borromeo ***palazzo*** provides a chance to explore opulently decorated rooms, including one where Napoleon and Josephine once slept. It's open daily late March to mid-October, 9am to 5:30pm. Admission is 13€ for adults and 5.50€ for children ages 6 to 15. Audio tours help make sense of it all for 3.50€ each or 5€ to rent two sets of headphones. For more details, call ✆ **0323-30-556.**

ISOLA SUPERIORE Most of Isola Superiore, also known as Isola Pescatori (10 min. from Stresa), is occupied by a not-so-quaint fishing village in which every one of the tall houses on this tiny strip of land seems to harbor a souvenir shop or pizza stand, and there are hordes of visitors to keep them busy. If you come when the crowds are absent, the visit is certainly worthwhile.

Homes on Isola Bella, one of the Borromean Islands.

Budgeting Your Time

To squeeze as much of Stresa's sights as you can into a day, note that the ferry back from the Isole Borromee stops first at the Mottarone cable-car area before chugging down the coast to the center of Stresa and the main docks. You can hop off at this first stop to either ride the cable car up the mountain or simply walk back into Stresa itself along a pretty lakeside promenade, past crumbling villas and impromptu sculpture gardens, in about 20 minutes.

ISOLA MADRE The largest and most peaceful of the islands is Isola Madre (30 min. from Stresa), every inch of which is covered with the exquisite flora and exotic colorful birds of the 3.2-hectare (8-acre) **Orto Botanico** (✆ **0323-31-261**). The map they hand out at the entrance/ticket booth details all the flora; you're on your own to identify the various peacocks, game fowl, exotic birds, funky chickens, and other feathered creatures that strut, flit, and roost amid the lawns around the central villa (1518–85), filled with Borromeo family memorabilia and some interesting old puppet-show stages. The botanical garden is open late March through mid-October daily 9am to 5:30pm, admission is 11€ for adults and 5.50€ for children ages 6 to 15. A joint 1-day ticket for the Isola Bella *palazzo* and the Isola Madre gardens costs 18€ for adults and 8€ for children.

Hiking & Biking in the Area

The forested slopes above Stresa are prime hiking and mountain biking terrain. To reach a network of trails, take the **cable car** (www.stresa-mottarone.it; ✆ **0323-30-295**) from near the lakefront at the north end of town up **Monte Mottarone;** it runs every 20 minutes from roughly 8am to 5:30pm (hours vary with the season). It costs 11€ one-way to take the cable car along with a bike, which you can rent at the station for 25€ for a half-day or 30€ for a full day. A round-trip ticket without a bike costs 14€ for adults and 8.50€ for children ages 4 to 12.

WHERE TO EAT & STAY

La Palma ★★ The Palma is one of the nicest of Stresa's luxury hotels and, given the high-level comfort and the amenities, one of the most reasonably priced. Most of the large rooms, done in rich floral fabrics and wood tones, open to balconies overlooking the lake, and all but a few of the spacious marble bathrooms have Jacuzzis. There's a rooftop sun terrace and fitness center, with a hot tub and sauna, but the most pleasant places to relax are in the flowery garden in front of the hotel and the terrace surrounding the lakeside pool.

Lungolago Umberto I, 33, 28838 Stresa. www.hlapalma.it. ✆ **0323-32-401.** Fax 0323-933-930. 128 units. 135€–150€ standard double; 160€–175€ superior double with lake view; 250€–320€ junior suite with lake view. Rates include buffet breakfast. AE, DC, MC, V. Free parking. Closed mid-Dec to mid-Feb. **Amenities:** Restaurant; bar; babysitting; bikes; concierge; exercise room; Jacuzzi; pool; room service; sauna; smoke-free rooms; tennis courts; Wi-Fi. *In room:* A/C, TV, hair dryer, minibar.

Taverna del Pappagallo ★ ITALIAN/PIZZERIA Most of Stresa seems to congregate in this pleasant restaurant for the most popular pizza in town. But just about all the fare here is delicious, including delectable homemade gnocchi and dishes such as grilled sausage. Weather permitting, ask for a table in the pleasant garden.

Via Principessa Margherita 46. ✆ **0323-30-411.** Reservations not necessary. Pizza 5.50€–15€; main courses 8€–17€. No credit cards. Thurs–Tues 11:30am–2:30pm and 6:30–10:30pm (daily in summer).

Verbano ★★ 🎁 This dusty-rose villa has one of the most envied positions on all of Lago Maggiore, sitting at the tip of the Isola dei Pescatori, overlooking the back side of Isola Bella. The flower-fringed terrace, with its excellent restaurant (reviewed separately below), enjoys great lake views in three directions. Each room is named after the flower that drives the villa's color scheme; all feature parquet floors, big old-wood furnishings, real beds with wrought-iron bedsteads, and large tiled bathrooms. Nos. 1 and 2, on the front of the villa with Isola Bella views, have working fireplaces; highly requested no. 2, on the corner, has a balcony on the front and a shared terrace on the side. Rooms on the first floor share a large terrace overlooking Isola Madre and the eastern shore of the lake.

Isola Superiore dei Pescatori, 28838 Stresa. www.hotelverbano.it. ✆ **0323-32-534.** Fax 0323-33-129. 12 units. 150€–185€ double; 190€–210€ triple. Rates include breakfast. Half board 140€ per person. AE, DC, MC, V. Closed end of Oct to mid-Mar. **Amenities:** Great regional restaurant (see review below); bar; babysitting; courtesy boat from the mainland in the evenings after public ferry service ends; concierge; room service. *In room:* Hair dryer, Wi-Fi.

Verbano ★★ ITALIAN Verbano offers a fairy-tale location on the point of the "Fisherman's Isle," taking up the jasmine-fringed gravelly terrace next to the hotel (reviewed above). The waters lap right up to the wall, and the views are over the back side of Isola Bella and the lake around you on three sides. The cooking needn't be anything special, given its location in a prime tourist spot, but it almost lives up to the setting. Among the tempting *primi* is *crema di patate e porri con code di gamberi,* a deliciously smooth potato-and-leek soup with fresh-water shrimp to give it a kick. The best *secondi* are based on the local lake fish (try grilled lake trout, or the *luccioperca,* a relative of perch, roasted in thyme and topped with black truffles), though there are always well-prepared pork, veal, and beef dishes on the menu.

Isola Superiore dei Pescatori. ✆ **0323-32-534.** Reservations recommended. Main courses 10€–25€. AE, DC, MC, V. Daily noon–2:30pm and 7–10pm (winter closed Wed). Closed Jan.

11
PIEDMONT
& VALLE
D'AOSTA

Loosely translated, Piedmont (Piemonte) means "at the foot of the mountains." Those mountains, of course, are the Alps, which define the region and are part of Italy's northern and western borders. These dramatic peaks are visible in much of the province, most of which rises and rolls over fertile foothills that produce a bounty that is as rich as the region is green. Piedmont is a land of cheeses, truffles, plump fruit, and wine—among which are some of Italy's most powerful, complex, and delicious reds, including **Barolo** and **Barbaresco,** lighter reds **Barbera** and **Dolcetto,** and one of Italy's most famous sparkling whites, **Asti Spumanti.**

Not that all of Piedmont is rural. **Turin,** Italy's car town, is the region's capital. But within its ring of industrialized suburbs, rather than an Italian Detroit lies an elegant city of mannerly squares, baroque palaces, and stunning art collections. The Torinesi and their neighbors from other parts of Italy often retreat to **Valle d'Aosta,** the smallest and most mountainous of Italian provinces.

THE BEST PIEDMONT & VALLE D'AOSTA EXPERIENCES

- **Lingering over coffee in Turin's Piazza San Carlo:** Coffee is an excuse, it could be tea, cookies, or anything else. What's important is that you stop and spend time here in what is without a doubt one of Italy's most beautiful squares. See p. 630.
- **Recharging in Parco del Valentino, Turin:** This long and narrow park flanking the Po river is where Torinesi come for a respite from the city and where visitors can slow down and recharge as Italy's longest river flows gently by. See p. 636.
- **Jumping back through time at the Sacra di San Michele:** Come to this hilltop abbey, outside of Turin, to be disabused of the notion that you need a time machine to travel back to the Middle Ages. See p. 642.
- **Sipping your way through Piedmont wine country:** Some of Italy's best wines get squeezed out of grapes that once called the hills south of Turin their home. As you sip your way through charming villages you'll also have ample opportunity to eat the tempting local specialties that include white truffles. See p. 642.
- **Ascending to new heights on the Mont Blanc Cable Car:** Just because you didn't bring your cords and pickax doesn't mean you can't make it to the upper reaches of the Mont Blanc massif. If you have the time (and deep pockets) you can hop all the way over to the French side and then take a bus back. See p. 655.

PREVIOUS PAGE: **Skiers relaxing beneath the Matterhorn.**

Piedmont & the Valle d'Aosta

TURIN (TORINO)

669km (415 miles) NW of Rome, 140km (87 miles) E of Milan

It's often said that Turin is the most French city in Italy or the most Italian city in France. The reason is partly historical and partly architectural. From the late 13th century to Italy's unification in 1861 (when the city served very briefly as capital), Turin was the capital of the **House of Savoy.** The Savoys were as French as they were Italian, and their holdings extended well into the present day French regions of Savoy and the Côte d'Azur, as well as Sardinia. The city's Francophile 17th- and 18th-century architects, inspired by the tastes of the French court, razed much of the existing city and replaced it with broad avenues, airy *piazze,* and grandiose buildings, enough of which are still around today to make Turin one of Europe's great baroque cities.

After Napoleon's occupation, Turin's intellectuals began percolating the ideas that would eventually blossom into the Risorgimento unification movement, with hometown king Vittorio Emanuele II of Savoy as its royal ruler. Italy's first prime minister was Turin native and the Risorgimento's political leader, Camillo Benso di Cavour. Later the Italian Communist Party was born here on the Fiat factory floor under the leadership of poet Antonio Gramsci, though that same factory floor also gave rise to the ultraradical Red Brigades terrorist group in the 1970s.

Thanks in part to a successful hosting of the 2006 Winter Olympics, and then another makeover ahead of the 2011 celebration of the 150th anniversary of Italian unification, Turin has transformed itself from a former industrial power into a vibrant city full of museums, enticing cafes, beautiful squares, and a riverside park that is perfect for relaxing after a day of heavy touring. Those who take the time to look around the historic center will find an elegant and sophisticated city with the charm of a place that, for all its Francophile leanings, is quintessentially Italian and perhaps the most pleasant big city in northern Italy.

Essentials

GETTING THERE **By Plane** Domestic and international flights land at the **Caselle International Airport** (www.aeroportoditorino.it; ✆ **011-567-6361**), about 15km (10 miles) north of Turin. Buses run between the airport and the city's main train stations, Porta Nuova and Porta Susa. The trip takes about 40 minutes. A **taxi** from the airport takes about 30 minutes and costs about 35€.

By Train Turin's main train station is **Stazione di Porta Nuova,** just south of the center on Piazza Carlo Felice, which marks the intersection of two of Turin's major thoroughfares, Corso Vittorio Emanuele and Via Roma. Porta Nuova was completely redone a few years ago making it a nice enough place to mingle before you catch a train or, alternatively, there is a nice park in front of the station (May–Sept 8am–11pm and until 7pm the rest of the year). From Porta Nuova, there are two dozen trains a day to and from Milan—the trip takes 1 hour each way on the fastest trains; otherwise, it can take as long as 2 hours (some trains to and from Milan also stop at Turin's other station, Stazione di Porta Susa). There are two direct trains a day to and from Venice (4½ hr.); otherwise with a change in Milan it actually takes less time if you take the fast trains on both legs (4 hr.). There are 15 trains a day to and from Genoa (2 hr.), and 15 trains a day to and from Rome (4½ hr.). **Stazione di Porta Susa,** west of the center on Piazza XVIII Dicembre, connects Turin with many outlying Piedmont towns; it is also the terminus for TGV service to and from Paris, with two trains a day making the trip in just under 6 hours.

By Bus Turin's main bus terminal is **Autostazione Terminal Bus,** Corso Vittorio Emanuele II 131 (near Stazione di Porta Susa; www.autostazionetorino.it). The ticket office is open daily from 9am to 1pm and 3 to 7pm. Buses connect Turin and Courmayeur (2½ hr.), Aosta (2 hr.), Milan (2 hr.), Chamonix (3½ hr.), and many smaller towns in Piedmont.

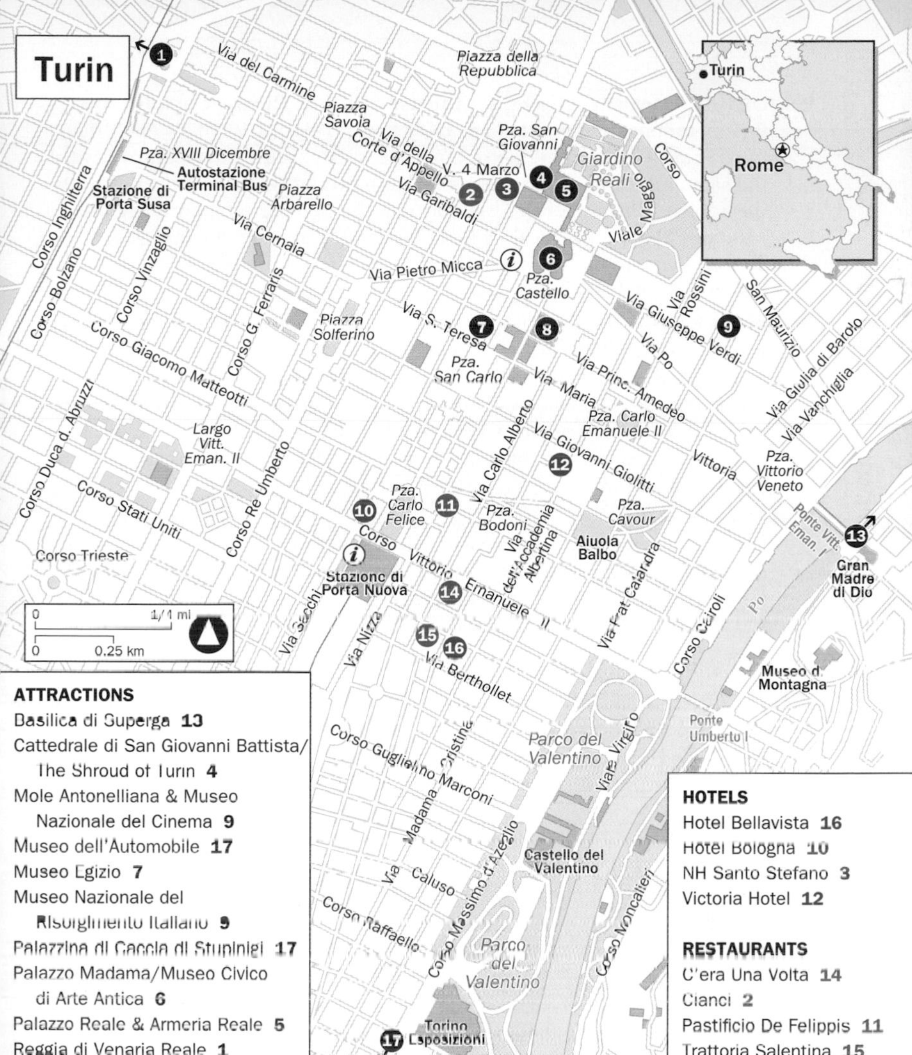

By Car Turin is at the hub of an extensive network of autostrade. A4 connects Turin with Milan, about an hour and a half; A6 connects Turin with the Ligurian coast (and, from there, with Genoa via A10, with a total travel time btw. the two cities of about 1½ hr.); A5 connects Turin with Aosta (about 1½ hr.); and A21 connects Turin with Asti and Piacenza, where you can connect with the A1 for Florence (about 4 hr. from Turin) and Rome (about 6½ hr. from Turin).

VISITOR INFORMATION There is a **tourist office** at **Piazza Castello** (www.turismotorino.org; ✆ **011-535-181;** fax 011-530-070) that's open daily from 9am to 7pm. There's also an office in **Stazione Porta Nuova** with the same hours. If you're coming to Turin on the weekend, check in with the tourist office's website, as you may be able to take advantage of a **"Torino Weekend"** deal, which offers 2 nights in a hotel plus two Torino+Piemonte Cards (see below), from 84€ to 195€ per person depending on the hotel chosen.

GETTING AROUND It's easy to get around central Turin **by foot.** There's also a vast network of GTT trams and buses as well as one metro line (www.comune.torino.it/gtt; ✆ **800-019-152** in Italy, or 011-57-641). Tickets on public transportation are available at newsstands for 1€ and are valid for 70 minutes. With the **Torino+Piemonte Card** (see "Exploring," below), you can ride the city's public transportation for free for 48 hours. Longer periods are available as well.

FESTIVALS & MARKETS Dance, opera, theater, and musical performances (mostly classical) are on the agenda all year long, but September is the month to really enjoy classical music—more than 60 classical concerts are held on stages around the city during the month-long **Settembre Musica** festival (www.mitosettembremusica.it; ✆ **011-442-4787**), which is hosted together with Milan.

Bric-a-brac of all kinds, be it household utensils, books, or used clothing, fills the stalls of the **Mercato del Balon,** held every Saturday at Piazza della Repubblica. **Gran Balon** fills the piazza the second Sunday of every month and is a larger affair, with some genuine antiques and artworks included in the mix. **Mercato della Crocetta,** at Largo Cassini, sells clothing at very low prices. For a look at the bounty of the surrounding farmlands, wander through the extensive **outdoor food market** at Porta Palazzo, open Monday through Friday from 8:30am to 1:30pm and Saturday until 6:30pm.

CITY LAYOUT You will get a sense of Turin's refined air as soon as you step off the train into the mannerly 19th-century Stazione di Porta Nuova. The stately arcaded Via Roma, lined with shops and cafes, proceeds from the front of the station through a series of *piazze* toward the Piazza Castello and the center of the city, about a 15-minute walk.

Directly in front of the station, the circular **Piazza Carlo Felice** is ringed with outdoor cafes and built around a garden. Walking farther along the street will lead you into the **Piazza San Carlo,** one of the most beautiful squares in all of Italy and home to two historic cafes as well as the twin churches of San Carlo and Santa Cristina. At the end of Via Roma, the **Piazza Castello** is dominated by the **Palazzo Madama,** so named for its 17th-century inhabitant Christine Marie. Just off the piazza is the **Palazzo Reale,** residence of the Savoys from 1646 to 1865, whose gardens now provide a pleasant respite from traffic and paving stones.

From here, a walk east toward the river along Via Po takes you through Turin's university district to one of Italy's largest squares, the much-elongated Piazza Vittorio Veneto and, at the end of this elegant expanse, the Po River. Two enjoyable streets to stroll that are closed to traffic are Via Garibaldi from Piazza Castello to Piazza Statuto and Via La Grange from Piazza Castello to Corso Vittorio Emanuele II.

[Fast FACTS] TURIN

Bookstores **Libreria Internazionale Luxemburg,** Via C. Battisti 7 (✆ **011-561-3896**), has a large selection of British books and a helpful English-speaking staff; it is open Monday through Saturday from 8am to 7:30pm, and Sunday from 10am to 1pm and 3 to 7pm. Another good bet for books in English is the chain **Feltrinelli,** Piazza Castello 19 (✆ **011-541-627**), and inside Stazione Porta Nuova (✆ **011-563-981**). Turin has many stores specializing in rare books and old prints, and many of these shops sell their wares from the secondhand-book stalls along the Via Po, which runs between Piazza Castello and the river.

Crime Turin is a relatively safe city, but use the same precautions you would exercise in any large city. Specifically, avoid the riverside streets along the Po after the revelers have gone home. In an **emergency,** call ✆ **113;** this is a free call. The **central police station** is near Stazione di Porta Susa at Corso Vinzaglio 10 (✆ **011-558-81**).

Drugstores A convenient late-night pharmacy is **Farmacia Boniscontro,** Corso Vittorio Emanuele 66 (✆ **011-538-271**); it is open most of the day and night, closing only between 12:30 and 3pm.

Emergencies The general emergency number is ✆ **113;** for an ambulance, dial ✆ **118.** Both are free calls.

Holidays Turin's patron saint, San Giovanni Battista (Saint John the Baptist), is honored on June 24. For a list of official state holidays, see the "Public Holidays" section, on p. 935.

Hospitals The **Ospedale Maggiore di San Giovanni Battista,** Via Cavour 31 at Piazza Cavour (✆ **011-633-1633**), offers a variety of medical services.

Internet For Internet access, **1PC4YOU,** at Via Verdi 20/G (✆ **011 026 8001**), is open Monday through Friday 9am to 9pm, Saturday 10am to 8pm, and Sunday 2 to 8pm. Or try the **FNAC superstore,** on Via Roma 56 (✆ **011-551-6711**), which is open daily 9:30am to 8pm.

Laundry **Lav@sciuga,** a laundromat/Internet point with seven locations across the city (www.lavasciuga.torino.it; ✆ **335-750-7813**), charges 7€ for a wash-and-dry of a small load. They're open daily from 8am to 10pm. The nearest location to the Porta Nuova train station is Via San Anselmo 9.

Luggage Storage Luggage storage is available at the Porta Nuova train station at the head of track 1: 4€ per bag for the first 5 hours, .60€ for each successive hour up to the 12th hour, and .20€ per hour after that. The office is open daily from 6:30am to 10pm.

Post Office Turin's main post office is just west of Piazza San Carlo at Via Alfieri 10 (✆ **011-506-011**); it is open Monday through Friday from 8:30am to 7pm and Saturday from 8:30am to 1pm. The postal code for Turin is 10100.

Taxis You can find taxis at cabstands; especially convenient in the central city are the stands in front of the train stations and around Piazza San Carlo and Piazza Castello. To call a taxi, dial ✆ **011-5737,** 011-5730, or 011-3399.

Telephone See "Fast Facts: Italy," p. 940. The area code for Turin is ✆ 011.

Exploring

The tourist office sells an extremely worthwhile **Torino+Piemonte Card** for 22€, valid for one adult plus one child 12 and under. The card grants you 48 hours of free public transport within Turin; access to more than 180 museums,

A Rare Glimpse: The Shroud of Turin

The Shroud of Turin—the garment that Christ was allegedly wrapped in when he was taken from the cross—is put on display about once a decade at the Cattedrale di San Giovanni Battista. The last viewing was in 2010.

monuments, castles, royal residences, and the like; and discounts on car rentals, ski lifts, theme parks, concerts, and sporting events. The card is also available in 3-, 5-, and 7-day versions. You can purchase the card at the tourist offices in Piazza Castello and Stazione Porta Nuova; visit www.turismotorino.org for more information.

In March 2011, **Turin's Automobile Museum** opened after a 4-year facelift that turned the already appealing museum into a true gem. Even the biggest car-skeptics are likely to find something interesting that will make them happy they took the small detour from downtown. For history buffs, the **Museo Nazionale del Risorgimento Italiano,** which chronicles the country's 19th-century push toward independence from foreign occupiers, has recently reopened after a 5-year renovation.

Basilica di Superga ★★ CHURCH As thanksgiving to the Virgin Mary for Turin's deliverance from the French siege of 1706, Vittorio Amedeo II commissioned Juvarra, the Sicilian architect who did his greatest work in Turin, to build this baroque basilica on a hill high above the city. The exterior, with a beautiful neoclassical porch and lofty drum dome, is more interesting than the gloomy interior, a circular chamber beneath the dome with six chapels. The church serves as a pantheon for the House of Savoy, whose tombs are scattered about, many in the Crypt of Kings beneath the main chapel. The building also includes some royal apartments. The name Superga, however, in the Italian memory will forever be associated with a plane crash there in 1949 that killed the members of the Torino soccer club, the reigning champions, who were flying home from Portugal. A small museum there about the "Grande Torino" squad is a fitting tribute to players who have become almost patron saints of the city. The trip up to the hilltop on a narrow railway through a verdant park is a favorite Torinese outing.

Strada della Basilica di Superga 73, about 6.5km (4 miles) northeast of the town center in Parco Naturale della Collina di Superga. www.basilicadisuperga.com. ✆ **011-899-7456.** Free admission. Grande Torino Museum admission 2€. Daily 9am–noon and 3–6pm (Nov–Mar until 5pm). Reached by rack railway (4€ round-trip) with a terminus at Stazione Sassi on Piazza Gustavo Modena (follow Corso Casale on east side of the River Po). Bus: 61 from side of Vittorio Emanuele I bridge opposite Piazza Vittorio Veneto to Stazione Sassi.

Cattedrale di San Giovanni Battista ★ CATHEDRAL When the controversial **Shroud of Turin (Sacra Sindone)** is put on display, it is in this otherwise uninspiring 15th-century church, one of the few pieces of Renaissance architecture in baroque-dominated Turin. When the shroud is not out for viewing, the church's main draw is the **Cappella della Santa Sindone,** the only problem being that the chapel has been closed since a 1997 fire (one of many the shroud has miraculously survived over the centuries) and there is little chance it will open anytime soon. While the only piece of the chapel that is visible is the black marble that somberly covers the part facing the inside of the church, the faithful still come in droves to venerate the shroud and its chapel.

The shroud, of course, is allegedly the one in which the body of Christ was wrapped when taken from the cross—and to which his image was miraculously affixed. The image is of a man 1.7m tall (5 ft., 7 in.), with bloodstains consistent with a crown of thorns, a cut in the rib cage, cuts in the wrists and ankles, and scourge marks on the back from flagellation. Recent carbon dating suggests that the shroud was manufactured sometime around the 13th or 14th century, but the mystery remains, at least in part, because no one can explain how the haunting image appeared on the cloth. Also, additional radio carbon dating has suggested that, since the shroud has been exposed to fire (thus affecting carbon readings), it could indeed date from around the time of the death of Christ. Regardless of scientific skepticism, the shroud continues to entice hordes of the faithful.

Around the corner at the **Museo della Sindone (Holy Shroud Museum),** Via San Domenico 28 (www.sindone.org; ✆ **011-436-5832**), open daily from 9am to noon and 3 to 7pm, you can find out more than you ever wanted to know about the shroud; admission is 6€ for adults and 5€ for those 12 and under or 65 and over and students 25 and under. Technically the shroud is put on display only in jubilee years, though it tends to pop up every 10 years more or less for special occasions. Otherwise, you'll have to content yourself with a series of dramatically backlit photos of the relic near the entrance to the cathedral, and another in the church of San Lorenzo. The museum houses a plethora of information (including photos, X-rays, and history) relating to the shroud.

In front of the cathedral stand two landmarks of Roman Turin—the remains of a theater and the **Porta Palatina,** a Roman-era city gate, flanked by twin 16-sided towers.

Piazza San Giovanni Battista. ✆ **011-436-1540.** Free admission. Mon–Sat 7:15am–12:30pm and 3–7pm (Sun open 8am). Bus: 11, 12, 19, 27, 50, 51, or 57. Tram: 3, 4, 7, or 16.

Mole Antonelliana & Museo Nazionale del Cinema (National Film Museum) ★★ ICON/MUSEUM Turin's most peculiar building—in fact, one of the strangest structures anywhere—comprises a squat brick base, which supports several layers of pseudo-Greek temples piled one atop the other, topped in turn by a steep conelike roof and a needlelike spire, all of it rising 167m (548 ft.) above the streets of the city center. Begun in 1863 and designed as a synagogue, the Mole, now a monument to Italian unification and architectural hubris, is home to Italy's **National Film Museum.**

The museum's first section tracks the development of moving pictures, from shadow puppets to kinescopes. The rest is more of a tribute to film than a true museum, offering clips and stills to illustrate some of the major aspects of movie production, from *The Empire Strikes Back* storyboards to the creepy steady-cam work in *The Shining*. Of memorabilia, masks from the original *Planet of the Apes, Satyricon,* and *Star Wars* hang together near *Lawrence of Arabia*'s robe, *Chaplin*'s bowler, and *What Ever Happened to Baby Jane*'s dress. Most of the clips (all in Italian-dubbed versions), as well as posters and other memorabilia, are heavily weighted toward American movies, with exceptions mainly for the major players of European/international cinema like Fellini, Bertolucci, Truffaut, and Wim Wenders.

Even if you skip the museum, you can (and should) still ascend to an observation platform at the top, an experience that affords a stunning view of Turin and the surrounding countryside backed by the Alps.

Via Montebello 20. www.museocinema.it. ✆ **011-813-8560.** Museum admission 7€; 5€ students 25 and under, and seniors 65 and over; 2€ children 6–18; free for children 5 and under. Observation platform 5€; 3.50€ students 25 and under, seniors 65 and over, and children 6–18; free for children 5 and under. Admission to both 9€, 7€ students 25 and under and seniors 65 and over, 4.50€ children 6–18, free for children 5 and under. Tues–Sun 9am–8pm (Sat until 11pm). Bus: 18, 55, 56, 61, or 68. Tram: 13, 15, or 16.

Museo dell'Automobile (Automobile Museum) ★ MUSEUM This shiny collection of mostly Italian automobiles—housed in a purpose-built, light-filled exhibition hall of classic 1960s design that reopened in 2011 after a 4-year makeover—draws car buffs from all over the world. Not too surprisingly, a century's worth of output from Fiat, which is headquartered less than a mile away, and the brands it owns are well represented. The collection includes most of the cars that have done Italy proud over the years, including Lancias, Alfa Romeos, and Ferraris, but you will also find the automobiles of many other manufacturers including a Ford Model T from 1916 and a Trabant, the signature car of the former German Democratic Republic. With unexpected exhibits, including a mock apartment filled with things made from car parts, the curator has gone out of his way to make the museum engaging for those who prefer to walk or bike. In a nod to the undeniably heavy environmental impact of the car industry, another peculiar exhibit shows a few burned-out cars in a desolate, black landscape strewn with tires and dead trees.

Corso Unità d'Italia 40. www.museoauto.it. ✆ **011-677-666.** Admission 7€ adults, 5€ children 15 and under and seniors 65 and over. Mon 10am–2pm; Tues 2–7pm; Wed–Sun 10am–7pm (Fri–Sat until 9pm). Bus: 1, 18, 34, 35, 55, or 74. Metro: Lingotto.

Museo Egizio (Egyptian Museum) ★★★ ☺ MUSEUM Turin's magnificent **Egyptian collection** is one of the world's largest. In fact, this was the world's first Egyptian museum, thanks to the Savoys, who amassed artifacts

The Royal Papyrus on display at the Egyptian Museum.

through most of their reign (the museum continued to mount collecting expeditions throughout the early 20th c.). The most captivating exhibits are in Area 2 on the ground floor. These include the **Rock Temple of Ellessiya,** from the 15th century B.C., which the Egyptian government presented to the museum in 1966 in gratitude for Italian efforts to save monuments threatened by the Aswan Dam. The two rooms nearby are staggering in the size and drama of the objects they house, most notably two sphinxes and a massive, richly painted statue of Ramses II. Smaller objects—mummies, funerary objects, and a papyrus *Book of the Dead*—fill the galleries on the next floor including palm leaf sandals found in the tomb of Queen Nefertari and what are thought to be her knees. Nothing beats a 4,000-year-old mummy to cheer up kids who are tired of touring (well, maybe a gelato would work even better).

Via Accademia delle Scienze 6. www.museoegizio.it. ✆ **011-561-7776.** Admission 7.50€ adults, 3.50€ ages 18–25, free for children 17 and under and seniors 65 and over. Tues–Sun 8:30am–7:30pm. Bus: 11, 12, 27, 55, 56, or 57. Tram: 13 or 15.

Museo Nazionale del Risorgimento Italiano (National Museum of the Risorgimento) MUSEUM An important slice of modern Italian history has been played out in Turin, and much of that in this *palazzo* that was home to the first king of a unified Italy, Vittorio Emanuele II, and the seat of its first parliament, in 1861. While any self-respecting town in Italy has a museum of the Risorgimento, the movement that launched Italian unification, this one is the best. Documents, paintings, and other paraphernalia recount the heady days when Vittorio Emanuele banded with Garibaldi and his Red Shirts to oust the Bourbons from Sicily and the Austrians from the north to create a unified Italy. The plaques that sum up each room are in English, and they will finally reveal to you the people behind the names of half the major streets and *piazze* in Italy—including Mazzini, Vittorio Emanuele II, Massimo d'Azeglio, Cavour, and Garibaldi. The last rooms house a fascinating collection that chronicles Italian Fascism and the resistance against it. Following a 5-year revamping, the museum reopened in March 2011, just in time to celebrate the 150th anniversary of Italy's unification.

Via Accademia delle Scienze 5. www.museorisorgimentotorino.it. ✆ **011-562-1147.** Admission 7€ adults; 5€ students 25 and under, and seniors 65 and over; 4€ high school students; 2€ middle and elementary school students; children 5 and under free. Tues–Sun 9am–7pm. Bus: 11, 12, 27, 55, 56, or 57. Tram: 13 or 15.

Palazzina di Caccia di Stupinigi ★ PALACE The other great work of the architect Juvarra (besides the Basilica di Superga) is this sumptuous, lavishly decorated hunting lodge that the Savoys commissioned in 1729. The main part of the lodge, to which the members of the House of Savoy retired for hunts in the royal forests that still surround it, is shaped like a Saint Andrew's cross (the lower arms extended and curved back inward like giant pincers), fanning out from a circular, domed pavilion topped with a large bronze stag. The lavish interior is filled with furniture, paintings, and bric-a-brac assembled from the many Savoy residences, technically comprising a **Museo d'Arte e Ammobiliamento (Museum of Art and Furniture).** Stroll through the acres of excessively decorated apartments to understand why Napoleon chose this for his brief residency in the region. Outstanding among the many, many frescoes are the scenes of a deer hunt in the King's Apartment and the triumph of Diana in the grand salon. The elegant gardens and surrounding forests provide lovely terrain for a jaunt.

Piazza Principe Amedeo 7, Stupingi-Nichelino, 8.5km (5¼ miles) southwest of the city center. ✆ **011-358-1220.** Admission 6.20€ adults, 5.15€ children 6–14. Tues–Sun 10am–6pm (late Oct to late Mar until 5pm). Bus: 63 from Porta Nuova train station to Piazza Caio Mario; change to bus 41.

Palazzo Madama—Museo Civico di Arte Antica (Civic Museum of Ancient Art) ★ MUSEUM Don't be misled by the baroque facade, added by architect Filippo Juvarra in the 18th century. If you walk around the exterior of the *palazzo* (named for its most popular resident, Christine Marie of France, the daughter of French King Henry IV and Marie de' Medici), you'll discover that the massive structure incorporates a medieval castle, a Roman gate, and several Renaissance additions. Juvarra also added a monumental marble staircase to the interior, most of which is given over to the far-reaching collections of the Museo Civico di Arte Antica. The holdings focus on the medieval and Renaissance periods, shown off against the castle's unaltered, stony medieval interior. One of Italy's largest collections of ceramics is here, as well as some stunning canvases, including Antonello da Messina's *Portrait of a Man.*

In the Palazzo Madama, Piazza Castello. www.palazzomadamatorino.it. ✆ **011-443-3501.** Admission 7.50€ adults, 6€ youths 18–25 and seniors 65 and over. Tues–Sat 10am–6pm; Sun 10am–8pm. Bus: 11, 12, 27, 51, 55, 56, or 57. Tram: 4, 13, 15.

Palazzo Reale (Royal Palace) & Armeria Reale (Royal Armory) ★ PALACE The residence of the House of Savoy, begun in 1645 and designed by the Francophile Amedeo di Castellamonte, reflects the ornately baroque tastes of European ruling families of the time—a fact that will not be lost on you as you pass from one opulently decorated, heavily gilded room to the next. (The Savoys had a keener eye for paintings than for decor, and most of the canvases they collected are in the nearby Galleria Sabauda.) Most notable here are some of the tapestries, including the Gobelins depicting the life of Don Quixote, in the Sala delle Virtù (Hall of Virtues), and the collection of Chinese and Japanese vases in the Sala dell'Alcova. One of the quirkier architectural innovations,

piazze & PARKS

Piazza San Carlo, Turin's most beautiful square, is the city's outdoor living room, surrounded by arcaded sidewalks that house the tables of the cafes for which Turin is famous (see "Cafes & Delicacy Shops," later). In the center is an equestrian statue of Duke Emanuele Filiberto of Savoy, and facing each other at the southern end of the piazza is a pair of 17th-century churches, San Carlo and Santa Cristina. The overall effect is one of elegant harmony.

At almost any time of day you will see the Torinesi out enjoying their beloved **Parco del Valentino,** a park flanking the Po river that is about 3 blocks wide and 1.6km (1 mile) long. The park is slightly displaced from the downtown area, but it is worth a visit because walking along the river immersed in green as you watch the rowers speed up and down the water is something that will remain with you for a long time. And for those who are up for a longish walk, in about 45 minutes by foot, and flanking the river the entire time, you can go from the top of the park (at the Umberto I bridge) to the Automobile Museum (p. 634).

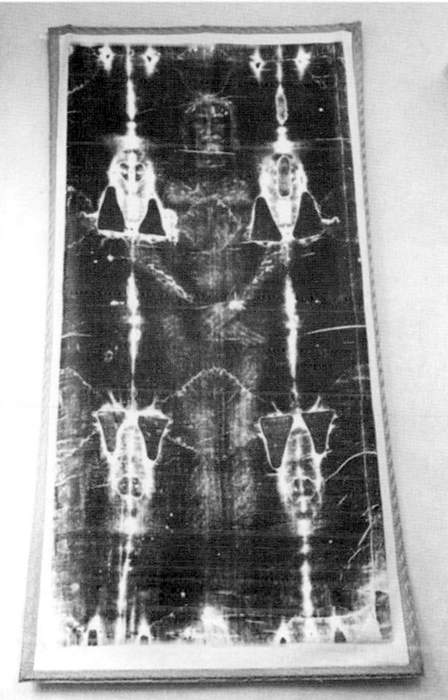
The Shroud of Turin.

though not open to the public, is an antidote to several monumental staircases, a manually driven elevator from the 18th century.

One wing houses the **Armeria Reale,** one of the most important arms and armor collections in Europe, especially of weapons from the 16th and 17th centuries. Behind the palace, and offering a refreshing change from its frippery, are the **Giardini Reali (Royal Gardens),** laid out by Le Nôtre, more famous for Paris's Tuileries park and the gardens at Versailles.

Piazzetta Reale Palazzo: ✆ **011-436-1455.** Admission 6.50€ adults, 3.25€ ages 18–25, free for children 17 and under and seniors 65 and over. Tues–Sun 8:30am–7:30pm. Armeria: ✆ **011-543 889.** Admission 4€, 2€ ages 18–25, free for children 17 and under and seniors 66 and over. Tues–Sun 8:30am–7:30pm. Bus: 11, 12, 27, 51, or 57. Tram: 4.

Reggia di Venaria Reale ★ PALACE Built in the mid–17th century on a design by Amedeo di Castellamonte, who had previously worked on Turin's Palazzo Reale (p. 636), this massive complex and surrounding park is Turin's answer to Versailles. The UNESCO heritage site reopened in 2011 following a royal makeover that brought the palace back to life after decades of work. The Savoys used Venaria as a hunting lodge, and what a lodge it was with two picturesque internal courtyards and impressive royal gardens. But it is the Venaria's stately rooms, the most noteworthy of which is the Salone di Diana, that will likely remain in your memory long after you've left.

Piazza della Repubblica, Venaria Reale, 10km (6¼ miles) northwest of the city center. www.lavenaria.it. ✆ **011-499-2333.** Admission 12€ adults, 8€ children 18 and under and seniors 65 and over, children 11 and under free. Tues–Fri 9am–6pm, Sat 9am–9:30pm, Sun 9am–8pm; shorter hours Nov–Apr. Royal gardens: Admission 4€ adults (5€ Sun and holidays), 3€ children 18 and under and seniors 65 and over (4€ Sun and holidays), children 11 and under free. Tues–Sun 9am–8pm (closed Oct and Mar at 7pm; Nov and Feb 6pm; Dec–Jan 5pm). Bus: 11 from Piazza Repubblica or 72 from northwest corner of downtown. There is also the Venaria Express bus that takes 40 minutes and runs Tues–Sun with stops downtown near Stazione Porta Nuova, on XX Settembre at corner of Via Bertola, and at Stazione Porta Susa.

Where to Eat

One of the great pleasures of being in Piedmont is sampling the region's unique cuisine. Two pastas you will encounter on menus are *agnolotti* (a type of ravioli often stuffed with an infusion of cheese and meat) and *tajarin,* a flat egg noodle that can be eaten with just butter as well as topped with porcini mushrooms or white truffles. While the Piemontesi love their grilled meat and game, there are enough vegetables in the local diet to make a meatless meal pretty easy to have; one of the favorite preparations is *bagna cauda* (hot dip), in which raw vegetables are dipped into a heated preparation of oil, anchovies, and garlic. If you have a sweet tooth, you will quickly discover that Turin and outlying towns can amply satisfy cravings for sweets, largely with pastries. Additionally, with wines as good as Piedmont produces (see "Visiting the Wine Villages," p. 647), even a carafe of the house red is likely to be memorable.

C'era Una Volta ★★★ PIEMONTESE A large, old-fashioned dining room filled with heavy, old tables and chairs and dark credenzas greets you as you enter "Once Upon a Time." While this is a quintessentially Torinese establishment that is committed to the heritage of the region's cuisine, you will also likely find some variations such as buttery spinach dumplings, and *tagliatelle* with fava beans. For *secondo,* if you are ready to turn your back on the usual Piemontese standbys (all done perfectly), you won't go wrong with the succulent grilled lamb chops or the local Toma cheese served with Speck (smoked ham) and orange marmalade. The menu, which changes monthly and is based on the availability of ingredients, almost always has one or two fish dishes, though you're much better off opting for the meat, cheese, and vegetables. You can accompany your meal with a fine Barolo or any other of the cellar's 300 local labels.

Corso Vittorio Emanuele II 41. www.ristoranteceraunavolta.it. ✆ **011-655-498.** Reservations recommended. Main courses 14€–17€; tasting menu 26€–28€. AE, MC, V. Mon–Sat 8–11pm (sometimes they will open if you call to reserve for Sun or for lunch during the week). Closed Aug.

Cianci ★★ 🎁 PIEMONTESE/TRATTORIA If you're disappointed at not having met a Torinese who invites you home for dinner, come to this friendly trattoria where the experience will be as close to a home-cooked meal as you are going to get at a restaurant. Marco, Gianni, and Danilo, who opened Cianci in 2010, are constantly changing the menu, which you will find displayed on a big chalkboard near the entrance to the restaurant. There is usually at least one Piemontese standby among the *primi* (often *tajarin* in some incarnation) and *secondi* (here it's anybody's guess, though if rabbit is on the menu that's always a good bet). The cheap prices are accompanied by an offering of Piemontese wine (the heavier ones like Barolo are only available in the winter) and the possibility to sit out in an enchanting little square if the weather permits.

Largo IV Marzo 9B. ✆ **338-876-7003.** Reservations recommended. Main courses 6€. MC, V. Daily noon–3pm and 7:30–11pm. Bus: 11, 12, 27, 51, or 57. Tram: 4.

Pastificcio De Felippis ★★ 🎁 ITALIAN This is pasta at its freshest. Since 1872, De Felippis has been making fresh pasta that the Torinesi take home, throw in boiling water, and serve up on special occasions. In 2007, they set out some tables on Via La Grange, which had just been closed to traffic, and started boiling the water themselves. All sauces, whether the pesto, fish, or *ragù,* are subtle because here it is all about the pasta and the idea is to make sure an overly aggressive sauce doesn't steal the show. There are a few *secondi* on the menu, but your best bet is to come here for a light lunch, order only a pasta (and perhaps one of the sumptuous desserts—vanilla crème brûlée, anybody?) and then save space for a large dinner. If you do go for dessert, avoid the *mattone,* the aptly named "brick," which is their interpretation of tiramisu.

Via La Grange 39. www.pastificiodefilippis.com. ✆ **011-542-137.** Reservations recommended. Main courses 9€–12€. MC, V. Daily noon–3pm and 7:30–11pm. Bus: 11, 12, 27, 51, or 57. Tram: 4.

Trattoria Salentina ★ PUGLIESE/TRATTORIA At a certain point, you'll need something lighter than Piemontese cuisine can offer. That's okay—it happens to everybody who comes to Turin and when it does, Trattoria Salentina with its southern Puglia cuisine is a good bet. The down-homey get-up of the trattoria (copper pots hanging from a yellow wall with a slightly ridiculous fresco) matches the food. Pugliese specialties such as *orecchiette con rape* and *ciceri e tria* (egg pasta cooked in a broth of tomatoes, celery, garlic, onion, carrot, and chickpeas and topped with a little bit of crunchy, fried pasta), are near perfect, not surprising since the trattoria is run by a family from Salento (the heel of the Italian boot). Fridays and Saturdays, there's a *fritto misto* (large pieces of fried fish) that's crispy yet light enough that you'll still have space for a homemade dessert.

Via Galliari 10bis/A. ✆ **011-427-0532.** Reservations not accepted. Main courses 5€–9€. Mon–Sat noon–2:30pm and 7–11:30pm (Sat closed for lunch). Bus: 1, 34, 35, 52, 67, or 68. Tram: 7 or 9.

CAFES & DELICACY SHOPS

Cafe sitting is a centuries-old tradition in sophisticated Turin. Via Roma and the *piazze* it widens into are lined with gracious salons that have been serving coffee to Torinese for centuries. Below are some of the city's classic cafes. While espresso and pastries are the mainstays of the menu at all of them, most also serve chocolates—including the mix of chocolate and hazelnuts known as *gianduiotti*—that are among the city's major contributions to culinary culture.

Keep in mind that as is the case all across Italy, in the fancier cafes the price of getting your drink served at a table can be three times what you will pay standing at the bar (in Caffè Torino, for example, a cappuccino costs 1.60€ at the bar and 5.50€ at a table, while in Caffè San Carlo the difference is 1.40€ vs. 4.50€). The same goes for pastries and sandwiches that can be consumed standing up or at a table.

Turin has a sizable sweet tooth, satisfied by any number of pastry and candy shops. One of the best chocolatiers in all of northern Italy is **Guido Gobino ★**, Via Lagrange 1/A (✆ **011-566-0707**), open daily 10am to 8 pm (Mon opens at 3pm). If Guido Gobino is not the best, that title very well might go to **Guido Castagna ★**, Via Maria Vittoria, 27/C (✆ **011-1988-6585**), open Tuesday through Saturday 10:30am to 7:30pm and Monday 3:30 to 7:30pm (June–July closed Mon, and 2 3pm other days). Walk into Guido Castagna and you are likely to think you've stumbled into a jewelry shop—such is the presentation and veneration afforded the chocolate. A wide variety of chocolates and other sweets, including sumptuous meringues, have been dispensed since 1836 at **Fratelli Stratta,** Piazza San Carlo 191 (www.stratta1836.it; ✆ **011-547-920**), open Monday through Friday 8am to 8pm, Saturday 9am to 8pm, and Sunday 10am to 7pm.

Caffè Confetteria al Bicerin ★ CAFE What claims to be Turin's oldest cafe, open since 1763 and still sporting the original 18th-century counter as well as marble-topped tables, is famous for its illustrious clientele, which has included Nietzsche, Dumas, and Puccini, as well as its signature drink—the Bicerin (local dialect for "small glass"). This calorie bomb combines coffee, hot chocolate, and cream and though it can be had in other cafes around town, if you are going to indulge you might as well have the best.

Piazza della Consolata 5. www.bicerin.it. ✆ **011-436-9325.** Bicherin 5€. MC, V. Thurs–Tues 8:30am–7:30pm.

Caffè San Carlo ★★ CAFE One of the essential stops on any tour of Turin is this classic cafe. The San Carlo opened its doors in 1837 and ever since has been accommodating patrons beneath a huge chandelier of Murano glass in a salon that is a remarkable assemblage of gilt, mirrors, and marble. An adjoining, frescoed tearoom is quieter and only a little less grand.

Piazza San Carlo 156. ✆ **011-532-586.** Sandwiches and pastries 2.50€–12€. AE, DC, MC, V. Daily 8am–midnight (Mon–Tues until 9pm).

Caffè Torino ★★ CAFE The mirrored and frescoed salons in Caffè Torino, opened in 1903, create an unforgettable atmosphere for one of the pastries or chocolates handsomely displayed in the main room. This place is great for a cheap, fast, light meal: At lunch and dinner, plates at the bar are loaded with bite-size sandwiches, pizzas, stuffed olives, fried cheese and veggies, and other goodies—all yours for the gobbling with the purchase of a drink.

Piazza San Carlo 204. www.caffe-torino.it. ✆ **011-545-118.** Sandwiches and pastries 2€–7€. AE, MC, V. Daily 7:30am–midnight.

Entertainment & Nightlife

Turin has a lively classical music and opera scene, and you can get info on these and other cultural events at the **Vetrina Infocultura** office at Piazza Castello 161, at the beginning of Corso Garibaldi (✆ **011-535-181**), open daily 9am to 7pm. This office also doubles as one of the two tourist offices in town. Aside from the city's much-attended summer festivals (see "Festivals & Markets," p. 630), there are regular classical concerts by the National Symphonic Orchestra at **Auditorium della RAI,** Via Rossini 15 (www.orchestrasinfonica.rai.it; ✆ **011-810-4653**). Other concerts, dance performances, and operas are staged at the city's venerable **Teatro Regio** (www.teatroregio.torino.it; ✆ **011-881-5241**), in the center of the city on Piazza Castello. If instead you are looking for an after-dinner drink in a hip yet relaxed atmosphere filled with Torinesi young and old, there is **La Drogheria** at Piazza Vittorio Veneto 18 (✆ **011-812-2414**), open daily until 2am (Fri–Sat until 3am).

Where to Stay

EXPENSIVE

NH Santo Stefano ★ Just a few steps from the cathedral and Piazza Castello, this is perhaps the best located of Turin's high-end hotels. A stunning wooden staircase circles above the lobby giving a medieval air to this very modern hotel. Most rooms are big, all are comfortable and sleek, and because the hotel opened just in time for the 2006 Olympics, everything is relatively new. All fifth-floor rooms and half of the fourth-floor rooms have sloped ceilings that lend a homey feel. The impressive breakfast can be consumed in the courtyard in good weather.

Via Porta Palatina 19, 10122 Torino. www.nh-hotels.com. ✆ **011-522-3311.** Fax 011-522-3313. 125 units. 160€–245€ double; 185€–265€ superior double. Rates include breakfast. AE, MC, V. Parking 20€ in garage. **Amenities:** Bar; concierge; room service; spa (not included in room rate). *In room:* A/C, TV, hair dryer, Wi-Fi (free), minibar.

Victoria Hotel ★★ Step through the doors of this somewhat plain-looking building between the Via Roma and the river, and you'll think you're in an English country house. That's the whole idea, and the Anglophile decor works splendidly. The lobby is decorated as a country-house drawing room, with floral sofas, deep armchairs, and a view onto a garden; the room doubles as a bar and is a pleasant place to enjoy a drink before setting out for one of the nearby restaurants. The glass-enclosed breakfast room, where a sumptuous buffet is served, resembles a conservatory. "Deluxe" accommodations, each with its own distinctive look, are oversize and furnished with carefully chosen antiques and such flourishes as canopied beds, richly covered divans, and marble bathrooms. Room 309 has the price of a standard double, but you also get a large terrace, while room 408, a suite, has a Jacuzzi in the room.

Via Nino Costa 4, 10123 Turin. www.hotelvictoria-torino.com. ✆ **011-561-1909.** Fax 011-561-1806. 106 units. 155€–245€ standard double; 180€–280€ deluxe double; 260€–325€ suite. Rates include breakfast. AE, MC, V. Parking 22€ at hotel (you must reserve a space) or 20€ in nearby garage. **Amenities:** Bar; bikes; concierge; pool; room service; smoke-free rooms; spa w/hot tub, sauna, and massage and facial services. *In room:* A/C, TV, hair dryer, minibar, Wi-Fi (free).

MODERATE

Hotel Bologna ★ Just across the street from the Porta Nuova train station (under the arcade to the left), this is a good option for affordable comfort. Each of the 45 rooms, spread over several floors of a gracious 18th-century apartment house, is different from the next. Some are quite grand, incorporating frescoes, fireplaces, and other original details (no. 52 hasn't changed since five time Italian prime minister Giovanni Giolitti stayed here at the turn of the 20th century, while 68 has a splendid painted ceiling). Other rooms have been renovated in sleek modern style, with laminated, built-in cabinetry and neutral carpeting. Still others fall in between, with well-maintained 1970s-style furnishings and linoleum flooring. Whatever the vintage, all the rooms are spotlessly clean and nicely maintained. It's key to ask for an internal room if the street traffic is going to bother you.

Corso Vittorio Emanuele II 60, 10121 Turin. www.hotelbolognasrl.it. ✆/fax **011-562-0193.** 45 units. 75€–100€ double. Rates include breakfast. MC, V. Free parking (call ahead for a space). **Amenities:** Bar; concierge; room service. *In room:* A/C (in some), TV, hair dryer, minibar, Wi-Fi (free).

INEXPENSIVE

Hotel Bellavista What will strike you first about this *pensione,* which occupies the sixth floor of an apartment house on a quiet street between the main train station and the river, is just how pleasant the surroundings are—step off the elevator and you will find yourself in a sun-filled corridor that's a garden of houseplants and opens onto a wide terrace. There's also a pleasant bar area. Rooms are airy and comfortable but a little less inspiring in decor, with banal, functional modern furnishings. Most, though, afford pleasant views over the surrounding rooftops—the best outlooks in the house are across the river toward the hills. What most rooms don't have is a private bathroom, though the several communal ones are well placed so most rooms are only a few steps away from a facility.

Via Galliari 15, 10125 Turin. www.bellavista-torino.it. ✆ **011-669-8139.** Fax 011-668-7989. 18 units. 40€–50€ double; 60€–70€ triple. Rates include breakfast. AE, MC, V. Free parking. **Amenities:** Bar; smoke-free rooms. *In room:* TV.

A Day Trip from Turin

SACRA DI SAN MICHELE ★★★

Perched high atop Monte Pirchiriano—part of it projecting over the precipice on an elaborate support system that was one of the engineering feats of the Middle Ages—this dramatically situated **abbey** (www.sacradisanmichele.com; ✆ **011-939-130**) dedicated to Saint Michael provides views and an astonishing look at medieval religious life. It may well remind you of Mont Saint-Michel monastery in France (Mont Saint-Michel, off the Normandy coast of France, was one of the 176 religious institutions that once fell under the jurisdiction of Italy's San Michele, which today is all but forgotten). But with its dizzying views and scary drops, it just as easily may remind you of the abbey in the novel and film *The Name of the Rose* (author Umberto Eco based his fictional abbey on this one). It was started in 983, but the extant church dates to the abbey's 12th-century heyday. A vast staircase hewn out of rock and clinging to the abbey's buttresses (known as Scalone dei Morti [Stairs of Death] because monks' corpses were once laid out here) leads to the massive carved doorway depicting the signs of the zodiac and the drafty Gothic and Romanesque church, decorated only with scraps of 16th-century frescoes by Secondo del Bosco di Poirino. Another stairway leads down to three tiny chapels, carved into the rock, that contain tombs of some of the earliest members of the House of Savoy.

On Saturday evenings (and some Fri) from March to December, the atmospheric church hosts **concerts** of everything from chant and liturgical music to Renaissance chamber pieces, gospel, and traditional Celtic airs; check the website for schedules.

The abbey is outside Avigliana, 15km (9¼ miles) west of Turin's ring road. Admission is 5€ adults, 4€ children 6 to 14 and seniors 65 and over. It's open Tuesday to Saturday 9:30am to 12:30pm and 2:30 to 5pm; Sunday 9:30am to noon and 2:40 to 5pm (mid-Mar to mid-Oct open an hour later; July–Sept open Mon).

GETTING THERE Take one of 20 trains a day from Turin to Avigliana (30 min.); from there, it's a 1½-hour trek up to the abbey from the Sant'Ambrogio station, or else you can get a taxi to take you the 13km (8 miles) from Avigliana train station. On Sundays from May to September, there is a shuttle that runs back and forth between the Avigliana train station and the abbey, but it sometimes gets cancelled so check with the tourist office in Turin if you are counting on it. By car, follow the A32 from Turin's western ring highway toward Bardonecchia/Frejus. Get off at the Avigliana Est exit and follow the brown signs to Sacra di San Michele; the trip takes about an hour.

THE PIEDMONT WINE COUNTRY

Asti: 60km (37 miles) SE of Turin, 127km (79 miles) SW of Milan; Alba: 60km (37 miles) S of Turin, 155km (96 miles) SW of Milan

South of Turin, the Po valley rises into the rolling Langhe and Roero hills, flanked by orchards and vineyards. You'll recognize the region's place names from the labels of its first-rate wines, among them **Asti Spumanti, Barbaresco,** and **Barolo.** Tasting these vintages at the source is one reason to visit the wine country, of course; another is to stroll through the medieval and Renaissance towns that rise from the vineyards and the picturesque villages that crown many a hilltop. And vines are not all that flourish in the fertile soil—truffles top the list of the region's

One of Piedmont's many vineyards.

gastronomic delights, which also include down-home country fare like rabbit and game dishes, excellent cheeses, and plump fruit.

Asti

The Asti of sparkling-wine fame is a bustling city more concerned with everyday business than with entertaining visitors, but there are many treasures to be found in the history-drenched Old Town—medieval towers (120 of them still stand), Renaissance palaces, and broad *piazze* provide the perfect setting in which to sample the town's famous product.

ESSENTIALS

GETTING THERE **By Train** One to four trains an hour link Asti with **Turin** (30–60 min.). There are 14 trains daily between Asti and Alba, some of which require that you change trains at Nizza Monferrato or occasionally at Castagnole delle Lanze (35 min.–1 hr.).

By Bus From Turin, **Arfea** (www.arfea.com; ✆ **0144-322-023**) runs two buses per day, one morning and one mid afternoon, on the hour-long ride to Asti. **Giachino** (www.giachino.it; ✆ **0141-937-510**) makes the hour-long trip to and from Alba, about once per hour.

By Car Asti, 60km (37 miles) east of Turin, can be reached from Turin in less than an hour via Autostrada 21.

VISITOR INFORMATION The **APT tourist office** is near the train station at Piazza Alfieri 34 (✆ **0141-530-357**). Hours are Monday to Saturday 9am to 1pm and 2:30 to 6:30pm, and Sunday 9am to 1pm. Among the office's offerings is a *Carta del Vini,* an annotated map that will point you to surrounding vineyards that provide wine tastings.

FESTIVALS & MARKETS In late June and early July, Asti stages **Astiteatro** (✆ **0141-399-111**), a theater festival with performances that incorporate dance and music. September, though, is the town's busy cultural month, with townsfolk and horses alike donning medieval garb for its famous **Palio** on the third Sunday (see the "Horses & Donkeys" box, p. 644). Local wine producers converge on the town the 2 weeks before the Palio for the **Douja d'Or** (www.doujador.it), an exhibition of local vintages accompanied by tastings; this is the perfect way to sample the products of the many wineries in the hills surrounding Asti and nearby Alba. On the second Sunday of September, surrounding villages mount feasts (almost always accompanied by a communal meal) known collectively as the **Pjasan.**

HORSES & donkeys

Asti and Alba, bitter rivals through much of the Middle Ages, each celebrate the autumn harvest with equine celebrations that are horses of a very different color.

The **Palio** (www.palio.asti.it; ✆ **0141-399-482**), Asti's annual horse race, is run the third Sunday of September. Like the similar but more famous horse race that the Tuscan city of Siena mounts, Asti's Palio begins with a medieval pageant through the town and ends with a wild bareback ride around the Campo del Palio. The race coincides with Asti's other great revel, the **Douja d'Or** (www.doujador.it), a weeklong fair-cum-bacchanal celebrating the grape.

On the first Sunday of October, Alba pulls a spoof on Asti with the **Palio degli Asini (Race of the Asses; ✆ 0173-362-806**). The event, which coincides with Alba's annual truffle fair, is not as speedy as Asti's slicker horseback Palio, but it's a lot more fun. Good-natured as the event is, though, it is rooted in some of the darkest days of Alba's history. In the 13th century, Asti, then one of the most powerful republics of northern Italy, besieged Alba and burned the surrounding vineyards. Then, to add insult to injury, the victors held their *palio* in Alba, just to put the humbled citizenry further in its place. Alba then staged a *palio* with asses, a not-so-subtle hint of what they thought of their victors and their pompous pageantry.

Being the agricultural center that it is, Asti has two **food markets.** The larger is held Wednesdays and Saturdays 7:30am to 1pm in the **Campo del Palio,** with stalls selling every foodstuff imaginable—seeds, herbs, flowers, farm implements, and no end of other merchandise—and spilling over to the Piazza della Libertà and Piazza Alfieri. Meanwhile, Asti's covered food market, the **Mercato Coperto,** is also located in this vicinity, on Piazza della Libertà, and is open Monday through Wednesday and Friday 8am to 1pm and 3:30 to 7:30pm, Thursday 8:30am to 1pm, and Saturday 8am to 7:30pm. There's also a small **antiques fair** on the fourth Sunday of every month except August.

EXPLORING ASTI

If you take the train to Asti, you will step right into the heart of the action—the town's lively clothing-and-food **markets** occupy three adjoining *piazze* just to the north of the station (Campo del Palio, Piazza Libertà, and Piazza Alfieri). If you're arriving by car, you're most likely to find parking in one of the lots in this area as well.

Walk through the *piazze* to **Corso Alfieri;** the town's Renaissance palaces are located on or just off this major thoroughfare, usually closed to traffic. This street and Asti's grandest piazza are named for the town's most famous native son, the 18th-century poet Vittorio Alfieri. His home, on the Corso at 375, houses a small, memento-filled museum.

Second to none in Asti is San Secondo, the town's patron saint. He was imprisoned at the western end of Corso Alfieri in the **Torre Rossa**—much of which dates to the 1st century (probably part of a Roman gate) with two levels tacked on in the 11th century—then beheaded on the spot just south of Corso

Alfieri, where the **Collegiata di San Secondo** (**© 0141-530-066**) now stands. Not only does this Romanesque-Gothic structure have the honor of housing the saint's remains in its eerie crypt, but it is also the permanent home of the coveted Palio Astigiano, the banner awarded to the horseman who wins the town's annual Palio (see the "Horses & Donkeys" box, above; Secondo is the patron saint of this event). The church is open daily from 10:45am to noon and 3:30 to 5:30pm (Sun morning for Mass only).

Asti's "other" church is its 14th-century, redbrick **Cattedrale** (**© 0141-592-924**), which you can reach by walking through Piazza Cairoli, at the western end of Corso Alfieri, into the nearby Piazza Cattedrale. Every inch of this brick church's cavernous interior is festooned with frescoes by late-18th-century artists, including Gandolfino d'Asti; trompe l'oeil vines climb many of the columns. The cathedral is open daily from 8:30am to noon and 3 to 5:30pm.

WHERE TO EAT & STAY

Hotel Rainero ★ ☺ The Rainero, which has been run by the same family for three generations and was being restructured in early 2012, enjoys a wonderful location just west of the Campo del Palio. Not only is this setting convenient, but since many of the surrounding streets are closed to traffic, the neighborhood is quiet. Room nos. 309 to 311 have terraces (views only of surrounding modern buildings), and nos. 153 and 155 have balconies looking onto a cobbled street; there's also a large roof terrace. Room 158 is large enough to be a quad and has a table and chairs on the walkway out front. Large room no. 161 gets one of those plant-filled courtyards all to itself.

Via Cavour 85, 14100 Asti. www.hotelrainero.com. **© 0141-353-866.** Fax 0141-594-985. 55 units. 85€–110€ double; 140€–150€ suite. Breakfast 8€. AE, DC, MC, V. Parking in lot in front of hotel 10€. Closed 1st week of Jan. **Amenities:** Bar; room service; Wi-Fi (2€/hr.). *In room:* A/C, TV, hair dryer, minibar.

Il Convivio ★★ PIEMONTESE The no-nonsense decor reflects the fact that the main business at this restaurant located on a small street just south of the Collegiata di San Secondo is to serve perfectly prepared food and accompany it with the region's best, but not necessarily most expensive, wines (these are dispensed from an extensive cellar that you can visit). Only a few starters, pasta dishes, and main courses are prepared daily. You'll always find wonderful fresh-made pastas such as *taglierini* in a light vegetable sauce, a soup incorporating vegetables bought that morning from Asti's markets, and serious meat dishes, such as a masterful *osso buco di vitello, brasato di cinghiale,* or *coniglio* sautéed with olives and white wine. Desserts, including a heavenly *panna cotta al cioccolato,* are as memorable as the rest of the dining experience.

Via G. B. Giuliani 4–6. **© 0141-594-188.** Reservations recommended. Main courses 10€–13€. AE, DC, MC, V. Mon–Sat noon–2:30pm and 8–10pm. Closed last 2 weeks of Aug and Dec 24–Jan 6.

Alba

Alba retains a medieval flavor that's as mellow as the wines it produces. It's a pleasure to walk along the Via Vittorio Emanuele and the narrow streets of the Old Town, visit the 14th-century Duomo, and peer into shop windows with lavish displays of Alba's wines; its other famous product, truffles; and its less noble, but enticing, *nocciolata,* a decadent spread of hazelnuts and chocolate.

ESSENTIALS

GETTING THERE **By Train** Only one direct train (in the evening, after 6pm) runs between Turin and Alba (1 hr.); otherwise, there's one per hour requiring a change either in Bra or Cavallermaggiore (1¼–2 hr.). There are 11 trains daily between Alba and Asti (30–60 min.).

By Bus Alba's Autostazione bus terminal (www.atibus.it; ✆ **0175-478-811**) is on Piazza Medford. Hourly GTT (www.comune.torino.it/gtt; ✆ **800-019-152**) buses make the trip between Alba and Turin in about 1¾ hours.

By Car The most direct way to reach Alba from Turin is to follow Autostrada A6 for 35km (22 miles) south to the exit near Bra, and from the Autostrada exit S231, go east for 24km (15 miles) to Alba. If you want to work Alba into a trip to Asti, take A21 to Asti and, from there, follow S231 southwest for 30km (19 miles) to Alba.

VISITOR INFORMATION Alba's **tourist office,** which also serves the surrounding area, is near the Duomo at Piazza Risorgimento 19 (www.langheroero.it; ✆ **0173-35-833;** fax 0173-363-878) and is open daily 9am to 6:30pm (Sat–Sun from 10am).

FESTIVALS & MARKETS October is Alba's big month. Its annual **truffle festival** is held the first week, and this, in turn, climaxes in the **Palio degli Asini** (see "Horses & Donkeys" box, above). On Saturday and Sunday mornings, from the second weekend in October through December, Alba hosts a **truffles market,** where you may well be tempted to part with your hard-earned cash for one of the fragrant specimens (the price of which depends on how much the local truffle hunters have managed to dig up; in particularly lean years it can top 1,500€ per lb.).

EXPLORING ALBA

Alba's two major sights face the brick expanse of **Piazza Risorgimento,** at the northern end of its major thoroughfare, **Corso Vittorio Emanuele.** The 14th-century brick **Duomo** is flanked by a 13th-century bell tower. Most of the interior and paintings hail from the late 19th century, save the two late baroque lateral chapels and the **elaborately carved and inlaid choir stalls ★** from 1512.

The town's two art treasures hang in the council chamber of the **Palazzo Comunale** across the square (go through the door on the right and up to the top of the stairs)—an early-16th-century portrait of the Virgin by Alba's greatest painter, Macrino d'Alba, and *Concertino,* by Mattia Preti, a follower of Caravaggio. It's open only during city office hours, Tuesday through Friday 8:15am to 12:15pm, Saturday 8:15am to noon.

From here, stroll the shopping promenade **Corso Vittorio** a few blocks to enjoy the low-key pace in the traffic-free heart of the town.

WHERE TO EAT & STAY

Enoclub ★ PIEMONTESE The evocatively chic brick-vaulted basement here is devoted to fine wine coupled with solid, slightly refined Piemontese cooking. The nice variety of rich pasta dishes includes *tajarin* (Piedmont's answer to *tagliatelle*) topped with a rich lamb sauce, and *fettuccine di farro* (noodles made from barley rather than wheat) tossed with pesto and served with potatoes and beans. Because this is Piedmont, the *secondi* are meaty: veal steak with aromatic herbs, rabbit cooked in red wine, and duck breast in a black-olive paste.

Up on the ground floor is the busy **Umberto Notte** bar (open evenings only), one of Alba's few late-night scenes, dispensing wines by the glass, from 3€. This is a fine place to sample the produce of the local vineyards as well as wines from all over the world.

Piazza Savona 4. ✆ **0173-33-994.** Reservations not necessary. Main courses 11€–17€; tasting menu 40€. AE, MC, V. Tues–Sun noon–2:30pm and 7:30pm–midnight. Closed Aug.

Hotel Savona ★ The simple yet spacious rooms in this hotel facing a shady piazza at the south edge of the Old Town have a slick, modern look. The rooms are pleasantly decorated in pastel shades and have contemporary furnishings and shiny new bathrooms, most with bathtubs and many with Jacuzzis. Many rooms open onto small terraces; the quietest face an interior courtyard. If you are looking for a thrill, the hotel sells package deals that include the use of a Vespa, the perfect way to explore the surrounding wine villages (2 nights for two people with the use of a Vespa for a day will cost you 310€). And if you have come to town to spend on shoes and shirts rather than truffles and Barolo, the hotel can hook you up with a personal shopper.

Via Roma 1 (just off Piazza Savona), 12051 Alba (CN). www.hotelsavona.com. ✆ **0173-440-440.** Fax 0173-364-312. 90 units. 105€–127€ double. Rates include breakfast. AE, DC, MC, V. Parking 6€ in courtyard. **Amenities:** Restaurant (local cuisine); bar; concierge; room service. *In room:* A/C, TV w/pay movies, hair dryer, minibar, Wi Fi (free).

La Libera ★★ PIEMONTESE The simple and wonderful *carne cruda* (raw veal) is something of a synthesis of this place, simple and wonderful. The chef, Marco Forneris, humbly says "it's not hard to make good food in Piedmont because the raw materials are excellent." Perhaps, but he has a special touch that makes this stylish *osteria* in the center of town as close to a must-visit as you are going to get for any place in Piedmont. Here you'll find slight variations on local cuisine, and you can watch it being prepared through the large window that sits between the dining room and kitchen. The *antipasto misto*—which often includes *insaltina di tacchino* (a salad of fresh greens and roast turkey breast), *vitello tonato* (the traditionally warm-weather dish of veal and tuna sauce), and *fiori di zucca* (zucchini flowers stuffed with a trout mousse)—will get you started right. As for *primi*, the *agnolotti* (pasta stuffed with cabbage and rice) are hard to beat.

Via E. Pertinace 24a. www.lalibera.com. ✆ **0173-293-155.** Reservations recommended. Main courses 13€–24€. AE, DC, MC, V. Tues–Sat noon–2pm; Mon–Sat 8–10pm. Closed 2 weeks in late Feb/early Mar and last 2 weeks of Aug.

Visiting the Wine Villages

Just to the south of Alba lie some of the region's, and Italy's, most enchanting wine villages. As you set out to explore the wine country, consider three words: **Rent a car.** While it's quite easy to reach some of the major towns by train or bus from Turin, setting out from those centers for smaller places can be difficult (there are some buses, but they are scarce and with your own wheels you'll see in a day what will take 3 days with public transport). In Turin, contact **Avis,** Via Lessona Michele 30 (www.avis.com; ✆ **011-774-1962**), or **Hertz,** at Corso Turati 37 (www.hertz.it; ✆ **011-502-080**). Before you head out on the labyrinth of small country roads, outfit yourself with a good map and a list of vineyards from the tourist office in Alba or Asti.

THE WINES While the wines of Chianti and other Tuscan regions are on the top of the list for many oenologically minded travelers, the wines of Piedmont are often less heralded among non-Italians, and unjustifiably so. Most are of exceptional quality and usually made with grapes grown only in the Piedmont and often on tiny family plots, making the region a lovely patchwork of vineyards and small farms. Below are some wines you are likely to encounter repeatedly as you explore the area.

Barolo is called the king of reds (and is considered one of Italy's top three wines, the others being Tuscany's Brunello and Sassicaia), the richest and heartiest of the Piedmont wines, and the one most likely to accompany game or meat. **Barbaresco,** like Barolo, is made exclusively from the Nebbiolo grape though it is less tannic and often more approachable. **Barbera d'Alba** is smooth and rich, the product of many of the delightful villages south of Alba. **Dolcetto** is dry, fruity, and mellow (not sweet, as its name leads many to assume). **Nebbiolo d'Alba** is rich, full, and dry (though remember that the best Nebbiolo grapes are used to make Barbaresco and Barolo).

Spumanti is the sparkling wine that has put Asti on the map for many travelers, and **Moscato d'Asti** is a floral dessert wine. You can taste and purchase these wines at cantinas and *enoteche* in almost all towns and villages throughout the region; several are noted below.

THE REGION The central road through the region and running between Alba and Asti is S231, a heavily trafficked and unattractive highway that links many of the region's towns and cities; turn off this road whenever possible to explore the region's more rustic backwaters.

One of the loveliest drives takes you south of Alba to a string of wine villages in what are known as the **Langhe hills** (from Corso Europa, a ring road that encircles the Old City in Alba, follow signs out of town for Barolo). After 8km (5 miles), you'll come to the turnoff for **Grinzane di Cavour,** a hilltop village built around a castle housing an enoteca (✆ **0173-262-159**), open daily 9am to 7pm, where you can enjoy a fine sampling of local wines from their more than 300 labels.

Continuing south another 4km (2½ miles), you'll come to the turnoff to **La Morra,** another hilltop village that affords stunning views over the rolling, vineyard-clad countryside from its central Piazza Castello (with parking). It has places to eat (see below) and to taste the local wines. The **Cantina Comunale di La Morra** (✆ **0173-509-204**), on the Piazza del Municipio, operates both as the local tourist office and as a representative for local growers, selling and offering tastings of Barolo, Nebbiolo, Barbara, and Dolcetto. You can also procure a map of hikes in the local countryside, many of which take you through the vineyards to the doors of local growers. It's open Wednesday to Monday 10am to 12:30pm and 2:30 to 6:30pm.

Barolo, a romantic place dominated by its 12th-century castle (about 5km/3 miles from La Morra), is directly across the valley from La Morra and enticingly in view from miles around. Here, too, are a number of restaurants (see our top choice, La Cantinetta, below) and shops selling the village's rich red wines. Among these outlets is the **Castello Falletti** ★ (www.barolo world.it; ✆ **0173-56-277**), which houses a small wine bar, enoteca (where you can taste), and tourist office in its cavernous cellars. A tasting of three of Barolo's wines (all from the same year but different zones, so you can more accurately compare labels) costs 5€. It's open Friday to Wednesday 10am to 12:30pm and 3 to 6pm, and 10am to 4:30pm in February, November, and December (closed Jan).

WHERE TO EAT & STAY

See "Visiting the Wine Villages," above, for information on how to get to the towns where the following hotels and restaurants are located.

La Cantinetta PIEMONTESE Brothers Maurilio and Paolo Chiappetto do a fine job of introducing guests to the pleasures of the Piemontese table in their cozy dining room grouped around an open hearth (in nice weather, book ahead for a table out on the tiny back terrace). The menu changes daily and, if you are lucky, will include: a wonderful country pâté, powerful *bagna cauda,* subtle ravioli in a truffle sauce, thick slabs of roast veal, and salad made with wild herbs. If you're not lucky, that's okay, too, because no matter what comes out of the kitchen here it's a good bet you won't be disappointed. The wonderful house wines come from the vines that run right up to the back door of this delightful restaurant (a bar/enoteca is located up front).

Via Roma 33, Barolo. ✆ **0173-56-198.** Reservations recommended. Main courses 12€–15€; tasting menu 37€, not including wine. AE, DC, MC, V. Fri–Wed 12:15–3pm; Fri–Tues 7:30–11pm. Closed Feb.

La Cascina del Monastero ★★ The main business at this delightful farm complex, just minutes away from La Morra toward Barolo (4km/2½ miles), is bottling wine and harvesting fruit. But Giuseppe and Velda di Grasso have converted part of the oldest and most character-filled building into a bed-and-breakfast. Guests can relax on a large covered terrace, furnished with wicker couches and armchairs, or on the grassy shores of a pond. A sumptuous breakfast of fresh cakes, yogurt, cheese, and salami is served in a vast brick-walled reception hall. The guest rooms, reached by a series of exterior brick staircases, have been smartly done with exposed timbers, golden-hued tile floors, and attractive antique bureaus, armoires, and brass beds. Bathrooms are sparkling and quite luxurious, with state-of-the-art stall showers and luxuriously deep basins.

Cascina Luciani 112A, Frazione Annunziata 12064 La Morra (CN). www.cascinadelmonastero.it. ✆/fax **0173-509-245.** 10 units. 100€–120€ double; 110€–130€ apt. Rates include breakfast. No credit cards. Free parking. Closed Jan and sometimes Feb. **Amenities:** Bike rental; small children's playground; small exercise room; outdoor pool; room service; sauna; Wi-Fi (free). *In room:* Hair dryer, kitchenette, minibar, no phone.

AOSTA & VALLE D'AOSTA

Aosta: 113km (70 miles) N of Turin, 184km (114 miles) NW of Milan; Courmayeur-Entrèves: 35km (22 miles) W of Aosta, 148km (92 miles) NW of Turin

Skiers, hikers, and outdoor enthusiasts, eager to enjoy one of Italy's favorite Alpine playgrounds, flock to this tiny mountainous region 1 hour by car north of Turin (and 2 hr. by train). At its best, **Valle d'Aosta** fulfills its promise: snowcapped peaks, among them the Matterhorn (Monte Cervino in Italian) and Mont Blanc (Monte Bianco), as well as verdant pastures, thick forests, waterfalls cascading into mountain streams, and romantic castles clinging to wooded hillsides.

Also plentiful in Valle d'Aosta are crowds—especially in August, when the region welcomes hordes of vacationing Italians, and January through March, the height of the winter ski season—and one too many overdeveloped tourist centers to accommodate them. You're best off coming at one of the nonpeak times, when you can enjoy the valley's beauty in relative peace and quiet.

Whenever you happen to find yourself in Valle d'Aosta, three must-sees are the town of **Aosta** itself, with its Roman and medieval monuments set dramatically against the backdrop of the Alps (and a fine place to begin a tour of the surrounding mountains and valleys), and the natural wonders of **Parco Nazionale del Gran Paradiso.** The third, more dramatic to-do is the thrilling cable-car ride from fashionable ski resort **Courmayeur-Entrèves** over the shoulder of **Mont Blanc** to France. While much of Valle d'Aosta is accessible by train or bus, you'll probably want a car to ease your exploration of the quieter reaches of the region.

Of course, recreation, not sightseeing, is what draws many people to Valle d'Aosta. Some of the best **downhill skiing,** accompanied by the best facilities, is on the runs at Courmayeur, Breuil-Cervinia (the town on the Italian side of the Matterhorn), and at the large Monte Rosa ski area that is centered around the towns of Champoluc and Gressoney. Valle D'Aosta also offers excellent **cross-country skiing** and **hiking** (see the "Into the Great Outdoors" box, below).

Aosta

GETTING THERE **By Train** Aosta is served by 20 trains a day to and from **Turin** (2 hr., with a change in Chivasso or Ivrea); there are 10 trains a day to and from **Milan** (3½–4 hr., with a change in Chivasso, and sometimes another in Ivrea).

By Bus Aosta's bus station, across the piazza and a bit to the right from the train station, handles about eight buses (only one or two direct; most change in Ivrea) to and from **Turin** daily; the trip takes 3 hours (2 hr. on the direct). Three daily buses run between Aosta and **Milan** (2½ hr.). Buses also connect Aosta with other popular spots in the valley, among them **Courmayeur,** where you can connect to the Palud cable car (see "Mont Blanc by Cable Car," p. 655) and **Cogne,** a major gateway to the Parco Nazionale del Gran Paradiso (see below). For information, call ✆ **0165-262-027.**

By Car Autostrada A5 from Turin shoots up the length of Valle d'Aosta en route to France and Switzerland via the Mont Blanc tunnel; there are numerous exits in the valley. The trip from Turin to Aosta normally takes about an hour and a half, but traffic can be heavy in high season, especially on Friday nights going into the valley and Sunday nights come back toward Turin and Milan.

View of the mountains surrounding Aosta.

VISITOR INFORMATION The **tourist office** in Aosta, Piazza Chanoux 2 (www.regione.vda.it/turismo; ✆ **0165-236-627**), dispenses a wealth of info on hotels, restaurants, and sights throughout the region, along with listings of campgrounds, maps of hiking trails, information about ski-lift tickets and special discounted ski packages, outlets for bike rentals, and rafting trips. It's open daily 9am to 8pm from mid-June to the end of September and from December 26 to January 6. The rest of the year the office closes at 6:30pm.

FESTIVALS & MARKETS Aosta celebrates its patron saint and warm winter days and nights with the **Fiera Sant'Orso** on the last 2 days of January. During the festival, the locals dance, drink vast quantities of mulled wine, and peruse the local crafts pieces, such as lovely woodcarvings and woven blankets, which vendors from throughout Valle d'Aosta offer for sale. Aosta's other major event is the **Bataille de Reines (Battle of the Queens).** The queens in question are cows, and these mainstays of the local economy lock horns; the main event is held the third Sunday in October, and preliminary heats take place throughout the spring and summer. Aosta's **weekly market** day is Tuesday, when stalls selling food, clothes, crafts, and household items fill the Piazza Cavalieri di Vittorio Veneto.

EXPLORING AOSTA

This mountain town, surrounded by snowcapped peaks, not only is pleasant but has soul—the product of a history that goes back to Roman times. While you're not going to find much in the line of pristine Alpine quaintness here in Valle d'Aosta's busy tourist and economic center, you can spend some enjoyable time strolling past Roman ruins and medieval bell towers while checking out the chic shops that sell everything from Armani suits to locally made Fontina cheese.

The "Rome of the Alps" sits majestically within its preserved walls, and the monuments of the empire make it easy to envision the days when Aosta was one of Rome's most important trading and military outposts. Two Roman gates arch gracefully across the Via San Anselmo, Aosta's main thoroughfare: the **Porta Pretoria,** the western entrance to the Roman town, and the **Arco di Augusto** (sometimes called Arco Romano), the eastern entrance, built in A.D. 25 to commemorate a Roman victory over the Celts. A **Roman bridge** spans the River Buthier while just a few steps north of the Porta Pretoria, you'll find the facade of the **Teatro Romano (Roman Theater)** and the ruins of the **amphitheater,** which once accommodated 20,000 spectators. The ruins of the **forum** are in an adjacent park. The theater and forum are open daily, in summer from 9:30am to noon and 2:30 to 6:30pm, in winter from 9:30am to noon and 2 to 4:30pm; admission is free. Architectural fragments from these monuments and a sizable collection of vessels and other objects unearthed during excavations are displayed in Aosta's **Archaeological Museum,** at Piazza Roncas 12 (✆ **0165-275-902**); it's open daily from 9am to 7pm, and admission is free.

SIDE TRIPS FROM AOSTA

BREUIL-CERVINIA & THE MATTERHORN You don't come to Breuil-Cervinia to see the town, a banal collection of tourist facilities—the sight to see, and you can't miss it, is the **Matterhorn** (**Monte Cervino** in Italian) ★. Its distinctive profile looms majestically above the valley, beckoning year-round skiers and those who simply want to savor a refreshing Alpine experience by ascending to its glaciers via cable car to the Plateau Rosa (26€ round-trip; closed Sept 10 to mid-Oct). An excellent trail also ascends from **Breuil-Cervinia** up the flank of the mountain. After a moderately strenuous uphill trek of 90 minutes, you come to a gorgeous mountain lake, **Lac du Goillet** ★, and from there,

INTO THE GREAT outdoors

Recreation is what draws most people to Valle d'Aosta. You'll find some of the best **downhill skiing** and facilities on the runs at **Courmayeur, Breuil-Cervinia,** and in the **Monte Rosa** ski area that centers around the towns of Champoluc and Gressoney. Multiday passes, providing access to the lifts and slopes of the entire valley, run 120€ for 3 days and 158€ for 4 days, with per-day rates sliding down a scale to 14 days at 434€. For more info, call ✆ **0165-238-871** or visit www.skivallee.it. Ski season starts in early December and runs through April, if the snow holds out.

One money-saving option is to take one of the ***settimane bianche* (white week) packages** that include room and board and unlimited skiing, and are available at resorts throughout Valle d'Aosta. The tourist board (www.regione.vda.it) is a good resource to start looking for availability.

Cross-country skiing is superb around Cogne in the Parco Nazionale del Gran Paradiso, where there are more than 50km (30 miles) of trails. Valle d'Aosta is also some of Italy's best **hiking** terrain.

it's another 90 minutes to the **Colle Superiore delle Cime Bianche ★**, a plateau with heart-stopping views.

PARCO NAZIONALE DEL GRAN PARADISO ★ The little town of Cogne is the most convenient gateway to one of Europe's finest parcels of unspoiled nature, the former hunting grounds of King Vittorio Emanuele that now make up this vast and lovely national park. The park encompasses five valleys and a total of 3,626 sq. km (1,414 sq. miles) of forests and pastureland where many Alpine beasts roam wild, including the ibex (a long-horned goat) and the chamois (a small antelope), both of which have hovered near extinction in recent years. Humans can roam these wilds via a vast network of well-marked trails. Cogne also offers some downhill skiing, but it is better regarded for its many cross-country skiing trails.

WHERE TO EAT & STAY

This is the land of mountain food—hams and salamis are laced with herbs from Alpine meadows; creamy cornmeal polenta accompanies meals; a rich beef stew, *carbonada,* warms winter nights; and buttery Fontina is the cheese of choice.

Many hotels in Valle d'Aosta require that guests take their meals on the premises and stay 3 nights or more. However, outside of busy tourist times, hotels often have rooms to spare and are willing to be a little more flexible with their policies. Rates vary almost month by month; in general, expect to pay the most for a room in August and at Christmas and Easter, and the least for a room in the fall. For the best rates, check with the local tourist boards for information on *settimane bianche* (white week) packages, all-inclusive deals that include room, board, and ski passes.

Belle Epoque Simple, very simple, but also cheap and well located in a quiet corner of the historic center. The stucco exterior has a cozy Alpine look to it, but the same can't be said of the somewhat stark interior. What is appealing about this hotel is the family-run atmosphere and the price. There is no elevator so you'll be taking the stairs to the spartan but clean rooms. A trattoria occupies most of the ground floor where you can arrange a half-board deal. Skip the breakfast and spend your money much more wisely in town, whether for a banana in the supermarket or a cappuccino and pastry at a bar.

Via d'Avise 18, 11100 Aosta. www.hotelbellepoqueaosta.it. ✆ **0165-262-276.** Fax 0165-261-196. 14 units, 11 with private bathroom. 46€–54€ double with shared bathroom; 50€–66€ double with private bathroom. Breakfast 6.50€. AE, MC, V. Free parking. **Amenities:** Restaurant; bar; room service. *In room:* A/C.

Caffè Nazionale CAFE This lovely fixture on Aosta's main square dates from 1886, and little has changed since then. For an almost sacred experience, try taking your coffee and pastry in the frescoed room that was once a chapel of the dukes of Aosta. It is said that Ava Gardner had romantic trysts here.

Piazza Chanoux 9. ✆ **0165-262-158.** Reservations not accepted. Pastries from 3€. AE, DC, MC, V. Tues–Sun 8am–2am.

Milleluci ★★★ 🎁 From its noticeably cooler perch on a hillside just above the town, this chaletlike hotel in a breezy garden offers pleasant views. Current owner Cristina's great-grandmother converted the family farm into a hotel 50 years ago, and it's been handed down from mother to daughter ever since. Downstairs, a large wood-beamed sitting area is grouped around an attractive hearth (always ablaze in winter) and bar. The spacious rooms (larger on the second floor; cozy on the first) sport some nice touches like traditional wood furnishings, beamed ceilings, canopied beds (in suites and in one double), rich fabrics, terrazzo floors, and handsome prints. The stupendous buffet breakfast, which in good weather can be had on the wraparound terrace overlooking the town, alone would be reason to stay here.

In Roppoz (off Via Porossan 1km/½ mile northeast of Arco di Augusto), 11100 Aosta. www.hotelmilleluci.com. ✆ **0165-23-5278.** Fax 0165-235-284. 31 units. 150€ double without balcony, 160€–250€ double with balcony. Rates include breakfast. AE, DC, MC, V. Free parking. **Amenities:** Babysitting; children's playground; concierge; Jacuzzi; outdoor heated pool; room service; sauna; smoke-free rooms. *In room:* TV/VCR, hair dryer, minibar, Wi-Fi (free).

Osteria da Nando VALDOSTAN The focus here is on hearty local cuisine: dishes such as *fonduta* (a creamy fondue made mostly with Fontina), *crepes à la Valdostana* (filled and topped with melted cheese), and *carbonada con polenta* (beef stew dished over polenta). Germana Scarpa has been running Osteria da Nando since 1957 and every night she still manages to give it a personal, family touch. Her son Corrado looks after guests and will suggest which of the many Valle d'Aosta wines on the list will pair best with what you're eating. And, if you must, you can get a pretty decent pizza. Dessert is not to be missed, especially the licorice and cinnamon panna cotta.

Via Sant'Anselmo 99. www.osteriadanando.it. ✆ **0165-44-455.** Reservations not accepted. Main courses 10€–20€. AE, DC, MC, V. Tues–Sun noon–3pm and 7:15–10pm. Usually closed 15 days in late June/early July.

Roma Tucked into a cul-de-sac near the Porta Pretoria, this place is not going to win you over with its charm, but it's clean and the location is superb (in the dead center of Aosta not far from the train station and the cable car to Pila). The paneled lobby and adjoining bar are pleasant places to relax and, with their plaid carpet and furnishings, are a little cozier than the nondescript guest rooms upstairs.

Via Torino 7, 11100 Aosta. www.hotelroma-aosta.it. ✆ **0165-41-000.** Fax 0165-32-404. 38 units. 87€–96€ double; 117€–129€ triple. Rates include breakfast. AE, DC, MC, V. Limited free parking. **Amenities:** Bar; room service. *In room:* TV, hair dryer, Wi-Fi (free).

Courmayeur-Entreves

The one-time mountain hamlet of **Courmayeur** is Valle d'Aosta's resort extraordinaire, a collection of traditional stone buildings, pseudo-Alpine chalets, and large hotels catering to a well-heeled international crowd of skiers. Even if you don't ski, you can happily while away the time sipping a grog while regarding the craggy bulk of Mont Blanc (Monte Bianco on this side of the border), which looms over this end of Valle d'Aosta and forms the snowy barrier between Italy and France. The Mont Blanc tunnel makes it possible to zip into France in just 20 minutes.

Entrèves, 3km (2 miles) north of Courmayeur, is the sort of place that the latter probably once was: a pleasant collection of stone houses and farm buildings surrounded by pastureland. Quaint as the village is in appearance, at its soul it is a worldly enclave with some nice hotels and restaurants catering to skiers and outdoor enthusiasts who prefer to spend time in the mountains in surroundings that are a little quieter than Courmayeur.

ESSENTIALS

GETTING THERE **By Bus** About a dozen daily buses connect Courmayeur with Aosta (1 hr.). At least hourly buses (more in summer; ✆ **0165-841-305**) run between Courmayeur's Piazzale Monte Bianco and Entrèves and La Palud (10 min.), just above Entrèves.

By Car Autostrada A5 from Turin to the Mont Blanc tunnel passes Courmayeur; the trip from Aosta to Courmayeur on this much-used route takes less than half an hour (lots of time in tunnels; for scenery, take the parallel S26, about 1 hr.), and total travel time from Turin is less than 2 hours.

VISITOR INFORMATION The **tourist office** in Courmayeur, Piazzale Monte Bianco 8 (www.regione.vda.it/turismo; ✆ **0165-842-060**), provides information on hiking, skiing, and other outdoor activities in the region, as well as hotel and restaurant listings. Mid-June through September, the office is open daily 9am to 7pm; October through mid-June, 9am to 1pm and 2 to 6pm.

WHERE TO EAT & STAY

Edelweiss ★ In winter, the pine-paneled salons and cozy rooms of this chalet-style hotel near the center of town attract a friendly international set of skiers, and in summer, many Italian families spend a month or two here at a time. The Roveyaz family extends a hearty welcome to all and provides modern mountain-style accommodations. Many rooms open onto terraces overlooking the mountains, and the nicest rooms are those on the top floor, tucked under the eaves. Basic, nonfussy meals are served in the cheerful main-floor

Skiing at Courmayeur.

MONT BLANC BY cable car

One of Valle d'Aosta's best experiences is to ride the series of cable cars from La Palud, just above Entrèves, across Mont Blanc to several ski stations in Italy and France and down into Chamonix, France. You make the trip in stages—first past two intermediate stops to the last aerie on Italian soil, **Punta Helbronner** (20 min. each way; 35€ round-trip or 96€ for a family pass valid for two adults and two children ages 6–11). At 3,300m (10,800 ft.), this ice-clad lookout provides stunning views of the Mont Blanc glaciers and the Matterhorn and other peaks looming in the distance. In summer, you may want to hop off before you get to Punta Helbronner at **Pavillon Frety** (14€ round-trip) and tour a pleasant botanic garden, Giardino Alpino Saussurea (www.saussurea.net; ✆ **333-446-2959**), open daily from the end of June through September; admission is 2.50€, or 1.50€ with your cable car ticket.

For sheer drama, continue from Punta Helbronner to **Aiguille du Midi ★★★** in France in a tiny gondola to experience the dramatic sensation of dangling more than 2,300m (7,500 ft.) in midair as you cruise above the Géant Glacier and the Vallée Blanche (30 min. each way; tack on another 20€ round-trip). From Aiguille du Midi, you can descend over more glaciers and dramatic valleys on the French flank of Mont Blanc to the resort town of **Chamonix** (50 min. each way; 50€). If you go all the way to Chamonix, the best way to return to Italy is to hop on a bus back through the tunnel, for a final 12€ per person. Buses take 45 minutes and leave Chamonix at 8:45 and 10:10am, and at 1:30, 3, 4, and 5:45pm.

Hours for these cable cars vary wildly, and service can be sporadic, depending on weather conditions (winds often close the gondola btw. Helbronner and Aiguille du Midi; this is, after all, the tallest mountain in western Europe), but in general, they run every 20 minutes from 7:20am (8:20am in fall and spring) to 12:30pm and 2 to 5:30pm (July 22–Aug 27 all day long; closed Nov 2–Dec 10). The last downward run is 5:30pm in summer and 4:30pm in winter. The Helbronner–Aiguille du Midi gondola is open only May through September. ***Note:*** Children 5 and under travel free, while those ages 6 to 11 get 50% off the prices above, and seniors 66 and older get a 10% discount. Hourly buses make the 10-minute run from Courmayeur to the cable car terminus at La Palud. For more info, call ✆ **0165-89-925** (www.montebianco.com). For a report of weather at the top and on the other side, dial ✆ **0165-89-961.**

dining room; you can arrange a half-board deal if you wish. The hotel also has a small exercise room for those who haven't done enough hiking or skiing during the day.

Via Marconi 42, 11013 Courmayeur. www.albergoedelweiss.it. ✆ **0165-841-590.** Fax 0165-841-618. 30 units. Summer 80€–140€ double per person, per day; winter 310€–420€ double per person, per week. Rates include breakfast. MC, V. Free parking. Closed Oct–Nov and May–June. **Amenities:** Regional restaurant; bar; a few free bikes; exercise room; sauna; smoke-free rooms; Wi-Fi (1st hr. free, then 5€/3 hrs.). *In room:* TV, hair dryer.

La Grange ★★ What may well be the most charming hotel in Valle d'Aosta occupies a converted barn and is ably managed by Bruna Berthold. None of the rooms are the same and all are decorated with a pleasing smattering of antiques and rustic furnishings; some have balconies overlooking Mont Blanc, which, quite literally, looms over the property. The stucco-walled, stone-floor lobby is a fine place to relax, with couches built around a corner hearth and a little bar area. A lavish buffet breakfast is served in a prettily paneled room off the lobby, and the hotel also has an exercise room and a sauna. The price-to-quality ratio of La Grange is outstanding if you don't come from about July 20 to August 20, when the prices, while still reasonable, are at their maximum.

Strada La Brenva 1, Entrèves. www.lagrange-it.com. ✆ **0165-869-733,** or 335-646-3533 in the off season. Fax 0165-869-744. 22 units. 80€–150€ double; 100€–180€ triple; 150€–230€ suite; there are discounts for stays of 3–5 days that don't include Fri–Sun. Rates include American breakfast. AE, DC, MC, V. Free parking. Closed May–June and Oct–Nov. **Amenities:** Bar; babysitting; bikes; concierge; exercise room; room service; sauna. *In room:* TV, hair dryer, minibar.

La Maison de Filippo ★★★ VALDOSTAN The atmosphere at this popular and cheerful restaurant in Entrèves is delightfully country Alpine, and the offerings are so generous you may not be able to eat again for a week. Daily menus vary but often include an antipasto of mountain hams and salamis, a selection of pastas filled with wild mushrooms and topped with Fontina and other local cheeses, and a sampling of fresh trout and game in season. Service is casual and friendly, and in summer you can choose between a table in the delightfully barn-like structure or one on the flowery terrace.

Loc. Entrèves. www.lamaison.com. ✆ **0165-869-797.** Reservations required. Fixed-price menu 48€ not including wine. MC, V. Wed–Mon 12:30–2:30pm and 7:30–10:30pm. Closed June and Nov.

Ristorante La Palud SEAFOOD/VALDOSTAN A table in front of the hearth in this cozy restaurant is just the place to enjoy the local specialties including creamy *polenta concia* (with Fontina cheese and butter folded in) and *cervo* (venison) in season. There is a selection of mountain cheeses for dessert, and the wine list borrows heavily from neighboring Piedmont but also includes some local vintages. On Fridays, you can enjoy a wide selection of fresh fish brought up from Liguria and you can always opt for one of the more than 200 types of pizza prepared in the wood-burning oven.

Strada la Palud 17, Courmayeur. www.lapalud.it. ✆ **0165-89-169.** Reservations recommended. Main courses 8.50€–21€; fixed-price menus 18€–25€ (the more expensive one includes wine). AE, MC, V. Thurs–Tues noon–3:30pm and 7:30–10:30pm.

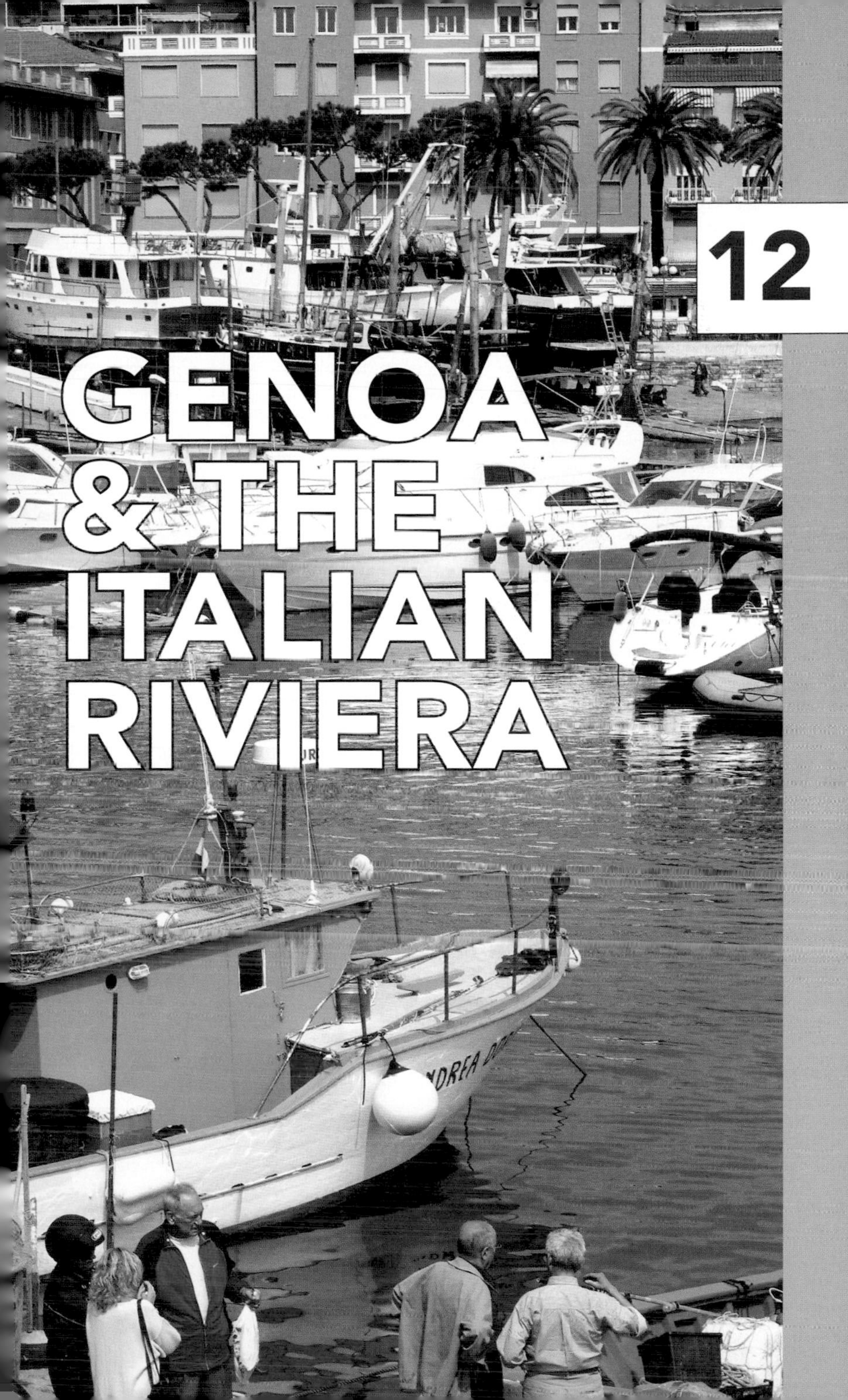

12

GENOA & THE ITALIAN RIVIERA

From the top of Tuscany to the French border, along the Ligurian Sea, Italy follows a crescent-shape strip of seacoast and mountains that make up the region of **Liguria.** The pleasures of this region are no secret. Ever since the 19th century, world-weary travelers have been heading for Liguria's resorts to enjoy balmy weather (ensured by the protective barrier of the Ligurian Alps) and turquoise seas. Beyond the beach, the stones and tile of fishing villages, small resort towns, and proud old port cities bake in the sun, and hillsides are fragrant with the scent of bougainvillea and pines.

Liguria is really two coasts. First, the beachier stretch west of Genoa known as the **Riviera di Ponente (Setting Sun),** is studded with fashionable resorts, many of which, like San Remo, have seen their heydays fade but continue to entice visitors with palm-fringed promenades and gentle ways.

The rockier, more colorful fishing-village-filled stretch to the southeast of Genoa, known as the **Riviera di Levante (Rising Sun),** extends past the posh harbor of Portofino to the remote hamlets of the Cinque Terre.

The province's capital, Genoa, is Italy's busiest port, an ancient center of commerce, and one of history's great maritime powers. However, though it is one of Italy's most historic places, it is also one of the country's least-visited large cities. But don't judge the area by its capital: Genoa's gritty feel and its brusque and clamorous elements are a world apart from the easygoing and charming seaside villages and resorts that populate the region as a whole.

THE BEST GENOA & RIVIERA EXPERIENCES

- **Visiting the Galata Museo del Mare (Museum of the Seas):** Many a metropolis offer you a "city museum" that helps decipher the past. For Genoa, a town that gave us Christopher Columbus, the honors are done by this museum that illustrates how the city and sea have always been intertwined. See p. 667.
- **Exploring Genoa by foot:** Many of Europe's great cities are best seen on foot, but in my humble opinion, none are more so than Genoa. It's the best way to experience the vibrancy of this old port town, and it's charming, too. As an added bonus, the more you walk the more focaccia you can eat.
- **Taking a ride through time:** Buy a 24-hour pass for the public transport system (4.50€, or 9€ for four people) and then go wild on Genoa's myriad of funiculars, elevators, and cog railways, which are fun in their own right and often whisk you up to beautiful belvederes. See p. 671.
- **Hiking Portofino's promontory:** Cinque Terre gets all the press, but excellent hiking can also be had here on this piece of Liguria that juts out into the sea between Camogli and Santa Margherita Ligure. Start at one, walk to the other, and enjoy the views (and Portofino) in between. See p. 685.

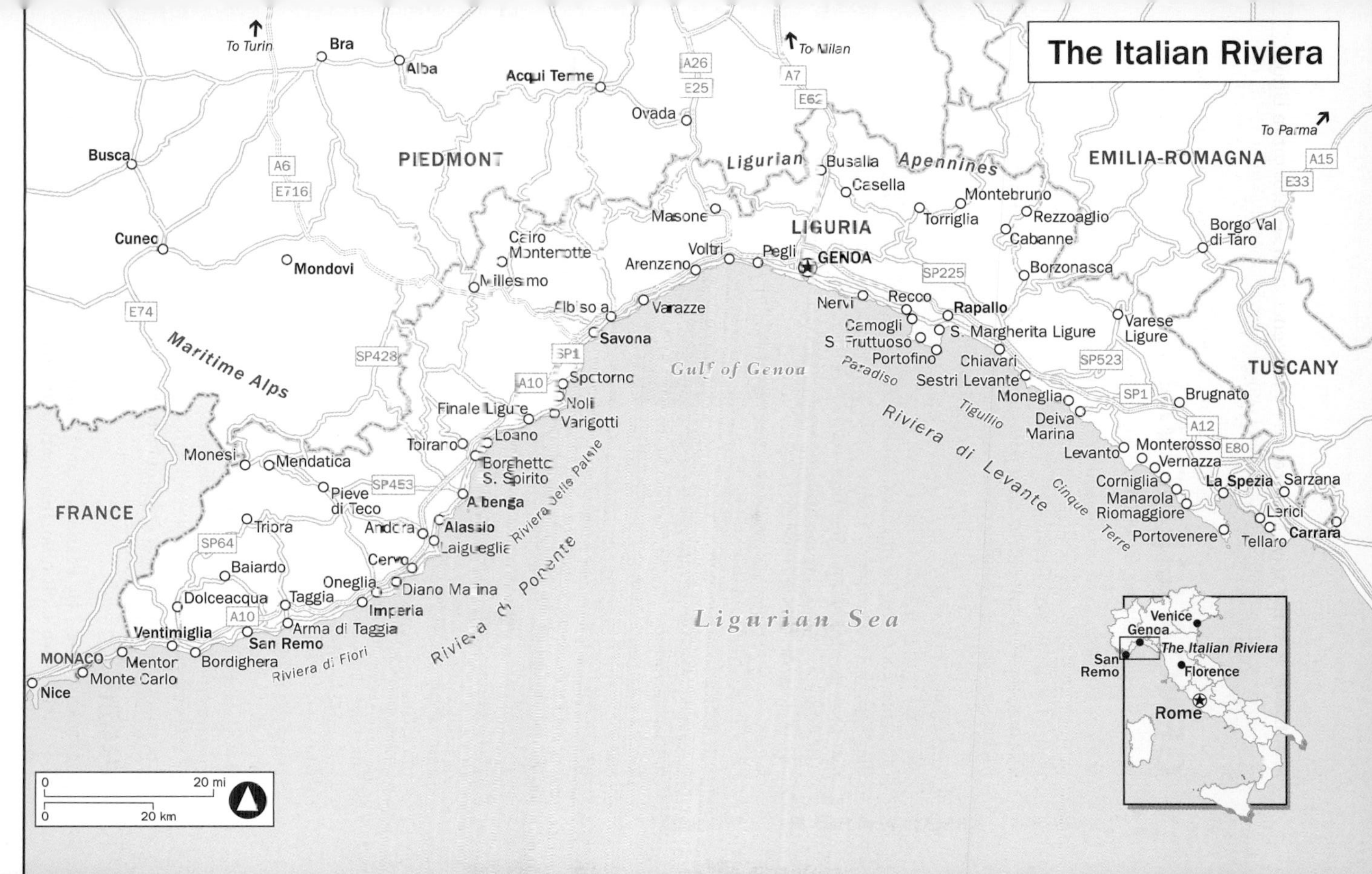

The Italian Riviera
To Turin
To Milan
To Parma
PIEDMONT
EMILIA-ROMAGNA
LIGURIA
TUSCANY
FRANCE
MONACO
Ligurian Apennines
Maritime Alps
Gulf of Genoa
Ligurian Sea
Riviera di Levante
Riviera di Ponente
Riviera delle Palme
Riviera di Fiori
Tigullio
Paradiso
Cinque Terre
Bra
Alba
Acqui Terme
Ovada
Busca
Cuneo
Mondovi
Cairo Montenotte
Millesimo
Masone
Busalla
Casella
Torriglia
Montebruno
Rezzoaglio
Cabanne
Borzonasca
Borgo Val di Taro
Varese Ligure
Brugnato
GENOA
Pegli
Voltri
Arenzano
Varazze
Albisola
Savona
Spotorno
Noli
Varigotti
Finale Ligure
Loano
Toirano
Borghetto S. Spirito
Albenga
Alassio
Laigueglia
Andora
Cervo
Diano Marina
Oneglia
Imperia
Taggia
Arma di Taggia
San Remo
Bordighera
Ventimiglia
Dolceacqua
Baiardo
Triora
Pieve di Teco
Mendatica
Monesi
Menton
Monte Carlo
Nice
Nervi
Recco
Camogli
S. Fruttuoso
Portofino
Rapallo
S. Margherita Ligure
Chiavari
Sestri Levante
Moneglia
Deiva Marina
Levanto
Monterosso
Vernazza
Corniglia
Manarola
Riomaggiore
Portovenere
La Spezia
Sarzana
Lerici
Tellaro
Carrara
A26
E25
A7
E62
A6
E716
A15
E33
E74
SP428
A10
SP1
SP453
SP64
SP225
SP523
A12
E80
Venice
Genoa
The Italian Riviera
San Remo
Florence
Rome
0
20 mi
0
20 km

- **Eating yourself silly at Sagra del Pesce:** Italy's town festivals, often based on a local food, are legendary and Camogli's sardine-based party is up there with the best of them. See p. 680.

GENOA (GENOVA)

142km (88 miles) S of Milan, 501km (311 miles) NW of Rome, 194km (120 miles) E of Nice

With its dizzying mix of the old and the new, **Genoa** is as multilayered as the hills it clings to. It was and is, first and foremost, a port city: an important maritime center for the Roman Empire, boyhood home of Christopher Columbus (whose much-restored house still stands near a section of the medieval walls), and, fueled by seafaring commerce that stretched to the Middle East, one of the largest and wealthiest cities of Renaissance Europe.

Genoa began as a port of the ancient Ligurian people at least by the 6th century B.C. and by the early Middle Ages had become a formidable maritime power, conquering the surrounding coast and the mighty outlying islands of Corsica and Sardinia. Genoa established colonies throughout North Africa and the Middle East, and made massive gains during the Crusades. With bigger success came new, bigger rivals, and Genoa locked commercial and military horns with Venice, which eventually took the upper hand in the late 14th century. Genoa increasingly fell under the control of outsiders, and though self-government returned for a while in the 16th century, by then sea trade was rapidly shifting to Spain and eventually to its American colonies, a trend exemplified by Genoa's most famous native son, Columbus, who had to travel to Spain to find the financial backing for his voyage of exploration across the Atlantic.

The mix of old and new in Genoa's harbor.

It's easy to capture glimpses of Genoa's former glory days on the narrow lanes and dank alleys of the portside Old Town, where treasure-filled palaces and fine marble churches stand next to laundry-draped tenements and brothels. In fact, some of the life within the old medieval walls doesn't seem to have changed since the days when Genovese ships set sail to launch raids on the Venetians, crusaders embarked for the Holy Land, and Giuseppe Garibaldi shipped out to invade Sicily in the 19th-century struggle to unify Italy. The other Genoa, the modern city that stretches for miles along the coast and climbs the hills, is a city of international business, peaceful parks, and breezy belvederes from which you can enjoy fine views of this colorful metropolis and the sea.

Essentials

GETTING THERE **By Plane** Flights to and from most European capitals serve **Cristoforo Colombo International Airport,** just 6.5km (4 miles) west

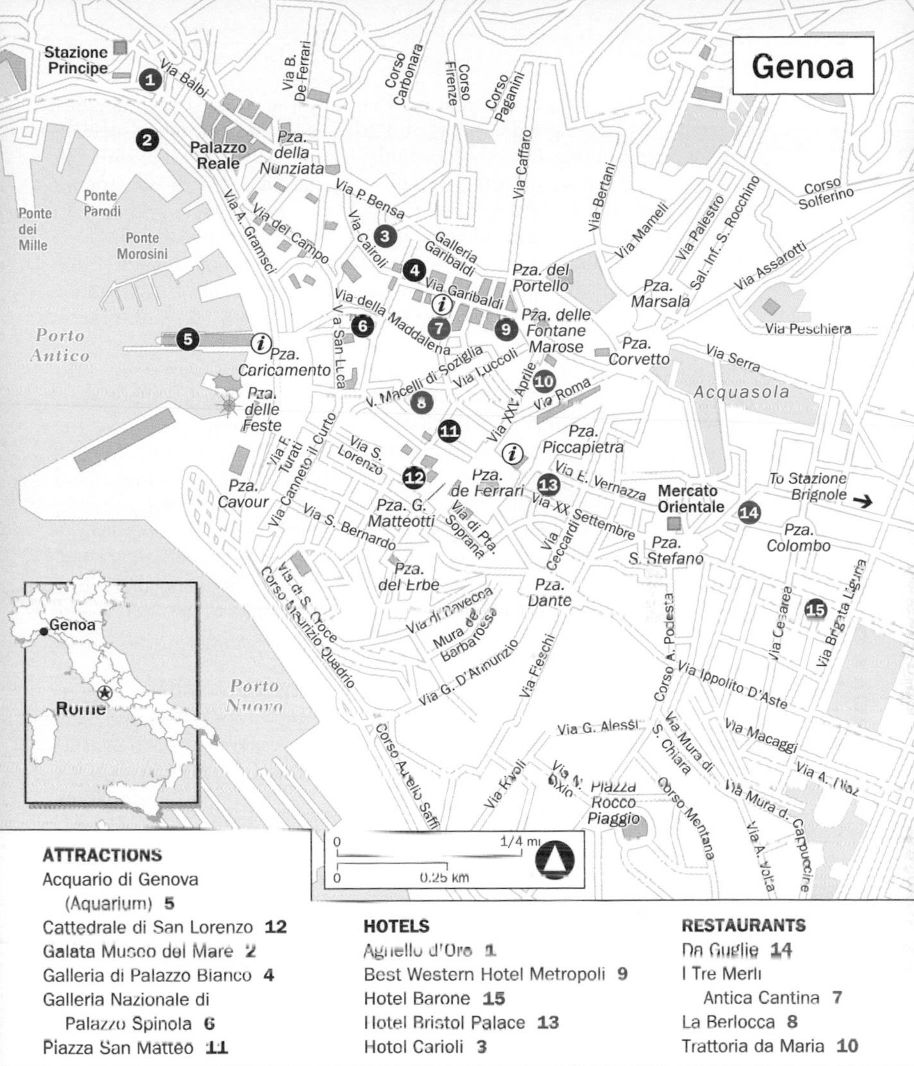

of the city center (www.airport.genova.it; ✆ **010-60-151**). **Volabus** (www.amt.genova.it; ✆ **010-558-2414** or 800-085-311 toll free from within Italy) connects the airport with the Principe and Brignole train stations, with buses running the 30-minute trip once or twice an hour from 5am to 10pm; buy tickets (6€, includes a transfer to or from the city transportation network) on the bus. The nearest airports handling overseas flights are at Nice, 188km (117 miles) west just over the border with France, and Milan, 136km (85 miles) to the north; both cities are well connected to Genoa by highways and train service.

By Train Genoa has two major train stations, **Stazione Principe** (designated on timetables as Genova P.P.), near the Old Town and the port on Piazza Acquaverde, and **Stazione Brignole** (designated on timetables as Genova BR.), in the modern city on Piazza Verdi. Many trains, especially those on long-distance lines, service both stations; however, some stop only at one, making it essential that you know the station at which your train is scheduled to arrive and from which it will depart. Trains (free, as they don't check tickets btw. the downtown stations) connect the two stations in 5 minutes and run about every 15 minutes. The city buses nos. 36 and 37 also run between the two train stations, leaving from the front of each station about every 15 minutes; the trip can take anywhere from 10 to 20 minutes depending on traffic.

Genoa is the hub for trains serving the Italian Riviera, with trains arriving from and departing for Ventimiglia on the French border about every half-hour, and **La Spezia,** at the eastern edge of Liguria, even more frequently, as often as every 15 minutes during peak times between 7am and 7pm (regional: 1½ hr.; high-speed: 1¼ hr.). The regional trains make local stops at almost all the coastal resorts while the faster trains stop at only a few of the towns (for towns covered in this chapter, see individual listings for connections with Genoa). Lots of trains connect Genoa with major Italian cities: **Milan** (one to two per hour; regional: 2 hr.; high-speed: 1½ hr.), **Rome** (hourly; 5–6 hr.), **Turin** (one per hour; regional: 2¼ hr.; high-speed: 1¾ hr.), **Florence** (hourly but always with a change, usually at Pisa; 3 hr.), **Pisa** (hourly; regional: 3 hr.; high-speed: 1½–2 hr.).

By Bus An extensive bus network connects Genoa with other parts of Liguria, as well as with other Italian and European cities, from the main bus station next to Stazione Principe. While it is easiest to reach seaside resorts by the trains that run up and down the coast, buses link to many small towns in the region's hilly hinterlands. For tickets and information, contact **PESCI,** Piazza della Vittoria 94r (✆ **010-564-936**).

By Car Genoa is linked to other parts of Italy and to France by a convenient network of highways. Genoa has lots of parking around the port and the edges of the Old Town, so you can usually find a spot easily, but it can be pricey (1.60€–2€ an hour) though in some lots you don't pay for the overnight hours.

By Ferry Genoa is linked to several other major Mediterranean ports, including Barcelona, as well as Sardinia and Sicily by ferry service (www.traghettitalia.it). Most boats leave and depart from the Stazione Marittima (✆ **010-089-8300**), which is on a waterfront roadway, Via Marina D'Italia, about a 5-minute walk south of Stazione Principe. For service to and from the **Riviera Levante,** check with **Tigullio** (www.traghettiportofino.it; ✆ **0185-284-670**); there's almost hourly service from 9am to 5pm daily in July and August.

VISITOR INFORMATION The **main tourist office** is on **Via Garibaldi 12r** across from the beautiful city hall (www.genova-turismo.it; ✆ **010-557-2903**), open daily 9am to 6:30pm. There are branches also in **Piazza de Ferrari** (✆ **010-806-6122**), open daily 9am to 1pm and 2:30 to 6:30pm; **Piazza Caricamento** near the aquarium (✆ **010-557-4200**), open daily 9:30am to 6:30pm; and **Cristoforo Colombo airport** (✆ **010-601-5247**), open daily 9am to 1pm and 1:30 to 5:30pm.

Genoa's twisting alleyways.

GETTING AROUND Given Genoa's labyrinth of small streets (many of which cannot be negotiated by car or bus), the only way to get around much of the city is on foot. This, however, can be a navigational feat that requires a good map. Sometimes the tourist office gives out terrific maps and other times they are a bit basic. Consider purchasing a more detailed map—preferably one with a good street index and a section showing the Old Town in detail—at a newsstand. Genovese are usually happy to direct visitors, but given the geography with which they are dealing, their instructions can be complicated. Also be aware of Genoa's unusual street numbering system: Addresses in red (marked with an *r* both below and in any literature you might pick up) generally indicate a commercial establishment; those in black are offices or residences. So two buildings on the same street can have the same number, one in black, one in red.

By Bus Bus tickets (1.50€) are available at newsstands and at ticket booths, *tabacchi* (tobacconists, marked by a brown-and-white T sign), and at the train stations; look for the symbol **AMT** (www.amt.genova.it; ✆ **010-558-2414**). Otherwise, they cost 2.50€ on board. You must stamp your ticket when you board. Bus tickets can also be used on the funiculars and public elevators that climb the city's steep hills surrounding the ancient core of the town (see "Public Transportation Has Never Been This Fun" box, p. 671). Tickets good for 24 hours cost 4.50€, or 9€ for four people (two people travel for free). You can also buy a pack of 10 single tickets for 14€.

By Taxi Metered taxis, which you can find at cabstands, are a convenient and safe way to get around Genoa at night if you are tired of navigating mazelike streets or trying to decipher the city's elaborate bus system. For instance, you may well want to consider taking a taxi from a restaurant in the Old Town to your hotel or to one of the train stations (especially Stazione Brignole, which is a bit farther). Cabstands at Piazza della Nunziata, Piazza Fontane Marose, and Piazza de Ferrari are especially convenient to the Old Town, or call a **radio taxi** at ✆ **010-5966.**

By Subway The city's nascent subway system is a work in progress, as there are still only seven stops on a single line between Piazza De Ferrari and a suburb to the northwest called Certosa (there are convenient stops in btw. at Stazione Principe and at Dinegro close to the ferry port). The tickets are the same as those used for the bus.

FESTIVALS & MARKETS In June, an ancient tradition continues when Genoa takes to the sea in the **Regata delle Antiche Repubbliche Marinare** (not to be confused with Venice's own **Regata Storica;** p. 466), competing against crews from its ancient maritime rivals, Amalfi, Pisa, and Venice, who host the event in turn. Another spectacular—though more modern—regatta takes place every April, the Millevele, or Thousand Sails, when Genoa's bay is carpeted with the mainsails and spinnakers of nautical enthusiasts from around the world.

Genoa adds a touch of culture to the summer season with an **International Ballet Festival** that attracts a stellar list of performers from around the world. Performances are held in the beautiful gardens of Villa Gropallo in outlying Nervi, a late-19th-century resort with lush parks and a lively seaside promenade. Contact the tourist office in Genoa for schedules and ticket information, as well as for the summer concerts staged at different venues, many of them outdoors, around the city.

The **Mercato Orientale,** Genoa's sprawling indoor food market, evokes the days when ships brought back spices and other commodities from the ends of the earth. Still a boisterous affair and an excellent place to stock up on olives, herbs, fresh fruit, and other Ligurian products, it is held Monday through Saturday 7:30am to 1pm and 3:30 to 7:30pm, with entrances on Via XX Settembre and Via Galata (about halfway btw. Piazza de Ferrari at the edge of the Old Town and Stazione Brignole). The district just north of the market (especially Via San Vincenzo and Via Colombo) is a gourmand's dream, with many bakeries, *pasticcerie* (pastry shops), and stores selling pasta and cheese, wine, olive oil, and other foodstuffs.

To enjoy what is probably the most delectable food court you have ever come across, take the elevators up to **Eataly ★★**, open daily 10am to 10pm, in the building right in front of the massive white Bigo (p. 668) in the Porto Antico. This is the same outfit that can be found on Fifth Avenue in New York City as well as in Milan (p. 561) and a few other Italian cities. There are five separate places to order food—including delicious pizza, salads, grilled meat, and fresh mozzarella—that you take to one of the tables and enjoy in an informal setting. You can also buy food in what is essentially a market of all the best Italian products and take it outside to eat on the benches facing the port. If you need a jar of pesto to bring home, this is a good place to get it, and if you need a cold drink, buying it up here will cost you a third of what you pay at the fast food joint downstairs. Even if you aren't going to eat, come up to have a look and enjoy the great free view of the harbor.

CITY LAYOUT Genoa extends for miles along the coast, with neighborhoods and suburbs tucked into valleys and climbing the city's many hills. Most sights of interest are in the **Old Town,** a fascinating jumble of old *palazzi,* laundry-festooned tenements, cramped squares, and tiny lanes and alleyways clustered on the eastern side of the old port. The city's two train stations are located on either side of the Old Town. As confusing as Genoa's topography is, wherever you are in the Old Town, you are only a short walk or bus or taxi ride from one of these two stations. **Stazione Principe** is the closest, just to the west; from **Piazza Acquaverde,** in front of the station, follow **Via Balbi** through **Piazza della Nunziata** and **Via Bensa** to **Via Cairoli,** which runs into Via Garibaldi (the walk will take about 15 min.). **Via Garibaldi,** lined with a succession of majestic *palazzi,* forms the northern flank of the Old Town and is the best place to begin your explorations. Many of the city's most important museums and other major monuments are on and around this street, and from here you can descend into the warren of little lanes, known as ***caruggi,*** that lead through the cluttered heart of the city and down to the port.

From **Stazione Brignole,** walk straight across the broad, open space to Piazza della Vittoria/Via Luigi Cadorna and turn right to follow broad **Via XX Settembre,** one of the city's major shopping avenues, due west for about 15 or 20 minutes to **Piazza de Ferrari,** which is on the eastern edge of the Old Town. From here, **Via San Lorenzo,** accessed by exiting the southwest corner of the square, will lead you past Genoa's cathedral and to the port. To reach Via Garibaldi, go north from Piazza de Ferrari on **Via XXV Aprile** to **Piazza delle Fontane Marose.** This busy square marks the eastern end of Via Garibaldi.

[Fast FACTS] GENOA

Bookstores Genoa's best source for English-language books and other media is **Feltrinelli,** Via Ceccardi 16, near Piazza De Ferrari, just off of Via XX Settembre (www.lafeltrinelli.it; ✆ **010-573-331**).

Crime Genoa is a relatively safe city, but some of the very small alleyways of the Old Town near the port can be sketchy at night, and even during the day they can sometimes make you feel unsafe. Violent crime in the city center is extremely rare, but use caution and good sense, and take the same precautions you would exercise in any large city. Wait for other people, preferably locals, before entering little-trafficked alleyways and avoid any streets that make you feel uneasy. In an **emergency,** call ✆ **113;** this is a free call. There is a **police station** on the cusp of the Old Town and the port at Via Balbi 38/B (✆ **010-254-871**).

Drugstores Pharmacies keep extended hours on a rotating basis; dial ✆ **192** to learn which ones are open late in a particular week. Several that are usually open overnight are **Pescetto,** Via Balbi 185r (✆ **010-246-2697**), across from Stazione Principe; **Ghersi,** Corte Lambruschini 16 (✆ **010-541-661**); and **Europa,** Corso Europa 676 (✆ **010-397-615**).

Emergencies The general emergency number is ✆ **113;** for an ambulance, dial ✆ **118.** Both are free calls.

Holidays Genoa's patron saint, San Giovanni Battista (Saint John the Baptist), is the same as Turin's and is honored on June 24. For a list of official state holidays, see p. 45.

Hospitals The **Ospedale San Martino,** Largo Rosanna Benzi 10 (✆ **010-5551**), offers a variety of medical services.

Internet **Fnac,** Via XX Settembre 46r (✆ **010-290-111**), charges 2€ for 30 minutes and 3€ per hour, and stays open daily 9:30am to 8pm (Sun open 10am). **Khairan Phone Center,** on the other side of town at Via Balbi 148r near Stazione Principe, is open daily 9am to midnight and charges 1€ an hour.

Laundry There is a self-service laundromat, **Lavanderia Self-Service,** at Via Gramsci 181R (✆ **340-235-1492**), open Monday to Saturday 9am to 6pm. Small washing machines and dryers are 3.50€ per load, large ones 6€.

Luggage Storage The luggage storage office in Stazione Principe is along track 11 and is open daily 7am to 11pm; the fee is 4€ per piece of baggage for the first 5 hours. It is an additional .60€ per hour for the next 7 hours and then an additional .20€ per hour after that. In Stazione Brignole the storage office is on the ground floor; it has the same hours and prices as its sister station.

Post Office Genoa's main post office is at **Piazza Dante 4** (✆ **010-591-762**). This office is open Monday through Saturday 8:10am to 7:40pm, while the other offices around town—including those at the two train stations and the airport—have shorter hours.

Telephone The area code for Genoa is ✆ **010.**

Travel Services **CTS,** Via Colombo 21R (✆ **010-564-366**), specializes in budget travel. It's open Monday to Friday 9:30am to 6:30pm.

Exploring Genoa

Acquario di Genova (Aquarium of Genoa) ★★★ ☺ AQUARIUM Europe's largest aquarium is Genoa's biggest draw and a must-see for travelers with children. The structure alone is remarkable, resembling a ship and built alongside a pier in the old harbor (the aquarium is about a 15-min. walk from Stazione Principe and about 10 min. from Via Garibaldi). Inside, more than 50 aquatic displays re-create Red Sea coral reefs, pools in the tropical rainforests of the Amazon River basin, and other marine ecosystems. These environments provide a pleasant home for sharks, seals, dolphins, penguins, piranhas, and just about every other known kind of creature that has lived in the sea, lakes, or near a major river. Look out for the tiny orange frogs from Madagascar the size of a thumbnail—you may find it hard to draw your gaze away from these tiny colorful creatures. During the day, playful seals and dolphins like to blow trick bubbles to entertain you, and there are small rays in a shallow pool that you can pet. All the descriptions are posted in English. There's also a 3-D film on ocean life (ask for a sheet with the narration in English).

Ponte Spinola (at the port). www.acquariodigenova.it. ✆ **010-234-5678.** Admission 18€ adults, 16€ for seniors 65 and over, 12€ children 4–12. Mon–Fri 9:30am–7:30pm; Sat–Sun 9:30am–8:30pm (July–Aug daily until 10:30pm). Bus: 1, 2, 3, 4, 5, 6, 7, 8, 12, 13, 14, or 15. Metro: Darsena.

Cattedrale di San Lorenzo ★ CATHEDRAL The austerity of this black-and-white-striped 12th-century structure is enlivened ever so slightly by the fanciful French Gothic carvings around the portal and the presence of two stone lions. A later addition is the bell tower, completed in the 16th century. In the frescoed interior, chapels house two of Genoa's most notable curiosities: Beyond the first pilaster on the right is a shell fired through the roof from a British ship offshore during World War II that never exploded, and in the Cappella di San Giovanni (left aisle), a 13th-century crypt contains what crusaders returning from the Holy Land claimed to be relics of John the Baptist. Fabled tableware of doubtful provenance appears to be a quirk of the adjoining treasury: the plate upon which Saint John's head was supposedly served to Salome, a bowl allegedly used at the Last Supper, and a bowl thought at one time to be the Holy Grail. The less fabled but nonetheless magnificent gold and bejeweled objects here reflect Genoa's medieval prominence as a maritime power. Entrance to the treasury is only by guided tour and though they are in Italian, it's interesting to see what is inside even if the extent of your Italian is gelato, pizza, and pasta al pesto.

Piazza San Lorenzo. ✆ **010-254-1250.** Admission to cathedral free; treasury 5.50€ adults, 4.50€ seniors 61 and over and students. Cathedral: Mon–Sat 9am–noon and 3–6pm. Treasury: By

The black-and-white marble facade of Cattedrale di San Lorenzo.

half-hour guided tour only (ask when you get there) Mon–Sat 9am–noon and 3–6pm. Bus: 1, 7, 8, 17, 18, 19, or 20.

Galata Museo del Mare (Museum of the Seas) ★★ ☺ MUSEUM Genoa's glory, past and present, has always been linked to the sea. For a taste of the sea's continued importance today, it is enough to take a walk around the port to see the massive cruise ships and smaller ferries; you can get a glimpse of the cargo docks, though most of those are farther up the coast. To appreciate what the sea has meant to Genoa in past centuries, there is no better place than this appealing four-floor museum. The first section is dedicated to the port and includes 17th century paintings that show you what was happening here all those years ago. Naturally, there is a large room dedicated to Christopher Columbus.

One of the best exhibits, and sure to get a few wows from the kids, is a full-scale reproduction of a Genovese galley, the attack ship the Genoa republic built in large numbers both to conquer far off corners of the Mediterranean, but also to protect their maritime trade. You'll see lots of props and panels, all with English translations, that describe the trials and tribulations of being a rower on one of these galleys and you can't help but walk away pleased to have your job, whatever it may be. There is also an interesting section dedicated to the overseas trip taken by the mass of Italians who from 1892 to 1914 left Genoa, having arrived from all corners of the country, for the United States via New York's Ellis Island.

Ponte Parodi (at the port). www.galatamuseodelmare.it. ✆ **010-234-5655.** Admission 11€ adults, 9€ for seniors 65 and over, 6€ children 4–12. Mar–Oct daily 10am–7pm; Nov–Feb Tues–Fri 10am–6pm, Sat Sun 10am–7:30pm (last entry 90 min. before closing). Bus: 1, 2, 3, 4, 5, 6, 7, 8, 12, 13, 14, or 15. Metro: Darsena (it's a 10-min. walk to the aquarium or else you can hop on the 1€ shuttle).

Galleria di Palazzo Bianco (White Palace) ★★ MUSEUM One of Genoa's finest palaces, built of white stone by the powerful Grimaldi family in the 16th century and reopened to the public in 2004 after an extensive renovation, the Palazzo Bianco houses the city's most notable collection of art. The paintings reflect the fine eye of Maria Brignole-Sale De Ferrari, the duchess of Galliera, who donated the palace and her art to the city in 1884, 4 years before her death. Her preference for painters of the northern schools, whom the affluent Genovese imported to decorate their palaces and paint their portraits, is obvious. Van Dyck and Rubens, both of whom came to Genoa in the early 17th century, are represented here as they are in the city's other major collections. One of the museum's most notable holdings is ***Portrait of a Lady,*** by Lucas Cranach the Elder. The collection also has works by other masters (Filippino Lippi, Veronese, and Caravaggio). Some local artists are also present such as Bernardo Strozzi, whose early-17th-century school made Genoa an important force in the baroque movement. The small rooftop terrace offers (for a fee) superb 360-degree views of the city.

Via Garibaldi 11. ✆ **010-557-2193.** Admission 8€ adults, 6€ for seniors 65 and over, free for E.U. citizens 18 and under; includes entrance to Palazzo Rosso and Palazzo Tursi. Tues–Thurs 9am–7pm; Fri 10am–11pm; Sat–Sun 10am–7pm. Bus: 18, 19, 20, 30, 35, 37, 39, 40, 41, or 42.

Galleria Nazionale di Palazzo Spinola ★ MUSEUM Another prominent Genovese family, the Spinolas, donated their palace and magnificent art collection to the city only recently, in 1958. One of the pleasures of viewing these works is seeing them amid the frescoed splendor in which the city's merchant/banking families once lived. As in Genoa's other art collections, you will find masterworks that range far beyond native artists like Strozzi and De Ferrari. In fact, perhaps the most memorable painting here is ***Ecce Homo,*** by the Sicilian master Antonello da Messina. Guido Reni and Luca Giordano are also well represented, as are Van Dyck (including his fragmentary ***Portrait of Ansaldo Pallavicino*** and four of the ***Evangelists***) and other painters of the Dutch and Flemish schools, whom Genoa's wealthy burghers were so fond of importing to paint their portraits.

Piazza Pellicceria 1. www.palazzospinola.it. ✆ **010-270-5300.** Admission 4€ adults, 2€ for those 18–25, free for those 18 and under or 65 and over, or pay 12€ for a Card Musei cumulative ticket (see box below). Tues–Sat 8:30am–7:30pm; Sun 1:30–7:30pm. Bus: 1, 3, 7, 8, 18, 20, or 34.

Il Bigo ★ ARCHITECTURE To get a new perspective on the city, take the elevator that lifts visitors to the top of **Il Bigo,** the modern, mastlike tower designed by Italian architect Renzo Piano to commemorate the Columbus quincentennial celebrations in 1992. This has become one of the centerpieces of the port and one of Genoa's signature landmarks—just don't try it after having had

A Cumulative Ticket

Admission to Genoa's major **palaces and art galleries** is grouped together on the **Card Musei** (12€ for 1 day, 16€ for 2; 14€ and 20€, respectively, also gets you unlimited use of the city's public transport), which includes entrance to the principal palaces, the Museo Sant'Agostino, San Lorenzo, the Galleria Nazionale di Palazzo Spinola, the Museo di Palazzo Reale, and a handful of other museums around town, plus a discount on admission to the aquarium and movie theaters. Pick it up at any city museum, the airport tourist office, or in one of several bookstores downtown (www.genova-turismo.it).

walk LIKE A GENOVESE

To **wander the squares and streets** of Genoa's **Old Town** is to get the essence of this incredible city. Via Garibaldi, Piazza Dante, and Piazza San Matteo (listed separately) are the absolute highlights, but your walk should take in a much larger swath of the historic center. One might start in **Piazza Banchi** near Piazza Caricamento at the port and follow **Via San Luca, Via Fossatello** (with a detour up Via Lomellini), and **Via del Campo,** one long shop-lined stretch, to the 12th-century **Porta dei Vacca** gate, once the western edge of town. You can continue along **Via di Prè,** cut up to **Via Balbi,** and follow that to **Via Garibaldi.** Following **Via Macelli di Soziglia,** which connects Via Garibaldi to Piazza Banchi, will bring you by many historic shops. Going a few blocks south from Piazza Banchi will bring you to the wide **Via San Lorenzo,** which goes by the cathedral, **Piazza Matteotti** (home to the Palazzo Ducale), and eventually up to Piazza de Ferrari (where you see another side of Palazzo Ducale) and Piazza Dante. Save time to explore the characteristic neighborhood south of Via San Lorenzo.

Add in a stroll along the Porto Antico from the Museo del Mare to the Bigo and the aquarium, with detours along the piers jutting out into the port.

too much to drink for lunch, as the constant rotation may go to your head. The observation platform provides an eagle's-eye view of one of Europe's busiest ports. Genoa also offers many cheaper (or free, if you are willing to do the steep climbs) ways to get great vistas; see the box above.

Ponte Spinola. Admission 4€ adults, 3€ children ages 4–12. Mon 2–6pm; Tues–Sun 10am–6pm (June–Aug until 11pm; Nov–Feb only Sat–Sun 10am–5pm).

Piazza Dante Though most of this square just south of Piazza de Ferrari is made of 1930s office buildings, one end is bounded by the twin round towers of the reconstructed **Porta Soprana ★★**, a town gate built in 1155. The main draw, though, is the small **house** (rebuilt in the 18th c.), still standing a bit incongruously in a tidy little park below the gate, said to have belonged to **Christopher Columbus's father,** who was a weaver and gatekeeper (whether young Christopher lived here is open to debate). To get there, take bus no. 14, 35, 42, 44, or 46.

Piazza San Matteo ★★ This beautiful little square 2 blocks off the northwest edge of Piazza de Ferrari is the domain of the city's most acclaimed family, the seagoing Dorias, who ruled Genoa until the end of the 18th century. The church they built on the piazza in the 12th century, **San Matteo,** contains the crypt of the Dorias's most illustrious son, Andrea, and the cloisters are lined with centuries-old plaques heralding the family's many accomplishments, which included drawing up Genoa's constitution in 1529. The church is open Monday to Saturday 8am to noon and 4 to 5pm, and Sunday 4 to 5pm. The **Doria palaces** surround the church in a stunning array of loggias and black-and-white-striped marble facades denoting the homes of honored citizens—Andrea's is at **no. 17.** To get there, take bus no. 18, 19, 20, 30, 32, 33, 35, 37, 40, or 41.

Via Garibaldi ★★ Many of Genoa's museums and other sights are clustered on and around this street, one of the most beautiful in Italy, where Genoa's

Some Antiques with Those Frescoes?

To see what very well might be the most beautiful inside of a shop anywhere, stop in at **Galleria Imperiale** (✆ **010-251-0086**) at Campetto 8 near Piazza San Matteo, where the vaulted ceilings are covered in 16th-century frescoes by Luca Cambiaso, whose work can also be seen in Palazzo Bianco (p. 667). Even if you aren't thinking of shipping home a 7,000€ antique table, this is worth a stop. Open Monday to Saturday 9am to 12:30pm and 3:30 to 7:30pm.

wealthy families built palaces in the 16th and 17th centuries. Aside from the art collections housed in the **Galleria di Palazzo Bianco** and **Galleria di Palazzo Rosso** (see above), the street contains a wealth of other treasures. The **Palazzo Podesta,** at no. 7, hides one of the city's most beautiful fountains in its courtyard, and the **Palazzo Tursi,** at no. 9, now housing municipal offices, proudly displays artifacts of famous locals: letters written by Christopher Columbus and the violin of Nicolo Paganini (which is still played on special occasions). Visitors are allowed free entry to the buildings when the offices are open: Monday through Friday 8:30am to noon and 1 to 4pm. To get there, take bus no. 19, 20, 30, 32, 33, 35, 36, 41, or 42.

Where to Eat

Also don't miss out on the good food at the wine bar **I Tre Merli,** recommended under "Entertainment & Nightlife," below.

Da Guglie LIGURIAN The busy kitchen here, with its open hearth, occupies a good part of this simple restaurant, which serves this neighborhood near Stazione Brignole with takeout fare from a counter and accommodates diners in a barebones little room off to one side. There's no attempt at all to provide a decorative ambience. The specials of the day (which often include octopus and other seafood) are displayed in the window; tell the cooks behind the counter what you want and they will bring it over when it's ready. Don't be shy about asking for a sampling of the reasonably priced dishes, because you could happily eat your way through all the greatest hits of Genovese cuisine here. You can accompany the warm *farinata* and the other dishes with Ligurian wines served by the glass or carafe.

Via San Vincenzo 64r. ✆ **010-565-765.** Reservations not necessary. Main courses 6€–13€. No credit cards. Daily noon–10pm.

La Berlocca GENOVESE Enrico Reboscio has turned this old pie and *farinata* shop, located between Via Garibaldi and the port, into an oasis of good food. Service can be a bit slow in the two tiny rooms of small, sturdy wooden tables under stuccoed ceilings, but the seasonal Ligurian menu marrying sea and garden is delicious. That coupling is nowhere more on display than with the *buridda,* a traditional dish of salted cod, tomatoes, and other vegetables. If you were thinking of trying this particular, yet tasty, dish this is as fine a place as any to do it. Otherwise you will find many other traditional Genovese favorites. There's a good wine selection, too.

Via dei Macelli di Soziglia 47r. ✆ **010-247-4162.** Reservations recommended. Main courses 12€–18€. AE, DC, MC, V. Tues–Sat noon–3pm and 7–11pm; Sun for lunch only with reservation. Closed last week of July to 3rd week of Aug.

Trattoria da Maria ★★ LIGURIAN Think simple, think good, think simple again, and you have all you really need to know about this Genovese institution. The cooking and the close-knit ambience of the two-floor restaurant on the cusp of the Old Town near Piazza delle Fontane Marose draw a crowd of neighborhood residents, students, businesspeople, and tourists of all nationalities. This unlikely mix sits side-by-side at long tables covered with red- or blue-checked tablecloths while the staff hurries about shouting orders up and down the shaft of a dumbwaiter. The stupendously cheap menu—which is listed on sheets of paper on the shiny pale green walls—has such simple main courses as

Public Transportation Has Never Been This Fun

Much like Lisbon, Portugal, through the years Genoa has sought to dominate its hilly geography through a combination of elevators, funiculars, and cog railways. Whether you care about getting splendid views of the city or not, it can be great fun to take these innovative modes of public transportation, some of which date back more than a century.

The **Ferrovia Principe-Granarolo,** a cog railway built in 1901, leaves from Via Legaccio, just behind the Piazza Principe railway station, and ascends 300m (980 ft.) to Porto Granarolo, one of the gates in the city's 17th century walls. At the top there's a belvedere. ***Note:*** The railway closed in early 2011 for a complete restructuring that is slated to take at least a year. The **Funicolare Zecca-Righi,** the first piece of which opened in 1895, takes 12 minutes and five intermediate stops to bring you from Largo della Zecca (once home to Genoa's mint or *zecca*) near Via Garibaldi to the Righi neighborhood from where you get a terrific view of the city. The **Funicolare Sant'Anna,** which came into service in 1891, making it the oldest funicular or public elevator in town, will take you from Piazza del Portello just above Via Garibaldi up to Via Bertani/Corso Magenta for another great view. Incredibly, this funicular used to work thanks to a counterbalanced system that made use of water. The conductor in the top carriage would take note of the number of people in the carriages at the top and the bottom of the funicular and would then add water to a tank in the top carriage. The extra weight of the water would make the top carriage descend and in the process it would pull up the other carriage.

You have your pick of 11 *ascensori* (public elevators), though the one not to miss is the **Ascensore di Castelletto Levante,** which connects Piazza del Portello with Belvedere Montaldo. The upper station, built in 1910, is a spectacular display of Art Nouveau architecture from where you can view the city and the surrounding hillside. The **Ascensore di Castelletto Ponente** also reaches the Belevedere Montaldo though any romanticism is lost as you have to access it from a traffic tunnel that connects Piazza del Portello with Largo della Zecca.

To ride the Ferrovia Principe-Granarolo and the Zecca-Righi funicular, you need a regular bus ticket that costs 1.50€ each way. The Sant'Anna Funicular and all the elevators cost .80€, or 2.80€ for four tickets. Your best bet though is to get a 24-hour public transport ticket for 4.50€ and take as many as you can manage. The funiculars generally run every 15 minutes and the elevators are continually going up and down.

Fast . . . and, Oh, So Good

All over Genoa you'll find shops selling **focaccia,** Liguria's answer to pizza, a sort of thick flatbread often stuffed or topped with cheese, herbs, olives, onions, vegetables, or prosciutto. Many of these *focaccerie* will also be selling ***farinata,*** a crepe made from chickpea flour that usually emerges from the oven in the shape of a big round pizza. Just point and make a hand gesture to show how much you want. Prices are by weight and in most cases a piece of either will cost about 1.50€ to 3€. Most focaccia, especially if it has cheese, and all *farinata* are better warm so if the piece you are getting looks like it has been there a while ask for it to be warmed up.

A favorite place for focaccia and *farinata,* and so close to Stazione Principe that you can stop in as soon as you step off the train, is **La Focacceria di Teobaldo ★**, Via Balbi 115r, open daily 8am to 8pm. **Focacceria di Via Lomellini ★**, on Via Lomellini 57/59 in the heart of the Old Town and open Monday to Saturday 8am to 7:30pm, has great *focaccia di Recco,* sometimes also called *focaccia al formaggio,* a super-thin focaccia filled with cheese that is the specialty of the nearby town of Recco. **Focaccia & Co.,** Piazza Macelli di Soziglia 91r, open Monday to Saturday 7am to 7:30pm, is across from Fratelli Klainguti (see below), so you can try some of the many focaccia offerings, all terrific, then take a few steps and continue with some sweets. If you are down at the Porto Antico and realize you need a focaccia fix, as happens often once you have tried this delicacy for the first time, **Il Localino** at Via Turati 8r, open Monday to Saturday 9am to 7pm, is your quickest road to bliss.

a filet of fish sautéed in white wine, or grilled sausages. The pasta with pesto is simply delicious. The *pansotti,* small ravioli covered with a walnut-cream sauce, are also tasty.

Vico Testadoro 14r (just off Via XXV Aprile). ✆ **010-581-080.** Reservations not necessary. *Primi* main courses 5€–9€. MC, V. Sun and Tues–Fri 11:45am–2:15pm and 7–9:15pm; Mon 11:45am–2:45pm.

PASTRY & GELATO

Fratelli Klainguti ★★, on Piazza Soziglia 98r–100r (✆ **010-860-2628**), is considered by most to be Genoa's best bakery, as well as its oldest—it was founded in 1828 by a Swiss family. One satisfied customer was the composer Giuseppe Verdi, who said the house's Falstaff (a sweet brioche) was better than his. This and a stupefying assortment of other pastries and chocolates, as well as light snacks (including panini), are served in a pretty rococo-style room or in the piazza out front. It's open Monday to Saturday 7am to 8pm.

For gelato in the Old Town, a good bet is **Excelsa,** on Via San Luca 88r right in the midst of the busy shop-lined street and open Monday to Saturday noon to 7:30pm. **Gelateria Balbi,** Via Balbi 165r, is very close to Stazione Principe and excels in rich cream flavors; it's open Monday to Saturday noon to 8pm. And then there is always **Grom,** on Via San Lorenzo 53r near the cathedral, as well as at Via San Vincenzo 81 near Stazione Brignole. Gromis open daily 11am to 11pm (Fri–Sat until midnight).

Entertainment & Nightlife

The Old Town, some parts of which are sketchy in broad daylight, is especially unseemly at night. Confine late-hour prowls in this area to the well-trafficked streets such as Via San Lorenzo and Via Garibaldi. On the edges of the Old Town, good places to walk at night are around the waterfront, Piazza Fontane Marose, Piazza de Ferrari, and Piazza delle Erbe, where many bars and clubs are located.

If you are looking for a nice walk to burn off some of your dinner, you could do some or all of a loop that starts in Piazza Caricamento at the waterfront. From there you take Via San Lorenzo (conveniently passing by Grom, where you can get dessert; see above) up to Piazza De Ferrari, then follow Via XXV Aprile up to Piazza Fontane Marose from where you can pass onto Via Garibaldi. Follow the continuation of Via Garibaldi (Via Cairoli and then Via Bensa) into Piazza della Nunziata where you can turn left onto Via delle Fontane, which will take you back to the waterfront.

PERFORMING ARTS Genoa has two major venues for culture: the restored **Teatro Carlo Felice,** Piazza de Ferrari (www.carlofelice.it; ✆ **010-589-329**), which is home to Genoa's opera company and also hosts visiting companies, and the modern **Teatro Stabile di Genova** (www.teatrostabilegenova.it; ✆ **010-53-421**), on Piazza Borgo Pila near Stazione Brignole, which hosts concerts, dance, and other cultural programs.

Teatro Carlo Felice.

BARS & CLUBS If you've had it with Ligurian white wine and really need a Guinness, **Brittania,** at Vico Casana (just off Piazza De Ferrari), serves pints Monday to Saturday from 11am to the wee hours (✆ **010-247-4532**). The pub closes for a month every year either in July or August.

New Yorkers will recognize the name and chic ambience in **I Tre Merli Antica Cantina,** at Vico Dietro il Coro della Maddalena 26r (www.itremerli.it; ✆ **010-247-4095**), which does a brisk business in Manhattan with four restaurants. Here in Genoa, I Tre Merli operates a couple of *enoteche* (wine bars), and this one, located on a narrow street just off Via Garibaldi, is delightful, even if the surrounding alleyways are sometimes seedy. It's open Tuesday to Sunday 7pm to 1am. I Tre Merli also has an enoteca in Camogli.

Where to Stay

Despite the draw of the aquarium and its intriguing Old Town, Genoa is still geared more to business than to tourism, and as a result, decent inexpensive rooms are scarce. On the other hand, just about the only time the town is booked solid is during its annual boat show, the world's largest, in October. It is best to avoid hotels in the heart of the Old Town, especially around the harbor, as many are a little sketchy. The upper end of the price range given in most cases is applied only the week of the boat show and the maximum the rest of the year is considerably lower, sometimes as much as 25%.

VERY EXPENSIVE

Hotel Bristol Palace ★ The majestic oval staircase and stained-glass dome of this historic late-19th-century *palazzo* set the tone for this oasis of comfort and calm in chaotic Genoa. It sits on the main shopping street one block off Genoa's main central piazza, halfway between the train station and the tangle of alleys that make up the center, but it is impressively quiet for the location. The recently renovated and soundproofed rooms have modern bathrooms, but still retain their period furnishings and classic air. A few choice rooms along the front of the hotel are larger, some with marvelous inlaid wood floors and Art Deco furnishings. The range for doubles below reflects a lower rate for most weekends.

Via XX Settembre 35, 16121 Genova. www.hotelbristolpalace.com. ✆ **010-592-541.** Fax 010-561-756. 133 units. 109€–450€ double; 199€–800€ junior suite. Buffet breakfast included. AE, DC, MC, V. Parking in garage 25€. **Amenities:** Restaurant; bar; babysitting; bikes; concierge; room service; smoke-free rooms. *In room:* A/C, TV w/pay movies, hair dryer, minibar, Wi-Fi.

EXPENSIVE

Best Western Hotel Metropoli ★★ Facing a lovely square, just around the corner from Via Garibaldi, the recently restored Metropoli brings modern amenities combined with a gracious ambience to the Old Town. No small part of the appeal of staying here is that many of the surrounding streets are open only to pedestrians, so you can step out of the hotel and avoid the onrush of traffic that plagues much of central Genoa. Guest rooms have somewhat banal and businesslike contemporary furnishings, but with double-pane windows and pleasing pastel fabrics, they provide an oasis of calm. Refurbished bathrooms are equipped with hair dryers, heated towel racks, and double sinks with lots of marble counter space.

Piazza delle Fontane Marose, 16123 Genova. www.hotelmetropoli.it. ✆ **010-246-8888.** Fax 010-246-8686. 48 units. 93€–246€ double; 99€–260€ triple. Rates include buffet breakfast. AE, DC, MC, V. Parking 20€ in nearby garage. **Amenities:** Bar; room service; smoke-free rooms. *In room:* A/C, TV, hair dryer, minibar, Wi-Fi.

MODERATE

Agnello d'Oro ★ ☺ This converted convent enjoys a wonderful location a few short blocks from Stazione Principe on the edge of the Old Town, which can be viewed from a nice terrace. A few of the lower-floor rooms retain the building's original 16th-century character, with high (rooms numbered in teens) or vaulted (rooms numbered under 10) ceilings. Those upstairs have been completely renovated in crisp modern style, with warm-hued tile floors and mostly modular furnishings; though many have only curtainless tubs with hand-held nozzles. Some top-floor rooms come with the added charm of balconies and views over the Old Town and harbor (best from no. 56). There is also a three-bedroom, two-bathroom apartment that can sleep up to six and is perfect for those traveling with a few kids. The friendly proprietor dispenses wine, sightseeing tips, and breakfast in the cozy little bar off the lobby.

Via Monachette 6 (off Via Balbi), 16126 Genova. www.hotelagnellodoro.it. ✆ **010-246-2084.** Fax 010-246-2327. 20 units. 70€–120€ double; 140€ for 4 people in 3-bedroom apt, 2 more people can be added for 20 E.U. each. Rates include breakfast. AE, DC, MC, V. Private parking 15€–25€. **Amenities:** Restaurant; bar; concierge; room service; smoke-free rooms, Wi-Fi. *In room:* A/C, TV, hair dryer (in some), minibar.

INEXPENSIVE

Hotel Cairoli ★★ Renovated in 2006, this pleasant family-run hotel on the third floor of an old building has an excellent location on the street that continues west from Via Garibaldi. The small rooms are extremely pleasant, with tasteful modern furnishings and tidy little bathrooms; double-pane glass keeps street noise to a minimum. The friendly management gives it the homey feel of an upscale youth hostel, leaving a little basket of snacks in your room. In good weather, you can relax on a terrace covered with potted plants (no. 9 opens onto it). They also have a small weight room, in case you feel the need to work off all that focaccia. The cost of a double usually maxes out at 105€, and the top price listed below is only during the boat show and a few other days a year.

Via Cairoli 14, 16124 Genova. www.hotelcairoligenova.com. ✆ **010-246-1524.** Fax 010-246-7512. 12 units. 75€–160€ double. Rates include breakfast. AE, DC, MC, V. Parking 15€ in nearby garage. Bus: 18, 19, 20, 30, 34, 35, 37, 39, 40, 41, or 100. **Amenities:** Bar; concierge; small exercise room; room service; smoke-free rooms. *In room:* A/C, TV, hair dryer, minibar, Wi-Fi.

THE RIVIERA DI PONENTE: SAN REMO

San Remo: 140km (87 miles) W of Genoa, 56km (35 miles) E of Nice

Gone are the days when Tchaikovsky and the Russian empress Maria Alexandrovna joined a well-heeled mix of titled Continental and British gentry in strolling along San Remo's palm-lined avenues. They left behind an onion-domed Orthodox church, a few grand hotels, and a casino, but **San Remo** is a different sort of town these days. It's still the most cosmopolitan stop on the Riviera di Ponente, as the stretch of coast west of Genoa is called, and caters mostly to sun-seeking Italian families in the summer and Milanesi who come down in the winter months to get away from the fog and chilly temperatures of their city.

In addition to the gentle ambience of days gone by, San Remo offers its visitors a long stretch of beach and a hilltop Old Town known as La Pigna. For cosmopolitan pleasures, the casino attracts a well-attired clientele willing to try their luck.

San Remo is an excellent base from which to explore the rocky coast and Ligurian hills. So is Bordighera, a quieter resort just up the coast. With excellent train and bus connections, both are within easy reach of a full itinerary of fascinating stops, including Giardini Hanbury, one of Europe's most exquisite gardens; the fascinating prehistoric remains at Balzi Rossi; and Dolceacqua, perhaps the most enticing of all the inland Ligurian villages.

The beach at San Remo.

Essentials

GETTING THERE **By Train** There are trains hourly in both directions between San Remo and **Genoa** (1¾–2½ hr.). Trains from Genoa continue west for another 20 minutes to **Ventimiglia** on the French border. Some trains continue on into France, otherwise you can cross the border on one of the twice-hourly trains to **Nice,** 50 minutes west.

By Bus **Riviera Trasporti** buses (www.rivieratrasporti.it; ✆ **0183-7001**) run every 15 minutes between San Remo and **Bordighera** (20 min.). Almost as many buses continue on to **Ventimiglia** (40 min. from San Remo).

By Car The fastest driving route in and out of San Remo is Autostrada A10, which follows the coast from the French border (20 min. away) to Genoa (about 45 min. away). The slower coast road, SS1, cuts right through the center of town and is the best option if you are not going very far (Bordighera and Ventimiglia are reached more quickly on the SS1, traffic permitting).

VISITOR INFORMATION The **APT tourist board** is at Largo Nuvoloni 1 (www.turismoinliguria.it; ✆ **0184-590-523**), at the corner with Corso Imperatrice/Corso Matteotti (cross the street from the old train station and go to the left a few hundred ft.). It's open Monday to Saturday 8am to 7pm and Sunday 9am to 1pm. In addition to a wealth of information on San Remo, the office dispenses information on towns up and down the nearby coast, known as the Riviera dei Fiori.

FESTIVALS August 15, the **Feast of the Assumption,** is celebrated with special flair in San Remo, with the festival of Nostra Signora della Costa (Our Lady of the Coast). The Virgin Mary allegedly saved a local sailor from drowning, and she is honored with fireworks and a procession in medieval garb to her shrine on a hillside high above the town.

Since the 1950s, the **Sanremo Festival** (in late Feb or early Mar) has been Italy's—and one of Europe's—premier music fests. It's sort of an Italian version of the Grammy Awards, only spread out over several days with far more live performances—by Italian pop stars, international headliners, and plenty of up-and-coming singers, songwriters, and bands. "Volare" was Sanremo's first-ever Best Recording, and today if you peruse the CD collections of most Italian households, you'll find at least a few of the yearly compilation albums the festival puts out. The festival has spawned many other contests/celebrations of film and music (international folk to *musica lirica*) throughout the year, but this is the big one, booking hotels up and down the coast months in advance. Call the tourist office if you want to try to score tickets.

Exploring San Remo

San Remo's underground railway station, buried into the coastal hills much like its counterpart in nearby Monaco, is sleek and clean, but there are a few disadvantages. For one thing, the walk from the tracks to the exit is formidable (***Note:*** Leave plenty of time to catch a train), and the walk from there to the center of town is also considerably longer than from the old station, which sits downtown, just by the coast. This leads to the final problem. Even today, more than a decade after the inauguration of the new station, some locals might give you directions to a hotel, restaurant, and such, referring to the "train station," when, in fact, they mean the former station.

To get downtown from the new train station, walk straight out of the exit, cross Corso Cavallotti, and continue downhill until you reach Corso Trento e Trieste. Take a right on that road, which hugs the shore and leads to the old port.

To the right of the old station are the beginnings of Via Roma and Corso Matteotti, San Remo's two main thoroughfares. Corso Matteotti will lead you past the **casino** (see below) and into the heart of the lively business district. Continue on that until it runs into Piazza Colombo and the flower market. If, instead, you turn left (north) on Via Feraldi about midway down Corso Matteotti, you will find yourself in the charming older precincts of town. Continue through Piazza degli Eroi Sanromesi to Piazza Mercato, where Via Montà leads into the old medieval quarter, **La Pigna.** The hill on which this fascinating district is located resembles a pine cone in its conical shape, hence the name. Aside from a few restaurants, La Pigna is a residential quarter, with tall old houses that overshadow the narrow lanes that twist and turn up the hillside to the park-enclosed ruins of a **castle** at the top.

VISITING THE CASINO

San Remo's white palace of a casino (✆ **0184-5951**), set intimidatingly atop a long flight of steps across from the old train station and enclosed on three sides by Corso degli Inglesi, is the hub of the local nightlife scene. You can't step foot inside without being properly attired (jacket for gents Oct–June) and showing your passport. You must be 18 or older to enter. There are poker tables starting at 2€ games, but there are more serious tables that attract high rollers from the length of the Riviera. Gaming rooms are open daily 2:30pm to 3am (weekends to 4am). Things are more relaxed in the rooms set aside for slot machines, where there is no dress code. They are open Sunday to Friday 10am to 3am.

Where to Eat & Stay

Hotel Sole Mare ★ Don't let the location on a drab side street near the train station put you off. This cheerful *pensione* on the upper floors of an apartment building is a delight and offers guests a friendly welcome, along with some of the best-value lodgings in the resort area. A lounge, bar area, and dining room are spacious and flooded with light, and have gleaming white-tile floors and open onto a wide terrace. The large guest rooms are also cheerful and equipped with the trappings of much more expensive hotels—pleasant modern furnishings, soothing pastel fabrics, and small but modern well-lit bathrooms—and almost all enjoy sea views, about half from wide balconies.

Via Carli 23, 18038 San Remo. www.solemarehotel.com. ✆ **0184-577-105.** Fax 0184-532-778. 21 units. 70€–136€ double. Half board 45€–75€ per person; full board 50€–80€ per person. Rates include breakfast. AE, DC, MC, V. Parking 7€ in nearby garage. **Amenities:** Restaurant (international); bar; babysitting; concierge; room service. *In room:* A/C, TV, hair dryer, minibar, Wi-Fi.

Hotel Villa Maria ★★ It's fairly easy to imagine San Remo's late-19th- to early-20th-century heyday in this charming hotel incorporating three villas on a flowery hillside above the casino. The promenade is only a short walk downhill, yet the hubbub of the resort seems miles away from this leafy residential district. A series of elegant salons and dining rooms with parquet floors, richly paneled ceilings, and crystal chandeliers spread across the ground floor, and many of these public rooms open to a nicely planted terrace. The bedrooms, too, retain the grandeur of the original dwellings, with silk-covered armchairs and antique beds; many have balconies facing the sea. Since rooms vary considerably in size and decor, ask to look around before you settle on one that strikes your fancy.

Corso Nuvoloni 30, 18038 San Remo. www.villamariahotel.it. ✆ **0184-531-422.** Fax 0184-531-425. 38 units, 36 with private bathroom. 70€–140€ double. For half board (required Easter, Christmas, and Aug 1–15), add 30€ per person. Rates include continental breakfast. AE, DC, MC, V. Free parking. **Amenities:** Restaurant (international); concierge; room service; smoke-free rooms. *In room:* TV, hair dryer.

Ristorante L'Airone ★ LIGURIAN/PIZZA With its pale gold walls and green-hued tables and chairs, this delightful, friendly restaurant in a pedestrian-only section of the city center looks as though it's been transported over the border from Provence. The food, though, is definitely Ligurian. There is a wide selection of pasta, including *spaghetti con le vongole,* which comes smothered in clams. For the *secondi* you are better off with the fish, perhaps a *grigliata mista* (mixed grilled fish) or grilled sole, rather than the meats that tend to disappoint. You can also get a pretty good light-crusted pizza (always available in the evening,

Is Board Necessary?

Many hotels offer room-and-board rates that include breakfast, lunch, and dinner (full board), or breakfast and one of these other two meals (half board or half pension). Only in the busy late July and early August beach season do many require you to take these meals, however. If you can procure a room without the meal plan, do so—San Remo has many excellent restaurants, and this is not a place where you have to spend a lot for a good meal.

THE CAFE & BAR scene

Agorà Cafè, on Piazza San Siro (no phone), which faces San Remo's cathedral, makes no claim other than to be a comfortable watering hole, a function it performs very well. For footsore travelers, the terrace out front, facing the pretty stone piazza and cathedral of San Siro, is a welcome oasis. Sandwiches and other light fare are served late into the night, when an after-dinner crowd tends to make this one of the livelier spots in town. It's closed Monday.

Wanderings through the center of town should include a stop at **Enoteca Bacchus ★★** (Via Roma 65; ✆ **0184-530-990**), a handsome wine bar open Monday to Saturday 10am to 9pm. Wine is served by the glass at a sit-down bar or at one of the small tables, and you can accompany your libations with fresh focaccia, cheeses, vegetable tarts, and even such substantial fare as *buridda*, a dish of salted cod, tomatoes, and other vegetables. If you find any particularly interesting wine, you can buy a bottle to take away.

though at lunchtime only on Tues and Sat). In good weather, meals are served in a small garden out back covered by a reed-thatched tent—and there are some tables on the piazza outside (which, admittedly, is nothing special).

Piazza Eroi Sanremesi 12. www.ristorantelairone.it. ✆ **0184-541-055.** Reservations not necessary. Main courses 7€–17€. DC, MC, V. Sat–Wed noon–2:30pm and 7:30–11:30pm (Fri only in the evening).

THE RIVIERA DI LEVANTE: CAMOGLI, SANTA MARGHERITA LIGURE & PORTOFINO

Camogli: 26km (16 miles) E of Genoa; Santa Margherita Ligure: 31km (19 miles) E of Genoa; Portofino: 38km (24 miles) E of Genoa; Rapallo: 37km (23 miles) E of Genoa

The coast east of Genoa, the **Riviera di Levante (Shore of the Rising Sun),** is more ruggedly beautiful than the Riviera Ponente, less developed, and hugged by mountains that plunge into the sea. Four of the coast's most appealing towns are within a few kilometers of one another, clinging to the shores of the Monte Portofino Promontory just east of Genoa: Camogli, Santa Margherita Ligure, Rapallo, and little Portofino.

Camogli

Camogli remains delightfully unspoiled, an authentic Ligurian fishing port with tall houses in various pastel colors facing the harbor and a nice swath of beach. Given also its excellent accommodations and eateries, Camogli is a lovely place to base yourself while exploring the Riviera Levante. This is also a restful retreat from which you can explore Genoa, which is only about 30 minutes away. One interpretation of Camogli's name is that it derived from "Ca de Mogge," or "House of the Wives" in the local dialect, and was named for the women who held down the fort while their husbands went to sea. Another possibility is that it comes from "Ca a Muggi," or "clustered houses," which will seem the perfect name when you are out swimming in the sea and turn to look up at the town's wonderful agglomeration of colorful buildings. Other interpretations of the name abound.

ESSENTIALS

GETTING THERE **By Train** One to three trains per hour ply the coastline, connecting Camogli with **Genoa** (30–45 min.), **Santa Margherita** (5 min.), **Monterosso** (50–60 min.), and other Cinque Terre towns.

By Bus There is at least one Tigullio (www.tigulliotrasporti.it; ✆ **0185-373-239**) bus an hour, often more, from **Santa Margherita;** since the bus must go around and not under the Monte Portofino Promontory, the trip takes quite a bit longer than the train—about half an hour.

By Boat In summer, boats operated by Golfo Paradiso (www.golfoparadiso.it; ✆ **0185-772-091**) sail from Camogli to **Portofino.**

By Car The fastest route into the region is Autostrada A12 from Genoa; exit at Recco for Camogli (the trip takes less than half an hour). Route SS1 along the coast from Genoa is much slower but more scenic. In the summer months, parking in Camogli can be a real challenge.

VISITOR INFORMATION The **tourist office** is across from the train station at Via XX Settembre 33 (www.prolococamogli.it or www.portofinocoast.it; ✆/fax **0185-771-066**). It's open Monday to Saturday 9am to 12:30pm and 3 to 7pm (Mar–Oct it closes at noon and 6:30pm, respectively), Sunday 9am to 12:30pm.

FESTIVALS & MARKETS Camogli throws a well-attended annual party, the **Sagra del Pesce ★★**, on the second Sunday of May, where the town fries up thousands of sardines in a 3.6m-diameter (12-ft.) pan and passes them around for free—a practice that is accompanied by an annual outcry in the press about health concerns and even accusations that frozen fish is used.

The first Sunday of August, Camogli stages the lovely **Festa della Stella Maris.** A procession of boats sails to Punta Chiappa, a point of land about 1.5km (1 mile) down the coast, and releases 10,000 burning candles. Meanwhile, the same number of candles is set afloat from the Camogli beach. If currents are favorable, the burning candles will come together at sea, signifying a year of unity for couples who watch the spectacle.

EXPLORING CAMOGLI

Camogli is clustered around its delightful waterfront, from which the town ascends via steep, staircased lanes to Via XX Settembre, one of the few streets in the town proper to accommodate cars (this is where the train station, tourist office, and many shops and other businesses are located). Adding to the charm of this setting is the fact that the oldest part of Camogli juts into the harbor on a little point (once an island) where ancient houses cling to the little **Castello Dragone** (now closed to the public) and the **Basilica di Santa Maria Assunta** (✆ **0185-770-130**), an originally 12th-century structure that has been much altered through the ages and now has an overwhelming baroque interior that's open daily 7:30am to noon and 3:30 to 7pm. Most visitors, though, are drawn to the pleasant **seaside promenade ★** that runs the length of the town. You can swim from the pebbly beach below, and should you feel your towel doesn't provide enough comfort, rent a lounge from one of the few beach stations for about 15€.

WHERE TO EAT & STAY

Albergo Augusta This is an acceptable alternative if La Camogliese (below) is full, and, more than a fallback, it's pleasant and convenient, with a handy location a short walk up a steep staircase from the harbor. The couple and their son who run this *pensione* also operate the ground-floor trattoria, which serves as a sitting room for the hotel guests and makes it easy to enjoy a cup of coffee or glass of wine. The clean guest rooms are extremely plain, with functional furnishings and drab decor, but most are large and have good-size bathrooms. You also get 15 minutes of free Internet access (in the reception area) per day. Ask for a room in front—those in back face the train tracks.

Via Schiaffino 100, 16032 Camogli. www.htlaugusta.com. ✆ **0185-770-592.** 14 units. 55€–110€ double; 90€–135€ triple. AE, DC, MC, V. Parking 12€. **Amenities:** Restaurant (local cuisine); bar; room service. *In room:* A/C, TV, Internet.

Bar Primula CAFE/LIGHT FARE If you need a light meal (a pasta dish and seafood plate or two are usually available, along with sandwiches, salads, omelets, and pizza), this is the most convenient spot, but many people come in simply for a cup of espresso and dessert, which presents a difficult choice between the delicious ice cream and pastries.

Via Garibaldi 140. ✆ **0185-770-351.** Reservations not accepted. Salads and other light fare, including pizza 9€–15€. AE, MC, V. Daily 9am–1am.

Hotel Cenobio dei Dogi ★★ This oasis sits just above the sea at the end of town and against the forested flank of Monte Portofino. The oldest part of the hotel incorporates an aristocratic villa dating from 1565. Converted to a hotel in 1956, the premises now include several wings that wrap graciously around a garden on one side and a series of terraces facing the sea on the other. There's a pool and a private beach as well as a lovely lounge area and a glass-enclosed breakfast room that hangs over the sea (the view from here is by itself almost worth whatever you happen to pay for a room). The guest rooms, 44 of which face the sea, vary considerably in size and shape, but all are furnished with a tasteful mix of

Focaccia by the Seaside

It might be the perfect seaside setting or perhaps there is something in the water, no matter the reason, Camogli has some of the best focaccia in all of Liguria. Along Via Garibaldi, the promenade above the beach, there are many *focaccerie* to choose from and though it is hard to go wrong with any of them, one stands out. At **Revello** (✆ **0185-770-777**) on Via Garibaldi 183 (the part closest to the church), Tino is carrying on the tradition passed down by his uncle, who first began pulling focaccia out of the oven here in 1964. It's likely they haven't messed up a batch once since then. Revello, which is open Wednesday to Monday 10am to 6pm (summer until 7pm), has a few benches outside where you can enjoy your loot while watching the kids play soccer in the little square overlooking the beach. **O'Becco** next door also makes some mean focaccia—special mention goes to the one with fresh anchovies, parsley, garlic, and olive oil—and **U Caruggiu** at the other end of Via Garibaldi has kamut (a type of wheat) focaccia on the weekends.

reproduction writing desks, contemporary glass-top tables, and island-style furnishings (bent bamboo headboards and the like).

Via Cuneo 34, 16032 Camogli. www.cenobio.it. ✆ **0185-7241.** Fax 0185-772-796. 105 units. 160€–230€ standard double with garden view; 220€–320€ standard double with sea view; 190€–270€ superior double with garden view; 300€–430€ superior double with sea view. Rates include buffet breakfast. AE, DC, MC, V. Free parking. **Amenities:** 2 Ligurian/international restaurants (1 at beach, which is only open in the summer); 2 bars; babysitting; concierge; nearby golf course; outdoor saltwater pool; outdoor lighted tennis courts; watersports equipment/rentals. *In room:* A/C, TV, hair dryer, minibar, Wi-Fi.

La Camogliese ★★ Genovese and Milanese come out to spend the weekend in this friendly, attractive little hotel near the waterfront, and they appreciate it for the same simple charms that will appeal to travelers from farther afield. (In fact, given the hotel's popularity, it's fundamental to reserve well in advance, especially on weekends and in the summer.) The large, bright rooms are decorated in modern furnishings that include comfortable beds. Some have balconies, and although the house isn't right on the waterfront, it faces a little river and is close enough to the beach that a slight twist of the head usually affords a view of the sea (best from rooms 3 and 16B). Rooms 4, 5, 14, 18, and 23 have balconies with side views of the sea. Bathrooms are small but adequate.

Via Garibaldi 55, 16032 Camogli. www.lacamogliese.it. ✆ **0185-771-402.** Fax 0185-774-024. 21 units. 80€–115€ double. Rates include breakfast. AE, DC, MC, V. Parking 15€, call ahead to alert them. **Amenities:** Babysitting; concierge; exercise room; outdoor pool; room service. *In room:* TV, hair dryer, Internet.

Lo Strufugio ★★ SEAFOOD What you give up in the view—the place is on the main drag up above the seaside promenade—you more than make up with the food. The intimate setting (there are only five tables), personal service, and an open kitchen create an enticing atmosphere that makes you happy even before your food arrives. And when it does, you'll soon be wondering if you can squeeze in another trip here before leaving town. The menu changes often, but if *gnocchi con gamberi, zucchine e bottarga* (gnocchi topped with tiny shrimp, zucchini, and shaved fish roe) is there your choice is made. The fried fresh anchovies are light, fluffy, and never enough, so don't share. Little or no English is spoken here and the menu is only in Italian, so bring your dictionary and be ready to interpret hand gestures.

Via della Repubblica 64. ✆ **0185-771-553.** Reservations highly recommended. Main courses 12€–24€. MC, V. Sun 12:30–2:30pm and Wed–Sun 5:30–10pm.

Santa Margherita Ligure

Santa Margherita had one brief moment in the spotlight, at the beginning of the 20th century when it was an internationally renowned retreat. Fortunately, the seaside town didn't let fame spoil its charm, and now that it's no longer as well known a destination as its glitzy neighbor Portofino, it might be the Mediterranean retreat of your dreams. A palm-lined harbor, a decent beach, and a friendly ambience make Santa Margherita a fine place to settle down for a few days of sun and relaxation.

ESSENTIALS

GETTING THERE **By Train** One to three trains per hour connect Santa Margherita with **Genoa** (25–30 min.), **Camogli** (5 min.), **Rapallo** (3 min.), and **Monterosso** (40–55 min.) of the Cinque Terre.

By Bus There is at least one Tigullio (www.tigulliotrasporti.it; ✆ **0185-373-239**) bus an hour to **Camogli** (30–35 min.) and to **Rapallo** (10 min.), leaving from Piazza Vittorio Veneto. Buses also follow the stunningly beautiful coast road to **Portofino,** leaving every 20 minutes from the train station and Piazza Vittorio Veneto (25 min.).

By Boat Tigullio ferries (www.traghettiportofino.it; ✆ **0185-284-670**) make hourly trips to **Portofino** (15 min.) and **Rapallo** (15 min.). In summer, there is a boat several days a week to the Cinque Terre. Hours of service vary considerably with the season; schedules are posted on the docks at Piazza Martiri della Libertà.

By Car The fastest route into the region is A12 Autostrada from Genoa; the trip takes about half an hour. Route SS1 along the coast from Genoa is much slower but more scenic.

VISITOR INFORMATION The **tourist office** is near the harbor at Via XXV Aprile 2B (www.turismoinliguria.it; ✆ **0185-287-485**). Summer hours are daily 9:30am to 12:30pm and 2:30 to 8pm; winter hours are Monday to Saturday 9am to 12:30pm and 2:30 to 5:30pm

FESTIVALS & MARKETS Santa Margherita's winters are delightfully mild, but even so, the town rushes to usher in spring with a **Festa di Primavera,** held on moveable dates in February. Like the Sagra del Pesce in neighboring Camogli, this festival also features food—in this case, fritters are prepared

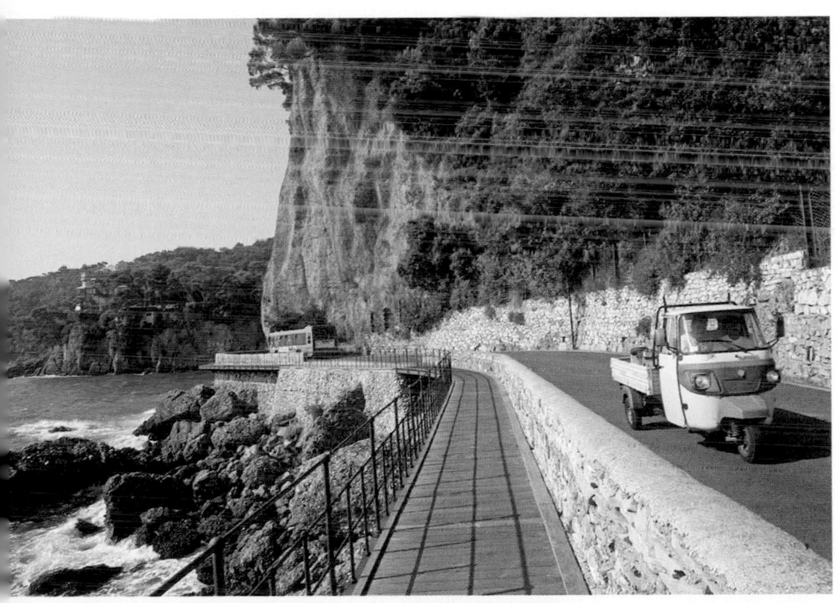

The Corniche Road from Portofino to Santa Margherita Ligure.

Along the waterfront in Santa Margherita.

on the beach and served around roaring bonfires. One of the more interesting daily spectacles in town is the **fish market** on Lungomare Marconi from 8am to 12:30pm. On Friday, Corso Matteotti, Santa Margherita's major street for food shopping, becomes an open-air **food market.**

EXPLORING SANTA MARGHERITA

Life in Santa Margherita centers on its palm-fringed **waterfront,** a pleasant string of marinas, docks for pleasure and fishing boats, and pebbly beaches, in some spots with imported sand of passable quality. Landlubbers congregate in the cafes that spill out into the town's two seaside squares, Piazza Martiri della Libertà and Piazza Vittorio Veneto.

The train station is on a hill above the waterfront, and a staircase in front of the entrance will lead you down into the heart of town. Santa Margherita's one landmark of note is its namesake **Basilica di Santa Margherita,** just off the seafront on Piazza Caprera. The church is open daily 7:30am to noon and 2:30 to 7pm and is well worth a visit to view the extravagant, gilded, chandeliered interior.

WHERE TO EAT & STAY

Grand Hotel Miramare ★★ This was one of the first grand hotels on this coast, converted in 1903 from a massive private villa a 10-minute walk from the town center along the road to Portofino. Rooms are enlivened by some modest stucco decorations on the walls and ceilings, from which hang chandeliers over parquet floors scattered with Persian rugs and slightly funky walnut and veneer furnishings. The first-floor suite, where Marconi stayed when conducting his radio experiments, has been kept in 19th-century style, while fifth-floor suites are more modernized. A very steep, pretty park rises behind the hotel, from which a trail leads over the headland to Portofino (it also makes for a pleasant view, especially if you don't get a room with that preferred sea vista). There's a small, private pebble beach/beach terrace across the busy road.

AN excursion TO SAN FRUTTUOSO

Much of the **Monte Portofino Promontory** can be approached only on foot or by boat (see below), making it a prime destination for hikers. If you want to combine some excellent exercise with the pleasure of glimpsing magnificent views of the sea through a lush forest, arm yourself with a map from the tourist offices in Camogli, Santa Margherita Ligure, Portofino, or Rapallo and set out. You can explore the upper reaches of the promontory or aim for the **Abbazia di San Fruttuoso** (✆ **0185-772-703**), a medieval abbey that is surrounded by a tiny six-house hamlet and two pebbly beaches. It is about 2½ hours away from Camogli and Portofino by a not-too-strenuous inland hike, or 3½ hours away by a cliff-hugging, up-and-down trail. En route, you can clamor down well-posted paths to visit San Rocco, San Niccolò, and Punta Chiappa, a string of fishing hamlets on the shore of the promontory.

Once you reach San Fruttuoso, you may well want to relax on the pebbly beach and enjoy a beverage or meal at one of the seaside bars. You can tour the stark interior of the abbey for 6€. It is open June to mid-September daily 10am to 5:45pm; in May Tuesday to Sunday 10am to 5:45pm; March, April, and October Tuesday to Sunday 10am to 3:30pm; and November to February Saturday and Sunday 10am to 3:30pm. Note, though, that despite these official hours, the abbey tends to close whenever the last boat leaves (see below). The abbey is just a plain, evocatively simple medieval monastic complex with a stellar setting on the coast. There's nothing really to "see" except how the monks lived. Should you happen to have your scuba or snorkeling gear along, you can take the plunge to visit Christ of the Depths, a statue of Jesus erected 15m (49 ft.) beneath the surface to honor sailors lost at sea.

You can also visit San Fruttuoso with one of the **boats** that run almost every hour during the summer months from Camogli. A round-trip costs 13€ (10€ one-way if you then plan to head southward from the abbey) and takes about 30 minutes. For more information, contact Golfo Paradiso (www.golfoparadiso.it; ✆ **0185-772-091**). ***Note:*** You can also reach it by hourly (in summer) Tigullio boats (www.traghettiportofino.it; ✆ **0185-284-670**) from Portofino (20 min.; 11€ round-trip), Santa Margherita (35 min.; 15€ round-trip), and Rapallo (50 min.; 15€ round-trip). Bear in mind that the seas are often too choppy to take passengers to San Fruttuoso, because docking there can be tricky. In that case, there are private boats you can take—smaller, rubber crafts capable of bad-weather landings—though they are expensive: From Portofino, you will likely be charged 100€ for up to 12 people.

Via Milite Ignoto 30, 16038 Santa Margherita Ligure (GE). www.grandhotelmiramare.it. ✆ **0185-287-013.** Fax 0185-284-651. 84 units. 255€–397€ double with park view; 305€–458€ double with sea view. AE, DC, MC, V. Parking 25€. **Amenities:** 2 restaurants (1 poolside lunch buffet; 1 international/regional); 2 bars (piano bar inside, pool bar); babysitting; concierge; nearby exercise room; nearby golf course; outdoor heated saltwater pool; room service; nearby sauna; nearby outdoor lighted tennis courts; watersports equipment/rentals. *In room:* A/C, TV, hair dryer, minibar, Wi-Fi.

Hotel Metropole ★★ ☺ This popular hotel is just above the port and a 5-minute stroll from the center. Accommodations are split between the main, modern building and the far-preferable Villa Porticciolo, a dusty red villa right on the beach; the rooms are smaller in the latter, but they're graced with 19th-century stuccoes, and the sea laps practically right up against the building. Six rooms up on the far end of the garden have large terraces. All other guest rooms have large balconies. The fourth floor is made up of junior suites and one double with sloped ceilings. Two suites on the lower floor of the main building open onto small private gardens. Several rooms can be joined to make family suites and there's day care at the beach, with a separate area of sand just for the kiddies. The small private beach includes a curving sunbathing terrace and a private boat launch.

Via Pagana 2, 16038 Santa Margherita Ligure (GE). www.metropole.it. ✆ **0185-286-134.** Fax 0185-283-495. 59 units. 100€–242€ double; 136€–286€ double with half board; 156€–306€ double with full board. Rates include buffet breakfast. AE, DC, MC, V. Parking 12€ outside or 18€ in private garage. **Amenities:** 2 restaurants (1 international/regional dining room; 1 beachside lunch restaurant); bar; babysitting; children's center (in summer); nearby golf course; small exercise room; swimming pool; sauna; watersports equipment/rentals. *In room:* A/C, TV, hair dryer, Internet, minibar, Wi-Fi.

Nuova Riviera ★ The Sabini family acts as if its sunny, early-20th-century Liberty-style villa in a quiet neighborhood behind the town center was a private home and guests were old friends. Every room is different, and though eclectically furnished with pieces that look like they may have passed through a couple of generations of the family, most rooms retain the high-ceilinged elegance of days gone by and have a great deal more character than you're used to finding in rooms at this end of the budget scale. The best rooms have expansive bay windows. Modular furnishings are mixed with antiques, the beds are springy (very springy), and a few rooms get balconies. Ask for an internal room as scooters cruise the street in front of the hotel at all hours. They also rent out rooms in another nearby structure (70€–125€ for two people with a 3-night minimum, no breakfast).

Via Belvedere 10–2, 16038 Santa Margherita Ligure (GE). www.nuovariviera.com. ✆/fax **0185-287-403.** 9 units. 85€–130€ double. Rates include breakfast. MC, V. **Amenities:** Restaurant (local cuisine, winter only); bar; smoke-free rooms. *In room:* TV, hair dryer, no phone.

Trattoria da Pezzi GENOVESE/LIGURIAN The two whitewashed, tile-floored rooms of this cozy little restaurant in the center of town near the market are usually filled with local workers and businesspeople who invite newcomers to share a table when no other place is available. Service is minimal—the chef puts what he's prepared for the day on a table near the front door, you tell him what you want, and one of the staff brings it to the table when it's ready. Focaccia, *farinata,* and other Genovese specialties are usually on hand, as are at least one kind of soup (the minestrone is excellent), a chicken dish, and grilled fresh fish.

Via Cavour 21. ✆ **0185-285-303.** Reservations not accepted. Main courses 6€–10€. MC, V. Sun–Fri 11:45am–2:15pm and 6–9:15pm. Closed the 2nd week of Sept and mid-Dec to mid-Jan.

Portofino

Portofino is almost too beautiful for its own good—in almost any season, you'll be rubbing elbows on Portofino's harborside quays with day-tripping mobs who join Italian industrialists, international celebrities, and a lot of rich-but-not-so-famous folks who consider this little town to be the epicenter of the good life. If you make an appearance in the late afternoon when the crowds have thinned out a bit, you are sure to experience what remains so appealing about this enchanting place—its untouchable beauty.

ESSENTIALS

GETTING THERE **By Train** Get off in Santa Margherita (see above) and catch the bus.

By Bus The **Tigullio** bus (www.tigulliotrasporti.it; ✆ **0185-373-239**) leaves from the train station and Piazza Vittorio Veneto in **Santa Margherita** every 20 minutes and follows one of Italy's most beautiful coastal roads (25 min.).

By Boat The best way to arrive in Portofino is on your private yacht. If you have left it at home for this visit to Italy, the next best thing is to sail in on one of the Golfo Paradiso ferries (www.golfoparadiso.it; ✆ **0185-772-091**) from **Camogli,** or on one of the Tigullio ferries (www.traghetti portofino.it; ✆ **0185-284-670**) from **Santa Margherita** or **Rapallo.**

By Car On a summer visit, you may encounter crowds even before you get into town, since traffic on the corniche from Santa Margherita, just a few kilometers down the coast of the promontory, can move at a snail's pace. In fact, given the limited parking space in Portofino, visitors must pay obscene rates to use the town garage. You would do well to leave your car in Santa Margherita and take the bus or boat.

VISITOR INFORMATION Portofino's **tourist office** is at Via Roma 35 (www.turism oinliguria.it; ✆ **0185-269-024**). Summer hours are Tuesday to Saturday 10am to 1pm and 2 to 6pm, Sunday 9:30am to 12:30pm and 3:30 to 6:30pm, winter hours are Tuesday to Saturday 9:30am to 1:30pm and 2 to 5pm

EXPLORING PORTOFINO

The one thing that won't break the bank in Portofino is the scenery. Begin with a stroll around the stunningly beautiful **harbor,** which is lined with expensive boutiques, eateries, and colorful houses set along the quay and steep green hills rising behind them. One of the most scenic walks takes you uphill for about 10 minutes along a well-signposted path from the west side of town just behind the harbor to the **Chiesa di San Giorgio** (✆ **0185-269-337**), built on the site of a sanctuary Roman soldiers dedicated to the Persian god Mithras. It's open daily 9am to 7pm.

From there, continue uphill for a few minutes more to Portofino's 15th-century **Castello Brown** (www.castellobrown.it; ✆ **0185-267-101**), which has a lush garden and offers great views of the town and harbor below. It costs 5€ (includes access to special exhibitions when they are going on) and is open daily 10am to 7pm from March to October, and the rest of the year on Saturday and Sunday from 10am to 5pm.

For more lovely views on this stretch of coast and plenty of open sea, go even higher up through lovely pine forests to the ***faro*** (lighthouse).

From Portofino, you can also set out for a longer hike on the paths that cross the **Monte Portofino Promontory** to the Abbazia di San Fruttuoso (see the box "An Excursion to San Fruttuoso," above), a walk of about 2½ hours from Portofino. The tourist office provides maps.

There's not much else to see in town, but most people are here to spend time on the water. If you're yachtless, one alternative is to take a dolphin-spotting cruise with **Delfini Metropolitani** (www.incomingliguria.it; ✆ **010-234-5666**). A 2-day tour, hotel accommodations in Genoa included, costs about 140€ per person, or 70€ for children 4 to 12 years old.

Portofino at night.

WHERE TO EAT & STAY

Portofino's charms come at a steep price. Its few hotels are expensive enough to put them in the "trip of a lifetime" category, and the harborside restaurants can take a serious chunk out of a vacation budget as well. An alternative is to enjoy a light snack at a bar or one of the many shops selling focaccia, and wait to dine in Santa Margherita or one of the other nearby towns.

Hotel Eden ★ Osta Ferruccio runs this cozy *pensione* in the heart of the tiny town, a long block up from the harbor. There are no views of the sea here, though those over the town's rooftops are pleasant enough. The most sought-after room is no. 7, which comes with a small terrace. The bathrooms are tight but well equipped, and there's a lovely small garden where Ligurian dishes are served in summer. While not exactly cheap, in Portofino this qualifies as a budget hotel and it's one of the few of any category that's open year-round.

Vico Dritto 18, 16034 Portofino (GE). www.hoteledenportofino.com. ✆ **0185-269-091.** Fax 0185-269-047. 12 units. 140€–290€ double. Rates include breakfast. AE, DC, MC, V. Parking 20€ in nearby lot. **Amenities:** Restaurant (Ligurian); bar; babysitting; concierge. *In room:* A/C, TV, hair dryer, Wi-Fi.

Hotel Nazionale ★★ It may be set smack in the middle of Portofino's harborfront square, amid some of the priciest real estate in Italy, but the Nazionale costs only one-third to one-half the price of its pricier neighbors. Decoration of the smallish to midsize rooms is minimal, but the pieces are a masterful mix of modern and antique, which adds to the relaxing elegance of the place. Several of the rooms are lofted suites with the bedroom upstairs. Only five rooms, all junior suites, enjoy views of the harbor.

Via Roma 8, 16034 Portofino (GE). www.nazionaleportofino.com. ✆ **0185-269-575.** Fax 0185-269-138. 12 units. 200€–275€ double without sea view; 300€–375€ junior suite with sea view.

Rates include breakfast. MC, V. Parking 20€ in nearby lot. Closed mid-Dec to Mar. **Amenities:** Restaurant (Italian); bar; concierge; room service. *In room:* A/C, TV, hair dryer, minibar, Wi-Fi.

Ristorante Puny ★★ LIGURIAN The gregarious owners make this a Portofino landmark, and also a difficult place to score a table in the summer. Right on the *piazzetta,* its tables enjoy views of the boats bobbing in the harbor and yachts having size contests beyond. Definitely book ahead to drink in those views and dig into *risotto al curry e gamberi* (curried rice embedded with tiny shrimp); *penne al puny* (pasta quills in a sauce of tomatoes, pancetta bacon, and mushrooms); fresh fish *al verde* (in a green sauce of parsley, lemon, and white wine) or *al sale* (baked under a thick salt crust); or *carne all'uccelletto* (diced veal sautéed in butter then cooked in white wine with bay leaves).

Piazza Martiri dell'Olivetta 5. ✆ **0185-269-037.** Reservations highly recommended. Main courses 14€–25€. AE, MC, V. Wed–Thurs and Sat–Sun 12:30–3:30pm; Wed–Fri 7:30–11pm.

THE CINQUE TERRE

Monterosso, the northernmost town of the Cinque Terre, 93km (58 miles) E of Genoa

Olive groves and vineyards clinging to hillsides, proud villages perched above the sea, hidden coves nestled at the foot of dramatic cliffs—the **Cinque Terre** is about as beautiful a coastline as you're likely to find in Europe. What's best about the Cinque Terre (named for the five neighboring towns of Monterosso, Vernazza, Corniglia, Manarola, and Riomaggiore) is what are *not* here—automobiles, large-scale development, or much else by way of 20th- and 21st-century interference. The pastimes in the Cinque Terre don't get much more elaborate than **walking ★★★** from one lovely village to another along trails that afford spectacular vistas, plunging into the Mediterranean, or basking in the sun on your own waterside boulder, and indulging in the tasty local food and wine.

Not too surprisingly, these charms have not gone unnoticed, and American tourists especially have been coming here in increasing numbers. In summer (weekends are worst), you are likely to find yourself in a long procession of like-minded, English-speaking trekkers making their way down the coast or elbow to elbow with day-trippers from an excursion boat. Even so, the Cinque Terre manages to escape the hubbub that afflicts so many coastlines, and even a short stay here is likely to reward you with one of the most memorable seaside visits of a lifetime.

Essentials

GETTING THERE **By Train** Cinque Terre towns are served only by local train runs. Coming from Florence or Rome you will likely have to change trains in nearby **La Spezia** (one or two per hour; 8 min.) at the coast's south tip or in **Pisa** (about six daily; 1¼ hr.). There are one or two direct trains per hour from **Genoa** to La Spezia that stop in Monterosso (1 hr., 40 min.) and sometimes Riomaggiore (15 min. farther south); often when coming from Genoa you will need to change in Levanto or Sestri Levante, both a bit farther north up the coast from Monterosso.

By Car The fastest route is via Autostrada A12 from Genoa, getting off at the Corrodano exit for Monterosso. The trip from Genoa to Corrodano takes less than an hour, while the much shorter 15km (9¼-mile) trip from Corrodano to Monterosso (via Levanto) is made along a narrow road and can take about half that amount of time. Coming from the south or Florence, get off Autostrada A12 at La Spezia and follow CINQUE TERRE signs.

By Boat **Navigazione Golfo dei Poeti** (www.navigazionegolfodeipoeti.it; ✆ **0187-732-987**) runs erratic service from the **Riviera Levante towns,** as well as from **Genoa,** mid-June to mid-September, though these tend to be day cruises stopping for anywhere from 1 to 3 hours in Vernazza (see description below) before returning (though you can usually talk them into not picking you up again for a day or three).

GETTING AROUND **By Foot** The best way to see the Cinque Terre is to devote a whole day and hoof it along the trails. See "Exploring the Cinque Terre," below, for details.

By Train Local trains make frequent runs (two to three per hour) between the five towns; some stop only in Monterosso and Riomaggiore, so check the posted *partenze* schedule at the station first to be sure you're catching a local. One-way tickets between any two towns are available, including one version that is good for 6 hours of travel in one direction, meaning you can use it to town-hop—or you can buy a day ticket good for unlimited trips.

By Car A narrow, one-lane coast road hugs the mountainside above the towns, but all the centers are closed to cars. Parking is difficult and, where available, expensive.

Riomaggiore and Manarola both have small **public parking facilities** just above their towns and minibuses to carry you and your luggage down. The cheapest option is the big open dirt lot right on the seafront in Monterosso. The priciest is the garage in Riomaggiore.

By Boat From the port in Monterosso, **Navigazione Golfo dei Poeti** (www.navigazionegolfodeipoeti.it; ✆ **0187-732-987**) makes 8 to 10 trips a day between Monterosso and Riomaggiore (a 25-min. trip), all stopping in Vernazza and half of them stopping in Manarola as well.

VISITOR INFORMATION The **tourist office** for the Cinque Terre is underneath the train station of Monterosso, Via Fegina 38 (www.turismoinliguria.it; ✆ **0187-817-506**). It's open Easter to the end of September daily 9am to 5pm; hours are reduced the rest of the year. Even when it's closed, you will usually find posted outside the office a handy display of phone numbers and other useful info, from hotels to ferries.

Useful websites for the region include www.cinqueterre.it, www.parconazionale5terre.it, and www.turismoinliguria.it.

Exploring the Cinque Terre

Aside from swimming and soaking in the atmosphere of unspoiled fishing villages, the most popular activity in the Cinque Terre is **hiking from one village to the next ★★★** along centuries-old goat paths. Trails plunge through vineyards and groves of olive and lemon trees and hug seaside cliffs, affording heart-stopping views of the coast and the romantic little villages looming ahead in the distance. The well-signposted walks from village to village range in difficulty and length, but as a loose rule, they get longer and steeper—and more rewarding—the farther north you go. Depending on your pace, and not including eventual stops for focaccia and *sciacchetrà,* the local sweet wine, you can make the trip between Monterosso, at the northern end of the Cinque Terre, and Riomaggiore,

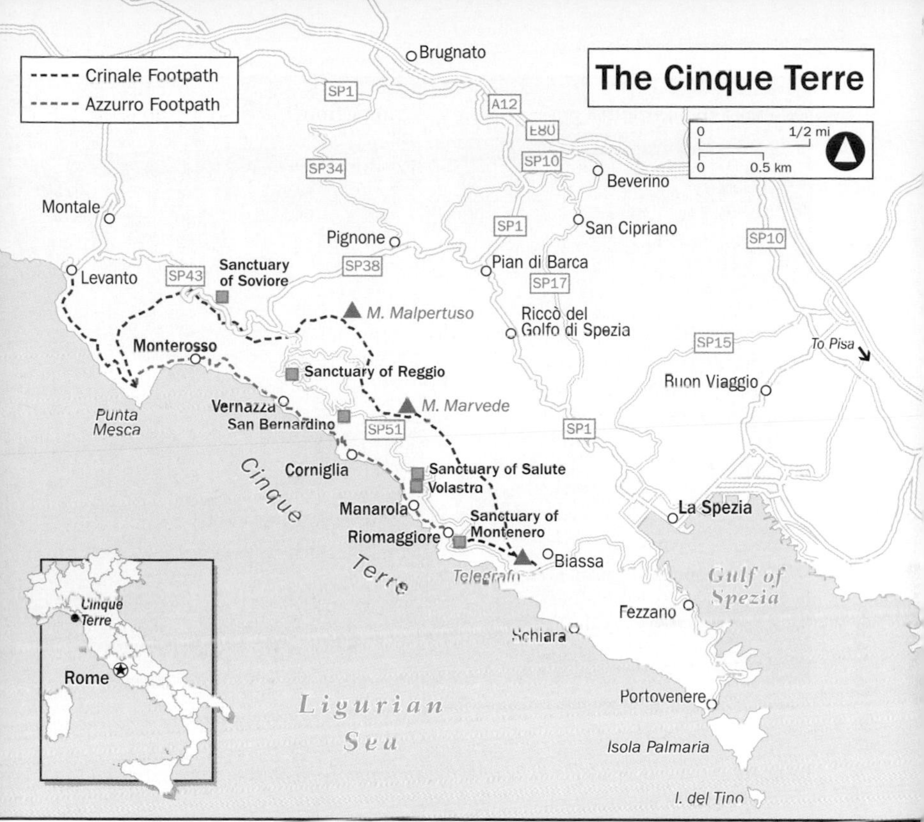

at the southern end, in about 4½ hours. You should decide whether you want to walk north to south or south to north. Walking south means tackling the hardest trail first, which you may prefer, because you'll get it out of the way and things will get easier as the day goes on and you start to tire. Heading north, the trail gets progressively harder between each town, so perhaps you might like this if you want to walk just until you get tired and then hop the train.

The walk from **Monterosso to Vernazza** is the most arduous and takes 1½ hours, on a trail that makes several steep ascents and descents (on the portion outside Monterosso, you'll pass beneath funicular-like cars that transport grapes down the steep hillsides). The leg from **Vernazza to Corniglia** is also demanding and takes another 1½ hours, plunging into some dense forests and involving some lengthy ascents, but is probably the prettiest and most rewarding stretch. Part of the path between **Corniglia and Manarola,** about 45 minutes apart, follows a level grade above a long stretch of beach, tempting you to break stride and take a dip. From **Manarola to Riomaggiore,** it's easy going for about half an hour along a partially paved path known as the Via dell'Amore, so named for its romantic vistas (great to do at sunset).

Because all the villages are linked by rail, you can hike as many portions of the itinerary as you wish and take the train to your next destination. Trails also cut through the forested, hilly terrain inland from the coast, much of which is protected as a nature preserve. The tourist office in Monterosso can provide maps.

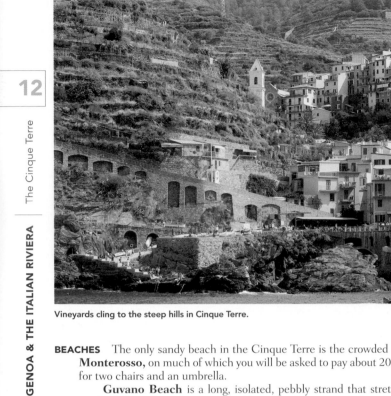

Vineyards cling to the steep hills in Cinque Terre.

BEACHES The only sandy beach in the Cinque Terre is the crowded strand in **Monterosso,** on much of which you will be asked to pay about 20€ per day for two chairs and an umbrella.

Guvano Beach is a long, isolated, pebbly strand that stretches just north of Corniglia and is popular with nudists (almost entirely men, many of whom are happy it's almost entirely men). You can clamber down to it from the Vernazza-Corniglia path, but the drop is steep and treacherous. A weird alternative route takes you through an unused train tunnel that you enter near the north end of Corniglia's train station. You must ring the bell at the gated entrance and wait for a custodian to arrive to unburden you of 2.50€, good for passage through the dank, dimly lit 1.5km-long (1-mile) gallery that emerges onto the beach at the far end.

There's also a long, rocky beach to the south of **Corniglia,** and it is easily accessible by some quick downhill scrambles from the Corniglia to Manarola path. **Riomaggiore** has a tiny crescent-shaped pebble beach reached by a series of stone steps on the south side of the harbor. Everywhere else, you'll be swimming off piers or rocks.

Monterosso

The Cinque Terre's largest village seems incredibly busy compared to its sleepier neighbors, but it's not without its charms. Monterosso is actually two towns—a bustling, character-filled Old Town built behind the harbor, as well as a relaxed resort that stretches along the Cinque Terre's only **sand beach** and is home to the train station and the tiny regional tourist office (upon exiting the station, turn left and head through the tunnel for the Old Town; turn right for the newer town and Il Gigante restaurant, see below).

The region's most famous art treasure is here: Housed in the **Convento dei Cappuccini,** perched on a hillock in the center of the Old Town, is a *Crucifixion* by Anthony Van Dyck, the Flemish master who worked for a time in nearby Genoa (you can visit the convent daily 9am–noon and 4–7pm). While you will find the most conveniences in citified Monterosso, you'll have a more rustic experience if you stay in one of the other four villages.

WHERE TO EAT & STAY

All the towns in the Cinque Terre have little shops like **Enoteca Internazionale ★★** on Via Roma 62 in Monterosso, where you can taste and purchase the local wines by the bottle, or simply enjoy a glass of Cinque Terre DOC (starting at about 3€) or *sciacchetrà* (3.50€) on the premises. The selection here, in the bustling part of old Monterosso, also includes olive oil pressed just down the street and jars of homemade pesto.

In terms of where to stay, aside from the traditional options below, you might try your luck at booking one of the rooms at **A Ca du Gigante** (Via IV Novembre; www.ilgigantecinqueterre.it; ✆ **0187-817-401;** 80€–180€ for a double with breakfast included).

Focacceria Il Frantoio LIGHT FARE Many patrons say this bustling shop, with a takeout counter and a few tables where you can dine on the premises, serves some of the best focaccia in Liguria. That's quite a claim, but suffice it to say that the freshly baked bread (especially when topped with fresh vegetables) is heavenly and provides one of the best fast meals around.

Via Gioberti 1 (off Via Roma). ✆ **0187-818-333.** Reservations not accepted. Pizza and focaccia from 1.50€. No credit cards. Fri–Wed 9am–2pm and 4–7pm. Closed Oct–Mar.

Hotel La Colonnina ★★ This friendly family-run gem is perfectly located in the heart of town just a few minutes from the beach. Sloped ceilings, marble bathrooms, small desks, and comfy chairs all make these large rooms seem as though they should be located in a much more expensive hotel. Some rooms come with a terrace, but even if you don't get one, all are welcome on the rooftop terrace that has a great view of the sea. The relatively rich buffet breakfast has mostly local items, some of which are organic. There is also a beautiful garden where you can relax and recoup after a day on the trails.

Via Zuecca 6, 19016 Monterosso al Mare (SP). www.lacolonninacinqueterre.it. ✆ **0187-817-439.** Fax 0187-817-788. 21 units. 120€–143€ double. Rates include buffet breakfast. MC, V. Parking 9€ in nearby public lot. Closed early Nov to Easter. **Amenities:** Wi-Fi *In room:* A/C, TV, hair dryer.

Hotel Pasquale ★★ The Pasquale gives you spectacular views for the money, and the family who runs it will make you feel extremely welcome. It's built into a cliff face—some of which shows through the walls inside—right at the port of the Old Town, so all rooms overlook the beach and sea. The green tile floors support simple beds and basic, built-in units. Rooms are midsize, but bathrooms are cramped. Families will appreciate quad no. 3, with its two separate bedrooms. Note that this room is also right next to the train tracks, though most of the noise can be held at bay by keeping the window closed. The owners of the Pasquale also run Hotel Villa Steno in Monterosso, another excellent option with doubles from 120€ to 200€ (www.villasteno.com; ✆ **0187-817-354**).

Via Fegina 4, 19016 Monterosso al Mare (SP). www.hotelpasquale.it. ✆ **0187-817-477.** Fax 0187-817-056. 16 units. 155€–200€ double; 185€–240€ triple. Rates include breakfast. AE, MC, V. Parking 9€ in nearby public lot. Closed Dec 6–26. **Amenities:** Bar; concierge; room service. *In room:* A/C, TV, hair dryer, minibar, Wi-Fi.

Ristorante Miky ★ ☺ SEAFOOD The first thing to strike you at this friendly and elegant restaurant is the giant scallop shells, loaded with *trenette alla pescatrice* (homemade pasta with mixed shellfish) that waiters carry out to hungry patrons. The shells are actually made of dough, and in fact, all of the dishes are served in pottery or some other sort of creative presentation. Adding to the charm is the restaurant's position right on the beach, set in a blooming garden. The specialty here is *pesce al sale,* which is your choice of seafood covered in coarse salt and slowly cooked in a wood-burning oven (the salt is removed before the fish is served).

Via Fegina 104. ✆ **0187-817-608.** Reservations recommended. Main courses 10€–20€. AE, DC, MC, V. Daily noon–3pm and 7:30pm to late. Closed Tues in winter.

Vernazza

It's hard not to fall in love with this pretty village. Tall houses cluster around a natural harbor (where you can swim among the fishing boats) and beneath a **castle** built high atop a rocky promontory that juts into the sea (this castle, which is nothing special, is open Mar–Oct daily 10am–6:30pm; admission 2€). The center of town is waterside **Piazza Marconi,** itself a sea of cafe tables. The only Vernazza drawback is that too much good press has turned it into the Cinque Terre's ghetto of American tourists, especially in summer.

WHERE TO EAT & STAY

There are plenty of nice places to stay here. Besides the Barbara (see below), you can rent one of **Trattoria Gianni Franzi**'s 23 rooms spread across two buildings; some come with a bathroom, some with excellent views up the coast, all with a steep climb up the streets of the town and then up the stairs within the building. No matter what room you get, it's worth the money. Rates are 65€ for a double with a shared bathroom, 80€ for a double with a shared bathroom and a sea view, 100€ for a double with a private bathroom and a sea view, and 140€ for a triple with all the luxuries. Call ✆ **0187-821-003** or fax 0187-812-228 to book, or when you arrive in town, stop by the trattoria's harborside bar at Piazza Marconi 5 (closed Wed, except during the busy summer months; if you arrive on a Wed when the trattoria is closed, there is usually somebody there in the afternoon to take care of new arrivals; ✆ **393-900-8155**). They're closed January 10 to March 10.

Albergo Barbara This is an exceedingly basic, but clean and cheap *pensione* in a stellar location at the center of the tiny harbor piazza with views over the fishing boats and Mediterranean. The *pensione* is on the two upper floors of a tall old house on the waterfront and you have to climb 63 steps to get there, and many of the rooms are reached by an additional climb up a spiral staircase. These efforts are rewarded by an eagle's-eye view of Vernazza's harbor from five of the rooms, and a partial view in others. Accommodations, though bare-bones, are not without charm—there's a pleasant smattering of homey furniture and cool tile floors. ***Note:*** The top floor can get especially hot in the summer, and the walls are thin so you might hear your neighbors. If no one answers the buzzer, inquire at the **Taverna del Capitano** restaurant across the square.

Piazza Marconi 30, 19018 Vernazza. www.albergobarbara.it. ✆ **0187-812-398.** 9 units. 55€ small double upstairs with shared bathroom; 65€ double with private bathroom down the corridor; 70€ double with private bathroom; 110€ large double with private bathroom and sea view. No credit cards. Closed early Dec to early Feb. *In room:* No phone, Wi-Fi.

Ristorante Gambero Rosso ★ LIGURIAN/SEAFOOD Enjoying the homemade pasta, fresh fish, and aromatic herbs on the terrace at this restaurant on the harbor is a pleasurable experience (though across the square at Taverna del Capitano, you can do it for cheaper and get better food to boot). At Gambero Rosso you can explore some hard-to-find dishes such as *acciughe* (fresh, local anchovies) baked with onions and potatoes, and *ravioli di pesce* (a delicate fish ravioli). Though the terrace is one of the main draws here—another being the *paccheri alla gambero rosso* (large, flattened tubular pasta served with tomato sauce and fish)—the stone-walled, stone-floored, timber-ceilinged dining room is a pleasant alternative when you can't eat outside. Gambero Rosso's owners also rent out four apartments (www.toninobasso.com; ✆ **335-269-436**).

Piazza Marconi 7. www.ristorantegamberorosso.net. ✆ **0187-812-265.** Reservations recommended. Main courses 16€–25€. AE, DC, MC, V. Tues–Sun 12:30–4pm and 7:15–10:30pm (summer sometimes open Mon). Closed Dec 15–Mar 1.

Taverna del Capitano ★★ LIGURIAN You'd have trouble finding a more pleasant way to take in the scene on Vernazza's lively harborside square than to do so while enjoying the seafood risotto and *muscoli ripieni* (*muscoli* is the Ligurian word for mussels, known as *cozze* elsewhere in Italy; here they are stuffed with fresh herbs). This place has been open since 1966, so they were serving their tasty cuisine way before Cinque Terre made it onto the tourist circuit. The service could use some polishing, but then again that's pretty much the case for most of the places around here when you come during the summer crush. Dish for dish this place beats Gambero Rosso across the square and it's also cheaper. The owners also rent out three rooms (70€–90€ for a double with private bathroom); ask at the restaurant for details.

Piazza Marconi 21/24. www.tavernavernazza.com. ✆ **0187-812-201.** Reservations recommended. Main courses 10€–20€. AE, DC, MC, V. Wed–Mon noon–3pm and 7–10:30pm. Closed mid-Nov to end of Dec.

Corniglia

The quietest village in the Cinque Terre is isolated by its position midway down the coast, its hilltop location high above the open sea, and its hard-to-access harbor. Whether you arrive by boat, train, or the trail from the south, you'll have to climb more than 300 steps to reach the village proper (arriving by trail from the north is the only way to avoid these stairs), which is an enticing maze of little walkways overshadowed by tall houses.

Once there, though, the views over the surrounding vineyards and up and down the coastline are stupendous—for the best outlook, walk to the end of the narrow main street to a belvedere that is perched between the sea and sky. Corniglia is the village most likely to offer a glimpse into life in the Cinque Terre the way it was decades ago.

WHERE TO EAT & STAY

Da Cecio ★★ 🎁 Elia and her son Carmelo rent out the second floor of their old stone house in the countryside just 2 minutes outside Corniglia (on the road to Vernazza) and offer what is one of the Cinque Terre's most pleasant inns. The rooms are big, bright, and stylish, with dark-wood veneer headboards and furnishings. Most feature great views over the sea, the olive groves, and the hilltop town (nos. 2 and 6 are on a corner with vistas out both windows). Bathrooms are on the small side. The sun-drenched rooftop deck or flowery terrace downstairs (which, at mealtimes, serves as an outdoor dining room for the restaurant) the perfect place to idle away an afternoon. If no rooms are available, one of the proprietors will take you down to their four pleasant rooms in the village. The church bell rings right near the annex so bring some earplugs.

Via Serra 58, 19010 Corniglia. www.cecio5terre.com. ✆ **0187-812-043.** Fax 0187-812-138. 12 units (4 are in a nearby building). 60€ double; 80€ triple. Breakfast 5€. MC, V. Closed Nov. **Amenities:** Ligurian restaurant; bar. *In room:* Hair dryer, no phone.

Osteria a Cantina de Mananan ★★ LIGURIAN The trek up to hilltop Corniglia is worth it anyway, but include a meal at this tiny restaurant carved into the stone cellars of an ancient house and you have a perfect combination. Agostino and Marianne, the husband-and-wife owners and chefs, draw on age-old local recipes and use only the freshest ingredients in their preparations. The results, posted on a blackboard in the one handsome vaulted room furnished with granite tables, are wonderful. Fresh vegetables from gardens just outside the village are grilled and mixed with herbs and smoked mozzarella as a simple appetizer. This can be followed by any of the hand-rolled pastas topped with homemade pesto or porcini. You can continue in this nonmeat direction with a plate of mussels, grilled fish, or fresh anchovies stuffed with herbs, but the few meat dishes on the menu are also excellent—especially the *coniglio* (rabbit) roasted in a white sauce.

Via Fieschi 117, Corniglia. ✆ **0187-821-166.** Reservations recommended. Main courses 9€–15€. No credit cards. Wed–Mon 12:30–2:30pm and 7:30–9:30pm. Closed Nov, Mon–Fri in Dec, and part of Jan–Feb.

Manarola

Not as busy as nearby Riomaggiore or as quaint as its neighbor Corniglia, Manarola is a near-vertical cluster of tall houses that seems to rise piggyback up the hills on either side of the harbor. In fact, in a region with no shortage of heart-stopping views, one of the most amazing sights is the descent into the town of Manarola on the path from Corniglia: From this perspective, the hill-climbing houses seem to merge into one another to form a row of skyscrapers. Despite these urban associations, Manarola is a delightfully rural village where fishing and winemaking are big business. The region's major **wine cooperative,** Cooperativa Agricoltura di Riomaggiore, Manarola, Corniglia, Vernazza e Monterosso, made up of 300 local producers, is here; call ✆ **0187-920-435** for information about tours of its modern (established 1982) facilities.

WHERE TO EAT & STAY

Manarola's **Ostello Cinque Terre** (www.cinqueterre.net/ostello; ✆ **0187-920-215;** fax 0187-920-218) offers cheap accommodations: 20€ to 25€ for beds in six-bed dorm rooms, 55€ to 70€ for a room with two single beds and private bathroom, or 126€ to 156€ for six-bed family rooms with private bathroom. The hostel, which is in the center of town near the church, offers services such as kayak, bike, and snorkel rental; Internet access; and cheap laundry. It's closed January 6 to February 15 and November 4 to December 6. Especially in high season, you must book a week in advance.

Aristide ★ LIGURIAN In this old house up the hill from the harbor (just below the train station), diners are accommodated on a couple of levels of small rooms, as well as on a covered terrace across the street. Many of Aristide's patrons live in the Cinque Terre or take the train here from nearby La Spezia, because this long-standing trattoria is known for its heaping platters of grilled fish, *gamberoni* (jumbo prawns), and *frittura di mare* (a selection of fried seafood). The *antipasto di mare* includes a nice selection of octopus, clams, sardines, and other local catches and serves well as a lighter meal. The house's white wine is from the hills above the town, and if the owner is in a good mood, he may come around after your dinner to offer a complimentary glass of *sciacchetrà*, the local dessert wine.

Via Discovolo 290. ✆ **0187-920-000.** Reservations recommended. Main courses 8€–20€; fixed-price fish menu 40€, including wine. AE, DC, MC, V. Tues–Sun noon–2:30pm and 7–9pm.

Marina Piccola ★★ Many of the rooms in this cozy inn on Manarola's harbor have a sea view and the decor in the whole establishment is a cut above that of most inns in the region. The charming rooms have old prints, faded floor tiles, and light pine-veneer furnishings. Rooms in the other building (the next one up the hill, containing the hotel lobby) are done in more of a country style, with nicer heavy wooden furnishings, flower-edged wallpaper, and fancy scrolled headboards. Service can occasionally be a bit rude and in the busy summer months you might be required to take half board.

Via Birolli 120, 19010 Manarola. www.hotelmarinapiccola.com. ✆ **0187-762-065.** Fax 0187-762-291. 13 units. 120€ double. Half board 90€ per person in double. Rates include breakfast. AE, DC, MC, V. Closed Nov. **Amenities:** Restaurant (local cuisine); bar. *In room:* A/C, TV.

Riomaggiore

Riomaggiore clings to the vestiges of the Cinque Terre's rustic ways while making some concessions to the modern world. The old fishing quarter has expanded in recent years, and Riomaggiore now has some sections of new houses and apartment blocks. This blend of the old and new works well—Riomaggiore is bustling and prosperous and makes the most of a lovely setting, with houses clinging to the hills that drop into the sea on either side of town. Many of the lanes end in seaside belvederes.

From the parking garage, follow the main drag down; from the train station, exit and turn right to head through the tunnel for the main part of town (or, from the station, take off left up the brick stairs to walk the Via dell'Amore to Manarola).

That tunnel and the main drag meet at the base of an elevated terrace that holds the train tracks. From here, a staircase leads down to a tiny fishing harbor, off the left of which heads a rambling path that, after a few hundred meters, leads to a pleasant little **beach** of large pebbles.

WHERE TO EAT & STAY

There are lots of folks renting out rooms illegally in the Cinque Terre, especially in Monterosso and Riomaggiore. These rooms are fine—usually—and

Seafood pasta at La Lanterna.

the price is right; it's just that they don't have the permits to do this, the properties are not inspected by the proper authorities, and of course it's all under the table so they don't pay taxes. It's a bit of a crapshoot if you rent one of these unpermitted rooms, though it should be kept as an option if you arrive late in the day in the summer.

One person renting rooms who has gone to the trouble of filing the paperwork with the authorities and submitting his rooms to oversight, meaning you'll be assured a certain guarantee of quality, is Mario Franceschetti. His rental room business, called **Mar Mar,** is run out of Via Malborghetto 8 (turn left when you come out of the tunnel from the train station; www.5terre-marmar.com; ✆/fax **0187-920-932**). Mario's very helpful business partner, Amy, is Californian and can be found in the office most days except Wednesday from 11am to 1:30pm. A bed in a coed dorm costs 15€ to 22€; double rooms cost 60€ to 80€. There are also eight apartments that sleep two to six people (65€–90€ for a double; 80€–120€ for the larger apartments with price depending on how many are in the room). Some of the rental units come with TV and private bathroom, and some have kitchenettes. Mar Mar's office is open daily from 9am to 5pm.

Hotel Villa Argentina The only full-fledged hotel in Riomaggiore is in the newer section of town, on a hillside about a 5-minute walk (up a lot of stairs) from the center. This location affords astonishing views, which you can enjoy from most of the guest rooms, and provides a nice retreat from the tourist-crowded main street and harbor. A breezy, arbor-shaded terrace and a bar area decorated by local artists off the lobby are the places to relax. And while the blandly furnished, tile-floored rooms upstairs will not overwhelm you with their character, they are large and pleasant, with ceiling fans and balconies (except room nos. 4–6 and 10) featuring views over the town to the sea. The hoteliers also offer apartments accommodating two to six people.

Via de Gaspari 187, 19017 Riomaggiore (SP). www.hotelvillargentina.com. ✆ **0187-920-213.** Fax 0187-760-531. 15 units. 94€–139€ double; 40€–60€ per person in apts. Rates include breakfast.

MC, V. Parking 10€. **Amenities:** Bar; concierge; room service; nearby sauna; watersports equipment/rentals; Wi-Fi. *In room:* TV, hair dryer, no phone.

La Lanterna ★ LIGURIAN/SEAFOOD From a table on the terrace here, perched only a few meters above Riomaggiore's snug harbor, you can hear the waves lap against the rocks and watch the local fishermen mend their nets. Seafood, of course, dominates the menu, with many Ligurian dishes such as *spaghetti allo scoglio* (spaghetti with mussels and shrimp in a white-wine sauce) or *spaghetti ai ricci di mare* (with sea urchins). The antipasto of shrimp, smoked tuna, and grilled swordfish is excellent and can suffice as an entree; you should, however, make room for one of the house specialties, *chiche*—homemade gnocchi filled with seafood and topped with a spicy tomato sauce.

Riomaggiore. ✆ **0187-920-589.** Reservations highly recommended. *Primi* 8.50€–11€; *secondi* 10€–22€. AE, DC, MC, V. Daily 11am–midnight. Closed Nov.

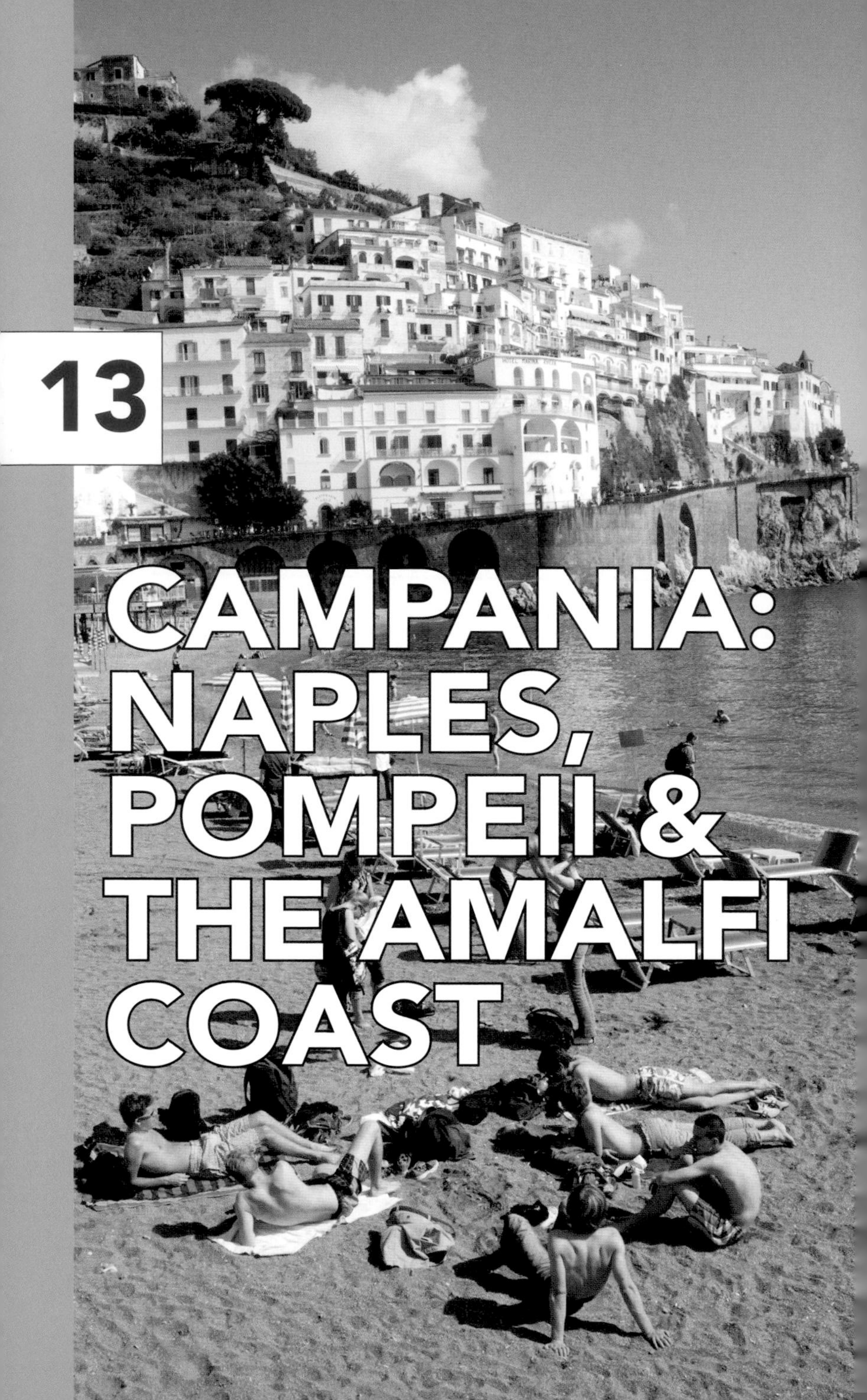

13

CAMPANIA: NAPLES, POMPEII & THE AMALFI COAST

Campania is one of Italy's most memorable and beautiful regions. It forms a fertile crescent around the bays of **Naples** and **Sorrento** and stretches inland to a landscape of rugged limestone hills dotted with patches of fertile soil. The geological oddities of Campania include mainland Europe's only active volcano (famous for having destroyed **Pompeii** and **Herculaneum**), sulfurous springs that belch steam and smelly gases, and lakes that the ancients believed to be the gateway to Hades. The road that hugs the southern shores of the **Sorrentine peninsula** is one of the most beautiful (and, some say, the most treacherous) in the world, combining danger at every hairpin bend with spectacular views. This captivating region is popular with Italians and visitors alike for its combination of earth, sea, and sky. Not only that, but Europe's densest collection of ancient ruins is here, each one celebrated by classical scholars as being among the very best of its kind.

The ancient Romans dubbed the land Campania Felix (Pleasant Countryside) and constructed hundreds of sumptuous villas there. In some ways, the beauty of Campania contributed to the decline of the Roman Empire; emperors, senators, and their courtiers spent more time pursuing its multiple pleasures than tending to Rome's administrative problems. Even today, seafront land is so desirable that hoteliers have poured their life savings into buildings that are sometimes bizarrely cantilevered above rock-studded cliffs, and despite an abundance of such hotels, they tend to be profitably overbooked in summer.

Along with other southern Italians, the Campanians enjoy their food and know how to make the most of their abundant, fresh produce. The proximity of sea and mountains is evident in local menus which feature fish and seafood, meat and vegetables, and wonderful cheeses, their flavors vibrant from the influence of sea and sun. Campanian wines have become much more sophisticated in recent years and pizza in the region is often memorable.

It's not a completely rosy picture, however, and today, parts of Campania typify the conditions that northern Italians label "the problem of the south." Although the inequalities are most pronounced in Naples, the entire region outside the coastal resorts has a lower standard of living, education, and health care and higher crime rates than in the more affluent north.

When the English say "see Naples and die," they mean the city and the bay, with majestic Vesuvius in the background. When the Germans use the expression, they mean the **Amalfi Drive.** Indeed, several motorists die each year on the dangerous coastal road, which is too narrow to accommodate the stream of

PREVIOUS PAGE: **One of the beaches dotting the Amalfi Coast.**

Campania is famous for its pizza.

summer traffic, especially the large tour buses that almost sideswipe one another as they try to pass. But as a driver, it's easy to be distracted by the view that André Gide remarked on as being "so beautiful that nothing more beautiful can be seen on this earth."

Sorrento and **Amalfi** are the principal towns with the widest range of facilities; glitzy **Positano** has more snob appeal and is popular with artists; and refined **Ravello** is still the choice of the discriminating few who desire relative seclusion. The gorgeous island of **Capri** (accessible by ferry from Sorrento or Naples) was known to emperors before international travelers discovered it. But the popularity of the resort-studded Amalfi Coast is a more recent phenomenon. It was discovered by German officers during World War II, and then later by American and English servicemen. When the war was over, many of these servicemen returned, often bringing their families. In time, the fishing villages became major tourism centers, with hotels and restaurants in all price ranges.

In addition to the stunning scenery and the lovely seaside towns, there are some world-class sightseeing attractions within easy access; the haunting ruins of **Pompeii** and the Greek temples of the ancient city of **Paestum** are among the most memorable sights in Italy.

THE BEST CAMPANIA TRAVEL EXPERIENCES

- **Taking in the coastal views:** "The Road of 1,000 Bends" as the **Amalfi Coast Drive** is sometimes known could also be called "the Road of 1,000 Views." The coastal panoramas from this world-famous road are magnificent; just make sure someone else is driving.

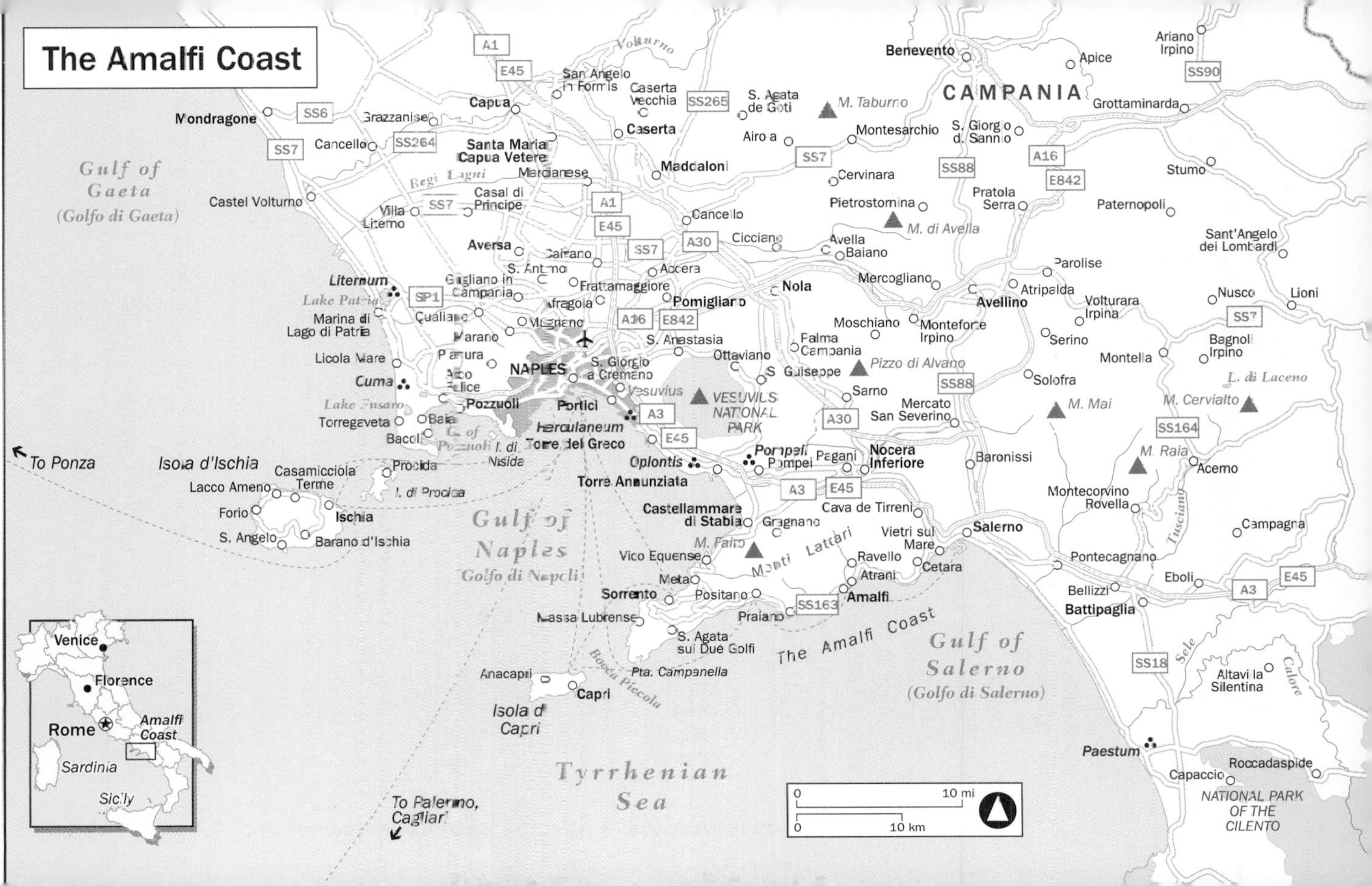

The Amalfi Coast
CAMPANIA
Gulf of Gaeta
(Golfo di Gaeta)
Gulf of Naples
Golfo di Napoli
Gulf of Salerno
(Golfo di Salerno)
Tyrrhenian Sea
The Amalfi Coast
Isola d'Ischia
Isola di Capri
NATIONAL PARK OF THE CILENTO
VESUVIUS NATIONAL PARK
To Ponza
To Palermo, Cagliari
Mondragone
Castel Volturno
Cancello
Capua
Santa Maria Capua Vetere
Casal di Principe
Marcianese
San Angelo in Formis
Caserta
Caserta Vecchia
Maddaloni
Airola
S. Agata de Goti
Benevento
Apice
Ariano Irpino
Grottaminarda
Montesarchio
S. Giorgio d. Sannio
Cervinara
Pietrostornina
Pratola Serra
Paternopoli
Stumo
Sant'Angelo dei Lombardi
Avellino
Atripalda
Parolise
Mercogliano
Avella
Baiano
Cicciano
Nola
Pomigliano
Acerra
Aversa
Literno
Liternum
Marina di Lago di Patria
Licola Mare
Cuma
Torregaveta
Baia
Bacoli
Pozzuoli
NAPLES
Portici
Herculaneum
Torre del Greco
Oplontis
Torre Annunziata
Castellammare di Stabia
Pompeii
Pagani
Nocera Inferiore
Sarno
Ottaviano
Mercato San Severino
Baronissi
Salerno
Montecorvino Rovella
Pontecagnano
Bellizzi
Battipaglia
Eboli
Campagna
Acerno
Paestum
Capaccio
Roccadaspide
Altavilla Silentina
Sorrento
Vico Equense
Meta
Positano
Praiano
Amalfi
Atrani
Ravello
Vietri sul Mare
Cetara
Cava de Tirreni
Gragnano
Massa Lubrense
S. Agata sui Due Golfi
Pta. Campanella
Bocca Piccola
Capri
Anacapri
Ischia
Procida
I. di Procida
Forio
Lacco Ameno
Casamicciola Terme
Barano d'Ischia
S. Angelo
M. Faito
Monti Lattari
Vesuvius
M. Taburno
M. di Avella
Pizzo di Alvano
M. Mai
M. Raia
M. Cervialto
L. di Laceno
Venice
Florence
Rome
Amalfi Coast
Sardinia
Sicily
10 mi
10 km

- **Visiting temples:** The three great Doric temples at **Paestum** are the best preserved outside Athens. Visit at sunset for the most romantic experience. See p. 786.
- **Buying Christmas cribs in Naples:** For festive atmosphere, head to the Via San Gregorio Armeno in the heart of Naples's historic district where shops sell traditionally crafted Christmas cribs and figurines in all shapes and sizes. See p. 723.
- **Rubbing shoulders with the rich and famous in Capri:** Capri simply oozes glamour, so put on your designer gear and splash out on an *aperitivo* at one of the pavement cafes in the famous Piazzetta to feel like one of the jet set, albeit temporarily. See p. 754.
- **Tucking into a seafood lunch:** There is still a thriving fishing industry in Campania which supplies coastal restaurants throughout the region with the freshest fish and seafood. What could be better than a beachside setting, a plate of sizzling hot *fritto misto,* and a jug of cold white wine?
- **Climbing mainland Europe's only active volcano: Vesuvius** looms dramatically over much of western Campania and they say it's a matter of "when" and not "if" the volcano will next blow its top. In spite of this sobering thought, climbing up to the wide crater and staring into its dark depths is a rare treat. See p. 730.

NAPLES ★★

219km (136 miles) SE of Rome, 263km (163 miles) W of Bari

Naples is Italy's most vibrant city, and in spite of continuing problems with garbage disposal and crime, it continues to attract visitors for its world-class sights, its natural setting, its food, and its sheer energy. Noisy, chaotic, traffic-clogged, and, at press time, dirty, Napoli is also fascinating and charming, but if it all becomes too much, you can easily escape.

The city and its immediate surrounding area boasts an extraordinary wealth of attractions with a lineup of artistic treasures that span millennia: There is enough here to keep a culture buff happy for weeks. Not only this, but nearby are some of the greatest **archaeological sites** in the world, while the magnificent natural beauty of **Vesuvius,** the **Bay of Naples, Capri,** and **Ischia** are a perfect contrast to the area's more intellectual attractions.

Shopping in the city is varied and interesting. Chic designer stores supply fashionistas with the latest styles, independent boutiques provide something a little more quirky, and respected, old-fashioned tailors' shops turn out superbly crafted bespoke suits, shirts, and ties for the city's best-dressed men. Looking for a souvenir to take home? Head to Via San Gregorio Armeno for intricately crafted Christmas cribs.

The variety of places to eat in Naples is stomach-challenging; the Neapolitans love their food and are proud of their culinary traditions. After all, this is home not only to pizza, one of the world's best-loved dishes, but also to Neapolitan ice cream, another universally celebrated culinary export. Restaurants range from elegant temples of creative gourmet cuisine to earthy, backstreet *trattorie* where you will find locals tucking into hearty traditional dishes.

The view from Naples's waterfront.

Essentials

GETTING THERE Naples's **Aeroporto Capodichino** (www.gesac.it; ✆ **081-7896259** and 081-7896255) is only 7km (4 miles) from the city center. It receives flights from Italian and European cities, plus a few intercontinental flights. From the airport, you can take a taxi into town (make sure it is an official white taxi with the Naples municipal logo); the flat rate for the 15 minute trip to the station is 16€ and to Molo Beverello for ferries to the islands 19€. There is a convenient bus service to Piazza Municipio and Piazza Garibaldi, the Alibus run by the **ANM bus company** (www.anm.it; ✆ **800-639525;** 3€ one-way). The bus runs every 30 minutes from the airport (6:30am–11:30pm) and from Piazza Municipio (6am–midnight).

Naples is on the main southern rail corridor and is served by frequent and fast **train service** from most Italian and European cities and towns. EuroStar trains (ES) make very limited stops, InterCity trains (IC) make limited stops, and AltaVelocità (AV) trains are expensive high-speed express trains. Regular trains take between 2 and 2½ hours between Rome and Naples, while the AV train takes only 87 minutes, making it by far the best method of transport between the two cities. The fare is 44€ one-way. The same journey on an InterCity train will cost 22€. Contact **Trenitalia** (www.trenitalia.it; ✆ **892021**) for reservations, fares, and information.

The city has two main rail terminals: **Stazione Centrale,** at Piazza Garibaldi, and **Stazione Mergellina,** at Piazza Piedigrotta. Most travelers will arrive at Stazione Central. Nearby is the **Stazione Circumvesuviana Napoli-Porta Nolana** (www.vesuviana.it; ✆ **800-053939**), on Corso Garibaldi. This is the starting point for commuter lines serving the Vesuvian and coastal area south of Naples, including Sorrento, Pompeii, and Ercolano.

ATTRACTIONS
Aquarium **41**
Cappella di Sansevero **19**
Castel dell'Ovo **51**
Castel Nuovo **35**
Catacombe di San Gennaro **7**
Certosa & Museo di San Martino **32**
Il Duomo-Cattedrale di Santa Maria Assunta **12**
Museo d'Arte Contemporanea Donna Regina (MADRE) **10**
Museo Nazionale Archeologico **9**
Museo Nazionale di Capodimonte **8**
Palazzo Reale **36**
San Domenico Maggiore **23**
San Lorenzo Maggiore **17**
Santa Chiara **26**
Teatro San Carlo **34**

HOTELS
Cappella Vecchia **39**
Chiaia Hotel de Charme **38**
Constantinopoli 104 **21**
Decumani Hotel de Charme **25**
Europeo/Europeo Flowers **24**
Grand Hotel Parker's **5**
Grand Hotel Vesuvio **43**
Hotel Excelsior **49**
Hotel Miramare **48**
Hotel Rex **47**
Il Convento **29**
Majestic **4**
Palazzo Alabardieri **40**
Piazza Bellini **22**
Romeo **28**
San Francesco al Monte **31**
Starhotel Terminus **14**
Suite Esedra **15**
Una Hotel **13**

RESTAURANTS
Acunzo **6**
Amici Miei **37**
Antonio & Antonio **42**
Da Michele **16**
Da Tonino **3**
Dora **2**
Ettore **45**
Europeo di Mattozzi **27**
George's **5**
Hostaria Toledo **30**
La Bersagliera **50**
La Cantinella **46**
La Stanza del Gusto **20**
Marino **44**
Mimi alla Ferrovia **11**
Rosiello **1**
San Ferdinando **33**
Scaturchio **18**

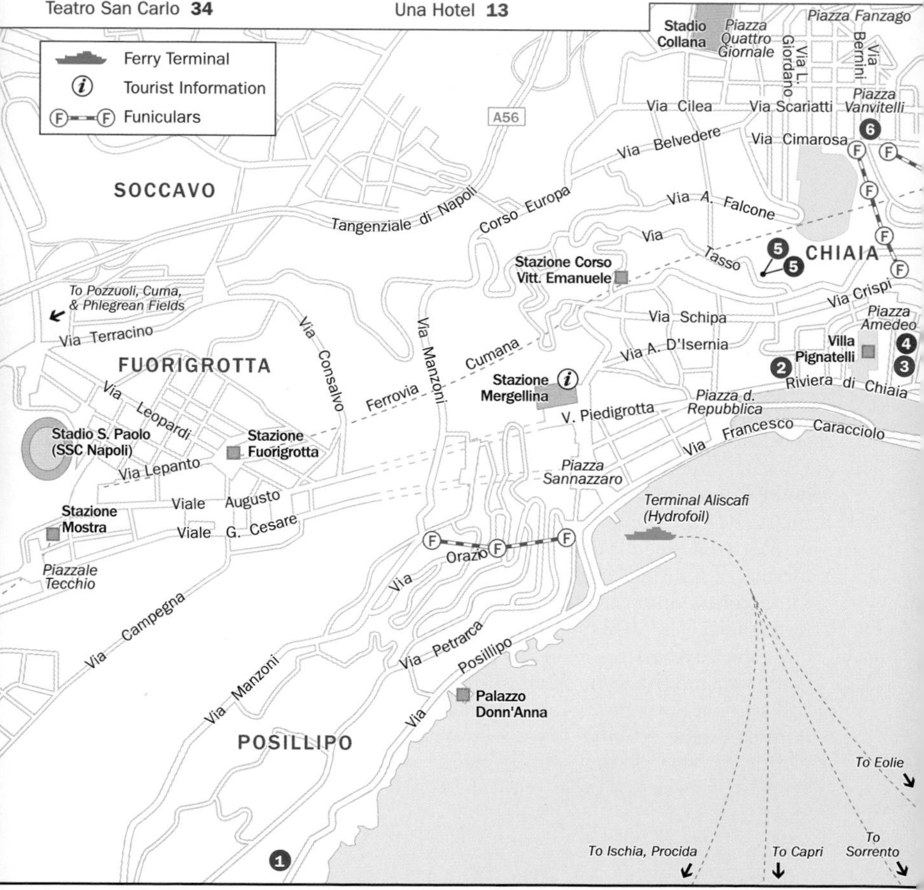

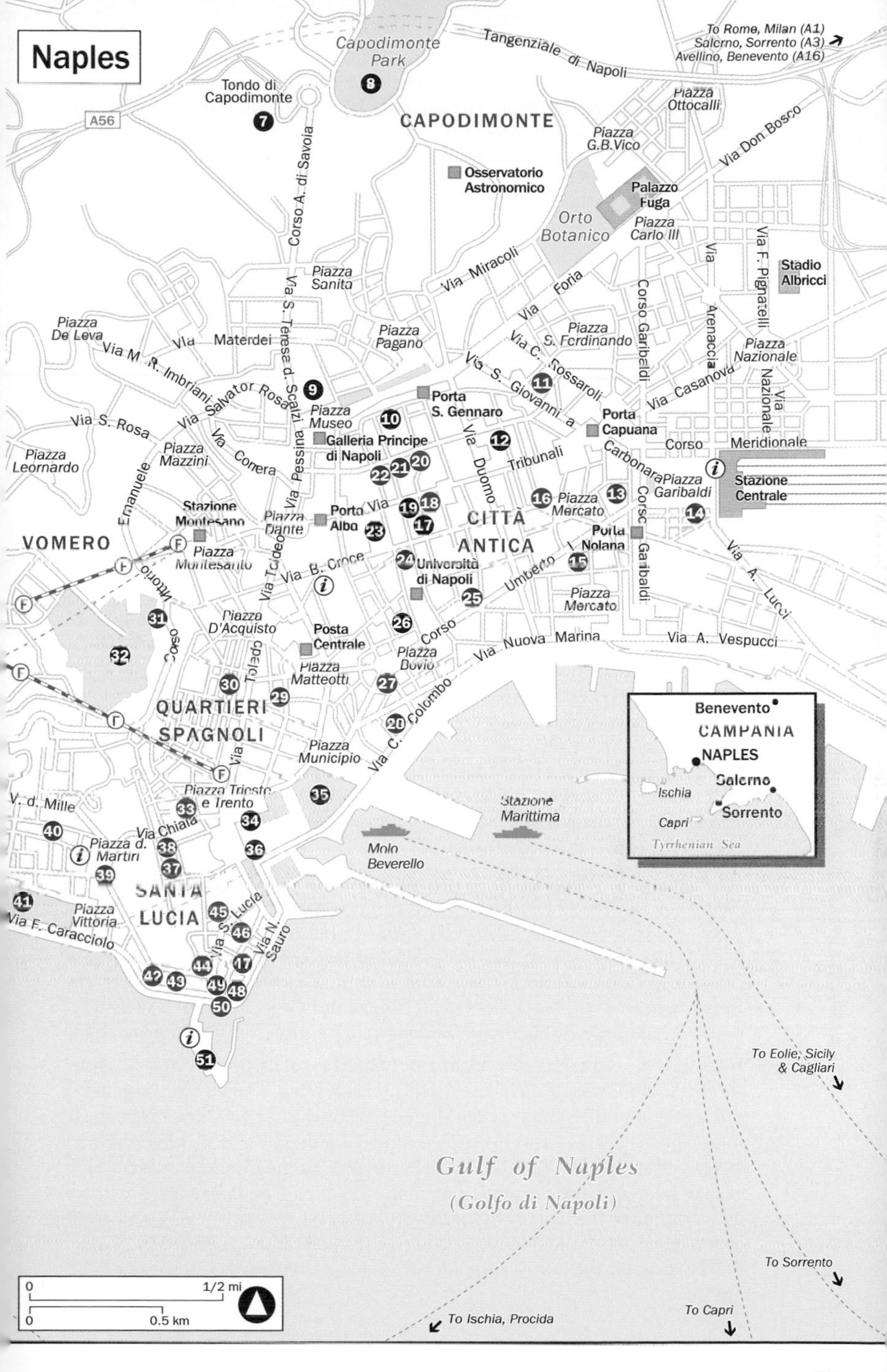
Naples
Capodimonte Park
Tangenziale di Napoli
To Rome, Milan (A1)
Salerno, Sorrento (A3)
Avellino, Benevento (A16)
Tondo di Capodimonte
A56
CAPODIMONTE
Piazza Ottocalli
Piazza G.B.Vico
Via Don Bosco
Osservatorio Astronomico
Palazzo Fuga
Orto Botanico
Piazza Carlo III
Corso A. di Savoia
Via Miracoli
Via Foria
Stadio Albricci
Piazza Sanità
Via S. Teresa d. Scalzi
Piazza De Leva
Via Materdei
Piazza Pagano
Piazza S. Ferdinando
Corso Garibaldi
Via Arenaccia
Via F. Pignatelli
Piazza Nazionale
Via M. R. Imbriani
Via Salvator Rosa
Via C. Rossaroli
Via S. Giovanni a Carbonara
Via Casanova
Via Nazionale
Porta S. Gennaro
Piazza Museo
Via S. Rosa
Porta Capuana
Corso Meridionale
Galleria Principe di Napoli
Via Duomo
Tribunali
Piazza Mazzini
Piazza Leornardo
Via Correra
Via Pessina
Piazza Garibaldi
Stazione Centrale
Emanuele
Stazione Montesano
Piazza Dante
Porta Alba
Via Tribunali
Piazza Mercato
CITTÀ ANTICA
Porta Nolana
VOMERO
Piazza Montesanto
Via Toledo
Via B. Croce
Università di Napoli
Corso Umberto I
Via A. Lucci
Vittorio
Piazza D'Acquisto
Posta Centrale
Via Nuova Marina
Via A. Vespucci
Piazza Bovio
Piazza Matteotti
QUARTIERI SPAGNOLI
Via C. Colombo
Piazza Municipio
Benevento
CAMPANIA
NAPLES
Salerno
Ischia
Sorrento
Capri
Tyrrhenian Sea
Piazza Trieste e Trento
V. d. Mille
Via Chiaia
Stazione Marittima
Piazza d. Martiri
Molo Beverello
SANTA LUCIA
Piazza Vittoria
Via F. Caracciolo
Via S. Lucia
Via N. Sauro
To Eolie, Sicily & Cagliari
Gulf of Naples
(Golfo di Napoli)
To Sorrento
0 1/2 mi
0 0.5 km
To Ischia, Procida
To Capri

Although driving *in* Naples is a nightmare, **driving** *to* Naples is easy. The Rome-Naples autostrada (A2) passes Caserta 29km (18 miles) north of Naples. The Naples–Reggio di Calabria autostrada (A3) runs by Salerno, 53km (33 miles) north of Naples.

From Palermo you can take a **ferry** to Naples that's run by **Tirrenia Lines,** Via Pontile Vittorio Veneto 1, Porto di Palermo (www.tirrenia.it; ✆ **892-123**), in the port area of the city. A one-way ticket costs 35€ to 55€ per person for an armchair in first class and 50€ to 70€ per person for a first-class cabin for the 11-hour trip.

GETTING AROUND The **Metropolitana** (subway) has two lines: line 1 from Piazza Dante to the Vomero and beyond and line 2 from Pozzuoli to Piazza Garibaldi and beyond. A new station, Università, in Piazza Bovia was inaugurated in March 2011 and another two stations are due to open in 2013. You can also use the urban section of the **Cumana** railroad from Montesanto, which is convenient to Mergellina and other coastal locations north of the city center.

Taxis are an excellent, relatively inexpensive way to get around the city, and these days are very reliable and strictly regulated. Official taxis are painted white and marked by the COMUNE DI NAPOLI. Inside, you'll find a sign listing official flat rates to the seaports, central hotels, and major attractions; don't fret if your driver doesn't use the meter—*not* using the meter is legal for all rides that have established flat rates. Taxis do not cruise but are found at the many taxi stands around town, or, for an extra 1€ surcharge, can be called by phone (✆ **081-444444** or 081-5555555).

As for **driving** around Naples, we have one word: *Don't.*

Funiculars take passengers up and down the steep hills of Naples. The **Funicolare Centrale** (www.metro.na.it; ✆ **800-568866**) connects the lower part of the city to Vomero. Daily departures (6:30am–12:30am) are from Piazzetta Duca d'Aosta just off Via Roma. Be careful not to get stranded by missing the last car back. The same tickets valid for buses and the Metro are good for the funicular.

VISITOR INFORMATION The **Ente Provinciale per il Turismo,** Piazza dei Martiri 58 (✆ **081-4107211;** bus: 152), is open Monday to Friday 9am to 2pm. There is another **office** at Stazione Centrale (✆ **081-268779;** Metro: Garibaldi), open Monday to Saturday 9am to 7pm. The **AASCT** (www.inaples.it) maintains two excellent tourist information points: **Via San Carlo 9** (✆ **081-402394**) and **Piazza del Gesù** (✆ **081-5512701**), both open Monday to Saturday 9:30am to 6:30pm, Sunday 9:30am to 2pm.

SPECIAL EVENTS **Maggio dei Monumenti (May of Monuments)** is sponsored by the Council of Naples, with events programmed every weekend during the month. Each year the theme is slightly different. One of the most interesting aspects of this event is a series of guided walks through the historic district that includes the city's fascinating underground passages. May is also the month for a variety of exhibits and fairs. Chamber music recitals, concerts, operettas, performances of classic Neapolitan songs, and even soccer matches and horse races add to the celebration. If you're in Naples in May, consult the tourist office for a full program of events, some of which are free.

[FastFACTS] NAPLES

Consulates The **U.S. Consulate** is on Piazza della Repubblica 1 (http://naples.usconsulate.gov; ✆ **081-5838111;** Metro: Mergellina, tram: 1). Its consular services are open Monday to Friday 8am to noon. The **U.K. Consulate** is at Via Dei Mille 40 (www.britain.it: ✆ **081-4238911;** Metro: Amedeo), open Monday to Friday 9:30am to 12:30pm and 2 to 4pm. The **Canadian Consulate** is at Via Carducci 29 (www.canada.it; ✆ **081-401338;** Metro: Amedeo), open Monday to Friday 9am to 1:30pm. Citizens of **Australia** and **New Zealand** will need to go to the embassies or consulates in Rome (see chapter 17).

Drugstores There are several pharmacies open weekday nights and taking turns on weekend nights. A good one is located in the Stazione Centrale (Piazza Garibaldi 11; ✆ **081-440211;** Metro: Piazza Garibaldi).

Emergencies If you have an emergency, dial ✆ **113** to reach the police. For medical care, dial ✆ **118,** but only in an emergency. To find the local **Guardia Medica Permanente,** ask for directions at your hotel.

Exploring Naples

If you arrive by train at Stazione Centrale, on **Piazza Garibaldi,** you'll want to escape fast. **Corso Umberto I** leads southwest toward the elegant Santa Lucia district which borders the seafront. Just to the east (but not within walking distance; you'll need to take a taxi) is the port area from where many of the ferries and hydrofoils serving the islands leave.

Many people confine their visit to **Santa Lucia** where most of the city's swankiest hotels are situated, only venturing farther afield to visit a museum or two. These hotels lie along seafront **Via Partenope,** which looks out on the Gulf of Naples and the Castel dell'Ovo. To the west is the **Mergellina** district, site of many restaurants and dozens of apartment buildings and, beyond that, lies **Posillipo.**

Naples grandest square is **Piazza del Plebiscito,** located just north of Santa Lucia and flanked on its eastern side by the Palazzo Reale. Adjacent is **Piazza Trento e Trieste,** with the magnificent Teatro San Carlo and entrance to the Galleria Umberto I. To the east lies busy, trafficked **Piazza Municipio** and Castel Nuovo. From Piazza Trento e Trieste, the city's main shopping street, **Via Toledo/Via Roma,** leads north. To the left is the notorious **Quartieri Spagnoli,** while to the right, just beyond Piazza Dante, lies the atmospheric historical center of the city, a crisscross of narrow lanes famously cut in two by the dead-straight street known as the **Spaccanapoli.** From Piazza Dante, a 10-minute walk north will bring you to Naples's celebrated Archaeological Museum.

THE TOP MUSEUMS

Carthusian Monastery of San Martino (Certosa di San Martino) & National Museum of San Martino (Museo Nazionale di San Martino) ★★ MUSEUM Originally built in 1325 and rebuilt in the 17th century, this great monastery complex has been restored to its original beauty. Entering from the courtyard, you first come to the church, a masterpiece of baroque decoration, from the marble floor to works of art by artists such as Jusepe de Ribera,

The Castel Sant'Elmo.

Giuseppe Sanmartino, and Battistello Caracciolo. Do not overlook the marble transenna of the presbytery, decorated with precious stones, and the Cappella del Tesoro, with a rich altar made of the same materials. The peaceful Chiostro Grande (the Great Cloister) encloses a smooth lawn; in the corner is the monk's graveyard, topped with creepy marble skulls. The Quarto del Priore contains a number of masterpieces, including a *Madonna col Bambino e San Giovannino* by Pietro Bernini. The monastery also houses the Museo Nazionale di San Martino, which has several sections including one housing *presepi* (Nativity scenes) some of which are extraordinarily complex. The Sezione Navale, or Maritime Museum, will appeal to kids who will love the displays of model ships and ship's instruments. In the Gothic cellars of the monastery, you will find sections dedicated to sculpture and epigraphy, while on the second floor is the library that houses the Prints and Drawings Collection, with over 8,000 pieces.

Next to the monastery is the star-shaped **Castel Sant'Elmo** (✆ **081-5784120**), built by the Angevins in a strategic position above the city from 1329 to 1343. It was enlarged in the 16th century and today offers a magnificent 360-degree panorama of Naples and its bay. Admission is 4€.

Largo San Martino 8. ✆ **081-5781769.** Admission 6€. Thurs–Tues 8:30am–7:30pm. Closed Jan 1 and Dec 25. Metro: Vanvitelli and then bus V1 to Piazzale San Martino.

National Archaeological Museum (Museo Archeologico Nazionale) ★★★ MUSEUM Naples's celebrated Archaeological Museum is home to the greatest collection of ancient art and artifacts in the world, both in terms of the quantity of the pieces on display and their quality. The museum occupies the huge Palazzo degli Studi, a former university that was remodeled to house the immense collection that King Ferdinand I had inherited from his grandmother, Elisabetta Farnese. The Farnese Collection, the core of the museum, was moved here in 1777 and enriched with treasures from the archaeological excavations of Pompeii, Herculaneum, Stabia, and the rest of the region.

The famed *Beware of the Dog* mosaic, taken from the ruins at Pompeii.

The superb **Farnese Collection** of Roman sculpture starts in Room 1 which is dominated by the two massively powerful ***Tyrannicides*** *(Tyrant Killers),* 2nd-century-A.D. marble copies of renowned bronzes cast in 477 B.C. The magnificent ***Ercole Farnese,*** a huge statue of Hercules, was unearthed at the Baths of Caracalla in Rome in the mid–16th century and is a signed copy by the Greek sculptor Lisippo of a 4th-century-B.C. bronze. The colossal ***Toro Farnese*** (Room 16) is one of the largest existing sculpture groups from antiquity and is another copy of a Greek original. Located behind the Hercules sculpture, the matchless **Gemme della Collezione Farnese** includes the unique, 2nd-century B.C. ***Tazza Farnese*** carved from a single piece of sardonyx agate into the shape of a drinking cup.

The mezzanine galleries are devoted to mosaics excavated from Pompeii and Herculaneum that include scenes of cockfights, dragon-tailed satyrs, and, finest of them all, the huge, million-plus-piece *Alexander Fighting the Persians.* On the top floor are the superb bronzes rescued from Herculaneum's **Villa dei Papiri.** Look out for the two lean ***Athletes*** poised for flight, the famous ***Drunken Satyr,*** the five life-size female bronzes known as the ***Dancers,*** and the celebrated bust of ***Seneca,*** the Roman philosopher, statesman, and dramatist.

Piazza Museo 19. www.marketplace.it/museo.nazionale. ✆ **081-4422149.** Admission 10€. Wed–Mon 9am–7:30pm. Closed Jan 1 and Dec 25. Metro: Museo or Cavour.

National Museum & Gallery of the Capodimonte (Museo e Gallerie Nazionale di Capodimonte) ★★★ MUSEUM Standing in the magnificent park that once was a hunting preserve of the Bourbon kings, this museum was created by Carlo III di Borbone in 1743 to house the art collection inherited from his mother, Elisabetta Farnese, and today, the imposing red and gray building houses one of Italy's most important art collections.

Together with the important Borghese Collection, Carlo III's inheritance makes up the core of the museum. Rooms 2 to 30 on the second floor make up the Farnese Gallery where the haul of art amassed by several generations of the Farnese family from Parma hangs. Here, the stars of the show include works by the greatest Italian artists such as **Tiziano, Raffaello, Masaccio, Botticelli, Perugino, Luca Signorelli, Sandro Botticelli, Correggio, Giovanni Bellini, Mantegna, Parmigianino, Guido Reni, Caravaggio**—and by a number of the best artists from the Flemish school, such as **Pieter Bruegel the Elder** and **Van Dyck.** Smaller but also worth a visit is the **Borgia Collection** which contains many precious Renaissance **ivory** and **enamel** pieces.

The **Royal Apartments** take up much of the second floor. The **Porcelain Gallery** houses objects and dinner plates from all the royal palaces of Naples,

A detail from Fra Filippo Lippi's *Annunciation and Saints* at the National Museum & Gallery of the Capodimonte.

including *bisquits* (a firing process) of **Sèvres** and **Vienna,** porcelains of **Meissen,** and, of course, the famous **Capodimonte** ceramics created in the local workshops. The **Armory** has interesting pieces, but is overshadowed by the famous **Salottino di Porcellana,** a small room completely inlaid with porcelain, made for Maria Amalia in the 18th century for the royal palace of Portici.

A **gallery** dedicated to painting in Naples from the 13th to the 19th centuries occupies the third floor, and provides a unique overview of artists who worked in Naples, such as **Sodoma, Vasari, Tiziano, Caravaggio,** and **Luca Giordano.** Here, too, are the seven beautiful 16th-century **tapestries** from the **d'Avalos Collection.** The contemporary art collection extends from the third to the fourth floor, with works by Alberto Burri, Jannis Kounellis, Andy Warhol, and Enzo Cucchi, among others.

Palazzo Capodimonte, Via Miano 1; also through the park from Via Capodimonte. http://museodicapodimonte.campaniabeniculturali.it/. ✆ **081-7499111.** Admission 7.50€; 6.50€ after 2pm. Thurs–Tues 8:30am–7:30pm. Closed Jan 1 and Dec 25. Bus: R4.

MORE ATTRACTIONS

Aquarium (Acquario) AQUARIUM The aquarium is housed in a building that stands in the Villa Comunale municipal park, between Via Caracciolo and the Riviera di Chiaia. Established by a German naturalist in the 1800s, it's the oldest aquarium in Europe and displays about 200 species of marine plants and fish found in the Bay of Naples. (They must be a hardy lot.)

Inside Villa Comunale, Viale Acquario 1. ✆ **081-5833111.** Admission 1.50€ adults, 1€ children ages 5–12. Mar–Oct Tues–Sat 9am–6pm, Sun 9:30am–6pm; Nov–Feb Tues–Sat 9am–5pm, Sun 9am–2pm. Bus: 140, 152, C9, or C10.

Cappella di Sansevero ★ MUSEUM In the 18th century, Prince Raimondo di Sangro of Sansevero remodeled his family's 16th-century funerary chapel—and lavishly decorated it with sculptures. Among these is one of the most celebrated works in Naples, Giuseppe Sanmartino's *Cristo Velato (Veiled Christ),* created by the Neapolitan sculptor in 1753, and still with the original patina. The challenge of depicting veiled figures in stone seems to have obsessed the prince: Other renowned sculptures here are the *Disinganno,* a technical virtuoso by Queirolo showing a standing figure of a man disentangling himself from a net, and *Pudicizia,* a masterpiece by Corradini showing a veiled naked woman. Prince Raimondo achieved fame as a master of the occult, and the decoration of the chapel has contributed to this reputation. The most striking (and weird) objects here are two actual human bodies conserved in the crypt, whose circulatory systems are perfectly preserved after 2 centuries.

The Castel dell'Ovo.

Via Francesco De Sanctis 19 (near Piazza San Domenico Maggiore). www.museosansevero.it. ✆ **081-5518470.** Admission 7€. Mon and Wed–Sat 10am–6pm; Sun 10am–1:30pm. Closed May 1 and Easter Monday. Metro: Dante.

Castel dell'Ovo CASTLE Built over the small island of Megaris, where the Greeks first settled in the 9th century B.C., this castle is one of Naples's most famous sites and its solid profile features in many pictures of the Bay. Its name, "Castle of the Egg," refers to the local legend that says that the classic poet Virgil placed an egg under the foundations predicting that when it broke, disaster would befall the city. The fortress evolved from the villa of the Roman Lucullus which was transformed into a castle by Frederick II. Enlarged and strengthened between the 16th and the 18th centuries, it remained a royal residence until the 20th century. Part of the castle now houses the Museum of Ethno-Prehistory, which is open only for special exhibits. You can visit the **Sala delle Colonne (Hall of the Columns)** and the Loggiato, plus the two towers, **Torre Maestra** and **Torre Normanna,** which offer great views. The island is connected to the shore by a solid bridge, a popular spot for wedding photos. Around it are the picturesque alleys and fishermen's houses of the Borgo Marinaro.

Borgo Marinari (off Via Partenope). ✆ **081-7954593.** Free admission. Mon–Sat 8am–6pm; Sun 8am–2pm. Bus: 152, C25, 140, or E5 to Via Santa Lucia.

Castel Nuovo ★★ CASTLE/MUSEUM An imposing fortress dominating the bay, this castle was created for the new king, Carlo I d'Angió, who wanted a more suitable residence than Castel dell'Ovo and Castel Capuano—both used by previous sovereigns. Finished in 1282, the Castel Nuovo (aka the Maschio Angioino) was enlarged in the 15th century by Alfonso I d'Aragona and has five towers and a facade graced by the grandiose **Triumphal Arch of Alfonso I of Aragona ★★**, a splendid example of early Renaissance sculpture.

Accessed through the courtyard is the magnificent **Sala dei Baroni ★★**, an enormous cube, 27m (89 ft.) wide and 28m (92 ft.) high, with a star-shaped vaulted ceiling: The room is still used for city council meetings today.

The **Museo Civico (Civic Museum) ★** holds a rich collection of artworks from the castle. The highlight is the **Cappella Palatine ★**, the only surviving segment of the Angevin castle. Note the carved portal from the 15th century and a lovely rose window. Giotto decorated the original chapel, but nearly all of his frescoes have vanished with time. But other art remains, including a **tabernacle ★★** by Domenico Gagini and two depictions of the *Virgin and Child* by Francesco Laurana.

Piazza Municipio. ✆ **081-7952003.** Admission 5€. Mon–Sat 9am–7pm. Bus: R1, R2.

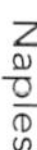

Frescoes in the Catacombs of San Gennaro.

Catacombs of San Gennaro (St. Januarius) ★ RELIGIOUS SITE A guide will show you through this two-story underground cemetery, dating from the 2nd century and boasting frescoes and mosaics. You enter the catacombs on Via di Capodimonte (head down an alley alongside the Madre del Buon Consiglio Church). These wide tunnels lined with early Christian burial niches grew around the tomb of an important pagan family; they became a pilgrimage site when the bones of San Gennaro himself were transferred here in the 5th century. Along with several well-preserved 6th-century frescoes, there's a depiction of San Gennaro (A.D. 400s), whose halo sports an alpha and an omega and a cross—symbols normally reserved exclusively for Christ's halo. The tour takes you through the upper level of tunnels, including several small early basilicas carved from the *tufo* rock. The cemetery remained active until the 11th century, but most of the bones have since been blessed and reinterred in ossuaries on the lower levels (closed to the public). The catacombs survived the centuries intact, but those precious antique frescoes suffered some damage when these tunnels served as an air-raid shelter during World War II.

Via Capodimonte 13. www.catacombedinapoli.it. ✆ **081-7443714.** Admission 8€. Tours are Mon–Sat on the hour 10am–5pm; Sun 10am–1pm. Bus: 24 or R4.

Il Duomo Cattedrale di Santa Maria Assunta ★★ CATHEDRAL King Carlo I d'Angio built Naples's great cathedral, dedicated to San Gennaro, in the 13th century on the site of a 6th century building that, in turn, stood next to the 4th century Basilica di Santa Restituta which is now part of the Duomo. Behind the fake Gothic facade, the grandiose interior, built on a Latin cross design supported by 110 ancient granite columns, is lavishly decorated. The most splendid chapel is the Gothic **Cappella Capece Minutolo,** with its beautiful 13th-century frescoes and mosaic floor.

The **Cappella di San Gennaro** is dedicated to the patron saint of Naples and is richly decorated with precious marbles, gold leaf, and frescoes. The famous reliquaries containing the skull and the blood of San Gennaro—which is said to miraculously liquefy three times a year—are housed over the main altar.

Don't miss the atmospheric basilica of **Santa Restituta** and, beyond it, the **Baptistery of San Giovanni in Fonte,** the oldest building of its kind in the Western world and decorated with dazzling (although partially damaged) 5th-century mosaics. From here you can also access the small but interesting archaeological zone.

Via del Duomo 147. www.duomodinapoli.it. ✆ **081-449097.** Free admission to the cathedral, but the archaeological zone is 3€. Mon–Sat 8am–12:30pm and 4:30–7pm; Sun 8am–1:30pm and 5–7:30pm. Metro: Piazza Cavour.

Museo d'Arte Contemporanea Donna Regina (MADRE) ★ ART MUSEUM This contemporary art museum has recently opened after a major renovation of the historical **Palazzo Regina,** in the heart of the historical district.

The rich collection of the museum comes both from the city's endowment, bestowed in recent decades, and from permanent loans from private collectors. Some of the world's best contemporary artists are represented, including Horn, Kapoor, and Lewitt, as well as a number of Italian artists such as Fabro, Clemente, and Serra. In addition to the permanent collection, the MADRE houses noteworthy temporary exhibits (check with the tourist office for current events). From the Cortile della Caffetteria, also called Cortile Banco dei Pegni, you can now access **Santa Maria di Donnaregina Vecchia,** a beautiful Gothic church that holds a monument to Queen Maria d'Ungheria carved by Tino da Camaino.

Via Settembrini 79 (btw. Via Duomo and Via Carbonara). www.museomadre.it. ✆ **081-19313016.** Admission 7€ Wed–Sun, free Mon. Mon and Wed–Sat 10:30am–7:30pm, Sun 10:30am–11pm. Bus: E1. Metro: Cavour.

Royal Palace (Palazzo Reale) ★ MUSEUM This royal palace was designed by Domenico Fontana in the 17th century, and the eight statues on the facade are of Neapolitan kings. Located in the heart of the city, it stands on Piazza del Plebiscito, one of Naples's most architecturally interesting squares, with a long, curving colonnade and a church, San Francesco di Paolo, that evokes the style of the Pantheon in Rome. Inside the Palazzo Reale you can visit the royal apartments, lavishly decorated in the baroque style with colored marble floors, paintings, tapestries, frescoes, antiques, and porcelain. Charles de Bourbon, son of Philip IV of Spain, became king of Naples in 1734. A great patron of the arts, he installed a library here, one of the finest in southern Italy, with more than 1,250,000 volumes.

Piazza del Plebiscito 1. www.palazzorealenapoli.it. ✆ **081-5808111.** Admission 4€; courtyard and gardens free. Thurs–Tues 9am–7pm. Bus: R2 or R3.

San Domenico Maggiore ★ CHURCH This massive Gothic edifice was built between 1289 and 1324 and then rebuilt in the Renaissance and early baroque eras. Upon entry from the apse end, you'll see that the body of the church was overhauled in neo-Gothic style in the 1850s. Walk down the left aisle (which is on your right because you're coming in from the wrong end) to the last chapel, where you'll find Luca Giordano's *Crowning of St. Joseph.* Now turn around to attack the church from the proper direction.

The first chapel on the right aisle is a Renaissance masterpiece of design and sculpture by Tuscans Antonio and Romolo da Settignano. The third chapel on the right contains frescoes from 1309 by Roman master Pietro Cavallini (a contemporary of Giotto). The seventh chapel on the right is the **Crucifixion Chapel (Cappella del Crocifisso),** with some Renaissance tombs and a copy of the 12th-century *Crucifixion* painting that spoke to St. Thomas Aquinas. Next door, the theatrical **sacristy** has a ceiling fresco by Francesco Solimena (1706) and small caskets containing the ashes of Aragónese rulers and courtiers, lining a high shelf. What acts like a right transept was actually a preexisting church grafted onto this one, the **Chiesa Antica di Sant'Angelo a Morfisa,** today an oversize chapel containing finely carved Renaissance tombs.

On Piazza San Domenico is another of Naples's baroque spires, this one a 1737 confection called the **Guglia di San Domenico** by Domenico Antonio Vaccaro.

Piazza San Domenico Maggiore. ✆ **081-459188.** Free admission. Daily 8:30am–noon and 3:30–7pm. Metro: Piazza Cavour.

San Lorenzo Maggiore ★ CHURCH The most beautiful of Naples's medieval churches, San Lorenzo is built over a basilica from the 6th century A.D. The church was rebuilt in 1270 by Carlo I d'Angiò and his successor in Gothic style; its facade is baroque as the original was partially destroyed by an earthquake. The interior is airy and holds innumerable works of art, including 13th- and 14th-century **frescoes,** as well as beautiful **altars** and monumental tombs. From the 14th-century cloister, enter the **Greek and Roman excavations** ★, where you'll see a slice of the city's layers of construction, from the Roman Macellum (the market), to a Paleo-Christian basilica, to a medieval building, to, finally, the existing buildings. It's a great place to visit with children in tow.

Piazza San Gaetano, Via Tribunali 316. www.sanlorenzomaggiorenapoli.it. ✆ **081-290580.** Free admission to church. Mon–Sat 8am–noon and 5–7pm. Excavations: Admission 4€. Mon–Sat 9:30am–5:30pm; Sun 9:30am–1:30pm. Metro: Piazza Cavour.

A detail from the exterior of San Lorenzo Maggiore.

Santa Chiara ★ CHURCH Standing on a *palazzo*-flanked street, this church was built on orders from Robert the Wise, king of Naples, in the early 14th century. It became the church for the House of Anjou. Although World War II bombers heavily blasted it, it has been restored to its original Gothic appearance. The light-filled interior is lined with chapels, each of which contains some leftover bit of sculpture or fresco from the medieval church. The best three pieces line the wall behind the High Altar. In the center is the towering multilevel tomb of Robert the Wise d'Angiò, sculpted by Giovanni and Pacio Bertini in 1343. To its right is Tino di Camaino's tomb of Charles, duke of Calabria; on the left is the 1399

Wine Tasting

The wines produced in the harsh, hot landscapes of Campania seem stronger, rougher, and, in many cases, more powerful than those grown in gentler climes. Among the most famous are the Lacryma Christi (Tears of Christ), a white that grows in the volcanic soil near Naples, Herculaneum, and Pompeii; Taurasi, a potent red; and Greco di Tufo, a pungent white laden with the odors of apricots and apples. One of the most frequently visited vineyards is **Mastroberardino,** Via Manfredi 75–81, Atripalda, Avellino (www.mastroberardino.com; ✆ **0825-614111**), which is reached by taking the A16 east from Naples. If you'd like to spend a day outside the city, driving through the countryside and doing a little wine tasting, call to make an appointment.

A typically narrow alley in Naples.

monument to Mary of Durazza. In the choir behind the altar are more salvaged medieval remnants of frescoes and statuary, including bits of a Giotto *Crucifixion*.

You have to exit the church and walk down its left flank to enter this next sight—the 14th-century **Cloisters of the Order of the Clares (Chiostri dell'Ordine di Santa Chiara)** ★★★. In 1742, Domenico Antonio Vaccaro lined the four paths to the center of the cloisters' courtyard with columns that are plated with colorfully painted majolica tiles. Interspersed among the columns are tiled benches. In the **museum** are a scattering of Roman and medieval remains.

On the piazza outside is one of Naples's several baroque spires, the **Guglia dell'Immacolata,** a tall pile of statues and reliefs sculpted in 1750.

Church: Via Santa Chiara 49. © **081-7971235.** Free admission. Mon and Wed–Sat 7:30am–1pm and 4:30–8pm. Cloisters and museum: Admission 5€. Mon and Wed–Sat 9:30am–5:30pm; Sun 10am–2:30pm. Metro: Dante.

Where to Eat

Neapolitans love to eat and love their traditions: Seafood and pizza dominate the scene, yet many traditional local dishes are vegetarian or meat based. Neapolitan desserts are famously sweet and more-ish; **Scaturchio,** Piazza San Domenico Maggiore 19 (www.scaturchio.it; © **081-5517031**), makes some of the best *sfogliatelle* (traditional warm, ricotta-filled pastries) in town and also serves excellent coffee. Naples's ice-cream parlors sell some of the best gelato in the country; try **Gelateria della Scimmia,** Piazza della Carità 4 (© **081-5520272**).

EXPENSIVE

Dora ★ NEAPOLITAN/FISH The prices at this tiny restaurant may be on the steep side, but it has something of a cult following among both locals and visitors and is well worth a visit if fish and seafood is your thing. Tables are always crammed with diners feasting on the freshest of the day's catch featured in simple local dishes such as *spaghetti alle vongole* (one of the best versions we have ever eaten) and the spectacular *linguine alla Dora* (with prawns, rock lobster, squid, clams, and cherry tomatoes), a meal in itself. For *secondo,* there is delicious *fritto misto* and perfectly grilled catch of the day.

Via Ferdinando Palasciano 30. ✆ **081-680519.** Reservations essential. *Secondi* 22€–40€. AE, DC, MC, V. Mon–Sat 1–3:30pm and 7:45pm–midnight (Sept–May open for Sun lunch and closed Mon lunch). Bus 27, 28, or 140.

George's ★★ GOURMET NEAPOLITAN A temple of good taste, located on the top floor of Grand Hotel Parker's, this place has a view second to none. You can watch the sun set on the gulf as your taste buds are pampered by Chef Baciòt's preparations, many of which are imaginative revisitations of traditional Neapolitan dishes. The seasonal menu might include *pizzelle foglia* (eggless homemade leaves of pasta with sautéed garden vegetables), *pezzogna arrosto in guazzetto di tartufi* (local fish in a light sauce with truffles), and *costolette d'agnello con le melanzane* (lamb with eggplants). The extensive wine list features only Italian wines including a large section devoted to Campania.

Corso Vittorio Emanuele 135. www.grandhotelparkers.com. ✆ **081-7612474.** Reservations required. *Secondi* 22€–30€. AE, DC, MC, V. Daily 12:30–2:30pm and 8–10:30pm. Bus: C24 or C27 to Via Tasso-Corso Vittorio Emanuele II. Metro: Piazza Amedeo.

La Cantinella ★ NEAPOLITAN/SEAFOOD A classic address in Naples, this local favorite attracts a chic clientele. The stylish old-fashioned nightclub atmosphere doubles with top-quality, mostly traditional Neapolitan food. *Primi* such as *pappardelle sotto il cielo di Napoli* (homemade pasta with zucchini, prawns, and green tomatoes) are delicious and we particularly enjoyed the creamy *risotto alla zucca, champagne e provola* (with pumpkin, champagne, and *provola* cheese). For your *secondo,* the *frittura* (deep-fried seafood) is a winner, but there are also classics such as steak and lobster. Don't miss the delicious homemade desserts such as superb chocolate soufflé. The huge tome of a wine list features wines from all over Italy and beyond. The adjacent piano bar stays open with live music well into the early hours.

Via Cuma 42. ✆ **081-7648684.** Reservations required. *Secondi* 19€–30€. AE, DC, MC, V. Mon–Sat 12:30–3pm and 7:30–11:30pm. Closed 3 weeks in Aug. Bus: C25, 140, or 152 .

La Stanza del Gusto ★★ CREATIVE NEAPOLITAN Extrovert chef Mario Avallone's double-face restaurant has become something of a temple of "new" Neapolitan cuisine and its dual identity means that you can eat either a modest meal for under 20€ or splash out on a gourmet experience. The casual, ground-floor cheese bar offers soups, salads, and the odd hot choice along with a wonderful selection of cheeses and cold cuts. In the first-floor Stanza del Gusto, the atmosphere is more serious and it is here that the chef's creative flair is on show. The inspired, regularly changing menus are strictly based around locally sourced ingredients which Avallone uses in new ways such as the *capesante e carciofi* (scallops and artichokes) and the *variazione di baccalà* (salt cod prepared in several different modes). If you are prepared to trust the chef, we recommend the 65€ tasting menu *a sopresa* (surprise).

Via Santa Maria di Costantinopoli 100. www.lastanzadelgusto.com. ✆ **081-401578.** Reservations required for the Stanza del Gusto (upstairs restaurant). *Secondi* (upstairs restaurant)

14€–20€. AE, DC, MC, V. Tues–Sat noon–11:30pm; Sun noon–3pm. Upstairs restaurant Tues–Sat 7–11pm. Closed 3 weeks in Aug. Metro: Piazza Dante.

Rosiello NEAPOLITAN/SEAFOOD This elegant restaurant is very popular not only for the quality of its cuisine, but also for the exceptional sea views from its terrace. Locals will line up for an outdoor table from spring to fall, so reserve in advance. You will delight in the excellent dishes such as *risotto alla pescatora* (with seafood) and *scialatielli con melanzane e provola* (fresh pasta with local cheese and eggplant), as well as the perfectly fried calamari and the *pezzogna all'acquapazza* (fish in a light tomato broth).

Via Santo Strato 10. www.ristoranterosiello.it. ✆ **081-7691288.** Reservations recommended. *Secondi* 10€–25€. AE, DC, MC, V. Thurs–Tues 12:30–4pm and 7:30pm–midnight (May–Sept daily). Closed 2 weeks each in Jan and Aug. Bus: C3 to Mergellina (end of line), and then 140.

MODERATE

Amici Miei ITALIAN/NEAPOLITAN If you are tired of seafood, this restaurant, located on the hill between Chiaia and the Quartieri Spagnoli, is for you. The menu focuses on meat—as in goose, lamb, pork—as well as on vegetarian choices. We recommend the homemade *fusilli alle melanzane* (with eggplant), the *pappardelle al sugo di agnello* (fresh large noodles with a lamb sauce), and the *costine e salsicce alla brace* (chargrilled lamb ribs and sausages), but anything on the seasonal menu is good. Just try not to fill up on the tasty homemade bread before your meal.

Via Monte di Dio 77. www.ristoranteamicimiei.com. ✆ **081-7646063.** Reservations required. *Secondi* 12€–13€. AE, DC, MC, V. Tues–Sat 12:30–3:30pm and 7:30–11:30pm; Sun 12:30–3:30pm. Closed July–Aug. Tram: 1 to Piazza dei Martiri.

Antonio e Antonio PIZZA/NEAPOLITAN Located on the beautiful *lungomare* (oceanfront), this restaurant is popular with locals, many of whom come for its youthful atmosphere. The two Antonios who created this restaurant grew up and were trained in two of Naples's most famous, historic restaurants, Zi Teresa and Giuseppone a Mare. The open kitchen zips out 40 types of pizza and all the great Neapolitan classics, including *fusilli di pasta fresca ai pomodorini del Vesuvio* (with super tasty cherry tomatoes from Mount Vesuvius) and *polipetti affogati in cassuola* (squid cooked in an earthenware pot with tomatoes and herbs). Appetizers and side dishes are served buffet style. A second location in Chiaia is located on the slopes of the Vomero, at Via Francesco Crispi 89 (✆ **081-682528**).

Via Partenope 24. www.antonioeantonio.net. ✆ **081-2451987.** Reservations recommended. *Secondi* 8€–17€; pizza 6€–13€. AE, DC, MC, V. Tues–Sun noon–1am. Bus: 152.

Ciro a Mergellina ★ NEAPOLITAN/PIZZA/SEAFOOD This historic restaurant is a favorite destination for tourists and locals alike, who come for the seafood—sautéed mussels and small clams, pasta dishes, and excellent pizza made with *mozzarella di bufala* (buffalo mozzarella)—and for the excellent service. We also love the seafood salad appetizer, *spaghetti alle vongole* (with baby clams), *pasta all'aragosta* (with lobster), and *spigola fritta* (deep-fried sea bass). The wonderful, homemade ice cream comes in a variety of flavors.

Via Mergellina 18. www.ciroamergellina.it. ✆ **081-681780.** Reservations recommended. *Secondi* 8€–18€. AE, DC, MC, V. Tues–Sun 11:30am–11:30pm. Bus: 140. Metro: Mergellina. Tram: 1.

Europeo di Mattozzi ★★ NEAPOLITAN/PIZZA/SEAFOOD This landmark of Neapolitan dining is one of our favorite places to eat in Naples. The chef/owner creates a welcoming atmosphere and offers a winning interpretation of traditional dishes. Among the *primi,* you can have a very tasty *zuppa di cannellini e cozze* (bean and mussel soup) or *pasta e patate con provola* (pasta and potatoes with melted local cheese); for a *secondo,* you could try *ricciola all'acquapazza* (a local fish in a light tomato and herb broth) or *stoccafisso alla pizzaiola* (dried codfish in a tomato, garlic, and oregano sauce). Pizza is also on the menu and is very well prepared, as are the desserts, including hometown favorites such as *babà* and *pastiera.*

Via Marchese Campodisola 4. www.mattozzieuropeo.com. ✆ **081-5521323.** Reservations required. *Secondi* 12€–18€. AE, DC, MC, V. Mon–Wed noon–3:30pm; Thurs–Sat noon–3:30pm and 8pm–midnight. Closed 2 weeks in Aug. Bus: R2 or R3 to Piazza Trieste e Trento.

La Bersagliera NEAPOLITAN/FISH The food at the elegant, Belle Epoque Bersagliera may not be the very best in town, but the setting is a total delight and we recommend it for that: With its waterside terrace overlooking the marina and Castel dell'Ovo, it is a perfect place for a lazy lunch in warm weather. The classic starter here is *zuppa di cozze e vongole* (mussel and clam soup) but the pasta with baby octopus, tomato, and olives is also good and you can follow this with an excellent *fritto misto* (deep-fried seafood medley).

Borgo Marinaro 10–11. www.labersagliera.it. ✆ **081-7646016.** Reservations recommended Fri–Sat. *Secondi* 10€–18€. AE, DC, MC, V. Wed–Mon noon–3:30pm and 7:30pm–midnight. Closed 1 week in Jan. Bus: 151.

Mimì alla Ferrovia ★ 🎁 NEAPOLITAN With its walls hung with the photos of past celebrity diners, this is another of Naples's historical landmark restaurants that has a faithful local following. The traditional menu is fish-based (although there is the odd meat choice) and the chef prepares excellent renditions of local favorites, varying according to the season. Depending on the time of year, you'll probably find *scialatielli ai frutti di mare* (eggless homemade pasta with seafood), *polipo alla Luciana* (squid cooked in a pocket with tomato and herbs), *in guazzetto* (squid in a light tomato sauce), and *sartù* (rice with baby meatballs and cheese). Desserts are traditional, too, and include *babà* and *pastiera.*

Via Alfonso d'Aragona 21. ✆ **081-5538525.** Reservations recommended Sat–Sun. *Secondi* 8€–15€. AE, DC, MC, V. Mon–Sat noon–3pm and 7–11:30pm. Metro: Piazza Garibaldi.

San Ferdinando 🎁 NEAPOLITAN The handwritten menu card at this delightful family-run restaurant changes daily but features superb *primi* such as *paccheri con calamaretti, caperi e olive nere* (pasta tubes with baby squid, capers, and black olives) or risotto with asparagus and prawns. Start your meal with the deliciously fresh house antipasti and swill it all down with the house Falanghina wine, served chilled in bright ceramic jugs. We really like the warm, friendly atmosphere of this place, and judging by the photos on the walls, so do the opera stars from nearby San Carlo.

Via Nardones 117 (off Piazza Triests e Trento). www.trattoriasanferdinando.net. ✆ **081-421964.** Reservations recommended. *Secondi* 10€–18€. AE, DC, MC, V. Mon–Sat 12:30–3:30pm; Wed–Fri 7:30–11pm. Bus: R2.

Vadinchenia 🎁 MODERN CAMPANIAN This restaurant, a favorite with local foodies, offers excellent food and professional service in a welcoming setting. The menu is large and varied and includes many unusual and surprisingly delicious offerings, such as the *ricotta farcita* (stuffed ricotta cheese) or deep-fried brie with a blueberry compote appetizers, the *fettuccelle ai totani in salsa agro dolce di agrumi* (pasta with squid in an orange and lemon sauce), and the *filetto di maiale al vin santo* (pork filet in a vin santo sauce). The food is well complemented by the moderately priced wine list.

Via Pontano 21 (off Corso Vittorio Emanuele). ✆ **081-660265.** Reservations required. *Secondi* 7€–15€. AE, DC, MC, V. Mon–Sat 12:30–3pm and 7:30–11:30pm; Sun 12:30–3pm. Closed Aug and Dec 25. Bus: C24 or C27 to Via Tasso-Corso Vittorio Emanuele II. Metro: Piazza Amedeo.

INEXPENSIVE

Acunzo ★ PIZZA This authentic neighborhood restaurant is often crowded with locals eating pizza with a variety of toppings—the 40-some different choices include *pizza con i fusilli* (with fusilli seasoned with tomatoes, peas, bacon, and mushrooms). Purists may prefer the typical Neapolitan dishes, such as *friarelli* (sautéed broccoli), superb eggplant parmigiano (Parmesan), and *zuppa di fagioli* (cannellini-bean soup). If you are not planning a visit to Sorrento, try the *gnocchi alla Sorrentina* (potato dumplings with tomato sauce and mozzarella)—it is superb.

Via Domenico Cimarosa 60 (off Via Lorenzo Bernini to the south). ✆ **081-5785362.** Reservations recommended for dinner. *Secondi* 6€–20€. AE, DC, MC, V. Mon–Sat 12:30–4pm and 6:30pm–midnight. Funicular: Vomero. Metro: Vanvitelli.

Da Tonino NEAPOLITAN One of the few authentic *osterie* left in Naples, Da Tonino has been run by the same family for over a century, and is consistently loved by locals—and an ever-increasing number of tourists. The interior is cramped and rustic and the menu short on choice, but the atmosphere is friendly and lively and the prices are rock bottom. You can't go wrong with the hearty dishes from the local tradition such as the tasty *ragù* or *seppie in umido* (cuttlefish stewed with tomato). There's also a small but excellent wine list. Prices at dinner are slightly higher than those at lunchtime.

Via Santa Teresa A Chiaia 47. ✆ **081-421533.** Reservations accepted only for large parties. *Secondi* 5€–9€. MC, V. Daily 1–4pm; Fri–Sat 8pm–midnight. Metro: Amedeo.

Ettore NEAPOLITAN/PIZZA This unpretentious, rustic restaurant has an authentic, neighborhood feel to it. It's so popular with locals, in fact, that we advise you to come early to get a seat; tables spill out onto the sidewalk in summer. The menu is simple but varies often, according to the season. The pizza is really excellent and their specialty is *pagnottiello*—calzone filled with mozzarella, ricotta, and prosciutto.

Via Santa Lucia 56. ✆ **081-7640498.** Reservations recommended. *Secondi* 6€–20€. AE, DC, MC, V. Mon–Sat 12:30–3:30pm and 7:30pm–midnight. Bus: C25, 140, or 152.

Hosteria Toledo NEAPOLITAN A picturesque restaurant with a lively atmosphere, the Hosteria Toledo has been serving tasty but inexpensive traditional Neapolitan food to locals and visitors since 1951. We recommend the *ziti al ragù* (pasta with meat and tomato sauce) or *tubettoni con fagioli e cozze* (with beans and mussels) maybe followed by *polipo in guazzetto* (squid in a tomato sauce), or *arrosto di maiale* (pork roast). If you have room left, try one of the luscious desserts, which often include such great classics as *babà* (a sort of brioche with rum) and *pastiera* (a sort of thick, custardy pie).

Vico Giardinetto a Toledo 78. www.hosteriatoledo.it. ✆ **081-421257.** *Secondi* 8€–15€. AE, DC, MC, V. Tues 12:30–3pm; Wed–Mon 12:30–3pm and 7pm–midnight. Bus: R2 to Piazza

Trieste e Trento. Coming from Piazza Trieste e Trento, it's off Via Toledo to the left, across from the Banco di Napoli.

Marino NEAPOLITAN/PIZZA Situated just a few minutes walk from some of the city's glitziest hotels, this homey place is a favorite of ours for its modest, old-fashioned atmosphere (complete with garish lighting), delicious pizza, and good, reasonably priced fish dishes. Antipasti of the day (including wonderfully fresh mozzarella) are served from a counter at the front of the restaurant; you can go up with the waiter and show him what you want. Follow this with one of the traditional *primi* such as spaghetti with mixed seafood or a dish of *polpo alla Luciana* (octopus in a punchy tomato sauce).

Via Santa Lucia 118. ✆ **081-7640280.** *Secondi* 7€–18€. AE, MC, V. Tues–Sun noon–3:30pm and 7:30pm–midnight. Bus: 151.

Pizzeria Da Michele ★★ PIZZA According to the locals, this no-frills place serves the best pizza in town. There are only two types (*margherita* or *marinara*) and the drinks menu runs to just beer, coca-cola, or water, but the *pizze* are enormous and simply delicious. Take a number at the door as you go in and join the inevitable queue; this place is always packed.

Via Sersale 1. www.damichele.net. ✆ **081-5539204.** Pizza 4€–5€. No credit cards. Mon–Sat 11am–11pm. Metro: Garibaldi.

Shopping

Naples is a great source for Italian designer clothes and accessories, as well as for antiques and traditional crafts.

Riviera di Chiaia, Via Calabritto, Via dei Mille, Via Filangeri, Via Poerio, and Piazza dei Martiri in **Chiaia** are where to go for the big-name **Italian fashion** labels, such as Valentino, Versace, Prada, and, of course, Salvatore Ferragamo—a Naples native. The area is also great for exploring the many smaller, independent boutiques and stores that sell men's and women's clothing and accessories.

In the vicinity are old-time local favorites, such as **Marinella,** Via Riviera di Chiaia 287 (✆ 081-7644214), famous for handmade classic and colorful ties; **Aldo Tramontano,** Via Chiaia 149 (✆ 081-414837), for his handbags; and **Mario Talarico,** Vico Due Porte a Toledo 4/b (✆ 081-401979), for his handcrafted umbrellas. You'll also find some of the most reputable **antiques** dealers, such as **Bowinkle,** Piazza dei Martiri 24 (✆ 081-7644344), and **Navarra,** Piazza dei Martiri (✆ 081-7643595), but also **Maurizio Brandi,** Via Domenico Morelli 9 (✆ 081-7643882). Good addresses for antique prints and books are **Libreria Colonnese,** Via San Pietro a Majella 32 (✆ 081-459858); **Dante e Descartes,** Via Mezzocannone 75 (✆ 081-5515368); and **Colonnese,** Via Carlo Poerio 92 (✆ 081-7642627).

In the **Vomero,** the best shopping is centered on Via Scarlatti.

For midprice fashions and some specialty stores, try the popular **Via Toledo/Via Roma** in the Quartieri Spagnoli/historical center. Here you will find the historic chocolate factory **Gay-Odin,** Via Toledo 214 and Via Toledo 427 (www.gay-odin.it; ✆ 081/417-843). Near here you will also find the elegant shops of the **Galleria Umberto I,** such as **Ascione 1855** (✆ 081-421111) and its **cameo** workshop, where you can observe the delicate process of carving agate and coral, and also purchase unique jewelry.

The best places to shop for traditional crafts are in the historic district. Head for **Via San Gregorio Armeno** if you are looking for a *presepio* or Christmas crib. Most of the traditional workshops are located in or around this street, but don't confuse the real thing with the mass-produced versions. Inevitably, the number of true artisans is in sharp decline, but it is worth seeking these craftsmen out and buying from them even though prices will be higher. The most reputable workshops are **Gambardella Pastori,** Via San Gregorio Armeno 40 (✆ 081-5517107); **Giuseppe Ferrigno,** Via San Gregorio Armeno 10 (✆ 081-5523148); and **Amendola,** Via San Gregorio Armeno 51 (✆ 081-5514899).

Entertainment & Nightlife

A warm southern city, Naples is best experienced outdoors, and the Neapolitans make the best of the balmy summer evenings by passing the time on the terraces of the city's many popular cafes. One of our favorites is the elegant **Gran Caffè Gambrinus,** Via Chiaia 1, in Piazza Trento e Trieste (**✆ 081-417582**). The oldest cafe in Naples, its original Liberty-style interior was decorated by Antonio Curri in the 1860s. Another very popular spot is **La Caffetteria,** Piazza dei Martiri 25 (**✆ 081-7644243**), frequented by a chic, local crowd who come here for evening *aperitivi.*

OPERA & CLASSICAL MUSIC Try and catch a performance at **Teatro San Carlo,** Via San Carlo 98/f (www.teatrosancarlo.it; **✆ 081-7972412** or 081-7972331), a world-class venue with a consistently high-level program. Performances take place Tuesday through Sunday, December through June. Tickets cost between 30€ and 100€; you'll get a 10% discount with an Artecard.

Classical music fans should also check out the **Associazione Alessandro Scarlatti,** Piazza dei Martiri 58 (www.associazionescarlatti.it; **✆ 081-406011**), which also organizes a concert series at Castel Sant'Elmo; ticket prices range from 15€ to 25€, with a 20% discount given to those with an Artecard.

BARS & CLUBS Naples is home to a growing number of excellent *enoteche,* or wine bars, where, aside from a good choice of wines both by the glass and by the bottle, you can also order food. We recommend the quiet **Berevino,** Via Sebastiano 62 (www.berevino.org; **✆ 081-0605688;** closed Mon), as well as **Barrique,** Piazzetta Ascensione 9 (**✆ 081-662721;** closed Mon), and **Enoteca Belledonne,** Vico Belledonne a Chiaia 18 (www.enotecabelledonne.com; **✆ 081-403162;** closed Sun).

This is a port, a cosmopolitan city, and a university town all rolled into one, so the Neapolitan nighttime scene is eclectic and lively. Trendy bars and cafes stay open at least until 2am every day of the week, while clubs stay open even later—usually until 4 or 5am—but often only from Thursday to Saturday. Good places to grab a drink include the sleek and exotic **Miami Bar Room,** Via Morghen 68C (**✆ 081-2298332**), while upmarket **S'move,** Vico dei Sospiri 10A (**✆ 081-7645813**), is a good place for drinks and dancing.

For jazz, head up to Vomero and the small but friendly **Around Midnight,** Via Bonito 32A (www.aroundmidnight.it; **✆ 333-7005230**). For live Neapolitan bands, check out **Vibes Cafè,** Via San Giovanni Maggiore

Pignatelli 10 (✆ **081-5513984**), where you can dance inside or outside on the terrace in summer. **Rising South,** Via San Sebastiano 19 (✆ **335-8790428**), and **Kestè,** Largo San Giovanni Maggiore 26 (www.keste.it; ✆ **081-5513984**), are favored by a younger crowd.

An elegant nightclub worth checking out is **Chez Moi,** Via del Parco Margherita 13 (✆ **081-407526**), in the Riviera di Chiaia. Nearby **La Mela,** Via dei Mille (✆ **081-4010270**), is also worth a visit.

In summer, the hottest clubbing action moves to the beach, and although these waterside nightspots are a bit of a way from the city center (the easiest way is by taxi), the cool factor justifies the effort to get there. In Bagnoli, the **Arenile,** Via Coroglio 14B (www.arenilereload.com; ✆ **338-8817715**), is open from May to October and is the nearest beach club to the city. **Vibes on the Beach,** Via Miseno 52, Capo Miseno (✆ **081-5232828**), is a cool, jazzy place open daily June to September, while **Nabilah,** at Via Spiaggia Romana 15, Fusaro (www.nabilah.it; ✆ **081-8689433**), is the chicest of them all and is open Friday to Sunday May through September.

For a more specifically gay-men-only spot, head for **Bar B,** Via Giovanni Manna, off Via Duomo (✆ **081-287681**), a famous gay sauna that turns into a disco on Thursday and Saturday nights. For a mixed/gay-male scene, check out **Sputnik Club** at Via Santa Teresa degli Scalzi 154 bis (✆ **081-19813222**).

Where to Stay

EXPENSIVE

Grand Hotel Parker's ★ A landmark building in Liberty (Italian Art Nouveau) style, this glorious villa retains most of its original architectural features and has splendid public spaces. The spacious guest rooms fronting the bay share the same spectacular views as the public areas and are furnished with elegant period pieces. The suites are really elegant duplex apartments on two levels but the back rooms are unremarkable and overlook the garage. The fine spa offers hydrotherapy treatments, all kinds of massages, and includes a sauna and Turkish bath. Elegant, rooftop **George's** is widely considered to be one of Naples's best restaurants.

Corso Vittorio Emanuele 135 (up the cliff from Riviera di Chiaia), 80121 Napoli. www.grandhotelparkers.com. ✆ **081-7612474.** 82 units. 300€ double; from 350€ suite. Rates include buffet breakfast. Children 1 and under stay free in parent's room. Internet specials available. AE, DC, MC, V. Parking 20€–30€. Bus: C24 or C27 to Via Tasso-Corso Vittorio Emanuele II. Metro: Piazza Amedeo. **Amenities:** Restaurant; bar; babysitting; concierge; health club; room service; smoke-free rooms; spa. *In room:* A/C, TV/VCR/DVD, fax, minibar.

Grand Hotel Vesuvio ★★ ☺ This elegant hotel may charge steep prices, but it is arguably the best in Naples. Superior rooms and suites have large balconies from which you can enjoy some of the best views in the city, and even the standard doubles are very roomy and come furnished with special details such as linen sheets and extra-firm mattresses. The breakfast buffet—served in a delightful bright room with a view of the harbor—is superb. There is a wonderful spa, and the hotel's gourmet restaurant, the recently refurbished Caruso Roof Garden, is a splendid place to enjoy both superb food and fabulous views.

Via Partenope 45 (off Via Santa Lucia by Castel dell'Ovo), 80121 Napoli. www.vesuvio.it. ✆ **081-7640044.** Fax 081-7644483. 160 units. 230€–460€ double; from 600€ suite. Rates include buffet breakfast. Children 2 and under stay free in parent's room. Internet specials available. AE, DC, MC, V. Parking 25€. Bus: C25, 140, or 152. **Amenities:** 2 restaurants; bar; babysitting; concierge; fitness center and spa; pool (for a fee); room service; smoke-free rooms. *In room:* A/C, TV/VCR/DVD, minibar, Wi-Fi (3€/30 min.; 10€/8 hr.).

Hotel Excelsior ★★ ☺ This Starwood property has more of a feeling of old-fashioned glamour than its sister hotel, the Vesuvius. Prices are slightly lower, but it shares the same spectacular waterfront location and gorgeous views and also has a splendid roof garden. The bedrooms are all a good size and come with all the amenities you would expect for this price, including fine linen sheets and marble bathrooms. Front-facing rooms overlook the Castel dell'Ovo while ones on the side have full-on views of Vesuvius. The rooftop Terrazza restaurant is a splendid place for a celebratory gourmet meal, and guests can use the spa facilities at the Vesuvius (for a fee).

Via Partenope 48 (off Via Santa Lucia, by Castel dell'Ovo), 80121 Napoli. www.excelsior.it. ✆ **081-7640111.** Fax 081-7649743. 121 units. 200€–400€ double; from 550€ suite. Rates include buffet breakfast. Children 2 and under stay free in parent's room. AE, DC, MC, V. Parking 23€. Bus: C25, 140, or 152. **Amenities:** Restaurant; bar; babysitting; concierge; health club; room service; smoke-free rooms. *In room:* A/C, TV/VCR/DVD, minibar.

Romeo If you like your luxury to come with a good dose of high-tech style, the sleek Romeo is the hotel for you. Situated on the edge of the old city, it is housed in a modern building overlooking the new tourist port, an area which is a bit shady at night but which is at present well on its way into a new development project. The open-plan public spaces on the ground floor are filled with the owner's impressive collection of contemporary art plus some priceless antiques. The super-contemporary bedrooms and slick, glassed-in bathrooms (some shower-only) come with every conceivable gadget including a sheet and pillow menu and Nespresso coffee machines. Dining options include a sushi bar and the top-notch Il Commandante restaurant. The fabulous new spa offers all sorts of treatments and there's a pool on the roof

Via Cristoforo Colombo 45, 80132 Naples. www.romeohotel.it. ✆ **081-0175008.** Fax 081-0175999. 83 units. 240€–300€ double. Rates include breakfast. AE, DC, MC, V. Parking 36€ in nearby garage. Metro: Univerista. **Amenities:** 2 restaurants; bar; concierge; fitness center and spa; pool; room service; smoke-free rooms. *In room:* A/C, TV/DVD, minibar, Wi-Fi (free).

MODERATE

Chiaia Hotel de Charme ★ Elder sister to the Decumani Hotel de Charme (see below), this cozy place enjoys an equally good, if a little more upmarket, location on smart, pedestrian-only Via Chiaia. It occupies the first floor of a building with a colorful past which stands on a quiet courtyard: It was once a brothel and the price list is still on display! The reception area, sitting areas, and breakfast room are done out in warm, welcoming colors and the bedrooms are equally inviting. Superior rooms have big bathrooms, some with Jacuzzi tubs (others, shower only). Breakfast is excellent and complimentary. Neapolitan pastries are laid out in the sitting room in the afternoon.

Via Chiaia 216, 80132 Napoli. www.hotelchiaia.it. ✆ **081-415555.** Fax 081-422344. 33 units. 145€–165€ double. Rates include buffet breakfast. Children 1 and under stay free in parent's room. AE, DC, MC, V. Parking 18€ in nearby garage. Bus: R2. **Amenities:** Bar; concierge. *In room:* A/C, TV, minibar, Wi-Fi (free).

Costantinopoli 104 ★ Located in the heart of the historical center, this charming small hotel is one of our favorites in the city, and occupies a 19th-century Italian Art Nouveau palace that once belonged to a marquis. Once inside the tall gates, you will find a true refuge from the city's noise and grime. Public spaces have the atmosphere of a palatial private home, from the living room with its fireplace to the private courtyard with palm trees, chaise longues, and a bean-shaped swimming pool. Some guest rooms open onto the terrace where breakfast is served in fair weather, and others have private balconies. All are individually decorated with modern furnishings and hardwood floors or hand-painted tiles: The suites have Jacuzzi tubs. Breakfast is a treat.

Via Santa Maria di Costantinopoli 104 (off Piazza Bellini), 80134 Napoli. www.costantinopoli104.com. ✆ **081-5571035.** Fax 081-5571051. 19 units. 160€ double; 210€ suite. Rates include buffet breakfast. AE, DC, MC, V. Parking 25€. Metro: Piazza Dante. **Amenities:** Babysitting; concierge; Internet (free); pool; room service; smoke-free rooms. *In room:* A/C, TV, Internet, minibar.

Decumani Hotel de Charme The palatial home of the last bishop of the Bourbon kingdom, Cardinal Sisto Riario Sforza, was recently renovated as an elegant and moderately priced hotel. The good-size rooms (some shower only) are furnished with period furniture and a few antiques, and many feature original architectural details and decorations. The location—just off the Spaccanapoli—is great if you want to be in the thick of things.

Via San Giovanni Maggiore Pignatelli 15 (off Via Benedetto Croce, btw. Via Santa Chiara and Via Mezzocannone), 80134 Napoli. www.decumani.it. ✆ **081-5518188.** Fax 081-5518188. 22 units. 124€–144€ double. MC, V. Rates includes breakfast. Children 4–12 and under 12€; children 3 and under stay free in parent's room. Internet specials available. AE, MC, V. Parking 25€ in nearby garage. Metro: Piazza Dante. *In room:* A/C, TV, minibar, Wi-Fi (free).

Hotel Majestic Popular with Italian businesspeople and travelers alike, this hotel is located at the end of the elegant shopping strip in the lower part of Chiaia and offers upscale accommodations. The large guest rooms are decorated with low-key elegance, sporting hardwood floors, streamlined modern furniture, and marble bathrooms. Many of the rooms afford great views of the bay. **La Giara,** the hotel's restaurant, serves good, creative food.

Largo Vasto a Chiaia 68 (off Riviera di Chiaia), 80121 Napoli. www.majestic.it. ✆ **081-416500.** Fax 081-410145. 112 units. 160€–300€ double; 300€–450€ suite. Rates include buffet breakfast. Children 2 and under stay free in parent's room. Internet specials available. AE, DC, MC, V. Parking 25€. Metro: Piazza Amedeo. **Amenities:** Restaurant; bar; babysitting; concierge; room service. *In room:* A/C, TV/VCR, minibar.

Hotel Miramare ★ Located on the waterfront overlooking the bay and Vesuvius and originally a private villa built in 1914, this small, elegant hotel offers excellent value and warm service. The public areas are still decorated in Liberty style, but guest rooms have been renovated, each with its own whimsical assortment of furniture. The attentive family management is reflected in such little touches as cool linen sheets in the summer, and you will be offered an *aperitivo* in the evening. The rooms overlooking the sea have splendid views: We recommend the large deluxe rooms with large balconies. In clement weather, breakfast is served on the roof terrace overlooking the bay.

Via Nazario Sauro 24 (off Via Santa Lucia, by Castel dell'Ovo), 80132 Napoli. www.hotelmiramare.com. ✆ **081-7647589.** Fax 081-7640775. 18 units. 185€–299€ double. Rates include buffet breakfast. Children 5 and under stay free in parent's room. Weekend and Internet specials available. AE, DC, MC, V. Parking 20€ in nearby garage. Bus: 152. **Amenities:** Bar; airport pickup (40€); babysitting; concierge; room service. *In room:* A/C, TV/VCR (free videos in lobby), minibar, Wi-Fi (free).

Hotel Palazzo Alabardieri ★ A stylish hotel with a great, central location, the Alabardieri is housed in the ancient cloister of what was once the convent of Santa Caterina a Chiaia. Sleek marble floors in the public areas contrast the warm hardwood floors in the guest rooms, which are furnished with period furniture and color coordinated in earth tones and pastel colors. We particularly like the junior suites with their stylish furnishings and designer accents. All units come with good-size marble bathrooms.

Via Alabardieri 38 (off Riviera di Chiaia), 80121 Napoli. www.palazzoalabardieri.it. ✆ **081-415278.** Fax 081-401478. 33 units. 190€–220€ double; 320€ junior suite. Rates include buffet breakfast. Children 2 and under stay free in parent's room; children ages 3–11 stay in parent's room for 20€ each. Internet specials available. AE, DC, MC, V. Parking 30€. Metro: Piazza Amedeo. **Amenities:** Bar; babysitting; concierge; room service. *In room:* A/C, TV, Wi-Fi (free), minibar.

San Francesco al Monte You cannot beat the atmosphere of this elegant hotel housed in an ex-Franciscan convent, nor the hillside location that overlooks the Riviera di Chiaia; the views are quite spectacular, particularly from the roof terrace with its heart-shaped swimming pool. The tastefully furnished guest rooms (some with just shower) overlook the bay and occupy the surprisingly roomy former monk's cells; they have tiled floors and lots of wood, and a few feature original architectural details. The hotel's restaurant, **Terrazza dei Barbanti,** offers a creative take on local dishes along with matchless views.

Corso Vittorio Emanuele 328 (up the cliff from Riviera di Chiaia), 80135 Napoli. www.sanfrancescoalmonte.it. ✆ **081-4239111.** Fax 081-4239471. 45 units. 195€–225€ double; 270€ suite. Rates include buffet breakfast. AE, DC, MC, V. Parking 25€. Metro: Piazza Amedeo. Amenities: Restaurant; bar; babysitting; pool; room service; smoke-free rooms. In room: A/C, TV/DVD, Internet (5€ for 30 min.), minibar.

Starhotel Terminus A member of the Italian Starhotel group, this hotel offers elegant accommodations with full amenities for both business and leisure travelers and excellent service. The spacious guest rooms are stylishly appointed, with warm wood, modern furniture, tasteful carpeting and fabrics, and elegant bathrooms. The "executive" doubles have extras such as trouser presses, a second TV in the bathroom, a cutting-edge CD/DVD system, and a complimentary tea/coffee/hot chocolate tray. The panoramic restaurant and bar on the roof garden have become quite a hit with Neapolitan socialites.

Piazza Garibaldi 91 (beside Stazione Centrale), 80142 Napoli. www.starhotels.it. ✆ **081-7793111.** Fax 081-206689. 173 units. 160€–210€ double; 250€ junior suite; 300€ suite. Rates include buffet breakfast. Internet specials available. Children 11 and under stay free in parent's room. AE, DC, MC, V. Free parking in garage. Metro: Garibaldi. Small pets accepted. **Amenities:** Restaurant; bar; babysitting; concierge; fitness room; room service. *In room:* A/C, TV, minibar, Wi-Fi (5.50€ per hour.).

Una Hotel Napoli ★ On the opposite end of Piazza Garibaldi to the Terminus (see above), this stylish, contemporary hotel occupies a 19th-century *palazzo.* Located near both the Stazione Centrale and the Circumvesuviana stations, its pleasant public spaces include a panoramic roof terrace with a trendy bar and restaurant. The spacious guest rooms are stylish, with a streamlined modern design and neutral color scheme. The good-size bathrooms are ultramodern.

Piazza Garibaldi 9 (opposite Stazione Centrale), 80142 Napoli. www.unahotels.it. ✆ **081-5636901.** Fax 081-5636972. 89 units. 115€–160€ double; 330€ suite. Rates include buffet breakfast. Internet specials available. AE, DC, MC, V. Free parking in garage. Metro: Garibaldi. **Amenities:** Restaurant; bar; concierge; room service. *In room:* A/C, TV, minibar, Wi-Fi (6€ per hour.).

INEXPENSIVE

Capella Vecchia 11 There is such a thing as a good value hotel in Chiaia as we found out when we visited this delightful little B&B situated just off elegant Piazza dei Martiti. Run by a young, superfriendly couple who will help you find your way around the city, it has six bright, comfortable bedrooms with mosaic bathrooms (shower only). You can choose to have breakfast in your room or at a big table in the communal area. There is an Internet point. This is a great choice if you are driving; there is a big car park almost next door.

Via Santa Maria a Cappella Vecchia 11, 80121 Napoli. www.cappellavecchia11.it. ✆ **081-2405117.** Fax 081-2455338. 6 units. 90€–100€ double. Rates include buffet breakfast. AE, MC, V. Parking 18€. Metro: Piazza Amedeo. **Amenities:** Internet. *In room:* A/C, TV, minibar, Wi-Fi (free).

Hotel Europeo/Europeo Flowers It would be difficult to find nicer budget-friendly accommodations in Naples. Close to Spaccanapoli and all the central sights, this modest hotel (technically two) offers good-size rooms that are adequate and tastefully appointed. The catch? It doesn't have public spaces, and it is on the fourth and fifth floors of a residential building. If you can do without breakfast and a lounge, the only drawback is that you'll need a small reserve of .10€ coins to operate the elevator. The Europeo Flowers has A/C and the largest rooms, which can accommodate up to four people.

Via Mezzocannone 109 and 109/c (btw. Corso Umberto and Via San Biagio dei Librai), 80134 Napoli. www.sea-hotels.com. ✆ **081-5517254.** Fax 081-5522212. 17 units. 105€ double; 110€ triple; 114€–130€ quad. Internet specials available. Children 6 and under stay free in parent's room. AE, DC, MC, V. Parking 25€ in nearby garage. Metro: Piazza Dante. Small pets accepted. **Amenities:** Concierge; Wi-Fi (free). *In room:* A/C, TV, minibar (in some).

Hotel Il Convento ★ ☺ This family-run hotel, housed in a 17th-century former convent, offers pleasant accommodations at moderate prices in the heart of Naples. The pastel-hued guest rooms feature original architectural details such as wooden beams and brick arches; two top-floor junior suites have delightful private roof gardens. There are also two family rooms with loft bedrooms. All have modern bathrooms.

Via Speranzella 137/a (2 short blocks west of Via Toledo/Via Roma), 80134 Napoli. www.hotelilconvento.com. ✆ **081-403977.** Fax 081-400332. 14 units. 83€–110€ double; 125€ junior suite. Rates include buffet breakfast. Children 2 and under stay free in parent's room. Internet and family specials available. AE, DC, MC, V. Parking 15€ in nearby garage. Bus: R2 to Piazza Municipio. Small pets allowed. **Amenities:** Bar; concierge; fitness room and sauna; room service. *In room:* A/C, satellite TV/VCR, minibar.

Hotel Piazza Bellini This stylish, contemporary hotel occupies an elegant gray-and-white 16th-century *palazzo* with a great location right on trendy Piazza Bellini. We like the minimalist yet welcoming rooms with their warm hardwood floors and designer furniture: Some have balconies overlooking the buzzy piazza,

Bags of dried pasta hang in the doorway of a Naples shop.

four others have big private terraces equipped with sun beds and showers. The duplex rooms are good for families. Bathrooms (some with shower only) are slick and modern. There are three Internet points in the sitting room, and in summer, you can sit out and enjoy breakfast or a drink in the lovely atrium.

Via Costantinioli 101, 80134 Napoli. www.hotelpiazzabellini.com. ✆ **081-451732.** Fax 081 4420107. 48 units. 100€–150€ double. AE, DC, MC, V. Metro: Piazza Dante or Piazza Cavour. **Amenities:** Bar; concierge; Wi-Fi (free). *In room:* A/C, TV, Internet (free), minibar.

Hotel Rex ☺ Housed in a 19th-century palace, steps from the top-notch hotels of Via Partenope (see above), this hotel offers spacious accommodations at moderate prices. Word has gotten out about this family-run spot, and it's very popular, especially with groups, so you must reserve well in advance. Guest rooms are simply but carefully decorated; some come with views over the harbor or Mount Vesuvio, and some come with private balconies. Bathrooms are modern and roomy. A simple continental breakfast, served in your room, is included in the rates. Up to two extra beds can be added to a room for no extra cost.

Via Palepoli 12 (off Via Santa Lucia, by Castel dell'Ovo), 80132 Napoli. www.hotel-rex.it. ✆ **081-7649389.** Fax 081-7649227. 33 units. 150€ double. Rates include continental breakfast. Children 3 and under stay free in parent's room. Internet specials available. AE, DC, MC, V. Parking 20€ in nearby garage. Bus: 152. **Amenities:** Bar; babysitting; concierge. *In room:* A/C, TV, minibar.

Suite Esedra This pleasantly cozy small hotel offers moderately priced rooms in a centrally located aristocratic palace that has been completely restored. Bedrooms with astronomy motifs are tastefully furnished, with excellent care to details; some have sweet little balconies. Of the two suites, Venus offers a fantastic private terrace equipped with a small pool. Breakfast is served in a pleasant common room. The drawback? The thundering traffic on nearby Corso Umberto I.

Via Arnaldo Cantani 12 (btw. Via Nuova Marina and Corso Umberto), 80134 Napoli. www.esedra.hotelsinnapoli.com. ✆/fax **081-5537087.** 17 units. 65€–70€ double. Rates include buffet breakfast. Internet specials available. Children 5 and under stay free in parent's room. AE, DC, MC, V. Parking 15€ in nearby garage. Metro: Piazza Garibaldi or Università. **Amenities:** Bar; concierge; health club. *In room:* A/C, TV, minibar.

THE PHLEGREAN FIELDS & HERCULANEUM

The Phlegrean Fields ★★

Named the "burning fields" thanks to their boiling mud craters, the area known as the Campi Flegrei was highly prized during Greek and Roman times for its hot springs, fertile soil, and secure harbors, and excavations here have brought to light many ruins and archaeological remains. Highlights are the Solfatara, with its lunar landscape and bubbling fumaroles; Pozzuoli, with its amphitheater and temples; Baia with its submerged Roman city; and Cuma, for its Sybilla Cave and Greek ruins.

TREADING LIGHTLY ON mount vesuvius

Stand at the bottom of the great market-place of Pompeii, and look up at the silent streets . . . over the broken houses with their inmost sanctuaries open to the day, away to Mount Vesuvius, bright and snowy in the peaceful distance; and lose all count of time, and heed of other things, in the strange and melancholy sensation of seeing the Destroyed and the Destroyer making this quiet picture in the sun.

—Charles Dickens, *Pictures from Italy*

A volcano that has struck terror in Campania for many centuries, the towering, pitch-black **Mount Vesuvius** looms menacingly over the Bay of Naples. August 24, A.D. 79, is the infamous date when Vesuvius blew its top and buried Pompeii, Herculaneum, and Stabiae under a toxic, molten mixture of ash and volcanic mud. Vesuvius has erupted periodically ever since: Thousands were killed in 1631 and in 1906 it blew the ring off its crater. The last spectacular eruption was on March 31, 1944. The approach to Vesuvius is dramatic, with the terrain growing increasingly foreboding as you near the top. Along the way, you'll see villas rising on its slopes, and vineyards: Excavations have revealed that the citizens of Pompeii enjoyed wine from grapes grown on these slopes, and today, the grapes produce an amber-colored wine known as Lacrimae Christi (Tears of Christ). Closer to the summit, the soil becomes puce colored and an occasional wildflower appears.

It might sound like a dubious invitation, but it's possible to visit the rim of the crater's mouth. As you look down into its smoldering core, you might recall that, a century before the eruption that buried Pompeii, Spartacus hid in the hollow of the crater, which was then covered with vines.

The **Parco Nazionale del Vesuvio** (www.parconazionaledelvesuvio.it; ✆ **081 8653911**) contains an **Observatory** at 608m (1,994 ft.) that is the oldest in the world, dating from 1841. Charging 8€, the park is open daily from 9am until sunset.

To reach Vesuvius from Naples, take the Circumvesuviana Railway and get off the train at Ercolano station, the 10th stop. From here, you can catch the shuttle bus to the entrance of the park (summer daily 9am–6pm; winter daily 9am–3pm). The cost is 18€. A taxi is a good alternative. For more information, call ✆ **081-7393666,** or go to www.vesuvioexpress.it. Once at the top, you must be accompanied by a guide, which will cost 10€. Assorted willing tour guides are found in the bus parking lot; they are available from 9am to about 4pm.

The Roman-era thermal baths at Baia.

The best base to use for exploring the area is **Pozzuoli,** reached from Naples by Line 2 of the Metropolitana (subway) or via the **Cumana Railroad** (✆ **800 053939**), starting from Piazza Montesanto. You can also catch the scenic no. 152 bus from Piazza Garibaldi. From Pozzuoli, SEPSA buses run to Baia (20 min.), Cumae, Solfatara, and Lago d'Averno.

SOLFATARA ★★ About 12km (7½ miles) west of Naples lies the **Vulcano Solfatara,** Via Solfatara 161 (www.solfatara.it; ✆ **081-5262341**), the dormant volcano crater that was called Forum Vulcani by the ancients who believed it to be the residence of the god Vulcan. Extinct it may be, but the lunar landscape spews sulfurous steam that hisses out of the ground in steaming jets, or fumaroles, that reach a temperature of 160°C (320°F). With the heavy stench of rotten eggs in the air, you can walk around the crater, stand in the clouds of steam, and marvel over the **Bocca Grande,** the largest fumarole. At the center of the crater is the **Fangaia,** an area of hot mud that gently bubbles away at a temperature of 140°C (284°F); you can understand why the ancient Romans believed this to be the entrance to Hades. You can visit the crater daily 8:30am to 1 hour before sunset for 6€.

POZZUOLI ★ Just 2km (1¼ miles) from Solfatara, the port of Pozzuoli opens onto a gulf screened from the Bay of Naples by a promontory. The ruins of the **Anfiteatro Flavio ★★**, Via Nicola Terracciano 75 (✆ **081-5266007**), which was built in the last part of the 1st century and once held 40,000 spectators, testify to past greatness. One of the finest surviving ancient arenas, it was the third largest in the Roman world and is distinguished by its "wings," which are in remarkably good condition. You can visit year-round Wednesday to Monday 9am to 1 hour before sunset. Admission is 4€. In another part of town, the **Tempio di Serapide ★** was really the Macellum (market square), and some of its ruined pillars still project upward. It was erected during the reign of the Flavian emperors. If you find it partially

The Cave of the Cumaean Sibyl, just outside of Naples.

submerged in water, that's because this area is subject to the geological phenomenon of bradyseism, where large tracts of land slowly subside beneath sea level, while others rise up.

BAIA ★★ In the days of imperial Rome, the emperors came here to frolic in the sun while enjoying the comforts of their luxurious villas and Roman baths. Emperor Claudius built a grand villa here for his first wife, Messalina, who spent her days and nights in debauched revelry and plotting to have her husband replaced by her lover (for which she was beheaded). And it was here that Claudius was poisoned by his last wife, Agrippina, the controlling mother of Nero. Nero is said to have had Agrippina murdered at nearby Bacoli, with its Pool of Mirabilis—after she had survived his first attempt on her life (a collapsing boat intended to send her to a watery grave). Parts of Baia's illustrious past have been excavated, including both the Temple of Baiae and the thermal baths.

You can explore this archaeological area (✆ **081-8687592**) Tuesday to Sunday from 9am to 1 hour before sunset. Admission is 4€. Ferrovia Cumana trains depart from Stazione Centrale for the 15-minute trip from Naples.

LAGO D'AVERNO ★ About 16km (10 miles) west of Naples, just north of Baia, lies a lake that fills an extinct volcanic crater. Known to the ancients as the **Gateway to Hades,** its vapors were said to provoke illness and death: Is this what they mean by "still waters run deep"? Facing the lake are the ruins of what has been known as the **Temple of Apollo** from the 1st century A.D. and what was once thought to be the Cave of the Cumaean Sibyl (see below). The Sibyl is said to have ferried Aeneas, son of Aphrodite, across the lake, where he traced a mysterious spring to its source, the River Styx. In the 1st century B.C., Agrippa turned it into a harbor for Roman ships by digging out a canal. Take the Napoli–Torre Gaveta bus from Baia to reach the site.

CUMA ★ It was on this site that the Greeks founded Cumae, their first stable colony in the western Mediterranean. It lies 19km (12 miles) west of Naples, and is of interest chiefly because it was home to the **Cave of the Cumaean Sibyl ★** where, according to legend, the famous oracle received her supplicants. The long, narrow trapezoidal tunnel was gouged from the rock by the Greeks in the 5th century B.C. and was a sacred spot to them. The archaeological area also includes the ruins of temples dedicated to Jupiter and Apollo (later converted into Christian churches) and is open daily 9am to 1 hour before sunset; admission is 2.50€ for adults (children 17 and under enter free). On Via Domitiana, to the east of Cuma, you'll pass the **Arco Felice,** an arch about 20m (64 ft.) high, built by Emperor Domitian in the 1st century A.D. Ferrovia Cumana trains run here, departing from Naples's Stazione Centrale.

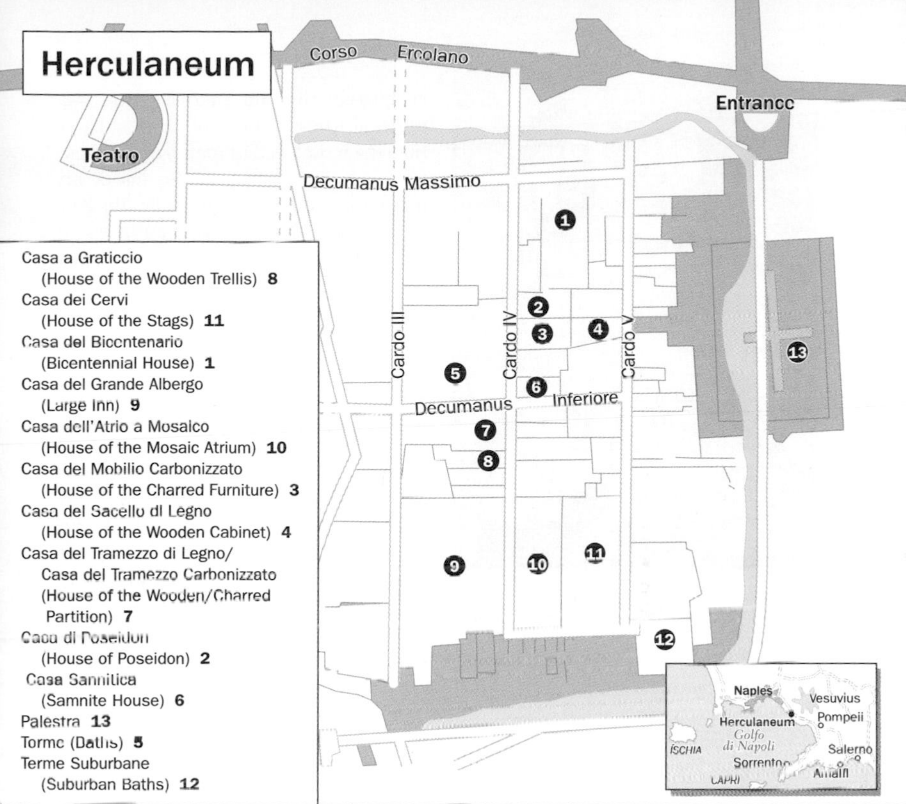

Herculaneum ★★

The volcanic mud that covered Herculaneum during the eruption of Vesuvius in A.D. 79 killed most of the town's estimated 5,000 inhabitants and quickly hardened to a semirock material, protecting the structures underneath but also making archaeological excavations much slower than at other sites. Herculaneum was discovered in 1709, and although excavations started shortly after and proceeded alongside those in Pompeii, the uncovered area here is much smaller than that of the more famous sibling site. Also, unlike at Pompeii, much of the ancient town lies under the modern one, making excavation even more difficult. The findings, however, have been stunning.

Researchers tell us that this town was about a third of the size of Pompeii and was a glitzy seaside resort for wealthy Romans. Most of the town was composed of elegant villas along with apartment blocks for poor laborers, while the middle class of merchants and artisans, which was so present in Pompeii, was almost completely absent here.

Much smaller than Pompeii, the archaeological remains of Herculaneum, the **Scavi di Ercolano** (Corso Resina; www.pompeiisites.org; ✆ **081-7324311**), may appear at first to also be less impressive. However, once you get down into the town from the entry ramp, you will soon be overtaken by the eerie sensation that, far from being a place of dusty ruins, the town was abandoned only recently rather than nearly 2,000 years ago. The particular quality of the volcanic mud that

The ruins at Herculaneum.

enveloped the site allowed for the unusual preservation of wood, from housing structures to room furnishings, allowing archaeologists to learn an incredible amount about daily life and building techniques in Roman times.

The excavated area stretches from the **Decumanus Maximus** (the town's main street) to what was once the shoreline (now a kilometer to the west); the rest of the Roman town remains inaccessible beneath the buildings of modern Ercolano. The archaeological area remains a work in progress, however, and finds, such as the boat discovered near the old shoreline in the 1990s, filled with the corpses of victims caught in frantic postures of escape, are still being revealed.

Highlights of the site include the **Sede degli Augustali Collegio degli Augustali (Hall of the Augustals) ★★**, with its marble floor and wall paintings, the elegantly decorated **Thermal Baths,** and the **Palestra,** a monumental sports arena used for competition and training. Among the private homes, the most interesting are the **Casa del Tramezzo di Legno (House of the Wooden Partition),** with its perfectly preserved facade, and the **Casa dei Cervi (House of the Stags) ★★**, the most elegant ruin in the excavated area, with terraces that would have overlooked the sea and magnificent decorations. The **Casa a Graticcio (House of the Latticework)** is one of the very few examples of working-class housing that has survived from antiquity; notice the partitions, cheaply made of interwoven cane and plaster. Another interesting house is the **Casa del Mosaico di Nettuno e Anfitrite (House of the Neptune and Anfitritis Mosaic) ★**, with its bright blue mosaic in the rear of the building; the annexed shop still has amphorae stacked on the shelves.

Elegant villas dotted what was the western seashore of Herculaneum, and one of the most famous is the **Villa dei Papiri ★★**, so-called because of the 1,000-odd badly charred papyrus scrolls (now in the library of the Plazzo Reale in Naples) that were revealed during excavations. The villa also yielded a treasure-trove of nearly 90 magnificent bronze and marble sculptures, Roman copies of Greek originals now housed in the Museo Archeologico Nazionale in Naples.

The ruins are open April to October daily 8:30am to 7:30pm and November to March daily 8:30am to 5pm (last admission 90 min. earlier). Admission is 11€. The site is a 20-minute ride on the Circumvesuviana Railway from Naples which also gets you to Vesuvius (same stop), Pompeii, and Sorrento. Otherwise, it's a 7km (4⅓-mile) drive on the autostrada to Salerno (exit at Ercolano). ***Note:*** A cumulative ticket for Herculaneum and Pompeii costs 20€, which is a good buy. You can purchase it at the Circumvesuviana Railway Station at Piazza Garibaldi in Naples.

POMPEII ★★★

24km (15 miles) S of Naples, 237km (147 miles) SE of Rome

Pompeii is Italy's most famous archaeological site and with good reason: With an excavated area of 44 hectares (109 acres) it is unique in the world, and no other ancient town has been brought to light so completely. Discovered by chance during excavations for a canal in the 16th century, the ruins of the ancient city of Pompeii were not recognized for what they were until further explorations in the 18th century. Formal excavations started only at the end of the 19th century, but continued steadily until most of the ancient town was uncovered and still continue today. Based on calculations of the city walls—only partly excavated—it is believed that Pompeii covered an area of 66 hectares (163 acres). Originally an Etruscan and then a Sannite town, it was colonized by the Romans in 80 B.C. At the time of the eruption, experts estimate the town was home to about 35,000 souls. Note that the ancient site is spelled Pompeii while the modern town is spelled Pompei; it can be confusing!

Essentials

GETTING THERE The **Circumvesuviana Railway** (www.vesuviana.it; ✆ **800-053939**) departs Naples every half-hour from Piazza Garibaldi. However, be sure you get on the train headed toward Sorrento and get off at Pompei/Scavi (*scavi* means "archaeological excavation"). If you get on the Pompei train, you'll end up in the town of Pompei and have to transfer there to the other train to get to the ruins. A ticket costs 2.80€ one way; trip time is 45 minutes each way. Circumvesuviana trains leave Sorrento several times a day for Pompeii, costing 2.10€ one-way. There's an entrance about 45m (150 ft.) from the rail station at the Villa dei Misteri. At the rail station in the town of Pompei, **bus** connections take you to the entrance to the excavations.

To reach Pompeii by **car** from Naples, take the 22km (14-mile) drive on the autostrada toward Salerno. If you're coming from Sorrento, head east on SS. 145, where you can connect with A3 (marked NAPOLI). Then take the signposted turnoff for Pompeii.

Pompeii's Stabian Baths.

VISITOR INFORMATION The **tourist office** is at Via Sacra 1 (www.pompeiturismo.it; ✆ **081-8507255**). It's open Monday to Friday 8am to 3:30pm (until 7pm Apr–Oct), and Saturday 8am to 2pm.

LOGISTICAL TIPS After you pay for your entrance, you'll find a **bookstore,** where you can purchase guidebooks to the ruins (available in English and complete with detailed photos) that will help you understand what you're seeing. We highly recommend that you purchase one before you set out.

If you're here on a sunny day, wear sunscreen and bring along a bottle of water. There's almost no place in Pompeii to escape the sun's rays, and it can often be dusty.

Exploring the Ruins

Most people visit the **Scavi di Pompeii,** Via Villa dei Misteri 1 (www.pompeiisites.org; ✆ **081-8610744**), the best preserved 2,000-year-old ruins in Europe, on a day trip from Naples (allow at least 4 hr. for even a superficial visit to the archaeological site).

The most elegant of the patrician villas is the **House of the Vettii (Casa dei Vettii) ★★★**, boasting a courtyard, statuary (such as a two-faced Janus), paintings, and a black-and-red Pompeian dining room known for its frescoes of delicate cupids. The house was occupied by two brothers named Vettii, both of whom were wealthy merchants. As you enter the vestibule, you'll see a painting of Priapus resting his gargantuan phallus on a pair of scales. The guard will reveal other erotic fertility drawings and statuary, although most such material has been removed to the Archaeological Museum in Naples. This house is the best example of a villa and garden that's been restored.

The second-most-important villa, the **House of the Mysteries (Villa dei Misteri) ★★**, near the Porto Ercolano, is outside the walls (go along Viale alla Villa dei Misteri). What makes the villa exceptional, aside from its architectural features, are its remarkable frescoes depicting scenes associated with the sect of Dionysus (Bacchus), one of the cults that flourished in Roman times. Note the Pompeian red in some of the backgrounds. The largest house, called the **House of the Faun (Casa del Fauno) ★★** because of a bronze statue of a faun found there, takes up a city block and has four dining rooms and two spacious peristyle gardens. It sheltered the celebrated *Battle of Alexander the Great* mosaic that's now in the Museo Archeologico Nazionale in Naples.

In the center of town is the **Forum (Foro) ★**. Rather small, it was nonetheless the heart of Pompeian life, known to bakers, merchants, and the aristocrats who lived in the villas. Parts of the Forum were severely damaged in an

A view of Pompeii's Forum, with its destroyer, Mount Vesuvius, in the background.

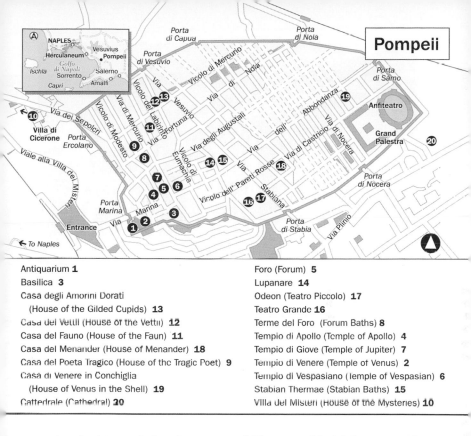

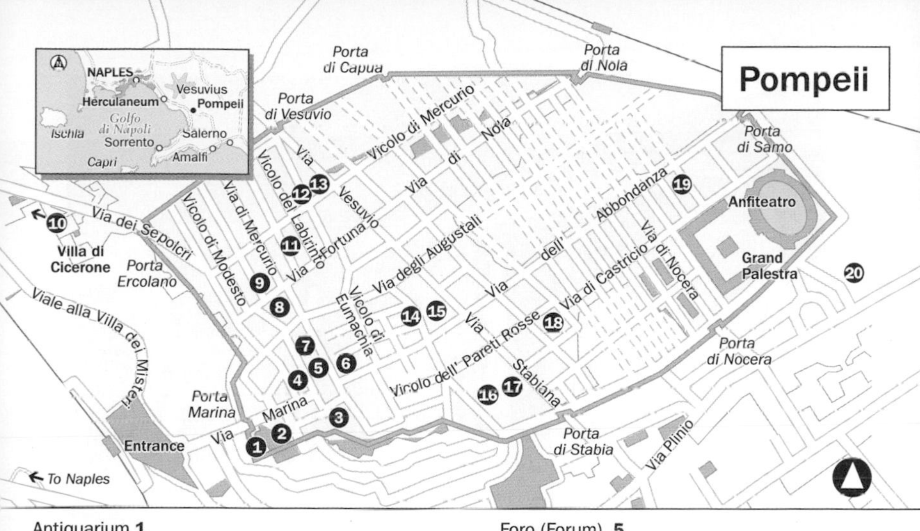

Antiquarium **1**
Basilica **3**
Casa degli Amorini Dorati (House of the Gilded Cupids) **13**
Casa dei Vettii (House of the Vettii) **12**
Casa del Fauno (House of the Faun) **11**
Casa del Menander (House of Menander) **18**
Casa del Poeta Tragico (House of the Tragic Poet) **9**
Casa di Venere in Conchiglia (House of Venus in the Shell) **19**
Cattedrale (Cathedral) **20**
Foro (Forum) **5**
Lupanare **14**
Odeon (Teatro Piccolo) **17**
Teatro Grande **16**
Terme del Foro (Forum Baths) **8**
Tempio di Apollo (Temple of Apollo) **4**
Tempio di Giove (Temple of Jupiter) **7**
Tempio di Venere (Temple of Venus) **2**
Tempio di Vespasiano (Temple of Vespasian) **6**
Stabian Thermae (Stabian Baths) **15**
Villa dei Misteri (House of the Mysteries) **10**

earthquake 16 years before the eruption of Vesuvius and hadn't been repaired when the final destruction came. Three buildings surrounding the Forum are the **basilica** (the city's largest single structure), the **Temple of Apollo (Tempio di Apollo)** ★★, and the **Temple of Jupiter (Tempio di Giove)** ★★. The **Stabian Thermae (baths)** ★★★—where both men and women lounged between games of knucklebones (a game played with knucklebones or jacks, once used the way gamblers use dice)—are in good condition, among the finest to survive from antiquity. Here you'll see some skeletons. In the **brothel (Lupanare)** are some erotic paintings (tip the guide to see them).

Other buildings of interest include the **Great Theater (Teatro Grande)** ★, built in the 5th century B.C. During the Hellenistic period from 200 to 150 B.C., it was largely rebuilt, as it was again by the Romans in the 1st century A.D. This open-air theater could hold 5,000 spectators, many of them bloodthirsty as they screamed for death in the battles between wild animals and gladiators. The **House of the Gilded Cupids (Casa degli Amorini Dorati)** ★ was a flamboyant private home; its owner is unknown, although he probably lived during the reign of Nero. Obviously he had theatrical flair, attested to by the gilded and glass cupids known as *amorini*. Even though it's badly ruined, the house contains a peristyle with one wing raised almost like a stage. The **House of the Tragic Poet (Casa del Poeta Tragico)** ★ gets its name from a mosaic discovered here

A detail from Pompeii's Stabian Baths.

(later sent to Naples). It depicts a chained watchdog on the doorstep with this warning: CAVE CANEM (Beware of the Dog).

An ancient **bathhouse** with erotic frescoes has been opened to the public for the first time, although the discovery was made back in the 1980s. The delay in opening was because of lack of funds for restoration. The 2,000-year-old thermal bathhouse was in remarkably good condition and was still adorned with elaborate mosaics, including an indoor waterfall. Controversy centers around eight frescoes in vivid green, reds, and golds. These frescoes depict graphic scenes of various sex acts. Some scholars have suggested that they were meant to advertise sexual services available on the upper floor of the baths; other archaeologists maintain they were intended merely to amuse.

The site is open April to October daily 8:30am to 7:30pm and November to March daily 8:30am to 5pm; last admission 90 minutes before closing. It costs 11€ for adults.

Where to Eat

Il Principe ★★ NEAPOLITAN/ANCIENT ROMAN With a dining room designed to emulate the luxury of ancient Pompeii, this is the best restaurant in the area and a perfect conclusion to a day spent visiting the ruins. Right in the center of town, it serves excellent food in a lively atmosphere with outdoor dining. The talented chef and owner is a real epicurean; the seasonal menu includes a choice of tasty ancient Roman recipes, such as the *lagane al garum* (homemade egg-free pasta with an anchovy-paste sauce). More modern choices include excellent *spaghetti alle vongole* (with baby clams) and delicious *maccheroni* with zucchini and prawns. The lounge bar with live music is extra reason to come here.

Piazza Bartolo Longo. www.ilprincipe.com. ✆ **081-8505566.** Reservations recommended. *Secondi* 12€–24€. AE, DC, MC, V. Tues–Sat 12:30–3pm and 8–11pm; Sun 12:30–3pm.

Ristorante President ★ NEAPOLITAN This is the most upscale place to eat in the area, offering gourmet food and great service. The sensational, seasonal food focuses on seafood, with such appetizers as smoked swordfish or tuna and delicious pasta dishes such as the *scialatielli allo scorfano* (homemade flat pasta with scorpion-fish). The *secondi* include a large choice of fish masterfully prepared au gratin, baked in a salt crust, or simply baked. We also recommend the tasting menus that explore the regional cuisine, from the modern to the ancient Roman (35€–55€ with wine pairings). Desserts are excellent and strictly homemade.

Piazza Schettini 12 (parking at back entrance, Via San Giuseppe 16). www.ristorantepresident.it. ✆ **081-8507245.** Reservations recommended Sat–Sun. *Secondi* 12€–25€. AE, DC, MC, V. Tues–Sat noon–3pm and 7pm–midnight; Sun noon–3pm (and 7pm–midnight in summer). Closed late Jan for 2 weeks.

Where to Stay

The once sketchy town of Pompei has notably improved, and there are several pleasant hotels located close to the archaeological area. You should still be careful, though, and avoid night strolls along deserted streets.

Hotel Diana ☺ This small family-run hotel is really welcoming, thanks to the efforts of the charming hosts. Guest rooms are well-appointed and pleasantly decorated, with all the expected amenities, although some are a little noisy. It isn't exactly convenient to the ruins, but it's reasonably close to the town center and right by the FS train station.

Vicolo Sant'Abbondio 12 (off Via Sacra, by the FS train station), 80045 Pompei. www.pompeihotel.com. ✆/fax **081-8631264.** 22 units. 110€ double; 130€ triple; 150€ quad. Rates include buffet breakfast. Children 2 and under stay free in parent's room. AE, DC, MC, V. Free parking. Pets accepted. **Amenities:** Bar; concierge; room service; smoke-free rooms. *In room:* A/C, TV, Internet (free).

Hotel Villa dei Misteri ☺ This old fashioned, family-run hotel has the advantage of being right by the main entrance to the excavations. Built in the 1930s, it has a certain charm and is an excellent choice if you don't need a huge range of amenities. Guest rooms are spacious and well-appointed, with modern quality furnishings and tiled floors; some have private balconies. Some overlook the amphora-shaped pool, while others have street views. If you want a room with A/C (for an additional 9€ per day), you must book well in advance. The staff is extremely accommodating, and the pool and good restaurant are great pluses, particularly if you have children.

Via Villa dei Misteri 11, 80045 Pompei. www.villadeimisteri.it. ✆ **081-8613593.** Fax 081-8622983. 34 units. 75€ double; 97€ triple. Half- and full-board plans available. Children 2 and under stay free in parent's room. DC, MC, V. Free parking. **Amenities:** Restaurant; bar; pool. *In room:* A/C (in some, 9€ fee), TV (in some), Wi-Fi (2€ per hour.).

Maiuri It's not located at the excavations, but this is one of the better recommendations in town. The accommodations are in up-to-date and soundproof rooms, most of which front a tranquil garden. The rooms are midsize and open in most cases onto small balconies. As an added convenience, a shuttle bus runs to and from the airport at Naples, but a fee is charged.

Via Acquasala 20, 80045 Pompeii. www.pompeiihotelmaiuri.com. ✆ **081-85622716.** Fax 081-8562716. 30 units. 85€–105€ double; 95€–120€ triple. Rates include buffet breakfast. AE, MC, V. Free parking. **Amenities:** Restaurant; bar; babysitting; concierge. *In room:* A/C, TV, hair dryer, minibar, Wi-Fi (free).

THE EMERALD ISLAND OF ISCHIA ★★

34km (21 miles) W of Naples

Ischia is the largest of Campania's islands, covering about 46sq. km (18 sq. miles). Its velvety slopes, green with pine woods and vineyards, have earned it the nickname **Isola Verde (Green Isle),** while its fame as a healthy retreat has earned it another nickname, **Island of Eternal Youth,** for its peaceful atmosphere and many spas. These are fueled by the widespread volcanic activity still present on the island, although its volcano, Mount Epomeo, has long been dormant. Hot springs, mineral-water springs, and steam and hot-mud holes dot the island's slopes while its shores are surrounded by sparkling waters that lap lovely, sandy beaches. Aside from its healthy hot springs and summer beach resorts, Ischia is known for its vineyards that produce the red and white Monte Epomeo, the red and white Ischia, and the white Biancolella.

Taking the waters at Ischia.

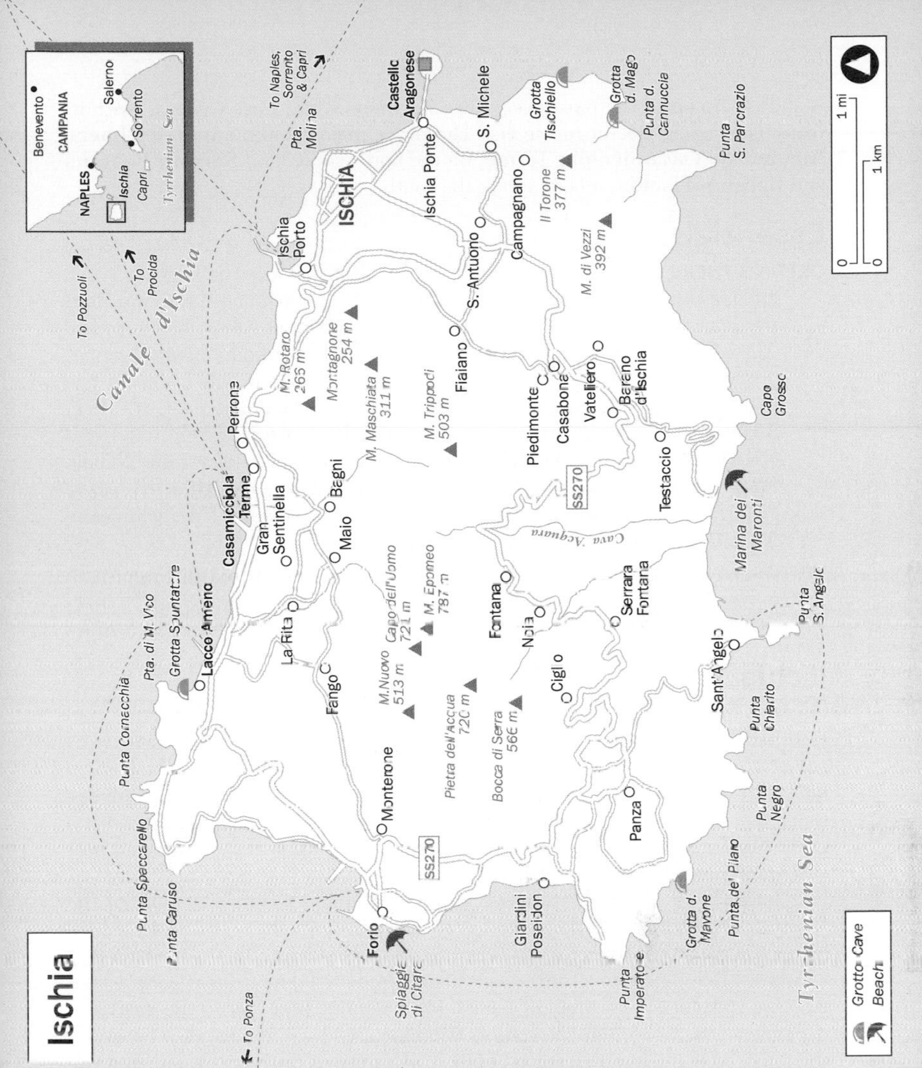

The Greeks first landed on Ischia in the 8th century B.C. but soon moved on to Cumae, near modern Pozzuoli, and it was under the Romans that the island became famous for its thermal waters with their curative properties. The first thermal establishment opened in Casamicciola Terme in 1604, and by the 19th century, the thermal waters of Ischia made a compulsory stopover on any Grand Tour itinerary. To this day, savvy travelers flock to the island's thermal baths and hotels for fabulous spa vacations, yet the atmosphere remains quieter and less glitzy than on Capri.

The largest community is at **Ischia Porto** on the eastern coast, a circular town seated in the crater of the extinct Monte Epomeo, which functions as the island's main port. The most lively town is **Forio** on the western coast, with its many bars along tree-lined streets. The other major communities are **Lacco Ameno** and **Casamicciola Terme,** on the north shore, and **Serrara Fontana** and **Barano d'Ischia,** inland and to the south.

Essentials

GETTING THERE Ischia's three main harbors—Ischia Porto (the largest), Forio, and Casamicciola—are very well connected to the mainland, with most ferries leaving from Pozzuoli and Naples's two harbors of Mergellina Terminal Aliscafi and Stazione Marittima. Both ferry and hydrofoil (*aliscafi*) services are frequent in summer but slow down during the winter, when some of the hydrofoil lines are suspended. **Medmar** (www.medmarnavi.it; ✆ **081-3334411**), **Caremar** (www.caremar.it; ✆ **199-116655** within Italy), and **SNAV** (www.snav.it; ✆ **081-4285555**) offer regular service from Napoli, Pozzuoli, and Procida to Ischia Porto and Casamicciola. **Alilauro** (www.alilauro.it; ✆ **081-4972222**) runs hydrofoils from Naples (Mergellina and Molo Beverello) to Ischia Porto and to Forio.

VISITOR INFORMATION In Porto d'Ischia, **Azienda Autonoma di Soggiorno e Turismo,** at Via Antonio Sogliuzzo 72 (www.infoischiaprocida.it; ✆ **081-5074231**), is open Monday to Saturday 9am to 1:30pm and 3 to 7:30pm.

Ischia Town

Once separate, **Ischia Porto** and **Ischia Ponte** have now merged into one, and together they make up the largest town on the island. The majority of activity is concentrated in **Ischia Porto,** around its naturally round harbor which is, in fact, an extinct volcano crater. Founded in the 18th century by the Bourbons, today it is a typically bustling and attractive Mediterranean port town with a yacht-filled marina, a busy commercial port, and plenty of restaurants and bars strung out along the water's edge.

Ischia Ponte is more attractive and is dominated by the vast bulk of the **Castello Aragonese ★★** (www.castellodischia.it; ✆ **081-992834**), which looms over the town from atop a rocky islet that is linked to the main island by a causeway. References to a fortress on this isolated rock date from as early as 474 B.C. and today it's the symbol of Ischia. We recommend a visit to the castle for the spectacular views from its terraces and ramparts; you can take the elevator to the top or walk up, but it's a steep climb. The fortress is privately owned, and you pay 10€ to get inside: It is open daily from 9am to 7pm in summer and until 4pm in winter.

WHERE TO EAT

Ristorante Damiano ★ ISCHITANO/NEAPOLITAN This charming restaurant, angled for the best sea views, is located about 1.6km (1 mile) southwest of the ferry terminal. Damiano Caputo infuses his cuisine with zest and very fresh ingredients. In the rustic setting—long communal tables and fresh flowers—you can select from an array of antipasti, homemade pasta, steamy bowls of minestrone, and some excellent veal and chicken dishes. Some especially savory specialties include fritters of arugula and shrimp, fresh mussels steamed in black pepper and garlic, or vermicelli pasta with seafood. Desserts include tiramisu and wonderful *gelati*.

Via delle Vigne 30. ✆ **081-983032.** Reservations recommended. Main courses 15€–28€. DC, MC, V. Daily 8pm–midnight. Closed Nov–Mar.

WHERE TO STAY

Albergo Il Monastero ★ 🎁 Housed in a former monastery inside Ischia's Aragonese Castle, this is the island's most spectacularly situated hotel and offers a unique atmosphere, a warm reception, and superb views. Guest rooms (former monk's cells) are spacious and stylishly spartan with whitewashed walls, tiled floors, and solid dark wood or wicker furniture. The bathrooms are small (some tiny) but tastefully designed. A few rooms boast small but delightful private terraces, while others open onto a common terrace. The restaurant, with tables on a scenic terrace in warm weather, serves excellent local specialties.

Castello Aragonese. www.albergoilmonastero.it. ✆ **081-992435.** Fax 081-991849. 20 units. 120€–160€ double. AE, DC, MC, V. Closed Nov–Mar. **Amenities:** Restaurant; concierge. *In room:* A/C.

Grand Hotel Excelsior ★ With a perfect location that is convenient to both Ischia Ponte and Ischia Porto, this hotel offers top-notch service and amenities, such as its own private beach. Posh public spaces—a pool with a view, elegant lounges, a spa with a beauty center—are complemented by beautiful, spacious guest rooms. Furnished with great taste and attention to detail, they have wrought-iron bedsteads, hand-painted tile floors, and designer-tiled bathrooms; each room has a private patio-terrace. It is definitely worth paying extra for a room with a view.

Via E. Gianturco 19, 80077 Ischia. www.excelsiorischia.it. ✆ **081-991522.** Fax 081-984100. 76 units. 160€–230€ double; from 380€ suite. Rates include buffet breakfast. Children 1 and under stay free in parent's room. AE, DC, MC, V. Closed mid-Oct to mid-Apr. **Amenities:** Restaurant; bar; concierge; health club; pool; room service; spa. *In room:* A/C, TV, minibar.

Hotel Continental Terme ★ The thermal springs at this sprawling complex are among the largest on the island. There are six thermal water pools (three covered), surrounded by the exotic greenery of 27,340 sq. m (294,285 sq. ft.) of gardens. The public spaces feature polished marble and terra-cotta floors, contemporary Italian seating, and wicker-and-glass tables, accented by cut flowers and plant life. The guest rooms are luxuriously furnished, set in a diverse collection of town-house villas scattered throughout the grounds.

Via M. Mazzella 74, 80077 Ischia Porto. www.continentalterme.it. ✆ **081-3336111.** Fax 081-3336276. 244 units. 120€–350€ double; 230€–430€ suite. Rates include breakfast and dinner. AE, DC, MC, V. Free valet parking. Closed Nov–Mar. **Amenities:** Restaurant; 2 bars; babysitting; children's center; exercise room; 5 thermal pools (2 indoor); room service; spa; outdoor tennis court (lit); Wi-Fi (3€ per hour, in lobby). *In room:* A/C, TV, hair dryer, minibar.

Hotel Il Moresco ★ This hotel sits in a sun-dappled park whose pines and palmettos grow close to its arched loggias. From some angles, the Moorish-inspired exterior looks almost like a cubist fantasy. Inside, the straightforward design re-creates a modern oasis in the southern part of Spain, with matador-red tiles coupled with stark-white walls and Iberian furniture. Each well-furnished guest room has a terrace or a balcony and a tidy bathroom.

Via Emanuele Gianturco 16, 80077 Ischia Porto. www.ilmoresco.it. ✆ **081-981355.** Fax 081-992338. 70 units. 230€–460€ double; 560€–760€ suite. Rates include buffet breakfast. AE, DC, MC, V. Closed Oct 18–Apr 23. **Amenities:** Restaurant; 2 bars; exercise room; 3 pools (1 thermal

Il Fungo, as seen from the beach at Lacco Ameno.

pool outside, 1 thermal pool in a grotto, 1 covered thermal pool); room service; spa. *In room:* A/C, TV/DVD/CD player (in some), hair dryer, minibar.

Hotel La Villarosa ★★ This is Ischia's finest *pensione,* set in a garden of gardenias and banana, eucalyptus, and fig trees. The dining room is in the informal country style, with terra-cotta tiles, lots of French windows, and antique chairs. What looks like a carriage house in the garden has been converted into an informal tavern with more antiques. The friendly staff maintains the personal atmosphere. The bright and airy guest rooms are well kept. Thermal treatments are available.

Via Giacinto Gigante 5, 80077 Ischia Porto. www.dicohotels.it. ✆ **081-991316.** Fax 081-992425. 37 units. 65€–110€ per person double. Rates include half board. AE, DC, MC, V. Closed Nov–Mar. **Amenities:** Bar; babysitting; thermal pool; room service; spa. *In room:* A/C, TV, hair dryer, minibar.

Lacco Ameno

Lacco Ameno's landmark is a rock named **Il Fungo (the Mushroom)** that juts from the sea in its sheltered bay. The town is the chicest resort on the island and is home to its best and most expensive hotels. People come from all over the world either to relax on the beach and be served top-level food or to take a cure. The mineral-rich waters at Lacco Ameno have led to the development of a modern spa with extensive facilities for thermal cures, everything from underwater jet massages to mud baths.

WHERE TO STAY

Hotel La Reginella ★ Set in a lush garden typical of the island's accommodations, this hotel boasts a Mediterranean decor that combines printed tile floors with light woods and pastel or floral fabrics. Although aging, the guest rooms are still very comfortable, with wood furnishings and well-kept bathrooms.

Piazza Santa Restituta 1, 80076 Lacco Ameno d'Ischia. www.albergolareginella.it. ✆ **081-994300.** Fax 081-980481. 90 units, shower only. 100€–190€ per person double; 170€–280€ per person suite. Rates include breakfast and dinner. AE, DC, MC, V. Free parking. Closed Nov 1–Apr 16. **Amenities:** 2 restaurants; babysitting; 5 pools (4 outdoor/1 heated indoor); room service; spa; outdoor tennis court (lit). *In room:* A/C, TV, hair dryer, minibar.

Hotel Regina Isabella ★★ This resort offers the finest accommodations and service in Lacco Ameno, plus a private beach. The refined setting successfully contrasts contemporary furnishings with rococo and less ornate antique styles. In the medium to spacious guest rooms, serene blues and greens are prevalent, and some printed tile floors are offset by earthy brown tiles and woodwork. Most have balconies.

Piazza Santa Restituta, 80076 Lacco Ameno d'Ischia. www.reginaisabella.it. ✆ **081-994322.** Fax 081-900190. 134 units. 460€–660€ double; from 900€ suite. Rates include breakfast and dinner. AE, DC, MC, V. Free parking. Closed Nov 8–Dec 27 and Jan 7–Mar 26. **Amenities:** 2 restaurants; 2 bars; babysitting; 4 pools (1 thermal covered); room service; spa; Wi-Fi (free, in lobby). *In room:* A/C, TV, hair dryer, minibar.

Hotel Terme di Augusto This hotel, 46m (151 ft.) from the shore, provides excellent service in a setting less ostentatious than that of many competing resorts. It combines prominent arched ceilings, patterned tile floors, and floral drapery and upholstery to create light, airy spaces. The guest rooms are comfortable, with well-maintained bathrooms.

Viale Campo 128, 80076 Lacco Ameno d'Ischia. www.termediaugusto.it. ✆ **081-994944.** Fax 081-980244. 119 units. 110€–165€ per person double; 165€–200€ per person junior suite. Rates include breakfast and dinner. AE, DC, MC, V. Free parking. Closed Nov 14–Dec 29 and Jan 6–23. **Amenities:** 2 restaurants; 3 bars; babysitting; exercise room; 4 pools (2 outdoor, 2 indoor); room service; spa; outdoor tennis court (lit); Wi-Fi (free, in lobby). *In room:* A/C, TV, hair dryer, minibar.

Hotel Terme San Montano ★★ This is an oasis of charm and grace, one of our favorite retreats on Ischia. The grounds spread out around the hotel in a luxuriant garden, leading to a private beach. Aged woods, leather, and brass are combined in the furnishings, and marine lamps shed light on almost every room. The headboards resemble a ship's helm, the windows are translated as portholes, and miniature ships and antiquated diving gear are decoratively scattered about. The guest rooms are well cared for and spacious. Rooms with sea views are the most requested.

Via Monte Vico, 80076 Lacco Ameno d'Ischia. www.sanmontano.com. ✆ **081-994033.** Fax 081-980242. 77 units. 140€–500€ double; 350€–600€ suite. Rates include buffet breakfast. AE, DC, MC, V. Free parking. Closed Nov–Apr. **Amenities:** Restaurant; 2 bars; babysitting; bikes; exercise room; 2 outdoor pools; room service; spa; outdoor tennis court (lit); limited watersports equipment. *In room:* A/C, TV, hair dryer, minibar (in some).

Forio

A short drive from Lacco Ameno, Forio stands on the west coast of Ischia, opening onto the sea near the Bay of Citara. Long a favorite with artists (filmmaker Luchino Visconti had a villa here), it now attracts a broader base of tourism. Locals produce some of the finest wines on the island. On the way from Lacco Ameno, stop at the **beach of San Francesco,** with its sanctuary. At sunset,

Santa Maria del Soccorso in Forio.

many visitors head for a rocky spur on which sits the church of **Santa Maria del Soccorso.** The lucky ones get to witness the famous "green flash" over the Gulf of Gaeta. It appears on occasion immediately after the sun sets.

WHERE TO EAT

Umberto a Mare ★★ CAMPANIAN/SEAFOOD This historic restaurant has been drawing diners for decades and is one of our favorites. The beautiful terrace—which affords a matchless panorama and is so romantic at sunset—combines with the gourmet cuisine for a perfect dinner. The menu changes daily according to market availability with a strong focus on seafood. From the copious choices of antipasti we loved the *insalatina di mare* (seafood salad) and the *tartare di palamito al profumo d'arancia* (tartar of local fish with citrus). We recommend you follow it with the delicious *pennette all'aragosta e agli asparagi* (short penne with lobster and asparagus) or with the catch of the day, either classically prepared on the grill or *all'acqua pazza* (in a light herb broth).

Via Soccorso 2, Forio. www.umbertoamare.it. ✆ **081-997171.** Reservations recommended. *Secondi* 25€–36€; prix-fixe menus 60€ and 70€. AE, DC, MC, V. Daily 12:30–3pm and 7–11:30pm. Closed Nov 5–Dec 28 and Jan 7 to late Mar.

WHERE TO STAY

Grande Albergo Mezzatorre ★★ The best hotel in Forio, this complex is built around a 16th-century villa whose stone tower once guarded against invaders; now it houses the least expensive of the doubles. The five postmodern buildings run a few hundred feet downhill to a waterfront bluff. A casual airiness prevails in the public spaces, which contrast soft lighting with terra-cotta floors. The decor in the guest rooms is contemporary, with wooden furniture, bright upholstered seating, and tiled bathrooms. Suites have a private garden and a whirlpool tub.

Via Mezzatorre 23, 80075 Forio d'Ischia. www.mezzatorre.it. © **081-986111.** Fax 081-986015. 59 units. 440€–580€ double; from 720€ suite. Rates include buffet breakfast. AE, DC, MC, V. Free parking. Closed Oct 24–Apr 21. **Amenities:** 2 restaurants; bar; babysitting; bikes; exercise room; saltwater heated pool; room service; thermal spa; 2 outdoor tennis courts (lit). *In room:* A/C, TV, hair dryer, minibar.

Sant'Angelo ★

The most charming settlement on Ischia, Sant'Angelo juts out on the southernmost tip. The fishing village is joined to the "mainland" of Ischia by a 91m long (300-ft.) lava-and-sand isthmus. Driving into the town is virtually impossible. And in summer you will probably have to park a long way off and walk. Its **beach** is among the best on the island.

WHERE TO STAY

Park Hotel Miramare Old-fashioned in style but not in spirit, this hotel was opened in 1923 and has been run by the same family ever since. Its real strength is the attached spa, **Aphrodite-Apollon,** which includes 12 different pools, extensive treatments and fitness programs, and a private beach. A portion of it is reserved only for nudists, one of the only such beach areas on the island. Guest rooms are bright and comfortable, furnished in an old-fashioned seaside style, with wicker and wrought-iron furniture plus antiques and quality reproductions. Bathrooms are modern (some with shower only), and all the rooms open onto private balconies or terraces overlooking the sea. The hotel also has a few rooms in two separate houses near the spa and beach; guests there have access to the hotel's facilities (192€ double).

Via Comandante Magdalena 29, 80070 Sant'Angelo d'Ischia. www.hotelmiramare.it. © **081-999219.** Fax 081-999325. 50 units. 250€–420€ double; from 660€ suite. Rates include buffet breakfast. AE, DC, MC, V. Closed mid Nov to early Apr. **Amenities:** 2 restaurants; bar; babysitting, children's program, concierge, spa, Wi-Fi (free). *In room:* A/C, TV, hair dryer, minibar.

SORRENTO ★★

50km (31 miles) S of Naples, 256km (159 miles) SE of Rome, 50km (31 miles) W of Salerno

The unique beauty of Sorrento's coast has inspired many myths. This is where the Sirens are said to have waylaid travelers with their irresistible song: Ulysses was forced to fill the ears of his sailors with wax and to tie himself to the mast of his ship in order to resist their call according to Homer's *Odyssey.*

Today, the pull of the sea and imposing rock-bound coast remain as compelling as in Homer's day, attracting coach-loads of tourists in the summer months. In spite of the crowds, however, Sorrento remains a charming and lively place and a good base from which to explore the whole of the Sorrentine peninsula.

Essentials

GETTING THERE Sorrento is connected to Naples by the **Circumvesuviana** railway (www.vesuviana.it; © **800-053939**), and the ride takes about 50 minutes. It leaves from one floor underground at Stazione Centrale (see "Essentials," earlier in this chapter).

By **car** from Naples, take the A3, then exit at Castellammare di Stabia and take the SS145.

VISITOR INFORMATION The **tourist office** is at Via de Maio 35 (www.sorrentotourism.com; ✆ **081-8074033**), off Piazza Tasso. It's open Monday to Friday from 9am to 4:15pm; in summer it's also open on Saturday mornings.

Strolling seaside in Sorrento.

Exploring Sorrento

Sorrento has few sandy beaches; most swimming spots are just piers or decks extending into the water where you can hire chaise longues and umbrellas. One exception is the stretch of sand at Marina Grande, but the best beach is **Punta del Capo,** reached by going along Corso Italia to Via del Capo.

If you'd like to go **hiking,** the hills around Sorrento are crisscrossed with some spectacular trails, many of which are well-marked. Ask in the tourist office for a walking map.

From Sorrento, confident drivers can undertake the spectacular but nerve-racking **Amalfi Drive.** If you want to leave the driving to someone else, you can take the blue SITA bus that runs between Sorrento and Salerno or Amalfi. In Sorrento, bus stops with timetables are outside the rail station and in the central piazza.

Although few visitors come to Sorrento to look at churches and monuments, there are some worth exploring. The **Chiesa di San Francesco,** Via San Francesco (✆ **081-8781269**), dates from the 18th century, but its charming **cloister ★**, with delicate arches and a garden dotted with flowering vines, predates it by 4 centuries and is a little oasis of calm in overcrowded Sorrento. The cloister is open daily 9am to 6pm, and admission is free.

Time permitting, visit the **Museo Correale di Terranova ★**, Via Correale 48 (✆ **081-8781846**), north of Piazza Tasso. This was once the home of the counts of Terranova—an old aristocratic family of Sorrento—who donated their villa and private collections to the public. The museum gives a unique overview of decorative art from the 16th to the 19th centuries: Stocked with its original furnishings, it houses some excellent Flemish paintings, a collection of Italian and foreign porcelain from reputedly the best 17th- and 18th-century manufacturers, and a number of unusual clocks. It is open from Wednesday to Monday 9:30am to 1:30pm and admission is 7€.

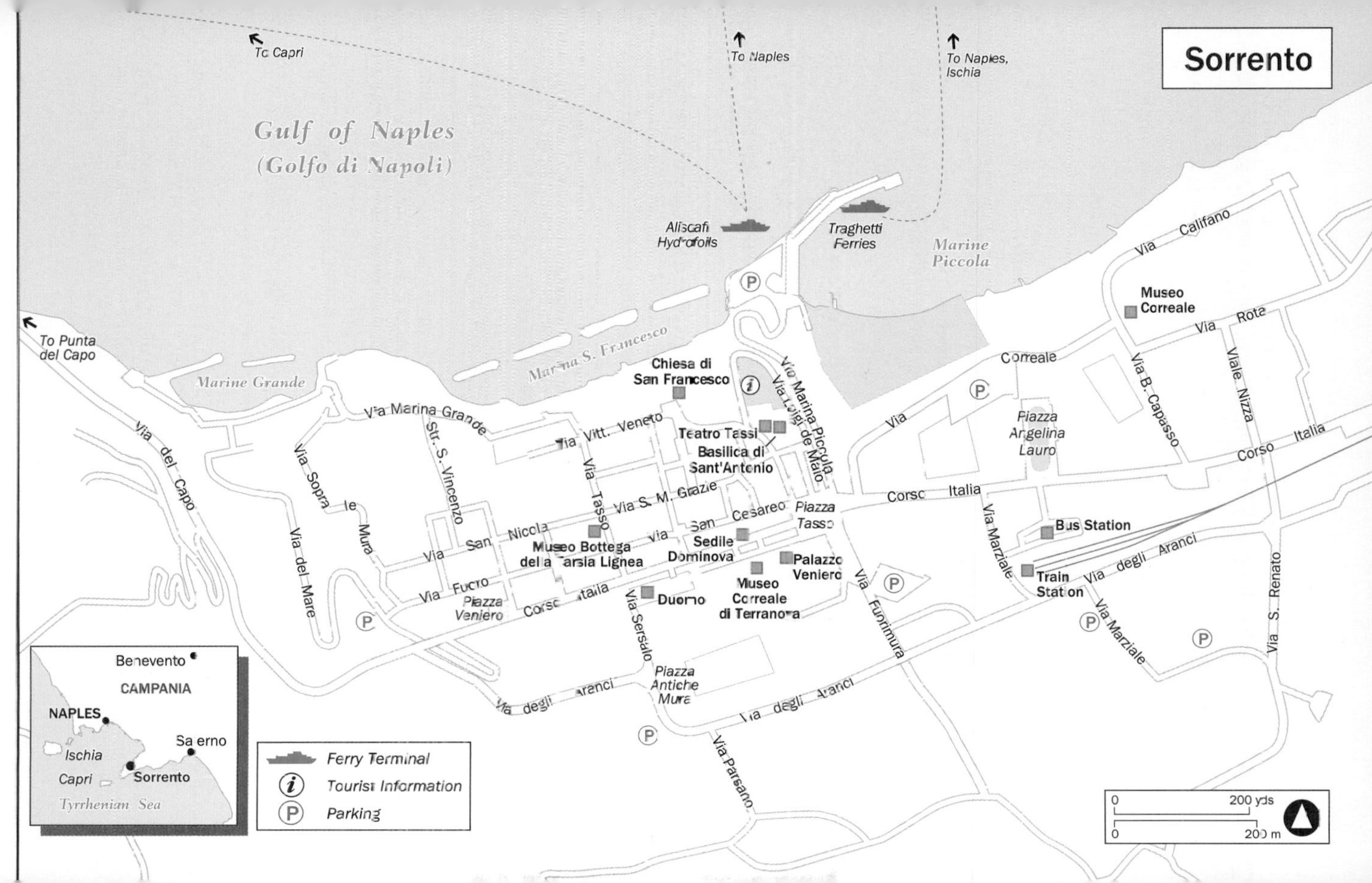

Sorrento
To Capri
To Naples
To Naples, Ischia
Gulf of Naples
(Golfo di Napoli)
Aliscafi
Hydrofoils
Traghetti
Ferries
Marine Piccola
To Punta del Capo
Marine Grande
Marina S. Francesco
Via Califano
Museo Correale
Via Rota
Via Correale
Via B. Capasso
Viale Nizza
Piazza Angelina Lauro
Corso Italia
Chiesa di San Francesco
Via Marina Piccola
Via Luigi de Maio
Teatro Tasso
Basilica di Sant'Antonio
Via Marina Grande
Via Vitt. Veneto
Str. S. Vincenzo
Via del Capo
Via Sopra le Mura
Via del Mare
Via Tasso
Via S. M. Grazie
Via San Cesareo
Piazza Tasso
Via San Nicola
Museo Bottega della Tarsia Lignea
Sedile Dominova
Palazzo Veniero
Via Fuoro
Piazza Veniero
Duomo
Museo Correale di Terranova
Via Fuorimura
Via Marziale
Bus Station
Train Station
Via degli Aranci
Via S. Renato
Via Sersale
Piazza Antiche Mura
Via Parsano
Benevento
CAMPANIA
NAPLES
Ischia
Salerno
Capri
Sorrento
Tyrrhenian Sea
Ferry Terminal
Tourist Information
Parking
0 200 yds
0 200 m

Via San Cesareo is Sorrento's main **shopping** street. Specialty shopping includes the bounty from local farms and groves—lemons and lemon products, walnuts, D.O.P. olive oil, and Penisola Sorrentina D.O.C. wine (some experts call it "the Beaujolais of Campania")—and the slowly disappearing local crafts: lace, embroideries, and wood intarsia and marquetry furniture.

For fresh ricotta formed in traditional handmade baskets and a sample of local products, head to one of **Apreda's** two locations: Via Tasso 27 (✆ **081-8782351**) or Via del Mare 20 (✆ **081-8074059**). You can find excellent limoncello and other specialties at **Sapori & Colori,** Via San Cesareo 57 (✆ **081-8784278**), and **Luigia Gargiulo,** Corso Italia 48 (✆ **081-8781081**), sells lovely, intricate embroideries. **Gargiulo & Jannuzzi,** Piazza Tasso 1 (✆ **081-8781041**), is right next to Bar Fauno and offers the best wood intarsia; you can visit the workshops for a demonstration of this ancient technique that follows centuries-old patterns. At the weekly **street market,** vendors sell everything from crockery to swimming suits (Tues morning, parking lot on Via San Renato).

Where to Eat

EXPENSIVE

Il Buco ★★ CREATIVE SORRENTINE Occupying the wine cellar of an ancient convent, this restaurant offers a menu of fine, imaginative cuisine that changes daily according to market availability. Only the best of local ingredients make their way to the kitchen. We loved the *mezzanelle con ragù di pesce in bianco* (pasta in a delicate seafood sauce flavored with black olives and wild fennel), and the *agnellodi paese al timo* (tender lamb served with rosemary roasted potatoes and savoy cabbage). The flower-filled outdoor terrace is delightful in summer.

2d Rampa Marina Piccola 5 (off Piazza Sant'Antonino). www.ilbucoristorante.it. ✆ **081-8782354.** Reservations recommended. *Secondi* 20€–30€; tasting menus 75€–85€; prix-fixe menu 55€. AE, DC, MC, V. Thurs–Tues 12:15–2:30pm and 7:30–11:30pm. Closed Jan.

MODERATE

O'Canonico 1898 ★ SORRENTINE This historic restaurant on Sorrento's main square has successfully maintained its popularity with tourists. Canonico offers professional service and a well-prepared traditional cuisine that incorporates only the freshest ingredients. We recommend the excellent *tagliatelle di pasta fresca con frutti di mare e zucchini* (fresh pasta with seafood and zucchini) and the *pescato del giorno* (fresh-caught fish of the day) in a potato crust. The wine list is extensive.

Piazza Tasso 5. ✆ **081-8783277.** Reservations recommended Sat–Sun. *Secondi* 16€–30€. AE, DC, MC, V. Daily noon–3:30pm and 7–11:30pm (closed Mon or Tues Nov–Mar).

INEXPENSIVE

Sant'Anna da Emilia ★ ☺ SORRENTINE This simple trattoria offers informal dining in an ancient boat shed in Marina Grande, complete with an outdoor terrace on a wooden pier. It is mobbed in summer, so be prepared to wait if you want to taste the great home-style cuisine that varies daily with the market offerings such as *spaghetti alle cozze* (with mussels), *gnocchi alla Sorrentina* (Sorrento-style potato dumplings), and *fritto misto* (deep-fried calamari and little fish). Order a jug of the excellent white house wine to go with your meal; it's chilled and refreshing.

Via Marina Grande 62. ✆ **081-8072720.** Reservations not accepted. *Secondi* 8.50€–14€. No credit cards. Daily noon–3:30pm and 7:30–11:30pm (closed Tues in winter). Closed Nov.

Entertainment & Nightlife

The narrow streets of Sorrento's *centro storico* are alive with cafes, clubs, and restaurants, which become positively crowded during the sweet nights of summer. Locals and visitors alike enjoy the lively terrace of the **Fauno Bar,** Piazza Tasso 13 (www.faunobar.it; ✆ **081-8781135**), for an *aperitivo* (aperitif) and people-watching till late into the evening.

Spring and summer are a special time in Sorrento, as music events are staged in venues throughout town. Some of the most popular are the concerts at the **Grand Hotel Cocumella,** Via Cocumella 7, Sant'Agnello (www.cocumella.com; ✆ **081-8782933**), and those in the **cloister of San Francesco,** Piazza Francesco Saverio Gargiulo. Contact the tourist office (p. 748) for a schedule of events.

For dancing and more lively entertainment for a more mature clientele (40s and up), head to Piazza Tasso and the nightclub **Fauno Notte Club** (www.faunonotte.it; ✆ **081-8781021;** cover 25€). It also offers a colorful **Tarantella Show,** the frenetic traditional folk dance, between stretches of DJ music (Mar–Oct; daily 9–11pm).

Sorrento Musical is a revue of Neapolitan songs hosted by **Teatro Tasso,** Piazza Sant'Antonino (www.teatrotasso.com; ✆ **081-8075525;** tickets about 25€ depending on show; 50€ including dinner). Live music (a varying menu of pop, folk, jazz, and so on) can also be heard at **Circolo dei Forestieri,** Via Luigi de Maio 35 (✆ **081-8773263;** closed Nov–Feb).

For more leisurely entertainment, try the laid-back **Chantecler,** Via Santa Maria della Pietà 38 (www.chanteclers.com; ✆ **081-8075868**); there's some dancing on weekends, and always some food. Other choices are **Chaplin's Video Pub,** Corso Italia 18 (✆ **081-8072551**), and the **English Inn,** Corso Italia 55 (✆ **081-8074357**); located across from each other, both stock a good selection of beers and maintain a lively atmosphere—sometimes even too lively on summer weekends.

Where to Stay

EXPENSIVE

Grand Hotel Excelsior Vittoria ★★★ ☺ Occupying an impressive villa and its estate right in the heart of town, this is a world-class hotel and one of our favorites. Owned by the same family since its opening in 1834, it offers exquisite, personalized service, superb facilities, and a charming Belle Epoque atmosphere. The elegant public spaces still have their original 19th-century furnishings and the huge, elegant guest rooms are finely decorated and furnished with many antiques along with all the modern comforts. They also have splendid marble bathrooms and most open onto a private balcony or terrace. From the hotel, elevators whisk guests down to the private beach-pier off Marina Piccola. In a splendid setting overlooking the gulf, the **Terrazza Bosquet** restaurant offers the most romantic gourmet dining in Sorrento.

Piazza Tasso 34, 80067 Sorrento. www.exvitt.it. ✆ **081-8777111.** Fax 081-8771206. 105 units. 390€–698€ double; from 660€ suite. Rates include buffet breakfast. Children 3 and under stay free in parent's room. Internet and family specials available. AE, DC, MC, V. Free parking. **Amenities:** 2 restaurants; bar; concierge; pool; room service; spa. *In room:* A/C, TV, minibar, Wi-Fi (free).

Parco dei Principi ★★ This retro stylish hotel is located just out of town at Sant'Agnello. Gio Ponti, the celebrated Milanese architect, designed the whole place (including the furniture, fittings, and lighting) in the 1960s and a stay here whisks you back to those heady, glamorous days. The modern building, with its clean white lines, sits on a cliff top with fabulous views over the Bay of Naples, and the '60s stylish blue-and-white color scheme throughout gives the place a nautical feel. Needless to say, the best rooms are the ones with sea views; each room has differently patterned blue and white floor tiles. There's a seawater pool, a private beach, a spa, and a lovely garden.

Via Rota 1, Sant'Agnello, 80067 Sorrento. www.hotelparcodeiprincipi.net. ✆ **081-8784644.** Fax 081-8783786. 96 units. 229€–279€ double; 400€–700€ suite. Rates include buffet breakfast. Children 2 and under stay free in parent's room. AE, DC, MC, V. Free parking. **Amenities:** 2 restaurants; bar; pool; room service; spa. *In room:* A/C, TV, minibar, Wi-Fi (free).

MODERATE

Grand Hotel Aminta ★★ ☺ In a dominant position above Sorrento (3km/2 miles away by free shuttle service), this modern hotel is an excellent choice for anyone wanting respite from the crowds and offers breathtaking views, professional yet friendly service, and good amenities. Public spaces are airy and welcoming and guest rooms are all bright and tastefully decorated with modern furnishings. They vary in size but all have contemporary bathrooms; most have balconies with magnificent sea views. For postsightseeing relaxation there is a large pool. The **restaurant** has a panoramic terrace where live music and dancing are often scheduled on summer evenings.

Via Nastro Verde 23, 80067 Sorrento. www.aminta.com. ✆ **081-8781821.** Fax 081-8781822. 81 units. 100€–300€ double; 250€–500€ junior suite. Rates include buffet breakfast. Internet specials available. Children 4 and under stay free in parent's room. AE, DC, MC, V. Free parking. **Amenities:** Restaurant; bar; concierge; pool; smoke-free rooms. *In room:* A/C, TV, minibar, Wi-Fi (free).

Hotel Antiche Mura ★ Situated in the heart of town, this lovely hotel is housed in an elegant Art Nouveau–style *palazzo* built on top of the defensive walls that give the place its name. Guest rooms are sunny and bright, decorated with Vietri-tile floors and Sorrentine marquetry furniture. "Comfort" rooms are more spacious, and we particularly liked the junior suites, which are large corner rooms with wraparound windows. All rooms are equipped with state-of-the-art bathrooms with tubs and special hydromassage showers. There's also a lovely garden where, among the lemon trees, there's a pool, lounge chairs, and snack bar serving drinks and light meals from 11am to 4pm.

Via Fuorimura 7 (entrance on Piazza Tasso), 80067 Sorrento. www.hotelantichemura.com. ✆ **081-8073523.** Fax 081-8071323. 46 units. 190€–250€ double; 290€ junior suite; 350€ suite. Rates include buffet breakfast. Internet specials available. Children 2 and under stay free in parent's room. AE, DC, MC, V. Parking 10€. **Amenities:** Bar; concierge; pool. *In room:* A/C, TV, minibar, Wi-Fi (free).

Hotel Imperial Tramontano ★ ☺ Another of Sorrento's historic hotels (past guests include Lord Byron and Henrik Ibsen), the Tramontano enjoys a dramatic position on a cliff overlooking the sea, a short distance from the center of town. Surrounded by a beautiful garden, the hotel offers the luxury of a patrician abode, with elegant public spaces and top-notch amenities. The spacious guest rooms are furnished with antiques and are bright and welcoming; some have private balconies and sea views. Guests have access to the hotel's private beach via elevator—or a hair-raising series of steps originally built by the Romans. The hotel's restaurant is one of the best in the area and music events are regularly staged on the terrace.

Via Vittorio Veneto 1, 80067 Sorrento. www.hoteltramonto.it. ✆ **081-8782588.** Fax 081-8072344. 116 units. 250€–380€ double; from 420€ suite. Rates include buffet breakfast. Family specials available. Children 3 and under stay free in parent's room. AE, MC, V. Free parking. Closed Jan–Feb. **Amenities:** Restaurant; bar; concierge; pool; room service. *In room:* A/C, TV, minibar.

Maison La Minervetta ★★★ La Minervetta started life in the 1950s as a popular seafood restaurant, but it's had a modern makeover. The result is a delightful boutique hotel that successfully combines contemporary design with bold Mediterranean colors. The upside-down building (car park and reception at the top, bedrooms underneath) clings to the cliffside and has fabulous views of the Bay of Naples and Vesuvius from public spaces and all the bedrooms. The huge living room has tables piled with magazines and arty books; it leads onto a wide sun terrace where an outstanding breakfast (one of the best we've come across) and drinks are served in warm weather. Far below is another terrace with a small Jacuzzi pool. The bedrooms all have bright fabrics, huge beds, and full-on sea views through floor to ceiling windows. The modern bathrooms are done out with colorful handmade tiles.

Via Capo 25, 80067 Sorrento. www.laminervetta.com. ✆ **081-8774455.** Fax 081-8784601. 12 units. 320€–420€ double. Rates include buffet breakfast. Internet specials available. Children 2 and under stay free in parent's room. AE, DC, MC, V. Free parking. **Amenities:** Concierge; Jacuzzi pool. *In room:* A/C, TV, minibar, Wi-Fi (3€ per hour).

Relais Villa Savarese 🎁 The perfect place to enjoy Sorrento as a 19th-century nobleman might have, this B&B/boutique hotel occupies a former patrician villa complete with garden and pool. The location along the road that leads out of Sorrento into adjacent Sant'Agnello is pleasant and quiet. Guest rooms are spacious and well-appointed. Bathrooms are good size and modern (some with shower only).

Corso M. Crawford 59, 80065 Sant'Agnello. www.relaisvillasavarese.com. ✆ **081-5324920.** Fax 081-8774187. 10 units. 240€–300€ double; 370€ junior suite. Rates include buffet breakfast. Internet specials available. AE, DC, MC, V. Parking 15€. Closed Nov–Mar. **Amenities:** Bar; concierge; fitness center (for a fee); Internet; pool. *In room:* A/C, TV, minibar.

INEXPENSIVE

Casa Astarita ★ 🏷 We really like this cozy little B&B which enjoys an excellent central location and is run like a private home by the Astarita sisters. Each of the seven bright bedrooms is different from the next, but all are stylish and comfortable with tiled bathrooms. Avoid the noisy room at the back of the building; those at the front are quieter. A delicious breakfast complete with homemade cakes is served around a communal table.

Corso Italia 7, 80067 Sorrento. www.casastarita.com. ✆ **081-8774906.** Fax 081-8071146. 7 units. 90€–110€ double. Rates include buffet breakfast. AE, MC, V. Parking 15€. *In room:* A/C, TV, Wi-Fi (free).

CAPRI ★★★

5km (3 miles) off the tip of the Sorrentine peninsula

Lying a few kilometers off the tip of the Sorrentine Peninsula, Capri (pronounced *Cap*-ry, not Ca-*pree*) is a rugged, mountainous island jutting dramatically from the sea. This chic playground for millionaires was the haunt of eccentrics and intellectuals in its past, and in spite of the daily invasion by thousands of tourists, it continues to beguile with its spectacular scenery, impossibly azure sea, and air of glamour. To get the best of the island, plan an overnight stay.

Touring the island is relatively simple. You dock at unremarkable **Marina Grande,** the port area. You can then take the funicular (or a taxi) up the steep hill to the town of **Capri** above, where you'll find the major hotels, restaurants, cafes, and shops. From Capri, a short bus ride will deliver you to **Anacapri,** perched at the top of the island near Monte Solaro. The only other settlement you might want to visit is **Marina Piccola,** on the south side of the island, with the major beach. There are also beaches at **Punta Carnea** and **Bagni di Tiberio.**

Essentials

GETTING THERE You can reach Capri from either Naples or Sorrento. From Naples's Molo Beverello dock (take a taxi from the train station), the **hydrofoil** *(aliscafo)* takes just 45 minutes. The hydrofoil leaves several times daily (some stop at Sorrento), and a one-way trip costs 19€. Regularly scheduled **ferry** *(traghetto)* service, departing from Porta di Massa, is cheaper but takes longer (about 1½ hr.). Fares are 17€ each way. For ferry schedules contact **Caremar** (www.caremar.it; ✆ **199-116655**); for hydrofoils, phone **SNAV** (www.snav.it; ✆ **081-4285555**). There's no need to check all the dock offices for the best price.

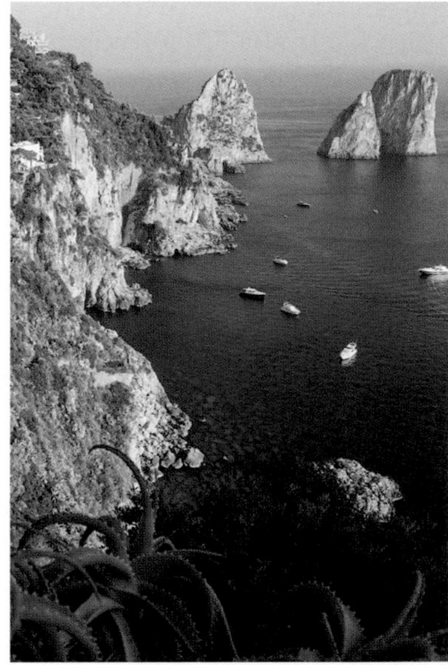

The Faraglioni rocks off the coast of Capri.

From Sorrento, go to the dock at Marina Piccola (just below Piazza Tasso), where you can board one of the **fast ferries** *(nave veloce)* run by Caremar or a hydrofoil run by **Gescab** (www.gescab.it; ✆ **081-8781430**). The hydrofoils are slightly faster and cost

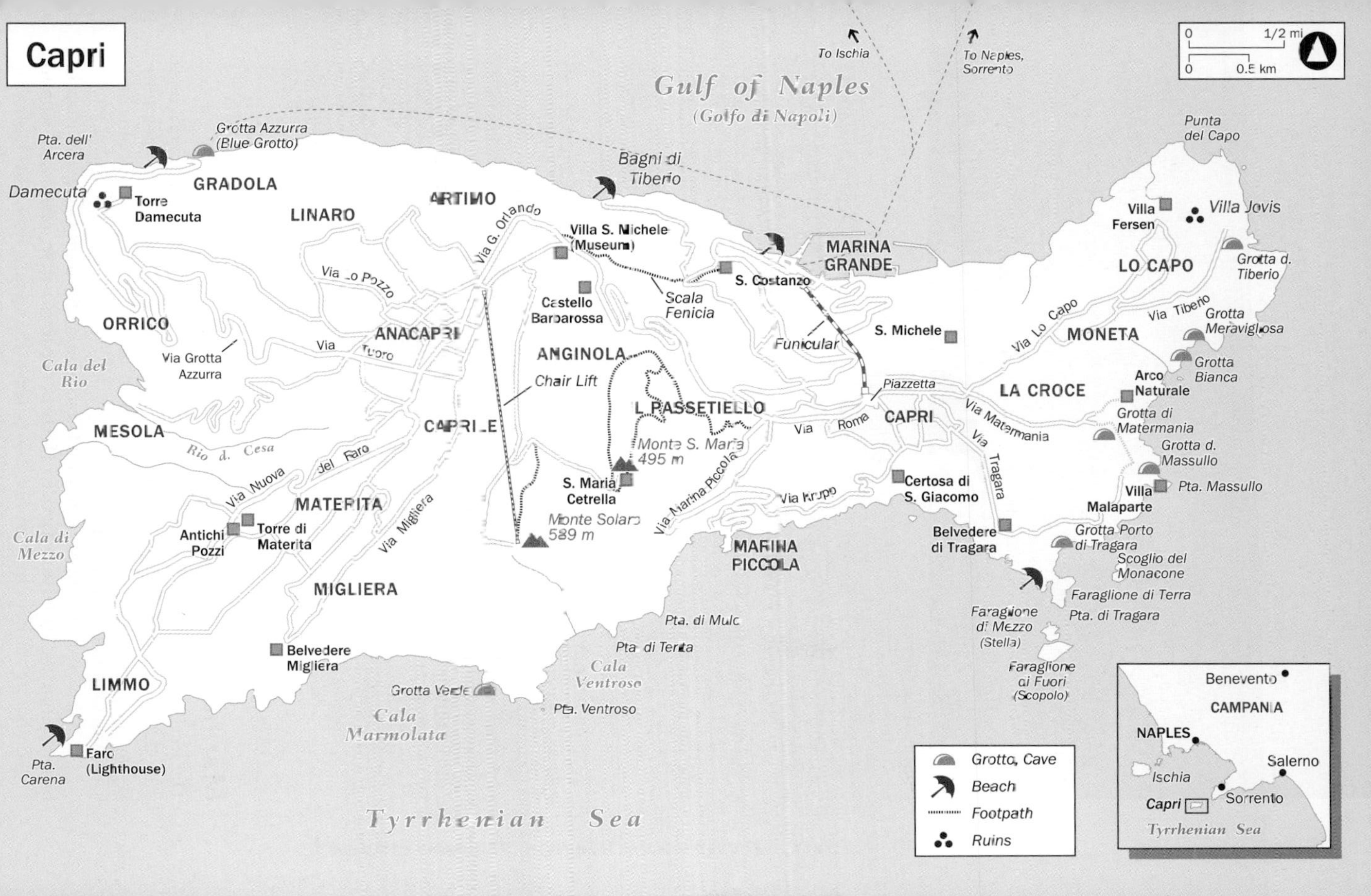

Capri
To Ischia
To Naples, Sorrento
0 1/2 mi
0 0.5 km
Gulf of Naples
(Golfo di Napoli)
Grotta Azzurra (Blue Grotto)
Pta. dell' Arcera
Bagni di Tiberio
Punta del Capo
Damecuta
Torre Damecuta
GRADOLA
LINARO
ARTIMO
Via G. Orlando
Villa S. Michele (Museum)
MARINA GRANDE
Villa Fersen
Villa Jovis
LO CAPO
Grotta d. Tiberio
Via Lo Pozzo
S. Costanzo
Castello Barbarossa
Scala Fenicia
ORRICO
ANACAPRI
Via Tuoro
S. Michele
Via Lo Capo
Via Tiberio
Grotta Meravigliosa
MONETA
Via Grotta Azzurra
ANGINOLA
Funicular
Grotta Bianca
Cala del Rio
Chair Lift
Piazzetta
LA CROCE
Arco Naturale
IL PASSETIELLO
Via Roma
CAPRI
Via Matermania
Grotta di Matermania
MESOLA
CAPRILE
Rio d. Cesa
Monte S. Maria 495 m
Via Tragara
Grotta d. Massullo
Via del Faro
S. Maria Cetrella
Via Marina Piccola
Certosa di S. Giacomo
Villa Malaparte
Pta. Massullo
Via Nuova
MATERITA
Via Krupp
Via Migliera
Monte Solaro 589 m
Antichi Pozzi
Torre di Materita
Cala di Mezzo
Belvedere di Tragara
Grotta Porto di Tragara
MARINA PICCOLA
Scoglio del Monacone
MIGLIERA
Faraglione di Terra
Pta. di Mulo
Faraglione di Mezzo (Stella)
Pta. di Tragara
Pta. di Terra
Belvedere Migliera
Cala Ventroso
Faraglione di Fuori (Scopolo)
LIMMO
Grotta Verde
Pta. Ventroso
Cala Marmolata
Faro (Lighthouse)
Pta. Carena
Tyrrhenian Sea
Grotto, Cave
Beach
Footpath
Ruins
Benevento
CAMPANIA
NAPLES
Salerno
Ischia
Sorrento
Capri
Tyrrhenian Sea

Inside the Blue Grotto.

15€ one-way; a one-way ticket for the fast ferry is 13€. Departures are 11 times per day from 7:15am to 7:15pm (the last boat back leaves Capri at 6:30pm).

Gescab (✆ **081-811986**) also runs a service between Positano and Capri from April through October. Hydrofoils cost 18€ one-way, and a ferry ticket goes for 16€ one-way.

VISITOR INFORMATION Get in touch with the **Tourist Board,** Piazzetta Italo Cerio (www.capritourism.com; ✆ **081-8375308**), at Capri town. From April to October, it's open Monday to Saturday 8:30am to 8:30pm, Sunday 8:30am to 2:30pm; November to March, hours are Monday to Saturday 9am to 1pm and 3:30 to 6:30pm.

GETTING AROUND There's no need for a car on tiny Capri. The island is serviced by funiculars, taxis, and buses. Capri's hotels are a long way from the docks, so we strongly recommend that you bring as little luggage as possible. You'll do best to hire a **porter** *(facchino)* for the climb from the ferry landing to your hotel; it is well worth the 6€ to 8€ per piece of luggage (depending on size). The service is perfectly trustworthy, so just leave your luggage and head to your hotel. If you like, you can save money by lugging your bags to the funicular or taxi and up into town, where the porters charge a little less per piece to the hotels not accessible by car.

Note that if you have reservations at one of the island's more upscale accommodations, your hotel might have its own porter on duty at the docks to help you with your luggage.

Marina Grande ★

The least attractive of the island's communities, Marina Grande is the port, bustling daily with the comings and goings of thousands of visitors. It has a little sand-cum-pebble beach, on which you're likely to see American sailors (on shore leave from Naples) playing ball.

If you're just spending the day on Capri, you might want to see the island's biggest attraction, the **Blue Grotto (Grotta Azzurra) ★★**, open daily 9am to 1 hour before sunset. In summer, boats leave frequently from the harbor at

Marina Grande to transport passengers to the entrance of the grotto for 25€ round-trip; this includes the fee for the small rowboat that takes you inside. Note that the grotto is closed during bad weather.

The Blue Grotto is one of the best-known natural sights of the region, although the way passengers are hustled in and out of it makes it a tourist trap. It's truly beautiful, however. Known to the ancients, it was later lost to the world until an artist stumbled on it in 1826. Inside the cavern, light refraction (the sun's rays entering from an opening under the water) achieves the dramatic Mediterranean cerulean color. The effect is stunning, as thousands testify yearly.

If you want, you can take a trip around the entire island, passing not only the Blue Grotto but the **Baths of Tiberius,** the **Palazzo al Mare** built in the days of the empire, the **Green Grotto** (less known), and the much-photographed rocks called the **Faraglioni.** Motorboats circle the island in about 1½ hours at 15€ per person.

Connecting Marina Grande with the town of Capri is a frequently running **funicular** charging 1.60€ one-way. However, the funicular, really a cog railway, doesn't operate off season. Buses also run year-round between Marina Grande and Capri town for the same price.

Swimming & Sunning

Capri is not strong on beaches. It's coastline is made up of sheer, soaring cliffs, rocky coves and the odd small stretch of sand, all surrounded by the bluest, clearest water you can imagine. The sea is tantalizingly close, but often difficult to get

Kayaking to the beach in Capri.

to, and most of the accessible "beaches" are run by private beach clubs called *stabilimenti balneari,* which you must pay to visit. Most people relax at their hotel pools and take in the gorgeous views from there.

For swimming, you might head for the **Bagni Nettuno,** Via Grotta Azzurra 46 (✆ **081-8371362**), a short distance from the Blue Grotto in Anacapri. Surrounded by scenic cliff sides, with an undeniable drama, it charges 35€. The price includes use of a cabana, towels, and deck chairs. Mid-March to mid-November, it's open daily 9am to sunset. From a point nearby, you can actually swim into the narrow, rocky entrance guarding the Blue Grotto, but this is advisable only after 5pm, when the boat services into the grotto have ended for the day, and only during relatively calm seas.

Another possibility for swimming is the **Bagni di Tiberio,** Via Palazzo a Mare (✆ **081-8370703**), a sandy beach a short walk from the ruins of an ancient Roman villa. To reach it, you have to board a motorboat departing from Marina Grande for the 15-minute ride to the site. Passage costs 18€ per person, unless you want to walk 30 minutes north from Marina Grande, through rocky landscapes with flowering plants and vineyards.

Closer to the island's south side is the **Marina Piccola,** a usually overcrowded stretch of sand extending between jagged lava rocks. You can rent a small motorboat here from the **Bagni le Sirene** (✆ **081-8370221**) for 100€ for 1 hour, 120€ for 2 hours, and 140€ for 3 hours.

The Town of Capri ★★★

Capri Town is the heart of the island. With its narrow streets hiding shops, a wide variety of restaurants and clubs, and some of the islands most exclusive hotels, this is Capri's most picturesque destination. Social life radiates from the famous **Piazzetta** (Piazza Umberto I), an open-air living room and a favorite spot for seeing and being seen.

One of the most popular walks from the main square is down Via Vittorio Emanuele, past the Quisisana hotel, to the **Giardini di Augusto park,** a choice spot for views and relaxation. From here you can see **I Faraglioni,** the iconic rocks once inhabited by the "blue lizard." At the top of the park is a belvedere overlooking emerald waters and Marina Piccola. Nearby you can visit the **Certosa,** a Carthusian monastery erected in the 14th century to honor St. James. It's open Tuesday to Sunday 9am to 2pm and charges no admission.

A statue amid the ruins of the Villa Jovis.

Back at Piazza Umberto I, head up Via Longano and then Via Tiberio, all the way to Monte Tiberio. Here you'll find the **Villa Jovis ★★**, the splendid ruin of the estate from which Tiberius ruled the empire from A.D. 27 to A.D. 37. Actually, the Jovis was one of a dozen villas that the depraved emperor erected on the island. Apparently, Tiberius had trouble sleeping, so he wandered from bed to bed, exploring his "nooks of lechery," a young girl one hour, a young boy the next. From the ruins, the views of the bays of Salerno and Naples plus the island itself are magnificent. You can visit the ruins of the imperial palace daily 9am to 1 hour before sunset for 2€. For information, call the tourist board at ✆ **081-8375308.**

WHERE TO EAT

Moderate

Al Grottino ★ CAPRESE/NEAPOLITAN Serving seafood and other Neapolitan dishes since 1937, this restaurant was a preferred hangout for VIPs in the 1950s. The food is still good, and you can choose from a variety of traditional Neapolitan comfort food, such as *frittura* (medley of deep-fried seafood) and *mozzarella in carrozza* (deep-fried mozzarella)—prepared in several different ways. We recommend the *sciaratelli* (local handmade pasta) with shrimp and zucchini flowers and the excellent *zuppa di cozze* (mussel soup) and *ravioli alla caprese* (with fresh mozzarella and marjoram), both Caprese specialties.

Via Longano 27, Capri. ✆ **081-8370584.** Reservations required for dinner. *Secondi* 13€–25€. AE, MC, V. Daily noon–3pm and 7pm–midnight. Closed Nov–Mar.

Aurora ★ CAMPANIAN/SEAFOOD One of the island's most consistently reliable restaurants, this traditional Caprese favorite lies in the historic center of Capri and is a celebrity favorite. The decor includes many elegant touches such as fine wooden furniture and terra-cotta floors and there is an outside terrace in summer. Aurora is also a pizzeria. Light, harmonious flavors go into the creation of the regional dishes such as mixed raw vegetables with lobster as a starter, followed by such main courses as fresh fish baked in a potato crust. The most imaginative homemade pasta is *pacchero,* a Neapolitan pasta with pumpkin flowers and Parmesan shavings, and the chef's pizza specialty *(all'acqua)* is made with mozzarella and chili peppers. Aurora also serves excellent pizza.

Via Fuorlovado 18, Capri. www.auroracapri.com. ✆ **081-8370181.** Reservations recommended. *Secondi* 18€–25€. AE, DC, MC, V. Daily 12:30–3pm and 7:30–11pm. Closed Jan–Mar.

Da Paolino ★★ CAPRESE Popular among locals, this restaurant serves deliciously simple food under a splendid lemon arbor terrace. The menu is traditional and down to earth, with a great array of grilled Mediterranean vegetables seasoned with the best local olive oil, and the freshest seafood. In addition to the great buffet of antipasti, we highly recommend the *sauté di cozze e vongole* (shellfish), and the *calamarata* (ring-shaped pasta with calamari).

Via Palazzo a Mare 11, Marina Grande. www.paolinocapri.com. ✆ **081-8376102.** Reservations required for dinner. *Secondi* 18€–32€. AE, DC, MC, V. Daily 7pm–midnight. Closed Nov–Mar.

La Savardina ★★ CAPRESE This historic address continues to lure both locals and visitors for its excellent traditional food, hospitable service, and delightful lemon and orange arbor terrace. We love it for the variety of its menu, including many vegetarian and meat-based dishes in addition to the typical seafood favorites. We recommend you start with a simple antipasto of grilled vegetables and local cured meat, followed by the very well-prepared *ravioli alla caprese* (filled with mozzarella), or with the linguine seasoned with capers, cherry tomatoes, and fresh herbs. For *secondo,* the *coniglio* (rabbit) is excellent, or try the excellent fish *all'acqua pazza.* The *torta caprese* (traditional chocolate and nut torte) is delicious.

Via Lo Capo 8, Capri. www.caprilasavardina.com. ✆ **081-8376300.** Reservations recommended. *Secondi* 12€–18€. AE, DC, MC, V. Mar–Apr and Sept–Oct Wed–Mon 12:30–3:30pm and 6:30–11pm; May–Aug daily 12:30–3:30pm and 6:30–11pm. Closed Nov–Easter.

Pulalli Wine Bar 🎁 CAMPANIAN You wouldn't think that there could be a culinary "discovery" to be had in the world-renowned Piazzetta, but this attractive wine bar and restaurant, with its delightful little terrace offering a bird's-eye view of the famed square, is just that. There's no obvious sign on the street; climb the steep steps that lead up from the right of the newsstand under the clock tower. The menu features the ubiquitous fish and seafood, but plenty more besides: We loved the tasty *pennette "aumm aumm"* (small pasta tubes with eggplant, tomato, mozzarella, and Parmesan) and the *risotto al limone* (lemon-flavored risotto) that is served in a half lemon. For *secondo,* go for one of the grilled meats (the filet steak is tender and delicious) accompanied by *polpettine di melanzane* (deep-fired eggplant croquettes), a Pulalli specialty.

Piazza Umberto I, 4, Capri. ✆ **081-8374108.** Reservations recommended. *Secondi* 10€–25€. AE, DC, MC, V. Wed–Mon noon–3pm and 7pm–midnight. Closed Nov to just before Easter.

Inexpensive

Grottelle 🎁 CAPRESE This small, off-the-beaten-track restaurant has a panoramic terrace just above the Arco Naturale and is a great place for sampling the local cuisine. The menu is centered on traditional Caprisian cuisine, and we highly recommend the *zuppa di fagioli* (bean soup) as well as the simple but delectable *spaghetti con pomodoro e basilica* (with fresh tomatoes and basil), followed by the perfect *frittura di paranza* (deep-fried seafood). The homemade desserts are very good.

Cafe in Capri.

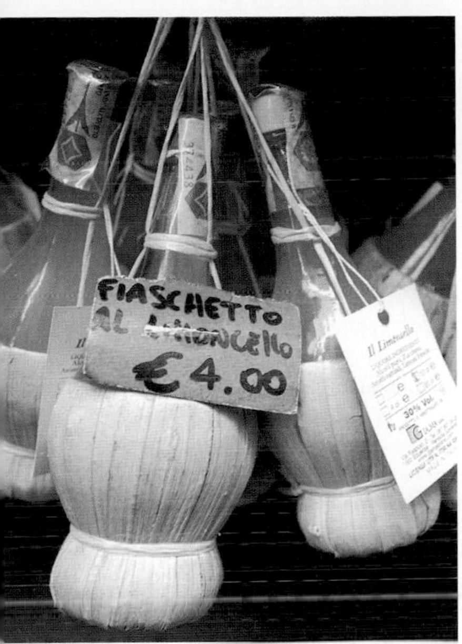

Bottles of limoncello for sale in Amalfi.

Via Arco Naturale 13, Capri. ✆ **081-8375719.** Fax 081-8389234. Reservations required for dinner. *Secondi* 15€–30€. AE, DC, MC, V. Fri–Wed noon–3pm and 7–11pm. Closed Nov–Mar.

SHOPPING

A little shop on Capri's luxury shopping street, **Carthusia-Profumi di Capri,** Via Camerelle 10 (www.carthusia.it; ✆ **081-8370529**), specializes in perfume made on the island from local herbs and flowers. Since 1948, this shop has attracted such clients as the late Elizabeth Taylor (before she started touting her own perfume). The scents are unique, and many women consider Carthusia perfumes collector's items.

Carthusia also has a **Perfume Laboratory,** Viale Matteotti 2D (✆ **081-8370368**), which you can visit daily 9:30am to 6pm. There's another **Carthusia shop** in Anacapri, at Via Capodimonte 26 (✆ **081-8373668**), next to the Villa Axel Munthe. The shops are closed November to March, but the laboratory remains open year-round.

Capri is famed for its **limoncello,** a liqueur whose recipe was conceived several generations ago by members of the Canali family. It consists of lemon zest (not the juice or pith) mixed with alcohol, sugar, water, and herbs to produce a tart kind of "hyper-lemonade" with a mildly alcoholic lift. It's consumed alone as either an aperitif or a digestive, or it's mixed with vodka or sparkling wines for a lemony cocktail. In 1989, the Canalis formalized their family recipe, established modern distilleries on Capri and in nearby Sorrento, and hired professionals to promote the product as far away as the United States and Japan. Limoncello is sold at **Limoncello di Capri,** Via Roma 79 (✆ **081-8375561**) in Capri, or at Via Capodimonte 27 (✆ **081-8372927**) in Anacapri, often in lovely bottles that make nice, affordable gifts.

Shoppers here also look for deals on sandals, cashmere, and jewelry, the town's big bargains. The cobblers at **Canfora,** Via Camerelle 3 (www.canfora.com; ✆ **081-8370487**), make all the sandals found in their shop. If you don't find what you need, you can order custom-made footwear. The store also sells shoes made elsewhere. The great sandal maker of Capri is Antonio Viva, holding forth for nearly half a century at **L'Arte del Sandalo Caprese,** Via Orlando 75 in Anacapri (www.sandalocaprese.it; ✆ **081-8373583**). In days of yore, Jackie O and Sophia Loren used to come here to purchase sandals. There are ready-made selections, but this cobbler will also design to order.

The eight talented jewelers at **La Perla Gioielli,** Piazza Umberto I 21 (✆ **081-8370641**), work exclusively with gold and gems and can design and create anything you want. Established in 1936 by a local matriarch, Mamma

Olympia, this is the most elegant and prestigious jeweler on Capri, with rosters of famous star-quality fans from around Europe and the New World. It's also the local branch of Buccellati, the prestigious silversmith based in Rome. Ask for Angela, or any of her charming children, Giorgio, Giuseppe, or Claudio. Another little charmer we recently stumbled upon quite by accident is **Grazia Vozza Gioielli,** Via Fuorlovado 38 (www.graziavozza.com; ✆ **081-8374010**), which sells freshwater pearls and a stunning collection of necklaces in peridot, jade, amber, and aquamarine.

ENTERTAINMENT & NIGHTLIFE

Warm, sweet summer nights in Capri are lively and long. The island of VIPs will not let you down, so prepare yourself for a trendy scene, with beautiful people dressing up and convening at the famous **Piazzetta** at nightfall. Fashionistas, take note: To compete with the local beauties, you'll have to learn how to walk on the steep cobblestone streets of Capri in your stilettos! Nightlife here centers on the elegant, trendy see-and-be-seen bars and restaurants. The **piano bars** in the **Grand Hotel Quisisana** and in the **Capri Palace** are the most exclusive venues, with prices to match; the newly opened **Rendez Vous,** in the **Grand Hotel Quisisana** (below), is more affordable. For a more relaxed scene, **Anema E Core,** Via Sella Orta 39/a, Capri (www.anemaecore.com; ✆ **081-8376461**), is a lively nightclub with live music; and the **Wine Bar,** Vico San Tommaso 1 (✆ **081-8370732**), in the historic restaurant **La Capannina,** is a cozy place to have a drink and listen to some music.

WHERE TO STAY

This is a ritzy resort, with correspondingly high prices. If you're really watching your wallet, you might have to visit for the day and return to the mainland for the night. Don't even think of coming in summer without a reservation.

Very Expensive

Grand Hotel Quisisana Capri ★★★ The island's grande dame since 1845, this is the favorite of a regular international crowd and a bastion of luxury. The sprawling buildings are painted a distinctive yellow and accented with vines and landscaping. Its guest rooms range from cozy singles to spacious suites—all opening onto wide arcades with a stunning view over the coast. They vary greatly in decor, with traditional and conservatively modern furnishings. All have a lovely, airy style, and all come with comfortable beds and tile or marble bathrooms. ***Note:*** Some rooms have a Jacuzzi.

Via Camerelle 2, 80073 Capri. www.quisisana.com. ✆ **081-8370788.** Fax 081-8376080. 148 units. 350€–600€ double; from 850€ suite. Rates include buffet breakfast. Children 3 and under stay free in parent's room. AE, DC, MC, V. Closed Nov–Easter. **Amenities:** 3 restaurants; 3 bars; babysitting; concierge; health club; pool; room service; spa; outdoor tennis courts. *In room:* A/C, TV, minibar.

Hotel Punta Tragara ★★ Standing high on a cliff with spectacular views over the famous Faraglioni, this hotel is in a quiet location slightly removed from the tourist madness of Capri town. Originally a luxurious private villa, it was designed by one of the greatest architects of the 20th century, Le Corbusier. Guest rooms have large windows and open onto private terraces, balconies, or small patios. They feature elegant modern furnishings, spacious bathrooms (some with shower only), and a restful ambience. The restaurant is worth a detour, even if you're not a guest.

Via Tragara 57, 80073 Capri. www.hoteltragara.com. ✆ **081-8370844.** Fax 081-8377790. 45 units. 500€–850€ double; from 920€ suite. Rates include buffet breakfast. Children 2 and under stay free in parent's room. Internet specials available. AE, DC, MC, V. Closed Nov–Easter. **Amenities:** Restaurant; bar; concierge; gym; pool; room service; spa. *In room:* A/C, TV, minibar.

JK Place Capri ★★ Great attention to detail, elegance, and beautiful views make this discreetly luxurious boutique hotel a winner, in spite of its less-than-desirable location on the main road from the harbor up to Capri and Anacapri. The cream-and-blue guest rooms are spacious and welcoming, decorated with a perfect mix of stylish elegance and comfort. The best have sea views and are filled with sunlight. Bathrooms are large (some with shower only). The hotel's restaurant serves excellent meals on the terrace or in the bar lounge.

Via Marina Grande 225 (up from the harbor), 80073 Capri. www.jkcapri.com. ✆ **081-8384001.** Fax 081-8376150. 22 units. 700€–900€ double; from 1,000€ suite. Rates include buffet breakfast. Internet specials available. AE, DC, MC, V. Closed Nov–Mar. **Amenities:** Restaurant service; bar; concierge; gym; pool; room service; spa. *In room:* A/C, TV, minibar, Wi-Fi (free).

La Scalinatella (Little Steps) ★★ This delightful hotel is built like a private villa above terraces offering a panoramic view. It's an exclusive pair of 200-year-old houses, with a vaguely Moorish design, run by the Morgano family (which also owns the Quisisana). The ambience is one of unadulterated luxury; all units include a phone beside the bathtub, beds set into alcoves, elaborate wrought-iron accents ringing the inner stairwell and the ornate balconies, and a sweeping view over the gardens and pool. Half of the accommodations boast two bathrooms each, one with a whirlpool tub. The hotel shares the facilities of the Quisi Club Spa at the Grand Hotel Quisisana, a 5-minute walk away.

Via Tragara 8, 80073 Capri. www.scalinatella.com. ✆ **081-8370633.** Fax 081-8378291. 45 units. 430€–560€ double; 700€ junior suite. Rates include buffet breakfast. Children 2 and under stay free in parent's room. AE, DC, MC, V. Closed Nov–Mar. **Amenities:** Restaurant; concierge; gym; pool; room service; outdoor tennis court. *In room:* A/C, TV, minibar.

Expensive

Casa Morgano ★★ This Morgano family property loses out by a hair to La Scalinatella, its next-door neighbor, but with prices much lower, you might not worry about the difference. Casa Morgano houses you in grand comfort in 20 of its rooms, which are spacious and deluxe; eight others are quite small. The best units are nos. 201 to 205 and 301 to 305. Most units contain good-size sitting areas along with terraces opening onto sea views. The bathrooms come with hydromassage bathtubs and showers.

Via Tragara 6, 80073 Capri. www.casamorgano.com. ✆ **081-8370158.** Fax 081-8370681. 28 units. 180€–490€ double; 450€–620€ junior suite. Rates include buffet breakfast. AE, DC, MC, V. Closed Nov–Mar. **Amenities:** Bar; babysitting; exercise room; heated pool; room service; outdoor tennis court (lit). *In room:* A/C, TV, hair dryer, minibar.

Hotel Luna ★ This first-class hotel stands on a cliff overlooking the sea and the rocks of Faraglioni. The guest rooms are a mix of contemporary Italian pieces and Victorian decor, most with recessed terraces overlooking the garden of flowers and semitropical plants. All are accompanied by tiled bathrooms.

Viale Matteotti 3, 80073 Capri. www.lunahotel.com. ✆ **081-8370433.** Fax 081-8377459. 54 units. 210€–480€ double; 380€–580€ suite. Rates include buffet breakfast. AE, MC, V. Closed Oct 24–Apr 20. **Amenities:** Restaurant; babysitting; Jacuzzi; pool; room service. *In room:* A/C, TV, hair dryer, minibar.

Moderate

Hotel La Vega This hotel began in the 1930s as the private home of the family that continues to run it today. It has a clear sea view and is nestled amid trees against a sunny hillside. The oversize guest rooms have decoratively tiled floors; each has a private balcony overlooking the water. Some beds have wrought-iron headboards. Below is a garden of flowering bushes, and on the lower edge is a free-form pool with a grassy border for sunbathing. Breakfast is served on your balcony or on a terrace surrounded by trees and potted flowers.

Via Occhio Marino 10, 80073 Capri. www.hotellavega.it. ✆ **081-8370481.** Fax 081-8370342. 24 units (some with shower only). 140€–320€ double; 320€–420€ suite. Rates include buffet breakfast. AE, DC, MC, V. Closed Nov–Easter. **Amenities:** Bar; babysitting; pool; room service. *In room:* A/C, TV, hair dryer, minibar.

Hotel Regina Cristina The white facade of the Regina Cristina rises four stories above one of the most imaginatively landscaped gardens on Capri. It was built in 1959 and has a sunny design of open spaces, sunken lounges, and cool tiles. Each guest room has its own balcony and is very restful. Their sizes range from small to medium, but each has a good mattress and a compact tiled bathroom. In general, the prices are high for what you get, but on Capri in July and August you're sometimes lucky to find a room at any price.

Via Serena 20, 80073 Capri. www.reginacristina.it. ✆ **081-8370744.** Fax 081-8370550. 55 units. 195€–450€ double. Rates include buffet breakfast. MC, V. **Amenities:** Restaurant; bar; Jacuzzi; pool; room service. *In room:* A/C, TV, hair dryer, minibar.

Villa Brunella 🎁 We particularly like the Brunella, set in a panoramic position, and a private villa until 1963, when it was transformed into its current incarnation as a pleasant family-run hotel. Guest rooms have a welcoming atmosphere and each double has its own flowered terrace or balcony with a sea view. Bathrooms are modest in size but come with modern fixtures and designer tiles. Guests have access to the beach club at Marina Piccola. The hotel's restaurant **Terrazza Brunella** ★ offers excellent food in a lovely setting and elegant service.

Via Tragara 24, 80073 Capri. www.villabrunella.it. ✆ **081-8370122.** Fax 081-8370430. 20 units. 270€–370€ double; 460€ junior suite. Rates include buffet breakfast. AE, DC, MC, V. Closed Nov–Apr. **Amenities:** Restaurant; bar; pool; room service. *In room:* A/C, TV, minibar.

Villa Sarah ★ 🎁 The modern Sarah, though far removed from the day-trippers from Naples, is still very central. A steep walk from the main square, it seems part of another world, with its private garden and good views. One of the bargains of the island, it's often fully booked, so reserve ahead in summer. The sea is visible only from the upper floors. Most of the guest rooms are quite small, but some of them make up for this with pleasant terraces. Bathrooms are a bit small as well. Breakfast is sometimes served on the terrace.

Via Tiberio 3A, 80073 Capri. www.villasarah.it. ✆ **081-8377817.** Fax 081-8377215. 20 units. 145€–220€ double; 290€ triple. Rates include buffet breakfast. AE, MC, V. Closed Nov 1–Mar 19. **Amenities:** Bar; babysitting; pool. *In room:* A/C, TV, hair dryer, minibar.

Inexpensive

Villa Krupp This is a longtime favorite known for its affordable prices. During the early 20th century, Russian revolutionaries Gorky and Lenin called this villa home. Surrounded by shady trees, it offers panoramic views of the sea and the Gardens of Augustus from its terraces. At this family-run place, the front parlor is all glass with views of the seaside and semitropical plants set near Hong Kong chairs, intermixed with painted Venetian-style pieces. Rooms are comfortable and vary in size, with spacious bathrooms.

Via Matteotti 12, 80073 Capri. hwww.villakrupp.com. ✆ **081-8377473.** Fax 081-8376489. 12 units, shower only. 140€–180€ double. Rates include buffet breakfast. MC, V. Closed Nov–Mar. **Amenities:** Bar; room service. *In room:* A/C, hair dryer.

Anacapri ★★★

Even nearer to the clouds than Capri is the idyllic town of Anacapri, which is more remote and secluded than the main resort. At one time, Anacapri and Capri were connected only by the Scala Fenicia, the Phoenician Stairs (which have been reconstructed a zillion times). Today, however, you can reach Anacapri on a daring bus ride more thrilling than any roller coaster. The fare is 2.80€ round-trip. One visitor remarked that all bus drivers to Anacapri "were either good or dead."

When you disembark at **Piazza della Vittoria,** you'll find a village of charming dimensions.

To continue your ascent to the top, hop aboard a chairlift (La Segiovia) to **Monte Solaro ★★**, the loftiest citadel on the island at 594m (1,950 ft.). The ride takes about 12 minutes and operates March to October daily 9:30am to sunset. A round-trip costs 9€. From the top, the panorama of the Bay of Naples is spread before you.

The Monte Solaro chairlift in Anacapri.

Back in the village below, you can head out on Viale Axel Munthe from Piazza Monumento for a 5-minute walk to the **Villa San Michele ★**, Capodimonte 34 (www.villasanmichele.eu; ✆ **081-8371401**). This was the home of Axel Munthe, the Swedish physician and author of *The Story of Villa San Michele.* Munthe was also a friend of Gustav V, king of Sweden, who visited him several times on the island. The villa has remained as Munthe (who died in 1949) furnished it, in a harmonious and tasteful way. It houses several marble sculptures which Munthe purchased from the ruins of Tiberius's imperial villa, located right under the Villa San Michele. Walk through the gardens for another in a series of sweeping views of the island. You can visit the villa daily January and February 9am to 3:30pm, March 9am to 4:30pm, April 9am to 5pm, May to September 9am to 6pm, October 9am to 5pm, and November to December 9am to 3:30pm. Admission is 6€.

WHERE TO EAT

Expensive

Il Riccio ★ CAPRESE Born from the proverbial ashes of the historic Add'o Riccio, this contemporary reinvention of the beach restaurant is part of the Capri Palace Hotel. The stylish club strikes the perfect balance between casual and chic with a fabulous location steps from the Blue Grotto, and a terrace overlooking the sea. The menu focuses on seafood and traditional dishes: From the classic Caprese salad to the *linguine all'astice* (with spiny lobster), everything is well prepared with only the freshest ingredients. For an extravagant treat, order the giant platter of *frutti di mare* (mixed seafood) to share with a friend. The secluded solarium carved in the rocks is available for private parties.

Via Gradola 4, Anacapri. www.ristoranteilriccio.com. ✆ **081-8371380.** Reservations recommended. *Secondi* 18€–25€. AE, DC, MC, V. Daily 12:30–3:30pm and 8–11pm. Closed Nov–Mar.

L'Olivo ★★ CREATIVE CAPRESE The double Michelin-starred restaurant of the Capri Palace Hotel, this is the perfect address for a truly exclusive experience. Stylish and pricey, it combines aesthetics (hand-blown glasses, silver cutlery, luxurious fabrics and details), perfect service, and gourmet haute cuisine. German chef Oliver Glowig has now moved on to pastures new, but L'Olivo is still considered to be among the best places to eat on the island and Glowig's successor, Andrea Migliaccio bases his light, innovative cuisine on regional and Mediterranean specialties. The menu is seasonal and best exemplified by the tasting menus.

Via Capodimonte 2, Anacapri. www.capri-palace.com. ✆ **081-9780111.** Reservations recommended. *Secondi* 35€–46€; tasting menus 150€ and 190€. AE, DC, MC, V. Daily noon–3pm and 7-10pm. Closed Nov–Mar.

Inexpensive

La Rondinella 🎁 CAPRESE/PIZZA This relaxed family-run restaurant is a good choice for a quiet, reasonably priced meal. In the evening, it prepares many varieties of brick-oven pizza. The menu is traditional and includes delicious *ravioli alla caprese* (mozzarella, fresh tomatoes, and marjoram), *pezzogna all'acqua pazza* (local fish in a light tomato sauce), and *frittura* (deep-fried seafood medley), which they prepare particularly well. In the evenings, there is a wide variety of pizza baked in a wood-burning oven. For dessert, local specialties such as *torta caprese* (chocolate and almond cake) are excellent.

Via G. Orlandi 245, Anacapri. ✆ **081-8371223.** Reservations required for dinner. *Secondi* 11€–16€; pizza 6€–10€. AE, DC, MC, V. Fri–Wed noon–3pm and 7–11pm. Closed Nov–Mar.

WHERE TO STAY

Very Expensive

Capri Palace ★★★ On the slopes of Monte Solaro, the contemporary, first-class Capri Palace sparkles. Its bold designer obviously loved wide-open spaces and vivid colors. The landscaped gardens with palm trees and plenty of bougainvillea have a large pool, which most guests use as their outdoor living room. Although it lacks the intimate charms of La Scalinatella in Capri (see earlier in this chapter), it's still a wonderful choice because of its setting. Each of the guest rooms is attractively and comfortably furnished, and from some on a clear day you can see smoking Vesuvius. Many beds (mostly twins) are canopied, and all of them feature quality linens. Children 9 years and under are not welcome from June to August. Each of the four special suites has a private pool and private garden.

Via Capodimonte 2, 80071 Anacapri. www.capri-palace.com. ✆ **081-9780111.** Fax 081-8373191. 79 units. 340€–1,250€ double; 720€–3,300€ suite. Rates include buffet breakfast. AE, DC, MC, V. Closed Oct 17–Mar 31. Children 9 years and under not accepted June–Aug. **Amenities:** 2 restaurants; bar; babysitting; heated pool; room service; spa. *In room:* A/C, TV, hair dryer, minibar

Moderate

Hotel Bella Vista A 2-minute walk from the piazza, this is a modern retreat with a panoramic view and a distinct sense of a family-run regional inn. Lodged into a mountainside, the hotel is decorated with primary colors and has large living and dining rooms and terraces with sea views. The breakfast and lunch terrace has garden furniture and a rattan-roofed sun shelter. The guest rooms are pleasantly contemporary (a few have a bed mezzanine, a sitting area on the lower level, and a private entrance). The tiled bathrooms are compact.

Via Orlandi 10, 80071 Anacapri. www.bellavistacapri.com. ✆ **081-8371463.** Fax 081-8382719. 15 units. 130€–240€ double; 180€–260€ triple. Rates include buffet breakfast. AE, DC, MC, V. Closed Nov 1–Easter. **Amenities:** Restaurant; room service; 3 outdoor tennis courts (lit). *In room:* TV, fridge, hair dryer.

Hotel San Michele di Anacapri This well-appointed hotel offers spacious cliffside gardens and unmarred views as well as enough shady or sunny nooks to please everybody. Guests linger in its private gardens, where the trees are softened by splashes of color from hydrangea and geraniums. The view includes the Bay of Naples and Vesuvius. The midsize bedrooms are tastefully and comfortably furnished.

Via Orlandi 1–3, 80071 Anacapri. www.sanmichele-capri.com. ✆ **081-8371427.** Fax 081-8371420. 60 units. 150€–230€ double; 250€–420€ suite. Rates include breakfast. AE, DC, MC, V. Closed Nov–Mar. **Amenities:** Restaurant; bar; babysitting; pool; room service. *In room:* A/C, TV, hair dryer.

Inexpensive

Il Girasole This series of four adjacent buildings with brick terraces opens onto views of the Bay of Naples. All the midsize to spacious bedrooms are handsomely decorated with padded headboards and tasteful modular furnishings and open onto terraces draped with bougainvillea. The best rooms are the suites,

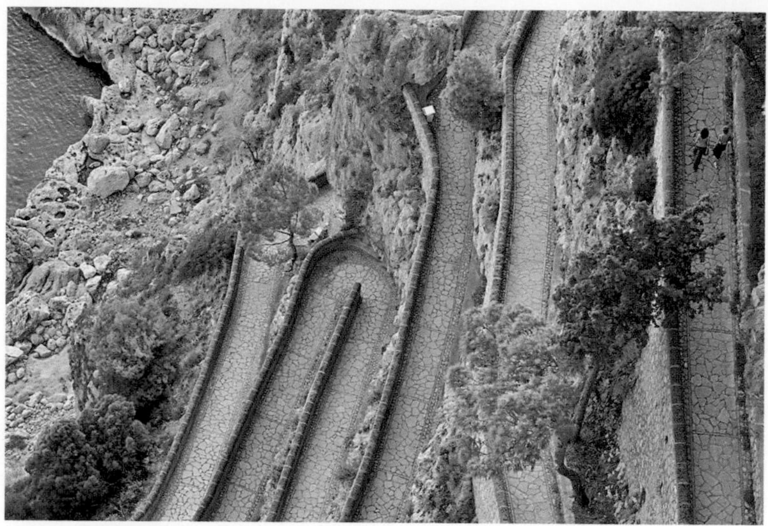

The winding walk from Capri to Marina Piccola.

Aurum and Raggio di Luna, which are decorated with reproduction antiques and painted motifs. Avoid room nos. 3 to 5 under the reception hall. The pool is a bit small, but otherwise this place is choice in every way.

Via Linciano 47, 80071 Anacapri. www.ilgirasole.com. ✆ **081-8372351.** Fax 081-8373880. 24 units. 78€–190€ double; 170€–230€ suite. MC, V. Closed late Oct to mid-Mar. **Amenities:** Bar; babysitting; pool; room service. *In room:* A/C, TV, hair dryer, minibar, Wi-Fi (5€ per 24 hr.).

Villa Eva ★ This was the childhood home of its owner, Eva Balestrieri, who was born in no. 5. Her husband, Vincenzo Parlato, an artist and craftsman, is the on-site gardener, builder, painter, and decorator. He even made the furniture scattered throughout the property. Artists, regular people, and what the owners call "eccentric characters" return year after year to this homelike place. Rooms are housed in a series of small cottages: Each cottage comes with a private bathroom with shower, and all units are tastefully decorated and furnished, with patios overlooking the charming garden. The focal point of the grounds is a pool shaped like a piano.

Via La Fabbrica 8, 80071 Anacapri. www.villaeva.com. ✆ **081-8371549.** Fax 081-8372040. 15 units. 70€–140€ double; 110€–180€ triple; 150€–210€ quad. Rates include buffet breakfast. AE, MC, V. Closed Nov–Feb. **Amenities:** Bar; Internet (free, in lobby); pool. *In room:* No phone.

Marina Piccola ★

It's a pleasant 20-minute walk from Capri down the hill to the little south-shore fishing village and beach of **Marina Piccola** (take a cab or a bus back up the steep hill to Capri). The village opens onto emerald-and-cerulean waters, with the Faraglioni rocks of the sirens jutting out at the far end of the bay. Treat yourself to lunch at **La Canzone del Mare,** Via Marina Piccola 93 (www.lacanzonedelmare.com; ✆ **081-8370104**), daily noon to 4pm (closed Nov–Mar). Seafood and Neapolitan cuisines are served.

POSITANO ★★

56km (35 miles) SE of Naples, 16km (10 miles) E of Sorrento, 266km (165 miles) SE of Rome

Hugging a semivertical rock formation, Positano is the quintessence of picturesque and its unique mix of seascapes, colors, art, and cultural life has fascinated famous artists, musicians, and writers from Picasso and Klee to Toscanini, Bernstein, and Steinbeck. Once part of the powerful Republic of the Amalfis and rival to Venice as a sea power, this one-time exclusive seaside resort has been thoroughly "discovered," but retains its character and charm in spite of a mass tourist invasion in the summer months. It remains a delightful place to visit, although we do recommend coming off season if possible. The village, you'll soon discover, is impossibly steep: Wear comfortable walking shoes.

Essentials

GETTING THERE SITA **buses** leave from Sorrento frequently throughout the day, more often in summer than winter, for the rather thrilling ride to Positano; a one-way fare is 1.40€. For information, call SITA at © **081-405145.**

Gescab (www.consorziolmp.it; © **089-811986**) runs hydrofoil and ferry services between Capri and Positano. Hydrofoils cost 18€ one-way, and a ferry ticket goes for 16€ one-way.

If you have a **car,** Positano lies along SS145, which becomes SS163 at the approach to the resort.

Positano.

VISITOR INFORMATION The **tourist office** (www.aziendaturismopositano.it; © **089-875067**) is at Via del Saracino 4. It is open Monday to Saturday 8:30am to 2pm, with additional hours (3:30–8pm) in July and August.

Where to Eat

EXPENSIVE

Buca di Bacco ★★ CAMPANIA/ITALIAN Right on the beach you'll find one of Positano's top restaurants, opened just days after the end of World War II. Guests often stop for a drink in the bar before heading up to the dining room on a big covered terrace facing the sea. On display are fresh fish, special salads, and fruit, such as luscious black figs and freshly peeled oranges soaked in caramel. An exciting opener is a fresh seafood salad; you might prefer the *zuppa di cozze* (mussels) in a tangy sauce. Other items not to miss are linguine with lobster and *grigliata del Golfo,* a unique mixed fish fry.

The pasta dishes are homemade and the meats are well prepared with fresh ingredients. Finish with a limoncello, the lemon liqueur celebrated along the Amalfi Drive.

Via Rampa Teglia 8. www.bucadibacco.it. ✆ **089-875699.** Reservations required. Main courses 13€–38€. AE, DC, MC, V. Daily noon–3:30pm and 7–11:30pm. Closed Nov–Mar.

La Cambusa AMALFITAN/SEAFOOD Baldo and Luigi created this beachfront restaurant in 1970 vowing to serve traditionally prepared fish of the highest quality, and they have stuck to their promise 40 years or so on. Only the freshest fish—brought in every morning by local fishermen—is prepared with techniques designed to bring out the natural flavors. Try *paccheri alla pescatrice* (thick pasta tubes with mixed seafood) or our favorite, *linguine agli scampi con pomodorini* (with shrimp and local cherry tomatoes). For the *secondo,* pick your fish from the display and have it simply grilled or cooked *all'acqua pazza* (with an herb broth).

Piazza Amerigo Vespucci 4, near Spiaggia Grande. www.lacambusapositano.com. ✆ **089-875432.** Reservations recommended. *Secondi* 16€–28€. AE, DC, MC, V. Daily noon–3pm and 7:30–11pm.

MODERATE

Da Adolfo ★ AMALFITAN/SEAFOOD You might like the challenge of reaching this picturesque beach restaurant from the SS 163 via the flight of 450 rugged steps down and then, unfortunately, up again. If not, a free water-shuttle service for the restaurant's guests is available at Marina Grande: You'll recognize the boat by the red fish symbol on the prow. This Positano classic has a laid-back atmosphere, and the menu includes many simple local dishes. The signature dish is mozzarella *alla brace* (grilled on fresh lemon leaves) and a truly special *zuppa di cozze* (mussel stew), but we also recommend the tasty *grigliata di pesce* (medley of fresh grilled seafood). Da Adolfo also offers **beach facilities** with changing rooms, showers, and chair-and-umbrella rentals.

Via Spiaggia di Laurito 40. www.daadolfo.com. ✆ **089-875022.** Reservations recommended. *Secondi* 10€–18€. AE, MC, V. Daily 1–4pm. Closed mid-Oct to early May.

Il Ritrovo 🎁 AMALFITAN/PIZZA This pleasant restaurant is located in the village of Montepertuso, high above Positano, and offers a great escape from the crowds, high prices, and summer heat below. There is a cool arbor-covered terrace with magnificent views, and a seasonal menu focused on meat and vegetables from the family farm. Both the *grigliata mista* (grilled meat medley) and the free-range chicken baked with herbs are excellent, as is homemade pasta such as ravioli served with cherry tomatoes, eggplant, and basil, or *tagliatelle* with local porcini mushrooms. The SITA bus stop from Positano is nearby, or you can call the restaurant for free pickup. There's live music on Friday and Saturday evenings and chef Salvatore also offers well-organized **cooking classes** year-round.

Via Montepertuso 77. www.ilritrovo.com. ✆ **089-812005.** Reservations recommended. *Secondi* 10€–20€; set-price menu 30€–40€. AE, DC, MC, V. Thurs–Tues noon–3:30pm and 7pm–12:30am (daily Apr to mid-Oct). Closed Jan.

Next 2 ★★ AMALFITAN We really like the classy, contemporary look of this buzzy wine bar and restaurant with its big terrace, and the food is great, too. Tanina Vanacore and her son-in-law turn out modern versions of local classics using fresh produce from their own garden. We loved the *fiori di zucchini ripieni di ricotta, mozzarella e basilico* (zucchini flowers stuffed with ricotta, mozzarella, and basil) served with a pesto sauce, the *ricciola scottata con le zucchine alla scapece* (local fish with mint and vinegar-flavored zucchini), and *tagliata di tonno con asparagi* (sliced tuna steak with asparagus). There's a comprehensive wine list, and a wine bar where you can order a plate of cheeses and mixed cold cuts if you want a lighter meal. After dinner, a young crowd moves in for late-night drinks.

Via Pasitea 242. www.next2.it. ✆ **089-8123516.** Reservations recommended in high season. *Secondi* 16€–25€. AE, DC, MC, V. Daily 7–11pm (closed Mon off season). Closed Nov–Mar.

Pupetto ★ ☺ AMALFITAN/PIZZA Right on the beach at Fornillo, this historic restaurant cannot be reached by car (an elevator will take you down from the parking lot off SS163), but is a moderately short walk away from Marina Grande along a seaside path. A 1950s vibe has been preserved, with the colorful and informal dining terrace and down-to-earth menu. The food is good, and your kids can run around on the beach outside (where you can rent umbrellas and chairs). We recommend the excellent *spaghetti alle vongole* (with fresh clams) and the *fritto misto* (deep-fried seafood medley). ***Note:*** Pizza is served only in the evening. Above the restaurant are 34 large **guest rooms** with basic amenities (170€–220€ double, including breakfast; parking 15€).

Via Fornillo 37, Spiaggia di Fornillo. www.hotelpupetto.it. ✆ **089-875087.** Fax 089-811517. *Secondi* 12€–22€; pizza 7€–10€. AE, DC, MC, V. Daily 12:30–3pm and 7:30–10pm. Closed Nov–Mar.

Shopping

The shop at the Hotel Le Sirenuse (see review below), **Emporio Le Sirenuse,** Via Cristoforo Colombo 103 (www.lesirenuse.it; ✆ **089-811468**), has the town's chicest merchandise, everything from ballerina slippers from Porselli (who designs them for Milan's La Scala) to sexy one-piece bathing suits.

The town is famous for its handmade sandals. Some of the artisan shops will make them for you while you wait. Try **D'Antonio,** Via Trara Genoino 13 (✆ **089-811824**); **Dattilo,** Via Rampa Teglia 19 (✆ **089-811440**), or **Safari,** Via della Taratana 2 (www.safaripositano.com; ✆ **089-811440**).

For the best collection of ceramics from the Amalfi town of Vietri sul Mare, head for **Ceramica Assunta,** Via Cristoforo Colombo 97 (www.ceramicassunta.it; ✆ **089-875008**), known for its colorful ceramics with fine artisanal decorations.

Entertainment & Nightlife

Music on the Rocks, Spiaggia Grande Via Grotte dell'Incanto 51 (www.musicontherocks.it; ✆ **089-875874**), is designed on two levels, one of which contains a quieter piano bar. It's owned by the same man who owns the chic Chez Black.

Similar in its choice of music, crowd, and setting is **L'Africana,** Via Torre a Mare 2 (✆ **089-874042**), near the resort of Praiano, about 7km (4½ miles) from Positano. Local fishermen come in during the most frenzied peak of the dancing. At a sinkhole at the edge of the dance floor, they lower their nets to pull up a catch of seafood for local restaurants. The contrast of New Age music with old-world folklore is as riveting as it is bizarre. Many chic guests from Positano

L'Africana nightclub in Praiano, near Positano.

arrive by boat. Both clubs open nightly at around 10pm June to August, but only Friday and Saturday in May and September, and they're closed the rest of the year.

Where to Stay

VERY EXPENSIVE

Hotel Le Sirenuse ★★ This striking red-and-white 18th-century villa with terraces overlooking the bay is a picturesque sight. Situated directly above the harbor, it was the residence of the Marchesi Sersale family (who still manage the hotel) until 1951, and the public spaces are palatial. The beautiful guest rooms are large and bright, with vaulted ceilings, antiques, hand-painted tile floors, and fine fabrics; all have private terraces and luxurious bathrooms. Most have matchless views of the bay. The hotel's swimming pool is perched on a terrace, and a state-of-the-art health club with an attached Aveda spa offers further relaxation. The buffet breakfast here is lavish, and the **restaurant La Sponda** is highly recommended for meals: It recently gained a Michelin star. Children 6 and under are not accepted in the hotel from May through September (the exact dates vary slightly each year, so check), or at the restaurant for dinner.

Via Cristoforo Colombo 30, 84017 Positano. www.sirenuse.it. ✆ **089-875066.** Fax 089-811798. 59 units. 500€–890€ double; from 1,260€ suite. Rates include buffet breakfast. AE, DC, MC, V. Parking 40€. Children 6 and under not accepted May–Sept. **Amenities:** Restaurant; 2 bars; concierge; health club; pool; room service; spa. *In room:* A/C, TV, minibar.

San Pietro ★★★ Offering luxurious accommodations and exceptionally professional service in a wonderful location just outside Positano near Laurito Beach, this family-run member of the Relais & Châteaux group is *the* place to stay on the Amalfi Coast. Elegant public areas have French windows opening onto the garden and the sea; spacious guest rooms have antiques, tiled floors, pink-marble bathrooms, and private terraces; some have huge picture windows. The hotel's private beach with its waterside restaurant **Carlino** is accessible by elevator, and there's a splendid panoramic swimming pool, tennis court, and a state-of-the-art fitness center with a wonderful spa. ***Note:*** The hotel welcomes children only age 10 and above.

The Michelin-rated **Il San Pietro** is unique not only for its exceptional food, but also for its magnificent views, cozy terrace, and lovely garden. The restaurant is closed November through March; reservations are required as well as formal dress for dinner.

Via Laurito 2, 84017 Positano. www.ilsanpietro.it. ✆ **089-875455.** Fax 089-811449. 60 units. 550€–680€ double; from 750€ suite. Rates include breakfast. 3 nights minimum stay in high season (May–Oct 18). AE, DC, MC, V. Free parking. Closed Nov–Mar. Only children 10 and above allowed. **Amenities:** Restaurants; bar; concierge; health club; pool; room service; sauna; spa; tennis court. *In room:* A/C, TV, minibar.

EXPENSIVE

Palazzo Murat ★★ This 18th-century baroque palace near the marina is said to have been built for Gioacchino Murat, Napoleon's brother-in-law who was to become king of Naples, and today, it's one of our favorite places to stay in the town center. The five large (and more expensive) guest rooms in the historical part of the building are decorated with antiques and original furnishings; the ones in the new wings are smaller but still very attractive and have private terraces. All units have good-size bathrooms, and most have ocean views. The rich buffet breakfast is served in the delightful garden under big white umbrellas when weather permits. The hotel's restaurant **Al Palazzo** offers alfresco gourmet dining in a charming setting.

Via dei Mulini 23, 84017 Positano. www.palazzomurat.it. ✆ **089-875177.** 31 units. 200€–450€ double. Rates include buffet breakfast. Children 2 and under stay free in parent's room. AE, DC, MC, V. Parking 25€ nearby. Closed Jan to week before Easter. **Amenities:** Restaurant; concierge; room service. *In room:* A/C, TV, minibar.

Villa Franca ★ 🎁 Situated at the top of the town, this delightful family-run hotel overlooking the sea is one of Positano's lesser-known, distinctive hotels. The common areas, with their neoclassical feel, are decorated with reproduction artwork and fine tiles: The motif continues in the elegant, comfortable guest rooms, all of which are decorated in Mediterranean style, with bright, tiled floors and bathrooms. Private balconies overlook the sea. The roof terrace has a swimming pool with a solarium and magnificent, 360-degree views over the town. There are 10 additional rooms in the rather less-inspiring annex. The hotel's restaurant serves good food in a romantic setting and there is a free shuttle bus to the center of Positano.

Via Pasitea 318, 84017 Positano. www.villafrancahotel.it. ✆ **089-875655.** Fax 089-875735. 38 units. 210€–410€ double. Rates include buffet breakfast. Children 2 and under stay free in parent's room. AE, DC, MC, V. Parking 21€. **Amenities:** Restaurant; bar; concierge; health club; pool; room service; spa. *In room:* A/C, TV, minibar.

MODERATE

Casa Albertina ★★ This small, family-run hotel in the upper part of Positano offers attentive service and great views. The famous Sicilian writer Luigi Pirandello was a regular guest: Maybe he found the beautiful bedrooms as cozy and welcoming as we did. Each is individually decorated, with carefully chosen furniture and a simple, monochromatic theme; French doors open onto private balconies with sea views. In good weather, breakfast is served on the terra-cotta tiled terrace. In the high season, rates include half board (breakfast and dinner).

Via della Tavolozza 3, 84017 Positano. www.casalbertina.it. ✆ **089-875143.** Fax 089-811540. 20 units. 180€–250€ double. Rates include breakfast. Children 2 and under stay free in parent's room. AE, DC, MC, V. Parking 20€–40€ nearby. **Amenities:** Restaurant; bar; concierge; room service. *In room:* A/C, TV, minibar.

Hotel Buca di Bacco Centrally positioned on the Marina Grande—a great choice if you don't mind a bit of noise—this excellent hotel boasts beautiful rooms that are all large and well furnished. Most have balconies facing the sea, and six superior rooms have full seafront terraces. The less-expensive rooms in the annexed buildings enjoy similar levels of comfort. The hotel's restaurant is extremely popular, as is the less-pricey snack bar.

Via Rampa Teglia 4, 84017 Positano. www.bucadibacco.it. ✆ **089-875699.** 54 units. 245€–450€ double. Rates include buffet breakfast. AE, DC, MC, V. No parking. Closed 2 weeks in winter. **Amenities:** Restaurant (see review, p. 769); bar; babysitting; concierge; room service; Wi-Fi (free). *In room:* A/C, TV, minibar.

INEXPENSIVE

Hotel Bougainville 🎁 This small, family-run hotel only has 14 rooms but is a good choice if you don't mind sacrificing amenities for location: It lies in the heart of Positano only steps from the beach, and rates are very reasonable. Some of the rear-facing guest rooms open onto flowery private terraces, where you can have breakfast in good weather, while others overlook the town. Try and avoid one of the few standard doubles with miniscule windows. All the rooms have good-quality simple, modern furniture, pastel-colored tiled floors, and good-size bathrooms (some with shower only).

Via Cristoforo Colombo 25, 84017 Positano. www.bougainville.it. ✆ **089-875047.** Fax 089-811150. 14 units. 125€–180€ double. AE, V. No parking. Closed Nov to mid-Mar. **Amenities:** Bar. *In room:* A/C, TV, minibar, Wi-Fi (3€ per hour).

Hotel Savoia ★★ Nestled in the heart of Positano, this quiet, well-run hotel is just steps away from shops and the beach. Guest units are spacious, bright, and comfortably furnished (think good beds and roomy cabinets), with cool tiled floors. Some of the rooms have sea views, while others overlook the village; bathrooms are good-size (some with shower only) and those in the best rooms have sauna showers or Jacuzzi tubs. This place has been run by the D'Aiello family since 1936, and they pride themselves on courteous service.

Via Cristoforo Colombo 73, 84017 Positano. www.savoiapositano.it. ✆ **089-875003.** Fax 089-811844. 42 units. 120€–190€ double; 240€ suite. Rates include buffet breakfast. AE, DC, MC, V. Parking 25€ nearby. **Amenities:** Bar; babysitting; concierge; room service; Wi-Fi (free). *In room:* A/C, TV, minibar.

AMALFI ★★

61km (38 miles) SE of Naples, 18km (11 miles) E of Positano, 34km (21 miles) W of Salerno, 272km (169 miles) SE of Rome

From the 9th to the 11th century, the seafaring Republic of Amalfi rivaled the great maritime powers of Genoa and Venice, and its maritime code, the Tavole Amalfitane, was followed in the Mediterranean for centuries. But raids by Saracens and a flood in the 14th century devastated the city. Amalfi's power and influence weakened, until its star rose again in modern times as the major resort on the Amalfi Drive.

From its position at the slope of the steep Lattari mountains, Amalfi overlooks the Bay of Salerno and the approach to the town is dramatic, whether you come from Positano or from Salerno. Today, Amalfi depends on tourism for its livelihood, and the hotels and *pensioni* are located right in the milling throng of vacationers. The finest and most highly rated accommodations are on the outskirts.

Essentials

GETTING THERE SITA **buses** run every 2 hours during the day from Sorrento, costing 2.50€ one-way. There are also SITA bus connections from Positano, costing 1.40€ one-way.

By **car** from Positano, continue east along the narrow hairpin turns of the Amalfi Drive (SS163).

VISITOR INFORMATION The **tourist office** (www.amalfitouristoffice.it; ✆ **089-871107**) is in Palazzo di Città, Corso delle Repubbliche Marinare 19. It is open Monday to Friday 9am to 1pm and 2 to 6pm, Saturday 9am to noon. In winter, it is only open in the mornings.

Exploring the Town

Amalfi lays some claim to being a beach resort, and narrow public **beaches** flank the harbor. In addition, between rocky sections of the coast, many of the first-class and deluxe hotels have carved out small stretches of sand reserved for their guests. However, better and more expansive beaches are adjacent to the nearby villages of **Minori** and **Maiori,** a short drive along the coast. Those beaches are lined with a handful of cafes, souvenir kiosks, and restaurants that thrive mostly during the summer. You can reach the villages by buses leaving from Amalfi's Piazza Flavio Gioia at 30-minute intervals during the day. Expect to pay 1€ each way.

The **Duomo ★**, Piazza del Duomo (✆ **089-871059**), evokes Amalfi's rich past. It is named in honor of St. Andrew (Sant'Andrea), whose remains are said to be buried inside the crypt (see below). Reached by climbing steep steps, the cathedral is characterized by its black-and-white facade and mosaics. The one nave and two aisles are all richly baroque. The cathedral dates from the 11th century, although the present structure has been rebuilt. Its bronze doors were made in Constantinople, and its campanile (bell tower) is from the 13th century, erected partially in the Romanesque style. The Duomo is open, and admission is free.

You can also visit the **Cloister of Paradise (Chiostro del Paradiso) ★★**, to the left of the Duomo, originally a necropolis for members of the Amalfitan "establishment." This graveyard dates from the 1200s and contains broken columns and statues, as well as sarcophagi. The aura is definitely Moorish, with a whitewashed quadrangle of interlaced arches. One of the treasures is fragments of Cosmatesque work, brightly colored geometric mosaics that once formed parts of columns and altars, a specialty of this region. The arches create an evocative setting for concerts, both piano and vocal, held on Friday nights July to September. The church and cloister are open from March to October daily 9am to 9pm

The Cloister of Paradise.

and in November to February daily 10am to 5pm. Admission is free to both. You reach the **crypt** from the cloister. Here lie the remains of St. Andrew—that is, everything except his face which the pope donated to St. Andrew's in Patras, Greece. The back half of his head has remained here, however.

A minor attraction, good for that rainy day, is the **Civic Museum (Museo Civico),** Town Hall Piazza Municipio (✆ **089-8736211**), which displays original manuscripts of the Tavole Amalfitane. This was the maritime code that governed the entire Mediterranean until 1570. Some exhibits relate to Flavio Gioia, Amalfi's most famous merchant adventurer. Amalfitani claim that he invented the compass in the 12th century. "The sun, the moon, the stars and—Amalfi," locals used to say. What's left from the "attic" of their once-great power is preserved here. The museum is open Monday to Friday 8am to 1pm. Admission is free.

For your most **scenic walk** in Amalfi, start at Piazza del Duomo and head up Via Genova. The classic stroll will take you to the **Valley of the Mills (Valle dei Mulini),** so called because of the paper mills that once thrived along its rocky reaches (the seafaring republic is said to have acquainted Italy with the use of paper). You'll pass by fragrant gardens and scented citrus groves. If the subject interests you, you can learn more details about the industry at the **Museum of Paper (Museo della Carta),** Via delle Cartiere 24 (www.museodellacarta.it; ✆ **089-8304561**), filled with antique presses and yellowing manuscripts from yesterday. It's open daily 10am to 6:30pm in summer and Tuesday to Sunday until 3pm from November to March. Admission is 4€. Guided tours are included.

Where to Eat

EXPENSIVE

La Caravella ★★★ MODERN AMALFITAN Do not expect sea views in this temple of cuisine, where guests are not to be distracted by such frivolities as a sunset. A successful advocate of the marriage between classic and modern

The Eerie Emerald Grotto

Five kilometers (3 miles) west of Amalfi is the millennia-old **Emerald Grotto (Grotta di Smeraldo) ★★**. This cavern, known for its light effects, is a chamber of stalactites and stalagmites, some underwater. You can visit daily 9am to 4pm, provided that the seas are calm enough not to bash boats to pieces as they try to land. The only way to get here is by boat from Amalfi's docks; it costs 10€ round-trip. For more information call the Amalfi tourist office (www.amalfitouristoffice.it; ✆ **089-871107**).

culinary traditions, Chef Antonio Dipino offers a seasonal menu with both elaborate and simple dishes prepared only with the freshest local ingredients; his skill earned him the first Michelin star to be awarded in southern Italy. Great attention is paid to service and setting, and you'll be surrounded by sober elegance in the dining hall of this 12th-century *palazzo*. Go with the tasting menu, or order a la carte: The seaweed fritters are excellent, followed by *tubetti di Gragnano al ragù di zuppa di pesce* (short pasta in a seafood sauce) and a superb *pezzogna* (fresh local fish). Those who prefer meat may favor *ziti di Torre Annunziata ripieni di carne alla Genovese* (pasta tubes filled with beef). The desserts and the wine list are on par with the rest of the menu. To celebrate its 50th year, La Caravella also opened an art gallery and wine bar near the restaurant.

Via Matteo Camera 12. www.ristorantelacaravella.it. ✆ **089-871029.** Reservations required. *Secondi* 25€–35€; tasting menu 90€. AE, DC, MC, V. Wed–Mon noon–2pm and 7:30–11pm. Closed Nov and Jan.

MODERATE

Da Gemma ★ SEAFOOD/AMALFITAN Located near the cathedral, Da Gemma is one of Amalfi's classic restaurants, with a strong emphasis on fresh seafood. It has been overseen by members of the Grimaldi family for many generations, a fact that caused a lot of fuss when Princess Caroline of Monaco (whose family name is also Grimaldi, but with a link that's very distant) came to dine. The kitchen sends out platefuls of savory pastas, grilled or sautéed fish, casseroles, and an enduring favorite—*zuppa di pesce,* a full meal in its own right and prepared only for two. The pasta specialty is *paccheri all'acquapazza,* made with shrimp and monkfish. For dessert, order the *crostata* (pie with jam), the best you're ever likely to have; it's made with pine nuts and homemade marmalades of lemon, orange, and tangerine.

Via Frà Gerardo Sasso 11. www.trattoriadagemma.com. ✆ **089-871345.** Reservations required. *Secondi* 16€–26€. AE, DC, MC, V. Daily 12:30–2:45pm and 7:30–11pm (closed Wed Nov to mid-Apr). Closed 6 weeks Jan to early Mar.

INEXPENSIVE

'a Paranza ★★ AMALFITAN This simple trattoria is our favorite restaurant in the area. Popular for its well prepared seafood and moderate prices, it is hidden away off the main street of Atrani—the village adjacent to Amalfi to the east—and does not have sea views or an outside terrace, but the wonderful food makes up for this. The traditional cuisine focuses on the best local ingredients. We recommend starting off with the house antipasti (almost a meal in itself) but other standouts include delicious *scialatielli alla paranza* (homemade pasta with small fish), *polipetti in cassuola* (baby octopus stewed in a terra-cotta pot), or *scampi al limone* (prawns in lemon sauce). Do not miss the homemade desserts such as the pear and ricotta tart. The wine list is short but includes excellent local labels.

Via Dragone 1-2, Atrani. www.ristoranteparanza.com. ✆ **089-871840.** Reservations recommended. *Secondi* 12€–23€. AE, DC, MC, V. Wed–Mon 12:30–3pm and 7:30–11:30pm (also Tues in summer). Closed 2 weeks in Dec.

Shopping

The coast has long been known for its **ceramics,** and the area at **Piazza del Duomo** is filled with hawkers peddling "regional" ware (which often means Asian). But the real thing is still made at nearby **Vietri sul Mare,** 13km (8 miles) west of Amalfi. The pottery made in Vietri is distinguished by its florid colors and sunny motifs. Vietri's best outlet is **Ceramica Solimene,** Via Madonna degli Angeli 7 (www.solimene.com; ✆ **089-210243**), which has been producing quality terra-cotta ceramics for centuries. It's fabled for its production of lead-free surface tiles, dinner- and cookware, umbrella holders, and stylish lamps.

In Amalfi itself, look for **limoncello,** a sweet lemon liqueur that tastes best chilled. It's manufactured in town by the **La Valle dei Mulini** factories. You can drop by its headquarters on Salita Chiarito 9 to buy a bottle or two (call ✆ **089-873211** for information). A bottle of limoncello costs about 15€. At **Antichi Sapori d'Amalfi,** Sottoportico Ferrara (www.antichisaporidamalfi.it; ✆ **089-872303**), you will find not only limoncello but a full array of local products, such as jams, honeys, lemon perfumes, and grappa.

At **La Grotta di Masaniello,** Largo Cesareo Console 7 (✆ **089-871929**), owner Francesco Mangieri (call him Mao) makes sculptures from ancient pieces of marble or a stalactite or stalagmite from one of the nearby grottoes.

Ceramics for sale in the Piazza del Duomo in Amalfi.

Where to Stay

VERY EXPENSIVE

Hotel Santa Caterina ★★★ This is the most luxurious hotel in Amalfi (and indeed one of the best of the coast), offering top-notch, family-run service and a superb cliffside location. Guests have access to a private beach, which you can reach by elevator or a winding garden path; the pleasant swimming pool is filled with seawater and is set in luscious gardens. Guest rooms are spread throughout the main building and three annexes. All are large and elegant, with antique furnishings, ceramic tiles from Vietri, and luxurious bathrooms (some with shower only). Each opens to a private balcony or terrace with views over the sea. Some of the suites are absolutely fantastic—we loved the luxurious Follia Amalfitana and Casa dell'Arancio in particular; they are independent bungalows immersed in a citrus grove, with a private garden and a small pool. At the Ristorante Santa Caterina you can sample sophisticated local dishes while the **Ristorante a Mare ★**, laid out on a terrace above the beach, offers more casual dining (open during the summer months only).

Via Nazionale 9, 84011 Amalfi. www.hotelsantacaterina.it. ✆ **089-871012.** Fax 089-871351. 49 units. 420€–790€ double; from 930€ suite. Rates include buffet breakfast. AE, DC, MC, V. Parking 15€. **Amenities:** 2 restaurants; bar; concierge; gym; pool; room service; spa. *In room:* A/C, TV, minibar, Wi-Fi (free).

EXPENSIVE

Hotel Belvedere ★ Below the coastal road outside Amalfi on the drive to Positano, the aptly named Belvedere has one of the best locations in the area. The house originated as a private villa in the 1860s and was transformed by its present owners into a hotel in 1962. The guest rooms have terraces overlooking the water. They range in shape and size, each with a tiled bathroom. The family owners see to it that guests are happy. There's a shuttle bus into Amalfi. An interior elevator will take you down to the pool and the path to the sea.

Via Smeraldo 19, Conca dei Marini, 84010 Amalfi. www.belvederehotel.it. ✆ **089-831282.** Fax 089-831439. 35 units. 160€–250€ double; 280€–350€ suite. AE, DC, MC, V. Free parking. Closed Oct 25–Apr 20. **Amenities:** Restaurant, 2 bars; saltwater pool; room service. *In room:* A/C, TV, hair dryer, minibar.

Hotel Luna Convento ★★ Transformed into a hotel in 1822, the Luna Convento occupies the ancient monastery, complete with beautiful original cloister and church, founded by Saint Francis in 1222 and Amalfi's watchtower dating from 1564. Situated on the promontory that protects Amalfi's harbor and only 273m (896 ft.) from the town's center, this family-run place counts Henrik Ibsen (who wrote *A Doll's House* here in 1879) among its famous guests. The space remains as artistically inspiring as ever: The hotel is surrounded by a garden, with sun terraces and a large seawater swimming pool carved out of the cliff. There is also a private, rather rocky beach and a highly praised gourmet restaurant, where you have to make reservations long in advance. The watchtower houses a disco and piano bar, as well as another restaurant with fantastic views. Guest rooms vary in size and decor, but all are bright and spacious, with sweeping vistas and spacious tiled bathrooms: We advise paying the extra for a private terrace.

Via Pantaleone Comite 33, 84011 Amalfi. www.lunahotel.it. ✆ **089-871002.** Fax 089-871333. 40 units. 250€–340€ double; from 440€ suite. Rates include buffet breakfast. Children 2 and under stay free in parent's room. AE, DC, MC, V. Parking 18€. **Amenities:** 2 restaurants; bar; babysitting; concierge; outdoor pool; room service. *In room:* A/C, TV, hair dryer, minibar.

MODERATE

Hotel Miramalfi Standing on a rocky point west of town, this family-run hotel offers attractive rooms and views in every direction. It has its own private beach, as well as a pool (accessible by elevator) and a cookery school. There is also a free shuttle bus service into town. Guest rooms are welcoming, modern in style, with good-size bathrooms (most with shower only); all have balconies and views overlooking the sea, but the best are the front-facing ones with large terraces. Lunch is served in a new restaurant set just above the beach.

Via Salvatore Quasimodo 3, 84011 Amalfi. www.miramalfi.it. ✆ **089-871588.** Fax 089-871287. 49 units. 270€–330€ double; 500€ suite. Rates include breakfast. Internet specials available. Children 2 and under stay free in parent's room. AE, DC, MC, V. Parking 15€. **Amenities:** Restaurant; bar; concierge; pool; room service; Wi-Fi (free). *In room:* A/C, TV, minibar.

Villa Lara In the heart of the resort, this restored villa from the late 19th century lies close to the Duomo and the water. It is perched on a cliff with views of Amalfi and the coast. The antique villa is surrounded by lemon trees and flowering bougainvillea. The furnishings are antiques but are combined with functional amenities, including such luxuries as a hydromassage shower. There is a high level of taste throughout, and much of the old has been retained, including the majolica tiles and the vaulted ceilings. Breakfast is taken on a panoramic terrace and is seasonally adjusted to take advantage of the typical products of the Amalfi coast, such as fresh fruit or freshly squeezed orange juice.

Via delle Cartiere 3, 84001 Amalfi. www.villalara.it. ✆ **089-8736358.** Fax 089-9830119. 7 units. 100€–195€ double; 175€–275€ suite. Rates include buffet breakfast. AE, DC, MC, V. Parking 18€. **Amenities:** Bar; babysitting; Internet (free, in lobby); room service. *In room:* A/C, TV, hair dryer, minibar.

INEXPENSIVE

Hotel Lidomare One of the best bargains in Amalfi, this pleasant small hotel is a few steps from the sea in a 13th-century building. The high-ceilinged guest rooms are airy and contain a scattering of modern furniture mixed with Victorian-era antiques. The Camera family extends a warm welcome. Breakfast is the only meal served, but you can order it until 10am.

Largo Piccolomini 9, 84011 Amalfi. www.lidomare.it. ✆ **089-871332.** Fax 089-871394. 15 units, 8 with shower only. 103€–145€ double. Rates include continental breakfast. AE, MC, V. Parking 18€. *In room:* A/C, TV, hair dryer, minibar, Wi-Fi (free).

RAVELLO ★★★

275km (171 miles) SE of Rome, 66km (41 miles) SE of Naples, 29km (18 miles) W of Salerno

Situated high up in the mountains, Ravello is like a terrace over the sea, overlooking the villages of Minori and Maiori. Long a refuge for VIPs (including Gore Vidal who only recently sold his villa here), it is worlds away from the clamor down on the coast, and its traffic-free status gives the town an air of classy tranquillity. Once the day-trippers leave, it reverts to being a sleepy, hilltop village and is a charming place to spend a couple of nights.

Essentials

GETTING THERE **Buses** from Amalfi leave for Ravello from the terminal at the waterfront at Piazza Flavio Gioia (✆ **089-871009** for schedules and information) almost every hour 7am to 10pm, costing 1.10€ one-way.

If you have a **car** and are in Amalfi, take the circuitous mountain road north of the town (the road is signposted to Ravello).

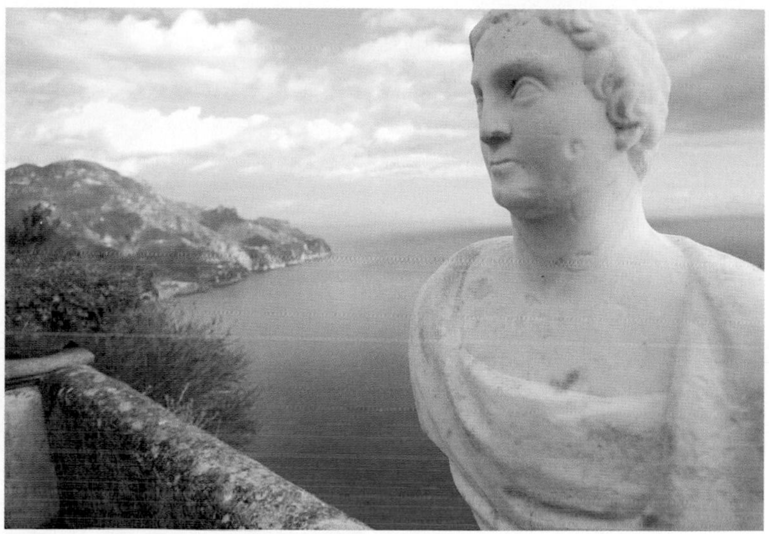

A view from Villa Cimbrone in Ravello.

VISITOR INFORMATION The **tourist office,** Via Roma 18 (www.ravellotime.it), is open daily 9am to 7pm, in November to May it closes at 6pm.

SPECIAL EVENTS The hilltop town is known for its summer **Ravello Festival.** Internationally famed artists sometimes appear. The venues range from the Duomo to the gardens of Villa Rufolo. Tickets, which you can buy at the tourist office, start at 20€.

Exploring Ravello

Although most of your time will be spent sunbathing, relaxing, strolling, and taking in the view, Ravello has a few outstanding sightseeing attractions, too.

Duomo It's unusual for such a small place to have a cathedral, but Ravello boasts one because it was once a major bishopric. The building dates from the 11th century, but its bronze doors are the work of Barisano da Trani and were crafted in 1179. Its **campanile** (bell tower) was erected in the 13th century. One of its major treasures is the pulpit of the Rufolo family, decorated with intricate mosaics and supported by spiral columns resting on the backs of half a dozen white marble lions. This is the work of Nicoló di Bartolomeo da Foggia in 1272. Another less intricate pulpit from 1130 features two large mosaics of Jonah being eaten and regurgitated by a dragonlike green whale. To the left of the altar is the **Chapel of San Pantaleone (Cappella di San Pantaleone),** the patron saint of Ravello to whom the cathedral is dedicated. His "unleakable" blood is preserved in a cracked vessel. The saint was beheaded at Nicomedia on July 27, A.D. 290. When Ravello holds a festival on that day every year, the saint's blood is said to liquefy. A museum of religious artifacts is also on-site.

Piazza Duomo. Duomo free admission; museum 2€. Duomo daily 9am–noon and 5:30–7pm. Museum Easter–Oct daily 9am–7pm; off season daily 9am–6pm.

Villa Cimbrone ★ The body of this grand villa dates from the 14th and 15th centuries but it was largely rebuilt in 1904 by its new owner, the eccentric Englishman Lord Grimthorpe (who also designed London's Big Ben). In the 1920s, the villa became a popular hangout for the literary Bloomsbury set, and Greta Garbo hid here in 1937 with her lover, the conductor Leopold Stokowski. Although today the villa is occupied by a luxury hotel and only accessible to hotel guests (unless you choose to eat in the restaurant), its **glorious grounds ★★★** are open to all. This grandiose garden, suspended high over the azure sea below, is one of the most beautiful in Italy and was also created by Lord Grimthorpe in 1905. Among the garden's many magical spots, the high point (both literally and figuratively) is the **Belvedere Cimbrone ★★★** which has dizzying views over the Bay of Salerno from between the neoclassical statues that grace the stone balustrade. Note that the villa is located some way from the center of town and can only be accessed by foot up a rather steep hill.

The gardens at Villa Rufolo in Ravello.

Via Santa Chiara 26. www.villacimbrone.it. ✆ **089-857459,** for reservations. Fax 089-857777. Admission 6€ adults, 4€ children. Daily 9am–sunset. Last admission 30 min. earlier.

Villa Rufolo ★★ The Villa Rufolo was named for the patrician family that founded it in the 11th century. Once the residence of kings and popes, such as Hadrian IV, it's now remembered chiefly for its connection with Richard Wagner. He composed an act of *Parsifal* here in a setting he dubbed the "Garden of Klingsor." He also lived and composed at Palazzo Sasso (see below). Boccaccio was so moved by the spot that he included it as background in one of his tales. The Moorish-influenced architecture evokes Granada's Alhambra, and the large tower was built in what's known as the Norman-Sicilian style. You can walk through the flower gardens leading to lookout points over the memorable coastline.

Piazza Duomo. www.villarufolo.it. ✆ **089-857621.** Admission 5€. Summer daily 9am–8pm; winter daily 9am–sunset. Last admission 15 min. earlier.

Where to Eat

Most guests take meals at their hotels. But the following are worth a special trip.

Cumpa' Cosimo AMALFITAN Here's where you're likely to find everyone from the electrician down the street to a movie star looking for the best home cooking in town. Pictures of Jackie O still decorate the walls, a reminder of a long-ago visit. The restaurant was opened in 1929 by a patriarch known affectionately as Cumpa' (Godfather) Cosimo and his wife, Cumma' (Godmother) Chiara. Today their daughter, Netta Bottone, runs the place, turning out well-flavored regional food in generous portions. Menu items include homemade versions of seven pastas, served with your choice of seven sauces. Any of these might be followed by a mixed grill of fish, giant prawns, roasted lamb seasoned with herbs, *zuppa di pesce, frittura di pesce* (fish fry), veal scaloppine, or beefsteak with garlic-and-wine sauce. Fresh local artichokes, asparagus, and mushrooms are among the vegetables available seasonally.

Via Roma 44. ✆ **089-857156.** Reservations recommended. *Secondi* 11€–18€; pizza 6€–10€. AE, DC, MC, V. Daily 12:30–3pm and 7:30–11pm. Closed Mon Nov–Feb.

Ristorante Pizzeria Vittoria 🎁 AMALFITAN/PIZZA This family-run place is a good choice for a moderately priced meal: The dining room is welcoming and the service is prompt. The pizza is top-notch and the menu includes many tasty choices such as *spaghetti alle vongole* (with clams), *risotto al limone e gamberi con bottarga di muggine* (with lemon and shrimp sprinkled with mullet roe), and the excellent *tagliata di tonno con aceto balsamico* (sliced, seared tuna steak with balsamic vinegar).

Via dei Rufolo 3. www.ristorantepizzeriavittoria.it. ✆ **089-857947.** Reservations recommended Sat–Sun. *Secondi* 15€–18€, pizza 6€–9€. AE, DC, MC, V. Wed–Mon 12:30–3pm and 7:30–11pm (also Tues Apr–Oct).

Rossellinis ★★★ MEDITERRANEAN In the Palazzo Sasso, this deluxe restaurant reigns supreme in the area. Visitors along the Amalfi Coast drive for miles just to sample the cuisine here. You dine like an aristocrat on stone floors under 12-foot ceilings. Under your feet is a vintage wine cellar.

Pino Lavarra, the chef, has mastered his art, with his sublime cuisine crafted from excellent raw materials. The food is inventive and the dishes are lightened for modern tastes. Specialties include deep-fried crab ravioli with zucchini and a creamed potato sauce, or else filet of cod crusted with a covering of black olives, tomatoes, and anchovy sauce. Filet of lamb is served with a rose liqueur and white asparagus, or else you might succumb to scorpion fish with an anchovy sauce.

Via San Giovanni del Toro 28 (in the Palazzo Sasso, p. 784). www.palazzosasso.com. ✆ **089-818181.** Reservations required. *Secondi* 28€–32€; tasting menu 120€. AE, DC, MC, V. Daily 7:30–11pm. Closed Nov–Mar.

Mosaics for sale at Ceramu.

Shopping

When Hillary Rodham Clinton came to visit and to call on former resident Gore Vidal, she also visited **Cammeo,** Piazza Duomo 9 (✆ **089-857461**), where owner Giorgio Filocamo designed a coral brooch for her. He can make one for you, too, or sell you any number of ready-made pieces. In the back of the shop, he has collected his most treasured pieces, all worthy of a museum.

Brothers Marco and Piero Cantarella are waiting for you at **Ceramu,** Via Roma 58 (✆ **089-858181**), where they'll sell you mosaics in majolica, and garden tables with wrought-iron or mosaic-bordered mirrors with wood.

Where to Stay

VERY EXPENSIVE

Hotel Caruso ★★ ☺ Housed in the splendid 11th-century Palazzo D'Afflitto, this hotel offers top-notch services and facilities and a unique and exclusive experience. Guest rooms are palatial yet welcoming, with baldaquin beds, heavenly linens, and large bathrooms. Most have sea views and open to private balconies, terraces, or small gardens. The hotel's facilities are crowned by a breathtaking outdoor infinity pool; we also recommend asking for a guided tour of the magnificent gardens. Guests enjoy access to two golf courses and a tennis court, though you do have to pay a fee. PlayStations, toys, and kids' bathrobes and slippers are available upon request.

Piazza San Giovanni del Toro 2, 84010 Ravello. www.hotelcaruso.com. ✆ **089-858801.** Fax 089-858806. 48 units. 760€–925€ double; from 1,200€ suite. Rates include American buffet breakfast. Children 12 and under stay free in parent's room. AE, DC, MC, V. Parking 20€. Closed Nov–Mar. **Amenities:** 2 restaurants; 2 bars; babysitting; concierge; gym; pool; room service; spa. *In room:* A/C, TV/DVD, minibar, Wi-Fi (free).

Palazzo Sasso ★★★ Housed in a 12th-century patrician palace, this opulent hotel enjoys a splendid location between plunging cliffs and steep mountainside. One of the best hotels in the world, it is *the* place to stay in Ravello. Guest rooms are luxuriously appointed with real antiques and handmade Vietri ceramic floors. Some afford gorgeous views—the best are from room numbers 1, 201, 204, and 301, and suite 304. Some of the suites are as big as a good-size apartment, and even the lower-priced rooms are spacious (a few have no view). Bathrooms are done out in marble, with large tubs. A free shuttle takes guests down to Sasso by the Sea (May–Sept), the hotel's beach club where there is a small outdoor pool, a waterside terrace with lounge chairs and umbrellas, and the casual Sasso restaurant. For more formal dining, book a table at the Michelin-rated Rossellinis in the main hotel.

Via San Giovanni del Toro 28, 84010 Ravello. www.palazzosasso.com. ✆ **089-818181.** Fax 089-858900. 44 units. 350€–710€ double; from 990€ suite. Rates include buffet breakfast. Children 2 and under stay free in parent's room. AE, DC, MC, V. Parking 34€. Closed mid-Oct to Mar. **Amenities:** Restaurant, Rossellinis (review, p. 783); bar; concierge; gym; Jacuzzi; pool; room service; spa. *In room:* A/C, TV, minibar, Wi-Fi (free).

EXPENSIVE

Hotel Palumbo ★★ This 12th-century palace is now a charming hotel. It has been favored by the famous since composer Richard Wagner persuaded the Swiss owners, the Vuilleumiers, to take in paying guests. If you stay, you'll understand why Humphrey Bogart, Ingrid Bergman, Tennessee Williams, and John and Jacqueline Kennedy found it ideal. D. H. Lawrence even wrote part of *Lady*

Chatterley's Lover while staying here. The hotel offers gracious living in its drawing rooms full of English and Italian antiques. Most of the snug but elegant guest rooms have their own terraces with glorious views. The original Hotel Palumbo contains the more glamorous accommodations; seven rooms are in the annex in the garden, but a few have sea views.

Via San Giovanni del Toro 16, 84010 Ravello. www.hotelpalumbo.it. ✆ **089-857244.** Fax 089-858133. 21 units. 295€–395€ double; 595€–795€ suite. Rates include buffet breakfast. AE, DC, MC, V. Parking 25€. **Amenities:** Open-air restaurant; bar; babysitting; Jacuzzi; room service; Wi-Fi (free, in lobby). *In room:* A/C, TV, hair dryer, minibar.

MODERATE

Hotel Rufolo ★ This family-run hotel is located in the heart of town overlooking the gardens of Villa Rufolo. Housed in a modern building decorated in a traditional style, it offers comfortable accommodations and friendly service. The views from the terrace gardens, the restaurant terrace, and the sun decks are superb. Guest rooms are spacious and attractive, with tiled Vietri floors and classic furnishings. Bathrooms are good-size and well maintained (some with shower only). Better rooms open onto private balconies and enjoy gorgeous views, while others overlook the town or garden. The hotel's restaurant, **Sigilgaida ★**, serves tasty cuisine prepared with produce from the hotel's organic gardens and select local ingredients (closed Jan–Feb).

Via San Francesco 1, 84010 Ravello. www.hotelrufolo.it. ✆ **089-857133.** Fax 089-857935. 30 units. 290€–350€ double; 550€ junior suite. Rates include buffet breakfast. Children 2 and under stay free in parent's room. AE, DC, MC, V. Free parking. **Amenities:** Restaurant; bar; babysitting; concierge; gym; pool; spa. *In room:* A/C, TV, minibar.

INEXPENSIVE

Hotel Giordano Not far from Villa Rufolo, guest rooms at this newly renovated, family-run hotel are on average a bit smaller than at the Rufolo, but there are some exceptions—the largest are good options for families and have private small terraces. The large swimming pool in the garden is very pleasant, and free use of the hotel's garage near Ravello's main square is included (porters collect your luggage). Guests enjoy access to the splendid gardens of **Villa Eva** and special rates for meals at Villa Maria.

Via Trinita 14, 84010 Ravello. www.giordanohotel.it. ✆ **089-857170.** Fax 089-857071. 30 units. 185€–300€ double; 355€ triple; 410€ quad; 450€ junior suite. Rates include breakfast. Children 2 and under stay free in parent's room. AE, DC, MC, V. Free parking. **Amenities:** Bar; concierge; pool. *In room:* A/C, TV, minibar.

Hotel Parsifal 🎁 In the northern part of town, this former 13th-century convent is a good budget option, with charming architectural details throughout. Guest rooms vary in size and shape—some with nice views over the sea; all are pleasantly done with bright Vietri tiled floors, whitewashed walls, and good-size bathrooms (some with shower only). The hotel's **restaurant ★** is very good.

Via Gioacchino D'Anna 5, 84010 Ravello. www.hotelparsifal.com. ✆ **089-857144.** 17 units. 135€–210€ double. Rates include buffet breakfast. Children 2 and under stay free in parent's room. AE, DC, MC, V. Parking 15€. **Amenities:** Restaurant; bar; concierge; Wi-Fi. (free). *In room:* A/C (in some), TV, minibar.

PAESTUM & ITS GLORIOUS GREEK TEMPLES ★★★

40km (25 miles) S of Salerno, 100km (62 miles) SE of Naples, 304km (188 miles) SE of Rome

The ancient city of Paestum (Poseidonia), founded by colonists from the Greek city of Sybaris, dates from 600 B.C. Lying just a short distance south of Salerno, its celebrated ruins more than fulfill expectations and are enormously evocative. The three majestic and remarkably well-preserved Greek temples sit on a grassy plain that really gives off the sense of an ancient, vanished city, enclosed in its still-standing boundary walls. The temples are a magical sight, especially at sunset, and in spring and fall when Paestum's famous roses—praised since antiquity—are in bloom. The archaeological area can be reached as a day trip from anywhere in Campania; plan on spending a minimum of 2 hours exploring the temples and an hour for the museum, but count on a whole day for a more in-depth visit.

Essentials

GETTING THERE You must go to Salerno to get to Paestum via public transport. Take a southbound **train,** which departs Salerno with a stop at Paestum about every 2 hours. For schedules, contact **Trenitalia** (www.trenitalia.it; ✆ **892021** toll-free in Italy). A one-way fare is 6€, and the journey takes around 30 minutes. The **bus** from Salerno leaves from Piazza Concordia (near the rail station) about every 30 minutes. Call ✆ **089-252228** for information. A one-way fare is 3€.

By **car,** from Salerno take SS18 south.

VISITOR INFORMATION The **tourist office,** Via Magna Grecia 887 (www.infopaestum.it; ✆ **0828-811016**), in the archaeological zone, is open daily from 9am to 1pm and 2 to 4pm.

Exploring the Temples

The **Tempio di Hera** (or Temple to Hera, aka the **Basilica**) is the oldest of the three structures and was built in 550 B.C. in Doric-Archaic style. The 50 columns of its monumental portico are still standing and show the pot-bellied profile typical of archaic temples, but the roof and the pediment collapsed long ago. The **Temple of Neptune (Tempio di Nettuno) ★★★** is the most impressive of the temples, and along with the Temple of Hephaestus ("Theseum") in Athens, it remains the best-preserved Greek temple in the world: Both date from around 450 to 420 B.C. Six columns in front are crowned by an entablature, and there are 14 columns on each side. The **Temple of Ceres (Tempio di Cerere) ★★**, from the 6th century B.C., has 34 columns still standing and a large altar for sacrifices to the gods.

The Archaeological Area is open daily 9am to sunset.

You can also visit the **National Archaeological Museum of Paestum (Museo Archeologico Nazionale di Paestum),** Via Magna Grecia 917 (✆ **0828-811023**), across from the Ceres Temple. It displays the metopes removed from the treasury of the Temple of Hera (Juno) and some of southern Italy's finest tomb paintings from the 4th century B.C. The Diver's Tomb is an extraordinary example of painting from the first half of the 5th century B.C. The museum is open daily 9am to 6:45pm. (It's closed the first and third Mon of every month.) Admission is 4€, but there is also a cumulative ticket, which includes the museum and the archaeological area, for 7.50€.

Recent discoveries have revealed hundreds of Greek tombs, yielding many Greek paintings, which archaeologists have called astonishing. In addition, other excavated tombs were found to contain clay figures in a strongly Impressionistic vein.

Where to Eat

Nettuno Ristorante SALERNITAN/SEAFOOD Nettuno's only drawback is that throughout most of the year it's open only for lunch. At the edge of Paestum's ruins, it's built from the same beige-colored limestone blocks used by the ancient Romans. Its core consists of an ancient tower built in the 2nd century B.C. Seated in the dining room or garden ringed with vines, oleander, and pines, you can order *crespolini,* a crepe stuffed with mozzarella and raw Parma ham; succulent pastas; a wide selection of fish; and veal, chicken, and beef dishes. Specialties include *pezzogna* (a local fish) baked with potatoes and olives, or risotto with lobster. Some of the best of the tantalizing appetizers are shrimp with wild arugula and Parmesan or else fresh asparagus and shrimp salad.

Via Nettuno 2 (by the secondary entrance to the archaeological area), Paestum. www.ristorante-nettuno.com. ✆ **0828-811028.** Reservations recommended. *Secondi* 12€–20€. AE, DC, MC, V. Daily noon–3:30pm. Closed 3 weeks Nov and Jan 7–Feb 7.

Where to Stay

Tenuta Seliano This pleasant *agriturismo* is a good choice if you want to stay in the countryside near the archaeological site. Set in a 19th-century hamlet, the picturesque buildings have been turned into lodgings with large, comfortable guest rooms with country-style elegance and good taste. A well-groomed garden with a swimming pool and some 91 hectares (225 acres) of land complete the property, part of which is dedicated to raising buffaloes (for mozzarella, of course). The cuisine prepared by Signora Bellelli—who also offers cooking classes—is wonderful and completes the service. You can choose to have all your meals at the farm, or only breakfast.

Via Seliano, Borgo Antico (Capaccio Scalo), 84063 Paestum. www.agriturismoseliano.it. ✆ **0828-723634.** Fax 0828-724544. 14 units. 120€ double. Rate includes breakfast. AE, DC, MC, V. Free parking. Closed Nov–Dec 27 and Jan 7–Feb. **Amenities:** Pool. *In room:* A/C, TV.

THE PONTINE ISLANDS

Scattered in the Tyrrhenian Sea between Rome and Naples, the Pontine Islands form an archipelago that is one of the undiscovered gems of Italy, known mainly to the Italians themselves who flock here in July and August. Only two of the islands are inhabited, **Ventotene** of volcanic origin, and **Ponza,** the site of a small tourist industry with some hotels and restaurants. Instead of a visit to pricey, overcrowded Capri, many visitors come to Ponza in the summer.

Ponza itself is a half-moon-shaped island, long and narrow, with Monte La Guardia at 279m (915 ft.), its highest point. The island is about 8km (5 miles) long with a jagged, cove-studded coastline.

Essentials

GETTING THERE If you're exploring Naples and want to extend your trip, **SNAV** operates hydrofoils departing from the Mergellina dock (www.snav.it; ✆ **0814-285555**). Departures are one time a day from mid-June to August, the trip taking 3 hours and costing 58€. The SNAV office in Ponza is at Via Banchina Nuova (✆ **077-180743**) in the port area.

More regular departures are from the port of Formia, lying along the coast between Rome and Naples. Formia is 153km (95 miles) south of Rome but more easily reached from Naples 86km (53 miles) to the south.

Caremar, at Via Banchina Azzurra in Formia (www.caremar.it; ✆ **892123**), operates ferries year-round, making the trip to Ponza in 2 hours, 30 minutes, and costing 17€ per person one-way. The cost of transporting a standard car is 70€. Ferries leave Formia daily at 9am, 2:30, and 5:30pm. The Caremar office in Ponza is at Molo Musco (✆ **892123**) at the port.

VISITOR INFORMATION The **Ponza Tourist Office** is at Via Molo Musco 2 (✆ **077-180031**) at the port, and it's open daily year-round from 9am to 1pm.

Exploring Ponza

The largest of the Pontine Islands, crescent-shaped Ponza was called Tyrrhenia in ancient times. Ponza is said to have been connected to the mainland of Italy by a narrow strip of land, which long ago sunk into the sea. Recent archaeological investigations have suggested that Ponza was once a large city that gave way to the sea. For example, Roman temples were found on a harbor floor that had sunk and risen several times in the past 5,000 years.

Ponza was once viewed as a place of exile for political dissidents, a tradition that lasted from Roman times until the Mussolini era. Il Duce himself was imprisoned on the island for several weeks in 1943. Settlements on Ponza were abandoned during the Middle Ages because of frequent raids by Saracens and pirates. When the pirate menace was wiped out, a newer generation of settlers returned.

The island is famed for its Blue Grottoes, the creation of the Etruscans. Built by the Romans, a tunnel connects the port of Ponza with the best large sandy beach on the island. Lying on the west side, it's called **Chiaia di Luna.**

The most spectacular site on island is the **Pilatus Caves ★**, with their maze of tunnels linked to the sea and each other and dug into the rocky bank to the southeast of the port. **Cooperativa Barcaioli** (www.barcaioliponza.it; ✆ **077-1809929**) offers year-round excursions to the caves, costing 15€ per person. The agency also features a circular tour of the island for 25€ per person. To contact the agency, go to Corso Pisacane (✆ **077-1809929**) in Ponza.

In summer the agency will also arrange tours of the other remote islands, including a visit to **Zannone** 11km (6½ miles) from the port of Ponza. This speck of an island is part of the **Circeo National Park.** The island is uninhabited (there are no tourist facilities). On the island you can see the ruins of a Benedictine convent dating from the 13th century, and you can follow well-marked paths along the upper ridge of the island to take in the scenic views. The cost of this tour is 25€ per person.

Exploring the Pilatus Caves on Ponza.

Except for the port of Ponza, the only other real village on island is **La Forna,** home of **Le Piscine Naturali ★**, a series of grottoes, enclosed pools of ocean water that have collected in lava rock basins. Take the bus from Ponza to Le Forna and walk down to the grottoes.

Where to Eat

Acqua Pazza ★★★ SEAFOOD/MEDITERRANEAN It comes as a complete surprise to find a Michelin-starred restaurant in this remote outpost. Patrizia Ronca and Gino Pesce have raised the culinary bar so high on the island that no other chef comes anywhere near meeting their standards. Their elegant restaurant is found on the main square of Ponza, right at the port. Tables with white napery and crystal open onto a view of the town and water. Start with some of their delectable specialties, including a pie made with artichokes and squid. You can then proceed to the mussel stew or else vermicelli with swordfish roe and a lime flavoring. The *tagliolini* with butter, anchovies, and capers is sublime, as is the grilled white fish with aromatic herbs of the Mediterranean.

Piazza Carlo Pisacane 10. www.acquapazza.com. ✆ **077-180643.** Reservations required. Main courses 18€–35€; fixed-price menu 70€. AE, MC, V. Daily 8–11:30pm. Closed Nov–Feb.

Gennarino a Mare MEDITERRANEAN/SEAFOOD In a small inn of the same name, this restaurant is a portside choice, a favorite of locals and visitors. The eatery stands on a wooden pile-work structure constructed on top of the water. The chefs essentially cook a Mediterranean cuisine with lots of fish, but they also serve some dishes based on old Ponza recipes. Start with one of their savory pasta dishes such as fettuccine alla Gennarino with shrimp and mussels or else *mezzemaniche,* a homemade pasta with shrimp, swordfish roe, and cherry tomatoes. The restaurant rents 12 very basic rooms, each with its own balcony overlooking the sea, costing 120€ to 170€ for a double.

Via Dante 64. www.gennarinoamare.com. ✆ **077-180071.** Reservations recommended. Main courses 15€–32€. AE, DC, MC, V. Daily 8–10:30pm. Closed mid-Oct to Easter.

Orestorante ★ MEDITERRANEAN/SEAFOOD This is a three-level restaurant in the center of town, standing on a cliff overlooking the sea with an open-air view terrace. It's long been a favorite with visitors who like the regional seafood, based on the harvest of the day and the well-chosen Mediterranean dishes prepared from fresh ingredients whenever possible. "We don't specialize in delicacies here," a waiter told us, "but we do serve the food of the people." That cuisine might start with a platter *tri trito,* three kinds of fish—shrimp, tuna, and sea bream—or else an appetizer of marinated red snapper on potato ice cream. The most recommendable pasta is spaghetti with clams and wild fennel, followed by a main dish of filet of sea bream stuffed with mozzarella and escarole sautéed with sultana and black olives.

Via Dietro La Chiesa 4. www.orestorante.it. ✆ **077-180338.** Reservations recommended. Main courses 20€–35€. MC, V. Daily 8:15–11:30pm. Closed Oct–Easter.

Where to Stay

Bellavista It's not as grand as the Grand Hotel (see below), but Bellavista is the second-best and most acceptable choice on Ponza. In the center of town, the four-story building is located on a cliff overlooking the sea. Rooms are utterly simple, yet comfortable, the grace note being in the most desirable accommodations that open onto small balconies with views of the sea. There is also a regional restaurant on-site, serving a Mediterranean cuisine, which consists mostly of seafood.

Via Parata 1, Ponza 04027. www.hotelbellavistaponza.it. ✆ **077-180036.** Fax 077-180395. 24 units. 140€–200€ double. Rates include buffet breakfast. AE, MC, V. **Amenities:** Restaurant; bar; room service. *In room:* A/C, TV, hair dryer, minibar.

Grand Hotel Santa Domitilla ★★ This is the best hotel in the entire archipelago. Lying 100m (328 ft.) from the beach, it brings a bit of style and a certain decorative flair to the island. In the heart of Ponza, the hotel is surrounded by beautiful gardens. The hotel offers a variety of rooms in different sizes and decor, and all of them are comfortable. Elegant suites have a Jacuzzi and a spacious outside terrace for sunbathing. Some of the accommodations feature twin bathrooms with steam showers. Units open onto a garden view or else a panorama of the sea. The hotel's amenities are the best on the island, including a seawater grotto where you can swim in a natural cove.

Via Panoramica 10, 04027 Ponza. www.santadomitilla.com. ✆ **077-1809951.** Fax 077-1809955. 57 units. 180€–370€ double; 300€–600€ suite. Rates include buffet breakfast. AE, DC, MC, V. Closed Nov–Mar. **Amenities:** Restaurant; bar; babysitting; 2 saltwater pools; room service; Wi-Fi (free, in lobby). *In room:* A/C, TV, hair dryer, minibar.

PUGLIA

14

Sunny, rural, and relaxing Puglia is not as well-known as some other Italian regions, but what it offers in spades—and what has become very hard to find in Rome, Florence, and Venice—is authenticity. Here among endless olive groves, picturesque whitewashed villages, and port towns, is traditional Mediterranean culture untainted by mass tourism. For travelers who've already done Italy's usual suspects, or who are more interested in getting to know the soul of a place than taking pictures in front of its monuments, Puglia should be at the top of the list.

On the map, it's the southeasternmost section of Italy, the stiletto heel of the boot. Puglia has already caught on among Brits and Northern Europeans as a less-discovered, and much less expensive, Italian alternative to the well-touristed central Italian regions of Tuscany and Umbria. But for North Americans, Puglia remains little known. Sights-wise, it's most famous for the *trulli,* those fairy-tale stone houses with cone-shaped roofs that only exist in this region, in Alberobello and the surrounding Valle d'Itria. But for the most part, Puglia isn't about ticking monuments and museums off a list. Instead, Puglia is about sleepy but lovely little hill towns like Martina Franca, the ebullient baroque architecture in elegant Lecce, the windswept Adriatic coast and sandy Ionian beaches, and above all, olive groves that look CGI-ed for their immense extent. It's about soaking up all this low-key loveliness with little to no agenda.

Trulli's unique beehive homes; PREVIOUS PAGE: **Trani's Duomo.**

Except for the rugged Gargano peninsula, Puglia is a mountainless territory with what appears to be soft, gray-green wall-to-wall carpeting. Olive trees are to Puglia as sheep are to New Zealand. There are six million specimens of olive trees here—some more than 500 years old—and after seeing how omnipresent they are, it's easy to understand why Puglia is the king of Italian olive oil regions, responsible for about 40% of the entire country's production. A lasting visual of any visit to Puglia is likely to be some composite of gnarled olive trunks growing out of red earth, dry stone country walls lining narrow country roads, and radiant architecture (whether the brilliant white of the *masserie* farmhouse or the sunshiny yellow of baroque churches), all

Puglia
Venice
Florence
Rome
Puglia
ADRIATIC SEA
Isole Tremiti
Peschici
Vieste
Gargano National Park
Gargano Peninsula
Rodi Garganico
Termoli
Lésina
Cagnano Verano
San Giovanni Rotondo
Mattinata
Monte Sant'Angelo
Manfredonia
S. Marco in Lamis
Gulf of Manfredonia
S. Severo
Foggia
Lucera
Troia
Barletta
Trani
Bari
Triggiano
Monopoli
Bitonto
Savelltri
Brindisi
Andria
Rutigliano
Conversano
SS379
Cerignola
Ruvo di Puglia
Castellana Grotte
Fasano
Ostuni
Castel del Monte
Alberobello
Cisternino
E90
SS613
E843
Locorotondo
Valle d'Itria
High Murgia National Park
Martina Franca
Ceglie Messapica
Lecce
E842
Gioia d. Colle
Appennino Campano
Candela
Le Murge
Grottaglie
A14
Massafra
Salento
Otranto
Maglie
Galatina
A16
Melfi
Matera
Taranto
Manduria
Benevento
Grottaminarda
Nardo'
Sta. Cesarea Terme
Gallipoli
E847
Lido di Metaponto
Marina de Leuca
Potenza
Avellino
Appennino Lucano
Capo S.M. de Leuca
Gulf of Taranto
Naples
Eboli
Salerno
E45
Gulf of Naples
Sorrento
Gulf of Salerno
Cilento and Vallo di Diano National Park
Pollino National Park
Amendolara
Capri
0
20 mi
0
20 km

against a pure and hale sky whose blue is somewhere between powder and cobalt.

And if a large part of what draws you to Italy is its food, you may just find that Puglia is your mother ship. The cuisine throughout the region is outstanding—perhaps my favorite in Italy on the strength of a few key staples: *burrata di Andria, orecchiette* pasta, *panzerotti,* rustic Pugliese bread, *capocollo di Martina Franca,* and abundant extra-virgin olive oil (did I mention the olive trees here?). Simple and fresh, full of flavor but not gut-busting, the food in Puglia represents all that modern foodies love about Italian gastronomy.

Certainly, Puglia's art and architecture is less spectacular than Rome's or Venice's, its natural beauty less amplified than the Amalfi Coast's, its charm less immediate than Tuscany's. (Several years ago, when Puglia was first being promoted to foreign tourists, some eager writers touted it as "the next Tuscany." Not only is this an inaccurate characterization, but it also sells Puglia short in failing to highlight just why Puglia is not Tuscany—or Umbria, or any other region—and why that is precisely part of its allure.) But that beauty and charm is there, in places largely free of bus-tour hordes. There has certainly been much development in Puglia to meet the growing number of tourists, most notably in the conversion of the region's many *masserie,* or fortified farmhouses, into chic country lodging. However, Puglia remains a region where you are often the only tourist around, the kind of place where the cafe or restaurant on the main piazza is a locals' haunt, not a tourist trap to be avoided like the plague. In a country like Italy that's been traipsed by tourists for centuries, that sense of intimacy and discovery is a treasure in itself.

Life is slower, quieter in Puglia. It's generally a more conservative and religious region with more traditional values than the central and northern parts of Italy, yet the Pugliese elected an openly gay man and communist, the charismatic Nichi Vendola, as president (equivalent to a U.S. governor) in 2005 and reelected him by a huge margin in 2010.

Strategies for Seeing the Region

The best way to visit Puglia is to fly from Rome to either Bari or Brindisi (either takes less than an hour), where you can rent a car to tour the region's highlights. Thankfully, most of Puglia's greatest hits are situated within manageable driving distance of each other between Bari and Lecce, themselves only 150km (93 miles) apart. If you have less than a week, pick one of the wonderful *masserie* (medieval fortified farmsteads, now mostly converted to boutique hotel-resorts with every possible amenity) south of Bari as your base. In 3 days, you can comfortably see the *trulli* of Alberobello, wander the lovely hill towns of Martina Franca and Ostuni, and venture south to soak up the sunny baroque splendor of Lecce—with time left over for relaxation, food and wine, and maybe even a beach excursion to the coast near Gallipoli or a spa treatment at your *masseria.* With a week to spend in Puglia, I recommend adding the Valle d'Itria towns of Locorotondo and Cisternino, a leisurely tour of the Salento peninsula (perhaps staying in Lecce itself a few nights for forays to Otranto, Santa Maria di Leuca, and beaches of the Ionian Coast), and a visit to handsome Trani and its magnificent seaside cathedral. Cap off the week with a full day in Puglia's waterfront capital city, Bari, to explore its equally compelling ancient and modern quarters.

THE BEST TRAVEL EXPERIENCES IN PUGLIA

- **Adopting a slow pace in a Valle d'Itria hill town:** In the surprisingly elegant Martina Franca, Locorotondo, and Ostuni (to mention the most famous ones), the main attraction is simply being there, surrounded by geraniums spilling from balconies, and stopping for coffee or wine, or browsing local products, or admiring the views that open up unexpectedly down narrow alleys. See p. 796.
- **Gorging yourself at the Pugliese table:** It's easy to adopt a five-meal-a-day plan in Puglia—the food is that good. Based on fresh and local ingredients and unfussy preparations, *la cucina pugliese* may be the best in Italy, from flavored *taralli* and focaccias to *orecchiette* pasta to *burrata* cheese to grilled meats to cured pork *capocollo*. All of it pairs beautifully with Pugliese wines like reds Primitivo and Negroamaro, lately gaining international renown.
- **Trulli-touring in Alberobello:** Cliché or not, there is something magical about those cone-topped cottages. Your camera's memory card may just crash from all the white-and-gray cuteness. See p. 797.
- **Walking wide-eyed from one astonishing baroque church to the next in Lecce:** Southern Italy's best-kept art secret is a revelation of sunny, intricate architecture, and a sophisticated vibe permeates the lively city center. See p. 808.
- **Staying at a masseria hotel:** The huge trend in Puglia of taking these formidable old white farmhouses and refitting them as boutique resorts is great news for tourists looking for pampered relaxation and rural charm. The fanciest *masserie* can cost a bundle, but there are plenty of moderately priced properties, too. Almost all have spas and fantastic on-site dining. See p. 806.

Taralli and biscotti.

THE VALLE D'ITRIA: *TRULLO* COUNTRY ★★

The most logical and best introduction to Puglia is the Valle d'Itria. A triangular swatch of land southeast of Bari, west of Brindisi, and north of Taranto, the Valle d'Itria is a lovely landscape of olive groves, roads bordered by low stone walls, elegant hill towns like Martina Franca, and most famously the fairy-tale-ish *trulli*.

Unique to Puglia, the *trullo* is a curious beehive-shaped structure with whitewashed limestone walls and conical fieldstone roofs that utilized the materials available in the area. *Trulli* are sprinkled over farms and fields throughout this part of Puglia, but for the ultimate in *trullo*-gawking, there's only one place to go: Alberobello. A handsome little town at the heart of the Valle d'Itria, Alberobello is Puglia's most famous tourist site and most obvious postcard attraction. Like something out of a children's storybook, Alberobello's amazing concentration of *trulli*—more than 1,500 of them line the hilly, winding streets—has earned the town UNESCO World Heritage Site status. Alberobello is also the only place in Puglia where you will encounter anything resembling tourist crowds.

But don't think for a minute that Alberobello and *trulli* are all there is to see and do in the Valle d'Itria. One of the great pleasures of this region is driving the back roads—and probably getting lost—that wend their way through secular olive groves. The Valle d'Itria is also packed with little towns, a bit less famous than Alberobello but equally enchanting, where simply being there, maybe sipping coffee or wine in some adorable whitewashed square with geraniums in every window, is the main attraction. There are often exquisite confections of baroque architecture to ogle, too. Martina Franca and Ostuni are the most famous of these towns, but if time permits, try to visit Locorotondo, Cisternino, and Ceglie Messapica, too.

Many visitors to this part of Puglia add a detour across the border into Basilicata to see the prehistoric rock dwellings known as the Sassi, in Matera. Matera is a doable half-day trip from any of these towns, although it's closest to Alberobello.

Although I list some accommodations options in each individual town in this section, my ultimate recommendation for lodging in the Valle d'Itria is in one of the *masseria* hotels, listed collectively on p. 806. Concentrated in the area around Fasano near the Adriatic coast, any of these countryside resorts puts you within easy driving distance of anywhere in the Valle d'Itria.

Essentials

GETTING THERE The sights of the Valle d'Itria are about equidistant from Bari and Brindisi airports (each about 1 hr. away by car), so if arriving by air, just go with whichever airport has the more convenient flights. Information for both can be found at www.aeroportidipuglia.it. For those arriving here by car from elsewhere in Italy, the Valle d'Itria is about 4 hours east of Naples (via the A16 and A14 autostrade to Bari, then southeast toward Alberobello), and about 5 hours southeast of Rome, following the A1 autostrada south to Naples and then the A16 and A14, as above, through Bari to the Valle d'Itria.

GETTING AROUND The Valle d'Itria is one part of Puglia where it's actually possible to see the highlights without a car. Regional trains are run by Ferrovia del Sud Est (www.fseonline.it), which depart from both Bari and Lecce and have stops in Alberobello, Martina Franca, Locorotondo, Cisternino, and Ceglie Messapica. Ostuni is not served by the Ferrovia del Sud Est local train but is along the main Adriatic line of the national rail system, Ferrovie dello Stato (www.trenitalia.com), and can be reached easily from Bari or Brindisi stations. Note that none of these train stations are located right in the center of these towns; they're usually a few kilometers away but linked with the town center by bus or inexpensive taxis. Otherwise, a car will serve you well for more freedom of movement, especially if you're also planning on visiting other parts of Puglia. Rent one from AutoEurope (www.autoeurope.com), which has desks at Bari and Brindisi airports and in downtown Bari.

VISITOR INFORMATION Puglia's official tourism website, www.viaggiareinpuglia.it, has a wealth of information about the Valle d'Itria. Smartphone and tablet users can install the Puglia Travel Guide app. The individual towns' tourist board offices are listed within each town section, below.

Alberobello ★★

Trulli charming, *trulli* one-of-a-kind . . . let the *trullo* puns begin! No matter what else you do in Puglia, Alberobello must be on your list. Wandering around the famed city of *trulli* is probably as close as you'll ever get to stepping into the pages of a fairy tale, or a scene from *The Hobbit*. You may have seen pictures of the *trulli*, but these odd, beehive-shaped houses are even more delightful in person. Alberobello has 1,620 *trulli*, a distinction that in 1996 won the town UNESCO World Heritage Site status. According to the official literature, Alberobello was inscribed to the list because its *trulli* are "an exceptional example of a form of building construction deriving from prehistoric construction techniques that have survived intact and functioning in the modern world." But come on, you know that the cuteness factor of the *trulli* had to have an effect on the UNESCO advisory board.

Although tourism is a major factor here, Alberobello remains elegant and clean, and still feels lived-in. In the back alleys of Alberobello's quiet Aia Piccola quarter, you'll smell vegetables sautéing and hear the banter of Italian talk shows from inside the *trulli*. For many years, the *trulli* within Alberobello were considered substandard peasant dwellings, and in the past century, the town's residents moved outside the old core of Alberobello into modern housing. But with the UNESCO stature, *trulli* have become fashionable again: Some have been converted into chic B&Bs, many are (tacky) souvenir shops or coffee bars, while some remain inhabited. Do be sure to check out the interiors of a few *trulli* to experience the true nature of this domestic architecture: The claustrophobic and damp feeling on the inside may just kill your dream of buying and fixing up a *trullo* for a vacation home.

You only need an hour or two to tour the *trulli*, so it's a good idea to plan your day to Alberobello in conjunction with another destination within the Valle d'Itria (Martina Franca is nearby, as are the Grotte di Castellana caves) or Matera (p. 800). However, if you're here around lunch or dinner, Alberobello has some impressive restaurants and even a chic *trullo* hotel.

ESSENTIALS

GETTING THERE FSE **trains** leave Bari every hour (every 2 hr. on Sun) heading to Alberobello. The trip takes about 1¾ hours and costs 4€. To find the *trulli*, follow Via Mazzini, which turns into Via Garibaldi, until you reach

trulli GENIUS

The architecture of Puglia's famous *trulli* is specific to the Valle d'Itria, where the conical-roofed dry stone huts were originally conceived as storage sheds or shelters in agricultural fields. This remarkable construction technique, in which no mortar is used, was later employed as a dwelling for the small farmer and his family. In the curious case of Alberobello, *trulli* became the standard house type. (Singular: *trullo,* from the Greek *troulos,* "dome.")

Even the gray roof "tiles" (slabs of limestone called *chiancarelle*) were dry-laid over an inner masonry cone. But some *trullari* (*trullo*-specialized masons) were more skilled than others: The smoother-roofed *trulli* are the work of A-list *trullari,* while jagged and sloppy courses of *chiancarelle* bear testimony to the quick and dirty jobs done by cut-rate masons or apprentices. The sculpted pinnacles or finials that top many *trulli*—there are globes, flat discs, and other, sometimes phallic polyhedrons—probably didn't have any real meaning or function besides being ornamental business cards for the particular *trullaro* who did that house. Some *trulli* have white, rather tawdry artwork on the side of their roofs. Often these are symbols from pagan, Jewish, and Christian traditions, but scholars believe these were purely decorative and can't be correlated with the dweller's religious affiliation.

Out in the countryside, *trulli* are typically a stand-alone, one-chamber affair, but in Alberobello, the *trulli* are clumped and clustered together to allow for multiroom residences. Because of the nature of *trullo* construction, each conical roof corresponds with a single room below. The cones rest on tremendously thick, almost windowless walls (up to 1m/3⅓ ft. thick) that are filled with rubble, causing a ton of wasted space in the *trullo*'s footprint.

Those thick walls become a nuisance, too, when it comes to buying a *trullo:* All that extra square footage is counted in the price. And yes, people do buy *trulli*—in fact, so many Brits have purchased and restored them as vacation properties that the Valle d'Itria has been dubbed Trullishire. In the countryside, where the *trulli* aren't under the UNESCO protectorate, owners can modernize and add windows.

Most of the *trulli* of Alberobello date from the mid–16th century to the late 18th century, and the best explanation for their proliferation has to do with the ease of dismantling the dry-laid houses: From the 1500s to the 1700s, Alberobello was locally controlled by the Counts of Conversano, who were trying to keep the population of Alberobello a secret to avoid paying taxes to the Kingdom of Naples. When the royal inspectors were on their way to Alberobello to assess its tax, the counts ordered the dismantling of the *trulli* and thus erased any evidence of its citizenry. After the inspectors left, citizens could rebuild their *trulli* and move back in fairly quickly. Far-fetched as this may seem, it's still experts' best theory for the proliferation of *trulli* in this specific town and time period.

Piazza del Popolo. Turn left on Largo Martellotta, which will take you to the edge of the popular tourist area. If you have a **car,** head south of Bari on S100 and then east (signposted) on S172.

VISITOR INFORMATION The **tourist office** in Alberobello is off the central square, Piazza del Popolo, at Piazza Ferdinando IV (✆ **080-4325171**). It's

The *trullo sovrano* in Alberobello.

open Monday, Wednesday, and Thursday 8:30am to 1pm, Tuesday and Friday 9am to 1pm and 4 to 7:30pm.

EXPLORING THE TOWN

Most visitors arrive in **Largo Martellotta,** Alberobello's pedestrian-only main square. Alberobello's *centro storico* has two primary zones for *trulli:* **Rione Monti** is the largest and heavier-trafficked area south of Largo Martellotta, while **Rione Aia Piccola,** lying on either side of Via Verdi north and east of Largo Martellotta, is smaller and quieter, where the ancient and surreal aspect of the *trulli* is less spoiled by tourism.

For your first encounter with the *trulli,* I recommend exploring the doglegging alleys of Aia Piccola first. Take Via Brigata Regina east (uphill) from the main square of Alberobello, and you'll soon be surrounded by *trulli.* Aia Piccola is almost entirely residential, with many *trulli* lying vacant or under restoration. Along the streets here you'll be able to see some of the variations in *trullo* construction such as pinnacle decoration and finely laid vs. roughly assembled roof tiles *(chiancarelle).* Aia Piccola occupies a gentle hill, and from here you'll get a great view across the valley to the other *trullo* quarter, Monti. Monti's hundreds upon hundreds of densely packed *trulli* make for quite a skyline. Photo ops abound from Aia Piccola's panoramic passageways.

Back across Largo Martellotta, in the busier and much more commercial Monti, the *trullo*-wandering is less intimate, but here you'll also find all manner of converted *trulli* that are now coffee bars, B&Bs, and of course, gift shops. It's hard to resist leaving Alberobello without a small-scale replica of a *trullo,* crafted in the same type of stone as the ancient builders used.

The grand pooh-bah of the *trulli* is a two-story affair known as the ***trullo sovrano* (sovereign *trullo*),** and it's not in Aia Piccola or Monti, but on the far northern edge of Alberobello in Piazza Sacramento. The 15m (50-ft.) structure, the only true two-story *trullo,* was built during the 19th century as headquarters for a religious confraternity and Carbonari sect. To find it, head down Corso Vittorio Emanuele until you get to a church, and then take a right. The *trullo sovrano* is open daily from 10am to 1pm and 3 to 7pm, charging no admission.

WHERE TO EAT & STAY

Alberobello has some fine restaurants and unique *trullo* accommodations that make spending a bit longer in town than the average tourist's half day plenty attractive. In addition to the full-service restaurants listed below, there are some great choices for quick bites on the main square. **La Fontana 1914 ★**, Largo Martellotta 55 (**© 080-4322789**), is a traditional *fornello,* or butcher shop, where they'll also cook your meats to order. The specialty there is the *bombette* **★★**, or pork shoulder wrapped around melted cheese and heavenly herbal seasonings. **Arte Fredda ★**, Largo Martellotta 47 (✆ **080-4324234**), makes the best gelato in town, with fresh, seasonal flavors made with local ingredients.

Il Poeta Contadino ★★ ITALIAN/PUGLIESE Alberobello's special occasion restaurant is one of the finest in Puglia, serving sophisticated reinterpretations of regional cuisine and fish. On the seasonal menu, antipasti might include pumpkin cream with prawns and wild rice, or *primi* like *cavatelli* with fava bean purée and mixed seafood. Art Nouveau furnishings fill the vaulted stone dining room, making for an elegant atmosphere.

Via Indipendenza 21. www.ilpoetacontadino.it. ✆ **080-4321917.** Reservations recommended. Main courses 14€–32€. AE, DC, MC, V. Winter Tues–Sun 12:30–2:30pm and 7:30–10:30pm; summer daily 12:30–2:30pm and 7–11pm. Closed Jan 7–22 and Mon Oct–June.

La Cantina ★★ Homey, traditional Pugliese food is cooked right before your eyes, and soul-warming *vino della casa* flows freely in this lively, intimate setting. On a street named for them, the Alberobello-native Lippolis family has been running this restaurant for more than 2 decades. Owner-chef Francesco puts on a nightly show for patrons from the open kitchen, where *cucina povera* (simple, "poor" food) with sensational flavor reigns supreme, from the fresh pastas to grilled meats, but the cheese and meat plates, with local *salumi* and *burrata,* are wonderful as well. There are only about 30 seats here, so booking is essential.

Vico Lippolis 8. www.ilristorantelacantina.it. ✆ **080-4323473.** Reservations recommended. Main courses 9€–15€. AE, MC, V. Wed–Mon 12:30–2:30pm and 7:30–10:30pm. Closed 2 weeks in Feb and 2 weeks in July.

Le Alcove ★★★ The top *trullo* lodging in town is this boutique "resort" with seven suites right on the main square of Alberobello (two more units are a short distance away). The *trulli* have been renovated with modern amenities and stylish furnishings that nevertheless capture the folk spirit of Puglia. Bathrooms—in a separate but privately connected *trullo*—are luxurious, with jetted tubs, designer toiletries, and thick terry robes. Proprietors Katia and Franco go the extra mile, and the chic, white-stone surroundings are cool and relaxing even on hot and crowded summer days.

Travel Back in Time to Matera

Another UNESCO World Heritage site lies just an hour away from Alberobello, in Matera (technically not Puglia but Basilicata). The attraction there is Matera's tremendously evocative Sassi quarter, a fantastically well-preserved rock-cut settlement dating back to the Paleolithic period. Here, houses were carved directly into the tufa ridge and "streets" run right over the rooftops of underlying houses on the steep slopes of the district. The Sassi (literally, "stones") are tremendously evocative of ancient Mediterranean civilization, so much so that the site has been used as a stand-in for ancient Jerusalem in many movies about the life of Christ—most notably by Mel Gibson in *The Passion of the Christ.* Allow a few hours to visit the Sassi, or spend the night in one of the rustic-chic boutique hotels set within the rock dwellings. The exquisite **L'Hotel in Pietra ★★**, Via San Giovanni Vecchio (www.hotelinpietra.it; ✆ **0835-344040**), occupies a converted 13th-century church and has six rooms with all the modern conveniences, from 110€ for a double.

Piazza Ferdinando IV 7, 70011 Alberobello. www.lealcove.it. ✆ **080-4323754.** Fax 080-2140999. 9 units. 220€–290€ suite. Rates include buffet breakfast. AE, MC, V. **Amenities:** Bar. *In room:* A/C, TV, hair dryer, Internet (free), minibar.

Trulli e Puglia B&B ★ In the heart of *trulli*-packed Monti quarter, Mimmo and his family run this comfortable B&B where units are independent converted *trulli,* some with kitchenette and lofts, and all with a cozy mix of rustic stone and wood. The *trulli* are big enough to accommodate families, but this is also an ideal place for solo travelers—Mimmo and his staff are the most enthusiastic, welcoming people in Alberobello.

Via Monte San Michele 58, 70011 Alberobello. www.trulliepuglia.com. ✆ **080-7558539** or 347-5538539. 6 units. 100€–180€ suite. Rates include buffet breakfast. AE, MC, V. **Amenities:** Bar; Internet station (free). *In room:* A/C, TV, minibar.

A SPELUNKING SIDE TRIP TO THE GROTTE DI CASTELLANA

If you need a break from the heat and/or are fascinated by stalactites and such, drive a few minutes north from Alberobello to the small town of Castellana Grotte, whose raison d'être is a series of caverns known, logically enough, as the **Grotte di Castellana ★★** (www.grottedicastellana.it; ✆ **080-4998221;** Nov–Mar daily 9:30am–12:30pm, Oct daily 9:30am–4:30pm, Apr–July and Sept daily 9:30am–7pm, Aug daily 9am–8pm; 15€). This immense network of caves has been carved out over the centuries by water streaming through the rocky soil. Once inside the *grotte,* a wide stairway leads you down through a tunnel into a grandiose, foyerlike cavern called the **Grave ★**. From here, a series of paths winds through other underground rooms filled with the strange shapes of stalagmites and stalactites. The culmination of the journey into the earth ends with the majestic **Grotta Bianca ★**, where alabaster concretions are the result of centuries of Mother Nature's work. The Grotte di Castellana are the most extensive caves in Europe. You can visit them only on guided tours, given once per hour until early afternoon. Bring an extra layer: It's 15°C (59°F) in the caves year-round.

Martina Franca ★★

Everyone falls in love with Martina Franca. This lively, friendly, handsome little hill town, with its baroque finery and whitewashed back alleys, is only 14km (8⅔ miles) from *trullo*-centric Alberobello but a world away in look and feel.

Martina Franca was founded in the 10th century when coastal residents fled inland to escape Saracen attacks (its position is equidistant from the Adriatic and Ionian seaside). Much of Martina Franca's medieval layout has been retained, and with it, a lot of cozy charm. Chief sights are the baroque Palazzo Ducale and the Basilica of San Martino, but Martina Franca's appeal lies mostly in its casually elegant atmosphere. Just walk around the labyrinthine *centro storico,* get lost in blind alleys, and let the town's sneaky charm soak in. Spend a few hours, or overnight, getting to know this very special Pugliese gem. And don't leave without sampling some of the town's prized *capocollo* (cured and smoked pork neck) at butcher/deli Romanelli (see "Where to Eat & Stay," below).

ESSENTIALS

GETTING THERE **By car** Martina Franca is an easy drive from anywhere in central or southern Puglia. From Bari (total: 77km/48 miles), follow the

SS16 south (toward Brindisi) for 56km (35 miles); at Fasano, go south (inland) for 18km (11 miles) on the SS172dir, through Locorotondo, to Martina Franca. From the Valle d'Itria towns of Alberobello (14km/8⅔ miles) or Locorotondo (9km/5½ miles), take the SS172 south to Martina Franca. From Lecce (total: 114km/71 miles), take the SS613 42km (26 miles) toward Brindisi and follow the SS379/E55 north (toward Bari) for 54km (33 miles) toward Bari; at Fasano, follow directions as above from Bari. You can't drive in Martina Franca's *centro storico* but you can park nearby in Via Giuseppe Aprile, Via Gabriele d'Annunzio, Piazza Francesco Crispi, Piazza Umberto, and Via Verdi (all within a few blocks of Piazza XX Settembre; see "Exploring," below).

By Train Martina Franca is served by the regional Ferrovie Sud Est (www.fseonline.it), from Bari (1 hr., 45 min.; 5.20€), from Alberobello (17 min.; 1€), and Locorotondo (6 min.; 1€). There's also a direct train between Martina Franca and Lecce (1¾ hr.; 7.10€), also run by Ferrovie Sud Est.

VISITOR INFORMATION The **APT (tourist office)** is in Piazza Roma (www.martinafrancatour.it; ✆ **080-4805702**), open Monday to Saturday 9am to 1pm. On Tuesday and Thursday it is also open 4 to 7pm.

EXPLORING

The natural place to begin your visit is in the long, pedestrianized esplanade **Piazza XX Settembre,** at the eastern edge of the historic center, where Via Valle d'Itria (SS172, the main road from Bari, Alberobello, and Locorotondo) turns into Corso Italia. Piazza XX Settembre was formerly the city market square and its local nickname is *u stradòn* (the big street). At its western end, a triumphal archway, the **Arco di Santo Stefano,** leads to the triangular, traffic-free Piazza Roma. There lies Martina Franca's grandest edifice, the mammoth **Palazzo Ducale ★**, built on top of the old castle in 1688. Today it is the *comune,* or city hall.

From here take the narrowing **Via Vittorio Emanuele** to the heart of the old town and **Piazza Plebiscito,** dominated by an 18th-century church, **Basilica di San Martino ★** (✆ **080-4306536**). Its facade is richly adorned with baroque relief sculptures depicting scenes from the life of St. Martin, and around back, a 14th-century bell tower still survives from a Romanesque church that once stood here. Inside the church, the exquisite inlaid marble work is well worth a peek. Admission is free; the church is open daily 8am to 12:30pm and 4:30 to 8pm. Also in the square is the municipal clock tower, erected in 1734, with a *meridiana* (sundial) inscribed on an eye-level plaque.

Continue west to the adjoining **Piazza Immacolata,** another pretty square with a neoclassical curved **portico ★** on one side. At the narrow end of the square, stop in at the atmospheric **Caffè Tripoli** (Via Garibaldi 25; ✆ **080-4805260**); the specialty of this 100-year-old coffee and pastry shop is *granita di caffè* (espresso slushy with whipped cream).

Next, take a stroll down **Via Cavour ★★**, the main street leading south from Piazza Immacolata. This is the best place in Martina Franca to admire the ensemble of smaller-scale, single-family baroque *palazzi,* with their fanciful architectural details and wrought-iron balconies.

After Via Cavour, set out on an aimless wander through Martina Franca's **tangle of whitewashed back streets ★**, some with impossibly narrow passageways and blind alleys. (A good area for this is just north and east of the basilica of San Martino.) The town's labyrinthine layout—Piazza Plebiscito and Piazza Immacolata are the only two really wide open areas in the old city—may seem haphazard but, in fact, was well thought out as a means to confuse and ambush invaders. Wealthy Martina was a natural target for Saracen plunderers, and by the 14th century it was necessary to build a defense wall circuit. Some of these walls and towers still exist around the old city's perimeter, and the streets just below them offer terrific views over the be-*trullo*-ed Valle d'Itria.

The baroque-style balconies on Via Cavour in Martina Franca.

WHERE TO EAT & STAY

The *case sparse* (scattered houses) agency **Villaggio In** (Via Arco Grassi 8, www.villaggioin.it; ✆ **080-4805911**) rents vacation apartments in the heart of Martina Franca. Rates start at 75€ a day for a double-occupancy studio.

Don't leave Martina without sampling some of the town's specialty: *capocollo* (cured pork). *Capocollo di Martina Franca* is meat cut from the top of the neck, where it meets the shoulder, and cured with local wine, herbs, and wood smoke. Butcher/deli **Romanelli ★★**, just off Piazza XX Settembre at Via Valle d'Itria 8–12 (✆ **080-4805385**), will let you sample its *capocollo* for free (often along with *taralli* and red wine in paper cups, depending on the time of day), and you can buy sliced *capocollo* there by the *etto* (¼ lb., 2.20€) or bring a full, 1kg (2¼ pounds) vacuum-sealed *capocollo* back home in your luggage.

La Tavernetta ★ The nice thing about Puglia is that you have restaurants like La Tavernetta—located on a prime thoroughfare of the old town, it could be a tourist trap, but instead it turns out solid, satisfying food with a lengthy menu where almost everything is under 10€. La Tavernetta has all bases covered from rigorously traditional Pugliese dishes like *fave e cicoria* and *orecchiette* to pan-Italian dishes (caprese salads, *spaghetti alla carbonara, scaloppine al limone*).

Tip: If they're closed or full, try **Piazzetta Garibaldi,** Via Giuseppe Garibaldi 17 (✆ **080-4304900**), just past Piazza Immacolata.

Via Vittorio Emanuele 30. ✆ **080-4306323.** Main courses 5.50€–15€. MC, V. Fri–Wed 12:30–3pm and 7:30–11pm.

Trattoria La Tana ★★ Set within the cozy vaults of the old stables of the Palazzo Ducale, La Tana specializes in traditional local *martinese* cuisine along with typical Pugliese seafood preparations. This is a place you'll want to go with a big appetite, because from the antipasti (don't miss the rustic veggies) to the *dolci* (order the ricotta-filled *bocconotto*), it's all sublime. Regulars rave about the *baccalà* (salt cod) and the *orecchiette* with *cime di rapa.* A loyal following of sophisticated locals speaks volumes about the quality of dining here. La Tana's only flaw, perhaps, is that you can find typical local cuisine elsewhere in Martina for significantly less money.

Via Mascagni 2-4-6 (right side of Palazzo Ducale). www.ristorantelatana.it. ✆ **080-4805320.** Reservations recommended. Main courses 10€–16€. MC, V. Mon–Sat 12:30–3pm and 7:30–11pm; Sun 12:30–3pm.

Villa San Martino ★★ A gracious air, attentive service, and a tranquil location make this villa the best lodging in Martina. (It's not in the old city, but a short 3km/2 miles south along the road to Taranto.) Throughout, the boutique hotel is luxuriously appointed, and the villa's relatively modern date means guest rooms and bathrooms are more ample than in a historic property. Villa San Martino's large garden, framed by umbrella pines and lush Mediterranean flora, has a pool and abundant areas for relaxing and sipping. The on-site restaurant, **Duca di Martina,** is one of the top gourmet addresses in the Valle d'Itria.

Via Taranto 59, Sud: 2.8km/1¾ miles, 74015 Martina Franca. www.relaisvillasanmartino.com. ✆ **080-4805152.** Fax 080-4801026. 21 units. 260€–395€ double; 365€–700€ suite. Rates include buffet breakfast. AE, DC, MC, V. Free parking. **Amenities:** Restaurant; bar; airport transfers (80€); babysitting; bikes; concierge; exercise room; Jacuzzi; pool; room service; sauna; spa. *In room:* A/C, TV, hair dryer, Jacuzzi (in some), minibar, Wi-Fi (free).

Ostuni ★★

Many other Valle d'Itria towns bill themselves as "white cities," but they're positively beige by comparison. Gleaming, practically blinding in summer, and perched atop a commanding hill near the Adriatic, only Ostuni is the capital-lettered White City. In Ostuni, the postcards are all of snow-white architecture against a bracing blue sky. In this town, you really know that you're getting close to Greece.

The "White City" of Ostuni.

Ostuni doesn't have any major individual attractions, but it's a wonderful place to spend a few hours walking up and down the lanes and taking in blissful vistas. Ostuni's main square is Piazza della Libertà, at the convergence of the higher, old city (where you'll want to spend your time), and modern Ostuni. From the piazza, Via Cattedrale winds its way up and up (north) through *la città bianca,* past the exceptionally gracious Gothic-style **cathedral ★** and under the lovely baroque **arched passageway ★** opposite, to the very top of Ostuni. Have lunch or dinner at one of the very good restaurants up here (two are reviewed below), then wind your way back down along any combination of quiet alleys leading back down to Piazza della Libertà.

WHERE TO EAT & STAY

The best hotel in the town proper is the **Ostuni Palace ★★**, Corso Vittorio Emanuele 218 (www.ostunipalace.com; ✆ **0831-338885;** 130€–260€ double), but another highly recommended place to stay in the vicinity is at **Masseria La Rascina** (p. 806).

Mela Bacata ★★ COCKTAIL BAR/SMOOTHIES In summer, the young and hip of Ostuni register a lot of Foursquare "check-ins" at this fabulous panoramic bar. Cushy, apple-green armchairs spill out from the bar itself (set within an evocative vaulted stone space) onto a stepped alley and a wide open terrace overlooking the Adriatic and Valle d'Itria.

Via G. Vitale, at Via Scipione Petrarolo.

Osteria del Tempo Perso ★★ PUGLIESE The *osteria* "of lost time" rewards those who hike to the very top of Ostuni to find it with a folksy dining room that's part 16th-century grotto and part museum of farm culture. Start with an antipasto of *burratina con melograno* (*burrata* with pomegranate—trust me on this one), and then try their unique *tegamino di funghi,* a sort of mushroom casserole with bread and zucchini flowers. *Secondi* include both meat and fish dishes, such as baked sea bass with clams, cuttlefish, tomatoes, parsley, garlic, and olive oil.

Via G. Tanzarella Vitale 47. ✆ **0831-304819.** Reservations recommended. Main courses 7€–16€. AE, MC, V. Tues–Sun 12:30–2:30pm and 7:30–10:30pm Oct–May. Mon–Sat dinner only and Sun lunch and dinner June–Sept.

Osteria Piazzetta Cattedrale ★★ PUGLIESE This small, cozy, and refined *osteria* directly opposite the cathedral offers local cuisine and seasonal ingredients at moderate prices. Among the specialties are the *riccia* (pastry tower) with eggplant and *scamorza* (similar to smoked mozzarella), and pasta dumplings with *scorfano* (scorpionfish). The place is small and much loved—reservations are a must or you risk major disappointment at the door.

Largo Arcidiacono. ✆ **0831-335026.** Reservations essential. Main courses 8€–16€. AE, MC, V. Wed–Mon 12:30–2:30pm and 7:30–10:30pm (also Tues in summer, with later evening hours).

Other Towns of the Valle d'Itria

If you love Alberobello, Martina Franca, and Ostuni, expand your exploration of the Valle d'Itria with visits to the also delicious nearby towns of Locorotondo, Cisternino, and Ceglie Messapica. The name **Locorotondo ★** means "round place" and the town, just 6km (3¾ miles) north of Martina Franca and 8km (5 miles) east of Alberobello, is in fact circular in shape. Besides its pleasant and pedestrian-friendly old center, standout features of Locorotondo are its eponymous white wine and its peculiar-for-Italy architecture, the *cummerse,* which are houses with steeply pitched, Baltic-looking gabled roofs. The local wine, a lightly fruity white called Locorotondo DOC, is a 50/50 blend of Verdeca and Bianco d'Alessano grapes. Virtually all of the wine is made at one winery just below the old city, **Cantina del Locorotondo,** Via Madonna della Catena 99 (www.locorotondodoc.com; ✆ **080-4311644**), which has a convivial tasting room and bottle shop. Along the road between Locorotondo (10km/6¼ miles) and Ostuni (14km/8⅔ miles), **Cisternino** is another, sunny whitewashed medieval town

THE BEST masseria hotels

An integral part of the Pugliese experience is spending a few days, preferably a week, at one of the region's wonderful *masseria* hotels. Offering boutique lodging, and often all-out luxury, in centuries-old farmhouses and outbuildings, *masserie* represent the best in comfy amenities and rural relaxation. Any of the properties listed here is a convenient base for travel through the Valle d'Itria and much of the Salento peninsula.

Borgo Egnazia ★★★ The latest project of hotelier Aldo Melpignano (of Masseria San Domenico) is a breathtakingly impressive resort. Entirely brand-new (opened in 2010) and massive, Borgo Egnazia has hotel rooms in the central building plus a vast number of suites, town houses, and private villas—all cleverly conceived with generous outdoor living areas and soothing white-stone built-in fixtures—strewn about an Arab-style "village," complete with picturesque lanes where you are bound to get lost (and quickly rescued and redirected by a hotel golf cart). The atmosphere here is dominated by clean white and dreamily luxurious, with a thousand different areas to make your own. As a full-service resort, Borgo Egnazia has just about everything on-site, from a superb spa to glorious pools, tennis, kids' programs, game room, and cooking schools. Borgo Egnazia, 72010 Savelletri di Fasano. www.borgoegnazia.com. ✆ **080-2255000.** 183 units. 260€–400€ double; 470€–1,040€ suite; 530€–1,200€ town house and villa. Rates include buffet breakfast. AE, MC, V. Free parking. **Amenities:** 7 restaurants; bar; babysitting; bikes; children's programs; 18-hole golf course; exercise room; saltwater pool; room service; spa; tennis courts. *In room:* A/C, TV, DVD player (some units), hair dryer, kitchenette (some units), minibar, Wi-Fi (free).

Masseria La Rascina ★★★ This is living! La Rascina is more B&B than full-service resort, an oasis of quiet that's convenient both to Ostuni and some of Puglia's best Adriatic beaches (both less than 10 min. away). Guest units are appointed with ethnic and contemporary furnishings, and the property's three apartment-suites have kitchenettes and outdoor dining areas. (The "B&B rooms" are simpler.) The *masseria*'s common terraces and sitting rooms are like an *Architectural Digest* spread, both rich and human-scale, with a tasteful Puglia-meets-the-Orient aesthetic. Proprietors Leonie and Paolo are a lovely couple and a big part of what makes staying at La Rascina such a treat. Strada Statale Adriatica (SP19, km 4.7), Rosmarina, 72017 Ostuni. www.larascina.it. ✆ **338-4331573.** 10 units. 800€–1,800€ per week double-occupancy; inquire about rates for shorter stays. No credit cards. **Amenities:** Babysitting; bicycle rentals; swimming pool; Wi-Fi (free). *In room:* A/C, TV/DVD (in self-catering suites), CD player (in self-catering suites), hair dryer, kitchenette (in self-catering suites), minibar.

Masseria San Domenico ★★★ (pictured at right) When the childhood home of owner Aldo Melpignano opened as a five-star hotel and spa in 1996, it set the gold standard for luxury *masseria* accommodations in Puglia. Set among mammoth, gnarled olive trees, this ancient coastal estate has been restored with a healthy respect for its past, but with the best modern amenities in the province, including a full-service spa with seawater piped directly into a massage pool. An irregularly shaped pool, encircled by rocks and plants, is an

oasis in the summer heat. You live like one of the Knights of Malta (except better) amid ultrarich fabrics, antique reproductions, and grand comfort in the vaulted, white-walled bedrooms, with their pillow menus and spacious bathrooms. The warm and worldly Melpignano presides over the whole thing with all his heart, and it shows. Strada Litoranea 379, 72010 Savelletri di Fasano (Brindisi). www.imasseria.com. ✆ **080-4827769.** Fax 080-4827978. 50 units. 300€–580€ double; from 600€ suite. Rates include buffet breakfast. AE, DC, MC, V. Free parking. Closed mid-Jan to mid Mar. No children 11 and under. **Amenities:** Restaurant; bar; babysitting; bikes; 18-hole golf course; exercise room; saltwater pool; room service; sauna; spa; 2 outdoor tennis courts (lit). *In room:* A/C, TV, DVD player (in some), hair dryer, minibar, Wi-Fi (free).

Masseria Torre Coccaro ★★★

The folk-chic Torre Coccaro may be the most romantic of the *masseria* hotels. The property even has its own delightful mini-piazza with an ochre-washed chapel and white lights strung around the olive trees. Beyond the usual spa and swimming pool, guests love the on-site cooking school, where you pick vegetables from the estate and learn how to make pastas, desserts, and *burrata.* The most unique unit here is the Orange Garden suite: Inside, it's cavernous, with exposed rock and rustic masonry, but its gorgeous, white-linen furnishings are a far cry from Bedrock; outside, the suite has its own private pool and deck set amid a walled grove of citrus trees. Contrada Coccaro 8, 72015 Savelletri di Fasano (Brindisi). www.masseriatorre coccaro.com. ✆ **080-4829310.** 39 units. 278€–510€ double; from 396€ suite. Rates include buffet breakfast. AE, DC, MC, V. Free parking. **Amenities:** Restaurant; bar; babysitting; bikes; exercise room; outdoor pool (heated Mar–Nov); room service; spa. *In room:* A/C, TV, hair dryer, minibar, Wi-Fi (free).

Masseria Torre Maizza ★★

Masseria meets Miami Beach at the sister property of Torre Coccaro, connected to it by a path through the olive trees. The overall look here is sleeker, more metropolitan and masculine than at Torre Coccaro, but amenities are comparable. The Aveda Spa occupies the farmhouse's central tower, but the pool is Torre Maizza's real showpiece, surrounded by an antique colonnade and teak decking where you can drift off into reveries of being Mediterranean royalty. Contrada Coccaro (no number), 72105 Savelletri di Fasano (Brindisi). www.masseriatorre-maizza.com. ✆ **080-4827838.** Fax 080-4414059. 26 units. 284€–537€ double; from 414€ suite. Rates include buffet breakfast. AE, DC, MC, V. Free parking. No children 9 and under in Aug. **Amenities:** Restaurant; bar; babysitting; bikes; exercise room; outdoor pool (heated Mar–Nov); room service; spa. *In room:* A/C, TV, hair dryer, minibar, Wi-Fi (free).

with a quiet and relaxing feel. In the countryside near Cisternino lies a highly recommended villa-style vacation property, **Sopra I Sassi ★★** (www.sopraisassi.it), with two *trulli* (one that sleeps six and another that sleeps eight) and a panoramic swimming pool, from 1,000€ per week. The town of **Ceglie Messapica** is slightly more out of the way (12km/7½ miles southwest of Ostuni and 18km/11 miles southeast of Martina Franca) but compelling for its several excellent restaurants, including the Michelin-starred yet totally down-to-earth **Fornello da Ricci ★**, Contrada Montevicoli (www.ricciristor.com; ✆ **0831-377104**).

LECCE & THE BEST OF THE SALENTO ★★

40km (25 miles) SE of Brindisi, 87km (54 miles) E of Taranto, 905km (561 miles) SE of Rome

Just when you think you've got Puglia pigeonholed—the blissfully endless olive groves, the *trulli*, the charming whitewashed alleyways of Martina Franca and Ostuni—along comes Lecce to wow you with something completely different. Surprisingly sophisticated Lecce is the *signora* (lady) of Pugliese cities, a trove of enchanting baroque architecture, urbane elegance, and typically southern Italian radiance.

The handsome old city center is clad almost entirely in the local yellow limestone, lending Lecce an irresistible warmth. That warmth becomes an ear-to-ear grin when, every few blocks or so, you encounter one of Lecce's fabulous baroque buildings. *Il barocco leccese* was a particularly ebullient version of the 17th-century Italian predilection for architectural embellishment. In part because this local limestone (a golden color that approximates Mediterranean sunshine) is relatively soft and easy to chisel, sculptors working in Lecce during the baroque period retooled church facades and civic palaces with as many extravagant flourishes and intricate details as if they were drawing them on paper. You don't have to be an architecture wonk to get a major kick out of Lecce's baroque; all you need are eyes and a sense of fun. (But save the best—the church of Santa Croce—for last.) Lecce's manageable scale and general atmosphere make it a delight to explore on foot. The city is filled with fashionable boutiques and sidewalk cafes, many of them concentrated on Lecce's monumental main square, Piazza Sant'Oronzo.

Lecce's Santa Chiara church.

Founded by Greeks more than 2,200 years ago, Lecce is also a city with

Lecce's limestone buildings.

tangible ancient history, and significant archaeological sites can be seen below street level around town. Puglia isn't known for its Roman ruins, but Lecce has both a theater and amphitheater, either from the Augustan or Trajanic-Hadrianic eras, lying within a few blocks of each other. The bastions of the 16th-century Castello Carlo V (Castle of Charles V, the Habsburg Holy Roman Emperor) house Lecce's culture bureau and temporary exhibitions.

And while Lecce's pedigree may be southern Italian through and through, it can sometimes feel like a prosperous midsize northern Italian city: The atmosphere might remind you a bit of Parma, albeit with a lot more sunshine. The city's longtime tourism slogan, "Florence of the South," is way off the mark artistically and architecturally, but you'll find some of the same aristocratic vibe as in the Tuscan capital. Unlike Florence, Lecce's economy isn't based on tourism at all, but on agriculture—in particular the sale and distribution of olive oil and wine. Local handicrafts, sold in galleries citywide, include papier-mâché (*cartapesta*) and ceramics, whose frequently monochrome dark glazes and minimalist silhouettes represent a marked departure from the folksier styles of other Italian ceramics.

In addition to its baroque splendor and shopping, Lecce also some excellent hotels, so if you've already done the country *masseria* thing elsewhere in Puglia and would like some city atmosphere for a night or two, it's an ideal base for day trips around the Salento, the highlights of which are described at the end of this section. Nothing in the peninsula—whether it's beaches or wine touring—is more than an hour's drive from Lecce.

Essentials

GETTING THERE Lecce is connected to Bari and Brindisi by **train** service on the state-run FS line. The journey from Bari takes about 2 hours and costs 10€ to 15€ one-way; from Brindisi it's a half-hour and 2.60€ to 7€ each way. Note that Lecce's train station is about 2km (1¼ miles) from the center of the old quarter; from the train station, you can take a bus to Piazza Sant'Oronzo in the heart of old Lecce. Visit www.trenitalia.com or call ✆ **892021** in Italy for train schedules and information.

If you have a **car** and are arriving from the north, follow signs to Brindisi then take state highway SS613 south to Lecce (38km/24 miles, or about a half-hour).

VISITOR INFORMATION There is a **tourist office** near the Duomo at Corso Vittorio Emanuele 16a (www.viaggiareinpuglia.it; ✆ **0832-332463**), open Monday to Friday from 8am to 2pm and 3 to 8pm, and an info-point at Castello Carlo V, Viale XXV Luglio, 2 blocks east of Piazza Sant'Oronzo (✆ **0832-246517;** Mon–Fri 9am–1pm and 5–9pm; Sat–Sun 9:30am–1pm and 5–9pm).

Capturing the Spirit of Lecce & the Salento Like a Local

Ylenia Sambati's Lecce-based boutique travel company, **Yltour ★★** (www.yltourcongressi.it; ✆ **0832-318536**), organizes weeklong itineraries in southern Puglia focused on food, relaxation, and hands-on, authentic cultural interfaces. Sambati is sunshine incarnate and personally involved in all aspects of your vacation: You'll learn to make pasta and bake bread in an actual Pugliese mama's country kitchen; photograph or paint idyllic olive groves; tour the region's best wineries, cheese makers, and food markets; and meet a lot of locals. It's like a backstage pass to the soul of the Salento. Packages start at 1,350€ for 1 week.

Exploring the Town

Monumental, social **Piazza Sant'Oronzo** is ground-zero of historic Lecce and the no-brainer place to begin a stroll through town. The 2nd-century-A.D. Roman column erected here, **Colonna Romana,** once stood near its mate in Brindisi; together they marked the end of the Appian Way. Lightning toppled this column in 1528, and the Brindisians left it lying on the ground until 1661, at which time the citizens of Lecce bought it and set up the pillar in their hometown. St. Oronzo, for whom the square is named, now stands atop it guarding the area. Oronzo is the patron saint of Lecce, feasted on August 26 and venerated particularly for his miraculous liberation of the Leccese from a plague in 1658.

At the southern side of the piazza are the remains of a **Roman amphitheater.** Archaeologists can't agree on the date of the structure—it's either Augustan (1st century B.C., thus predating the Roman Colosseum), or Trajanic-Hadrianic (2nd century A.D.), but it would have accommodated 20,000 fans, who came to watch bloody fights between gladiators and wild beasts.

Perhaps the most striking element in Piazza Sant'Oronzo is the odd but gracious **Palazzo del Seggio,** or Il Sedile, along the northwest curve of the amphitheater. It's the delicious little quadrifrons building with ogival arches on each side, capped by an arcaded loggia. Erected in 1592, Il Sedile was originally the seat *(sede)* of the municipal government and has also served as the city munitions deposit, a museum, and an exhibition space (its current vocation).

North of the piazza, Via Umberto I leads to the stunning Basilica di Santa Croce, but I recommend you save that for last, as its over-the-top facade is the crowning glory of the *barocco leccese* and a sight for even the sorest tourist's eyes.

So, instead of going north from Piazza Sant'Oronzo, head west down Via Vittorio Emanuele. On the way, you'll encounter smart shops, including the handy cafe **All'Ombra del Barocco** at Corte dei Cicala 9 (www.allombradelbarocco.it; ✆ **0832-245524**)—it has wine and free Wi-Fi. Opposite the cafe is the baroque **church of Sant'Irene,** built in 1591 for the then-patron of Lecce. (Poor Irene was demoted to regular saint status when Oronzo saved Lecce from the plague the following century.)

One block farther down (west) Via Vittorio Emanuele, the **Duomo ★**, Piazza del Duomo (✆ **0832-308557**), stands in an almost completely enclosed square. The cathedral, which has two facades (on the north, at the end of the transept, and on the west, at the end of the nave), was reconstructed between 1659 and 1670 by Zingarello. To the left of the Duomo, the **campanile** towers

64m (210 ft.) above the piazza. The cathedral is open daily from 7am to noon and 4 to 7pm, and admission is free. On the opposite side of the Duomo is the **Bishop's Palace (Palazzo Vescovile),** where Lecce's archbishop still lives today. Also in the courtyard is a **seminary,** built between 1694 and 1709 by Giuseppe Cino, who was a student of Zimbalo. Its decorations have been compared to those of a wedding cake. A baroque well, extraordinarily detailed with garlands and clusters of flowers and fruit, stands in the courtyard. To continue your walking tour, exit the Duomo via its "secret" door at the south end of the transept.

Outside the Duomo, walk south down Via Guglielmo Paladini and then turn left (east) on Via Marco Basseo; then, make your first left (north) onto the narrow Via del Teatro Romano, which leads directly to the remains of Lecce's **Roman Theater,** tucked between the surrounding buildings. Like the amphitheater in Piazza Sant'Oronzo (above), its date is uncertain but was constructed sometime between the late 1st century B.C. and the early 2nd century A.D. The theater was much smaller than the amphitheater—and only a half-round versus a full ellipse—housing only about 5,000 spectators for plays and concerts.

For a selection of local crafts, including *cartapesta* (papier-mâché), ceramics, and terra-cotta, go to **Mostra dell'Artigianato,** Via Francesco Rubichi 21 (www.mostrartigianato.le.it; ✆ **0832-246758**). And if you're interested in any of the wines and foodstuffs of the region, head for a food emporium that's been here as long as anyone can remember, **Enoteca,** Via Cesare Battisti 23 (✆ **0832-302832**). Usually they'll let you taste a glass of whatever wine you're interested in before you buy a bottle.

Where to Eat

For *aperitivo* or after-dinner, the ultrastylish **Hea 180,** Via Federico d'Aragona 1a (www.hea180.com; ✆ **0832-241761**), has refined small plates and the best regional wine.

Alle Due Corti ★★ PUGLIESE It's in all the guidebooks, but don't worry, this is some superauthentic *cucina salentina* (the menu is even in dialect) that the Leccese love and patronize as much as tourists do, and the location up the street from baroque stunner Santa Croce is ideal. Try the *ricciareddhe* pasta with cherry tomatoes, garlic, and cheese and the *agnellu te li signuri* (lamb cooked with flour, onions, and white wine)

Corte dei Giugni 1. ✆ **0832-242223.** Reservations recommended. Main courses 9€–15€. AE, MC, V. Mon–Sat 1–2:30pm and 8–11:30pm.

Trattoria Cucina Casareccia (Le Zie) ★ PUGLIESE The owner and chef, Mrs. Anna Carmela, claims that she serves *cucina povera,* which translates as "cooking of the poor." Don't get the wrong idea. At her rustic family trattoria, you are served some of the most authentic ingredients of the region. Begin with one of my favorite dishes—purée of fava beans parboiled and mashed with a little olive oil and salt and served with sautéed chicory. I also am fond of her potato pie with mussels and her beef meatballs with a white-wine sauce. Only for aficionados do I suggest the filet of horse in a light spicy sauce.

Via Costadura 19. www.lezietrattoria.com. ✆ **0832-245178.** Reservations recommended. Main courses 8€–14€. MC, V. Tues–Sun 1–2:30pm and 7–10pm. Closed last week of Aug and 1st week of Sept.

Where to Stay

With the long-awaited reopening of the five-star Risorgimento (see below), as well as the addition of boutique properties like the **Santa Chiara Suites** (www.santachiaralecce.it), Lecce now has a fine range of accommodations options, from the simple and economical to the luxurious.

Eos ★ A winning combination of slick design and friendly atmosphere, the stylish and affordable Eos is managed by the same people who run the fancier Risorgimento in the heart of town. The hotel is a modern white cube about a 10-minute walk from central Lecce; inside, the rooms aren't vast, but they're cleverly designed with smart shelving and storage. Taking inspiration from the landscape of Puglia, but with a decidedly contemporary spin, the rooms' aesthetics are cool, relaxing, and functional. The bathrooms (also with a bold design) have a surprising amount of space as well as sexy Italian fixtures. Breakfast here is wonderful, with a huge array of local, artisanal products. Guests can also utilize the roof terrace for wine drinking and hanging out.

Viale Alfieri 11, 73100 Lecce. www.hoteleos.it. ✆ **0832-230030.** Fax 0832-347840. 30 units. 80€–100€ double. Rates include buffet breakfast. AE, DC, MC, V. Free parking. **Amenities:** Bar; babysitting; bikes; concierge; room service. *In room:* A/C, TV, hair dryer, minibar, Wi-Fi (10€ per hour).

Patria Palace Hotel ★★ The top choice in Lecce for timeless elegance (if not luxury), the Patria Palace enjoys a lively location in the midst of the baroque monuments of the old city. The stunning facade of Santa Croce is straight out the front door. Once the *palazzo* of rich family landowners, it was turned into an inn in 1797, and remains a bastion of good taste. Much of its clientele are Italian businesspeople, which lends the property a chic, dynamic air. The smallish but perfectly comfortable bedrooms are furnished in the Liberty style, each with its own original decorative paintings. The best rooms are on the third floor—307, a "superior" double, has a fantastic private terrace.

Piazzetta Riccardi 13, 73100 Lecce. www.patriapalacelecce.com. ✆ **0832-245111.** Fax 0832-245002. 67 units. 255€–305€ double. Rates include buffet breakfast. AE, DC, MC, V. Parking 15€. **Amenities:** Restaurant; bar; babysitting; bikes; concierge; room service. *In room:* A/C, TV, hair dryer, minibar, Wi-Fi (free).

Risorgimento Resort ★★ The luxurious Risorgimento is the only five-star hotel in the center of Lecce, and it's surprisingly reasonable for a hotel of such class. It reopened in 2007 after a lengthy restoration which returned its historic exterior to its original splendor while refitting the interior with contemporary design. Bold red and clean lines dominate throughout the common areas and guest rooms, although the sleek modern-imperial look is softened here and there by traditional Pugliese accents, such as papier-mâché dioramas in the lobby. Rooms are spacious and filled with pampering amenities (though no designer bath products—odd for a five-star), and internationally trained staff graciously meet the needs of the most demanding travelers.

Via Augusto Imperatore 19, 73100 Lecce. www.risorgimentoresort.it. ✆ **0832-246311.** Fax 0832-245976. 47 units. 160€–270€ double. Rates include buffet breakfast. AE, DC, MC, V. Parking 10€. **Amenities:** 3 restaurants; bar; babysitting; concierge; fitness room; room service; Turkish bath; spa; Wi-Fi (free, in lobby only). *In room:* A/C, TV, hair dryer, minibar.

Beyond Lecce: Best of the Salento

The Salento peninsula has much to offer beyond Lecce. Along the coast, there are delightful port towns, beautiful white-sand beaches, thermal waters, and sea caves to explore. Inland, take time to visit the Grecia Salentina, where a version of ancient Greek is still spoken by elders, and handsome towns hide treasures both architectural and culinary. Presented in a clockwise tour from Otranto, on the Adriatic coast, to Manduria, at the upper west corner of the peninsula, here are the highlights of the Salento.

The major port town on the Salento's east coast, and the easternmost town in all of Italy, is **Otranto ★★**. Here, two colors dominate: the electric turquoise of the sea and the gleaming white of the old quarter. Otranto is well-kept and lively, and simply walking around the maze of streets in the medieval *borgo* and gazing out over the Adriatic are attractions enough, but the city also has two compelling art-historical landmarks.

The first is the 11th-century **Cathedral ★★**, Piazza Basilica (✆ **0836-802720;** daily 7am–noon and 3–5pm, also until 8pm June–Sept; free admission), the largest church in Puglia and famous for its stupendous **floor mosaic ★★★** (1163), in which a tree of life motif tells the story of humankind as it stood then, interweaving imagery from classic mythology, Arthurian legend, the Old Testament, the zodiac, and more. The pictures are amazingly vivid, having survived even the brutal Ottoman sack of Otranto in 1480, in which 800 citizens were killed by beheading. As a reminder of that grisly event, the skulls of those *beati martiri* are displayed inside the cathedral.

Otranto's other major monument is the **Castello Aragonese ★**, Piazza Castello (✆ **0836-871308;** Jan–Feb and Nov–Dec Tues–Sun 10am–1pm and 3–5pm, Mar and Oct Tues–Sun 10am–1pm and 3–6pm, Apr–May daily 10am–1pm and 3–7pm, June and Sept daily 10am–1pm and 3–10pm, July–Aug daily 10am–midnight; 2€), a 15th-century sea fortress, complete with a moat filled with appropriately scary looking green water. You can walk all over the castle, parts of which are now exhibition galleries, and there are great views from the battlements.

The historic center of Otranto has several good restaurants, the fanciest of which is **Peccato di Vino**, Via Rondachi 7 (✆ **0836-801488;** lunch and dinner Wed–Mon year-round). In summer, you might prefer to take your meal at one of the casual pizza-and-panini spots along the town beach, north of the castle and cathedral.

The **tourist office** of Otranto is at Piazza Castello 8 (✆ **0836-801436**).

Heading south from Otranto on SS173, the coast is quite rugged and the driving scenic. The town of **Santa Cesarea Terme ★** is a highlight along this route. It's been a spa town for more than 500 years, exploiting the sulfuric waters emerging from the rock beneath. (The waters, though stinky, are purported to heal all kinds of maladies, mostly rheumatic.) Even if you don't have time for a treatment at the **Terme di Santa Cesarea** spa facility, Via Roma 40 (www.termesantacesarea.it; ✆ **0836-944070;** 60-min. massages from 60€), the town is a kick for the eclectic architecture of the villas that rich spa patrons built here over the centuries.

Just south of Santa Cesarea begins a stretch of coastline rich in caves. The largest and most impressive of these is the **Grotta Zinzulusa ★**, 160m (525 ft.) deep and filled with stalactites whose resemblance to rags *(zinzi)* hanging from the ceiling earned the cavern its name. The cave's entrance is along the water (and swimming here is unforgettable) but for real spelunking, you must use a footpath, accessible by water or by land—just outside the town of Castro Marina, follow the Via Zinzulusa down to the water.

The very tip of the Salento's stiletto heel is **Santa Maria di Leuca.** The classic experience here is climbing up to the lighthouse and adjacent basilica, called De Finibus Terrae (End of the World), for a bracing, almost 360-degree **panorama ★★** of the Adriatic and Ionian Seas. Below this perch, the town of Leuca itself has handsome Art Nouveau villas and a busy tourist port offering boat excursions to the many caves between here and Otranto.

Rounding the tip of the Salento and heading back north up the Ionian coast, which has none of the Adriatic's rugged and rocky geography, you begin to enter the prime **beach territory ★★** of Puglia. The shores near Ugento have some excellent sandy beaches, like **Torre Pali,** and closer to Gallipoli, **Punta della Suina** and **Baia Verde.**

Gallipoli ★ is the chief harbor on the Salento's Ionian coast. The old town, set upon an island of limestone and connected to the modern city by a Renaissance bridge, is a tranquil fishing village where it's a pleasure to stroll the back alleys and admire baroque palaces and churches that proudly line the seafront. One word of caution: The restaurants and cafes along the sea walls attract many with their romantic settings, but I'd recommend stopping only for a drink or light snack here instead of overpaying for a mediocre seafood meal.

Slightly north of Gallipoli is the city of **Nardò,** the second most populous in the Salento, and a sort of mini-Lecce with some equally delicious baroque architecture. Here you're also in proximity to several more lovely beaches, starting with **Porto Selvaggio** (a nature reserve with a wild aspect), **Sant'Isidoro,** and finally the broad sandy expanses around **Porto Cesareo,** a resort town heavy on beach club/discos that are loud and packed in summer.

North of here, the handsome inland town **Manduria ★** is a magnet for oenophiles. It's home to the DOC appellation Primitivo di Manduria, arguably Puglia's finest red wine. Stop in at the **Enoteca del Primitivo ★**, Vico Primo Senatore Giacomo Lacaita (www.enotecadelprimitivo.it; ✆ **099-9711523**), a bottle shop and wine bar with small plates. Before heading back to Lecce, it's worth the short detour north from Manduria to **Oria ★**, with its imposing cathedral and Swabian castle.

BARI ★

268km (168 miles) E of Naples, 459km (287 miles) SE of Rome

Surprisingly captivating Bari is Puglia's largest city (the ninth largest in Italy; pop. 320,475) and the region's capital, whose history as a principal Adriatic seaport and fishery goes back thousands of years. Many Puglia-bound visitors skip Bari, seeing only its airport before heading out into the countryside in a rental car, and admittedly, most travelers to Puglia are here for the countryside and small towns, not busy cities, but Bari is well worth an afternoon detour or overnight stay. In the medieval quarter of Bari Vecchia—a warren of twisty streets on a peninsula between the city's two harbors—lie two important churches, the splendid and much-venerated basilica of San Nicola (in the crypt are the bones of "Santa Claus" himself), and the cathedral of San Sabino. Bari Vecchia is an increasingly fashionable district with chic cafes and boutiques tucked into the seafront promenades, but in the back streets you'll still find traditional workshops and street-level apartments where women sell their homemade *orecchiette*.

Outside the enclave of Bari Vecchia, the city's look is modern. To the south, shoppers will be thrilled by the concentration of fashion, design, and home boutiques in the grid of the Murat quarter and its principal, pedestrianized street, Via Sparano da Bari. To the east, Bari's attractive *lungomare* is an immaculate stretch of white stone seafront promenade—with what appear to be enough Adriatic-facing benches for everyone in the city—backed by crisp Fascist-era apartments and government buildings. Bari is clean, safe (just see my warning about Bari Vecchia at night, below), and small enough that you can get everywhere on foot.

The **tourist office** is at Piazza Aldo Moro 33/a (✆ **080-9909341**), near the train station.

Essentials

GETTING THERE **Bari-Palese airport** (www.aeroportidipuglia.it), about 7km (4⅓ miles) west of downtown, is well served by domestic and international flights, including nonstops from London, Paris, and Frankfurt. By **car,** Bari is a 5-hour drive from Rome (take the A1 to Naples then head east on the A16/A14). You can also take the **train** to Bari from anywhere in Italy—from Rome, as an example, it's 4 hours and 51€ on the Eurostar (fast train), or upwards of 6 hours on the InterCity (from 36€) or even slower *regionale* or *diretto* trains.

GETTING AROUND You can easily walk everywhere within Bari's city center, including the old quarter of Bari Vecchia and the shops, restaurants, and hotels of the newer Murat quarter.

VISITOR INFORMATION The **tourist office** is at Piazza Aldo Moro 33/a (✆ **080-9909341**), near the train station, or visit www.viaggiareinpuglia.it for more information about Bari.

Exploring

In a few hours' walking tour you can get a good feel for Bari's two distinct halves. Start at the **Castello Normanno-Svevo,** Piazza Federico II di Svevia (no phone, not open to the public), architectural symbol of Bari and right on the line between the old and new parts of the city. Much of the castle was built in the 12th (by the Norman king Roger II) and 13th (under Swabian emperor Frederick II) centuries, though the remains visible today are largely 16th-century reinforcements. From the castle, take one of the little roads leading into the old quarter of Bari Vecchia. Along these tiny streets, like Arco Basso and Arco Alto, you'll find women selling homemade *orecchiette* and other goods from tables in front of their apartments. Once inside the twisty alleyways of Bari Vecchia, it's a labyrinth where even a good map may not be of much use. Ask a local to point you toward your next stop, the Cattedrale. The **cathedral of San Sabino ★**, Piazza dell'Odegitria 1 (✆ **080-5210605;** daily 8am–7pm; free admission), is one of two major historical churches in Bari Vecchia. Built from 1170 to 1178 out of the almost iridescent local white stone, it has splendid Romanesque architectural details on all sides. From here, continue north along Strada del Carmine to Bari Vecchia's other main church, the even more interesting **Basilica di San**

Nicola ★★, Largo Abate Elia (© **080-5737111;** Mon–Sat 7am–8:30pm, Sun 7am–10pm; free admission). The cult of St. Nicholas—a catch-all patron saint of sailors, merchants, thieves, students, and children (especially around Christmas)—is a big deal in Bari, and this basilica, where his bones are kept in a poignant **tomb in the crypt ★**, is an important pilgrimage site for both Roman Catholics and Eastern Orthodox Christians. The 12th-century San Nicola has a rather fortresslike appearance, with square towers at each corner: Indeed, the relics of San Nicola were a hotly contested item over the centuries and as such the church had to act as his posthumous castle on more than one occasion.

After visiting San Nicola, head east, toward the water, along the left outer wall of the church. Then, climb the short stairs that lead to **Via Venezia ★**, Bari Vecchia's panoramic promenade, which lies atop the old city battlements, facing the water. Walk right (south, back toward the harbor) down Via Venezia, which eventually places you back in the social heart of Bari Vecchia, **Piazza del Ferrarese ★**, the expansive esplanade where Bari Vecchia meets the Murat quarter near the harbor. Here, and in the adjoining Piazza Mercantile, you'll find lots of cafes and some cool little shops. In the evenings, especially, Piazza del Ferrarese heaves with activity. (Do, however, avoid the inner core of Bari Vecchia at night, where petty crime can be a problem.)

Directly south of Piazza del Ferrarese is the intersection of Corso Vittorio Emanuele and Corso Cavour, the two main streets of modern downtown Bari. The rectangle to the south and west of them is the Murat quarter, filled with excellent shops and restaurants. Pedestrianized **Via Sparano da Bari ★** is a **prime retail corridor** jampacked with big-name fashion boutiques. But some of the best shops lie just down the side streets in this area, such as **Experya ★**, at the corner of Via Principe Amedeo and Via Argiro, one of those brilliant, only-in-Italy leather goods stores with chic, well-made bags and shoes for a third of the price of Prada. At Via Marchese di Montrone 7 (corner of Via Putignani), **Vinarius ★** is a fantastic enoteca (wine bar) and liquor store. Serious shoppers will want to comb the grid of the Murat quarter, but avoid visiting between 2 and 5pm, when almost all the stores in Bari are closed.

If you still have time after strolling in Bari Vecchia and shopping in the Murat quarter, take a walk—or just sit and relax on one of the myriad benches—along the modern ***lungomare*** **★** (waterfront) to the east. Here, serried ranks of gleaming Fascist-era *palazzi* make for a formidable backdrop to the busy harbor.

Where to Eat & Stay

If you spend the night in Bari, you'll want to be within walking distance of both Bari Vecchia and the shopping district: My hotel choices below both fit that bill. A good general destination for a casual bite or drink is at one of the bars on Piazza Ferrarese.

Ai Due Ghiottoni ★ PUGLIESE/SEAFOOD "The Two Gluttons" is a long beloved address in Bari for reliably tasty food in a stylish, happening setting. The menu is extensive but focuses on fish. Opulent presentations deliver fabulous flavor, and service is a well-oiled machine of efficient and cordial black-clad waiters. Ai Due Ghiottoni is also a great place to go if someone else is paying—the fashionable surroundings (you might feel at times like you're at a trendy club) and prime seafood don't come cheap. (However, the restaurant has a more casual, less expensive spinoff for pizzas and roast meats, a few kilometers south of here at Via Amendola 197h; © 080-5467134).

Via Niccolò Putignani 11. www.ai2ghiottoni.it. ✆ **080-5232240.** Reservations recommended. Main courses 14€–30€. AE, MC, V. Mon–Sat 12:30–3pm and 8pm–midnight.

Oriente ★★ Located along Corso Cavour just steps from the elegant government buildings, theaters, and luxury boutiques of the Murat quarter, the Oriente occupies the 1920s Palazzo Marroccoli. Extensive renovations in 2010 gave the Art Nouveau hotel a face-lift, with some bold accents in the lobby and common areas (and an especially lovely, more contemporary roof bar). Guest rooms, although refitted with modern technology, retain a prewar luxury, with marble-clad bathrooms and Liberty-style furniture. ***Tip:*** An adjacent parking lot offers much cheaper rates than the hotel's own on-site lot.

Corso Cavour 32, 70122 Bari. www.orientehotelbari.com. ✆ **080-5255100.** Fax 080-5255777. 75 units. 220€–300€ double. Rates include buffet breakfast. AE, DC, MC, V. Parking 35€. **Amenities:** Restaurant; bar; babysitting; bikes; concierge; fitness room; room service. *In room:* A/C, TV, hair dryer, minibar, Wi-Fi (free).

Palace ★ The classic four-star hotel of downtown Bari has comfortable rooms, many with small balconies. Even if the Palace isn't all that stylish (for that, see the more expensive Oriente), it's handsome enough, and the comings and goings of businesspeople and other eventgoers daily in the lively lobby lend a happening vibe. The on-site dining is surprisingly good, and staff are stellar all around, from the joyous Mimma at reception to the professional waitstaff at the seventh-floor restaurant.

Via Francesco Lombardi 13, 70122 Bari. www.palacehotelbari.it. ✆ **080-5216551.** 195 units. 140€–290€ double. Rates include buffet breakfast. AE, DC, MC, V. Parking 20€. **Amenities:** Restaurant; bar; concierge; room service; Wi-Fi (free, in common areas). *In room:* A/C, TV, hair dryer, minibar.

Terranima ★★ PUGLIESE In homey surroundings that evoke grandma's house (that is, your boho-chic grandma who lived in Paris yet never forgot her Pugliese roots), Terranima serves classic, absolutely delicious local cuisine. There's a loving hand in everything that comes out of the kitchen, and the best way to dine here is to let them choose for you. Your meal will most likely include antipasti with Pugliese cheeses, cured meats, rustic *torton*, and savory *sformatini* (like a dense soufflé), and to-die-for primi like capunti (canoe-shaped pasta) with a creamy sauce of ricotta, mint, and sun-dried tomatoes. Terranima isn't fancy (for example, there's no sophisticated wine list), but it's friendly and satisfying.

Via Niccolò Putignani 215. www.terranima.com. ✆ **080-5219725.** Reservations recommended. Main courses 10€–16€. AE, MC, V. Thurs–Tues 12:30–2:30pm and 7:30–10:30pm.

NORTH OF BARI

While many travelers to Puglia tend to focus their time in areas farther south, like the Valle d'Itria and Salento peninsula, there are several sights north of Bari worth visiting if you can spare the time. Seaside Trani, with its famous cathedral and lively atmosphere is the easiest and perhaps most rewarding of them, a short drive up the coast from Bari. Architecture buffs may want to swing inland to see Castel del Monte, the curious and lonely 13th-century fortress that is one of Puglia's four UNESCO World Heritage sites. Finally, the northernmost part of Puglia is the Gargano Promontory, the spur of Italy's boot and a rugged paradise for nature lovers. As you tour around northern Puglia, you may drive through towns with familiar food names like Cerignola (the town's green *bella* olives are a popular gourmet export) and Andria (*burrata* was invented here and is still the main industry)—just another reminder that when in Puglia, you are in foodie country.

Essentials

GETTING THERE Use Bari as your gateway to visit Trani and Castel del Monte; each of these sights lies less than an hour away from the Pugliese capital by **car** on well-signed and well-maintained highways. The Gargano promontory lies at the northern tip of Puglia and can be reached in 2½ hours from Bari (take the A14 north to Foggia then bear east on the SS89, toward Manfredonia). If driving to the Gargano from Rome (4 hr.) or Naples (2¾ hr.), do not go as far south as Bari; instead follow signs to Foggia and then Manfredonia. You can also fly into **Foggia's airport** (www.aeroportidipuglia.it).

GETTING AROUND You can reach Trani by train (2€) or car from Bari in 45 minutes. For other destinations north of Bari, you'll need a car. Bear in mind that roads in the Gargano are tortuous and slow going.

VISITOR INFORMATION Visit www.viaggiareinpuglia.it for detailed information and media about Trani, Castel del Monte, and the Gargano. In Trani, there's a tourist office at Piazza Trieste 10 (✆ **0883-588830**). On the Gargano, Vieste's tourist office is at Piazza J.F. Kennedy (✆ **0884-708806**), and Peschici has an office at Via Magenta 3 (✆ **0884-915362**).

Trani ★★

If you can only visit one place north of Bari, make it Trani. Trani's water's-edge cathedral is one of the most memorable sights in Puglia, and among Italy's best examples of Romanesque architecture, period. The town itself is also beautiful: Immaculate streets are paved with the local white limestone and lined with *nobiliar palazzi* and castles, while the crescent-shaped harbor is cafe central and one of Puglia's most popular, picturesque places to hang out and socialize.

To reach Trani by car from Bari (52km/32 miles), take the A14 autostrada north, toward Foggia, then follow signs east to Trani. It's also easy to reach Trani by train from Bari. The trip takes about 40 minutes and costs 2€.

EXPLORING

Trani's main draw by far its **Cathedral ★★**, Piazza Duomo 9 (✆ **0883-494210;** daily 9am–8pm; free admission). Perched dramatically at the edge of the Adriatic, it's a towering, gleaming, gorgeous example of Romanesque style. There is something powerful and exquisitely harmonious about this basilica, the consummate dramatic set-piece of ecclesiastical architecture. The cathedral is dedicated to San Nicola Pellegrino (St. Nicholas the Pilgrim), a Greek boy who washed ashore, drowned, in Bari in 1094. Just 5 years later, Nicholas was canonized and work began on his church, which was completed, minus the bell tower, in 1143. The 59m-high (194-ft.) **campanile ★★** (bell tower) was added in the 13th century and is the element that makes the Trani cathedral such a stunner, breaking up the sober symmetry of the facade and lifting the entire tableau skyward. The interior of the church, divided into three naves, is a splendid play of arches, columns, and vaults where the local limestone, not ornate sculptures, painting, or marble inlay, is the star. The church's original **bronze door ★★**, the work of

12th-century sculptor Barisano da Trani, is also on display here, having been moved inside after restoration. Thirty-two intricate panels feature illustrations of biblical figures as well as dragons, lions, archers, and jugglers more fitting with the popular imagery of the medieval period—an interesting mix of the sacred and "profane." The **crypt** ★ of the cathedral consists of several interconnected, atmospheric spaces, including the tomb of San Nicola Pellegrino.

After touring the cathedral, stroll Trani's port, chockablock with attractive cafes and restaurants. For an excellent local meal, try **Gallo** ★★, Via Statuti Marittimi 48 (www.gallorestaurant.it; ✆ **0883-487255**), where owner-manager Alessandro Gallo is as beautiful as the refined seafood dishes. If you'd like to spend the night in Trani, book a room at the **Regia** ★, Piazza Monsignor Addazi 2 (www.hotelregia.it; ✆ **0883-584444;** doubles 100€–140€), a pint-size *palazzo* with modern rooms and an optimal location directly behind the cathedral.

Castel del Monte ★

Spend any time in Italy, anywhere at all, and you'll see Castel del Monte—it's the monument that adorns the reverse side of the Italian-minted 1-cent euro coin. Built by Swabian emperor Frederick II, the 13th-century castle is a mash-up of classical, Islamic, and Cistercian Gothic architecture and was declared a UNESCO World Heritage site in 1996.

Castel del Monte is a bit out of the way (54km/33 miles west of Bari and 31km/19 miles west of Trani) and somewhat forlorn-feeling, but the site is absolutely unique in the world for its strange octagonal shape, with octagonal towers attached to each of the eight corners of the edifice. With all its elegant and mathematical details, Castel del Monte hardly seems like a fortress that ever saw battle and was most likely conceived by Frederick II, a particularly prolific builder of show-castles, as an architectural experiment and entertainment venue.

Castel del Monte.

The castle (✆ **0883-569997**) is open 10:15am to 7:45pm March through September and 9:15am to 5:45pm October through February; admission is 5€.

The Gargano Peninsula ★★

Puglia's ace in the hole for nature lovers is the Promontorio del Gargano national park. The thumb-shaped promontory is the "spur" of Italy's famous boot and the only part of Puglia with dramatic topography. Its mountainous interior is densely wooded with maples, ashes, cedars, and chestnuts, as well as the ancient oak and beech forest known as the Foresta Umbra. The Foresta Umbra once covered much of Central Europe, and the only surviving part of it in Italy is here on the Gargano.

The coast offers stunning scenery that switches between cliffs, rocks, caves, islets, and sandy beaches. In addition to well-equipped coastal resort towns Vieste, Peschici, and Mattinana, you'll find pristine salt lakes at Lesina and Varano, where you can enjoy swimming and watersports in the mild climate and calm waters. Italy's only Adriatic archipelago, the **Tremiti islands ★★**, lie just north of the Gargano. These tiny islands are rustic and little known outside Italy. Boat service to the Tremiti is primarily from Termoli, in Molise to the north, though ferries also run from Vieste and Peschici in summer.

The Gargano is also home to two important Catholic pilgrimage sites, the **cave of St. Michael the Archangel in Monte Sant'Angelo** and the **sanctuary of Padre Pio in San Giovanni Rotondo,** where the beloved saint's body can be viewed. (Incredibly, the latter is the second-most-visited Catholic pilgrimage site in the world, after Mexico City's Our Lady of Guadalupe, with seven million pilgrims per year.)

It is admittedly a bit of a trek to reach the Gargano from elsewhere in Puglia (allow 2 hr. from Bari to Gargano gateway city Manfredonia), and getting around the Gargano once you're there is also time-consuming. It'll take a leisurely 7 hours just to drive around the Gargano, but the highways that skirt the rugged coastline here are among the most scenic drives in Italy. (Train service is limited to a private spur along the northwestern coast.) For these reasons, consider spending at least 1 night somewhere on the promontory. The resort towns Vieste and Peschici have plenty of accommodations options, though many of these close in winter.

The swimming and beach season runs from May through September (Aug is the busiest month), but for all-around beauty, the best time to come is autumn, just after the beach clubs have been shuttered, when you can enjoy the colors of the Foresta Umbra, along with a tranquil sense of timelessness.

WHERE TO EAT & STAY

La Locanda della Castellana ★★ This place offers the ultimate in relaxation. This charming family-run inn in the hills just outside Peschici makes you feel at home from the moment you arrive. The Locanda has a delightful colonial-retreat look and feel, against a backdrop of fragrant local trees and shrubs, with sublime views across the hills to the sea. Rooms are simple, spacious, and spotless, and those on the first floor have large balconies. Breakfast is a farm-to-table feast served until late morning.

Località Valle Castellana, 71010 Peschici. ✆/fax **0884-963020.** 14 units. 58€–152€ double. AE, MC, V. Free parking. **Amenities:** Restaurant; bar; free bikes; fitness center; pool; Wi-Fi (free, in common areas). *In room:* A/C, TV, hair dryer, minibar.

Piccolo Paradiso ★★ ITALIAN/SEAFOOD My top pick for dining in Peschici is this large, friendly restaurant with an ample terrace overlooking the Adriatic and the Tremiti islands. The menu runs the gamut from *carpaccio di pesce* to simple wood-fired pizzas to rustic Pugliese *stuzzicheria* (small plates), all at surprisingly reasonable prices.

Viale Kennedy 29, Peschici. www.ristorantepiccoloparadisopeschici.com. ✆ **0884-964122.** Entrees 8€–16€. MC, V. Thurs–Tues noon–3pm and 7–11pm (daily in summer, with later evening hours).

SICILY

15

Exotic, sunbaked Sicily is the biggest island in the Mediterranean Sea and Italy's largest region by area. Sicily's multi-cultural pedigree, thanks to thousands of years as a stepping stone for empires and conquests, has as much Greek, Arab, and Northern European flavor as it does Italian. Though it's only separated from the mainland by the 4km-wide Stretto di Messina, Sicily has a palpable, captivating sense of otherness. It also offers the full package of Italian travel experiences: evocative towns with compelling art and architecture, outstanding ruins older than anything in Rome, and a geographic palette that goes from the sere, chalky southeast to the brooding slopes of Mt. Etna to the brawny headlands of Palermo and the gentle, agricultural landscapes of the east—all surrounded by cobalt seas and beaches where you can swim from May to October. True to international stereotypes, Sicilians are a passionate people, and their warmth and hospitality make even everyday transactions memorable. Food lovers have an entirely new culinary world to explore in Sicily, whose regional cuisine is both unique and accessible, drawing on the bounty of the Med, a long tradition of pastry making, and an increasingly sophisticated collection of local wines.

Sightseeing Often remarkably well-preserved within their original context, Sicily's main attractions are stellar ruins (noble Greek temples, spectacularly situated ancient theaters, and the wonderful Roman mosaics at Piazza Armerina), theatrical Baroque towns like Siracusa and Noto where ebullient architectural details become an operatic chorus to the simple act of walking down the street, Arab-Norman glories in and around Palermo, and the exhilarating opportunity to be up-close-and-personal with active volcanoes like Etna and Stromboli. In summer, you'd be crazy not to include a few sea-oriented days, whether in the dramatic Aeolian islands or just at the gorgeous "people's beach" of Mondello, outside Palermo.

Eating & Drinking Swordfish, mint, pistachios, ricotta, eggplant, juicy and sweet pachino tomatoes all become part of your diet in Sicily. Seafood lovers can salivate over red Mazara prawns and sea urchin pasta (trust me), and sweet tooths just may find their mothership in Sicily. No other Italian region can compete with Sicily when it comes to desserts, which include the famous cannoli (you haven't had a cannolo until you've had one here), cassata, and countless other cakes and confections. You'll also find North-African-inflected dishes, both in the widely popular fish couscous and in Palermitan street foods, like the

PREVIOUS PAGE: **The Temple of Hercules in the Valley of the Temples.**

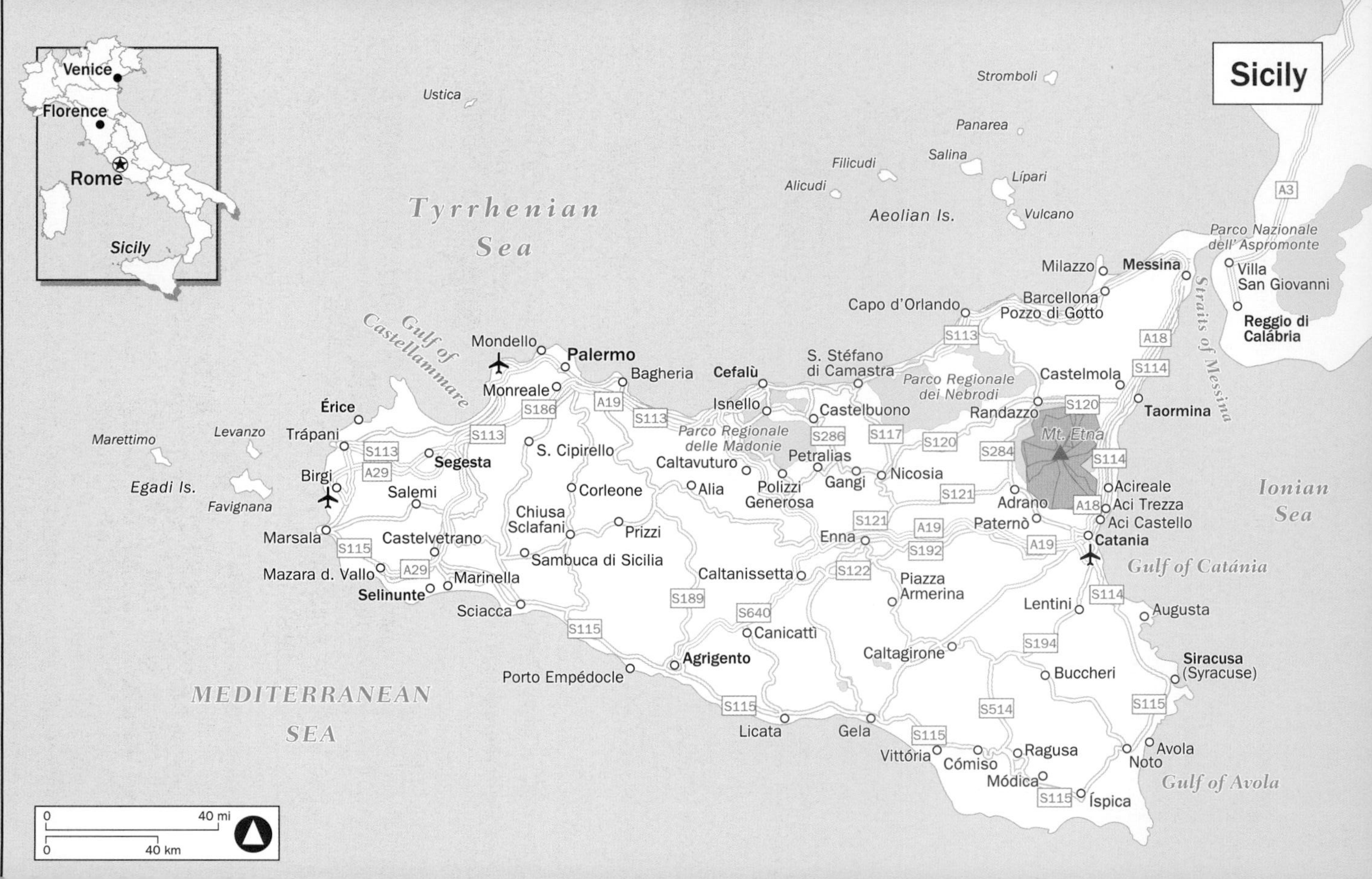
Sicily
Venice
Florence
Rome
Sicily
Ustica
Stromboli
Panarea
Salina
Filicudi
Alicudi
Lípari
Aeolian Is.
Vulcano
Tyrrhenian Sea
Parco Nazionale dell' Aspromonte
Villa San Giovanni
Reggio di Calábria
A3
Milazzo
Messina
Straits of Messina
Barcellona Pozzo di Gotto
Capo d'Orlando
S113
A18
S114
Gulf of Castellammare
Mondello
Palermo
Bagheria
Cefalù
S. Stéfano di Camastra
Parco Regionale dei Nebrodi
Castelmola
Taormina
Monreale
A19
S186
S113
Isnello
Castelbuono
Randazzo
S120
Érice
Marettimo
Levanzo
Trápani
S113
S. Cipirello
Parco Regionale delle Madonie
S286
S117
S120
Mt. Etna
S284
S114
Segesta
Caltavuturo
Petralias
Gangi
Nicosia
Birgi
A29
Egadi Is.
Salemi
Corleone
Alia
Polizzi Generosa
S121
Adrano
Acireale
Ionian Sea
Favignana
Chiusa Sclafani
Prizzi
A18
Aci Trezza
Aci Castello
S121
A19
Paternò
Marsala
S115
Castelvetrano
Enna
A19
Catania
S192
Sambuca di Sicilia
A29
Mazara d. Vallo
Marinella
Caltanissetta
S122
Gulf of Catánia
Piazza Armerina
Selinunte
S189
Lentini
S114
Sciacca
S640
Augusta
S115
Canicattì
Caltagirone
S194
Agrigento
Siracusa (Syracuse)
Porto Empédocle
Buccheri
MEDITERRANEAN SEA
S115
S514
S115
Licata
Gela
S115
Vittória
Cómiso
Ragusa
Avola
Noto
Módica
Gulf of Avola
S115
Íspica
0
40 mi
0
40 km

addictive *panelle* (chickpea fritters). Sicilian wine has really come into its own in recent years, and in addition to internationally known varietals like the red Nero d'Avola, there are tons of flinty and refreshing whites—meet grillo, insolia, and grecanico—that go perfectly with local veggies and seafood, while Etna Rosso—a silky Sicilian cousin of pinot noir—pairs beautifully with more substantial meat dishes that are also common on Sicilian menus.

History Talk about a checkered past! When you're the largest island in the Mediterranean, and strategically positioned between two continents, expect some cross-cultural trampling. In its more than 10,000-year recorded history, Sicily has been conquered, settled, and abandoned by virtually dozens of civilizations, from the Phoenicians, Greeks, and Carthaginians in antiquity, to the Arabs, Berbers, Moors, and Normans in the Middle Ages, to the Spanish and Bourbons in the Renaissance, and finally, finally the (at least nominally) Italian modern era. It's an intricate and violent story that nonetheless left a fascinating physical legacy—touring the relics of Sicily's past can feel like visiting several different countries at once—and a surprisingly mixed gene pool. Blue-eyed, natural blondes aren't as rare here as you might think.

THE BEST TRAVEL EXPERIENCES IN SICILY

- **Standing humbled, and often mystically transported, before the great Greek ruins:** The ruins of ancient Akragas—commonly known as the Valley of the Temples, in Agrigento—are justifiably Sicily's most celebrated archaeological site. The 2,500-year-old temples, their simple Doric columns striking a timeless figure against the cobalt sky, have come to be a calling card for Sicilian tourism itself, but smaller and more intimate sites like Selinunte and Segesta are also impressive. See p. 856.
- **Living the good life in Taormina:** Sicily's most glamorous town, and one of the poshest resorts in Italy, has long been a destination for international tourism. It wears its popularity surprisingly well, and the preposterously gorgeous hill town above the Ionian Sea (and with omnipresent views of Mount Etna) welcomes one and all with its easy-going, elegant holiday atmosphere. See p. 830.
- **Cross-cultural sightseeing in Arab-Norman Palermo:** Sicily's complicated history is riddled with influences from north, south, east, and west. Nowhere on the island is this illustrated better than in fascinating Palermo, where street markets evoke Middle Eastern souks and the most famous monuments bear the striking, exotic artistic signature of the Arab-Norman 12th century, when Palermo was one of Europe's greatest cultural and intellectual centers. See p. 863.
- **Adopting la dieta siciliana:** Local specialties like cannoli, *arancine,* Mazara prawns, and *pesto alla trapanese* only taste this good on this island—and some exist here only. Accompanying it all is a new world of lovely Sicilian wines, from the flinty white *grillo* to the velvety reds of Mount Etna, that you can't find anywhere else. See "Where to Eat" throughout the chapter.
- **Cooling off in the Sicilian Mediterranean:** Nothing washes away the grime of ruin-traipsing and city-touring like a dip in the clear, refreshing waters of the Sicilian coast. For cerulean scenes that scream "vacation in paradise," seek

ORGANIZING YOUR time

If you want to see most of Sicily's highlights, plan on spending at least a week and moving a few times. Renting a car is essential if you want to see a lot in a relatively short amount of time. Otherwise, buses are excellent in Sicily and connect all major cities and tourist attractions. The trains here, unlike the rest of Italy, are slow and antiquated—don't bother going by rail anywhere in Sicily. For a first visit, focus on the eastern half of the island, including Palermo and Agrigento (the Valley of the Temples), Taormina, Siracusa, and maybe Piazza Armerina (the Roman mosaics at Villa del Casale). Remember that everything is very spread out (Sicily is the largest Italian region and the largest island in the Mediterranean, 178km/110 miles north to south and 282km/175 miles wide), and even though distances may look short on a road map, driving can be slow-going on all lesser highways. The autostrade (motorways), however, are fast, smooth, and virtually empty. Even with the best-laid travel plans, expect at least one item to fall off your itinerary as you adopt a Sicilian pace and tire of running around like a manic culture vulture.

Taormina is the most popular resort in Sicily. With its stunning beauty, excellent hotels, and tourist infrastructure, Taormina is a great place to relax and play for a couple of days; from here you can also visit Mount Etna. However, the town is isolated in the east, so it's not a good base for seeing the island's other major highlights. The quickest and most efficient way to see most of Sicily is to fly into Palermo, rent a car, and travel east to Taormina; then return your car and fly back to the mainland from Catania. (Conversely, you can fly into Catania, perhaps from Rome, and end your itinerary in Palermo, returning the car there before flying back to Rome.) If you have more than a week to spend in Sicily, consider adding some of the highlights of western Sicily, including the archaeological areas of Selinunte (also a beach area) and Segesta, the medieval hill town of Erice, wine tasting in Marsala, the sugary beach of San Vito lo Capo, and the Zingaro Nature Reserve. If your 10- to 14-day Sicilian vacation falls during the summer, it would be even more tempting to forgo some of the above "sights" and park yourself in some seaside locale for several days, perhaps a villa near Siracusa, or, for a real Mediterranean paradise experience, a rental cottage somewhere in the Aeolian Islands.

out the volcanic coves of the Aeolian Islands, and for a spectacular turquoise bay only a stone's throw from a maddening city, go to Palermo's summertime haven, Mondello. Because of Sicily's southern position, beach days are possible from April to October. See p. 882 and 889.

ESSENTIALS

Arriving

BY PLANE By far the easiest way to reach Sicily is to fly there. With Sicily's increasing popularity as a summer holiday destination, flights to the island from mainland Italy and elsewhere in Europe are now frequent and usually quite inexpensive. Sicily has three airports, in Palermo, Catania, and Trapani, that are linked with many Italian mainland airports and European hubs. Palermo's airport is the largest and best connected, with dozens of daily flights to Rome (50 min.) and Milan (1 hr., 15 min.), and nonstops to airports throughout Europe. The **Aeroporto di Palermo** (www.gesap.it; ✆ **091-7020111**), known as Falcone e Borsellino (after the two anti-Mafia magistrates who were assassinated in the early 1990s) or Punta Raisi for the spit of coastal land it occupies beneath spectacular headlands, is 31km (19 miles) west of Palermo on the A29 highway. Over in eastern Sicily, the **Aeroporto di Catania,** also known as Fontanarossa (www.aeroporto.catania.it; ✆ **095-7239111**), also has myriad domestic flights and European connections; you can even fly here nonstop from Beirut and Tel Aviv. On the western Sicilian coast, the **Aeroporto di Trapani-Birgi** (aka Vincenzo Florio; www.airgest.it; ✆ **0923-842502**) has flights to and from mainland Italy and a handful of European cities, as well as Malta and the island of Pantelleria. Note than many of the European flights to and from Catania and Trapani, and a few for Palermo, are operated by low-cost airlines that use those European cities' lesser airports (for example, Paris's Beauvais instead of Charles De Gaulle), so be careful of that when planning connections.

BY TRAIN Trains to Sicily are operated by Italy's national rail company, **Ferrovie dello Stato** (www.trenitalia.com). The trains from mainland Italy come down from Rome and Naples through Calabria—the "toe" of the boot-shaped peninsula—and across the Strait of Messina to Sicily on ferries equipped with railroad tracks on the cargo deck. It's a novel way to arrive in Sicily, though not very efficient.

From Rome to Palermo, there are three direct trains daily—at 7:39 and 11:39am, and 9:20pm—that arrive in Palermo 12 to 14 hours later. Fares start at 66€ for a second-class ticket.

Many more Sicily-bound trains originate in Naples (trip time to Palermo: 9–10 hr.). But if you're in Naples and trying to get to Sicily without flying, it's more comfortable and fun to take the ferry.

BY CAR Yes, you can drive to the island of Sicily. No, there's no bridge—the much-discussed Straits of Messina bridge has not yet materialized. However, the northeastern tip of Sicily is only separated from mainland Italy by a very narrow waterway, the 5km-wide (3-mile) Stretto di Messina (Strait of

Safety in Sicily

Sicily is attracting ever greater numbers of foreign tourists, especially British and German sun seekers on villa holidays. Many Americans who are otherwise enamored of Italy continue to skip Sicily, though, often because they harbor a media- and pop-culture-propagated fear of the Mafia. Put those fears to rest! However much a part of Sicilian society the Cosa Nostra has been, the Mafia doesn't concern itself with tourists. It still exists and affects Sicilian society, but in weakened form today thanks to decades of work by relentless anti-Mafia law enforcement agencies. As a casual visitor, you will be completely unaware of the Mafia's presence. As for other safety matters, pickpocketing can be a problem on crowded streets or buses in Palermo and Catania, and parts of those cities can seem menacing after dark, but if you take the usual safety precautions that apply to any big Italian city (be alert, hold bags and valuables in front of your body in crowded areas, and don't flash jewelry; women keep to busier thoroughfares if walking alone in the evening), you'll be fine.

Messina), which is crossed by regular car ferries between the Calabrian port of Villa San Giovanni (just north of Reggio Calabria, essentially the "toe" of the Italian peninsula's boot shape) and the Sicilian city of Messina. From Messina, which lies on the well-maintained A20 and A18 autostrade, it's a straight shot west to Palermo (233km/145 miles; about 2 hr.) or south to Taormina (52km/32 miles; 45 min.), Catania (97km/60 miles; 1 hr., 15 min.), and Siracusa (162km/100 miles; about 2 hr.).

If you're planning to drive down from Naples or Rome, as many visitors do, prepare yourself for a long ride: 721km (448 miles) south from Naples or 934km (580 miles) south from Rome.

BY SEA Palermo's large port is served by passenger ferries from the Italian mainland cities of Naples, Civitavecchia (near Rome), Livorno, and Genova, and from the Sardinian city of Cagliari. Nearly all of these are nighttime crossings, departing between 7 and 9pm and arriving the next morning between 6 and 8am. Some of these ferries are tricked out like miniature cruise ships, with swimming pools, salons, discos, gyms, and presidential suites. Ferries from Naples are the most numerous, operating daily year-round. The Naples-Palermo route is run by **SNAV** (www.snav.it; ✆ **081-4285555**) and **Tirrenia Lines** (www.tirrenia.it; ✆ **892123** or 02-26302803). With either company, the ferry trip takes 11 hours, although there is also a faster, more expensive daytime hydrofoil service that takes 6 hours (summer only). Fares for ferries to Sicily vary widely depending on whether you opt for a seat or a berth in a semiprivate cabin, and whether you bring a car aboard. Expect to pay between 50€ and 75€ for a *poltrona* (seat) and from 100€ to 180€ per person for a berth in a four-person cabin with a sea view. A car will cost an extra 25€ or so. From Civitavecchia, which is the port that cruise ships use when visiting Rome, Grandi Navi Veloci has ferries to Palermo that depart at 8pm, arriving in Palermo the next morning at 8am. Schedules vary depending on weather conditions, so always call on the day of departure even if you've already confirmed your reservation the day before.

Getting Around

In a region as spread out and varied in its offerings as Sicily, renting a car gives you the freedom and flexibility to see as much of the island (and especially its less touristed pockets) as possible in what will inevitably be a limited amount of time. It means you can arrive and depart whenever you like and make last-minute itinerary changes stress-free. Having a car as extra storage throughout your trip is also a huge convenience, as is, of course, the ability to drive right into your hotel parking lot. Driving in Sicily is a pleasure on the whole and helps get you into the culture a little bit more. Negotiating traffic in the cities can feel like a video game, so drivers need to keep their peripheral vision on high alert and be prepared for all kinds of variables. If that sounds more like stress than adventure, simply plan your itinerary around the numerous, efficient, and inexpensive bus lines that serve Sicily.

Bus travel in Sicily is excellent and another highly recommended means of getting around the island. Buses here are clean and modern coaches with comfortable upholstered seats, air-conditioning, and smooth suspensions. (They're not the dusty third-world vehicles you might be picturing.) The network of bus service in Sicily covers all corners of the island, with the fastest and most frequent lines connecting major tourist destinations like Palermo, Siracusa, Agrigento, and Taormina. However, some careful planning and attention to bus schedules is key. If you miss the 8am bus from Palermo to Siracusa, the next one doesn't leave until 2pm. Still, on a first tour of Sicily's highlights, buses may be the way to go.

Deciding between car rental and bus travel in Sicily can come down to a matter of budget. Consider the following numbers: With a prepaid booking through a low-cost company like AutoEurope, you can get a compact car (four-door, decent trunk space) for 35€ to 40€ per day. (Note that the overwhelming majority of rental cars in Italy have manual transmission, so if you can't drive a stick shift, you'll pay a huge premium to rent a car with automatic transmission.) Also factor in the high price of gas in Europe: It costs about 60€ to fill up the tank of that compact car, and you'll probably fill up twice on a 10-day tour of Sicily. Compare that with some typical bus fares: The 2-hour run from Palermo to Agrigento is 8.30€; the 3¼-hour trip from Palermo to Siracusa is 11€.

Once arrived at your destination, by car or by bus, you'll almost always get around on foot. In Palermo, a few handy bus lines can relieve your feet while sightseeing.

The main bus companies in Sicily are **Interbus** (www.interbus.it; ✆ **091-6167919;** also goes by the names **Etna Trasporti, Segesta,** and **Sicilbus,** depending on which part of Sicily you're in), and **Cuffaro** (www.cuffaro.info; ✆ **091-6161510**), which operates the buses between Palermo and Agrigento.

Trains (www.trenitalia.com) do exist in Sicily, but passenger rail service on the island is generally spotty and slow, with antiquated, dirty coaches. (This is of course in marked contrast to the rest of Italy, where trains are usually a tourist's best friend.) The bus is always a better option, so think of the train as a last resort when your desired route is not covered by a bus.

If you opt for car rental, **AutoEurope** (www.autoeurope.com; ✆ **888/223-5555** toll-free in North America) consistently has the best rates—a good 25% lower than other "budget" companies and up to 50% lower than big agencies like Hertz and Avis, and you can prepay the rental for even greater savings. (Do note that AutoEurope requires a deposit, in the form of a hold of a certain amount of funds—usually twice the rental charge—on your credit card, to be lifted when you return the vehicle.) AutoEurope has offices in all Sicilian airports, major train stations, and tourist city centers. Otherwise, you can also find all the other major rental agencies around Sicily.

Anyone taking the wheel in Sicily will want to acquire a good road map *(carta stradale),* such as that published by Touring Editore (7.90€, available at newsstands and bookshops). For covering longer distances, use the autostrada (marked with green signs) whenever possible, even if it looks like you're making a significant detour (or face a high-blood-pressure situation when you discover that 200km on a lesser, yet more "direct" highway takes 5 hr.). Sicily has four autostrada routes: the A18 (along the east coast, from Messina to Noto); the A19 (Palermo to Catania); the A20 (on the north coast, from Palermo to Messina, overlapping with the A19 near Palermo); and the A29 (Palermo to Mazara del Vallo, in the southwest). The A29 *diramazione* branches off from the A29 at Alcamo (near the temple of Segesta) and goes west to Trapani and its airport. You can go 120 to 140 kmph (74–89 mph) on the autostrada, shredding the miles and saving a lot of time traversing spread-out Sicily. For local jaunts, the *strade statali* (state roads, labeled as "SS+number," and marked with blue signs) are your only option and often quite scenic; they're just not very fast (average 60 kmph/37 mph), as they typically pass through trafficky town centers. There are some

The Rules of the Autostrada

Sicily's well-maintained autostrade (motorways) make for smooth, swift, and nearly traffic-free driving. However, there is a very clear code of etiquette to autostrada travel (this goes for all of Italy, by the way) that visitors must obey in order to avoid incurring the wrath of local speed demons. For each direction of travel on the autostrada, there are two lanes. The left lane is for passing only. I repeat, unless you are actively passing another vehicle, YOU MUST STAY IN THE RIGHT LANE. Simply cruising along in the left lane, admiring the scenery, is a big no-no. You will quickly learn this because if you don't get out of the way, there will be an aggressive German-made sedan zooming at about 150 kmph (95 mph) to within 10 inches of your rear bumper and belligerently flashing its headlights. That's a local driver's not-so-subtle reminder that you need to guide your buggy back into the right lane, pronto. Even if you're not an aggressive driver, expect to do plenty of passing yourself on the autostrada, as you will certainly encounter slow-going trucks, buses, and underpowered Fiats in the right lane that you'll want to move around. Just be very, very vigilant before entering the left lane: Those speed demons come out of nowhere.

exceptions to the rule, like the wide-open, fast-moving stretch of the SS115 between Agrigento and Sciacca.

Sicilian roads, as in the rest of Italy, are generally signposted well and abundantly. As you drive along, though, you may encounter intersections with two signs for your destination, a blue sign saying TAORMINA and a green sign saying TAORMINA, let's say, pointing in opposite directions. The green sign leads you to the autostrada and will invariably be the faster route. And sometimes there are two green signs for the same destination, pointing in opposite directions: In that case, it's up to careful map-reading to determine the more direct route. You're bound to make a few wrong turns, but hey, that small town where you have to pull over and ask directions at a lively cafe—where, incidentally, you end up eating the best cannoli you've ever had in your life—may end up being a memorable part of your journey.

TAORMINA ★★★

53km (33 miles) N of Catania, 53km (33 miles) S of Messina, 250km (155 miles) E of Palermo

Welcome to Sicily's enchantress. Despite being discovered, well-touristed, and often crowded, lofty Taormina is the belle of the island and still provides plenty of magic for visitors. For all you may have already heard about Taormina's charms, it's a place that makes newcomers and even repeat visitors, as they approach the town via a series of breathtaking hairpin curves, say, "Oh, *wow.*" I might offend some Amalfi Coast lovers here, but it's an even lovelier town than Positano. Typical of a medieval Italian village, Taormina has its historic churches, *palazzi,* city gates, and captivating alleyways. The fact that it has all of those things—plus a stunningly situated Greco-Roman theater—resting precariously on a steep cliff halfway between the sinister slopes of Mount Etna and the glittering Ionian Sea is what makes Taormina the glamorous movie star of Sicily.

Taormina is small, however, and has been well-known to the international travel industry for more than a century. For much of the year, tourists far

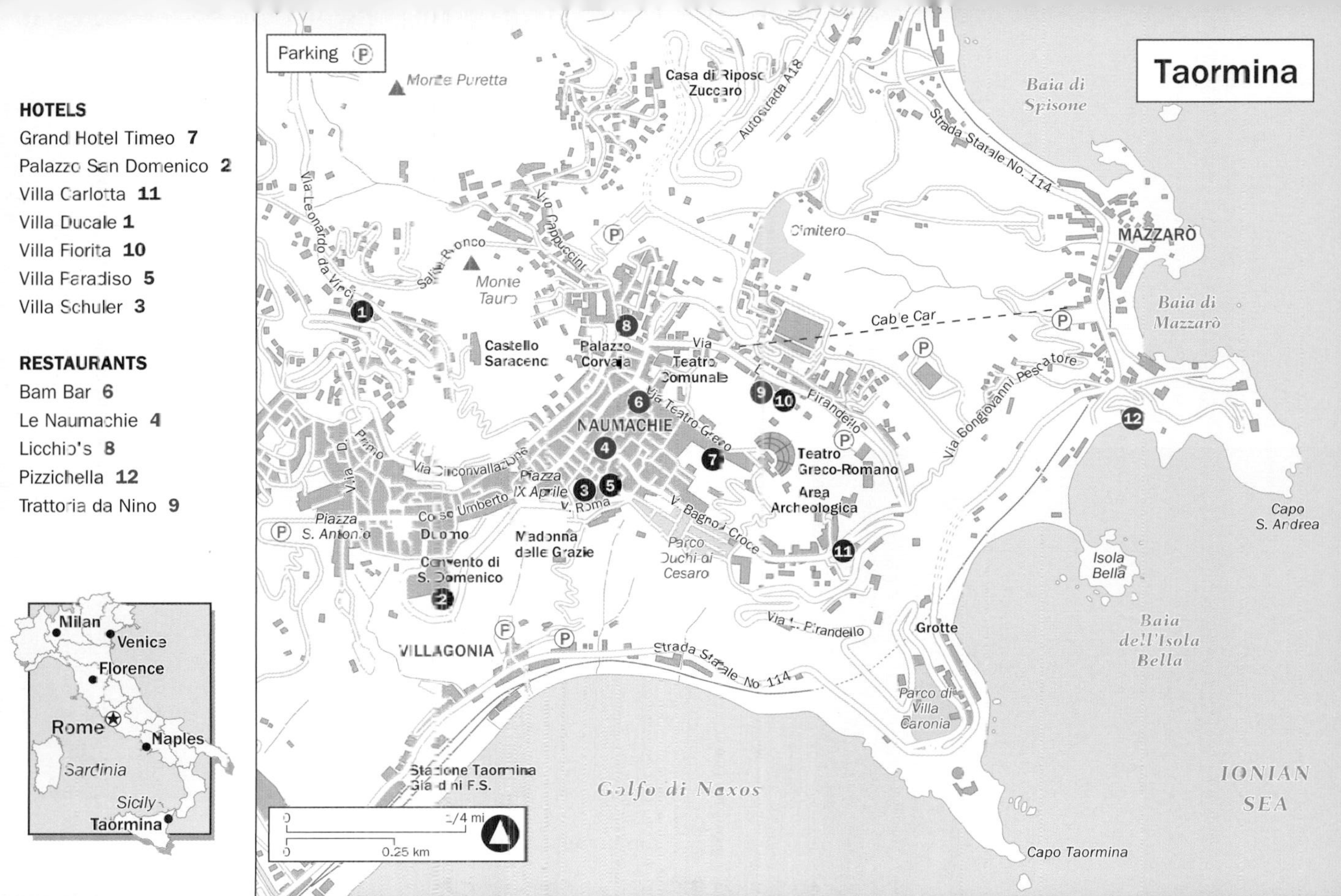
Taormina
Parking
HOTELS
Grand Hotel Timeo 7
Palazzo San Domenico 2
Villa Carlotta 11
Villa Ducale 1
Villa Fiorita 10
Villa Paradiso 5
Villa Schuler 3
RESTAURANTS
Bam Bar 6
Le Naumachie 4
Licchio's 8
Pizzichella 12
Trattoria da Nino 9
Milan
Venice
Florence
Rome
Naples
Sardinia
Sicily
Taormina
Monte Puretta
Casa di Riposo Zuccaro
Autostrada A18
Strada Statale No. 114
Baia di Spisone
MAZZARÒ
Baia di Mazzarò
Via Leonardo da Vinci
Via Cappuccini
Cimitero
Monte Tauro
Castello Saraceno
Palazzo Corvaja
Via Teatro Comunale
Cable Car
Via Bongiovanni Pescatore
Via Teatro Greco
NAUMACHIE
Pirandello
Teatro Greco-Romano
Area Archeologica
Via Circonvallazione
Via D. Primo
Piazza IX Aprile
Corso Umberto
V. Roma
V. Bagnoli Croce
Piazza S. Antonio
Duomo
Madonna delle Grazie
Parco Duchi di Cesaro
Convento di S. Domenico
Capo S. Andrea
Isola Bella
Baia dell'Isola Bella
Grotte
Via L. Pirandello
VILLAGONIA
Strada Statale No 114
Parco di Villa Caronia
Stazione Taormina Giardini F.S.
Golfo di Naxos
IONIAN SEA
Capo Taormina
1/4 mi
0.25 km

Taormina, below looming Mount Etna.

outnumber locals. Yet there's still a relaxed, small-town feel all over Taormina, and people who do call Taormina home aren't jaded by their town's popularity, and they avidly maintain that it's still an authentic place, and an ideal base from which to explore the highlights of northeastern Sicily, whether as a resident or a vacationer. Upsides to being such an established resort include an amazing range of accommodations options, and tons of services and amenities catering to foreigners, from world-class shopping to Babel-like newsstands and bookstores to excellent dining and hip nightspots. Taormina has been welcoming outsiders for a very long time and does it with an easy elegance that's infectious.

So what do you do in Taormina? After all, perched high above the Ionian Coast, it's a sea resort that isn't technically on the sea. Beaches, however, lie just below town and are easily accessed by cableway, bus, or car. But there's a surprising amount to do in town, too, after your token visit to the Greek theater: Take in the views from Piazza IX Aprile, shop, stop for a *granita,* breathe in the salubrious marine air and the heady scent of eucalyptus, wander stepped side streets, and let the undeniably jolly, true vacation spirit of Taormina relax you.

In the packed summer months, you can always escape the throngs during the day by seeking out adventures like a day trip to Mount Etna or the Alcantara Gorges.

Essentials

GETTING THERE Taormina is well served by **buses,** most of which connect through Catania. From Catania's Fontanarossa airport, there are nine

Taormina's stunning Teatro Greco.

Taormina-bound buses per day, stopping in downtown Catania before heading up the coast to Taormina. Travel time by bus from Catania to Taormina is about 1½ hours; tickets are about 5€ one-way. Full schedules are available from **Interbus** (www.interbus.it; ✆ **095-530396,** or 0942-625301 for the local Taormina ticket office). Taormina's bus station is on Via Pirandello, near Porta Messina, on the north end of town.

If you're arriving by **car** from Messina, head south along A18, following signs for Catania. From Catania, take the A18 north, toward Messina. Exit the autostrada at the Taormina exit, which lies just north of a series of highway tunnels. If you're arriving by car, find out if your hotel has parking and if there's a fee, and get very clear instructions about how to arrive—Taormina is a mind-boggling maze of tiny one-way streets and hairpin turns. Otherwise, take advantage of the large public **parking garages** just outside the old town, both clearly signposted with blue *P*s on all roads that approach Taormina. On the north side of town, **Parking Lumbi** (✆ **0942-24345**) charges 14€ per day (16€ per day in Aug) and has a free shuttle from the garage to the Porta Messina gate of Taormina proper. On the south end of town, **Parking Porta Catania** (✆ **0942-620196**) is another multilevel garage with slightly higher rates than Lumbi (15€ per day, 17€ per day in Aug) but with the advantage of being practically in town (it's just 100m/328 ft. from the Porta Catania city gate). Down by the beach at Mazzarò, in the vicinity of the lower cable car station, is **Parking Mazzarò** (14€ per day, 16€ in Aug).

It's also possible to take the **train** to Taormina. The nearest rail hubs are Messina and Catania, each between 40 minutes and 1½ hours away, depending on the speed of your train. Tickets from either Messina or Catania to Taormina cost about 4€. See www.trenitalia.com for complete schedules. Keep in mind that Taormina's train station, which is shared with the seaside town of Giardini-Naxos, lies down the hill from town, 1.6km (1 mile) away. From the station, you have to take a bus up the hill to Taormina proper (9am–9pm, every 15–45 min.; 2€ one-way), or a taxi (about 15€).

VISITOR INFORMATION The **tourist office** is in Palazzo Corvaja, Piazza Santa Caterina (✆ **0942-23243** or 0942-24941); it's open Monday to Thursday 8:30am to 2pm and 4 to 7pm, and Friday 8:30am to 2pm. Here you can get a free map, hotel listings, bus and rail timetables, and a schedule of summer cultural events staged at the Teatro Greco (Greek Theater).

SPECIAL EVENTS The summer-long **TaorminaArte** festival includes opera and ballet in the ancient setting of the Teatro Greco (see below), as well as theatrical performances, concerts of all kinds in the Villa Comunale, churches, and other venues. Check with TaorminaArte's headquarters, Corso Umberto 19 (www.taoarte.it; ✆ **0942-21142**), or at the tourist office for exact dates and showtimes.

Exploring Taormina

Just about everything to see in Taormina unfolds from the main pedestrian drag, Corso Umberto I, which slices through town from Porta Messina, in the north, to Porta Catania, in the south. In theory, it only takes about 10 minutes to walk the length of Corso Umberto I, but in practice, allowing for shopping at boutiques both upscale and down-home, stopping for a drink or ice cream at a panoramic bar, or visiting one of the countless side streets, you could spend days getting to know Taormina. Taormina is also a handy base for day trips to Mount Etna—the high-altitude visitor areas are only about 1 hour away by car.

Teatro Greco (Teatro Antico) ★★★ RUINS This ancient Greek theater is Taormina's most visited attraction and its only bona fide, admission-charging monument. In the Hellenistic period, the Greeks hewed the theater out of the rocky slope of Mount Tauro; the Romans remodeled and modified it greatly. What remains today dates from the 2nd century A.D. The conquering Arabs, who seemed intent on devastating the town, slashed away at it in the 10th century, leaving us with a rather sparse and dusty ruin, less intact than the Greek theater in Siracusa. However, what Taormina's theater boasts are unparalleled views of the seacoast and Mount Etna, framed by evocative columns and fragmented brick walls. (Climb to the top of the *cavea,* or curved seating area, for the best photo-ops and breathtaking vistas.) Today, the Teatro Antico is the site of the annual TaorminaArte cultural festival (summer opera and concerts), and films are projected here during the Taormina Film Festival.

Via del Teatro Greco. ✆ **0942-23220.** Admission 8€. Apr–Sept daily 9am–7pm; Oct–Mar daily 9am–4pm.

Villa Comunale ★★★ PARK/GARDEN In a verdant, panoramic setting just below the densest part of town, the splendid Villa Comunale (city park) may be Taormina's ultimate treasure. Also known as **Parco Duca di Cesarò,** it has 3 hectares (7½ acres) of beautifully groomed terraces filled with luxuriant Mediterranean vegetation, geometrically cobblestoned walkways linked by picturesque stone stairways, and a sinuous path lining the park's eastern rim that has superb views over the sea. Not even the fanciest hotel gardens in Taormina can rival the romance of the Villa Comunale. The gardens were the creation of Lady Florence Trevelyan in the late 19th century. This Scottish lady was "invited" to leave Britain after a well-publicized romance with the future king, Edward VII, son of Victoria. She built various amusements in the gardens, including a fanciful stone-and-brick pavilion for bird-watching and other charming architectural follies. The Villa Comunale is an ideal spot for a picnic, a portrait session, or a

Taormina's Piazza del Duomo.

MEET MIGHTY mount etna

Warning: Always get the latest report from the tourist office before setting out for a trip to Mount Etna. Adventurers have been killed by surprise "belches" (volcanic explosions). Mount Etna remains one of the world's most active volcanoes, with sporadic gas, steam, lava, and ash emissions from its summit.

Looming menacingly over the coast of eastern Sicily, **Mount Etna ★★★** is the highest and largest active volcano in Europe—and I do mean active. The peak changes in size over the years but is currently in the neighborhood of 3,324m (10,906 ft.). Etna has been active in modern times (in 1928, the little village of Mascali was buried under its lava), with powerful eruptions in 1971, 1992, 2001, and 2003 causing extensive damage to facilities nearby. Throughout the year, episodes of spectacular but usually harmless lava fountains, some hundreds of meters high, are not uncommon.

Etna has figured in history and in Greek mythology. Empedocles, the 5th-century-B.C. Greek philosopher, is said to have jumped into its crater as a sign that he was being delivered directly to Mount Olympus to take his seat among the gods. It was under Etna that Zeus crushed the multiheaded, viper-riddled dragon Typhoeus, thereby securing domination over Olympus. Hephaestus, the god of fire and blacksmiths, made his headquarters in Etna, aided by the single-eyed Cyclops. The Greeks warned that when Typhoeus tried to break out of his prison, lava erupted and earthquakes cracked the land. That must mean that the monster nearly escaped on March 11, 1669, one of the most violent eruptions ever—it destroyed Catania, about 27km (17 miles) away.

Gazing upon Etna from a distance is one thing, but it's a whole different experience to meet Etna up close and personal. The volcano isn't beautiful, per se, but it's a must for nature lovers and a highlight of any trip to Sicily. Visibility is generally better before noon.

Etna lies 31km (19 miles) north of Catania and is easy to reach by car from Taormina. The fastest way is to take the E45 autostrada south to the Acireale exit. From here, follow the brown ETNA signs west to Nicolosi, passing through several smaller towns along the way. From Nicolosi, keep following the ETNA signs up the hill toward Rifugio Sapienza (1,923m/ 6,307 ft.), the starting point for all expeditions to the crater. Here there's a faux-Alpine hamlet with tourist shops and services, cheap and ample parking, as well as the base station of the **Funivia del Etna** cable car (www.funiviaetna.com, ✆ **095-914141;** daily 9am–4:30pm), which takes you to the Torre del Filosofo (Philosopher's Tower) station at 2,900m (9,514 ft.). Otherwise, this is a strenuous hike that takes about 5 hours. To reach the authorized crater areas at about 3,000m (9,843 ft., as close to the summit as visitors are allowed), you'll then climb into white, *Star Wars*-ish off-road vehicles that make the final ascent over a scrabbly terrain of ash and dead ladybugs (dead ladybugs are *everywhere* on Mount Etna). Conditions at the crater zone are thrilling, but the high winds, exposure, and potential sense of vertigo are not for the faint of heart.

The round-trip cost of going to the top of Etna, including the cable car ride, the off-road vans, and the requisite authorized guide at the crater zone, is about 55€. Etna is not a complicated excursion to do on your own, but if you'd prefer to go with a tour, Taormina is chock-full of agencies that organize Etna day trips.

Hiking around Mount Etna.

peaceful stroll; the limited size of the park makes it less practical as a place to jog, but you'll see some locals and tourists doing laps. A bell tolls just before the rigorously enforced closing time, at which point all the local kids can be heard shouting, in theatrical unison, *"Sta chiudendo la villaaaaaaa!"* ("The villa is cloooosing!"). A custodian makes the rounds to shoo out any lingerers before sliding the big iron gates on Via Bagnoli Croce closed.

Via Bagnoli Croce. No phone. Free admission. Daily 8:30am to 7pm (6pm in winter).

Outdoor Pursuits

See also the "Meet Mighty Mount Etna" box, on the previous page.

Many visitors to Taormina come for the beach, although the sands aren't exactly at the resort. To reach the best and most popular beach, **Lido Mazzarò ★★**, you have to go south of town via a cable car (**© 0942-23605**) that leaves from Via Pirandello every 15 minutes. A round-trip ticket costs 3€. This soft, finely pebbled beach is one of the best equipped in Sicily, with bars, restaurants, and hotels. You can rent beach chairs, umbrellas, and watersports equipment at various kiosks from April to October. To the right of Lido Mazzarò, past the Capo Sant'Andrea headland, is the region's prettiest cove, where twin crescents of beach sweep from a sand spit out to the minuscule **Isola Bella** islet. You can walk here from the cable car in a few minutes, but it's more fun to paddle a boat from Mazzarò around Capo Sant'Andrea, which hides a few grottoes with excellent light effects on the seaward side. Don't miss a meal at Isola Bella's Pizzichella restaurant (see below).

North of Mazzarò are the long, wide beaches of **Spisone** and **Letojanni,** more developed but less crowded than **Giardini,** the large, built-up resort beach south of Isola Bella. A local bus leaves Taormina for Mazzarò, Spisone, and Letojanni, and another heads down the coast to Giardini.

Where to Eat

Not surprisingly, many Taormina restaurants trade on cliff's-edge, panoramic locations more than the quality of their food. This isn't true across the board, but generally speaking, the better the view, the more you'll pay, and the lazier the kitchens are.

The ultimate address for the ultimate Sicilian summer refreshment, the sorbetlike *granita,* is **Bam Bar,** not far from the Grand Hotel Timeo at Via di Giovanni 45 (✆ **0942-24355**). Specialties are the almond *(mandorla)* or white fig *(fico bianco),* but there are usually more than a dozen flavors to choose from.

Le Naumachie ★★ CREATIVE SICILIAN Exquisite and inventive dishes like gnocchi with pistachio pesto and Mazara prawns, or tuna "bites" with onion jam and chocolate or foie gras, and an equally delicious setting in the shadows of a Roman aqueduct make Le Naumachie many Taormina regulars' top insider choice for dining out, especially when they want something a bit more avant-garde than the typical steaming plate of penne alla norma. This is an intimate, family-run place, and the young chef owner, Francesco Aversa, personally welcomes every party and goes out of his way to ensure an enjoyable meal. Food presentation is contemporary, and Aversa's unique combinations of ingredients are often revelations that you'll remember forever. Portion size, however, in keeping with the modern aesthetic of the place, is small.

Via Giardinazzo 8. www.ristorantelenaumachie.com. ✆ **0942-625145.** Reservations recommended. Main courses 10€–16€. AE, MC, V. Mar–June Wed–Sun noon–3pm, daily 6:30–11:30pm; July–Sept Tues, Thurs, and Sat noon–3pm, daily 6:30–11:30pm; Oct daily noon–3pm and 6:30–11:30pm; Nov Wed–Mon noon–3pm and 6:30–11:30pm. Closed Dec–Feb.

Licchio's ★★ SICILIAN Licchio's does not need any Taormina clichés (rapturous view, street-side alfresco seating) to earn your business. The food is so good, and the whole experience of dining here so lovely that you should devote at least one evening meal to Licchio's. (Ignore the less-than-attractive entrance, just up from Porta Messina; it gets much more charming inside, where there's a pretty terrace enveloped by lush greenery.) The cuisine here is smart Sicilian. The chef knows when to leave the classics as-is and when to add just a touch of creative flair. Recommended first courses are the pasta fresca con verdurine in crema di parmigiano (fresh pasta with small vegetables in a creamy Parmesan sauce—your plate will be bare in minutes) and Licchio's perfectly executed version of the classic Italian spaghetti con vongole veraci (with fresh clams). Among the second courses, the lamb chops have sensational flavor and texture (my 2-year-old son recently ate two whole orders by himself), but seafood lovers should try the millefogli di pesce, fish filet between layers of grilled eggplant and drizzled with balsamic vinegar. Service is attentive, well-informed (especially about local wines), and well-timed.

Via C. Patricio 10. www.licchios.it. ✆ **0942-625327.** Reservations recommended in high season. Main courses 10€–18€. AE, MC, V. Fri–Wed 8–11:30pm.

Pizzichella ★★ 🎁 SICILIAN/SEAFOOD Sicily sometimes has a way of hiding some of its best food in the most unassuming places. Pizzichella may look like a beach club (and it is, located on the rocky north edge of the Isola Bella inlet), but the on-site restaurant does killer pastas and seafood at fair prices and with the most genuinely warm hospitality you can imagine. Try not to be put off by the stairs and rocky beach you must navigate to reach this place for an evening meal. A dinner here, overlooking Isola Bella and its sense of rugged tranquillity, is magical. At lunch and throughout the day, beachgoers can also fill up on Pizzichella's hearty panini, made with fresh vegetables and high-quality meats and cheeses. Note that it's open daily only in summer and has much more restricted hours in the off season.

On the north end of the bay of Isola Bella (below Taormina town; take the cable car to Mazzarò; at the bottom of the long staircase down to Isola Bella, the restaurant will be to your left). ✆ **0942-625189.** Reservations for dinner essential. Main courses 8€–16€. MC, V. June 15–Aug 31 daily 9am–11pm; other times of the year, weekends and holidays only 9am–7pm. Closed mid-Jan to mid-Mar.

Trattoria da Nino ★ SICILIAN Look no further for Sicilian *cucina casalinga* (home-cooking) in a bustling, bright, fun atmosphere. Right across from the upper station of the cable car, Nino's is the unassuming yet always-packed restaurant with the yellow sign. It's not that you'll necessarily have a transcendent culinary experience here—although the menu is a tantalizing array of everything from house-made pasta to the most prized fresh seafood available—it's that Nino's just kind of feels like a gathering of old friends and family. In the mood for meat? Trattoria da Nino can cook your veal scaloppine 15 different ways. Everyone from host Nino himself to veteran waiter Sebastiano sees to customers' needs in swift fashion (this could come in the form of one of the friendly staff observing that your kids are getting antsy during a multicourse meal and solving the problem by asking them to help take orders from other parties around the restaurant). Everything is handled with the ease and charm that comes naturally to Sicilians, the kind of place you leave with your soul and your palate smiling. Nino's is also one of few Taormina restaurants open every day for lunch and dinner all year-round. Reservations for parties smaller than six are not accepted.
Via Pirandello 37. www.trattoriadanino.com. ✆ **0942-21265.** Reservations not accepted for parties smaller than 6. Main courses 8€–18€. AE, MC, V. Daily noon–3pm and 6:30–11pm.

Shopping

Shopping is all too easy in Taormina—just find **Corso Umberto I** and go. The trendy shops here sell everything upscale, from sunglasses to handbags and boots to lacy linens and beachwear to winter coats to antique furniture and jewelry. It's definitely way more than the repetitive range of resort apparel in places like Positano. A dangerous feature of the Taormina retail scene is that the shops stay open well after midnight (that is, after you've probably had a bit of wine) in summer.

More curious shoppers will want to veer off the Corso and search out the little shops on the side streets; I like to come down here and browse the authentic hardware and grocery stores and then get my hair styled (for less than 15€) at one of the many *parrucchieri* (hair salons) hidden in these alleyways—you'll meet locals *and* look fabulous for dinner!

Ceramics are one of Sicily's most notable handicrafts, and Taormina's shops are among the best places to buy them on the island as the selection is excellent and they're very experienced with international shipping. Just know that the good stuff doesn't come cheap, but you can certainly pick up fun, packable ceramic souvenirs for less than 10€. **Giuseppa di Blasi,** Corso Umberto I 103 (✆ **0942-24671**), has a nice range of designs and specializes in the highly valued "white pottery" from Caltagirone. Mixing the new and the old, **Carlo Panarello Antichità,** Corso Umberto I 122 (✆ **0942-23910**), offers Sicilian ceramics (from pots to tables) and also deals in eclectic antique furnishings, paintings, and engravings.

Entertainment & Nightlife

Go ahead, be a tourist and begin your evening at the **Caffè Wunderbar,** Piazza IX Aprile 7 (www.wunderbar.it; ✆ **0942-625302**). Beneath a vine-covered arbor on Taormina's main square, and perched as close to the edge of the cliff as safety allows, it was once a favorite watering hole of Tennessee Williams. It's definitely an old-school place with a full selection of cocktails and a piano bar. However, you come to the Wunderbar for the location. A better bar on the same piazza, just not as breathtakingly situated, is the **Mocambo** (Piazza IX Aprile 9; www.mocambobar.com; ✆ **0942-23350**), with elegant inside and outside seating, friendly service, and prices that don't gouge quite as much.

The beautiful people favor **Morgana Bar,** Scesa Morgana 4 (✆ **0942-620056**), named after the seductive fairy (Morgan la Fée) of Camelot days, who lured valiant knights to their doom. It is a sophisticated yet friendly lounge (with DJ inside and open-air seating in a lovely candlelit courtyard outside) that's tucked into one of the narrow alleyways running downhill from the Corso Umberto I.

The above are all fairly mellow options; hard-core partiers looking for more of a scene will have to head down the hill, to the thumping bass of the big discos in Giardini-Naxos.

Where to Stay

The hotels in Taormina are the best in Sicily. All price ranges are available, with accommodations ranging from army cots to sumptuous suites.

If you're driving to a hotel at the top of Taormina, call ahead to see what arrangements can be made for your car. Ask for exact driving directions as well as instructions on where to park—the narrow, winding, one-way streets can be bewildering once you get here.

Grand Hotel Timeo ★★★ Hidden in a tranquil private park just below the Teatro Greco, the Timeo is a 19th-century baronial villa that has gracefully entered the modern era. Comparisons are often made between the Timeo and the San Domenico, and the key difference is the vibe: The Timeo is social, sunny, with a lived in elegance, while the San Domenico's refinement is sober, even ecclesiastical. Old-world glamour is here in spades, and you get the feeling that the Timeo was built purely for pleasure; staff provide a warm welcome. All rooms are spacious and well outfitted, with sumptuous marble bathrooms and balconies, and the Timeo's strategically terraced layout takes full advantage of sweeping views from Mount Etna down to the Ionian Sea. Some rooms in the main villa abut the 2,000-year-old ruins of the Teatro Greco—you simply can't ask for a more privileged setting than this. Even nonguests can avail themselves of the Timeo's panoramic and popular bar, a lovely place to be at sunset. The hotel has a private beach (at its sister property in Mazzarò, the Villa Sant'Andrea) and a full spa on-site.

Via Teatro Greco 59, 98039 Taormina. www.grandhoteltimeo.com ✆ **0942-6270200.** Fax 0942-6270606. 87 units. 480€–700€ double; from 890€ suite. Rates include buffet breakfast. AE, DC, MC, V. Free parking. **Amenities:** Restaurant; piano bar; babysitting; exercise room; heated pool; room service; spa. *In room:* A/C, TV/DVD, hair dryer, minibar, Wi-Fi (free).

Palazzo San Domenico ★★★ An air of hushed luxury reigns at one of the most prestigious hotels in Italy. The San Domenico is a converted 14th-century convent, with magnificent grounds that seem unchanged—just very well maintained—since that time. The entire property, set within private walls at the northern edge of Taormina, looks like something out of a period film, complete with evocative archways, porticoes, and grand common areas outfitted with museum-quality antiques. The extensive gardens, splendidly illuminated in the evening, are an especially romantic treat. Guest rooms are located in either the old monastery part of the hotel, where furnishings are dignified and very comfortable, or in the somewhat more opulent wings added in 1897, which evoke the Gilded Age. Rooms have all been updated with modern conveniences while still preserving the historic character that suffuses the San Domenico. The only downside to all this cinematic perfection is that the San Domenico can seem a little standoffish (and certainly when compared to the also luxurious but more approachable Timeo, above); the ultraprofessional staff can come across as too formal for this sunny Mediterranean milieu, but if you wanted to be treated like royalty, this is the best place in town to put on those airs.

Piazza San Domenico 5, 98039 Taormina. www.amthotels.it/sandomenico. ✆ **0942-613111.** Fax 0942-625506. 105 units. 203€–666€ double; from 640€ suite. Rates include buffet breakfast. AE, DC, MC, V. Free parking. **Amenities:** 4 restaurants; piano bar; babysitting; concierge; exercise room; heated pool; room service. *In room:* A/C, TV, hair dryer, minibar.

Villa Carlotta ★★★ Only Villa Ducale and Grand Hotel Timeo enjoy the same tranquil and romantic position as this house, situated in a mock castle at a busy corner in Taormina town. Chic owners Andrea and Rosaria Quartucci (who also own and manage Villa Ducale) really know how to run a hotel. The property was updated in 2007 with strikingly sophisticated and varied interiors that never sacrifice style for comfort. Secluded back gardens (with swimming pool) add to the wonderful sense of privacy, given the hotel's central location. As at Villa Ducale, the staff are unbelievably warm and helpful, and are a big part of what makes a stay here so special. Both Villas Carlotta and Ducale are extremely popular; book well ahead for a stay in high season. ***Note:*** The Quartuccis recently opened Taormina Luxury Apartments, a collection of sumptuous apartments just up the street from Villa Carlotta. Absolutely no expense was spared in creating these fabulous Mediterranean homes-away-from-home, which sleep from two to four (call for pricing).

Via Pirandello 81. www.hotelvillacarlottataormina.com. ✆ **0942/626058.** 23 units. 200€–350€ double. AE, DC, MC, V. **Amenities:** Restaurant; concierge; health club; pool. *In room:* A/C, TV/DVD player, hair dryer, minibar, Wi-Fi (free).

Villa Ducale ★★★ This is the ultimate in Sicilian boutique accommodations, and couples looking for real romance might find this even more attractive than the showy Timeo and San Domenico down in town. The sister property of Andrea and Rosaria Quartucci's Villa Carlotta, this villa—restored with luxurious and cosmopolitan touches while preserving an appealing amount of Sicilian country flair—sits on a hillside, a 10-minute walk up from the center. The entire, low-slung property boasts magnificent views of the Mediterranean, the town, and Mount Etna. Each guest room has a veranda, terra-cotta floors, a wrought-iron bed, and a compact bathroom with a tub/shower combination. Service is exceedingly warm and personalized yet discreet. Breakfast is served on an outdoor terrace with a gorgeous view. At 6pm every day, guests gather on the terrace for a complimentary sunset cocktail, accompanied by a spread of typical Sicilian appetizers.

Via Leonardo da Vinci 60, 98039 Taormina. www.villaducale.com. ✆ **0942-28153.** Fax 0942-28710. 15 units. 240€–400€ double; from 350€ suite. Rates include buffet breakfast. AE, MC, V. Parking 10€. Closed Jan 18–Mar 4. **Amenities:** Jacuzzi; room service. *In room:* A/C, TV, hair dryer, minibar, Wi-Fi (free).

Villa Fiorita ★ This small inn stretches toward the Teatro Greco from its position beside the road leading to the top of this cliff-hugging town. Its imaginative decor includes a handful of ceramic stoves, which the owner delights in collecting. A well-maintained garden lies alongside an ancient but empty Greek tomb whose stone walls have been classified a national treasure. The guest rooms are arranged in a steplike labyrinth of corridors and stairwells, some of which bend to correspond to the rocky slope on which the hotel was built. Each unit contains antique furniture and a shower-only bathroom; most have private terraces.

Via Luigi Pirandello 39, 98039 Taormina. www.villafioritahotel.com. ✆ **0942-24122.** Fax 0942-625967. 26 units, shower only. 105€–125€ double; 145€–165€ junior suite. Rates include continental breakfast. AE, MC, V. Parking 12€. **Amenities:** Outdoor pool; room service. *In room:* A/C, TV, hair dryer.

Villa Paradiso ★ This charming boutique hotel originated in 1921 when the grandfather of the present owner bought a villa originally built in 1892. Set within a warren of narrow streets adjacent to the town's most beautiful public gardens, the Paradiso contains tastefully furnished public rooms outfitted with antiques and fine art. Each of the cozy, individually decorated guest rooms has a balcony, conservative furnishings, and a tiled bathroom. Between June and October, the hotel offers free shuttle service and free entrance to the Paradise Beach Club, about 6km (4 miles) to the east, in the seaside resort of Letojanni.

Via Roma 2, 98039 Taormina. www.hotelvillaparadisotaormina.com. ✆ **0942-23921.** Fax 0942-625800. 37 units. 130€–210€ double; 175€–230€ junior suite. AE, DC, MC, V. Parking 15€. **Amenities:** Restaurant; bar; room service; Wi-Fi (8€ per hour, in lobby). *In room:* A/C, TV, hair dryer.

Villa Schuler ★★ This lovely pastel *palazzo* hearkens back to a gentler era of Taormina tourism. Immersed in lush gardens below the madness of Corso Umberto and filled with the fragrance of jasmine, the family-run hotel is a haven of tranquillity with airy rooms (many with dramatic sea views) and huge bathrooms (many with Jacuzzi tubs). The most luxurious way to stay here is to book the garden villa suite with its own private access. It's spacious and beautifully furnished, with two bathrooms (one with a Jacuzzi). The villa comes with a kitchenette, patio, private garden, and veranda.

Piazzetta Bastione, Via Roma, 98039 Taormina. www.villaschuler.com. ✆ **0942-23481.** Fax 0942-23522. 26 units, most with shower only. 145€–150€ double. Rates include continental breakfast. AE, MC, V. Parking 15€ in garage, free outside. Closed Nov 21–Mar 4. **Amenities:** Bar; babysitting; bikes; room service. *In room:* A/C, TV, hair dryer, Wi-Fi (free).

Side Trips from Taormina

A worthwhile little outing from Taormina is a jaunt up to the village of **Castelmola** ★, which sits like an eagle's nest 3km (2 miles) northwest of Taormina. Perched even higher than Taormina, it's one of the most panoramic places in eastern Sicily, with a magnificent view of Mount Etna on clear days. Castelmola's **Bar Turrisi** (Piazza Duomo 19; ✆ **0942-28181;** 10am–1am, and until 3am weekends and holidays) is famed both for its *vino alla mandorla* (almond wine) and for its collection of phalluses—on display for purely artistic and cultural reasons, of course—so be sure to stop in for a drink and an eyeful of Sicilian, uh, prowess. You might also visit the ruined *castello* (castle) on the summit of **Mount Tauro** (390m/1,280 ft.). You can drive up to Castelmola or take an orange local bus (2.20€ round-trip, approx. once per hour) from Porta Messina.

To see a unique, canyonlike landscape of limpid green waters and gray basalt rock walls sculpted by a happy accident of nature, head outside of town to the **Gole dell'Alcantara** ★ (www.parcoalcantara.it; ✆ **0942-985010**), a series of gorges on the Alcantara (Al-*cahn*-ta-rah) river. Several thousand years ago, a lava flow from Mount Etna blocked the riverbed. The river was forced to find a new way around the obstacle but in the process encountered molten rock, which was cooled and crystallized by the river water in quick and dramatic fashion. Lava meeting icy water created the stunning, fractured facets of basalt here today. On entering the site, which is almost comically overproduced with random turnstiles everywhere and signage galore, first hike the short orientation trail, which overlooks the river and some of the gorges. Then, you can pay to take the elevators down to water level for a more intimate exploration. Down here is a series of "beaches" (rock platforms and other flattish areas) along the river, where you can simply hang out, wade, and sunbathe, or embark on a **scenic hike up the riverbed ★★**, which is the best way to fully appreciate the beauty of the gorge's geological formations. From May to September, when visitors are allowed down here, the river is only a foot or so deep in most areas, but the waters are extremely cold—about 6°C (42°F) even in the height of summer—but quite refreshing under the often scorching Sicilian sun, and there are deeper swimming holes along the gorge if you want a full-immersion swim. The gorge walk, if you elect to do it, involves about an hour of wading in the shade on uneven, sometimes slippery surfaces; save your feet some misery by renting heavy-duty rubber boots from the park entrance. From October to April, only the upper area of the park, above the gorge, is open, but the view is always stunning. It costs 5€ to enter the gorge, which is open daily from 7am to 7:30pm. Onsite are a gift shop, cafeteria, picnic areas, and toilets. You can reach the Gole dell'Alcantara by car from Taormina (a drive of about 35 min.) or you can take **Interbus** (**✆ 0942-625301**) for the 1-hour trip departing from Taormina at 9:15, 11:45am, 1:15, and 4:45pm daily. Buses from Gole dell'Alcantara return to Taormina at 9:25am, 12:35, 2:35, and 3:45pm. The round-trip fare is 6€. Organized excursions (from 25€) to the gorges are also offered by many bus tour operators in Taormina, often in conjunction with a visit to Mount Etna.

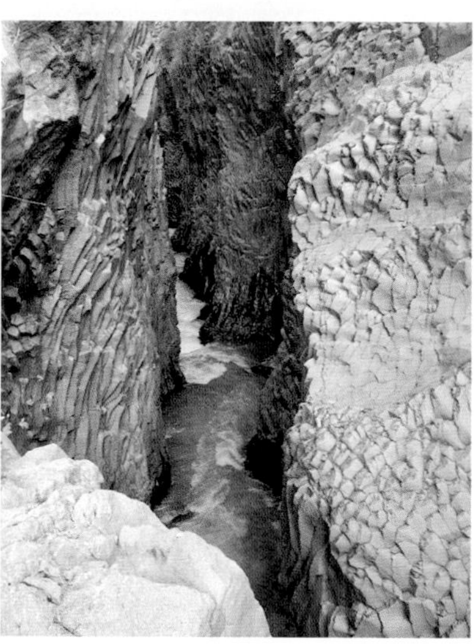

A gorge at Gole dell'Alcantara.

SIRACUSA ★★

One of the centers of ancient Western civilization, Siracusa (sometimes called Syracuse by English-speakers), was one of the most important cities of the ancient world of Magna Graecia (Greater Greece), rivaling even Athens in its cultural and military muscle. In the 18th century, following the devastating earthquake of 1693, the entire town was rebuilt in the ebullient baroque style that still characterizes Ortigia Island, Siracusa's irresistibly charming *centro storico*. When people talk about how much they love Siracusa, they're really talking about Ortigia and of course those glorious Greek ruins.

The heart of "old" (though not ancient Greek) Siracusa is the island of Ortigia, an impossibly picturesque village whose main square, Piazza del Duomo, is among the prettiest public spaces in Sicily. The side streets, lined with balconied baroque *palazzi* and opening onto narrow views of the sea, ooze Sicilian flair. While Ortigia spent much of the late 20th century crumbling, energetic restorations of those sultry *palazzi* have been underway for the past decade, and Ortigia is now brighter and cleaner than ever. (Although you can save money by staying at hotels in the modern town, I highly recommend staying somewhere on Ortigia, since this is where all the best dining, street life, and shopping are.)

The greatest single historical attraction of Siracusa is the **Parco Archeologico della Neapolis,** one of the most impressive archaeological gardens in Italy. The park is on the mainland of Siracusa, a half-hour walk or cab/bus ride north of Ortigia, and drips with the atmosphere of ancient times. It contains a massive Greek theater, a Roman amphitheater, and a quarry, once used as a prison, where lush vegetation has taken root. An adjacent museum contains artifacts from the entire region. Dedicated antiquities enthusiasts should also make it to the **Castello Eurialo,** a fun-to-explore Greek fortress, where native son Archimedes first uttered "Eureka!"

Some of the most memorable cultural events in Sicily are staged in May and June, when ancient Greek plays are produced by Siracusa's **Istituto Nazionale del Dramma Antico** (Via Cavour 48; www.indafondazione.org; ✆ **0931-487248;** ticket office Mon–Fri 10am–1pm and 3–5pm). Performances, strictly from the ancient oeuvre of Euripides, Aeschylus, and their contemporaries, take place in the Teatro Greco (Greek Theater) in the Parco Archeologico della Neapolis (archaeological park). Tickets cost from 30€ to 62€.

Taking in the rich sights and local flavor of Siracusa is a breeze and enormously satisfying—no wonder it's so many visitors' favorite destination in Sicily. And as word has gotten out about Siracusa, it has drawn exponentially more visitors each year. Unfortunately, the town hasn't handled its boom in popularity as gracefully as it might have, which is why I've given Siracusa as a whole a two-star rating as opposed to the three stars it's historically carried. But if you can seek out the quieter corners of Ortigia and give the ancient ruins the time and careful exploration they deserve, you'll come away with that three-star experience.

Though it's on the water, Siracusa proper doesn't have any sand, but some great beaches lie just a short distance away. Siracusa is also a convenient base for visiting the other celebrated baroque hill towns of southeastern Sicily, including Noto. Allow 2 full days to see the principal sights of Siracusa alone, a few more if you're adding in side trips and beach days.

Essentials

GETTING THERE Siracusa is 1½ hours south of Taormina on the A18. It's 3 hours southeast of Palermo on the A19 and A18, and 3 hours east of Agrigento on the SS540, A19, and A18. Siracusa is also well connected with the rest of Sicily by bus and train, though buses are generally more efficient and frequent than trains.

GETTING AROUND You won't need a car, just your own two feet and perhaps a few bus or cab rides to see the best of Siracusa proper. However, because Siracusa is a common base for exploring southeastern Sicily, many travelers arrive here by car and use it to get around the region. In that case, inquire about parking with your hotel or rental agency before arriving.

VISITOR INFORMATION The **tourist office** is at Via San Sebastiano 43 (✆ **0931-481232**), open Monday to Friday 8:30am to 1:30pm and 3 to 6pm, Saturday 8:30am to 1:30pm. There's another office in the historic center at Via della Maestranza 33 (✆ **0931-65201**), open Monday to Friday 8:15am to 2pm and 2:30 to 5:30pm, Saturday 8:15am to 2pm.

SPECIAL EVENTS Some of the most memorable cultural events in Sicily are staged in May and June, when actors from the Instituto Nazionale del Dramma Antico present **classical plays** by Aeschylus, Euripides, and their contemporaries. The setting is the ancient Teatro Greco (Greek Theater) in the Archaeological Park. Tickets cost 30€ to 70€. For information, contact **INDA,** Corso Matteotti 29, 96100 Siracusa (www.indafondazione.org; ✆ **0931-487200**).

Exploring Siracusa

With splendors both ancient and baroque, this cheerful coastal town is a one-two punch of architectural delights. Ortigia Island is Siracusa's *centro storico,* a mostly pedestrian zone where narrow alleys lined with romantic 18th-century *palazzi* spill onto such visual treats as Piazza del Duomo—in my opinion, the prettiest square in Sicily. The ancient ruins lie a good half-hour walk north of Ortigia. The walk, along grimy Corso Gelone, is flat but not very attractive (although there are some decent mainstream shops along the way); in summer especially, it's best to take a bus or taxi to the Parco Archeologico. You'll find the bus stop and taxi rank on Ortigia at Piazza Pancali, the tree-lined square directly opposite the central bridge, Ponte Umbertino.

Siracusa's waterfront.

ORTIGIA ISLAND ★★★

Simply **wandering around Ortigia ★★★**, allowing yourself to get tangled up in the back streets, is a great way to pass a few hours. You'll never get very lost—the island is only about 1 sq. km (¾ sq. mile)—and without even trying, you're likely to hit the major sights discussed below. Ortigia is roughly rectangular in shape, with three bridges on the western edge of the island leading over a narrow waterway to the "mainland." A 500m-long (1,640-ft.) spur of land, culminating in the Castello Maniace fortress and lighthouse (not all of which is accessible to the public), juts into the harbor on the southern side of Ortigia. Corso Matteotti is the main north-south drag that leads into the heart of Ortigia, ending at the round Piazza Archimede; this thoroughfare, planned in the Fascist era, is more modern than the rest of Ortigia (stick to the parallel side streets for more atmosphere), but it is nevertheless clean and attractive and has some nice boutiques and handy main-street services like ATMs and a pharmacy.

About halfway down the western edge of Ortigia and a few blocks back from the water is **Piazza del Duomo ★★★**, the first "big" thing you'll want to see when visiting Siracusa. The theatrical baroque perfection of Sicily's most beautiful piazza seems ripped from the illustrated pages of a Sicilian folklore tome. Dominating the square is the **Duomo ★★** (daily 8am–noon and 4–7pm) a sunny baroque cathedral built on top of the ancient Greek Temple of Athena. On the northwest side of the piazza is the delightful **Palazzo Beneventano del Bosco ★★**, a baroque confection with convex, wrought-iron balconies. On the south side of the square is the sultry-looking church of **Santa Lucia alla Badia ★**. The many, interchangeable cafes on the square provide wonderful respite and people-watching—avoid mid-afternoon, when no one is here, but do make an effort to be here around sunset.

Also on Piazza del Duomo is an entrance to the **Hypogeum ★★** (no phone; admission 3€; Tues–Sun 9am–1pm and 4–8pm), a network of underground chambers and corridors dug as air-raid shelters in World War II. The hypogeum visit exit is on Foro Vittorio Emanuele II, a tree-shaded seafront promenade that is pleasant to look at if not to smell—the birds love the green canopy here and they poop everywhere.

South of Piazza del Duomo and along the seafront is the lovely **Fonte Aretusa ★★**. This natural fountain near the harbor is one of Siracusa's most unique sights. Papyrus grows in the shallow pool, and the freshwater spring beneath once served as the city's main water supply. Fonte Aretusa is sunken about 6m (20 ft.) below street level and encircled by an iron-and-stone parapet. At night, the cafes and sidewalks here are a breeding ground for the hot and bothered teens and 20 somethings of Siracusa.

A few blocks inland from Fonte Aretusa is the elegant **Galleria Regionale Palazzo Bellomo ★** (Via Capodieci 16; ✆ **0931/69511;** admission 8€; Tues–Sat 9am–7pm, Sun 9am–1pm), a recently overhauled 13th-century building that houses one of the great art collections of Sicily, dating from the high Middle Ages through the 20th century. The standout pieces here are Caravaggio's ***Burial of St. Lucia*** **★★** (1608) and Antonello da Messina's ***Annunciation*** **★** (1474). Caravaggio, bad boy of the baroque and a master of light, created a stunning canvas of grieving figures, illuminated from the right as if by a ray of sunlight.

Toward the opposite shore of Ortigia, in a ladder of streets between Via della Giudecca and Via Alagona, is where the old **Jewish Ghetto** of Siracusa was, and parts are still visible. The recently unearthed **Miqwe** (Via Alagona 52; ✆ **0931-22255;** admission 6€; daily 10am–7pm) consists of three freshwater pools, used for ritual bathing, and a private pool for the rabbi.

Back toward modern Siracusa and mainland Sicily, just off Piazza Pancali, are the ruins of the **Temple of Apollo ★**, the oldest Doric temple in Sicily, dating back to the 6th century B.C. The Apollion would have measured 58m×24m (190 ft.×79 ft.) when it was built. The massive ruins—of the temple platform, a fragmentary colonnade, and an inner wall, all in brown limestone—are not open to the public but visible and impressive enough from the street.

To see Ortigia from the sea, motor launches operated by a number of outfits along Ortigia's waterfront will take you on a panoramic *gita in barca*, or **boat trip around Ortigia ★★**. Go at twilight, when the monuments of the old city are floodlit, but not when it's completely dark, as there are some sea caves along the route that you'll need a bit of daylight to see. Tours, offered by numerous outfits at Molo Zanagora pier, on the northwest tip of Ortigia (near the Grand Hotel), last about an hour and cost 10€ per person. Boat sizes vary but it's often more fun to go in one of the smaller skiffs.

THE ANCIENT RUINS ★★★

Walk north along Corso Gelone (or better yet, take bus 1, 3, or 12, or a cab from Ortigia's Piazza Pancali) to reach Siracusa's sprawling collection of Greek and Roman ruins, the excellent archaeological museum adjacent, and some evocative Christian catacombs. The city's other ancient attraction, Castello Eurailo (see below), lies about 6km (3¾ miles) west of Siracusa proper—without a car, the simplest way to reach it is by taxi. Otherwise, you can take bus 11, 25, or 26 from the front of Siracusa's central train station.

Castello Eurialo ★ RUINS This 4th-century-B.C. fortress on the outskirts of Siracusa is the best-preserved example of a Greek castle anywhere in the Mediterranean. It's also one of those great, undervisited Italian archaeological sites where you can romp all over everything, from the towers to the tunnels, without getting yelled at. Legend has it that Castello Eurialo is where Greek mathematician Archimedes famously cried "Eureka!" having discovered the law of water displacement while taking a bath.

Piazza Eurialo 1, off Viale Epipoli in the Belvedere district. ✆ **0931-481111.** Admission 4€; 10€ when combined with Parco Archeologico and Museo Archeologico. Daily 9am–5:30pm.

Catacombe di San Giovanni ★★ RUINS Similar to the more famous Christian burial grounds along Rome's Appian Way, the Catacombs of St. John contain some 20,000 ancient tombs (long emptied by grave robbers), in honeycombed tunnels. In Roman times, Christians were not allowed to bury their dead within the city limits, so they went outside the boundaries of Syracuse to create burial chambers in what had been used by the Greeks as underground aqueducts. The early Christians recycled these into chapels. Some faded frescoes and symbols etched into stone slabs can still be seen. You enter the "world of the dead" from the **Chiesa di San Giovanni,** once the cathedral of Siracusa, now

Siracusa's Duomo, on Ortigia Island.

Baroque details in the Piazza del Duomo in Ortigia.

a ruin. St. Paul is said to have preached on this spot, so the early Christians venerated it as holy ground. ***Warning:*** Make sure that you exit the catacombs well before closing. Two readers who did not were accidentally locked in.

Piazza San Giovanni, at end of Viale San Giovanni. No phone. Admission 5€. Tues–Sun 9:30am–12:30pm and 2:30–4:30pm. Closed Feb.

Museo Archeologico Regionale Paolo Orsi (Paolo Orsi Regional Archaeological Museum) ★★★ MUSEUM One of the most important archaeological museums in southern Italy surveys the Greek, Roman, and early Christian epochs. Crafted from glass, steel, and Plexiglas, and designed as an ultramodern showcase for the objects unearthed from digs throughout Sicily, this is the kind of museum that reinvigorates an appreciation for archaeology. Its stunning modernity is in direct contrast to the sometimes startling portrait busts and vases unearthed from around the island. Laid out like a hexagon, the museum is set in a garden dotted with ancient sarcophagi.

Section A takes us back before the dawn of recorded history. I'm always fascinated by the skeletons of prehistoric animals found here, including dwarf elephants. Many artifacts illustrate life in Paleolithic and Neolithic times. Look for the stunning red-burnished **Vase of Pantalica ★**.

Section B is devoted to Greek colonization. The celebrated **Landolina Venus ★★** is here, without a head but alluring nonetheless. After all these centuries, the anatomy of this timeless Venus is still in perfect shape. A Roman copy of an original by Praxiteles, the statue was found in Siracusa in 1804. When he visited the town in 1885, Guy de Maupassant fell in love with this Venus and left a vivid description of her. Although it's not the equal of the Landolina Venus, the singular limestone block of a **Mother-Goddess ★** suckling twins dates from the 6th century B.C. and was recovered from a necropolis.

Section C brings the subcolonies and Hellenistic centers of eastern Sicily alive once more. It's a hodgepodge of artifacts and fragments, including votive terra cottas, sarcophagi, and vases from Gela. Interspersed among some rather dull artifacts are stunning creations such as an enthroned male figure from the 6th century B.C., a horse and rider from the same era, a terra-cotta goddess from the late 6th century B.C., and a miniature 6th-century-B.C. altar with a relief depicting a lion attacking a bull. You can also seek out three rare wooden statues from the 7th century B.C. (found near Agrigento).

In the gardens of the Villa Landolina in Akradina, Viale Teocrito 66. ✆ **0931-464022.** Admission 8€ or 14€ with combo ticket that includes Parco Archeologico della Neapolis. Tues–Sat 9am–6pm; Sun 9am–1pm.

Parco Archeologico della Neapolis ★★★ RUINS Siracusa's Archaeological Park contains the town's most important attractions, all on the mainland at the western edge of town, immediately north of Stazione Centrale. The entrance to the park is down Via Augusto.

The main draw at Siracusa's wonderfully enjoyable archaeological park is the gigantic **Teatro Greco ★★★** (Greek Theater), whose 16,000-capacity *cavea* (seating area) was hewn right out of bedrock in the 5th century B.C. This bowl of blazing white stone is a heat trap in summer, but there are some *nymphaea* (alcoves with pools) at the top of the theater where you can splash yourself with water. Also in summer, the Italian Institute of Ancient Drama presents classical plays by Euripides, Aeschylus, and Sophocles in the ancient theater.

The thickly vegetated area next to the theater (behind and below the nosebleed section) is the **Latomia del Paradiso ★★** (Quarry of Paradise), a lush and primeval garden where a stegosaurus would not look out of place. It's one of four or five quarries from which stones were hauled to erect the great monuments of Siracusa in its glory days. Down here, follow the tour groups into the **Orecchio di Dionisio ★** (Ear of Dionysius), a tall and vaguely ear-shaped cave where the Greek tyrant Dionysius supposedly kept and eavesdropped on prisoners. But what an ear: It's nearly 60m (200 ft.) long. You can enter the inner chamber of the grotto, where the tearing of paper sounds like a gunshot. Nearby is the **Grotta dei Cordari,** where rope makers plied their craft.

An evocative site lies on the path down into the Roman amphitheater. The **Ara di Ierone,** or "Altar of Heron," was once used by the Greeks for sacrifices involving hundreds of animals at once. A few pillars still stand, along with the mammoth stone base of this 3rd-century-B.C. monument. The longest altar ever built, it measured 196m×23m (643 ft.×75 ft.).

The **Anfiteatro Romano ★** (Roman Amphitheater) was created at the time of Augustus. It ranks among the top five amphitheaters left by the Romans in Italy. Like the Greek Theater, part of it was carved from rock. Unlike the Greek Theater with its classical plays, the Roman Amphitheater tended toward gutsier fare. Gladiators faced each other with tridents and daggers, and slaves were whipped into the center of a battle to the death between

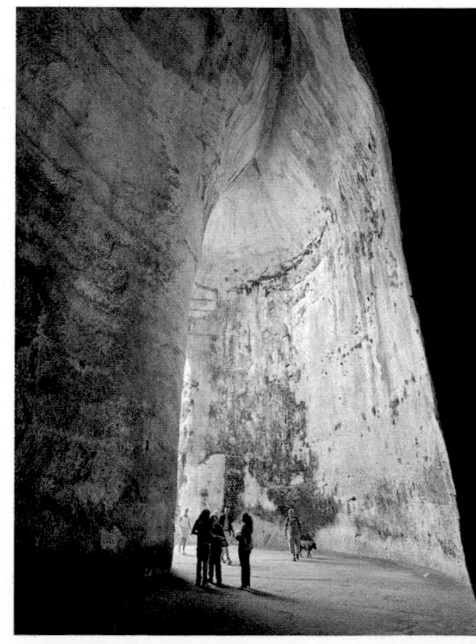

The Ear of Dionysius cave at Parco Archeologico della Neapolis.

A GIGANTIC teardrop RUNS THROUGH IT

The tallest building in Siracusa is the bizarre **Santuario della Madonna delle Lacrime** (Our Lady of Tears Sanctuary, Via Santuario 33; ✆ **0931-21446;** free admission; daily 8am–noon and 4–7pm), a monstrous cone of contemporary architecture (built in 1993) halfway between Ortigia and the archaeological zone. Meant to evoke a sort of angular teardrop and rising 74m (243 ft.) with a diameter of 80m (262 ft.), it houses a statue of the Madonna that supposedly wept for 5 days in 1953. Alleged chemical tests showed that the liquid was similar to that of human tears. Pilgrims still flock here, and you'll see postcards of the weepy Virgin around Siracusa. Although criticized by architectural purists, the **interior** ★ is rather amazing. You might get dizzy looking up at the vertical windows stretching skyward to the apex of the roof. A charlatan TV evangelist and his rapt congregation would not look out of place here.

wild beasts. There's also some historical evidence to suggest that the arena could be flooded and used to stage mock sea battles called *naumachiae*. The amphitheater is near the entrance to the park, but you can also view it in its entirety from a belvedere on the road.

Via Del Teatro (off the intersection of Corso Gelone and Viale Teocrito), Viale Paradiso. ✆ **0931-66206.** Admission 10€ or 14€ with combo ticket that includes archaeological museum. Daily 9am–6pm (until 4:30pm on certain summer evenings when performances are held in the theater).

Where to Eat

Castello Fiorentino ★ PIZZA You can't get the full Italian dining picture without going to a great pizzeria—and this is one of the best in Sicily. Everyone, from teenagers to older couples, waits in the alley outside for a table (waits can be long, but that's part of the fun) and then sits down in an energetic, unpretentious room to stuff his or her face with the local comfort food. The lengthy menu includes fritters, bruschetta, pizza, and pasta. Warm service makes you feel like a regular, and it's all yours for one very inexpensive tab.

Via Crocifisso 6. ✆ **0931-21097.** Pizzas from 6€. AE, DC, MC, V. Tues–Sun 7:30pm–midnight.

Don Camillo ★★ SEAFOOD Its slightly formal dining room—high-vaulted stone ceilings, polished antiques along the walls—strikes an odd note in laid-back Ortigia, but this is the place to splurge on exquisite renditions of Sicilian specialties, including spaghetti with *ricci* (sea urchin—trust me, it's wonderful). It's a special night out, where the focus is on the food, not Sicilian theatrics and brio.

Via Maestranza 96. www.ristorantedoncamillosiracusa.it. ✆ **0931-67133.** Reservations recommended. Main courses 14€–24€. AE, DC, MC, V. Mon–Sat 12:30–3pm and 7:30–10:30pm.

L'Ancora ★★ ☺ SIRACUSAN/SEAFOOD The full bounty of the sea plus lots of fresh local vegetables and herbs are employed at this bustling local favorite near the main post office on Ortigia. Decor isn't much to write home about, but there's an ample veranda, and the food is the absolute apex of freshness and Mediterranean tradition. It's best to book a table for weekend lunches, as the spot is a Siracusan go-to for family get-togethers, baptism parties, and the like.

Via G. Perno 7. www.ristoranteancora.com. ✆ **0931-462369.** Main courses 10€–18€. AE, DC, MC, V. Tues–Sun 12:30–3pm and 7:30–10:30pm.

PADDLING AMONG THE papyrus

Just south of Ortigia is a nature reserve where dense papyrus grows along the banks of the *Fiume Ciane* (Ciane River). Boat tours up this gentle waterway are a rustic and peaceful way to step back in time. You can also walk the path that follows the river course, past an ancient temple. Take Via Elorina (SS. 115) a few kilometers south to the bridge that crosses both the Anapo and Ciane rivers. Boats are usually stationed on the far (Ciane) side. Guided tours cost between 8€ and 15€ per person, depending on the number of passengers. For tickets and information on departure times, call ✆ **0931-69076.** To reach the departure site by bus, take line 21, 22, or 23 from Piazza della Posta and get off at Ponte delle Fiane.

Perbacco ★ SICILIAN/CREATIVE Somewhere between the fancy splurge of Don Camillo and the bare-bones bustle of L'Ancora lies Perbacco. The atmosphere here is the perfect mix of contemporary style and laid-back Sicilian, and the clientele is international. On the menu, look for mostly Sicilian classics, reinvented here and there with a few creative touches. Seafood is the main event here, and the seafood pastas are especially memorable: If it's available, order the spaghetti ai pappani di mare (a large type of local crab) e tartufo biano (white truffle). Seating is either in a tight but charming little courtyard area or inside a sleek, lounge-type dining room, whose air-conditioning you'll need in summer.
Via Roma 120. ✆ **0931-449046.** Main courses 12€–20€. AE, DC, MC, V. Mon–Sat 7pm–midnight.

Entertainment & Nightlife

For nightlife with a little more edge than people-watching on Piazza del Duomo, walk 1 minute south to **San Rocco,** Piazza San Rocco 3/5 (✆ **333-9854177**), a sleek indoor/outdoor enoteca (wine bar) and cocktail bar with a great *aperitivo* spread and a young crowd. Next door, the dive-y **Doctor Sam,** Piazza San Rocco 4 (✆ **0931-483598**), is perfectly friendly but big on tattoos, piercings, and reggae. Down the street, the English-style **Vecchio Pub,** Via delle Vergini 9 (✆ **0931-464692**), is where tourists and expats of all ages come to tie one on among their own species.

Where to Stay

The best place to stay in the Siracusa area is on Ortigia. The island has far more character and charm than "mainland" Siracusa. All the choices below are on Ortigia. However, the countryside near Siracusa is an increasingly popular zone for villa rentals, which are a great way to enjoy this region, especially if you are traveling with kids or other couples. The feverish restoration work on historic buildings all over Ortigia has also resulted in a surfeit of short-term holiday lets and B&Bs with lots of character. A good agency for apartments in Ortigia is **Case Sicilia** (www.casesicilia.com; ✆ **339-2983507**). For villas, **Think Sicily** (www.thinksicily.com; ✆ **800/490-1107** in the U.S. and Canada or 44/020/7377-8518 in the U.K.) has a carefully edited list of well-equipped properties in the Siracusa region.

Algilà Ortigia Charme Hotel ★★ 🎁 In a stately old building in the historic heart of Ortigia, this hotel opens onto panoramic views of the ancient Ortigia Sea. The latest restoration in 2010 has preserved its antique architecture while installing the latest amenities. Each of the rooms is furnished differently with antiques, four-poster beds, and elegant decoration, and each contains a colorfully tiled bathroom. Rooms open onto a blissful inner courtyard. Both a Mediterranean and an international cuisine are served in the hotel restaurant, with a special menu for vegetarians.

Via Vittorio Veneto 93, 96100 Siracusa. www.algila.it. ✆ **0931-465186.** Fax 0931-463889. 30 units. 174€–400€ double; 224€–560€ junior suite. AE, MC, V. **Amenities:** Restaurant; room service; Wi-Fi (free, in lobby). *In room:* A/C, TV, hair dryer.

Approdo delle Sirene ★★ The modern and immaculate "Mermaid's Landing," ideally situated near the entrance to Ortigia Island, was opened in 2004 by a mother and son team, Fiora and Friedrich, from Rome. The nautical decor features dark wood floors and striped linens in bold colors. Rooms with water view are considerably more spacious than standards, but all have contemporary bathrooms. The hosts can arrange all kinds of tours and excursions and also have bikes available for guests' use (no charge).

Riva Garibaldi 15, 96100 Siracusa. www.apprododellesirene.com. ✆ **0931-24857.** 8 units. 80€–130€ double. 2-night minimum stay June–Aug. AE, DC, MC, V. **Amenities:** Bikes. *In room:* A/C, TV, hair dryer, minibar, Wi-Fi (free).

Hotel Gutkowski ★ On the quieter "back side" of Ortigia, this robin's-egg blue *palazzo* is a haven of minimalist, spalike style. Some rooms (and especially bathrooms) are quite small, but all are equipped with minibar and TV. There's a roof terrace and informal wine bar on-site.

Lungomare Vittorini 26, 96100 Siracusa. www.guthotel.it. ✆ **0931-465861.** 25 units. From 100€ double. AE, DC, MC, V. **Amenities:** Bar. *In room:* A/C, TV, minibar, Wi-Fi (free).

Side Trips from Siracusa

You could easily spend weeks making short forays into the countryside around Siracusa, discovering wonders both historic and natural, but if your time in Siracusa itself is limited, my number-one day-trip choice is the 18th-century *centro storico* of **Noto** (an easy half-day from Siracusa), whose line-up of ebullient *palazzi* represent the Sicilian baroque at its sunniest. From May to September, a beach outing may be very compelling, and several seaside areas offer diverse settings at which to enjoy the coast of southeastern Sicily.

NOTO ★★★

The *centro storico* of this hill town is Sicily's crown jewel of baroque delights. An earthquake leveled most of Noto in 1693, clearing the way for the fanciful *barocco* style to establish a foothold in the early 18th century. In 2002, Noto was inscribed, along with seven other towns in the area, in the "Late Baroque Towns of the Val di Noto" UNESCO World Heritage Site for "outstanding testimony to the exuberant genius" of that period of art and architecture, which represented the "culmination and final flowering of baroque art in Europe."

Whether with your own car or on a bus, it's about a 35-minute drive from Siracusa: If you're driving yourself, take the A18 autostrada south for 27km (17 miles), then exit and head north and up the hill, following blue signs toward Noto; once near town, be sure to follow the yellow signs toward Noto's *"centro storico,"* not the brown signs to "Noto Antica," which is an archaeological site (it's the ruins of the old city destroyed by the earthquake) quite some distance from town. It's also easy to reach Noto by bus (55 min. each way; 6€ round-trip) from

A detail from one of Palazzo Villadorata's balconies in Noto.

Siracusa. Two companies, AST and Interbus, serve the route, offering about a dozen buses per day from Ortigia or Siracusa train station. In Noto, both bus companies arrive at the Piazzale Marconi bus station, a 5-minute walk from the *centro storico.* To get your bearings, stop at the **tourist office** at Via Gioberti 13 (✆ **0931-836503**), to pick up a map and some tips about exploring the town on foot. The office is open from May to September daily from 9am to 1pm and 3:30 to 6:30pm, and from October to April Monday through Friday from 8am to 2pm and 3:30 to 6:30pm.

Noto's pedestrian-only main strip, Corso Vittorio Emanuele III, cuts east-west through a stage-set of honey-colored limestone confections, most of which are centered on Piazza Municipio. Curvaceous and curvilinear accents and potbellied wrought-iron balconies adorn the facades of all the buildings on the square. The most photographed spot in Noto, however, is hidden away on Via Corrado Nicolaci (a cross street of Corso Vittorio): About halfway up, on the left, is **Palazzo Villadorata** (or **Palazzo Nicolaci**) ★★★, with its diminutive but wonderful balcony supports carved with the heads of cheeky maidens, dwarves, lions, and horses—the individual figures' expressions are fabulous. For a fabulous (and expensive) overnight stay in the building that is the hallmark of *Noto barocca,* book a room at the new guesthouse inside the *palazzo,* **Seven Rooms Villadorata** (Via Nicolaci 18; www.7roomsvilladorata.it; ✆ **338-5095643;** inquire about rates).

Noto is even more bewitching when the sun goes down. If you're in Noto at mealtime, your best bet is **Al Buco** ★ (Via G. Zanardelli; ✆ **0931-838142;** main courses 8€–14€; MC, V), which serves mostly seafood and vegetables at lunch and dinner but is closed on Saturdays. Alternatively, for a snack, seek out one of Noto's celebrated pastry shops—**Mandorlo in Fiore** ★★ (Via Ducezio 2; ✆ **0931-836615**) is famous for its *cassata,* while **Pasticceria La Fontana Vecchia** (Corso Vittorio Emanuele 150; ✆ **0931-839412**) specializes in *pan di spagna* (sponge cake filled with sweet ricotta) and has great gelato, too.

BEACHES NEAR SIRACUSA ★

Some of the best unspoiled shoreline in all of Italy is on Sicily's southeastern coast. The color palette is lighter down here—the water is more pastel than cerulean, and the sand is white and sugary. From north to south, **Fontane Bianche** ★★ is the classic beach detour for those who stay in Siracusa, 15 minutes away. It's an almost-square bay with laid-back beach clubs and luxurious deep sand. **Lido di Noto,** 15 minutes from the baroque hill town, is a lively beach with great waterfront restaurants. Half the beach is private beach clubs (where you pay around 10€ for day use of a lounge chair, umbrella, and shower facilities), and half is free public access. Between Noto and Pachino is the **Vendicari Nature Reserve,** where beaches are small and hard to find but the scenery is beautiful. Thousands of migratory birds nest here every year. A few miles south of the autostrada on SP19, park at the Agriturismo Calamosche to reach **Calamosche ★★**, favored by local teens and 20-somethings. It's a 15-minute walk down a nature path to reach the intimate cove, framed by rock cliffs and sea caves. The water is a calm, perfectly dappled teal. **Isola delle Correnti ★★**, at the southeastern tip of the island, is one of the best beaches on Sicily. It's a bit more windswept and wavy than the other spots, which can be nice when you tire of perfectly still turquoise water and searing sunshine. On a clear day, you can even see Malta, which is just 100km (60 miles) to the south.

PIAZZA ARMERINA ★★★

158km (98 miles) SE of Palermo, 134km (83) miles NW of Siracusa

The city of Piazza Armerina, situated in the dead-center of Sicily, is graced with impressive but decaying *palazzi,* but no one would make the trek here if it weren't for the world-famous mosaics at the Villa del Casale, a UNESCO World Heritage archaeological site in the countryside just 5km (3 miles) outside of town.

The extraordinary mosaics at the 4th-century-A.D. villa, the former country retreat of a wealthy Roman citizen, are some of the most important Roman pictorial art in the world. And I'm not talking precious, restrained imagery of emperors and the like: This is like an uncut, down-and-dirty Roman reality show about gladiators and wild animal fights, hunting parties, alcohol and sex, skimpy gym clothes, and more. Few archaeological sites brush the dust off our notions of "antiquity" quite like the mosaics of Villa Romana del Casale. This is without exaggeration the richest collection of Roman mosaics anywhere and is one of the top 10 Roman sites anywhere in Italy. If, after ogling the mosaics, you have the time and energy, the town of Piazza Armerina itself is worth a quick visit. Set on a plateau some 700m (2,297 ft.) above sea level, the city was founded during the Norman era, and today it's filled with mansions showing both baroque and Renaissance architectural influences. Its historic **medieval quarter ★** is graced with many beautiful churches, the most impressive of which is the **Duomo** (Via Cavour; **✆ 0935-680214;** daily 8:30am–noon and 3:30–7pm), crowning the highest point in town at 720m (2,364 ft.).

Essentials

GETTING THERE To reach the villa by car from Palermo, take the A19 east and south. Where the highway turns east toward Enna, take the Caltanissetta

An Important Note on Visiting the Villa Romana del Casale

As this update is being written, the site is still in the midst of a massive and much-needed cleaning and restoration project, which includes the construction of a new shelter of wood and copper to replace the awful greenhouselike enclosure erected in the 1960s. Until the work is complete, only part of the villa (currently 30%–50% of the rooms) is open to visitors at any given time. As work progresses, different parts of the villa open up, while others are roped off, but site officials do their best to make sure visitors can see as many of the really spectacular mosaics as possible. (The work began in 2007 and was initially supposed to be finished by mid-2011; with any luck, it might wrap up sometime in early 2013. You can check www.villaromanadelcasale.org for updates.)

exit, then immediately look for signs Piazza Armerina. The route is SS626 south to SS122 east to SS117bis. From Taormina, Siracusa, or anywhere in the east, take the A19 from Catania west, exit at Dittaino and head south following blue signs for Piazza Armerina (a few stretches of this route are practically dirt roads, but don't be discouraged, you'll be on better surfaces soon). From Agrigento, take the SS640 toward Caltanissetta. Just before Caltanissetta, bear right, following blue signs to Piazza Armerina. Once in the vicinity of Piazza Armerina town, follow the yellow or brown signs saying VILLA DEL CASALE, VILLA ROMANA, MOSAICI, and the like, west along the SP15 (down the hill from town), about 5km (3 miles). The entrance to the park will be on the left.

Exploring Piazza Armerina

Villa Romana del Casale ★★★ RUINS This is one of the most wonderful archaeological sites in the world: You're not here to see evocative columns and arches, but to look down and see mosaics, mosaics, and more mosaics. Some 3,535 sq. m (38,050 sq. ft.) in total, the mosaics are all polychrome marble and all on display *in situ* on the floors of 40 rooms that made up the private countryside mansion and hunting lodge of a rich and powerful Roman patrician who lived, or at least vacationed, in Sicily in the late 3rd or early 4th century A.D. The original roof of the villa is long gone (at press time, the site is getting a brand-new shelter to replace the plastic-panel enclosure from 1967 that became a furnace in summer) and visitors view the mosaics from carefully placed walkways above the ancient floors.

Among the thoroughly engrossing scenes, animal, hunting, sporting, and mythological themes predominate. Unsurprisingly for a men's weekend getaway pad, gore and blood abound in the artwork, though there are also some tender vignettes captured in the mosaics and even a dash of slightly racy erotica. Do yourself a favor and acquire a site map before setting out—there are many, many rooms in all different directions here, and you wouldn't want to miss any of these treasures. Make a note of which mosaics interest you the most and plot them on your map so that you don't accidentally skip over them. The walkways can be crowded with tour groups (which linger in the best viewing spots for the best mosaics and sometimes try to push you out of the way), but try not to let this frustrate you into rushing through, and out of, the site.

The villa's central architectural feature was a garden courtyard, or peristyle, from which all the other rooms branch out. After parking along the road and walking south toward the actual villa grounds, you will most likely enter from the northwest corner of the structure and tour the mosaics in a sort of clockwise fashion. Among the first discernible rooms you'll encounter are the **Terme,** or steam baths (Rooms 1–7), which supplied water and also heated the villa with steam circulating through cavities (now exposed) in the floors and walls. In the **Sala delle Unzioni** (Anointment Room, Room 4), a slave is oiling up his master for a shoulder massage.

The corridors of the peristyle (Room 13) contain the splendid **Peristyle mosaic ★★**, which can be viewed on all sides of the portico. It's a romp of birds, plants, wild animals, and more domesticated creatures such as horses. Adjoining it to the baths is the **Palestra ★★** (exercise area, Room 15). In these highly detailed mosaics, a chariot race at Rome's Circus Maximus is depicted.

Along the north side of the peristyle are a few rectangular rooms with fragmentary mosaics of mostly geometrical motifs. The **Sala delle Quattro**

Stagioni (Room 23) contains mosaic medallions representing allegories of the four seasons. Next to it, the **Sala degli Eroti Pescatori ★** (Room of the Fishing Cupids, Room 24) is a busy scene of little winged men harpooning, netting, even underwater-wrestling various species that are destined to become ancient Roman seafood.

Just past those rooms is one of the highlights of the villa, the **Sala della Piccola Caccia ★★★**, Room 25. *Piccola caccia* means "small hunt," referring to the type of game being captured—fowl, deer, rabbits, and the like. Spend some time studying all the action in the various registers of this mosaic and all the individual creatures and facial expressions.

The long hall to the east of here (it's where all the crowds tend to gather) is the villa's most spectacular feature, the **Corridoio della Grande Caccia ★★★**, or Corridor of the Great Hunt (Room 28), measuring 65m (197 ft.) in length. The mosaics here, depicting big game—exotic African beasts here, not the common European fauna you see in the Small Hunt mosaics of room 25—are arguably the most splendid from the ancient world. From panthers to camels to ostriches, the animals are all captured alive and shown in various stages of transport across land and sea to the port of Rome, where they will be part of the games in the Colosseum.

A cluster of three rooms east of the north (right-hand side) end of the Grande Caccia corridor includes the **Vestibolo di Ulisse e Polifemo ★** (Vestibule of Ulysses and Polyphemus, Room 47), where the Homeric hero proffers a *krater* of wine to the Cyclops (here with three eyes instead of one, and a disemboweled ram draped casually over his lap) in hopes of getting him drunk. Adjacent is the **Cubicolo con Scena Erotica ★** (Bedroom with Erotic Scene, Room 46)—despite the titillating name, it's a very tame affair. Most of the mosaic is geometric patterns, but at the center is a seductress, with vampy side gaze and a nicely contoured rear end for all to see, embracing a young man.

Off the southwest side of the Grande Caccia corridor is one of the most amusing rooms of all, the **Sala delle Palestrite ★★**, Room of the Gym Girls, formerly known as the Room of the Girls in Bikinis, Room 30. Their skimpy strapless bikinis would be appropriate for a beach in the 21st century, but ancient literary sources tell us that this was actually standard workout apparel 1,700 years ago—the bandeau top was called the *strophium,* and the bikini bottom the *subligar.* (They're also wearing a lot of jewelry and have voluminous up-dos—proto-Snookis, perhaps, minus the tan?) The girls are engaged in various exercises—curling dumbbells, tossing a ball, and running.

South of the central block of the villa and peristyle is the trefoil-shaped **Triclinium ★★★**, Room 33, a large dining room known for a magnificent rendition of the Labors of Hercules. In the central apse, the mosaics depict the **Gigantomachy ★★★** (Battle of the Giants), five mammoth creatures in their death throes after being pierced by Hercules's arrows, poisoned with the blood of the Lernaean hydra.

As you pore over the mosaics at Villa del Casale, it's easy to forget that the villa itself, architecturally, must have been splendid—an enormous space, it was replete with fancy water features, marble-clad walls, and opulent vaulted ceilings. There are other, more intact Roman villas in Italy where you can get a more complete picture of the architecture, but nowhere else are there mosaics like these.

Strada Provinciale 15, Piazza Armerina. www.villaromanadelcasale.org. ✆ **0935-680036.** Admission during the restoration work is 5€ but will go up to 10€ when the project is completed. Daily 9am until 1 hr. before sunset.

AGRIGENTO & THE VALLEY OF THE TEMPLES ★★★

129km (80 miles) S of Palermo, 175km (109 miles) SE of Trapani, 217km (135 miles) W of Siracusa

Agrigento's amazing Valley of the Temples is one of the most memorable and evocative sights of the ancient world. It's hard to describe the near-mystical experience of being among these ruins, majestically arranged as they are on a long ridge, their honey-colored columns and pediments the embodiment of classical dignity, their immediate surroundings remarkably unspoiled by modern intrusions, the air of antiquity thick all around. Like Pompeii, it's a site that really transports you. You could go nowhere else in Sicily but the Valley of the Temples, and the trip would be worth it. (And that's good to know, because Agrigento is pretty much in the middle of nowhere.)

Greek colonists established a beachhead here the 6th century B.C., calling the settlement Akragas. In fact, the name "valley of the temples" is a misnomer, as everything is set on a ridge with olive and almond trees and commanding views of the sea. In time, Akragas grew to become one of the most prosperous cities in Magna Graecia. But like Selinus (113km/70 miles to the west), the wealth of Akragas drew the attention of the war-waging Carthaginians, who attacked as early as 406 B.C., eventually wresting control from the Greeks here. In the 3rd century B.C., the city changed hands between the Carthaginians and the Romans until it finally succumbed to Roman domination by 210 B.C.

Meanwhile, the temples fell into varying degrees of ruin, having been toppled by earthquakes, or quarried and pillaged over the turbulent centuries of Sicilian history. It wasn't until the 19th century that methodical archaeological excavation and restoration of the temples and their surroundings began. The entire site of the Valley of the Temples was inscribed to the UNESCO list of World Heritage Sites in 1997. A lengthy cleaning of the temples was concluded quite recently—be grateful you weren't one of the thousands of visitors who came all the way down to Agrigento during the restoration years only to find the Temple of Concordia shrouded in scaffolding. Some have criticized the restoration, however, saying the ancient patina was stripped in the process, changing the color of the stone from the familiar sun-bleached yellow-beige to a darker, Dijon-mustard tone. (Most postcards sold at the site still show the old version.)

You come to Agrigento for the temples, not the town itself. It's a bustling place, but heavy Allied bombing during World War II necessitated much rebuilding, and the result is, for the most part, uninspired architecture, but there are tourist shops galore and good people-watching at the cafes along Via Atenea. When it gets too hot (as it so often does), flee to a beach at nearby San Leone.

I highly recommend visiting the temples either late in the afternoon or early in the morning for the best light effects and fewer crowds—though the temples are never fully deserted. If you're here in summer or on a weekend, you can even tour the temples at night, a tremendously evocative experience (though one that's hard to photograph) you'll never forget. Spend the night at the excellent Villa Athena hotel, which occupies an unbelievable position just below the marquee sight of the area, the Temple of Concordia.

Essentials

GETTING THERE By **car** from Palermo, cut southeast on the SS121, which becomes SS189 before it finally reaches Agrigento. Allow 2½ hours. From

Siracusa, take the A18 autostrada north to Catania and then the A19 west toward Enna. Just past Enna, exit the A19 and follow signs south through Caltanissetta and down to Agrigento. This trip is about 2½ hours. The "coastal route" from Siracusa—taking the SS115 all the way—may look more direct on the map but is much more time-consuming, up to 5 hours on an often very curvy, two-lane road.

Bus connections between Palermo and Agrigento are fairly convenient: **Cuffaro** (www.cuffaro.info; ✆ **0922-403150**) runs nine buses per day each way and drops you right in front of the entrance to the archaeological site; the trip takes 2 hours and costs 8.30€ one-way or 13€ round-trip. Bus service is also possible from Siracusa, but it's a long haul of at least 4 hours each way.

Taking the **train** to Agrigento is a hassle. The main rail station, **Stazione Centrale,** is at Piazza Marconi (✆ **892021**); from there you then have to take a cab or local bus (lines 1, 2, or 3) to the temples, 10 minutes away. The train trip from Palermo takes 2 hours and costs 8€; there are 12 trains daily. From Siracusa, you must change in Catania; the full 6-hour trip costs 20€ one-way.

VISITOR INFORMATION The **tourist office,** in the modern town at Piazzale Aldo Moro 7 (✆ **0922-20454**), is open Sunday through Friday 8am to 1pm and 3 to 8pm, Saturday 8am to 1pm. Another tourist office is at Via Empedocle 73 (✆ **0922-20391**), open Monday to Friday 8am to 2:30pm and Wednesday 3:30 to 7pm.

Exploring the Ruins

You've seen them on countless postcards as you've traveled around Sicily, and now here they are before you: the evocative skeletons of seven temples that together comprise the most important Greek ruins outside Greece itself. The weathered podiums, colonnades, and architraves of these magnificent buildings are the poignant legacy of the once-powerful city of Akragas, founded in the 6th century B.C. as a beachhead. Sadly, the temples were systematically quarried for their stone throughout the Middle Ages, and many went on to live new lives in the mundane structures of coastal towns nearby, such as Porto Empedocle.

While the temples deservedly get top billing here, there are other elements of ancient city life, such as houses, streets, and tombs, whose outlines can be discerned. As you wander the site, imagine the glorious beacon that the temples, embellished with gold sculptural details, must have been for those approaching by sea.

Ticket booths are found at the west and east entrances (www.lavalledeitempli.eu; ✆ **0922-621611**). Admission is 8€. Hours are daily from 8:30am to 7pm. On Saturdays year-round it's also open from 8am to 11:30pm, and from July 8 to August 31, the site is open for evening visits daily from 7:45am to 9:30pm, and until 11pm on Saturday and Sunday. Note that your daytime admission ticket is not valid for the evening hours; you'll pay another 8€ to walk around the temples at night—and it's worth it.

Day or night, allow several hours to tour the ruins. It's such a special place, however, you might want to spend all day just soaking up the atmosphere. If you have only have limited time, start from the east, as that's where the oldest and most impressive temples are found, like the postcard-perfect Temple of Concordia. Otherwise, start from the western end and check out the humbler ruins there before working your way east to the site's more stellar attractions. Overall, your route through the ruins will be linear, as they all sit atop a straight ridge.

The Temple of Concordia.

In the western zone (the less overtly impressive part of the Valley of the Temples), the four extant columns of the **Temple of Castor and Pollux ★** still carry a corner of the entablature and pediment, making them among the most evocative and photographed ruins in Agrigento. Just east of here, the **Temple of Zeus ★** would have been the largest ever built, with 20m-high (66-ft.) Doric columns, but it was never completed (war with Carthage and an earthquake sealed its unfinished fate). This is where you'll find one of the famous 8m-tall (26-ft.) *telamones* (atlases) meant to support the structure.

Across Via dei Templi is the eastern zone of the archaeological park and the reason you came all the way down to Agrigento: It's where the real heavy-hitters lie. The first ruin you'll encounter is the **Temple of Hercules ★★**, which once ranked in size with the Temple of Zeus to the west, but today only eight fluted columns still stand along the temple's flank. Incredibly, scorch marks from fires set by Carthaginians over 2,000 years ago are still visible. After the Temple of Hercules, you're pulled irresistibly up the hill to the most impressive temple at the site—the "Don" of the Valley of the Temples—the **Temple of Concordia ★★★**. Preservation-wise, this golden giant is on par with the Temple of Hephaestus in Athens. Unlike the other temples here, it was spared destruction and pillaging by later occupants of Agrigento because its *cella,* or cult chamber, was reconsecrated as a Christian basilica in the 4th century A.D. It's not clear to which deity the temple was dedicated in antiquity: It was only named the Temple of Concordia in 1748, when its 34 columns were picked up and restored to the state you see today. The last of the major temples in this zone is the **Temple of Juno ★★**, with a romantically skeletal look despite its 30 re-erected columns and sections of entablature. It was likely used for wedding ceremonies and sacrificial offerings. The view from the eastern end of the stylobate (temple platform), past the flank of columns to the sea, is splendid.

Between the ruins and Agrigento town, the **Museo Archeologico** (Via dei Templi; **✆ 0922-40111;** admission 6€ or 10€ with archaeological park combo ticket; Mon 9am–1:30pm, Tues–Sat 9am–7:30pm) has detailed explanations in both Italian and English of the many artifacts unearthed in this area. However, after a long and dusty outing at the ruins, this isn't a necessary stop unless your thirst for all things Akragas is stronger than your thirst for a cold beer, water, anything, back at your hotel or at a bar somewhere in town.

Where to Eat & Stay

The place to stay in Agrigento is the Villa Athena, both for its incomparable and privileged setting within spitting distance of the temples and its handsomely remodeled rooms.

With few exceptions, the dining in town is forgettable. This is one place where eating at the hotel (yours or another) may be your best option; otherwise, pick up picnic fare from a local deli or supermarket.

Colleverde Park Hotel ★★ Sheathed in a layer of ocher colored stucco, this is one of our favorite hotels in Agrigento, partly for its verdant garden, partly for its helpful staff, and partly for its location convenient to both the ancient and the medieval monuments of Agrigento. The decor throughout is discreetly elegant, providing refuge from the hysteria that sometimes permeates Agrigento, particularly its roaring traffic. Guest rooms have tiled bathrooms (all with tub/shower combinations), lots of exposed wood, charming artwork, and big windows that in some cases reveal views of the temples of Concordia and Juno.

Via Panoramica dei Templi, 92100 Agrigento. ✆ **0922-29555.** Fax 0922-29012. www.colleverdehotel.it. 48 units. 135€–190€ double; 160€–210€ junior suite. Rates include continental breakfast. AE, DC, MC, V. Free parking. Bus: 1, 2, or 3. **Amenities:** Restaurant; bar. *In room:* A/C, TV, hair dryer, minibar, Wi-Fi (6€ per hour).

Villa Athena ★★★ 📷 No hotel has a right to be this close to the most outstanding collection of Greek temples in the world, yet here it is, the Villa Athena, tucked gracefully into the valley directly below the Temple of Concordia, with views that'll widen the eyes of even the most experienced world travelers. The hotel, an 18th-century villa with pretty gardens and grounds, recently underwent extensive remodeling, rendering formerly tired guest rooms supremely comfortable and stylish. Ask for a room with a view of the temples, preferably one with a balcony. The perfect choice would be the Presidential Suite, whose ample terrace affords a million-dollar panorama of the Temple of Concordia, seemingly floating atop the olive-covered slope that separate the hotel from the archaeological park. (Even the bathrooms have glorious vistas—porthole windows above the bathtubs frame perfect little art prints of the Temple of Concordia.) The on-site garden restaurant (again with that insane temple view), where you're likely to dine at least once given the isolation of the hotel and your fatigue after touring the ruins, is excellent if a bit pricey. As gracious and romantic as it is, the Villa Athena is definitely no secret find; be sure to reserve at least a month in advance.

The Temple of Hercules.

wine TOURING BETWEEN THE RUINS

A visit to the **Planeta winery** is a fun inland detour on the way from Agrigento to Selinunte. Planeta makes some of the best Sicilian wines, including exquisite chardonnay and syrah, and their Cantina dell'Ulmo estate in Sambuca di Sicilia has a 16th-century farmhouse set up for tastings and tours (by appointment).

To get there, exit the SS115 a few kilometers east of Menfi and follow the SS624 and SS188 to Sambuca di Sicilia. In Sambuca, follow signs that say AZIENDA AGRICOLA PLANETA-TERRE SICANE (www.planeta.it; ✆ **091-327965;** Tues–Sat 9am–3pm). Book visits at least 3 days in advance; e-mail visits@planeta.it or fax 091-6124335.

Via Passeggiata Archeologica 33, 92100 Agrigento. www.hotelvillaathena.it. ✆ **0922-596288.** Fax 0922-402180. 40 units. 220€–380€ double; from 400€ suite. Rates include continental breakfast. AE, DC, MC, V. Free parking. **Amenities:** Restaurant; 2 bars; concierge; pool; room service. *In room:* A/C, TV/DVD, CD player, minibar, Wi-Fi (free).

SELINUNTE ★★

122km (76 miles) SW of Palermo, 113km (70 miles) W of Agrigento, 89km (55 miles) SE of Trapani

First-time visitors to Sicily may find it hard to understand which of Sicily's many notable ruins they should visit and why; the fact is they all have quite different characters. Without a doubt, Agrigento's Valley of the Temples has the biggest "wow" factor, but it's packed with busloads of tourists. For a true sense of exploration, the chance to commune almost privately with behemoth stones, not to mention phenomenal photo ops thanks in part to a killer seaside position and few gates and fences to obstruct the beauty of the ruins, serene Selinunte should be at the top of your list.

The splendid jumble of ruins here are the more-or-less intact remains of five 6th-century-B.C. temples, divided into two areas across an immense archaeological site, one that could take hours to traverse if it weren't for the handy trams that shuttle visitors from one end of the park to the other. Selinunte is vast, yet it's also the most intimate of Sicily's big-time Greek sites. The scenic pathways around the western Acropolis section, which seem poised to spill you right into the Med, are often deserted, and you can climb all over fallen columns and temple pediments and feel that you are the first to discover dusty details like ancient water basins and millstones.

One of the superb cities of ancient Greece, ancient Selinus traces its history from the 7th century B.C., when immigrants from Megara Hyblaea (Siracusa) set out to build a new colony. (The ancient name, Selinus, means "wild celery," which grew extensively in the area.) They succeeded, erecting a city of power and prestige adorned with many temples. In fact, the site's most impressive group of temples sat on a promontory east of the actual city and served as a kind of billboard advertising the might and wealth of the colony. That boasting evidently created envy: Much of Selinunte's history involves seemingly endless conflicts with the Elymi people of Segesta (see "Segesta," later in this chapter). Siding with Selinunte's rival, the Carthaginians virtually leveled the city in 409 B.C. And halting construction of what would have been Selinunte's largest temple, the so-called Temple G. The city never recovered its former glory and ultimately fell into decay.

The ruins at Selinunte.

Before or after touring Selinunte, don't miss the easy detour to the Cave di Cusa, an atmospheric ancient quarry where the stones for the temples were hewn; dozens of raw column drums, intended for the never-finished Temple G, have lain here since 409 B.C.

Essentials

GETTING THERE Selinunte is on the southern coast of Sicily and is best reached by **car** because public transportation is awkward (you must make connections in the town of Castelvetrano, 23km from Selinunte). If you're driving from Agrigento, take SS115 northwest into Castelvetrano; then follow the signposted secondary road marked SELINUNTE, which leads south to the sea. From Palermo, take the A29 to Castelvetrano and follow directions as above. Allow at least 2 hours to drive here from either Palermo or Agrigento.

By **train or bus:** You can take the train from Palermo, Trapani, or Marsala to Castelvetrano. **Lumia buses** (www.autolineelumia.it; ✆ **0922-20414**) run to Castelvetrano from Agrigento. Once at Castelvetrano, you board a bus, operated by **Autoservizi Salemi** (www.autoservizisalemi.it; ✆ **0923-981120**) for the final push to Selinunte. The 20-minute ride costs 2€ each way.

Exploring the Archaeological Garden

Selinunte's temples lie in scattered ruins, the honey-colored stone littering the ground as if an earthquake had struck (as one did in ancient times). Some sections and fragments of temples still stand, with great columns pointing to the sky. From 9am to 1 hour before sunset daily, you can walk through the monument zone. Some of it has been partially excavated and reconstructed. Admission is 6€ for adults, free for children 17 and under.

The temples, in varying states of preservation, are designated by letters, not deities, although they were certainly dedicated to such mythological figures as Apollo and Hera (Juno). Most date from the 6th and 5th centuries B.C.

Confusingly, you'll encounter the lettered temples in reverse alphabetical order. Temples E, G, and F are in the so-called "eastern section" near the parking lots and ticket office, while temples A and C lie several hundred meters away in the Acropolis section of the park, to the east and overlooking the sea.

Hogging all your attention in the eastern group of temples, **Temple E ★★**, less frequently called the Temple of Hera, is the showiest structure at Selinunte and was heavily reconstructed in the early 20th century. Its 38 towering Doric columns of tawny stone and the fairly intact temple *cella,* or inner sanctuary, make for a marvelous encounter with ancient architecture. You can climb all over everything and get a real sense of just how big these stones are, and what sophisticated engineering it took to put them together. **Temple G,** in scattered ruins north of Temple E, was one of the largest erected in Sicily and was also built in the Doric style. The ruins of the less impressive **Temple F** lie between temples E and G. Not much remains of Temple F, and little is known about it.

As you wander around temples E, F, and G, you'll catch sight of another picturesque temple and surrounding cluster of ruins in the distance, toward the sea. Those are the ruins of Selinunte's Acropoli, or citadel. To reach it, you can avail yourself of one of the electric trams that shuttle visitors from the eastern temples to the western part of Selinunte, or walk there in about 30 minutes.

The **Acropoli** was enclosed within defensive walls and built from the 6th century to the 5th century B.C. The actual town of Selinus, now flattened and mostly buried, lay to the north of here. With its quiet pathways and sea views framed by evocative fragments of archaeology, the Acropoli is a particularly romantic corner of Sicily that doesn't get as much traffic as Selinunte's eastern temples; treasure your time here. The most impressive single element here is **Temple C ★★**. In 1925, 14 of the 17 north flank columns of Temple C were re-erected. This is the earliest surviving temple of ancient Selinus, built in the 6th century B.C. and probably dedicated to Apollo. The pediment, ornamented with a clay Gorgon's head, lies broken on the ground.

Also here is **Temple A,** which, like the others, remains in scattered ruins. The streets of the Acropoli were laid out along classical lines, with a trio of principal arteries bisected at right angles by a grid of less important streets. The Acropoli was the site of the most important public and religious buildings, and it was also the residence of the town's aristocrats. Be slow and detective-like as you explore the Acropolis, as remnants of everyday life—wash basins, millstones—lie scattered in the scrubby vegetation. If you look down below the hill to the water, you can see the site of the town's harbor, now overgrown.

Where to Eat & Stay

The nearest town is the modern Marinella di Selinunte, with some pleasant beach bars and restaurants where you can have a casual lunch, such as **Pierrot,** Via Marco Polo 108 (✆ **0924-46205**), but not much in the way of compelling lodging.

A bit farther away, the lively fishing town of **Mazara del Vallo ★** (whence the famed red prawns of Mazara hail) is a good overnight base for seeing Selinunte and the Cave di Cusa (as well as Erice and Segesta, discussed in Palermo's "Side Trips" section). Consider staying at the ultrapampering **Kempinski Giardini di Costanza ★★★**, Via Salemi Km 7, 100, Mazara del Vallo (www.kempinski.com/en/sicily; ✆ **0923-675000**), in the countryside near Mazara. Our favorite restaurant in Mazara is **Cafe Garibaldi,** Via Garibaldi 53/55 (www.cafegaribaldi.it; ✆ **347-4440170**), with outdoor seating on a charming courtyard in the heart of this surprisingly attractive town.

Side Trips

The perfect complement to touring the ruins of Selinunte is going to visit the Cusa quarries, about 10km (6¼ miles) away and only reachable by car, where the stones to build the temples came from. The **Cave di Cusa ★★** is a wonderful, undervisited site (✆ **0924-46540;** daily 9am–2pm; admission is 2€ or free with Selinunte ticket) with tons of ancient atmosphere, where you can walk a fascinating "landscape" of unfinished column drums (this is great hide-and-seek, burn-off-energy stuff if you have kids in tow) and other curious carvings. The stone here, a resistant and fine-grained tufa, was quarried for more than 150 years, beginning in the first half of the 6th century B.C. and grinding to a halt when Selinunte was defeated in 409 B.C. To reach the site from Selinunte, take the SP56 east toward Campobello di Mazara, and follow signs carefully to Cave di Cusa.

PALERMO ★★★

233km (145 miles) W of Messina, 721km (447 miles) S of Naples, 934km (579 miles) S of Rome

As you arrive in Palermo, you start spotting blond, blue-eyed bambini all over the place. Don't be surprised. If fair-haired children don't fit your concept of what a Sicilian should look like, remember that the Normans landed here in 1060 and launched a campaign to wrest control of the island from the Arabs. Today you can see elements of both cultures, notably in Palermo's architecture—which is a unique Norman-Arabic style.

The city is Sicily's largest port, its capital, and a jumble of contradictions. Whole neighborhoods remain bombed out and not yet rebuilt from World War II, yet Palermo boasts some of the greatest sights and museums in Sicily. Unemployment, poverty, traffic, crime, and crowding are rampant, and city services just don't run as they should. If you come to Palermo after having traveled elsewhere in slow-paced, user-friendly Sicily, the difficulties presented by this city come down like a ton of bricks. Yet there is magic in its madness, and those who brave it are rewarded with the discovery of artistic gems and memorable vignettes of street life. I can't guarantee you'll love every inch of this alluring yet hectic place, but what I can promise is that giving Palermo the significant effort it demands of tourists pays dividends in indelible travel experiences. And in the meantime, you'll get closer to the soul of Sicily.

The combination of distinctive sights in Sicily's capital—the result of more than a thousand years and countless Western and Eastern cultural influences—simply doesn't exist anywhere else. Not to be missed are the stunning Byzantine mosaics at the Norman Palace's Cappella Palatina or the cathedral of Monreale, and the eye-popping rococo stuccoes at the *oratori* of San Domenico and San Lorenzo. Witness Palermo's striking Islamic-inflected architecture in the bulbous red domes of San Giovanni degli Eremiti and San Cataldo. In the crumbling, captivating Kalsa district, visit Palazzo Abatellis, the masterpiece of Catalonian-Gothic architecture that houses Sicily's best art museum. Palermo's Museo Archeologico Regionale is the island's most comprehensive repository of ancient artifacts—a helpful complement to all the open-air ruins on Sicily.

Essentials

GETTING THERE Most people arrive via Palermo's dramatically situated **Falcone-Borsellino airport** (aka Punta Raisi; www.gesap.it; ✆ **091-7020273**), on the sea among tall headlands 25km (16 miles) northwest of the city center. Palermo is well served by flights from all over Italy and many European cities, too. All the major rental car companies have operations here. If you won't be driving into Palermo with a rental car (and if you do, get clear directions and parking information from your hotel), an easy way to reach the center from the airport is with the shuttle bus run by **Prestia e Comandè** (✆ **091-580457**). The buses depart every half-hour from 5am to 11pm; the trip takes 45 minutes and costs 6€ one-way. In central Palermo, the bus stops at the main train station, at Via Emerico Amari (port), and at Teatro Politeama. There's also a direct train called the **Trinacria Express** (www.trenitalia.com; ✆ **091-7044007;** 1 hr.; 6€) from Palermo airport to Palermo central station. Otherwise, taxis are plentiful; expect to pay about 45€ from the airport to town.

If you're arriving in Palermo from another place in Sicily by **rail,** all trains come into Palermo Stazione Centrale, just south of the historic center. **Buses** from elsewhere in Sicily arrive at a depot adjacent to the train station.

GETTING AROUND Walking is the best way to get around Palermo, since distances are never great within the historic center. To reach greater Palermo destinations (like the catacombs) or farther-flung locales (such as Mondello and Monreale), buses run by **AMAT** (✆ **091-350111**) cost 1.20€ per ride or 3.50€ for a full-day ticket. **City Sightseeing** (www.city-sightseeing.com/tour-palermo; ✆ **091-589429**) operates two different **double-decker bus tours** (20€ for adults; 10€ children 5–15 years) that do loops of some of the main sights and have prerecorded commentaries in several languages. I normally wouldn't recommend something this blatantly touristy and passive, but in demanding Palermo, this chance to rest your feet and have someone else do the navigating might save you some urban overload. Board the buses

Palermo's Duomo.

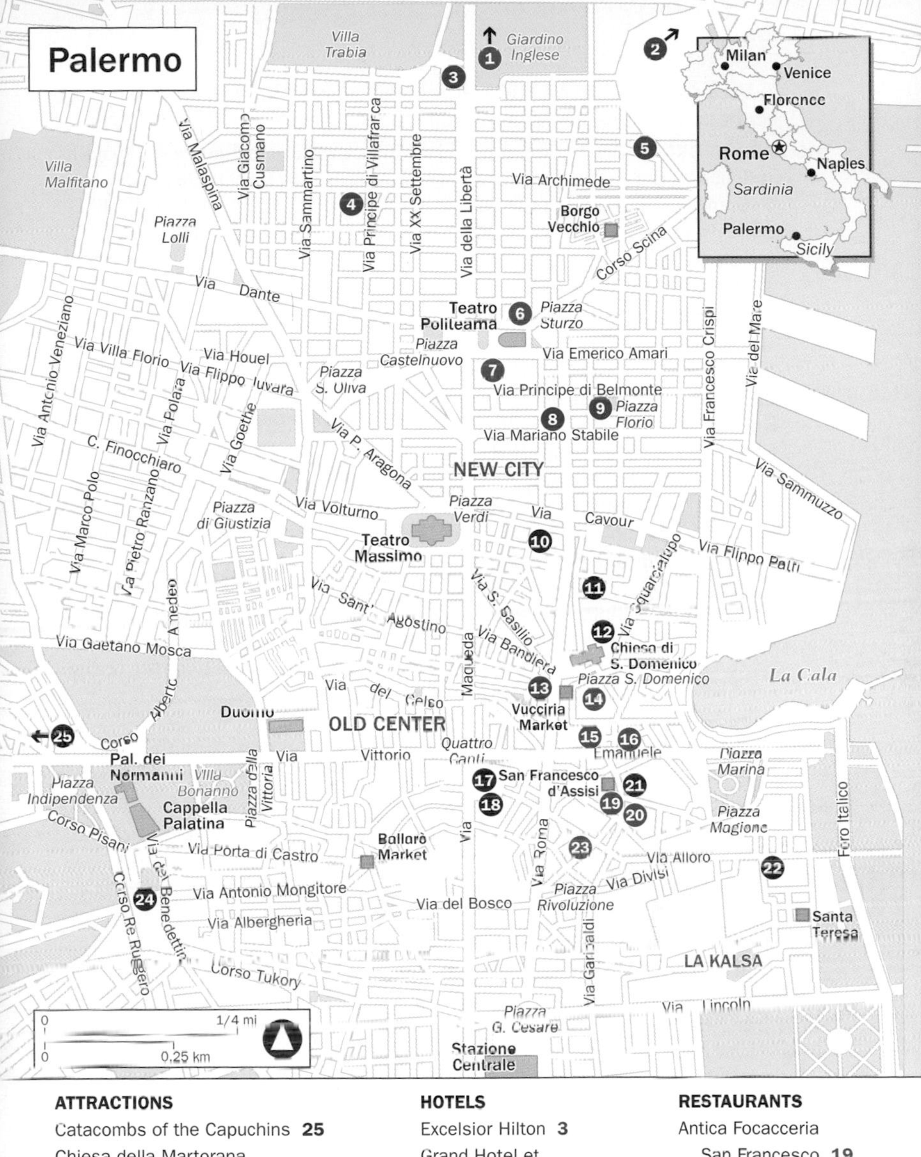

ATTRACTIONS

Catacombs of the Capuchins **25**
Chiesa della Martorana & San Cataldo **18**
Fontana Pretoria **17**
Galleria Regionale della Sicilia - Palazzo Abatellis **22**
Museo Archeologico Regionale **10**
Oratorio di Santa Cita **11**
Oratorio di San Domenico **12**
Oratorio di San Lorenzo **21**
San Giovanni degli Eremiti **24**

HOTELS

Excelsior Hilton **3**
Grand Hotel et des Palmes **8**
Joli **9**
Moderno **13**
Principe di Villafranca **4**
Ucciardhome **5**
Villa Igiea **2**

RESTAURANTS

Antica Focacceria San Francesco **19**
Antico Caffe' Spinnato **7**
Casa del Brodo **15**
Il Baro **1**
Le Delizie di Cagliostro **16**
Lo Scudiero **6**
Mi Manda Picone **20**
Osteria dei Vespri **23**
Santandrea **14**

at Via Emerico Amari 142 (near Piazza Politeama); they leave at least once per hour.

VISITOR INFORMATION Official **tourist information offices** are located at Falcone-Borsellino (Punta Raisi) airport (✆ **091-591698;** Mon–Sat 8:30am–7:30pm), and in the city center at Piazza Castelnuovo 35 (✆ **091-6058351;** Mon–Fri 8:30am–2pm and 2:30–6:30pm; yes, they close for a collective half-hour lunch break). The website of Palermo's tourism board is www.palermotourism.com.

FESTIVALS & MARKET You can't do justice to Palermo without swinging through one of its street markets, if only for 15 minutes. Nowhere is Palermo's multicultural pedigree more evident than at the stalls of **Vucciria ★★** (on Via Argenteria, north of Via Vittorio Emanuele and east of Via Roma), **Ballarò ★★** (in Piazza Ballarò), and **Capo ★★** (from Via Porta Carini south toward the cathedral). These open-air markets go on for blocks and blocks, hawking everything from spices to seafood to sides of beef to toilet paper to handicrafts to electronics and meat snacks of questionable provenance. Ballarò and Capo, west and north of the train station, are where more real Palermitans shop, but the twinkling lights of Vucciria (from the French *boucherie,* or butcher shop) and its covered souklike atmosphere is irresistibly charming. The vendors' colorful theatrics are very much for your benefit, so feel free to photograph away as they ham it up with swordfish heads and the like. Delve even deeper into Palermo's market culture at the neighborhoody **Borgo Vecchio** market (along Via Ettore Ximenes to Via Principe di Scordia), in the newer part of the city, northwest of Piazza Politeama. Antiques vendors with many unusual buys lie along the **Piazza Peranni,** off Corso Vittorio Emanuele.

SAFETY Be especially alert. Palermo is home to some of the most skilled pickpockets on the continent. Don't flaunt expensive jewelry, cameras, or wads of bills. Women who carry handbags are especially vulnerable to purse snatchers on Vespas. It's best to park your car in a garage rather than on the street; wherever you leave it, don't leave valuables inside. Police squads operate mobile centers throughout the town to help combat street crime.

Exploring Palermo

Apart from the spectacle of amped-up humanity that Palermo is, it's also one of the great art cities of Europe, and ideally, you should give it at least 3 days. However, most people don't build that much Palermo time into their Sicily itineraries. Even if you only have a day to see Palermo, you can pick and choose from the sights listed below—they'll only whet your appetite for the next trip.

The gritty corner known as the **Quattro Canti,** where Via Maqueda meets Via Vittorio Emanuele, is the approximate geographic center from which the old town of Palermo radiates. This 5-sq.-km (2-sq.-mile) pocket of busy roads, quiet alleys, splendid monuments, and hidden treasures is where the lion's share of the city's tourist attractions is located. Everything listed here, except the Catacombe dei Cappuccini, is within walking distance of the Quattro Canti. Southeast of Quattro Canti is **Piazza Pretoria ★**, Palermo's most famous square. Its Renaissance fountain, **Fontana Pretoria ★**, originally intended for a Tuscan villa, is bedecked with nude statues and mythological monsters—thus, it was called Fontana della Vergogna, or "Fountain of Shame," by outraged churchgoers.

If you don't want to bother with admission fees and museum crowds, the most atmospheric neighborhood for an unstructured walking tour is **La Kalsa ★★**. The key to understanding the contrasts of Palermo—if that's even possible—is this tangle of streets south of the main harbor, and northeast of the train station (Via Alloro is the main east-west street). The name is derived from the Arabic *khalisa,* or "pure," which the Kalsa is anything but. In the oldest and most intriguing part of the city, tarnished baroque gems like **Palazzo Gangi** (Piazza Croce dei Vespri), **Palazzo Ajutamicristo** (Via Garibaldi), and **Palazzo Mirto** (Via Merlo 2, off Piazza Marina; ✆ **091-6167541;** 3€; Mon–Sat 9am–7pm, Sun 9am–1pm) evoke Palermo's princely heyday, while entire blocks of the neighborhood are crumbled, never rebuilt after Allied air raids in 1943. Some of the bombed-out buildings are makeshift homes for families (and their livestock), who live together in a few rooms and sleep on simple pallets, while other scarred buildings have been repurposed as avant-garde art exhibition spaces. La Kalsa is quite an eye-opening place. Nearby, **Santa Maria dello Spasimo ★★** (Via dello Spasimo; ✆ **091-6161486**) is a swoon-inducing skeleton of a church, where mature trees grow out of broken Gothic vaults into the Palermitan sky. After your walking tour, have a drink at stylish outdoor bar **Qvivi,** Piazza della Rivoluzione (see "Entertainment & Nightlife," later in this section).

Tip: La Kalsa is safe during the day, but don't walk around the narrower streets of the districts alone at night. If in doubt, just stick to Via Alloro or Piazza Marina

Catacombs of the Capuchins (Catacombe dei Cappuccini) ★★★

CEMETERY Palermo's unforgettable "Library of Corpses" is the most bizarre final resting place in Italy, downright creepy to some, oddly clinical to others. Mummified, fully dressed cadavers hang from the walls, cantilevering eerily toward you as you walk the corridors of this ostensibly holy place. From the 16th to the 20th century, some 8,000 souls were "buried" here, most of them having elected while alive to be displayed thus—though the campy poses of some look more like a mortician's creative license.

Some 350 years ago, it was discovered that the catacombs contained a mysterious preservative that helped mummify the dead. As a result, Sicilians from nobles to maids demanded to be buried here. The oldest corpses date from the late 16th century. The last corpse to be buried here was that of 2-year-old Rosalia Lombardo, who died in 1920. She still appears so lifelike that locals have dubbed her "Sleeping Beauty." Giuseppe Tommasi, prince of Lampedusa and author of one of the best-known works of Sicilian literature, *The Leopard,* was buried here in 1957. His body was not embalmed, but buried in the cemetery next to the catacombs instead.

Capuchins Monastery, Piazza Cappuccini 1. ✆ **091-212117.** Admission 3€. Daily 9am–noon and 3–5pm (until 7pm in summer). Closed holidays. Bus: 327.

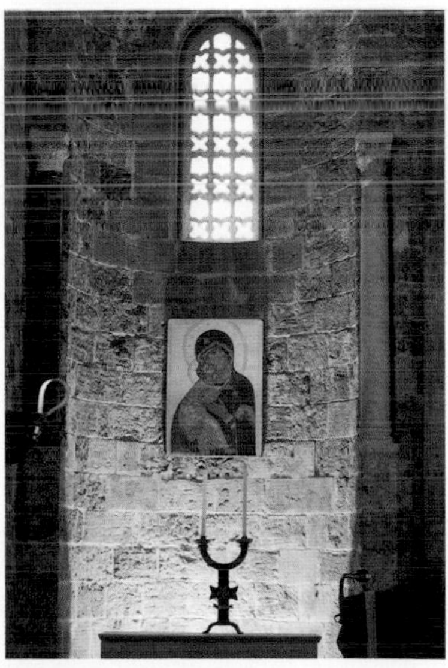

Interior of San Cataldo.

Chiesa della Martorana/San Cataldo ★★ CHURCH These two Norman churches stand side by side, separated by a sultry little garden of tropical plants and trees. If you have time for only one, make it La Martorana, as it is the most celebrated church in Palermo remaining from the Middle Ages. Visit it if only to see its series of spectacular **mosaics ★★**.

Named for Eloisa Martorana, who founded a nearby Benedictine convent in 1194, this church is dedicated not to her, but to Santa Maria dell'Ammiraglio (St. Mary of the Admiral). History was made here as well: It was in this church that Sicily's noblemen convened to offer the crown to Peter of Aragón.

Today's baroque facade regrettably conceals a Norman front. You enter through a beautiful combined portico and bell tower with a trio of ancient columns and double arch openings. The bell tower is original, dating from the 12th century. Once you go inside, you'll know that your time spent seeking out this church was worthwhile. The stunning mosaics were ordered in 1143 by George of Antioch, the admiral of King Roger and a man of Greek descent. He loved mosaics, especially when they conformed, as these did, to the Byzantine iconography of his homeland. It's believed that the craftsmen who designed these mosaics also did the same for the Cappella Palatina. The mosaics are laid out on and around the columns that hold up the principal cupola. They're at their most beautiful in the morning light when the church opens.

Dominating the dome is a rendition of Christ, surrounded by a bevy of angels with the Madonna and the Apostles pictured off to the sides. Even with the passage of centuries the colors remain vibrantly golden, with streaks of spring green, ivory, azure blue, and what one art critic called "grape-red."

On a visit to La Martorana, you can obtain a key from the custodian sitting at a tiny table to your right as you enter the chapel. This key allows entry into the tiny **Chiesa di San Cataldo** next door. Also of Norman origin, it was founded by Maio of Bari, chancellor to William I. But because he died in 1160, the interior was never completed. The church is much more famous for its exterior, with the red domes and the lacy Moorish crenellation around the tops of the walls.

Piazza Bellini 2, adjacent to Piazza Pretoria. ✆ **091-6161692.** Free admission. La Martorana: Mon–Sat 9:30am–1pm and 3:30–6:30pm; Sun 8:30am–1pm. San Cataldo: Tues–Fri 9am–5pm; Sat–Sun 9am–1pm. Bus: 101 or 102.

Duomo ★ CATHEDRAL A few blocks east of the Norman Palace, the Arab-Norman Duomo is a 12th-century structure much reworked and muddled in subsequent eras. As you enter, the first chapel on the right contains the tomb of Roger II, the first king of Sicily, who was crowned here in 1130 and died in 1154. Several of his descendants are also buried here. Accessed from the south transept, the Tesoro, or "Treasury," is a repository of rich vestments, silverware, chalices, holy vessels, altar cloths, and ivory engravings of the 17th century. The cathedral's grassy square is a welcome stop along one of the most maniacal roads in the city.

Piazza Cattedrale. ✆ **091-334373.** Duomo: free admission; crypt and treasury: 1€ each. Mon–Sat 9:30am–1:30pm and 2:30–5:30pm. Bus: 101, 104, 105, 107, or 139.

Galleria Regionale della Sicilia (Regional Gallery)/Palazzo Abatellis ★★★ MUSEUM This is the greatest gallery of regional art in Sicily and one the finest art galleries in all of Italy. It's housed in the **Palazzo Abatellis ★**, itself an architectural treasure, a Catalan-Gothic structure with a Renaissance overlay designed by Matteo Carnelivari in 1490. Carnelivari

ESCAPING THE madness

Believe it or not, Palermo has plenty of genteel (and kid-friendly) places where one can go to escape the chaos of the *centro storico* and the tourist sights there. The modern part of town starts north of Via Mariano Stabile, where broad, tree-lined avenues like Via della Libertà make for pleasant strolling. The Arabs, a people who knew the joy of a green oasis, were the ones who introduced gardens into Palermo. The Normans extended the idea by creating parklands and summer palaces to escape the heat. Today, you can wander among the greenery and encounter incredible banyan trees and other exotic plantings. The most rewarding Palermitan parks are the **Orto Botanico** ★★ (Via Abramo Lincoln 2B, just south of La Kalsa; ✆ **091-6238241**) and the **Giardino Inglese** ★ (off Via della Libertà in north-central Palermo).

To mix with Palermo's upper crust (and its wannabes), free from the menace of motorized traffic, strut your stuff down pedestrian-only **Via Principe di Belmonte,** home to **Antico Caffè Spinnato** ★★, Via Principe di Belmonte 107/115 (✆ **091-329229**), the best coffee bar in town. Alternatively, get out of the city altogether with a day on the woodsy slopes of Monte Pellegrino or at the beach in Mondello (see "Side Trips from Palermo," below).

constructed the building for Francesco Abatellis, the praetor of Palermo. After World War II bombings, the architect Carlo Scarpa restored the *palazzo* in 1954.

The superb collection shows the evolution of the arts in Sicily from the 13th to the 18th centuries. Sculpture predominates on the main floor. Beyond Room 2, the former chapel contains the gallery's most celebrated work, the ***Triumph of Death*** ★★★, dating from 1449 and of uncertain attribution (though it's sometimes credited to Pisanello). In all its gory magnificence, it portrays a horseback-riding skeleton (representing Death, of course) trampling his victims. The painter depicted himself in the fresco, seen with a pupil praying in vain for release from the horrors of Death. The modernity of this extraordinary work, including the details of the nose of the horse and the men and women in the full flush of their youth, is truly amazing, especially for its time.

The second masterpiece of the gallery lies at the end of the corridor exhibiting Arabic ceramics in Room 4: the white-marble, slanted-eyed bust of ***Eleonora di Aragona*** ★★, by Francesco Laurana, who created it in the 15th century. This was Laurana's masterpiece.

The second-floor galleries are filled mainly with paintings from the Sicilian school, including a spectacular ***Annunciation*** ★★, the creation of Antonello da Messina, in Room 11.

In the salon of Flemish paintings rests the celebrated ***Triptych of Malvagna*** ★★, the creation of Mabuse, whose real name was Jean Gossaert. His 1510 work depicts a Madonna and Bambino surrounded by singing angels with musical instruments.

Via Alloro 4, Palazzo Abatellis. ✆ **091-6230011.** Admission 8€ adults, 4€ children. Tues–Sun 9am–1:30pm and 2:30–6:30pm. Bus: 103, 105, or 139.

Museo Archeologico Regionale ★★★ MUSEUM This is one of the grandest archaeological museums in Italy, stuffed with artifacts from prehistoric times to the Roman era. Spread over several buildings, the oldest from the 13th century, the museum's collection includes major Sicilian finds from the

THE oratories OF GIACOMO SERPOTTA: PALERMO'S *PUTTI*-PALOOZA

You'll quickly notice that among Palermo's artistic attractions, there's a lot of talk about *oratorio* this or *oratorio* that. These private places for prayer at several churches around town are justly famous for their fantastic rococo decorations, alive with delightful and remarkably three-dimensional stuccoes, executed by native son Giacomo Serpotta in the early 18th century. In the case of the three listed below, the attached church is far less interesting than its *oratorio*. Admission to all three is free, but pay attention to the limited opening hours.

The **Oratorio di San Lorenzo ★★** (Via dell'Immacolatella; ✆ **091-332779;** Mon 3–6pm, Tues–Fri 9am–1pm and 3–5:30pm, Sat 9am–1pm) was his earliest such work—the walls are filled with playful white *putti* (cherubs) blowing bubbles or kissing over the architectonic elements, which are also in white stucco. The effect is disarmingly dynamic, like the whole place is inhaling and exhaling around you. At the more polychrome **Oratorio del Rosario di San Domenico ★★** (Via dei Bambinai; ✆ **091-332779;** same hours as Oratorio di San Lorenzo), another profusion of charming *putti* frames more introspective statues of the Christian virtues. Lastly, the all-white **Oratorio di Santa Cita ★★★** (Via Valverde 3; ✆ **091-332779;** Mon–Sat 9am–1pm) is Serpotta's crowning achievement. His cherubs and angels romp with abandon, delightfully climbing onto the window frames or spreading garlands of flowers in their path. They can also be seen sleeping, eating, and simply hugging their knees deep in thought, like a day care full of the most adorable toddlers imaginable.

Phoenician, Punic, Greek, Roman, and Saracen periods, with several noteworthy treasures from Egypt. Even though some of the exhibitions appear shabby and the museum is definitely not state of the art, its treasures are worth wading through the dust to see.

You'll pass through small **cloisters ★** on the ground floor, centered on a lovely hexagonal 16th-century fountain bearing a statue of Triton. In Room 3 is some rare Phoenician art, including a pair of **sarcophagi** that date from the 5th century B.C.

In Room 4 is the ***Pietra di Palermo,*** a black diorite slab known as the Rosetta Stone of Sicily. Dating from 2700 B.C., and discovered in Egypt in the 19th century, it was intended for the British Museum. Somehow, because of red tape, it got left behind in Palermo. It contains carved hieroglyphics detailing information about the pharaohs, including the delivery of 40 shiploads of cedar to Snefru.

The most important treasures of the museum, in Room 13, are the **metopes of Selinunte ★★**. These finds were unearthed at the temples of Selinunte, once one of the major cities of Magna Graecia (Greek colonies along the coast of southern Italy). The Selinunte sculptures are remarkable for their beauty, casting a light on the brilliance of Siceliot sculpture in general. Displayed are three magnificent metopes from Temple C, a quartet of splendid metopes from Temple E, and, in the center, a 5th-century bronze statue, **Ephebe of Selinunte ★**. These decorative friezes cover the period from the 6th century B.C. to the 5th century B.C., depicting such scenes as Perseus slaying Medusa, the rape of Europa by Zeus, and Actaeon being transformed into a stag.

Etruscan antiquities grace Rooms 14 to 17. Discoveries at the Tuscan town of Chisu, such as the unearthing of funereal *cippi* (stones), shed more light on these mysterious people. The **Oinochoe Vase,** from the 6th century B.C., is one of the most detailed artifacts of Etruscan blackened earthenware (called *bucchero*).

Other exhibit halls on the ground floor display underwater archaeology, with the most complete collection of **ancient anchors,** mostly Punic and Roman, in the world.

Finds from Greek and Roman sites in western Sicily are to be seen on the second floor in Rooms 2 and 12. Here are more artifacts from Selinunte and other ancient Sicilian sites such as Marsala, Segesta, Imera, and Randazzo. These include **funereal aedicules** (openings framed by two columns, an entablature, and usually a pediment), **oil lamps,** and **votive terra cottas.**

In Room 7 is a remarkable and rare series of large Roman bronzes, including the most impressive, a supremely realistic **bronze ram ★★**, a Hellenistic work from Siracusa. It's certainly worth the climb up the steps. Another notable work here is ***Hercules Killing the Stag*** **★**, discovered at Pompeii, a Roman copy of a Greek original from the 3rd century B.C. In Room 8, the most remarkable sculpture is ***Satyr Filling a Drinking Cup*** **★**, a Roman copy of a Praxitelean original.

On the third floor is a prehistoric collection along with Greek ceramics, plus Roman mosaics and frescoes. The highlight of the collection is panels illustrating ***Orpheus with Wild Animals*** **★**, from the 3rd century A.D.

Piazza Olivella 24. ✆ **091-6116805.** Admission 4€ adults, 3€ children. Tues–Sat 8:30am–2pm and 2:30–6:30pm; Sun–Mon 8:30am–1:30pm. Bus: 101, 102, 103, 104, or 107.

Palazzo dei Normanni ★★ and Cappella Palatina ★★★ PALACE

This is Palermo's greatest attraction and Sicily's finest treasure-trove. Allow 1½ hours and visit this site if you have to skip all the rest. The history goes back to the days of the Arab emirs and their harems around the 9th century, but they in time abandoned the site. Discovered by the conquering Normans, the palace was restored and turned into a sumptuous residence. Today it is the seat of Sicily's semiautonomous regional government. If you enter from Piazza Indipendenza you'll be directed to the splendid **Cappella Palatina ★★★**, representing the apex of the Arab-Norman collective genius and built from 1130 to 1140 by Roger II when it was adorned with extraordinary Byzantine mosaics. Along with the much-larger cycle of mosaics up the hill at Monreale cathedral (see "Side Trips from Palermo," later in this section), these are on par with the world-class mosaics in Ravenna or Istanbul.

The interior of Palermo's Cappella Palatina.

Chiesa di Santa Cita.

At the entrance to the nave is a royal throne encrusted in mosaics. Note the towering **Paschal Candelabrum ★** carved with figures, wild animals, and acanthus leaves, a masterpiece from the 12th century. Covering the central nave is a honeycomb stalactite wooden ***muqarnas* ceiling ★★**, a masterpiece and the creation of Arab artisans brought in from North Africa. They depicted scenes from daily life, including animal hunts and dances.

Expect tight security as you wander around the **Royal Apartments ★★** above, because this is still a seat of government. On some days you may not gain entrance at all. When visits are possible, you enter Salone d'Ercole from 1560, the chamber of the Sicilian Parliament. The most intriguing room of the apartments is the Sala di Ruggero II, where King Roger himself slumbered. The room is decorated with 12th-century mosaics like the chapel just visited.

Piazza del Parlamento. www.ars.sicilia.it. ✆ **091-626833.** Admission 8.50€, free for children 17 and under. Admission 7€ Tues–Thurs, when the Royal Apartments are closed due to Parliamentary meetings. Mon–Sat 8:15am–5pm; Sun 8:15am–12:15pm. Bus: 104, 105, 108, 109, 110, 118, 304, or 309.

San Giovanni degli Eremiti ★ CHURCH This is one of the most famous of all the Arab-Norman monuments still standing in Palermo. It is certainly the most romantic building remaining from the heyday of Norman Palermo. Since 1132, this church with its series of five red domes has remained one of the most characteristic landmarks on the Palermo skyline. It is located on the western edge of the Albergheria district.

With an atmosphere appropriate for the recluse it honors, St. John of the Hermits (now deconsecrated), this is one of the most idyllic spots in Palermo. A medieval veil hangs heavily in the gardens, with their citrus blossoms and flowers, especially on a hot summer day as you wander around the cloister.

A single nave divides the simple interior into two bays, surmounted by a dome. A small cupola tops the presbytery. The right-hand apse is covered by one of the red domes. Surrounding the left-hand apse is a bell tower with pointed windows; it, too, is crowned by one of the church's red domes.

The small late Norman **cloister ★**, with a Moorish cistern in the center, was part of the original Benedictine monastery that once stood here. It has little round arches supported by fine paired columns.

Via dei Benedettini 3. ✆ **091-6515019.** Admission 6€ adults; 3€ students, seniors, and children. Tues–Sat 9am–1pm and 3–7pm; Sun 9am–6:30pm. Bus: 109 or 318.

Villa Malfitano ★★ HISTORIC HOME One of Palermo's great villa palaces, built in the Liberty style, sits within a spectacular **garden ★★**. The villa was constructed in 1886 by Joseph Whitaker, grandson of the famous English gentleman and wine merchant Ingham, who moved to Sicily in 1806 and made a fortune producing Marsala wine. Whitaker had trees shipped to Palermo from all over the world to plant around his villa. These included such rare species as Dragon's Blood, an enormous banyan tree and the only one found in Europe. Local high society flocked here for lavish parties, and even British royalty visited. In World War II, Gen. George Patton temporarily stayed here as he planned the invasion of southern Italy. The villa today is lavishly furnished with antiques and artifacts from all over the world. The **Sala d'Estate (Summer Room)** is particularly stunning, with *trompe l'oeil* frescoes covering the walls and ceiling.

Via Dante 167. ✆ **091-6816133.** Admission 6€. Mon–Sat 9am–1pm. Bus: 103, 106, 108, 122, 134, 164, or 824.

Where to Eat

Sometimes, Palermo can leave you so drained that you lose your motivation to seek out the best restaurants. Thankfully, there are also plenty of options for informal, cafe, or take-away fare that can be just as authentic, and certainly a whole lot less expensive, than dining out in the traditional sense. Two pillars of the Palermitan food scene that fit this bill, Antico Caffè Spinnato and Antica Focacceria San Francesco, are listed below. Dirt-cheap, locally revered street food can be found at **I Cuochini,** near Piazza Politeama (see the "Street Eats" box, below). The gourmet wine and food shop **Cibus,** in the Shopping section, has a dining room/cafeteria, and legendary pastry shops like **Mazzara ★**, Via Generale Magliocco 19 (✆ **091-321443**), will fill you up with cassata, cannoli, *frutta martorana* (marzipan sweets), and gelato. There's no shame in doing a hotel room picnic after a chaotic day of negotiating Palermo.

Antica Focacceria San Francesco.

MEN OF dishonor

In Sicily, they don't call it the Mafia (from the Arabic *mu'afah*, or "protection"). They call it Cosa Nostra, literally "our thing," but, more accurately, "this thing we have." Its origins are debated, but the world's most famed criminal organization seemed to grow out of the convergence of local agricultural overseers working for absentee Bourbon landowners—hired thugs, from the peasant workers' point of view.

Members of the Sicilian Mafia (or "Men of Honor," as they like to be called) traditionally operated as a network of regional bosses who controlled individual towns by setting up puppet regimes of thoroughly corrupt officials. It was a sort of devil's bargain with the national Christian Democrat Party, which controlled Italy's government from World War II until 1993 and, despite its law-and-order rhetoric, tacitly left Cosa Nostra alone as long as the bosses got out the party vote.

The Cosa Nostra trafficked in illegal goods, of course, but until the 1960s and 1970s, its income was derived mainly from low-level protection rackets, funneling state money into its own pockets, and ensuring that public contracts were granted to fellow *mafiosi* (all reasons why Sicily has experienced grotesque unchecked industrialization and modern growth at the expense of its heritage and the good of its communities). But the younger generation of Mafia underbosses got into the highly lucrative heroin and cocaine trades in the 1970s, transforming the Sicilian Mafia into a world player on the international drug-trafficking circuit—and raking in the dough. This ignited a clandestine Mafia war that, throughout the late 1970s and 1980s, generated headlines of bloody Mafia hits. The new generation was wiping out the old and turning the balance of power in their favor.

This situation gave rise to the first Mafia turncoats, disgruntled ex-bosses and rank-and-file stoolies who told their stories, first to police prefect Gen. Carlo Alberto Dalla Chiesa (assassinated 1982) and later to crusading magistrates Giovanni Falcone (killed May 23, 1992) and Paolo Borsellino (murdered July 19, 1992), who staged the "maxitrials" of *mafiosi* that sent hundreds to jail. The magistrates' 1992 murders, especially, garnered public attention to the dishonorable methods that defined the new Mafia and, perhaps for the first time, began to stir true shame.

On a broad and culturally important scale, it is these young *mafiosi,* without a moral center or check on their powers, who have driven many Sicilians to at least secretly break the unwritten code of *omertà,* which translates as "homage" but means "silence," when faced with harboring or even tolerating a man of honor. The Mafia still exists in Palermo, the small towns south of it, and the provincial capitals of Catania, Trapani, and Agrigento. Throughout the rest of Sicily, its power has been slipping. The heroin trade is a far cry from construction schemes and protection money, and the Mafia is swiftly outliving its usefulness and its welcome.

Antica Focacceria San Francesco ★ ☺ SICILIAN/SNACKS All visitors need to make at least one stop at this local favorite, a tradition since 1834, in the Palazzo Reale/Monte di Pietà district. Nearly every kid in Palermo has feasted on its stuffed focaccia sandwiches and other inexpensive eats. High ceilings and marble floors evoke the era in which the eatery was born; the food has changed little since. You can still get *panino con la milza* (real hair-on-your-chest fare: a bread roll stuffed with slices of boiled spleen and melted cheese). The *panelle* (deep-fried chickpea fritters) are marvelous, as are the *arancini di riso* (rice balls stuffed with tomatoes and peas or mozzarella). Try the specialty, *focaccia farcita* (flat pizza baked with various fillings). AFSF also has a proper sit-down restaurant with tables in the lovely piazza out front.

Via A. Paternostro 58. www.afsf.it. ✆ **091-320264.** Sandwiches 3€–5€; main courses 8€–16€. AE, DC, MC, V. Apr–Sept daily 11am–11pm; Oct–Mar Wed–Mon 11am–11pm. Bus: 103, 105, or 225.

Antico Caffè Spinnato ★★ SICILIAN/SNACKS Established in 1860, this is the most opulent cafe in its neighborhood. Set on a quiet, pedestrian-only street, it's the focal point for residents of the surrounding Via della Libertà district, thanks to its lavish displays of sandwiches, pastries, and ice creams. Buy coffee at the bar and be tempted by the elaborate cannoli and almond cakes. If you're hungry, sit at a tiny table—either indoors or out—for one of the succulent *piatti del giorno*. (These include fresh salads, grills, and succulent pastas such as spaghetti with sea urchins.) In the evenings, the focus shifts from coffee to cocktails, and from pastries to platters. Live music entertains the nighttime crowd.

Via Principe di Belmonte 115. www.spinnato.it. ✆ **091-583231.** Pastries 1.50€–3€; platters 4€–12€. AE, DC, MC, V. Daily 7am–1am. Bus: 101, 104, 107, or 806.

Casa del Brodo ★ SICILIAN For more than a century, this Palermitan institution in the Palazzo Reale/Monte di Pietà neighborhood has handsomely fed some of the island's most discerning palates, such as the late Count Giuseppe Tasca of Almerita, once Sicily's premier vintner. In its two intimate, plainly decorated rooms, it attracts an equal number of locals and visitors, its atmosphere unchanged over the years.

With a name like "House of Broth," you could well imagine that broth is its specialty. And in truth, there is no kettle of broth finer in all of Sicily than that served here. But Casa del Brodo has many other dishes, too, including *macco di fave* (meatballs and tripe), a recipe that seems long forgotten in the kitchens of most Sicilians today. The one specialty we always order is *carni bollite* (boiled meats). Trust us: It may not sound enticing, but it is a tantalizing assortment of tender, herb-flavored meats, especially good when preceded by a savory risotto with fresh asparagus.

Corso Vittorio Emanuele 175. www.casadelbrodo.it. ✆ **091-321655.** Reservations recommended. Main courses 8€–16€; fixed-price menus from 20€. DC, MC, V. Wed–Mon 12:30–3pm and 7:30–11pm (closed Sun June–Sept). Bus: 103, 104, 105, 118, or 225.

Il Baro ★ SICILIAN/PIZZA North of the old quarter, just off Via della Libertà, Il Baro is like an old friend, a shelter in the storm of crazy Palermo where you can count on a solid, satisfying meal at a reasonable price. Come to this comfortable and unpretentious restaurant—with its rustic exposed wooden beams, bricks, and terra cotta—for a huge menu of traditional Sicilian pastas, meats, and fish dishes, and 12 different kinds of pizza! Try the linguine Bronte (with prawns and pistachios). They also have meal-size salads—a rarity at Palermo restaurants.

Via Mario Rutelli 20. www.ilbaro.net. ✆ **091-303110.** Main dishes 8€–16€; pizzas from 5€. AE, MC, V. Tues–Sun 7:45pm–midnight.

Le Delizie di Cagliostro ★ 🎁 SICILIAN/INTERNATIONAL The restaurant that bears his name celebrates the dubious achievements of Sicily's most successful (and, ultimately, tragic) swindler, Giuseppe Balsamo (alias Count Cagliostro; 1743–95). His mystical mumbo jumbo and sleight of hand looted the purses and pride of commoners and aristocrats alike (including Marie Antoinette), earning him a respected place in the pantheon of noteworthy Sicilian rogues.

STREET eats

Are you steely of stomach? Is the phrase "barbecued goat intestines" more appetizing than revolting? If so, you'll definitely want to try out some of the street food *(cibo di strada)* in markets like Capo, Ballarò, and Vucciria. Real Palermitans go crazy for this stuff, and you'll earn major street cred if you step up to the challenge.

Slaughterhouse leftovers play a starring role on the "menu" at these stands, so you might be better off not asking what's in there. No matter what stewed organ they're hawking—all organs and medleys thereof are fair game—Palermo's colorful *cibo di strada* vendors will unfailingly tell you it's the most *pregiato* (prized) piece of the animal. Sure, many of these nondescript meats will tempt you with their aromas, but it's only fair to disclose that *stigghiola* is essentially barbecued goat intestines, and that *pane con milza* sandwich consists of chopped spleen on a roll of bread. (You go in thinking, "Piece of cake, it's just a modified Sloppy Joe," but those decommissioned red blood cells are an acquired taste.) At Antica Focacceria San Francesco, the spleen bits are churned in a huge, ominous-looking cauldron.

On the less daring side, try *sfincione,* a typical Palermitan pizza with tomatoes, anchovies, onion, and grated cheese, but you'll get bonus points for ordering *babaluci,* baby snails with olive oil, garlic, and fennel. Craving stadium food? Have *pane con salsiccia,* an herb-y Sicilian riff on bratwurst on a roll. If you are vegetarian, try a delicious *pane e panelle* sandwich. *Panelle* are discs of fried chickpeas and universally adored by *cibo di strada* newbies. Least bizarre of all, *arancine* are another typical Sicilian snack and easy to eat on the go. These deep-fried rice balls with mozzarella or meat inside will cost you about 1€ each. Where to find the best *arancine* in town is highly debatable, but a surefire bet is **I Cuochini,** Via Ruggero Settimo 68 (✆ **091-581158;** closed Sun), which also does excellent renditions of a number of the aforementioned street treats.

Set on a busy boulevard in a commercial neighborhood, the restaurant boasts vaulted 18th-century ceilings covered with *trompe l'oeil* frescoes. Once you get past the overweening presence of the ghost of the count, you can sit back and enjoy the cuisine. Market-fresh ingredients go into dishes such as risotto with shrimp, cream, and curry; mushroom-stuffed crepes; and that Palermo favorite, pasta with fresh sardines. The platter of grilled vegetables, their flavors enhanced with olive oil and balsamic vinegar, is succulent.

Corso Vittorio Emanuele 150. www.ledeliziedicagliostro.it. ✆ **091-332818.** Reservations recommended. Main courses 7€–15€. AE, DC, MC, V. Daily noon–2pm and 7pm–midnight. Bus: 101, 102, or 105.

Lo Scudiero ★★ SICILIAN Set directly across the busy street from the Teatro Politeama Garibaldi (site of the Galleria d'Arte Moderno) is this cozy restaurant and brasserie (its name translates as "the Shield Bearer"). Do not confuse it with the grander and more expensive restaurant with a roughly similar name out in the suburbs near the soccer stadium. Honest, straightforward, and unpretentious, it's favored by locals, many of whom work or live in the nearby Libertà neighborhood. Fine raw materials and skilled hands in the kitchen produce such tempting dishes as grilled swordfish flavored with garlic and a touch of mint. The fish served here is really fresh, as the owner buys it every day at the market. This place gets our vote for some of Palermo's best roulades, grilled veal rolls with a stuffing of ground salami and herbs. Vegetarians can opt for the medley of grilled vegetables with balsamic vinegar and olive oil.

Via Turati 7. ✆ **091-581628.** Reservations recommended. Main courses 8€–18€. AE, DC, MC, V. Mon–Sat 12:30–3pm and 7:30–11pm. Closed Aug 10–20. Bus: 101 or 107.

Mi Manda Picone ★★ WINE BAR I like to come here for three reasons: to sample the excellent and well-chosen Sicilian wines, to enjoy the tasty food at affordable prices, and to admire the facade of that Romanesque gem, Chiesa di San Francesco. The specialty here is wine, mostly from Sicily (450 kinds), accompanied by platters of hearty, robust food. Sit on the terrace in front of the church or retreat to the woodsy, medieval-style interior, which once functioned as a stable. Light snacks include stuffed and deep-fried vegetables; a marvelous flan of fava beans and pecorino cheese; fresh salads; and antipasti platters. More substantial fare includes grilled tuna or swordfish steaks with capers and black pepper. The famous Antica Focacceria San Francesco is across the street.

Via Alessandro Paternostro 59 (Piazza San Francesco d'Assisi). ✆ **091-6160660.** Main courses 9€–16€; wine 4€–10€ per glass. AE, MC, V. Mon–Sat 7–11pm. Bus: 103, 108, or 164.

Osteria dei Vespri ★★ SICILIAN/ITALIAN This consistently delicious and atmospheric spot, on the ground floor of the elegant baroque Palazzo Gangi, is where Palermitans take out-of-towners for well crafted twists on local cuisine in an intimate, old-fashioned setting. The pasta dish that merits the most raves is ravioli with ricotta and fresh basil, homemade tomato sauce, eggplant, and crispy onion. An imaginative use of ingredients continues with such delights as swordfish Cordon Bleu, with almonds, oregano, and ginger, or the braised beef with Nero d'Avola red wine and wild fennel on a potato purée with glazed onions. The wine list, with literally hundreds of vintages, is the best in town.

Piazza Croce dei Vespri 6. www.osteriadeivespri.it. ✆ **091-6171631.** Reservations recommended. Main courses 10€–18€; fixed-price menu 45€. AE, DC, MC, V. Mon–Sat 1–3pm and 8:30pm–midnight. Closed 2 weeks in Aug. Bus: 103 or 105.

Santandrea ★★ SEAFOOD/SICILIAN More chic than those restaurants listed above, this spot has alfresco and inside tables and daily specials on its menu. Thanks to its location in the heart of the Vucciria market, Santandrea features only the freshest vegetables and seafood. The waiter will recite the day's specials with obvious pleasure; go with the mixed antipasti, which always features fresh seafood. The pasta dishes are excellent, notably spaghetti prepared with sea urchins, a local delicacy, or spaghetti with fresh sardines. A friend describes Santandrea as "just the place you are always looking for—the right combination of great inventive dishes with amazing ingredients and a relaxed, hip setting."

Piazza Sant'Andrea 4. ✆ **091-334999.** Reservations required. Main courses 9€–18€. AE, MC, V. Mon–Sat 8–11:30pm. Closed Aug 13–17. Bus: 101, 103, 104, or 107.

Shopping

Like any big Italian city, the shopping in Palermo is great, from upscale housewares and designer shoes to street-market trinkets. The national brand names—Benetton, Frette, Max & Co., and the like—are along Via Roma and Via Ruggero

Shopperse at Vucciria, one of Palermo's main markets.

Settimo, while more independent, often fancy boutiques are tucked into a lot of the side streets between Piazza Politeama and Teatro Massimo.

Epicures can pay homage to Sicilian food and wine at the excellent gourmet shop **Cibus ★★**, Via Emerico Amari 64, just east of Piazza Politeama (www.cibus.pa.it; ✆ **091-6122651**), which also serves top-notch hot food in a rear dining area. If you've been traveling the island and discovering all of Sicily's wonderful wines, Cibus sells the best from each region and grape.

For ceramics, **De Simone,** Via Gaetano Daita 13B (www.lafabbricadellaceramica.it; ✆ **091-6119867**), a family-run business, has been producing quality majolica stoneware since the 1920s. It also offers some of the most tasteful ceramics and some of the finest tiles in Palermo.

Entertainment & Nightlife

The liveliest squares at night, and relatively safe because lots of people are there, are Piazza Castelnuovo and Piazza Verdi. Another "safe zone" is a pedestrian strip flanked by bars and cafes, many with sidewalk tables, along Via Principe di Belmonte, lying between Via Roma and Via Ruggero Settimo. On warm summer evenings, the people of the town can be seen parading along the beach of Mondello (see below) to cool off at one of its myriad waterfront bars.

The young, hip, beautiful, intellectual crowd hangs out in the Kalsa district, an up-and-coming area that has gotten safer and cleaner in recent years. In the Kalsa's Piazza della Rivoluzione, try the ultracool lounge bar **Qvivi ★★** (✆ **091-6168595**), with tables on the square and the most delicious, exotic-inflected buffet, which comes free with the purchase of an *aperitivo* (happy hour drink).

If you're interested in the arts and cultural venues, go by the tourist office (see "Essentials," earlier in this section) and pick up a copy of *Agenda,* which lists cafes or other venues offering live music in summer.

THE ARTS

Palermo is a cultural center of some note, with an opera and ballet season running from November to July. The principal venue for cultural presentations is the restored **Teatro Massimo ★★**, Piazza G. Verdi (www.teatromassimo.it; ✆ **091-6053111**), across from the Museo Archeologico. It boasts the third largest indoor stage in Europe. Francis Ford Coppola shot the climactic opera scene here for *The Godfather: Part III*. The theater was built between 1875 and 1897 in a neoclassical style and reopened after a restoration in 1997 to celebrate its 100th birthday. Ticket prices range from 10€ to 125€. The box office is open Tuesday to Sunday 10am to 3pm. ***Note:*** The Teatro Massimo can be visited Tuesday through Sunday from 10am to 3pm. Visits cost 5€. Guided tours in English are given Tuesday through Saturday from 10am to 3pm (bus: 101, 102, 103, 104, 107, 122, or 225).

Where to Stay

Choose your hotel carefully in Palermo. Safe, central locations are an important consideration in this town. Luckily, even the ritziest hotels in Palermo will cost you about 50% less than the same standard of accommodations in Rome or Florence.

Excelsior Hilton ★ Even though it was completely restored in 2005, this nostalgic favorite still exudes much of the aura of the 19th century. It was built for the National Exhibition of 1891, when it was called Hotel de la Paix. Much of the Art Nouveau style of that elegant era remains, at least in the public rooms with their atmosphere of Palermitan Belle Epoque. The location is in a quiet neighborhood at the northern end of Via della Libertà. Bedrooms range from midsize to large and have been completely modernized, with a well-equipped private bathroom. Many rooms open on a view of the hotel garden. The formal restaurant, where the staff is elegantly uniformed, serves first rate Sicilian and International dishes.

Via Marchese Ugo 3, 90141 Palermo. www.excelsiorpalermo.it. ✆ **091-7909001.** Fax 091-342139. 117 units. 110€–270€ double; from 275€ junior suite. Rates include buffet breakfast. AE, DC, MC, V. Parking 20€. Bus: 101, 104, 107, 108, or 806. **Amenities:** Restaurant; bar; babysitting; concierge, exercise room; room service. *In room:* A/C, TV, minibar, Wi-Fi (5€ per hour).

Grand Hotel et Des Palmes ★ The top address for reliving bygone Palermitan glamour, this was once the city's prime setting for trysts and intrigue. A recent sprucing up of the property has taken away some of the nostalgia—but made rooms much more modern and comfortable. Budget travelers needn't shy away from this place—even suites can be had for close to 200€. Even if you don't stay here, step in for a gander at the lobby or a drink at the bar. It's decadent and sultry, and as one Sicilian friend describes it, *palermitano da morire* ("ridiculously Palermitan").

Via Roma 398. www.amthotels.it/despalmes. ✆ **091-6028111.** 180 units. 115€–193€ double; 250€–315€ suite. AE, DC, MC, V. Free parking. **Amenities:** Restaurant; bar; concierge; fitness room; room service. *In room:* A/C, TV, hair dryer, minibar, Wi-Fi (17€ per day).

Hotel Joli Not to be confused with the Jolly chain, this is an inexpensive hotel on the beautiful old Piazza Ignazio Florio. It's got a prime location in the historic center of Palermo, a few blocks away from Piazza Castelnuovo and the pedestrianized hangout Via Principe di Belmonte. Small to midsize guest rooms are a bit boxy, with cramped bathrooms, but if you're looking to save money and you don't demand elegance, the Joli is a good choice due to its convenient location and cheery staff. Superior rooms are worth the extra euros, as they're almost twice the size of standards and have balconies, some overlooking the square.

Via Michele Amari 11, 90139 Palermo. www.hoteljoli.com. ✆/fax **091-6111765.** 30 units. 62€–98€ double; 115€–128€ junior suite. Rates include buffet breakfast. AE, DC, MC, V. Parking 12€. Bus: 103, 106, or 108. **Amenities:** Bar; babysitting; bikes; room service. *In room:* A/C, TV, hair dryer, Wi-Fi (free).

Hotel Moderno From fussy chandeliers to a preponderance of lugubrious gilt-framed oil paintings, this basic hotel right off the Quattro Canti doesn't live up to its name, but this is nevertheless a cool and comfortable choice for budget travelers. The Moderno has the most central Palermo location possible, but light sleepers beware: This corner sees whizzing traffic at all hours.

Via Roma 276 (at Via Napoli), 90133 Palermo. www.hotelmodernopa.com. ✆/fax **091-588683.** 38 units. 80€ double. AE, DC, MC, V. Parking 15€. Bus: 101, 102, 103, or 107. **Amenities:** Bar. *In room:* A/C, TV.

Principe di Villafranca ★★★ This charming 1998 property is the finest boutique-style hotel in Palermo. Stylish, intimate, and evocative of an elegant, unfussy private home, it occupies two floors of what was originally built as a low-rise apartment house. Its Sicilian theme includes enough antiques and architectural finesse to make you think the place is a lot older than it really is. Grace notes include Oriental rugs, marble floors, vaulted ceilings, and a baronial fireplace. The hotel and some of its neighbors were built within what was once one of Palermo's most beautiful gardens, the Ferriato. Guest rooms are midsize to spacious, with tile, granite, and travertine bathrooms.

Via G. Turrisi Colonna 4, 90141 Palermo. www.principedivillafranca.it. ✆ **091-6118523.** Fax 091-588705. 34 units. 230€–297€ double; 363€ suite. Rates include buffet breakfast. AE, DC, MC, V. Free parking. Bus: 101 or 102. **Amenities:** Restaurant; bar; babysitting; exercise room; room service. *In room:* A/C, TV, hair dryer, minibar, Wi-Fi (4€ per hour).

Ucciardhome ★★ At Palermo's "it" hotel for modernist aesthetes, dark wenge wood furniture contrasts with ivory fabrics for an ultrarelaxing, masculine feel. The comfortable rooms are filled with techno-gadgetry, and the sleek bathrooms are done up in metallic mosaics. The boutique Ucciardhome is in the less chaotic modern side of town, across from the Carcere Ucciardone, a prison and the hotel's namesake. For a contrasting dose of Palermo color, the lively Borgo Vecchio street market, along Via Ettore Ximenes, is just around the corner.

Via Enrico Albanese 34-36. www.hotelucciardhome.com. ✆ **091-348426.** 14 units. 140€–200€ double. AE, DC, MC, V. **Amenities:** Wine bar; babysitting; concierge; gym. *In room:* A/C, TV, CD player/radio, hair dryer, minibar, Wi-Fi (free).

Villa Igiea ★★★ Newly acquired by Hilton, this consummately Mediterranean property, a peach-toned castle surrounded by fragrant gardens and the sea, is the most luxurious stay in Palermo. Recently updated and spacious guest rooms have understated Art Nouveau decor and all mod-cons. Graceful columns of a Greek temple ruin stand alongside the hotel's kidney-shaped swimming pool, beyond which there's a sheer drop to the sea. The hotel can organize sailing tours of the coast for guests. The Villa Igiea is not in the center of town or near any transportation hubs, which guarantees the utmost tranquillity, but you'll need a car or taxi to go anywhere in the rest of Palermo.

Once the private villa of the Fiorio family, whose claim to fame was coming up with the notion of putting tuna fish into a tin can, the seaside villa hosts the moneyed elite of Sicily when they're in town for business or pleasure.

Salita Belmonte 43, Acquasanta, 90142 Palermo. www.hilton.com. ✆ **091-6312111.** Fax 091-547654. 124 units. 200€–450€ double; 495€–600€ suite. Rates include continental breakfast. AE, DC, MC, V. Free parking. Bus: 139. **Amenities:** Restaurant; bar; airport transfers (95€); babysitting; concierge; saltwater pool; room service; tennis court (lit). *In room:* A/C, TV, hair dryer, minibar, Wi-Fi (20€ per day).

Side Trips from Palermo

MONREALE ★★

10km (6 miles) S of Palermo

The Arab-Norman cathedral of Monreale, famous for its monumental cycle of glittering mosaics, is the classic cultural day trip from Palermo. This site is often compared with Cappella Palatina (p. 871), in Palermo's Palazzo Normanni: Bear in mind that Monreale has the far more extensive mosaics, and you can spend as long as you want looking at them, while in the Cappella Palatina, the scale is smaller and tour groups are sometimes rushed through.

Normans under William II founded a Benedictine monastery at Monreale in the 1170s. Eventually a great cathedral was built near the monastery's ruins. Like the Alhambra in Granada, Spain, the **Duomo di Monreale ★★**, Piazza Guglielmo il Buono (www.cattedraledimonreale.it; ✆ **091-6404413**), has a relatively drab facade, giving little indication of the riches inside. The interior is virtually covered with shimmering **mosaics ★★★** illustrating scenes from the Bible. The artwork provides a distinctly original interpretation of the old, rigid Byzantine form of decoration. The mosaics have an Eastern look despite the Western-style robed Christ reigning over his kingdom. On the north and west facades are two bronze doors depicting biblical stories in relief. The cloisters are also of interest. Built in 1166, they consist of twin mosaic columns, and every other pair bears an original design (the lava inlay was hauled from Mount Etna). Admission to the cathedral is free; if you visit the cloisters, there's a charge of 6€, free for children 17 and under. For 2€ you can climb to terraces on top of the church, all the way up to the bell tower, where there are phenomenal views over the Conca d'Oro (the headlands-framed plain of Palermo) and the sea. The cathedral is open daily 8am to 6pm. From May to September, the cloister is

Detail from the mosaics at Duomo di Monreale.

open daily 9am to 6:30pm; off-season hours are Monday to Saturday from 9am to 6:30pm, Sunday from 9am to 1pm.

Monreale itself is a fun, "real" town despite the constant tourist influx, with a lively main drag, Via Roma. Before or after your visit to the cathedral, drop in at **Bar Italia,** Piazza Vittorio Emanuele (✆ **091-6402421**), near the Duomo. The plain cookies are wonderfully flavorful and fresh; if you go early in the morning, order one of the freshly baked croissants and a cup of cappuccino, Monreale's best.

From Palermo, take bus no. 389 from Piazza Indipendenza, which drops you off at Monreale's Piazza Vittorio Emanuele 45 minutes to 1½ hours later, depending on traffic. During the day, three buses per hour leave for Monreale, costing 1.30€ one-way.

Where to Eat

Taverna del Pavone ★ SICILIAN/ITALIAN The most highly recommended restaurant in Monreale faces a small cobblestone square, about a block uphill from the cathedral. Inside, you're likely to find a friendly greeting, an artfully rustic environment that's akin to an upscale tavern, and tasty Sicilian food. I delighted in the zucchini flowers braised in a sweet-and-sour sauce; a delightful *pennette* with fava-bean sauce; and the house-made *maccheroni,* which was loaded with country cheese and absolutely delicious. For dessert, the most soothing choice might be *semifreddo*—whipped cream folded into ice cream, given extra flavor with baked almonds.

Vicolo Pensato 18. www.tavernadelpavone.eu. ✆ **091-6406209.** Reservations recommended. Main courses 9€–18€. AE, DC, MC, V. Tues–Sun noon–3:30pm and 7:30–11:30pm.

MONDELLO ★★

11km (7 miles) N of Palermo

A crescent bay with shallow, Caribbean-esque water and 2km (1¼ miles) of white sand, an Art Nouveau bathhouse, and a festive atmosphere make Mondello Lido a glorious retreat from crazy Palermo. In summer, and if you have kids especially, it'd be a crime not to spend at least half a day at Mondello. Between the wars, Mondello was a snobbish retreat for the upper crust, evoking the most fashionable parts of the French Riviera. After World War II, it became more democratic, though posh villas can still be seen among the trees in town. Windsurfing and snorkeling are popular here, and the grand **Stabilimento Balneare** (bathing club, now the elegant Le Terrazze restaurant), built on a pier in the middle of the bay in 1913, is a fabulous nugget of the old-fashioned European good life. Mondello is an easy 15-minute bus ride (no. 806 from Piazza Sturzo, near Teatro Politeama) or drive from Palermo.

MONTE PELLEGRINO ★

6km (4 miles) N of Palermo

The parkland and nature preserve of the crown-shaped Monte Pellegrino, what Goethe called "the most beautiful headland on earth," looms over north Palermo. This green oasis and haven from the heat is where Palermitani not bound for Mondello retreat on a summer day (and on Sun, when it's overcrowded and best avoided).

You can reach the mountain with bus no. 812 from Piazza Sturzo (Politeama) in Palermo (30 min.), or with your own car (15–20 min.), following signs to Monte Pellegrino or Santuario Santa Rosalia.

Along the way to the top, you'll be rewarded with some of Sicily's most **panoramic views ★★★**, taking in the old city of Palermo and a sweeping vista of the coastline. Families use the grounds and trails on Pellegrino as a picnic site, but the chief attraction of Monte Pellegrino is the **Santuario di Santa Rosalia** (✆ **091-540326**), a cave where the patron saint of Palermo lived. (Kitschy souvenir hawkers mar the scene somewhat.) Note the little pathway leading to the left of the chapel. If you take it, after about 30 minutes, you'll be at a cliff-top promontory with a view and a statue of the saint. The pathway to the right of the sanctuary leads to the top of Pellegrino, a leisurely hike of about 40 minutes.

SEGESTA ★★

77km (48 miles) W of Palermo

Just west of the town of Alcamo, the A29 spur for Trapani spans an idyllic valley. Drinking in the view, your eyes might wander over to, and then fixate upon in amazement, a certain hilltop south of the roadway. The scene looks fake: Is that a . . . *Greek temple* up there? You squint your eyes, and logic tells you it's either a mirage or some modern reconstruction. Ruins are never that perfect. But Segesta's single, preposterously picturesque Doric temple, sitting like an ornament atop a lonely crest amid forested vales, is 100% authentic. Segesta may be a one-trick pony, but the temple is so well preserved and so romantically situated that it's reason enough to add this pocket of western Sicily to your itinerary. It takes about an hour to get here from Palermo, and because it's so close to the highway, it makes a good brief stop en route to **Erice** (see below).

Segesta was the ancient city of the Elymi, a people of mysterious origin who are linked by some to the Trojans. As the major city in western Sicily, it was brought into a series of conflicts with the rival power nearby, Selinus (Selinunte). From the 6th to 5th centuries B.C., there were near-constant hostilities. The Athenians came from the east to aid the Segestans in 415 B.C., but the expedition ended in disaster, eventually forcing the city to turn to Hannibal of Carthage.

The *teatro* atop Mount Barbaro.

Twice in the 4th century B.C., Segesta was besieged and conquered, once by Dionysius, again by Agathocles (a brutal victor who tortured, mutilated, or made slaves of most of the citizenry). Segesta, in time, turned on its old but dubious ally, Carthage. Like all Greek cities of Sicily, it ultimately fell to the Romans.

The main sight in Segesta is its remarkable **Doric temple ★★★** from the 5th century B.C. Although never completed, it's in an excellent state of preservation. (The entablature still remains.) The temple was far enough away from the ancient town to escape being leveled during the "scorched earth" days of the Vandals and Arabs. From its position on a hill, the Doric temple commands a majestic setting. Although you can scale the hill on foot, you may encounter boys trying to hustle you for a donkey ride. (I advise against it—some of these poor animals have saddle sores and seem to be in pain when ridden.)

The site is open daily from 9am to 5pm (ticket office closes at 4pm); admission costs 6€.

After visiting the temple, you can take a bus (2€) to the large 3rd-century-B.C. ***teatro*** **★** (theater), at the top of Mount Barbaro at 431m (1,414 ft.). There's no further admission charged at the theater; you can also theoretically walk up there, though it's a steep hike. (If you're on the fence about doing the theater, keep in mind that the heights of Monte Barbaro are what allow you to get those priceless postcard **views of the temple below ★★★**, otherwise hard to photograph from right in front.) The theater was constructed in a semicircle with a diameter of 63m (207 ft.) and hewn right out of the side of the mountain, its stage area facing to the north. In antiquity, the theater could hold as many as 4,000 spectators, and the site is still used for the staging of both modern and classical plays presented from mid-July to early August every other year.

There are approximately four **trains** per day between Palermo and Segesta, and buses leave almost hourly. The station is about a 1km (½-mile) walk to the ancient site. Special bus service is usually offered in conjunction with the evening plays. For information, contact the tourist office in Palermo. By **car,** drive 57km (35 miles) west from Palermo along A29, then take the A29 *diramazione* (branch) toward Trapani; after 7km (4⅓ miles) take the Segesta exit and follow the signs to the archaeological site.

ERICE ★★

112km (70 miles) W of Palermo

The town of Erice commands an aerie-like position just inland from Trapani; in just minutes, you can be whisked via cable car away from the bustle of that busy port city and up a rugged slope to the gates of medieval Erice. From its thrilling mountaintop setting, two sheer cliffs drop 755m (2,478 ft.) to vistas across the plains of western Sicily and down the coast. On a clear day, you can see Cap Bon in Tunisia, but Erice is often shrouded in a mist that only adds to the mystique (or, in winter, the misery; temperatures can plummet below Sicilian norms and snow and hail are not uncommon).

Sleepy Erice is a lovely place to spend an afternoon wandering the medieval streets, with their baroque balconies and flowering vines, and drinking in the vistas. The southwest corner of town contains the Villa Balio gardens, originally laid out in the 19th century. Beyond the gardens, a path winds along the cliff edge up to Erice's highest point, the **Castello di Venere ★**, today little more than crumbling Norman-era walls surrounding the sacred site where a temple to

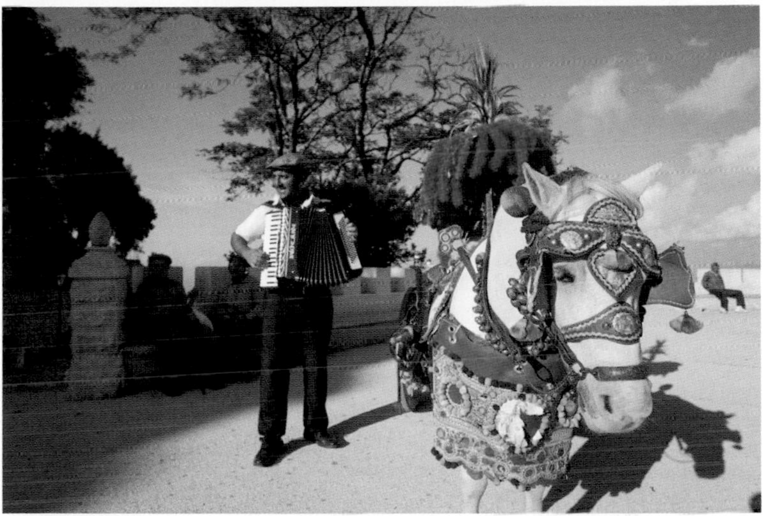

A traditionally dressed street musician and his horse in Erice.

Venus once stood. Piercing the walls are several windows and doorways with spectacular views across the countryside.

You probably don't need to spend the night here—Erice is easy to visit not only from Palermo but from anywhere you might be based in western Sicily.

Erice is noted for its pastries. Stop off at **Pasticceria Grammatico,** Via Vittorio Emanuele 14, near Piazza Umberto (www.mariagrammatico.it; ✆ **0923-869390**), to sample sugary almond treats flavored with lemon. For lunch, try the homey and delicious **Ristorante Monte San Giuliano ★**, Vicolo San Rocco 7 (www.montesangiuliano.it; ✆ **0923-869595**), and order the *busiati San Giuliano*.

It's most fun to reach Erice by means of the **Funivia Trapani-Erice** cable car (www.funiviaerice.it; ✆ **0923-569306;** 6.50€ round-trip). The 10-minute ride covers 3.1km (2 miles) in length and a vertical distance of 663m (2,175 ft.). The lower station is in Trapani at the corner of route SP31 and Via Capua, in the Casa Santa district, where you can find free street parking. (The Funivia is sometimes closed in the winter for maintenance, so check the website or call first.) However, you can also drive yourself all the way to Erice: Follow the A29 southwest from Palermo or Segesta to the first Trapani exit, then continue along the switchback road up the mountain. The least attractive option is by rail: First take a train to Trapani, which is 14km (8½ miles) to the southeast of Erice. Then, from Trapani station, AST buses (www.aziendasicilianatrasporti.it; ✆ **840-000323**) depart from Piazza Montalto in Trapani, but these only run every few hours and can take up to an hour to reach Erice.

CEFALÙ ★★

68km (42 miles) E of Palermo, 213km (132 miles) NW of Taormina

Picturesque Cefalù, east of Palermo on the northern coast of Sicily, is where Giuseppe Tornatore shot most of 1988's *Cinema Paradiso* (rent it before you go), and despite a considerable influx of northern European sun seekers in summer, it's still a working fishing village where everyone seems to be named Salvatore. The seaside town is a great place to dip your toes in the Med as well as see one of the most imposing Norman churches in Sicily. Cefalù's 1131 **Duomo** (Piazza del Duomo; **© 091-922021;** daily 8am–noon and 3:30–7pm; free admission), supposedly ordered built by the Norman King Roger II when he landed on a nearby beach after surviving a terrible storm at sea, has a fortresslike facade, emphasized by the two spired and mullioned towers that flank it. Immediately behind the cathedral is the Rocca, a towering, 278m (912-ft.) rock cliff that enhances the Duomo's formidable aspect. The Greeks thought the Rocca evoked a head, so they named the village Kephalos, which in time became Cefalù.

The swimming and sunbathing part of Cefalù is its western, modern end, along Lungomare Giardina, where gentle breakers lap at a narrow but well-used strip of white sand. Farther east, the beach is packed with European vacationers, while it's a bit broader and less crowded to the west.

Cefalù is 1 hour (68km/42 miles) from Palermo, making it a popular day-trip destination. Take the E90 east to the A20 east, toward Messina. Exit at Cefalù and follow signs to the *"centro."* You can also take the train (1 hr.) or a bus (1½ hr.) from Palermo. A few hours' tour of the town is also a nice way to break up the drive between Palermo and Taormina (another 2 hr. east and south), though an overnight stay may be more satisfying.

Hitting the Beach

Cefalù's crescent-shaped beach is one of the best along the northern coast. Regrettably, it's always packed in summer. In town, I prefer **Lido Poseidon,** where you can rent an umbrella and beach lounger from any number of clubs (May–Sept) for 10€. Other recommended beaches are found west of town at Spiaggia Settefrati and Spiaggia Mazzaforno.

Where to Eat & Stay

Al Porticciolo ★ SICILIAN At the seafront of the old town, adjacent to the old port, this restaurant is set within a cavelike room that used to be a storage point for fish before the days of refrigeration. During the day, dine in air-conditioned comfort to avoid the heat, but at night, opt for an outdoor table. The pasta with sardines is well prepared here, but I'm also fond of the *tagliatelle* of octopus, the addictive grilled radicchio, and the country-style kettle of mussel soup—just

CLIMBING THE crag

During the dog days of August, it's a long, hot, sweaty climb up to the top of Cefalù's Rocca, but once you're there, the view is panoramic, one of the grandest in Sicily. If you're stout-hearted, count on 20 minutes to approach the ruins of the so-called Temple of Diana and another 45 huffing and puffing minutes to scale the pinnacle. From Piazza Garibaldi, along Corso Ruggero, a sign—ACCESSO ALLA ROCCA—will launch you on your way. In summer, I recommend taking this jaunt either in the early morning or when evening breezes are blowing.

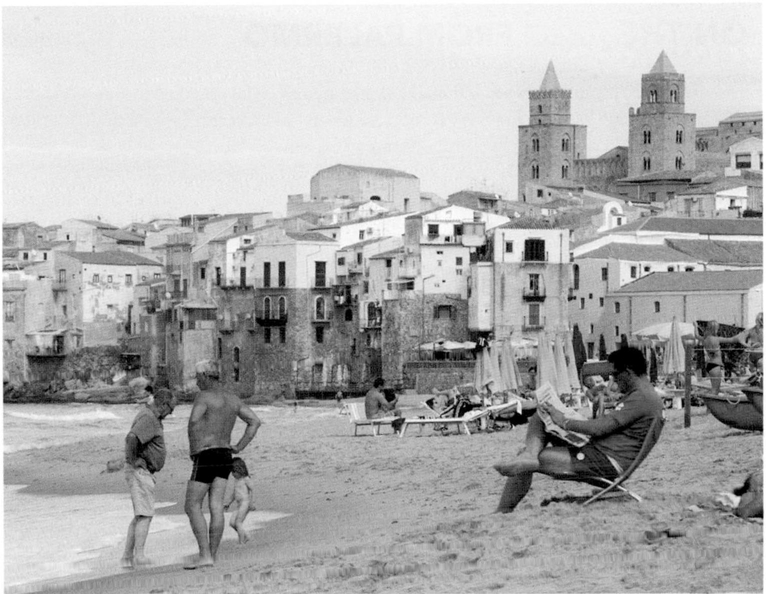

Cefalù's beach.

right for a seafaring town. Their *cassata Siciliana* (layered sponge cake filled with ricotta, chocolate, and candied fruits) is among the best I've tasted.

Via Carlo Ortolani di Bordonaro 66. ✆ **0921-921981.** Main courses 8€–17€. AE, DC, MC, V. Thurs–Tues noon–3pm and 7pm–midnight. Closed Nov to mid-Dec.

Osteria del Duomo ★★ SICILIAN/INTERNATIONAL The hippest, most sophisticated restaurant in Cefalù is right in front of the town's famous cathedral, at the bottom of steps that have been trod upon by Norman knights and *la dolce vita* movie stars alike. Many tables sit in the open air on cobblestones, others under the vaulted ceiling of the air-conditioned interior. The chefs enthrall you with their smoked fish, their seafood salads are the town's best (and the ideal food on a hot summer day), and their truly excellent *carpaccio* of beef will appeal to serious carnivores. Count on freshly made salads and desserts as well.

Via Seminario 3. ✆ **0921-421838.** Reservations recommended Sat–Sun. Main courses 10€–18€. AE, DC, MC, V. Tues–Sun noon–midnight. Closed mid-Nov to mid-Dec.

Riva del Sole ★ The town's finest accommodations are in a three-story building rising along the seafront. Completely refurbished, it has its own discreet charm and harmonious styling in both its public and private rooms. Run by the Cimino family since it opened in 1966, it offers both attentive service and a welcoming atmosphere. Special features include a graceful garden, a solarium, a panoramic terrace, and an intimate bar. Bedrooms are midsize, tastefully furnished, and well-equipped, each with a private balcony or veranda opening onto the water.

Lungomare G. Giardina 25. www.rivadelsole.com. ✆ **0921-421230.** 28 units. 105€–230€ double. AE, DC, MC, V. Free parking. Closed Oct to mid-Dec. **Amenities:** Bar; babysitting; all nonsmoking rooms; room service. *In room:* A/C, TV, minibar.

ON THE road FROM PALERMO

The excursions listed below are within an hour's drive of Cefalù but can just as easily be done while en route on the coastal road between Palermo and Taormina.

Since 1989, some 39,679 hectares (98,049 acres) of the most beautiful land in Sicily has been set aside as the **Parco Naturale Regionale Delle Madonie ★★**. The park contains more than half of the 2,600 plant species known in Sicily. Some of the most ancient rocks and mountains on the island are found here, along with some of the most spectacular peaks. Among them, **Pizzo Carbonara,** at 1,979m (6,493 ft.), is the highest mountain in Sicily outside of Mount Etna.

The park is far from a wilderness—it is inhabited and contains any number of charming villages. To reach it from Cefalù, follow the road directions south for 14km (8¾ miles) to the **Santuario di Gibilmanna.** From the belvedere at this town, in front of the little 17th-century church, you can take in a **panoramic view ★★** of the Madonie, including the peak of Pizzo Carbonara.

The Santuario di Gibilmanna is a shrine to the Virgin Mary. The Madonna is said to have shown signs of life in the 18th century when she was restoring sight to blind pilgrims and speech to a mute. Since the Vatican confirmed this claim, Gibilmanna has been one of the most important shrines in Sicily, drawing the devout.

After taking in the view, continue southeast, following the signs to **Castelbuono,** an idyllic town that grew around a *castello* (castle) constructed in the 1300s. You can stop over to visit its historic core, **Piazza Margherita.** The church, **Madrice Vecchia,** dates from the 14th century, and was built on the ruins of a pagan temple.

If you arrive during the lunch hour, your best bet for a bite to eat is **Romittaggio,** Località San Guglielmo Sud (✆ **0921-671323**), 5km (3 miles) south of Castelbuono. Specializing in simple mountain food, the restaurant is installed in a monastery from the Middle Ages. In summer, you can request a table in the arcades of the cloister. Meals range in price from 8€ to 16€. The restaurant is closed from June 15 to July 15 and on Wednesdays year-round.

The road continues south to **Petralia Soprana ★★**, at 1,147m (3,763 ft.) the loftiest town in Madonie and one of the best-preserved medieval villages of Sicily, with narrow streets and houses of local stone. A grand belvedere is found at Piazza del Popolo, with a **stunning vista ★★** toward Enna in the east.

At Capo Tindari, approximately 85km (53 miles) east from Cefalù, stand the **ruins of Tyndaris** (✆ **0941-369023;** daily 9am to 1 hr. before sunset; 2.10€), on a lonely, rocky promontory overlooking Golfo di Patti. The view alone is reason enough to go; it stretches from Milazzo in the east to Capo Calavà in the west. On a clear day, there are stunning vistas of the Aeolian Islands, with Vulcano the nearest. Though Tyndaris goes back to the Greek era, most of what you see dates to the Roman Empire, including the basilica, beyond which is a **Roman villa** in rather good condition, with some original floor mosaics. Cut into a hill at the end of town is a 4th-century-B.C. **Greek theater.** The ***insula romana,*** an apartment building with ground-floor shops, contains the ruins of baths, patrician villas with fragments of mosaics, and what may have been taverns or drinking halls.

THE AEOLIAN ISLANDS ★★★

Lipari: 30km (19 miles) N of Milazzo; Stromboli: 81km (50 miles) N of Milazzo; Vulcano: 20km (12 miles) N of Milazzo

The Sicilian mainland has so much to offer that you may find it hard to tear yourself away, but off the northeast coast of Sicily, the extraordinary and evocative Aeolian Islands are quite a compelling detour for anyone seeking an unforgettable island vacation. The archipelago is made up of seven islands: Lipari, Vulcano, Salina, Panarea, Stromboli, Filicudi, and distant Alicudi—the visible part of a volcanic system on the cusp of the Eurasian and African plates. The tectonic activity far below has left a major geological legacy, and volcanic activity reigns supreme. Whether in the form of the extinct verdant twin peaks of Salina, the disconcerting rumbling mass of still-active Stromboli, or the bubbling sulfurous mud at Vulcano, each island has its own geographical and geological quirks and its own very distinct character and atmosphere.

Lipari, the main island, offers the widest range of accommodations and most of the nightlife, and as such, is especially favored by young travelers and backpackers. Stromboli and Vulcano are the main draws for geology buffs, but also the focus of the mass tourism of the archipelago, and hordes of German and Italian groups descend in high season. Salina offers relaxation, glorious settings, and spectacular hikes, but little in the way of nightlife. Beautiful Panarea is adored by the very chic in-crowd, while those seeking isolation and communion with nature make for Filicudi and Alicudi.

The rugged terrain of the volcanoes means that the Aeolians are not the spot for the traditional beach holiday; there are few sandy beaches for idle lounging, and wherever you go you tend to be walking uphill. However, for those who like to explore, there are countless coves, inlets, and peaks to investigate both from land and sea, all set off against the blue sky by glorious and rampant vegetation.

Tip: Do not set out for the Aeolians in July or August without accommodations booked.

Essentials

GETTING THERE Milazzo, on the northeast coast of Sicily, is the main port for ferries to the Aeolians, though seasonal service is available from Naples as well. From Milazzo, you can choose between ferries and hydrofoils run by **Siremar** (www.siremar.it; ✆ **91-7493111**) and hydrofoils run by **Ustica Lines** (www.usticalines.it; ✆ **090-9287821**). As per usual, ferries take a little longer (2–4 hr. from Milazzo; from 10€), and cost a little less than hydrofoils (45 min.–2 hr. from Milazzo; from 15€). Because schedules change without notice,

A cove in Salina.

it's best to call or check online for current crossings and prices. It is a good idea to buy tickets in advance, especially in high season (July–Aug) and on weekends throughout the summer.

If you're driving from Messina in the east, take S113 west to Palermo until you come to the turnoff for the port at Milazzo.

GETTING AROUND Island-hopping is easy thanks to frequent ferry and hydrofoil connections operated by **Siremar** and **Ustica Lines** (contact info above). Schedules vary from season to season and are known to change with little notice. For the most up-to-date planning info, especially for your inter-island journeys, consult each company's website.

If you prefer to explore the islands from one base rather than island-hop, Lipari is a good choice. While not the most attractive of the islands, it has a wide range of accommodations at all price ranges and abundant services. However, Salina's position at the heart of the archipelago makes it a charming and practical choice. As far as getting around each island itself, most are small enough to get around on foot, but on Lipari and Salina, local buses shuttle visitors from the port to the main beach areas and other attractions.

VISITOR INFORMATION The **tourist office** in Lipari is at Via Vittorio Emanuele 202 (✆ **090-9880095**). In July and August, it is open Monday to Friday 8:30am to 1:30pm and 4:30 to 7:30pm, Saturday 8am to 2pm. From September to June, hours are Monday to Friday 8:30am to 1:30pm and 4:30 to 7:30pm. There's no information center in Stromboli or Vulcano.

Lipari ★

The largest and most populated island in the Aeolians, and the effective "hub" of the archipelago, Lipari is the administrative center for all of the islands with the exception of Salina, which is autonomous. Lipari town is the only reasonably sized town of the archipelago. While not the most picturesque Italian burg you'll ever clap eyes on, it nevertheless has a small-city feel, and, beyond the gaudy souvenir shops, its historical center has a certain charm, dominated by a 16th-century **Spanish castle.**

Excellent artifacts from the Stone and Bronze ages, as well as relics from Greek and Roman acropolises that once stood here, are housed in the **Museo Archeologico Eoliano ★★**, Via del Castello (✆ **090-9880174**), one of Sicily's major archaeological museums. It houses one of the world's finest Neolithic collections. The oldest discoveries date from 4200 B.C. Lustrous red ceramics, done in what is known as the "Diana style," come from the last Neolithic period, 3000 to 2500 B.C. Other exhibits are reconstructed necropolises from the Middle Bronze Age and a 6th-century-A.D. depiction of Greek warships. Some 1,200 pieces of painted terra cotta from the 4th and 3rd centuries B.C., including stone theatrical masks, are on exhibit. The museum also houses the only Late Bronze Age (8th-c.-B.C.) necropolis found in Sicily. It's open daily 9am to 1:30pm and 3 to 6pm. Admission is 6€.

The most popular **beaches** are at **Canneto,** about a 20-minute walk north of Lipari on the eastern coast, and, just north of it, **Spiaggia Bianca** (named for the white sand, an oddity among the region's black sands). To reach the beach from Canneto, take the waterfront road, climb the stairs of Via Marina Garibaldi, and then veer right down a narrow cobbled path for about 300m (984 ft.).

Acquacalda (Hot Water) is the island's northernmost city, but it's not noted for beaches (the black sand is rocky and unpleasant for walking or lying on). The town also is known for its obsidian and pumice quarries. West of Acquacalda at Quattropani, you can make a steep climb to the **Duomo,** where the point of interest isn't the cathedral but the panoramic view from the church grounds. On the west coast, 4km (2½ miles) from Lipari, the island's other great view is available by making another steep climb to the **Quattrocchi Belvedere.**

Twenty-nine kilometers (18 miles) of road circle the island, connecting all its villages and attractions. Buses run by Lipari's **Autobus Urso Guglielmo,** Via Cappuccini 9 (www.ursobus.com; ✆ **090-9811262**), make 10 circuits of the island per day. Tickets costing 2€ are purchased onboard from the driver. Along the way you'll pass the highlights of Lipari's scenery. It's also possible to summon one of the independently operated taxis, most of which are found at Marina Corta.

WHERE TO EAT & STAY

Filippino ★★ SICILIAN/AEOLIAN The most famous restaurant on the island, Filippino celebrated its centenary in 2010. Very much a family affair, the dining room is run by Filippino's grandson, Antonio Bernardi. The atmosphere is traditionally elegant, with a large covered terrace full of wrought-iron lamps and crisp white linen. The accent is on local produce, fresh fish, and traditional dishes produced with flair. Sicily's Arab influence comes through in couscous with prawns, eggplant, and zucchini, and many of the seafood offerings, like the *mupa,* are specific to the deep waters around the volcanic islands. Finish with that great Sicilian classic, cassata, and a drop of Malvasia. The heavily Sicilian wine list is well priced, and it's possible to escape with a bill of 35€ a head if you're careful; otherwise, with fresh lobster and top-end wines, the sky's the limit.

Piazza Mazzini, Lipari. ✆ **090-9811002.** Reservations required July–Aug. Main courses from 12€. AE, DC, MC, V. Daily noon–2:30pm and 7:30–10:30pm. Closed Nov 10–Dec 26.

Hotel Tritone ★★ ☺ Opened in 2004 by the Bernardi family, who also run the celebrated restaurants Filippino (see above) and E' Pulera, the newly built hotel is a 10-minute walk from the Lipari town center. Rooms, each with a patio and balcony looking over the volcanically heated pool, are comfortably furnished with all mod cons and nice bathrooms. Service is prompt and polite, and the family's strong culinary tradition makes itself felt in wonderful breakfasts. The hotel **restaurant** is also excellent, with the emphasis on local produce and fish. When weather permits, meals are served on the terrace.

Via Mendolita, 98055 Lipari. www.hoteltritonelipari.com. ✆ **090-9811595.** 39 units. 120€–240€ double. Rates include breakfast. AE, DC, MC, V. **Amenities:** Restaurant; bar and pool bar (July–Aug); babysitting; pool; smoke-free rooms. *In room:* A/C, TV, hair dryer, minibar.

Villa Meligunis ★ The Villa Meligunis is in the old fisherman's quarter behind the port of Marina Corta, which is also very close to the ferry port. The 32 rooms have terra-cotta-tiled floors and heavy cream-colored bed linens; the superior rooms have private terraces, and the nearby Residence Agave, run by the same management, houses six self-catering apartments. The hotel's finest feature is its panoramic roof garden. It also offers a restaurant, pool, bar, and splendid views.

Via Marte 7, 98055 Lipari. www.villameligunis.it. ✆ **090-9812426.** Fax 090-9880149. 32 units. 160€–325€ double; 225€–395€ suite. Rates include continental breakfast. AE, DC, MC, V. Free parking. Closed Nov 7–Dec 25. **Amenities:** Restaurant; 2 bars; babysitting; saltwater pool; room service. *In room:* A/C, TV, hair dryer, minibar, Wi-Fi (8€ per hour).

Salina ★★★

The richly verdant twin mounts of Salina are at the center of the Aeolian Islands making it a good, and infinitely classier, alternative to Lipari if you prefer to do your island-hopping from a fixed base. If your idea of island life is dancing till dawn to pounding bass, Salina is definitely *not* for you; this is about as far as you can get from Ibiza. If, however, smart hotels, a couple of tiny towns, good food, and soaking in gorgeous scenery are your style, this is the Aeolian island for your relaxing and romantic break. Explore the inland mountains by renting a small car, or putter around the island's bulk seeking out crystalline coves in a boat—or just admire the view and sigh.

At Salina's heart are two extinct volcanoes—the island was known in antiquity as Didyme (meaning "Twin"), when the mountains were interpreted as the breasts of a goddess. These twin mountains are now a protected nature reserve. The taller peak, **Monte Fossa delle Felci** (Mountain of the Valley of Ferns), is to the east of the island. At 962m (3,156 ft.), it is the highest point in the Aeolian Islands; the slightly smaller **Monte Porri** (Mountain of Leeks) is to the west.

The island's modern name is more pragmatic, and was given by the Romans in reference to the abundant quantities of salt extracted from the brackish lake at **Lingua,** on the southeast of the island. For the Romans, this salt export was fundamental, but nowadays the major exports are Malvasia wine and capers. The popularity of Malvasia saw a massive boom in merchant activity on Salina in the 19th century, but the boom came to a dramatic end with the outbreak of phylloxera, a disease that destroyed the Malvasia vines. The resulting famine saw a mass emigration from which the island never recovered; the population today is 2,400 in contrast to a late-1800s population of 9,000. The **Museum of Emigration** at Malfa commemorates this extraordinary turn in the island's fortunes.

For excursions to the verdant center of the island, best undertaken in spring and autumn, take the road to **Valdichiesa,** just north of Leni, where you can take one of the routes to the top of the **Monte Fossa dei Felci,** passing through paths rich in the ferns that give the mountain its name. The crater of the extinct volcano is 100m (328 ft.) deep, with a diameter of over 600m (1,969 ft.). From the rim of the crater, **spectacular views ★★★** take in the entire archipelago in a setting rich in centuries-old chestnuts, oaks, and pines.

WHERE TO EAT & STAY

Hotel Signum ★★★ One of the star hotels in the Aeolian Islands, the Hotel Signum is down an alley off Malfa's main drag. It was opened in the 1980s by Malfa native Clara Rametta, who restored a jumble of long abandoned small village houses connected by open staircases. The crisp, cool rooms are all different in size and aspect, but all have elegantly rustic furniture. Some have sea views; others are set under the shade of lemon trees and open onto the garden. The infinity pool is undoubtedly one of the hotel's highlights and offers views across to the belching silhouette of Stromboli, as does the beautiful terrace where the abundant breakfasts are served under the vine-covered pergola. A spa at Hotel Signum exploits the naturally warm waters of the island. Massages and various other treatments are offered, and they're only too happy to bring you an aperitif to enjoy in the Jacuzzi as you ponder the great verdant mass of the volcano rising above after a hard day by the pool. Staff are courteous and knowledgeable, and anything Clara Rametta doesn't know about Salina isn't worth knowing.

Via Scalo 15 Malfa, 98050 Salina. www.hotelsignum.it. ✆ **090-9844222** or 090-9844375. 30 units. 130€–450€ double. Rates include breakfast. MC, V. Closed early Nov to mid-Mar. **Amenities:** Restaurant; bar. *In room:* A/C, TV, minibar, Wi-Fi (free).

Porto Bello ★★ SEAFOOD The *porto* of Santa Marina is indeed *bello,* and, overlooking it since 1977, Porto Bello has since become an institution. Founded by the Cataffo family—who take their food very seriously indeed—it offers a romantic terrace that is frequented in high season by yachting types whose boats bob about by the pier below. As to be expected, fish is the order of the day, the freshness advertised by a number of raw dishes such as the *cassata del tonno,* a layering of tuna, mint, and tomatoes, finished with slices of orange. If you fancy a break from fish, try the house pasta, spaghetti *al fuoco* (on fire), a fusion of tomato, basil, garlic, chili, and ricotta.

Lungomare Giuffrè, Santa Marina Salina. portobellosalina@tin.it. ✆ **090-9843125.** Reservations advised. Main courses 10€–18€. AE, MC, V. Mar–Nov daily noon–3pm and 7:30–11pm.

Panarea ★★

15

The smallest of the Aeolians, Panarea is an island paradise of whitewashed walls dripping with Mediterranean flora, and a coastline dotted with preposterously gorgeous cerulean coves. The fauna, however, may be an acquired taste: It's a popular haunt for the *figli di papà* (rich kids) and Peter Pans from Italy's bigger cities who overrun it in July and August. Petite Panarea is chic, and it definitely isn't cheap. Book your stay in advance, especially in high season. Prices in late May, June, or September are much more bearable, and you'll have the island almost to yourself.

Resist the temptation to visit Panarea as a day trip from another island; when the boats offload day-trippers in high season, the island is swamped and loses its sleepy Mediterranean charm. If you're going to "do" Panarea, you should stay at least 1 night. During the day, avoid the throng and hire a boat to putter around the gorgeous coves: Cooling off in the crystalline waters, having a floating picnic as you bob around, is the way to enjoy Panarea. As the sun goes down, and the last boats have whisked away the day-visit hordes, the island takes on its chic evening mantle.

Where to Eat & Stay

Da Adelina ★★★ 🎁 CREATIVE AEOLIAN Right on the seafront, chef Giovanni Sorano, a native of Messina and previously of Filomena in Washington, D.C., conjures up sophisticated reworkings of traditional Aeolian dishes using local ingredients in the cozy dining room overlooking the port. The wild fennel so characteristic of these islands crops up again and again, as do home-salted anchovies. The menu changes regularly to accommodate seasonal produce, much of which comes from the restaurant's own garden. I enjoyed gnocchi made with squid ink and served with artichoke hearts and mussels, and crispy *lasagnette* (minilasagna) with seafood.

Via Comunale del Porto 28. ✆ **090-983277.** Reservations recommended. Main courses 14€–20€. AE, MC, V. Daily 8–11pm. Closed mid-Oct to late May.

Hycesia ★★ AEOLIAN In the tangle of streets above the port, the Hycesia has been providing beautifully cooked fresh fish to the beautiful people on its elegantly rustic and splendidly charming covered terrace since 1979. First opened by Maria Maisano, it is now run by her sons Marcello and Gaetano, and Gaetano's wife, Andrea. The emphasis is on the innovative use of high-quality, fresh ingredients, and the menu varies constantly. Specialties include the simple marine flavors of spaghetti *ai ricci di mare* (with sea urchins), and the wildly delicious *scorfano* (scorpion fish) with wild fennel. The proprietors will be happy to guide you through their excellent selection of Sicilian wine.

Via San Pietro. www.hycesia.it. ✆ **090-98304** or 090-983226. Reservations advised. Main courses from 15€. AE, MC, V. Daily 8–11pm. Closed late Oct to Apr.

Lisca Bianca ★★ Despite being part of the Best Western franchise, the Lisca Bianca remains very much a family affair. Directly opposite the jetty at San Pietro, all rooms have a terrace or small patio. Three price levels—standard, superior, and executive—reflect room size and whether views are of the sea or the garden. Breakfast is served on the cool tiled terrace with views toward Stromboli, beyond the hulk of Basiluzzo rock. Come sundown, the terrace with its blue-cushioned iron chairs and tiled tables becomes one of the island's *aperitivo* hot spots. The hotel also has an annex at the next village over, **Ditella,** with sea views and a double and triple room, two bathrooms, sitting room, and small kitchen that can be booked as a family unit. The hotel's diving center and boat rental will set you up for exploring the seas.

Via Lani 1, 98050 Panarea. www.liscabianca.it. ✆ **090-983004** or 090-983005. Fax 090-983291. 35 units. 180€–540€ double; 420€–750€ suite. Rates include breakfast. AE, DC, MC, V. Closed Nov–Mar. **Amenities:** Restaurant; bar; babysitting; room service. *In room:* A/C, TV, hair dryer, minibar, Wi-Fi (fee).

ENTERTAINMENT & NIGHTLIFE

As the sun begins to set, it is time for an *aperitivo*. The most fashionable spot is the rooftop terrace at the **Hotel Raya** (www.hotelraya.it; ✆ **090-983013**). Or start the evening off at the loosely Moroccan-themed **Bar Banacalli,** on the wooden veranda overlooking the port, at the **Hotel Lisca Bianca:** The best tables are upstairs on the elegant terrace. The rich, under-25 set flocks with religious devotion to a "sushi bar" above the port called the **Bridge** for *aperitivo*. A little farther afield, **Da Nunzio** at Zimmari is a good spot for a sun-downer overlooking the beach. Equally pleasant, but with much less flash, there are a few more "normal" Italian bars (where you can get an iced coffee or a beer, simple cocktails, or a smoothie) on the port opposite the jetty. Panarea's only nightclub is at the **Hotel Raya,** where the key word is *posh*.

Stromboli ★★★

The most isolated of the archipelago, Stromboli (the accent is on the first syllable) is at the northeast extremity of the Aeolians, and is Europe's most active volcano. Its name derives from the Greek *strongyle,* meaning "circular," and seen from afar it is a child's drawing of what a volcano should look like. Its single cone rises 926m (3,038 ft.) out of the sea, belching clouds of white smoke you can set your watch by. A recurring feature in classical literature, Stromboli is sometimes identified with the treacherous "wandering rocks" described to Ulysses, by the sorceress Circe.

The Slope of Fire on Stromboli.

In fact, the island can serve as a fantasyland for those who have volcanomania. For active types, the evening trek to the **Sciara del Fuoco** (Slope of Fire) ★★★ will be the highlight of traveling to the Aeolians. To reach the summit of the volcano, the **Gran Cratere** ★★★ at 915m (3,000 ft.), you need to go with an accredited guide in groups of no more than 20; various companies offer guided walks, including **Magmatrek,** Via Vittorio Emanuele (www.magmatrek.it; ✆ **090-9865768**), and **Stromboli Adventures,** corner of Piazza San Vincenzo and Via Vittorio Emanuele (www.stromboliadventures.it; ✆ **090-986264**). Book in advance in high season to be sure of a spot. The group tours cost 35€ and take 5 to 6 hours—including between 30 minutes and an hour at the summit—and start from either Stromboli or Ginostra. Reasonable physical condition is required, children 9 and under are not allowed.

In spite of the volcano and its sloped terrain, there are two settlements. **Ginostra** is on the southwestern shore, little more than a cluster of summer homes with only 15 year-round residents. **Stromboli** is on the northeastern shore, a conglomeration of the villages of Ficogrande, San Vincenzo, and Piscita, where the only in-town attraction is the black-sand beach.

Do remember that the island is an active volcano, bubbling and belching away under your feet. The black soil is rich in minerals and produces bigger, brighter, bolder vegetation. This rampant fecundity, combined with the intermittent rumbling of the beast beneath, and a distinct sense of isolation, can be extremely disquieting. It has been known for visitors to arrive in the morning only to set sail the same evening in search of somewhere a little less unnervingly wild. If you do opt to stay, join the masses for sunset *aperitivi* at the island's most popular bar, **Bar Ingrid,** at Via Michele Bianchi 1 (✆ **090-986385**).

WHERE TO EAT & STAY

La Sirenetta Park Hotel ★★ These are the island's finest accommodations, a well-maintained, government-rated four-star hotel. It's the best equipped, with a scenic terrace, a nightclub, and a restaurant serving the best cuisine of any

Hiking the Gran Cratere on Vulcano.

hotel here. It also has an idyllic location on the Ficogrande Beach in front of Strombolicchio, the towering rock that rises out of the waters at San Vincenzo. Guest rooms are attractively furnished, with tiled floors and an airy feel. All come with private bathrooms—half with showers, half with tubs. The hotel is justly proud of having the island's best pool as well, complete with hydromassage. Facilities include a fitness center and a dive center that also offers water-skiing, sailing, and windsurfing.

Via Marina 33, 98050 Ficogrande (Stromboli). www.lasirenetta.it. ✆ **090-986025.** Fax 090-986124. 60 units. 120€–310€ double. Rates include continental breakfast. AE, DC, MC, V. Closed Nov–Mar. **Amenities:** Restaurant; 2 bars; exercise room; Internet (free, in lobby); saltwater pool; room service; tennis court; limited watersports equipment. *In room:* A/C, TV, hair dryer, minibar.

Punta Lena ★★ AEOLIAN The island's best cuisine is served at this old Aeolian house tastefully converted into a 17-seat restaurant, with a terrace opening onto the sea. The restaurant lies on the beach, a 10-minute walk from the center of town. There is a genuine effort here to cook with fresh products whenever possible. Stick to whatever the fishermen have brought in that day. The *gnocchi alla Saracena,* with white fish, capers, olives, and tomatoes, is also excellent. The restaurant stocks the island's widest selection of wines.

Via Marina Garibaldi 8 (Località Ficogrande). ✆ **090-986204.** Reservations recommended. Main courses 10€–18€. AE, DC, MC, V. Daily noon–2:30pm and 7–11pm. Closed Nov–Mar.

Vulcano ★

The island closest to Milazzo and the mainland, Vulcano, with its still-active **Vulcano della Fossa,** was thought to be not only the home of Vulcan, but also the gateway to Hades. Three dormant craters also exist on the island, but a climb to the rim of the active **Gran Cratere ★★** (Big Crater) draws the most attention. It hasn't erupted since 1890, but one look inside the sulfur-belching hole makes you understand how it could've inspired the hellish legends surrounding it. The 418m (1,372-ft.) peak is an easier climb than the one on Stromboli, taking just about an hour—though it's just as hot, and the same precautions prevail. Avoid midday, load up on sunscreen and water, and wear good hiking shoes.

The **Laghetti dei Fanghi ★** (Little Lakes of Mud), famous free mud baths that reputedly cure every known ailment, are along Via Provinciale a short way from the port. Be warned that the mud discolors everything from cloth to jewelry, which is one explanation for the prevalent nudity. Expect to encounter muddy pools brimming with naked, package-tour Germans. Within sight, the *acquacalda* features hot-water jets that act as a natural Jacuzzi. Either can scald you if you step or sit on the vents that release the heat, so take care if you decide to enter.

The island offers one of the few smooth beaches in the entire chain, the **Spiaggia Sabbie Nere ★** (Black Sands Beach), with dark sand so hot in the midday sun that flip-flops or wading shoes are suggested if you plan to while away your day along the shore. You can find the beach by following signs posted along Via Ponente.

Having knowledge of street names is worthless, really, because there are no signs. Not to worry—the locals who gather at the dock are friendly and experienced at giving directions to tongue-tied foreign visitors, especially because all they ever have to point out are the paths to the crater, the mud baths, and the beach. You'll need to spend little time in the village center itself. This is a drab 1970s eyesore filled with souvenir shops and fast-food snack bars.

Vulcano is best visited as a day trip from one of the other islands (Lipari is the closest) or on your way to or from Milazzo. If you're here at mealtime, try **Vincenzino ★**, Via Porto di Levante (www.ristorantevincenzino.com; **© 090-9852016;** daily noon–3pm and 7–10pm).

Serious gourmands and lovers of casual, unforgettable dining experiences will have no problem packing on a few extra kilos while in Sardinia. Food is generally high quality no matter where you go, and the island's regional cheeses, breads, and pastries are famous nationwide. Sardinian menus can at first be difficult to navigate, but they're not that far from "continental" Italian cuisine; they just have slightly odd names for everything. For example, a common dish is *malloreddus.* Sounds exotic, but it's just shell pasta flavored with a hint of saffron, usually tossed with something simple and hearty like tomato and meat sauce. And this being an island caressed by the seafood-rich Mediterranean on all sides, fish of all kinds is almost always available at any restaurant. But go inland, and the classic dish is *porceddu,* roast pig.

Even with all of Sardinia's enticing attributes—Caribbean waters and Italian food—the island can be a bit of an aloof soul, and for seasoned Italian travelers, it can feel like a piece of the sensuous package you've come to expect from Italy is missing. But for water- and sun-themed relaxation seekers, Sardinia is paradise.

THE BEST SARDINIA TRAVEL EXPERIENCES

- **Finding your own perfect beach:** Sardinia, for most who travel here, is all about the coast—where soft shimmering sand meets the perfectly cerulean water of the Med. The island has hundreds, even thousands, of beaches: Some of our favorites, for their otherworldly, stunning beauty, are La Pelosa, Tuerredda, and Cala Sinzias. See p. 912, 918, and 919.
- **Exploring La Maddalena archipelago:** If all the glitz on the Costa Smeralda seems a bit much, immediately to the west is the much more laid-back, equally gorgeous La Maddalena island group. Only La Maddalena itself is inhabited, but group boat tours take you to the idyllic coves of pristine islands like Spargi and Budelli, a stone's throw from Corsica. See p. 907.
- **Dining with your feet in the sand at a seaside restaurant on the island's southeastern coast:** Utter relaxation plus fresh seafood—what else could you want from your Sardinian holiday? Several ideal places for this can be found between Villasimius and the Costa Rei. See p. 919.
- **Pretending to be royalty along the luxurious playground of the Costa Smeralda:** Gaze nonchalantly at the world's most expensive yachts in the harbor at Porto Cervo, shop designer boutiques and sip cocktails at glamorous clubs, and look out for the paparazzi on the celeb-packed beaches La Celvia and Liscia Ruja. See p. 904.
- **Strolling the atmospheric streets of Alghero:** Between centuries-old cobblestones, Catalan-style Renaissance architecture, and a prime waters-edge position, this city on the northwest coast is Sardinia's loveliest. A walk along the city's sea-facing bastions, followed by some *vino sardo* at one of the romantic cafes there, completes the Alghero experience. See p. 907.

ESSENTIALS

Sardinia is big, and simply covering the distances here is time-consuming. A car is essential, and unless you have 2 weeks to spend here, try to pick one half of the island to explore. Most travelers find the north of Sardinia more satisfying than the south. If you have a long weekend, say 3 or 4 days, limit yourself to one

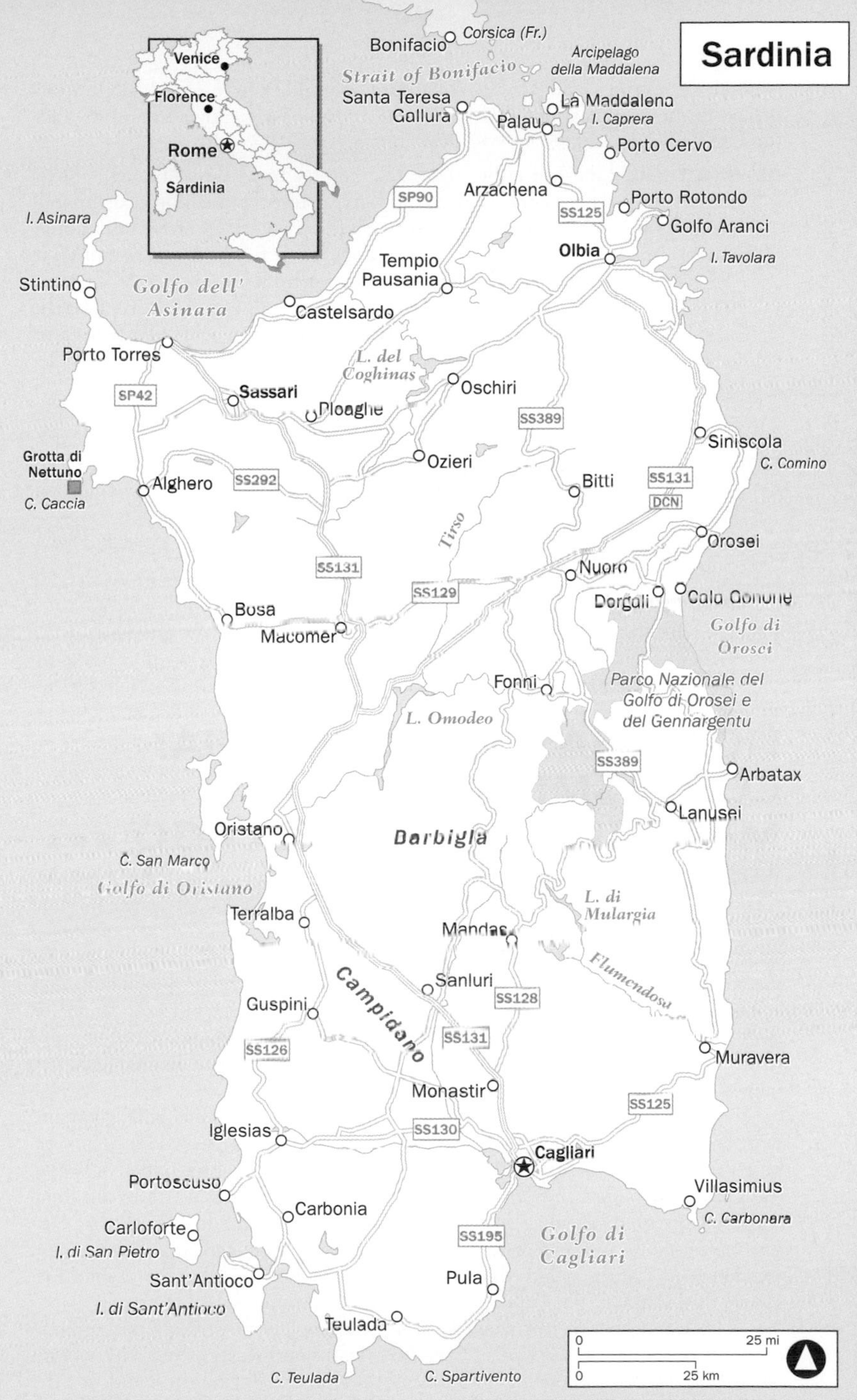
Sardinia
Venice
Florence
Rome
Sardinia
Bonifacio
Corsica (Fr.)
Strait of Bonifacio
Arcipelago della Maddalena
Santa Teresa Gallura
La Maddalena
I. Caprera
Palau
Porto Cervo
Arzachena
SP90
SS125
Porto Rotondo
Golfo Aranci
I. Asinara
Olbia
I. Tavolara
Tempio Pausania
Stintino
Golfo dell' Asinara
Castelsardo
Porto Torres
L. del Coghinas
Oschiri
SP42
Sassari
Ploaghe
SS389
Siniscola
C. Comino
Grotta di Nettuno
C. Caccia
Alghero
SS292
Ozieri
Bitti
SS131
DCN
Tirso
Orosei
SS131
Nuoro
SS129
Dorgali
Cala Gonone
Golfo di Orosei
Bosa
Macomer
Fonni
Parco Nazionale del Golfo di Orosei e del Gennargentu
L. Omodeo
SS389
Arbatax
Lanusei
Oristano
Barbigia
C. San Marco
Golfo di Oristano
L. di Mulargia
Terralba
Mandas
Flumendosa
Campidano
Sanluri
SS128
Guspini
SS131
SS126
Muravera
Monastir
SS125
Iglesias
SS130
Cagliari
Portoscuso
Villasimius
C. Carbonara
Carbonia
Carloforte
I. di San Pietro
SS195
Golfo di Cagliari
Sant'Antioco
Pula
I. di Sant'Antioco
Teulada
0
25 mi
0
25 km
C. Teulada
C. Spartivento

general area of the island, such as the Costa Smeralda and the Maddalena archipelago in the northeast or Villasimius in the southeast, or Alghero and its environs, in the northwest.

GETTING THERE You can either fly or take a ferry to Sardinia. Flying is faster and usually just as economical as the ferry, as ferry connections exist mainly for Italians who want their own cars with them once they arrive in Sardinia. Flight time from Italy is about 45 minutes, while ferries can take from 5 to 15 hours. The main airports are **Cagliari-Elmas** airport (www.sogaer.it; ✆ **070-211211**), 3km (2 miles) from the capital, and **Alghero Fertilia** airport (www.aeroportodialghero.it; ✆ **079-935282**), while **Olbia airport** (Aeroporto Costa Smeralda; www.olbiairport.it; ✆ **0789-563444**) handles summer traffic to the Costa Smeralda.

By sea, myriad options exist for reaching Sardinia from the Italian mainland. Sardinia's principal ferry terminals are at **Olbia** (www.mobylines.com), **Golfo Aranci** (www.corsica-ferries.it), **Arbatax** (www.gnv.it and www.mobylines.com), and **Cagliari** (www.tirrenia.it). Fares range from 25€ to 100€ per person, depending on the season and specials.

You can book ferries through the U.K.-based **Direct Ferries** (www.directferries.co.uk), which has a handy summary of all passenger/vehicle boat connections to Sardinia on its home page.

VISITOR INFORMATION The multilingual main **website for tourism** in the Regione Sardegna, www.sardegnaturismo.it, has a wealth of information for trip-planning, history and culture, and brochures for various special interests.

NORTHEASTERN SARDINIA: COSTA SMERALDA & MADDALENA ARCHIPELAGO ★★★

When I first lived in Italy in my 20s, my beach reading of choice was *Chi,* Italy's version of *Us Weekly.* Invariably, the hot-actress-and-star-soccer-player fling du jour was always photographed somewhere off the northern coast of Sardinia—the dateline would be Porto Cervo, or Palau, or La Maddalena—canoodling for the paparazzi on the back of someone's yacht, romping in the turquoise waters of some sugary beach that looked like the Caribbean, or partying at Flavio Briatore's infamous disco, Billionaire. To me, that part of Italy, Sardinia's Costa Smeralda (Emerald Coast), represented the ultimate in Italian fabulosity. Everyone was so tanned and radiant. I had to see it for myself.

When I got there, it wasn't quite what I expected, in ways both good and bad. The scenery blew me away; the superficial things that passed for "glamour" here turned me off of celebrity-life daydreaming forever. But for better or worse, the Costa Smeralda is foremost in my mind when I think of a trip to Sardinia. Most Sards would cringe at that, because admittedly there's little authentic Sardinian culture up in these parts, but the Costa Smeralda is such a stunning and rarefied pocket of the world (that just happens to be in Sardinia) that it's a must-see on this island.

The landscape on this coast is drop-dead gorgeous—striking pink granite outcrops recalling the red rocks of the American Southwest, mixed with vibrant oleanders, gnarled juniper trees, and umbrella pines bent by the wind. It's the desert meets the Med, and it's rapture for the eyes. The coast is riddled with mostly small, though pretty, sandy beaches with calm bays for swimming, and although you can certainly drive from beach to beach, regulars putter around these glittering waters in boats.

As impressive as the natural setting and the cleanliness of it all is, the developed areas feel utterly fake and un-Italian. Of course, the fake feel should come as no surprise, because the Costa Smeralda was built up only a few decades ago, and marketed from the get-go as a hideaway for the international jet set. The Aga Khan purchased this 56km (35-mile) stretch of then-virgin coastline in the 1960s. The area was dubbed Costa Smeralda (Emerald Coast), and ersatz villages sprouted up around the natural harbors and gated villa compounds went up on the promontories. Sure enough, the package attracted the rich and famous, and became the international luxury playground it is today.

The main developments along the Costa Smeralda are Porto Cervo and Porto Rotondo, each with a requisite jumble of new pastel buildings that is really just a cleverly disguised outdoor mall with a *Vogue*-perfect lineup of designer boutiques arranged around a simulated piazza. You can get expensive drinks at sterile cafes, and gleaming sailboats bob in the modern harbors. Between the two of them, Porto Cervo and Porto Rotondo have about 2 grams of soul. Yet in July and August, the entire coast is chockablock with sun seekers and revelers, oligarchs and skippers, and the Costa Smeralda is, out of all Italian seaside locales, *the* place to be. No contest.

The scenic and friendly Maddalena archipelago, an easy hop from anywhere along the Costa Smeralda, is perhaps the most compelling attraction in northeastern Sardinia. The vibe is low-key and the nature is lovely—lots of exposed peach-toned rock, maritime pines, and quiet sandy coves, and almost all of it is protected as parkland of the Parco Nazionale dell'Arcipelago della Maddalena.

ESSENTIALS

GETTING THERE The northeast is well served both by air (Olbia airport) and sea (ports of Olbia and Golfo Aranci). The **Maddalena archipelago** is exclusively reached by sea. Regularly scheduled ferries leave from Palau every 15 minutes and arrive at La Maddalena 20 minutes later. If arriving by car from elsewhere in Sardinia, the fastest route is the SS131 highway north, past Olbia.

GETTING AROUND A car is essential on the Costa Smeralda. Rental agencies abound; you'll find the best deals with **AutoEurope** (www.autoeurope.com), which has an office at Olbia airport.

VISITOR INFORMATION Sardinia's **tourism website,** www.sardegnaturismo.it, has information in English about the northeastern part of the island, including the Costa Smeralda and La Maddalena archipelago.

Costa Smeralda ★★

Loosely speaking, the Costa Smeralda is the coastal zone between Porto Rotondo and Baja Sardinia. Along the roads of the Costa Smeralda, giant granite boulders engraved with *Pirates of the Caribbean*–style lettering announce the various swanky subdivisions, like Cala di Volpe and Romazzino.

EXPLORING THE REGION

The principal activities on the Costa Smeralda and its environs are beach-going, boating, shopping, posing, and partying. Beaches are abundant and almost all of them are free to the public. The waters here are universally gorgeous, shallow, and calm, and afford gorgeous views of the surrounding granitic promontories.

Ground zero of the Costa Smeralda is **Porto Cervo,** which essentially has two nuclei: On the south side, the **Piazzetta** mall is the hub of all high-fashion, high-end retail action (get your 400€ Versace bikini here). The north end of Porto Cervo, accessible via a panoramic road or by free boat shuttle from the old marina below the Piazzetta, is dominated by the modern **marina ★**, complete with a fancy yacht club and the latest in seaborne behemoths moored in the harbor. Be sure to have a good look around.

BEACHES

In the zone around Porto Rotondo, the best beach is **Spiaggia Ira ★★** (follow signs toward Porto Rotondo, then Rudargia). Fringed by sugary white sand, the bay here is a swimming pool of electric turquoise water, and facilities include a snack bar and boat rentals. Near Porto Cervo, **Liscia Ruja ★★** (just south of Cala di Volpe, off the SP94), also referred to as Long Beach by Costa Smeralda regulars, is the see-and-be-seen beach for the fashion set. It's also Porto Cervo's biggest and best equipped beach, so if you only have time for one Costa Smeralda sun and sand day, you can't go wrong with Liscia Ruja. Continuing through Cala di Volpe and back south along the east side of the bay, **La Celvia ★★** is an intimate sandy beach enveloped by *macchia mediterranea* and the most amazing private villas in the area. Keep your eyes peeled—this is where a lot of Italian showbiz personalities hang out. Another great spot, though it involves a bit of a walk, is the **Spiaggia del Principe ★★** (from Cala di Volpe, follow signs to Romazzino, then turn right on Via degli Asfodeli; park at the end of this road, then follow a 600m/1,969-ft. pedestrian path to the beach). This is a perfect crescent of bleach-white sand, neon blue water, and a little granite reef in the middle of the beach.

In the Baja Sardinia area, though a bit removed from the town center, is a highly recommended outdoor bar/club called **Phi Beach ★★** (see "Entertainment & Nightlife," below). The actual beach here is scant, but the setting is divine, and it's a fun place where vacationers of all stripes gather on big sun beds and sip communal mojitos while a DJ spins summer anthems. Phi Beach has a full bar and restaurant, serving stylish delicacies like seafood *carpaccio.* To get there, follow signs from Baja Sardinia west to Forte Cappellini.

Liscia Ruja beach at Porto Cervo.

BOATING

Part and parcel of the Costa Smeralda experience is *la barca.* Motorboating or sailing around the jigsaw-puzzle-piece coves is practically a religion here, so the nautically inclined will be in hog heaven. You don't have to be a yacht owner to get out on the water—myriad charters operate out of Porto Cervo and Porto Rotondo and the secondary marinas nearby, whether you want a big or small boat, sails or motor, a

The Cala di Volpe resort, near Porto Cervo.

day trip or a weeklong tour with a skipper. In Portisco (btw. Porto Rotondo and Porto Cervo), **Boomerang Charter** (www.boomerangcharter.com; ✆ **0789-24293**) has good rates for weeklong tours on a variety of sailboats. Prices start at around 1,500€ per week for self-piloted vessels that can sleep six people. If your party is only one or two, and you don't mind a little less privacy, they also organize group cruises for 8 to 10 people. In Porto Cervo, **Sea World Services** (Piazzetta Clipper, Porto Cervo; www.swsportocervo.com; ✆ **0789 91693**) is a higher-end agency that arranges all kinds of boat charters (though no rentals), from 600€ per day, crew included, for an eight-person boat.

Group boat tours to the Maddalena archipelago are much more affordable than private charters from the Costa Smeralda and are an easy day trip from just about anywhere in northeastern Sardinia.

Still want to be your own captain? No problem: The mainstays of Italian island do-it-yourself boat tourism, *gommoni* (rubber Zodiac motorboats), can be rented easily at any port and many beaches along the Costa Smeralda, from 100€ for a half-day.

ENTERTAINMENT & NIGHTLIFE

The Costa Smeralda has no shortage of trendy places to party among the beautiful people. However, if you're traveling outside of high season, you can skip this section. The places listed here are only open in summer. If you do plan to hit the bars and clubs, prepare for lots of traffic, even after midnight.

Any discussion of Costa Smeralda nightlife has to include Flavio Briatore's infamous nightclub, **Billionaire** (Località Sottovento; www.billionairelife.com; ✆ **0789-94192**). The most hyped nightspot in Italy is ridiculously expensive and selective.

If you'd like to have some actual fun (as opposed to just ogling glamazons), head instead to the outdoor water's edge bar and *aperitivo* hot spot of **Phi Beach ★★** (www.phibeach.com; ✆ **0789-955012;** late May to mid-Sept only 10am–late), attached to the Forte Cappellini bungalow village west of Baja Sardinia. The crowd here is much more diverse and laid-back—families with kids are just as welcome as sporty singles. Though Phi Beach doesn't have much sand (it's mostly granitic boulders around here), the multilevel decks are equipped with dozens of white-cushioned platform sun beds and shell-shaped wicker furniture that fully look the part of a trendy Miami-inspired beach bar. Phi is open all day as a beach club and restaurant, but the best time to come is for happy hour (6pm onward), when the action heats up and the sunset over the water is truly spectacular.

WHERE TO EAT & STAY

There are a number of wildly expensive five-star resorts along the Costa Smeralda, like the **Cala di Volpe,** the **Romazzino,** and the **Pitrizza** (all near but not directly in Porto Cervo), that bill themselves as exclusive luxury retreats where all the VIPs go. However, none of them offers a setting or services quite splendid enough to justify their rates, which can be upwards of 1,000€ per night; it's hard to recommend them on cache alone. Almost all the fancy hotels in the area, including those listed above, are Starwood properties, so if you have a bunch of extra rewards points, it might be an option to consider.

Sardinian Villas (www.sardinianvillas.com) has a number of lovely properties (many very exclusive and expensive) on the Costa Smeralda and also handles bookings for the **Le Case della Marina ★**, attractive and modern apartments with sweeping views, shared pool, and ample outdoor living space, conveniently situated on the hill directly behind the harbor.

Clipper ★★ ITALIAN/SEAFOOD Set within one of the hairpin turns on the road leading down to Porto Cervo marina, Clipper does a brisk business with resort habitués and serves very good Mediterranean cuisine at slightly more honest prices than other places in town. The seafood on offer is displayed on ice, so you can pick exactly which fish or lobster you want and how you want it cooked. The house specialty pasta, the *spaghetto Clipper,* is a tasty blend of shrimp, cherry tomatoes, avocado, and curry. An extensive wine list includes dozens of Sardinian wines at good prices. As the name would suggest, decor here is maritime themed, but the result—lots of varnished mahogany, artsy and oversize photos of sailboats, and nautical striped upholstery—is handsome, not tacky. Request a table outside or at one of the large picture windows inside.

Via della Marina, Porto Cervo. ✆ **0789-91644.** Reservations essential July–Aug. Entrees from 14€. AE, DC, MC, V. May–Oct daily 7:30pm–1:30am.

Gianni Pedrinelli ★★★ SARDINIAN For a gourmet splurge, look no further than this institution of Costa Smeralda gastronomy. This is quite an elegant spot, despite the rustic framework of the old farmhouse it occupies in the hills above Porto Cervo, but thankfully it's mostly free of the flash and pretense that pervades other famous restaurants in the region. The scene and cuisine are country-chic, and the food tends more to turf than surf, although fish is present in starters like seafood *carpaccio* and grilled octopus. The artisanal antipasti table is enough to warrant a meal here, but among the *primi,* try the ravioli in fresh *ragu;* for a *secondo,* choose from chicken, pork, or beef dishes in rich and delectable reductions. Consider dining here at the end of your trip, because you might not want to put on a bathing suit after you've had an indulgent meal at Gianni Pedrinelli.

Località Piccolo Pevero, on the road btw. Porto Cervo and Abbiadori. www.giannipedrinelli.it. ✆ **0789-92436.** Reservations essential. Entrees from 16€. AE, DC, MC. V. Daily 7:45–10:45pm and for lunch by reservation only. Closed Nov–Feb.

Le Ginestre ★★ Fabulously positioned amid dense Mediterranean greenery about 1km (¾ mile) south of Porto Cervo center, this resort offers generously sized rooms and plenty of amenities. It's the kind of place where you'll want to unpack your entire suitcase and hole up for a week. All rooms in the low-slung peach stucco villa feature clean, contemporary furnishings and fixtures, and have ample terraces. The hotel's private beach lies 250m (820 ft.) away. A swimming pool and tennis court (no fee) are also directly on the hotel grounds. Le Ginestre's helpful and unobtrusive staff can arrange all kinds of activities.

Località Pevero, near Porto Cervo. www.leginestrehotel.com. ✆ **0789-92030.** 80 units. 180€–300€ double. AE, DC, MC, V. **Amenities:** Restaurant; bar; fitness room; pool; room service; spa; tennis. *In room:* A/C, satellite TV, hair dryer, minibar, Wi-Fi (free).

Papillo ★★ Formerly known as the Borgo Antico, this yellow stucco retreat in the inland village of San Pantaleo (btw. Porto Rotondo and Porto Cervo) is an oasis of friendliness and relaxation. Almost all units have a balcony overlooking the inner courtyard and swimming pool. The Papillo is an immaculate and convenient base for touring the Costa Smeralda. One drawback is that it's not directly on the water, but in summer, the hotel runs a free shuttle to Rena Bianca, one of the prettiest and largest beaches in the area.

Via la Petra Sarda, San Pantaleo. www.borgoanticohotel.com. ✆ **0789-65400.** 27 units. 110€–220€ double. AE, DC, MC, V. Closed mid-Oct to Mar. **Amenities:** Restaurant; bar; pool. *In room:* A/C, satellite TV, hair dryer, minibar, Wi-Fi (free).

A SIDE TRIP TO LA MADDALENA ARCHIPELAGO ★★★

A stone's throw from the Costa Smeralda, the Maddalena archipelago consists of one main inhabited island, **La Maddalena,** which has a cute port town and is connected to the rural island of **Caprera** by a short causeway, and about 60 other islands and islets, the most visited of which are **Spargi, Budelli,** and **Razzoli.** Boat excursions to the Maddalena archipelago can be arranged at any of the small ports and through most hotels, or you can take the 20-minute car ferry (recommended, so you'll have wheels once you get there) from Palau to La Maddalena, and from there you drive all over La Maddalena (lots of beaches and pretty scenery) and then over to Caprera. The other islands in the Maddalena group are nearby but only accessible by private boat.

Daylong group boat tours are the cheapest and easiest way to get an overview of the entire archipelago. In high season, these can be arranged through any hotel and at any of the marinas along the coast of northeastern Sardinia, from Olbia to Palau. Palau is where the lion's share of these tours are based, and there you'll find dozens of outfits all offering the same basic itinerary, which starts at 10am, ends at 5pm, and includes at least two long stops for swimming (you'll have 2 hr. at Cala Corsara on Spargi, the loveliest beach in the archipelago), lunch on board, and coastal tours of Budelli, La Maddalena, and Caprera. Prices range from 35€ to 45€, lunch included.

In summer, these excursions can be organized ad hoc on the day of travel, but from October to May, there are far fewer options for boating the Costa Smeralda or reaching the lesser islands of the Maddalena archipelago: Be sure to inquire with your hotel before arrival about tour availability if this is something that's important to you.

Alghero ★★

If you've been traveling up and down Sardinia, enjoying the beaches and relaxation but secretly pining for something more reminiscent of the Italy you know and love back across the Med, Alghero will have you exclaiming "finally!" Here, at last, is a historical center with picturesque architecture and an air of nobility that feels very much lived in. However stereotypically Italian the atmosphere, Alghero is more Catalan than anything else. When the people of Alghero rebelled against their Aragonese/Catalan rulers in the 15th century, the population was summarily replaced by Catalans, who remained ever since. Only a century ago did Alghero's Catalan purity begin to be diluted by intermarriage with Sards and adoption of the Italian language.

Surrounded by imposing sea walls—the *bastioni,* which make for romantic strolling—the cobblestoned *centro storico* is chock-full of great cafes, restaurants, and shops. In recent years, low-cost flights into Alghero's Fertilia airport have brought a flood of British and Northern European vacationers to this area, but so far Alghero has weathered the crowds gracefully and untainted by mass tourism.

ESSENTIALS

GETTING THERE Alghero has its own **airport,** Alghero-Fertilia (www.aeroporto dialghero.it; ✆ **079-935282**), which is linked with dozens of Italian and European cities, mostly by low-cost carrier RyanAir. By **car,** take the SS131 toward Sassari then follow blue highway signs west to Alghero.

GETTING AROUND While Alghero itself is a pleasure to walk around, you'll need a car to do all the excellent side trips in this section. Rent one from AutoEurope (www.autoeurope.com) at Alghero airport. You can't drive into the *centro storico,* so park at the free marina lot, from which it's a 5-minute walk to the heart of town.

VISITOR INFORMATION The **tourist information office** is just outside the city walls at Piazza Porta a Terra 9 (www.alghero-turismo.it; ✆ **079-979054**), open Monday to Saturday 9am to 7pm.

EXPLORING

The nondescript outskirts of Alghero belie the charm and beauty of the old city that lies on the tip of the promontory. Within the old city walls, wander the old

Alghero.

streets (whose signs are bilingual—in Italian and Catalan), still lined with patrician palaces from the Spanish period, shop at hip and elegant boutiques, and stop in at the Gothic-Catalan **cathedral of Santa Maria** (daily 9am–6pm; free admission), but above all in Alghero, don't miss a **walk along the bastions ★★** that run between the western edge of the old town and the sea below. The views from here are panoramic any time of day, but it's especially captivating at night when the promenade and walls are floodlit. You can also "do the walls" from a seated position—at one of the stylish cafes along the bastions.

ATTRACTIONS

While Alghero's old city is a major attraction in itself, the most compelling individual sites are actually a bit out of town. Just a short drive to the north are several places of significant historical, cultural, and naturalistic interest, including a *nuraghe,* a Neolithic necropolis, and an international-level winery. The cliffs of Capo Caccia, also to the north, conceal the splendid cave of Grotta di Nettuno.

Anghelo Ruiu Necropolis ★★ With 38 tombs in the form of miniature houses called *domus de janas* (fairy dwellings) built inside caves and outfitted with sophisticated stone carvings, this site is totally worthy of Indiana Jones. Artifacts from the site are at the archaeological museum in Cagliari, but there are fine replicas at the Sella e Mosca winery (see below).

SP42 (road to Porto Torres), 10km (6 miles) north of Alghero. ✆ **079-980040.** Admission 3€. Apr–Oct daily 9am–7pm; Nov–Mar daily 9:30am–4pm.

Grotta di Nettuno ★★ One of the greatest natural attractions of Sardinia is Neptune's Cave, set inside the base of the cliffs of Capo Caccia. It is, however, a bit expensive and can be chaotic in summer, and if you've seen stalactites and stalagmites elsewhere, you might want to think twice before you commit. You can arrive by boat, with one of the regularly organized excursions from Alghero's marina, or by land, down the legendary **Escala del Cabirol ★★**: This hand-cut "stairway of goats" has 656 stone steps leading down the cliff face. Either way you get there, this spectacular cavern has a 120m-wide (394-ft.) saltwater lake, a forest of stalactite columns, and concretions in the form of "organ pipes." Guided tours of the cave are included in the admission fee and last about 30 minutes. For those who wish to brave the stone stairs, a public bus marked Nettuno runs here from Alghero, costing 4€ round-trip. Allow 20 minutes to descend the stairs, and longer for the trip back. For the boat trip crowd, excursions depart from Bastione della Maddalena in Alghero several times daily, though not in rough weather. The boat tour of the caves takes 2½ hours total, costing 10€ to 14€ per person, depending on the company.

Capo Caccia, 27km (17 miles) northwest of Alghero (the top of the staircase to the grotto is clearly signposted). ✆ **079-946540.** Admission 12€. Apr–Sept daily 9am–7pm; Oct–Mar daily 9am–4pm.

Nuraghe Palmavera ★ If you missed Su Nuraxi (p. 916), this is the best place on the island to see a prehistoric stone-built *nuraghe,* some 50 individual dwellings crowded close together. A central tower surrounds these huts, forming a limestone complex from 1500 B.C. Built with huge blocks of stone, the truncated cone tower is in the shape of a beehive and opens onto a panorama of the countryside. The remains of a 14th-century-B.C. "palace" can also be seen.

SS. 127bis, km 45; from Alghero follow signs to Porto Conte. ✆ **079-980040.** Admission 3€. Apr–Oct daily 9am–7pm; Nov–Mar daily 9:30am–4pm.

Sella e Mosca Winery ★★ This is one of the oldest and biggest wine estates in Sardinia, with beautifully maintained grounds, multilingual tours of the cellar, a wine shop and tasting room, and a surprisingly good museum. Don't let the moderate prices in the wine shop (bottles from 4€) mislead you: Sella e Mosca is a serious winemaker; the Cannonau D.O.C. is well balanced, spicy, and herbal—even fuller-bodied are the cab-Cannonau blend, Tanca Farrà, and the 100% cabernet Marchese di Villamarina. Also, try the wonderfully versatile and hot-weather-friendly Terre Bianche. It's made from the white *torbato*, a temperamental but lovely grape that isn't grown anywhere else in Italy.

Località I Piani, on the SP42, 11km (7 miles) north of Alghero. www.sellaemosca.com. ✆ **079-997700.** Free tours Mon–Sat at 5:30pm June–Sept, call for times in other months. Shop June–Sept daily 8:30am–8pm; Oct–May Mon–Sat 8:30am–1pm and 3–6:30pm.

BEACHES

The best beaches near Alghero all lie to the north of the city. For a quick dip near the center, the city beach of San Giovanni will do in a pinch, but far better is the beach of **Maria Pia ★★** (4km/2½ miles north of Alghero). Here, a strip of truly flourlike sand is caressed by gentle turquoise waves, a pinewood behind the beach provides some respite from the sun, and the trees emanate a fragrance that, blended with the marine air, should be bottled and sold as Acqua di Sardegna!

Alghero's most beloved beach, **Le Bombarde ★★**, lies at the top of the bay that extends north of the city, 7km (4⅓ miles) away. Le Bombarde has lots of amenities, soft sand, and clean turquoise water. It's also the main beach hangout for the young and socially inclined locals and vacationers. Just west of here, past some dense vegetation (take the inland road; don't try to bushwhack your way through) is **Lazzaretto ★**, a sort of a smaller cousin of Le Bombarde, with the same fine sand, crystal-clear water, and ample services.

ENTERTAINMENT & NIGHTLIFE

The cafes along the sea walls draw a lively crowd in summer. The hippest is **Cafe Latino ★** (Bastioni Magellano; ✆ **079-976541**), where you can sip coffee or cocktails on outdoor tables facing the marina. Another good bet is the **Bar Mirador ★**, attached to the restaurant of the same name (see below). For the young crowd, if you can get past the overwrought name, the party is at **Buena Vista Sunset Club** (Via Cavour 15).

WHERE TO EAT & STAY

Most hotels are located on the outskirts of old Alghero, in high-rises on the beach in the modern town. Consider renting a vacation apartment in old Alghero—Casa Maiorca Apartments (Via Maiorca 24; ✆ **349-8060989**) consists of two totally renovated units with modern fixtures and historic charm, from 85€ to 175€ per night (sleeps four to six).

Andreini ★★ CREATIVE SARDINIAN A modish eye has gone into everything at this chic restaurant—the garden, the exposed stone in the dining room, the menu font—that just walking by, you want to love it. Luckily, the food holds its own with the overt style of the place. The kitchen, helmed by Cristiano Andreini, turns out clever combinations of seafood and vegetables with haute presentations, but if you're not a fish person, steer clear—nearly everything served here has some sort of sea creature, whose names you might not always recognize. In addition to a la carte offerings, the chef has two set menus (60€ and 70€ per person, excluding wine), but the entire table must participate.

Via Ardoino 45. ✆ **079-982098.** Reservations recommended. Entrees 13€–22€. AE, DC, MC, V. Tues–Sun 7:30–11pm.

Carlos V ★ A less expensive alternative to the Villa Las Tronas, which it's opposite, this large sea resort hotel on the waterfront is surrounded by well-landscaped gardens and terrace. It's been around since 1971 but was completely renovated in 2006. Rated five stars by the government, its front rooms open onto the Bay of Alghero. If possible, try for a room with a view and avoid the units in the rear. Bedrooms are midsize to spacious and tastefully and comfortably furnished with modern pieces.

Lungomare Valencia 24. www.hotelcarlosv.it. ✆ **079-9720600.** 179 units. 100€–427€ double. AE, DC, MC, V. **Amenities:** Restaurant; bar; babysitting; pool; room service; tennis. *In room:* A/C, TV, hair dryer, minibar, Wi-Fi (free).

La Lepanto ★★ SEAFOOD This is Alghero's go-to address for a special night of feasting on fish. The setting is contemporary-elegant, complete with artful lobster tanks and panoramic windows overlooking the water. While there are great meals to be had here, service seems to have gone a bit downhill recently. Still, most people love it, and if you love classic Mediterranean seafood in all its various species and unfooled-around-with preparations, you'll love it, too.

Via Carlo Alberto 135. ✆ **079-979116.** Reservations required. Entrees 14€–28€. AE, DC, MC, V. Tues–Sun noon–2:30pm and 7:30–11pm.

Mirador ★ ALGHERESE/SEAFOOD With terrace seating on the bastions of old Alghero, Mirador has a lengthy menu of Algherese standards (paella, pastas with crustaceans and local herbs and spices) and Italian seafood classics. Among a handful of nonfish dishes, the *tagliata di manzo* (sliced rib-eye steak) with balsamic vinegar, arugula, and parmigiano, is outstanding. The setting is lovely, and the restaurant itself is quite handsome. Prices are surprisingly moderate, and the attached bar is one of the nicest spots in town for a drink, before or after dinner.

Bastioni Marco Polo 63. ✆ **079-9734018.** Reservations recommended. Entrees 12€–20€. Tues–Sun 11:30am–1:30pm and 7–11pm.

Villa Las Tronas ★★★ The top choice for luxury in the Alghero area, this is the most romantic and elegant hotel in northeastern Sardinia, a place where Italian royalty used to spend their summer vacations. Built in the 1800s, the villa remained in private hands until 1940. It is erected on a private promontory virtually surrounded by the sea, but only a short walk from Alghero. Piers and terraces attract sun worshippers. Much of the aristocratic atmosphere remains, including marble floors, tall ceilings, crystal chandeliers, and antiques. Bedrooms are elegantly styled with traditional pieces, and the hotel has the best facilities in Alghero.

Lungomare Valencia 1. www.hotelvillalastronas.it. ✆ **079-981818.** 25 units. 259€–470€ double. AE, DC, MC, V. **Amenities:** Restaurant; bar; babysitting; fitness center; pool; room service; spa. *In room:* A/C, TV, hair dryer, minibar, Wi-Fi (free).

SIDE TRIPS

The Panoramic Road to Bosa

The **Alghero-Bosa *strada litoranea* (corniche road)** ★★, a 45km (28-mile) stretch of cliff-hugging, curving highway, ranks right up there with the most breathtaking drives in Italy. From either city, follow signs to *strada litoranea;* the highway numbers are SP105 and SP49. There's another road between Bosa and

Alghero, slightly inland and parallel to the *litoranea* (following the SP12), so I recommend taking that inland route south from Alghero and then returning from Bosa to Alghero on the *litoranea.* Forty-five kilometers (28 miles) of perpetual drop-offs to the sea are beautiful, but stressful to have to negotiate twice.

North to La Pelosa & Asinara Island

At the northeast tip of Sardinia, past the village of Stintino, is the stunning beach of **La Pelosa ★★★** (4km/2½ miles north of town), which looks like it might have been concocted by Mother Nature after she took some hallucinogenic substances. A broad expanse of soft, crystalline white sand gently gives way to a veritable wading pool of perfectly clear water that goes on and on and on for hundreds of meters without getting deeper than about knee height. The color effects in the water are absolutely breathtaking, floating between palest gray-aqua to brilliant tourmaline. Depending on how the clouds and sun are behaving, the colors can look even more electric.

From the beach of La Pelosa, you can see the island and national park of **Asinara ★** (www.parcoasinara.org; ✆ **079-503388**), about 10km (6 miles) to the northeast. Once a penal colony and closed to the public for a century, Asinara has recently reopened to the public, who come primarily to catch a glimpse of the **albino donkeys** that roam the island's scrubby contours. To reach Asinara, take an authorized boat from Stintino or Porto Torres; these usually leave around 10am, so plan to be at the marinas around 9:30am. There are no car ferries to Asinara, but once there you can take a tram around the island (www.trenino asinara.it; 40€ including boat transfer from Stintino; on Asinara there are stops to visit the old prison, view wildlife, and swim), rent bikes, or set out on any number of hiking trails.

CAGLIARI ★

The capital of Sardinia lies on the southern tier of the island, surrounded by sea and hills. Cagliari is modern-looking except for an evocative medieval quarter, Castello, built up on fortification walls of sun-bleached stone. Its narrow, picturesquely dilapidated streets are filled with *palazzi* from the 1300s and 1400s and several churches, including the city's atmospheric Duomo. Most people visit Cagliari only because they have a few hours or a night to kill when flying in or out of its airport, but chances are they're pleasantly surprised by Cagliari's often cosmopolitan vibe and manageable quantity of sights. You can easily see the city's highlights in the space of an overnight stay.

ESSENTIALS

GETTING THERE **Cagliari-Elmas airport** (www.sogaer.it; ✆ **070-211211**) is just 3km (2 miles) from the city center. It's also Sardinia's busiest airport and served from most major Italian and European cities. By **car,** Cagliari lies at the southern end of the main highway running through Sardinia, the SS131.

GETTING AROUND Within Cagliari, it's best to get around on foot, by bus, or by taxi. Driving in the city is a hassle. Buses are operated by **CTM** (www.ctm cagliari.it) and cost 1.20€ for a single ride. For cabs, call **Radio Taxi 4 Mori** (✆ **070-400101**). If you're staying near the Castello area, Cagliari's major tourist draw, you can walk everywhere. For the recommended side trips to Nora and the Su Nuraxi *nuraghe,* a car is essential. All the major rental agencies have offices in the city center and at the airport; try **AutoEurope** (www.autoeurope.com) for the most competitive rates.

VISITOR INFORMATION The **tourist office** is at Piazza Matteotti (near the waterfront, across from the main bus station and taxi rank; www.visit-cagliari.it; **© 070-669255**), open Monday to Saturday from 9am to 1pm and 5 to 8pm.

Exploring

If, like most people who visit the capital, you only have a few hours to explore, make a beeline for the Castello district, the city's richest trove of architectural and historic sights. Situated high above the rest of town, Castello is a district of panoramic piazzas, quaint alleys, and aging *palazzi*. To reach this area, simply walk straight inland from the port up the gentle slope of shopping street Largo Carlo Felice. Near the top of Largo Carlo Felice, bear right on Via Marino, then take a slight left onto Via Giovanni Spano, where you'll see signs for the elevator (free, always open) that whisks you up through the fortification walls to the heights of Castello and to the top of the bastions of this quarter. This is the southern end of Castello, where the **Porta dei Leoni** (Lion's Gate) dovetails with the splendid Bastione Saint Remy and Terrazza Umberto I above. (There are also free elevators from "lower" Cagliari to the northern end of Castello, at Porta S'Avanzada and the Torre di San Pancrazio. If you can't find the elevator entrances, just ask a local, *"Ascensore?"*) Castello is just as much fun to explore, and perhaps even more so, in the evening as during the day.

The Porta dei Leoni elevator will deposit you before the **Bastione Saint Remy ★★** (sometimes referred to as Terrazza Umberto I), the piazza-like southeast corner of the citadel walls that affords 270-degree views over Cagliari and its harbor. This is the beating heart of Castello and a favorite meeting place, day or night, for Cagliaritani. At the north end of the square is the very hip **Caffè degli Spiriti ★★** (**© 070-655884**), with an alfresco terrace and tables under a tented and glassed-in dining area. Grab a seat and an iced coffee here while you drink in the view from this lofty position.

Heading west from Bastione Saint Remy, up Via dell'Università, you soon reach the Pisan-era **Torre dell'Elefante ★**, which impresses with its original wooden portcullis still *in situ*. The tower is named for the sculpture of a marble elephant sitting on a ledge on one of the tower walls. (Like the Torre San Pancrazio a few blocks north, the Torre dell'Elefante only has one solid facade—that which faces "intruders" on the Castello district; the inside of the tower, with its wooden stairs and landings, is left exposed to the elements.) At the northern, higher end of Castello is the tallest monument and architectural symbol of the city, the Pisan **Torre di San Pancrazio ★** (Piazza Indipendenza; **© 070-6776400;** Apr–Oct Tues–Sun 9am–1pm and 3:30–7:30pm, Nov–Mar Tues–Sun 9am–4:30pm; 2€). Dating from 1305, this Pisan defense tower is a sort of twin to the Torre dell'Elefante at the southeast edge of Castello. Climb the steps for a wonderful view of the city and its bay—the same view watchmen saw while looking for enemies approaching from the sea.

Adjacent to the Torre San Pancrazio is the **Cittadella dei Musei ★** (Piazza Arsenale; **© 070-662496;** Tues–Sun 9am–8pm; individual admissions 2€–4€), a recently restructured conglomerate of museums and **panoramic grounds ★** in the former Piedmontese arsenal.

Right in the middle of Castello, the **cathedral ★** (*cattedrale,* or *duomo;* Piazza Palazzo, off Via Martini; **© 070-663837;** Mon–Fri 8am–12:30pm and 4:30–8pm, Sat–Sun 8am–1pm and 4–8pm; free admission) was constructed in the 13th century in the Pisan style. Inside, there are splendid **pulpits ★** by Maestro Guglielmo that illustrate the life of Christ.

Cagliari's promenade.

Shopping

As Sardinia's biggest city, Cagliari also has plenty of good shopping. The main retail thoroughfares in the city center are palm-lined Via Roma, facing the port, and the perpendicular Largo Carlo Felice, which leads north and uphill toward the Castello district.

For only-in-Sardinia gifts and home furnishings, your best bet is **ISOLA ★**, Via Bacaredda 176 (www.isola-cagliari.com; ✆ **070-492756**), a government-run exhibition of the finest arts and crafts on the island. This is high-quality stuff that doesn't come cheap, but the pieces are exquisite.

Entertainment & Nightlife

The best place to soak up what nightlife there is in the Sardinian capital is atop the ramparts of the Castello district. Ground zero of the action is Bastione Saint Remy and the **Caffè degli Spiriti ★★** (see "Exploring," above), whose open-air bar is abuzz with scenesters well into the wee hours. Not far away, the cavelike bar **Librarium Nostrum ★** (Via Santa Croce 33; ✆ **070-650943**) is a hip hideaway with nice views from its outdoor tables.

Where to Eat & Stay

Dal Corsaro ★ SARDINIAN One of Cagliari's preeminent dining addresses, this restaurant is classically elegant, catering to both locals out for a special occasion or tourists out for a bit of a splurge. The Deidda family has been in charge since 1967, and they are ambassadors of Sardinian regional cuisine, using only the freshest ingredients. They excel in their fresh fish dishes, including filet of red tuna with an onion fondant, black olives, and tomatoes, and in their filet of white fish with mussels and caramelized eggplant. Especially delicious is their homemade spaghetti with calamari and fresh lemon.

Viale Regina Margherita 28. ✆ **070-664318.** Reservations required. Entrees 15€–30€. AE, DC, MC, V. Mon–Sat 12:30–3:30pm and 8–11pm. Closed first 2 weeks of Jan.

Due Colonne ★ You won't find a more strategic location in Cagliari—the Due Colonne occupies the prime real estate where Via Roma intersects Largo Carlo Felice, in the heart of Cagliari's Marina district, putting guests within steps of the city's most vibrant shopping and dining and the portside promenade. Rooms are classic and comfortable, with big bathrooms; many units have a view over the busy harbor, though these are also a bit noisier.

Via Sardegna 4. www.hotel2colonne.it. ✆ **070-658710.** 23 units. 110€–130€ double. AE, DC, MC, V. **Amenities:** Breakfast room; Internet (30 min. free; 2€ per 12 hr. after that). *In room:* A/C, TV, hair dryer, minibar.

Opera Prima ★★ SARDINIAN Even better (and less expensive) than Dal Corsaro is this friendly spot along the water just east of the main port area. Opera Prima is the rare dining establishment that does fish and meat equally well, so feel free to toggle back and forth between the *mare* and *terra* selections on the menu. Everything, from the antipasti to the dessert, is mouth-wateringly memorable.

Via Campidano 9. ✆ **070-684619.** Reservations required. Entrees 10€–18€. AE, DC, MC, V. Tues–Sun 12:30–3:30pm and 8–11:30pm.

T Hotel ★ A cylindrical skyscraper with a showy contemporary lobby, the T makes quite a statement and is without a doubt the "cool" address in this town. The T has a slick ground floor cafe (tables are set on catwalks surrounded by shallow pools) that draws the dashing and trendy of the city for business lunches and after-work drinks. The lower level houses a futuristic looking spa. Once off the elevator on the guest unit floors, however, the T disappoints somewhat: Standard rooms, while done up in bold colors and equipped with the latest in "design" fixtures, are on the small side. The king-size mattresses are ridiculously comfortable, however. The staff is eager to please, and there's definitely an appealing energy to the place that's hard to find elsewhere in Cagliari. Note that the hotel

The shopping arcade along Via Roma in Cagliari.

is in an anonymous modern neighborhood, about a 10-minute cab or bus ride to the historic district.

Via dei Giudicati 66. www.thotel.it. ✆ **070-47400.** 207 units. 120€–200€ double. AE, DC, MC, V. **Amenities:** 2 restaurants; bar; concierge; pool; room service; spa. *In room:* A/C, TV, hair dryer, minibar, Wi-Fi (free).

Side Trips

In addition to the ideas below, you can also theoretically use Cagliari as a base for daylong forays to the beaches of Chia (p. 917) or Villasimius (p. 919). Each is only about a 90-minute drive from the capital; however, most beach-minded vacationers prefer to base themselves in those resort areas, which are well equipped with accommodations and dining.

NORTH TO SU NURAXI *NURAGHE* & THE GIARA DI GESTURI

The most celebrated of Sardinia's unique *nuraghi* (and Sardinia's only UNESCO World Heritage site) is **Su Nuraxi ★★** (✆ **070-9368128;** daily 9am–sunset; 8€ includes obligatory guided tour, offered every half-hour), near the town of Barumini. Su Nuraxi, which just means "the *nuraghe,*" is an easy half-day trip from Cagliari (90-min. drive each way). About 40km (25 miles) north of Cagliari, exit the highway and follow SS. 197 to Barumini for 20km (12 miles), then follow brown signs to SU NURAXI or NURAGHE. Within the 1500-B.C. *nuraghe,* which is dominated by a conical central tower, or *mastio,* 19m (62 ft.) high, there are all sorts of mystical-feeling corridors and stairs, and guides will point out ingenious engineering touches.

Immediately north of Su Nuraxi is the basalt plateau called the **Giara di Gesturi ★★**. This is an idyllic area for hiking, with cork oak woods alternating with savannah and little mirrorlike ponds. The Giara di Gesturi is home to a species of miniature horse, *is quaddeddus,* which is only about 1m (3 ft.) tall and unique to this habitat. The easiest way to reach the area is from Gesturi, north of Barumini.

WEST TO THE RUINS AT NORA

Sardinia's most important Roman ruins are at the **archaeological area of Nora ★★** (✆ **070-921470;** daily 9am–8pm, in winter until 5:30pm; 5.50€), with ruins of theaters, baths, markets, and houses scattered along the water at Capo di Pula promontory, an easy 36km (22-mile) drive from Cagliari. Follow highway signs to Pula; after about 25km (16 miles) on the SS. 195, follow brown signs to Nora, CITTÀ ROMANA or ZONA ARCHEOLOGICA.

Nora is part of a larger town, **Pula ★**, which is a fun detour in its own right. The main piazza is always lively and there are good restaurants and shopping.

SOUTHWESTERN SARDINIA ★★

Unless you're heading for one of the cushy "resort-villages" in Santa Margherita di Pula, southwestern Sardinia feels remote and offbeat. Brawny foothills, shady pinewoods, and windswept dunes predominate on this largely uncontaminated stretch of coast; hotels and resorts are oases unto themselves, and there isn't much in the way of village life. If you're looking for a social atmosphere and "action," this probably isn't where you want to be. On the flipside, the atmosphere in the southwest is utterly romantic and relaxing, and the top attractions here—the beaches—are plenty compelling for anyone in search of a place to chill and unwind. The best stretches are along the Costa del Sud, around Chia and Teulada. Completing the beach vibe, there are even pink flamingos living in a marsh behind the beaches of Chia. This part of the island gets a lot of wind, making it a destination for windsurfers and kitesurfers, but nearly all of the beaches have calm, kid-friendly waters.

Essentials

GETTING THERE All the places listed here are less than a 2-hour drive from Cagliari's Elmas airport, and most are only about an hour away, along highway SS195.

GETTING AROUND One of the main roads in southwestern Sardinia, the coastal SP71 highway between Chia and Teulada, ranks as one of the most spectacular drives in Italy. Many hotels here provide bicycles for their guests, which are a viable option for getting from beach to beach and for experiencing the panoramic SP71. But you'll also need a car in almost all cases to explore this part of the island.

VISITOR INFORMATION Sardinia's **official tourism website,** www.sardegnaturismo.it, has information about Chia and the southwest.

Chia & the Costa del Sud ★★

Virgin dunes and stunning white-sand beaches lapped by waters in amazingly variegated shades of turquoise make the seaside around Chia and Capo Teulada the most popular zone in southwest Sardinia. Santa Margherita, which you'll drive through on the way down here from Cagliari, is almost entirely private beach, either belonging to all-inclusive resorts (like the way overrated and overpriced Forte Village— don't even consider it) or vacation homes. The beaches of Santa Margherita di Pula are nowhere near as pretty as those near Chia and Teulada, so don't let those snobby gated properties make you feel like you're missing out!

It may be difficult to tear yourself away from the beaches, but this area also boasts an inland natural treasure in the **Is Cannoneris forest ★★** (Località Sedda Is Tovus; ✆ **070-9270285**), an easy half-hour detour from Chia. At 4,768 hectares (11,782 acres), it's one of the largest holm oak forests in Europe and is home to many examples of endemic fauna, like the Sardinian deer. An extensive network of well-maintained paths makes this a hiker's dream and a great option when you've had too much sun. (To reach Is Cannoneris, drive to the town of Domus de Maria, then follow signs to Sedda Is Tovus and Is Cannoneris.)

BEACHES

The prime beach zone begins just before (east of) the Torre di Chia, an old Spanish watchtower. (From the SP71 highway, follow signs to Torre di Chia.) The beach directly below the tower is called **Su Portu,** a perfectly rounded sickle of the kind of brilliant and fine white sand that is the hallmark of this part of Sardinia. Along the access road to Su Portu, another road branches off to the left and to the longer beach of **Sa Colonia ★**. Sa Colonia is backed by the Stagno di Chia (Chia Pond), which is full of **pink flamingos,** herons, and cormorants.

Back on SP71, continue west for another 1.7km (1 mile) to reach the turnoff for Su Giudeu. In fact, this road leads to several beaches (and several hotels), including Campana, Su Giudeu, and Cala Cipolla. Each of these is signposted, but drive slowly so as not to miss them; Cala Cipolla is the farthest away, though it's only 2km (1¼ miles) in from the main highway. **Campana ★** is the first one you'll come to, and it's essentially an extension of the larger beach to the west, **Su Giudeu ★★**; together, they form a wide expanse of gently sloping golden sand and placid water that is generally regarded as the best beach in Cagliari province. Su Giudeu has all the facilities you need. At the far western end of Su Giudeu, follow a short stretch of dirt road to **Cala Cipolla ★★**, a delightful cove set within a narrow bay, framed by granitic promontories and dense *macchia mediterranea.*

After Cala Cipolla and Capo Spartivento promontory, Chia ends and the coast becomes rather squiggly and mostly rocky, with no beach access for several kilometers. Return to the SP71, following signs for Teulada, and go west about 5km (3 miles); turn left where you see signs for Tuerredda, the most celebrated sunning and swimming locale of the Costa del Sud. **Tuerredda ★★★** is a south-facing cove, within a larger and protected bay of powdery sand and quasi-Polynesian sea. In the middle of the bay, accessible by a short swim through crystalline blue-green waters, is the Isolotto di Tuerredda, an islet where you can dry off on the smooth, sun-warmed rocks or sand. Tuerredda has a snack bar, a restaurant, and boat rentals. Spread your towel on the sand or rent a beach chair from one of the vendors.

WHERE TO EAT & STAY

Even the simplest hotels in this area are rather pricey in high season. For something more affordable, try the **Locanda Sa Colonia** (www.sacoloniachia.it; **✆ 070-9230001;** doubles 140€–220€), on the beach in Chia.

Aquadulci ★★ Discreet luxury is the hallmark of this hotel near the beach of Su Giudeu. The Aquadulci features minimalist, eco-friendly style in its airy, contemporary guest rooms and common areas. Within steps of your room is the hotel's subtropical garden, where hammocks are suspended between palms, and its swimming pool. The whole place has the feel of a spa, and in fact there is an on-site *centro benessere* with the full gamut of massages and body treatments. The famous beaches of Chia are less than a 10-minute walk away, on a boardwalk over the dunes. Guests are mostly Italian, especially young families and honeymooners. ***Tip:*** Classic rooms are really too small; opt for a superior or junior suite if budget allows.

Località Capo Spartivento, Chia. www.aquadulci.com. **✆ 070-9230555.** 41 units. 180€–500€ double. AE, DC, MC, V. **Amenities:** Restaurant; bar; babysitting; bike rentals; concierge; pool; room service; spa. *In room:* A/C, TV, hair dryer, minibar, Wi-Fi (free).

Ristorante Mirage ★ SARDINIAN/SEAFOOD Seafood reigns at what many regard as the best free-standing restaurant in Chia. It's not cheap, but the cuisine is to die for and a dinner here the perfect way to cap off a day of rest and relaxation on the beach. The word is out—it's a must to book your table in advance. The place is open year-round, which is a good sign: Long after the tourists have gone home, a dedicated customer base of locals keeps the Mirage in business.

Viale Chia 10. www.miragechia.it. **✆ 070-9230249.** Reservations recommended. Entrees 12€–20€. AE, DC, MC, V. Wed–Mon noon–3pm and 7:30–11:30pm.

SOUTHEASTERN SARDINIA: VILLASIMIUS & THE COSTA REI ★★

When waxing rhapsodic about Sardinia's Caribbean-like seas, island aficionados are usually talking about the southeast part of the island. This beach paradise—namely around Villasimius and the Costa Rei—is mighty tempting for the weekend sun seeker or anyone looking for complete relaxation. Only an hour's drive from Cagliari, this stretch of the island has a gorgeous landscape that feels like somewhere between the South Pacific and the Costa Smeralda, full of turquoise coves fringed by fine sandy beaches, lush vegetation, and granite outcrops where pirate ships wouldn't look out of place. This Mediterranean idyll can be yours for prices considerably lower than what you'll pay on the Costa Smeralda or even in the southwest, around Chia. If there's a downside to all this, it's that parts of the southeast have been developed recently and quite rapidly as a sort of more democratic, family-oriented cousin of the Costa Smeralda.

Essentials

GETTING THERE Use Cagliari's Elmas airport to reach Villasimius and the Costa Rei, which are only about an hour's drive from the capital. If arriving here by car from elsewhere on the island, take the main highway SS131 south to Cagliari-Quartu Sant'Elena, and follow the SS125 to Villasimius or Costa Rei (sometimes signposted as Costa Rey).

GETTING AROUND Given the variety of hidden coves on this stretch of the island, your own car is a must. You can rent one at Cagliari airport from any of the major carriers, including budget-friendly **AutoEurope** (www.autoeurope.com).

VISITOR INFORMATION There is a **tourist information office** in Villasimius at Piazza Giovanni XXIII (www.villasimiusweb.com; ✆ **070-7930271**), open Monday to Saturday 8am to 2pm and also from 3 to 5pm Monday and Thursday.

Exploring

The best beach in Villasimius is **Porto Giunco ★**, sometimes called the "beach of two seas" because the Mediterranean on the eastern side and the Notteri pond on the western side are separated by a tongue of sand just a few dozen meters wide. Porto Giunco's very white, fine sand and striking looks have made it a popular location for Italian TV spots promoting the glamorous beach life. A bit north of here, **Splaggia Simius ★** is the well-equipped town beach of Villasimius, with a wide band of superfine sand—great for long beach walks.

Leaving some of that development behind, head north to **Punta Molentis ★★** and the eponymous beach there, a little peninsular promontory with sea on both sides (sand to the west, rocks to the east) and a charming little thatched-roof *ristoro* (casual restaurant) called I Due Mari (by reservation only, see "Where to Eat & Stay," below), accessible by a boardwalk over the rocks. Punta Molentis is hardly ever crowded, nor is the excellent beach at **Cala Sinzias ★★★**, about 15km (9⅓ miles) north of here. Cala Sinzias is one of those vacation-in-paradise poster-child beaches—a smooth expanse of pale golden pink sand lapped by gin-clear turquoise water. This paradisiacal setting is the beginning of the Costa Rei, which refers to the long parenthesis of sandy shore between Cala Sinzias and Capo Ferrato. However, farther north, the Costa Rei gets a lot more crowded and its beaches much more prone to strong winds, especially the *maestrale* from the north that can blow sand all over you and make it difficult to enjoy the gorgeous setting unless you're a windsurfer. The flourlike sand of **Costa Rei ★★** beach goes on for 8km (5 miles), backed by thousands of cookie-cutter vacation homes, most of which have been erected in the past 20 years.

Where to Eat & Stay

Vacation houses abound in coastal southeastern Sardinia; an agency with comprehensive listings for modern, well-appointed villas is **Rent Sardinia** (www.rent-sardinia.com; ✆ **848580081** toll-free in Italy or 070-684545). A property that sleeps six can range from about 800€ per week in low season to upwards of 3,000€ per week in high season, depending on the location, distance from the water, and amenities.

Hotel Garden Beach Cala Sinzias ★★ The setting alone, between the eucalyptus woods and gorgeous sands of Cala Sinzias beach, is enough of a selling point, but the Garden Beach is also a very well-run, attractive hotel with comprehensive services and amenities. Guest rooms are in low-slung Spanish-style buildings and decorated with charming Sardinian flair. Handsome pavilions around the property house bars and restaurants, though nothing makes as big an impression as the swimming pool, as big as a small sea. A robust lineup of kids' club activities (soccer camps, dance) will keep the little ones busy.

Strada Panoramica Villasimius-Costa Rei, Cala Sinzias. www.hotelgardenbeach.it. ✆ **070-995037.** 106 units. 160€–348€ double. AE, MC, V. **Amenities:** 3 restaurants; bar; babysitting; kids' programs; fitness room; pool; tennis; watersports equipment. *In room*: A/C, satellite TV, hair dryer, minibar, patio.

I Due Mari ★SEAFOOD On the far outer curve of Punta Molentis beach, this open-air cafe is open by reservation only for lunch and dinner. The set menu includes an appetizer, loads of grilled fish, dessert, wine, water, espresso, and a *digestivo*. It's not a gourmet experience but the intimate setting in this quiet cove, weathered fishing boats bobbing within spitting distance, is sublime.

Punta Molentis, 3km (2 miles) east of Villasimius. ✆ **393-4077632** or 346-5221679. Reservations essential. Prix-fixe lunch 20€; dinner 40€. No credit cards. June–Sept at 1pm for lunch; 9pm for dinner.

Il Miraggio ★★★ ☺ 📷 SEAFOOD/SARDINIAN Torchlight flickering around you, your toes in the sand, feast on amazing seafood pastas and grilled fish at this wonderful beach restaurant near Villasimius. During the day, it's a kiosk that sells *panini* to beachgoers and serves quick lunches, but at dinner, the food gets a bit more serious and all tables are moved out on the sand and under the stars. When booking your table, specify *prima fila* (front row) so that you can gaze out past the dwarf palms and flaming Tiki torches to the sea—and perhaps also keep an eye on your kids, who are welcome at this informal place and often play in the sand between courses. As low-key and family-friendly as it is, Il Miraggio is also a bit trendy; I've even spotted a few Italian celebrities here.

Località Campus, Villasimius. ✆ **070-798021.** Reservations essential. Entrees 10€–18€. AE, DC, MC, V. Apr–Oct daily 11:30am–3:30pm (snack bar/lunch) and 8–11pm.

17

PLANNING YOUR TRIP TO ITALY

With so many historical treasures, epicurean pleasures, and opportunities for outdoor leisure, it will be a challenge deciding where to spend your time.

As with any trip, a little preparation is essential before you start your journey to Italy. This chapter provides a variety of planning tools, including information on how to get there, tips on accommodations, and the inside track regarding local resources.

Getting around Italy can range from very easy in the north (minus the city and highway traffic and the occasional jampacked train) to sometimes impossible without a car in the south. Getting to and from Italy is exceedingly easy with well-served international airports in Rome and Milan and an extensive network of local airports all up and down the peninsula.

For certain things—including getting a nice hotel room in Milan, especially during the spring and fall fashion weeks and the design trade show in April—it is key to plan ahead. Many mountain resorts fill up months prior to the first snowfall, and the choicest spots on the Riviera (especially the Cinque Terre) as well as on the Amalfi Coast are snapped up before it starts getting hot. As for Venice, it's a general mob scene in any month not containing an *R* and during any of its spectacular festivals. Ditto for Florence, though ever so slightly less intense.

If you do your homework on special events, pick the right place for the right season, and pack for a variety of climates, preparing for a trip to Italy should be pleasant and uncomplicated.

GETTING THERE

By Plane

If you're flying across an ocean, you'll most likely land at Milan's **Malpensa Airport** (MXP; www.seamilano.eu; ✆ **02-232-323**), 45km (28 miles) from downtown, or Rome's **Leonardo da Vinci-Fiumicino Airport** (FCO; www.adr.it; ✆ **06-659-51**), 40km (25 miles) from downtown.

Milan From **Malpensa** Terminal 1, you have the choice of a 50-minute train ride with **Trenitalia** to Stazione Centrale (leaves hourly and costs 7€), the city's main train station, or a 30-minute trip with **Malpensa Express** that costs 11€ and heads half-hourly to Cadorna train station (also in central Milan, but toward the western side of town). From Cadorna, a short Metro or taxi ride will bring you to Stazione Centrale from which trains depart for all corners of northern Italy. There are also two **bus** companies calling in at both Terminal 1 and Terminal 2 that make the 50-minute run to the east side of Stazione Centrale and that between them have a departure about every 10 minutes. In both cases, you can buy the tickets on the bus for no extra charge. **Malpensa Shuttle** costs 7.50€, as does **Autostradale,** though the latter also has a three-tickets-for-the-price-of-two deal

PREVIOUS PAGE: **A woman biking in Lucca, Tuscany.**

(you don't have to use all three tickets at the same time so you can save one or two for your trip back to Malpensa). A **taxi** to the city center has a fixed price of 85€.

For flights to Milan from within Europe, you might also fly into the ridiculously convenient **Linate Airport** (LIN; www.seamilano.eu; ✆ **02-7485-2200**), about 8km (5 miles) east of the city. From **Linate, Starfly** shuttles (✆ **02-5858-7237**) make the 30-minute trip from 6am to midnight to Milan's Stazione Centrale for 4€. **City bus no. 73** leaves every 10 minutes for the San Babila Metro stop downtown (1€ for a regular bus ticket bought from any newsagent inside the airport, 1.50€ onboard and you must have exact change) and takes about 25 minutes. The **express no. 73X** is faster, though there is only one an hour. The trip into town by **taxi** costs about 15€.

Rome From **Leonardo da Vinci,** you can opt for the Leonardo Express, a somewhat dilapidated **train** that in 35 minutes takes you to the city's Termini train station. The tickets, which must be validated before boarding at the machines on the platforms, cost 14€. Trains run from about 6am to 11pm. There are also several **bus lines** to the city center. For a flat fee of 40€, up to four people and their bags can be taken by **taxi** to any address in the city center.

Rome's much smaller **Ciampino Airport** (CIA; www.adr.it; ✆ **06-6595-9515**) serves low-cost airlines connecting to European cities and other destinations in Italy. **Bus** options from the airport include a short bus ride (1€) which will bring you to the Ciampino train station from where you can connect to Rome's Termini train station in about 15 minutes. You can also bus directly to the center (40 min., 4€) or walk out to the road in front of the airport to catch a local bus to the Anagnina stop of the Rome Metro that passes three times an hour (20 min., 1.50€). For a flat fee of 30€, up to four people and their bags can be taken by **taxi** to any address in the city center.

FLYING DIRECTLY TO GENOA, BERGAMO, VENICE, BOLOGNA, PISA, OR BARI

Budget carriers within Europe fly to a number of Italian cities, six of the most popular are Genoa's **Cristoforo Colombo Airport** (www.airport.genova.it), Bergamo's **Orio al Serio Airport** (www.sacbo.it), Venice's **Marco Polo Airport** (www.veniceairport.it), Bologna's **Marconi Airport** (www.bologna-airport.it), Pisa's **Galileo Galilei Airport** (www.pisa-airport.com), and Bari's **Palese Airport** (www.aeroportidipuglia.it).

In Venice, **ATVO** buses (www.atvo.it) run every 30 minutes between Piazzale Roma and the airport for 5€, and also run more frequently to the busy train station in nearby Mestre. Bergamo's airport is easily reached from Milan with a shuttle that leaves every 30 minutes from Stazione Centrale, takes about an hour, and costs 9.90€. Genoa's airport is very close to the downtown, taking 20 minutes on the bus (4€) that runs to the Stazione Principe. From Bologna's airport, it's a 20-minute ride to the center of town or you can bus directly to Ferrara, Modena, and Siena. Pisa's airport is a 40-minute train ride from Florence and is also connected to most of Tuscany's other tourist destinations. From the Bari airport, you can connect easily to the city center as well as directly with most of the nearby big cities, including Lecce, Brindisi, Taranto, Matera, and Foggia.

By Car

Italy's superhighways connect so seamlessly with their counterparts in France, Switzerland, Austria, and Slovenia that, besides the road signs, you might not even realize that you have entered Italy. Some of northern Italy's major cities—specifically Milan, Turin, Genoa, and Trieste—are very close to the border, making them logical stopping points on your first day if you arrive from abroad by car.

For more information on driving in Italy, from road rules to gasoline, see "Getting Around," below.

By Train

Traveling to Italy by train probably only makes sense if you are coming into Milan or another major city in the north. You can arrive in Milan on direct trains from Barcelona, Nice, Paris, and Lyon. Direct trains from central and Eastern Europe arrive at Verona, Venice, and Trieste.

For more information about train travel in Italy, see "Getting Around," below.

GETTING AROUND

By Plane

If you are sticking to the northern half of the country, the only flight vaguely worth considering is Milan-Trieste, which takes an hour. Though Alitalia has a pretty good lock on the route, you can sometimes find cheap deals so it might be worth considering starting your trip in Milan, working your way with the train or a car slowly east all the way to Trieste and then taking a flight back to Milan, where you will probably have your international flight back home.

Internal flights are a good option if you are planning to visit both the north and the south of the country in the same trip. Both Alitalia and several low-cost airlines serve most of the major tourist destinations, including on the islands of Sicily and Sardinia.

By Car

Much of Italy is accessible by public transportation, but to explore vineyards, ski resorts, and smaller towns, a car will save you tons of time.

If you're planning to rent a car, you'll get the **best rental rate** if you book your car from home instead of renting direct in Italy—in fact, if you decide to rent once you've arrived, it's worth it to call home to have someone arrange it all from there. You must be 25 or older to rent from most agencies (although some accept ages 21 and up).

The legalities and contractual obligations of renting a car in Italy (where accident and theft rates are very high) are more complicated than those in almost any other country in Europe. You must have nerves of steel, a sense of humor, and a valid driver's license or International Driver's Permit. Insurance on all vehicles is compulsory, though what kind and how much is up to you and your credit card company: Ask the right questions and check with your credit card company before leaving home.

Note: If you're planning to rent a car in Italy during high season, you should book well in advance. It's not at all unusual to arrive at the airport in Milan in June and July to find that every last agent is all out of cars, perhaps for a week. Although the 21% IVA value-added tax is unavoidable, you can do away with the government airport tax of 19% by picking up your car at an office in town (the tax is 9% at most big train stations).

The autostrada, or superhighway, that runs the length of the Po valley from Turin to Trieste is the A4. Other autostrade you are likely to use if you rent a car are the A1 connecting Milan to Rome and Naples and the A14, which links Bologna with Rimini and then runs the length of the Adriatic coast to Bari. It can sometimes be tricky to get to the autostrada from the city center so insist on specific, detailed directions from the car rental agencies and make use of a co-pilot who knows how to use a map. In the bigger cities you will first have to get to the *tangenziale,* or "beltway," which will eventually lead to your highway of choice. Just to make things more confusing, the beltway in Rome is known as the Grande Raccordo Anulare, or "Big Ring Road."

Unless you are planning to drive the length of Italy, you will find that the distances are manageable and that the country's various macro-areas are rather compact. Genoa to Milan, for example, is 130km (81 miles) on a highway where people regularly drive in excess of 130 kmph (81 mph). But don't think it will take you only an hour to drive from Milan to Genoa as you have to budget for the potentially slow-going from downtown to the *tangenziale* and then the highway. Milan to Verona is about 160km (100 miles), and Verona to Venice is another 121km (75 miles). Coast to coast, then, is only 4 hours, even at North American driving speeds (if traffic isn't bad). The first part of the A4 heading east from Milan toward Verona and Venice is the most traveled highway in Europe, so the going can get slow, especially on Friday afternoons leaving the cities and Sunday nights on the way back into town, and rush hour around the cities any day of the week can be epic. Plan to travel midweek and midday, if possible. Rome to Bari is 455km (282 miles) and should take under 5 hours, while Rome to Siena is 240km (150 miles) and takes less than 3 hours. See **www.autostrade.it** for live traffic updates.

Tolls can get expensive, costing about 1€ for every 16km (10 miles), which means that it would cost about 15€ for a trip from Milan to Venice. Add in the gasoline and the car rental, and it's often cheaper to take the train from city to city, even with two people.

Driving in Italy can be nerve-racking—for both the winding roads and the Italian penchant for always driving as if you absolutely had to be home 10 minutes ago. Both rental-car and gas prices are as high as they get in all of Europe. Before leaving home, you can apply for an **International Driving Permit** from the American Automobile Association (AAA; www.aaa.com; ✆ **800/622-7070** or 650/294-7400). In Canada, the permit is available from the Canadian Automobile Association (CAA; www.caa.ca; ✆ **416/221-4300**). In the U.K., contact the British Automobile Association (AA; www.theaa.com; ✆ **08706/000-371**). Technically, you need this permit and your actual driver's license to drive in Italy, though in practice your license itself often suffices.

Italy's equivalent of AAA is the **Automobile Club d'Italia (ACI),** a branch of the Touring Club Italiano. They're the people who respond when you place an emergency call to ✆ **803-116** for road breakdowns, though they do charge for this service if you're not a member. You may join at the border as you're driving into Italy, at one of the club's regional offices (in Milan, Viale Sarca 189; ✆ **02-643-2142**), or online at **www.aci.it**.

DRIVING RULES Italian drivers aren't maniacs; they only appear to be. Well, some actually are maniacs and with those the best you can do is just get out of their way. Spend any time on an Italian highway and you will have the experience of somebody driving up insanely close to you from behind while

Travel Times Between the Major Cities

CITIES	DISTANCE	(FASTEST) TRAIN TRAVEL TIME	DRIVING TIME
Florence to Milan	298km/185 miles	1¾ hr.	3½ hr.
Florence to Venice	281km/174 miles	2 hr.	3¼ hr.
Milan to Venice	267km/166 miles	2½ hr.	3 hr., 10 min.
Rome to Florence	277km/172 miles	1½ hr.	3 hr.
Rome to Milan	572km/355 miles	3 hr.	5½ hr.
Rome to Naples	219km/136 miles	1 hr., 10 min.	2½ hr.
Rome to Venice	528km/327 miles	3¾ hr.	5½ hr.
Rome to Genoa	501km/311 miles	5 hr.	5¼ hr.
Rome to Torino	669km/415 miles	4½ hr.	6½ hr.

flashing his or her headlights. The first time this happens, it will cause an immediate hot sweat and will make the heart of even the most stoic of drivers miss a beat. Take a deep breath and don't panic; this is the rather aggressive signal for you to move to the right so he can pass and until you do he will stay mind-bogglingly close to you. On a two-lane road, the idiot passing someone in the opposing traffic who has swerved into your lane expects you to veer obligingly over into the shoulder so three lanes of traffic can fit—he would do the same for you. Many Italians seem to think that using their blinkers is optional, so be aware that the car in front of you could be getting ready to turn at any time.

Autostrade are toll highways, denoted by green signs and a number prefaced with an *A*, like the A1 from Milan to Rome. A few aren't numbered and are simply called *raccordo,* a connecting road between two cities (such as Florence-Siena and Florence-Pisa). ***Strade statali*** (singular is *strada statale*) are state roads, usually without a center divider and two lanes wide (though sometimes they can be a divided four-way highway), indicated by blue signs. Their route numbers are prefaced with an *SS*, as in the SS11 from Milan to Venice. On signs, however, these official route numbers are used infrequently. Usually, you'll just see blue signs listing destinations by name with arrows pointing off in the appropriate directions. Even if it's just a few kilometers from the *strada statale,* often the town you're looking for won't be mentioned on the sign at the appropriate turnoff. It's impossible to predict which of all the towns that lie along a road will be the ones chosen to list on a particular sign. Sometimes the sign gives only the first minuscule village that lies past the turnoff, at other times it lists the first major town down that road, and some signs mention only the major city the road eventually leads to, even if it's hundreds of kilometers away. It pays to study the map before coming to an intersection. The *strade statali* can be frustratingly slow due to traffic, traffic lights, and the fact that they cross through countless towns, so when possible opt to pay for the autostrade.

The **speed limit** on roads in built-up areas around towns and cities is 50 kmph (31 mph). On rural roads it's 90 kmph (56 mph) and on the highway its 130 kmph (81 mph). Italians have an astounding disregard for these limits, mostly because they're enforced only if the offense is egregious. However, police can ticket you and collect the fine on the spot. The blood-alcohol limit in Italy is 0.05%, often achieved with just two drinks; driving above the limit can result in a fine, driving ban, or imprisonment. Safety belts are obligatory in both the front and the back seats.

As far as ***parcheggio*** (parking) is concerned, on streets, white lines indicate free public spaces, blue lines are pay public spaces, and yellow lines mean only residents are allowed to park. Meters don't line the sidewalk; rather, there's one machine on the block where you punch in how long you want to park. The machine spits out a ticket that you leave on your dashboard. Sometimes streets will have an attendant who'll come around and give you your time ticket (pay him or her when you get ready to leave). If you park in an area marked PARCHEGGIO DISCO ORARIO, root around in your rental car's glove compartment for a cardboard parking disc (or buy one at a gas station). With this device, you dial up the hour of your arrival and display it on your dashboard. You're allowed *un'ora* (1 hr.) or *due ore* (2 hr.), according to the sign. **Parking lots** have ticket dispensers, but booths are not usually manned as you exit. Take your ticket with you when you park; when you return to the lot to get your car and leave, first visit the office or automated payment machine to exchange your ticket for a paid receipt that you then use to get through the automated exit.

ROAD SIGNS Here's a brief rundown of the road signs you'll most frequently encounter. A **speed limit** sign is a black number inside a red circle on a white background. The **end of a speed zone** is just black and white, with a black slash through the number. A red circle with a white background, a black arrow pointing down, and a red arrow pointing up means **yield to oncoming traffic,** while a point-down red-and-white triangle means **yield ahead.** Many city centers are closed to traffic and a simple white circle with a red border, or the words *zona pedonale* or *zona traffico limitato,* denotes a **pedestrian zone** (you can drive through only to drop off baggage at your hotel); a white arrow on a blue background is used for Italy's many **one-way streets;** a mostly red circle with a horizontal white slash means **do not enter.** Any image in black on a white background surrounded by a red circle means that image is **not allowed** (for instance, if the image is two cars next to each other, it means no passing; a motorcycle means no Harleys permitted, and so on). A circular sign in blue with a red circle-slash means **no parking.**

Gasoline (gas or petrol), *benzina,* can be found in pull-in gas stations along major roads and on the outskirts of town, as well as in 24-hour stations along the autostrade. Almost all stations are closed for the *riposo* and on Sundays (except for those on the autostrade), but the majority have a pump fitted with a machine that accepts cash so if you have bills in your wallet you can fill up at any time of day. Gasoline is very expensive in Italy and even a small rental car guzzles 40€ to 60€ for a fill-up. Unleaded gas is *senza piombo.*

By Train

Italy, especially the northern half, has one of the best train systems in Europe and you'll find most destinations connected, thus the train is an excellent option if you're looking to visit the major sites without the hassle of renting and driving a car. The vast majority of lines are run by the state-owned **Ferrovie dello Stato,** or **FS** (www.trenitalia.com; © **892-021** for info and to buy tickets).

Almost all towns in Italy have a train station. The major train hubs are in Milan, Genoa, Turin, and Verona in the north; Bologna, Florence, and Rome in the center; and Naples in the south. The travel times and the prices of the tickets vary considerably depending on what type of train you are traveling on.

Along the major east-west train line in northern Italy, from Turin to Milan it will take you an hour (32€ second class) on the nicest and fastest train and 2 hours (9.55€) on the sometimes slightly grimy local. Milan to Verona ranges in price from 9€ to 19€. Verona and Padua are 40 to 90 minutes apart by train, and the trip costs 5€ to 16€. The train continues east to Venice; from Padua, it will take 25 to 50 minutes to get to Venice and will cost 3€ to 15€. The fastest connection onto Trieste from Venice costs 18€ and takes about an hour and a half.

The major north-south train lines in northern Italy are Milan-Genoa (1½ hr. and 18€ on the fastest train) and Trento-Verona (1 hr. and 6€). The country's principal north-south line links Milan to Bologna, Florence, Rome, and Naples. Milan to Rome takes 3 hours on the fastest train (98€, though the price on this and all fast trains drops by as much as 40% if you buy ahead of time and especially if you travel in off-peak hours). ***Note:*** Some Milan-Rome trains are nonstop, skipping even the important Bologna and Florence stations. Rome to Naples takes 70 minutes and costs 45€ on the fast train, or you can spend half as much for a trip that takes twice as long.

The speed, cleanliness, and overall quality of **Italian trains** vary enormously. *Prima classe* (first class) is usually only a shade better than *seconda classe* (second class) and the only real benefits of first class come if you're traveling overnight (in which case you'll often have four berths per compartment rather than six), or the train is overcrowded and there are seats available only in first class.

The **Frecciarossa** is the nicest of the nice and the fastest of the fast (Italy's bullet train), while the **Frecciabianca** uses the same hardware but is a bit slower. They are both also generically called **Eurostar (ES)** and are up to the standard of the best trains in northern Europe, zipping between Italy's biggest cities including on the Milan-Naples line with stops in Bologna, Florence, and Rome (there are also trains doing Milan-Rome nonstop). The Eurostar also runs on the Milan-Venice line—with stops at Verona, Vicenza, and Padua along the way—and does Milan-Turin in an impressive 63 minutes (a trip that takes almost 2 hr. on the slower trains). Speed and cleanliness come at a price with tickets for the Eurostar trains costing as much as three times the cheapest regional train. With the Eurostar you must make a reservation for a particular train when you buy a ticket.

Intercity (IC) trains are a step down from the Eurostar, both in speed and comfort, but are an extremely valid option and are unlikely to provide any shocks. The slower Regionale (R) and Regionale Veloce (RV) make many stops and can sometimes be on the grimy side of things, but they are also ridiculously cheap (a Milan-Turin second-class ticket will put you back only 9.55€ compared with 32€ on the Eurostar). **Espresso** trains are the cheap option if you are traveling long distances, though in terms of comfort and speed you'll be somewhere between a Regionale and Intercity.

Few visitors are prepared for how **crowded** Italian trains can sometimes get, though you can count your blessings that, with the increase in automobile travel, they're not as crowded as they were in times gone by. An Italian train is full only when the corridors are packed solid and there are more than eight people sitting on their luggage in the little vestibules by the doors. Overcrowding is often a problem on Friday evenings, weekends, and holidays, especially in and out of big cities, or just after a strike. In summer, the crowding escalates, and any train going toward a beach in August all but bulges like an overstuffed sausage.

When buying a **regular ticket,** ask for either *andata* (one-way) or *andata e ritorno* (round-trip). If the train you plan to take is an ES or IC, ask for the ticket *con supplemento rapido* (with speed supplement) to avoid on-train penalty charges. The best way to avoid presenting yourself on the train with the wrong ticket is to tell the person at the ticket window exactly what train you are going to take, for example, "the 11:30am train for Venice."

If you don't have a ticket with a reservation for a particular seat on a specific train, then you must **validate you ticket by stamping it in the little yellow box** on the platform before boarding the train. If you board a train without the correct ticket, or without having validated your ticket, you'll have to pay a hefty fine on top of the ticket or supplement, which the conductor will sell you. If you knowingly board a train without a ticket or realize once onboard that you have the wrong type of ticket, your best bet is to search out the conductor who is likely to be more forgiving because you found him and have as such made it clear you weren't trying to ride for free.

Schedules for all trains leaving a given station are printed on yellow posters tacked up on the station wall (the equivalent white poster lists all the arrivals). These are good for getting general information, but you must keep your eye on the electronic boards/television screens throughout the stations that are updated with delays and track (*binario*) changes. You can also get official schedules (and more train information, also in English) and buy tickets at **www.trenitalia.com**.

In the big cities (especially Milan and Rome) and the tourist destinations (above all, Venice and Florence), the lines can be dreadfully long. There is a solution though: **automatic ticket machines.** They are easy to navigate, allow you to follow instructions in English, accept cash and credit cards, and can save your life by cutting down on the stress that comes with waiting on an interminably slow line as you see the minutes tick away until your train is set to leave. ***Note:*** You can't buy international tickets at the automatic machines.

With ticket in hand, the next step is **finding your track.** This is easy at small towns, but can become a challenge in big cities, especially Milan where there are more than two dozen tracks and trains leaving every few minutes. All trains to Venice and Milan's main station (Stazione Centrale) terminate there so all you have to do is look on the electronic boards for those cities, but if you are traveling from Milan to Verona, for example, you must know the terminus station, which might be Verona, but also could be Venice, Trieste, or even Munich in Germany. This information is easily consultable on the aforementioned yellow posters or you can ask the conductors who stand at the head of trains coming close to departure time.

Stations tend to be well run, with luggage storage facilities at all but the smallest and usually a good bar attached that serves surprisingly palatable food. If you pull into a dinky town with a shed-size station, find the nearest bar or *tabacchi,* and the man behind the counter will most likely sell you tickets.

SPECIAL PASSES & DISCOUNTS To buy the **Eurail Italy Pass,** available only outside Italy and priced in U.S. dollars, contact **Rail Europe** (www.raileurope.com). You have 2 months in which to use the train a set number of days; the base number of days is 3, and you can add up to 7 more. For adults, the first-class pass costs $278, second class is $227. Additional days cost roughly $30 more for first class, $25 for second class. For youth tickets (25 and under), a 3-day pass is $183 and additional days about $20 each. Saver passes are available for groups of two to five people traveling together at all times, and amount to a savings of about $40 off each adult pass.

There are also Italy-Greece, Italy-Spain, and Italy-France combinations, in addition to a **rail-and-drive pass.** This is valid for 2 months, during which you can use 3 rail days and 2 car days (and add more car or rail days cheaply). Prices start at $361 for second-class tickets and an economy car with unlimited miles from Hertz.

When it comes to regular tickets, if you're **25 and under,** you can buy a 40€ **Carta Verde (Green Card)** at any Italian train station that gets you a 10% discount for domestic trips and 25% on international connections for 1 year. Present it each time you buy a ticket. A similar deal is available for anyone **61 and over** with the **Carta d'Argento (Silver Card):** 15% off domestic and 25% off international, for 30€ (the Carta d'Argento is free for those 76 and over). Children 11 and under ride half-price while kids 3 and under don't pay (though they don't have the right to their own seat).

By Bus

Although trains are quicker and easier, you can get just about anywhere through a network of dozens of local, provincial, and regional bus lines (see below). **Schedules** in cities are posted in a little box on the pole of the large orange or yellow signs that demarcate the stops. Keep in mind that in smaller towns, buses exist mainly to shuttle workers and schoolchildren, so the most runs are on weekdays, early in the morning, and usually again in midafternoon.

In a big city, the **bus station** for trips between cities is usually near the main train station, while a small town's **bus stop** is usually either in the main square on the edge of town or the bend in the road just outside the main city gate. You should always try to find the local ticket vendor—if there's no office, it's invariably the nearest newsstand or *tabacchi* (signaled by a sign with a white T), or occasionally a bar—but you can usually also buy tickets on the bus. You can sometimes flag down a bus as it passes on a country road, but try to find an official stop (a small sign tacked onto a telephone pole). Tell the driver where you're going and ask him courteously if he'll let you know when you need to get off. When he says *"È la prossima fermata,"* that means yours is the next stop. *"Posso scendere?"* (*Poh*-so *shen*-dair-ay?) is "Can I get off?"

One of the leading bus operators is **SITA,** Viale dei Cadorna 105, Florence (www.sitabus.it; ✆ **055-47-821**). SITA buses serve most parts of the country, especially the central belt, including Tuscany, but not the far frontiers. Among the largest of the other companies, with special emphasis in the north and central parts of the country, is **Autostradale,** with an office in Piazza Castello, Milan (www.autostradale.it; ✆ **02-7200-1304**). It offers regular service to Aosta, which is difficult to get to by train, and to the non-trainable Dolomite ski resorts of Madonna del Campiglio and Cortina d'Ampezzo. **Lazzi,** Via Mercadante 2, Florence (www.lazzi.it; ✆ **055-363-041**), goes through Tuscany, including Siena, and much of central Italy.

Where these nationwide services leave off, **local bus companies** operate in most regions, particularly in the hill sections and the Alpine regions where rail travel isn't possible. For information, see "Getting There" in the city, town, and village sections.

TIPS ON ACCOMMODATIONS

The cheap, family-run *pensione* with the shared bathroom and personal attention does still exist in Italy, but it is increasingly hard to find, especially in the northern half of the country. Not to fear though, in the past decade the country's stock of accommodations has increased and improved to the point that in most spots you are likely to visit you will have a wide array of choices.

Hotels are **rated** by regional boards on a system of one to five stars. Prices aren't directly tied to the star system, but for the most part, the more stars a hotel has, the more expensive it'll be—but a four-star in a small town may be cheaper than a two-star in Venice. The number of stars awarded a hotel is based strictly on the amenities offered and not how clean, comfortable, or friendly a place is, or whether it's a good value for the money overall.

A few of the four- and five-star hotels have their own private **garages,** but most city inns have an agreement with a local garage. In many small towns, a garage is unnecessary because public parking, both free and pay, is widely available and never too far from your hotel. In this book, parking costs and procedures are indicated under the reviews for each hotel, and the rates quoted are per day (overnight). It should go without saying that there are no garages in Venice, as there are no cars.

The **high season** throughout most of Italy runs from May to early September—peaking June through August—and from December 24 to January 6. You can almost always bargain for a cheaper rate if you're traveling in the shoulder season (early spring and late fall) or winter off season (not including Christmas). The reviews usually quote a range of prices; if there is only one figure, it represents the maximum. Prices vary so wildly, depending entirely on availability, that sometimes the only dependable figure is the highest the hotel is allowed to charge. The moral of the story: If it seems like availability is high, you should be getting a discount from the prices you see here.

Most hotels include **breakfast** automatically in the room rate. With very few exceptions, which include most high-end accommodations, Italian hotel breakfasts tend to consist of a *brioche* (croissant) and coffee/cappuccino, occasionally with juice and fresh fruit as well. If it's not included in the room rate, it's rarely worth the 5€ to 15€ charged for it, since you can get the same breakfast—and freshly made instead of packaged—for around 3€ at the bar down the block. It's always worth asking what kind of breakfast is offered and for your room quote without breakfast: *prezzo senza colazione* (*pretz*-zoh *sen*-zah coal-lat-zee-*oh*-nay).

Agriturismo (Farm Stays)

The number of *agriturismi,* working farms or agricultural estates that offer accommodations to visitors who want to stay out in the countryside, has exploded in recent years. You can find excellent *agriturismi* all over Italy. An operation can call itself *agriturismo* only if it offers fewer than 30 beds total, and the agricultural component of the property brings in a larger share of sales than the hospitality part—in other words, the property has to remain a farm and not become just a rural hotel. That's why you'll almost always be offered homemade sausages, home-pressed olive oil, and so on, either because they've been doing it that way for years or because these country barons essentially have been required to become farmers by law.

Agriturismi are generally a crapshoot. The types of accommodations can vary dramatically. Most, though, are miniapartments, sometimes rented out only with a minimum stay of 3 days. Sometimes you're invited to eat big country dinners at the table with the family; other times you cook for yourself. Rates can vary from 60€ for two per day to 250€ and beyond—as much as a board-rated four-star hotel in town. A few choice *agriturismi* are included throughout this book.

There are three independent national organizations that together represent almost all *agriturismi*.

The website of **Terranostra** (www.terranostra.it) lets you refine your search by region (there are more than 150 listed for Lombardy), price, services, and products produced at the farm.

At the site of **Turismo Verde** (www.turismoverde.it), click on *"Scegli il tuo Agriturismo,"* and choose from a list of regions and then provinces (for example, click on Liguria and then La Spezia for something in or near Cinque Terre); this will give you a list of local *agriturismi*. Another useful website is **Agriturist** (www.agriturist.it), which is easy to navigate and offers its text in English. You can find hundreds upon hundreds of individual properties via a search engine.

Villa Rentals

Each summer, thousands of visitors rent an old farmhouse, or "villa," a marketing term used to inspire romantic images of manicured gardens, a Renaissance mansion, and rolling green hills, but in reality this term guarantees no more than four walls and most of a roof.

Actually, finding your countryside Eden isn't that simple, and if you want to ensure a romantic and memorable experience, brace yourself for a lot of research and legwork. Occasionally, you can go through the property owners themselves, but the vast majority of villas are rented out via agencies (see below).

Shop around for a trustworthy agent or representative. Often several outfits will list the same property but charge radically different prices. At some, you sign away any right to refunds if the place doesn't live up to your expectations. Make sure the agency is willing to work with you to find the right property. Always ask to see lots of photos: Get the exterior from several angles to make sure the railroad doesn't pass by the back door, as well as pictures of the bedrooms, kitchen, and bathrooms, and photos of the views out each side of the house.

Ask to see a floor plan to make sure access to the bathroom isn't through a bedroom. Find out if this is the only villa on the property—some people who rent the villa for the isolation find themselves living in a small enclave of foreigners all sharing the same small area. Ask whether the villa is purely a rental unit or if the owners live there during winter but let it out during summer. Renting a

House-Swapping

House-swapping is becoming a more popular and viable means of travel; you stay in their place, they stay in yours, and you both get a more authentic and personal view of a destination—the opposite of the escapist retreat many hotels offer. Try **HomeLink International** (www.homelink.org), the largest and oldest home-swapping organization, founded in 1952, with more than 13,000 listings worldwide ($119 to list a house for a year). **InterVac.com** ($100 for over 10,000 listings) is also reliable. **Craigslist.org** also has an extensive list of housing swap options in Italy, as many Italians are eager to find a cheap vacation alternative in American cities. As with any transaction on Craigslist, do some serious due diligence so you know you are dealing with a reputable person.

lived-in place offers pretty good insurance that the lights, plumbing, heat, and so on will all be working.

One of the best agencies to call is **Rentvillas.com,** 700 E. Main St., Ventura, CA 93001 (www.rentvillas.com; © **800/726-6702** or 805/641-1650; fax 805/641-1630). It has almost 1,000 villas and apartments on offer in Italy and its agents are very helpful in tracking down the perfect place to suit your needs. Marjorie Shaw's **Insider's Italy** (www.insidersitaly.com; © **914/470-1612;** fax 914/470-1612), is a small, upscale outfit run by a very personable agent who's thoroughly familiar with all of her properties and with Italy in general.

The **Parker Company Ltd.,** Seaport Landing, 152 Lynnway, Lynn, MA 01902 (www.theparkercompany.com; © **800/280-2811** or 781/596-8282; fax 781/596-3125), handles overseas villa rentals and offers properties all over Italy.

For some top properties, call **Cottages to Castles,** Tuscany House, 10 Tonbridge Rd., Maidstone, Kent ME16 8RP, U.K. (www.cottagestocastles.com; © **0044/1622-775-217**).

Villas and Apartments Abroad, Ltd., 183 Madison Ave., Ste. 1111, New York, NY 10017 (www.vaanyc.com; © **212/213-6435;** fax 212/213-8252), has almost 200 properties in Italy.

Homelidays (www.homelidays.com) is an excellent choice for everything from villas to apartments by the sea and chalets in the Dolomites. You deal directly with the owner and the listings contain copious amounts of information, photos, and testimonials from people who have stayed before you.

[Fast FACTS] ITALY

Area Codes The **country code** for Italy is **39. City codes** (for example, Milan's is 02, Venice's is 041, Rome's is 06) are incorporated into the numbers themselves. Therefore, you must dial the entire number, ***including the initial zero,*** when calling from *anywhere* outside or inside Italy and even within the same town. To call Milan from the States, you must dial **011-39-02,** then the local phone number. Phone numbers in Italy can range anywhere from 6 to 12 digits in length.

Business Hours General open hours for **stores, offices,** and **churches** are from 9:30am to noon or 1pm and again from 3 or 3:30pm to 7:30 or 8pm. The early afternoon shutdown is the *riposo,* the Italian siesta (in the downtown area of large cities stores don't close for the *riposo*). Most stores close all day Sunday and many also on Monday (morning only or all day). Some shops, especially grocery stores, also close Thursday afternoons. Some services and business offices are open to the public only in the morning. Traditionally, **museums** are closed Monday, and though most of the biggest stay open all day long, many close for *riposo* or are only open in the morning (9am–2pm is popular). Some churches open earlier in the morning, but the largest often stay open all day. **Banks** tend to be open Monday through Friday 8:30am to 1:30pm and 2:45 to 4:15pm.

Car Rental See "By Car" under "Getting Around," p. 924.

Cellphones See "Mobile Phones," p. 936.

Customs Italy's *Guardia di Finanza* is in charge of checking what people bring into and out of Italy. Foreign visitors can bring along most items for personal use duty-free, including merchandise up to $800. If you are planning to mail items to Italy, you can mail only merchandise costing up to $200. For information on what you're allowed to bring home, contact your country's customs agency.

Disabled Travelers In Italy, a few of the top museums and churches have installed ramps at their entrances, and some hotels have converted first-floor rooms into accessible units by widening the doors and bathrooms. Other than that, don't expect to find much of Italy easy to tackle. Builders in the Middle Ages and the Renaissance didn't have wheelchairs or mobility impairments in mind when they built narrow doorways and spiral staircases, and preservation laws keep modern Italians from being able to do much about this.

Many buses and trains can cause problems as well, with high, narrow doors and steep steps at entrances (notably, the Malpensa Express train from the airport to Milan is wheelchair accessible). For those with disabilities who can make it on to public transportation, there are usually seats reserved for them and Italians are quick to give up their place for people who look like they need it more than them.

Accessible Italy (www.accessibleitaly.com; ✆ **378-0549-941-111**) provides travelers with information about accessible tourist sites and places to rent wheelchairs, and also sells organized "Accessible Tours" around Italy.

Drinking Laws People of any age can legally consume alcohol in Italy, but a person must be 16 years old in order to be served alcohol in a restaurant or a bar. Laws in other countries that exist in order to stamp out public drunkenness simply aren't as necessary in Italy, where binge-drinking is unusual. Noise is the primary concern to city officials, and so bars generally close at 2am at the latest, though alcohol is commonly served in clubs after that. Supermarkets generally carry beer, wine, and sometimes spirits.

Driving Rules See "Getting Around," p. 924.

Electricity Italy operates on a 220 volts AC (50 cycles) system, as opposed to the United States' 110 volts AC (60 cycles) system. You'll need a simple adapter plug to make the American flat pegs fit the Italian round holes and, unless your appliance is dual-voltage (as some hair dryers, travel irons, and almost all laptops are), an electrical currency converter. You can pick up the hardware at electronics stores, travel specialty stores, luggage shops, and airports.

Embassies & Consulates The **Australian Embassy** is in Rome at Via Antonio Bosio 5 (www.italy.embassy.gov.au; ✆ **06-852-721**). Australia's consulate in Milan is at Via Borgogna 2 (✆ **02-777-041**), open Monday through Thursday 9am to noon and 2 to 4pm.

The **Canadian** Embassy is in Rome at Via Zara 30 (www.canadainternational.gc.ca/italy-italie; ✆ **06-854-443-937**). The Canadian consulate in Milan is at Via Vittor Pisani 19 (✆ **02-67-581**), open Monday through Friday 8:30am to 12:30pm and 1:30 to 4pm.

The **New Zealand Embassy** is in Rome at Via Clitunno 44 (www.nzembassy.com/italy; ✆ **06-853-7501**). New Zealand's Milan consulate is at Via Terragio 17 (✆ **02-7217-0001;** fax 02-4801-2577), open Monday through Friday 8:30am to 12:30pm and 1:30 to 5pm.

The **U.K. Embassy** is in Rome at Via XX Settembre 80a (http://ukinitaly.fco.gov.uk/it; ✆ **06-4220-0001;** fax 06-4220-2334). The **U.K. consulate in Milan** is at Via San Paolo 7 (✆ **02-723-001;** fax 02-869-2405). It's open Monday to Friday 9:30am to 12:30pm and 2:30 to 4:30pm.

The **U.S. Embassy** is in Rome at Via Vittorio Veneto 121 (http://italy.usembassy.gov; ✆ **06-46-741;** fax 06-488-2672 or 06-4674-2217). The **U.S. consulate in Milan**—for passport and consular services but *not* for visas—is at Via Principe Amadeo 2/10 (http://milan.usconsulate.gov; ✆ **02-2903-5333;** fax 02-2903-5273). It's open for drop-ins Monday through Friday 8:30am to noon for emergencies, otherwise only by appointment.

Emergencies The best number to call in Italy (and the rest of Europe) with a **general emergency** is ✆ **112,** which connects you to the military-trained ***carabinieri*** who will transfer your call as needed. For the **police,** dial ✆ **113;** for a **medical emergency** and to call an **ambulance,** the number is ✆ **118;** for the **fire department,** call ✆ **115.** If your car breaks down, dial ✆ **116** for **roadside aid** courtesy of the Automotive Club of Italy. All are free calls.

Family Travel Italy is a family-oriented society, and kids have free rein just about anywhere they go. A crying baby at a dinner table is greeted with a knowing smile rather than with a stern look. Children under a certain age almost always receive discounts, and maybe a special treat from the waiter.

Gasoline See "By Car" under "Getting Around," p. 924.

Health There are no special health risks you'll encounter in Italy. The country's public health care system is generally well regarded. If you do need medical attention, keep in mind that the richer north tends to have better **hospitals** (see below) than the south.

While Italy offers universal health care to its citizens and those of other European Union countries, others should be prepared to pay medical bills upfront. Before leaving home, find out what medical services your **health insurance** covers. ***Note:*** Even if you don't have insurance, you will be treated in an emergency room.

Pharmacies offer essentially the same range of generic drugs available in the United States, plus a lot of them that haven't been approved yet by the U.S. Food and Drug Administration. **Pharmacies** are ubiquitous (look for the green cross) and serve almost like miniclinics, where pharmacists diagnose and treat minor ailments, like flu symptoms and general aches and pains, with over-the-counter drugs. Carry the generic name of prescription medicines, in case a local pharmacist is unfamiliar with the brand name. Pharmacies in cities take turns doing the night shift; normally there is a list posted at the entrance of each pharmacy informing customers which pharmacy is open each night of the week.

Holidays Banks, government offices, post offices, and many stores, restaurants, and museums in Italy are closed on the following legal national holidays: January 1 (New Year's Day), January 6 (Epiphany), Easter Sunday and the following Monday (called Pasquetta, or Little Easter), April 25 (Liberation Day), May 1 (Labor Day), June 2 (Republic Day), August 15 (Feast of the Assumption), November 1 (All Saints' Day), December 8 (Immaculate Conception), and December 25 and December 26 (Santo Stefano).

For more information, see "Public Holidays," p. 45.

Hospitals In Milan, the **Ospedale Maggiore Policlinico** (www.policlinico.mi.it; ✆ **02-5503-3103**) is centrally located a 5-minute walk southeast of the Duomo at Via Francesco Sforza 35 (Metro: Duomo or Missori). In Venice, the **Ospedale Civile Santi Giovanni e Paolo** (✆ **041-785-111**), on Campo Santi Giovanni e Paolo, has English-speaking staff and provides emergency service 24 hours a day (*vaporetto:* San Toma). In Rome, the Ospedale San Giovanni-Addolorata (www.hsangiovanni.roma.it; ✆ **06-77-051**), is right on Piazza San Giovanni in Laterano on the southern edge of the city center.

Insurance Italy may be one of the safer places you can travel in the world, but accidents and setbacks can and do happen, from lost luggage to car crashes. For information on traveler's insurance, trip cancellation insurance, and medical insurance while traveling, please visit www.frommers.com/tips.

Internet Access Internet cafes are in healthy supply in most Italian cities, though don't expect to find them in smaller towns. If you are traveling with your own computer or smartphone, you will find wireless access in many hotels in the bigger cities throughout the country, but if this is key for your stay make sure you ask before booking and certainly don't expect to find a connection in a rural *agriturismo* (disconnecting is part of their appeal). In a pinch, hostels, local libraries, and often pubs will have some sort of terminal for access. Several spots around Milan, Venice, Bologna, Florence, Rome, and other big cities are covered with free Wi-Fi access provided by the local administration, but at these and any other Wi-Fi spots around Italy, anti-terrorism laws make it obligatory to register for an access code before you can log on. Milan's two airports as well as Rome's Leonardo da Vinci-Fiumicino Airport offer wireless Internet access for a fee.

Language Italians may not be quite as polished with their English as some of their European counterparts, but they've been hosting Anglophones for a long time, and English is a regular part of any business day. In very rural parts, slow and clear speech, a little gesticulating, and a smile will go a long way. In Venice, you will probably be the 20th English-speaking tourist they've spoken with that day. Italians love it when foreigners speak their language, no matter how pathetically, so you can earn lots of good will and smiles by familiarizing yourself with the useful terms and phrases in "Molto Italiano" (p. 943).

Legal Aid Your embassy or consulate can provide a list of foreign attorneys, should you encounter legal problems in Italy. In criminal cases, if you cannot afford an attorney, the local court will provide one for you.

LGBT Travelers Italy as a whole and northern Italy in particular, is gay-friendly. Homosexuality is legal, and the age of consent is 16. Luckily, Italians are already more affectionate and physical than Americans in their general friendships, and even straight men occasionally walk down the street with their arms around each other—however, kissing anywhere other than on the cheeks at greetings and goodbyes will certainly draw attention. As you might expect, smaller towns tend to be less permissive than cities. Milan has the largest and most visible homosexual population, and during fashion week especially, gay travelers will feel particularly at home.

Italy's national association and support network for gays and lesbians is **ARCI-Gay/ARCI-Lesbica.** The national website is **www.arcigay.it**, and most cities have a local office (though not Venice). In **Trieste,** it is found at Via Pondares 8 (www.arcigay.it/comitati/trieste; ✆ **040-630-606**); in **Verona,** Via Nichesola 9 (www.arcigayverona.org; ✆ **346-9790553**); in **Milan,** Via Bezzecca 3 (www.arcigaymilano.org; ✆ **02-5412-2225**); in **Genoa,** Via Mezzagalera 3 (http://nuke.arcigaygenova.it; ✆ **010-565-971**); in **Turin,** Via Fratelli Faà di Bruno 2 (www.arcigaytorino.it; ✆ **333-713-8813**); in **Florence,** Via di Mezzo 39/r (www.arcigayfirenze.it; ✆ **393-401-0237**); and in **Rome,** Via Zabaglia 14 (www.arcigayroma.it; ✆ **06-64501102**).

Mail Sending a postcard or letter up to 20 grams, or a little less than an ounce, costs .75€ to other European countries, 1.60€ to North America, and a whopping 2€ to Australia and New Zealand.

Medical Requirements

There are no special medical requirements for entering Italy. For more information on staying healthy while over there, see "Health" above.

Mobile Phones **GSM** (Global System for Mobile Communications), is a cellphone technology used by most of the world's countries that makes it possible to turn on a phone with a contract in Australia, Ireland, the U.K., Pakistan, or almost every other corner of the world and have it work in Italy without missing a beat. (In the U.S., some service providers use a technology different from GSM, and phones used with those networks won't work in Italy.)

Any phone that works in the U.K., Ireland, Australia, or New Zealand will work in Italy, where coverage is excellent just about everywhere, but if you are coming from the U.S. or Canada you might need a multiband phone. In some cases you might have to activate "international roaming" on your account, so check with your service provider at home before leaving.

Using your cellphone in a different country can be very expensive so another option, once you arrive, is to buy an Italian SIM card (the fingernail-size removable plastic card found in all GSM phones that is encoded with your phone number and account information). This is not difficult and an especially good idea if you will be in Italy for more than a few weeks. You can **buy a SIM card** at one of the many cellphone shops you will see around every city (the biggest service providers are TIM, Vodafone, Wind, and 3). If you have an Italian SIM card in your phone, local calls may be as low as .10€ per minute, and incoming calls are free. ***Note:*** Some cellphones are "locked" and will only work with the SIM card provided by the service provider back home, so check to see that you have an unlocked phone.

Buying a phone is another option, and in the bigger cities in northern Italy you shouldn't have too much trouble finding one that won't put you back more than about 40€. Another, usually more expensive, option is to **rent a phone** from kiosks at airports, car-rental agencies, or in a number of places in Milan and Rome.

Money & Costs

Frommer's lists exact prices in the local currency. The currency conversions quoted below were correct at press time. However, rates fluctuate, so before departing, consult a currency exchange website, such as **www.oanda.com/convert/classic**, to check up-to-the-minute rates.

Like many other European countries, Italy uses the euro as its currency. Euro coins are issued in denominations of .01€, .02€, .05€, .10€, .20€, and .50€, as well as 1€ and 2€; bills come in denominations of 5€, 10€, 20€, 50€, 100€, 200€, and 500€.

The aggressive evolution of international computerized banking and consolidated ATM networks has led to the triumph of plastic throughout the Italian peninsula—even if cold cash is still the most trusted currency, especially in smaller towns or cheaper mom-and-pop joints, where credit cards may not be accepted. Traveler's checks, while still the safest way to carry money, are going the way of the Stegosaurus.

You'll get the best rate if you **exchange money** at a bank or one of its ATMs. The rates at "Cambio/change/wechsel" exchange booths are invariably less favorable but still a good deal better than what you'd get exchanging money at a hotel or shop (a last-resort tactic only). The bill-to-bill changers you'll see in some touristy places exist solely to rip you off.

The easiest and best way to get cash away from home is from an ATM (automated teller machine), referred to in Italy as a ***bancomat.*** ATMs are very prevalent in Italian cities and while every town usually has one, it's good practice to fuel up on cash in urban centers before traveling to smaller towns.

THE VALUE OF THE EURO VS. OTHER POPULAR CURRENCIES

€	Aus$	Can$	NZ$	UK£	US$
1	A$1.32	C$1.37	NZ$1.74	£0.85	$1.33

Be sure to confirm with your bank that your card is valid for international withdrawal and that you have a four-digit PIN. (Some ATMs in Italy will not accept any other number of digits.) Also, be sure you know your daily withdrawal limit before you depart. ***Note:*** Many banks impose a fee every time you use a card at another bank's ATM, and that fee can be higher for international transactions (up to $5 or more) than for domestic ones (where they're rarely more than $2). In addition, the bank from which you withdraw cash may charge its own fee, although this is not common practice in Italy.

If at the ATM you get a message saying your card isn't valid for international transactions, don't panic: It's most likely the bank just can't make the phone connection to check it (occasionally this can be a citywide epidemic) or else simply doesn't have the cash. Try another ATM or another town.

Credit cards are widely accepted in northern Italy and the bigger urban centers of the south, especially in hotels and larger establishments. However, it is always a good idea to carry some cash, as small businesses may accept only cash or may claim that their credit card machine is broken to avoid paying fees to the credit card companies.

Visa and **MasterCard** are almost universally accepted at hotels, plus most restaurants and shops; the majority of them also accept **American Express. Diners Club** is gaining some ground.

Finally, be sure to let your bank know that you'll be traveling abroad to avoid having your card blocked after a few days of big purchases far from home. ***Note:*** Many banks assess a 1% to 3% "transaction fee" on **all** charges you incur abroad (whether you're using the local currency or your native currency).

Multicultural Travelers Many Italians are still grappling with the new reality that theirs is no longer the homogenous society that it was for centuries. You will see nonwhite immigrants everywhere you travel in Italy, with the exception of mountain villages. But because most of the immigrants that you, and most Italians, will meet are working as street vendors and not bankers means that travelers with darker skin may feel—correctly at times—as if they're being looked at or in some way singled out.

Pockets of outright racism do exist in Italy, especially in Veneto and the Northeast in general. There, African and South Asian workers fill the need for low-paid labor and, according to outfits like the Northern League, are responsible for all crime that occurs. Skinhead violence is extremely rare, but you might expect the occasional slur from a soccer hooligan and maybe some sideways glances from a few provincial old men.

Newspapers & Magazines The *International Herald Tribune* (published by the *New York Times* and with news catering to Americans abroad) and *USA Today* are available at most newsstands in the big cities, and sometimes even in smaller towns. You can find the *Wall Street Journal Europe,* European editions of *Time* and *Newsweek*, the *Economist,* and most of the major European newspapers and magazines at the larger kiosks in the bigger cities.

Sports daily *La Gazzetta dello Sport* is Italy's best-selling newspaper while *Corriere della Sera* is the best selling general-interest daily. Both are based in Milan and can be found on any newsstand across Italy.

Parking See "By Car" under "Getting Around," p. 924.

Passports Anyone traveling to Italy from outside the 25 Schengen Agreement countries (which essentially comprises all of Western Europe except the U.K. and Ireland) will need a passport to enter. You're required to present a passport at hotel desks in Italy.

Citizens of the United States, Canada, the U.K., Australia, and New Zealand are allowed to stay in Italy for 90 days; after that period, they are required to have a visa.

See www.frommers.com/tips for information on how to obtain a passport. See "Embassies & Consulates," above, for whom to contact if you lose yours while traveling in Italy. For other information, please contact the following agencies:

For Residents of Australia Contact the **Australian Passport Information Service** at ✆ **131-232,** or visit the government website at www.passports.gov.au.

For Residents of Canada Contact the central **Passport Office,** Department of Foreign Affairs and International Trade, Ottawa, ON K1A 0G3 (www.ppt.gc.ca; ✆ **800/567-6868**).

For Residents of Ireland Contact the **Passport Office,** Setanta Centre, Molesworth Street, Dublin 2 (www.foreignaffairs.gov.ie; ✆ **01/671-1633**).

For Residents of New Zealand Contact the **Passports Office** at ✆ **0800/225-050** in New Zealand or 04/474-8100, or log on to www.passports.govt.nz.

For Residents of the United Kingdom Visit your nearest passport office, major post office, or travel agency, or contact the **United Kingdom Passport Service** at ✆ **0870/521-0410,** or search its website at www.homeoffice.gov.uk/agencies-public-bodies/ips.

For Residents of the United States Call the **National Passport Information Center** toll-free number (✆ **877/487-2778**) for automated information or visit http://travel.state.gov/passport.

Petrol See "By Car" under "Getting Around," p. 924.

Police For emergencies, call ✆ **112** or ✆ **113.** Italy has several different police forces, but there are only two you'll most likely ever need to deal with. The first is the *carabinieri* (✆ **112**), who normally only concern themselves with more serious crimes or problems, but point you in the right direction. The *polizia* (✆ **113**), whose city headquarters is called the *questura,* is the place to go for help with lost and stolen property or petty crimes.

Safety Italy is a remarkably safe country. The worst threats you'll likely face are the pickpockets who sometimes frequent touristy areas and public buses; keep your hands on your camera at all times and your valuables in an under-the-clothes money belt. Don't leave anything valuable in your rental car overnight, and leave nothing visible in it at any time to avoid tempting a would-be thief. If you are robbed, you can fill out paperwork at the nearest police station *(questura),* but this is mostly for insurance purposes and perhaps to get a new passport issued—don't expect them to actually spend any resources hunting down the perpetrator.

In general, avoid public parks at night and public squares in the wee hours of the morning. The square in front of Milan's main train station is pretty dodgy after hours and travelers—especially women—should avoid Genoa's port area after dark. Be careful in the poorer neighborhoods of Naples, for example the Quartieri Spagnoli, where nothing is likely to happen to you during the day, but where you will stand out and perhaps be looked at. Avoid these neighborhoods altogether at night. Other than that, there is a remarkable sense of security in Italy.

Senior Travel Seniors and older people are treated with a great deal of respect and deference throughout Italy, but there are few specific programs, associations, or concessions made for them. The one exception is on admission prices for museums and sights, where those ages 60 or 65 and older will often get in at a reduced rate or even free. There are also special train passes and reductions on bus tickets and the like in many towns (see "Getting Around," p. 924). As a senior in Italy, you're *un anziano* (if you're a woman: *un'anziana*, *"una"* contracts to *"un"* so the pronunciation is the same for both sexes), or "elderly"—it's a term of respect, and you should let people know you're one if you think a discount may be in order.

Single Travelers On package vacations, single travelers are often hit with a "single supplement" to the base price. To avoid it, you can agree to room with other single travelers on your tour.

Smoking Smoking has been eradicated from restaurants, bars, and most hotels in Italy. Naturally, many smokers remain, and they tend to take the outside tables at bars and restaurants. Be aware that if you are keen for an outdoor table, you are essentially choosing a seat in the smoking section, and requesting that your neighbor not smoke may not be politely received.

Student Travelers The World Youth Student & Educational Travel Confederation (WYSE; www.wysetc.org) seeks to make travel around the world more affordable for students. The website gives comprehensive travel services information and details on how to get an **International Student Identity Card (ISIC),** which qualifies students for substantial savings on rail passes, plane tickets, entrance fees, and more. It also provides students with basic health and life insurance and a 24-hour help line. The card is valid for 1 year. You can apply for the card online or in person at **STA Travel** (www.statravel.com; ✆ **800/781-4040** in North America), the biggest student travel agency in the world; check out the website to locate STA Travel offices worldwide. If you're no longer a student but are still 25 and under, you can get an **International Youth Travel Card (IYTC)** from the same agency, which entitles you to some discounts. **Travel CUTS** (www.travelcuts.com; ✆ **800/592-2887**) offers similar services to Canadians and U.S. residents alike. Irish students can turn to **USIT** (www.usit.ie; ✆ **01/602-1904**), an Ireland-based specialist in student, youth, and independent travel.

In Italy, students will find many university cities that offer ample student discounts and inexpensive youth hostels.

Taxes There's no sales tax added onto the price tag of your purchases in Italy, but there is a 21% value-added tax (in Italy: IVA) automatically included in just about everything except basic foodstuffs like milk and bread. For major purchases, you can get this refunded. Some four- and five-star hotels don't include the 13% luxury tax in their quoted prices. Ask when making your reservation.

Telephones **To call Italy:** (1) Dial the international access code: 011 from the U.S.; 00 from the U.K., Ireland, or New Zealand; or 0011 from Australia. (2) Dial the country code 39. (3) Dial the city code (for Milan: 02) and then the number. (Do not drop the initial 0 as you might in other European countries.) Even when calling within Italy, you always need to dial the city code first.

To make international calls: To make international calls from Italy, first dial 00 and then the country code (U.S. or Canada 1, U.K. 44, Ireland 353, Australia 61, New Zealand 64). Next, dial the area code and number. For example, if you wanted to call the British Embassy in Washington, D.C., you would dial 00-1-202-588-6500.

For directory assistance: Each cellphone carrier has its own directory assistance number, which is listed automatically in the address book of your SIM card. For Telecom Italia, and its mobile carrier, TIM, the directory assistance number is ✆ **1254.**

For operator assistance: For operator assistance in making either a domestic or an international call from a Telecom Italia land line, call ✆ **187.**

Toll-free numbers: Numbers in Italy beginning with 800 or 877, and a few others beginning with 8, are toll-free, but calling a 1-800 number in the States from Italy is not toll-free. In fact, it costs the same as an overseas call.

Throughout Italy you'll find public telephones that accept **Telecom Italia phone cards** *(scheda telefonica)*, which you can purchase at tobacco shops in various denominations. With the ubiquity of cellphones, public phones are rapidly disappearing so actually finding one in which to use your phone card can be a challenge.

You can also buy phone cards with special fixed rates to the United States, Canada, Australia, and other countries *(una carta telefonica prepagata per chiamare gli Stati Uniti, Canada, . . .)* that can be used from any phone. The rates on these phone cards, which can be found at newsstands and tobacconists, are heavily discounted from what you would pay from a land line and far less expensive than calling abroad from a cellphone.

Time Italy is in the same Western European time zone as Paris, Brussels, and Berlin—that is, GMT plus 1 hour.

Tipping In **hotels,** a service charge is usually included in your bill. In family-run operations, additional tips are unnecessary and sometimes considered rude. In fancier places with a hired staff, however, you may want to leave a .50€ daily tip for the maid, pay the bellhop or porter 1€ per bag, and tip a helpful concierge 2€ for his or her troubles. In **restaurants,** a 1€ to 3€ service charge is automatically added to the bill and in some tourist areas, especially Venice, another 10% to 15% is tacked on (except in the most unscrupulous of places, this will be noted on the menu somewhere; to be sure you can ask, *è incluso il servizio?*). It is not necessary to leave any extra money on the table though it is not uncommon to leave up to 5€, especially for good service. At **bars and cafes,** you can leave something very small on the counter for the barman (maybe 1€ if you have had several drinks), though it is hardly expected; there is no need to leave anything extra if you sit at a table, as they are probably already charging you double or triple the price you'd have paid standing at the bar. It is not necessary to tip **taxi** drivers, though it is common to round up the bill to the nearest euro or two.

Toilets Aside from train stations, where they cost about .50€ to use, and gas/petrol stations, where they are free (with perhaps a basket seeking donations), public toilets are few and far between in northern Italy. Standard procedure is to enter a cafe, make sure the restroom is not *fuori servizio* (out of order), and then order a cup of coffee before bolting to the facilities. In Venice, the price of using a toilet is a little steeper: about 1.50€ in the major squares and parking garages, and they usually close at 8pm. It is advisable to always make use of the facilities in the hotel, restaurant, and bar before a long walk around town.

VAT See "Taxes," earlier in this section.

Visas Travelers from Australia, Canada, New Zealand, the U.S., and the U.K. can visit Italy for up to 90 days without a visa, though they need a valid passport. Visits of more than 90 days may require a visa, but the requirements vary depending on the purpose of your visit.

For more information on visas to visit or stay in Italy, go to the Foreign Ministry's English-language page at **www.esteri.it/visti**.

Visitor Information In Milan, the main **Azienda di Promozione Turistica (APT) office** is at Piazza Castello 1, on the south side of the square where it meets Via Beltrami (www.visitamilano.it; ✆ **02-7740-4343**). Hours are Monday to Friday 9am to 6pm, Saturday 9am to 1:30pm and 2 to 6pm, Sunday 9am to 1:30pm and 2 to 5pm. There is also an office in Stazione Centrale (✆ **02-7740-4318**), in front of tracks 13 and 14, with the same hours.

In Rome, there are tourist information points at the two airports, Termini train station, and sprinkled around town, including at Castello Sant'Angelo and just off Piazza Navona in Piazza delle Cinque Lune. They are open daily from 9am to 6:30pm.

In Venice, the main tourist office is on Fondamenta San Lorenzo, 5 minutes from Piazza San Marco (www.turismovenezia.it; ✆ **041-529-8711**); it's open daily 10am to 6pm. There is also a small, private tourist office in Venice's train station.

See "Visitor Information," in each of the chapters, for more information.

Water Though Italians take mineral water with their meals, tap water is safe everywhere. Unsafe sources, for example on trains, will be marked ACQUA NON POTABILE. The water from fountains in public parks is not only potable, but it's often the best water you've ever tasted.

Wi-Fi See "Internet Access," earlier in this section.

Women Travelers

Women feel remarkably welcome in Italy—sometimes a bit too welcome, actually. It seems every young Italian male is out to prove himself the most irresistible lover on the planet; remember, this is the land of Romeo and Casanova, so they have a lot to live up to. And with most every Italian woman playing the especially hard-to-get Juliet, well, you see what's coming next for foreign women.

It should be noted that the culture in northern Italy feels a lot more like that in neighboring Austria and Switzerland than what you'll find in southern Italy, especially Sicily, in that the divide between the sexes is not quite as deep, it is a lot more egalitarian, and perhaps it is less chivalrous, but naturally attractive women everywhere will, er, attract attention.

The attention is mostly kept to verbal flirtation (but should there be inappropriate touching, immediately speak up and report it to police). These men want to conquer you with their charm, not their muscles. Rape is much rarer in Italy than in the United States, but it does happen (mostly by non-Italian men, if you believe the newspapers). Use common sense: Don't walk through poorly lit city parks alone late at night, especially in Milan, Turin, Genoa, Rome, and Naples.

18

MOLTO ITALIANO

BASICS

USEFUL ENGLISH-ITALIAN PHRASES

English	Italian	Pronunciation
Thank you	Grazie	*graht*-tzee-yey
You're welcome	Prego	*prey*-go
Please	Per favore	*pehr* fah-*vohr*-eh
Yes	Si	see
No	No	noh
Good morning or Good day	Buongiorno	bwohn-*djor*-noh
Good evening	Buona sera	*bwohn*-ah *say*-rah
Good night	Buona notte	*bwohn*-ah *noht*-tay
It's a pleasure to meet you.	Piacere di conoscerla.	pyah-*cheh*-reh dee *koh*-nohshehr-lah
My name is ____.	Mi chiamo ____.	mee *kyah*-moh
And yours?	E lei?	eh lay
Do you speak English?	Parla inglese?	*pahr*-lah een-*gleh*-seh
How are you?	Come sta?	*koh*-may *stah*
Very well	Molto bene	*mohl*-toh *behn*-ney
Goodbye	Arrivederci	ahr-ree-vah-*dehr*-chee
Excuse me (to get attention)	Scusi	*skoo*-zee
Excuse me (to get past someone)	Permesso	pehr-*mehs*-soh

GETTING AROUND

English	Italian	Pronunciation
Where is . . . ?	Dovè . . . ?	*doh*-vey
the station	la stazione	lah stat-tzee-*oh*-neh
a hotel	un albergo	oon ahl-*behr*-goh

English	Italian	Pronunciation
a restaurant	un ristorante	**oon reest-ohr-*ahnt*-eh**
the bathroom	il bagno	**eel *bahn*-nyoh**
I am looking for . . .	Cerco . . .	***chehr*-koh**
a porter	un facchino	**oon fahk-*kee*-noh**
the check-in counter	il check-in	**eel check-in**
the ticket counter	la biglietteria	***lah beel-lyeht-teh-ree-ah***
arrivals	l'area arrivi	***lah*-reh-ah ahr-*ree*-vee**
departures	l'area partenze	***lah*-reh-ah pahr-*tehn*-tseh**
gate number	l'uscita numero	**loo-*shee*-tah *noo*-meh-roh**
the waiting area	l'area d'attesa	***lah*-reh-ah daht-*teh*-zah**
the men's restroom	la toilette uomini	**lah twa-*leht* *woh*-mee-nee**
the women's restroom	la toilette donne	**lah twa-*leht* *dohn*-neh**
the police station	la stazione di polizia	**lah stah-*tsyoh*-neh dee poh-lee-*tsee*-ah**
a security guard	una guardia di sicurezza	***ooh*-nah *gwahr*-dyah dee see-koo-*ret*-sah**
the smoking area	l'area fumatori	***lah*-reh-ah foo-mah-*toh*-ree**
the information booth	l'ufficio informazioni	**loof-*fee*-choh een-*fohr*-mah-*tsyoh*-nee**
a public telephone	un telefono pubblico	**oon teh-*leh*-foh-noh *poob*-blee-koh**
an ATM/cashpoint	un bancomat	**oon *bahn*-koh-maht**
baggage claim	il ritiro bagagli	**eel ree-*tee*-roh bah-*gahl*-lyee**
a luggage cart	un carrello portabagagli	**oon kahr-*rehl*-loh *pohr*-tah-bah-gahl-lyee**
a currency exchange	un cambiavalute	**oon *kahm*-byah-vah-*loo*-teh**
a cafe	un caffè	**oon kahf-*feh***
a restaurant	un ristorante	**oon ree-stoh-*rahn*-teh**
a bar	un bar	**oon bar**
a bookstore	una libreria	***oo*-nah lee-breh-*ree*-ah**
a duty-free shop	un duty-free	**oon duty-free**
To the left	A sinistra	**ah see-*nees*-tra**
To the right	A destra	**ah *dehy*-stra**
Straight ahead	Avanti (*or* sempre diritto)	**ahv-*vahn*-tee (*sehm*-pray dee-*reet*-toh)**

DINING

English	Italian	Pronunciation
Breakfast	Prima colazione	**pree-mah coh-laht-tzee-ohn-ay**
Lunch	Pranzo	**prahn-zoh**
Dinner	Cena	**chay-nah**
How much is it?	Quanto costa?	**kwan-toh coh-sta**
The check, please	Il conto, per favore	**eel kon-toh pehr fah-vohr-eh**

A MATTER OF TIME

English	Italian	Pronunciation
When?	Quando?	**_kwan_-doh**
Yesterday	Leri	**ee-_yehr_-ree**
Today	Oggi	**_oh_-jee**
Tomorrow	Domani	**doh-_mah_-nee**
What time is it?	Che ore sono?	**kay _or_-ay _soh_-noh**
It's one o'clock.	È l'una.	**_eh loo_-nah**
It's two o'clock.	Sono le due.	**_soh_-noh leh _doo_-eh**
It's two-thirty.	Sono le due e mezzo.	**_soh_-noh leh _doo_-eh eh _mehd_-dzoh**
It's noon	È mezzogiorno.	**eh mehd-dzoh-_johr_-noh**
It's midnight.	È mezzanotte.	**eh mehd-dzah-_noht_-teh**
It's early.	È presto.	**eh _prehs_-toh**
It's late.	È tardi.	**eh _tahr_-dee**
in the morning	al mattino	**ahl maht-_tee_-noh**
in the afternoon	al pomeriggio	**ahl poh-meh-_reed_-joh**
at night	alla notte	**dee _noht_-the**

DAYS OF THE WEEK

English	Italian	Pronunciation
Monday	Lunedì	**loo-nay-_dee_**
Tuesday	Martedì	**mart-ay-_dee_**
Wednesday	Mercoledì	**mehr-cohl-ay-_dee_**
Thursday	Giovedì	**joh-vay-_dee_**
Friday	Venerdì	**ven-nehr-_dee_**
Saturday	Sabato	**_sah_-bah-toh**
Sunday	Domenica	**doh-_mehn_-nee-kah**

MONTHS & SEASONS

English	Italian	Pronunciation
January	gennaio	**jehn-*nah*-yoh**
February	febbraio	**fehb-*brah*-yoh**
March	marzo	***mahr*-tso**
April	aprile	**ah-*pree*-leh**
May	maggio	***mahd*-joh**
June	giugno	***jewn*-nyo**
July	luglio	***lool*-lyo**
August	agosto	**ah-*gohs*-toh**
September	settembre	**seht-*tehm*-breh**
October	ottobre	**oht-*toh*-breh**
November	novembre	**noh-*vehm*-breh**
December	dicembre	**dee-*chehm*-breh**
spring	la primavera	**lah pree-mah-*veh*-rah**
summer	l'estate	**lehs-*tah*-teh**
autumn	l'autunno	**low-*toon*-noh**
winter	l'inverno	**leen-*vehr*-noh**

NUMBERS

English	Italian	Pronunciation
1	uno	***oo*-noh**
2	due	***doo*-ay**
3	tre	**tray**
4	quattro	***kwah*-troh**
5	cinque	***cheen*-kway**
6	sei	**say**
7	sette	***set*-tay**
8	otto	***oh*-toh**
9	nove	***noh*-vay**
10	dieci	**dee-*ay*-chee**
11	undici	***oon*-dee-chee**
20	venti	***vehn*-tee**
21	ventuno	**vehn-*toon*-oh**
22	venti due	***vehn*-tee *doo*-ay**
30	trenta	***trayn*-tah**
40	quaranta	**kwah-*rahn*-tah**
50	cinquanta	**cheen-*kwan*-tah**

Index

D

E

N

O

S

T

W

Z

PHOTO CREDITS

p. i, © Raffale Capasso; p. 1, © Riccardo De Luca; p. 3, © Tom Weber / Frommers.com Community; p. 4, left, © Riccardo De Luca; p. 4, right, © Riccardo De Luca; p. 5, © Vanessa Berberian; p. 6, © Raffaele Capasso; p. 7, © Riccardo De Luca; p. 9, © Vanessa Berberian; p. 10, top, © Riccardo De Luca; p. 10, bottom, © Giuseppe Piazza; p. 11, top, © Vanessa Berberian; p. 11, bottom, © Cristina Fumi; p. 12, © Giuseppe Piazza; p. 13, © Vanessa Berberian; p. 14, © Riccardo De Luca; p. 15, © Vanessa Berberian; p. 16, © Vanessa Berberian; p. 18, © Vanessa Berberian; p. 19, © Vanessa Berberian; p. 20, © Riccardo De Luca; p. 230, © Jayne Ilene Hanlin / Frommers.com Community; p. 24, © Vanessa Berberian; p. 255, © Raffaele Capasso; p. 26, © Vanessa Berberian; p. 28, © Riccardo De Luca; p. 310, © Carolyn Marczak / Frommers.com Community; p. 32, © Riccardo De Luca; p. 34, top, © mauritius images GmbH / Alamy; p. 34, bottom, © LOOK Die Bildagentur der Fotografen GmbH / Alamy; p. 39© E.J. Baumeister Jr. / Alamy; p. 42, © Riccardo De Luca; p. 499, © Vanessa Berberian; p. 52, © Vanessa Berberian; p. 53, © Sandro Di Fatta; p. 56, © Riccardo De Luca; p. 57© Riccardo De Luca; p. 58, © Riccardo De Luca; p. 59, © Riccardo De Luca; p. 60, © Raffaele Capasso; p. 66, © Riccardo De Luca; p. 68© Vanessa Berberian; p. 70, © Vanessa Berberian; p. 71, © Vanessa Berberian; p. 76, © Riccardo De Luca; p. 83, © Vanessa Berberian; p. 86, © Riccardo De Luca; p. 92, © Riccardo De Luca; p. 93, © Riccardo De Luca; p. 94, © Vanessa Berberian; p. 96, © Michele Falzone / Alamy; p. 97, © Vanessa Berberian; p. 98, © Riccardo De Luca; p. 100, © Vanessa Berberian; p. 107, © Riccardo De Luca; p. 112, © Kelly Regan; p. 115, © Vanessa Berberian; p. 116, © Vanessa Berberian; p. 117, © Vanessa Berberian; p. 118, © Riccardo De Luca; p. 119, © Riccardo De Luca; p. 123, © Vanessa Berberian, p. 125, © Riccardo De Luca; p. 148, left, © Vanessa Berberian; p. 148, right, © Riccardo De Luca; p. 149, © Riccardo De Luca; p. 150, © Vanessa Berberian; p. 152, © Riccardo De Luca; p. 153, © Riccardo De Luca; p. 156, left, © Riccardo De Luca; p. 156, right, © Vanessa Berberian; p. 181, © Vanessa Berberian; p. 182, © Cristina Fumi; p. 188, © Riccardo De Luca; p. 189, © Jon Arnold Images Ltd / Alamy; p. 190, © Vanessa Berberian; p. 191, © Vanessa Berberian; p. 195, © Vanessa Berberian; p. 196, © Philip Game / Alamy; p. 202, © Vanessa Berberian; p. 203, © Vanessa Berberian; p. 204, top, © Vanessa Berberian; p. 204, bottom, © Vanessa Berberian; p. 206, © Vanessa Berberian; p. 207, © Vanessa Berberian; p. 209, © Superstock; p. 211, © Art Kowalsky / Alamy; p. 212, © Vanessa Berberian; p. 215, © Kirsten Scully; p. 216, © Vanessa Berberian; p. 217, © Vanessa Berberian; p. 221, © Vanessa Berberian; p. 222, © Vanessa Berberian; p. 227, © Vanessa Berberian; p. 230, © Vanessa Berberian; p. 239, © Riccardo De Luca; p. 243, © Riccardo De Luca; p. 245, © Vanessa Berberian; p. 263, © Vanessa Berberian; p. 265, © Vanessa Berberian; p. 267, © Stock Connection / SuperStock; p. 272, © Vanessa Berberian; p. 273, © Vanessa Berberian; p. 274, © Vanessa Berberian; p. 282, © Vanessa Berberian; p. 286, top, © Giulio Andreini / Marka / Alamy; p. 286, middle, © Steven Gillis hd9 imaging / Alamy; p. 288, left, © Vanessa Berberian; p. 288, right, © Vanessa Berberian; p. 295, © Riccardo De Luca; p. 298, © Riccardo De Luca; p. 308, © Riccardo De Luca; p. 309, © Riccardo De Luca; p. 316, © Riccardo De Luca; p. 317, © Vanessa Berberian; p. 318, © Vanessa Berberian; p. 321, © Riccardo De Luca; p. 325, © Vanessa Berberian; p. 329, © Riccardo De Luca; p. 330, © Vanessa Berberian; p. 332, © Vanessa Berberian; p. 334, © Vanessa Berberian; p. 337, © Vanessa Berberian; p. 338, © Vanessa Berberian; p. 341, © PRISMA ARCHIVO / Alamy; p. 345, © Vanessa Berberian; p. 349, © Vanessa Berberian; p. 354, © Vanessa Berberian; p. 362, © Riccardo De Luca; p. 364, © Riccardo De Luca; p. 367, © Riccardo De Luca; p. 368, © Riccardo De Luca; p. 373, © Riccardo De Luca; p. 375, © Riccardo De Luca, p. 378, © Riccardo De Luca; p. 379, © Riccardo De Luca; p. 381, © Riccardo De Luca; p. 387, © Sando Di Fatta; p. 392, © Sando Di Fatta; p. 396, © Riccardo De Luca; p. 397, © De Agostini / SuperStock ; p. 398, © Sando Di Fatta; p. 402, © Riccardo De Luca; p. 404, © Riccardo De Luca; p. 405, © Riccardo De Luca; p. 410, © Riccardo De Luca; p. 411, © Riccardo De Luca; p. 413, © Riccardo De Luca; p. 416, © Riccardo De Luca; p. 421, © Cristina Fumi; p. 424, © Krys Bailey / Alamy; p. 426, © Riccardo De Luca; p. 432, © Riccardo De Luca; p. 433, © Riccardo De Luca; p. 439, © Riccardo De Luca; p. 443, © Riccardo De Luca; p. 444, © Riccardo De Luca; p. 446, © Riccardo De Luca; p. 447, © Sergio Pitamitz / Robert Harding Picture Library Ltd / Alamy; p. 450, © Riccardo De Luca; p. 451, © Riccardo De Luca; p. 452, © Riccardo De Luca; p. 454,

© Riccardo De Luca; p. 455, © Riccardo De Luca; p. 456, © Sandro di Fatta; p. 457, © Riccardo De Luca; p. 459, © Riccardo De Luca; p. 460, © Riccardo De Luca; p. 461, © Sandro Di Fatta; p. 462, © Sandro Di Fatta; p. 465, © Riccardo De Luca; p. 470, © Riccardo De Luca; p. 471, © Riccardo De Luca; p. 481, © Riccardo De Luca; p. 482, © Riccardo De Luca; p. 483, © Riccardo De Luca; p. 485, © Riccardo De Luca; p. 486, © Arco Images GmbH / Alamy; p. 490, © Riccardo De Luca; p. 502, © Jon Arnold Images Ltd / Alamy; p. 504, © Sandro Di Fatta; p. 506, © MELBA PHOTO AGENCY / Alamy; p. 511, © Riccardo De Luca; p. 514, © Riccardo De Luca; p. 517, top, © Riccardo De Luca; p. 517, bottom, © Courtesy Settimane Musicali al Teatro Olympico; p. 523, © Riccardo De Luca; p. 524, © Cristina Fumi; p. 526, © Cristina Fumi; p. 529, © MARKA / Alamy; p. 534, © Riccardo De Luca; p. 535, © Gaetano Barone / Corbis Cusp / Alamy; p. 536, © Riccardo De Luca; p. 540, © Riccardo De Luca; p. 542, © Riccardo De Luca; p. 544, © Riccardo De Luca; p. 546, © G Roli / De Agostini Editore / AGE Fotostock; p. 548, © Ian Dagnall / Alamy; p. 553, © Alberto Campanile / CuboImages / Alamy; p. 557, © Cristina Fumi; p. 564, © Riccardo De Luca; p. 571, © Riccardo De Luca; p. 575, © National Geographic Image Collection / Alamy; p. 581, © Riccardo De Luca; p. 582, © Riccardo De Luca; p. 584, © Allen Brown / dbimages / Alamy; p. 593, © Riccardo De Luca; p. 600, © Marka / SuperStock ; p. 602, © Cristina Fumi; p. 603, © Sandro Di Fatta; p. 610, © Cristina Fumi; p. 615, © Cristina Fumi; p. 619, © Cristina Fumi; p. 620, © Cristina Fumi; p. 622, top, © Cristina Fumi; p. 622, bottom, © Cristina Fumi; p. 625, © Cristina Fumi; p. 634, © Riccardo De Luca; p. 637, © Riccardo De Luca; p. 643, © Riccardo De Luca; p. 650, © Cristina Fumi; p. 654, © Cristina Fumi; p. 655, © Cristina Fumi; p. 657, © Ray Roberts / Alamy; p. 660, © Riccardo De Luca; p. 663, © Riccardo De Luca; p. 667, © Sandro Di Fatta; p. 673, © Sandro Di Fatta; p. 676, © Riccardo De Luca; p. 683, © Riccardo De Luca; p. 684, © Riccardo De Luca; p. 685, © Riccardo De Luca; p. 688, © Riccardo De Luca; p. 692, © Riccardo De Luca; p. 698, © Riccardo De Luca; p. 700, © Raffaele Capasso; p. 702, © Raffaele Capasso; p. 705, © Raffaele Capasso; p. 710, © Raffaele Capasso; p. 711, © Raffaele Capasso; p. 712, © Raffaele Capasso; p. 713, © Raffaele Capasso; p. 714, © Raffaele Capasso; p. 716, © Raffaele Capasso; p. 717, © Riccardo De Luca; p. 729, © Riccardo De Luca; p. 731, © Raffaele Capasso; p. 732, © Raffaele Capasso; p. 743, © Riccardo De Luca; p. 735, © Riccardo De Luca; p. 736, © Riccardo De Luca; p. 738, © Riccardo De Luca; p. 740, © Raffaele Capasso; p. 744, © Riccardo De Luca; p. 746, © Riccardo De Luca; p. 748, © Raffaele Capasso; p. 754, © Raffaele Capasso; p. 756, © Raffaele Capasso; p. 757, © Raffaele Capasso; p. 758, © Raffaele Capasso; p. 760, © Raffaele Capasso; p. 761, © Raffaele Capasso; p. 765, © Raffaele Capasso; p. 768, © Raffaele Capasso; p. 769, © Raffaele Capasso; p. 772, © Raffaele Capasso; p. 776, © Raffaele Capasso; p. 778, © Raffaele Capasso; p. 781, © Raffaele Capasso; p. 782, © Raffaele Capasso; p. 783, © Raffaele Capasso; p. 789, © donato r / Alamy; p. 791, © Calabria / Frommers.com Community; p. 792, © Riccardo De Luca; p. 795, © Karla666 / Frommers.com Community; p. 799, © Riccardo De Luca; p. 803, © Riccardo De Luca; p. 804, © Wesso / Frommers.com Community; p. 807, © Courtesy Masseria San Domenico; p. 808, © CuboImages srl / Alamy; p. 809, © Riccardo De Luca; p. 819, © Calabria / Frommers.com Community; p. 822, © Jessica Hauf; p. 832, top, © Guiseppe Piazza; p. 832, bottom, © Guiseppe Piazza; p. 834, © Jessica Hauf; p. 836, © Guiseppe Piazza; p. 844, © Jessica Hauf; p. 846, © Guiseppe Piazza; p. 847, © Jessica Hauf; p. 848, © Guiseppe Piazza; p. 852, © Guiseppe Piazza; p. 858, © Jessica Hauf; p. 859, © Jessica Hauf; p. 861, © Jessica Hauf; p. 864, © Guiseppe Piazza; p. 867, © Guiseppe Piazza; p. 871, © Jessica Hauf; p. 872, © Guiseppe Piazza; p. 873, © Guiseppe Piazza; p. 878, © Guiseppe Piazza; p. 881, © Guiseppe Piazza; p. 883, © Guiseppe Piazza; p. 885, © Guiseppe Piazza; p. 887, © Guiseppe Piazza; p. 889, © Jessica Hauf; p. 895, © C.Mueller-Planitz / Frommers.com Community; p. 896, © imagebroker.net / SuperStock ; p. 898, © Luca Spano; p. 904, © Luca Spano; p. 905, © Luca Spano; p. 908, © Giles Longhurst / Frommers.com Community; p. 914, © Luca Spano; p. 915, © Luca Spano; p. 921, © Riccardo De Luca.